Central America

THE ROUGH GUIDE

There are more than one hundred Rough Guide titles
covering destinations from Amsterdam to Zimbabwe

Forthcoming titles include
Chile • Indonesia • New Orleans • Toronto

Rough Guide Reference Series
Classical Music • European Football • The Internet • Jazz
Opera • Reggae • Rock Music • World Music

Rough Guide Phrasebooks
Czech • Egyptian Arabic • French • German • Greek
Hindi & Urdu • Hungarian • Indonesian • Italian • Japanese
Mandarin Chinese • Mexican Spanish • Polish • Portuguese
Russian • Spanish • Swahili • Thai • Turkish • Vietnamese

Rough Guides on the Internet
www.roughguides.com

ROUGH GUIDE CREDITS

Text editors: Kate Berens and Samantha Cook
Series editor: Mark Ellingham
Editorial: Martin Dunford, Jonathan Buckley, Jo Mead, Amanda Tomlin, Ann-Marie Shaw, Paul Gray, Chris Schüler, Helena Smith, Judith Bamber, Kieran Falconer, Orla Duane, Olivia Eccleshall, Ruth Blackmore, Sophie Martin, Jennifer Dempsey, Sue Jackson, Geoff Howard, Claire Saunders, Anna Sutton, Gavin Thomas Alexander Mark Rogers (UK); Andrew Rosenberg, Andrew Taber (US)
Production: Susanne Hillen, Andy Hilliard, Link Hall, Helen Ostick, James Morris, Julia Bovis, Michelle Draycott, Cathy Edwards

Cartography: Melissa Flack, Maxine Burke, Nichola Goodliffe
Picture research: Eleanor Hill, Louise Boulton
Online editors: Alan Spicer, Kate Hands (UK); Geronimo Madrid (US)
Finance: John Fisher, Celia Crowley, Neeta Mistry, Katy Miesiaczek
Marketing & Publicity: Richard Trillo, Simon Carloss, Niki Smith (UK); Jean-Marie Kelly, SoRelle Braun (US)
Administration: Tania Hummel

....

PUBLISHING INFORMATION

This first edition published February 1999 by Rough Guides Ltd, 62–70 Shorts Gardens, London WC2H 9AB.
Distributed by the Penguin Group:
Penguin Books Ltd, 27 Wrights Lane, London W8 5TZ.
Penguin Books USA Inc., 375 Hudson Street, New York, NY 10014, USA.
Penguin Books Australia Ltd, 487 Maroondah Highway, PO Box 257, Ringwood, Victoria 3134, Australia.
Penguin Books Canada Ltd, 10 Alcorn Avenue, Toronto, Ontario, Canada M4V 1E4.
Penguin Books (NZ) Ltd, 182–190 Wairau Road, Auckland 10, New Zealand.
Typeset in Linotron Univers and Century Old Style to an original design by Andrew Oliver.
Printed in England by Clays Ltd, St Ives plc.
Illustrations in Part One and Part Three by Edward Briant.

Illustrations on p.1 and p.749 by Henry Iles.
© The Rough Guides Ltd 1999
No part of this book may be reproduced in any form without permission from the publisher except for the quotation of brief passages in reviews.
816pp – Includes index.
A catalogue record for this book is available from the British Library.
ISBN 1-85828-335-3

....

Central America

THE ROUGH GUIDE

written and researched by
**Peter Eltringham, Jean McNeil,
James Read, Iain Stewart and
Dominique Young**

with additional research by
David Claughton

THE ROUGH GUIDES

THE ROUGH GUIDES

TRAVEL GUIDES • PHRASEBOOKS • MUSIC AND REFERENCE GUIDES

 We set out to do something different when the first Rough Guide was published in 1982. Mark Ellingham, just out of university, was travelling in Greece. He brought along the popular guides of the day, but found they were all lacking in some way. They were either strong on ruins and museums but went on for pages without mentioning a beach or taverna. Or they were so conscious of the need to save money that they lost sight of Greece's cultural and historical significance. Also, none of the books told him anything about Greece's contemporary life – its politics, its culture, its people, and how they lived.

So, with no job in prospect, Mark decided to write his own guidebook; one that aimed to provide practical information that was second to none, detailing the best beaches and the hottest clubs and restaurants, while also giving hard-hitting accounts of every sight, both famous and obscure, and providing up-to-the-minute information on contemporary culture. It was a guide that encouraged independent travellers to find the best of Greece, and was a great success, getting shortlisted for the Thomas Cook travel guide award,

and encouraging Mark, along with three friends, to expand the series.

The Rough Guide list grew rapidly and the letters flooded in, indicating a much broader readership than had been anticipated, but one which uniformly appreciated the Rough Guide mix of practical detail and humour, irreverence and enthusiasm. Things haven't changed. The same four friends who began the series are still the caretakers of the Rough Guide mission today: to provide the most reliable, up-to-date and entertaining information to independent-minded travellers of all ages, on all budgets.

We now publish more than a hundred titles and have offices in London and New York. The travel guides are written and researched by a dedicated team of more than a hundred authors, based in Britain, Europe, the USA and Australia. We have also created a unique series of phrasebooks to accompany the travel series, along with an acclaimed series of music guides, and a best-selling pocket guide to the Internet and World Wide Web. We also publish comprehensive travel information on our Web site:

www.roughguides.com

HELP US UPDATE

We've gone to a lot of effort to ensure that this edition of *The Rough Guide to Central America* is accurate and up-to-date. However, places get "discovered"; telephone numbers change; restaurants, hotels and other tourist facilities raise prices or lower standards. If you feel we've got it wrong or left something out, we'd like to know, and if you can remember the address, price, the time, the phone number, so much the better.

We'll credit all contributions, and send a copy of the next edition (or any other Rough Guide if you prefer) for the best letters.

Please mark letters: "Rough Guide Central America" and send to: Rough Guides Ltd, 62–70 Shorts Gardens, London WC2H 9AB, or Rough Guides, 375 Hudson St, 9th Floor, New York, NY 10014. Or send email to: mail@roughguides.co.uk Online updates about this book can be found on Rough Guides' Web site at www.roughguides.com

ACKNOWLEDGEMENTS

Editorial thanks go to Maxine, Nichola and Melissa for their dedicated work on the maps; Narrell Leffman and Melanie Cook for additional Basics research; Sophie for help with Guatemala; Cathy for diligent typesetting; Matthew Teller for proofreading; and to the authors for their hard work and enthusiasm.

Peter: Selecting just a few people to thank out of the hundreds who've provided absolutely invaluable support in Belize is not easy, but top of the list are Matt and Marga at Monkey Bay, and thanks too to Deborah for the long hours spent typing the entire first draft. Many thanks to Jean Shaw MBE in Belize City, Lori Reed in San Pedro, Doris and Terry Creasey in Caye Caulker, Martha and John August in San Ignacio, Derek and Debbie Jones in Dangriga, Wende Bryan in Placencia, and Charles Wright in Punta Gorda.

Jean: In Costa Rica I would like to thank Helena Chaverria and Mauricio Hernandez and their exceptionally helpful staff at Camino Travel. My thanks also go to the all-knowing Dieter Jungblut and Karola Tipperman for their hospitality in Tres Rios. San José would not be home without Flor Ugalde, Marta and Jorge at Casa Rigeway and the Centro de los Amigos para la Paz. In Nicaragua thanks to David Claughton, Tania Pesce and their daughter Francesca for being a home in Managua, and to David especially for his help in the research and writing of the chapter. At Rough Guides my thanks go to Sam Cook and Kate Berens for their careful editing and for their continual support.

James: Thanks to Aris Anibal Acosta, Ivy Vergara y Correa and José Thomas of IPAT, Gustavo Pinzón of INRENARE, Karl Burrows, Francisco Acosta, Alberto Vergara and Bibi for all their assistance and insights, and to Thomas Read for inspiration.

Iain: Thanks to the Utila crew at the Mango Inn and UDC, Tammy Ridenour and Maya Expeditions, Phillipa and the Rainbow staff, Geovanny Mendoza, all at the Iguana Perdida, Mike Shawcross, Tony Oswold, Oliver Morgan and CIAO, the Central America Report and Mark Whatmore.

Dominique: For Laurent, in loving memory, and with much love to Julienne and Geoffrey. Many thanks to everyone I met in El Salvador and Honduras, and who gave so much help along the way. In particular (in no particular order): Prof Angel Iraheta, José Cañas, Elsie Alvarenga, Sra Gloria Contreras, Juan José Torres, Maria Peña, Jörg Mauelshagen, Joaquín Muñoz, José Sigüenza, Carlos Tenorio and Olivier Rogard. And, of course, hats off to the patience and support of Sam Cook and Kate Berens.

THE AUTHORS

Peter Eltringham's first visit to Belize was when he volunteered to do a tour of duty in what was considered a "hardship posting" by the Royal Air Force. After returning briefly to the UK, he set off once again for Central America to co-write the first edition of the **Rough Guide to Guatemala and Belize**. Since then he has researched and co-authored Rough Guides to Mexico, Belize and the Maya World, spending several months each year in the region and contributing articles on Belize to a number of newspapers and magazines. This year he promises to return to Portsmouth University to finish his Latin American Studies degree.

After completing a degree in International Relations and Latin American Studies, **Jean McNeil** took the rash step of leaving her native Canada for London in 1991; she has been based there ever since, interspersed with long periods spent living and working in Mexico, Central America and Brazil. She has been a journalist and a book editor, and currently works for the environmental pressure group Friends of the Earth. Author of the *Rough Guide to Costa Rica*, she is also a novelist – her first novel, *Hunting Down Home*, was published in the UK and Canada in 1996 and is forthcoming in the US.

James Read first travelled to Latin America in 1991. Expecting to be there for three months, he stayed for three years, working on the reconstruction of pre-Columbian irrigation systems in the high Peruvian Andes. Since then, he has travelled widely in the region, writing sporadically. He currently works for the BBC World Service as a researcher and writer on Latin America.

After two years of travelling the world, **Iain Stewart** ended up in Guatemala and liked it so much that he stayed. Now co-author of Rough Guides to Guatemala and the Maya World, he takes every opportunity to return to this part of the world. Based in South London, he combines being a Rough Guide author with other work as a journalist and restaurant critic.

After a year spent in Japan and four years at university, **Dominique Young** got caught again by the travel bug and moved to Latin America to live and work for eighteen months. Now back in London and working as a researcher, she takes any and every opportunity to go back there and has contributed to Rough Guides to Guatemala, Belize and the Maya World.

HURRICANE MITCH

In late October 1998, as this book went to press, **Hurricane Mitch** hit Central America. Initially exciting little international media interest, in the days and weeks that followed it gradually became clear that a disaster of gigantic proportions was unfolding. A true figure for the numbers killed by the hurricane, or in the widespread floods that followed, will never be known. Conservative estimates suggest that nine thousand people died in the immediate aftermath of the storm, with about the same number remaining unaccounted for. Across the region around two million were left homeless, with millions more severely affected. It seemed to some to be the final blow for a region only just recovering from decades of civil war.

Worst hit were Honduras and Nicaragua. Floods of biblical proportions across **Honduras** destroyed three-quarters of the country's agricultural capacity and much of its civil infrastructure. At least seven thousand people died outright, with eleven thousand registered missing one week after the disaster struck. Major highways, bridges, in some cases whole villages, were simply washed away. Large sections of the capital, Tegucigalpa, were destroyed when the Río Choluteca burst its banks. In neighbouring **Nicaragua**, as many as four thousand people were killed in a mud slide around the Casitas volcano, in the northwest of the country, while destitute refugees from villages and hamlets across the region struggled to make contact with the outside world. The estimated costs of repairing the damage in these two countries, two of the poorest in Latin America, are at least US$4 billion, over one-third of their economic output. Elsewhere in Central America, damage in **El Salvador**, **Guatemala** and **Belize** was not as widespread, though affected areas suffered the same catastrophic destruction of roads, crops and villages.

The timescale for physical reconstruction is realistically likely to be decades rather than months or years. These economically impoverished republics simply do not have the money required to fund reconstruction programmes. How quickly rebuilding moves ahead is dependent on the levels, and form, of international aid; the lifting of the countries' international debt burden is seen by many as an important step. It is also impossible to gauge how long is needed for people who witnessed the death of their families, their homes being destroyed and livelihoods wiped out to begin to come to terms with what has happened.

In the UK, the **aid agencies** Christian Aid, Oxfam, Action Aid and twelve other charities formed a joint Disasters Emergency Committee in response to the crisis; the committee's work is focused as much on ongoing reconstruction as on emergency relief. In the US, the American Red Cross and CARE have been at the forefront of the aid campaign. Get in touch with one of the agencies if you have skills you wish to volunteer, or simply want information about projects being run in Honduras, Nicaragua and the other countries.

In terms of **this guide**, much of the information on Honduras and Nicaragua, particularly, is likely to be redundant. In neighbouring countries, in the areas most affected, reconstruction of the tourist infrastructure – like everything else – will take time. Travel through the region and across borders, previously relatively uncomplicated, will now be dependent upon the pace of reconstruction. It's therefore important to find out the latest information before making any travel plans. Either call the relevant embassies, listed in the guide, or if you have access to the Internet, check out the UK's Foreign and Commonwealth Office Web site at *www.fco.gov.uk* or the US State Department site at *travel.state.gov*. Updates will be posted on the Rough Guides Web site.

CONTENTS

Introduction xii

LIST OF MAPS

MAP SYMBOLS

Symbol	Description	Symbol	Description
══(CA 1)══	Carretera Interamericana	△	Campsite
══(CA 5)══	Other major highways and roads	⚲	Border crossing
──────	Minor highways and roads (paved)	◔	Cave
─ ─ ─ ─	Unpaved highways	⌣	Bridge
══════	Pedestrianised street (town maps)	⚲	Church (regional maps)
──────	Seasonal track	▓	Built up area
- - - - -	Footpath	⊞	Cemetery
══ ◇ ══	Railway	▓	Building
▬ ▬ ▬ ▬	National boundary	▣	Cathedral/church (town maps)
▬ ▬·· ▬	State boundary	♯	Castle
▬ ▬ ▬ ▬	Chapter division boundary	♦	Museum
─ ─ ─	Ferry route	⚘	Public gardens
──────	River	✈	International airport
▨	National park	✗	Domestic airport
▨	Biological Reserve	⚑	Lighthouse
▨	Park	◉	Hotel
⌃⌃⌃	Mountain range	▣	Restaurant
▲	Mountain peak	⊞	Hospital
⫰	Volcano	E	Embassy
ᐟᐟᐟᐟ	Escarpment	ⓟ	Fuel station
⸰⸰⸰⸰	Reef	★	Bus/taxi stop
⩢	Marshland	⊠	Post office
⫰	Waterfall	ⓘ	Information centre
⚲	Ruin	ⓒ	Public telephone

INTRODUCTION

C orrugated by mountains and studded by volcanoes, **Central America** reaches
from Mexico towards South America like a hooked, tentative finger. Its geography – seven piecemeal nations stacked on top of each other in a narrowing isthmus – is in many ways its destiny: a distinct region caught between two larger
realities. The archeological term used for the region is Mesoamerica (Middle
America), and for millennia it has been just that: the meeting point of the landmasses,
plants, animals and people of the giant continents to the north and the south.

This clash of tropical and temperate zones has created a startling, often surreal **landscape** in which dense, humid rainforests abound with the yelps of oropendola birds
and the chattering of monkeys; somewhere inside the forest's dark mesh, the antediluvian form of the tapir lumbers and the endangered jaguar steals quietly through cobalt
shadows. Carpeting the eastern halves of Honduras and Nicaragua are the impenetrable swamp-jungles of Mosquitia, whose curlicued lagoons harbour mirror-surfaced
mangroves where shellfish and manatees breed among the gnarled roots. Beaches,
coves, cayes and island archipelagos hem the coral-laced coasts, while volcanoes –
some active – form a chain of fire that stretches from Guatemala to Costa Rica.

Central America had, until recently, receded in the public consciousness, as the
"news" (read: war and revolution) spotlight moved elsewhere; now, however, it's experiencing something of a **tourism** renaissance. Ten or fifteen years ago, visitors to the
region largely consisted of the college backpacker contingent and groups on socialist-
minded "education" tours. Since the beginning of the 1990s, though, a wider variety of
people, some with little knowledge of or interest in the region's turbulent past, have
come here to experience its startling natural beauty on the back of another kind of revolution – this time in tourism.

Perhaps more than anywhere else in the world, Central America seems to have
been designed with the ecotourist in mind. **Costa Rica** draws nature-lovers by the
plane-load with its impressive system of National Parks, while English-speaking
Belize, for much of its history a forgotten fragment of the British Empire, has reinvented itself as a prime diving and snorkelling destination, thanks to its offshore
national treasury: the second-longest barrier reef in the world. The best place to experience the region's pre-Conquest culture is **Guatemala**, which has the strongest
indigenous traditions, not to mention a stunning landscape of velvet volcanoes and
amethyst lakes. **Panamá** and **Honduras** are just waking up to the potential – at least
in tourism terms – of their rainforests, rugged mountain cloudforests, mangroves and
beaches. Tourists still tend to avoid **Nicaragua** and **El Salvador** – a misguided
manoeuvre, as neither is more dangerous for visitors than its neighbours, and despite
considerable poverty, the people are welcoming and the basic tourist infrastructure
good; plus, they too have the volcanoes, beaches and rainforests that draw travellers
to their more popular neighbours.

Amidst all the hype about the region's natural beauty, it's easy to forget that this
rugged, humid part of the world was home (along with Mexico and Peru) to the most
sophisticated pre-Columbian cultures of the Americas. The splendid **Maya** civilization,
with its diaphanous pyramids and neurotic pursuit of time-keeping, flourished in
Guatemala and to a lesser extent in modern-day Belize, Honduras and El Salvador
between the years of 300 and 900 AD (although the Maya have been in existence for
over 4000 years). During this time, termed the Classic period, the region was made up
of independent, and often mutually antagonistic city-states – Tikal in Guatemala,
Copán in Honduras and El Salvador's San Andrés being three of the more prominent

– which fought each other for prestige and economic dominance. As their civilization declined, the Maya became increasingly interested in blood-letting and the ritualizing of pain and death, while paradoxically setting their greatest minds the task of predicting the future through one of the most precise understandings of time in history. You can see shadows of their huge achievements in science and the arts by visiting the ruined cities and viewing their displays on calendrics, ceramics and the Maya's wildly illustrative glyphic scripts.

In sharp contrast to the Maya, further south in lower Costa Rica and Panamá, peoples from the **Chibcha** group dominated. Thought to have come originally from Colombia, the Chibcha were largely agrarian, without the talent for urban planning or numerology obsession of the Maya, and have left little or nothing behind in the way of monuments or artefacts.

Central America was "discovered" by the Spanish on **Christopher Columbus**'s fourth and last voyage to the Americas in 1502–4. Columbus himself barely set foot in Central America, preferring to anchor offshore and write florid letters back home to his sovereign, packed with references to maidens and gold (of which the Spaniards unhappily discovered there was little). Nearly ten years later, an incredible sight met the eyes of **Vasco Nuñez de Balboa**, the first real conquistador of the region, who in 1513 slashed and clambered his way over the scaly mountain spine of Panamá to become the first European to set eyes on the American side of the Pacific Ocean.

Within a few years of Balboa's thrilling sight, the Spanish had established Panamá City, in 1519; León, Nicaragua, followed in 1524; and in 1527, in Guatemala, they built their most important capital, the future colonial seat of the Empire, from which the region was administered. Still, Central America remained a backwater of the Spanish Empire in the New World: gold-poor, stuffed with venomous serpents, impenetrable jungles and often hostile natives. In human terms, the ensuing **colonial period** was characterized by waves of yeoman farmers emigrating from Spain, followed by waves of deaths of indigenous people from diseases to which they had no immunity. Slave labour was taken from Costa Rica and Nicaragua to work the mineral mines in Peru; in Guatemala the conquerors, led by the handsome blond adventurer with a taste for massacre, Pedro de Alvarado, set about a systematic, if drawn-out, destruction of the Maya peoples, who have, against all the odds, maintained their culture to this day, albeit in much reduced numbers.

In the early 1800s, nearly 300 years after Spain's first incursions in the isthmus, the region was caught up in a fervour of **independence**; in part this was fuelled by the growing anger of the *criollos* (Spanish people born in the New World), who were thwarted from advancement and political office by Spain's snobbish insistence on promoting only those born on Spanish soil and their descendants. By 1823 the collective drive towards autonomy was strong enough for the Central American states all to declare themselves independent, forming a loose federation amongst themselves (with the exception of Panamá, by then part of Colombia). In many of the countries, separate but eerily similar internal conflicts erupted between the self-styled educated, Europhile Liberals (demanding egalitarianism and "democracy") and the moneyed, land-owning Conservatives. With a few refinements to encompass the middle classes, the neo-liberals and the newly rich, this rift between the right and the left, still intact today, remains the most divisive, destructive and dynamic presence in Central American **politics**.

When it comes to relations between the countries, Central America is rather like a family where there's little love lost, but they recognize that sticking together is their best chance for economic survival. Amongst themselves, the nations have oscillated between surprising regional solidarity to outright war, sometimes in the form of incomprehensible and arbitrary conflicts, such as El Salvador and Honduras's infamous "Football War" of 1969, a five-day border war ostensibly sparked by a soccer match. National **stereotypes** are bandied back and forth with relish (Costa Ricans think Nicaraguans are intrinsically

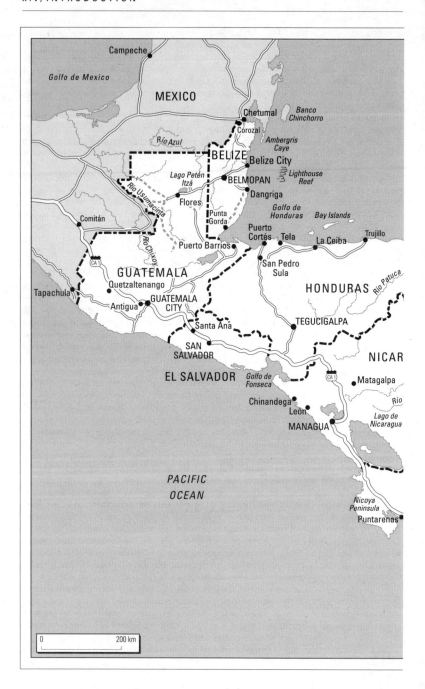

Campeche

Golfo de Mexico

MEXICO

Chetumal
Banco Chinchorro

Corozal

Río Azul
Ambergris Caye

BELIZE Belize City

Lago Petén Itzá
BELMOPAN
~ *Lighthouse Reef*

Flores
Dangriga

Río Usumacinta
Punta Gorda
Golfo de Honduras *Bay Islands*

Comitán
Puerto Cortés
Tela
La Ceiba
Trujillo

Río Chixoy
Puerto Barrios

CA 1
San Pedro Sula

GUATEMALA
Río Patuca

Quetzaltenango
HONDURAS

Tapachula
Antigua
GUATEMALA CITY

Santa Ana
TEGUCIGALPA

SAN SALVADOR
NICAR

EL SALVADOR
Golfo de Fonseca
CA 1
Matagalpa

Chinandega
Río

León
Lago de Nicaragua

MANAGUA

PACIFIC OCEAN

Nicoya Peninsula

Puntarenas

0   200 km

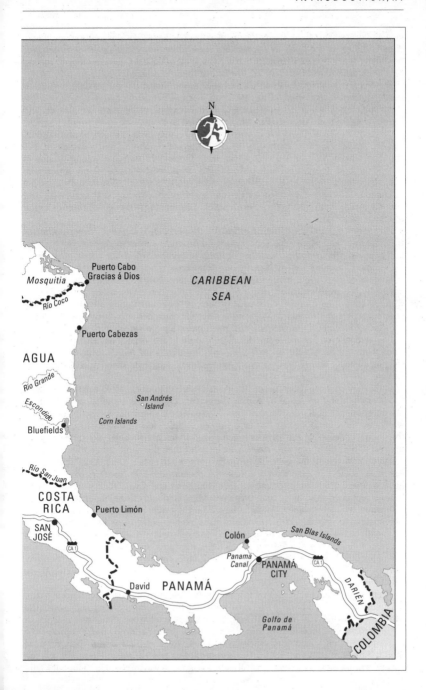

violent, Nicaraguans think Costa Ricans placid opportunists, virtually everybody thinks Hondurans wrote the book on corruption) even while the region's politicians describe neighbour nations as *hermanos* (brothers) and seek to build a Central American trading bloc to neutralize the effect NAFTA has had on their economies.

However, it was internal conflicts and relations with the US, rather than any cross-border tensions, that sparked the ravaging **wars** of the 1970s and 80s, a time when Central America was seen as a place of brutal conflict where nuns were raped and priests slaughtered. Nicaragua notably succeeded in its attempt to shake off its dictator, Anastasio Somoza, and the cynical, corrupt regime he had spawned around him, with its galvanizing – if ultimately failed – internal revolution and subsequent US-sponsored Civil War (1981–1990). El Salvador, too had its own devastating version of war throughout the 1980s. Now peace reigns, or at least a certain kind of peace-in-name-between-governments. Less conspicuous conflicts persist, however, for example in Guatemala, where the state's long-running campaign of repression against its own (mostly indigenous) inhabitants shows signs of continuing, despite the recent signing of official peace accords.

Nowadays, generally speaking, Central America is keen to shake off its reputation for machine guns and earthquakes. Most Central Americans want to forget about the past and look towards the future, and they're likely to succeed: these are young countries – for example, around half of Nicaragua's population is under thirty, and 26-year-old politicians or 20-year-old mothers of three are commonplace. Travellers are often surprised by the **multicultural** nature of Central American cities: there are families of Chinese restaurateurs (who have usually been in the country for generations), Syrian shopkeepers, and Brazilian hotel-owners; Catholic churches sit side-by-side with their tin shack Evangelical equivalents, and most cities have a synagogue; and you'll also notice evidence of European immigration, if only in the occasional blond, blue-eyed Central American. Equally apparent, though, are traditional *ladino* values – of family, religion (usually Catholic), hard work, shrewdness, suspicion when necessary, and a sardonic, even biting, sense of humour.

In these years of so-called peace, the region has had to work out its relationship with the overwhelming presence of **North American culture**. Whether it be four-wheel drives, shopping malls, fast-food outlets or credit-card spending, American culture is wholeheartedly embraced by the urban upper middle classes, and trickles down into the poorer echelons in the form of much-prized baseball hats and Nike trainers; as in the rest of the world, any *ropa americana* is better than the homespun equivalent. This relatively new yen for the good life through T-shirts and cars is one reason why Central American society is described – at least by economists – as **"modernizing"**. Times have changed from when countries like Honduras and Costa Rica were bona fide banana republics, little more than hosts providing land and cheap labour for the huge, US-owned fruit companies. Manufacturing and service industries are increasingly **investing** in the region: communications giant Intel recently opened a factory in Costa Rica, with other new arrivals belonging to the biodiversity, resource management and pharmaceutical industries. Piecework factories churning out women's clothing or face cloths for the US market, called *maquiladoras*, still provide many people – particularly women – with employment, but there's a feeling that NAFTA is already forcing these countries to diversify.

There's not much evidence that this new-found investment is trickling down into the pockets of the poorest Central Americans: income differentials here are still among the widest in the world, and much of the population lives in **poverty**, sometimes abjectly so – you don't need to look further than the faces of begging children on street corners or at border crossings, asking to relieve you of your extra *menudo* (small change), or at the high rates of common crimes like pickpocketing and burglary. These are still the sort of **crimes** most travellers, as well as locals, have to worry about, although it's true that violent crimes against tourists are becoming more common. Certain cities, like Managua and Panamá City, have always had bad reputations: where dangers are real – mostly in cities – they are well-publicized, and locals will often volunteer warnings and advice. Travelling in Central America is hardly risk-free, and visitors should read up on the various dangers before arriving.

Wherever you go, it's easy to get around. **Travel networks** in the region are well-developed, with reliable air and road transport systems. Flying from Guatemala City to San José or Panamá City can save you a lot of time, as what looks like a short hop on the map is often a lengthy road journey thanks to the (often bad) state of the highways and the effects of weather. In the riverine waterways of Mosquitia, boats are the only way to get around, along with light planes – if you can stump up the cash. Most of the time, though, you'll be going by **bus** – cheap, frequent and cheerful, and the quintessential Central American experience, where you'll find yourself seated among knitting grand-mothers, travelling evangelists, gum-popping teenagers and perhaps the odd chicken. The other inescapable Central American reality is **bureaucracy** (in Spanish, *trámites*), which in Central America has taken on the character of a grotesque social art: witness the unhappy queues of locals trying to get drivers' licences or any other kind of permit. For travellers, crossing borders will illustrate the eccentricity of the local interpretation of paperwork – lots of it, and each piece will cost you a couple of dollars.

What to see

The archetypal image of Central America is of the grey-white pyramids of the ruined Maya city of **Tikal**, rising smokily above the rainforest canopy. Almost everyone who comes to Central America makes tracks for these haunting, rainforest ruins: Tikal is the best known, but there are other popular sites at Copán in Honduras, San Andrés in El Salvador and Lamanai in Belize. Even if you don't visit the ruins, everywhere in the isth-mus you can appreciate the **craftsmanship** of the Maya peoples, in their technicolour textiles (which are not just decorative but a visually encoded social history), exquisite wood carvings and jewellery made from local or imported jade, turquoise and silver.

Life on the **Caribbean coast** of Central America is a sharp shock for those who are used to the formal, rather staid code of good manners and appearance that are so dear to the highland *ladino* culture. The atmosphere in these slightly rancid coastal towns – Livingston, Bluefields, Limón and Colón, to name a few – can be raffish; certainly the machete-feuds and drug-running are real. On the Caribbean coast it's Marley, not marimba, you'll hear; English, cricket and herbal teas make an appearance, too. Immigration from Jamaica and Barbados to work on banana plantations and railroads in the late nineteenth and early twentieth century transformed this coast into an anthro-pological Galapagos, more Caribbean than Latin American, dominated by West Indian accents, subsistence agriculture, and a quaint allegiance to the Queen (even if they don't always know which Queen is in at the moment).

Overall, though, it is the natural rather than cultural attractions of the isthmus that entice travellers, especially as ecotourism becomes ever more popular. In Central America, the term can encompass the more traditional pleasures of palm-draped Caribbean **beaches**, or diving and snorkelling off the coral atolls of Belize, lolling with the tourists on picture-perfect beaches of Costa Rica's Pacific coast, or exploring the sand-fringed islands of Panamá's San Blas archipelago.

For wildlife enthusiasts, Guatemala's Biotopo del Quetzal and the Monteverde Reserve in Costa Rica, high in the misted **cloudforests** of the Cordillera Central, will be high on the itinerary. In the pristine forests of Nicaragua's Matagalpa region, the shimmering quetzal, the sacred bird of the Maya, is still abundant; while in Costa Rica's Tortuguero region you can take steamy boat-journeys through mirror-still canals, and watch sea turtles nest by night. Commentators struggle to represent this staggering **biodiversity** in spiralling numbers: 3000 species of moth in Costa Rica's Guanacaste province alone, 850 species of bird (more than in the whole of North America) and literally millions of plants, some as yet uncatalogued.

For most travellers the **cities** of Central America are not much of a draw in themselves, with their pothole-scarred, traffic-choked streets, cheap skyscraper architecture and gutters full of soapy water and rotting fruits. Yet in each of them, if you can get beyond the initial ugliness – on sunny days even Panamá City and San José can look enticing – you'll find a vibrant, if hectic, urban life with enough cafés, bars, galleries and museums to keep you busy for at least a few days. True city-lovers will want to indulge in spates of salsa dancing, join ice-cream-eating teenagers lolling on the benches of the local park, or improve their Spanish by watching the latest subtitled blockbuster American movie in a theatre filled with sighing matrons and buzzing boys.

When to go

Although located firmly within the tropics, altitude, rather than latitude, governs **climate** in Central America. Between sea level and 3000m the temperature can vary by as much as twenty degrees. The year is divided into just two seasons: a **"rainy season"**, which lasts roughly from May to October and is often called "winter" (*invierno*), and a **"dry season"** – or "summer" (*verano*) – from November to April, although the distinction between the two varies wildly, even within small areas. In the highlands of Guatemala or Costa Rica, rainy-season downpours (*aguaceros*) are common in September and October, the mountains helping to condense the clouds into dense water-filled balloons that don't rain so much as plummet their cargo all at once. Meanwhile, on the Caribbean coastline, you'll find it's mostly wet year-round and almost supernaturally humid.

Where there is a rainy season, don't assume it will rain all the time; a common pattern is a fine, sunny dry morning until about noon or 1pm, then a clouding over and an afternoon downpour that sometimes extends into evening showers. It's true that **travelling** in the rainy season can be a little more problematic, due to washed-out roads and swollen creeks on some of the more backroads routes. But more than likely, it just means feeling uncomfortably damp, having your shoes go a little mouldy, and travelling with good-quality rain gear. The advantages to coming to Central America in the rainy season are many: lower accommodation prices (especially in heavily touristed areas like Costa Rica), fewer tourists, and the relief of a cooling shower or two.

Yearly average **temperatures** in the region change little, with daytime temperatures in the lowlands the hottest, averaging anywhere from 28 to 32°C. The coastal areas or the low inland plains are where you will feel the heat most uncomfortably. The mountains the weather can be cooler, fresh, and surprisingly like a fine late spring day in the temperate zone, with temperatures more like 22 to 25°C. For more specific climate details, see the individual country introductions.

AVERAGE TEMPERATURES AND MONTHLY RAINFALL

	Jan	Feb	Mar	Apr	May	Jun	Jul	Aug	Sept	Oct	Nov	Dec
Belize (Belize City)												
Max °C	27	28	29	30	31	31	31	31	31	30	28	27
Min °C	19	21	22	23	24	24	24	24	23	22	20	20
Rainfall (mm)	137	61	38	56	109	196	163	170	244	305	226	185
Guatemala (Guatemala City)												
Max °C	23	25	27	28	29	27	26	26	26	24	23	22
Min °C	12	12	14	14	16	16	16	16	16	16	14	13
Rainfall (mm)	8	3	13	31	152	274	203	198	231	173	23	8
El Salvador (San Salvador)												
Max °C	32	33	34	34	33	31	32	32	31	31	31	32
Min °C	16	16	17	18	19	19	18	19	19	18	17	16
Rainfall (mm)	8	5	10	43	196	328	292	297	307	241	41	10
Honduras (Tegucigalpa)												
Max °C	25	27	29	30	30	28	27	28	28	27	26	25
Min °C	14	14	15	17	18	18	18	17	17	17	16	15
Rainfall (mm)	12	2	1	26	180	177	70	74	151	87	38	14
Nicaragua (Managua)												
Max °C	31	32	34	34	34	31	31	31	31	31	31	31
Min °C	20	21	22	23	23	23	22	22	22	22	21	20
Rainfall (mm)	5	1	5	5	76	296	134	130	182	243	59	5
Costa Rica (San José)												
Max °C	24	24	26	26	27	26	25	26	26	25	25	24
Min °C	14	14	15	17	17	17	17	16	16	16	16	14
Rainfall (mm)	15	5	20	46	229	241	211	241	305	300	145	41
Panamá (Panamá City)												
Max °C	32	33	33	34	31	30	31	31	30	30	30	31
Min °C	23	23	24	24	24	23	23	23	23	22	22	23
Rainfall (mm)	30	10	20	55	200	210	205	200	205	245	250	120

PART ONE

THE

BASICS

GETTING THERE FROM NORTH AMERICA

Getting to Central America from the USA and Canada is simplest and usually cheapest by air. The main US and Central American airlines have daily flights to all the Central American capitals from US gateways. The great variety of possible destinations, routes and prices makes any comprehensive listing virtually impossible, but most non-stop flights leave from Miami, Houston, LA, Atlanta and New Orleans; airlines serving these hubs have excellent connections throughout the USA and Canada (where gateways are Toronto, Montreal and Vancouver). In addition, several Mexican airlines fly direct from more than twenty cities in the USA and Canada to Mexico, with onward connections to Central America; it's particularly easy and cheap to fly to Cancún and continue from there.

You can also travel **overland** inexpensively by bus through Mexico, and often in considerable comfort, though this can take between two and four days. From Tapachula and Chetumal, in southern Mexico, buses from Guatemala and Belize respectively (some luxury services) take you safely across the border.

SHOPPING FOR AIR TICKETS

In general, the **price** you pay for a ticket to any of the Central American countries depends more on how and when you book your flight and how long you plan to stay than on a particular season. However, prices to most destinations do go up in the **high seasons** of July and August (due mainly to the cost of flights within the US; ironically, this is the rainy season in much of Central America), and Easter and Christmas, when seat availability can become a problem: it certainly pays to book ahead.

The cheapest of the airlines' published **fares** is usually an Apex ticket, generally for a maximum stay of three months, which needs to be booked and paid for at least 14 days before departure. Being a student or under 26 can also help, though you may be subject to eccentric booking conditions.

You can cut costs further by going through a **specialist flight agent** – either a consolidator, who buys up blocks of tickets from the airlines and sells them at a discount, or a discount agent, who in addition to dealing with discounted flights may also offer special student and youth fares and a range of other travel-related services. Bear in mind, though, that penalties for changing your plans can be stiff. Remember too that these companies make their money by dealing in bulk – don't expect them to answer lots of questions. Some agents specialize in **charter flights**, which may be cheaper than scheduled flights, but again departure dates are fixed and withdrawal penalties are high (check the refund policy). **Open-jaw tickets**, where you fly into one city and out of another, are readily available, and, depending on which airline you use, often cost little more than a return to one city, particularly if combined with an airpass (for more on which, see p.29).

The companies listed on p.5 are a good place to begin your search and if you've got access to the Internet then the **eXito website** (see p.5) is the best place to start.

ROUTES AND FARES

Though correct at the time of going to press, the following **fares**, quoted by the airlines, should be taken as an indication only – at peak times they may well be higher, while if you hunt around, the specialist agents will almost certainly offer better deals.

Flying to **Belize**, **American**'s non-stop flight from Miami costs $450 year-round. Though American could connect you to Miami from any major American city, to give you an idea, fares from NY and Chicago are $600, around $50 more

AIRLINES IN NORTH AMERICA

In addition to the destinations listed below most airlines also have frequent departures for Mexico City, Cancún and other cities in **Mexico**. The routes detailed below are all **non-stop**; for fares, and information on direct routes and possible connections, see "Routes and Fares" below. And for details of **air passes**, see p.29.

Aeroméxico (☎1-800/237-6639). Direct flights from many US gateways to Mexico City. Tickets can be linked to the Mex-AmeriPass for connections throughout Mexico, on Mexicana Airlines to Guatemala, San José and Panamá, and on Aeroperu to destinations in South America.

American (☎1-800/433-7300). Daily non-stops from Miami (and some from Dallas/Ft Worth) to all Central American capitals. Non-stop from Toronto to Miami and Vancouver to Dallas for connections.

Aviateca (☎1-800/327-9832). Non-stop flights to Guatemala from Houston, Miami and LA.

Canada 3000 (☎416/674-2661). Inexpensive charter flights (Nov–April) from Toronto to Belize and San José.

Continental (☎1-800/231-0856). Daily non-stops from Houston (and some from Newark) to all Central American capitals, and to San Pedro Sula, Honduras. Route-sharing with Air Canada means good connections from Canada.

Copa (☎1-800/359-2672). Daily non-stop flights from Miami to Panamá City, with connections to other capitals. Tickets can be used in conjunction with the Visit Central America Airpass.

Delta (☎1-800/241-4141). Non-stop daily flights from Atlanta to San Salvador, Guatemala City, San José and Panamá.

Iberia (☎1-800/772-4642). Daily non-stop flights from Miami to all Central American capitals except Belize.

Lacsa (☎1-800/225-2272). Non-stop flights to Costa Rica from Miami, Dallas and Havana.

Mexicana (☎1-800/531-7921). Frequent flights from Chicago, Denver, LA, New York, San Francisco, Montreal and Toronto to México City, with connections to Guatemala, San José and Panamá. Tickets can be linked to the "Mex-AmeriPass" and flights on subsidiary airline Aerocaribe from airports in Yucatán to Flores, Guatemala and Belize City.

Nica (☎1-800/831-6422). Non-stop to Nicaragua from Miami, with connections to other capitals.

Taca (☎1-800/535-8780). Information and reservations for four of the national airlines of Central America: Aviateca (Guatemala), Lacsa (Costa Rica), Nica (Nicaragua) and Taca (El Salvador). Regular non-stop flights from Houston, Miami and New York to all the Central American capitals and frequent service from Chicago, New Orleans, LA and San Francisco to the capitals and many other cities; many via San Salvador gateway. Tickets can be linked to the "Visit Central America Airpass".

United (☎1-800/531-7921). Daily non-stop flights from Chicago, Washington and LA to Guatemala, San Salvador and San José.

from LA. **Taca** has three non-stop flights to Belize, all of which leave four times a week: from Houston they cost $480; from Miami $500; and from New Orleans $455. **Continental**'s non-stop flight from Houston costs $500.

To **Costa Rica**, national airline **Lacsa** offers the best fare from Miami non-stop to San José at $372. They also fly from Dallas at $469. **American**'s non-stop flight from Dallas is a little higher at $525. **Continental**'s flight from Houston ranges from $322 to $599, while **Delta** non-stop from Atlanta is $585.

American's non-stop from Miami to San Salvador is the cheapest fare to **El Salvador**, at $535. **Taca**'s non-stop flight from LA costs $660, while **Continental**'s non-stop from Houston costs

$620 and **Delta**'s non-stop from Atlanta costs $625. **United**'s non-stop from LA costs anywhere between $396 and $610.

To **Guatemala City**, **Iberia** has the best non-stop from Miami at $392, but **American** and **Aviateca** are not far behind at $500. Aviateca's fare from Houston is especially good, at $245. From LA, Aviateca's fare is $620, as is **Taca**'s, which costs the same as from San Francisco. **United**'s is slightly higher at $670 – the same as from Chicago. Taca's direct flight from Washington DC is $700, with a stop in San Salvador. **Delta** non-stop from Atlanta costs $535.

American or **Taca** do the best deals to **Honduras**, flying non-stop from Miami to San Pedro Sula or Tegucigalpa for $539. **Iberia** non-stop from Miami costs around $20 more. Taca also has direct flights from NY, which leave four times a week, and stop in Cancún; the fare is $700. **Continental** flies non-stop from Houston to Tegucigalpa or San Pedro Sula for around $563.

To **Nicaragua**, **Nica**'s non-stop flight to Managua from Miami ranges from $250 to $600. They also fly direct from NY, Washington, New Orleans, Houston, Dallas, LA and San Francisco, stopping in either San Salvador or San José. **American**'s and **Iberia**'s non-stop flight from Miami costs $535, while **Continental**'s non-stop to Managua is from Houston at $596.

Iberia's non-stop flight from Miami to **Panamá City** costs $385–510; **Copa**'s around $430. **American**'s fare for the same route costs $480; they also fly from Dallas ($650). **Continental** flies non-stop from NY for around $580, and **Delta** from Atlanta for $550.

FROM CANADA

There are no non-stop flights **from Canada** to Central America. Your best bet is to fly to Miami or Houston on either **American** or **Continental** and change there. Non-stop flights from Toronto to Miami with American go as low as CAN$236, while Continental can fly you from Vancouver to Houston for CAN$538. Continuing on to Miami from there costs CAN$604. Toronto to Miami on Continental, stopping in Cleveland, costs CAN$540. There are also **charter flights** with Canada 3000.

PACKAGES AND ORGANIZED TOURS

The range of **package tours** available to Central America increases every year. Specialist companies organize ecsorted group trips to Maya ruins,

colonial towns, markets and beaches (some trips include a visit to Mexico's Yucatán peninsula), with options of biking, diving, birdwatching and the like. If time is short these can be very good value, especially for first-time visitors to the region, and the tour companies often have special arrangements with airlines for seat prices. Though in many cases you could organize the same or very similar itineraries yourself for less, some knowledge of Spanish would certainly help and you'd probably need longer to do the trip. But expeditions to remote jungle ruins and rivers, and sea-kayaking trips are more difficult (or even impossible) to organize on your own, and these are best done in a group, where you get expert leaders and emergency back-up.

Budget groups usually travel by van, stay at comfortable, family-run hotels and call at the main tourist attractions as well as some lesser-known places. More **expensive tours** can take you rafting or sea-kayaking, caving or on expeditions with archeologists and scientists to remote sites and nature reserves.

ROUTES THROUGH MEXICO

It's a long haul **overland** to Central America from the US; however, if you want to see something of Mexico on the way, it might be worth considering. There are numerous possible routes (the quickest way is always through Mexico City), combining bus and train travel or taking an internal flight. For those needing a **visa** to visit Central America there are Guatemalan consulates in Tapachula and Comitán and a Belize consulate in Chetumal; for more on entry requirements see p.16. The possible routes and

SPECIALIST TOUR OPERATORS IN THE USA

Backroads, 1516 5th St, Berkeley, CA 94710-1740 (☎1-800/462-2848). Walking, biking, hiking and snorkelling vacations in Belize and Costa Rica. Eight-day trip to Costa Rica costs $2398 excluding air fare.

Bahia Tours, 105 S Federal Hwy, Dania, FL 33004 (☎1-800/443-0717). Diving specialists. Horseback riding, diving and canoeing trips in the Honduras Bay Islands, and adventure tours (including birdwatching, canoeing and hiking) in Panamá. Seven-day trips start at $825 excluding air fare.

Eco-Adventures Special Interest Tours and Travel, 960 N San Antonio Rd, Suite 201, Los Altos, CA 94022 (☎1-800/227-3026). Nature and wildlife tours in Costa Rica, Belize and Guatemala, with rafting, camping and birdwatching. From one to three weeks.

Elderhostel, 75 Federal St, Boston, MA 02110 (☎617/426-8056). Twelve-day natural study trips and 2-week educational trips studying environment and history in Costa Rica. Also Maya-related tours in Honduras, Guatemala and Belize. Must be over 55 (companions may be younger).

Far Horizons, PO Box 91900, Albuquerque, NM 87199-1900 (☎1-800/552-4575; *journey@ farhorizon.com; www.farhorizon.com*). Superb yearly archeological trips to remote Maya sites in Guatemala, Belize and Honduras, led by the archeologists directing the projects or renowned experts in the field. Around $3200 for a 9-day expedition to Belize, including air fare. Highly recommended.

Green Tortoise Adventure Travel, 494 Broadway, San Francisco, CA 94133 (☎1-800/867-8647 or 415/956-7500; *info@ greentortoise.com; www.greentortoise.com*). Tours from November through April on converted buses with sleeping space which explore "cool places off the beaten path". The "Southern Migration" is a very popular 23-day journey from San Francisco to Antigua, Guatemala. Leaves Dec; $900 including food.

Guatemala Unlimited, PO Box 786, Berkeley, CA 94701 (☎1-800/733-3350, fax 415/661-5364; *Guatemala@aol.com*). As the name suggests, an extensive array of set or custom arranged tours of obscure and better known Maya ruins as well as jungle trekking, river-rafting, mountain biking and volcano tours.

Imagine Travel Alternatives, PO Box 13219, Burton, WA 98103 (☎1-800/777-3975). Arrangements for independent travellers; escorted small-group tours in Belize and Costa Rica.

International Expeditions Inc, 1 Environs Park, Helena, AL 35080 (☎1-800/633-4734). Top-notch group or independent all-inclusive tours in Costa Rica, Belize and Honduras. "Natural Quest" 11-day tour of Belize includes guided natural walks, horseback riding, canoeing and snorkelling ($2598 including air fare from Miami). "Maya heartland" tour concentrates on archeological ruins in all three countries.

Journeys, 4011 Jackson Rd, Ann Arbor, MI 48103-1825 (☎1-800/255-8735 or 734/665-4407, fax 665-2945; *info@journeys-intl.com; www. journeys-intl.com*). Superb nature- and culture-oriented tours to Belize, Guatemala, Costa Rica and Panamá; some for women only. Around $1600 for a week in Costa Rica; $1500 for Guatemala. Highly recommended.

Nature Expeditions International, 474 Willamette St, PO Box 11496, Eugene, OR 97440 (☎1-800/869-0639). Excellent, varied small-group adventure expeditions led by anthropology, biology and natural history specialists in Belize, Honduras, Costa Rica and Belize. Fifteen-day Costa Rica wildlife expedition costs $2590 excluding air fare.

Questers Worldwide Nature Tours, 257 Park Ave South, New York, NY 10010 (☎1-800/468-8668). Upmarket nature tours emphasizing birds and cultural history in Costa Rica and Belize.

REI Adventures, PO Box 1938, Sumner, WA 98390-0800 (☎1-800/622-2236). Excellent small group adventure tours including 9-day camping trips to Costa Rica and Belize with snorkelling, kayaking, whitewater rafting; also stays in jungle camps and ruin exploration ($1950 excluding air fare). Eight-day trips to Honduras explore the undeveloped coast and islands with an emphasis on outdoor activities ($1750 excluding air fare).

Slickrock Adventures, PO Box 1400, Moab, UT 84532 (☎1-800/390-5715, fax 801/259-6996; *slickrock@slickrock.com*). One of the very best companies, offering sea kayaking, jungle and river (some whitewater) expeditions in Belize, Guatemala and Honduras: $1800 for 9-day adventure "week" in Belize.

South American Fiesta, 3774 Swallow Way, Marietta, GA 30066 (☎1-800/793-5841). Trips to Belize, Costa Rica, Panamá and Honduras. Eight-day tours explore inland areas, ruins, mountains and forests and include watersports such as diving in the islands off Honduras ($779 excluding air fare) and Panamá ($859 excluding air fare). Belize tours also include inland ruins and diving in the keys.

Toucan Adventure Tours, PO Box 1073, Cambria, CA 93428 (☎805/927-5885, fax 927-0929; *www.toucanadventures.com*). Inexpensive camping tours through northern Central America. Three-week "Ruta Maya" trip through Guatemala, Honduras and Belize emphasizing ruins and rainforest ($1245 excluding air fare), and 21-day camping trips to Belize and Guatemala which explore the keys, ruins and rainforests in rougher style ($1960 excluding air fare).

Travel Loves Company, 430 1st Ave North, Suite 216, Minneapolis, MN 55401 (☎612/824-4313). Group tours and individual itineraries to any Central American country. Emphasis is on "a people to people angle". Tours can be escorted by one of six female experts.

Tread Lightly Limited, PO Box 329, 37 Juniper Meadow Rd, Washington Depot, CT 06794 (☎1-800/643-0060 or 860/868-1710, fax 868-1718; *info@treadlightly.com*; *www.treadlightly.com*). Wide selection of top-notch "low impact" natural history and cultural trips to Belize, Guatemala, Honduras, Costa Rica and Panamá. Tours to Guatemala emphasize natural history and culture as well as kayaking, rafting and hiking. In Belize and Honduras there are inland natural/cultural tours and watersports in their bays/islands (6-day Honduras trip is $895 excluding air fare). Nature and wildlife tours in Costa Rica start at $1298, while birdwatching in Panamá starts at $900; all excluding air fare.

Tropical Travel, 5 Grogans Park, Suite 102, Woodlands, TX 77380-2190 (☎1-800/451-8017 or 713/688-1985). Tailor-made trips to Belize, Costa Rica, Guatemala and Honduras, taking in ruins and rainforests. Diving packages available also.

White Magic Unlimited, PO Box 5506, Mill Valley, CA 94942 (☎1-800/869-9874 or 415/381-8889). Top of the line trips to Guatemala (whitewater rafting and Maya sites), Belize (the reef), Panamá (whitewater rafting) and Costa Rica.

SPECIALIST TOUR OPERATORS IN CANADA

Adventures Abroad, 1037 W Broadway, Suite 202, Vancouver, BC, V6H 1E3 (☎1-800/321-2121). Excellent small-group tours, which focus on archeology, culture, nature and relaxation, to all the countries except Panamá. Tours last 1–4 weeks. An 18-day Belize/Tikal tour is CAN$2251 excluding air fare.

Eco-Summer Expeditions, 1516 Duranleau St, Vancouver, BC, V6H 3S4 (☎1-800/465-8884 or 604/669-7741, fax 465-3244; *trips@ecosummer.com*; *www.ecosummer.com*). Wildlife tours, whale-watching and sea-kayaking in Mexico and Belize; around US$1300 a week. Highly recommended.

Fun Sun Adventures, 10316-124 St, #201, Edmonton, AB, T5N 1R2 (☎403/482-2030). Hotel-based holidays, mainly in Costa Rica and Belize, but also tours to Guatemala and Panamá. Around CAN$1100–1600 for 2 weeks. Highly recommended.

Gap Adventures, 266 Dupont St, Toronto, ON, M5R 1V7 (☎1-800/465-5600 or 416/922-8899, fax 922-0822; *adventure@gap.org*; *www.gap.ca*). Good group trips (some camping) with diving and kayaking in Guatemala, Belize,

Honduras, Nicaragua and Costa Rica. Individual trips are also available to Panamá and El Salvador. Around CAN$1700 (excluding air fare) for a 29-day journey from Cancún to San José, taking in the main archeological sites. "Hummingbird Highway" (CAN$1595) and "Kayak Belize" (CAN$1195) focus on birdwatching, canoeing, exploring jungles and ruins, and island-hopping. All trips can be mixed and matched – more trekking, for example – and proceed via public bus and private van. Highly recommended.

Pacific Sun Spots Tours, 201–196 W Third Ave, Vancouver, BC, V5Y 1E9 (☎1-800/663-0755 or 604/606-1750; *res@pacsun.com*). Hotel-based holidays focusing on Costa Rica and Belize, but also some hotels in Guatemala, Honduras and Panamá. CAN$520–1000 for a week in Belize; CAN$440–660 in Costa Rica (excluding air fare).

Quest Nature Tours, 36 Finch Ave W, Toronto, ON, M2N 2G9 (☎416/221-3000). Wildlife tours to Belize and Costa Rica led by naturalists. CAN$1600 for 8 days in Costa Rican reserves; CAN$1700 for reefs and rainforests in Belize. Recommended.

attractions on the way south are all fully covered in *The Rough Guide to Mexico*. Note that Mexico and the USA observe Daylight Saving Time, while Central America does not.

Greyhound (☎1-800/231-2222) runs regularly to all the major border crossings; some of their buses will take you over the frontier and into the Mexican bus station and in many cases you can reserve tickets with their Mexican counterparts. Mexican buses similarly cross the border into US bus stations. **Green Tortoise** (see p.6) run cheap and cheerful long haul trips through Mexico to Guatemala using buses dubbed "hostels-on-wheels".

From every Mexican border crossing there are constant buses to the capital (generally 18–24 hours away), and beyond Mexico City there are good **bus connections** to all the main Guatemala and Belize border crossings. Probably the best **route into Guatemala** takes you along the Carretera Interamericana through Oaxaca to San Cristóbal de las Casas, and then on to Huehuetenango in Guatemala. The other main road crossings are on the Pacific coast, through Tapachula, from where you can take an international bus to Guatemala City, and on the Caribbean coast, from Chetumal into Belize. An interesting option is to visit the Maya sites of Palenque and Yaxchilán in Chiapas, and from there travel on the Río Usumacinta to a remote border crossing in the department of Petén in Guatemala, about five hours by bus from Flores.

Driving south may give you a lot more freedom, but does entail a great deal of bureaucracy. You need separate **insurance** (sold at the border); Sanborns (☎1-800/222-0158) arranges insurance for Mexico and Central America and much more besides, offering legal assistance, road maps and guides and a 24hr emergency hotline. You and the car will also require separate **entry permits**, possibly valid for different lengths of time, and you'll need to show the registration and your licence. Everywhere there are strict controls to make sure you're not importing the vehicle to sell – if you attempt to leave without it (even if it's been destroyed in a crash) you'll face a massive duty bill. US, Canadian, EU, Australian and New Zealand **driving licences** are valid in Mexico and throughout Central America, but it's a good idea to arm yourself with an International Driving Licence – available for a nominal fee from the American Automobile Association (☎1-800/222-4357) – if you run into problems with a traffic cop for any reason, show that first, and if they abscond with it you at least still have your own, more difficult to replace, licence. For more on driving around Central America, see p.29.

Obviously the simplest way to get to Central America from Mexico is to **fly**. There are daily flights from Mexico City to a number of destinations in southern Mexico, Yucatán and all the Central American capitals. A popular option is to fly to Palenque or Cancún, and from there fly to Flores and Belize City on Aerocaribe. If you're thinking of doing a number of journeys by air, it may be worth contacting Aeroméxico, Mexicana or Taca in advance about their **air passes**, which must be bought from outside the country. For more on this see "Getting Around", p.29.

GETTING THERE FROM THE UK AND IRELAND

There is just one non-stop flight from the UK to Central America (to Costa Rica on British Airways); as a rule, the journey will involve changing aircraft (and sometimes airline),

usually in the USA. That said, it's possible to reach most of the Central American capitals (except Belize City and Tegucigalpa) in one day from London – the best connections are on Continental and American. While no airport in Britain offers the same degree of choice as London, most of the main carriers to the USA have two or three regional options available, often at the same fares as you would pay from the capital.

Fares to Central America are almost always higher than those to **Mexico**, so you might want to consider travelling down overland from Mexico City or Cancún (see p.5). Several European airlines fly to Mexico City, although the only direct flights from London are on British Airways, which has three flights a week to Mexico City and a weekly departure to Cancún. For a complete list of carriers see the box below. It's also worth checking if your

AIRLINES IN THE UK

Aeroflot ☎0171/355-2233
Aeroméxico ☎0171/823-5231
American Airlines ☎0345/789789
British Airways ☎ 0345/222111
Continental ☎0800/776464
Delta ☎0800/414767

Iberia ☎0171/830-0011
KLM ☎0990/750900
Mexicana ☎0171/284-2550
Taca Group ☎01293/23330: representatives for four Central American airlines
United ☎0845/844-4777
Virgin Atlantic ☎01293/747747

SPECIALIST FLIGHT AGENTS

Usit Campus, 52 Grosvenor Gardens, London SW1W 0AG (☎0171/730-2101); 53 Forest Rd, Edinburgh EH1 2QP (☎0131/668-3303); 166 Deansgate, Manchester M3 3FE (☎0161/833-2046); *www.campustravel.co.uk* Student/youth travel specialists. Branches in YHA shops, in cities, and on university campuses all over Britain.

Journey Latin America, 12–13 Northfield Terrace, London W4 4JE (☎0181/747-3108, fax 747-8315); Barton Arcade, 51–63 Deansgate, Manchester M3 2BH (☎0161/832-1441); *sales@journeylatinamerica.co.uk* The leaders in the field on air fares and tours to Latin America; some of the best prices on high-season flights.

STA Travel, 86 Old Brompton Rd, London SW7 3LH; 117 Euston Rd, London NW1 2SX (☎0171/361-6262; *enquiries@sta.travel.co.uk*; *www.statravel.co.uk*). Student/youth travel specialists with an international help desk if you have problems while abroad; dozens of branches throughout the UK, and many more worldwide.

Trailfinders, 42–50 Earls Court Rd, London W8 6FT (☎0171/938-3366). Air fare specialists; also tailor-made packages for independent travellers. Offices throughout the UK and in Dublin.

Travel Cuts, 295a Regent St, London W1R 7YA (☎0171/255-2082; *sales@travelcuts.co.uk*; *www.travelcuts.co.uk*). Air fare and independent travel specialists.

transatlantic carrier has an airpass which links flights in the US and Mexico (usually only Mexico City) – most major US airlines do – for details of the "Mex-AmeriPass" from Aeromexico and the "Visit Central America" pass from Taca, see p.29.

Another option for same-day arrival is to fly on one of the main **European carriers**: KLM (via Amsterdam) has good connections from throughout the UK and Ireland, with flights to Mexico City, Guatemala (arriving early next morning) and Panamá at least three or four times a week. On Iberia from London (via Madrid and Miami) you can reach all the capitals (except Belize City and Tegucigalpa) daily.

SHOPPING FOR TICKETS

Flights to Central America fill up early, so **book as far ahead** as you can. Official **fares**, quoted by the airlines, are generally more expensive than those booked through a travel agent; wherever you book, **peak season** rates apply in July, August and December and at Easter. If you simply want a plain return ticket, the best deal you'll get is usually an Apex, which means booking at least two weeks ahead and committing yourself to flight dates that you cannot change without paying a hefty penalty. Tickets are usually valid for between three and six months; you'll pay more for one that allows you to stay for up to a year. There's always some deal available for young people or students, though don't expect massive reductions.

In November 1998, British Airways began a **weekly direct flight** to San José for around £450 low season/£550 high season; the only route that doesn't entail changing planes, and a very reasonable price. Otherwise, for scheduled return flights from London or Manchester to Guatemala City or

SPECIALIST TOUR OPERATORS

Dragoman, Camp Green, Kenton Rd, Debenham, Suffolk, IP14 6LA (☎01728/861133; *100344.1342@compuserve.com; www. dragoman.co.uk*). Eight-week overland camping expeditions through Mexico to Panamá; around £1400, plus food kitty. Other trips available.

Encounter Overland, 267 Old Brompton Rd, London, SW5 9JA (☎0171/370-6845; *adventure@encounter-overland.co.uk*). Three- to six-week overland camping and hotel trips through Mexico to Panamá, including Darien. From Mexico City via Yucatán to Guatemala (42 days) costs £1800 excluding air fare.

Exodus, 9 Weir Rd, London, SW12 0LT (☎0181/673-0859; *sales@exodustravels.co.uk; www.exodustravels.co.uk*). Fifteen-day escorted tours, staying at hotels, through the Maya region (around £1400) and Costa Rica (£1750). Prices include air fare.

Explore Worldwide, 1 Frederick St, Aldershot GU11 1LQ (☎01252/344161; *info@explore.co.uk; www.explore.co.uk*). Wide range of 2-to-3-week hotel-based tours to Mexico and all Central America (except Panamá). Some tours run year-round. About £1100 for 15 days in Mexico, Guatemala and Belize; £1400 for a 16-day tour of volcanos and rainforest in Nicaragua, including air fare.

Global Travel Club, 1 Kiln Shaw, Langdon Hills, Basildon, Essex, SS16 6LE (☎01268/541732, fax 542275; *info@global-travel.co.uk*). Small compa-ny specializing in individually arranged diving and other tours to Mexico, Belize and Panamá.

Journey Latin America, 12–13 Heathfield Terrace, London, W4 4JE (☎0181/747-3108, fax 742-1312; *tours@journeylatinamerica.co.uk*). Wide range of high-standard tours and individual itineraries from the acknowledged experts. Around £1700 (fully inclusive) for 10 days' superb birdwatching in Costa Rica.

Reef and Rainforest Tours, Prospect House, Jubilee Rd, Totnes, Devon, TQ9 5BP (☎01803/866965, fax 865916; *reefrain@ btinternet.com*). Individual itineraries from a very experienced company, focusing on nature reserves, research projects and diving in Belize, Honduras and Costa Rica.

Travelbag Adventures, 15 Turk St, Alton, Hants, GU34 1AG (☎01420/541007, fax 541022; *mail@travelbag-adventures.co.uk; www. travelbag-adventures.co.uk*). Small group hotel-based tours through Yucatán and Central America. "Realm of the Maya", an 18-day trip from Cancún through Guatemala and Belize costs around £950 excluding air fare; others available.

Trips, 9 Byron Place, Clifton, Bristol BS8 1JT (☎0117/987-2626, fax 987-2627; *trips@trips.demon.co.uk*). Friendly, experienced company with an inspired range of tailor-made itineraries to all Mexican and Central American destinations.

USEFUL ADDRESSES IN IRELAND

AIRLINES

Aer Lingus Dublin: ☎01/705-3333

British Airways Belfast: ☎0345/222111;
Dublin: ☎01-800/626747

British Midland Belfast: ☎0345/240-530;
Dublin: ☎01/283-8833

Delta Dublin: ☎01-800/768080

KLM Belfast: ☎0990/750900

Ryanair Dublin: ☎01/609-7800; Belfast:
☎0541/569569

FLIGHT AND TOUR AGENTS

Maxwell's Travel, D'Olier Chambers, 1 Hawkins St, Dublin 2 (☎01/677-9479, fax 679-3948). Very experienced in travel to Latin America, and Ireland's representatives for many of the British specialist tour operators in the box opposite.

Trailfinders, 4–5 Dawson St, Dublin 2 (☎01/677-7888). Irish branch of the air fare and independent travel experts.

Usit, 19–21 Aston Quay, O'Connell Bridge, Dublin 2 (☎01/602-1700); Fountain Centre, College St, Belfast BT1 6ET (☎01232/324073); *www.usit.ie*. All-Ireland student travel agents, with 17 offices (mainly on campuses) in the Republic and the North.

San José for example, you should expect to pay around £635–£740 high season, £525–555 at other times. To Mexico City prices are lower but even more variable, ranging from £370 to £500.

If you want to travel through several countries in Central America, or continue into South America, then it's worth considering an **"open jaw"** ticket (which lets you fly into one city and out of another), or an **airpass** (see p.29).

Websites in the UK are not geared so directly to Central American destinations as their US counterparts but a check through *www. cheapflights.co.uk* will allow some comparisons on fares from various UK airports to North America and Mexico, and there are good links to travel agents and other sources of information. Usit CAMPUS webpage also has a reasonable farefinder.

PACKAGES AND INCLUSIVE TOURS

Many companies offer **package tours** to Central America, which save hassle and can be good value. They're generally relaxed and friendly, usually led by someone from the UK who knows the area well; in many cases there may also be a local guide. Transport can vary from local buses to comfortable minibuses, from fast launches to light aircraft. The list opposite covers the best and most experienced UK operators. Prices quoted are a guide only; some tours also require a local pay-

ment for meals. Most operate through the winter only, but several run year-round.

FLIGHTS FROM IRELAND

No airline offers **direct flights** from Ireland to Central America but there is a direct flight to Mexico City – once weekly with Aeroflot via Shannon. The cheapest way to get to Central America is to take one of the numerous daily flights from Dublin or Belfast to London, and then connect with one of the transatlantic flights detailed on p.9. You can, however, take direct flights from Ireland to the **USA** or **Europe** for easy onward connections to Mexico and Central America. Delta has the widest range of direct flights from Dublin (and several from Shannon) to JFK and Atlanta, with daily connections to Mexico City, Guatemala and Panamá. On Aer Lingus from Dublin (and some from Shannon) you can get same-day connections to Mexico City and San José for example, by flying to New York (JFK); and you can also fly with them from Dublin to Amsterdam and pick up KLM's flights to Mexico and Central America from there. BA also fly from Dublin to meet their connections in London to Mexico City and Cancún. KLM's flights from Belfast connect with their services from Amsterdam to Mexico City and Central America.

Discount fares from Dublin or Belfast to Mexico range from £430 to £588 return; from Dublin to Guatemala from around IR£572.

GETTING THERE FROM AUSTRALIA AND NEW ZEALAND

There are no direct flights from Australasia to Central America, and consequently you've little choice but to fly via the US or Mexico. For most airlines, low season is from mid-January to the end of February and October to the end of November; high season mid-May to the end of August and December to mid-January. Seat availability on international flights out of Australia and New Zealand is often limited, so it's best to book several weeks ahead.

The **best deals** are with Air New Zealand–Continental and United Airlines, who have daily scheduled fares via LA, at around A$2299/NZ$2499 during their low seasons; at other times the cheapest fare is JAL's at A$1550–1850/NZ$1850–2250 to either LA or Mexico City via Tokyo, plus an add-on to the country's gateway city. Qantas–Continental also have daily scheduled fares to Central America, but these are a little more expensive, starting at A$2399 low season.

If you want to **stop off** in North America before travelling on, then you may want to look into some of the **air passes** that can be booked before you leave (see p.29). United Airlines, Taca and Aviateca all offer flight coupons for single flights to Central America.

Few **round-the-world** tickets include Central American countries, but it is possible to visit them on a side trip (at extra cost) with Cathay Pacific–UA's "Globetrotter" and Air New Zealand–KLM–Northwest's "World Navigator"; prices are A$2699–3299/NZ$3189–3699.

Note that tickets bought direct from the airlines are usually at published rates. The **discount agents** listed in the box opposite offer better deals on fares and have the latest information on limited special offers.

AIRLINES IN AUSTRALIA AND NEW ZEALAND

Air New Zealand Australia: ☎13 2476; New Zealand: ☎09/357-3000. Daily from Sydney, Brisbane, Melbourne and Adelaide to LA, either direct or via Honolulu/Tonga/Fiji/Papeete. Onward connections to all Central American capitals with Continental.

Continental Airlines Australia: ☎02/9321-9242. No NZ office. Teams up with Qantas and Air New Zealand to offer a through service to Central America from LA.

Garuda Australia: ☎02/9334-9944 or 1-800/800-873; New Zealand: ☎09/366-1855. Several flights a week to LA from major Australasian cities, with a stopover in Denpasar or Jakarta.

JAL Australia: ☎02/9272-1111; New Zealand: ☎09/379-9906. Several flights a week from Sydney, Brisbane, Cairns and Auckland to LA and Mexico City with a stopover in Tokyo or Osaka.

Philippine Airlines Australia: ☎02/9262-3333. No NZ office. Several flights a week to LA from Sydney, Melbourne or Brisbane, with a transfer or overnight in Manila.

Qantas Australia: ☎13 1211; New Zealand: ☎09/357-8900 or 0800/808767. Daily flights to LA from major Australasian cities with onward connections to all Central American capitals with Continental.

Taca and **Aviateca** Australia: ☎03/9329-5211. No NZ office. Air passes from LA to Guatemala City and San José.

Singapore Airlines Australia: ☎13 1011; New Zealand: ☎09/379-3209. Twice a week to LA from major Australian cities and once a week from Auckland via Singapore.

United Airlines Australia: ☎13 1777; New Zealand: ☎09/379-3800. Daily direct to LA from Sydney, Melbourne and Auckland with onward connections to all Central American capitals; also air passes to these cities

AUSTRALASIAN DISCOUNT AGENTS

Anywhere Travel, 345 Anzac Parade, Kingsford, Sydney (☎02/9663-0411).

Brisbane Discount Travel, 260 Queen St, Brisbane (☎07/3229-9211).

Budget Travel, 16 Fort St, Auckland, plus branches around the city (☎09/366-0061 or 0800/808040).

Destinations Unlimited, 3 Milford Rd, Auckland (☎09/373-4033).

Flight Centres Australia: 82 Elizabeth St, Sydney (☎13 1600), plus branches nationwide; New Zealand: 205 Queen St, Auckland (☎09/309-6171), plus branches nationwide.

Northern Gateway, 22 Cavenagh St, Darwin (☎08/8941-1394).

STA Travel, Australia: 702 Harris St, Ultimo, Sydney; 256 Flinders St, Melbourne; other offices in state capitals and major universities (nearest branch ☎13 1776; fastfare telesales ☎1300/360-960); New Zealand: 10 High St, Auckland (☎09/309-0458; fastfare telesales ☎09/366-6673), plus branches in Wellington, Christchurch, Dunedin, Palmerston North, Hamilton and at major universities; *traveller@statravelaus.com.au; www.statravelaus.com.au*

Thomas Cook, Australia: 175 Pitt St, Sydney; 257 Collins St, Melbourne; plus branches in other state capitals (local branch ☎13 1771; telesales ☎1800/063-913); New Zealand: 96 Anzac Ave, Auckland (☎09/379-3920).

Tymtro Travel, Level 8, 130 Pitt St, Sydney (☎02/9223-2211 or 1300/652-969).

FLIGHTS AND FARES

The cheapest way to get to **LA** or **Mexico City** is via Asia. Currently JAL flies from Sydney, Brisbane and Cairns to both cities, with an overnight stop in Tokyo (included in the fare) from A$1550/NZ$1850 low season. Garuda flies to LA via either Jakarta or Denpasar, and Philippine Airlines flies to LA via Manila. Both start at around A$1750 low season. United Airlines flies direct to LA, while Qantas and Air New Zealand fly either direct or via stopovers in the Pacific (from A$1850 low season). Air Pacific costs around the same and includes a stopover in Fiji. From New Zealand, Singapore Airlines offers a good connecting service via Singapore to LA for NZ$2099 low season. For the same price you can take the faster Air New Zealand flight (non-stop, or via Honolulu, Fiji, Tonga or Papeete), or United Airlines non-stop. All the above fares are from Auckland – expect to pay an extra NZ$150 for Christchurch or Wellington departures.

Continental and United Airlines have daily scheduled through fares to all the **Central American capitals** via LA, at around ,A$2140/NZ$2499 low season. Qantas–Continental's fares

are a little more expensive, starting at A$2365 to Guatemala, Costa Rica and Panamá and A$2420 to Belize, El Salvador, Honduras and Nicaragua.

If you're flying **via Asia** the cheapest add-ons are from Mexico City (year-round flat rates of US$349 to El Salvador and Honduras, US$399 to Nicaragua, US$440 to Belize and Costa Rica, US$425 to Guatemala and Panamá), while from LA you'll pay anything between US$429 and US$660 (year-round flat rates)

SPECIALIST TOURS

If you prefer to have all the arrangements made for you before you leave, then the **specialist agents** on p.14 can help you plan your trip. Most can do anything from booking a few nights' accommodation to arranging fully escorted archeological-cultural tours. Some of the "adventure" specialists can also help organize activities such as diving and jungle treks. Most agents concentrate on Belize, Guatemala and Costa Rica, though there are other options. Note that few of the tour prices include air fares from Australasia; the same agents can usually assist with flight arrangements. Many of the tours listed can also be arranged through your local travel agent.

SPECIALIST TOUR OPERATORS

Adventure Associates, 197 Oxford St, Bondi Junction (☎02/9389-7466). Two- to twelve-day jungle, archeological and cultural tours in Guatemala and Belize; tours, city stopovers and cruises, trekking, mountain biking, whitewater rafting, canal trips and sportsfishing in Costa Rica; independent and escorted small-group tours and city stopovers in Panamá.

Adventure Specialists, 69 Liverpool St, Sydney (☎02/9261-2927 or 1800/634465). Variety of adventure travel options to Central America, specializing in Guatemala and Belize, plus adventure trips (8–22 days) in Costa Rica, including whitewater rafting, rainforest hikes, National Park tours and horse riding.

Adventure World, Australia: 73 Walker St, N Sydney (☎02/9956-7766 or 1800/221931), plus branches in Melbourne, Brisbane, Adelaide and Perth; New Zealand: 101 Great South Rd, Remuera, Auckland (☎09/524-5118). Variety of tours, including trips to Tikal and Chichicastenango from Guatemala City, reef-river cruises in Belize, 5-day packages and rainforest tours in Costa Rica.

Contours, 466 Victoria St, N Melbourne (☎03/9329-5211). Specialists in tailored city stopover packages to Central America.

Exodus, Top Deck Adventure, 350 Kent St, Sydney (☎02/9299-8844 or 1800/800724); in New Zealand contact Adventure World. Eight-week overland tours trucking between Mexico City and Panamá City.

Padi Travel Network, 4/372 Eastern Valley Way, Chatswood, NSW (☎1800/678100) with agents throughout Australasia. Dive packages to the prime sites of the Belize coast.

Peregrine Adventures, 258 Lonsdale St, Melbourne (☎03/9663-8611), plus offices in Brisbane, Sydney, Adelaide and Perth. Extended overland-sea adventures from southern Mexico through Guatemala and Belize and from Honduras to Panamá City.

Surf Travel Company, Australia: 12 Cronulla Plaza, Cronulla Beach, Sydney (☎02/9527-4722); Kirra Surf Centre, cnr Gold Coast Highway and Coolangatta Rd, Kirra, Queensland (☎07/5599-2818); New Zealand: 6 Danbury Drive, Torbay, Auckland (☎09/473-8388). Fly–4WD–accommodation surfing packages to Costa Rica; also overland surfing tours from LA.

Wiltrans/Maupintour, 189 Kent St, Sydney (☎02/9255-0899). All-inclusive guided tours in Costa Rica. Also US–Central American cruises, some including stopovers in Costa Rica.

INSURANCE

Wherever you go in Central America, medical insurance is essential. You should have coverage of at least US$2million, which should include provision for repatriation by air ambulance. Specialist travel policies also offer cover for loss or theft of personal possessions and travel delay, though on some this is optional. Whether you take this part depends on how valuable your equipment is; be warned that theft is rife in Central America and expensive-looking luggage attracts attention.

Before **buying a policy**, check to see if you're already covered for certain eventualities. **Credit and charge cards** (particularly American Express and Visa) often have certain levels of medical or other insurance included, especially if you use them to pay for your trip. This can be quite comprehensive, anticipating anything from lost or stolen baggage and missed connections to charter companies going bankrupt. That said, however, the medical cover offered is usually insufficient for Central America, so check the small print carefully, as you should for any policy.

If you plan to participate in **watersports**, including scuba diving, you'll probably have to pay an extra premium. Note also that very few insurers will arrange on-the-spot payments in the event of a major expense or loss; you will usually be reimbursed only after going home. In all cases of loss or theft of goods, you will have to contact the local police to have a report made out so that your insurer can process the claim.

NORTH AMERICAN COVER

Canadian provincial health plans typically provide some overseas medical coverage, although they are unlikely to pick up the full tab in the event of a mishap. Holders of official **student/teacher/youth cards** are entitled to accident coverage and hospital in-patient benefits – the annual membership is far less than the cost of comparable insurance. Students may also find that their student health coverage extends during the vacations and for one term beyond the date of last enrollment. **Homeowners' or renters' insurance** often covers theft or loss of documents, money and valuables while overseas.

After exhausting the possibilities above, you might want to contact a **specialist travel insurance company**; your travel agent can usually recommend one, or see the box below. Policies vary:

some are comprehensive while others cover only certain risks (accidents, illnesses, delayed or lost luggage, cancelled flights, etc). In particular, ask whether the policy pays medical costs up front or reimburses you later, and whether it provides for medical evacuation home. For policies that include lost or stolen luggage, check exactly what is and isn't covered, and make sure the per-article limit will cover your most valuable possessions.

The best premiums are usually to be had through **student/youth travel agencies** – *ISIS* policies, for example, cost US$60 for fifteen days, US$110 for a month, US$165 for two months, US$665 for a year for any of the Central American countries. There is no coverage for adventure sports of any kind, including underwater activities.

Most North American travel policies apply only to items lost, stolen or damaged while in the custody of an identifiable, responsible third party. Even in these cases you will have to contact the local police within a certain time limit.

BRITISH COVER

If you have a good "all risks" home insurance policy it may well cover your possessions against loss or theft even when overseas, and many private medical schemes also cover you when abroad – make sure you know the procedure and the helpline number. Otherwise, **comprehensive travel insurance** is sold by almost every travel agent (many will offer insurance when you book your flight or holiday) but you'll almost certainly be

---

TRAVEL INSURANCE COMPANIES

IN NORTH AMERICA

Access America ☎1-800/284-8300

Carefree Travel Insurance ☎1-800/323-3149

International Student Insurance Service (ISIS) – sold by STA Travel ☎1-800/777-0112

Travel Assistance International ☎1-800/821-2828

Travel Guard ☎1-800/826-1300

Travel Insurance Services ☎1-800/937-1387

IN THE UK

Columbus Travel Insurance ☎0171/375-0011

Endsleigh Insurance ☎0171/436-4451

Frizzell Insurance ☎01202/292333

Marcus Hearn ☎0171/739-3444

IN AUSTRALIA

Cover More Australia: ☎02/9202-8000 or 1800/251881

Ready Plan Australia: ☎03/9791-5077 or 1800/337462; New Zealand: ☎09/379-3208

better off arranging your own from a specialist company. The growing number of travel insurance companies, especially those offering multi-trip or year-round cover, makes shopping for a policy ever more time-consuming, but competition means that prices are keen. When phoning for a quote, apart from asking about the level of cover, check if it includes insurance premium tax – now 17 percent.

AUSTRALASIAN COVER

Travel insurance is available from most travel agents, some banks or direct from insurance com-panies, for periods ranging from a few days to a year or even longer. All are fairly similar in premi-um and coverage, which includes medical expens-es, loss of personal property and travellers' cheques, cancellations and delays, as well as most adventure sports. If you plan to indulge in high-risk activities, such as mountaineering, bungee jump-ing or scuba diving, check the policy carefully to make sure you'll be covered – it may be necessary to tailor a policy to suit your requirements. A nor-mal policy for Central America costs around A$100/NZ$120 for 2 weeks, A$170/NZ$200 for 1 month, A$250/NZ$300 for 2 months.

RED TAPE AND ENTRY REQUIREMENTS

Information on the entry requirements of the seven Central American countries, while correct at the time of going to press, is liable to sudden change. Before travelling, it's cru-cial to contact a consulate to check what's required of you – even when you've checked and armed yourself with the correct paper-work you may find the requests of the immi-gration officer at variance with the official policy.

That said, **visas** and/or **tourist cards** (with a few notable and perhaps idiosyncratic excep-tions) are usually not needed by citizens of the US, Canada, EU, Australia and New Zealand to enter Central America as tourists. These visitors are usually permitted a stay from thirty to ninety days, depending on the country; again, check with your consulate.

In **Mexico**, all the countries have consulates in the capital; there's also a Guatemalan con-sulate in Comitán; Guatemalan and El Salvadorean consulates in Tapachula; and a Belize consulate in Chetumal.

If you're flying in on a **one-way ticket** (pro-viding the airline lets you board – some countries, Costa Rica for example, refuse travellers with no return tickets) you may have to prove your inten-tion to leave the country; additionally you may

VISAS/TOURIST CARDS NEEDED

If you need a **visa** it's always best get one in advance; don't bank on picking one up at the bor-der. Apply to the Consular Department of the country you want to visit, preferably before you leave home, though you will usually be able to get one at the relevant consulate in any other country. Visas are **valid** for at least thirty days, and generally allow you to stay in the country for up to ninety days, depending largely on the mood of the immigration official when you arrive.

Citizens of the USA, Canada, Australia and New Zealand need a visa to enter **El Salvador**.

Citizens of Germany, France, Canada, Australia and New Zealand need a visa for **Nicaragua**.

Citizens of Ireland (Eire), USA, Canada, Australia and New Zealand need a visa for **Panamá**.

have to show "sufficient funds" for your stay, though these conditions are rarely enforced.

Even if you don't officially require a visa or tourist card to enter a particular country, the immigration official may ask you to "buy" one, or pay some form of unspecified "fee" – usually equivalent to a dollar or five (exceptions are Belize and El Salvador, where you'll never be asked for illegal entry or exit fees). How you deal with this depends on how good your Spanish is, the amount of hassle you're willing to put up with and the attitude of the official. It's certain-ly annoying to have to pay these **bribes** and, if you know the rules, and stick to the "won't pay" line you'll probably get waved through – eventu-ally. However, in places like Guatemala and Honduras where there's a semi-institutionalized requirement to pay officials Q10/L20 (around US$1.50) it's usually more bother than it's worth to kick up a fuss. Once you get your stamp (and visa/tourist card if required) you should keep your **passport** with you at all times, or at the very least carry a photocopy, as you may be asked to show it.

CENTRAL AMERICAN EMBASSIES AND CONSULATES

IN NORTH AMERICA

Belize 2535 Massachusetts Ave NW, Washington DC 20009 (☎202/332-9636); Honorary Consul, Suite 3800, South Tower, Royal Bank Plaza, Toronto, ON, M5J 2JP (☎416/865-7000, fax 865-7048; in Quebec ☎514/871-4741).

Costa Rica 2114 S St NW, Washington DC 20008 (☎202/234-2945).

El Salvador 2308 California St NW, Washington DC 20008 (☎202/265-9671).

Guatemala 2220 R St NW, Washington DC 20008 (☎202/745-4952).

Honduras 3007 Tilden St NW, Washington DC 20008 (☎202/966-7702).

Nicaragua 1627 New Hampshire Ave NW, Washington DC 20009 (☎202/939-6570).

Panamá 2862 McGill Terrace NW, Washington DC 20008 (☎202/483-1407).

IN THE UK

Belize 22 Harcourt House, 19 Cavendish Square, London W1M 9AD (☎0171/499-9728, fax 491-4139).

Costa Rica Flat 1c, Lancaster Gate, London W2 3LH (☎0171/706-8844, no fax).

El Salvador Tennyson House, 159 Great Portland St, London W1N 5FD (☎0171/436-8282, fax 436-8181).

Guatemala 13 Fawcett St, London SW10 9HN (☎0171/351-3042, fax 376-5708).

Honduras 115 Gloucester Place, London W1H 3PJ (☎0171/486-4880, fax 486-4550).

Nicaragua Vicarage House, Kensington Church St, London W8 4DB (☎0171/938-2373, fax 937-0952).

Panamá Panamá House, 40 Hertford St, London W1Y 7TG (☎0171/409-2255, no fax).

IN AUSTRALASIA

Belize Australia: British High Commission, Commonwealth Ave, Yarralumla, Canberra (☎06/6270 6666); New Zealand: British High Commission, 44 Hill St, Wellington (☎04/495-0889).

Costa Rica Australia: Consulate-General, 30 Clarence St, Sydney (☎02/9261-1177); New Zealand: contact consulate in Australia.

El Salvador Australia: Honorary Consulate, 3 Donnington St, Carindale, Brisbane,

(☎07/3398-8658); New Zealand: contact con-sulate in Australia.

Guatemala The nearest representative is in the USA.

Honduras Australia: Consulate-General, Level 7, 19–31 Pitt St, Sydney (☎02/9350-8121); New Zealand: contact consulate in Australia.

Nicaragua The nearest representative is in the US.

Panamá The nearest representative is in Singapore (☎+65/221-8677).

Extensions to the permitted period of stay – whether you need a visa/tourist card or not – can be obtained at the immigration department (**migración**) in the country concerned, sometimes only in the capital. The process often takes a full day, so you may choose to use the services of a *tramitador*, an agency that, for a fee, will deal with the red tape. In many cases it's often easier to leave the country for a few days and re-enter with a new stamp.

COSTS AND MONEY

By European or North American standards the cost of living in Central America is low, and with most currencies in a gradual slide in value against the dollar (not to mention the pound), you can live quite cheaply here.

Belize and Costa Rica are the most expensive, while Nicaragua, Guatemala and Honduras are probably the cheapest. There are, of course, exceptions and variations – in El Salvador, for example, one of the cheaper countries overall, accommodation is surprisingly expensive for the region.

The **US dollar** is the most widely accepted foreign currency in Central America – Panamá's balboa *is* the US dollar – and, in one form or another, this is the one you should take. Though you can pay for some things by **plastic** – and, more usefully, use it to withdraw currency from bank ATMs – some countries are less geared up for this than others, and it's always a good idea to have some **travellers' cheques** (though again, these aren't accepted everywhere; see below) or **cash dollars**, in case you run short of local currency a long way from the nearest bank. You'll get the best rate for your dollars if you change them for local currency in the country you're in or entering. Most international airports have a bank for **currency exchange**, while at the main land border crossings there might be a bank, or more likely a swarm of moneychangers, who'll give fair rates for cash and occasionally travellers' cheques. At even the most remote border crossing you can usually depend on finding some entrepreneur willing to change dollars, though rates worsen significantly the further you are from a bank.

As all local currencies float against the US dollar, (with the exception of Panamá, and Belize, which has fixed exchange rates of Bz$2 to US$1) prices quoted in the guide are in **US dollars**.

PLASTIC, TRAVELLERS' CHEQUES AND WIRING MONEY

Credit cards are widely accepted in Central America – though you shouldn't rely on them in Nicaragua or Honduras – and increasingly even in smaller hotels and restaurants. Visa is the most useful, followed by Mastercard. In most countries there will usually be one or more particular bank which accepts either (sometimes both); we've detailed these in the Guide. You can use your card to get cash (except

---

EXCHANGE RATES

Though the following **exchange rates** were correct at time of going to press, inflation and devaluation in some countries will mean that they may change somewhat over the course of this edition of the guide.

Belize (Belizean dollar) Bz$2 = US$1
Costa Rica (colón) 250c = US$1
El Salvador (colón) 8.1c = US$1
Guatemala (quetzal) Q6.50 = US$1
Honduras (lempira) L13 = US$1
Nicaragua (córdoba) C$10.17 = US$1
Panamá (dollar/balboa) $1 = US$1

when crossing land borders, which is where travellers' cheques and cash dollars come in handy) from ATMs, and over the counter at banks. Although most ATMs are in service 24 hours it's wiser to use them when the bank is open; firstly you can see a bank employee if something goes wrong and the machine keeps your card (though this is very rare), and secondly you benefit from the added security in daytime. Using your debit card means you don't have to buy and countersign travellers' cheques and, though you pay a handling charge each time you use it, the amount may be less than the commission on cheques and you may benefit from a better exchange rate.

Travellers' cheques (though very hard to use in Nicaragua, and difficult in El Salvador outside the capital) are a safe way to bring money, as they offer the added security of a refund if they're stolen. To facilitate this you want to make sure that you have cheques issued by one of the big names, which are also more readily accepted. You should also always carry your proof of purchase when trying to change travellers' cheques, as some places will refuse to deal with you otherwise.

Having money **wired from home** is never convenient or cheap, and should be considered a last resort. Funds can be sent via **Western Union** or **American Express MoneyGram**. Both companies' fees depend on the destination and the amount being transferred. The funds should be available for collection at Amex's or Western Union's local office within minutes of being sent.

It's also possible for a fee to have money wired directly from a bank in your home country to a bank in Central America, although this is somewhat less reliable because it involves two separate institutions, and can take between a couple of days and several months. If you go this route, the person wiring the funds to you will need to know the routing number of the bank the funds are being wired to.

COSTS

Under most circumstances, life in Central America is **cheaper** than in North America and Europe (though travellers are often surprised by the expense of Belize and Costa Rica, where prices are not that different from in the US). As a general rule, locally produced goods are cheap and anything imported is overpriced.

To an extent, what you spend will obviously depend on where, when and how you choose to travel. **Peak tourist seasons**, such as Christmas and Easter, tend to push up hotel prices, and certain tourist centres are notably more expensive. **Public transport**, geared to locals, is invariably a bargain – though bear in mind that in some places foreigners are routinely charged more in what's effectively an institutionalized two-tier price system. Travelling by car is expensive, and the cost of renting a car is higher in Central America than it is in the USA, as is the cost of fuel – although this is still cheaper than in Europe.

If you have a **student card** it may be worth carrying, as it sometimes opens the way for a reduction, but it won't save you a great deal and, unless you need one to clinch a deal on air fare, it's not worth buying one for the trip.

HEALTH

It's always easier to become ill in a country with a different climate, different food and different germs, still more so in a poor country with lower standards of sanitation than you might be used to. Most visitors, however, get through Central America without catching anything more serious than a dose of "traveller's diarrhoea", and the most important precaution is to be aware of health risks posed by poor hygiene, untreated water, insect bites, undressed open cuts and unprotected sex.

Above all, it's vital to get the best **health advice** you can before you set off; pay a visit to your doctor or a travel clinic (see p.23) as far in advance of travel as possible. Many clinics also sell travel-related accessories, malaria tablets, mosquito nets, water filters and the like. Regardless of how well-prepared you are medically, you will still want the security of **health insurance** (see "Insurance" on p.14).

VACCINATIONS, INOCULATIONS AND MALARIA PRECAUTIONS

If possible, all **inoculations** should be sorted out at least ten weeks before departure. The only obligatory jab for certain Central American countries is a **yellow fever** vaccination if you're arriving from a "high-risk" area – northern South America and much of central Africa – in which case you need to carry your vaccination certificate. You'll also need a yellow fever jab if travelling in Panamá south of the canal. **Diphtheria** vaccinations are considered essential, and long-term travellers should look at the combined **hepatitis A and B** and the **rabies** vaccines (though see p.22 for a caveat on that one). And all travellers should check that they are up to date with **polio**, **tetanus**, **typhoid** and hepatitis A jabs.

North Americans can get inoculations at any immunization centre or at most local clinics, and will have to pay a fee. Most GPs in the **UK** have a travel surgery where you can get advice and certain vaccines on prescription, though they may not administer some of the less common immunizations. Note too that though some jabs (diphtheria, typhoid) are free, others will incur quite a hefty charge, and it can be worth checking out a

travel clinic, where you can receive vaccinations almost immediately, some of them (hepatitis, rabies) at lower prices than at the doctor's. In **Australasia**, vaccination centres are always less expensive than doctors' surgeries.

Malaria is endemic in many parts of Central America, especially in the rural lowlands. The recommended prophylactic west of the Panamá Canal is Chloroquine; Mefloquine to the east of the canal, including the San Blas Islands. However, as Mefloquine (also known as Larium) can have upsetting side effects, it's worth checking with a medical practitioner as to its suitability for you. You need to begin taking the tablets one week before arrival and for four weeks after leaving the area. You should still take precautions to avoid getting bitten by insects altogether: sleep in screened rooms or under nets, burn mosquito coils containing permethrin (available everywhere), cover up arms and legs, especially around dawn and dusk when the mosquitoes are most active and use insect repellent containing over 35 percent Deet. Also prevalent throughout Central America (usually occurring in epidemic outbreaks), **dengue fever** is a viral infection transmitted by mosquitoes also active during the day. There is no vaccine or specific treatment, so you need to pay great attention to avoiding bites.

OTHER SIMPLE PRECAUTIONS

What you **eat or drink** while you're travelling is crucial: a poor diet lowers your resistance. Be sure to drink clean water and eat a good balanced diet. Eating plenty of peeled fresh fruit helps keep up your vitamin and mineral intake, but it might be worth taking daily multi-vitamin and mineral tablets with you. It is also important to eat enough and get enough **rest**, as it's easy to become run-down if you're on the move a lot, especially in a hot climate. Don't try anything too exotic in the first few days, before your body has had a chance to adjust to local microbes, and avoid food that has been on display for a while and is not freshly cooked. You should also steer clear of raw shellfish, salads, and don't eat anywhere that is obviously dirty. In addition to the hazards mentioned under "Intestinal Troubles", below, contaminated food and water will also transmit the hepatitis A virus, which can lay a victim low for several months with exhaustion, fever, diarrhoea, and can even cause liver damage. For advice on **water**, see below.

More serious are **hepatitis B**, and **HIV** and **AIDS**, all transmitted through blood or sexual contact; you should take all the usual, well-publicized precautions to avoid them. To contemplate casual sex without a condom would be madness; condoms also offer protection from other sexually transmitted diseases.

Two other common causes of problems are **altitude** and the **sun**. The answer in both cases is to take it easy; allow yourself time to acclimatize before you leap up a volcano, and build up exposure to the sun gradually – only a few minutes on the first day. Use a strong sunscreen and, if you're walking during the day, wear a hat and try to keep in the shade. Avoid dehydration by drinking enough – water or fruit juice rather than beer or coffee. Overheating can cause heatstroke, which is potentially fatal. Lowering body temperature (by taking a tepid shower, for example) is the first step in treatment.

Finally you might want to consider carrying a **travel medical kit**. These range from a box of band-aids to a full compact sterilized kit, complete with syringes and sutures; you can buy them from pharmacies and the specialist suppliers in the box on p.23.

INTESTINAL TROUBLES

Despite all the dire warnings, a bout of **diarrhoea** is the medical problem you're most likely to encounter. No one, however cautious, seems to avoid it altogether. Its main cause is simply the change of diet: the food in Central America contains a whole new set of bacteria, as well as perhaps rather more of them than you're used to. The best cure is the simplest one: take it easy for a day or two, drink lots of bottled water, and eat only the blandest of foods – papaya is good for soothing the stomach and also crammed with vitamins. Only if the symptoms last more than four or five days do you need to worry. **Cholera** is an acute bacterial infection, recognizable by watery diarrhoea and vomiting, and an epidemic has recently swept through Central America, though many victims may have only mild or even no symptoms. However, risk of infection is considered low, particularly if you're following the health advice above, and symptoms are rapidly relieved by prompt medical attention and clean water.

If you're spending any time in rural areas you also run the risk of picking up various **parasitic infections**: protozoa – amoeba and giardia – and intestinal worms. These sound (and can be) hideous, but they're easily treated once detected. If you suspect you have an infestation take a stool sample to a good **pathology lab** and go to a

WHAT ABOUT THE WATER?

Contaminated **water** is a major cause of sickness in Central America, and even if it looks clean, all drinking water should be regarded with caution. That said, however, it is also essential to increase fluid intake to prevent dehydration. Bottled water is widely available, but stick with known brands and always check that the seal is intact since refilling empties with tap water for resale is not unknown (carbonated water is generally a safer bet in that respect). Many restaurants use purified water (*agua purificada*), but always check; many hotels have a supply and will often provide bottles in your room. There are various methods of treating water while you are travelling, whether your source is from a tap or a river: boiling for a minimum of five minutes is the most effective method of sterilization, but it is not always practical, and will not remove unpleasant tastes.

Water filters remove visible impurities and larger pathogenic organisms (most bacteria and parasites). The Swiss-made Katadyn filter is expensive but extremely useful (various sizes available from outdoor equipment stores). To be really sure your filtered water is also purified however, **chemical sterilization**, using either chlorine or iodine tablets, or a tincture of iodine liquid, is advisable. Both chlorine and iodine leave a nasty aftertaste (though it can be masked with lemon or lime juice), and iodine is more effective in destroying amoebic cysts. Pregnant women or people with thyroid problems should consult their doctor before using iodine sterilizing tablets or iodine-based purifiers. Inexpensive iodine removal filters are recommended if treated water is being used continuously for more than a month or is being given to babies.

Any good outdoor equipment shop will stock a range of **water treatment products**; their experts will give you the best advice for your particular needs.

doctor or pharmacist with the test results (see "Getting Medical Help", below). More serious is **amoebic dysentery**, which is endemic in many parts of the region. The symptoms are more or less the same as a bad dose of diarrhoea but include bleeding. On the whole, a course of Flagyl (metronidazole or tinidozole) will cure it; if you plan to visit the far-flung corners of Central America then it's worth carrying these, just in case. If possible get some, and some advice on their usage, from a doctor before you go.

BITES AND STINGS

Taking steps to avoid getting bitten by **insects**, particularly mosquitoes (above), is always good practice. Sandflies, often present on beaches, are tiny but their bites, usually on feet and ankles, itch like hell and last for days. Head or body lice can be picked up from people or bedding, and are best treated with medicated soap or shampoo; very occasionally, they may spread typhus, characterized by fever, muscle aches, headaches and eventually a measles-like rash. If you think you have it, seek treatment.

Scorpions are common; mostly nocturnal, they hide during the heat of the day under rocks and in crevices. If you're camping, or sleeping in a village cabaña, shake your shoes out before putting them on and try not to wander round barefoot. Their sting is painful (occasionally fatal) and can become infected, so you should seek medical treatment. You're less likely to be bitten by a **spider**, but the advice is the same as for scorpions and venomous insects – seek medical treatment if the pain persists or increases.

You're unlikely to see a **snake**, and most are harmless in any case. Wearing boots and long trousers will go a long way towards preventing a bite – walk heavily and they will usually slither away. Exceptions are the fer-de-lance (which, thankfully, lives on dense, mountainous territory, and rarely emerges during the day) and the bushmaster (which can be found in places with heavy rainfall, or near streams and rivers), both of which can be aggressive, and whose venom can be fatal. If you do get bitten remember what the snake looked like (kill it if you can), immobilize the bitten limb as far as possible and seek medical help immediately: antivenoms are available in most hospitals.

Swimming and snorkelling might bring you into contact with potentially dangerous or venomous **sea creatures**. You're extremely unlikely to be a victim of shark attack (though the dubious practice of shark-feeding as a tourist attraction is growing, and could lead to an accidental bite), but jellyfish are common and all corals will sting. Some jellyfish, like the Portuguese man-o'-war, with its distinctive purple, bag-like sail, have very long tentacles with stinging cells, and an encounter will result in raw, red weals. Equally painful is a brush against fire coral: in each case clean the wound with vinegar or iodine and seek medical help if the pain persists or infection develops.

Rabies does exist in Central America; the best advice is to give dogs a wide berth, and not to play with animals at all, no matter how cuddly they may look. Treat any bite as suspect: wash any wound immediately with soap or detergent and apply alcohol or iodine if possible. Act immediately to get treatment – rabies is fatal once symptoms appear. There is a **vaccine**, but it is expensive, serves only to shorten the course of treatment you need anyway and is effective for no more than three months.

GETTING MEDICAL HELP

For minor medical problems, head for the **farmacia** – look for a green cross and the *Farmacia* sign. Pharmacists are knowledgeable and helpful, and many may speak some English. They can also sell drugs over the counter (if necessary) which are only available by prescription at home. Every capital city has **doctors** and dentists, many trained in the US, who are experienced in treating visitors and speak good English. Your embassy will always have a list of recommended doctors, and we've included some in our "Listings" for the main towns. Health insurance (see p.14) is essential and for anything serious you should to go to the best **private hospital** you can reach; again, these are located mainly in the capital cities. If you suspect something is amiss with your insides, it might be worth heading straight for the local **pathology lab** (all the main towns have them), before seeing a doctor, as the doctor will probably send you anyway. Many rural communities have a **health centre** (*centro de salud* or *puesto de salud*), where healthcare is free, although there may be only a nurse or healthworker available and you can't rely on finding an English-speaking doctor. Should you need an injection or transfusion, make sure that the equipment is sterile (it might be worth bringing a sterile kit from home) and ensure any blood you receive is screened.

MEDICAL RESOURCES FOR TRAVELLERS

IN NORTH AMERICA

Center for Disease Control, 1600 Clifton Rd NE, Atlanta, GA 30333 (☎404/639-3311; *netinfo@cdc.gov, www.cdc.gov/travel/camerica*). Current information on health risks and precautions. Clear and comprehensive web pages covering Mexico and Central America; check these first if you can.

International Association for Medical Assistance to Travellers (IAMAT), 417 Center St, Lewiston, NY 14092 (☎716/754-4883); 40 Regal Rd, Guelph, ON, N1K 1B5 (☎519/836-0102). Non-profit organization supported by donations. Can provide climate charts and leaflets on various diseases and inoculations.

Medic Alert, 2323 Colorado Ave, Turlock, CA 95381 (☎1-800/432-5378; in Canada ☎1-800/668-1507). Sells bracelets engraved with the traveller's medical requirements in case of emergency.

Travel Medicine, 351 Pleasant St, Northampton, MA 01060 (☎1-800/872-8633). Sells first-aid kits, mosquito netting, water filters and other health-related travel products.

Travellers Medical Center, 31 Washington Square, New York, NY 10011 (☎212/982-1600). Consultation service on immunizations and treatment.

IN THE UK AND IRELAND

British travellers should pick up a copy of the free booklet *Health Advice for Travellers*, published by the Department of Health; it's available from GP's surgeries, many chemists, and most of the agencies listed below.

British Airways Travel Clinic, 156 Regent St, London W1R 5TA (Mon–Fri 9am–4.15pm, Sat 10am–4pm; ☎0171/439-9584); and over 30 other clinics throughout UK: call ☎01276/685040 or check *www.british-airways.com* to find your nearest branch. Excellent medical advice, vaccinations and a comprehensive range of travel health items – and you even get air miles. No appointments necessary at Regent St; call ahead at other clinics.

Hospital for Tropical Diseases Travel Clinic, Mortimer Market Centre, Capper St, London WC1 (Mon–Fri 9am–5pm; ☎0171/530-3454). Recorded message service on ☎0839/337722 gives hints on hygiene and illness prevention as well as lists of appropriate immunizations; will fax back area-specific health information.

MASTA (Medical Advisory Service for Travellers Abroad), London School of Hygiene and Tropical Medicine, Keppel St, London WC1E 7HT (☎0171/631-4408; calling this number will auto-matically refer you to the premium rate Travellers' Health Line (☎0891/224100) which operates round the clock, giving written information tailored to your journey by return of post; *dspace.dial.pipex.com/masta/index.html*

Trailfinders Travel Clinic, 194 Kensington High St, London W8 6BD (☎0171/338-3999); 254–284 Sauchiehall Street, Glasgow G2 3EH (☎0141/353-0066). Expert medical advice and a full range of travel vaccines and medical supplies. No appointments necessary in London. Discounts on vaccinations for clients.

Travel Medicine Services, PO Box 254, 16 College St, Belfast 1 (☎01232/315220). Operates a travel clinic (Mon 9–11am & Wed 2–4pm) which can give inoculations after referral from a GP, but primarily administers yellow fever vaccine.

Tropical Medical Bureau, Grafton St Medical Centre, Dublin 2 (☎01/671-9200; *tmb@iol.ie; www.tmb.ie*),

IN AUSTRALIA

Travellers' Medical and Vaccination Centre, 7/428 George St, Sydney (☎02/9221-7133); 3/393 Little Bourke St, Melbourne (☎03/9602-5788); 6/29 Gilbert Place, Adelaide (☎08/8212-7522);

6/247 Adelaide St, Brisbane (☎07/3221-9066); 1 Mill St, Perth (☎08/9321-1977); Level 1, Canterbury Arcade, 170 Queen St, Auckland 1 (☎09/373-3531); *www.tmvc.com.au*

INFORMATION AND MAPS

Information about Central America is available from a number of sources, though much of the promotional puff provided by the official tourist offices is pretty to look at but of little practical use. However, the quality of such information is improving, and if you have specific questions you could try contacting some of the official organizations listed below.

INFORMATION

When digging out information on Central America, don't forget the **specialist travel agents** (see p.6, 7 and 10) and the **embassies** (see p.17). Best of all for practical details, bookmark the recommended **Internet sites**.

CENTRAL AMERICAN TOURIST OFFICES: WEB SITES AND EMAIL ADDRESSES

Belize *www.belizenet.com*

Costa Rica *www.tourism-costarica.com*

El Salvador no tourist Web site: *www.elsalvador.nv* is a government page with some information.

Guatemala *www.travel-guatemala.org.gt* email: *inguat@guate.net*

Honduras *www.hondunet.net/turis.html*

Nicaragua *www.mitur.gob.ni*

Panamá email: *ipat@panaminfo.com*
See also the list of useful Internet sites on p.26.

Current political analysis and an interesting and informative overview of the society, economy and environment of each Central American country is provided by two **specialist publishers**; the Resource Center in the USA who produce the *Inside* series covering each country; and the Latin America Bureau in UK, an independent, non-profit research organization, whose *In Focus* series so far covers Belize, Guatemala and Costa Rica in Central America, as well as Mexico and much of South America. Though detailed, the books are not large, around 100–200 pages, and if you're going to spend any length of time in the region it's worth having a look at these before you go.

The **Latin American Travel Advisor** is a quarterly newsletter with a comprehensive report on every Central American country, covering safety, health, politics and the economy, along with a special feature on a relevant topic. One issue costs US$15, or you can pay US$39 for a year's subscription. Send a cheque to Latin American Travel Consultants, PO Box 17-17-908, Quito, Ecuador (fax 593/2-562-566). Headlines and excerpts are published on their Web site: *www.amerispan.com/latc/*

Anyone who has an interest in **working or volunteering** in Central America should contact Amerispan, PO Box 40007, Philadelphia, PA 19106-0007 (☎1-800/879-6640; *info@amerispan.com*; *www.amerispan.com*), which has a wide range of resources for learning Spanish and volunteer opportunities in Central America, selecting language schools and providing excellent support and information.

IN THE UK

In London you can freely visit **Canning House Library**, 2 Belgrave Square, SW1X 8PJ (☎0171/235-2303), which has the UK's largest publicly accessible collection of books and periodicals on Latin America (you have to be a member to take books out and receive the twice-yearly *Bulletin*, a review of recently published books on Latin America).

Citizens of the UK who are thinking of **working or volunteering** in Central America should take a look at the publications of the Central Bureau for Educational Visits, 10 Spring Gardens, London SW1A 2BN (☎0171/389-4880; *books@centralbureau.org.uk*) particularly *Working Holidays* (updated annually) and *Volunteer Work*, both packed with essential information, including contacts in Mexico and Central America.

For general information on **independent travel** pick up a copy of the excellent *Everything You Need to Know Before You Go* (Abroadsheet Publications, from specialist bookshops); author Mark Ashton has managed to compile an enormous amount of essential advice and tips onto one amazingly well-organized (large) glossy sheet. Finally, if you're planning an expedition from the UK, you can (and should) avail yourself of the services of the **Expedition Advisory Centre**, at the Royal Geographic Society, 1 Kensington Gore, London SW7 2AR (☎0171/581-2057; *eac@rgs.org*). As well as expedition planning seminars, the EAC also publishes a range of specialist books.

IN CENTRAL AMERICA

While you're in Central America you'll find **government tourism offices** in each capital city, and sometimes in the main tourist centres. The information they're able to give is variable, but they can usually provide at the very least a city map, a bus timetable and perhaps a list of hotels (and may possibly even call them for you). The addresses (and an idea of how useful a particular office will be) are given throughout the guide. In addition there are some locally run initiatives, often set up by an association of tourism businesses; any tour and travel agents we've mentioned in the guide will be reliable sources of information.

TOURIST INFORMATION

IN NORTH AMERICA

Belize USA: ☎212/563-6011 or 1-800/624-0686.

Costa Rica No tourist office in the US or Canada, but calling ☎1-800/343-6332 will reach an English speaker at the tourist office in San José at no extra charge to you.

El Salvador USA: ☎212/889-3608; Canada: ☎613/238-2939.

Guatemala USA: ☎212/689-1014 or 1-800/742-4529, fax 305/442-1013; Canada: ☎613/233-2339.

Honduras USA: ☎1-800/410-9608.

Nicaragua USA: ☎202/939-6531.

Panamá email them (see box opposite) or call the embassy (p.17).

IN THE UK AND IRELAND

Only Guatemala has a tourist office in the **UK**, at the same address as the embassy (☎0171/349-0346; Mon–Fri 10am–3pm). This office and the consular representatives of the other countries (addresses are listed on p.17) will send you information on their respective countries if you send an SAE with a 39p stamp; best give them a call first to check what they have:

Belize	☎0171/499-9728	**Honduras**	☎0171/486-4880
Costa Rica	☎0171/706-8844	**Nicaragua**	☎0171/938-2373
El Salvador	☎0171/436-8282	**Panamá**	☎0171/409-2255

IN AUSTRALASIA

It's difficult to find official tourist information about Central America in **Australia** or **New Zealand**; your best bet is to contact the websites, Bushbooks (see opposite), the consulate (listed on p.17) or specialist travel agents (p.14).

MAP OUTLETS

USA

Rand McNally, 444 N Michigan Ave, Chicago, IL 60611 (☎312/321-1751); 150 E 52nd St, New York, NY 10022 (☎212/758-7488); 595 Market St, San Francisco, CA 94105 (☎415/777-3131); 1201 Connecticut Ave NW, Washington DC 20003 (☎202/223-6751).

For other locations, or for maps by mail order, call ☎1-800/333-0136 (ext 2111).

UK

Stanfords, 12–14 Long Acre, London WC2E 9LP (☎0171/836-1321); 52 Grosvenor Gardens, London SW1W 0AG; 156 Regent St, London W1R 5TA.
For mail order maps call the Long Acre branch.

AUSTRALASIA

Specialty Maps, 58 Albert St, Auckland (☎09/307-2217).
Travel Bookshop, Shop 3, 175 Liverpool St, Sydney, (☎02/9261-8200).

THE INTERNET

The number of pages devoted to Central America on the **Internet** is growing daily. The first place to look is the comprehensive and logically laid-out homepage of the **Latin American Information Center** (LANIC; *www.lanic.utexas.edu*), which has a seemingly never-ending series of superb links for each country. You can reach almost anywhere and anything in Central America connected to the net from here. **Green Arrow**'s pages (*www.greenarrow.com*) while concentrating on Costa Rica, are a good source of travel and environmental information and volunteering opportunities throughout Central America. It's also worth checking the web page of the **Latin American Travel Advisor** (see p.24). The **Central Index of Appointments Overseas** (CIAO; *www.ciao-directory.org*) has links with dozens of organizations accepting volunteers with specialist skills in Central America. Finally, the ever-helpful members of the **newsgroup** *rec.travel.latin-america* will answer any query about travel in the region. Most have been asked already so there's a huge (and generally accurate) information base to dip into.

MAPS

The best **map of Central America**, covering the region at a scale of 1:1,800,000, is produced by International Travel Map Productions (736A Granville St, Vancouver, BC, V62 1G3, Canada). They also publish **individual maps** of each country at a scale of 1:750,000 (Belize at 1:350,000), but these tend to have a few mistakes. Specialist map shops should sell them and it's wise to try to get what you need before you go, although they are available in many Central American capitals.

ACCOMMODATION

Central American hotels come in all shapes and sizes and it's usually not hard to find somewhere reasonable. Accommodation comes under a bewildering range of names; *hotel*, obviously, but you'll frequently see *pensión*, *casa de huéspedes*, *hospedaje*, *posada*, *rancho* and *campamento* – the last two usually refer to some form of camping. The different names don't always mean a great deal: in theory a *casa de huéspedes* is less formal than a *hotel* but in reality the main difference will be the price. You'll soon get used to finding what's on offer in your preferred price and style of accommodation.

Most countries have some form of price (and in theory, quality) regulation and there's sometimes also a **hotel tax** to pay: always check if this is included in the rate you're quoted. It's a good idea to have a look at the room before you take it; make sure the light and fan work, and if you've been told there's hot water, see just what that means.

BUDGET HOTELS

There's so much variety in standards for even a budget hotel that to list every possible permuta-tion of types and furnishings would be impossi-ble. However, a **basic room** in a town will have a light and a fan in addition to the bed, though don't expect a reading light or anywhere to put clothes, and all but the rock bottom places will also supply a towel, soap and toilet paper. You'll often have the option of a private **bathroom** (ie a toilet and basic shower); worth paying the small amount extra, especially if you're travelling as a couple. If the **price** seems a little high for the type of establishment it's worth asking if there's less expensive room (*¿Tiene un cuarto más bara-to, por favor?*) – you'll often get the same room at a lower price. It's always better to get a room at the back, away from the noise of the street, and upstairs you're more likely to benefit from a breeze. Most small hotels will be family run, and the owners usually take pride in the cleanliness of the rooms. There will usually be a place to hand-wash clothes (a *pila*); ask first before you use it.

In **lowland areas** a fan (*ventilador*) will be more important than hot water (*agua caliente*), but in the mountains you'd probably prefer a hot shower, though there will rarely be any form of heating (*calefacción*); make sure you have enough blankets. The term "hot shower" in Central America can be a bit misleading; the water tem-perature may just be tepid rather than really hot. And sometimes the "heating element" will be a couple of wires running into a contraption above the shower nozzle – touching this is likely to give you an electric shock.

As a rule budget hotels in the **capital cities** tend to be less attractive than those in smaller towns and tourist areas, though we've listed the exceptions in the relevant chapters. In the bigger cities it's worth paying a little more, or even mov-ing to one grade of hotel higher than you might otherwise, to stay in a more secure place – par-ticularly for your first night. Cheap hotels are

---

ACCOMMODATION PRICE CODES

All accommodation reviewed in this guide has been graded according to the following price scales, which represent the cost of a double room in high season excluding any taxes.

① up to US$5	④ US$15–25	⑦ US$60–80
② US$5–10	⑤ US$25–40	⑧ US$80–100
③ US$10–15	⑥ US$40–60	⑨ US$100 and over

often crowded around bus stations and markets; some of these can be very dismal, many of them being used by prostitutes and their clients. However, in every capital there are at least one or two hotels where other travellers congregate (as well as plenty where they don't) to offer company and perhaps security.

Budget hotels in **rural areas** or **coastal locations** which are not touristy are often quite basic; a ramshackle building or perhaps a stick and thatch cabaña. These can be delightful – you'll be less of a guest and more an extra member of the family – but they can also be very uncomfortable, with lumpy mattresses and poor ventilation. This is where serviceable insect proofing can make the difference between misery and a good night's sleep.

Booking ahead for a budget room is not usually necessary (and often not possible, because of the difficulty of paying in advance), though it might be worth trying at busy times like Christmas and Easter. Otherwise arriving early at your destination will give you a better selection.

RESORTS AND LODGES

Bigger hotels in cities will have similar facilities to those at home, though often in a more attractive setting and sometimes in a wonderfully restored colonial building. They will almost certainly have air conditioning (*aire acondicionado*); a feature increasingly offered in less expensive places. You'll pay a good deal more for this than you would for a room with a fan and, other

things being equal, it may not be worth the extra. Some of the best accommodation in the region, however, is offered by the **resorts**, in beach areas, or **jungle-lodges**, often in beautiful, remote locations in or near national parks. Here you'll often have a private thatched cabaña, with a balcony overlooking the forest, lake, beach or other natural attraction. Obviously you'll be paying extra for this, but the experience of a rainforest dawn chorus and the chance of getting close to wildlife makes it worthwhile. These lodges are often used by the adventure and nature tour operators and occupancy varies with the season – if the lodge is open out of season, ask about possible discounts.

YOUTH HOSTELS AND CAMPING

In a region so full of inexpensive hotels you need rarely consider staying in **youth hostels**. In any case, only Costa Rica has a useful hostel network, with many located near national parks. The situation is similar with respect to **camping**. Few places outside Costa Rica offer formal campsites. Elsewhere, you'll usually only need a tent if you're hiking really off the beaten track – though you'll probably have a guide who knows where there are shelters to hang a hammock, a tent offers better protection from rain and, more importantly, from insects. Some volcanos are too high to climb and descend in one day and if camping on the top you'll need some protection from the cold as well; a good sleeping bag is essential.

GETTING AROUND

Travel within Central America is a varied as the region itself. Since most locals don't own a car, buses are the most common form of public transport, and if you're travelling independently without your own vehicle you'll be spending a lot of time in (and waiting for) them.

You're also likely to travel by **boat** – out to and between islands, along rivers, and as the main form of transport in areas like the Mosquito coast of Honduras and Nicaragua. The craft themselves range from precarious-looking dugout canoes and old tubs for ferries, to fast, modern launches, capable of long-distance sea travel.

Each country has one or more domestic **airline**, usually relatively inexpensive, and often saving hours of road travel over the region's diffi-cult terrain. If you're covering a lot of territory, air-passes can be very good value; see below.

Taxis are readily available in all the main towns; some routes (from airports to city centres for example) have set prices, but meters are a rarity – always fix a price before you set off. Taxis can also be a good substitute for a rental car; you have the advantage of your own transport without the responsibility, and could even work out cheaper.

Prices vary for **car rental** throughout Central America. The cheapest rate for a week in Belize, for example, where companies only offer sport/utility vehicles, is with Budget at around US$400. However, in Costa Rica, one week's car rental costs around US$170 per week with Avis. Dollar's rates for Panamá, El Salvador and Honduras are around US$100, US$200 and US$270 respectively, per week. In Guatemala rates don't vary between companies; expect to pay around US$250 a week for a standard car, or US$320 for 4WD. If you plan to rent a car make sure you get a good **map** (see p.24) and bear in mind that Central America has some of the highest **accident rates** in the world – and as a foreigner any collision is likely to be construed as your fault. Always take full-cover insurance. If you've suc-ceeded in getting your own car to Central America, any further problems you face are likely to seem fairly minor. If you belong to a **motoring organi-zation** at home, it's worth calling to see if they'll offer advice, maps and even help from reciprocal organizations in Central America. **Security** is a

AIRPASSES

If want to visit the whole region in a fairly short time, the **"Visit Central America Airpass"** can cut costs considerably. For example, a routing Miami–San José–Managua–Guatemala City–LA will cost US$699 low season/US$749 high season – at least one-third less than flying the same route on a normal ticket. The pass links North American gateways with all the capitals and some other cities in Central America, and some destinations in South America and the Caribbean; the possible routes are mind-boggling. You have to buy the pass – in the form of coupons for each flight – before leaving home, enter the region on one of the participating airlines (Aviateca, Copa, Lacsa, Nica and Taca) and book your route in advance. Free date changes are allowed if space is available (within the 60-day validity of the pass) but a change of route will cost US$50.

The **"Mex-AmeriPass"** combines the exten-sive networks of Aeroméxico and Mexicana, link-ing destinations throughout Mexico with several Central and South American cities.

The best way to find out how (or if) an airpass will benefit you is to call JLA in the UK (☎0181/747-3018; *sales@journeylatinamerica.co .uk*); or contact eXito in the USA (☎1-800/655-4053 or 510/655-2154; *exito@wonderlink.com*; *www.wonderlink.com/exito*)

major headache – always park in a safe place and never leave your car in the street overnight. **Traffic** is generally light outside the main cities and major routes are paved. **Fuel** is marginally more expensive than in the US and cheap by European standards, but filling stations are scarce outside the main cities.

Bicycles are very common in Central America, and increasing numbers of visitors bring their own. If you do (or if you rent a bike) you'll find a repair shop in every town. Some buses can carry bikes on the roof, giving greater flexibility. In the UK, membership of the Cyclists' Touring Club (69 Meadrow, Godalming, Surrey GU7 3HS ☎01483/417217; *cycling@ctc.org.uk*; *www.ctc.org.uk*) means you can access trip reports from and information geared to cyclists who've taken bikes in the region.

GETTING AROUND BY BUS

Cheap, convenient, often crowded and sometimes wildly entertaining, Central American **buses** come in a variety of forms, from first-class, air-conditioned luxury liners with videos and reclining seats, to ramshackle, third-class, third-hand, recycled US schoolbuses. They're often garishly painted, carrying villagers, their shopping and their animals to and from market – the original and ubiquitous "chicken bus". They ply the main routes regularly, and some form of service connects the most remote villages to the provincial and national capitals – provided even a rudimentary road exists. In places where the bus does not reach, drivers of pickup trucks will load passengers in the back; you pay the driver a small fee. How to make best use of each country's bus service is detailed in the guide. The best **international bus service** is the Ticabus, running from Guatemala City to Panamá City, calling at San Salvador, Managua and San José. The whole journey takes two and a half days, including overnights (at your own expense) at San Salvador and Managua.

At many **land borders**, buses from the adjacent country will cross the border to drop off and pick up passengers in the other country's terminal, which simplifies transport and immmigration, especially if the immigration posts and terminals are some distance apart.

MAIL, PHONES AND THE INTERNET

Mail and telecommunication services in Central America run the gamut from extremely efficient (Belize and Costa Rica) to chronically temperamental (Guatemala). Postal services are generally inexpensive and postcards and letters mailed home do usually get through, however. Local calls (and many long-distance internal calls) from payphones are fairly cheap but international calls are comparatively more expensive than at home. A number of private communications agencies operate in the capitals and some tourist areas, generally offering better service – at a price.

MAIL

Throughout the region the best way to ensure speed(ier) delivery is to use the **main post office** in a capital city; this will also be the best place to send parcels. **Post boxes** are rare – you'll find them in the lobbies of big hotels and some tourist shops – but the best bet is to take mail to a post office. As a rule of thumb, an **airmail letter** to the USA takes about a week; to Europe about ten days or so. **Receiving mail** is less certain, but you can generally rely on the service in main post offices; have letters sent to you (with your surname underlined), *Lista de Correos* ("General Delivery" in Belize), *Correo*

Central, name of city, country, and finishing with "Central America". When looking to see if mail has arrived ask to see the *Lista de Correos*, which is usually typed up each day, and search for your name (check whether mail is being held under your forename or surname). You'll need identification; a passport is best.

Always use some form of registration for **parcels** (the exact name differs from country to country); it won't cost much extra above the postage and you'll get a certificate to give you some peace of mind. You can send parcels via surface mail but this literally takes months. Be prepared for the parcel to undergo some form of inspection, and there may be some quaint labelling and wrapping regulations to observe.

PHONES

Although Central America's **telephone system** is gradually improving, and telephone charge and calling cards are widely accepted, much of it still leaves a lot to be desired. Sending a **fax** from a public telephone office is often easier than mak-

ing a phone call. A number of **communication businesses** have opened in tourist areas throughout the region, often offering email and Internet services also. **Calling home collect** (*llamar por cobrar*) is simple to those countries which receive collect calls from the country you're in – but not all do. Before leaving home, it's worth checking whether a phone company in your country has a number to call abroad to connect you with the operator – this is usually the easiest way to call home collect.

THE INTERNET

With the exception of Nicaragua, Central America's capitals and main towns are well connected to the **online services**, and it's becoming easier every month to access the Internet yourself. Most of the big towns will have a **cybercafé**; if you've got a service provider which allows you to pick up email anywhere you can check your mail at these. Before you go, look at *www.netcafeguide.com* and click on the Latin America map to see where they are.

CRIME AND PERSONAL SAFETY

While political violence has decreased over recent years, crime rates in Central America are rising alarmingly, and in many popular tourist locations you or your belongings will be targeted by determined thieves. The majority of crime is petty theft – bag-snatching or pickpocketing for example – but some

criminals operate in gangs and are prepared to use extreme violence to rob you.

Though it is commonly accepted that **Guatemala** tops the list for tourist crime, it's closely followed by the north of **Honduras** and **El Salvador** – and given the relatively small number of tourists in these countries, the probability of coming across trouble is that bit higher. Wherever you go you should take commonsense precautions; relax, but don't get complacent. If you've got valuables, insure them properly (see p.14).

AVOIDING CRIME

You're more likely to be a **victim** of crime when you've just arrived, especially when you're looking for a room after dark – getting to your hotel in daylight will add greatly to your safety. Keep your most valuable possessions on you (but don't wear expensive jewellery) in a moneybelt under your outer clothes, though this isn't as easy as it sounds, as you'll have to get your passport and money out at border crossings. Trousers with zipped pockets are an idea to deter pickpockets. Border crossings, where you'll often have to change money, surprisingly enough aren't that dangerous; the moneychanger is unlikely to shortchange you (though getting the right exchange rate is another matter), and the presence of armed officials generally discourages thieves in the immediate area of the immigration post. Do the transaction and put your money away out of sight of other people if at all possible. Once away from the post however, you need to be on your guard; beware of people "helping" you find a bus and offering to carry your luggage. In many cases they will genuinely be offering a service in return for a tip, but at times like this you're easily distracted and you should never let your belongings out of sight unless you're confident they're in a safe place.

TRAVEL AND HOTELS

Travelling on **public transport**, particularly by bus, you'll usually be separated from your main bag – it will go either in the luggage compartment underneath or in the rack on top. This is usually safe enough (and you have little option in any case) but keep an eye on it whenever you can. Although the theft of the bag itself is uncommon, opportunist thieves may dip into zippers and outer pockets. You can get small padlocks for backpacks but for greater security you can put your pack into a coffee or flour sack (*costal*) and put

that into a net (*red*). It might look a little outlandish but it's the way the locals transport goods and keeps it clean and dry too – sacks and nets are sold in any market. Once on the bus it's best to keep your small bag on your lap. If you do put it on the inside luggage rack keep it in sight and tie it (or preferably clip it with a carabiner) onto the rack to deter thieves who may try to snatch it and throw it out of the window to an accomplice.

In your **hotel**, make sure the lock on your door works; from the inside as well as out. In many budget hotels the lock will be a small padlock in the outside, and it's a good idea to buy your own (*candado* – readily available on street stalls) so you're the only one with keys. Many hotels will have a safe or secure area for valuables. It's up to you whether you use this; most of the time it will be fine, but make sure whatever you do put in is securely and tightly wrapped; a spare, lockable moneybelt is good for this.

You're less likely to be a victim of a mugging or armed robbery, but when it happens there's little you can do about it, so prevention is essential. Avoid obviously dangerous areas – deserted city centres and bus stations late at night – just like you would at home. A ploy to watch out for is for someone to surreptitiously throw an obnoxious liquid over your pack or clothes – a "passer by" kindly offers to help you clean it up, while another member of the gang snatches your bag. Much worse are the planned armed robberies on tourist

---

TRAVEL WARNINGS AND SAFETY INFORMATION

For **British travellers** the **Foreign Office Travel Advice Unit** (☎0171/238-4503, Mon–Fri 9.30am–4pm; ☎0374/500900 for automated service; *www.fco.gov.uk/*) issues travel advice notices, which give a broadly accurate overview of the dangers facing visitors to Central America. They also produce a worthwhile leaflet for backpackers and independent travellers, which gives good advice and explains what a consul can and cannot do for you when you're abroad. The **US equivalent** is the **State Department's Consular Information Service** (*travel.state.gov/travel_warnings.html*), which publishes information sheets about each country, again listing fairly accurately the main dangers to US citizens. If any country is considered particularly dangerous, a travel warning will be issued, though this may in fact simply indicate an isolat-

ed incident involving a US visitor. The advice contained in these pages is worth heeding, but don't be put off travelling completely – you could get into more danger in any big city at home than you're likely to encounter travelling wisely in Central America.

You can always register at your **embassy** when (or even before) you arrive – we've listed phone numbers in the guide. This is advisable if you're spending a long time in or travelling to remote areas of the region, though it's not necessary if you're on an organized tour. Always take photocopies of your passport and insurance documents and try to leave them in a secure place; leave a copy with someone at home too. A second credit card, kept in a very safe location and only to be used in emergencies, will be invaluable if your other cards or funds get stolen.

minibuses in Guatemala; usually the robbers will go through the passengers collecting money and valuables but occasionally victims are taken away and assaulted, and even raped. For this reason some tour groups in Guatemala are accompanied by an armed guard.

POLICE

If you have anything stolen, report the incident immediately to the **police** – if there is a tourist police force, try them first – if only to get a copy of the report (*denuncia*) for insurance purposes (see p.14). The police in Central America are poorly paid and you can't expect them to do much more than make out the report – often you'll have difficulty getting them to do even this. You may have to dictate it to them (and sometimes they'll demand a fee

for their services); unless you're fluent, try to take someone along who speaks better Spanish than you do. And if you can, also report the crime to your **embassy** – it helps the consular staff build up a higher-level case for better protection for tourists.

Obviously you want to avoid any **trouble** with the police whatsoever. Practically every capital city has foreigners incarcerated for drug offences who'd never do it again if they knew what the punishment was like. Drugs of all kinds are readily available but if you indulge be very discreet. The pusher may have a sideline reporting clients to the police, and catching "international drug smugglers" gives the country concerned brownie points with the DEA. If you are arrested your embassy will probably send someone to visit you, and maybe find an English-speaking lawyer, but certainly can't get you out of jail.

PART TWO

BELIZE

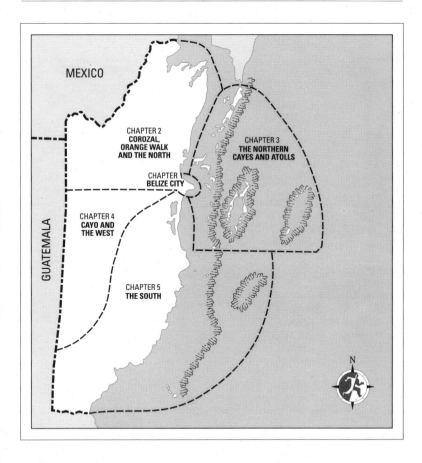

MEXICO

GUATEMALA

CHAPTER 2
**COROZAL,
ORANGE WALK
AND THE NORTH**

CHAPTER 1
BELIZE CITY

CHAPTER 3
**THE NORTHERN
CAYES AND ATOLLS**

CHAPTER 4
**CAYO AND
THE WEST**

CHAPTER 5
THE SOUTH

N

Introduction

Wedged into the northeastern corner of Central America by the Yucatán peninsula and the rainforests of Guatemala's Petén, **Belize** offers some of the most breathtaking scenery anywhere in the Caribbean. This small country consists of marginally more sea than land, with the dazzling turquoise shallows and cobalt depths of the longest **barrier reef** in the Americas just offshore. Here, beneath the surface, a brilliant, technicolour world of fish and corals awaits divers and snorkellers. Scattered along the entire reef, a chain of islands (known here as "**cayes**") protect the mainland from the ocean swell and offer more than a hint of tropical paradise. Beyond the reef lie the real jewels in Belize's natural crown – three of only four **coral atolls** in the Caribbean.

These reefs and islands are among the most diverse marine ecosystems on the planet, but, like all coral reefs, face numerous threats. Belize, however, is at the forefront of practical research to develop effective protection for the entire coastal zone, which for visitors means a chance to explore some of the best **marine reserves** in the world.

Belizeans recognize the importance of conservation and their country boasts a higher proportion of protected land (over 35 percent) than any other. This has allowed the **densely forested interior** to remain relatively untouched, boasting abundant natural attractions, including the highest waterfall in Central America and the world's only jaguar reserve. Rich tropical forests support a tremendous range of **wildlife**, including howler and spider monkeys, tapirs and pumas, jabiru storks and scarlet macaws; spend any time inland and you're sure to see the national bird, the very visible keel-billed toucan. To see the more reticent animals, you should make every effort to visit what is easily the best **zoo** in Central America.

Despite being the only Central American country without a volcano, Belize does have some rugged uplands in the south-central region, where the **Maya Mountains** rise to over 1100m. The country's main rivers rise here, flowing north or east to the Caribbean, along the way forming some of the largest **cave systems** in the Americas, few of which have been fully explored. These caves often bear traces of the **Maya civilization** that dominated the area from around 2000 BC until the arrival of the Spanish. The most obvious remains of this fascinating culture are the ruins of dozens of **ancient cities** rising out of the rainforest.

Officially **English-speaking**, and only gaining full independence from Britain in 1981, Belize is as much a Caribbean nation as a Latin one, but one with plenty of distinctively Central American features, above all a blend of cultures and races that includes Maya, *mestizo*, African and European. Spanish is at least as widely spoken as English, but the rich, lilting **Creole** is the spoken language understood and used by almost every Belizean, whatever their first tongue. You'll hear this everywhere – and though based on English, it's less comprehensible to outsiders than it might first appear.

With far less of a language barrier to overcome than elsewhere in the region, uncrowded Belize is the ideal first stop on a tour of the isthmus. And, although it's the second-smallest country in Central America (slightly larger than El Salvador), the wealth of national parks and reserves, the numerous small hotels and restaurants, together with plenty of reliable public transport make Belize an ideal place to travel independently, giving visitors plenty of scope to explore little-visited Caribbean islands as well as the heartland of the ancient Maya.

■ Where to go

Almost every visitor will have to spend at least some time in **Belize City**, even if only passing through, as it's the hub of the country's transport system. First-time visitors may be shocked by the decaying buildings and the pollution of the Belize River, but it's possible to spend several pleasant hours in this former outpost of the British Empire. In contrast, Belize's capital, **Belmopan**, is primarily an administrative centre with little to offer visitors.

Northern Belize is relatively flat and often swampy, with a large proportion of agricultural land, though as everywhere in Belize there are Maya ruins and nature reserves. **Lamanai**, near Orange Walk, is one of the most impressive Maya sites in the country, and lagoons here and at **Sarteneja** (Shipstern Nature Reserve) and **Crooked Tree** offer a superb protected habitat for wildlife. Adjacent to the Guatemalan border is the vast **Rio Bravo Conservation Area.**

The largest of the cayes, **Ambergris Caye**, draws more than half of all tourists to Belize, their

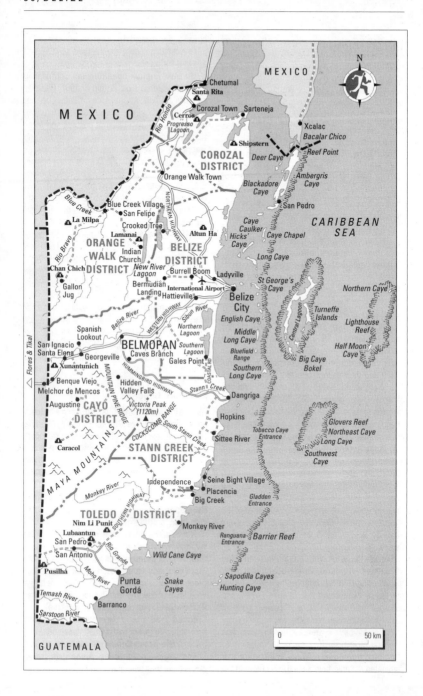

main destination the resort town of **San Pedro**. To the south, **Caye Caulker** is the most popular of the islands with independent travellers. Many of the less developed cayes are becoming easier to reach, and organized trips are available to the atolls of **Lighthouse Reef** and **Glover's Reef**.

In the west **San Ignacio** has everything for the ecotourist: Maya ruins and rainforest, rivers and caves, and excellent accommodation in every price range. **Caracol**, the largest Maya site in Belize, is now a routine day-trip from here, while the magnificent ruin of **Xunantunich** is also within easy reach, on the road to the Guatemalan border.

Dangriga, the main town of the south-central region, serves as a jumping-off point for visitors to the central cayes and atolls (still little developed at present) and for trips to the **Cockscomb Basin Wildlife Sanctuary**. Further south along the coast, the quiet Garífuna village of **Hopkins** sees more visitors every year, while the delightful, laid-back **Placencia**, at the tip of a long, curving peninsula, has some of the country's best **beaches**. Most visitors to **Punta Gorda**, the main town in the far south of Belize, are on their way to or from Puerto Barrios in Guatemala. If you venture inland, however, you'll come across the **villages** of the Mopan and Kekchi Maya, set in some of the most stunning countryside in Belize and surrounded by the only true **rainforest** in the country, dotted with caves, rivers and ruins.

■ When to go

Belize lies in a **subtropical** latitude, so the weather is always warm by European standards. The immediate climate is largely determined by **altitude**, with the Maya Mountains pleasantly cool and the lowland jungles usually steamy and humid, no matter what the time of year. The coast and offshore cayes can be sweltering, but most of the time the heat is tempered by cooling ocean breezes. Humidity is most marked in the **rainy season** – officially from May to November – when mornings are generally clear and afternoons often drenched by downpours. The worst of the rain falls in September and October, when in the more remote southern parts of the country roads can be flooded and journeys delayed, though the rains often continue through to December, when **cold fronts** push down from the north, lowering temperatures to around 10°C. The **best time of year** to visit is

from December to March, when the vegetation is lush and the skies are generally clear. This coincides with the peak tourist season, though many people also visit during the summer. Late March to May, before the onset of the first rains, can often be stiflingly hot.

Perhaps the most serious weather threat is from **hurricanes**, which occasionally sweep through the Caribbean in the late summer and autumn. If you're on the coast or the cayes, you'll hear about it long before the storm hits. Wind speeds can exceed 120km per hour, but rest assured that the country has an efficient warning system and a network of shelters.

Getting around

Despite having just four main roads, and only two – the Northern and Western highways – that are as yet truly all-weather, Belize is well served by **public transport**. The main roads, and even most unpaved side roads, are generally kept in good repair and are usually passable except in the very worst rainstorms. Anywhere you can't reach by bus, you can generally get there by water taxi or light aircraft, which can be less expensive than you might expect.

■ Buses

The vast majority of buses are **second-class**, although on the Northern and Western highways there are also a couple of luxury **express buses**, crossing into Chetumal in Mexico and Melchor in Guatemala. These express buses stop only in the towns, while regular buses will pick up and drop off anywhere along the roadside. The Hummingbird and Southern highways, to Dangriga, Placencia and Punta Gorda, are not quite so well provided for, though there are at least eight daily buses to Dangriga and three or four to Placencia and Punta Gorda (a good eight hours from Belize City). On all of these routes tickets can be bought in advance from the offices in Belize City; pay the conductor if you get on along the route. **Fares** are very reasonable (roughly US$5 from Belize City to Chetumal and US$11 to Punta Gorda).

Heading away from the main highways you'll be relying on the slower **local bus services**, often with just one bus a day. Be warned that most services are reduced on Sunday, when local buses often don't run at all.

■ Taxis

All **taxis** in Belize are licensed and easily identifiable by their green number plates. They operate from special ranks in the centre of all mainland towns and, particularly in Belize City, drivers will call out to anyone they suspect is a foreigner. There are no meters so you'll need to establish rates in advance, though within the towns a US$2.50 fixed rate applies.

■ Driving and hitching

Driving in Belize is subject to the same limitations as bus travel. The Northern and Western highways offer easy motoring and smooth roads, as does most of the Hummingbird Highway, but in the south the roads are rough and distances are long. If you want to head off the beaten track or make your way down south, then you'll need high clearance and four-wheel drive. **Unleaded petrol** is easily available, but it can be difficult to get hold of spare parts for your own car. **Insurance** is available from an agent just inside either of the land border crossings or in Belize City. Under Belize's new **seatbelt law**, you'll be fined US$12.50 for not belting up.

All the main **car rental companies** offer cars, Jeeps and four-wheel drives for between US$75 and US$100 a day, plus US$15 per day for insurance. You'll usually have to be over 25 and will need to leave either a credit card, travellers' cheques or a large cash deposit. Many outfits do not offer comprehensive insurance, so the renter is likely to be held liable for any damage to the vehicle, however caused. Note that some companies consider driving a car on minor dirt roads (especially in the south) to be taking the vehicle "off-road", which may invalidate your insurance. Check carefully before signing anything.

In the more remote parts of Belize the bus service will probably only operate once a day, if at all, and unless you have your own transport, **hitching** is the only option. The main drawback is the shortage of traffic, but if cars or, more likely, pickup trucks, do pass they'll usually offer you a lift, though you may be expected to offer the driver some money.

■ Cycling

Seeing Belize from a **bike** is fairly straightforward and you'll find repair shops in all the towns. Increasingly bikes are available for **rent**, especially in San Ignacio and Placencia. Few Belizean buses have the roof racks that are such a familiar sight in Guatemala; if there's room, the driver might let you take the bike onto the bus.

■ Boats

Most **boats** you're likely to use will be fast **skiffs**, usually open boats with two powerful outboard motors (though some are covered), carrying around twenty passengers from Belize City and mainland destinations out to the **cayes**; some also cover the **international** routes from Punta Gorda to Puerto Barrios in Guatemala and from Dangriga to Puerto Cortés in Honduras. The service is fast, reliable and safe – all registered boats should carry lifejackets and most also carry marine radios. Times and destinations are covered in the text and you'll only need to book ahead for international departures, though it's worthwhile buying your ticket the day before for early departures from the cayes.

Travel to more remote cayes will usually be part of a tour or package, but boats can be chartered for travel along the rivers and amongst the islands.

■ Planes

Maya Island Air (☎02/31362) and Tropic Air (☎02/45671) offer a **scheduled service** from Belize International airport and Belize City's Municipal airport to all of the main towns (except Belmopan and San Ignacio) and out to San Pedro and Caye Caulker; there are also several **charter airlines**. A flight from Belize City to San Pedro costs around US$23, to Punta Gorda US$70.

There have been regular **regional flights** to **Flores** and **Guatemala City** and to **San Pedro Sula**, and **Roatán** in the Bay Islands, Honduras, for years. Flights to Mexico, however, are plagued by interruptions in service. Currently Aerocaribe fly three times a week to **Cancún**, usually calling at Chetumal.

Costs, money and banks

Belize has the unfortunate but generally well-deserved reputation as being one of the more expensive countries in Central America and even on a tight budget you'll spend at least forty percent more than in, say, Guatemala. Perhaps as compensation for the general cost of living you can travel in the sure knowledge that you'll be paying the same fares as the locals and you'll never be subjected to mysterious (and sometimes illegal) border crossing charges.

■ Currency, exchange and banks

The national currency is the **Belize dollar**, firmly and very conveniently fixed at two to one with the US dollar (**US$1=Bz$2**) which, in cash notes or travellers' cheques, is accepted (sometimes preferred) everywhere as legal tender. This apparently simple dual currency system can be problematic: it's all too easy to assume the price of your hotel room, or trip for example, is in Belize dollars, only to find payment is demanded in the same number of US dollars – a common cause of misunderstanding and aggravation. All Belizean notes (divided into 100 cents) and coins carry the British imperial legacy in the form of a portrait of Queen Elizabeth – and quarters are called "shillings".

You'll find at least one **bank** (generally open Mon–Thurs 8am–2.30pm, Fri 8am–4.30pm) in every town in the country, and there's also one on Caye Caulker. Although the exchange rate is fixed, banks in Belize will give slightly less than Bz$2 for US$1 for both cash and travellers' cheques; on the other hand, **moneychangers** at the borders will often give slightly higher rates, especially for larger sums; anywhere else beware of rip-offs. You can readily buy cash US$ from the banks and sometimes from hotels or restaurants.

Credit and debit cards are widely accepted in Belize, and increasingly even in smaller hotels and restaurants, though always check what the charge will be for using it – most places will add an extra 5 or even 7 percent for the privilege. Although banks can give you a Visa/Mastercard **cash advance** over the counter, Barclays is the only bank which doesn't impose an extra charge to use plastic and also has the only **ATMs** which accept foreign-issued cards.

■ Costs

Even travelling as a couple it's difficult to survive on less than US$20 a day per person – though it can be done – but US$25 a day will cover a decent budget hotel, meals and drinks, bus travel and a short taxi ride for example. For a **simple room** you can expect to pay at least US$7.50 single, US$14 double, whereas a night in an upmarket lodge will set you back anything from US$65 to US$150. Food and drink are fairly pricey too, with an average breakfast costing around

US$3–5, lunch US$5–7, and dinner US$6–8. A small bottle of Belikin **beer**, the only local brew, costs at least US$1.65; imported cans cost over twice as much.

Bus travel is much more reasonable, with the longest journey in the country, from Belize City to Punta Gorda, costing US$11. A **taxi** ride within a town costs US$2.50 for one or two people; for more passengers and longer rides agree a price beforehand.

Hotel rooms are subject to a seven percent **tax**, usually added separately (and many of the more expensive places will also impose a **service charge** of around ten percent); in restaurants the tax is almost always included in the price. The fifteen percent VAT, which is applied to most goods and services, does not apply to hotel rooms, though some package operators will slap it on illegally – always check carefully what you're paying for.

Leaving Belize you must pay a US$11.25 **exit tax** at the international airport. In addition there's a conservation exit tax, the **PACT**, an extra US$3.75, payable at **all exit points**.

Information

The country's official sources of tourist information are the **Belize Tourist Board** (BTB) offices in Belize City and Punta Gorda, plus an information booth open at the airport for incoming flights. The staff are generally quite helpful, handing out maps, brochures and local information. The **Tourist Police** are also part of the BTB and you should report any tourism-related crime here if you can.

The **Belize Tourist Industry Association** (BTIA) also has numerous offices and representatives around the country and, although they are really an industry organization, they do try to help with information and will deal with complaints about hotel standards or service. Additionally, and perhaps of more practical use, most of the hotels and all of the travel agents mentioned in the guide will be able to give excellent recommendations on local guides and attractions.

For the latest information on the growing number of reserves, **national parks** and associated visitor centres call or visit the **Belize Audubon Society** in Belize City, which adminsters many of the country's protected areas, or check with the Conservation Division of the Belize Forestry Department in Belmopan (☎08/22709), which has overall responsibility for Belize's conservation policy and management of protected areas.

For in-depth information on social, cultural, political and economic matters concerning Belize, the place to look is the Society for the Promotion of Education and Research (SPEAR; on the corner of Pickstock St and New Rd, Belize City; ☎02/31668, fax 32367), which has an excellent library and video collection.

Accommodation

Most Belizean **accommodation** is expensive by Central American standards. Fortunately there are budget hotels in all towns except Belmopan and Orange Walk, and the most popular tourist destinations, like Caye Caulker, San Ignacio and Placencia, have a great deal of choice.

A simple double room in Belize usually costs at least US$12.50 (just over half that for a single), for facilities little better than a cheap Guatemalan hotel. On a budget, you're most likely to end up in a basic room with a shared bathroom; for the luxury of a private bathroom expect to pay at least US$17.50. If you've a lot more money to spend, you could try one of the delightful, family run lodges, usually set in a spectacular natural location, with rooms in the house or in private cabañas. Some of these offer **bed and breakfast**, a style of accommodation which is growing in popularity.

Finding a room is no problem in Belizean towns: even in Belize City most options will be within ten minutes' walk of your point of arrival. On the whole there's always accommodation available, but during the peak season, from December to April and especially at Christmas and Easter, you may have to look a little longer; calling ahead to book is easy.

■ Camping

Although there are few proper **campsites** in Belize, you'll easily be able to find somewhere to pitch a tent or sling a hammock in rural areas and coastal villages like Placencia and Hopkins. Camping is not really possible (or recommended) on Caye Caulker or in San Pedro. You can also camp in the area around San Ignacio and in the Mountain Pine Ridge, where several lodges have campsites, some very economical, some surprisingly expensive. Down south a tent will enable you to spend some time wandering inland, around the Maya villages and ancient ruins.

Eating and drinking

Belizean food is a distinctive mix of Latin America and the Caribbean, with Creole "rice and beans" dominating the scene but with plenty of other influences playing an important part. Mexican *empanadas* are as common as pizza, chow mein and hamburgers. In a few places Belizean food is a real treat, and the seafood is particularly good, but in all too many it's a neglected art.

■ Where to eat

The quality of the food rarely bears much relation to the appearance of the restaurant, whether you're eating in a **bar**, a **café** or a smart-looking **restaurant**. Out on the islands and in small seashore villages some restaurants are little more than thatched shelters, with open sides and sand floors, while you'll just as often find upmarket hotels with polished floors, tablecloths and napkins. Only in Belize City and San Pedro though, is there much choice, with fast-food and snack bars sprouting on street corners but a few surprisingly elegant restaurants as well. Most places, however, are somewhere between the two, serving up good food without too much concern for presentation. You'll soon become accustomed to the fact that **lunch hour** (noon–1pm) is observed with almost religious devotion. Abandon any hope of getting anything else done and tuck in with the locals.

ACCOMMODATION PRICE CODES

All accommodation reviewed in this guide has been graded according to the following price scales, which refer to the cost of a double room in high season. Rates exclude Belize's hotel tax of 7 percent and, in the case of the higher-priced resorts, any service charge.

① up to US$5
② US$5–10
③ US$10–15
④ US$15–25
⑤ US$25–40
⑥ US$40–60
⑦ US$60–80
⑧ US$80–100
⑨ US$100 and over

Travelling, you'll find that food sometimes comes to you, as street traders offer up *tamales*, *empanadas*, ham-burgers (literally a slice of canned ham served in a bun) and fruit to waiting bus passengers, although the practice isn't nearly as common as elsewhere in Central America.

■ What to eat

The basis of any Creole meal is **rice and beans**, and this features heavily in smaller restaurants. In many cases it means just that, with the rice and beans cooked together in coconut oil and flavoured with *recado* (a mild ground pepper) and often with a chunk of salted pork thrown in for extra taste, but usually it's served with chicken, fish or beef, and backed up by some kind of sauce. Vegetables are scarce in Creole food but there's often a side dish of potato salad and **fried plantains**, and sometimes **flour tortillas**. At its best Creole food is delicious, taking the best from the sea and blending it with coconut and spices. But all too often what you get is a stodgy mass, with little in the way of flavour.

Vegetarians will find the pickings slim. There are no specifically vegetarian restaurants, but in the main tourist resorts there's often a meat-free choice on the menu. Otherwise, you're likely to be offered chicken or ham if you say you don't eat meat. The fruit is good and there are some locally produced vegetables but they are rarely served in restaurants. Your best bet outside the main tourist areas will be a Chinese restaurant.

Seafood is almost always excellent. **Red snapper** is invariably fantastic, and you might also try a **barracuda** steak, **conch fritters** or a plate of fresh (though usually farmed) shrimps. On San Pedro and Caye Caulker the food is often exceptional, and the only worry is that you might get bored with **lobster**, served in an amazing range of dishes: pasta with lobster sauce, lobster and scrambled eggs, lobster chow mein, or even lobster curry. The closed season for lobster is from February to June. **Turtle** is still on the menu in a few places, in theory only during the short open season, but note that this is a threatened species, and by even tasting it – or any other wild animal – you'll be contributing to its extinction.

Chinese food will probably turn out to be an important part of your trip, and when there's little else on offer Belize's many Chinese restaurants are usually a safe bet. Other Belizean ethnic minorities are now starting to break into the restaurant trade: there's a **Garífuna** restaurant in Dangriga and an excellent **Sri Lankan** curry restaurant in San Ignacio.

■ Drinks

The most basic **drinks** to accompany food are water, beer and the usual soft drinks. Belikin, the only brand of **beer** produced in Belize, comes in four varieties: lager-type bottled and draught beer; bottled **stout** (a rich, dark beer); and Premium and Supreme, more expensive bottled beers and often all you'll be able to get in upmarket hotels and restaurants. Cashew-nut and berry **wines**, rich and full-bodied, are bottled and sold in some villages, and you can also get hold of imported wine, which is far from cheap. Local **rum**, in both dark and clear varieties, is the best deal in Belizean alcohol. The locally produced gin, brandy and vodka are poor imitations – cheap and fairly nasty.

Non-alcoholic alternatives include the predictable array of soft drinks. Despite the number of citrus plantations, **fruit juices** are rarely available, though you can sometimes get orange juice. **Tap water**, in the towns at least, though safe, is highly chlorinated, and many villages (though not Caye Caulker) now have a potable water system. Pure **rainwater** is usually available in the countryside and on the cayes. Filtered bottled water and mineral water are sold almost everywhere.

Coffee, except in the best establishments, will almost certainly be the instant variety. **Tea**, due to the British influence, is a popular hot drink, as are Milo and Ovaltine (malted milky drinks). One last drink that deserves a mention is **seaweed**, a strange blend of seaweed, milk, cinnamon, sugar and cream. If you see someone selling this on a street corner, give it a try.

Opening hours, holidays and festivals

It's difficult to be specific about **opening hours** in Belize but in general most shops are open 8am–noon and 3–8pm. The lunch hour – noon to 1pm – is almost universally observed and it's hopeless trying to get anything done then. Some shops and businesses work a half-day on Wednesday and Saturday, and everything is liable to close early on Friday. Banks and government offices are only open Monday to Friday. Watch out for Sundays, when everybody takes it easy; shops,

PUBLIC HOLIDAYS

January 1	New Year's Day
March 9	Baron Bliss Day
Good Friday	
Holy Saturday	
Easter Monday	
May 1	Labour Day
May 24	Commonwealth Day
September 10	National Day
September 21	Independence Day
October 12	Columbus Day
	(Pan America Day)
November 19	Garífuna Settlement Day
December 25 & 26	Christmas

and sometimes restaurants, are closed, and fewer bus services and internal flights operate. Archeological sites, however, are open every day.

The main **public holidays**, when virtually everything will be closed, are shown above.

In Belize it's only in the outlying areas, such as around San Ignacio and Corozal, and in the Maya villages of the south, that you'll find traditional village **fiestas**. Elsewhere, national celebrations are the main excuse for a day-long party, and the rhythms of the Caribbean dominate the proceedings. But here you'll feel less of an outsider and will be welcome to dance and drink with the locals. **Traditional dance** is still practised by two ethnic groups in Belize: the Maya and the Garífuna. The best time to see Garífuna dances is November 19, Garífuna Settlement Day, in either Dangriga or Hopkins. Maya dances are still performed at fiestas in the south and west, and in many ways resemble their counterparts in Guatemala. Dance is very much a part of Creole culture and all national celebrations are marked by open-air dances.

Mail and telecommunications

Belizean postal services are perhaps the most efficient (and most expensive) in Central America. **Sending letters**, cards and parcels home is straightforward: a normal airmail letter takes around four days to reach the US, eight days to Europe, and around two weeks to Australia; **parcels** have to be wrapped in brown paper and tied with string.

Belize has a modern (albeit expensive) phone system with **payphones** an increasingly common sight throughout the country. Rural areas are served by **community telephones** (nowadays often fixed cellular phones), usually located in a private house; you pay the person who operates the phone. Two types of pre-paid **phonecards** are in use: the **Telecard**, which you can use at any touch-tone phone (public or private), uses a PIN number, while the **Payphone card** is slotted into payphones. Both of these are sold at BTL (Belize Telecommunications Limited) offices, and increasingly at hotels, shops and gas stations. **Calling home collect** is easy using Home Country Direct, available at BTL offices, most payphones and larger hotels. Simply dial the access code (printed on some payphones and in the phone book) to connect with an operator in your home country. **Area codes** in Belize range from ☎02 for Belize City to ☎09 for San Ignacio, while ☎01 signifies a cellular phone, either fixed or mobile; all area codes are included with numbers given in the text. Calling Belize from abroad, the **international country code** is ☎501.

Most hotels and businesses now have **fax** machines and any BTL office will have a public fax you can use. Fax numbers are listed in the pink pages in the telephone directory. Belizean businesses and individuals are also avid users of **email** and the **Internet**; at present, there's only one Internet café, in San Ignacio, but you can go online at BTL's Belize City office (US$3 for 30min), with other BTL offices likely to offer the same facilities in the near future. Some of the most useful **Web sites** covering Belize are listed in Basics, p.24.

The media

Although Belize, with its English-language media, can make a welcome break in a world of Spanish, this doesn't necessarily mean that it's very easy to keep in touch with what's happening in the rest of the world. In the **national newspapers** (published weekly on Friday) local news takes pride of place and international stories receive very little attention. In Belize City, San Pedro and some other main towns you should be able to get hold of **foreign publications**, including *The Miami Herald*, *Time* and *Newsweek*.

There are two national **television** stations, channels 5 and 7, which show mainly imported American shows, with a few local news programmes. Cable TV, however, is the nation's preferred viewing medium, giving saturation coverage of American soaps, CNN and sports. There are three **radio** stations. Radio Belize is talk-based, with plays and cultural and educational programmes, plus the World Service daily from midnight to 6am, while Friends is primarily a music station; both are operated by the Broadcasting Corporation of Belize and partly sponsored by the government. The third station, KREM, is privately owned and plays mostly music.

Shopping

Compared to its neighbours, Belize has less to offer in terms of traditional **crafts** or neighbourhood **markets**. The latter are purely food markets, but in several places you'll come across some impressive local crafts. **Wood and slate carvers** are often to be found at the Maya sites, and their work, especially the reproductions of glyphs and stelae on slate, is high quality; **ceramics** are less good, but improving. In the Maya villages in southern Belize you'll come across some attractive **embroidery**, though it has to be said the quality of both the cloth and the work is better in Guatemala. Garífuna and Creole villages produce good basketware and superb **drums**; Dangriga, Hopkins and Gales Point are the places to visit for these.

The excellent **National Handicrafts Center** in Belize City (see p.58) is the best place to buy souvenirs if time is short, with a wide range of genuine Belizean crafts, including paintings, prints and music recordings as well as the items mentioned above. The craftspeople are paid fair prices for their work and no longer have to hawk it on the streets. There are often exhibitions by Belizean artists here too, but the best place for contemporary **Belizean art** is The Image Factory in Belize City (see p.58).

SOUVENIRS

Some souvenirs you'll see are dependent on the destruction of the reef and wildlife, so think twice before you buy. These include black coral, often made into jewellery, and turtle shells, which look far better on their rightful owners. The turtle-fishing season in Belize is now very much restricted and it is against the law to take turtle products out of the country. You will certainly have them (and most items made from wild animals) confiscated on entering the USA, Canada or Europe, and may face a fine as well.

For **everyday shopping** you'll find some kind of shop in every village in Belize, however small, and if you have the time to hunt around, most things you'd find at home are also available in Belize. Luxury items, such as electrical goods and cameras, tend to be very expensive, as do other imported goods. Film is a little more expensive than at home, but easy to get hold of.

One tasty souvenir everyone likes to take home is a bottle (or three) of **Marie Sharp's Pepper Sauce**, made from Belizean habañeros in various strengths, ranging from "mild" to "fiery hot". This spicy accompaniment to rice and beans graces every restaurant table in the country – and visits to the factory near Dangriga can be arranged.

Safety and the police

Belize has earned itself a reputation for criminal activities, and while it's true that Belize City has a high crime rate, it certainly doesn't live up to some of the stories. The atmosphere on the streets is much less intimidating since the introduction of the **tourist police** and on the whole petty crime is the most you need to worry about. Nevertheless, it pays to be aware of the dangers.

In Belize City, theft is now fairly common, the majority of cases involving **break-ins** at hotels: bear this in mind when you're searching for a room. Out and about there's always a slight danger of **pickpockets**, but certainly no greater than in the surrounding countries, and with a bit of common sense you've nothing to fear. There's also a chance of something more serious happening, such as a **mugging**. During the daytime there's little to worry about. However, at night you should stick to the main streets and avoid going out alone, especially if you're a woman. If you arrive in Belize City at night, take a taxi to a hotel, as the bus stations are in a particularly derelict part of town – though not bad enough to worry about daylight arrivals. Having said all this, muggings are really not that common, and your greatest fear is likely to be the mood of intimidation on the streets, which makes Belize City feel far more dangerous than it actually is. If you do need to **report a crime**, your first stop should be the tourist police, where they exist – crime against tourists is taken very seriously in Belize. The **emergency** number for the police is ☎911 nationwide.

Verbal abuse is not uncommon, especially in Belize City, where there are always plenty of people hanging out on the streets, commenting on all that passes by. For anyone with a white face, the inevitable "Hey, white boy/white chick – what's happening?" will soon become a familiar sound. At first it can all seem very threatening, but if you take the time to stop and talk, you'll find the vast majority of these people simply want to know where you're from, and where you're heading – and perhaps to offer you a deal on boat trips, money exchange, or bum a dollar or two. Once you realize that they mean no harm the whole experience of Belize City will be infinitely more enjoyable. Obviously, the situation is a little more serious for women, and the abuse can be more offensive. But once again, it's unlikely that anything will come of it and it's usually possible to talk your way out of a dodgy situation without anyone losing face.

Overtly **gay** couples are another likely target for verbal abuse, though with a little discretion you're unlikely to get any more hassle than anyone else. Although homosexuality is, in fact, illegal in Belize, no one's been prosecuted for years and it's extremely unlikely that the authorities are going to begin any proceedings against tourists. There's no openly gay community and no exclusively gay bars, though gay cruise ships have visited Belize recently, provoking a minor protest at the quayside but no further problems for the tour members once they left the dock.

■ Drugs

Belize has long been an important link in the chain of supply between the drugs producers in South and Central America and the users in North America, with minor players often being paid in kind, creating a deluge of illegal drugs. **Marijuana**, **cocaine** and **crack** are all readily available in Belize, and whether you like it or not you'll receive regular offers. All such substances are **illegal**, and despite the fact that dope is smoked openly in the streets, the police do arrest people for possession of marijuana and they particularly enjoy catching tourists. If you're caught you'll probably end up spending a couple of days in jail and paying a fine of several hundred US dollars: expect no sympathy from your embassy.

Work and study

There's virtually no chance of finding paid temporary work in Belize as half the population is under-

employed. Work permits are only on offer to those who can prove their ability to support themselves without endangering the job of a Belizean, or to wealthy investors.

There are, however, a growing number of opportunities for **voluntary work** – mainly as a fee-paying member of a conservation expedition – or **study**, at an archeological field school. These options generally mean raising at least a thousand pounds or dollars and committing yourself to weeks (or months) of hard work, often in difficult conditions. The rewards are personal satisfaction and (sometimes) a genuine contribution to scientific research. Many of these expeditions, aimed at gap-year students, work on rural infrastructure projects such as schools and health centres, or building trails and visitor centres in nature reserves. Organizations with projects in Belize are listed below. If you find the initial cost a deterrent, and if you're dedicated, self-motivated and self-supporting, you can always volunteer independently: contact the Belize Audubon Society or ask at any of the reserves.

You don't have to raise money to work for **Voluntary Service Overseas**, which sends people with the required skills on long-term postings – mainly teaching, though they also look for agricultural and health specialists – and you even get a small allowance. Similarly the **Peace Corps** sends American volunteers to Belize to work in education, agriculture and conservation.

At least twenty academic **archeological groups** undertake research in Belize each year, and many take paying students in field schools;

VOLUNTARY WORK AND STUDY CONTACTS

Belize Audubon Society PO Box 1001, Belize City; ☎02/35004.

Coral Cay Conservation UK ☎0171/498-6248. Marine conservation research.

Earthwatch UK ☎01865/311600; USA ☎617/926-8200; Australia ☎03/9600-9100. Archeological and conservation reseach.

Peace Corps USA ☎703/235-9191.

Raleigh International UK ☎0171/371-8585. Youth development through community and conservation projects.

Trekforce Expeditions UK ☎0171/824-8890. Archeological and conservation projects.

Voluntary Service Overseas (VSO) UK ☎0181/780-2266.

you don't have to be a student, but payment is required. Lack of space prevents listing all the possibilities here, but look in *Archaeology* magazine, specialist college literature or at the Lanic Web site (see p.26).

History

Belize is the youngest nation in Central America, gaining full independence from Britain only in 1981, and its history has been markedly different from the Latin republics in the isthmus since at least the mid-seventeenth century. Although all the Central American countries were colonized by European powers, beginning in the early sixteenth century, it is the colonial entanglement with Britain that has given Belize its present cultural, social and political structures.

After crossing the **Bering land bridge** the early peoples rapidly spread southwards, developing the **Clovis** hunter-gatherer culture by 11,000 BC. Worked stone flakes from this era have been found at Richmond Hill, a site in northern Belize. Gradually the hunters turned to more intensive use of plants, particularly the newly domesticated **maize** and **beans**, settling into primarily agricultural societies in Belize during the **Archaic** or **Proto-Maya period**, lasting from around 7500 BC until later than 2000 BC. Few visible remains from that period can be seen today, however, and it is only during the subsequent **Preclassic** period (1500 BC–300 AD) that the culture that we recognize as **Maya** became distinct.

City-states emerged whose populations gathered into cities with larger and more elaborate buildings. Temples and palaces were built of stone, using the famous Maya corbelled arch, and characteristic stepped-pyramids rose dozens of metres above enormous plazas. Ceramics found at **Cuello**, near Orange Walk, dating from around 1000 BC, are amongst the earliest in the Maya lowlands. **Cerros**, at the mouth of the New River, and **Lamanai**, on the New River Lagoon, expanded into great trading centres, probably continuing in this role right through the Classic and into the Postclassic period.

■ The Classic and Postclassic periods

Whatever the original construction dates of the Maya sites in Belize, most of what you can see today dates from the **Classic period** (300–900

AD), the greatest phase of Maya achievement. Elaborately carved **stelae**, bearing dates and emblem-glyphs, tell of actual rulers and of historical events in their lives – battles, marriages, dynastic succession and so on. The best example in the country is at **Nim Li Punit**, north of Punta Gorda.

Developments in the Maya area were powerfully influenced by cultures to the north, above all that of **Teotihuacán**, which dominated central Mexico during the early Classic period; Teotihuacán's collapse in the seventh century caused shockwaves throughout the Maya world. However, as the new Maya rulers in Belize gradually established dynasties free of Teotihuacán's military or political control, their cities flourished as never before.

The entire Belize River valley was thickly populated during Classic times, with powerful cities such as **El Pilar** and **Xunantunich** in the west of Cayo District controlling this important trade route. Many Maya centres were much larger than contemporary Western European cities, then in their "Dark Ages": **Caracol**, in southern Cayo District, had an estimated 150,000 people.

Exactly how the various centres related to one another is unclear, but it appears that three or four main centres dominated the Maya region through an uncertain process of alliances. Calakmul, in Campeche, Mexico, and Tikal in Petén, Guatemala, were the nearest of these "**superstates**" to Belize, but in 562 AD Caracol defeated Tikal, as shown by a Caracol ball-court marker. Detailed carvings on wooden lintels and stone monuments at the site depict elaborately costumed lords trampling on bound captives.

The end of the Classic Maya civilization, when it came, was abrupt. By 750 AD political and social changes began to be felt; alliances and trade links broke down, wars increased and stelae were carved less frequently. Most cities rapidly became depopulated and new construction ceased over much of Belize after about 830 AD. By the end of the Classic period there appears to have been strife and disorder throughout Mesoamerica. But not all Maya cities were deserted: those in northern Belize, in particular, survived and indeed prospered, with Lamanai and other cities in the area remaining occupied throughout the **Postclassic** period (900–1540 AD). In the years leading up to the Spanish Conquest, the Yucatán and northern Belize consisted of over a dozen rival provinces, bound up in a cycle of competition and conflict.

■ The Conquest

The general assumption that Belize was practically deserted by the time Europeans arrived is now widely discredited. In fact the Maya towns and provinces were still vigorously independent, as the Spanish found to their cost on several occasions.

Northern Belize was part of the wealthy Maya province of **Chetumal**, with its capital probably **Santa Rita**, near Corozal. Trade, alliances and wars kept Chetumal in contact with surrounding Maya states up to and beyond the Spanish conquest of Aztec Mexico. Further south was the province known to the Maya of Chetumal as *Dzuluinicob* – "land of foreigners" – whose capital was **Tipu**, probably located at Negroman, on the Macal River south of San Ignacio. The Maya here controlled the upper Belize River valley and put up strenuous resistance to attempts by the Spanish to subdue and convert them. The struggle was to continue with simmering resentment until 1707, when the population of Tipu was forcibly removed to Lago de Petén Itzá, near Tikal.

The first **Europeans** to set eyes on the mainland of Belize were Spanish sailors in the early 1500s, but they didn't attempt a landing. In 1511 a small group of shipwrecked Spanish sailors managed to reach land on the southern coast of Yucatán: five were immediately sacrificed but the others were taken as slaves. One of them, **Gonzalo Guerrero**, later married the daughter of Nachankan, the chief of Chetumal, and became a crucial military adviser to the Maya in their subsequent resistance to Spanish domination. The archeologist Eric Thompson calls him the first European to make Belize his home.

In Mexico and Peru it had proved relatively simple to capture and eventually kill the "living god", leader of a militaristic, unified and highly organized society, but in Belize the Spanish found the leaders of independent Maya city-states were accustomed to dealing with enemies and fighting to retain their independence. By 1544 however, **Gaspar Pacheco** had subdued Maya resistance sufficiently to found a town on Lake Bacalar, and a mission was established at Lamanai in 1570. Maya resentment that was always present beneath the surface, however, boiled over into total rebellion in 1638, forcing Spain to abandon the area. The whole region from southern Yucatán to Honduras was never completely pacified by the Spanish, nor were administrative boundaries clearly defined, but it is likely that the Maya of Belize were under some form of Spanish influence, even if they were not under Spanish rule.

■ The arrival of the British

The failure of the Spanish authorities to clearly delineate the southern boundary of Yucatán subsequently allowed **buccaneers** or pirates (primarily British) preying on the Spanish treasure fleets to find refuge along the coast of Belize. When Spain attempted to take action on various occasions to expel the British there was confusion over which Spanish captain-general maintained jurisdiction in the area. Consequently the pirates were able to flee before the Spanish arrived and could return in the absence of any permanent Spanish outposts.

Treasure wasn't always easy to come by and sometimes they would plunder the piles of **logwood**, cut and awaiting shipment to Europe. Worth £90–110 a ton, the hard and extremely heavy wood was used in the expanding British textile industry to dye woollens black, red and grey. The various treaties signed between Britain and Spain from the late seventeenth to mid-eighteenth centuries, initially designed to outlaw the buccaneers, eventually allowed the British to establish logwood camps along the rivers in northen Belize, though they were never intended to permit permanent British settlement of a territory which Spain clearly regarded as its imperial domain. Thus the **British settlements** in Belize periodically came under attack whenever Spain sought to defend its interests. But the attention of the European powers rarely rested upon the humid and insect-ridden swamps where the logwood cutters, who became known as **Baymen**, worked and lived. The British government, while wishing to profit from the trade in logwood, preferred to avoid the question of whether or not the Baymen were British subjects. For the most part they were left to their own devices.

Spanish attacks on the settlements in Belize occurred throughout the eighteenth century, with the Baymen being driven out on several occasions. Increasingly though, Britain began to admit a measure of responsibility for the protection of the settlers and occasionally sent troops to aid the Baymen. Decades of Spanish attacks had fostered in the settlers a spirit of defiance and self-reliance, and the realization that British rule was preferable to Spanish, as long as they could choose which of its institutions to accept.

The final showdown between the waning Spanish empire and the Bay settlers (supported this time by a British warship and troops), the **Battle of St George's Caye**, came as a result of the outbreak of war between Britain and Spain in 1796. The Governor of Yucatán assembled ships and troops, determined to drive out the British settlers and occupy Belize. But this time the Baymen had time to prepare and voted (by a small margin) to stay and fight. A **Lieutenant-Colonel Barrow** was despatched to Belize as Superintendent, to command the settlers in the event of hostilities, and the Baymen, now under martial law, prepared for war, albeit grudgingly. A few companies of troops were sent from Jamaica and **slaves** were released from woodcutting to be armed and trained. The sloop **HMS Merlin** was stationed in the bay, local vessels were armed, gun rafts built and an attack was expected at any time.

The **Spanish fleet**, reported to include 16 heavily armed men-of-war and 12,000 troops, arrived just north of St George's Caye in early September 1798, making several attempts to capture the caye and force a passage to Belize. Each time they were beaten back by the Baymen with their small but highly manoeuvrable fleet, with the Baymen's slaves at least as eager to fight the Spanish as their masters were. During the final attack, on the morning of **September 10**, the Spanish fleet, already weakened by desertions and yellow fever, suffered heavy losses before sailing for Yucatán.

■ From settlement to British colony

Though a victory was won, the Battle of St George's Caye was not by itself decisive. However, in purely practical terms the power of the Spanish Empire was waning while the British Empire was consolidating and expanding. But in Belize the slaves were still slaves; even though they had fought valiantly alongside the Baymen, their owners expected them to go back to cutting mahogany. **Emancipation** came no earlier than elsewhere in the British Empire. Indeed contoversy still exists over the fact that the battle was fought between two European powers to establish rule over a colony. It created the conditions for Belize to become an integral part of the British Empire and enabled the slave owners to claim that the slaves were willing to fight on behalf of their masters. Whatever its legacy, the 1798 expedition was the last time that Spain attempted to gain control over Belize and Britain gradually assumed a greater role in the government of the settlement. Government House, built in Belize Town (later City) in 1814, housed the **Superintendent** (always an army officer) until 1862, when Belize became the colony of **British Honduras**, then serving as home to the **Governor**, head of government under British colonial policy.

■ Towards independence

By 1900, free for the moment from worries about external threats, Belize was an integral, though minor, colony of the British Empire. Comfortable complacency set in and the predominantly white property owners could foresee no change to their rule. The workers in the forests and on the estates were mainly black, the descendants of former slaves, and known as "Creoles". Wages were low and the colonial government and employers maintained strict controls over the movement of workers, repressing any labour organizations.

Belizeans rushed to defend the "Mother Country" in both **world wars** but each time the returning soldiers faced humiliation and poverty. In 1919 veterans rioted in Belize City, an event that marked the onset of black consciousness and the beginning of the **independence movement**. Even in 1946 political power lay with a wealthy elite and with the governor, a Foreign Office appointee, and the devaluation of the British Honduras dollar at the end of 1949 caused greater hardship. The days of the British Empire were numbered, however, and in 1954 elections were held in which all literate adults over the age of 21 could vote. These elections were won with an overwhelming majority by the **Peoples' United Party** (PUP), led by **George Price**.

However, **Guatemala**, as the inheritor of the Spanish colonial territory of that name, had never entirely let go of its claim to the territory of Belize, regarding colonial treaties giving the British settlers rights to cut wood but not to own the land as still applicable in law. These interminable disputes, particularly the 1859 treaty which Britain, despite failing to fulfil the provision to build a road allowing Guatemala access to the Caribbean, regarded as the final settlement of the boundary dispute, rumbled on in the background. The British government never took the Guatemalan claim very seriously and Belize was allowed to proceed down the road to full independence by becoming an **internally self-governing** colony in 1964.

The prospect of what was (notionally at least) the department of "Belice" becoming independent outraged Guatemalan national pride and at

ETHNIC BELIZE

ETHNIC BELIZE

Belize has a very mixed cultural background, with the two largest ethnic groups, **Creoles**, descendants of enslaved Africans and early British settlers, and **Mestizos**, descended from Amerindians and Spanish colonial settlers, forming about 75 percent of the population. The **Maya** in Belize are from three separate groups: Yucatec, who fled from the Caste Wars in the mid-nineteenth century; Mopan, who arrived in southern and western Belize from Petén in the 1880s; and Kekchi, who came to Toledo in southern Belize from Alta Verapaz from the late 1800s onward. Together they form around 11 percent of the total population.

The **Garífuna** (or **Caribs**), descended from enslaved Africans shipwrecked on St Vincent who mingled with the last Caribs there, settled in Belize in the nineteenth century, and now form around 7 percent of the population.

Since the 1980s, the arrival of an estimated 40,000 **Central American immigrants**, refugees from war and poverty, have boosted Belize's population to around 220,000. These refugees, together with the existing population of predominantly Spanish-speaking *mestizos*, have dramatically altered the demographic balance, and are now the majority ethnic group in Belize. Though they are treated with tolerance and encouraged to integrate into Belizean society, the recent arrivals are the source of slight racial tension, often referred to as "aliens" and blamed for a disproportionate amount of crime. Some Creoles feel marginalized now that Spanish is the most widely spoken first language, though English, taught in all schools, is certain to remain the official language for the foreseeable future.

least twice, in 1972 and 1977, Guatemala moved troops to the border and threatened to invade, but prompt British reinforcements were an effective dissuasion. The situation remained tense but international opinion shifted gradually in favour of Belizean independence.

The most important demonstration of worldwide endorsement of Belize's right to self-determination was the **UN resolution** passed in 1980, which demanded secure independence, with all territory intact, before the next session. Further negotiations with Guatemala began but complete agreement could not be reached: Guatemala still insisted on some territorial concessions. On March 11, 1981, Britain, Guatemala and Belize released the "Heads of Agreement", a document which would, they hoped, eventually result in a peaceful solution of the dispute. Accordingly, on September 21, 1981, Belize became an **independent member of the British Commonwealth**, with Queen Elizabeth II as head of state.

The territorial dispute remains a stumbling block in relations between Belize and Guatemala, however, with President Arzú restating the claim to Belize soon after his election in 1996. Despite this, the outlook is probably brighter than any time in history; Arzú claims to be committed to resolve the dispute though negotiation and the countries exchange ambassadors.

■ Modern Belize

Belize's **democratic credentials** are beyond dispute: at each general election since independence the voters have kicked out the incumbent government and replaced it with the opposition. So far this has meant that the slightly left-of-centre PUP has alternated with the more market-led, United Democratic Party (UDP) under Manuel Esquivel. The neo-liberal policies adopted by Esquivel (under pressure from the World Bank to reduce government spending and widen the revenue base) by slashing thousands of public sector jobs and imposing a highly unpopular VAT led directly to the UDP's resounding defeat in the August 1998 general election. With campaign pledges to repeal the "killer" VAT, the **PUP** captured 25 out of 29 seats in the National Assembly in an unprecedented landslide – though it's extremely unlikely that the new government, under prime minister **Said Musa**, will be able to keep such rash promises.

Despite a booming **tourist industry**, bringing in almost US$100 million a year, **agriculture** remains the mainstay of Belize's economy, accounting for 25 percent of GNP – around US$135 million a year. Sugar is the most important agro-export, followed by bananas and citrus products. Figures are obviously not available for Belize's income from the lucrative **drug transshipment** business, but this illicit economy is as least as large as the official one.

Per capita **income** is high for Central America, at over US$2500, boosted by the money many Belizeans receive from relatives abroad, mainly in the USA. This apparent advantage is offset by the fact that many of the brightest and most highly trained leave the country, finding it easy to settle in English-speaking North America.

Though traditional links with Britain and the Commonwealth countries in the West Indies remain strong, Belize is being inexorably drawn into the proposals for a Free Trade Area of the Americas. The initial step, the imminent signing of a **Free Trade Agreement** with Mexico, is viewed with alarm by many Belizean workers, who fear that an end to all tariffs will further depress agricultural prices and drive the small manufacturing base into bankruptcy. Even worse in many peoples' eyes, these proposals signal an end to the fixed rate of exchange with the US dollar leading to potentially catastrophic **devaluation** of the Belizean currency.

CHAPTER 1

BELIZE CITY

The narrow, crowded streets of **BELIZE CITY** can initially be daunting to anyone who has been prepared by the usual tales of crime-ridden urban decay. Admittedly, at first glance the city is unprepossessing. Its buildings – many of them dilapidated wooden structures – stand right at the edge of the road, and few sidewalks offer refuge to pedestrians from the ever-increasing numbers of cars and trucks. The hazards of Belize City, however, are often reported by those who have never been here. If you approach the city with an open mind and take some precautions with your belongings, you may well be pleasantly surprised.

The city has a distinguished history, a handful of sights, and, particularly if you visit during the **September celebrations**, an astonishing energy. The sixty thousand people of Belize City represent every ethnic group in the country, with the **Creole** descendants of former slaves and Baymen forming the dominant element, generating an easy-going Caribbean atmosphere.

Belize City is divided neatly into north and south halves by the **Haulover Creek**, a delta branch of the Belize River. The pivotal point of the city centre is the **Swing Bridge**, always busy with traffic and opened twice a day to allow larger vessels up and down the river. **North** of the Swing Bridge is the slightly more upmarket part of town, home to the most expensive hotels. **South** of the Swing Bridge is the market and commercial zone, the location of all the city's banks and a couple of supermarkets. The city is small enough to make **walking** the easiest way to get around.

Some history

Exactly how Belize came by its name is something of a mystery; it could be a corruption of Wallace, a Scotsman and probably a pirate, reputed to have settled here in 1620. Those preferring a more ancient origin believe the name to be derived from *beliz*, a Maya word meaning "muddy", or from the Maya term *belekin*, meaning "towards the east".

What is known is that by the late seventeenth century, buccaneers were cutting **logwood** (used for textile dyes in Europe) in this region, and were settled in a mangrove swamp consolidated with wood chips, loose coral and rum bottles at the mouth of today's Haulover Creek. The settlement became known as **Belize Town**, and by the 1700s it was well established as a centre for logwood cutters, their families and their slaves. The seafront contained the houses of the **Baymen**, as the settlers called themselves; the slaves lived in cabins on the south side of Haulover Creek, with various tribal groups occupying separate areas. After the rains had floated the logs downriver the men returned here to drink and brawl, with riotous Christmas celebrations going on for weeks.

Spain was the dominant colonial power in the region and mounted several expeditions aimed at demonstrating control over the territory. In 1779 a Spanish raid captured many of the settlers and the rest fled, but most returned in 1783, when Spain agreed to recognize the rights of the British settlers, and Belize Town grew into the main centre of the logwood and mahogany trade on the Bay of Honduras. Spanish raids continued, however, until the Battle of St George's Caye in 1798, when the settlers achieved victory with British naval help – a success that reinforced the bond with the British government.

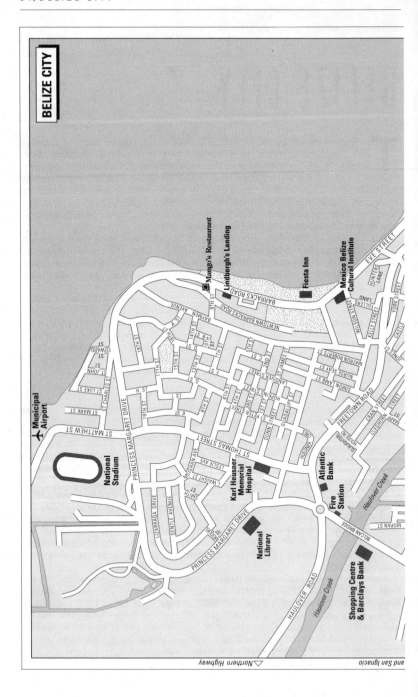

BELIZE CITY

Municipal Airport

National Stadium

National Library

Karl Heusner Memorial Hospital

Atlantic Bank

Fire Station

Shopping Centre & Barclays Bank

Mango's Restaurant

Lindbergh's Landing

Fiesta Inn

Mexico Belize Cultural Institute

ST MATTHEW ST
ST MARK ST
ST LUKE ST
ST JOHN ST
ST EDWARD ST
ST CHARLES ST
PRINCESS MARGARET DRIVE
IZARRAGA DRIVE
GENTLE AVENUE
18TH ST
17TH ST
19TH ST
15TH ST
BAYMEN AVENUE
16TH ST
14TH ST
13TH ST
12TH ST
11TH ST
10TH ST
9TH ST
8TH ST
7TH ST
6TH ST
5TH ST
4TH ST
3RD ST
2ND ST
1ST ST
H ST
I ST
J ST
K ST
BARRACKS ROAD
NEWTOWN BARRACKS ROAD
ST THOMAS STREET
LANDIVER STREET
HOPKINS STREET
ST PETER STREET
ST JAMES ST
DUNN STREET
GUADALUPE ST
MAHON ROBERTS ST
NURSE SEAY ST
SIMON LAMB ST
WILSON STREET
CULLEN ST
KELLS STREET
CASTLE ST
JONES ST
YORK STREET
HUNTERS LANE
EVE STREET
WAIGHT ST
SMITH ST
MCFIELD ST
LESLIE AVE
FREETOWN ROAD
SLAUGHTERHOUSE RD
CLEGHORN
CRAIG STREET
MAPP ST
MORAN ST
BELCAN BRIDGE
Haulover Creek
HAULOVER ROAD
HAULOVER ROAD

Northern Highway

and San Ignacio

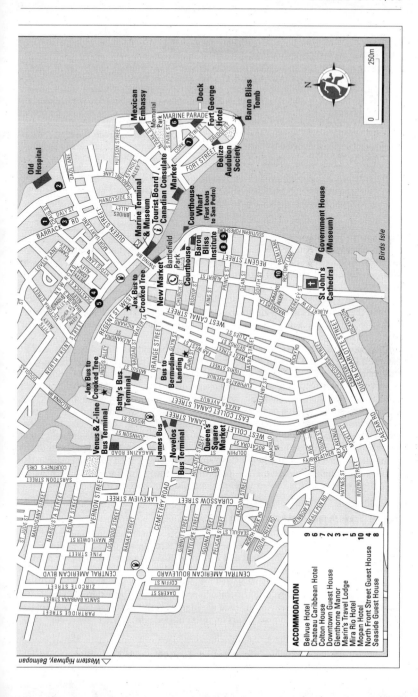

△ Western Highway, Belmopan

N

0   250m

Old Hospital

Mexican Embassy

Memorial Park

MARINE PARADE

Dock

Fort George Hotel

Baron Bliss Tomb

Belize Audubon Society

Marine Terminal & Museum

Tourist Board / Canadian Consulate

Market

Courthouse Wharf (Fast boats to San Pedro)

Government House (Museum)

Birds Isle

New Market

Battlefield Park

Courthouse

Baron Bliss Institute

SOUTHERN FORESHORE

St John's Cathedral

Jex Bus to Crooked Tree

Jex Bus to Crooked Tree

Bus to Bermudian Landing

Batty's Bus Terminal

Venus & Z-line Bus Terminal

James Bus

Novelos Bus Terminal

Queen's Square Market

Collet Canal

WEST CANAL STREET

EAST COLLET CANAL STREET

WEST COLLET CANAL STREET

CENTRAL AMERICAN BOULEVARD

CENTRAL AMERICAN BLVD

ACCOMMODATION

Bellvue Hotel	9
Chateau Caribbean Hotel	6
Colton House	7
Downtown Guest House	2
Glenthorne Manor	3
Marin's Travel Lodge	1
Mira Rio Hotel	5
Mopan Hotel	10
North Front Street Guest House	4
Seaside Guest House	8

HASSLE

Walking in Belize City **in daylight** is perfectly safe if you observe common-sense rules. The introduction of specially trained **tourist police** in 1995, coupled with the legal requirement for all tour guides to be licensed, has driven away the hustlers and reduced street crime considerably. You'll soon learn to spot dangerous situations and in the city centre you can always ask the tourist police – instantly recognizable by their baseball caps and green T-shirts – for advice or directions; they'll even walk you back to your hotel if it's near their patrol route. That said, it's still sensible to proceed with caution: most people are friendly and chatty, but quite a few may want to sell you drugs or bum a dollar or two. The best advice is to stay cool. Be civil, don't provoke trouble by arguing too forcefully, and never show large sums of money on the street. Women wearing short shorts or skirts will attract verbal abuse from local studs.

The virtual absence of nightlife outside the more expensive hotel bars means there's little reason to walk the streets **after dark**; if you do venture out, bear in mind that anyone walking alone is in danger of being mugged. It's a good idea to travel at night by taxi.

The nineteenth century saw the increasing influence of **British expatriates**, colonial-style wooden housing dominating the shoreline as the "Scots clique" began to clean up the town's image and take control of its administration. Despite fires and epidemics in the the nineteenth century the town and settlement grew with immigration from the West Indies and refugees from the Caste Wars in the Yucatán. In 1862 Belize became the colony of **British Honduras**, with Belize City as the administrative centre, and in 1871 Belize was officially declared a Crown Colony, with a resident governor appointed by Britain.

On September 10, 1931, the city was celebrating the anniversary of the Battle of St George's Caye when it was hit by a massive **hurricane** that uprooted houses, flooded the entire city and killed about a thousand people – ten percent of the population. Disaster relief was slow to arrive and many parts of the city were left in a state of squalid poverty. In 1961 the city was again ravaged by a hurricane: 262 people died, and the damage was so serious that plans were made to relocate the capital inland to Belmopan. (Hattieville, on the Western Highway, began life as a refuge for those fleeing the hurricane.) The official attitude was that Belize City would soon become a redundant backwater as Belmopan grew, but in fact few people chose to leave for the sterile "new town" atmosphere of Belmopan, and Belize City remains by far the most populous place in the country. Since independence the rise of foreign investment and tourism has made an impact, and Belize City is now experiencing a major construction boom.

Arrival and information

The four main **bus companies** in Belize have their terminals in the same western area of the city, around the Collet Canal and Magazine Road, a fairly derelict part of town known as Mesopotamia. It's only 1km from the centre and you can easily walk – or, especially at night, take a taxi – to any of the hotels listed below. **Taxis**, identified by green licence plates, charge US$2.50 for one or two passengers within the city limits. **Boats** returning from the cayes pull in at the Marine Terminal on the north side of the Swing Bridge, or at Courthouse Wharf on the south side, from where it's a short walk

For an explanation of **accommodation price codes**, see p.42.

or taxi ride to any of the hotels or bus depots. Belize City has two **airports**. International flights land at the **Phillip Goldson International Airport**, 17km north-west of the city; taxis into town cost US$15, or you could walk to the Northern Highway (25min) and try to flag down a bus. Domestic flights come and go from the **municipal airport**, a few kilometres north of town on the edge of the sea; taxis charge US$2.50.

The Belize **tourist board** is upstairs at 83 North Front St, just past the Marine Terminal (Mon–Fri 8am–5pm; ☎02/77213). The staff give out free bus timetables, a hotel guide and a city map.

Accommodation

Accommodation in Belize City is generally more expensive than elsewhere in the coun-try, and prices for even budget rooms can come as quite a shock. The selection below covers all price ranges and you can be confident of cleanliness and security in the hotels listed. There's no need to book unless you're desperate to stay in a particular hotel – you'll always be able to get something in the price range you're looking for.

Most of the city's hotels are located **north of the river**, and so a little further from the bus stations but closer to the Marine Terminal, with budget places clustered on or near **North Front St**. The more upmarket hotels are generally located in the historic **Fort George area** or along the **seafront** either side of the river mouth, where the res-idents can benefit from the sea breezes.

North of the river

Chateau Caribbean, 6 Marine Parade (☎02/30800, fax 30900). Luxurious, a/c, colonial-style hotel with cable TV and some sea views. ⑦.

Colton House, 9 Cork St (☎02/44666, fax 30451). Beautifully kept colonial house and the best guest house in Belize. All rooms have a balcony and an immaculate private bathroom, and the own-ers have a wealth of information on Belize – with discounts on tours. ⑥.

Downtown Guest House, 5 Eve St, near the end of Queen St (☎02/39012, fax 32057). Best value budget place in the city. Small, very friendly, clean and secure; even the shared bathrooms have reliable hot water. Breakfast available. ③.

Glenthorne Manor, 27 Barrack Rd, off Queen St (☎02/44212). Pleasant, individually designed rooms in a large, colonial-style house. Kitchen facilities available; breakfast included. ⑤.

Marin's Travelodge, 6 Craig St (☎02/45166). Clean, comfortable, secure and really quiet. The rooms are well furnished and the showers excellent. ③.

Mira Río Hotel, 59 North Front St (☎02/39947). Reasonable rooms, with washbasin and toilet but shared showers, set above a riverfront bar. ③.

North Front Street Guest House, 124 North Front St (☎02/77595). Clean, secure and good for information. Small rooms all with shared bath. ③.

South of the river

Bellevue Hotel, 5 Southern Foreshore (☎02/77051, fax 72353). The top hotel on the south side of the Swing Bridge. A/c, colonial-style rooms, and a relaxing courtyard with palms and a pool. The disco here is a focal point of the city's nightlife, with live music at weekends. ⑦.

Mopan Hotel, 55 Regent St (☎02/77351, fax 75383). Large wooden building run by avid conserva-tionist Jean Shaw – a mine of information on Belize – and popular with naturalists, writers and sci-entists. Rooms have private bath, but some are dimly lit. Jean can arrange flights to Guatemala and tours in Belize. ⑥.

Seaside Guest House, 3 Prince St, half a block from the southern foreshore (☎02/78339). A clean, well-run, very secure hotel with hot showers – and you really can see the sea. Meals can be ordered, and there's a beer and wine licence. Email service for guests: *friends@btl.net* Dorm beds US$10, rooms ④.

The City

Richard Davies, a British traveller in the mid-nineteenth century, wrote of the city: "There is much to be said for Belize, for in its way it was one of the prettiest ports at which we touched, and its cleanliness and order . . . were in great contrast to the ports we visited later as to make them most remarkable."

Most of the features that elicited this praise have now gone. In some other cities, **wooden colonial buildings** would be preserved as heritage showpieces, but here their only chance of escaping decrepitude is to be turned into a hotel or restaurant. Yet even in cases where the decay is too advanced for the paintwork, balconies and carved railings to be restored, the old wooden structures remain more pleasing than the concrete blocks that have replaced so many of them.

Before the construction of the first wooden bridge in the early 1800s, cattle were winched over the waterway that divides the city – hence the name **Haulover Creek**. Its replacement, the **Swing Bridge**, focal point of the city centre, was made in Liverpool and opened in 1923. Today it is the only manually operated swing bridge left in the Americas. Every day at 5.30am and 5.30pm the endless parade of vehicles and people is halted and the process of turning begins: using long poles inserted into a capstan, four men gradually lever the bridge around until it's pointing in the direction of the harbour mouth.

If walking around the sights sounds too tiring, then take a **bus tour** with Captain Nicolas Sanchez (mobile ☎014/877), whose historical knowledge is phenomenal. Daily tours leave punctually from the Marine Terminal at 9am and 3pm (2hr 30min; US$12.50).

The north side

Immediately on the **north side** of the Swing Bridge is the **Marine Terminal**, the place to catch boats for the northern cayes. In the same building are two of Belize's new museums, both superbly designed. The **Coastal Zone Museum** contains fascinating displays and explanations of reef ecology, the highlight being a 3-D model of the entire reef system, including the cayes and atolls; upstairs, the **Marine Museum** exhibits a collection of models and documents relating to Belize's maritime heritage (both Mon–Sat 8am–4.30pm; US$2). Opposite the Marine Terminal is the vast wooden **Paslow Building**, which houses the post office on the ground floor. A block east of the Marine Terminal, at 91 North Front St, **The Image Factory** (Mon–Fri 9am–6pm; ☎02/34151; free but donations welcome) is home to Belize's hottest contemporary artists. The gallery puts on outstanding, often provocative exhibitions and you often get a chance to chat with the artists themselves.

Continuing east, past the "temporary" market, which often has a greater variety of produce than the official market south of the Swing Bridge, you pass the **National Handicrafts Center**, which sells high-quality Belizean crafts at fair prices (Mon–Fri 8am–5pm); beyond is the lighthouse and the tomb of Baron Bliss, Belize's greatest benefactor (see opposite). Natural history enthusiasts will benefit from a visit to two of Belize's foremost conservation organizations, the **Belize Audubon Society** at 12 Fort St and the **Programme for Belize** at 2 South Park St, a block north on Memorial Park; here you can pick up all the latest information on access and developments in Belize's protected areas. Walking north around the shoreline, you pass the *Fort George* hotel and **Memorial Park**, which honours the Belizean dead of World War I. In this area you'll find several well-preserved colonial mansions, many of the finest now taken over by embassies and upmarket hotels.

The south side

The **south side** is generally the older section of Belize City: in the early days the elite lived in the seafront houses while the backstreets were home to the slaves and labourers. These days it's the city's commercial centre, containing the ugly new market building just over the Swing Bridge, the main shopping streets, banks and travel agencies. **Albert Street**, running south from the Swing Bridge, is the main commercial thoroughfare. On the parallel **Regent Street** are the former colonial administration and court buildings, known together as the **Court House**. These well-preserved examples of colonial architecture, with their columns and fine wrought iron, were completed in 1926 after an earlier building on the same site was destroyed by fire. The Court House overlooks a patch of grass and trees with an ornamental fountain in the centre, ambitiously known as Central Park until it was renamed Battlefield Park (an earlier unofficial name) in the early 1990s, commemorating the noisy political meetings that took place there before independence.

A block behind the Court House, on the waterfront, is the **Bliss Institute**, which is in many ways the cultural centre of Belize City. The Institute was funded by the legacy of **Baron Bliss**, a moderately eccentric Englishman with a Portuguese title. A keen fisherman, he arrived off the coast of Belize in 1926 after hearing about the tremendous amount of game fish in local waters. Unfortunately, he became ill and died without ever having been ashore. Despite this he left most of his considerable estate to the colony and, in gratitude, the authorities declared March 9, the date of his death, Baron Bliss Day. The Bliss building is the home of the **National Arts Council** and, as well as a small permanent exhibit from the national art collection, hosts temporary exhibitions, concerts and plays.

At the end of Albert Street is **St John's Cathedral**, the oldest Anglican cathedral in Central America and one of the oldest buildings in Belize. Looking like a large English parish church, it was begun in 1812, its red bricks brought over as ballast in British ships. Here, between 1815 and 1845, the kings of the Mosquito Coast were crowned amid great pomp, taking the title to a British Protectorate that extended along the coast of Honduras and Nicaragua.

On the way to the seafront from the cathedral, you'll come to the well-preserved white-painted, green-lawned **Government House** (Mon–Fri 8.30am–4pm; US$2.50), built in 1814, which served as the residence of the governor when Belize was a British colony. A plush red carpet leads down the hall to the great mahogany staircase, the walls lined with prints and photos of sombre past governors.

Eating, drinking and nightlife

The multitude of **restaurants** in Belize City don't offer much in the way of variety. There's the tasty but monotonous **Creole** fare of rice and beans, plenty of seafood and steaks, and a preponderance of **Chinese** restaurants, usually the best bet for **vegetarians**. Greasy fried chicken is available to take away from small restaurants all over the city. The big **hotels** have their own restaurants, naturally quite expensive but with much more varied menus. Be warned that many restaurants are closed on Sunday.

Restaurants

The Ark, 109 North Front St (☎02/77820). Very tasty Belizean dishes at great prices; already cooked so it's a good choice for a quick meal. Also does deliveries. Mon–Sat 7am–11pm.

Macy's, 18 Bishop St. Tiny, long-established Creole restaurant that's popular with locals and extremely busy at lunchtimes.

Mangos, 164 Newtown Barracks Rd (☎02/34021). Away from the centre, near the *Fiesta* hotel, this is one of the best restaurants in the city. Seafood is a speciality, but there are also well-prepared steak dishes and there's always a vegetarian option.

Pepper's Pizza, 2215 Baymen Ave (☎02/35000). Decent pizza restaurant that delivers. Mon–Thurs 5–11pm, until midnight Fri & Sat.

Pop'n'Taco, corner of King St and Regent St. Inexpensive restaurant serving cheap Chinese food, despite the name.

River Side Patio, at the rear of the new market. Good place to relax with a snack and a drink as you watch the bridge swing.

Sea Rock, 190 Newtown Barracks Rd. Extremely good Indian food in a quiet, clean restaurant. Unfortunately it's a long way from the centre – you need to take a taxi.

Drinking, nightlife and entertainment

Belize City's more sophisticated, air-conditioned **bars** are found in the most expensive establishments, and there aren't many of those. At the lowest end of the scale are dimly lit dives, effectively men-only, where there's the possibility that you'll be offered drugs or robbed. There are several places between the two extremes, most of them in restaurants and hotels. One of the best is *Lindbergh's Landing*, a quiet, open-air bar with sea views located at the spot where Charles Lindbergh landed in Belize in 1928, just past the *Fiesta Inn*, next to *Mango's*. **Nightlife**, though not as wild as it used to be, is becoming more reliable and the quality of live bands is improving all the time. The *Radisson Fort George* and the *Bellevue* hold regular dances, and if you're after **live music**, there's reggae at the *Lumba Yaad Bar*, on the riverbank just out of town on the Northern Highway.

Listings

Airlines Aerocaribe (☎02/77185); Aerovias, *Mopan Hotel*, 55 Regent St (☎02/75446); American, corner of New Rd and Queen St (☎02/32522); Continental, 32 Albert St (☎02/78309; airport ☎025/2488); Maya Island Air, Municipal Airport (☎02/31140 or 026/2345); TACA, at Belize Global Travel, 41 Albert St (☎02/77185; airport ☎025/2163); Tropic Air, Municipal Airport (☎02/45671 or 026/2012).

American Express Belize Global Travel, 41 Albert St (☎02/77363).

Banks and exchange All the banks have branches on Albert St (generally open Mon–Thurs 8am–2pm, Fri 8am–4.30pm). Barclays, opposite the park at no. 21, does cash advances (Belize or US dollars) on Visa and MasterCard without a surcharge, and also has an ATM.

Books The Book Centre, 2 Church St (opposite the BTL office), has the best selection of titles, including *Rough Guides*.

Car rental All the following have desks at the International Airport: Avis ☎02/34619; Budget ☎02/32435; Crystal ☎02/31600; and National ☎02/31650.

Embassies and consulates Though the official capital is at Belmopan, some embassies remain in Belize City and are normally open Mon–Fri mornings. Current addresses and phone numbers can be checked in the green pages of the telephone directory. Canada, 83 North Front St (☎02/31060, fax 30060); Guatemala, 8 A Street, Kings Park (☎02/33150, fax 35140); Honduras, 91 N Front St (☎02/45889, fax 30562); Mexico, 20 North Park St (☎02/30194, fax 78742); USA, 29 Gabourel Lane (☎02/77161, fax 30802).

Immigration The Belize Immigration Office is in the Government Complex on Mahogany St, near the junction of Central American Blvd and the Western Highway (Mon–Fri 8am–noon & 1–4pm; ☎02/24620). Extensions of permitted stay cost US$12.50.

Laundry Central America Coin Laundry, 114 Barrack Rd (Mon–Sat 8.30am–9pm, reduced hours on Sun).

Medical care Dr Gamero, Myo-On Clinic, 40 Eve St (☎02/45616); Karl Huesner Memorial Hospital, Princess Margaret Drive, near junction with the Northern Highway (☎02/31548).

Photography For prints, slides and fast passport photos, try Spooners, 89 North Front St.

Police On Queen Street, a block north of the Swing Bridge (☎02/72210). Or contact the Tourist Board (see p.57) during opening hours. The emergency number is ☎911.

Post office In the Paslow Building, on the corner of Queen St, immediately north of the Swing Bridge (Mon–Fri 8am–noon & 1–4.30pm).

Supermarkets Brodies and Romacs are opposite each other on Albert St, just beyond the park.

Telephones There are payphones and cardphones for local and international calls dotted around the city; or use the main BTL office, 1 Church St (Mon–Fri 8am–6pm, Sat 8am–noon), where there are also fax and email services.

Travel agents The largest, and the best for booking international flights, is Belize Global Travel, 41 Albert St (☎02/77185, fax 75213). Jal's, 148 North Front St (☎02/45407, fax 30792), can book domestic and international flights.

Moving on from Belize City

Moving on from Belize City by **bus** couldn't be simpler. Most of the bus **companies** are in the same area, along the Collet Canal and Magazine Rd, a short walk from the centre of town. The box overleaf lists all the routes from Belize City, including frequencies and duration.

Tours

Most inland **day tours** from Belize City visit two or more of the following: The Belize Zoo, Bermudian Landing Baboon Sanctuary, Crooked Tree Wildlife Sanctuary, Lamanai ruins and Altun Ha ruins. All but the last of these places are very easy to visit independently, though in some cases you'll need to stay overnight. Even when you include the cost of accommodation you're still likely to save money doing by it on your own. If time is short and you'd prefer a guided tour then contact Mopan Travel and Tours, 55 Regent St (☎02/77351, fax 75383), or David Cunningham, an independent naturalist tour guide (☎02/31153), or Belize Travel Adventures, 168 N Front St (☎02/33064, fax 33196).

Bus companies and depots

While the main bus companies have their own depots, there are numerous smaller operators with regular departures but no contact address or phone number. The abbreviations used in the box overleaf follow the name of the company.

Batty (BA), 15 Mosul St (☎02/72025).

James Bus (JA) leaves for Punta Gorda (via Belmopan) from Shell station, Cemetery Rd, near Collet Canal daily at 7am.

Jex Bus (JX) departs for Crooked Tree from Regent St West and Pound Yard, Collet Canal (☎025/7017).

McFadzean's Bus (MF) leaves for Bermudian Landing from the corner of Cemetery Rd and Mosul St, near the Batty bus depot.

Novelos (NV), 19 West Collet Canal (☎02/77372).

Perez bus (PE) leaves for Sarteneja from Texaco station on N Front St at noon.

Ritchie's Bus (RI) leaves from Collet Canal, near Cemetery Rd.

Russell's Bus (RU) leaves for Bermudian Landing from Cairo St, near the corner of Cemetery Road and Euphrates Ave.

Venus (VE), Magazine Rd (☎02/73354).

Z-Line (ZL), Magazine Rd (☎02/73937).

BUS SERVICES FROM BELIZE CITY

Where express services are available (exp), these are faster and a fraction more expensive than regular services. For bus company addresses, see p.61.

DESTINATION	FREQUENCY	COMPANY	DURATION
Belmopan	hourly 5am–8pm (exp)	BA, NV	1hr 15min
Bermudian Landing	Mon–Sat noon & 4.30pm	MF, RU	1hr 15min
Chetumal, Mexico	hourly 4am–7pm (exp)	BA, VE	3hr 30min
Corozal	hourly 4am–7pm (exp)	BA, VE	2hr 30min
Crooked Tree	Mon–Sat 4 daily, 1 on Sun: BA Mon–Fri 4pm, Sat noon, Sun 9am; JX Mon–Sat 10.30am, 4.30pm & 5.30pm.	BA, JX	1hr 30min
Dangriga	10 daily 6am–5pm	RI, JA, ZL	2hr via Coastal Road; 3hr 30min via Belmopan
Gales Point	few direct; buses pass junction 3km away	RI, ZL	1hr40min to junction
Melchor, Guatemala	hourly 5am–6pm	BA, NV	3hr 30min
Orange Walk	hourly 4am–7pm	BA, VE	1hr 30min
Placencia	3–4 daily, all via Dangriga; direct at 2.30pm.	RI, ZL	4hr 30min; 6–7hr via Belmopan
Punta Gorda	5 daily, all via Dangriga	JA, ZL	8–10hr
San Ignacio	hourly 5am–8pm (exp), all via Belmopan	BA, NV	3hr
Sarteneja	2 daily, via Orange Walk: PE noon, VE 12.30pm	PE, VE	3hr 30min

travel details

BUSES
For bus routes, see the box opposite.

INTERNATIONAL FLIGHTS
Belize international airport to: San Salvador; San Pedro Sula and Roatán; Flores and Guatemala City; Cancún; plus US destinations.

DOMESTIC FLIGHTS
Tropic Air (☎02/45671 or 026/2012) and Maya Island Air (☎02/31140 or 026/2345) operate flights from both airports to: **Caye Caulker** (15–20min) and **San Pedro** (10min from Caye Caulker), at least hourly from 7am to 5pm; to **Dangriga** (8–10 daily; 25min), **Placencia** (a further 20min) and **Punta Gorda** (another 25min).

BOATS
Most boats to Caye Caulker leave from the Marine Terminal on North Front St, by the Swing Bridge (☎02/31969); for Ambergris Caye, boats also leave from Courthouse Wharf, south of the river.

Caye Caulker (every 2hr 9am–5pm; 45min).

Ambergris Caye (3 daily from 9am, calling at Caye Caulker; 1hr 25min).

CHAPTER 2

COROZAL, ORANGE WALK AND THE NORTH

Northern Belize is an expanse of relatively level land, where swamps, savannahs and lagoons are mixed with rainforest and farmland. The largest settlement in the north is **Orange Walk**, the country's main centre for sugar production. Further north is **Corozal**, a small and peaceful Caribbean town with a strong Mexican element – scarcely surprising as it lies just fifteen minutes from the border. Most of the original settlers in the north were refugees from the Caste War in Yucatán, thus Spanish is as common as Creole.

Most visitors to northern Belize are here to see the **Maya ruins** and **wildlife reserves**. The largest site, **Lamanai**, served by regular boat tours along the **New River Lagoon**, features some of the most impressive pyramids in the country. East of Lamanai, **Altun Ha**, reached via the old Northern Highway, is usually visited as a part of a day-trip from Belize City or San Pedro. The smaller sites include **Cuello**, west of Orange Walk, and **Santa Rita** and **Cerros**, both near Corozal.

The most northerly of the wildlife reserves is the **Shipstern Nature Reserve**, close to the village of Sarteneja. Further south, at the **Crooked Tree Wildlife Sanctuary**, a network of rivers and lagoons offers protection to a range of migratory birds, and at the **Bermudian Landing Community Baboon Sanctuary** a group of farmers have combined agriculture with conservation to the benefit of the black howler monkey. By far the largest and most ambitious conservation project, however, is the **Rio Bravo Conservation Area**, comprising 960 square kilometres of tropical forest and river systems in the west of Orange Walk district.

Travelling around the north is fairly straightforward if you stick to the main Northern Highway. Venus and Batty between them operate bus services every hour from 4am to 7pm between Belize City and Chetumal in Mexico, calling at Orange Walk and Corozal on the way.

Crossing from Mexico

It's only a four-hour bus journey from the Mexican town of **Chetumal**, along the Northern Highway via Orange Walk and Corozal to Belize City. At the **Santa Elena** border crossing, 12km from Chetumal, Mexican immigration and customs posts are on the northern bank of the River Hondo; when you're finished there, the bus will pick you up again to take you across to Belizean immigration. Border formalities take just a matter of minutes. **Moneychangers** on the Belize side won't rip you off; you get the standard rate of Bz$2 for US$1.

For an explanation of **accommodation price codes**, see p.42.

Corozal and around

Continuing south from the border, the road meets the sea at **COROZAL**, just thirty minutes from Chetumal. Corozal's location near the mouth of the New River enabled the ancient **Maya** to prosper here by controlling river and seaborne trade, and two sites, Santa Rita and Cerros are within easy reach. The present town was founded here in 1849 by refugees from the massacre in Bacalar, Mexico, who were hounded south by the Caste Wars. Today's grid-pattern town is a neat mix of Mexican and Caribbean, its appearance largely due to reconstruction in the wake of Hurricane Janet in 1955. There's little to do in Corozal, but it's an agreeable place to spend the day on the way to or from the border, and is hassle-free, even at night. The breezy shoreline park is good for a stroll, while on the tree-shaded main plaza, the **town hall** is worth a look inside for a vivid depiction of local history in a mural by Manuel Villamar Reyes. In two corners of the plaza you can see the remains of a small fort, built to ward off Maya attacks in the late 1800s.

Arrival and information

All **buses** between Belize City and Chetumal pass through Corozal, roughly hourly in each direction. The Venus bus depot is near the northern edge of town, opposite the

Shell station; Batty buses stop on 4th Ave, north of the park. Maya Island Air and Tropic operate daily **flights** between Corozal and San Pedro on Ambergris Caye. Jal's travel agency (☎04/22163), at the the southern end of town, beyond *Tony's*, can organize **international flights**. For reliable tourist **information**, visit the **Corozal Cultural Centre** (Tues–Sat 9am–noon & 1–4.30pm; ☎04/23176), housed in the restored colonial market building in the waterfront park, just past the new market. The centre also holds a **museum** (US$1.50) with imaginative displays depicting episodes in Corozal's history.

Scotia Bank, on the southeast side of the main plaza, offers the best value for **cash advances**. The **post office** is on the west side of the plaza. For domestic flights and **organized tours** to local nature reserves and archeological sites, contact Henry Menzies at *Caribbean Village* (☎04/22725). Stephan Moerman (☎04/22833), a French biologist, arranges tours to Cerros and Bacalar Chico National Park, at the north end of Ambergris Caye (see p.78).

Accommodation, eating and drinking

Corozal has plenty of **accommodation** in all price ranges and you'll always be able to find a suitable room. *Nestor's*, on 5th Ave South, between 4th and 5th streets (☎04/22354; ③), is a centrally located budget hotel, with private showers and a popular sports bar and restaurant. The *Hotel Maya*, on the main road at the south end of town, facing the sea (☎04/22082, fax 22857; ④–⑤), is clean and well-run with private bathrooms; new rooms have a/c. Just beyond the *Maya*, the *Caribbean Village Resort* (☎04/22045, fax 23414; ④) offers good-value whitewashed thatched cabins with hot water, set among the palms, facing the sea. There's also a trailer park (US$12) and camping (US$5). For more luxury, head 1km south from town to *Tony's Inn and Beach Resort* (☎04/22055, fax 22829; ⑥–⑦), where spacious a/c rooms overlook landscaped gardens and a pristine beach bar in a superb seaside location with secure parking.

Whatever your budget, the best **meals** in Corozal are to be found in the hotels. The popular bar at *Nestor's* serves American and Belizean food, while *Hotel Maya* serves very good Belizean and Jamaican food in a quieter environment. There's a wonderful restaurant at *Tony's*, and *Haley's* in *Caribbean Village* is renowned locally for its fine, inexpensive food. Authentic French pastries can be had at *Le Cafe Kela*, on the seafront just north of the centre.

Around Corozal: Santa Rita and Cerros

Of the two small Maya sites within reach of Corozal, the closest is **Santa Rita** (daily 8am–4pm; US$2.50), about fifteen minutes' walk northwest of town. To get there, follow the main road in the direction of the border and where it divides take the left-hand fork. Founded around 1500 BC, Santa Rita was in all probability the powerful Maya city known as Chetumal. It was still a thriving settlement in 1531 AD, when the conquistador Alonso Davila entered the town, only to be driven out almost immediately by Na Chan Kan, the Maya chief, and his Spanish adviser Gonzalo Guerrero. The main remaining building is a small pyramid. Excavations here have uncovered the burial sites of an elaborately bejewelled elderly woman and a Classic Period warlord.

The remains of the late Preclassic centre of **Cerros** (daily 8am–4pm; US$2.50), are just 5km across the bay from Corozal and best reached by **boat** with a guide from the town, though in the dry season it's possible to drive there through the villages of Progresso and Copper Bank. Built in a strategic position at the mouth of the New River, this was was one of the earliest places in the Maya world to adopt the rule of kings.

Despite initial success, however, Cerros had been abandoned by the Classic Period. The site includes three large acropolis structures, ball courts and plazas flanked by pyramids. The largest building is a 22-metre-high temple, whose intricate stucco masks represent the rising and setting sun.

Sarteneja and the Shipstern Reserve

Across Chetumal Bay from Corozal, the largely uninhabited **Sarteneja peninsula**, jutting out towards the Yucatán in the northeast of Belize, is covered with dense forests and swamps that support an amazing array of wildlife. The only village is **SARTENE-JA**, a quiet lobster-fishing centre populated by Spanish-speaking *mestizos*, and only just beginning to experience tourism. A couple of new hotels have been built (there's also accommodation at the reserve; see below), and **guides** are available to take you to the lagoons and beyond. *Fernando's Guest House* (☎04/32045; ⑤), on the seafront, has thatched rooms with private bath, and *Sayab Cabañas* (④), by the water tower, has two thatched cabins surrounded by plants.

To get there by **bus**, you need to go via Orange Walk. From Belize City the Perez bus leaves the Texaco station on North Front St at noon, and the Venus bus at 12.30pm (Mon–Sat; 4hr; US$6). They all pass through Orange Walk, stopping at Zeta's store on Main St ninety minutes later. Buses return from Sarteneja at 5am and 6am.

The **Shipstern Nature Reserve** (daily 8am–5pm; US$5 including guided walk), established in 1981, covers an area of eighty square kilometres. The bulk of the reserve is made up of what's technically known as "tropical moist forest", although it contains relatively few mature trees, since the area was wiped clean by Hurricane Janet in 1955. It also includes some wide belts of savannah – covered in coarse grasses, palms and broad-leaved trees – and a section of the shallow Shipstern Lagoon, dotted with mangrove islands. Taking the superb guided walk along the **Chiclero Trail**, you'll encounter more named plant species in an hour than on any other trail in Belize. Shipstern is a birdwatcher's paradise: the lagoon system supports blue-winged teal, American coot, thirteen species of egret and huge flocks of lesser scaup, while the forest is home to fly-catchers, warblers, keel-billed toucans, collared aracari and at least five species of parrot; and in addition there are crocodiles, coatis, jaguars, peccaries, and an abundance of wonderful butterflies.

All **buses** to Sarteneja pass the **entrance** to the reserve, 5km before the village. You can **stay** at the headquarters near the visitor centre; there are two neat four-bed dorms (US$10 per person) with cooking facilities, and a two-roomed house for rent (US$40).

Orange Walk and around

With a population approaching twenty thousand, **ORANGE WALK** is the largest town in the north of Belize and the centre of a busy agricultural region. Like Corozal, less than an hour away along the Northern Highway, it was founded by *mestizo* refugees fleeing from the Caste Wars in Yucatán in 1849, who chose as their site an area that had long been used for logging camps and was already occupied by the local Icaiché (Chichanha) Maya.

Orange Walk traditionally thrived on the sugar and citrus industries, but a fall in sugar prices has seen it depend more heavily on the profits from marijuana. Recently, however, pressure from the US government has forced Belizean authorities to destroy many of the marijuana fields. The town itself boasts few tourist attractions,

MENNONITES IN BELIZE

The **Mennonites** arose from the radical Anabaptist movement of the sixteenth century and are named after the Dutch priest Menno Simons, leader of the community in its formative years. Recurring government restrictions on their lifestyle, especially regarding their pacifist objection to military service, forced them to move repeatedly. Having removed to Switzerland they travelled on to Prussia, and in 1663 a group emigrated to North America. After World War I they migrated from Canada to Mexico, eventually arriving in Belize in 1958. Perseverance and hard work made them successful farmers, and in recent years prosperity has caused drastic changes in their lives. The Mennonite Church in Belize is increasingly split between a modernist section – who use electricity and power tools, and drive trucks, tractors and even cars – and the traditionalists, who prefer a stricter interpretation of their beliefs. Members of the community, easily recognizable in their denim dungarees, can be seen trading their produce and buying supplies every day in Orange Walk and Belize City.

and Corozal (see p.66) is a preferable place to spend the night. The centre of town is marked by a distinctly Mexican-style formal plaza, and the town hall across the main road is actually called the Palacio Municipal, reinforcing the town's strong historical links to Mexico. The tranquil, slow-moving New River, a few blocks east of the centre, was a busy commercial waterway during the logging days. Now, however, it's a lovely starting point for visiting the ruins of **Lamanai**, and several local operators now offer tours (see p.69).

Practicalities

Hourly **buses** from Belize City and Corozal pull up on the main road in the centre of town, offically Queen Victoria Avenue but always referred to as the Belize–Corozal road. Services to and from Sarteneja stop at Zeta's Store on Main St, two blocks to the east, while local buses to the surrounding villages leave from near the crossroads by the fire station in the centre of town.

The Belize–Corozal road is lined with hotels, restaurants and filling stations, so there's no need to walk far. There are no recommended budget **hotels**; if you do have to stay, then the best options are either the *Victoria*, 40 Belize–Corozal Rd (☎03/22518, fax 22847; ⑤), where most of the rooms have balconies, some are a/c, and there's a pool, or the new *St Christopher's*, 10 Main St (☎ & fax 03/21064; ⑤), which has beautiful new rooms (some a/c) with private bath, set in grounds sweeping down to the New River. The best place to **change money** and get cash advances on credit cards is the Scotia Bank, just east of the plaza. The **post office** is at the north end of town on the Belize–Corozal road.

The majority of **restaurants** in Orange Walk are Chinese, though there are a few Belizean-style places serving simple "Mexican" food or rice and beans. *Lover's Restaurant*, tucked away in the far corner of the park at 20 Lover's Lane, offers the best Belizean food, while *Juanita's*, on the side street by the Shell station, has the best Mexican dishes. Nightlife boils down to the weekend **discos** in the *Mi Amor* and *Victoria* hotels.

Maya sites around Orange Walk

Although the **Maya sites** in northern Belize have been the source of a number of the most important archeological finds in the Maya world, they are not (with the exception of Lamanai) as monumentally spectacular as some in the Yucatán. The area around Orange Walk has some of the most productive arable farmland in Belize, and this was also the case in Maya times – aerial surveys in the late 1970s revealed evidence of raised fields and a network of irrigation canals, showing that the Maya practised skilful intensive agriculture. In the Postclassic era this region controlled the trade in cacao beans (used as currency by the Maya) that were grown in the Hondo and New river valleys. For a while the Maya here were even able to resist the conquistadors, and Maya rebellions continued long after nominal Spanish rule had been established in 1544.

Cuello and Nohmul

Cuello lies about 5km west of Orange Walk. Discovered in 1973 by Norman Hammond, until recently the site was thought to be one of the earliest in the Maya region, originating in 1500 BC. However, new research suggests that it in fact dates back only to 1000 BC. The site itself isn't very impressive, with little to see except a single small pyramid and several earth-covered mounds. The ruins are behind a factory where Cuello rum is made; the site is on their land, so you should call beforehand for permission to visit (☎03/22141). Taxis here from Orange Walk cost around US$10.

Situated on the Orange Walk–Corozal district boundary, **Nohmul** (Great Mound) is a major ceremonial centre with origins in the Middle Preclassic, between 900 and 400 BC. During the Classic period it was abandoned, but reoccupied during the Early Postclassic. The ruins cover a large area, comprising two groups connected by a causeway, with several plazas around them. The main structure is an acropolis platform surmounted by a later pyramid: the highest point in the area. Nohmul lies amid sugar-cane fields, 2km west of the village of **San Pablo**, which is 17km north of Orange Walk on the Northern Highway. You'll need to get permission to enter the site from the landowner, Estevan Itzab, who lives on the west side of the highway, directly opposite the village water tower.

Lamanai

Though they can't match the scale of the great sites in Mexico and Guatemala, the **ruins of Lamanai** (daily 8am–4pm; US$5) are the most impressive in Belize, and their setting on the New River Lagoon – in the 4-square-kilometre Archeological Reserve, now the only jungle for miles around – gives them a special quality that is long gone from sites served by a torrent of tourist buses.

Lamanai is one of only a few sites whose original Maya name is known – it translates as "Submerged Crocodile", hence the numerous representations of crocodiles. *Lamanai*, however, is the seventeenth-century mistranslation of *Lamanyan*, and actually means "Drowned Insect". The site was occupied up until the sixteenth century, when Spanish missionaries built a church alongside to encourage the Maya to abandon their heathen ways. Troops of **black howler monkeys** make Lamanai their home and you're certain to see them peering down through the branches as you wander the trails.

The site's most impressive feature is the prosaically named N10-43, a massive **Late Preclassic pyramid**, the largest structure from the period in the Maya region. The view across the surrounding forest from the top of the temple is magnificent. North from here, structure N9-56 is a sixth-century pyramid with two stucco masks of a deity (probably the sun god) carved on different levels. The lower mask, 4m high, is particularly well-preserved, showing a clearly humanized face bordered by decorative columns, wearing a crocodile headdress. There are a number of other well-preserved and clearly defined glyphs. Traces of later settlers can be seen around the nearby village of **Indian Church** (see below): to the south of the village are the ruins of two churches built by Spanish missionaries. The site's small **archeological museum** at the site houses an amazing collection of artefacts arranged in chronological order, mostly figurines depicting gods and animals. Nazario Ku, the caretaker, is very knowledgeable about Maya culture and the best guide at the site.

Practicalities

Getting to Lamanai from Orange Walk is relatively straightforward. Three **buses** a week (Mon, Wed & Fri, returning Mon, Wed & Fri; 2hr) leave from the side of the fire station, in the centre of town, for the village of **Indian Church** (community phone ☎031/2015); the 4pm departure time means you'll have to stay overnight. The most pleasant way to get here, though, is by river, and a number of operators now organize **day-trips** for US$30–50 per person. By far the most informative are those operated by Jungle River Tours, run by the knowledgeable Antonio and Herminio Novelo and based at the *Lover's Restaurant* in Orange Walk (☎03/22293, fax 23749). On the way they will point out lurking crocodiles and the dozens of species of birds, including snail kites, that you might otherwise miss. For independent travellers on a budget, the best bargain can usually be arranged by Barbara or Tanya at Tower Hill Maya Tours (☎03/23839), by the **toll bridge**, 11km south of Orange Walk. To make your own way to the toll bridge, take the Batty bus that leaves Belize City at 7am for Chetumal.

If you want to **stay** (and you'll have to if you're travelling by bus) there are a couple of places offering **rooms** (④) in Indian Church, though they're rather overpriced. Speak to Nazario at the site and he'll let you **camp** at his house or rent you a hammock very cheaply; you can eat with the family. More **upmarket accommodation** is available nearby in the thatched cabañas at *Lamanai Outpost Lodge* (☎ & fax 02/33578; ⑦), set in extensive gardens sweeping down to the lagoon.

Rio Bravo Conservation Area

In the far northwest of Orange Walk district is the **Rio Bravo Conservation Area**, a 960-square-kilometre tract designated for tropical forest conservation, research and sustained-yield forest harvests. This conservation success story actually began with a disastrous plan in the mid-1980s to clear the forest, initially to fuel a wood-fired power station and later to provide Coca-Cola with frost-free land to grow citrus. Environmentalists were alarmed, and their strenuous objections forced Coca-Cola to drop the plan.

An imaginative project to save the threatened forest, the **Programme for Belize**, was initiated by the Massachusetts Audubon Society in 1988. Funds were raised from corporate donors and conservation organizations but the most widespread support was generated through an ambitious "adopt-an-acre" scheme. Coca-Cola itself, anxious to distance itself from the charge of rainforest destruction, has donated more than 90,000 acres (360 square kilometres). Today rangers patrol the area to prevent illegal logging and to stop farmers encroaching onto the reserve with *milpas* (slash and burn fields). Thanks to the ban on hunting, the forest teems with **wildlife**, including all five of Belize's cat species, plus more than 300 species of bird. The guarded boundaries also protect dozens of **Maya sites**, most of them unexcavated and unrestored, though many have been looted.

There's no **public transport** to Rio Bravo, but if you're staying at La Milpa field station (see below) you can get a bus (Mon–Sat 10am) from the side of the fire station in Orange Walk to San Felipe, 37km away, and arrange to be picked up there.

La Milpa and Hill Bank field stations

Set in a former *milpa* clearing in the forest, **La Milpa Field Station** offers comfortable dorm and cabaña **accommodation** in a tranquil, studious atmosphere (dorms US$75, cabañas US$90 per person, including three meals and two excursions or lectures a day). Guests are mainly students on tropical ecology courses, though everyone is welcome, and the facilities utilize the latest green technology. Deer and ocellated turkeys feed contentedly around the cabins. Adjacent to the station is the huge Classic Maya city of **La Milpa**, the third largest in Belize, where several royal tombs have recently been uncovered. A day visit, which includes a guided tour of La Milpa or one of the trails, costs US$20. At the southern end of the New River Lagoon is **Hill Bank Field Station**, where a former logging camp has been adapted to undertake scientific research. Similar dorm accommodation is on offer (US$75). For **information** and bookings for either station, contact the PFB office, 2 South Park St, Belize City (☎02/75616, fax 75635), who may be able to arrange transport; or write to PFB, Box 749, Belize City.

Gallon Jug and Chan Chich Lodge

Forty kilometres south of La Milpa, the former logging town of **Gallon Jug** is the home of Barry Bowen, reportedly the richest man in Belize. In the 1980s, his speculative land deals led to an international outcry against threatened rainforest clearance. The experience apparently proved cathartic; Bowen is now an ardent conservationist and most of the 500 square kilometres here are strictly protected. The focal point is the luxurious **Chan Chich Lodge** (☎02/75634, fax 76961; ⑨), with twelve large thatched cabañas set in the plaza of the Classic Maya site of Chan Chich, surrounded by forest. It is a truly awe-inspiring setting: grass-covered temple walls crowned with jungle tower up from the lodge, and the forest explodes with a cacophany of bird calls at dawn. You can drive here, but most guests fly in on a charter from Belize Municipal airport to the **airstrip** at Gallon Jug.

Crooked Tree

Heading south from Orange Walk along the Northern Highway, after 38km you pass the branch road for the **Crooked Tree Wildlife Sanctuary**, a reserve that takes in a vast area of wetlands, covering four separate lagoons. It provides an ideal resting place for thousands of **migrating and resident birds**, such as snail kites, tiger herons, snowy egrets, ospreys and black-collared hawks. The reserve's most famous visitor is the **jabiru stork**, the largest flying bird in the New World, with a wingspan of 2.5m. Belize has the biggest nesting population of jabiru storks at any one site: they arrive in November, the young hatch in April or May, and they leave just before the rainy season gets under way. The **best months** for birdwatchers to visit are from late February to June, when the lagoons shrink to a string of pools, forcing wildlife to congregate for food and water.

In the middle of the reserve, straggling around the shores of a lagoon, 5km from the main road, is the village of **CROOKED TREE** – effectively an island in the lagoons but linked to the mainland by a **causeway**. One of the oldest inland villages in the country, its existence is based on fishing and farming – some of the mango and cashew trees are reckoned to be more than a hundred years old. Near the end of the causeway is the **Sanctuary Visitor Centre**, where you pay the US$4 entrance fee.

Practicalities

There are four daily **buses** to Crooked Tree from Belize City. The Jex service (☎025/7017) leaves once daily from Regent St West (Mon–Sat 10.30am) and twice on weekdays from the Pound Yard (Mon–Fri 4.30pm & 5.30pm). There's also one Batty service a day (Mon–Fri 4pm, Sat noon & Sun 9am; returning Mon–Sat between 6am and 7am, Sun 4pm).

Note that at present the community telephone (☎021/2084) is the main communication link, but private phones are now coming on line. There's a **payphone** in the village centre.

Most of the **accommodation** at Crooked Tree is in resort-type lodgings, with meals included, though there is also some reasonably priced **bed and breakfast** accommodation in private houses (③) – ask at the visitor centre. Several of the resorts have camping space. Anyone offering accommodation can also arrange boats and guides for **tours**. *Bird's Eye View Lodge* (☎02/32040, fax 24869; ⑥ including breakfast), on the lakeshore at the south end of the village, has comfortable private rooms in a two-storey concrete building; there's also an inexpensive dorm room (US$10) and camping (US$5). *Crooked Tree Resort* (☎02/75819, fax 74007; ⑤) consists of neat wood-and-thatch cabins on the lakeshore near the village centre. Though not on the lake, *Sam Tillet's Hotel* (☎021/2026; ④) has comfortable rooms which are the best value in the village and its garden attracts a variety of birds. *Paradise Inn* (☎02/44101 or 44333; ⑤) has beautiful thatched cabins in a lovely, quiet location, just steps from the lake at the north end of the village.

The ruins of Altun Ha

Fifty-five kilometres north of Belize City and just 9km from the sea is the impressive Maya site of **Altun Ha** (daily 8am–4pm; US$5), which was occupied for around twelve hundred years until abandoned in 900 AD. Its position close to the Caribbean coast suggests that it was sustained as much by trade as by agriculture – a theory upheld by the discovery of trade objects such as obsidian and jade, neither occurring naturally in Belize and both very important in Maya ceremony. The jade would have come from the Motagua valley in Guatemala and much of it would probably have been shipped onwards to the north..

The core of Altun Ha is clustered around two Classic period plazas, both dotted with palm trees. Entering from the road, you come first to Plaza A. Large temples enclose it on all four sides, and a magnificent tomb has been discovered beneath Temple A-1, the **Temple of the Green Tomb**. Dating from 550 AD, this yielded a total of three hundred pieces, including jade, jewellery, stingray spines, skin, flints and the remains of a Maya book. The adjacent Plaza B is dominated by the site's largest temple, the **Temple of the Masonry Altars**. Several tombs have been uncovered within the main structure, though only two were found intact. In one, archeologists discovered a carved jade head of **Kinich Ahau**, the Maya sun god. Standing just under 15cm high, it is the largest carved jade to be found anywhere in the Maya world; today it's kept hidden away in the vaults of the Belize Bank.

Outside these two main plazas are several other areas of interest, though little else has yet been restored. A short trail leads south to **Rockstone Pond**, which was dammed in Maya times (and today is home to a large crocodile), at the eastern edge of which stands another mid-sized temple. Built in the second century AD, this contained offerings that came from the great city of Teotihuacán in the Valley of Mexico.

From Cinderella Plaza in Belize City, a daily afternoon **bus** runs along the Old Northern Highway to the village of **MASKALL** (call ☎03/22041 to check times), passing within 3km of Altun Ha. Any travel agent in Belize City will arrange a **tour** (see p.61) and increasing numbers visit as part of a day-trip from San Pedro (see p.79). There's no accommodation at the site but you can ask the caretaker for permission to camp.

Bermudian Landing to Belize City

West off the Northern Highway, the **Community Baboon Sanctuary** is one of the most interesting conservation projects in Belize. It was established in 1985 by Dr Rob Horwich and a group of local farmers (with help from the World Wide Fund for Nature), who adopted a voluntary code of practice to harmonize their own needs with those of the wildlife. A mixture of farmland and broad-leaved forest along the banks of the Belize River, the sanctuary coordinates eight villages and more than a hundred landowners in a project combining conservation, education and tourism.

The main focus of attention is the **black howler monkey** (locally known as a baboon). They generally live in groups of between four and eight, and spend the day wandering through the leaf canopy feasting on leaves, flowers and fruits. At dawn and dusk they let rip with the famous howl: a deep and rasping roar that carries for miles. The sanctuary is also home to around two hundred bird species, plus iguanas, peccaries and coatis. The **visitor centre** (US$5, includes a short guided walk), at the west end of Bermudian Landing (see below), is home to Belize's first natural history museum, with exhibits and information on the riverside habitats and animals you're likely to see.

Practicalities

The Sanctuary comprises eight villages along the Belize River, from Flowers Bank to Big Falls. All of them welcome visitors and you'll find plenty of places where you can rent canoes or horses. Probably the most convenient base is the village of **BERMU-DIAN LANDING** at the heart of the area, an old logging centre that dates back to the seventeenth century.

You can **camp** at the visitor centre for a small fee and a number of local families offer bed and breakfast (③). Behind the visitor centre, *Baboon Guest House* (☎014/2186; ④) has two rooms in a lovely thatched cabin. The best place to stay in the village, howev-er, is the friendly *Jungle Drift Lodge* (☎014/9578, fax 02/78160; ④–⑤), set right above the riverbank, shaded by trees, and with a profusion of tropical plants in the gardens – you're practically guaranteed close-up views of the baboons. Accommodation is in neat cabañas, some with deck and private bath, and there's hot water in the shared bath-rooms; camping costs US$5 per person. Meals are eaten with the family and the food is excellent. The lodge also rents canoes, and organizes float trips 22km downriver to the village of Isabella Bank. There are several **shops** in the village and *Edna's Cool Spot* serves simple meals of beans and rice.

At least two **buses** daily (Mon–Sat), leaving early in the morning, run between Belize City and the sanctuary, a journey of an hour and a quarter; see the Belize City chapter, p.61, for departure points and times.

On to Belize City

Back on the Northern Highway, there's not much else to stop for before Belize City. At **Ladyville** you pass the turn-off to the **International Airport**. From here it's just 15km to Belize City, with the road running very close to the river, crossing the river mouth over the Haulover Bridge. Beyond this point you begin to enter the spreading suburbs of Belize City, where expensive houses are constructed on reclaimed mangrove swamps.

travel details

BUSES

Addresses and times of services from Belize City are given in the box on p.62.

Bermudian Landing to: Belize City (2–3 Mon–Sat; 1hr 15min).

Chetumal to: Belize City (hourly; 3hr 30min, express services 3hr) via Corozal (1hr 30min) and Orange Walk (2hr 30min); Sarteneja (1 daily at 1.30pm), via Orange Walk (3hr 30min).

Corozal to: Belize City (hourly; 2hr 30min); Orange Walk (hourly; 1hr).

Crooked Tree to: Belize City (4 daily; 1hr 30min).

Orange Walk to: Belize City (hourly; 1hr 30min); Corozal (hourly; 1hr).

Sarteneja to: Belize City (2 daily; 3hr 30min), via Orange Walk.

FLIGHTS

Tropic Air and Maya Island Air (for both see p.40) operate three daily flights each between **Corozal** and **San Pedro**.

CHAPTER 3

THE NORTHERN CAYES AND ATOLLS

B elize's spectacular **Barrier Reef**, with its dazzling variety of underwater life and string of exquisite islands – known as cayes – is the main attraction for most first-time visitors to the country. Forming part of the longest barrier reef in the western hemisphere, it runs the entire length of the coastline at a distance of 15 to 40km from the mainland.

Most of the **cayes** (pronounced "keys") lie in shallow water behind the shelter of the reef. A limestone ridge forms larger, low-lying islands to the north, while smaller, less frequently visited outcrops are clustered toward the southern end of the chain – often these are no more than a stand of palms and a strip of sand. Though the 450 cayes themselves form only a tiny proportion of the country's total land area, and only around three dozen have any kind of tourism development, Belize has more territorial water than it does land, and the islands' tourism and lobster fishing accounts for a substantial amount of foreign currency earnings.

In recent years the town of **San Pedro**, on **Ambergris Caye**, has undergone a transition from a predominantly fishing economy to one geared to commercial tourism. There are still some beautiful spots here, however, notably the protected sections of reef at either end of the caye: the **Bacalar Chico National Park** to the north and **Hol Chan Marine Reserve** to the south. South of Ambergris Caye, **Caye Caulker** is less – but increasingly – developed, and remains popular with budget travellers. Fifteen kilometres east of Belize City, **St George's Caye**, Belize's first capital, occupies a celebrated niche in the nation's history and still has some fine colonial houses.

Beyond the chain of islands and the coral reef are two of Belize's three **atolls**, the **Turneffe Islands** and **Lighthouse Reef**, regularly visited on day-trips from San Pedro and Caye Caulker. Here the coral reaches the surface, enclosing a shallow lagoon, with some cayes lying right on top of the encircling reef. Lighthouse Reef encompasses two of the most spectacular diving and snorkelling sites in the country – **Half Moon Caye Natural Monument** and the **Great Blue Hole**, an enormous collapsed cave.

A brief history of the cayes

The earliest inhabitants of the cayes were **Maya** peoples or their ancestors. By the Classic period (300–900 AD) the Maya had developed an extensive trade network stretching from the Yucatán to Honduras, with evidence of settlements and trading centres on several of the islands.

Probably the most infamous residents of the cayes were the **buccaneers**, usually British, who lived here in the seventeenth and eighteenth centuries, taking refuge in the shallow waters after plundering Spanish treasure ships. In time the pirates, now calling themselves **Baymen**, settled more or less permanently on some of the northern and central cayes, establishing their first capital on St George's Caye. In 1779 a Spanish

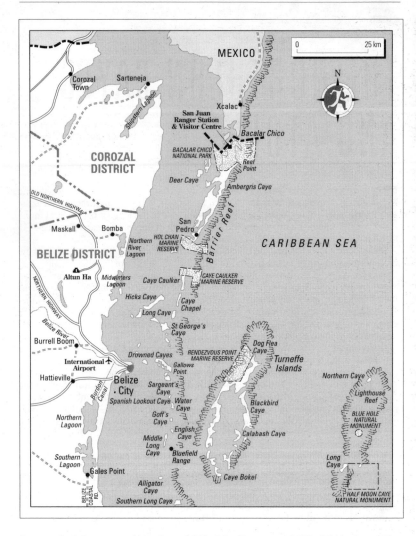

force sacked the caye and imprisoned 140 of the Baymen and 250 of their slaves. The Baymen returned in 1783 and took revenge on the Spanish fleet in 1798, during the celebrated **Battle of St George's Caye**.

Fishermen and turtlers continued to use the cayes as a base for their operations, and refugees fleeing the Caste Wars in the Yucatán towards the end of the nineteenth century also settled on the islands in small numbers. During the twentieth century the island population has increased steadily, and the establishment of the **fishing cooperatives** in the 1960s brought improved traps, ice plants, and access to the export market. There's now the possibility that the lobster-fishing industry will destroy itself by overfishing. At around the same time came another boom, as the cayes of Belize, particularly Caye Caulker, became a hangout on the hippy trail, and then began to attract more lucrative custom. The islanders generally welcomed these visitors and a new-found prosperity began to transform life on the cayes.

Ambergris Caye

The most northerly and by far the largest of the cayes is **Ambergris Caye**, separated from Mexico by the narrow Bacalar Chico channel, dug by the ancient Maya. The island's main attraction is the former fishing village of **SAN PEDRO**, facing the reef just a few kilometres from the southern tip, 58km northeast of Belize City. If you fly into San Pedro, which is the way most visitors arrive, the views are breathtaking: the sea appears so clear and shallow as to barely cover the sandy bed.

San Pedro is not a large town, but its population of two thousand is the highest of any of the cayes. Although you're never more than a stone's throw from the Caribbean – the town takes up the whole width of the island – in the built-up area most of the palms have died or been cut down, and traffic has increased in recent years, creating deep ruts (which become mud holes after rain) in the sandy streets. San Pedro is the main destination for most visitors to Belize, and the tourist industry here caters mainly for North Americans – almost all prices are quoted in US dollars. Some of the most exclusive hotels, restaurants and bars in Belize are here; the only budget places are in the original village of San Pedro.

Getting to Ambergris Caye from Belize City is simple. As well as half-hourly **flights**, there are regular **fast boats**, which take around ninety minutes to reach San Pedro; full transport details are given on p.86.

Arrival and information

Arriving boats usually dock at the Texaco pier on the front (reef) side of the island, though the *Thunderbolt* docks at *Cesario's* at the back of the island; head down Black Coral Street to Rock's supermarket, roughly in the centre of town. Arriving at either **dock,** you're pretty much in the centre. If you land at the **airport,** there are golf buggies and taxis to take you to your hotel, though it's only a short walk to anywhere in town. Formerly called Front, Middle and Back streets, the town's three **main streets,** running parallel to the beach, have been given names in keeping with the new upmarket image – Barrier Reef Drive, Pescador Drive and Angel Coral Drive – but in any case, it's impossible to get lost.

Despite being Belize's premier tourist destination, San Pedro has only recently gained an official **tourist office,** which shares a building with the new Ambergris Museum on Barrier Reef Drive (see p.78). For arranging international flights and trips throughout the country, try Travel and Tour Belize, on Coconut Drive just north of the airstrip (☎026/2031). It's always worth picking up a copy of *San Pedro Sun*, the island's weekly paper, available free in most hotels and restaurants.

You needn't worry about **changing money,** as travellers' cheques and US dollars are accepted – even preferred – everywhere. San Pedro's **post office** (Mon–Fri 8am–4.30pm) is in the Alijua building opposite the Atlantic Bank (best for cash advances). There are two **laundries** on Pescador Drive.

For an explanation of **accommodation price codes**, see p.42

Accommodation

Most of the hotels in San Pedro are just a short walk or taxi ride from the airport. All but a couple are outside the reach of budget travellers, who should stroll down Front or Middle streets to find the bargains; there's nowhere to **camp** legally.

It's risky turning up at Christmas or Easter unless you've **booked** a room; at other times in high season (Dec–Easter) you should be OK. If you haven't booked somewhere in advance, use the phone in the airport to call hotels; you'll often receive a worthwhile discount.

Caribbean Villas Hotel, just over 1km along the road south from town (☎026/2715, fax 2885). Spacious, very comfortable rooms, all with sea views. Plenty of peace and quiet and the best value smaller hotel in this range. ⑦.

Changes in Latitudes, south of town, near the Belize Yacht Club (☎ & fax 026/2986). Very friendly small B&B half a block from the beach. Immaculately clean rooms, some a/c. Canadian owner Lori is a mine of information. ⑦.

Del Rio Cabañas, ten minutes' walk north of the centre (☎ & fax 026/2286). A friendly place with very comfortable wood-and-thatch cabins facing the sea. Also new budget rooms with shared bath, plus pricier a/c rooms. ⑤–⑦.

Hideaway Sports Lodge, south of town, just past the Texaco station (☎026/2141, fax 2269). Large rooms with fan or a/c, especially good value for groups. Relaxing pool area and on-site restaurant serving tasty fish and chips and European dishes. ⑥.

Martha's, Pescador Drive across from *Elvie's Kitchen* (☎026/2053). Clean, comfortable rooms with fan and private bath with hot water. Rooms have better views and increased rates the higher up they are. ⑤.

Milo's, at the end of Barrier Reef Drive, on the left just before the *Paradise Hotel* (☎026/2033, fax 2198). The best-value budget hotel on the island; basic but clean rooms, some with private bath. Shared bathrooms have hot water. ③–④.

Ruby's, Barrier Reef Drive, a short walk from the airstrip (☎026/2063, fax 2434). Clean, comfortable, family-run hotel on the seafront. Rooms on the higher floors cost more but all are good value. ③–④.

The caye and the reef

The **water** is the focus of daytime entertainment on Ambergris Caye, from sunbathing on the docks to windsurfing, sailing, fishing, diving and snorkelling, and even taking trips on glass-bottomed boats. Many hotels will rent equipment and there are several specialist **dive shops** offering instruction. A **warning**: there have been a number of accidents in San Pedro where speeding boats have hit people swimming off the piers. A line of buoys, clearly visible, indicates the "safe area", but speedboat drivers can be a bit macho; be careful when choosing where to swim.

Before going snorkelling or diving, whet your appetite with a visit to the excellent **Hol Chan Marine Reserve office** (Mon–Sat 8.30am–5pm; ☎026/2247) on Caribeña Street, near the Texaco station on the lagoon side. They have photographs, maps and other displays on the reserve (see p.80), and the staff are happy to answer any questions. Equally worthwhile is a visit to the new **Ambergris Museum** on Barrier Reef Drive (daily from 2pm; US$2.50, Sun US$1.25), run by the local Ambergris Historical Society. Maya pottery comprises some of the earliest exhibits, with weapons and old photographs continuing to illustrate the island's history right up to the 1960s.

Bikes, mopeds and very expensive golf carts can be rented for exploring the caye on the rough track that runs north and south from town. Try any of the travel agents. Heading **south**, you could ride at least part of the way to **Marco Gonzalez**, a Maya ruin near the southernmost tip of the island, though there's not much to see. **North**, after about ten minutes' walk you'll come up against the **Boca Del Rio**, a channel crossed by a ferry (US$1.50), though with transport you can continue to some secluded resorts and beaches. A **fast ferry**, the *Island Express* (US$4 each way) runs several times a day from Fido's dock, in the centre of town, to the resorts in the north.

You might also take a guided day-trip to some of the **Maya sites** on the northwest coast of the island – Daniel Nuñez (☎026/2314) is one of the best guides. On **San Juan** beach you'll be scrunching over literally thousands of pieces of Maya pottery, but perhaps the most spectacular site is **Chac Balam**, a ceremonial and administrative centre with deep burial chambers. On the way back, you navigate **Bacalar Chico**, the channel separating Belize from Mexico, which is now a **national park** and marine reserve with a new visitor centre and some great snorkelling. At the mouth of the channel the reef is close to the shore; the boat has to cross into the open sea, re-entering the lagoon as you approach San Pedro and so completing a circumnavigation of the island.

Diving

For anyone who has never dived in the tropics before, the **reefs near San Pedro** are fine, but more experienced divers may be disappointed. This is a heavily used area which has long been subject to intensive fishing, and much of the reef has been plundered by souvenir hunters. To experience the best diving in Belize, you need to take a trip out to one of the **atolls**.

Among the best local **operators** are Amigos Del Mar, just north of the centre (☎026/2706). In general, **open water certification**, which takes novices up to the standard of a fully qualified sport diver, costs around US$350, and a more basic, introductory course at one of the resorts around US$125. For qualified divers a two-tank dive costs around US$45, including tanks, weights, air and boat. To book the local dive operators or offshore dive boats contact Chris Allnatt at the Blue Hole Dive Center, on Front Street, near the *Spindrift Hotel* (☎ & fax 026/2982).

Two **live-aboard** dive boats, the *Caye Explorer* (☎026/5019) and the *Offshore Express* (☎026/2982), are based in San Pedro and you'll usually need to book well in advance. A typical two-day trip costs around US$250, including meals and five dives, and you may well have the chance to camp on remote islands such as Half Moon Caye. They can be booked direct or at any travel agent on the island, where you'll be able to see photos of the boats and what the trips offer; you can be picked up from Caye Caulker at no extra cost.

The best dive shops in San Pedro recommend you make a voluntary contribution of US$1 per tank to help fund the town's **hyperbaric chamber**: this covers you for treatment if you need it, so make sure you fill out the agreement when you sign on to dive.

Snorkelling and other trips

Just about every hotel in San Pedro offers **snorkelling** trips, costing around US$15 for three hours, plus about US$4 to rent equipment. Generally, trips take you either north to the spectacular Mexico Rocks or Rocky Point, or, more commonly, south to the Hol Chan Marine Reserve (see below). **Night snorkelling**, a truly amazing experience, is also available. Several boats take snorkellers out for an utterly relaxing day-trip to Caye Caulker, employing a mix of motor and sail. The popular, safe *Rum Punch* (sail) and the *Winnie Estelle* (motor) are probably the best overall value, and can be booked through any travel or tour agent.

Day-trips from San Pedro to the ruins of **Altun Ha** (see p.72) are increasingly popular. Rounding the southern tip of the island in a fast skiff, you head for the mainland at the mouth of the Northern River, cross the lagoon and travel up the river to the tiny village of Bomba, where a van waits to take you to the site. With a good guide this is an excellent way to spot wildlife, including crocodiles and manatees, and the riverbank trees are often adorned with orchids. The best guide is Daniel Nuñez (☎026/2314).

SAFEGUARDING THE BARRIER REEF

Coral reefs are among the most complex and fragile ecosystems on earth. Colonies have been growing at a rate of less than 5cm a year for thousands of years; once damaged, the coral is far more susceptible to bacteria, which can quickly lead to large-scale irreversible damage. Remember to follow these **simple rules** while snorkelling, diving or in a boat:

- Never anchor boats on the reef – use the permanently secured buoys.
- Never touch or stand on corals – protective cells are easily stripped away from the living polyps on their surface, destroying them and thereby allowing algae to enter.
- Don't remove shells, sponges or other creatures from the reef, or buy reef products from souvenir shops.
- Avoid disturbing the seabed around corals – quite apart from spoiling visibility, clouds of sand settle over corals, smothering them.
- If you're either a beginner or an out-of-practice diver, practise away from the reef first.
- Don't use suntan lotion in reef areas – the oils remain on the water's surface; wear a T-shirt to protect yourself from the sun.
- Check you're not in one of the new marine reserves before fishing.
- Don't feed or interfere with fish or marine life – this can harm not only sea creatures and the food chain, but snorkellers too – large fish may attack, trying to get their share!

The Hol Chan Marine Reserve

The **Hol Chan Reserve**, 8km south of San Pedro, at the southern tip of the caye, takes its name from the Maya for "little channel", and it is this break in the reef that forms the focus of the reserve. Its three zones – covering a total of around thirteen square kilometres – preserve a comprehensive cross-section of the marine environment, from coral reef through seagrass beds to mangroves. All three habitats are closely linked: many reef fish feed on the seagrass beds, and the mangroves are a nursery area for juvenile fish. As your boat approaches, you'll be met by a warden who explains the rules and collects the entry fee (US$2.50).

A great deal of damage has already been caused by snorkellers standing on the coral or holding onto outcrops for a better look – on all the easily accessible areas of the reef you will clearly see the white, dead patches, especially on the large brain coral heads. **Never touch** the coral – not only does it damage the delicate ecosystem (see box above), it can also sting and cause agonizing burns, and even brushing against the razor-sharp ridges on the reef top can cause cuts that are slow to heal.

Eating drinking and nightlife

There are plenty of places to eat in San Pedro, and **prices** are generally higher than elsewhere in Belize, though you'll usually get good service – a comparative rarity in much of the country. **Seafood** is prominent at most restaurants; you can also rely on plenty of steak, shrimp, chicken, pizza and salads. There are several **Chinese** restaurants, too, the cheaper ones representing the best value on the island. **Buying your own food** isn't much of a bargain here: there's no market and the grocery stores are stocked with imported canned goods. Rock's on Pescador and Milo's at the north end of Barrier Reef Drive offer the best value.

Restaurants

Duke's, Coconut Drive, across from *Ramon's* resort, just south of the airstrip. Excellent, family-run restaurant serving great fish, steaks and Mexican food at bargain prices (dinner includes a drink and dessert), surrounded by John Wayne memorabilia. Breakfast and dinner only.

El Patio, towards the southern end of the town, next to the second Rock's supermarket. Fine dining at very reasonable prices in a lovely courtyard.

Elvie's Kitchen, across the road from *Martha's* hotel. The place for seafood, burgers and fries, accompanied by delicious, licuado-like fruit drinks. Slick service and upmarket prices.

Jade Garden, Coconut Drive, south of town. The best Chinese restaurant – good value, too.

Little Italy, next to the *Spindrift Hotel* (☎026/2866). The finest Italian restaurant in San Pedro; excellent food and service, and a good wine list. You may have to book for dinner in high season. Great-value Mexican-style lunch buffet (11.30am–2pm).

Ruby's Cafe, Barrier Reef Drive, next to *Ruby's Hotel*. Delicious home-made cakes, pies and sandwiches, and freshly brewed coffee. Open at 6am, so it's a good place to order a packed lunch if you're going on a trip.

The Reef, near the north end of Pescador. Good Belizean food, including delicious seafood, at great prices.

Bars and clubs

Some of the hotels have fancy bars, several of which offer happy hours, while back from the main street are a couple of small **cantinas** where you can buy a beer or a bottle of rum and drink with the locals. *Sandals Bar*, on the side street between *Martha's Hotel* and the park, is a friendly, long-established bar serving tasty ceviche and barbecue in the evenings.

Entertainment in San Pedro becomes more sophisticated every year. *Big Daddy's* **disco**, in and around a beach bar near the main dock, has early evening piano, and a lively reggae band later on; happy hour runs from 5 to 9pm. *Tarzan's Disco and Nite Club*, opposite the park, has the best dance floor. The *Crazy Canuk Bar* at the *Playador Hotel*, south of the airport, has a happy hour from 5 to 7pm, with live music.

Caye Caulker

South of Ambergris Caye and 35km northeast of Belize City, **Caye Caulker** is the most accessible island for the budget traveller. Until recently, tourism existed almost as a sideline to the island's main source of income, **lobster fishing**. Now, however, new hotels and bars are being built, older ones improved, and prices – low for years – have begun to rise. For the moment, though, Caye Caulker remains relaxed and easy-going. As yet there is little air-conditioning on the island, which is fine most of the time, when a cooling breeze blows in from the sea, but **sandflies and mosquitoes** can cause almost unbearable irritation on calm days.

Flights on the San Pedro run stop at Caye Caulker's airstrip; however, most visitors still arrive by **boat**. The establishment of the Caye Caulker Water Taxi Association means you no longer have to run the gauntlet of hustlers; simply go to the Marine Terminal in Belize City, from there boats leave every two hours (for full details, see p.86).

Arrival and information

The **airstrip** is about 1km south of the centre, within easy reach of the hotels south of the main dock; alternatively, you can take a golf-cart taxi. If you arrive at either the "front" dock or the "back" dock (easily recognizable, as they are longer than the others), simply follow your nose to the **water taxi office**, effectively the centre of the village. They can give **information** and will hold your luggage while you look for a place to stay.

There are no street names here, but the street running along the shore at the front of the island is effectively "**Front Street**", with just one or two streets running behind it in the centre of the island. The Atlantic Bank, just south of the centre, gives Visa **cash advances** (for a US$5 fee), and an increasing number of businesses accept plastic for

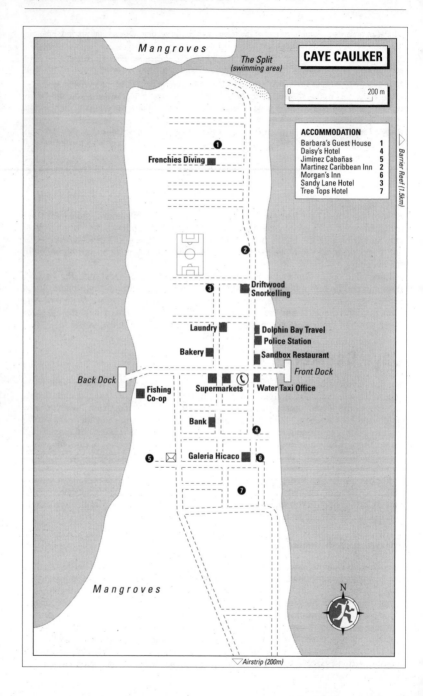

Mangroves

The Split
(swimming area)

CAYE CAULKER

0   200 m

Barrier Reef (1.5km)

ACCOMMODATION

Barbara's Guest House	1
Daisy's Hotel	4
Jiminez Cabañas	5
Martinez Caribbean Inn	2
Morgan's Inn	6
Sandy Lane Hotel	3
Tree Tops Hotel	7

Frenchies Diving

Driftwood
Snorkelling

Laundry

Dolphin Bay Travel

Police Station

Bakery

Sandbox Restaurant

Back Dock

Front Dock

Fishing
Co-op

Supermarkets

Water Taxi Office

Bank

Galeria Hicaco

Mangroves

N

Airstrip (200m)

payment. The **post office** is on the back street, south of the centre, and the **BTL** office on the corner leading to the main dock. Ilna and Tina Axillou, who run Caye Caulker's **travel agency**, Dolphin Bay Travel (☎ & fax 022/2214), just north of the centre on Front St, have outstanding local knowledge, and can arrange international flights and boat trips. Next door, Seaing is Belizing offer slide shows on reef ecology and sells books and gifts.

Accommodation

Most of the year it's easy enough to find an inexpensive room, but to arrive at Christmas or New Year without a **reservation** could leave you stranded. Even the furthest **hotels** are no more than ten minutes' walk from the front dock and places are easy to find: the following listings are given roughly in the order you'd come to them walking from the dock.

North from the front dock

Sandy Lane Hotel (☎022/2217). Small, clean and inexpensive, with rooms in the original wooden buiding and new ones in the concrete building at the back. ③.

Martinez Caribbean Inn, on the seafront (☎022/2133). Secure and well run; all rooms with private bath and hot water. ③–⑤.

Barbara's Rooms, towards the north end, near the split (☎022/2025). Friendly, Canadian-run place, with simple, clean rooms, away from the bars and secure for women. ③.

South from the front dock

Daisy's (☎022/2150). Simple, budget rooms run by a friendly family. ③.

Morgan's Inn, opposite Galería Hicaco (☎022/2178, fax 2239). Quiet, private houses set just back from the beach; no cooking facilities. ④–⑤.

Tree Tops Hotel, just beyond the cemetery (☎022/2008, fax 2115). Easily the best hotel on the island, just 50m from the water. Five comfortable rooms, with fridge, cable TV and powerful ceiling fans; booking advisable. ⑤.

Jiminez Cabañas (☎022/2175). Clean, comfortable wood-and-thatch cabins – the best value on the island, surrounded by a delightful garden. ④.

The reef and the caye

Caye Caulker is a little over 7km long, with the southern, inhabited end curving away west like a hook. At the northern end of the village you come to **"The Split"**, a narrow (but widening) channel cut by Hurricane Hattie in 1961 and a popular place to relax and swim. It's also a glaring example of what happens when mangroves are cut down – the original owner of the beach bar here removed them to build a dock and the subsequent erosion now threatens to wash the bar away.

Although a couple of houses are being built across the channel, the larger northern part of the island is almost uninhabited, and the very northern tip is included in the recently designated **Caye Caulker Marine Reserve**.

The **reef** is certainly an experience not to be missed: swimming along coral canyons accompanied by an astonishing range of fish, with perhaps even the odd shark or two (these will almost certainly be harmless nurse sharks). Here as everywhere, snorkellers should be aware of the fragility of the reef and be careful not to touch any coral – even sand stirred up by fins can cause damage (see p.80 for reef etiquette).

Trips to the reef by skiff (US$7.50–10 per person; around 3hr) are easily arranged; contact Barbara at *Barbara's Guest House*, Meldie at Driftwood Snorkeling (☎022/2011), on the front north of the centre, or Carlos Tours (☎022/2093) at *Cindy's Cafe*, opposite the basketball court. One of the best day outings is offered by Ras Creek, in his dory *Heritage* (US$12.50), which sails from the main dock in the morning – you're almost certain to encounter nurse sharks and eagle rays. An extended **sailing trip** to the uninhabited reefs and islands is not cheap, but better value here than in Belize City – try Seaing is Belizing, next to Dolphin Bay Travel (☎022/2189). **Kayaks** are available too: try *Daisy's* hotel or ask at the Galería Hicaco.

Diving is available from Frenchie's, towards the northern end of the village (☎022/2234, fax 2074), who offer enthusiastic, knowledgeable local trips, with some great reef diving and coral gardens, plus day-trips to the Blue Hole (see opposite). Caye Caulker School of Scuba (☎022/2292, fax 2239) has the best value PADI **dive courses** in the country, with excellent instruction.

For a really well-informed **tour of the reef**, contact marine biologist Ellen at the Galería Hicaco (☎022/2178). She can explain exactly what it is you're seeing in this amazing underwater world. She also conducts **Audubon bird walks**, an introduction to the dozens of bird species that inhabit the caye, and has been the driving force behind the creation of the new Caye Caulker Marine Reserve, designed initially to protect the caye littoral forest, habitat of the endangered black catbird.

Caye Caulker is a good base for **day-trips** to the **other cayes**, especially Goff's, English and Sergeant's cayes for dolphin and manatee spotting; ask at Driftwood. One of the best snorkelling trips is Jim and Cindy Novelo's expedition to the exquisite Half Moon Caye (see opposite), the most easterly of Belize's islands, on the *Sunrise*. After meeting the red-footed booby (and the huge hermit and land crabs) face to face, it's back in the boat for the unique splendour of the Blue Hole. Rates (US$65) include lunch but not snorkel gear.

Eating, drinking and entertainment

Good home cooking, large portions and very reasonable prices are features of all the island's restaurants. **Lobster** (in season) is served in every imaginable dish, from curry to chow mein; **seafood** generally is good value, accompanied by rice or potatoes. Otherwise, evening entertainment mostly consists of relaxing in a restaurant over dinner or a drink, or gazing at the tropical night sky. You can buy food at several **shops** and supermarkets on the island. Also, many houses advertise banana bread, coconut cakes and other home-baked goodies, and there's a good **bakery** on the street leading to the football field.

Restaurants, cafés and bars

Along the main street, one block back from the shore, is *Marin's Restaurant*, with a shady outdoor dining area, great for breakfasts and seafood. At the back of the island, *Glenda's* is a favourite breakfast meeting place, serving great cinnamon rolls. On the middle street, call in at *Cindy's* for superb fresh fruit, yoghurt, carrot cake and home-made bagels. Serving Italian/American food, the *Sand Box*, by the main dock, is the best restaurant on the island, and often packed. Walking north along the waterfront, you'll come to a proliferation of **beach bars and restaurants**: *Oceanside*, by *Martinez*, has good food and service and sometimes live music. Further on, the *Rainbow Restaurant*, on a deck over the water, and *Sobre Las Olas*, are the best of the restaurants this end of the island.

Other northern cayes

Although Caye Caulker and San Pedro are the only villages anywhere on the reef, there are a couple of dozen other inhabited islands, some of them supporting fishing camps or upmarket resorts – called **lodges** – on a few reefs and cayes. **Prices** are not low, but include transport from Belize City or the international airport, accommodation, all meals, and usually diving or fishing. The attraction of these lodges is the "simple life" scenario. Buildings are low-key, wooden and sometimes thatched, and the group you're with will probably be the only people staying there. There are no phones (most are in radio contact with Belize City), electricity comes from a generator, and views of palm trees curving over turquoise water reinforce the sense of isolation.

St George's Caye

Tiny **St George's Caye**, around 15km from Belize City, was capital for the Baymen of the eighteenth century, but doesn't offer much for the casual visitor. The island, home today to a few fishermen, boasts a couple of hotels and luxury holiday villas and acts as an adventure training centre for the British forces in Belize. Independent travellers can **stay** at the luxurious *Cottage Colony* (☎02/77051, fax 73253; ⑧), a collection of extremely comfortable colonial-style wooden houses with a dining room overlooking the Caribbean.

The Bluefield Range

In the **Bluefield Range**, a group of around half a dozen mangrove cayes 35km southeast of Belize City, you can stay on a remote fishing camp. *Ricardo's Beach Huts* (☎02/78469; US$165 per person for 3 days, 2 nights; price includes transport from Belize City, meals, use of canoe and a trip to tiny Rendevous Caye) offer simple, comfortable accommodation in huts built on stilts over the water. Ricardo Castillo is a reliable, expert fishing guide, scrupulously practising conservation of the reef.

The Turneffe Islands

The virtually uninhabited **Turneffe Islands**, 40km from Belize City, are an oval archipelago of low-lying mangrove islands around a shallow lagoon 60km long, enclosed by a beautiful coral reef. You can visit as part of a day-trip from Caye Caulker, or stay – for a price. The construction of resorts on this remote, fragile island has meant cutting down mangroves, the cause of much controversy among conservationists: a proposed **marine reserve** has yet to be designated.

Calabash Caye, on the eastern side of the atoll, was at the time of writing the base for Coral Cay Conservation, where volunteers take part in a research project to complete a systematic investigation of the entire atoll. Participants stay in dorm cabins at the University College of Belize Marine Research Centre in dorm cabins.

Lighthouse Reef, the Blue Hole and Half Moon Caye

About 80km east of Belize City is Belize's outer atoll, **Lighthouse Reef**, with the Great Blue Hole and Half Moon Caye Natural Monument as the main attractions for divers. The **Blue Hole**, technically a karst-eroded sinkhole, is a shaft about 90m in diameter and 145m deep, which drops through the bottom of the lagoon and opens out into a complex network of caves and crevices; its depth gives it an astonishing deep blue colour. Several **shipwrecks** form artificial reefs. You can visit the atoll as either a day or overnight trip from San Pedro (p.79) or Caye Caulker (p.83).

The **Half Moon Caye Natural Monument**, the first marine conservation area in Belize, was declared a national park in 1982 and became one of Belize's first World Heritage Sites in 1996. The 180,000-square-metre caye is divided into two distinct ecosystems. In the west, guano from thousands of seabirds fertilizes the soil, allowing the growth of dense vegetation, while the eastern half has mostly coconut palms growing in the sand. A total of 98 bird species has been recorded here, including frigate birds, ospreys, and a resident population of four thousand **red-footed boobies**, one of only two nesting colonies in the Caribbean. The boobies came by their name because they displayed no fear of humans, moving only reluctantly when visitors stroll among them. Their nesting area is accessible from a platform built by the Belize Audubon Society and rebuilt by Raleigh Expeditions volunteers. The resident **reserve wardens** will collect the US$4 visitor fee and can give permission to **camp** (US$2.50 per person).

travel details

FLIGHTS

Maya Island Air (☎02/31362) and Tropic (☎026/2012 in San Pedro) between them operate flights between Belize City and San Pedro, calling at Caye Caulker on request, every hour from 7am to 5pm (25min).

BOATS

All boats to and from San Pedro stop at Caye Caulker on the way. Note that services are reduced on Sunday and during September and October.

Belize City to San Pedro (1hr 25min; US$12.50): the *Triple J* (☎02/44375) leaves Courthouse Wharf at 9am; *Andrea* (☎026/2578) leaves Courthouse Wharf at 3pm; *Thunderbolt* leaves the Swing Bridge at 1pm.

San Pedro to Belize City (1hr 25min; US$12.50): *Triple J* at 3pm; *Andrea* and *Thunderbolt* at 7am; other boats leave at 8am & 2.30pm.

Belize City to Caye Caulker (45min; US$7.50): from the Marine Terminal every 2hr from 9am to 5pm.

Caye Caulker to Belize City (45min; US$7.50): departures every 2hr between 6.30am and 3.30pm. It's best to book a day ahead at the water taxi office by the main dock (☎022/2992).

CHAPTER 4

CAYO AND THE WEST

H eading west from Belize City towards the Guatemalan border, you travel through a wide range of landscapes, from open grassland to rolling hills and dense tropical forest. A fast paved road, the **Western Highway**, runs to the border, a route that takes you from the heat and humidity of the coast to the lush foothills of the Maya Mountains. Before reaching Belize's tiny, almost lifeless capital, **Belmopan**, the road passes several places of interest: the **Belize Zoo**, the **Monkey Bay Wildlife Sanctuary**, and **Guanacaste National Park**, at the junction with the Hummingbird Highway.

Heading further west, following the Belize River valley, you start to climb into the foothills of the Maya Mountains, a beautiful area where the air is clear and the land astonishingly fertile. South of the road, **Mountain Pine Ridge** is a pleasantly cool region of hills and pine woods traversed by good dirt roads. **San Ignacio**, on the Macal River, is the busy main town of **Cayo District** and the ideal base for exploring the forests, rivers and ruins of western Belize. The ruins of **Caracol**, the largest Maya site in Belize, lie deep in the jungle of the Vaca plateau, south of San Ignacio.

Between San Ignacio and the Guatemalan border, the road climbs past the hilltop ruins of **Cahal Pech** then descends, following the valley of the Mopan River 15km to the frontier bridge. A few kilometres before the border, at the village of **San José Succotz**, an ancient ferry crosses the river, allowing access to the Maya site of **Xunantunich**, from the top of which you can view the Guatemalan department of Petén.

Belize City to San Ignacio

Leaving Belize City through the cemetery, the well-paved Western Highway skirts the shoreline, running behind a tangle of mangrove swamps. After 26km the road passes through **HATTIEVILLE** (named after the 1961 hurricane), where an unpaved turning north to **Burrell Boom** is used as a short cut to the Northern Highway, bypassing Belize City. If time permits you should allow an hour or two vist the **Belize Zoo**, one of the finest in Latin America. You'd need to stay at least overnight to fully appreciate the **Monkey Bay Wildlife Sanctuary**, but **Guanacaste National Park** is another worthwhile stop right by the roadside. For most people the capital, **Belmopan**, is no more than a break in the bus ride, though if you're heading south for Dangriga or Placencia this is the place to change buses. Beyond Belmopan the landscape becomes a little more hilly and a few unpaved **side roads** head south into the uplands, leading to some of Belize's most spectacular scenery. However, you're better off continuing to the delightful riverside town of San Ignacio (see p.90) for a night or two's stay, to get your bearings and pick up the latest information.

For an explanation of **accommodation price codes**, see p.42.

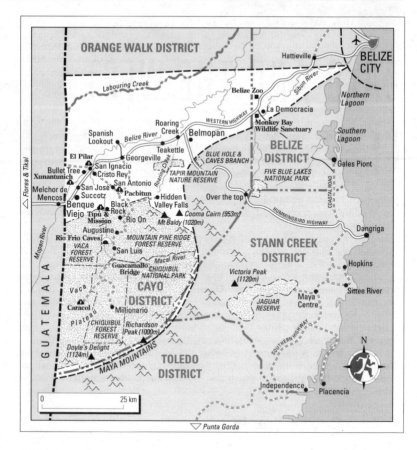

The Belize Zoo

The first point of interest out this way is the **Belize Zoo**, at Mile 29 (daily 9am–4.30pm; ☎081/3004; US$7.50). Set up in 1983 by Sharon Matola, after an ambitious wildlife film left her with a collection of semi-tame animals, the zoo is organized around the theme of "a walk through Belize". The residents include all the Belizean cats, some of which, including the jaguars, have bred successfully here. The zoo is actively involved in conservation and captive breeding, and runs a series of touring outreach programmes. To **get to the zoo** take any bus between Belize City and Belmopan and ask the driver to drop you; there's a sign on the highway. A 200-metre walk brings you to the entrance and visitor centre.

One kilometre past the zoo the **Manatee Road** (or Coastal Road) provides an unpaved short cut (marked by a sign and a couple of bars) to Gales Point and **Dangriga** (see p.101). The road is in good condition and is served by buses; hitching is also relatively easy. A kilometre or so past the junction, on the left, is *Cheers*, a friendly **bar** run by a Canadian family, where you can get good food at reasonable prices, and reliable **information**.

Monkey Bay Wildlife Sanctuary and Guanacaste Park

Half a kilometre past *Cheers* on the Western Highway is the **Monkey Bay Wildlife Sanctuary** (☎08/23180), a 44-square-kilometre protected area extending to the Sibun River, which offers birding and nature trails through five distinct vegetation and habitat types. Adjoining the sanctuary is the Monkey Bay National Park, which extends a biological corridor south through karst limestone hills to connect with the Manatee Forest Reserve. Facilities include a field research station for visitors and student groups with an excellent library and small museum. Apart from being a relaxing **place to stay**, either in a bunkhouse (US$7.50) or camping (US$5) on raised platforms, Monkey Bay is a viable experiment in green living, utilizing solar power, rainwater catchment, biogas for cooking fuel and growing food in organic gardens.

Next is *JB's Bar*, with comfortable, well-priced **rooms** (④) enjoying views over the forested Sibun valley. It's an old favourite with the British Army, whose mementoes deck the walls. Just 2km before the turning for Belmopan, a 2.5-km track leads off right to the *Banana Bank Lodge* (☎081/2020, fax 2026) on the north bank of the Belize River, whose beautifully furnished wood-and-thatch cabañas offer sweeping views (⑧ including breakfast).

At the junction for Belmopan and the Hummingbird Highway, 73km from Belize City, is **Guanacaste National Park** (US$2.50), where you can wander through a superb area of lush tropical forest, at the confluence of Roaring Creek and the Belize River. The main attraction is a huge **guanacaste** or tubroos tree, a 40-metre-high, spreading hardwood that supports some 35 species: hanging from its limbs are a huge range of bromeliads, orchids, ferns, cacti and strangler figs. The trunk of the guanacaste is traditionally favoured for making dugout canoes. As the park is so close to the road, your chances of seeing any four-footed **wildlife** are fairly slim, but recently a small number of howler monkeys have been using the park as a feeding ground. Birds, however, abound, with over fifty species, among them blue-crowned motmots, parrots and squirrel cuckoos.

There's a visitor centre near the entrance, with an orchid display, as well as four or five short **trails** to take you on tours through the park and along the banks of the Belize River.

Belmopan

From Guanacaste Park the Western Highway pushes on towards San Ignacio and the Guatemalan border; the **Hummingbird Highway** heads south 2km to the junction for **BELMOPAN**, then continues to Dangriga on the coast. Belmopan was founded in 1970 after Hurricane Hattie swept much of Belize City into the sea. The government decided to use the disaster as a chance to move to higher ground and, in a Brasília-style bid to focus development on the interior, chose a site in the geographical heart of the country. The name of the city combines the words Belize and Mopan, the language spoken by the Maya of Cayo. The layout of the main government buildings, designed in the 1960s, is modelled on a Maya city, grouped around a central plaza. In classic new-town terms Belmopan was meant to symbolize the dawn of a new era, with tree-lined avenues, banks, a couple of embassies and telecommunications worthy of a world centre. Today it has all the essential ingredients bar one – people. Arriving in the market square or bus station, the first thing that strikes you is a sense of space. Unless you've come to visit the government's archeology or immigration departments, there's no reason to stay any longer than it takes your bus to leave.

Practicalities

Buses from Belize City to San Ignacio, Benque Viejo and Dangriga all pass through Belmopan, so there's at least one service an hour in either direction; the last bus from

Belmopan to San Ignacio leaves at 10pm. The nearest **restaurant** is the *Caladium*, beside the Novelos bus terminal. Nearby you'll also find *The International Cafe* and *Moms Place*, both friendly places where you can always get a vegetarian meal. There are also banks close to where the buses stop (including Barclays, for cash advances), a bakery and a small market. The **British High Commission** is situated on the North Ring Road (☎08/22146, fax 22761); there are also embassies here for El Salvador (2, 3rd St, Picini Site; ☎ & fax 08/23404) and Costa Rica (60 Orange St; ☎08/23801, fax 23805). A new archeological exhibit designed to display the astonishing range of Maya artefacts found in Belize is currently under construction – check with the Archeology Department on ☎08/22106.

Belmopan to San Ignacio

Beyond Belmopan the scenery becomes more rugged, with thickly forested ridges always in view to the south. The road stays close to the valley of the Belize River, passing through a series of villages. There's been something of an accommodation boom along this route, with a couple of long-established cottage-style lodges now joined by several newer enterprises. One of the best is *Pook's Hill Jungle Lodge* (☎081/2017, fax 08/23361; ⑧ including breakfast), 9km along a clearly signposted track from **TEA KETTLE**, itself 8km from the Belmopan junction. Nine cabañas are set in a small clearing above a hillside terraced by the Maya, in a private nature reserve overlooking the thickly forested Roaring River valley, with breathtaking views across the strictly protected **Tapir Mountain Nature Reserve** (no public access) to Mountain Pine Ridge. Superb **horseriding** across farmland and along forest trails is available.

At Mile 54, about 4km beyond, just across Warrie Head Creek, is the entrance to *Warrie Head Ranch and Lodge* (☎02/75317, fax 75213; ⑦), formerly a logging camp but now a working farm, offering comfortable rooms. On Barton Creek, at Mile 60, is *Caesar's Place*, a café and guesthouse with comfortable, attractive **rooms**, trailer hookups, space for camping and a fabulous gift shop (☎09/22341, fax 23449; ⑥).

At **GEORGEVILLE**, 26km from the Belmopan junction, the Chiquibul Road heads south from the highway to **Mountain Pine Ridge** (see p.95), reaching deep into the forest and crossing the Macal River at the Guacamallo Bridge. The road is well used by villagers, foresters and tourists, making it relatively easy to hitch from here to **Augustine/Douglas Silva**, headquarters of the Mountain Pine Ridge Forest Reserve.

The highway continues for 9km to **SANTA ELENA**, San Ignacio's sister town on the eastern bank of the Macal River, which is crossed by the Hawksworth Bridge, built in 1949 and still the only road suspension bridge in Belize. Though quite a large town, Santa Elena has none of the attractions found in San Ignacio, but it is the site of the turn-off to the **Cristo Rey road** towards Augustine/Douglas Silva and the Mountain Pine Ridge.

San Ignacio and Cayo district

On the west bank of the Macal River, about 35km from Belmopan, **SAN IGNACIO** is a friendly, relaxed town that draws together the best in inland Belize. Surrounded by fast-flowing rivers and forested hills, it's an ideal base from which to explore the region, offering good food, inexpensive hotels and frequent bus connections. The evenings here are usually cool and the days fresh – a welcome break from the sweltering heat of the coast.

The name originally given to this area was **El Cayo**, the same word that the Spanish used to describe the offshore islands. (San Ignacio town is usually referred to as **Cayo** by locals, and this is the name you'll often see indicated on buses.) It's an apt description of the area, in a peninsula between two converging rivers. The early wave of the

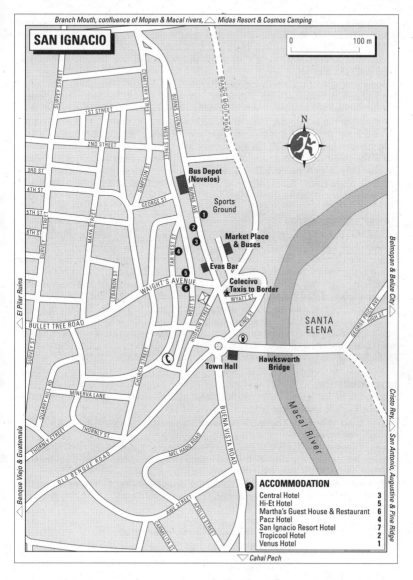

Branch Mouth, confluence of Mopan & Macal rivers, △ Midas Resort & Cosmos Camping

SAN IGNACIO

0   100 m

N

SURVEY STREET

CEMETERY STREET

1ST STREET

BURNS AVENUE

BRANCH MOUTH ROAD

WEST STREET

2ND STREET

3RD ST

4TH ST

SIMPSON ST

GEORGE ST

BURNS AVE

Bus Depot (Novelos)

5TH ST

MAYA STREET

FAR WEST ST

Sports Ground

6TH ST

SURVEY STREET

LEBANON ST

WAIGHT'S AVENUE

❶
❷
❸
❹

Market Place & Buses

WEST ST

Evas Bar

El Pilar Ruins

BULLET TREE ROAD

❺
❻

HUDSON STREET

Colecivo Taxis to Border
WYATT ST

KING ST

SANTA ELENA

Belmopan & Belize City △

GEORGE PRICE AVE

HIGH ST

SURVEY ST

CHURCH STREET

QUARRY HILL RD

MINERVA LANE

☎

Town Hall

ℹ

Hawksworth Bridge

George Price Hwy

Macal River

Cristo Rey, △ San Antonio, Augustine & Pine Ridge

Benque Viejo & Guatemala

THORNLY STREET

THORNLY ST

BUENA VISTA ROAD

MELHADO ROAD

OLD BENQUE ROAD

ANE STREET

APOLLO STREET

CARMELITA ST

❼

ACCOMMODATION

Central Hotel	3
Hi-Et Hotel	5
Martha's Guest House & Restaurant	6
Pacz Hotel	4
San Ignacio Resort Hotel	7
Tropicool Hotel	2
Venus Hotel	1

▽ Cahal Pech

Spanish conquest, in 1544, made little impact here, and the area was a centre of rebellion in the following decades. **Tipu**, a Maya city that probably stood at Negroman on the Macal River, about 9km south of the present-day town, was the capital of the province of Dzuluinicob, where for years the people resisted attempts to convert them to Christianity. **Spanish friars** arrived in 1618, but a year later the entire population was still practising idolatry. Four years later, Maya from Tipu worked as guides in an expedition against the Itzá, in Guatemala, and in 1641 the friars returned, determined to christianize the inhabitants. To express their defiance of the Spanish clerics the Maya priests conducted a mock mass and then threw out the friars. Tipu retained a measure of independence until 1707 when the population was forcibly removed to Lago de Petén Itzá.

Some time after this **British loggers** (Baymen) arrived seeking mahogany and, like many places in modern Belize, San Ignacio probably started life as a logging camp. Spanish influence, never great, was by now in permanent decline, and the British were not interested in converting the remaining Maya – a map drawn up in 1787 simply states that the Indians of this general area were "in friendship with the Baymen".

In addition to logging, San Ignacio became a centre for the shipment of **chicle**, the sap of the sapodilla tree and basis of chewing gum. The self-reliant *chicleros*, as the collectors of chicle were called, knew the forest intimately, including the location of most, if not all, Maya ruins. When the demand for Maya artefacts sent black-market prices rocketing, many of them turned to looting.

Arrival and information

Buses stop in the marketplace, behind the *Hotel Belmoral*. Batty and Novelos run regular services from Belize City, most of which continue to the border and Melchor in Guatemala (30min). A shared **taxi** to the border costs only US$2 per person. **Car rental** is offered by Western Auto Rental (☎09/23134). Bob Jones, owner of the long-established *Eva's Bar* on Burns Avenue, is renowned for providing first-class **tourist information** and *Eva's* is still the only **Internet café** in Belize (*evas@btl.net*). Most other facilities are also on Burns Avenue, including the **banks**, though if you're crossing into Guatemala, it's easiest to use the services of the reliable moneychangers who'll approach you. The **post office** is next to Courts furniture store in the centre of town. **Laundry** can be done at *Martha's* on West Street, behind *Eva's*. For international **air tickets**, go to Universal Travel, 8 Mossiah St (☎09/23884, fax 23885).

Accommodation

The **hotels** in San Ignacio offer the best value budget accommodation in the country and you'll almost always find space.

Central Hotel, 24 Burns Ave (☎09/22253). Reasonable hotel with hot water and shared baths and a balcony with hammocks overlooking the street. ③.

Cosmos Campground, 15min walk from town along the road to Branch Mouth (☎09/22116). Full camping facilities, including showers, flush toilets and a kitchen. In addition to tent space, there are also clean, simple cabins, some with private bath. ①–②.

Hi-Et Hotel, West St, behind *Eva's* (☎09/22828). Family-run hotel with four basic rooms upstairs, each with a tiny balcony, all sharing a cold-water bathroom; easily the best in the rock-bottom price range. ②.

Martha's Guest House, West St, behind *Eva's* (☎09/23647). Very comfortable rooms at great prices in a homely atmosphere. The restaurant is a favourite meeting place. ④.

Midas Resort, Branch Mouth Rd (☎09/23172, fax 23845). Very comfortable Maya-style thatched cabañas with private bath, set on the riverbank; camping also available. ④.

PACZ Hotel, 4 Far West St, two blocks behind *Eva's* (☎09/22110, fax 22972). Five clean, comfortable rooms at bargain rates, sharing two hot-water showers. ④.

San Ignacio Resort Hotel, 18 Buena Vista St (☎09/22034, fax 22134). In a superb location, just ten minutes' walk uphill from the town centre, with views over the Macal River valley. San Ignacio's premier hotel with spacious, comfortable rooms (some with balcony and a/c) and a dining room terrace overlooking a pool. ⑦.

Tropicool Hotel, Burns Ave, 75m past *Eva's* (☎09/23052). Bright, clean budget rooms with shared hot-water bathrooms, and a sitting room with TV. ③.

Eating

Along with its budget hotels, San Ignacio has several good, inexpensive **restaurants**. The Saturday **market** is worth a visit; it's the best in Belize, with local farmers bringing in fresh-picked produce. For general groceries Celina's Store, on Burns Avenue, has the widest selection of goods. You can pick up good fresh **bread** and baked goods at the La Popular Bakery in West Street.

Eva's Bar, 22 Burns Ave. Good, reasonably priced, filling meals. Usually busy, it's a great place to meet travellers and local tour operators.

Martha's Kitchen, West St, behind *Eva's*. Under the guest house of the same name and just as well-run. Great breakfasts, local coffee, pizza and traditional Creole food. There's usually a vegetarian choice and always delicious cakes for dessert.

Maxim's, Far West St, behind *Martha's*. One of the best of San Ignacio's numerous Chinese restaurants, serving large portions.

Serendib Restaurant, 27 Burns Ave. Excellent Sri Lankan curries and seafood at very reasonable prices. Good service too.

Around San Ignacio

San Ignacio's best feature is its location. The river and the surrounding countryside are equally inviting, and there are many ways to enjoy them – on foot, by boat or even on horseback. You can easily use the town as a base for day-trips, but if you'd prefer to stay in the countryside, numerous resorts in the area offer **cottage-style accommodation**. The countryside around Cayo is ideal for exploring on **horseback**, with one of the best deals offered by Charlie Collins, who runs Easy Rider (☎014/8276). A **mountain bike** is a great way to explore Cayo and you can take a bike on the bus to San Antonio (for the Pine Ridge); ask at *Eva's* for details. **Caving** is growing in popularity and the most experienced caving guide around is Pete Zubrzycki at *PACZ Hotel* (☎09/22110), who leads truly amazing trips into the realm of the Maya underworld. For **canoe trips** above ground, see the Macal River account below, but for an awe-inspiring paddle along an **underground river** through **Barton Creek Cave**, viewing Maya burials surrounded by pottery vessels, contact David Simpson at *Martha's* (☎09/23647).

Cahal Pech

Twenty minutes out of town, clearly signposted along the Benque road, lie the ruins of **Cahal Pech** (daily 8am–4pm; US$2.50). The name means "place of ticks" in Mopan Maya, and is certainly not how the elite families who ruled here in Classic times would have known it. Cahal Pech was the royal acropolis-palace of an elite Maya family during the Classic period, and there's evidence of monumental construction from at least as early as 400 BC, in the Middle Preclassic. There's also a **visitor centre** with exhibits from the site, but the opening hours are unpredictable. The best of the nearby **accommodation** choices are the neat, comfortable wood and thatch cabins of *Cahal Pech Village* (☎09/23203, fax 22225; ⑥).

The Macal River

If the idea of a day or more on the river appeals, Tony's River Adventures offer the best value **guided canoe trip** (☎09/23292, or check at *Eva's*). For US$12.50 per person you will be expertly paddled upriver in the morning and float down in the afternoon. Although it is also possible to get there by road, a canoe trip is by far the best way to visit the **Rainforest Medicine Trail** (☎09/23870), a botanical version of the Belize Zoo, taking you through the forest along the Macal riverbank to seek out many of the plants and explain their medicinal properties. The trail is dedicated to Don Eligio Panti, a Maya bush doctor or *curandero*, who passed on his skills to Dr Rosita Arvigo at Ix Chel Tropical

Research Station, where the trail begins. The medical knowledge of the Maya was extensive, and the trail is fascinating: among the plants you'll see are vines that provide fresh water like a tap, and the negrito tree, whose bark was once sold in Europe for its weight in gold as a cure for dysentery. The more mundane but equally effective products of the forest range from herbal teas to blood tonic; Traveller's Tonic, a preventative for diarrhoea, really works, as does Jungle Salve, for soothing insect bites.

A visit to the marvellous **Chaa Creek Natural History Centre**, next to the Medicine Trail (daily 8am–5pm; US$5), is the best introduction to Cayo's history, geography and wildlife. If you're spending more than a couple of days in the area try to see this first. There are fascinating and accurate displays of the region's flora and fauna, vivid archeological and geological maps, and a scale model of the Macal Valley.

ACCOMMODATION

All accommodation on the Macal River is in upmarket cabaña-style resorts; beautifully located but outside the reach of budget travellers. Any of them will give discounts out of season (Dec–Easter). We have listed them in the order you approach them travelling upriver.

Crystal Paradise Resort, in the village of Cristo Rey, on the east bank of the river (☎09/22823, fax 22772). Cabañas, rooms and a lovely thatch-roofed dining room. Two delicious meals a day included. Electricity and hot water, and some cabins have private baths. Buses to San Antonio pass by; alternatively, owner Victor Tut will pick you up in San Ignacio or you could take a taxi for about US$12.50. ⑥–⑧.

Chaa Creek Cottages, on an unpaved turnoff, signed 10km along the road to Benque; also easily reached by river (☎09/22037, fax 22501). Whitewashed wood and stucco cabañas (⑨) in beautiful grounds high above the Macal River, with a justly deserved reputation for luxury and ambience. Chaa Creek also run the *Macal River Safari Campsite* (⑦) just downstream from the resort: this is camping in comfort – hot water, clean, tiled bathrooms and big meals.

du Plooy's, further along the *Chaa Creek* track (☎09/23101, fax 23301). Private luxury bungalows and jungle lodge rooms, each with a private porch. The Pink House has six rooms and can be rented by groups. Great for birdwatching. ⑥–⑨.

Guacamallo Jungle Camp (contact David or Connie at *Martha's Restaurant* in San Ignacio). Simple cabins high above the river (which you cross in a canoe), located on the edge of a huge Maya site. US$20 per person, including transport, dinner and breakfast.

El Pilar Ruins and the Mopan River

The village of **BULLET TREE FALLS** on the **Mopan River** is 5km west of San Ignacio. From here you can visit **El Pilar**, the largest Maya site in the Belize River valley, by a rough road climbing the escarpment, 15km from Bullet Tree; there's no public transport, but if archeologists are working at the site you may be able to get a lift – ask at *Eva's*. Teo, the caretaker, will show you around the site, which covers almost half a square kilometre and includes seventy major structures grouped around 33 plazas. El Pilar's long sequence of construction began in the Preclassic era and continued right through to the Terminal Classic, when some of the largest existing temples were completely rebuilt. A causeway runs west into Guatelmala, and the area is now the focus of an **international archeological park**.

Rushing down from the Guatemalan border, the Mopan River offers excellent possibilities for **whitewater rafting** – contact Pete Zubrzycki at *PACZ Hotel* in San Ignacio (☎09/22110).

ACCOMMODATION

There is less **accommodation** along the Mopan branch of the Belize River than there is along the Macal, but what's available is more within reach of the budget traveller. The resorts below are listed in order of distance from San Ignacio.

Parrot Nest, just past Bullet Tree Falls, 5km from San Ignacio (☎09/23702). Fantastic thatched cabins; one sits very securely up a tree. Shared bathroom with hot shower. ④.

Clarissa Falls, along a signed track to the right off the Benque road, just before the *Chaa Creek* turnoff (☎09/23916). Restful place with simple, clean, stick-and-thatch cabins and camping; shared hot water showers. The restaurant serves fantastic home cooking. ④.

Nabitunich, off the Benque Road, down a track on the right, just beyond the *Chaa Creek* turnoff (☎09/32309, fax 33096). The best of the resorts on the Mopan River; simple cabins set in beautiful gardens with spectacular views of El Castillo at Xunantunich ruins (see p.97). ⑤–⑦.

The Mountain Pine Ridge

South of San Ignacio, running parallel to the border with Guatemala, the **Mountain Pine Ridge Forest Reserve** is a spectacular range of rolling hills and jagged peaks, formed from some of the oldest rocks in Central America. Sections of limestone are riddled with superb caves, the most accessible being the **Rio Frio Caves** in Augustine/Douglas Silva. For the most part the landscape is semi-open, a mixture of grassland and pine forest growing in nutrient-poor, sandy soil, although in the warmth of the river valleys the vegetation is thicker gallery forest, giving way to rainforest south of the Guacamallo Bridge. The rains feed a number of small streams, most of which run off into the Macal and Belize rivers. One of the most scenic is the **Rio On**, rushing over cataracts and forming a gorge – a sight of tremendous natural beauty within view of a picnic shelter. On the northern side of the ridge are the **Thousand-Foot Falls**, actually over 1600ft (488m) and the highest in Central America.

The Pine Ridge is virtually uninhabited but for a few tourist lodges and one small settlement, **Augustine/Douglas Silva**, site of the reserve headquarters. The whole area is perfect for **hiking** and **mountain biking**, but **camping** is allowed only at Augustine/Douglas Silva and at the Mai Gate.

Getting to the reserve

There are two **entrance roads** to the Mountain Pine Ridge reserve, one from the village of **Georgeville**, on the Western Highway (see p.90), and the other from Santa Elena, along the **Cristo Rey** road and through the village of **San Antonio**. The cheapest way to explore the reserve is by **hitching** on either road; there are also four Mesh **buses** a day from San Ignacio to San Antonio, or you could check with the conservation officer in Belmopan (☎08/22079) to see if you can get a ride with the transport for forestry workers.

The best way to get around is to rent a **mountain bike** in San Ignacio, which you can take on the bus to San Antonio. **Organized tours** can also be arranged: contact Rafael at *Martha's* or Tommy at *Eva's* for the best prices. If you are **driving**, always check road conditions and heed the advice of the forestry officials.

San Antonio

The villagers of **SAN ANTONIO** are descendants of Maya refugees (Uxcawal is their name, in their own language) who fled the Caste Wars in Yucatán in 1847; many people still speak Yucatec. Their story is told in a fascinating account of the village's oral history, *After 100 Years*, by Alfonso Antonio Tzul. Nestled in the Macal River valley, surrounded by scattered *milpa* farms, with the forested Maya Mountains in the background, this is a superb place to learn about traditional Maya ways. The Garcia sisters, who grew up in the village determined not to let Maya culture be swamped by outside influences, run the **Tanah Museum** and the simple but comfortable *Chichan Ka Guest House* (☎09/23310, fax 22057; ③) at the approach to the village (buses from San Ignacio stop outside). It's a very relaxing place to stay; traditional meals are served and courses are offered in the gathering and use of medicinal plants. The sisters are also renowned for their slate carvings, and their **gift shop** has become a favourite tour -group stop.

If you're driving in from Santa Elena, you'll pass the excellent *Maya Mountain Lodge* (☎09/22164, fax 22029; ⑤–⑦), run by Bart and Suzi Mickler, 2km along the Cristo Rey road. As well as regular cabañas, with private bath, electricity and hot water, there's a larger cabin, ideal for groups, and families are particularly welcome.

The forest reserve

Not far beyond San Antonio, the roads meet and begin a steady climb to the **reserve**. One kilometre beyond the junction is a **campsite** (①) run by Fidencio and Petronila Bol, who also operate Bol's Nature Tours; Fidencio can guide you to several nearby caves. About 5km uphill from the campsite is the **Mai Gate**, a forestry checkpoint with reserve information as well as toilets and drinking water. Once you've entered the reserve, the dense, leafy forest is quickly replaced by pine trees.

After 3km a branch road heads off to the left, running for 7km to a point which overlooks the **Thousand-Foot Falls** (US$1.50). The setting is spectacular, with rugged, thickly forested slopes across the steep valley – almost a gorge. The waterfall itself is about 1km from the viewpoint, but try to resist the temptation to climb around for a closer look: the slope is a lot steeper than it first appears and, if you do make it down, getting back up again is very difficult.

One of the reserve's main attractions has to be the **Rio On Pools** – a gorgeous spot for a swim – where the river forms pools between huge granite boulders before plunging into a gorge. Another 8km from here and you reach the reserve headquarters at **AUGUSTINE/DOUGLAS SILVA**. If you're heading for Caracol (see opposite), check road conditions with the Forestry Department here. You can **stay** in Augustine/Douglas Silva, either at the campsite or the **bunkhouse** (①), for which you need camping gear. There's a **shop** selling basic supplies and cold beer.

The **Rio Frio Caves** are a twenty-minute walk from Augustine, following the signposted track from the parking area through the forest to the main cave, beneath a small hill. The Rio Frio flows right through and out of the other side of the hill here, and if you enter the foliage-framed cave mouth, you can scramble over limestone terraces the entire way along into the open again. Sandy beaches and rocky cliffs line the river on both sides.

Accommodation

The **resorts** in Mountain Pine Ridge include some of the most exclusive accommodation in the interior of Belize. These lodges, mostly cabins set amongst the pines, surrounded by the undisturbed natural beauty of the Forest Reserve, and with quiet paths to secluded waterfalls, provide ideal places to stay if you're visiting Caracol.

Three kilometres beyond the Mai Gate, the Cooma Cairn Road heads left for 5km to *Hidden Valley Inn* (☎ 08/23320, fax 23334; US$180 double, including breakfast, dinner, tax and service charge; ⑨). Rooms are in twelve spacious, well-designed cottages with log fireplaces, set in a private reserve which includes Thousand-Foot Falls (p.95). Back on the main (Chiquibul) road to Augustine, just past the Cooma Cairn junction, *Pine Ridge Lodge* (☎09/23310, fax 22267; ⑦ including breakfast), on the banks of Little Vaqueros Creek, has accommodation in Maya-style thatched cabins or more modern ones with red-tiled roofs. The grounds and trees are full of orchids and trails lead to pristine waterfalls. A kilometre beyond here, a side road heads right 2km to *Blancaneaux Lodge* (☎09/23878, fax 23919; ⑨ including breakfast), with sumptuous rooms, cabins and villas decorated with Guatemalan and Mexican textiles set in lovely gardens among the pines; owned by Francis Ford Coppola, this is the most luxurious place to stay in the Mountain Pine Ridge. Finally, *Five Sisters Lodge* (☎09/23134, fax 2081; rooms ⑥, cabañas ⑨, including breakfast), at the end of the road past *Blancaneaux*, has the finest location in the Pine Ridge, with palmetto-and-thatch cabañas and lodge rooms set on a hillside overlooking the Five Sisters Falls.

The ruins of Caracol

Beyond Augustine the ridges of the Maya Mountains rise up to the south, while to the west is the wilderness of Vaca plateau. Here the ruins of **Caracol**, the largest Maya site in Belize, and one of the largest in the Maya world, were lost for several centuries until their rediscovery in 1936. Two years later they were explored by A.H. Anderson, who named the site Caracol – Spanish for "snail" – because of the large numbers of snail shells found there. In 1985 the first detailed, full-scale excavation of the site, the "Caracol Project", began, and research continues today, unearthing artefacts relating to everyday life at all levels of Maya society.

The site is open daily (8am–4pm; US$5) and you'll be guided on your visit by one of the guards or, if excavation is in progress, by an archeology student. Only the core of the city, comprising thirty-two large structures and twelve smaller ones grouped round five main plazas, is open to visitors. At its greatest extent, around 700 AD, during the Late Classic period, Caracol covered 88 square kilometres and had a population estimated to be around 150,000. The largest pyramid, **Canaa**, is still the tallest building in Belize at 42m. Glyphs carved on altars tell of war between Caracol and Tikal, when control over a huge area alternated between the two great cities. One altar dates Caracol's victory over Tikal at 562 AD – a victory that set the seal on the city's rise to power. Archeological research has revealed some superb tombs, with lintels of iron-hard sapodilla wood supporting the entrances and painted texts decorating the walls. Caracol has been designated a Natural Monument Reserve, an absolute haven for wildlife as well as archeologists, and the new **visitor centre**, built by Raleigh volunteers, should be fully open now.

Succotz and the ruins of Xunantunich

Back on the Western Highway, around 10km west of San Ignacio, the village of **SAN JOSÉ SUCCOTZ** lies right beside the Mopan River, just before Benque Viejo. It's a quiet village, and the main reason most people visit outside fiesta times is to see the ruins of **Xunantunich** (pronounced Shun-an-tun-ich), "the Stone Maiden", a Classic-period centre, just across the river. An old chain ferry crosses the river on demand (daily 8am–5pm, lunch break around noon; free Mon–Sat, US$1.50 Sun). If you're carrying luggage, you can safely leave it at the *Plaza Restaurant* (also a good source of information), opposite the ferry.

Xunantunich

From the riverbank a steep track leads through the forest for a couple of kilometres to the ruins, where an **entrance fee** is charged (US$5). The **site**, located on top of an artificially flattened hill, includes five plazas, although the remaining structures are grouped around just three of them. Recent investigations have found evidence of Xunantunich's role in the power politics of the Classic period. It seems most likely that it joined Caracol in an alliance with the regional superpower Calakmul, against Tikal. By the Terminal Classic period, Xunantunich was already in decline, though still apparently populated until around 1000 AD, after the so-called Classic Maya "collapse".

The track from the entrance brings you out into plaza A-2, with large structures on three sides. Plaza A-1, to the left is dominated by **El Castillo**, at over 40m the city's tallest structure. It was originally ringed by a decorative stucco frieze, now extensively restored, of abstract designs, human faces and jaguar heads, depicting a king performing rituals associated with assuming authority. The climb up El Castillo can be daunting, but the views from the top are superb, with the forest stretching out all around and the rest of the ancient city mapped out beneath you.

The new **visitor centre** is the best at any Maya site in Belize, with a scale model of the city and an explanation of the symbols on the frieze on El Castillo. Another room has several fairly well preserved stelae from the site. For an interpretation of their glyphs, ask Eduardo Alfaro, one of the caretakers; if he's not busy he'll also be your guide.

Benque Viejo and the Guatemalan border

The final town before the Guatemalan border is **BENQUE VIEJO DEL CARMEN**, less than half an hour from San Ignacio, where Guatemala and Belize combine in almost equal proportions and Spanish is certainly the dominant language. It's a quiet place, served by a constant stream of taxis to and from the border post.

The border itself is a little under 2km beyond Benque Viejo. Most **buses** continue all the way to the market in Melchor. The border is open from 6am to midnight and there is an exit charge of US$3.75 (the PACT) to leave Belize; Guatemala charges a Q10 (US$1.50) entry (and exit) tax, even if you already have a visa – you can try and protest if you feel up to it. Guatemalan **tourist cards** (which should be free but rarely are) and even visas (US$10) can be issued here. It's always best to cross the border in daylight – Guatemalan immigration closes at around 8pm. There are a couple of restaurants and cantinas at the border; they're not up to much but then nor are the ones in Melchor itself. However, just over the border, *Hotel Frontera Palace*, right on the riverbank, has comfortable cabins with hot water (④).

Buses on to **Flores** (see p.244) will call at the immigration post to pick up passengers, and you'll certainly be approached by drivers of the minibuses which shuttle between the border and **Tikal** (US$10) and Flores.

travel details

BUSES

The Western Highway **from Belize City to the Guatemalan border** is served by hourly buses from 5am to 8pm, most of which continue over the border to **Melchor de Mencos**. Bus companies and main destinations are covered in the Belize City chapter (see pp.61–62), with Batty operating until 10am and Novelos' services taking over at 11am; each has **express** buses on some journeys.

From Benque and the border to Belize City buses leave hourly 4am–4pm; the last bus **from San Ignacio to Belize City** leaves at 5pm; all call

at **Belmopan**. To check **bus times** in San Ignacio call Batty on ☎09/22058 or Novelos on ☎09/32054. Additionally Shaws run a service **between Belmopan and San Ignacio** (Mon–Fri 7am–5pm).

Belize City to: Belmopan (hourly; 1hr 15min); San Ignacio (hourly; 3hr); Benque Viejo and the border (hourly; 3hr 30min).

San Ignacio to: San Antonio (Mon–Sat 4 daily 10.30am–5pm; 1hr), returning from San Antonio between 6am and 1.30pm.

CHAPTER 5

THE SOUTH

o the **south of Belmopan** Belize is at its wildest. Here the central area is dominated by the **Maya Mountains**, which slope down towards the coast through a series of forested ridges and valleys carved by sparkling rivers. As you head further south, the climate becomes more humid, promoting the growth of dense rainforest, rich in wildlife.

Population density in this part of Belize is low, with most of the towns and villages located on the coast. **Dangriga**, the largest settlement, is home to the **Garífuna** people, descended from Carib Indians and shipwrecked, enslaved Africans. The villages of **Gales Point**, on Southern Lagoon, north of Dangriga, and **Hopkins**, on the coast to the south, are worth visiting to experience their tranquil way of life. Further south, **Placencia** has become established as the focus of coastal tourism in southern Belize and allows access to a number of idyllic **cayes**, some of which sit right on the top of the Barrier Reef.

Inland, the Maya Mountains remain unpenetrated by roads, forming a solid barrier to land travel except on foot or horseback. The Belize government, showing supreme foresight, has placed practically all of the mountain massif under some form of legal protection, whether as national park, nature reserve, wildlife sanctuary or forest reserve. The most accessible area of rainforest, though still little-visited by tourists, is the **Cockscomb Basin Wildlife Sanctuary**, a reserve designed to protect the sizeable jaguar population. The Southern Highway comes to an end in **Punta Gorda**, a final outpost, from where you can head south to Guatemala or visit Maya villages and ruins in the southern foothills of the Maya Mountains.

The Hummingbird Highway

The **Hummingbird Highway**, heading southeast from Belmopan to Dangriga, passes through magnificent scenery as it rises steadily over the hills and through lush forest, with the eastern slopes of the **Maya Mountains** visible on the right. These hills form part of a ridge of limestone mountains, riddled with underground rivers and **caves**, several of which are accessible.

St Herman's Cave to Five Blues Lake National Park
About 19km out of Belmopan the road crosses the **Caves Branch River**, a tributary of the Sibun River. Just beyond, by the roadside on the right, is **St Herman's Cave** (US$4, includes entrance to the Blue Hole), one of the most accessible caves in Belize. Follow the marked trail behind the **Visitor Centre** (daily 8am–4pm) for ten minutes to the cave entrance, beneath a dripping rock face; you'll need a flashlight to enter, down steps that were originally cut by the Maya. Inside, you clamber over the rocks and splash through the river for about thirty minutes, admiring the stunning formations, before the cave appears to end. To continue beyond, and emerge from one of the other entrances, you need to go on an tour – one of the best is organized by Pete Zubrzycki of *PACZ Hotel* in San Ignacio (see p.92).

For an explanation of **accommodation price codes**, see p.42.

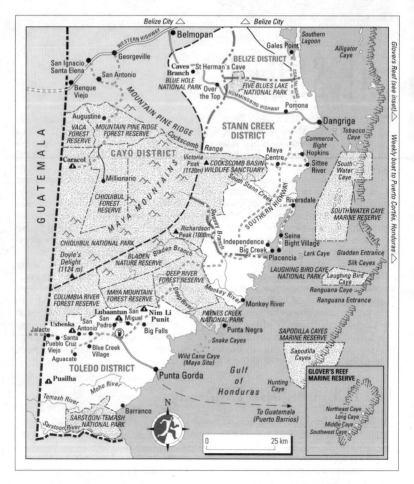

Two kilometres past the cave, signed from the roadside, is the **Blue Hole National Park**, its focus a beautiful pool whose cool, fresh turquoise waters, surrounded by dense forest and overhung with vines, mosses and ferns, are perfect for a refreshing dip. The Blue Hole is actually a short but deep stretch of underground river, whose course is revealed by the collapse of a karst cavern, flowing on the surface for about 50m before disappearing beneath another rock face. New trails are being cut, allowing you to explore the dense forset, and a **campsite** is being built; check at the Visitor Centre for the latest information.

Any bus between Belmopan and Dangriga will drop you at the cave or the Blue Hole, but to really appreciate the mysteries of caving in Belize you can **stay** nearby at *Caves Branch Jungle Lodge* (☎ & fax 08/22800; cabañas ⑥, bunkhouse US$15 per person, camping US$5), halfway between St Herman's Cave and the Blue Hole and about 1km from the highway. The **guided cave trips** run by the lodge are not cheap (on average about US$70 per person), but well worth the cost. All the caves contain Maya artefacts – ceramics, carvings and the like – with abundant evidence of Classic period ceremonies.

Beyond the Blue Hole the Hummingbird Highway is well paved, undulating smoothly through the increasingly hilly landscape and eventually crossing a low pass. The downhill slope is appropriately, if unimaginatively, called **Over the Top**. On the way down, the road passes through **ST MARGARET'S VILLAGE**, where a women's cooperative arranges bed and breakfast **accommodation** in private houses (☎081/2005; ③).

A few kilometres past the village, the *Over the Top Restaurant* stands on a hill at Mile 32, overlooking the junction of the track to **Five Blues Lake National Park**, seventeen square kilometres of luxuriantly forested karst scenery, centred on a lake. Named for its constantly changing colours, the lake was created by a cavern collapsing. Continuing south for 3km on the Hummingbird Highway from Over the Top there's cabaña accommodation at *Palacio's Mountain Retreat* (⑤ including breakfast), overlooking a river; it's great for swimming and there's a ten-metre waterfall just upstream.

Palacio's marks the start of the **Stann Creek valley**, the centre of the Belizean citrus fruit industry. Bananas were the first crop to be grown here, but the banana boom came to an abrupt end in 1906, when disease destroyed the crop, and the government set out to foster the growth of **citrus fruits**. Between 1908 and 1937 the valley was even served by a small railway, and by 1945 the citrus industry was well established. Today it accounts for about thirteen percent of the country's exports and is heralded as one of the nation's great success stories – although for the largely Guatemalan labour force, housed in rows of scruffy huts, conditions are little better than on the oppressive coffee fincas at home. The Hummingbird Highway officially comes to an end at **Middlesex**, 18km past Over the Top, and continues as the Stann Creek Valley Road.

Gales Point and the Southern Lagoon

At Melinda, 27km past Middlesex and only 14km from Dangriga, an improved dirt road heads north to the small Creole village of **GALES POINT**, which straggles along a narrow peninsula jutting into the Southern Lagoon, connected by creeks to Northern Lagoon, an even larger body of shallow water. These lagoons are an essential breeding ground for rare wildlife, including jabiru storks, turtles, manatee and crocodiles. The area is bounded on the west by the limestone Peccary hills, riddled with caves, and the shores of the lagoons are cloaked with mangroves.

Several houses offer simple bed and breakfast **accommodation** (③), or try the café *Gentle's Cool Spot*, which also has a few simple, clean rooms (③); a couple of basic **campsites** have opened recently, too. The most luxurious accommodation is at *Manatee Lodge* (☎08/23320; ⑨, including tax), a two-storey colonial-style building right at the tip of the peninsula, where the US$180 room charge includes breakfast and dinner. Gales Point is only infrequently served by **buses** on the Belize City–Dangriga route, though buses using the Manatee (Coastal) Road pass within 4km of the village and will drop you at the junction.

Dangriga

The last stretch of the Hummingbird Highway is flat and relatively uninteresting; from the junction with the **Southern Highway** to Punta Gorda, it's another 10km further to **DANGRIGA**, the district capital (formerly known as Stann Creek) and the largest town in southern Belize. Though Dangriga is the cultural centre of the **Garífuna**, a people of mixed indigenous Caribbean and African descent, who overall make up about eleven percent of the country's population, it is not the most exciting of places unless you're here during a festival. However, the town is home to some of the country's most popular artists, including painters, drum-makers, the Waribagabaga Dancers and the Turtle Shell Band, and you may catch an exhibition or performance. It's also a useful base for visiting south-central Belize, its offshore cayes and the mountains and jaguar reserve inland.

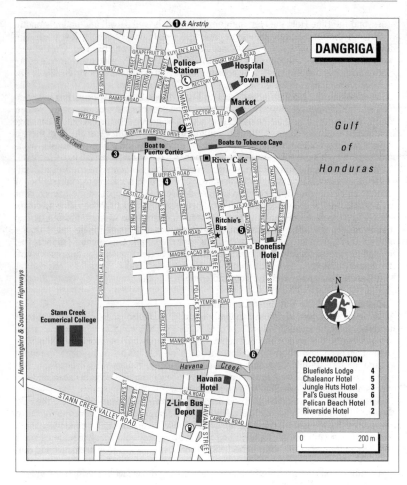

Since the early 1980s Garífuna culture has undergone something of a revival, and as a part of this movement the town was renamed Dangriga, a Garífuna word meaning "standing waters". The most important day in the Garífuna calendar is November 19, **Garífuna Settlement Day**, in Dangriga a time of wild celebration, when the town erupts with music, dance, drink and dope. A group of local people re-enact the arrival from Roatán, landing on the beach in dugout canoes.

A brief history of the Garífuna

The Garífuna trace their history back to the island of **St Vincent**, in the eastern Caribbean, when two Spanish ships, carrying slaves from Nigeria to their colonies in America, were wrecked off the coast in 1635. The survivors took refuge on the island, which was already inhabited by **Caribs**, themselves recent arrivals from South America, who had subdued the original natives, the **Kalipuna**, from whom it is likely the Garífuna derived their own name. At first there was conflict between the Native

Americans and the Africans, but the Caribs had been weakened by wars and disease and eventually the predominant race was black with some indigenous blood, becoming known by the English as the **Black Caribs**.

For most of the seventeenth and eighteenth centuries St Vincent was nominally under British control, though in practice it belonged to the Caribs, who successfully fended off British attempts to gain full control of the island until 1796. The British colonial authorities, however, could not allow a free black society to survive amongst slave-owning European settlers, so the Carib population was hunted down and transported to **Roatán**, off the coast of Honduras (see p.423), where the British abandoned them. The Spanish Commandante of Trujillo, on the Honduran mainland, took the 1700 surviving Black Caribs to Trujillo, where they were in demand as free labourers, fishermen and soldiers. Their intimate knowledge of the rivers and coast also made them expert smugglers, evading the Spanish laws that forbade trade with the British in Belize.

In the early **nineteenth century** small numbers of Garífuna moved up the coast to Belize, and they were already there when European settlers arrived in Stann Creek in 1823. The largest single migration to Belize took place in 1832 when thousands fled from Honduras (then part of the Central American Republic) after they supported the wrong side in a failed revolution to overthrow the Republican government. It is this arrival which is today celebrated as Garífuna Settlement Day, though it seems likely many arrived both before and after.

Arrival and information

Dangriga's airstrip, served by daily **flights** from Belize City, is on the shore just north of the *Pelican Beach Hotel*; for flights onward, check the schedules at Treasured Travels, 64 Commerce St (☎05/22578). All **buses** enter Dangriga at the south end of town: Z-Line buses from Belize City have a terminal around 1km south of the centre, while Ritchie's buses stop further north on St Vincent Street. Dangriga's centre is marked by the **road bridge** over the South Stann Creek, with the main street leading north as Commerce Street and south as St Vincent Street. Almost everything you're likely to need, including **hotels**, **restaurants** and **banks**, is on or near this road. For reliable **tourist information**, call in at the *River Café* (☎05/29908), by the bridge on the south bank of the river. The **post office** is on Caney Street, in the southern half of town, a block back from the sea.

Accommodation

Dangriga has experienced something of a hotel-building boom in the last few years, resulting in an ample choice of **places to stay**, with some real bargains, so there's no need to stay in a cheap dive – though there are a few of these, too.

Bluefield Lodge, 6 Bluefield Rd, south side of town (☎05/22742). Very clean, good value rooms, some with private bath. ④.

Chaleanor Hotel, 35 Magoon St (☎05/22587, fax 23038). New hotel with very clean, spacious rooms, all with private bath, plus a rooftop restaurant. The best value at this price. ⑤.

Jungle Huts, on the riverbank to the south of town (☎05/23166). Thatched cabañas and hotel rooms with private bath and hot and cold water. ⑤.

Pal's Guest House, 868 Magoon St, by the bridge over Havana Creek (☎ & fax 05/22095). Good-value accommodation in two buildings: the budget rooms (some with shared bath) are in the older part; beachfront rooms all have TV and private baths. ④.

Pelican Beach Hotel, on the shore north of the town, next to the airstrip (☎05/22024, fax 22570). The most expensive hotel in town. Ask for a discount – it's only worth paying full price if you get a beachfront room. ⑦.

Riverside Hotel, right beside the bridge (☎05/22168). Clean rooms with a vantage point over the river. ③.

Eating and drinking

On the south bank of the river, just over the bridge, the *River Café* serves good meals (including vegetarian) to visitors waiting for boats to Tobacco Caye (see below). At the south end of town, *Pola's Kitchen*, 25 Tubroose St, serves good value Garífuna special-ities and has a no-smoking policy that is probably unique in Belize. Of the several good Chinese restaurants on the main street, the *Starlight* is the best value.

There's no shortage of **bars** in Dangriga, though some, particularly those calling themselves clubs, like *The Culture Club* and the *Harlem Club*, are particularly dubious-looking, both inside and out. North along the shore the *Round House* is a good spot to meet the locals.

Moving on from Dangriga

Returning **to Belize City**, Z-Line (☎05/22732) have eight daily departures. If you're heading **south** bear in mind that the four daily buses to **Punta Gorda** don't necessar-ily originate here; the first leaves Dangriga at noon. All buses to Punta Gorda stop at **Independence** – where you can pick up boats to Placencia (see p.109).

Buses from Dangriga to **Placencia** (at least one calls at **Hopkins** and **Sittee River**) depart daily at 11.30am (Ritchies ☎05/23132); and 12.30pm and 4.30pm (Z-Line). The James line also runs a daily service between Belize City and Punta Gorda, calling at Dangriga.

Tropic and Maya Island operate regular **flights** between Dangriga and Belize Municipal airport; there are also flights south to Placencia and Punta Gorda, departing roughly every two hours from 6.30am to 4.30pm.

For **Puerto Cortés** in **Honduras** (see p.401) a fast skiff leaves each Saturday at 9am (around 3hr; US$50) from the north bank of the river, two blocks up from the bridge; be there an hour before departure with your passport so that the skipper, Carlos Reyes (☎05/23227), can take care of the formalities.

Offshore from Dangriga: Tobacco and South Water Cayes

About 20km offshore from Dangriga is **Columbus Reef**, a superb section of the Barrier Reef with tiny **Tobacco Caye** perched on its southern tip. From here **Tobacco Reef** stretches south for 8km, with the slightly larger **South Water Caye** at its southern end.

Ideally situated right in the middle of the reef, **Tobacco Caye** is easy to reach and has the better value accommodation. **Boats** (40min; US$15) leave daily from near the bridge, but there are no scheduled departures; ask at your hotel or the *River Café*. The island is tiny: if you stand in the centre you're only a couple of minutes from the shore in any direction, with the unbroken reef stretching north for miles. Sunsets can be breathtakingly beautiful, outlining the distant Maya Mountains with a purple and orange aura. **Diving** here is great, one of the highlights being a dive to nearby caves harbouring sharks. The island's dive shop, Second Nature Divers (☎05/37038), run by an English couple, is excellent, charging around US$25 for a single-tank local dive (plus equipment); a PADI open-water course costs US$225.

The least expensive **place to stay** is *Gaviota Coral Reef Resort*, which offers cabins on the sand and more expensive rooms in the main building, all with shared bath (☎014/9763, fax 05/23477; ⑨, including meals). The owner can arrange discounted boat fares for guests. Alternatively, try simple *Island Camps* (☎014/7160; ⑥), which has seven small double cabins and three larger cabins, one with private bath.

Eight kilometres south and slightly larger, **South Water Caye** is arguably one of the most beautiful – and exclusive – islands in Belize; it is now part of a **marine reserve**. Like Tobacco Caye it sits right on the reef and offers fantastic snorkelling and diving in crystal-clear waters. The island's **accommodation** is upmarket and expensive and has to be booked in advance, generally as an all-inclusive package. Overnight rates are available, but this entails paying at least US$125 one-way for a skiff from Dangriga. The *Pelican Beach* in Dangriga (☎05/22024) owns some idyllic wooden houses built on stilts over the white sand and shaded by palms (⑨), plus a two-storey hotel with five rooms (⑨). Prices range from US$150 to US$170, including meals.

The Southern Highway to Placencia

To the **south of Dangriga** the country becomes more mountainous, with development restricted to the coastal lowlands. The road is unpaved for the most part and the towns and villages are increasingly isolated. However, work on paving the surface has begun and the highway is generally passable except during the very worst rainstorms. For its entire length the road is set back from the coast, running beneath the peaks of the Maya Mountains, passing through pine forest and vast citrus and banana plantations. Several branch roads lead off to idyllic coastal villages such as **Hopkins**. From the village of Maya Centre, 36km by road from Dangriga, another road leads west into the **Cockscomb Basin** and its wildlife reserve.

Hopkins, Sittee River and Glover's Reef

Stretching for more than 3km along a shallow, gently curving bay, the village of **HOPKINS** is home to around a thousand Garífuna people; Garífuna Settlement Day, November 19, is celebrated enthusiastically here. A few kilometres south of the Hopkins turnoff, a road heads east to **Sittee River**, a pleasant place in its own right, but most useful as a jumping-off point for **Glover's Reef** (see p.106).

Hopkins practicalities

There's a Ritchies **bus** to Hopkins from Dangriga daily at 12.30pm, and usually a Z-line service at 4.30pm, both continuing to Sittee River. The best way to get here, though, is by **boat**; ask around where the boats tie up by the bridge in Dangriga. There are no street names in Hopkins, but the main point of reference is the point where the road from the Southern Highway enters the village – this divides the place into north and south. Private phones are new in Hopkins; for now you can make calls on the **community telephone** (☎05/22033) in the Nuñez store at the roadside in the south of the village.

There's plenty of **accommodation** in the village. At the north end, *Lebeha* has a clean, brightly painted cabin (③), and *Swinging Armadillos* (☎05/37016; ④), on the beach 150m north of the centre, has two small but comfortable rooms perched over the sea alongside its bar and restaurant (see below). South of the centre, the *Hopkins Inn* (☎05/37013) offers two immaculate white cabins (⑥, including breakfast) with hot showers and fridge. The *Sandy Beach Lodge*, on the beach at the south end (☎05/37006; ③), has simple, spacious rooms in wood-and-thatch cabins, most with private bath.

A few simple **restaurants** and **bars** have opened up in Hopkins in recent years. *Over the Waves*, on the beach in the village centre, is recommended, as is *Swinging Armadillos*, a great little "hammock lounge", where you can enjoy the sea breeze while sipping a cold drink. *Ronnie's Kitchen*, north of the centre, serves filling snacks and fresh fruit juices; for a more substantial dinner, you need to book.

Sittee River

The 5km sandy road heading south from Hopkins is the "back way" to **SITTEE RIVER**. Most visitors are on their way to *Glover's Atoll Resort* (see below), but there are a couple of places to **stay**. The great-value *Toucan Sittee* (☎05/37039; ④) is by far the best option, set in a beautiful riverbank location and graced by toucans most mornings. As well as rooms, it offers dorm accommodation (US$8 per person) and camping space (US$2 per person). The food is really good, with lots of fresh fruit and vegetables, and they rent **canoes**. In the village there's the basic *Glover's Guest House* (③). Sandflies in Sittee River can be atrocious and the mosquito nets provided are essential.

Glover's Reef

The southernmost of Belize's three coral atolls, **Glover's Reef** lies between 40 and 50km off Sittee River. Named after a British pirate, the reef is roughly oval in shape, about 35km north to south, and its only cayes are in the southeastern section. The whole atoll is a **marine reserve**, with a research station on Middle Caye. What makes Glover's Reef so unusual among the remote atolls is that it offers **accommodation** within the reach of budget travellers, at the *Glover's Atoll Resort* (☎014/8351). There are nine simple **beach cabins** (US$149 per person per week, including transport from Sittee River) overlooking the reef on **Northeast Caye**, plus camping space (US$80 per week). Unless you're here on a group package, you'll need to bring your own food. Activities include sailing, sea kayaking, fishing, snorkelling and scuba diving, which is spectacular, thanks to a huge underwater cliff and some tremendous wall diving. The resort's boat drops off visitors at Sittee River on Saturday afternoon and collects the new guests on Sunday morning for the four-hour trip to the atoll.

Two other cayes offer more exclusive accommodation: **Long Caye**, just south of Northeast Caye, is the base camp for Slickrock Adventures for sea kayaking and diving, (see p.6 for details) and **Southwest Caye** serves the same purpose for Vancouver-based Island Adventures.

The Cockscomb Basin Wildlife Sanctuary

The jagged peaks of the **Maya Mountains** rise to the west of the Southern Highway, their lower slopes covered in dense rainforest. The tallest summits are those of the Cockscomb range, which includes Victoria Peak (1120m), the second highest mountain in Belize. Beneath the ridges is a sweeping bowl, part of which was declared a jaguar preserve in 1986; today, the **Cockscomb Basin Wildlife Sanctuary** has expanded to cover an area of more than four hundred square kilometres. The sanctuary is reached via a rough ten-kilometre track that branches off the main highway at the village of **Maya Centre**, running through towering forest and fording a couple of fresh, clear streams before crossing the Cabbage Hall Gap and entering the Cockscomb Basin. This area was inhabited in Maya times, and the ruins of **Chucil Balam**, a small Classic period ceremonial centre, still lie hidden in the forest.

The basin's luxuriant vegetation (technically tropical moist forest) is home to a sizeable percentage of Belize's plant and animal species. Among the **mammals** are tapir, otter, anteater, armadillo and, of course, jaguar. Over 290 species of **bird** have also been recorded, including the endangered scarlet macaw, the great curassow and the king vulture, and there's an abundance of **amphibians** and **reptiles**, including the red-eyed tree frog and the deadly fer-de-lance. Trails have been cut to give visitors a taste of the forest's diversity. These take you along the riverbanks, through the forest and even, if you're suitably prepared, on a three-day hike to Victoria Peak. Although the basin could be home to as many as fifty of Belize's 600-strong jaguar population, your chances of seeing one are very slim.

Practicalities

All **buses** heading south from Dangriga pass **MAYA CENTRE** (45min). You need to stop here to sign in and pay the reserve's entrance fee (US$5) at the **craft centre** on the Southern Highway. A small shop here sells basic supplies and cold drinks and is also a good place to find out about guides and transport. If you want to stay, try Aurora and Ernesto Saqui's *Nu'uk Che'il Cottages* in Maya Centre (☎051/2021; ④): simple but delightful thatched cabañas, with shared bathroom and good food.

You can arrange transport here (US$12.50), or walk the 10km downhill to the **reserve headquarters**, where there's an excellent **visitor centre** and some simple but comfortable **dorm accommodation** (US$7.50–15); the **campground** (US$2.50) is a little further on. You'll have to bring your own food, but the cabins do have a gas stove.

Beyond Maya Centre

Three kilometres past Maya Centre you'll reach the turnoff for the privately owned **Sapodilla Lagoon Wildlife Refuge** (signed on the left-hand side of the road), stretching along both sides of the highway, from the eastern foothills of the Maya Mountains to the coast. *Black Cat Lodge*, a 25-minute walk from the road, provides the only nearby **accommodation** and is run like a very relaxed youth hostel, with bunk beds and hammocks. The price (US$22.50 per person) includes three meals, which guests cook themselves. If you're **camping**, you pay only for food.

The Placencia peninsula

Shaded by palm trees, cooled by the sea breeze, and perched on the tip of a narrow, sandy peninsula 75km south of Dangriga, **Placencia** is light-years from the hassle of Belize City. A good dirt road cuts east from the Southern Highway for 13km, reaching the sea at Riversdale, before heading south down the peninsula for 26km, through **Maya Beach** and the Garífuna village of **Seine Bight** to Placencia village. Travelling down the peninsula, you'll pass around a dozen upscale **resorts**, most of them owned and operated by expatriate North Americans, where accommodation is usually in cabins with private bathrooms and electricity. In addition to the pleasures of a Caribbean beach just a few steps away, most of the resorts also have access to **Placencia Lagoon**, a few metres away on the other side of the road.

Halfway along the peninsula, on the beautiful stretch of coast called **Maya Beach**, are the *Green Parrot Beach Houses* (☎ & fax 06/22488; ⑨). Raised on stilts, the beach houses sleep up to five people: each has a spacious deck, kitchen and a loft bedroom. There's also an excellent restaurant. Just south of the *Green Parrot* are the six wood-and-thatch cabins of *Singing Sands Inn* (☎ & fax 06/22243; ⑨).

Some 3km further, the small, previously little-visited Garífuna village of **SEINE BIGHT** now has several (mostly overpriced) resorts and hotels. One of the best is the *Hotel Seine Bight* (☎06/23536, fax 23537; ⑨), with thatched rooms and suites around a beachfront pool. The village, reputed to have been founded by privateers in 1629, is worth a visit even if you're not staying; you can play pool in the *Sunshine Bar*, listen to Garífuna music in the *Kulcha Shak* or visit *Lola's Art Gallery and Cafe*, where Lola Delgado displays her superb (and affordable) oil and acrylic paintings of village life.

Beyond Seine Bight another series of resorts offers upscale **accommodation**. *Kitty's Place*, just south of Placencia's airstrip (☎06/23227, fax 23226; ⑥–⑧), is the best, a convenient 3km north of the village and offering a variety of accommodation including apartments, beach cabañas and garden rooms. The restaurant serves delicious Belizean and international food.

Placencia village: practicalities

Placencia is one of the few places on mainland Belize with proper beaches, and this, together with the abundant, inexpensive accommodation makes it a great place to relax. Unfortunately its remote location and distance from the reef put many of the available tours beyond the reach of travellers on a low budget. The easiest way to get to **Placencia** village is on one of the regular **flights** from Belize City (about 45min). The airstrip is about 3km north of the village; taxis are usually waiting – or it's a five-minute walk to *Kitty's*, where you can phone. There are two **direct buses** a day from Belize City, both of them passing through Dangriga, plus at least one starting in Dangriga. You can also hop over easily from Independence/Mango Creek, just across the lagoon, on the *Hokey Pokey* (☎06/22376; 10am & 4pm; 30min).

Buses from Dangriga end up at the beachfront gas station, right at the end of the peninsula, but if you're looking for budget rooms you should get off when you see the sign for the *Sea Spray Hotel*, about halfway through the village. Head left for **the sidewalk**, a concrete walkway that winds through the palms, and you'll be at the centre of a cluster of budget hotels and restaurants.

There's no tourist office, but locals are glad to answer questions and the Orange Peel Gift Shop supplies hand-drawn maps. A couple of good sources of **information** are the tour office next to the gas station and the *Jay Byrd Bar*, just beyond. The **post office**, without a permanent home, is currently across from Olga's Store, near the gas station. The nearest **bank** is in Independence (see opposite; Friday mornings only) and, while travellers' cheques are readily accepted, you may find them difficult to cash.

Accommodation

In Placencia village proper there's a wide choice of **accommodation**, and you should have no problem finding a room provided you don't arrive at Christmas, New Year or Easter without a booking. Possibilities begin at the sidewalk, and as you wend your way down it seems as though every family is offering **rooms**.

Barracuda and Jaguar Inn, towards the south end of the village (☎06/23330, fax 23250). Two varnished wooden cabins and a large deck with lounge chairs and a hammock, set in tropical gardens; the best value in this range. ⑤.

Coconut Cottage, on the beach south of the centre (☎ & fax 06/23234). Two gorgeous, well-decorated cabins in a quiet location, with fridge and hot water. ⑥.

Conrad and Lydia's Rooms, near the north end of the sidewalk (☎06/23117). Very good value, clean, secure rooms run by a friendly family. ④.

Deb & Dave's Last Resort, on the road, near the centre (☎06/23207). The nicest budget place in the village; lovely rooms with shared hot-water bathroom. ③.

Julia's Rooms, in the centre of the village, just south of the *Seaspray* (☎06/23185). Small hotel, with clean, basic rooms, between the sidewalk and the sea. ③.

Seaspray Hotel, on the beach in the centre of the village (☎06/23148). Popular hotel, with a range of accommodation, all with private bath and hot water. ④–⑥.

Trade Winds, on the south point (☎06/23122, fax 23201). Cabins and rooms with hot water and deck on a spacious, secluded plot, facing sea breezes. ⑥.

Traveller's Inn, signed from the sidewalk, just south of the centre (☎06/23190). Five basic rooms – cheapest in the village – with shared bath, and some in a separate building with private bath. ③.

Eating and drinking

There are plenty of good **restaurants** in Placencia, but even more than elsewhere in Belize, places change management fast, so it's worth asking around. Most places close early; you'll certainly have a better choice if you're at the table by 8pm. Fresh **bread** is available from John The Bakerman, signed from the sidewalk, and from a number of local women who bake Creole bread and buns.

Daisy's Ice Cream Parlour, set back from the sidewalk, just south of the *Seaspray*, has long been deservedly popular for its **ice cream**, **cakes** and **snacks**, and now serves full meals. The *Pickled Parrot Bar & Grill*, at the *Barracuda and Jaguar Inn*, is consistently the best restaurant in the village, serving fresh **seafood** and international dishes. At the south end (turn right past the gas station), *Merlene's Restaurant* (☎06/23264) is usually the first to open, serving great breakfasts, good coffee and fantastic home-made bread and cakes. Lunch and dinner are equally good, especially for fish, but the place is tiny so you may have to book. A few steps beyond here, built over the water, *Tentacles* is in a superb location for enjoying the sunset, though the food – mainly steaks, pasta and seafood – can be variable.

Travel connections: Independence (Mango Creek)

Just across the lagoon from Placencia, **Independence** (also called Mango Creek) is a useful travel hub. The *Hokey Pokey* boat runs from here to Placencia twice daily, at 8.30am and 2.30pm (30min).

Heading north, Z-Line buses leave for **Dangriga** (2hr) at 8am, noon and 3pm, and south to **Punta Gorda** (3hr) at 3pm, 6pm and 9pm. The James bus also passes through once daily. Z-Line buses take a rest/meal stop at the *Cafe Hello* in Independence; the James bus stops nearby at *Marita's Restaurant*, on Hercules Ave. The **food** at these places is fine, but try not to get stuck **overnight** here. If you do, the *Hello Hotel* (☎06/22428; ⑤), mainly used by business people, has some a/c rooms; you could also try the clean, simple *Ursula's Guest House* (③) on Gran Main St. The Barclays **bank** in Independence, open Friday mornings, gives cash advances.

Around Placencia

In general, trips from Placencia can be tailor-made to your preference and your pocket, and you can arrange anything from an afternoon on the water to a week of camping, fishing, snorkelling and sailing. Placencia **lagoon** is ideal for exploring in a canoe or kayak; you may even spot manatee, though it's more likely to be a series of ripples as the shy giant swims powerfully for cover. **Canoes** (US$10 per day) are available from Dave Dial at the gas station, who also rents out a **sailboat** (US$25 per day). **Kayaks** (US$15 per day) and **bikes** (US$7.50) can be rented from Sundowner Tours (current-ly located in the post office).

One of the best **day-trips** from Placencia takes you by boat 20km southwest to the almost pristine **Monkey River**, which teems with fish, bird life and, naturally enough, howler monkeys. Dave Dial, of Monkey River Magic, runs the best tours (☎06/23209, fax 23291; US$40), his wildlife expertise complemented by the experienced local guides from Monkey River village. A thirty-minute dash through the waves is followed by a leisurely glide up the river and a walk along forest trails. If your trip doesn't include a packed lunch you can get a meal in *Alice's Restaurant* in the village.

Snorkelling and **diving** trips commonly include a visit to uninhabited **Laughing Bird Caye**, a recently expanded National Park and Marine Reserve. Beyond here lie the exquisitely beautiful **Silk Cayes**, where the Barrier Reef begins to break into several smaller reefs and cayes. Diving here is excellent, with fringing and patch reefs, but you have to bear in mind that the distance to the dive sites means that trips here are a little more expensive than elsewhere. Booking your dive through a dive shop (rather than an independent dive guide) is usually the least expensive option. Placencia Dive Shop, at the southern end of the sidewalk (☎06/23313), offers the best value, at US$60 for a two-tank dive, including all equipment and breakfast. Also worth trying, especially for PADI instruction, is Aquatic Adventures, on the dock at the end of the village (☎06/23182).

The far south

Beyond the Placencia and Independence junctions, the Southern Highway leaves the banana plants and the small, grim settlements squashed beside the plantation roads, twisting at first through pine forests, and crossing numerous creeks and rivers. There are few villages along the way, and new citrus plantations are almost always in view, the neat ranks of trees marching over the hills.

About 73km from the Placencia junction, just off the highway, is **Nim Li Punit**, a Late Classic Maya site, possibly allied to nearby Lubaantun. Eight carved stelae were found here, including one that measured 9m in height, the tallest yet found in Belize. The site is about 1km west of the Southern Highway, surrounded by the fields of the nearby Maya village of **Indian Creek**.

A little further south, just before the highway comes to an end in Punta Gorda, a road branches off west to **Silver Creek**. With your own transport, you can use this route to explore the southern foothills of the Maya Mountains, home to some delightful Maya villages with ruins scattered in the surrounding hills.

Punta Gorda

The Southern Highway eventually comes to an end in **PUNTA GORDA**, the last town in Belize and the heart of the isolated Toledo District, an area that has always been hard to reach, though work has now begun on paving the highway north from Punta Gorda. Today's town is populated by a mixture of Garífuna, Maya – who make up more than half the population of the district – and Creoles, and is the focal point for a large number of villages and farming settlements. The busiest day is Saturday, when people from the surrounding villages come into town to trade. Despite the recent minor building boom, Punta Gorda remains a small, unhurried, friendly town and you won't encounter any hassle. Its position on low sea cliffs allows cooling breezes to reduce the worst of the heat but there's no denying that this is the wettest part of Belize, the trees here heavy with mosses and bromeliads.

Arrival and information

Buses from Belize City, via Dangriga, take around eight hours to reach Punta Gorda; Z-Line buses use a depot at the south end of José María Nuñez Street, while James buses stop at an office near the dock. **Skiffs** from Puerto Barrios in **Guatemala** use the main dock, roughly in the centre of the sea front; **immigration** is nearby. There are three or four daily **flights** from Belize City, landing at the small airstrip five blocks west of the main dock.

Despite having relatively few visitors, Punta Gorda is practically awash with **information centres**: the Toledo Visitors Information Center (TVIC), by the ferry dock, offers information and bookings for accommodation in the local area, and there's the Belize Tourist Board on Front Street (☎07/22351). The group of government buildings a block back from the ferry dock house the **post office**, the BTL office and a public phone. The only **bank** is the Belize Bank, at the top corner of the main square, across from the Civic Center (Mon–Fri 8am–2pm).

Accommodation

During the last couple of years there has been a spate of **hotel** building in the town, but although visitor numbers have increased, few people spend long here, and there are plenty of bargains. For an alternative to staying in town, contact the **Toledo Ecotourism Association** in *Nature's Way*, 65 Front St (☎07/22119), which operates an award-winning programme of guesthouse accommodation in surrounding villages.

Charlton's Inn, 9 Main St (☎07/22197, fax 22471). Two-storey concrete building; rooms have private bath and hot water and some are a/c. Safe parking. ④.

Mahung's, corner of North and Main streets (☎07/22044). Cheap and basic but does have hot water and some private baths. Bike rental. ③.

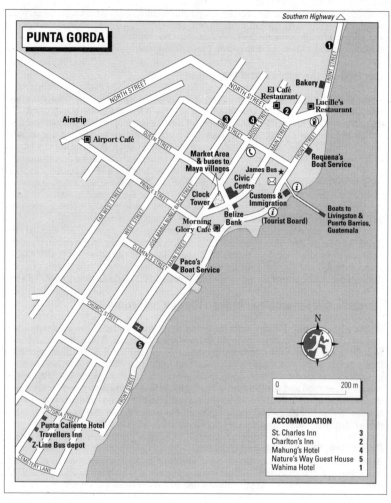

PUNTA GORDA

Southern Highway △

❶

NORTH STREET

FRONT STREET

NORTH STREET

Bakery

El Café Restaurant ❷

Lucille's Restaurant

Airstrip

KING STREET

QUEEN STREET

❸

❹

MIDDLE STREET

MAIN STREET

FRONT STREET

■ **Airport Café**

Market Area & buses to Maya villages

James Bus ★

Civic Centre ✉

Requena's Boat Service

PRINCE STREET

BACK STREET

ℂ

ⓘ

Clock Tower

Customs & Immigration

Boats to Livingston & Puerto Barrios, Guatemala

FAR WEST STREET

WEST STREET

JOSE MARIA NUNEZ

MAIN STREET

Belize Bank

Morning Glory Café ■

ⓘ **(Tourist Board)**

CLEMENT'S STREET

Paco's Boat Service ■

CHURCH STREET

✚

❺

N

0   200 m

VICTORIA STREET

FRONT STREET

Punta Caliente Hotel
Travellers Inn
Z-Line Bus depot

CEMETERY LANE

ACCOMMODATION

St. Charles Inn	3
Charlton's Inn	2
Mahung's Hotel	4
Nature's Way Guest House	5
Wahima Hotel	1

Nature's Way Guest House, 65 Front St (☎07/22119). The best budget place in Punta Gorda; renowned as a meeting place and information point. Dorm accommodation overlooking the sea, and a couple of private rooms. Good meals are served in the wholefood restaurant. Dorms US$8, rooms ③.

St Charles Inn, 23 King St (☎07/22149). Clean and quiet carpeted rooms with TV. At the top end of the scale for Punta Gorda, and recommended. ④.

Wahima, 11 Front St. Inexpensive, basic and friendly; a small bar/restaurant next door provides local colour. ③.

Eating

Restaurants tend to be rather basic in Punta Gorda, but there are a couple of newer places where the quality is somewhat higher, and certainly it's easy to get a filling meal at a reasonable price. On Front Street the *Morning Glory Cafe* (closed Sun) serves seafood, burgers and snacks in clean, bright surroundings. *Lucille's*, by the Texaco station at the corner of North and Front streets, serves the good old Creole staples of rice and beans. *El Cafe*, behind *Charlton's Inn*, does the best coffee in town and opens for breakfast at 6am. There's a **bakery** on Front Street, past the Texaco station.

Out to sea: the cayes and the coast

From Punta Gorda you can see range upon range of mountains in Guatemala and Honduras, but the Belizean **coastline** south of here is flat and sparsely populated. The cayes and reefs here mark the southern end of Belize's barrier reef, and the main reef has started to break up, leaving several clusters of islands, each surrounded by a small independent reef. The closest to Punta Gorda are the **Snake Cayes**, hundreds of tiny islands in the mouth of a large bay, where the shoreline is a complex maze of mangrove swamps. On Wild Cane Caye here archeologists have found evidence of a Maya coastal trade centre. Further out, in the Gulf of Honduras, are the **Sapodilla Cayes**, now a marine reserve, of which the largest caye, **Hunting Caye**, is frequented by Guatemalan as well as Belizean day-trippers. Though visited by specialist sea-kayaking tours, the whole area receives relatively little attention from foreign visitors and is fascinating to explore.

In the far south rivers meander across a coastal plain covered with thick tropical rainforest. The Temash River is lined with the tallest mangrove forest in the country and the Sarstoon River forms the border with Guatemala. The only village here is **BARRANCO**, a small, traditional Garífuna settlement of two hundred people, which you can visit through the village guesthouse programme operated by Toledo Ecotourism (see p.110).

Towards the mountains: Maya villages and ruins

Heading inland from Punta Gorda towards the foothills of the Maya Mountains, you meet yet another uniquely Belizean culture. Here **Mopan Maya** are mixed with **Kekchí** speakers from the Verapaz highlands of Guatemala. For the most part each group keeps to its own villages, language and traditions, although both are partially integrated into modern Belizean life and most people speak English. The villages are connected by road and while there's a basic bus service from Punta Gorda (check with the information offices for times), moving around isn't that easy: in many places you'll have to rely on hitching – and traffic is sparse – or walking. The easiest village to reach is **San Antonio**, served by regular buses from Punta Gorda.

Blue Creek, San Antonio and Uxbenka

About 4km before you reach San Antonio, at *Ray's Cool Spot*, where you can get a meal and a drink, a branch road heads off south and west to the village of **BLUE CREEK**, where the main attraction is the village's namesake – a beautiful stretch of water that runs through magnificent rainforest. Whether you're walking or driving you won't miss the river, as the road crosses it just before it enters the village. To get to the best swimming spot, walk upriver along the right-hand bank (facing upstream), and in about ten minutes you'll come to a lovely turquoise pool. The source, the **Hokeb Ha** cave, is about another fifteen minutes' walk upriver through the privately owned **Blue Creek Rainforest Reserve**. A guide can take you to Maya altars deep in the cave.

Perched on a small hilltop, the Mopan Maya village of **SAN ANTONIO** has the advantage of *Bol's Hill Top Hotel* (community phone ☎07/22144; ③), which offers simple **rooms** and superb views, and is a good place for **information** on local natural history and archeology. The area is rich in wildlife, surrounded by jungle-clad hills and swift-flowing rivers. Further south and west are the villages of the **Kekchí Maya**. The founders of San Antonio were from the village of **San Luis**, just across the border in Guatemala, and they maintain many age-old traditions. Among other things the people of San Luis brought with them their patron saint – opposite *Bol's* hotel is the church of San Luis Rey. The Maya also adhere to their own pre-Columbian traditions and fiestas – the main one takes place on June 13, and features marimba music, masked dances and much heavy drinking.

Seven kilometres west from San Antonio, towards the village of **Santa Cruz**, are the ruins of **Uxbenka**, a fairly small Maya site, superbly positioned on an exposed hilltop, with great views towards the coast. As you climb the hill before the village you'll be able to make out the shape of two tree-covered mounds and a plaza, and there are several badly eroded stelae, protected by thatched shelters. Trucks and buses continue 13km further west to **Jalacte**, near the Guatemalan border, used regularly used as a crossing point by nationals of both countries, though it's not currently a legal entry point for tourists.

San Pedro Columbia and the ruins of Lubaantun

To visit the ruins of Lubaantun from San Antonio, head back along the road to Punta Gorda and after 8km turn left at the track leading to **SAN PEDRO COLUMBIA**, a Kekchí village 4km along the road. Head through the village and cross the Columbia River, just beyond which you'll see the track to the ruins, a few hundred metres away on the left.

Lubaantun, which means "Place of the Fallen Stones" – not its original name – is a major Late Classic ceremonial centre, which at one time covered a large area. The site is on a high ridge and from the top of the tallest building you can (just) see the Caribbean, over 30km away. Maya architects shaped and filled the hillside, with retaining walls as high as 10m, and the pyramids are quite impressive, as is the surrounding forest.

It now seems that the site was only occupied briefly, from 700 to 890 AD, very near the end of the Classic period. The architecture is unusual in a number of ways: there are no stelae or sculpted monuments other than ball court markers, and the whole site is essentially a single acropolis, constructed on a series of low ridges. Another unusual feature is the absence of mortar. In this case the stone blocks are carved with particular precision and fitted together, Inca style, with nothing to bind them.

Perhaps Lubaantun's most enigmatic find came in 1926, when the famous **Crystal Skull** was unearthed here. Carved from pure rock crystal, the skull was apparently found beneath an altar by Anna Mitchell-Hedges (who still has it in her possession), the adopted daughter of the British Museum expedition's leader, F.A. Mitchell-Hedges. The skull was given to the local Maya, who in turn presented it to Anna's father as a token of their gratitude for the help he had given them.

Several places around San Pedro offer **accommodation**. The best are *Dem Dats Doin* (☎07/22470; ④), a sustainable technology farm with one guest room, 2km from the turn-off on the San Antonio road, and the comfortable wooden cabins of *Fallen Stones Butterfly Ranch* (☎07/22167; ⑨), in a fantastic hilltop location 3km beyond the turn for the ruins.

travel details

BUSES

Dangriga to: Belize City (at least 8 daily; 2–3hr); Hopkins (1–2 daily; 50min); Independence (5 daily; 2hr); Placencia (3 daily; 2hr); Punta Gorda (3 daily; 5hr).

Placencia to: Belize City (2 daily; 5hr); Dangriga (3 daily; 2hr).

Punta Gorda to: Belize City (5 daily; 8hr); Dangriga (5 daily; 5hr).

FLIGHTS

Maya Island (☎02/31362) and Tropic (☎026/2012) have flights from **Belize City to Dangriga** (35min), most continuing to **Placencia** and **Punta Gorda**. All flights from Punta Gorda to Belize City call at Placencia and Dangriga.

INTERNATIONAL BOATS

Dangriga to: Puerto Cortés, Honduras (1 weekly on Sat; 3hr).

Punta Gorda to: Puerto Barrios, Guatemala (3 daily; 1hr).

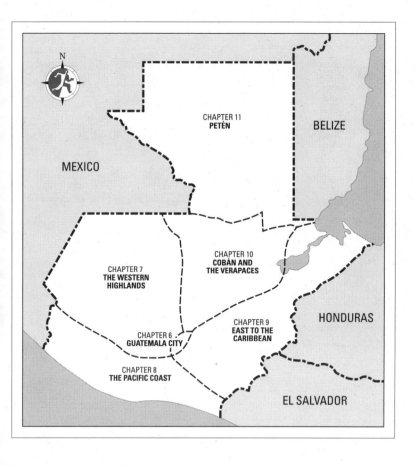

Introduction

Situated across a verdant chunk of mountainous Central American land, **Guatemala** is endowed with simply staggering natural, historical and cultural interest. Though the giant **Maya** temples and rainforest cities have been long abandoned, ancient traditions remain very much alive throughout the Guatemalan highlands. Uniquely in Central America, at least half the population of Guatemala is still Native American, and this rural indigenous culture is far stronger than anywhere else in the region. Countering this is a powerful **ladino** society, characteristically urban and commercial in its outlook. All over the country you'll come across remnants of Guatemala's **colonial** past, with the graceful former capital, Antigua, providing a stunning architectural showcase.

It is this outstanding cultural legacy, combined with Guatemala's mesmeric natural beauty, that makes the country so compelling for the traveller. The Maya temples of **Tikal** would be magnificent in any arena but set inside the pristine jungle of the Mayan Biosphere Reserve, with attendant toucans and howler monkeys, they are bewitching. Similarly, the genteel cobbled streets and plazas of colonial **Antigua** gain an extra dimension with the looming presence of the three giant volcanoes that encircle the town. This architectural wealth is scattered to a lesser degree throughout the country – almost every large village or town boasts a giant whitewashed colonial church and a classic Spanish-style plaza. Though most of the really dramatic Maya ruins lie deep in the jungles of **Petén**, interesting sites are scattered throughout the land, along the Pacific coast and in the foothills of the highlands.

The diversity of the Guatemalan **landscape** is astonishing. Perhaps most arrestingly evident are the backbone of **volcanoes** (some smoking) that divide the flat, steamy *ladino*-dominated Pacific coast from the cool air and pine trees of the largely indigenous western highlands. Most of these volcanoes can be climbed, while there's also less demanding hiking in the highlands: a lovely mixture of green sweeping valleys, tiny cornfields, gurgling streams and sleepy traditional villages. Further east towards the **Caribbean**, the scenery and the people have more of a tropical feel and at Lívingston, life beside the mangrove and coconut trees swings to reggae rhythms and punta rock.

The **rainforests** of Petén, among the best preserved in Latin America, harbour a tremendous array of **wildlife**, including jaguar, lumbering tapir, spiders, howler monkeys, jabiru storks and scarlet macaws. Further south, you may be lucky and catch a glimpse of the elusive quetzal in the cloud forests close to Cobán or see manatee in the Río Dulce. On the Pacific coast three kinds of sea turtle nest in the volcanic sand beaches of Monterrico.

All of this exists against the nagging background of Guatemala's turbulent and bloody **history**. Over the years, the huge gulf between the rich and the poor, between indigenous and *ladino* culture and the political left and right has produced bitter conflict. With the signing of the **1996 Peace Accords** between the government and the ex-guerrillas, the armed confrontation has ceased and things have calmed down considerably, though many of the country's deep-rooted inequalities remain. At the heart of the problem is the red-hot issue of **land reform** – in Guatemala it's estimated that close to seventy percent of the cultivable land is owned by less than five percent of the population. There is also a chronic lack of faith in the **justice system**, which has led to the public lynching of suspected thieves, and general discontent with the high cost of living. Guatemala has very little industry except the foreign-owned export-exclusive *maquila* factories that typically pay their assembly line workers $3–4 for a twelve-hour day.

Despite these structural inequalities, you'll find most Guatemalans are extraordinarily courteous people, eager to help a lost foreigner catch the right bus or find the local post office. Guatemalans tend to be less extrovert than other Central Americans and are quite formal in social situations. Many will automatically assume you are wealthy, since very few Guatemalans ever get to visit another country. Though you may hear complaints about the cost of living, the endemic corruption and the lack of decent jobs, this is not to say that Guatemalans are not patriotic and sensitive to criticisms from outsiders.

■ Where to go

Perhaps the most fascinating part of the entire country is the **western highlands**, where not only is the scenery wildly beautiful, but you'll also find the most interesting Maya villages and amazing fiestas and markets. **Lago de Atitlán** is unmissable, a large highland lake, ringed by sentinel-like volcanoes, whose shores are dotted

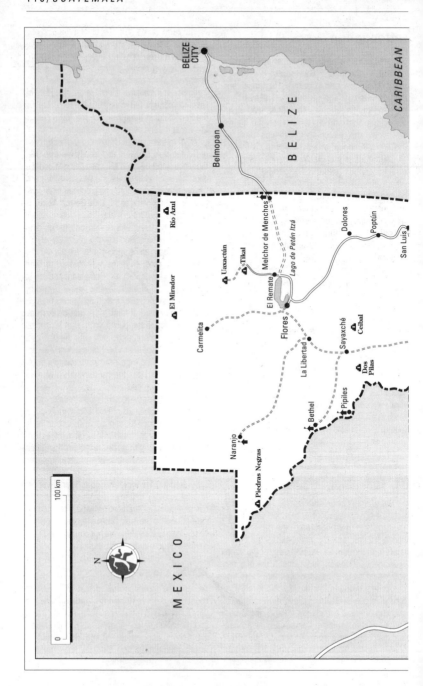

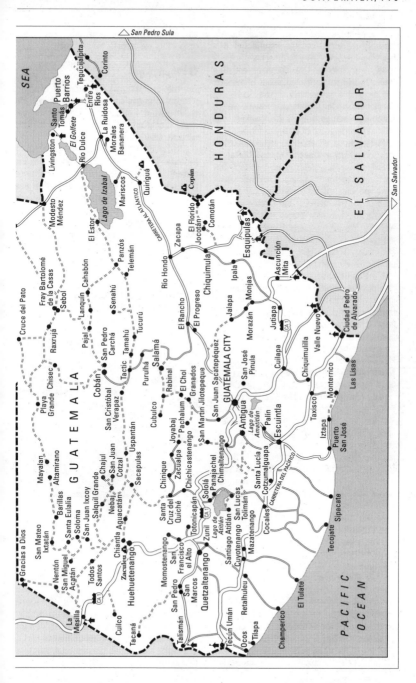

with some of the most traditional indigenous villages in the entire country. **Panajachel** is a booming lakeside town with some excellent restaurants, cafés and textile stores and **San Pedro la Laguna**, on the other side of the lake, has more of a bohemian travellers' scene. For handicrafts, the famous twice-weekly **Chichicastenango market** is unrivalled, with an incredible selection of weavings for sale.

Further scenic excesses lie around the country's second city of **Quetzaltenango (Xela)**, an excellent base for a series of day-trips to nearby hot springs, market towns and volcanoes. Finally, there are the isolated and traditional villages deep in the mountains of the **Cuchumatanes**: perhaps the two best places to head for are **Nebaj** in the Ixil triangle and **Todos Santos** to the north of Huehuetenango. Both are intensely rewarding places to visit with superb scenery, excellent walking and cheap guesthouses.

The **Pacific coast** is generally hot and dull, a strip of black volcanic sand with a smattering of mangrove swamps behind it that blend into the country's most productive farmland. The area is devoted to commercial agriculture and dotted with bustling urban centres; points of interest are thin on the ground. The **beaches** are not as you imagine a Pacific beach to be, except at the wildlife reserve of **Monterrico**, where there is a fine stretch of sand and a maze of mangrove swamps to explore.

If it's real adventure and exploration you seek, nothing can compete with the hidden archeological wonders of **Petén**. This unique lowland area, which makes up about a third of the country, is covered with dense rainforest – only recently threatened by development – that is alive with wildlife and dotted with superb Maya ruins. The only town of any size is **Flores**, from where you can easily reach **Tikal**, the most impressive of all Maya sites. Other dramatic sites like the monumental **El Mirador** require days of tough travel to reach.

In the **east** of the country are the spectacular gorge systems of the **Río Dulce**, the ruins of **Quiriguá** and on the Caribbean coast the funky town of **Lívingston**, home to Guatemala's only black community. Dividing this eastern area from the Petén is another highland region, the **Verapaces**, where there is more stunning alpine scenery and the sleepy coffee centre of **Cobán**.

Guatemala City is of little interest to the traveller except for a couple of museums; it's much better to stay in the colonial capital **Antigua**, just

an hour away, where there are great hotels, restaurants and cafés for every budget.

■ When to go

The bulk of Guatemala enjoys one of the most pleasant **climates** on earth, with typically warm or hot days and mild or cool evenings all year round – only in the lowlands does it get really uncomfortably hot and humid.

The immediate climate is largely governed by **altitude**. The Guatemala tourist board calls the country "the land of eternal spring", and since most places of interest are between 1300 and 1800m (including Guatemala City and Antigua, Lago de Atitlán, Chichicastenango and Cobán), there's some justification in this. However, in Quetzaltenango and the Cuchumatanes mountains the climate can be cool and damp and nights distinctly cold. In low-lying Petén it's a different world, with sticky, steamy conditions most of the year. The Pacific and Caribbean coasts are equally hot and humid, but here at least you can usually rely on the welcome relief of sea breezes.

There is also a **rainy season**, roughly from May to October, which Guatemalans call winter, though the rain is usually confined to the late afternoon and the rest of the day is often warm and pleasant. As a rule it's only in remote parts that rain can affect your travel plans. This is especially so in Petén, where the rainy season extends into December and it's advisable to delay any real exploration until February.

The busiest time for **tourism** is between December and March, when many North Americans seek respite from the cold; and again in July and August – this is also the busiest time for the language schools.

Getting around

For most people, travelling in Guatemala means using the anarchic fume-belching **bus system**: a chaotic mix of fun, frustration and discomfort. While it's possible to remove yourself from this chaos to a certain degree by taking **tourist shuttles** and **flights**, you risk missing out on one of Guatemala's essential experiences. Though in remote areas many buses leave in the dead of night in order to reach the morning markets, we strongly recommend **not travelling after dark**.

Despite a concerted governmental campaign to improve things, Guatemala's road network is still alarmingly inadequate and you'll constantly find yourself stuck behind smoking trucks as you climb up the Carretera Interamericana to Lago de Atitlán or drive down to the Caribbean. Fortunately, whatever the pace of your journey, you always have the spectacular Guatemalan countryside to wonder at.

■ Buses

Buses are cheap and convenient, and can be wildly entertaining. There are two types of service. **Second-class** buses, known as *camionetas* to Guatemalans and "chicken buses" to foreigners are by far the most numerous and easily distinguished by their trademark clouds of thick black fumes. If they look familiar to North Americans that's because they're old school buses (mainly Bluebirds). Second-class buses will usually stop for every possible passenger, cramming their seats, aisles and occasionally roofs: journeys are certainly never dull. Chickens cluck, merengue assaults your eardrums, snack vendors tout for business and the locals gossip and laugh. Almost all second-class buses operate out of **bus terminals**, often adjacent to the local market. Tickets are bought on board and cost around US$1 per hour's journey, though ripping off gringos does go on – check out what the locals are paying.

First-class or **pullman** buses, usually old Greyhounds, are faster and more expensive (around $1.50 an hour) than regular buses and make fewer stops. Each passenger will be sure of a seat to him or herself, and tickets can be bought in advance. They only serve the main routes such as the Carretera al Atlántico and Interamericana, but they will usually stop for you en route if they have space aboard. Pullmans usually leave from the bus company's office rather than the main bus terminal.

■ Taxis

Taxis are available in all the main towns and their rates are fairly low. Except in Guatemala City, meters are nonexistent, so it's essential to **fix a price** before you set off. Local taxi drivers will almost always be prepared to negotiate a price for a half-day or day's excursion to nearby villages or sites.

■ Driving and hitching

On the whole, **driving** inside Guatemala is pretty straightforward and it certainly offers unrivalled freedom as traffic is rarely heavy outside the capital. **Parking and security** are the main problems and in the larger towns you should always get your car shut away in a guarded car park. Most of the main routes are paved but minor roads are often extremely rough. **Fuel** is extremely cheap by European standards, marginally more expensive than in the US. If you plan to head up into the mountains or along any of the smaller roads in Petén, you'll need high clearance and four-wheel drive.

Renting a car takes some of the worries out of driving but is expensive: generally at least US$50 a day (around US$250 a week) by the time you've added the extras. If you do rent, make sure to check the details of the insurance, which often does not cover damage to your vehicle at all.

If you plan to visit the more remote parts of the country then it is almost inevitable that you will **hitch** a ride with a pick-up or truck from time to time. You'll usually have to pay for your lift – around the same as the bus fare. Rule number one is **safety**: it's not a good idea for women to hitch alone and if you don't feel comfortable about getting in someone's vehicle, don't do it.

■ Bikes and motorbikes

Bikes are pretty common in Guatemala and cycling is a popular sport, so you'll be well received and should be able to find a repair shop in most towns. Though cycling is the most exhilarating way to see Guatemala, the country is very mountainous and roads are poor. Most buses will carry bikes on the roof if it all gets a bit too much. You can rent **mountain bikes** in Antigua and Panajachel: see the relevant listings.

Motorbikes can also be an excellent way of getting around and since many locals ride them it's not too hard to locate parts and expertise. There are rental outlets in Guatemala City, Panajachel and Antigua, charging around US$25 a day or US$120 for a week.

■ Boats

The main **ferry** routes are between Puerto Barrios and Lívingston and across Lago de Izabal from Mariscos to El Estor. The two definitive **boat trips** in Guatemala are through the Río Dulce gorge system, starting in either Lívingston or the town of Río Dulce, and across Lago de Atitlán, usually beginning in Panajachel.

■ Planes

The only internal **flight** most people are likely to take is from the capital to **Flores** (from US$60 return), with five airlines offering rival services (see p.153 for further details). However, a new domestic airline, Inter (part of the Taca group), has started flying to various different destinations within Guatemala, and if time is extremely tight you may want to take advantage of their services. Unfortunately, Inter has already gained a poor reputation, with flights being cancelled at very short notice and timetable and fare changes almost monthly. These could be early teething problems but it's essential to check the latest schedules first with a good travel agent like Monarcas (☎8324305) or Rainbow (☎8324202), or with the airline direct (☎3347722).

In theory, Inter operates daily return services between Guatemala City and Puerto Barrios, Santa Cruz del Quiché, Quetzaltenango, Retalhuleu, Cobán and Huehuetenango, plus weekend return flights to the Río Dulce. Fares hover around US$40 to US$60 one-way.

Costs, money and banks

Guatemala is an extremely cheap country to travel in, and the currency, the **quetzal**, has remained remarkably stable throughout the 1990s. The **exchange rate** at the time of writing was Q6.50 to US$1.

It's certainly possible for **budget travellers** to survive on around US$100 a week in Guatemala by sleeping in simple hospedajes, eating at comedores, travelling by local bus and going easy on the beers. Your wallet will suffer in tourism-driven towns like Antigua and Panajachel, and you'll pay for any weaknesses for wine, taxis or shuttle buses. The extremely self-disciplined or fiscally challenged could survive in somewhere like San Pedro la Laguna (see p.188) for as little as US$60 a week. If you can afford to burn a few more quetzales, however, and desire a hotel room with private bath, more varied food and want to take the odd shuttle bus, reckon on US$200 a week. Guatemala has some spectacular hotels at the luxury end of the market – to travel in **real style**, reckon on paying on around US$80 a day, for which you can expect accommodation with period character (plus modern amenities), shuttle buses and the best food in town. Remember that leaving the country you'll be charged an **airport tax** of US$25, payable in cash (either dollars or quetzales).

Travellers' cheques are one of the safest ways to carry money, with American Express, Thomas Cook, Mastercard, and Citibank being accepted in most banks. It's not a sensible idea to take cheques issued in any currency other than US$ – though Lloyds Bank (branches in Guatemala City, Antigua, Puerto Barrios and Escuintla) will cash sterling travellers' cheques.

Credit cards are widely accepted in upmarket hotels, selected restaurants and most travel agencies. You'll need to pay by cash in most smaller hotels and restaurants. Cards may also be used in the country's network of ATMs; if you've a **Visa** card (by far the most useful) Banco Industrial is the first place to head for. **Mastercard** holders will have more of a problem finding functional ATMs, though all branches of Banco G & T should give you an advance.

Finally, a few dollar bills are always handy as many hotels, travel agents and gift shops will cash a greenback when the banks are closed.

Information

Branches of the national tourist board, **Inguat**, are to be found in Guatemala City, Panajachel, Antigua, Flores and Quetzaltenango. They give out glossy brochures and will try to help you with your travel plans. In **Petén**, two Flores-based organizations, CINCAP and ProPetén, provide essential support for jungle trekking (see p.245).

Accommodation

Though Guatemala is undoubtedly a budget travellers' dream, there are plenty of possibilities if you desire a little more comfort. **Accommodation** in Guatemala comes in a multitude of different guises: pensiones, huéspedes, posadas, hospedajes and even hotels. The names don't actually mean that much, though most hotels tend to be towards the top end of the price scale and most hospedajes and pensiones towards the bottom. Breakfast is almost never included in the price. As most small towns have a hospedaje or two, staying in peoples' houses is rare, but at fiesta time many families are keen to rent out a room for a little extra cash.

At the **top end** of the scale (above US$80 a night) you'll find magnificent colonial hotels with authentic interiors in most of the main tourist centres, especially Antigua. In the **mid-range** bracket (US$15–80) there are some brilliant deals available: you can still expect character and comfort, and a private bathroom, but perhaps without any extra facilities. Even at the **budget** end of the scale you should be able to find a clean double room for under US$10 in any town in the country, and in some places this can drop as low as US$2 a person. Usefully, **prices** are all fixed by Inguat, the tourist board; there should be a price posted behind the door of your room. Despite this, it's well worth trying to **haggle** a little, or asking if there are any cheaper rooms. There are no official youth hostels in Guatemala, but you will find the odd dormitory.

It's only on the Pacific and Caribbean coasts and in Petén that you'll need a **fan** or **air-conditioning**; in the highlands you'll sometimes find a logwood fire in the luxury hotels, and heavy-duty blankets in the cheaper places. **Mosquito nets** are very rarely provided, even in the lowland areas, so if you plan to spend some time in Petén or on either coast, it's well worth investing in one, and essential if you plan to so some jungle trekking.

Campsites are extremely thin on the ground in Guatemala. The main cities certainly don't have them and the only places with any decent formal provision for camping are Panajachel and Tikal. However, if you decide to set off into the wilds then a **tent** is certainly a good idea, although even here it's by no means essential as most villages have a simple hospedaje – if not, ask for the mayor (*alcalde*), who should allow you to sleep in the town hall (*municipalidad*).

Eating and drinking

Food doesn't come high in the list of reasons to visit Guatemala. In general Guatemalans are unadventurous eaters and seem to survive on a strict diet of eggs, beans and tortillas – in most towns a pizza is considered extremely exotic. However, in the main tourist centres there's much more choice, and in Antigua you'll be able to feast on numerous different European cuisines, several Asian ones, all-American menus and even Middle Eastern dishes.

Traditionally, Guatemalans eat a **breakfast** of tortillas and eggs, accompanied by the inevitable beans. **Lunch** is the main meal of the day, and this is the best time to fill up as restaurants often offer *comidas corridas*, a set two- or three-course meal that sometimes costs as little as a dollar. It's always filling and occasionally delicious. **Evening meals** are generally more expensive.

■ Where to eat

The first distinction in Guatemala is between the **restaurant** and the **comedor**. Comedores are basic eateries that serve simple food at cheap prices – expect to pay around US$2 for a good feed. In contrast, restaurants are a purely urban phenomenon, and more formal and expensive (US$4 a head and upwards). There are, however, plenty of restaurants with comedor-like menus, and vice versa.

In the larger towns you'll also find **fast-food** joints, modelled on the American originals and often part of the same chains. When you're travelling you'll also come across the local version of fast food: at junctions, buses are besieged by vendors offering a huge selection of drinks, sweets, local specialities and complete meals. Many of these are delicious but you do need to treat this kind of food with a degree of caution and bear in mind the general lack of hygiene.

In most towns there's some kind of pizzeria and a Chinese restaurant: they can make a welcome break from eggs and beans but don't expect anything very authentic. Cakes and pastries are also widely available but tend to be pretty dull and dry.

Vegetarians are hardly catered for specifically, except in the tourist restaurants of Antigua and Panajachel and at a handful of places in Guatemala City. It is, however, fairly easy to get by eating plenty of beans and eggs, which are always on the menu, accompanied by freshly made tortillas. The **markets** also offer plenty of superb fruit and snacks like *tostadas* and *pupusas* (see below).

■ What to eat

Maya cuisine is at the heart of Guatemalan cooking. Maize is an essential – in Maya legend, humankind was originally created from maize – and it appears most commonly as a thin corn pancake, the **tortilla**. The maize is traditionally ground by hand and shaped by clapping it between two hands then toasted on a **comal**, a flat pan of clay placed over the fire. Tortillas are eaten while warm and usually brought to the table wrapped in cloth. The very best have a slightly burnt, smoky taste and a pliable texture. Mexican-style **tamales** (steamed cornmeal often stuffed with meat, wrapped in a banana leaf) are not that common but when you can get them usually delicious.

Beans (*frijoles*) are served as they are in the rest of Central America, either refried (*volteados*) or whole (*parados*) in their own black juice. Almost all truly Guatemalan meals include a portion of beans. In the highlands you'll come across **mosh** (porridge) from time to time. To a lesser extent, **chillies**, usually served in the form of a spicy sauce (*salsa picante*), are the final ingredient in a Maya meal.

Combined with this essentially Maya culinary style, you'll find **ladino-style** food everywhere, often on the same menu. *Bistek* (steak), *pollo frito* (fried chicken) and *hamburguesas* are popular with all Guatemalans. *Chiles rellenos* (stuffed peppers) make a healthy change from other cholesterol saturated dishes and *pepián* (meat stew with vegetables) and *caldos* (meat broths) are usually excellent.

Popular **market snacks** include *pupusas* (thick tortillas topped with crunchy grated salad vegetables) and *tostadas* (corn crisps smeared with avocado, cheese and other toppings).

Finally, on the Caribbean coast there is a distinct **Creole cuisine**, heavily based on fish, seafood, coconuts, plantain and banana.

■ Drinks

To start off the day most Guatemalans drink a cup of weak **coffee**, which is usually loaded with sugar. It's almost impossible to get a decent cup – even in tourism-geared towns you're much more likely to be served brown-coloured slops rather than anything resembling the real thing. Through the day locals drink water or *refresco*, which is a thirst-quenching water-based drink with some fruit flavour added. *Coca-Cola*, *Pepsi*, *Sprite* or *Fanta* (all called *aguas*) are also common and popular. For a healthy treat, order a *licuado*: a thick fruit-based drink with either water or milk added

(milk is safer). **Bottled water** (*agua mineral* or *agua pura*) is almost always available.

Guatemalan **beer** tends to be bland and unexciting and is very rarely available on tap. Woefully, one characterless brew has a near monopoly – the ubiquitous **Gallo** – a medium-strength lager-style beer that comes in 33cl (around US$1) or litre (around US$2) bottles. More interesting but not as widespread is *Moza*, a dark brew with a slight caramel flavour. The best of the lagers is the premium beer *Montecarlo*, which is worth the extra quetzal or two when you can get it. You'll also come across *Dorada Draft*, another dull lager brew, and occasionally *Cabro* which has a little more flavour. Imported brands are very rare.

As for **spirits**, rum (*ron*) and *aguardiente*, a clear and lethal sugarcane spirit, are very popular and correspondingly cheap. *Ron Botran Añejo* is a good rum (around $4 a bottle) while hard drinkers will soon get to know *Quetzalteca*, a local *aguardiente* sold and drunk everywhere, whose power is at the heart of many a fiesta.

Guatemalan **wine** does exist but it bears little resemblance to the real thing. Chilean wines are the best value, with decent bottles available from around US$5 in supermarkets and double that in restaurants.

Opening hours, festivals and holidays

Most offices, shops, post offices and museums are **open** between 8.30am and 5pm, though some take a break for lunch. Bank hours are extremely

---

PUBLIC HOLIDAYS

January 1 New Year's Day

Semana Santa Easter Week

May 1 Labour Day

June 30 Army Day, anniversary of 1871 revolution

August 15 Guatemala City fiesta (capital only)

September 15 Independence Day

October 12 Discovery of America (banks only closed)

October 20 Revolution Day

November 1 All Saints' Day

December 24 from noon

December 25 Christmas

December 31 from noon

convenient, with many opening until 7pm (and some as late as 8pm) from Monday to Friday and until 12.30pm or 1pm on Saturdays.

Archeological **sites** are open every day, usually from 8am to 5pm, though **Tikal** is open from 6am to 6pm (until 8pm with permission). Principal public holidays, when almost all businesses close down, are listed opposite; in villages most shops will be shut during fiestas (see box below).

■ Fiestas

Traditional **fiestas** are one of the great excitements of a trip to Guatemala, and every town and village, however small, devotes at least one day a year to celebration.

Guatemalan fiestas can be divided into two basic models: *ladino* and Maya. **Ladino** towns

and villages celebrate with daytime processions, beauty contests and perhaps the odd marching band with dance halls by night. In the highlands, however, where the bulk of the population is **Maya**, you'll see a blend of religious and pre-Columbian secular celebration. The very finest ceremonial costumes are usually dusted down and worn, and you can expect to see some hugely symbolic traditional dancing, including the *Baile de la Conquista*, which reenacts the Spanish victory over the Maya. Whether *ladino* or Maya, festivals tend to be chaotic, drunken affairs with plenty of dancing and fireworks. If you can join in the mood, there's no doubt that fiestas are wonderfully entertaining as well as offering a real insight into both sides of Guatemalan culture.

GUATEMALAN FESTIVALS

JANUARY
1–5 **Santa María de Jesús**, near Antigua (main action on the 1st and 2nd).
19–25 **Rabinal**, in the Verapaces (main day 21st).
22–26 **San Pablo La Laguna**, Lago de Atitlán (main day 25th).

MARCH
Second Friday in Lent **Chajul**, in the Ixil triangle.

APRIL
24 **San Jorge La Laguna**, Lago de Atitlán.
25 **San Marcos La Laguna**, Lago de Atitlán.

MAY
6–10 **Uspantán** (main day 8th).
8–10 **Santa Cruz La Laguna** (main day 10th).

JUNE
12–14 **San Antonio Palopó**, near Panajachel (main day 13th).
21–25 **Olintepeque**, near Quetzaltenango.
22–25 **San Juan Cotzal**, near Nebaj.
22–26 **San Juan Atitán** (main day 24th).
27–30 **San Pedro La Laguna** (main day 29th).
28–30 **Almolongo**, near Quetzaltenango (main day 29th).

JULY
21–Aug 4 **Momostenango** (most interesting on July 25 and Aug 1).
23–27 **Santiago Atitlán** (main day 25th).
25 **Antigua**.
25 **Cubulco**, in the Verapaces.
31–Aug 6 **Cobán**.

AUGUST
1–4 **Sacapulas** (main day 4th).
9–15 **Joyabaj**, west of Santa Cruz del Quiché (main day 15th).
12–15 **Nebaj** (main day 15th).
15 **Guatemala City**.

SEPTEMBER
12–18 **Quetzaltenango** (main day 15th).
17–21 **Salamá** (main day 17th).
24–30 **Totonicapán** (main day 29th).

OCTOBER
1–6 **San Francisco el Alto** (main day 4th).
2–6 **Panajachel** (main day 4th).
29–Nov 1 **Todos Santos**.

NOVEMBER
1 (All Saints' Day) Celebrations all over, but most dramatic in **Todos Santos** and **Santiago Sacatepéquez**, where massive paper kites are flown.
23–26 **Nahualá** (main day 25th).
22–26 **Zunil** (main day 25th).
25 **Santa Catarina Palopó**, Lago de Atitlán.
30 **San Andrés Xecul**, near Quetzaltenango.
30 **San Andrés Iztapa**, near Antigua.

DECEMBER
7 Bonfires (the Burning of the Devil) throughout the country.
7 **Ciudad Vieja**, near Antigua.
13–21 **Chichicastenango** (main day 21st).

Many of the **best fiestas** include some specifically local element, such as the giant kites at **Santiago Sacatepéquez**, the religious processions in **Antigua** and the horse race in **Todos Santos**. At certain times virtually the whole country erupts simultaneously: **Easter week** is perhaps the most important, particularly in **Antigua** and **Santiago Atitlán**, but All Saints' Day (November 1), when people gather in cemeteries to honour the dead, and Christmas are also marked by celebrations across the land. The festivals listed in the box on p.125 are the pick of the lot.

Mail and telecommunications

Even in small towns, you'll find there's normally a branch of **Telgua**, the national phone company, where you can make international phone calls. Most are open daily from 7am to midnight. Telgua tariffs are ridiculously high, however, and in Antigua, Flores, Panajachel and Quetzaltenango you'll be able to find a shop, hotel or travel agency offering cheaper rates (and no queues). From Guatemala you can only make **collect calls** (reverse charges) to the USA, Canada, Mexico, Italy, Spain, Japan, Switzerland and other Central American countries – not to the UK. Dial ☎171 for the **international operator**. Calling Guatemala from abroad, the **country code** is ☎502. **Local** calls in Guatemala are very cheap, and phone boxes are quite common.

Faxes can be sent or received from any Telgua branch in the country, or often more cheaply through travel agencies, some shops and languages schools. The cheapest method of all for sending a fax is via the **Internet** (see below).

Outgoing Guatemalan postal services are fairly efficient by Latin American standards, and you can **send mail** easily from even the smallest of towns – though it's probably safer to send anything of importance through a private firm. The regular mail service is also extremely **cheap** but not very speedy; airmail letters generally take around a week to the US, a couple of weeks or more to Europe. Alternatively, UPS, DHL and Federal Express all operate in Guatemala. **Sending parcels** through the standard mail service is problematic as there are complex regulations about the way in which they should be wrapped. You may want to use a specialized shipping agency instead: see the

Antigua and Panajachel listings for recommended companies.

Post coming into Guatemala is less reliable. Letters and postcards are normally fine but don't get anyone to send anything valuable or bulky through the regular mail – use a courier service instead. **American Express** on Av la Reforma 9–00, Zona 9, Guatemala City, Central America (☎3311311) will keep mail for card- or chequeholders, though any post office in the country can hold poste restante for you (have it marked Lista de Correos); alternatively, if you've studied with a language school they'll usually keep your mail for you.

Cybercafés are mushrooming throughout the country, though they are largely a foreign-fuelled phenomenon. You'll find them in Antigua, Flores, Quetzaltenango, Guatemala City, Cobán and Panajachel – don't expect to be able to send email from Escuintla or Jalapa. There are also frequent connection problems, what with Guatemala's antiquated phone system. Increasingly, many language schools are getting online and many offer their students cheaper rates to send and receive email than the cybercafés.

The media

After a couple of decades when being a journalist in Guatemala was one of the most dangerous professions on the entire continent, things have cooled down somewhat. The nation's **newspapers** have expanded in both volume and coverage and, in theory, there is little restriction on their freedom, although pressures are still exerted and journalism remains to many in authority a "subversive" profession.

Guatemala has a number of daily newspapers with extensive national coverage and a more limited international perspective. Best of the **dailies** are the forthright and outspoken *El Periódico*, which is often tricky to find, and the more widely distributed *Siglo Veintiuno*. The most popular paper is the *Prensa Libre*, a conservative business-driven institution, though it does have a reasonable sports section. *El Gráfico* is also to the right of centre and broadly supportive of the economic, military and big business elite. Look out for a good **weekly** paper called *El Regional*, which is published in both Spanish and Maya languages. As for the **periodicals**, *La Crónica* is usually a decent read, concentrating on Guatemalan current political affairs and business news with a smattering of foreign coverage.

Not surprisingly for a country so dependent on tourism, there is a substantial **English-language** press in Guatemala. All three of the publications listed below are available free in hotels, bookstores and cafés, and are well worth picking up, both for their features and to keep up to date with the current security situation. Top of the pile is the excellent *Siglo News*, a sister to the daily Spanish-language *Siglo Veintiuno*. This weekly paper is an essential aid to the foreign traveller, offering concise, independent coverage of the main Guatemalan news stories. Other Central American stories are covered, in less detail, and there's also a classified section and news about fiestas and cultural events. The *Siglo's* main rival is the *Guatemala Weekly*, a more lightweight publication, though it does carry some excellent Central America Report stories and comprehensive cultural listings. Finally, the monthly *Revue* magazine, published in Antigua, doesn't seek to cover much political stuff but there's often something interesting in it, with a regional Guatemalan focus and a "volcano of the month" column.

For really reliable, in-depth reporting, *Central America Report* excels, with proper journalistic investigation of controversial news stories like the plight of street children in Guatemala City. It's published by Inforpress Centroamericana and available from their offices at 7 Av 2-05, Zona 1, Guatemala City (☎ & fax 2329034).

As for **foreign publications**, *Newsweek*, *Time* and *The Economist* are all sold in the streets of Guatemala City, particularly on the south side of the main plaza. Some American newspapers are also available: check in the *Camino Real Hotel* bookstore in Guatemala City.

Guatemala has an abundance of **radio stations**, though variety is not their strong point. Most transmit a turgid stream of Latin rock and cheesy merengue, which you're sure to hear plenty of on the buses. There is a host of religious stations, too, broadcasting an onslaught of rabid evangelical lectures, services, "miracles", and so on. If you're visiting Guatemala City, it's worth twiddling your FM dial – there can be some interesting stuff broadcast over the capital's airwaves at weekends, including European techno.

Television stations are also in plentiful supply. Viewers can choose from five local channels and over a dozen cable stations, all of them dominated by American programmes, either subtitled or dubbed into Spanish. Many upmarket hotels and some bars in tourist areas also have direct satellite links to US stations, which can be handy for catching up with the news on *CNN*. The only thing that is seemingly impossible to see is English premier league football action.

Shopping

Guatemalan **craft traditions**, locally known as **artesanía**, are very much a part of modern Maya culture, stemming from practices that in most cases predate the arrival of the Spanish. Many of these traditions are highly localized, with different regions and even different villages specializing in particular crafts. It makes sense to visit as many **markets** as possible, particularly in the highland villages, where the colour and spectacular settings are like nowhere else in Central America

As for **everyday goods**, you'll find that both slide and print film is available in most towns in the country, though monochrome is much less common. Camcorder videotapes are also widely on sale though DV tapes are difficult to find.

■ Crafts

The best place to buy Guatemalan **crafts** is in their place of origin, where prices are reasonable and the craftsmen and women get a greater share of the profit. If you haven't the time to travel to remote highland villages, the best places to head for are Chichicastenango on market days (Thurs & Sun) and the shops and street hawkers in Antigua and Panajachel.

The greatest craft in Guatemala has to be **textile weaving**. Each Maya village has its own traditional designs, woven in fantastic patterns and with superbly vivid colours. All the finest weaving is done on the **backstrap loom**, using complex weft float and wrapping techniques. Chemical dyes have been dominant in Guatemala for over a century now and virtually no natural colourings are used.

One of the best places to start looking at textiles is in Antigua's Nim Po't, 5 Av Norte (☎ & fax 8322681), a large store with an excellent collection of styles and designs. Guatemala City's Museo Ixchel (see p.148) is another essential visit.

You should bear in mind that while most Maya are proud that foreigners find their textiles attractive, for them clothing has a spiritual significance – so it's not wise for women travellers to wear men's shirts or men to wear *huipiles*.

Alongside Guatemalan weaving most **other crafts** suffer by comparison. However, if you hunt around you'll also find good ceramics, baskets, mats, silver and jade. Antigua has the most comprehensive collection of shops. For anything woollen, particularly blankets, head for Momostenango Sunday market (see p.198).

■ Markets

For shopping – or simply sightseeing – the **markets** of Guatemala are some of the finest anywhere in the world. The large markets of Chichicastenango, Sololá and San Francisco el Alto are all well worth a visit, but equally fascinating are the tiny weekly gatherings in remote villages like San Juan Atitán and Chajul, where the atmosphere is hushed and unhurried. In these isolated settlements market day is as much a social event as a commercial affair, providing the chance for villagers to catch up on local news, and perhaps enjoy a tipple or two, as well as selling some vegetables and buying a few provisions. Most towns and villages have at least one weekly event; for a comprehensive list, see p.157.

Safety and the police

Personal safety is a serious problem in Guatemala, partly due to a recent nationwide rise in crime that has also affected tourists. There is little pattern to these attacks, but some areas can be considered safer than others. It's wise to register with your embassy on arrival, try to keep informed of events by reading newspapers, and avoid travelling at night.

Though Guatemala attracts around 600,000 tourists a year and relatively few have any trouble, it's essential that you try to minimize the chance of becoming a victim. **Petty theft** and **pickpockets** are likely to be your biggest worry. Theft is most common in Zona 1 and the bus stations of Guatemala City, but you should also take extra care when visiting markets popular with tourists (like Sololá and Chichicastenango) and during fiestas. Avoid wearing flashy jewellery or waving your money around. When **travelling**, there is actually little danger to your pack when it's on top of a bus; it's the conductor's responsibility alone to go up the roof and collect luggage.

Muggings and **violent crime** are on the increase in Guatemala City. There's not too much danger in the daylight hours but don't amble around at night, especially if you don't know your way around. Stick to the main streets and use buses and taxis. There have also been a few cases of armed robbery in Antigua and attacks on tourists on the Pacaya volcano.

If you are robbed you'll have to report it to the police, which can be a very long process and may seem like little more than a symbolic gesture; however, most insurance companies will only pay up if you can produce a police statement.

Machismo is very much a part of Latin American culture, and many Guatemalan men consider it their duty to put on a bit of a show to impress the Western *gringas*. It's usually best to ignore any such hassle. *Ladino* towns and *cantinas* are the worst places. Indigenous society is more deferential so you're unlikely to experience any trouble in the western highlands. **Homosexuality** is publicly strongly frowned upon – although not theoretically illegal – so it's sensible to be discreet. There's a small gay community in Guatemala City but few clubs or public meeting places. Call the low-key gay helpline on ☎2323335 for more details.

■ The police

For Europeans and North Americans expecting to enter a police state, Guatemala may come as something of a surprise. Though there are a lot of police and soldiers on the streets, there's rarely anything intimidating about their presence. You may even find them gratifyingly helpful.

Guatemala has had a new civilian **police force** since July 1997, trained by experts from Spain, the USA, France and Chile. Monthly pay has been doubled (to US$400) and working shifts cut in an effort to eradicate corruption, but most people have little confidence that crime or corruption will be reduced. Antigua also has a new **tourist police force**, who are being taught English. They will accompany you if you want to visit the Cross overlooking Antigua for a view of the city. There are plans to expand the force to other tourist towns like Panajachel.

If for any reason you do find yourself in **trouble with the law**, be as polite as possible. Remember that bribery is a way of life here, and that corruption is widespread.

■ Drugs

Drugs are increasingly available as Guatemala is becoming a centre for both shipment and production. Marijuana and cocaine are both readily available and cheap heroin is also to be found on the streets.

Remember that **drug offences** are dealt with severely. Even the possession of marijuana could land you in jail – a sobering experience in Guatemala. If you do get into a problem with drugs, it may be worth enquiring with the first policeman if there is a "fine" (*multa*) to pay, to save expensive arbitration later. At the first possible opportunity, get in touch with your embassy and negotiate through them: they will understand the situation better than you. The addresses of embassies and consulates in Guatemala City are listed on p.152. Officially you should **carry your passport** (or a photocopy) at all times.

Work and study

Guatemala is one of the best – and most popular – places in the continent to **study Spanish**. The language school industry is big business, with around fifty well-established schools and many more less reliable set-ups. Thousands of foreigners from all over the world study each year in Guatemala – mainly travellers, but also college students, airline crew and business people.

As for **work**, teaching English is the best bet, though there are always opportunities for committed **volunteers**.

■ Studying Spanish

Most schools offer a weekly deal that includes four or five hours one-on-one tuition a day, plus

---

RECOMMENDED LANGUAGE SCHOOLS

ANTIGUA

Tecún Umán Linguistic School, 6 C Poniente 34 (☎ & fax 8312792).

Proyecto Lingüístico Francisco Marroquín, 7 C Poniente 31 (☎8322886).

Centro Lingüístico Maya, 5 C Poniente 20 (☎ & fax 8320656).

Christian Spanish Academy, 6 Av Norte 15 (☎ & fax 8320367).

Sevilla, 1 Av Sur 8 (☎ & fax 8320442).

La Unión, 1 Av Sur 21 (☎ & fax 8320424).

Probigua, 6 Av Norte 41B (☎ & fax 8320860).

Note that the *Rigoberta Menchú* school has a bad reputation and has no connection at all with Rigoberta or her foundation.

QUETZALTENANGO

La Paz, 2 C 19–30, Zona 1 (☎7614243).

Popwuj, 1 C 17–72, Zona 1 (☎7618286).

Desarrollo del Pueblo, 20 Av 0–65, Zona 1 (☎7622932, ☎ & fax 7616754).

Escuela Juan Sisay, 15 Av 8–38, Zona 1 (☎ & fax 7631684).

Guatemalensis, 19 Av 2–14, Zona 1 (fax 7632198).

Casa de Español Xelajú, 9 C 11–26, Zona 1 (☎7612628).

English Club International Language School, Diagonal 4 9–71 (☎7632198).

Proyecto Lingüístico Quetzalteco de Español, 5 C 2–40, Zona 1 (☎7612620).

HUEHUETENANGO

El Portal, 1 C 1–64, Zona 3 (☎ & fax 7641987).

Xinabajul, 6 Av 0–69 (☎ & fax 7641518).

PETÉN

Eco-Escuela, San Andrés, Lago de Petén Itzá. Contact *ProPetén*, C Centro América, Flores (☎9261370, fax 9260495), or call ☎9288106 (Spanish) or ☎9261370 (Spanish and English). In the USA you can contact Conservation International Eco-Escuela (☎202/973-2264, fax 887-5188).

COBÁN

Instituto Cobán Internacional, 2 C 6–23, Zona 2 (☎ & fax 9521727).

TODOS SANTOS

Language school reservations through Proyecto Lingüístico Quetzalteco de Español (see above).

CHIMALTENANGO

Spanish and Mayan Language School of Chimaltenango, 9 C final, Lote 23, Quintas los Aposentos 1 (☎ & fax 8391492).

full board with a local family, at an inclusive **cost** of around US$130 a week. It's important to bear in mind that the success of the exercise is dependent both on your personal commitment to study and on the enthusiasm and aptitude of your teacher – if you are not happy with the teacher you've been allocated, ask for another. Insist on knowing the number of other students that will be sharing your family house; some schools pack as many as ten foreigners in with one family. Virtually all schools have a student liaison officer, usually an English-speaking foreigner who acts as a go-between for students and teachers, so if you're a complete beginner there will usually be someone around who you can communicate with.

The first decision to make is to choose where you want to study. By far the most popular choices are the towns of Antigua and Quetzaltenango. **Antigua** is undoubtedly an excellent place to study Spanish: a beautiful, relaxed town with several superb schools, a vibrant social scene and plenty of cultural activities. The major drawback is that there are so many other students and tourists here that you'll probably end up spending your evenings speaking English. **Quetzaltenango** (Xela) has a very different atmosphere, with a much stronger "Guatemalan" character and far fewer tourists. Despite it being one of the most popular places in the world to study Spanish, it's still possible to really immerse yourself in the language and local culture. If you already speak some basic Spanish, you could study somewhere where you're unlikely to be able to speak any English at all, such as Huehuetenango, Petén, Cobán and Chimaltenango.

■ Paid and volunteer work

There's always a demand for **volunteers** in Guatemala, and several agencies can help you find work. **CIAO** (Central Index for Appointments Overseas), at present solely devoted to Guatemala, is the first place to start looking – it lists companies looking for professional and semi-skilled volunteers on its Web site at *www.ciao-directory.org*. Alternatively, Central Bureau, 10 Spring Gardens, London SW1A 2BN (☎0171/389 4880), has a section on Guatemala in its book *The Complete Voluntary Service*. Another excellent organization is the UK-based **Guatemala Accompaniment Group**, 1B Waterlow Rd, London N19 5NJ (☎0171/281 4052, fax 272 9243; email *cahrc@gn.apc.org*), who send volunteers to

act as observers in refugee camps holding those who were exiled during the civil war. Potential accompanees need to be able to speak reasonable Spanish and must commit themselves to a minimum of six weeks.

In Guatemala, El Arco, 5 Av Norte 25B, Antigua (☎8320162), is a good walk-in resource centre set up to direct volunteers to projects. In Quetzaltenango, the Escuela Español Xelajú, 9 C 11–26 (☎7612628), runs community projects and encourages its students to help out. Casa Alianza runs a shelter for streetchildren in Guatemala City; volunteers can contact them at Apartado Postal 2704, Guatemala (☎2532965, fax 2533003; email *bruce@casaalianza.org*); in the USA at SJO 1039, PO Box 025216, Miami FL 33102-5216; or in the UK at The Coach House, Grafton Underwood, Northants, NN14 3AA.

Finally, if you'd rather get involved with **wildlife** projects, the ARCAS organization runs two excellent programmes. Near Santa Elena, Petén, is a rescue service for animals taken illegally as pets from the forest; and on the Pacific coast near Monterrico they run a sea turtle hatchery. Volunteers are needed for both projects: the work is demanding and you'll have to commit yourself to a minimum of three weeks. Contact ARCAS first at 1 C 50–37, Zona 11, Guatemala City (☎ & fax 591 4731) or email them at *arcas@pronet.net.gt*

As for **paid work**, teaching English is the best bet; check the English schools in Guatemala City (listed in the phone book). In Antigua there are always a few vacancies for staff in the gringo bars and sales positions in jade showrooms. Many language schools also employ an English speaker as a student co-ordinator. The English language press (*Siglo News*, *Guatemala Weekly* and *The Revue*) and noticeboards in the popular bars and restaurants in Antigua and Quetzaltenango also occasionally advertise vacancies. To work anywhere in Guatemala you'll need to speak some Spanish.

History

The very first humans to inhabit the land we know today as Guatemala were nomadic hunters, who by around 1500 BC had settled to farm maize, beans, squash and chillies – the staples of today's Central American diet. These early farmers, who built villages of thatched roofed houses on the Pacific coast and made pottery, are regarded as the first of the **Maya**, and it's thought that most people spoke a proto-Maya language. In the period after 1500 BC, known as the **Preclassic**, the population steadily began to increase throughout the Maya region (encompassing today's Guatemala and Belize, Mexico's Chiapas, Tabasco and Yucatán peninsula, and western El Salvador and Honduras).

There is little evidence that the early Maya were anything but subsistence farmers until more advanced cultures, the Mexican **Olmec** and **Izapa**, began to filter down the Pacific coast. These Mexican peoples were hugely influential on the Maya region, introducing the Long Count calendar, an early writing system and a polytheistic religion. Evidence of their sculptural skills can be seen at the Pacific coast sites around Santa Lucía Cotzumalguapa and Abaj Takalik, and at the great urban centre of **Kaminaljuyú**, on the outskirts of Guatemala City, where there are substantial Preclassic temple mounds and granite stelae with calendric glyphs.

By the **Middle Preclassic** (1000–300 BC) similar pottery and artefacts, including red and orange jars, dishes and stone *metates*, for grinding corn, were to be found throughout the Guatemalan Maya lands. Temple mounds remained basic and the entire culture was village-based. It is thought that language and religion bonded communities together and that increased harvests enabled more ambitious constructions to be undertaken and initial probes into the science of astronomy to be made. By about 400 BC the settlement of **Nakbé** in Petén had evolved into the most advanced centre in the northern lowlands, a state or chiefdom with over eighty structures, including pyramids and the earliest recorded stelae in the region.

Real advances in architecture came in the **Late Preclassic** (300 BC–300 AD), when large pyramids and temple platforms at numerous sites throughout Guatemala were built in what amounted to an explosion of Maya culture. The principal centres at this time were the cities of Kaminaljuyú, which dominated the central highlands, and the great early settlements in Petén: El Mirador, Nakbé, Uaxactún and Tikal. Traditionally, the early Maya were painted as peaceful peasant farmers and traders, led by astronomer-priests, but in fact these new cities were bloodthirsty, warring rivals fighting for hegemony.

Of all the sites dating from this era, it is the colossal triadic structures of **El Mirador** that are the most astounding. Though almost entirely late Preclassic, the temples are the highest ever built in the entire Maya world, rising to over seventy metres above the forest and connected by a complex system of raised causeways to distant settlements. The scale of El Mirador – covering around sixteen square kilometres – was immense and the city undoubtedly supported of tens of thousands of inhabitants, including engineers, architects, farmers, labourers, and priests. This first great Maya city traded with centres as far away as the Gulf of Mexico, the Pacific and Caribbean coasts and the Guatemalan highlands.

■ The Classic Maya

The development that separates the Late Preclassic from the early **Classic period** (300–900 AD) is the introduction of the Long Count calendar in the Petén lowlands and the development of a recognizable form of writing, which included phonetic glyphs. This appears to have taken place by the fourth century AD and marks the beginning of the greatest phase of Maya achievement.

During the Classic period all the cities we now know as ruined or restored sites were built, almost always over earlier structures. Elaborately carved **stelae**, bearing dates and emblem-glyphs, were erected at regular intervals. These tell of actual rulers and of historical events in their lives – battles, marriages, dynastic succession and so on. As these dates have come to be deciphered they have provided confirmation (or otherwise) of archeological evidence and offered a major insight into the nature of Maya dynastic rule.

Developments in the Maya area were still powerfully influenced by events to the north. The overbearing presence of the Olmecs was replaced by that of **Teotihuacán**, which dominated central Mexico during the early Classic period. Armed merchants, called *pochteca*, operated at this time, spreading the influence of Teotihuacán as far as Petén and the Yucatán. They brought new styles of ceramics and alternative religious beliefs and perhaps preceded a complete military invasion. Whatever happened around 400 AD, the overwhelming power of Teotihuacán radically altered life in Maya lands. Influence spread south, via the Pacific coast, first to Kaminaljuyú on the site of modern Guatemala City and thence to Petén, where **Tikal**'s rise to power must have been helped by close links with Teotihuacán. Both cities prospered greatly: Kaminaljuyú was rebuilt in the style of Teotihuacán, and Tikal has a stela depicting a lord of Tikal on one side and a warrior from Teotihuacán on the other.

Exactly how the various centres related to one another is unclear, but it appears that large cities dominated specific regions though no city held sway throughout the Maya area. Broadly speaking, the culture was made up of a federation of city states, bound together by a coherent religion and culture and supporting a sophisticated trade network. The cities jostled for power and influence, a struggle that occasionally erupted into open warfare.

Intense wars were fought as rival cities sought to dominate one another, with no ruler appearing to gain ascendancy for very long. There were clearly three or four main centres that dominated the region through an uncertain process of alliances. Tikal was certainly a powerful city, but at one time Caracol in Belize defeated Tikal, as shown by a Caracol ball-court marker. Detailed carvings on wooden lintels and stone monuments depict elaborately costumed lords trampling on captives and spilling their own blood at propitious festivals, staged according to the dictates of the intricate and the precise Maya calendar. Copán and Quiriguá were certainly important centres in the southern area, while the cities of the highlands were still in their infancy.

At the height of Maya power, advances were temporarily halted by what is known as the **Middle Classic Hiatus**, a period during which there was little new building at Tikal and after which many smaller centres, once under the control of Tikal, became independent city states. The victory of Caracol over Tikal, some time around 550 AD, may have been a symptom or a cause of this, and certainly the collapse of Teotihuacán in the seventh century caused shock waves through all the civilizations of Mesoamerica. In the Maya cities no stelae commemorating events were erected, and monuments and statues were defaced and damaged. In all likelihood the Maya centres suffered revolts, and warfare raged as rival lords strove to win political power.

However, as the new kings established dynasties, now free of Teotihuacán's military or political control, the Maya cities flourished as never before. Architecture, astronomy and art reached degrees of sophistication unequalled by any other pre-Columbian society. Trade prospered and populations grew: Tikal had an estimated 40,000 people. Many Maya centres were larger than contemporary Western European cities, then in their "Dark Ages".

The prosperity and grandeur of the **Late Classic** (600–800 AD) reached all across the Maya lands: from Bonampak and Palenque in the west, to Labná, Sayil, Calakmul and Uxmal in the north, Altun Ha and Cerros in the east, and Copán and Quiriguá in the south, as well as hundreds of smaller centres. Masterpieces of painted pottery and carved jade (their most precious material) were created, often to be used as funerary offerings. Shell, bone and, rarely, marble were also exquisitely carved; temples were painted in brilliant colours, inside and out. Most of the pigments faded long ago, but vestiges remain, enabling experts to reconstruct vivid images of the appearance of the ancient cities.

■ The Maya in decline

The glory days were not to last very long, however, and by 750 AD political and social changes began to be felt: alliances and trade links broke down, warring increased and stelae were carved less frequently. Cities gradually became depopulated and new construction ceased in present-day Guatemala after about 830 AD. It is uncertain what factors precipitated the downfall of the Maya but it's thought that there may have been peasant revolts against the ruling elite. An increase in population probably put great strains on food production, possibly exhausting the fertility of the soil. Climate changes could also have been influential. By the tenth century, the Maya had abandoned their cities in Petén and those few Maya that remained were reduced to a fairly primitive state.

By the **Postclassic** period (900 AD to the Spanish Conquest) all the city states in Guatemala had collapsed. The decline of Maya civilization in the heartland of Petén brought about a rapid depopulation which prompted an influx of people into the Guatemalan highlands to the south. Along with the Yucatán, this area, formerly a peripheral region of relatively little development, now contained the last vestiges of Maya culture. Small settlements remained scattered throughout the highlands, usually built on open valley floors and supporting large populations with the use of terraced farming and irrigation. Little was to change in this basic village structure for several hundred years.

■ Pre-conquest: the highland tribes

Towards the end of the thirteenth century there was an invasion of the central Guatemalan highlands by a group of **Toltec-Maya** who had controlled the Yucatán until this time. Their numbers were probably small but their impact was profound and following their arrival life in the highlands was radically altered.

What once had been a relatively settled, peaceful and religious society became, under the influence of the Toltecs, fundamentally secular, aggressive and militaristic. The well-organized Toltec quickly established themselves as a ruling elite, presiding over a series of competing tribes. The greatest of these were the **Quiché**, who dominated the central highlands and had their capital, **Utatlán**, to the west of the modern town of Santa Cruz del Quiché. Next in line were the **Cakchiquel**, centred around **Iximché**. On the slopes of the San Pedro volcano on Lago de Atitlán were the **Tzutujil**, while in the west, the **Mam** occupied the area around the modern town of Huehuetenango, with their capital at **Zaculeu**. A number of smaller tribes controlled the high Cuchumatanes mountain region.

To the east, around the modern city of Cobán, were the notoriously fierce **Achi** nation with the **Kekchi** to their north, while around the modern site of Guatemala City the land was controlled by the **Pokoman**. Finally, the **Pipil** occupied the stretch along the Pacific coast. The sheer number of these tribes gives an impression of the extent to which the area was fragmented, and it's these same divisions, now surviving on the basis of language alone, that still shape the highlands today.

The Toltec rulers probably controlled only the dominant tribes – the Quiché, the Tzutujil, the Mam and the Cakchiquel – initially terrorizing the local highlanders and gradually establishing themselves at the top of a new, rigidly hierarchical society. It was the Quiché tribe, with strong Toltec influence, that grew to become the dominant power in the highlands, conquering the neighbouring Mam and Cakchiquel tribes under their great ruler, **Quicab**. After his death in 1475, their empire lost much of its authority and for the next fifty years the tribes were in a state of almost perpetual conflict, fighting for access to the inadequate supplies of farmland. The tribal capitals from this period – Iximché, Zaculeu and Utatlán – are all fortified hilltop sites, surrounded by ravines and man-made ditches.

When the Spanish arrived, the highlands were in crisis. The population had grown so fast that it had outstripped the food supply leaving a situation that could hardly have been more favourable to the conquistadors.

■ The Spanish Conquest

While the tribes of highland Guatemala were warring amongst themselves to the north, in what is now Mexico, the Spanish conquistadors had captured the Aztec capital at Tenochtitlán. Amidst the horrors of the Conquest there was one man, **Pedro de Alvarado**, whose evilness stood out above the rest. He could hardly have been better suited to the job – ambitious, cunning, intelligent, dashingly handsome and ruthlessly cruel.

In 1523, Alvarado arrived in Guatemala via the Pacific coast with a very modest force of a few hundred horsemen, soldiers and Mexican allies. After some minor skirmishes Alvarado confronted the Quiché army, said to be 30,000-strong, at **Xelajú** (present-day Quetzaltenango). Despite the huge disparity in numbers, sling-shot and foot soldiers were no match for cavalry and gunpowder, and the Spanish were able to wade through the Maya ranks. Legend has it that the battle was brought to a close when Alvarado himself slew the Quiché leader **Tecún Umán** in hand-to-hand combat.

By a series of tactical alliances and brilliant, utterly ruthless military manoeuvres, Alvarado's small Spanish force had overpowered all the main highland tribes by 1525. First the Quiché capital, Utatlán, was sacked, then the Tzutujil were defeated on the shores of Lago de Atitlán with the aid of the Cakchiquel, followed by the Pipil of the Pacific coast. Finally, the last of the major highland tribes, the Mam, were conquered after a siege of their fortified capital, Zaculeu. The support of the **Cakchiquel** during this string of relatively easy gains was probably invaluable; the Spanish in fact used the Cakchiquel capital, Iximché, as the base for their campaigns.

Dealing with the more remote tribes proved more difficult and it wasn't until the 1530s that Alvarado managed to assert control over the Ixil and Uspantec. In 1526, the Cakchiquel also revolted and waged a guerrilla war against their former partners, forcing the Spanish from Iximché to a site near the modern town of Antigua (now called Ciudad Vieja). Here, at the base of the Agua volcano, they established their first permanent capital on November 22, 1527.

Meanwhile, one thorny problem remained. Despite all his efforts, Alvarado had been unable to conquer the **Achi** and **Kekchi** tribes who occupied what are now the Verapaz highlands. In the end, Dominican priests under Fray Bartolomé de Las Casas succeeded where gunpowder had failed, and the last of the highland tribes were brought under colonial control in 1540. Thus did the area earn its name of Verapaz – "true peace".

■ Colonial rule

The early years of colonial rule were marked by a turmoil of uprisings, political wrangling and natural disaster. In 1541, following a massive earthquake, a great wall of mud and water swept down the side of Agua volcano, burying the capital. The surviving colonial authorities moved up the valley to a new site (at present-day Antigua), where a new city was established. The new capital controlled the provinces of the **Audiencia de Guatemala** (Costa Rica, Nicaragua, El Salvador, Honduras, Guatemala and Chiapas in Mexico) and was the region's centre of political and religious power for two hundred years. By the mid-eighteenth century its population had reached some 80,000 and the city boasted some of the finest buildings in the hemisphere, until another huge earthquake destroyed the city in 1773 and the capital was moved again to its present-day site.

Colonial society was rigidly structured along racial lines, with pure-blood Spaniards at the top, indigenous slaves at the bottom, and a host of carefully defined racial strata in between. There was very little in the way of instant plunder in Central America – certainly none of the gold and silver of Mexico and Peru – and the **economy** was based on agriculture: livestock, cacao, tobacco, cotton and, most valuable of all, indigo were all farmed. At the heart of the colonial economy was the system of *repartamientos*, whereby the ruling classes were granted the right to extract labour from the indigenous population. It was this that established the process whereby the Maya population were transported to the Pacific coast to work the plantations, a pattern (if no longer state-enforced) that continues to this day.

Perhaps the greatest power in colonial times was the **Church**, whose wealth from sugar, wheat and indigo concessions, based on the exploitation of a Maya labour force, fostered the construction of some eighty churches, plus schools, convents, hospitals, hermitages, craft centres and colleges.

In the countryside, scattered native communities were merged into new Spanish-style towns and villages, making exploitation that much easier. Though Maya social structures were also profoundly altered, in the distant corners of the highlands priests were few and far between and *cofradía* (brotherhood) groups and *principales* (village elders) developed a religion of Catholic and Maya traditions that has persisted to this day.

Even more brutal than the social changes were the **diseases** that arrived with the conquistadors. Waves of plague, typhoid and smallpox swept through a people without any natural resistance to them. It was the devastating impact of these diseases that ensured that the small Spanish invading force was able to maintain control in Guatemala: around ninety percent of the Maya population was wiped out within a few years of the arrival of Alvarado.

Two centuries of colonial rule totally reshaped the structure of Guatemalan society, giving it new cities, a new religion, a transformed economy and a racist hierarchy. Nevertheless, the impact of colonial rule was perhaps less marked than in many other parts of Latin America. Only two sizeable cities had emerged and many outlying areas had received little attention from the colonial authorities. While the indigenous population had been ruthlessly exploited and suffered enormous losses at the hands of foreign weapons and imported diseases, its culture was never eradicated. There was little profit for the Spanish in the mountains – no gold, very little silver and harsh terrain – so the colonists concentrated instead on developing agriculture in more profitable regions like the Pacific coast. In the relative isolation of the highlands, the Maya simply absorbed the symbols and ideas of the new Spanish ideology, fusing Maya and Catholic traditions to create a unique synthesis of old and new world beliefs.

■ Independence

The racist nature of colonial rule had given birth to deep dissatisfaction amongst many groups in Central America. A fundamental issue was Spain's determination to keep wealth and power in the hands of those born in the motherland, a policy that left growing numbers of subjects hungry for power and change. The spark that precipitated independence was Napoleon's invasion of Spain, after which a mood of reform swept through the colonies, including Central America.

Brigadier Don Gabino Gainza, the Captain General of Central America, bowed to liberal demands for independence but still hoped to preserve the colonial power structure when he signed the **Act of Independence** on September 15, 1821. Mexico promptly sent troops to annex Guatemala but by 1823 Guatemala had joined a **Central American federation** with a US-style liberal constitution. Religious orders were abolished, the death penalty and slavery done away with, and trial by jury, a general school system, civil marriage and the Lívingston law code were all instituted.

The liberal era was soon overthrown by a revolt from the mountains. The indigenous population, hit hard by a cholera epidemic and seething with discontent, marched on Guatemala City behind a charismatic leader, the 23-year-old **Rafael Carrera**. Carrera respected no authority other than that of the Church, and upon seizing power he reversed all the liberal reforms with the support of conservative religious and landowning lobbies. Carrera then fought a bitter war against the rest of the Central American federation and Guatemala declared itself a an **independent republic** in 1847. In 1865 Carrera died, at the age of 50, leaving the country ravaged by the chaos of his tyranny and inefficiency. He was succeeded by **Vicente Cerna**, another conservative, who was to rule for the next six years.

Meanwhile, the opposition was gathering momentum yet again and 1867 saw the first **liberal uprising**, led by **Serpio Cruz**. His bid for power was unsuccessful but it inspired two young liberals, Justo Rufino Barrios and Francisco Cruz, to follow suit. In the next few years they mounted several other unsuccessful revolts, and in 1870 Serpio Cruz was captured and hanged.

■ Coffee and bananas

A major turning point in Guatemalan politics came in 1871, when Rufino Barrios departed Mexico with an army of just 45 men and started a **liberal revolution**.

Rufino Barrios was a charismatic leader with tyrannical tendencies (monuments throughout the country testify to his sense of his own importance), who regarded himself as the great reformer and was intent on making sweeping changes. He was undoubtedly a man of action: he restructured the education system, attacked the power of the Church and modernized the University of San Carlos in Guatemala City.

Underneath the new liberal perspective lay a deep arrogance, however. Barrios would tolerate no opposition and developed a network of secret police and an army academy that became an essential part of his political power base.

Alongside all this, Barrios set about reforming agriculture, particularly **coffee farming**. Cultivation had increased fivefold by 1884, creating an economic boom. The railway network was expanded, ports developed and a national bank established. Between 1870 and 1900, the volume of foreign trade increased twenty times. Much of the coffee trade was bound for Germany and many of the plantations owned by an immigrant German elite – reflecting Barrios's perspective that foreign ideas were superior to indigenous ones; the Maya population were regarded as hopelessly inferior.

Maya society was also deeply affected by the coffee boom as Barrios instituted a system of **forced labour** to safeguard harvests. Up to one quarter of the male population were despatched to work on the fincas, where conditions were appalling and the workforce treated with utter contempt. Many lost not only their freedom but also their **land**. From 1873, the government began confiscating land and selling it to the highest bidder, sparking village revolts throughout the western highlands that continued into the twentieth century. The loss of their most productive land also ensured that the Maya became dependent on seasonal labour.

By the early twentieth century, a new and exceptionally powerful player was becoming involved in Guatemala: the **United Fruit Company**. It first moved into Guatemala in 1901 after previous successes in Costa Rica and initially bought a small tract of land on which to grow **bananas**. Soon after, it was awarded railway contracts and built its own port, Puerto Barrios, giving it a virtual monopoly over transport. Large-scale banana cultivation took off and United Fruit got very rich very quickly.

The power of the United Fruit Company was by no means restricted to agriculture, and its influence was so pervasive that the company earned itself the nickname "El Pulpo" (The Octopus). In 1919, President Carlos Herrera threatened to terminate United Fruit Company contracts. He lasted barely more than a year.

Jorge Ubico became president in 1930, inheriting financial disaster. Guatemala had been badly hit by the Depression and though he got trade agreements signed that exempted coffee and bananas from US import duties, he steadfastly supported the United Fruit Company at home.

Internally, Ubico embarked on a radical programme of reform, including a sweeping drive against corruption and a massive road-building effort which won him great popularity in the provinces. Despite his liberal pretensions, however, Ubico sided firmly with big business when the chips were down, always offering his assistance to the United Fruit Company and other sections of the land-owning elite. Peasants were still compelled to work the fincas by a **vagrancy law** and there were more revolts in the late 1930s and early 1940s.

But while Ubico tightened his grip on every aspect of government through internal security and repression, the rumblings of opposition grew louder. In 1944 discontent erupted in a wave of student violence, and Ubico was finally forced to resign after 14 years of tyrannical rule.

■ Ten years of "spiritual socialism"

The overthrow of Jorge Ubico released a wave of opposition that had been bottled up throughout his rule. Students, professionals and young military officers demanded democracy and freedom. The transformation of Guatemalan politics was so extreme a contrast to previous governments that the handover was dubbed **the 1944 revolution**. A new constitution was drawn up, the vote given to all adults and the president prevented from running for a second term.

Juan José Arévalo, a teacher, won the 1945 presidential elections with 85 percent of the vote. His political doctrine was dubbed **"spiritual socialism"** and he immediately set about effecting much-needed structural reforms. Extensive social welfare programmes were introduced: schools and hospitals were built, an ambitious literary campaign launched, the vagrancy law was abolished, and workers were granted the right to union representation and to strike. Some state-owned fincas were turned into cooperatives, and there were other policies to stimulate industrial and agricultural development, though land reform was not seriously tackled. Unsurprisingly, these sweeping reforms angered conservative interests (the army, Church leaders and large landowners) and there were repeated coup attempts.

The next president, **Jacobo Arbenz**, won the election with ease and immediately set out **land reform** proposals in a direct challenge to the US

corporations that dominated the economy. Arbenz enlisted the support of peasants, students and unions to break the foreign dominance and began a series of suits against foreign corporations, seeking unpaid taxes.

In July 1952, the **law of agrarian reform** was passed, stating that idle and state-owned land would be distributed to the landless. The big landowners were outraged. Between 1953 and 1954, around 8840 square kilometres was redistributed to the benefit of some 100,000 peasant families – the first time since the arrival of the Spanish that a government had responded to the needs of the indigenous population. The United Fruit Company lost about half of its property, provoking the US government to accuse the new Guatemalan government of being a communist beach-head in Central America.

In 1954, the CIA (whose director was on the United Fruit Company's board) set up a small **military invasion** of Guatemala to depose Arbenz and install an alternative administration more suited to US tastes. A ragtag invasion army of exiles and mercenaries was put together in Honduras and under CIA supervision invaded the country, prompting Arbenz to resign after failing to get the support of the Guatemalan military. The US approved a new "government" and flew to it to Guatemala aboard a US Air Force plane. Guatemala's "spiritual socialism" adventure had ended.

■ Military rule and guerrilla war

Following the overthrow of Arbenz, it was **the army** that rose to fill the power vacuum, with US support; they were to dominate politics for the next thirty years, sending the country into a spiral of violence and economic decline.

Castillo Armas, the new president, immediately swept away all the reforms of the previous ten years: the 1945 constitution was revoked, all illiterates were disenfranchised, left-wing parties were outlawed, and large numbers of unionists and agrarian reformers were simply executed. All the land that had been confiscated was returned to its previous owners. Hardest hit was the indigenous population as the old order of *ladino* rule was firmly reinstated.

In the following years, corruption, incompetence, outrageous patronage, and economic decline caused by a fall in coffee prices brought Guatemala to its knees. Arevalo even threatened to return to Guatemala and contest the 1963 elections. The possibility was too much for the Guatemalan establishment and the United States and John F. Kennedy authorized another coup in 1963.

The 1960s saw the start of **guerrilla war** – initially confined to the eastern highlands and ruthlessly fought by the army. Though there was a centre-left government in power until 1970, it was the army that really controlled affairs. Political assassination became commonplace as "**death squads**" operated with impunity, killing peasant leaders, students, unionists and academics.

In the 1970 elections the power of the military and the far right was confirmed. **Colonel Arana Osorio** was elected president with the support of just four percent of the population (bearing in mind that only a small percentage was enfranchised). Once in power he set about eradicating armed opposition, declaring that "if it is necessary to turn the country into a cemetery in order to pacify it, I will not hesitate to do so". The reign of terror reached unprecedented levels: students, academics, opposition politicians, union leaders and agrarian reformers were particularly targeted. Some estimate that there were 15,000 political killings in the first three years of Arana's rule.

The limited reforms of the Laugerund government, elected in 1974, were interrupted by a massive **earthquake** on February 4, 1976. The quake left around 23,000 dead, 77,000 injured and a million homeless. The poor suffered the most, while subsistence farmers were caught out just as they were about to plant their corn. On the Caribbean coast, Puerto Barrios was almost totally destroyed and remained cut off from the capital for several months.

In the wake of the earthquake, during the process of reconstruction, many of the victims felt the time had come to take action. New trade unions and a new guerrilla organization, the **EGP**, emerged with predictable army reactions: daily disappearances, murders and atrocities. In 1977 President Carter suspended all military aid to Guatemala because of the country's appalling human rights record. Guatemala continued to press its longstanding claim to **Belize**, but failed to gain international support.

In 1978 elections were again dominated by the army, who procured a victory for **Lucas García**, the most murderous of all Guatemala's leaders. All opposition groups met with severe repression. The economy took a battering, while several guerrilla armies started developing strongholds in the highlands. There was a major massacre within a month in the village of Panzós, Alta Verapaz – a

hundred villagers were shot by the army. Political opponents, including rival Christian Democrat politicians, were assassinated by death squads and **Vinicio Cerezo**, the party's leader, was forced into hiding. A peaceful occupation of the Spanish embassy by demonstrators ended with the security forces burning the building to the ground, resulting in the death of 39 people. Spain broke off diplomatic relations for over five years.

The rural guerrilla war intensified. Army casualties rose to 250 a month, and the demand for conscripts grew rapidly. Israeli military aid replaced American. The guerrilla groups had an estimated 6000 combatants and some 250,000 unarmed collaborators. Peasants were massacred in their thousands while in the towns victims included students, journalists, academics, politicians, priests, lawyers, teachers and unionists. Tens of thousands fled to become **refugees** in Mexico. The Catholic Church withdrew all its clergy from Quiché after a number of priests were murdered. It's estimated that around 25,000 Guatemalans were killed during the four years of the Lucas regime.

In 1982 a successful coup was engineered by **Ríos Montt**, who even today remains one of the most powerful political figures in Guatemala. Ríos Montt was a committed evangelical Christian who was, above all, determined to restore law and order, eradicate corruption, and defeat the guerrillas. Repression dropped overnight in the cities, corrupt police and army officers were forced to resign, and trade and tourism began to return.

However, in the highlands the war intensified as Ríos Montt declared that he would defeat the guerrillas by Christmas. By a highly successful (and locally detested) programme, villagers were organized into **Civil Defence Patrols** (PACs), armed with ancient rifles, and told to patrol the countryside. The guerrillas' support infrastructure was immediately undermined and villagers were forced to take sides, caught between the attraction of guerrilla propaganda and the sheer brutality of the armed forces. Significant gains were made against the guerrillas, but as fighting intensified thousands of highland Maya fled into Mexico.

Little progress was made towards democratic reform, however. The Catholic church had become alienated and in 1983 Ríos Montt was overthrown by yet another military coup – this one backed by a US government keen to see Guatemala set on the road to democracy. Although the rural repression, death squads and disappearances continued under the new president, General Mejía Víctores, elections were held for an 88-member Constituent Assembly in July 1984. GAM, a new mutual support group for families of the "disappeared", brought the human rights abuses in Guatemala to international media attention. In November 1985, the first legitimate elections in thirty years were held.

■ Civilian rule

The elections were won by **Vinicio Cerezo**, a Christian Democrat who was not associated with the traditional ruling elite. In the run-up to the election he offered a programme of reform that he claimed would rid the country of repression.

Once in office, however, Cerezo declared that the army still held 75 percent of power and throughout his six-year rule he adopted a non-confrontational approach. Above all he avoided upsetting big business interests, landowners and generals. Political killings did drop but murder was still a daily event in Guatemala in the late 1980s and the guerrilla war continued to rage in remote corners of the highlands.

In many ways the Cerezo administration was a bitter disappointment to the Guatemalan people and by the time the decade drew to a close it was clear that the army was still actively controlling political opposition. The fate of the disappeared remained unsolved. Human rights leaders became victims of death squads. Land reform had yet to be tackled and 65 percent of the population remained below the poverty line. Acknowledging that his greatest achievement had been to survive, Cerezo organized the country's first civilian transfer of power for thirty years in 1990.

The 1990 elections were won by **Jorge Serrano**, an engineer and evangelical with a centre-right economic position. His administration once again proved both uninterested and incapable of effecting any real reform or bringing to an end the civil war. The level of human rights abuse remained high, death squad activity continued, the economy remained weak and the army was still a powerful force, using intimidation and murder to stamp out opposition. Economic activity was still controlled by a tiny elite: less than two percent of landowners owned more than 65 percent of the land, leaving some 85 percent of the population living in poverty, with little access to health care or education.

Nevertheless, Guatemala's dispossessed and poor continued to clamour for change. Maya peasants became increasingly organized and influential, denouncing the continued bombardment of villages and rejecting the presence of the army and the system of civil patrols. Matters were brought into sharp focus in 1992 when **Rigoberta Menchú** was awarded the Nobel Peace Prize for her campaigning work on behalf of Guatemala's indigenous population. In spite of the efforts of the Serrano administration, the country's civil war still rumbled on and three main guerrilla armies, united as the **URNG**, continued to confront the army.

Small groups of refugees began to return from exile in Mexico and start civil communities, though an estimated 45,000 still remained. The territorial dispute with **Belize** was officially resolved when the two countries established full diplomatic relations in 1991; but the decision to recognize Belize as an independent country provoked hostility with ultra-nationalists and the Guatemalan military.

By early 1993 Serrano's reputation had plummeted following a series of **scandals** involving corruption and his backing of a casino and race track development that had suspected links with Colombian drug cartels. Despite his membership of no fewer than four evangelical churches, Serrano had supported a venture dependent on gambling and alcohol consumption that was probably financed by cocaine barons.

In **May 1993** Serrano responded to the wave of popular protest with a **self-coup**, declaring he would rule by decree because the country was endangered by civil disorder and corruption. He also argued that the drug mafia planned to take over Guatemala; few were convinced and the US responded by suspending its annual $67 million of aid. Basically he wanted to hang onto power and talked the generals into supporting him. Protests from the left and right got Serrano removed after just two days and another army appointee was also rejected through popular protest. The whole sorry affair revealed much about Guatemala: that the army (backed by big business and landowners) allowed civilians to run the government so that they could get on with the more serious business of running the country. Guatemala still retained its hopelessly unbalanced structure but the army were now susceptible to the force of popular protest.

Congress finally appointed **Ramiro León de Carpio**, the country's human rights ombudsman, as the new president. One of his first moves was a reshuffle of the senior military command, although he rejected calls for revenge, declaring that stability was the main goal. There was great early optimism at Carpio's appointment but public frustration quickly grew as the new government failed to address fundamental issues: crime and land ownership, tax and constitutional reform. Some progress was made in peace negotiations with the URNG guerrilla leadership but the question of indigenous rights remained unsolved.

■ Arzú and the peace accords

The **1996 presidential elections** demonstrated above all the country's increasing lack of faith in the electoral process, which had failed to bring any real change after the return to civilian rule in 1986. Some 63 percent of registered voters stayed at home and it was only a strong showing in Guatemala City, where **Alvaro Arzú** had previously served as mayor, that ensured his election. Arzú represents Guatemala's so-called modernizing right, his party (**PAN**, the National Advancement Party), has strong oligarchic roots and is committed to private-sector-led growth and the free market. Nevertheless, many were surprised as he quickly adopted a relatively progressive stance, shaking up the armed forces in bold early manoeuvres that left seasoned political observers holding their breath in anticipation.

Arzú moved quickly to bring an end to the 36-year civil war, meeting the URNG guerrilla leaders, and working towards a final settlement. The **Peace Accords**, signed on December 29, 1996, concluded almost a decade of talks and terminated a conflict that had claimed over 150,000 lives. The core purpose of the Peace Accords is to investigate previous human rights violations through a Truth Commission overseen by MINUGUA (the UN mission to Guatemala), to recognize the identity of indigenous people and to eliminate discrimination and promote socio-economic development for all Guatemalans. Though the aims of the peace accords are undeniably ambitious, there has been little real progress as yet – Guatemalans are weary of such promises and for many the rhetoric appears all too familiar. The cards are, as ever, heavily stacked against progressive change, though happily there has at least been a remarkable transformation of the political landscape with extremely few recent cases of politically related violence. The left wing and Maya rights groups have become much more confident in pursuing the freedom of organization, protest and participation that has been denied for centuries.

By 1998, the early enthusiasm for the initial changes the Arzú administration had ushered through had waned somewhat within Guatemala and the same fundamental problems remain. **Land reform** and **Maya issues** are perhaps the most delicate (and potentially explosive) political topics. Somewhat inevitably given the grotesquely unequal land ownership within the country, bitter land disputes have arisen resulting in deaths as squatters have clashed with security forces. Large swathes of the Petén jungle continue to be cut down by campesinos and timber companies, and more and more marginal plots are being farmed throughout the land. The indigenous Maya people, who number over half of Guatemala's population, are still grossly disadvantaged, subject to institutionalized racial discrimination and, despite the Indigenous Rights Accord of 1995, seem likely to remain so for the foreseeable future.

The **rising cost of living** is another problem for virtually the entire population – many day-to-day essentials cost little less than they do in the USA or Europe. **Unemployment** and underemployment are also rising: Guatemala has very little industry to speak of except for foreign-owned *maquila* factories where garments are assembled for export to the USA and Korea. These factories typically pay no tax or import-export duty and pay their workers a daily wage of around three or four dollars. Around 70,000 Guatemalans (mainly women) were working in these factories in 1997.

Partly fuelled by this lack of opportunity, there has been a nationwide rise in the **crime rate**. Guatemala, despite its small population of 12 million, has the fourth-highest incidence of kidnapping in the world (around 1000 people in 1997). Petty theft, muggings and armed robbery are all on the increase, affecting every social class including the super wealthy and, of course, tourists. Finally, **corruption** is still endemic, despite the introduction of a new **police force**.

Guatemala's immediate future is extremely precarious. On the positive side there has been a visible liberalization of the political landscape, as the left, human rights groups, trade unions and indigenous rights organizations have felt confident enough to become involved in mainstream national politics. A sharp reduction in politically related violence since the signing of the Peace Accords enabled the left to participate in political debate with a freedom not evident for over forty years.

This mood of optimism was shattered when **Bishop Juan Gerradi** was murdered in April 1998, two days after publishing a long-awaited human rights investigation that blamed the military for most of the deaths and atrocities of the previous thirty years. Though Guatemalans have been long accustomed to horrific levels of political violence, the bishop's assassination stunned the nation. Most had believed that the days of disappearances and death squads were over; as one newspaper put it, "This wasn't supposed to happen. Not any more."

Whether Bishop Gerradi's murder represents an incident of isolated brutality or a return of more sinister times remains to be seen, but it certainly demonstrated the acute fragility of Guatemalan democracy. Most observers reason that it was an action sanctioned by a military intent on preserving its dominant power base under the growing challenge from myriad different pressure groups, which are increasingly well organized and less easily intimidated. The public support is there: hundreds of thousands attended a silent protest in the capital following Gerradi's murder. In communities throughout the country, there is an intense desire for a new start, for some stability after more than thirty years of conflict, as ex-guerrillas and ex-military settle to start new lives, living together as neighbours. Huge obstacles remain, though, and in many ways the work to reshape Guatemala has just begun.

CHAPTER 6

GUATEMALA CITY

Guatemala's capital sprawls across a sweeping highland basin, surrounded on three sides by low hills and volcanic cones. Chaotic, congested and polluted, **GUATEMALA CITY** is, in many ways, the antithesis of the rest of the country. The capital was moved here in 1776, after the seismic destruction of Antigua (see the Western Highlands chapter), but the site had been of importance long before the arrival of the Spanish. These days, its shapeless and swelling mass, ringed by shantytowns, ranks as the largest city in Central America. It's home to around three million people – about a quarter of Guatemala's population – and is the undisputed centre of politics, power and wealth.

The city has an intensity and vibrancy that are both its fascination and its horror, and for many travellers a trip to the capital is an exercise in damage limitation, struggling through a swirling mass of bus fumes and crowds. The centre is now run-down and polluted and the affluent middle classes have long since fled to the suburbs. It is certainly not somewhere you visit for its beautiful architecture but it does have a sight or two and a couple of good museums.

Like it or not – and many travellers don't – Guatemala City is the crossroads of the country, and you'll certainly end up here at some time, if only to hurry between bus terminals or negotiate a visa extension. Once you get used to the pace, it can offer a welcome break from life on the road, with cosmopolitan restaurants, cinemas, shops and metropolitan culture. And if you really can't take the city, it's easy enough to escape: buses leave every few minutes, day and night.

Some history

The pre-conquest Maya city of **Kaminaljuyú**, whose ruins are still scattered amongst the western suburbs, was well established here two thousand years ago. As a result of an alliance with the great northern power of Teotihuacán (near present-day Mexico City) in early Classic times (250–550 AD), Kaminaljuyú came to dominate the highlands and eventually provided the political and commercial backing that fostered the rise of Tikal (see p.249). The city was situated at the crossroads of the north–south and east–west trade routes and at the height of its prosperity it was home to a population of some fifty thousand; however, following the decline of Teotihuacán around 600 AD, Kaminaljuyú was surpassed by the great lowland centres that it had helped to establish. Soon after their rise, some time between 600 and 900 AD, the city was abandoned.

Seven centuries later, when Alvarado entered the country, the fractured tribes of the west controlled the highlands and preoccupied the conquistadors. The Spanish ignored the possibility of settling here until the devastating **1773 earthquake** that forced them to flee disease-ridden Antigua and establish a new capital. The new city was named Nueva Guatemala de la Asunción by royal decree and was officially inaugurated on January 1, 1776.

The splendour of the former capital was hard to re-establish and the new city's growth was steady but by no means dramatic. An 1863 census listed just 1206

For an explanation of **accommodation price codes**, see p.123.

residences and the earliest photographs show the city was still little more than a large village with a theatre, a government palace and a fort. One of the factors retarding the city's growth was the existence of a major rival, Quetzaltenango. When it too was razed to the ground by a massive earthquake in 1902, many wealthy families moved to the capital, finally establishing it as the country's primary city.

Since 1918, Guatemala City has grown at an incredible rate, mainly due to an influx of rural immigrants. The steady flight from the fields, characteristic of developing countries, was aided and abetted by a chronic shortage of land and, in the 1970s and 1980s, by internal refugees escaping rural violence. Many of these displaced people, for the most part Maya, feel unwanted and unwelcome in the city. The divisions that cleave Guatemalan **society** are at their most acute in the capital's crumbling streets. While the wealthy elite sip coffee in air-conditioned shopping malls and plan their next visit to Miami, Zona 1, the heart of the city, has been left to disintegrate into a threatening treeless tangle of fume-choked streets, largely devoid of any kind of life after dark. A small army of **street children** live rough, scratching a living from begging, prostitution and petty crime, and there is strong evidence of "social cleansing" by the security forces. Glass skyscrapers rise alongside colonial churches and shoeless widows peddle cigarettes and sweets to designer-clad nightclubbers. Guatemala City has, in many ways, much more in common with Cairo or Bogotá than with the rest of the country.

Arrival and information

Arriving in Guatemala City for the first time, it's easy to feel overwhelmed by its scale, with suburbs sprawled across some nineteen **zones**, but you'll find that the central area, which is all that you need to worry about, is really quite small.

Broadly speaking, the city divides into two distinct halves. The northern section, centred on **Zona 1**, is the old part of town, containing the **parque central**, most of the budget hotels, shops, restaurants, cinemas, the post office, and many of the bus companies. This part of the city is cramped, congested and polluted but bustling with activity. The two main streets are 5 and 6 avenidas, both thick with street traders, fast-food joints and copious neon.

To the south, acting as a buffer between the two halves of town, is **Zona 4**, home of the administrative centre or Centro Cívico, the **tourist office** and the national theatre. The other great landmark is the Zona 4 **bus terminal**, a crazy world of peripatetic humanity and exhaust fumes.

The southern half of the city, **Zona 9** and **Zona 10**, is the modern, wealthy part of town, split in two by **Avenida la Reforma**. Here you'll find exclusive offices, apartment blocks, hotels and shops and Guatemala's most expensive nightclubs, restaurants and

GUATEMALA CITY: CENTRE

ZONAS 9 & 10
ACCOMMODATION

Camino Real	3
Holiday Inn	4
Hotel Carillon	1
Hotel Casa Santa Clara	5
Hotel el Dorado	2

See 'Guatemala Zona 1' Map

ADDRESSES IN GUATEMALA CITY

The system of street numbering in the capital may seem a little confusing at first and it is complicated by the fact that the same calles and avenidas can exist in several different zones. Always check the zone first and then the street. For example "4 Av 9–14, Zona 1" is in Zona 1, on 4 Avenida between 9 and 10 calles, house number 14.

cafés. Many of the embassies and two of the country's finest museums are also here. Continuing south, the neighbouring zonas 13 and 14 are rich leafy suburbs and home to the airport, zoo and more museums and cinemas.

By air
Aurora airport is on the edge of the city in Zona 13, some way from the centre. The domestic terminal, though in the same complex, is separate and entered from Av Hincapié. Inside the airport there's a Banco del Quetzal for **exchange**, a **tourist office** (daily 6am–9pm), and a **Telgua** office for making phone calls (open 24hr). Much the easiest way to get to and from the airport is by **taxi**: you'll find plenty of them waiting outside the terminal. The fare to or from Zona 1 costs around US$10, to Antigua around US$25. Buses also leave from directly outside the terminal, across the concrete plaza, dropping you in Zona 1, either on 5 Av or 9 Av.

By bus
If you're travelling by **first-class** (pullman) bus you'll arrive either at the bus company's own terminal – most of them are in Zona 1 – or at one of the two new terminals, which should be fully functioning by 1999. The new **Meta del Norte** terminal in Zona 6 will serve all routes to Petén, Cobán and the Caribbean; the **Central de Mayoreo** terminal in Zona 12 will be the base for routes to the Western Highlands, the Pacific coast and Mexico. Brand-new Volvo cross-city buses will connect the two with each other and the centre of town.

If you've arrived by **second-class** "chicken bus" from Antigua you'll arrive in Zona 1 at the junction of 18 C, between 4 and 5 Av. The **Zona 4 terminal** operates second-class buses to the Western Highlands and the Pacific and the **Zona 1** terminal near the old train station continues to send second-class services to the east of the country.

Information
Inguat, the **tourist office**, is at 7 Av 1–17, Zona 4 (Mon–Fri 8.30am–4.30pm, Sat 8.30am–1pm; ☎3311333, fax 3318893). At the information desk, on the ground floor, you can buy a half-decent **map** of the country and city. There's usually someone who speaks English. For detailed hiking maps, go to the Instituto Geográfico Militar, Av las Américas 5–76, Zona 13 (Mon–Fri 8am–4pm).

City transport

As in any big city, coping with the public transport system takes time. Even locals can be bamboozled by Guatemala's seemingly anarchic web of **bus routes**. In Zona 1 buses #82 and #83 stop on **10 Av**, while buses to many different parts of the city run along **4 Av**. Destinations are posted on the front of the bus. Buses run from around 6 or 7am

The main **bus companies**, their addresses and routes are all given at the end of this chapter on p.154.

USEFUL BUS ROUTES

#71 Connects 10 Av, Zona 1, the Centro Cívico and the immigration office on Av la Castellana.

#82 Starts in Zona 2 and continues through Zona 1 along 10 Av, then past the Centro Cívico in Zona 4 and on to Av la Reforma before turning left at the Obelisco. The route passes many of the embassies, the American Express office, the Popol Vuh and Ixchel museums and the Los Próceres shopping centre.

#83 To and from the airport from Zona 1 on 10 Av.

Terminal Any bus marked "terminal", and there are plenty of these on 4 Av in Zona 1, will take you to the main bus terminal in Zona 4.

Bolívar/Trébol Any bus marked "Bolívar" or "Trébol" will take you along the western side of the city, down Av Bolívar and to the Trébol junction – for connections to the Western Highlands.

until about 10pm. Guatemala City has a ferocious **rush hour** and many roads throughout the city are jammed between 7.30 and 9am and from 4.30 to 7pm.

There are currently both metered and non-metered **taxis**. If you can't face the complexities of the bus system, or it's late at night, the excellent new metered taxis are comfortable and cheap; Amarillo (☎3321515; 24hr) are highly recommended and will pick you up from anywhere in the city. The fare from Zona 1 to Zona 10 is US$4–5. There are plenty of non-metered taxis around too – you'll have to use your bargaining skills with these and fix the price beforehand. You may also see the odd **Thai tuk-tuk** buzzing around the city streets, Bangkok-style – these are very quick and cheap.

Accommodation

The luxury **hotels** are mostly in a cluster in Zona 10, with the majority of the budget and mid-range places conveniently grouped in central and eastern Zona 1. Zona 1 is not a great place to be wandering around in search of a room. Book ahead and be sure to take a taxi if you arrive after dark.

Budget hotels

Hotel Fenix, 7 Av 15–81, Zona 1 (☎2516625). Safe, friendly and vaguely atmospheric, set in an old, warped, wooden building. Café downstairs and some rooms with private bathroom. ②.

Hotel Hernani, corner 15 C and 6 Av A, Zona 1 (☎2322839). Comfortable old building with good, clean rooms, all with their own shower. Close to being the best budget deal in town. ②.

Pensión Meza, 10 C 10–17, Zona 1 (☎2323177 or 2534576). Infamous budget travellers' hang-out; cheap and laid-back, with plenty of 1960s-style decadence. Fidel Castro and Che Guevara stayed here – the latter in room 21. Dorms and doubles, some with private shower. Noticeboard, ping-pong, music all day, and the owner, Mario, speaks good English. ①–②.

Hotel Monteleone, 18 C 4–63, Zona 1 (☎2382600, fax 2382509). Rooms are attractively decorated, with quality mattresses and bedside lamps, and some with private bath. The best value in town, extremely clean and safe and right by the Antigua terminal, but not the best area to be in after dark. ②–③.

Hotel San Martin, 16 C 7–65, Zona 1 (☎2380319). Very cheap, clean and friendly, this is among the best deals at the lower end of the scale. Some rooms with private bath. ②.

Hotel Spring, 8 Av 12–65, Zona 1 (☎2326637, fax 2320107). Excellent deal, though usually full of Peace Corps volunteers. Rooms are set around a pretty colonial courtyard and some have private bath. Safe location, free mineral water, breakfast available. ②–③.

Mid-range hotels

El Aeropuerto Guest House, 15 C A 7–32, Zona 13 (☎3323086). Five minutes' walk from the international airport: call for a free pick-up or else walk across the grass outside and follow the road to the left. A pleasant, convenient and very comfortable hotel; all rooms have private showers, hot water and fluffy towels. ⑤.

Hotel Carillon, 5 Av 11–25, Zona 9 (☎ & fax 3324036). If you'd rather not enter the turmoil of Zona 1, this place is good value for the location. It is wood-panelled throughout and the rooms are well appointed. ⑤.

Hotel Hincapié, Av Hincapié 18–77, Zona 13 (☎3327771, fax 3374469). Under the same management as the *El Aeropuerto* and conveniently located for the domestic terminal. Rates include local calls, continental breakfast, and transport to and from the airport. ⑤.

Hotel PanAmerican, 9 C 5–63, Zona 1 (☎2326807, fax 2518749). The city's oldest smart hotel, very formal and civilized, with a strong emphasis on Guatemalan tradition. Cable TV, continental breakfast and airport transfer included. Brilliant for Sunday breakfast. ⑥.

Hotel Posada Belén, 13 C A 10–30, Zona 1 (☎2534530, fax 2513478). Tucked down a side street in a beautiful old building. Supremely quiet, safe and very homely, with its own restaurant. No children under five. ⑥.

Chalet Suizo, 14 C 6–82, Zona 1 (☎2513786, fax 2320429). Friendly, comfortable and very safe, as it's right opposite the police headquarters. Nicely designed, spotlessly clean and all very Swiss and organized, with left luggage and a new café that's open all day. No double beds. ④–⑤.

Luxury hotels

Camino Real, Av la Reforma and 14 C, Zona 10 (☎4484633, fax 3374313). The favoured address for visiting heads of state and anyone on expenses, this hotel continues to lead in the luxury category, in spite of increasing competition from newer places. Rooms costs US$180. ⑨.

Hotel Casa Santa Clara, 12 C 4–51, Zona 10 (☎3391811, fax 3320775). Small, beautifully appointed hotel that also boasts a quality in-house Middle Eastern restaurant. ⑦.

Hotel el Dorado, 7 Av 15–45, Zona 9 (☎3317777, fax 3321877). In the same category as the *Camino Real*; luxurious and comfortable rooms cost US$140. ⑨.

Holiday Inn, 1 Av 13–22, Zona 10 (☎3322555, fax 3322584). First-class hotel, within walking distance of the city's best upmarket shops, bars and restaurants. Best value in this category, with rooms for US$140. ⑨.

Hotel Royal Palace 6 Av 12–66, Zona 1 (☎ & fax 3324036). Comfortable, Best Western-owned landmark right in the heart of Zona 1; avoid the noisy streetside rooms. Seasonal bargain rates. ⑦.

The City

Though few people come to Guatemala City for the sights, there are some places well worth visiting while you're here. The Ixchel and Popol Vuh **museums** are particularly good; there's the odd impressive building in **Zona 1** and, dotted across the southern half of the city, some more outlandish modern structures.

Zona 1: the old city

The hub of the old city is **Zona 1**, which is also the busiest and most claustrophobic part of town. This is a squalid world of faceless concrete blocks, broken pavements, parking lots and plenty of noise and dirt. However, 5 and 6 avenidas, the city's principal shopping area, harbour a certain brutal fascination and are the most exciting part of the capital, thick with street vendors and city bustle.

The heart of the capital, the windswept **Parque Central**, is also the country's political and religious centre. All distances in Guatemala are measured from here. A soulless place patronized by bored taxi drivers, *limpiabotas* (shoeshiners) and pigeons, it only really comes alive on Sundays and public holidays, when a tide of Guatemalans descend on the

GUATEMALA CITY: ZONA 1

ACCOMMODATION

Chalet Suizo	5	Hotel Posada Belén	10	
Hotel del Centro	2	Hotel Royal Palace	3	
Hotel Fenix	7	Hotel San Martin	8	
Hotel Hernani	5	Hotel Spring	9	
Hotel Monteleone	1	Pensión Meza	11	
Hotel Pan American	4			

0   200 m

RESTAURANTS & CAFÉS

Altuna	B
Café León	F
Europa Bar	C
Las Cien Puertes	E
Long Wah	A
Rey Sol	D

parque to stroll, chat and snack. There is a new spirit of Guatemala detectable here as soldiers chat with Maya girls, and you may even hear politics being discussed. Next to the giant Guatemalan flag is a small box containing an **eternal flame** dedicated to "the anonymous heroes for peace". For many Guatemalans this is a place of pilgrimage.

The most striking building here is the **Palacio Nacional**, a grandiose stone-faced structure started in 1939 under President Ubico. For decades it housed the executive branch of the government, and from time to time its steps have been fought over by assorted coupsters. The palace is currently undergoing conversion into an interactive **museum** of the history of Guatemala.

On the east side of the plaza, the blue tile-domed **Cathedral** (daily 8am–1pm & 3–7pm) was completed in 1868. Its solid, squat design was intended to resist the force of earthquakes and has, for the most part, succeeded. Inside there are three main aisles, all lined with arching pillars, austere colonial paintings and intricate altars supporting an array of saints.

Around the back of the cathedral is the **mercado central**, housed in three sickly blue- and yellow-painted layers of sunken concrete; a structure which the architect apparently modelled on a nuclear bunker, sacrificing any aesthetic concerns to the need for strength. Inside, the top floor sells textiles, leatherware and jewellery; there are flowers, fruit and vegetables and snack stalls in the middle; and **handicraft** sellers at the bottom – mainly selling basketry and *típica* clothing.

Heading south from the parque central are **6 and 7 avenidas**, thick with clothes shops, fast-food joints and neon signs. On the corner of 6 Av and 13 C is the **Iglesia de San Francisco**, dating from 1780, a church famous for its carving of the Sacred Heart. It's said that cane syrup, egg whites and cow's milk were mixed with the mortar to enhance its strength against earthquakes. Another block to the south is the **police headquarters**, an outlandish-looking mock castle with imitation medieval battlements. The next block is taken up by the **Parque Concordia**, a leafy square with some of Zona 1's very few trees. Plenty of people spend their time hanging out here, and there's always a surplus of shoeshine boys, taxi drivers and rabid preachers on weekends. More disturbingly, this is where many of Guatemala's street children spend the night.

As you head south from the Parque Concordia, things go into a slow but steady decline as the pavements become increasingly swamped by temporary stalls, finally emerging in the madness of **18 Calle**, a distinctly sleazy part of town day or night, and probably best avoided. An assorted collection of grimy nightclubs and "streap-tease" joints, this is the street that most of the city's petty thieves, prostitutes and low-life seem to call home.

At the southern end of the old city, separating it from the newer parts of town, the **Centro Cívico** marks the boundary between Zonas 1 and 4. Here you'll find the main office of Inguat (see p.144) and the lofty **teatro nacional**, one of the city's most prominent and unusual structures. Designed along the lines of a huge ship and painted blue and white, with portholes as windows, it has superb **views** across the city.

The new city

The more spacious southern half of the city, with its broader streets, is, roughly speaking, divided into two by 7 Avenida. To the south of the Centro Cívico, at the junction of 7 Av and 2 C, in Zona 4, is the landmark **Torre del Reformador**, Guatemala's answer to the Eiffel Tower. The steel structure was built in honour of President Barrios, whose liberal reforms transformed the country between 1871 and 1885. Unfortunately you can't go up it.

A block east from the Torre is **Av la Reforma**, the new city's main transport artery, which divides zonas 9 and 10. Many of the city's important sites and buildings are to be found on or just off this tree-lined boulevard, including the **Jardín Botanico** (Mon–Fri 8am–5pm) of the San Carlos University, whose entrance is on 0 C. Inside you'll find a beautiful little garden with quite a selection of species, all neatly labelled in Spanish and Latin. There's also a small, not terribly exciting **natural history museum**, with a collection of stuffed birds, including a quetzal and an ostrich, along with geological samples, wood types, live snakes and some horrific pickled rodents.

Far more worthwhile are the two privately owned **museums** in the campus of the University Francisco Marroquín, reached by following 6 C Final off Av la Reforma to the east. **Museo Ixchel** (Mon–Fri 8am–5.50pm, Sat 9am–12.50pm; US$2) is strikingly housed in its own purpose-built cultural centre. Probably the capital's best museum, the Ixchel is dedicated to Maya culture, with particular emphasis on traditional weaving. There's a stunning collection of hand-woven fabrics, including some very impressive examples of ceremonial costumes, with explanations in English. There's also information about the techniques, dyes, fibres and weaving tools used and the way in which costumes have changed over the years. Don't miss the miniature *huipil* collection next to the basement café.

Right next door, on the third floor of the auditorio building, is the city's other private museum, the excellent **Popol Vuh Archeological Museum** (Mon–Fri 9am–5pm, Sat 9am–1pm; US$2), with an outstanding collection of artefacts from sites all over the country. The small museum is divided into Preclassic, Classic, Postclassic and Colonial rooms and all the exhibits are top quality. In the Preclassic room are some stunning ceramics, stone masks and *hongo zoomorfo* (mushroom heads). The Classic room has an altar from Naranjo, some lovely incense burners, and a model of Tikal; the Postclassic a replica of the Dresden code. The colonial era is represented with some ecclesiastical relics and processional crosses.

Back on Av la Reforma, the smart part of town is to the south, a collection of leafy streets filled with boutiques and travel agents, the American Embassy, banks, office blocks and sleek hotels. This part of town has clearly escaped the Third World. A little to the east, around 10 C and 3 Av, is the so-called **Zona Viva**, a tight bunch of upmarket hotels, restaurants and nightclubs and, at the bottom of La Reforma, the upmarket Los Próceres shopping mall. To get to Av la Reforma from Zona 1, take bus #82, which runs along 10 Av in Zona 1, past the Yurrita Church and all the way along Av la Reforma, which is a two-way street so you can return by the same means.

West of 7 Avenida

Out to the west of 7 Avenida it's quite another story, and while there are still small enclaves of upmarket housing, and several expensive shopping areas, things are really dominated by commerce and transport, including the infamous **Zona 4 bus terminal**, at 1 C and 4 Av. This area is probably the country's most impenetrable and intimidating jungle, a brutish swirl of petty thieves, hardware stores, bus fumes and sleeping vagrants. Around the terminal the largest **market** in the city spreads across several blocks. To get to the bus terminal from Zona 1, take any of the buses marked "terminal" from 4 Av or 9 Av, all of which pass within a block or two.

Further to the south, in **Zona 13**, the **Parque Aurora** houses the city's remodelled **zoo** (Tues–Sun 9am–5pm; US$1.40) with a collection that includes African lions, Bengal tigers, crocodiles, giraffes, Indian elephants, hippos, monkeys and all the Central and South American big cats, including some well-fed jaguar. Most of the larger animals have a reasonable amount of space, many smaller animals do not.

On the other side of the Parque Aurora is a collection of state-run **museums** (all Tues–Fri 9am–4pm, Sat & Sun 9am–noon & 1.30–4pm). The best of these is the **Museo Nacional de Arqueología y Etnología** (US$5), with a selection of Maya artefacts to rival the Popul Vuh. The collection includes some fantastic stelae, as well as a display on indigenous culture, with traditional masks and costumes. There are several vast pieces of Maya stonework on show, some of them from more remote sites like Piedras Negras. In comparison, the city's **Museo Nacional de Arte Moderno** (US$1.70) is a little disappointing, though there are some impressively massive murals, as well as an abundance of twee images of Maya life. The **Museo Nacional de Historia Natural** (US$1.70) seems the most neglected, featuring a range of mouldy-looking stuffed animals from Guatemala and elsewhere, and a few mineral samples. Beside the park there's a **bullring**, and a running track, while to the south is Aurora airport. To get here, take bus #63 from 4 Av or #83 from 10 Av.

Kaminaljuyú

Way out west on the edge of the city, beyond the stench of the city rubbish dump, is the long thin arm of Zona 7, which wraps around the ruins of **Kaminaljuyú** (Mon–Fri 8am–4pm, Sat 8am–1pm; US$4). Archeological digs on this side of the city have revealed the astonishing proportions of a Maya city that once housed around fifty thousand people and includes more than three hundred mounds and thirteen ball courts. Unlike the massive temples of the lowlands, these structures were built of adobe, and most of them have been lost to centuries of erosion and a few decades of urban sprawl. Today, the archeological site, incorporating only a tiny fraction of the original city, is little more than a series of earth-covered mounds, a favourite spot for football and romance. Unfortunately it's virtually impossible to get any impression of Kaminaljuyú's former scale and splendour.

To get to the ruins, take bus #29 or #72 from the parque central or any bus that has a small "Kaminaljuyú" sign in the windscreen.

Eating, drinking and entertainment

Despite its role as the country's economic centre, Guatemala City isn't a great place for indulging. Most of the population hurry home after dark and it's only the very rich who eat, drink and dance until the small hours. There are, however, restaurants everywhere in the city, invariably reflecting the type of neighbourhood they're in. Movie-watching is also popular and there is a good selection of cinemas. Nightclubs and bars are concentrated in Zona 10.

Restaurants and cafés

When it comes to eating cheaply in Guatemala City, stick to **Zona 1**, where there are some good comedores and dozens of fast-food chains. In the smarter parts of town, particularly **Zonas 9** and **10**, the emphasis is more on upmarket cafés and glitzy dining, though there is more choice, including Mexican, Middle Eastern, Chinese and Japanese options.

Zona 1

Altuna, 5 Av 12–31, Zona 1. Spanish/Basque food in a wonderfully civilized, old-fashioned atmosphere. Very strong on fish and seafood. Not cheap, but affordable.

Café Astoria, 10 C 6–72, Zona 1. Very German deli and café – excellent sausages and ham.

Café León, 8 Av 9–15, Zona 1. Spanish-owned café in the heart of things, ideal for *café y churros*.

Café Penalba, 6 Av 11–71, Zona 1. Inexpensive set meals.

Europa Bar, 11 C 5–16, Zona 1. The most popular expat hangout in Zona 1, set inauspiciously beneath a multistorey car park. Primarily a bar, with CNN and sports on screen, but there are also cheapish eats. Owner Judy is a mine of local information. You can change dollars here and make local calls. Closed Sun.

Fu Lu Sho, 6 Av and 12 C, Zona 1. Popular, inexpensive Chinese restaurant with an Art Deco interior, opening onto the bustle of 6 Av.

El Gran Pavo, 13 C 4–41, Zona 1; 6 C 3–09, Zona 9; and 15 Av 16–72, Zona 10. Three restaurants all serving massive portions of genuinely Mexican, moderately priced food.

Long Wah, 6 C 3–75, Zona 1, west of the National Palace. Good Chinese restaurant, not at all expensive.

Rey Sol, south side of Parque Centenario. "Aerobic" breakfasts (sic), very good selection of vegetarian dishes and licuados. Wholemeal bread, granola and veggie snacks are sold from the shop.

Tao Restaurant, 5 C 9–70, Zona 1. The city's best value three-course veggie lunch. There's no menu; you just eat the meal of the day at tiny tables around a plant-filled courtyard.

Zonas 9 and 10

Los Alpes, 10 C 1–09, Zona 10. A haven of peace, where superb pastries and a fine range of drinks make for the best place to relax in the city. Closed Mon.

Los Antojitos, Av la Reforma 15–02, Zona 9. Good, moderately priced Central American food – try the *chile relleno* or guacamole.

Antro's, 4 Av 15–53, Zona 10. Excellent vegetarian restaurant with some Middle Eastern dishes. Closed Sun.

El Arbol de la Vida, 7 Av 13–56, Zona 9. The city's best vegetarian restaurant; reasonably priced.

Burger Warehouse, 4 Av 15–70, Zona 10. Well-priced burgers, fried chicken dishes and pitchers of beer.

Jake's, 17 C 10–40, Zona 10. Lunch and dinner from an international menu, very strong on fish and with terrific desserts. Pleasant, candle-lit atmosphere, excellent service, and correspondingly high prices. Closed Sun & Mon.

Luigi's Pizza, 4 Av 14–20, Zona 10. Very popular, moderately priced Italian restaurant, serving delicious pizza, pasta and baked potatoes.

Maitreya's Deli, 13 C 4–44, Zona 10. Top quality, delicious sandwiches, freshly prepared in house. Wide range of drinks and full meals also offered. Expensive.

Olivadda, 12 C 4–51, Zona 10. Very smart, authentic Middle Eastern fare. Feast on falafel, hummus and tabbouleh for around US$10 a head.

Palace, 10 C 4–40, Zona 10. Pasta and snacks, cakes and pastries, in a cafeteria atmosphere.

Piccadilly, Plaza Espana, 7 Av 12–00, Zona 9. One of the most popular continental restaurants with tourists and Guatemalans alike. Decent range of pastas and pizzas, served with huge jugs of beer. Moderate prices. Also at 6 Av and 11 C in Zona 1.

Puerto Barrios, 7 Av 10–65, Zona 9. Excellent, pricey seafood in a boat-like building.

Sushi, 2 Av 14–63, Zona 10. Very popular Japanese restaurant, which rather bizarrely advertises itself as a "rock café". Reasonable prices.

Vesuvio Pizza, 18 C 3–36, Zona 10. Huge pizzas with plenty of mouthwatering toppings cooked in traditional, wood-burning ovens.

Nightlife and entertainment

Despite appearances, Guatemala City quietens down very quickly in the evenings, and **nightlife** is certainly not one of its strengths. The best bet for a night out in Zona 1 is to start at somewhere like *Las Cien Puertes* (see below) or one of the bars nearby and then check out what's on at *La Bodeguita*. In the **Zona Viva** (Zona 10), there are several Western-style nightclubs and bars. If you crave the low life, then stroll on down 18 C, to the junction with 9 Av, and you're in the heart of the **red light district**, where the bars and clubs are truly sleazy.

Zona 10 is where the wealthy go to have fun and it's anything but an egalitarian experience. **Techno** has now hit Guatemala, though you'll be lucky to get anything other than the standard, commercial "handbag" strain. Most city DJs spin a mix of pan-Latin and Eurohouse sounds, with the merengue of the Caribbean often being spiced up with raggamuffin vocals; plus there are specialist clubs for **salsa** fanatics. The city's greatest **reggae club** is *La Gran Comal* on Via 4 between 6 Av and Ruta 6, Zona 4. Radiating rhythm, it's relaxed, but not as worn-out as the clubs of Zona 1. It's a favourite haunt of black Guatemalans from Lívingston and the Caribbean coast, and well worth a visit.

Guatemala City's **gay nightlife** is mostly underground and concentrated around two (almost entirely male) clubs: *El Metropole*, 6 C and 3 Av, Zona 1, and *Pandora's Box*, Via 3 and Ruta 3, Zona 4. There are no specifically lesbian clubs or bars in the city. For more information on the scene, call OASIS on ☎2323335.

Bars and clubs

La Bodeguita del Centro, 12 C 3–55, Zona 1 (☎2302976). Large, leftish venue with live music, comedy, poetry and all manner of arty events. Free entry in the week, around US$4 at weekends. Definitely worth a visit for the Che Guevara memorabilia alone.

Crocodilo's, 16 C and 2 Av, in the Los Próceres shopping mall in Zona 10. A restaurant that doubles up as a cocktail bar, with happy hour daily 6–9pm.

El Establo, Av la Reforma 14–34, Zona 9. Cosy bar with polished wood interior, bookstore, good food and pool tables round the back.

Kahlua, 15 C and 1 Av, Zona 10. Currently the most happening club in town with two dance floors and a chill-out room. Music is reasonable mix of dance and Latin pop.

Las Cien Puertes, Pasaje Aycinena, 9 C between 6 and 7 Av. Funky, leftfield bar in a beautiful run-down colonial arcade. Good Latin sounds, very moderate prices and some of the best imaginative cooking in Guatemala. Highly recommended.

Shakespeare's Pub, 13 C 1–51, Zona 10. Small basement bar catering to middle-aged North American expats.

Tapioca Azul, 3 Av & 13 C, Zona 10. Stylish bar with a convivial atmosphere and good food.

Cinemas

Most movies are shown in English with Spanish subtitles. There are four **cinemas on 6 Av** between the main plaza and Parque Concordia. Elsewhere, the very best for sound quality is the Magic Place on Av las Américas, Zona 13. Also recommended are **Cine las Américas**, Av las Américas, between C 8 and 9, Zona 13, and **Cine Tikal Futura**, Tikal Futura, Calzada Roosevelt, Zona 11. Programmes are listed in the two main newspapers, *El Grafico* and *Prensa Libre*.

Listings

Airlines Airline offices are scattered throughout the city, with many along Av la Reforma. It is fairly straightforward to phone them and there will almost always be someone in the office who speaks English. Aerovias, Av Hincapié 18 C, Zona 13 (☎3325686; airport ☎3327470); Air Canada 12 C 1–25, Zona 10 (☎3353341); American Airlines, Av la Reforma 15–54, Zona 9 (☎3347379); Aviateca (also for Taca, Lacsa and Nica), Av Hincapié 12–22, Zona 13 (☎3347722); British Airways, 1 Av 10–81, Zona 10, 6th floor of Edificio Inexa (☎3327402); Continental, 12 C 1–25, Zona 10, Edificio Geminis 10, Torre Norte (☎3313341); Delta, 15 C 3–20, Zona 10, Centro Ejecutivo building (☎3370642); Iberia, Av la Reforma 8–60, Zona 9 (☎3370911; airport ☎3325517); Lacsa, see Aviateca above; Mexicana, 13 C 8–44, Zona 10, Edificio Edyma (☎3336001); Nica, see Aviateca above; TWA, Av la Reforma 12–81, Zona 10 (☎3346240); Taca, see Aviateca above; United Airlines, Av la Reforma 1–50, Zona 9, Edificio el Reformador (☎3322995, fax 3323903).

American Express Main office in the Banco del Café, Av la Reforma 9–00, Zona 9 (Mon–Fri 8.30am–4.30pm; ☎3340040, fax 3311928). Take bus #82 from 10 Av, Zona 1.

Banks and exchange Opening hours vary wildly, with some banks shutting as early as 3pm, and others staying open until after dark. At the airport, Banco Del Quetzal (Mon–Fri 7am–8pm, Sat & Sun 8am–8pm) gives a good rate and also takes most European currencies. For cashing travellers' cheques, try Banco Industrial, 7 Av 11–52, Zona 1 (Mon–Fri 8.30am–7pm, Sat 8.30am–5.30pm; Visa cash advances); or Lloyds Bank, 8 Av 10–67, Zona 1 (Mon–Fri 9am–3pm). Visa and Mastercard cash advances are available at Credomatic, on the corner of 5 Av and 11 C (Mon–Fri 8.30am–7pm, Sat 9am–1pm).

Books For a reasonable selection of English fiction, try Arnel, in the basement of the Edificio el Centro on 9 C, corner of 7 Av, in Zona 1; Librería del Pensativo, 7 Av and 13 C, Edificio la Cúpula, Zona 9 (Mon–Fri 10am–7pm, Sat 10am–1.30pm); Geminis, 6 Av 7–24, Zona 9; and Sol y Luna, 12 C and 3 Av, Zona 1. A selection of secondhand English books can be bought from the El Establo, Av la Reforma 14–34, Zona 10, and the Europa Bar on 11 C 5–16, Zona 1.

Car rental Renting a car in Guatemala is expensive and you should always keep a sharp eye on the terms. Jeeps can be rented for a little under US$100 a day and cars start from US$70. Avis, 12 C 2–73, Zona 9 (☎3312734, fax 3321263); Budget, Av la Reforma 15–00, Zona 9 (☎3322591, fax 3342571); Dollar, airport (☎3317185); Hertz, 7 Av 14–76, Zona 9 (☎3322242, fax 3317924); National Car Rental, 14 C 1–24, Zona 10 (☎3664670, fax 3370221); Rental, 12 C 2–62, Zona 10 (☎3610672, fax 3342739) – the only company to rent **motorbikes**; Tabarini, 2 C A 7–30, Zona 10 (☎3319814, fax 3341925).

Embassies Most of the embassies are in the southeastern quarter of the city, along Av la Reforma and Av las Americas, and they tend to open weekday mornings only. Belize, Av la Reforma, Edificio el Reforma 1–50, Zona 9, 8th Floor, Suite 803 (☎3345531 or 3311137, Mon–Fri 9am–1pm & 2–5pm); Brazil, 18 C 2–22, Zona 14 (☎3370949; Mon–Fri 9am–1pm); Canada, 13 C 8–44, Zona 10, Edificio Edyma Plaza (☎3336102; Mon–Thurs 8am–4.30pm, Fri 8am–1.30pm); Chile, 14 C 15–21, Zona 13 (☎3321149; Mon–Fri 8.30am–1pm); Colombia, 12 C 1–25, Zona 10 (☎3353602; Mon–Fri 9am–1pm); Costa Rica, Av la Reforma 8–60, 3rd floor, Zona 9, Galerias Reforma Torre 1 (☎ & fax 3320531; Mon–Fri 9am–2pm); Ecuador, 4 Av 12–04, Zona 14 (☎3372902; Mon–Fri 9am–1pm); El Salvador, 4 Av 13–60, Zona 10 (☎3662240; Mon–Fri 8am–2pm); Honduras, 9 Av 16–34, Zona 10 (☎3374344; Mon–Fri 9am–2pm); Mexico, 15 C 3–20, Zona 10 (☎3337254–8; Mon–Fri 9am–1pm & 3–6pm); Nicaragua, 10 Av 14–72, Zona 10 (☎3680785, 9am–1pm); Panamá, 5 Av 15–45, Zona 10 (☎3372445; Mon–Fri 8.30am–1.30pm); Peru, 2 Av 9–67, Zona 9 (☎3318558; Mon–Fri 9am–1pm); UK, Torre II, 7 Av 5–10, 7th floor, Zona 4 (☎3321604; Mon–Fri 9am–noon & 2–4pm); USA, Av la Reforma, 7–01, Zona 10 (☎3311541; Mon–Fri 8am–5pm); Venezuela, 8 C 0–56, Zona 9 (☎3316505; Mon–Fri 9am–1pm).

Immigration Main immigration office (*migración*) is at 41 C 17–36, Zona 8 (☎4751302, fax 4751289; Mon–Fri 8am–4pm). Come here to extend your tourist card up to a maximum of ninety days, or extend a visa for a month. Take bus #71 from 10 Av in Zona 1 or 6 Av in Zona 4.

Laundry Lavandería Obelisco, Av la Reforma 16–30, next to Samaritana supermarket (Mon–Fri 8am–6.45pm, Sat 8am–5.30pm).

Libraries The best library for English books is in the IGA (Guatemalan American Institute) at Ruta 1 and Via 4, Zona 4. There's also the National Library on the west side of the Parque Central, and specialist collections at the Ixchel and Popol Vuh museums.

Medical care Your embassy should have a list of bilingual doctors, but for emergency medical assistance, dial ☎125 for the Red Cross, or there's the Centro Médico, a private hospital with 24-hour cover, at 6 Av 3–47, Zona 10 (☎3323555). Central Dentist de Especialistas, 20 C 11–17, Zona 10 (☎3371773), is the best dental clinic in the country, and superb in emergencies.

Pharmacies Farmacia Osco, 16 C & 4 Av, Zona 10.

Photography Colour transparency and both colour and monochrome print film is easy to buy, though expensive. There are several camera shops on 6 Av in Zona 1. Foto Sittler, 12 C 6–20, Zona 1 and La Perla, 9 C and 6 Av, Zona 1, repair cameras and offer a three-month guarantee on their work.

Police Main police station is in a bizarre castle-like structure on the corner of 6 Av and 14 C, Zona 1. In an emergency dial ☎120.

Post office The main post office, 7 Av and 12 C (Mon–Fri 9am–5.30pm) has a lista de correos, where they will hold mail for you.

Telephone You can make long-distance phone calls and send faxes from Telgua, one block east of the post office (daily 7am–midnight).

Travel agents Flights can be arranged at any of the many agents in the centre and along Av la Reforma in Zonas 9 and 10. For tours, see p.154.

Moving on from Guatemala City

There are frequent **international** flights from Guatemala City's Aurora airport to Mexico, Central America and North America, and four daily flights to **Flores** in Petén, the only other international airport in the country. Three of these leave at around 7am, and one at about 4pm. Tickets for the fifty-minute flight can be bought from virtually any travel agent in the capital, and cost from US$60 return. To get to the **international terminal** of Aurora **airport** from Zona 1, either take **bus** #83 from 10 Av (30min) or a taxi (around US$8); from Zona 10 a taxi costs around US$5. There's a US$25 **departure tax** on all international flights, payable in either quetzals or dollars.

A new **domestic** airline, Inter (☎3347722), in theory fly daily return services between Guatemala City and Puerto Barrios (US$60 each way; 1hr), Santa Cruz del Quiché (US$55; 25min), Quetzaltenango (US$40; 30min), Retalhuleu (US$40; 35min), Coatepeque (US$55; 1hr), Cobán (US$45; 30min) and Huehuetenango (US$55; 50min), plus return flights to the Río Dulce at weekends (US$50; 1hr). Note, however, that their schedules are subject to change and cancellation. For the **domestic terminal**, in the same complex as the international terminal but only reached via Av Hicapié, you'll need to take a taxi.

If you're leaving by **first-class bus**, departures are either from the office of the bus company or from the new purpose-built terminals on the edge of the city. These new terminals are due to become fully operational in 1999, but as most companies have refused to move out of the centre you will probably find there's a terminal in the city and another outside. The new **Zona 12 Centro de Mayoreo** terminal will serve routes to Mexico, the Pacific Coast (and El Salvador) and the Western Highlands via the Carretera Americana. The **Meta del Norte** terminal in the northeast of the city is to serve routes east and north including Petén (for Belize), the Caribbean and Cobán. Presently, the **Zona 1 terminal**, spread out around the streets surrounding the old train station at 18 C and 9 Av, has departures to Puerto Barrios, Cobán, the Pacific highway, the Mexican border and Petén.

Moving on by **second-class bus** the main centre is the chaotic **Zona 4 terminal**, where services run to all parts of the country. To get there take any city bus marked "terminal"; you'll find these heading south along 4 Av in Zona 1.

Tours

If you'd prefer someone else to organize your escape from the capital, particularly if time is short, the following companies offer some excellent adventure, ecotourism and sightseeing trips.

Clarke Tours, Diagonal 6 10–01, Zona 10, Las Margaritas Torre 2, 7th floor (☎3392888, fax 3392909). City tours and trips to many parts of the country.

Discovery Tours, 12 C 2–04, Zona 9, Edificio Plaza Del Sol (☎3392281, fax 3392285). Ecotourism adventure trips.

Jungle Flying, Av Hincapié and C 18, domestic terminal, Hangar 21, Zona 13 (☎3604917, fax 3314995). Flight tours to Copán in Honduras and other Maya sites.

Maya Expeditions, 15 C 1–91, Zona 10 (☎3634955, fax 3634164). Leading ecotourism specialists, especially for rafting trips.

Mesoamerica Explorers, 7 Av 13–01, Zona 9 (☎3325045). Nature and archeological trips around Petén and Alta Verapaz.

BUSES FROM GUATEMALA CITY

Note that there are two **new terminals** being built on the outskirts of town, which will no doubt affect bus departure points (see p.144 for more details). The abbreviations we've used for the bus companies are as follows:

KQ	King Quality	**TB**	Ticabus
L	Lituega	**TA**	Transportes Alamo
LA	Líneas Américas	**TD**	Transportes Dulce María
LD	Línea Dorada	**TE**	Transportes Escobar y Monja Blanca
LH	Los Halcones	**TG**	Transportes Galgos
MI	Melva International	**TM**	Transportes Marquensita
RO	Rutas Orientales	**TR**	Transportes Rebuli
SJ	San Juanera	**TV**	Transportes Velásquez

DESTINATION	COMPANY	BUS STOP	FREQUENCY	DURATION
Antigua	various (2nd)	18 C & 4 Av, Zona 1	15min	1hr
Chichicastenango	various (2nd)	Zona 4 terminal	30min	3hr 30min
Chiquimula	RO	19 C & 9 Av, Zona 1	15 daily	3hr 30min
Cobán	TE	8 Av 15–16, Zona 1	14 daily	4hr 30min
Cubulco	TD (2nd)	19 C & 9 Av, Zona 1	13 daily	5hr
Escuintla	various (2nd)	Zona 4 terminal	30min	1hr 15min
Esquipulas	RO	19 C & 9 Av, Zona 1	15 daily	4hr
Flores	various (1st/2nd)	17 C & 8 Av, Zona 1	12 daily	12–14hr
	LD (1st)	16 C 10–55, Zona 1	1 daily	12hr
Huehuetenango	LH (1st)	7 Av 15–27, Zona 1	3 daily	5hr
	TV (1st)	20 C 1–37, Zona 1	11 daily	5hr

DESTINATION	COMPANY	BUS STOP	FREQUENCY	DURATION
La Mesilla	TV (1st)	20 C 1–37, Zona 1	5 daily	7hr
Monterrico	various (2nd)	Zona 4 terminal	5 daily	4hr 30min
Panajachel	TR (2nd)	21 C 1–54, Zona 1	11 daily	3hr
Puerto Barrios	L (1st)	15 C 10–40, Zona 1	19 daily	5hr 30min
Quetzaltenango	LA (1st)	2 Av 18–74, Zona 1	6 daily	4hr
	TA (1st)	21 C 1–14, Zona 1	5 daily	4hr
	TM (1st)	1 Av 21–31, Zona 1	8 daily	4hr
	TG (1st)	7 Av 19–44, Zona 1	6 daily	4hr
	SJ (2nd)	Zona 4 terminal	9 daily	4hr 30min
Rabinal	TD (2nd)	19 C & 9 Av, Zona 1	13 daily	4hr 30min
Salamá	TD (2nd)	19 C & 9 Av, Zona 1	13 daily	3hr 30min
San Salvador	MI (1st)	3 Av 1–38, Zona 9	11 daily	5hr
	TB (1st)	11 C 2–72, Zona 9	1 daily	5hr
	KQ (1st)	16 C 1–30, Zona 10	2 daily	5hr
Santa Cruz del Quiché	various (2nd)	Zona 4 terminal	30min	4hr
Tecún Uman	various (1st)	19 Av & 8 C, Zona 1	30min	5hr
Talismán	various (1st)	19 Av & 8 C, Zona 1	30min	5hr
Zacapa	RO	19 C & 9 Av, Zona 1	15 daily	3hr

CHAPTER 7

THE WESTERN HIGHLANDS

Guatemala's **western highlands**, stretching from Guatemala City to the Mexican border, are perhaps the most captivating and beautiful part of the entire country. The area is defined by two main features: the chain of awesome volcanoes that lines the southern side, and the high mountain ranges that dominate the northern boundaries. The greatest of these are the **Cuchumatanes**, whose granite peaks rise to over 3800m. Between the two is a bewitching pattern of twisting, pine-forested ridges, lakes, gushing streams and deep valleys.

It's an astounding landscape, blessed with tremendous fertility but cursed by instability. The hills are regularly shaken by earthquakes and occasionally showered by volcanic eruptions. Of the thirteen cones that loom over the western highlands, three volcanoes are still active: **Pacaya**, **Fuego** and **Santiaguito**. Two major **fault lines** also cut through the area, making earthquakes a regular occurrence. The most recent major quake, in 1976, centred on **Chimaltenango** – it left 25,000 dead and around a million homeless. But despite its sporadic ferocity, the countryside is outstandingly beautiful and the atmosphere calm and welcoming, with irrigated valleys and terraced hillsides carefully crafted to yield the maximum potential farmland.

The highland landscape is controlled by many factors, all of which affect its appearance. Perhaps the most important is **altitude**. At lower levels the vegetation is almost tropical, supporting dense forests, **coffee**, **cotton**, **bananas** and **cacao**, while higher up, the hills are often wrapped in cloud and the ground is sometimes hard with frost. Here trees are stunted by the cold, and **maize** and potatoes are grown alongside grazing land for herds of sheep and goats. The **seasons** also play their part. In the rainy season, from May to October, the land is superbly green, with young crops and lush forests of pine, cedar and oak, while during the dry winter months the hillsides gradually turn to a dusty yellow.

Some history

The western highlands are home to one of the American continent's largest groups of indigenous people, the **Maya**, who have lived in this land continuously for over two thousand years. Despite the catastrophe of the Spanish conquest, their society, languages and traditions remain largely intact and in these highlands they continue to form the vast majority of the population.

The highlands are still divided up along traditional tribal lines. The **Quiché** language is spoken by the largest number of people, centred on the town of Santa Cruz del Quiché and reaching west into the Quetzaltenango valley. The highlands around Huehuetenango are **Mam**-speaking, the **Tzutujil** occupy the southern shores of Lago de Atitlán, and the **Cakchiquel** are to the east. **Smaller tribal groups**, with distinct languages and costumes, such as the Ixil and the Aguateca, also occupy clearly defined areas in the Cuchumatan mountains.

Though pre-conquest life was certainly hard, the **arrival of the Spanish** in 1523 was a total disaster for the Maya population. In the early stages, **Alvarado** and his army met with a force of Quiché warriors in the Quetzaltenango basin and defeated them in open warfare. Legend has it that Alvarado himself slew the great Quiché warrior, **Tecún Umán**, in hand-to-hand combat. The Spanish made their first permanent base at **Iximché**, the capital of their Cakchiquel Maya allies, but this uneasy alliance was to last only a few years. Alvarado then moved to a site near the modern town of Antigua, from where the Spanish gradually brought the rest of the highlands under a degree of control. The damage done by Spanish swords, however, was nothing when compared to that of the **diseases** they introduced. Waves of smallpox, typhus, plague and measles swept through the indigenous population, reducing their numbers by as much as ninety percent in the worst-hit areas.

In the long term, the **Spanish administration** of the western highlands was no gentler than the Conquest, as indigenous labour became the backbone of the Spanish empire. Guatemala offered little of the gold and silver that was available in Peru or Mexico, but there was still money to be made from **cacao** and **indigo**. As well as being at the heart of Spanish Guatemala, **Antigua** also served as the administrative centre for the whole of Central America and Chiapas (now in Mexico). In 1773, however, the city was destroyed by a massive earthquake and the capital was subsequently moved to its modern site.

The departure of the Spanish in 1821 and subsequent **independence** brought little change at village level. *Ladino* authority replaced that of the Spanish, but Maya were still required to work the coastal plantations and when labour supplies dropped off, they were simply press-ganged and forced to work, often in horrific conditions. It's a state of affairs that has changed little even today, and remains a major burden on the *indígena* population.

In the late 1970s, **guerrilla movements** began to develop in opposition to military rule, seeking support from the indigenous population and establishing themselves in the western highlands. The Maya became the victims in this process, caught between the guerrillas and the army. A total of 440 villages were destroyed; thousands died and thousands more fled the country, seeking refuge in Mexico. Indigenous society has also been besieged in recent years by a tidal wave of American **evangelical churches** whose influence undermines local hierarchies, dividing communities and threatening to destroy Maya culture.

Today, with the signing of the 1996 **peace accords**, tensions have lifted and there is evidence of a new spirit of self-confidence within the highland Maya population. Some fundamental problems still remain, such as poverty, racism, and the still unsettled issue of **land reform**, but there is a reawakened sense of pride in Maya identity. Despite

---

MARKET DAYS

Make an effort to catch as many market days as possible – they're second only to local fiestas in offering a glimpse of a traditional way of life.

Monday: Antigua; San Juan Atitán; Zunil.

Tuesday: Chajul; Patzún; San Lucas Tolimán; San Marcos; Totonicapán.

Wednesday: Cotzal; Huehuetenango; Momostenango.

Thursday: Aguacatán; Antigua; Chichicastenango; Jacaltenango; Nebaj; Panajachel; Sacapulas; San Mateo Ixtatán; San Pedro Sacatepéquez; Santa Cruz del Quiché; Soloma; Totonicapán; Uspantán.

Friday: Chajul; San Francisco el Alto; Santiago Atitlán; Sololá.

Saturday: Antigua; Cotzal; Santa Clara la Laguna; Santa Cruz del Quiché; Todos Santos; Totonicapán.

Sunday: Aguacatán; Chichicastenango; Huehuetenango; Jacaltenango; Joyabaj; Momostenango; Nebaj; Nahualá; Panajachel; Sacapulas; San Juan Comalapa; San Pedro Sacatepéquez; Santa Cruz del Quiché; Santa Eulalia; Soloma; Uspantán.

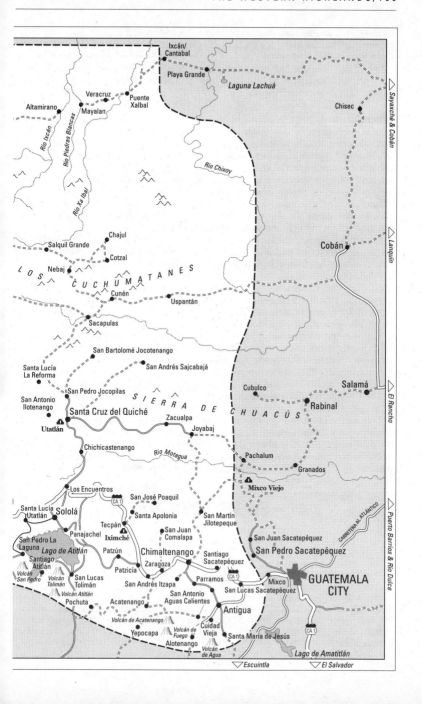

intense pressure, the traditional structures of society are still in place. Rejecting *ladino* commercialism, the Maya see trade as a social function as much as an economic one. Conservative and inward-looking, they live in a world centred on the village, with its own civil and religious hierarchy. Subsistence farming of maize and beans remains at its heart, and the land is its life-blood. It is this unique culture, above all else, that is Guatemala's most fascinating feature.

Where to go

Almost everywhere in the western highlands is of interest to the traveller. The landscape is exceptionally beautiful, dotted with highland villages of adobe houses and whitewashed colonial churches. **Antigua**, the former capital, is unmissable: a beautiful colonial city nestling in the shadow of giant volcanoes, it also has the most cosmopolitan restaurant scene in Central America. **Lago de Atitlán** is another jewel – a lake of astounding natural beauty, ringed by volcanoes and some of the most traditional Maya villages in all Guatemala. With perhaps the most famous market in the country, **Chichicastenango** is a sleepy highland town steeped in Maya/Catholic ritual. There are tremendous markets, too, at **Sololá** and **San Francisco el Alto**.

For real adventure, spectacular scenery and myriad hiking possibilities, the **Ixil triangle** in northern Quiché and the countryside around **Todos Santos** in the Cuchumatanes are unmatched. Both are remote, intensely traditional areas that lie at the end of tortuous bus journeys; both suffered terribly in the civil war. Much easier to get to are the villages around **Quetzaltenango** (Xela), Guatemala's second city. Though Xela itself is a fairly unexciting provincial centre, close by you'll find the villages of Zunil, San Francisco el Alto, the hot springs of Fuentes Georginas and the climbable near-perfect cone of Volcán Santa María.

The scenery, villages and living Maya culture are the main attractions in the highlands but there are also interesting **historical Maya ruins**: the pre-conquest cities of **Iximché**, **Utatlán** and **Zaculeu**, and assorted smaller sites, many still actively used for Maya religious ritual and ceremony. These ancient cities don't bear comparison to Tikal, Copán and the lowland sites, but they're fascinating nevertheless.

The **Carretera Interamericana** runs through the middle of the western highlands, served by a constant flow of buses, some branching off along minor roads to more remote areas. Travelling in these areas can sometimes be a gruelling experience, particularly in northern Huehuetenango and Quiché, but the scenery makes it well worth the discomfort. The most practical plan of action is to base yourself in one of the larger places and then make a series of day-trips to markets and fiestas, although even the smallest of villages will usually offer some kind of accommodation.

TOURIST CRIME

While there is no need to be paranoid, visitors to the heavily touristed areas around Antigua and Lago de Atitlán should be aware that **crime against tourists** – including robbery and rape – is a problem. Pay close attention to security reports from your embassy and follow the usual precautions with extra care. In particular, avoid walking alone, especially at night or to isolated spots during the day. If you want to visit viewing spots like the *cruce* overlooking Antigua, inform the newly formed Tourist Police and they will accompany you or even give you a ride there on one of their motorbikes. Though there have been very few attacks on hikers in the Lago de Atitlán area recently, it's still safer to walk in a group. Similarly, don't amble around Panajachel alone late at night. In the more remote highlands, where foreigners are a much rarer sight, attacks are extremely uncommon.

For an explanation of **accommodation price codes**, see p.123.

Antigua

Superbly sited in a sweeping highland valley and suspended between the cones of Agua, Acatenango and Fuego volcanoes is one of Central America's most enchanting colonial cities – **ANTIGUA**. In its day, it was one of the great cities of the Spanish empire, ranking alongside Lima and Mexico City and serving as the administrative centre for all of Central America and Mexican Chiapas. Built by Spanish architects and Maya labourers, it is a classically designed city of elegant squares, churches, monasteries and grand houses and this magnificent colonial legacy has ensured Antigua's continuing prosperity as one of Guatemala's premier tourist attractions.

Antigua was actually the third capital of Guatemala. The Spanish settled first at the site of Iximché in July 1524 and then at a site a few kilometres from Antigua, now called Ciudad Vieja, but when this was devastated by a massive mudslide from Volcán Agua in 1541, the capital came to rest in Antigua. Antigua grew slowly but steadily as religious orders established themselves one by one, competing in the construction of schools, churches, monasteries and hospitals, all largely built by the sweat and blood of conscripted Maya labourers.

The city reached its peak in the middle of the eighteenth century, after the 1717 earthquake prompted an unprecedented building boom, and the population rose to around fifty thousand. By this stage Antigua was a genuinely impressive place, with a university, a printing press and a newspaper. But, as is so often the case in Guatemala, **earthquakes** brought all of this to an abrupt end. For the best part of a year the city was shaken by tremors, with the final blows delivered by two severe shocks on September 7 and December 13, 1773. The damage was so bad that the decision was made to abandon the city in favour of the modern capital. Fortunately, despite endless official decrees, many refused to leave and Antigua was never completely deserted.

Since then, the city has been gradually repopulated, particularly in the last hundred years or so, and as Guatemala City has become increasingly congested, many of the conservative middle classes have moved to Antigua. They've been joined by a large number of resident and visiting foreigners, attracted by its relaxed and sophisticated atmosphere, lively cultural life, the benign climate and largely traffic-free streets.

Efforts have been made to preserve the architectural grandeur of the past in recent years and although some of the buildings of the colonial period lie in splendidly atmospheric ruin or else are steadily decaying, many more have been impeccably restored as hotels or restaurants. Local conservation laws also protect the streets from the intrusion of overhanging signs and extensions to houses.

Thanks to its relaxed atmosphere, Antigua is a favoured hangout for jaded travellers to refuel and recharge. The bar scene is always lively and there's an extraordinarily cosmopolitan choice of restaurants. If you can make it here for **Semana Santa** (Easter week) you'll witness the most extravagant and impressive processions in all Latin America. Another attraction are the city's **language schools**, some of the best and cheapest in all Latin America, drawing students from around the globe. Expats from Europe, North and South America and even Asia contribute to the town's cosmopolitan air, mingling with the Guatemalans who come here at weekends to eat, drink and enjoy themselves. The downside of this settled, comfortable affluence is perhaps a loss of vitality – this civilized, isolated world can seem almost a little too smug and comfortable. After a few days of sipping cappuccinos and munching cake, it's easy to forget that you're in Central America at all.

Arrival and information

Antigua is laid out on the traditional grid system, with avenidas running north–south, and calles east–west. Each street is numbered and has two halves, either a north and south (*norte/sur*) or an east and west (*oriente/poniente*), with the plaza, the **parque central**, regarded as the centre. Despite this apparent simplicity, poor street lighting and the lack of street signs combine to ensure that most people get lost here at some

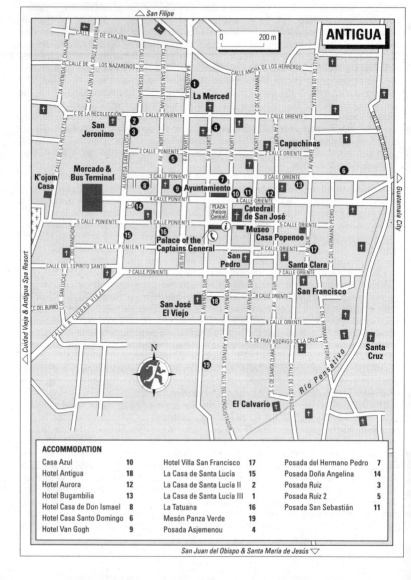

ACCOMMODATION					
Casa Azul	10	Hotel Villa San Francisco	17	Posada del Hermano Pedro	7
Hotel Antigua	18	La Casa de Santa Lucía	15	Posada Doña Angelina	14
Hotel Aurora	12	La Casa de Santa Lucía II	2	Posada Ruiz	3
Hotel Bugambilia	13	La Casa de Santa Lucía III	1	Posada Ruiz 2	5
Hotel Casa de Don Ismael	8	La Tatuana	16	Posada San Sebastián	11
Hotel Casa Santo Domingo	6	Mesón Panza Verde	19		
Hotel Van Gogh	9	Posada Asjemenou	4		

San Juan del Obispo & Santa María de Jesús ▽

stage. If you get confused, remember that Volcán Agua, the one that hangs most immediately over the town, is to the south.

Arriving by bus, you'll end up in the main **bus terminal**, a large open space beside the market. The street opposite (4 C Poniente), leads directly to the plaza. The city is easy to **get around** on foot but should you need a taxi, you'll find one around on the east side of the plaza close to the cathedral; alternatively you can call one on ☎8320526. Mountain bikes and cars can be rented in town – see p.168.

The **tourist office** (daily 8am–6pm; ☎8320763) on the south side of the plaza dispenses reasonable if overcautious information. **Noticeboards** in various tourist venues advertise everything from private language tuition to apartments, flights home and shared rides. Probably the most read are those at *Doña Luisa's* restaurant, 4 C Oriente 12, and the Rainbow Reading Room, 7 Av Sur 8. For a fascinating **city tour** looking at Maya influence on Antiguan architecture and the flora around the city, contact Geovany at Monarcas, 6 Av Norte 34 (☎8323343). Elizabeth Bell, author of the *Antigua Guatemala* guide, also leads excellent historical walking tours around the town (☎8320140 ext 341). Antigua is one of the most popular places in Latin America to **study Spanish**. For a full list of recommended schools, see p.128.

Accommodation

Hotels in Antigua are in plentiful supply, although like everything else they can be a bit hard to find due to the absence of overhanging signs. Be warned that rooms get scarce (and prices increase) around Semana Santa.

Casa Azul, 4 Av Norte 5 (☎8320961 or 8320962, fax 8320944). One of the best locations in town, just off the plaza, with huge, atmospheric rooms in a converted colonial mansion. Facilities include sauna, jacuzzi and a small swimming pool. ⑧.

La Casa de Santa Lucía, Alameda Santa Lucía Sur 5 (☎8326133). Secure, spacious and attractive rooms done out in dark wood, all with bathrooms and hot water. Best value in town in this price category, hence very popular. You'll have to ring the bell to get in; guests are given a key. ②.

La Casa de Santa Lucía 2, Alameda Santa Lucía Norte 21, & **La Casa de Santa Lucía 3**, 6 Av Norte 43A (no phones). Almost carbon copies of the original. Spacious rooms all with hot showers and extremely well priced. Neither is signposted. Ring the bell for entry. ②.

Hotel Antigua, 8 C Poniente 1 (☎8320288, fax 8320807). Tasteful colonial decor with a ruined church practically on the premises. Swimming pool, excellent restaurant, beautiful gardens and pleasant rooms with open fires to ward off the chill of the night. US$132 including breakfast. ⑨.

Hotel Aurora, 4 C Oriente 16 (☎ & fax 8320217). Attractive colonial building with rooms set around a pleasant grassy courtyard and fountain. Rooms are a little old-fashioned, but comfortable enough. ⑥.

Hotel Bugambilia, 3 C Oriente 19 (☎8325780). Quiet location, clean and safe, but rooms are a little plain. The English-speaking owners are very helpful and hospitable. Snacks available. ③.

Hotel la Casa de Don Ismael, 3 C Poniente 6 (☎8321932). Attractively presented rooms with towels and soap provided, free mineral water and free tea or coffee in the morning. Communual bathrooms are brightly painted and kept spotless and there's a lovely little garden. Very fair prices. ②.

Hotel Casa Santo Domingo, 3 C Oriente 28 (☎8320140, fax 8320102). Spectacular colonial convent, sympathetically converted into a hotel and restaurant. Rooms and corridors are bedecked in ecclesiastical art and there's no lack of luxury. Probably the most atmospheric hotel in Guatemala. Off-season discounts of up to fifty percent. Doubles US$150. ⑨.

Hotel Van Gogh, 6 Av Norte 14 (☎ & fax 8320376). Homely atmosphere, attractive rooms, a nice bar/TV lounge with log fires in winter, a café, and email and fax services. ④.

Hotel Villa San Francisco, 1 Av Sur 15 (☎8323383). Well run, Swiss-owned hotel with secure, pleasant rooms, a rooftop terrace and very competitive email, fax and phone services. ②–③.

Mesón Panza Verde, 5 Av Sur 19 (☎ & fax 8322925). Small, immaculately furnished hotel in a colonial-style building that is also home to one of Antigua's premier restaurants. Supremely comfortable suites, some with four-poster beds. Faultless service. Breakfast included. ⑥–⑧.

Posada Asjemenou, 5 Av Norte 31 (☎8322670, fax 8322832). Comfortable rooms with colonial feel. Good value, either with or without private bathroom. ④–⑤.

Posada de Doña Angelina, 4 C Poniente 33 (☎8325173). Popular budget option. Rooms are a bit gloomy, but there are plenty of them, some with private bath. Close to the bus terminal, so not the most tranquil place in town. Run by a dynamic señora. ②–③.

Posada del Hermano Pedro, 3 C Oriente 3 (☎8322089, fax 8322087). Comfortable hotel in a tastefully converted colonial mansion. Good location. When the rooftop bar opens, the views will be stunning. ⑥.

Posada Ruiz 2, 2 C Poniente 25 (no phone). Small rooms with no frills but extremely cheap rates and just a short stumble from the bus terminal. Its sister hotel, *Posada Ruiz 1*, at Alameda Santa Lucia 17, is similar. ①.

Posada San Sebastian, 3 Av Norte 4 (☎ & fax 8322621). Charming establishment. Each room is individually decorated with antiques; there's a gorgeous little bar and the location is very convenient. Excellent value. ⑥.

La Tatuana, 6 Av Sur 3 (☎8320537). Small hotel with imagintively decorated rooms, all with private bath. Extremely good value for the price. ④.

The City

Antigua has an incredible number of ruined and restored **colonial buildings**, and although these constitute only a fraction of the city's original architectural splendour, they do give an idea of its former extravagance. However, the prospect of visiting them all can seem overwhelming; if you'd rather just see the gems, make La Merced, Las Capuchinas, Casa Popenoe and San Francisco your targets.

The Parque Central

The focus of the colonial city was its central plaza, the **Parque Central**. For centuries it served as the hub of the city, bustling with constant activity. A huge market spilled out across it, cleared only for bullfights, military parades, floggings and public hangings. The calm of today's shady plaza, with its risqué fountain, is relatively recent.

The most imposing of the surrounding structures is the **Catedral de San José**, on the eastern side. The first cathedral was begun in 1545 but an earthquake brought down much of the roof and, in 1670, it was decided to start on a new cathedral worthy of the town's role as a capital city. The scale was astounding: a vast dome, five naves, eighteen chapels and an altar inlaid with mother-of-pearl, ivory and silver. But in 1773, it was destroyed yet again by an earthquake. Today, two of the chapels have been restored, and inside is a figure of Christ by the colonial sculptor, Quirio Cataño. Behind the church, entered from 5 C Oriente, are the remains of the rest of the original structure, a mass of fallen masonry and some rotting beams, broken arches and hefty pillars. Buried beneath the floor are some of the great names of the Conquest, including Alvarado, his wife Beatriz de la Cueva, Bishop Marroquín and the historian Bernal Díaz del Castillo.

Along the entire south side of the square runs the squat two-storey facade of the **Palace of the Captains General**, with a row of 27 arches along each floor. It was originally constructed in 1558 but rebuilt after earthquake damage. The palace was home to the colonial rulers and also housed the barracks of the dragoons, the stables, the royal mint, law courts, tax offices, great ballrooms, a large bureaucracy, and a lot more besides. Today it contains the local government offices, the headquarters of the Sacatepéquez police department and the tourist office. Directly opposite is the **Ayuntamiento**, the city hall, which dates from 1740 and remained undamaged until the 1976 earthquake. It holds a couple of minor museums, the **Museo de Santiago** (Tues–Fri 9am–4pm, Sat & Sun 9am–noon & 2–4pm; US$1.60), which holds a collection of colonial artefacts, and the **Museo del Libro Antiguo** (same hours; US$1.60), in the rooms that held the first printing press in Central America. A replica of the press is on display, alongside some copies of the works produced on it.

South and east of the Parque Central

Across the street from the ruined cathedral, in 5 C Oriente, is the **Museo de Arte Colonial** (Tues–Fri 9am–4pm, Sat & Sun 9am–noon & 2–4pm; US$4), formerly the site of a university. The deep-set windows and beautifully ornate cloisters make it one of the finest architectural survivors in Antigua. The museum contains a good collection of dark and brooding religious art, sculpture, furniture and murals depicting life on the colonial campus.

On the corner of 5 C Oriente and 1 Av Sur is the **Casa Popenoe** (Mon–Sat 2–4pm; US$1), a superbly restored colonial mansion, which gives an interesting insight into domestic life in colonial times. Originally owned by a Spanish judge, it was abandoned for some time until its painstaking restoration by Dr Wilson Popenoe, a United Fruit Company scientist. Among the paintings are portraits of Bishop Marroquín and the menacing-looking Alvarado himself. The kitchen and servants' quarters have also been carefully renovated and you can see the original bread ovens, the herb garden, and the pigeon loft which would have provided the occupants with their mail service.

A little further down 1 Av Sur is the imposing church of **San Francisco** (daily 8am –6pm). One of the oldest churches in Antigua, dating from 1579, it grew into a vast religious and cultural centre that included a school, a hospital, music rooms, a printing press and a monastery. All of it was lost, though, in the 1773 earthquake. Inside the church are buried the remains of **Hermano Pedro de Betancourt** (a Franciscan from the Canary Islands who founded the Hospital of Belén in Antigua). Pilgrims come here from all over Central America to ask for the benefit of his powers of miraculous intervention. The **ruins** of the monastery, which are among the most impressive in Antigua, have pleasant grassy verges with good picnic potential.

VOLCANO TOURS FROM ANTIGUA

A number of outfits in Antigua run guided tours to climb **Volcán Pacaya** near Guatemala City. These trips cost around US$12–15 per person and also enable you to visit the volcano at night without having to camp out. Though the spectacle is astounding, there is an element of danger involved and not just from falling rocks and ash. A number of cowboy operators offer trips to Pacaya and some occasionally set up "robberies" of their own tourists. Though there is a small risk of trouble no matter who you go with, try Quetzal Volcano Expeditions, who advertise in *Doña Luisa's*; Gran Jaguar Tours, 4 C Poniente 30 (☎8322712); or Adventuras Vacacionales, 5 Av Sur 11B (☎8323352).

North and west of the Parque Central

At the junction of 2 C Oriente and 2 Av Norte is the site of **Las Capuchinas** (Tues–Sun 9am–5pm; US$1.60), the largest and most impressive of the city's convents, dating from 1726, whose ruins are some of the best preserved but least understood in Antigua. The Capuchin nuns who lived here were not allowed any visual contact with the outside world: food was passed to them by means of a turntable and they could only speak to visitors through a grille. The ruins are the most beautiful in Antigua, with fountains, courtyards and massive earthquake-proof pillars. The most unusual point is the tower or "retreat" with eighteen tiny cells set into the walls on the top floor and a lower floor incorporating seventeen small recesses, some with stone rings.

A couple of blocks to the west, spanning 5 Av Norte, is the arch of **Santa Catalina**, all that remains of the original convent founded here in 1609. The arch was built in order for the nuns to walk between the two halves of the establishment without being exposed to the pollution of the outside world. Somehow it has managed to defy the constant onslaught of earthquakes.

Walking under the arch and to the end of the street, you reach the church of **La Merced**, which boasts one of the most intricate facades in the entire city. Look closely and you'll see the outline of a corn cob, a design not normally used by the Catholic church and probably added by the original Maya labourers. The church is still in use, but the cloisters and gardens lie in ruins, exposed to the sky.

Continue west down 1 C Poniente to the junction of the tree-lined Alameda Santa Lucía, and you reach the spectacular remains of **San Jeronimo**, a school built in 1739. Well-kept gardens are woven between the huge blocks of fallen masonry and crumbling walls. On the other side of the bus station is an imposing monument to **Rafael Landivar** (1731–93), a Jesuit composer who is generally considered to be the finest poet of the colonial era. Behind the bus station at C de Recoletos 55, the **K'ojom Casa de la Música** (Mon–Fri 9am–12.30pm & 2–5pm, Sat closes at 4pm; US$1) is a small but delightful museum devoted to indigenous music and ceremony, with some fascinating photographs of Maya life.

Eating and drinking

In Antigua the choice of **food** is even more cosmopolitan than the population. You can munch your way around the world in a number of reasonably authentic restaurants for a few dollars a time, or dine in real style for around US$10 a head. The only thing that seems hard to come by is authentic Guatemalan comedor food – which will be quite a relief if you've been subsisting on eggs and beans in the mountains.

Cafés

Bagdad Café, 1 C Poniente 9. Simple courtyard café that bakes its own bread. Healthy snacks and tasty sandwiches and cakes. Also has in-house email, fax and phone facilities.

Café Condesa, west side of plaza, through the Casa del Conde bookshop. Extremely civilized place to enjoy an excellent breakfast, coffee and cake, or full lunch. Gurgling fountain and period charm create a nice tone for the long, lazy Sunday brunches favoured by Antiguan society.

Café la Fuente, in *La Fuente*, 4 C Oriente 14. Vegetarian restaurant/café where you can eat stuffed aubergine and falafel or sip coffee in one of the most attractive restored courtyards in the city.

Jugocentre Peroleto, Alameda Santa Lucía 36. Brilliant hole-in-the-wall cabin with excellent and cheap healthy breakfasts, fruit juices and delicious cakes.

Restaurants

El Asador de Don Martín, 4 Av Norte 16. Superb colonial setting. Beautiful dining rooms and a lovely roof terrace with some of the finest views in Antigua. Three ambitious menus and a huge wine list. Well worth a splurge.

Café-Pizzeria Asjemenou, 5 C Poniente 4. A favourite for its legendary breakfasts. Also very strong on pizza and calzone, but the service can be erratic. Daily 9am–10pm.

Beijing, 6 Av Sur and 5 C Poniente. Antigua's best Chinese and East Asian food, prepared with a few imaginative twists. Good noodle dishes, soups and Vietnamese spring rolls. Fairly expensive.

Doña Luisa's, 4 C Oriente 12. One of the most popular places in town. The setting is relaxed but the menu could do with a revamp – the basic line-up of chilli con carne, baked potatoes, salads and hamburgers is looking a little tired. An adjoining shop sells bread and pastries baked on the premises.

La Escudilla, 4 Av Norte 4. Tremendous courtyard restaurant, usually extremely busy on account of the excellent quetzal/quality food exchange. The pasta is good, the US$3 all-day, all-night set meal is exceptional value and the delicious salads are unequalled in Antigua. Vegetarians have plenty of tasty choices too. You may have to wait, though, when it's busy.

Café Flor, 4 Av Sur 1. Highly commendable Thai, Indonesian and Indian cuisine. While the cooking is not a hundred percent authentic, dishes are still well executed and the atmosphere relaxed and convivial. Reasonable prices.

La Fonda de la Calle Real, upstairs at 5 Av Norte 5; and a smarter new restaurant in a beautiful colonial house at 3 C Poniente 7. Probably the most famous restaurants in Antigua. Try the excellent Guatemalan specialities, including *pepián* (spicy meat stew) and *caldo real* (chicken soup). Moderate to expensive. Closed Wed.

Frida's, 5 Av Norte 29. Lively atmosphere and the best Mexican food in town – a tasty selection of enchiladas, fajitas etc. Decorated with Fifties Americana.

Café Panchoy, 6 Av Norte 1B. Good-value cooking with a real Guatemalan flavour – top steaks and some traditional favourites like *chiles rellenos*. Excellent margaritas. Closed Tues.

Panza Verde, 5 Av Sur 19. One of Antigua's most exclusive restaurants. Exemplary European cuisine, professional service and a nice setting, with well-spaced tables grouped around a courtyard garden. Try the trout or sea bass meunière.

Los Pollos, 7 Av and 4 C Poniente. The restaurant everyone loves to hate, home to assorted nocturnal Antiguan low-life. The soggy fries and deep-fried chicken may not seem that tempting, but wait until you stumble out of a bar at midnight. Open 24hr.

Rainbow Café, 7 Av Sur 8. Relaxed bohemian crowd in this favourite travellers' hangout. Great vegetarian menu of creative salads and pasta dishes, epic smoothies and decent cappuccinos matched by friendly, prompt service. Also home to one of Antigua's best travel agents, a good secondhand bookshop, and regular musical jams.

Nightlife and entertainment

Evening activity is officially curtailed in Antigua by a "**dry law**" which forbids the sale of alcohol after 1am. The places listed below on 5 and 7 Av Norte are particularly popular with the gringo crowd and all open at around 7pm. Antigua's club scene is limited to two venues; both tend to be quiet Monday to Wednesday, busy Thursday and heaving at weekends.

There are a number of small **video cinemas** that show a range of Western films on a daily basis – *Trainspotting*, *Salvador* and *Reservoir Dogs* are on almost permanently. Fliers with weekly listings are posted on noticeboards all over town. The main cinemas are Cinemaya, 2 C Oriente 2; Cinema Bistro, 5 Av Norte 28; Cinema Tecún Umán, 6 C Poniente 34a; and Proyecto Cultural el Sitio, 5 C Poniente 15.

Bars

La Chimanea, 7 Av Norte 7. One of the more popular bars, though the music selection is very eclectic – expect everything from Rod Stewart to Black Sabbath.

Macondo's, 5 Av Norte and 2 C Poniente. Probably the closest thing Antigua has to a pub, though the constant visual barrage of music videos spoils things somewhat. Closed Mon.

Picasso's, 7 Av Norte 16. Good drinking hole that can get quite lively in high season. Usually closed Sun.

Riki's Bar, 4 Av Norte 4. Unquestionably the most happening place in town due to the excellent site inside *La Escudilla*, the jazz-only policy and the unrivalled happy hour (7–9pm) which means this place is packed most nights.

Clubs

La Canoa, 5 C Poniente between 4 Av and 5 Av. A small, unpretentious club where people come to dance to mainly Latin sounds. Merengue is the main ingredient, spiked with a dash of salsa and reggae; they also play a few tracks of western and Latin pop/rock. Good mix of locals and foreigners and reasonable drink prices. US$2 at weekends, free other nights.

La Casbah, 5 Av Norte 30. The most controversial place in town and seen as positively subversive by the old school, including the tourist office. It is undeniably pretentious and primarily attracts a well-heeled crowd from Antigua and Guatemala City. The venue, in the ruins of an ancient church, is spectacular and the music can occasionally match the site, with deep bassline-driven dance mixes. Drinks are expensive. Mon–Thurs free, Fri & Sat around US$4.

Listings

Banks and exchange Banco Industrial, 5 Av Sur 4, just south of the plaza (Mon–Fri 8.30am–7pm, Sat 8am–5pm), has a 24hr Visa ATM. Other convenient banks include Banco del Agro, north side of the plaza (Mon–Fri 9am–8pm, Sat 9am–6pm), and Lloyds, in the northeast corner of the plaza (Mon–Fri 9am–5pm), which changes sterling travellers' cheques.

Bookstores Casa Andinista, 4 C Oriente 5A; Casa del Conde, on the west side of the plaza; Un Poco de Todo, also on the west side of the plaza. The Rainbow Reading Room, 7 Av Sur 8, has by far the largest selection of secondhand books.

Car and bike rental Tabarini, 2 C Poniente 19A (☎ & fax 8323091), and Avis, 5 Av Norte 22 (☎ & fax 8322692), both rent cars from around US$60 a day, and jeeps from US$80, including unlimited mileage and insurance. Mountain bikes can be rented at *Posada San Vincente*, 6 Av Sur 6 (☎ & fax 8323311), and Aviatur, 5 Av Norte 27 (☎ & fax 8322642), for around US$8 a day or US$25 a week. For motorbikes, try Jopa, 6 Av Norte 3 (☎8320794).

Laundry Rainbow Laundry, 6 Av Sur 15 (Mon–Sat 7am–7pm).

Libraries and cultural institutes El Sitio, 5 C Poniente 15 (☎8323037), has an active theatre, library and art gallery, and regularly hosts exhibitions and concerts; see the *Revue* or *Guatemala Weekly* papers for listings.

Medical Care 24hr emergency service at the Santa Lucía Hospital, Calzada Santa Lucía Sur 7 (☎8323122). Doctor Aceituno, who speaks good English, has his surgery at 2 C Poniente 7 (☎8320512).

Pharmacies Farmacia Santa María, west side of plaza (8am–10pm).

Police The Police HQ is on the south side of the plaza, next to the tourist office (☎8320572). The tourist police are just off the plaza on 4 Av Norte.

Post office Alameda de Santa Lucía opposite the bus terminal (Mon–Fri 8am–4.30pm). DHL are at 6 C Sur 16 (☎8323718 or 8323732) and Quick Shipping is at 3 Av Norte 26 (☎8322595).

Supermarkets La Bodegona on 4 C Poniente, close to Alameda Santa Lucía.

Telephones The Telgua office is half a block south of the plaza on 5 Av Sur (daily 7am–10pm) but rates are higher here than anywhere else and you'll have to queue. For all communication services, including email, Conexion in the La Fuente cultural centre on 4 C Oriente 14 (☎8323768) is probably the most well organized place in town. *Hotel San Francisco*, 1 Av Sur 15 (24hr; ☎8323383), also has competitive rates for email, fax and overseas calls. The very cheapest place to make international calls is the CSA language school on 6 Av Norte 15 (☎8323922). Several offices, cafés, hotels and language schools will send email – try the internet café *Cybermannia* at 5 Av Norte 25B (☎8320162).

Travel agents There are dozens of travel agents in Antigua; the following are the most professional and reliable: The Rainbow Travel Center, 7 Av Sur 8 (Mon–Sat 9am–6pm; ☎8324202 or 8324203, fax 8324206); Tivoli, 5 Av Norte 10A, on the west side of the plaza (Mon–Sat 9am–1pm & 3–5.30pm; ☎8323041); Monarcas, 6 Av Norte 60A (☎ & fax 8323343), runs Maya culture and ecology tours, and trips to Semuc Champey and Copán; Adventure Travel Center Viareal, 5 Av Norte 25B (☎ & fax 8320162), organizes adventure and sailing trips, plus shuttle buses.

Around Antigua

The countryside around Antigua is superbly fertile and breathtakingly beautiful. The valley is dotted with small villages, ranging from the *ladino* coffee centre of Alotenango to the traditional *indígena* village of Santa María de Jesús. None of them is more than an hour or two away and all make interesting day-trips. For the more adventurous, the volcanic peaks of Agua, Acatenango and Fuego offer strenuous but superb hiking, best done through a specialist agency.

Santa María de Jesús and Volcán Agua

Up above Antigua, a smooth new sealed road snakes through the coffee bushes and past the village of San Juan del Obispo before arriving in **SANTA MARÍA DE JESÚS**, starting point for the ascent of Volcán Agua. Perched high on the shoulder of the volcano, the village is some 500m above Antigua, with magnificent views over the Panchoy valley and east towards the smoking cone of Pacaya. The village was founded at the end of the sixteenth century and is of little interest, though the women wear beautiful purple *huipiles*. **Buses** run from Antigua to Santa María every hour or so from 6am to 5pm, and the trip takes thirty minutes.

Agua is the easiest and by far the most popular of Guatemala's big cones to climb: on some Saturday nights hundreds of people spend the night at the top. The trail starts in Santa María de Jesús: head straight across the plaza, between the two ageing pillars, and up the street opposite the church doors. Take a right turn just before the end, and then continue past the cemetery and out of the village. From here on it's a fairly simple climb on a clear path, cutting across the road that goes some of the way up. The climb can take anything from four to six hours, and the peak, at 3766m, is always cold at night. There is shelter (though not always room) in a small chapel at the summit, however, and the views certainly make it worth the struggle.

San Andrés Itzapa

The main road from Antigua to Chimaltenango ascends from the Panchoy valley, past dusty farming villages, before a dirt track branches off to **SAN ANDRÉS ITZAPA**, one of the many villages badly hit by the 1976 earthquake. San Andrés is home to to the cult of **San Simón** (or Maximón), the "evil saint", who is housed in his own pagan chapel. Despite San Andrés being just 18km from Antigua, few tourists visit this shrine, and you may feel less intrusive and more welcome here than his other places of abode, which include Zunil (see p.197) and Santiago Atitlán (p.187).

To pay San Simón a visit, head for the central plaza from the dirt road into the village, turn right when you reach the church, walk two blocks, then up a little hill and you should spot street vendors selling charms, incense and candles. If you get lost, just ask for the "Casa de San Simón". Once you've tracked him down, you'll find that Maximón lives in a fairly strange world, his image surrounded by drunken men, cigar-smoking women and hundreds of burning candles, each symbolizing a request: red for love, white for health, and so on. Local stores stock candles and incense and there are also books on witchcraft for sale. Uniquely in Guatemala, this San Simón attracts a largely *ladino* congregation and he is particularly popular with prostitutes. Inside the dimly lit shrine, the walls are adorned with hundreds of plaques from all over Guatemala and Central America, thanking San Simón for his help. You may be offered a *limpia* or **soul cleansing**, which involves being beaten by one of the resident women workers with a bushel of herbs. A bottle of the firewater *aguardiente* is also demolished: some is offered to San Simón, some of it you'll have to drink yourself and the rest is consumed by the attendant, who sprays you with alcohol (from her mouth) for your sins – all in all, quite an experience. If you want to visit San Simón you have to do so between sunrise and sunset, as he's believed to be asleep at other times.

To get to San Andrés Itzapa from Antigua, take any **bus** heading to Chimaltenango from the terminal (every 20min, 5.30am–7pm) and get the driver to drop you off where the dirt road leaves the highway. From there you can hitch or else it's a thirty-minute walk.

The Carretera Interamericana

Leaving Guatemala City to the west, the serpentine **Carretera Interamericana** cuts right through the central highlands as far as the border with Mexico. In its entirety, this road stretches from Alaska to Chile (with a short break in southern Panamá), and here in Guatemala it forms the backbone of transport in the highlands. As you travel around, the highway and its junctions will inevitably become all too familiar since, wherever you're going, it's invariably easiest to catch the first local bus to the Carretera Interamericana and then flag down one of the buses heading along the highway.

Heading west from the capital, you'll climb steadily up a three-laned highway to **San Lucas Sacatepéquez**, from where a well maintained side road descends to Antigua. There are other major junctions on the Interamericana which you'll soon get to know well. The first of these is **Chimaltenango**, an important town and capital of its own department. From its ugly sprawl along the highway you can also make connections to or from Antigua. Continuing west, **Los Encuentros** is the next main junction, where one road heads off to the north for Chichicastenango and Santa Cruz del Quiché and another branches south to Panajachel and Lago de Atitlán. Beyond this, the highway climbs high over a mountainous ridge before dropping to **Cuatro Caminos**, from where side roads lead to Quetzaltenango, Totonicapán and San Francisco el Alto. The Interamericana continues on to Huehuetenango before reaching the Mexican border at

La Mesilla. Virtually every bus travelling along the highway will stop at all of these junctions and you'll be able to buy fruit, drink and fast food from a resident army of vendors, some of whom will storm the bus looking for business, while others are content to dangle their wares outside your window.

Leaving Guatemala City, the first place of interest is **SANTIAGO SACATEPÉQUEZ**, 1km or so to the north of the highway. The road branches off from San Lucas Sacatepéquez and buses shuttle back and forth along the branch road. The best time to visit Santiago is on November 1, for a local fiesta to honour the **Day of the Dead**. Massive kites made from paper and tobacco are flown in the cemetery to release the souls of the dead from their agony. The festival is immensely popular, and hundreds of Guatemalans and tourists come every year to watch the spectacle. Teams of young men struggle to get the kites aloft while the crowd looks on with bated breath, rushing for cover if a kite comes crashing to the ground. There is also a **market** in Santiago on Tuesday and Sunday.

Chimaltenango

Founded by Pedro de Portocarrero in 1526, on the site of the Cakchiquel centre of Bokoh, **CHIMALTENANGO** was later considered as a possible site for the new capital. It has the misfortune, however, of being positioned on a continental divide and it suffered terribly from the earthquake in 1976 which shook and flattened much of the surrounding area. Today's town, its centre just to the north of the main road, is dominated by that fact, with dirt streets, breeze-block walls and an air of weary desperation. The town extracts what little business it can from the stream of traffic on the Interamericana, and the roadside is crowded with cheap comedores, mechanics' workshops, and sleazy bars that become brothels by night. "Chimal" is also home to a good new **Spanish school** where you can live and study away from the gringo scene of Antigua, but within firing range if you need to catch a film or have a meal (see p.129). **Buses** passing through Chimaltenango run to all points along the Carretera Interamericana. For Antigua they leave every twenty minutes between 5.30am and 6.30pm from the market in town – though you can also wait at the turnoff on the highway.

Tecpán and the ruins of Iximché

Continuing west along a fast section of the Carretera Interamericana, the next site of interest lies close to the small town of **TECPÁN**, ninety minutes or so from Guatemala City. This may well have been the site chosen by Alvarado as the first Spanish capital, to which the Spanish forces retreated in August 1524, after they'd been driven out of Iximché. Today it's a place of no great interest, though it has a substantial number of restaurants and guest houses. It caters for a mainly Guatemalan clientele who come to picnic at the ruins and drink and eat in town.

The **ruins of Iximché** (daily 8am–5pm; US$4), the pre-conquest capital of the Cakchiquel, are about 5km south of Tecpán on a beautiful exposed hillside, protected on three sides by steep slopes and surrounded by pine forests. From the early days of the Conquest, the Cakchiquel allied themselves with the conquistadors, so the structures here suffered less than most at the hands of the Spanish. Since then, however, time and weather have taken their toll and the majority of the buildings that housed a population of ten thousand have disappeared, leaving only a few stone-built pyramids, clearly defined plazas and a couple of ball courts. Nevertheless, the site is strongly atmospheric and its grassy plazas, ringed with pine trees, are marvellously peaceful, especially during the week, when you may well have the place to yourself. The ruins are still actively used as a focus for Maya worship: sacrifices and offerings take place down a small trail through the pine trees behind the final plaza.

To get there, take any bus travelling along the Carretera Interamericana between Chimaltenango and Los Encuentros and ask to be dropped at Tecpán. To get to the ruins, simply walk through Tecpán and out the other side of the plaza, passing the Centro de Salud, and follow the road through the fields for about 5km – an hour or so on foot. With any luck you'll be able to hitch some of the way, particularly at weekends when the road can be fairly busy. There's **camping** at the site but bring your own food as the small shop sells little other than drinks. Iximché's shady location is perfect for a picnic or barbecue. If you're not planning to camp, be back on the Carretera Interamericana before 6pm to be sure of a bus.

Chichicastenango

The road for Chichicastenango and the **department of El Quiché** leaves the Carretera Interamericana at the **Los Encuentros** junction, another thirty kilometres past the Iximché turnoff. Heading north from Los Encuentros, the highway drops down through dense, aromatic pine forests, plunging into a deep ravine before bottoming out by a tributary of the Río Motagua.

Continuing upwards around endless switchbacks, the road eventually reaches **CHICHICASTENANGO**, Guatemala's "mecca del turismo". If it's market day, you may get embroiled in one of the country's very few traffic jams – a rare event outside the capital — as traders, tourists and locals all struggle to reach the town centre. In this

CHICHICASTENANGO

△ Santa Cruz del Quiché (19km)

N

Buses to Santa Cruz
Buses to CA1 & Guatemala City

Banco Industrial
Banco Del Ejercito

Centro Comercial

El Calvario
Plaza

Museo Rossbach
Former Monastery
Santo Tomás

Mask Shop

Pascual Abaj

ACCOMMODATION

Hospedaje El Salvador	5
Hospedaje Girón	1
Hotel Chugüilá	2
Hotel Posada Belen	6
Hotel Santo Tomás	3
Maya Inn	4

0   200 m

Los Encuentros & Guatemala City ▽

compact and traditional town of cobbled streets, adobe houses and red-tiled roofs, the calm of day-to-day life is shattered on a twice-weekly basis by the **Sunday and Thursday markets** – Sunday is the busiest. The market attracts myriad tourists and commercial traders, as well as Maya weavers from throughout the central highlands.

The market is by no means all that sets Chichicastenango apart, however. For the local Maya population it's an important centre of culture and religion. The area was inhabited by the Cakchiquel long before the arrival of the Spanish, and over the years Maya culture and folk Catholicism have been treated with a rare degree of respect – although inevitably this blessing has been mixed with waves of arbitrary persecution and exploitation. Today, the town has an incredible collection of Maya artefacts, parallel *indígena* and *ladino* governments, and a church that makes no effort to disguise its acceptance of unconventional pagan worship. Traditional weaving is also adhered to here and the women wear superb, heavily embroidered *huipiles*. The men's costume of short trousers and jackets of black wool embroidered with silk is highly distinguished, although it's very expensive to make and these days most men opt for western dress. However, for the town's fiesta (December 14–21) and on Sundays, a handful of *cofradías* (elders of the religious hierarchy) still wear traditional clothing and carry spectacular silver processional crosses and incense burners.

Arrival and information

There's no bus station in Chichi, but the corner of 5 C and 5 Av operates loosely as a terminal. **Buses** heading between Guatemala City and Santa Cruz del Quiché pass through Chichicastenango every half-hour, stopping in town for a few minutes to load up with passengers. In Guatemala City, buses leave from the terminal in Zona 4, from 4am to about 5pm. Coming from Antigua, you can pick up a bus easily in Chimaltenango. From Panajachel, you can take any bus up to Los Encuentros and change there; or on market days there are several direct buses, supplemented by a steady flow of special tourist shuttles run by various companies. There are also special shuttle services from Antigua on market days.

If you're bitten by market fever and need to **change money**, there's no problem in Chichi, even on a Sunday. Try Banco Ejercito on 6 C (Tues–Sun 9am–5pm) or, almost opposite, Banco Industrial (Mon 10am–2pm, Wed–Sun 10am–5pm), which does Visa transactions. *Hotel Santo Tomás* also offers exchange. The **post office** (Mon–Fri 9am–5.30pm) and **Telgua** (daily 7am–8pm) are both on 6 Av, up behind the church.

Accommodation

Hotels can be in short supply on Saturday nights before the Sunday market, but you shouldn't have a problem on other days. Prices can also be inflated on market days, though at other times you can usually negotiate a good deal.

Hospedaje el Salvador, 5 Av 10–09 (☎7561329). Best budget deal in town, with a vast warren of rooms, a bizarre external colour scheme, and cheap prices. Insist that the owners turn on the hot water. ②.

Hospedaje Girón, 6 C 4–52 (☎7561156). Rooms are pretty, clean and well priced, either with or without private bath. Good value for single travellers. ③.

Hotel Chugüilá, 5 Av 5–24 (☎ & fax 7561134). Attractive rooms, all on different levels and some with fireplaces. Lovely greenery and pot plants everywhere. Secure parking. ④–⑤.

Hotel Posada Belen, 12 C 5–55 (☎7561244). Not the most attractive rooms, though half have private bathrooms; the views are good from the back. ②.

Hotel Santo Tomás, 7 Av 5–32 (☎7561061, fax 7561306). Very comfortable, well-appointed rooms set around two colonial-style courtyards. Rooms 29–37 are the ones to book if you can – they have great mountain views. Restaurant, swimming pool, sauna and jacuzzi. ⑦.

Mayan Inn, 8 C & 3 Av (☎7561176, fax 7561212). Chichi's oldest tourist hotel offers very comfortable rooms with old-fashioned period charm. Though its character is undeniable, prices are a bit steep. ⑨.

The Town

Though most visitors come here for the market, Chichicastenango also offers an unusual insight into traditional religious practices in the highlands. At the main **Iglesia de Santo Tomás**, in the southeast corner of the plaza, the Quiché Maya have been left to adopt their own style of worship, blending pre-Columbian and Catholic rituals. The church was built in 1540 on the site of a Maya altar, and rebuilt in the eighteenth century. It's said that indigenous locals became interested in worshipping here after Francisco Ximénez, the priest from 1701 to 1703, started reading their holy book, the **Popul Vuh**.

Before entering the church, it's customary to make offerings in a fire at the base of the steps or to burn incense in perforated cans, a practice that leaves a cloud of thin, sweet smoke hanging over the entrance. Inside is an astonishing scene of avid worship. A soft hum of constant murmuring fills the air as the faithful kneel to place candles on low-level stone platforms for their ancestors and the saints. For these people, the entire building is alive with the souls of the dead, each located in a specific part of the church. Don't enter the building by the front door, which is reserved for *cofrades* and senior church officials; use the **side door** instead and be warned that taking photographs inside the building is considered deeply offensive – don't even contemplate it.

Beside the church is a former monastery, now used by the parish administration. It was here that the Spanish priest Francisco Ximénez became the first outsider to be shown the Popol Vuh. His copy of the manuscript is now housed in the Newberry Library in Chicago: the original was lost some time later in the eighteenth century. The text itself was written just to the north of here, in Utatlán, shortly after the arrival of the Spanish, and is a brilliant poem of over nine thousand lines that details the cosmology, mythology and traditional history of the Quiché.

On the south side of the plaza, the **Rossbach Museum** (Tues, Wed, Fri & Sat 8am–noon & 2–4pm, Thurs & Sun 8am–1pm & 2–4pm; US$0.20) houses a broad-ranging collection of pre-Columbian artefacts, mostly small pieces of ceramics, some as much as two thousand years old, that had been kept by local people in their homes.

THE CEMETERY AND THE SHRINE OF PASCUAL ABAJ

The town **cemetery**, down the hill behind El Calvario, offers further evidence of the strange mix of religions that characterizes Chichicastenango. The graves are marked by anything from a grand tomb to a small earth mound, and in the centre is a Maya shrine where the usual offerings of incense and alcohol are made.

The church and cemetery are certainly not the only scenes of Maya religious activity: the hills that surround the town, like so many throughout the country, are topped with shrines. The closest of these, **Pascual Abaj**, is less than a kilometre from the plaza and regularly visited by tourists, but it's important to remember that any ceremonies you may witness are deeply serious – you should keep your distance and be sensitive about taking photographs. The shrine is laid out in a typical pattern with several small altars facing a stern pre-Columbian sculpture. Offerings are usually overseen by a *brujo*, a type of shaman, and range from flowers to sacrificed chickens, always incorporating plenty of incense, alcohol and incantations.

To get to Pascual Abaj, walk down the hill beside Santo Tomás, take the first right, 9 Calle, and follow this as it winds its way out of town. You'll soon cross a stream and then a well-signposted route takes you through the courtyard of a workshop that churns out wooden masks. If you look up, you may see a thin plume of smoke if there's a ceremony in progress. The path continues uphill for ten minutes through a dense pine forest.

Eating

If you've come from Panajachel or Antigua, the dining scene here may come as a bit of a shock to the system. You won't find sushi or Thai curries in Chichi, just simple, good-value Guatemalan comedor food. The plaza on **market day** is the place to come for authentic highland eating: try one of the makeshift food stalls, where you'll find cauldrons of stew, rice and beans.

Café la Villa de los Cofrades, in the Centro Commercial on the north side of the plaza. Good set meals – soup, a main dish and salad, fries and bread costs under US$4. The breakfasts are also superb.

Buenadventura, upper floor, inside the Centro Comercial. Bird's-eye view of the vegetable market; simple, no-nonsense food and the breakfasts are the cheapest in town.

La Fonda del Tzijolaj, upper floor in the Centro Comercial. Yes, the name's unpronounceable, but the food is probably the best in town and the balcony views of the church of Santo Tomás and the market are excellent. Try the *chiles rellenos*.

Comedor Gumarcaj, opposite the *Hotel Santo Tomás*. Simple, cheap and friendly comedor that serves up a mean chicken and chips and lush licuados.

Santa Cruz del Quiché and around

The capital of the Department of El Quiché, **SANTA CRUZ DEL QUICHÉ** lies half an hour north of Chichicastenango. A good paved road connects the two towns, running through pine forests and ravines, and past the **Laguna Lemoa**, a lake which, according to local legend, was originally filled with tears wept by the wives of Quiché kings after their husbands had been slaughtered by the Spanish.

On the central **plaza**, there's a large colonial **church**, built by the Dominicans with stone from the ruins of Utatlán. The Catholic church suffered terribly in Quiché in the late 1970s and early 1980s, when priests were singled out and murdered for their connections with the cooperative movement. The situation was so serious that, in 1981, Bishop Juan Gerardi (who was himself assassinated in April 1998) withdrew all his priests from the department, although they've since returned to their posts.

Beside the church, the large clock tower is also said to have been built from Utatlán stone stripped from the temple of Tohil, and in the middle of the plaza, a defiant **statue** of the Quiché hero, Tecún Umán, stands prepared for battle. His position is undermined somewhat by an ugly urban tangle of hardware stores, bakeries and trash that surrounds this corner of the square and the spectacularly ugly, looming presence of the tin-roofed, breezeblock **market** building.

Arrival and information

The **bus terminal**, a large, open affair, is about four blocks south and a couple east of the central plaza. Connections are generally excellent from Quiché. There's a constant stream of second-class **buses** to Guatemala City, going every half-hour between 3.30am and 5pm (3hr 30min); all pass through Chichicastenango (30min) and Los Encuentros (1hr). There are also regular services to Nebaj between 8.30am and 4pm (every 1hr 30min; 4hr), to Uspantán four times a day between 9am and 2pm (5hr), and to Quetzaltenango between 3am and 1pm (3hr). Inter airlines also serve Quiché with daily **flights** from Guatemala City (25min; US$55 one-way). The airstrip is 4km south of the town centre.

The street directly north of the terminal is **1 Av**, which takes you up into the heart of the town. Two **banks** will change your travellers' cheques: Banco G&T, 6 A 3–00 (Mon–Fri 9am–7pm, Sat 9am–1pm), and Banco Industrial, at the northwest corner of the plaza (Mon–Fri 8.30am–5.30pm, Sat 8.30am–12.30pm), which also advances cash on Visa. If you're heading into the Ixil triangle (see p.178), you may need to stock up on **film**: try Kodak or Fuji, both one block northeast of the central church.

Accommodation

There's a limited range of **hotels** in Quiché and nothing luxurious. The cheapest are some extremely basic dives right beside the bus terminal. Most of the others are between the terminal and the plaza.

Hotel Rey K'iche, 8 C 0–39, Zona 5 (☎2325834). Two blocks north and one east from the terminal. Well-run, extremely clean and welcoming. Most of the 26 rooms have cable TV and private bath. ③–④.

Hotel Maya Quiché, 3 Av 4–19, Zona 1 (☎7551464). A friendly place with big clean rooms, some with bathroom. ②–③.

Posada San Antonio, 2 Av, two blocks from the terminal (no phone). Brand new in 1997 and the best budget deal in town. Rooms are smallish but very clean and the bathrooms (with hot water) are scrubbed with evangelical zeal. Decent in-house restaurant. ②.

Hotel San Pascual, 7 C 0–43, Zona 1 (☎7551107). Walk up 1 Av, and turn left into 7 C. Large, clean rooms and equally well kept communal bathrooms. ②–③.

Hospedaje Tropical, 1 Av and 9 C. Extremely basic place; no hot water but dirt cheap. ①.

Eating and drinking

There's very little to get excited about in Quiché. Most restaurants and cafés are grouped around the plaza. **El Torito Steakhouse**, 7 C 1–73, just southwest of the plaza, is the smartest place in town with kitsch cowboy decor and a menu that's a real carnivore's delight – try the sausages or fried chicken. On the west side of the plaza is **La Pizza de Ciro**, which dispenses reasonable pizzas that taste fine if you've come from remote Nebaj and pretty poor if you've journeyed from cosmopolitan Antigua. Close by are several uninspiring bakeries with dry pastries and cakes and also **Café la Torré**, a friendly place for a coffee, snack or a delicious piece of cheesecake. For no-nonsense comedor meals, try **Restaurante las Rosas**, 1 Av 1–28.

The ruins of Utatlán (K'umarkaaj)

Early in the fifteenth century, riding on the wave of successful conquest, the Quiché king Gucumatz (Feathered Serpent) founded a new capital, K'umarkaaj. A hundred years later, the Spanish arrived, renamed the city **Utatlán**, and then destroyed it. Today you can visit the ruins, about 4km to the west of Santa Cruz del Quiché.

According to the Popol Vuh, Gucumatz was a lord of great genius, assisted by powerful spirits, and there's no doubt that his capital was once a great city, with several separate citadels spread across neighbouring hilltops. It housed the nine dynasties of the tribal elite, including the four main Quiché lords, and contained a total of 23 palaces. The splendour of the city embodied the strength of the Quiché empire, which at its height boasted a population of around a million.

By the time of the Conquest, however, the Quiché had been severely weakened and their empire fractured. They first made contact with the Spanish on the Pacific Coast, suffering a heavy defeat at the hands of Alvarado's forces near Quetzaltenango, with the loss of their hero, Tecún Umán. The Quiché then invited the Spanish to their capital, but the suspicious Alvarado captured the Quiché leaders, burnt them alive and then destroyed the city.

The site (8am–5pm; US$2) is not as dramatic as some of the ruins in Guatemala, but impressive nonetheless, surrounded by deep ravines and pine forests. This setting and its fascinating historical significance make up for the lack of huge pyramids and stellae. There has been little restoration since the Spanish destroyed the city and only a few of the main structures are still recognizable, most buried beneath grassy mounds and shaded by pine trees. The small **museum** has a scale model of what the original city may once have looked like.

The central plaza is almost certainly where Alvarado burned alive the two Quiché leaders in 1524. Nowadays, it's where you'll find all the remaining three **temple buildings**, the great monuments of Tohil, Auilix and Hacauaitz, all of which were simple pyramids topped by thatched shelters. In the middle of the plaza there used to be a circular **tower**, the Temple of the Sovereign Plumed Serpent, and its foundations can still be made out. The only other feature that is still vaguely recognizable is the **ball court**, which lies beneath grassy banks to the south of the plaza.

Beneath the plaza is a long **tunnel** that runs underground for about 100m. Inside are nine **shrines**, perhaps signifying the nine levels of the Maya underworld, Xibalbá. Each is the subject of prayer and attention, but it is the ninth, housed inside a chamber that is the most actively used for sacrifice, incense and alcohol offerings. Why the tunnel was constructed remains uncertain, but some local legends have it that it was dug by the Quiché to hide their women and children from the advancing Spanish whom they planned to ambush at Utatlán.

Perhaps the most interesting thing about the site today is that *brujos*, traditional Maya priests, still come here to perform **religious rituals**, practices that predate the arrival of the Spanish by thousands of years. The entire area is covered in small burnt circles – the ashes of incense – and chickens are regularly sacrificed in and around the plaza. If there is a ceremony taking place you'll hear the mumbling of prayers and smell incense smoke as you enter the tunnel, in which case it's wise not to disturb the proceedings by approaching too closely.

You can walk or take a taxi here from Santa Cruz del Quiché. To walk, head south from the plaza along 2 Av, and then turn right down 10 C, which will take you all the way out to the site – it's a pleasant forty-minute hike. You're welcome to **camp** close to the ruins, but there there are no facilities or food. A taxi there and back with an hour at the ruins costs around US$8.

To the Cuchumatanes: Sacapulas and Uspantán

The land to the north of Santa Cruz del Quiché is sparsely inhabited and dauntingly hilly. About 10km out of town, the single rough road in this direction passes through San Pedro Jocopilas, and from there struggles on without tarmac, eventually dropping to the isolated town of **SACAPULAS**, two hours from Quiché. In a spectacular position on the Río Negro, beneath the foothills of the Cuchumatanes, Sacapulas has a small colonial church, and a good market every Thursday and Sunday beneath a huge ceiba tree in the plaza.

With its strategic position, Sacapulas should be a transport hub but, alas, it's not. To **get to Sacapulas** is not too difficult; you can catch any of the buses that leave Santa Cruz del Quiché for Uspantán or Nebaj. **Leaving Sacapulas** is far more difficult: buses leave at 1am and 3am so you'll probably have to **hitch**. Wait by the bridge as traffic heading for Quiché can turn left or right after crossing the river. There are also buses to Huehuetenango and to Uspantán but all services in this remote region are erratic and subject to delays and cancellations. Hitchhike whenever possible and expect to pay the same rate as you would on the bus.

At least if you get stuck there's a half decent place to **stay**; the *Restaurant Río Negro* offers basic but clean rooms (①). The cook, Manuela, serves good **meals** and excellent banana, pineapple and papaya milkshakes.

East of Sacapulas, a dirt road rises steeply, clinging to the mountainside and quickly leaving the Río Negro far below. As it climbs, the views are superb, with tiny Sacapulas dwarfed by the sheer enormity of the landscape. Eventually the road reaches a high valley and arrives in **USPANTÁN**, a small town lodged in a chilly gap in the mountains and often soaked in steady drizzle. Rigoberta Menchú, the Quiché Maya woman who won the 1992 Nobel Peace Prize, is from Chimel, a tiny village in this region. But probably the only reason you'll end up here is in order to get somewhere else. With the **buses for Cobán** and San Pedro Carchá leaving at around 3am, the best thing to do is go to bed. (The return buses leave San Pedro Carchá for Uspantán at 10am and noon.) There are two friendly pensiones, the *Casa del Viajero* (①) and the *Galindo* (①). **Buses for Uspantán**, via Sacapulas, leave Quiché at 9am, 11am, noon and 2pm, returning at 7pm, 11.30pm, 1am and 3am – a five-hour trip.

The Ixil triangle

High up on the spine of the Cuchumatanes, in a landscape of steep hills, bowl-shaped valleys and gushing rivers, is the **Ixil triangle**. Here the three small towns of Nebaj, Chajul and Cotzal, remote and extremely traditional, share a language spoken nowhere else in the country. This triangle of towns forms the hub of the **Ixil-speaking region**, a massive highland area which drops away towards the Mexican border and contains at least 100,000 inhabitants. These lush and rain-drenched hills are hard to reach and notoriously difficult to control, and today's relaxed atmosphere and highland charm conceal a bitter history of protracted conflict. It's an area that embodies some of the very best and the very worst characteristics of the Guatemalan highlands.

On the positive side is the beauty of the landscape and the strength of indigenous culture, both of which are overwhelming. When Church leaders moved into the area in the 1970s they found very strong communities with women included in the process of communal decision-making. The people were reluctant to accept new authority for fear that it would disrupt the age-old structures. Counterbalancing these strengths are the horrors of the human rights abuses that took place here over the last few decades, which must rate as some of the worst anywhere in Central America.

Before the arrival of the Spanish, the town of Nebaj was a sizeable centre, producing large quantities of jade and possibly allied in some way to Zaculeu (see p.200). The **Conquest** was particularly brutal in these parts, however. After many setbacks, the Spanish managed to take Nebaj in 1530, and by then they were so enraged that not only was the town burnt to the ground but the survivors were condemned to slavery as punishment for their resistance. Things didn't improve with the coming of independence, when the Ixil people were regarded as a source of cheap labour and forced to work on the coastal plantations. Many never returned. Even today large numbers of local people are forced to migrate in search of work and conditions on many of the plantations remain appalling. In the late 1970s and early 1980s, the area was hit by waves of horrific violence as it became the main theatre of operation for the **EGP** (the Guerrilla Army of the Poor). Caught up in the conflict, the people have suffered enormous losses, with the majority of the smaller villages destroyed by the army and their inhabitants herded into "protected" settlements. With the peace accords, a degree of normality has returned to the area and new villages are being rebuilt on the old sites.

Despite this terrible legacy, the fresh green hills are some of the most beautiful in the country and the three towns are friendly and accommodating, with a relaxed and distinctive atmosphere.

Nebaj

NEBAJ is the centre of Ixil country, a beautiful old town, by far the largest of the three, with white adobe walls and cobbled streets. The weaving done here is unusual and intricate, the finest examples being the women's *huipiles*, which are an artistic tangle of complex geometrical designs in superb greens, yellows, reds and oranges, worn with brilliant red *cortes* (skirts). On their heads, the women wear superb headcloths decorated with pompom tassles that they pile up above their heads; most men no longer wear traditional dress. You'll find an excellent shop, selling goods produced by the Ixil weaving cooperative, on the main square.

The small **market** is worth investigation, a block to the east of the church. On Thursday and Sunday the numbers swell as traders visit from out of town with second-hand clothing from the USA, stereos from Taiwan and Korea and chickens, eggs, fruit and vegetables from the highlands. The town church is also worth a look, although it's fairly bare inside. If you're here for the second week in August, you'll witness the **Nebaj fiesta**, which includes processions, dances, drinking and fireworks.

Arrival and information

The **plaza** is the focal point for the community with the major shops, municipal buildings and police station all encircling the square. The market and brand new **bus terminal** are on 7 C nearby. There is a **bank**, Bancafe, 2 Av 46, near the market (Mon–Fri 8.30am–4pm, Sat 8am–1pm), which exchanges both cash and travellers' cheques.

Getting to Nebaj is straightforward with **buses** from Santa Cruz del Quiché every hour and a half between 8.30am and 4pm (4hr), plus a daily service from Huehuetenango every morning (6hr), or you can take a bus to Sacapulas and change there. **Leaving Nebaj** is more problematic with the schedules being subject to frequent changes, so check at the terminal before you want to leave. **Pickups and trucks** supplement the buses; the best place to hitch south is on the road out of town, a little further past the Hotel Ixil.

Accommodation

You'll find little in the way of luxury in Nebaj, although what there is does have an inimitable charm and prices here are some of the lowest in the country. There are few street signs, so you'll probably have to rely on the gang of children who act as guides – none of the hotels in town is more than a few minutes' walk from the terminal.

Hospedaje Esperanza, northwest of the plaza. Friendly, simply and basic. Ask the owner's daughter if you want to learn to weave. ①.

Hospedaje Ilebal Tenam, three minutes from the plaza on the road to Chajul/Cotzal. Tremendous hospedaje with a double deck of very simple but very clean rooms. The showers are exhilaratingly hot. Brand new in 1997, may be signposted. ①.

Hospedaje las Tres Hermanas, a block northwest of the plaza. Despite its damp rooms, ancient mattresses and shabby apperance, this is one of the most famous hotels in Guatemala and still has real character. During the troubles of the 1970s and 80s this place put up a virtual Who's Who of international and Guatemalan journalists including Victor Perera, George Lovell and Ronald Wright. It is still run by two of the original three sisters. ①.

Hotel Posada de Don Pablo, one block west of the plaza, opposite *Irene's* comedor. Another new hotel, this is one of the smartest in town with spotless, pine-trimmed rooms, comfortable beds, private bathrooms and safe parking. ③.

Hotel Ixil, on the main road south out of town. Large, bare rooms are a little on the damp side though the setting is pleasant, around a courtyard in a nice old colonial house. Functional, warmish shower and friendly staff. ②.

Eating

The best **comedor** in town is *Irene's*, just off the main square, with several others in the plaza itself. The *Maya-Inca* on 5 C is owned by a friendly Peruvian/Guatemalan couple and serves delicious Peruvian and local dishes, though the portions are small. In addition, there is always something to eat at the market. For entertainment, most of the raving in town is courtesy of Nebaj's burgeoning neo-Pentecostal church scene, with four-hour services involving much wailing and gnashing of teeth.

Walks around Nebaj

In the hills that surround Nebaj there are several beautiful **walks**, with one of the most interesting ones taking you to the village of **ACUL**, two hours away. Starting from the church in Nebaj, cross the plaza and turn to the left, taking the road that goes downhill between a shop and a comedor. At the bottom of the dip it divides and here you take the right-hand fork and head out of town along a dirt track. The track switchbacks up a steep hillside, and heads over a narrow pass into the next valley, where it drops down into Acul.

The village was one of the original so-called "model villages" into which people were herded after their homes had been destroyed by the army. If you walk on through the village and out the other side, you arrive at the Finca San Antonio, run by an Italian family who have lived here for more than fifty years, making some of the country's best cheese, which they sell at pretty reasonable prices.

A second, shorter walk takes you to a beautiful little **waterfall**, La Cascada de Plata, about an hour from Nebaj. Take the road to Chajul and turn left just before it crosses the bridge, a kilometre or two outside Nebaj. Don't be fooled by the smaller version you'll come to shortly before the main set of falls.

San Juan Cotzal and Chajul

To visit the other two towns in the Ixil triangle, it's best to coincide your visit with **market days**, when there is more traffic on the move: Cotzal is on Wednesday and Saturday; Chajul on Tuesday and Friday; and Nebaj on Sunday. **Buses** run to an irregular schedule, but on Sunday transport returns to both Cotzal and Chajul from Nebaj after 10am. Pickups supplement the buses. Look out too for aid agency and MINUGUA (United Nations) four-wheel drives. It's certainly possible to visit both towns on a daytrip from Nebaj if you get an early start.

SAN JUAN COTZAL is closer to Nebaj, up to an hour and a half away, depending on the state of the road. The town is set in a gentle dip in the valley, sheltered somewhat beneath the Cuchumatanes and often wrapped in a damp blanket of mist. Cotzal attracts very few Western travellers so you may find that many people assume you're an aid worker or attached to an evangelical church.

Intricate turquoise *huipiles* are worn by the Maya women in Cotzal, who also weave bags and rope from the fibres of the maguey plant. There is little to do in the town itself but there is some great hill-walking close by. If you want to **stay**, there is a small, very basic unmarked pensión called *Don Polo* (②) two blocks from the church, or you may find the *farmacia* in the corner of the plaza will rent you a room. The *La Maguey* **restaurant** in someone's front room, a block behind the church, serves up reasonable, if bland, food. **Buses** should return to Nebaj daily at 6am and 1am; at other times you'll have to hitch.

Last but by no means least of the Ixil settlements is **CHAJUL**. Made up almost entirely of old adobe houses, with wooden beams and red-tiled roofs blackened by the smoke of cooking fires, it is also the most determinedly traditional and least bilingual of the Ixil towns. The women of Chajul wear earrings made of old coins strung up on lengths of wool and dress entirely in red, filling the streets with colour – you'll see them washing their scarlet *cortes* and *huipiles* at the stream that cuts through the middle of the village. Here boys still use blowpipes to hunt small birds, a skill that dates from the earliest of times but is now little used elsewhere.

The colonial church, a massive structure with huge wooden beams and gold leaf decoration, is home to the **Christ of Golgotha** and the target of a large pilgrimage on the second Friday of Lent – a particularly good time to be here. The dirty *Hospedaje Cristina* (①) is a depressing option if you want somewhere to **stay** for the night; ask instead at the post office where one of the workers rents out rooms. Some other families also rent out beds in their houses to the steady trickle of travellers now coming to Chajul; you won't have to look for them, they will find you.

A number of unscheduled trucks bump along the two-hour route between Nebaj and Chajul, and on **market** days (Tuesday and Friday) there are regular morning **buses** from 4am. Return buses leave at 11.30am and 12.30pm and there's usually a **truck** at 3.30pm. (You'll share the covered trailer with firewood and vegetables – not recommended for anyone who is claustrophobic.) You can also **walk** here from San Juan Cotzal, two to three hours away through the spectacular Ixil countryside. Follow the unpaved road that branches off to the main Nebaj–Cotzal road just before you enter Cotzal. The final uphill part of the walk is quite tough, especially if the sun is shining.

Lago de Atitlán

Lake Como, it seems to me, touches the limit of the permissibly picturesque; but Atitlán is Como with the additional embellishments of several immense volcanoes. It is really too much of a good thing. After a few days of this impossible landscape one finds oneself thinking nostalgically of the English Home Counties.

Aldous Huxley, *Beyond the Mexique Bay* (1934).

Whether or not you share Huxley's refined sensibilities, there's no doubt that **Lago de Atitlán** is astonishingly beautiful. Most people find themselves captivated by its scenic excesses. Indeed, the effect is so overwhelming that a handful of gringo devotees have been rooted to its shores since the 1960s. The lake itself is an irregular shape, with three main inlets. It measures 18km by 12km at its widest point, and shifts through an astonishing range of blues, steely greys and greens as the sun moves across the sky. Hemmed in on all sides by steep hills and massive volcanoes, it's at least 320m (nearly 1000 feet) deep.

Another astonishing aspect of Atitlán is the strength of Maya culture still evident in the lakeside villages. Despite the thousands of tourists that pour in here from Europe and North America every year, you can still find some of the most intensely traditional villages in Guatemala here. **San Antonio Palopó**, **Santiago Atitlán** and, above the lake, **Sololá** are some of the very few villages in the entire country where Maya men still wear *traje* – traditional costume. Two languages, **Tzutujil** and **Cakchiquel**, are spoken on the shores.

There are thirteen villages on the shores of the lake, with many more in the hills behind, ranging from the cosmopolitan resort-style **Panajachel** to tiny, isolated **Tzununá**. The villages are mostly subsistence farming communities and it's easy to hike and boat around the lake staying in a different one each night. The area has only recently attracted large numbers of tourists and for the moment things are still fairly undisturbed but some of the new pressures are decidedly threatening. The increase in population has also had a damaging impact on the shores of the lake, as the desperate need to cultivate more land leads to deforestation and accompanying soil erosion.

You'll probably reach the lake through Panajachel, which makes a good base for exploring the surrounding area. "Pana" has an abundance of cheap hotels and restaurants and is well served by buses. To get a real sense of a more typical Atitlán village, however, travel by boat to Santiago Atitlán or San Antonió Palopó. **San Pedro de la Laguna** is now the village with the most established travelling "scene", and a surplus of extremely cheap hotels. **Santa Cruz** and **San Marcos** are the places to head for if you're seeking real peace and quiet, and there are good hikes on this side of the lake.

Sololá

Perched on a natural balcony overlooking the lake, **SOLOLÁ** is a fascinating place, overlooked by the majority of travellers. In common with only a few other towns, it has parallel *indígena* and *ladino* governments and is probably the largest Maya town in the country, with the vast majority of the people still wearing traditional costume.

LAGO DE ATITLÁN

0   5 km

Cocales (25 km) & Carretera del Pacífico ▽

The town itself isn't much to look at: a wide central plaza with a recently restored clock tower on one side and a modern church on the other. However, its **Friday market** is one of Central America's finest – a mesmeric display of colour and commerce. From as early as 5am the plaza is packed, drawing traders from all over the highlands, as well as thousands of local Sololá Maya, the women covered in striped red cloth and the men in their outlandish "**space cowboy**" shirts, woollen aprons and wildly embroidered trousers. There's another smaller market on Tuesday. Another interesting time to visit Sololá is on Sunday, when the **cofradías**, the elders of the Maya religious hierarchy, parade through the streets in ceremonial costume to attend the 10am Mass.

Panajachel

Ten kilometres beyond Sololá, separated by a precipitous descent, is **PANAJACHEL**. Over the years, what was once a small Maya village has become something of a resort, with a sizeable population of long-term foreign residents whose numbers are swollen in the winter by an influx of North American seasonal migrants and a flood of tourists.

Panajachel was a premier hippie hangout back in the 1960s and 70s and developed a bad reputation amongst some sections of Guatemalan society as a haven for drug-taking gringo drop-outs. Today "Pana" is much more integrated into the tourism mainstream and is as popular with Guatemalans as Westerners. The lotus-eaters and crystal-gazers have not all deserted Panajachel, however. Many have reinvented themselves as (vaguely) conscientious capitalists who own restaurants and export *típica* clothing. In many ways, it's this **gringo** crowd that gives the town its modern character and identity.

Not so long ago (although it seems an entirely different age) Panajachel was a quiet little village of **Cakchiquel** Maya, whose ancestors were settled here after the Spanish crushed a force of Tzutujil warriors on the site. Today the old village has been enveloped by the new building boom, but it still retains a traditional feel, and most of the Maya continue to farm in the river delta behind the town. The Sunday market, bustling with people from all around the lake, remains oblivious to the tourist invasion.

For travellers, Panajachel is one of those inevitable destinations, as it's a comfortable base for exploring the lake and central highlands, and, although no one ever owns up to actually liking it, everyone seems to stay for a while. The old village is still attractive and although most of the new building is fairly nondescript, its lakeside setting is superb. The main **daytime activity** is hanging out, either wandering the streets, shopping, eating and drinking, or swimming and sunbathing at the **public beach**, where you can also rent a kayak and explore the lake for a few hours (mornings are usually much calmer). Scuba divers can also dive the lake with ATI Divers (see p.191). **Weaving** from all over Guatemala is sold with daunting persistence in the streets here. Prices can be high, so bargain hard.

Arrival, information and accommodation

The bus drops you beside the Banco Inmobiliario, very close to the main drag, C Santander, which runs down to the lake shore. Straight ahead, up C Principal, is the old village. The **tourist office** is on C Santander (Mon–Sat 9am–5pm; ☎7621392). **Boat and bus schedules** are posted on the door. **Taxis** usually wait outside the post office, or you can call one on ☎7621571.

The streets of Panajachel are overflowing with cheap **hotels**, and there are plenty of "**rooms**". If you have a tent, first choice is the new **campsite** (☎7622479; US$2 per person), on the corner of the road to Santa Catarina and C del Cementerio, over the river bridge. Here happy campers will find kitchen and storage facilities and there are also sleeping bags and tents for hire. Don't bother camping at the public beach: your stuff will be ripped off.

Casa Linda, down an alley off the top of C Santander. Popular backpackers' retreat where the central garden is undeniably beautiful but the rooms are a shade pricey for a hospedaje. ②.

Casa Loma, C Rancho Grande, near the lake (☎7621447). New place with very inviting pine-trimmed rooms, some with kitchen and TV. Best value in town in this price category. ③–④.

Las Casitas, at the back of the old village, near the market (☎7621224). Very clean, friendly, safe and quiet. Rooms have private bathrooms and hot water. ③.

Hospedaje Eli, Callejeón del Pozo, off C de los Arboles (☎7620148). Eight clean, cheap rooms overlooking a pretty garden in a quiet location. ①.

Hospedaje García, C el Chali (☎7622187). Plenty of featureless but perfectly reasonable budget rooms. ②.

Hospedaje Santander, C Santander (☎7621304). Leafy courtyard, friendly owners and clean, cheap rooms, some with private bathrooms. Recommended. ①–②.

Hotel Atitlán, on the lakeside, 1km west of the centre (☎ & fax 7621441 or 7621416). The nicest hotel in Panajachel with a stunning lakeside location, lovely gardens and a swimming pool. Rooms are very comfortable and tastefully decorated. A double costs US$120. ⑨.

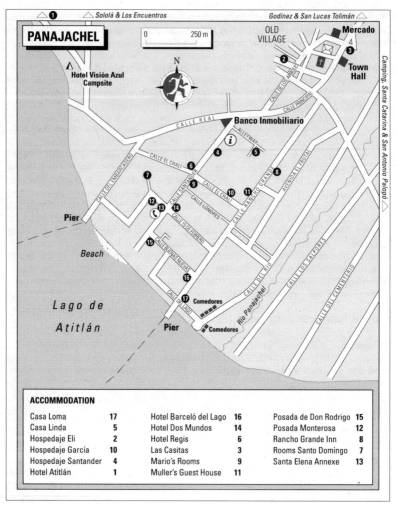

PANAJACHEL

0   250 m

OLD VILLAGE

Mercado

Town Hall

Camping, Santa Catarina & San Antonio Palopó △

Hotel Visión Azul Campsite

Banco Inmobiliario

CALLE REAL

CALLE EL CHALI

CALLE SANTANDER

CALLE EL CHALI

CALLE LONDRES

CALLE 15 DE FEBRERO

CALLE BUENAS NUEVAS

CALLE RANCHO GRANDE

AVENIDA EL FRUTAL

CALLE LOS ÁRBOLES

CALLE PRINCIPAL

CALLE DEL EMBARCADERO

Pier

Beach

Lago de Atitlán

Pier

Comedores

Comedores

Río Panajachel

CALLE DEL RÍO

CALLE LOS SALPORES

CALLE DEL CEMENTERIO

CALLE DEL LAGO

ACCOMMODATION

Casa Loma	17	Hotel Barceló del Lago	16	Posada de Don Rodrigo	15
Casa Linda	5	Hotel Dos Mundos	14	Posada Monterosa	12
Hospedaje Eli	2	Hotel Regis	6	Rancho Grande Inn	8
Hospedaje García	10	Las Casitas	3	Rooms Santo Domingo	7
Hospedaje Santander	4	Mario's Rooms	9	Santa Elena Annexe	13
Hotel Atitlán	1	Muller's Guest House	11		

Hotel Barceló del Lago, right on the lakeshore (☎7621555, fax 7621562). Luxury colossus complete with pool, jacuzzi and gym. Very corporate "international" flavour though great volcano views help remind you you're in Guatemala. US$110 double. ⑨.

Hotel Dos Mundos, C Santander (☎ & fax 7622078). Italian-owned hotel, just off the main drag, offering comfortable rooms set in a private garden, where there's also a small swimming pool. The attached *Lanterna* restaurant is recommended for authentic Italian cuisine at moderate prices. ⑤.

Hotel Posada de Don Rodrigo, C Santander, facing the lake (☎ & fax 7622322 or 7622329). Colonial-style hotel where the rooms, though on the small side, have a little more character than most. Pool and ugly waterslide overlook the lake. ⑧.

Hotel Regis, C Santander 3–47 (☎7621149, fax 7621152). Age-old establishment with lovely outdoor thermal pools. Individual bungalows are pleasant and come with cable TV. ⑥.

Mario's Rooms, C Santander (☎7621313). Basic, clean rooms, some with private bathrooms. Hot water on request for a few quetzales. ②–③.

Muller's Guest House, C Rancho Grande (☎7622442). Extremely tasteful Swiss-owned luxury guest house with quality modern European furnishings and a garden. Recommended. ⑤.

Posada Monterosa, C Monterrey (☎7620055). Brand new in 1997, this small place has spotless rooms with bathrooms and safe car parking. ④.

Rancho Grande Inn, C Rancho Grande (☎7621554, fax 7622247). A long-standing Panajachel institution with very attractive, nicely appointed bungalows, superbly kept gardens and helpful staff. Breakfast included. ⑤–⑥.

Rooms Santo Domingo, down a path off C Monterrey. One of the very cheapest places in town, set well away from the hustle. Wooden rooms all face a charming little garden or else there are more expensive options upstairs with private baths. ①–③.

Santa Elena Anexe, C 15 de Febrero. Safe, pleasant and ramshackle place with an abundance of children and parrots. One of the cheapest places in Pana, though hot showers are extra. ①.

Eating, drinking and entertainment

Panajachel has an abundance of **restaurants**, all catering to the cosmopolitan tastes of its floating population. You'll have no trouble finding tasty Chinese, Indian, Italian, Mexican and Mediterranean dishes. For really cheap and authentically Guatemalan food there are plenty of comedores on and just off the new beach promenade and close to the market.

CAFÉS AND RESTAURANTS

Bombay, in the shopping arcade just past *Al Chisme*, C de los Arboles. Eclectic vegetarian food which, despite the name, has nothing Indian about it. Indonesian *gado-gado*, epic pitta bread sandwiches (try the falafel), and organic coffee. Closed Mon.

TRANSPORT ON THE LAKE

There are two **piers** in Panajachel. The pier near the *Hotel Barceló del Lago* serves Santa Catarina, San Antonio Palopó, San Lucas Tolimán, Santiago Atitlán and lake tours. The second pier at the end of C del Embarcadero is for all villages on the northern side of the lake: Santa Cruz, San Marcos, San Juan and San Pedro. Confusing matters somewhat, some of the boats for the northern lakeside start from the *Hotel Barceló del Lago* pier, but all will call at the C del Embarcadero pier to pick up passengers. Unfortunately, **ripoffs** are the rule for tourists. You'll be asked for triple or quadruple what the locals normally pay, particularly if it's the last boat of the day. The Inguat office has a list of official boat schedules and prices.

Tours of the lake, run by the Santa Fe company, leave the *Hotel Barcelo del Lago* pier at 8.30am and Santiago at 10.30am. Both visit San Pedro, Santiago Atitlán and San Antonio Palopó.

Panajachel to Santiago Atitlán (1hr) at 5.45am, 8.35am, 9.30am, 10.30am, 1pm, 3pm and 4.30pm. Returning at 6am, 7am, 11.45am, 12.30pm, 2pm, 3pm and 4.30pm.

Panajachel to San Pedro (1hr 30min) at 6am, 7am, 8.20am, 10am, 11am, noon, 2pm, 3pm, 4pm, 6pm and 7pm. Returning at 4.45am, 5.30am, 6am, 8am, 8.45am, 10am, noon, 12.30pm, 2pm, 3.45pm and 5pm.

Panjachel to Santa Catarina (20min) **San Antonio** (40min) and **San Lucas** (1hr 30min) at 9.30am & 2pm. Returning from San Lucas at 12.15pm, San Antonio 1pm, Santa Catarina 1.30pm.

Santiago Atitlán to San Pedro (40min) at 7am, 9am, 10am, 11am, noon, 1pm, 2pm, 3.30pm and 5pm. Returning nine times daily from 6am until 3pm.

Comedor Costa Sur, near the church in the old town. Clean and attractive comedor, loudly bedecked with Mexican blankets. Great breakfasts, lunchtime dishes and licuados.

Las Chinitas, halfway down C Santander. Excellent pan-Asian cuisine in a pretty patio. Menu raids Indonesia, China, Thailand, and Japan for influence. Moderate prices. Closed Mon.

Al Chisme, C de los Arboles. A smart, European-style restaurant and bar adorned with black and white photographs of former customers that is very popular with gringos. Delicious food including sandwiches, crêpes, steaks, curried shrimps, and pasta, but all a little pricey. Closed Wed.

Deli, C Principal. Excellent range of salads, sandwiches, pastries, bagels, cakes, wine and tea. Also a nice garden and classical music. Two more branches on C Santander, *Deli 2* and *Delicafé*.

Restaurante Jhanny, halfway down C Rancho Grande. Ignore the fairy lights and head inside for a superb Guatemalan-style menú del día (US$2.50); tables are nicely arranged around a little garden.

The Last Resort, C el Chali. Looks vaguely like an English pub but serves the best American buffet breakfasts in town. Also a vast menu of pasta, steaks and vegetarian dishes – portions are huge.

Mario's, C Santander. A limited range of low-cost food: huge salads, delicious yoghurt and pancakes.

La Terraza, above Inguat at the top of C Santander. This is the finest restaurant on the lake and one of the best in the country, serving a captivating collection of European and Asian influenced cuisine. Expensive.

Yalanki, C Santander. Pana's best streetside bar/café, with good snacks, barbecued meats, beer and musical vibes.

NIGHTLIFE

There are three **video bars**, each showing English-language films: the *Grapevine* on C Santander, one in the *Carrot Chic* restaurant at the top end of C de los Arboles and, on the same street, *Cafe Cinema*. For **drinking**, try *The Last Resort* on C el Chali, where you can also play table tennis, or *Ubu's Cosmic Cantina*, behind the *Sevananda* restaurant on C de los Arboles, where there's a big screen for sports fans, movie buffs and news addicts. On C de los Arboles you'll also find the long-running *Circus Bar* and the new *El Aleph* bar/café for **live music**, and across the road the *Chapiteau* **nightclub**. Other clubs have a habit of opening and closing rapidly. Finally there's a **pool hall** in the old village, near the post office.

Listings

Bike and motorbike rental Moto Servicio Queche, C de los Arboles and C Principal, rents mountain bikes for US$1 an hour, US$5 a day; and 185cc motorbikes for US$6 an hour, US$25 for 24 hours, US$100 for the week.

Banks and exchange Banco Inmobiliario at the junction of C Santander and C Principal (Mon–Fri 9am–7pm, Sat 9am–noon) or Banco Industrial on C Santander, which has a 24hr ATM for Visa card holders. Try the AT travel agency or *Hotel Regis*, both on C Santander, for Mastercard transactions.

Bookstores Delante, down an alley off C Buenas Vistas, has a comprehensive selection of secondhand titles. Galería Bookstore, upper floor, C de los Arboles, stocks a reasonable selection of secondhand books and a few interesting new books in English.

Car rental Dalton Rent-a-Car, C de los Arboles (☎7622251, fax 7621275), charges from US$50 a day, including unlimited mileage.

Laundry Lavandería Automatico, C de los Arboles (Mon–Sat 7.30am–6pm).

Medical care Dr Edgar Barreno speaks good English; his surgery is down the first street that branches to the right off C de los Arboles (☎7621008).

Pharmacy Farmacia la Union, C Santander.

Police On the plaza in the old village (☎7621120).

Post office In the old village, down a sidestreet beside the church (Mon–Fri 8am–4.30pm).

Telephone Check first with businesses in C Santander for the best rates; many advertise discounted calls. Otherwise Telgua (daily 7am–midnight) is near the junction of C Santander and C del Chali. *C@fenet*, in the same building as Telgua, at street level, will send or receive email.

The eastern shore

On the eastern shore of the lake, backed up against the slopes, are a couple of villages, the first of which, **SANTA CATARINA PALOPÓ**, is just 4km from Panajachel. The people of Santa Catarina used to live almost entirely by fishing and trapping crabs but the introduction of black bass into the lake to create a sport-fishing industry has put an end to all that as the bass eat the smaller fish. They've now turned to farming and migratory work, with many of the women travelling to Panajachel and Antigua to peddle their weaving. The women wear stunning *huipiles*, in vibrant turquoise and purple zigzags.

Much of the shoreline as you leave the village has been bought and developed, and great villas, ringed by impenetrable walls and razor wire, have come to dominate the village. Very much a part of this invasion is the new hotel *Villa Santa Catarina* (☎7621291; ⑦) which has opened on the lakeshore, complete with 32 rooms, two banqueting halls, a pool and superb views of the lake.

Another 5km brings you to **SAN ANTONIO PALOPÓ**, a larger and more traditional village, squeezed in beneath a steep hillside. Because it is on the tour group itinerary, the villagers have become a bit pushy in selling their weavings. But, despite this, the village is quite interesting and certainly very traditional. The hillsides above San Antonio are well irrigated and terraced, reminiscent of rice paddies, and most men wear the village *traje* of red shirts with vertical stripes and short woollen kilts. Women wear almost identical shirts, made of the same fabric with subtle variations to the collar design. The whitewashed central church is also worth a look; just to the left of the entrance are two ancient bells.

A single **bus** leaves Panajachel for San Antonio at 9.15am, but a number of pickups also ply the route approximately hourly (last one back to Panajachel at 5pm) and of course there are **boats** (see p.185).

If you decide **to stay** in San Antonio there are two options: the fairly upmarket *Hotel Terrazas del Lago* (☎7621288; ⑤), down by the water, with beautiful views, or the very simple but clean pensión (①) owned by Juan Lopez Sanchez near the entrance to the village. Try the comedor below the church for a cheap **meal**.

Santiago Atitlán

On the other side of the lake from Panajachel, **SANTIAGO ATITLÁN** is set to one side of a sheltered horseshoe inlet, overshadowed by the cones of the San Pedro, Atitlán and Tolimán volcanoes. It's the largest and most important of the lakeside villages, and also one of the most traditional, being the main centre of the Tzutujil-speaking Maya. At the time of the Conquest, the Tzutujil had their fortified capital, **Chuitinamit-Atitlán**, on the slopes of San Pedro, while the bulk of the population lived spread out around the site of today's village. Alvarado and his crew, needless to say, destroyed the capital and massacred its inhabitants, assisted this time by a force of Cakchiquel Maya, who arrived at the scene in some three hundred canoes.

Today, Santiago is an industrious but relaxed sort of place. During the day the town becomes fairly commercial, its **main street**, which runs from the dock to the plaza, lined with weaving shops. There's nothing like the Panajachel overkill, but the persistence of underage gangs here can still be a bit much. By mid-afternoon, once the ferries have left, things revert to normal and the whole village becomes a lot more friendly. There's not a lot to do in Santiago other than stroll around soaking up the atmosphere or go to the market on Friday morning.

The old colonial Catholic **church** is well worth a look, however. The huge altarpiece which was carved when the church was under *cofradía* control culminates in the shape of a mountain peak and a cross. The cross symbolizes the Maya world tree, which supports the source of all life, including people, animals and the corn ears that you can see on the cross. In the middle of the floor is a small hole which Atitecos believe to be the centre of the world. The church is also home to a stone memorial commemorating Father Stanley Rother, an American priest who served in the parish from 1968 to 1981. Father Rother was a committed defender of his parishioners in an era when, in his own words, "shaking hands with an Indian has become a political act". Branded a Communist by President García, he was assassinated by a paramilitary death squad like hundreds of his parishioners before and after him. His body was returned to his native Oklahoma for burial but his heart was removed and buried in the church.

As is the case in many other parts of the Guatemalan highlands, the Catholic Church in Santiago is locked in bitter rivalry with several evangelical sects, who are building churches here at an astonishing rate. Their latest construction, right beside the lake, is the largest structure in town. Folk Catholicism also plays an important role in the life of Santiago and the town is well known as one of the few places where Maya still pay homage to **Maximón**, the drinking and smoking saint. Any child will take you to see him; just ask for the "Casa de Maximón".

The traditional **costume** of Santiago, still worn a fair amount, is both striking and unusual. The men wear long shorts which, like the women's *huipiles*, are striped white and purple and intricately embroidered with birds and flowers. The women also wear a *xk'ap*, a band of red cloth approximately 10m long, wrapped around their heads, which has the honour of being depicted on the 25 centavo coin. Sadly this headcloth is going out of use and on the whole you'll probably only see it at fiestas and on market days, worn by the older women.

Practicalities

Daily **boats** to Santiago leave Panajachel seven times a day between 5.45am and 4.30pm, returning between 6am and 4.30pm – the trip takes about an hour. The village is also astonishingly well connected by **bus** with almost everywhere except Panajachel (see below).

As for **accommodation**, a backpackers' favourite is the *Hotel Chi-Nim-Ya* (☎7217131; ②), on the left as you enter the village from the lake. The good value *Hotel Tzutuhil*, in the centre of town (☎7217174; ②), is a five-storey concrete building with spectacular views from the top floor and a restaurant. For something special there are two good options. The *Posada de Santiago*, on the lakeshore 1km south of the town (☎7028462, fax 7217167; ⑥), is a fine American-owned luxury hotel and restaurant with rooms in stone cabins, each with its own log fire; they'll also rent you a bike. The new *Hotel Bambú* (☎2018913; ⑤) is a second comfortable option, with beautiful thatched-roofed stone bungalows and rooms, plus an excellent restaurant with Spanish specialities; the hotel is a ten-minute walk north of the main Santiago dock.

There are three **restaurants** at the entrance to the village, just up from the dock, all fairly similar. In the centre of the village you can eat at the *Hotel Tzutuhil* or, if you really want to dine in style, head out to the restaurant in the *Posada de Santiago*.

Leaving Santiago, buses depart from the central plaza and head via San Lucas Tolimán and Cocales towards Guatemala City, leaving six times daily between 2.30am and 2pm. For San Pedro, seven boats leave Santiago every day from 7am until 4pm (40min).

San Pedro la Laguna

Around the other side of Volcán San Pedro is the village of **SAN PEDRO LA LAGUNA**, which has now usurped Panajachel to become the pivotal centre of Guatemala's travelling "scene". Generally, this status involves little more than playing host to the few dozen colourful foreigners who have set up home here, and providing a plentiful supply of marijuana to keep the young gringo visitors happy. It isn't Goa but it does have a distinctively bohemian feel about it. Things certainly seem very mellow here but it hasn't always been so. Crack cocaine arrived in San Pedro in the early 1990s and the locals got so fed up with wasted gringos that they wrote to a national newspaper demanding that the freaks get out of town. Today things seem to have settled down again and, despite the obvious culture clash between locals (most of whom are evangelical) and travellers, everyone seems to get on reasonably well.

Again, the setting is spectacular, with Volcán San Pedro rising to the east and a ridge of steep hills running behind the village. To the left of the main beach, as you look towards the lake, a line of huge white boulders juts out into the water – an ideal spot for an afternoon of swimming and sunbathing.

Volcán San Pedro, which towers above the village to a height of some 3020m, is largely coated with tropical forest and can be climbed in four to five hours. Any of the underage guides will be able to show you the trail. Andres Adonias Cotuc Cite, who makes a living collecting wood on the volcano, is highly recommended. Get an early start in order to see the views at their best and avoid the worst of the heat. If you'd rather do something a little more relaxing, **horses** can be rented for around US$2.50 an hour and **canoes** for a great deal less.

Accommodation

San Pedro has some of the cheapest accommodation in all Latin America, with a number of basic, clean guest houses that almost all charge less than US$2 a person per night. There's nothing in the way of luxury. If you plan to stay around for a while then you might want to consider **renting a house**, which works out incredibly cheap.

Hotel Puerto Bello, turn left after *Nick's Place*, by the docks. Excellent budget hotel with really cheap rates, hot showers and a friendly owner. Good deal for solo travellers. ①.

Hotel Sakari, between the piers. The smartest place in town – modern and clean with four tiled rooms all with private bath and hot water. ②.

Hotel San Pedro, close to the Santiago dock, next door to the *Villa Sol*. Clean rooms grouped around a central courtyard, some with private bath. ②.

Hotel Ti'Kaaj, near the Santiago dock. Rooms are the same as everywhere else but they are set in a beautiful garden with orange trees and hammocks. ①.

Hotel Valle Azul, turn right at the Panajachel dock. Ugly new addition on two floors, but the views are excellent and the rooms are plain, clean and good value, some with private bathrooms. ①.

Hotel Villa Sol, beside the Santiago Atitlán dock. Twin deck concrete block with plain clean rooms, some with bathroom. Palm trees and a nice lawn add a little green relief. ①–②.

Hospedaje Xocomil, turn left from the Panajachel dock and it's on the right. Spotless rooms around a little garden. ①.

Eating and drinking

The steady flow of gringo travellers has given San Pedro's **cafés** and **restaurants** a decidedly international flavour and most places are excellent value for money. Vegetarians are well catered for, especially at the **thermal baths** between the two docks where, after a revitalizing soak, you can eat some fine organic food (late afternoon and early evening only). There are a few typical Guatemalan comedores in the centre of the village and by the Santiago dock. For a **drink**, try *Nick's Place* (with upstairs café), or the *Ti'Kaaj*.

Restaurant Ti'Kaaj, opposite the eponymous hotel. Stunning views of the lake and volcanoes from the upper floor and a lovely garden out front too. Great breakfasts, pasta and a bar.

Comedor Francés, between the docks. Reasonably priced Gallic fare – coq-au-vin at less than US$2 and delicious crêpes.

Pinocchio, between the two docks. Good Italian where you can feast on bruscetta and pasta.

Restaurant al Mesón, close to the Panajachel dock. Thatched cabañas shelter a good restaurant serving chicken platters and sandwiches. Favoured daytime haunt where you can sit on the grassy verges and watch the boats come and go.

Nick's Place, by the Pana docks. Free movies upstairs and good value grub (chicken and chips at US$2) make this the most popular place in town.

Restaurant Valle Azul, overlooking the lake. Popular daytime place for snacks and drinks.

Restaurant Rosalinda, a short walk uphill from Santiago dock. Excellent comedor – fresh lake fish, grilled meats and a warm welcome.

The western shore

The **western side** of the lake is the only part that remains largely inaccessible to cars. From San Pedro, a rough dirt road runs as far as Tzununá and from there a spectacular path continues all the way to Sololá. Most of the boats between San Pedro and Panajachel call at all the villages en route but the best way to see this string of isolated settlements is **on foot**: it makes a fantastic day's walk. A narrow strip of level land is wedged between the water and the steep hills most of the way, but where this disappears the path is cut into the slope providing dizzying views of the lake below. To walk from San Pedro to Santa Cruz takes between five and six hours and if you want some real peace and quiet this is the section of the lake to head for. There are also some excellent **places to stay** in both San Marcos and Santa Cruz.

From San Pedro you follow a dirt road to **SAN JUAN**, just 2km or so away at the back of a sweeping bay surrounded by shallow beaches. The village of San Juan specializes in the weaving of *petates*, mats made from lake reeds, and there's a large weaving co-op, Las Artesanas de San Juan, where you can buy them; if you walk from the dock it's signposted on the left. On the other side of the street a brand new hospedaje has been built.

After San Juan, you'll pass the small settlement of **San Pedro**. After this, the villages start shrinking considerably. At **SAN MARCOS**, about two hours from San Pedro, a group of hotels have been sensitively established amongst a thick foliage of banana, mango, jocote and avocado trees. San Marcos has a decidedly New Age feel, thanks to the influence of the *Pirámides* yoga and meditation retreat (fax 7622080; US$8 per person per day for courses and accommodation). The grounds of the retreat are beautiful, the pyramid cabañas comfortable and the vegetarian food delicious.

There are a number of other **accommodation** possibilities in San Marcos including the excellent *Posada Schumann* (Guatemala City ☎3604049 or 3392683, cell phone 2022216; ④), run by the charming Olga Robinson. It is solar-powered and has four rooms and three beautiful stone bungalows with some stupendous volcano and lake views. *Hotel Paco Real* (fax 7629168; ②) also has a superb choice of well-priced chalets and rooms, a restaurant and immaculate communal bathrooms with hot water. The cheapest beds in the San Marcos jungle are at the *Hotel San Marcos* (②), where you'll find six perfunctory rooms in a concrete block; or at the *Unicornio* (①), where there are basic huts, a kitchen and a sauna. For somewhere **to eat**, though there are no comedores, most of the hotels above have restaurants and there is also a brilliant **bakery** that pumps out wholemeal bread and supplies many of the hotels. To **get to** any of the places listed above, turn left (west) from the jetty and walk along the lakeshore path for 300m until the *Posada Schumann*; signposts will direct you from here.

In the next lakeside village, **Tzununá**, the women often run from oncoming strangers, sheltering behind the nearest tree in giggling groups. Here the road indisputably ends, giving way to a narrow path cut out of the steep hillside which can be a little hard to follow as it descends to cross small streams and then climbs up again around the rocky outcrops. The next village is **Jaibalito**, a ragged-looking place lost amongst the coffee bushes; from here it's two more hours to Santa Cruz along a glorious, easy-to-follow path that grips the steep hillside.

Set well back from the lake on a shelf 100m or so above the water, **SANTA CRUZ** is the largest of this line of villages. If you arrive by boat it may appear to be just a collection of hotels, as the main village is higher up above the lake. There are **no phones** in Santa Cruz; if you want **to stay**, use the communal fax number (7621196) to book a few days ahead. There isn't much to see in the village apart from a fine sixteenth-century church and most people spend their time here walking, swimming or just chilling out with a book.

On the shore, opposite a line of wooden jetties, you'll find the *Iguana Perdida* (①–②), owned by Mike and Deedle, a very special place with undoubtedly the most convivial atmosphere around the lake. The rooms are fairly basic, ranging from a dorm to twin doubles, but it's the gorgeous, peaceful site overlooking the lake and volcanoes that really makes this place. Dinner is a three-course communal affair (US$5) and the *Iguana* is also home to Lago de Atitlán's only **dive school**, ATI Divers, a professional PADI outfit that can train all levels up to assistant instructor. Next door is another good place, the *Hotel Arca de Noé* (④), slightly more expensive and comfortable with attractive rooms and excellent home cooking. Just behind the *Iguana* are the simple, clean rooms at the *Hospedaje García* (②); and on the other side, the *Posada Abaj* (③), which has a beautiful peaceful garden but lacks atmosphere.

Beyond Santa Cruz there are two ways to reach Panajachel. **Boats** travelling between San Pedro and Panajachel stop at Santa Cruz hourly in the day, or you can rent a boat to Panajachel for around US$4. The path that runs directly to Panajachel is very hard to follow, and distraught walkers have been known to spend as long as seven hours scrambling through the undergrowth. Alternatively, you could **walk to Sololá**, up through the village along a spectacular and easy-to-follow path that takes around three hours, and from there catch a bus back to Panajachel.

Quetzaltenango (Xela) and around

To the west of Lago de Atitlán, the highlands rise to form a steep-sided ridge topped by a string of forested peaks. On the far side of this is the **Quetzaltenango basin**, a sweeping expanse of level ground that forms the natural hub of the western highlands. It was here that the conquistador Pedro de Alvarado first struggled up into the highlands and came upon the abandoned city of Xelajú (near Quetzaltenango), entering it without any resistance. Six days later, he and his troops fought the Quiché in a decisive battle on the nearby plain, massacring the Maya warriors. Legend has it that Alvarado himself killed the Quiché king, Tecún Umán, in hand to hand combat.

Totally unlike the capital and only a fraction of its size, Guatemala's second city, **QUETZALTENANGO**, has the subdued provincial atmosphere that you might expect in the capital of the highlands, its edges gently giving way to corn and maize fields. Bizarre though it may seem, Xela's character and appearance is vaguely reminiscent of an industrial town in northern England – grey, cool, slightly dour and culturally conservative. Ringed by high mountains and bitterly cold in the early mornings, the city wakes slowly, only getting going once the warmth of the sun has made its mark.

Some history
Under colonial rule, Quetzaltenango flourished as a commercial centre, benefiting from the fertility of the surrounding farmland and good connections to the port at Champerico. When the prospect of independence eventually arose, the city was set on deciding its own destiny and Quetzaltenango declared itself the capital of the independent state of **Los Altos**. But the separatist movement was unsuccessful and the city has had to accept provincial status ever since. During the coffee boom at the end of the last century, Quetzaltenango's wealth and population grew so rapidly that it began to rival the capital in status.

QUETZALTENANGO

▽ Almolonga

All this, however, came to an abrupt end when the city was almost totally destroyed by the massive **1902 earthquake**. Rebuilding took place in a mood of high optimism: all the grand Neoclassical architecture dates from this period. A new rail line was built to connect the city with the coast but after this was washed out in 1932–33 the town never regained its former glory, gradually falling further and further behind the capital.

Today Quetzaltenango has all the trappings of wealth and self-importance: the grand imperial architecture, the great banks, and a list of famous sons. But it is completely devoid of the rampant energy that binds Guatemala City to the all-American twentieth century. The city has a calm and dignified air and Quetzaltecos have a reputation for formality and politeness so if the chaos of Guatemala City gets you down then Quetzaltenango is an ideal antidote.

Arrival and information

Unhelpfully for the traveller, virtually all buses arrive and depart Quetzaltenango from nowhere near the centre of town. If you arrive by **second-class bus** you'll almost certainly end up in the chaotic **Minerva bus terminal** on the city's western edge. Walk through the covered market place to 4 C and catch a local bus marked "parque" to get to the plaza from there. An extremely useful transport hub is a roundabout called the **rotunda** at the far end of Calzada Independencia, where virtually all long-distance buses stop on their way to and from the city. Three main companies operate **first-class buses** between Xela and the capital: Líneas Américas, just off Calzada Independencia at 7 Av 3–33, Zona 2 (☎7612063 & 7614587; 6 buses daily); Alamo buses, 14 Av 3–76, Zona 3 (☎7612964; 4–5 buses daily); and Galgos, C Rodolfo Robles 17–43, Zona 1 (☎7612248; 7 buses daily). There are also **daily flights** to and from the capital with Inter airlines (30min; US$55 one-way); the airstrip is 5km east of the town centre.

The official **tourist office** is on the main plaza (Mon–Fri 8am–1pm & 2–5pm, Sat 8am–noon; ☎7614931). They are helpful and have maps and local information. Xela is an excellent place to **study Spanish**, with dozens of schools, many of a high standard. For a list of recommended language schools, see p.129.

Quetzaltenango is laid out on a standard grid pattern, somewhat complicated by a number of steep hills. The oldest part of the city, focused around the plaza, is made up of narrow streets, while in the newer part, reaching out towards the Minerva terminal, the blocks are larger. The city is also divided up into **zones**, although for the most part you'll only be interested in 1 and 3, which contain the plaza area and the bus terminal respectively. When it comes to **getting around**, most places are within easy walking distance (except the terminal). To get to the Minerva terminal you can take any bus that runs along 13 Av between 8 C and 4 C in Zona 1. To head for the eastern half of town, along 7 Av, catch one of the buses that stops in front of the Casa de la Cultura, at the bottom end of the plaza.

Accommodation

A bit like the town, most accommodation in Quetzaltenango tends to be dour and gloomy. Once you've made it to the plaza, all the places listed below are within ten minutes' walk.

Casa Argentina, 12 Diagonal 8–37, Zona 1 (☎7612470). Probably the best budget place in town with comfortable rooms, a reasonable dorm, kitchen and very friendly owners who are an excellent source of information. Home of Quetzaltrekkers (see p.196) and assorted long-term gringos. ②.

Casa Internacional, 3 C 10–24, Zona 1 (☎7612660). Excellent budget choice and often booked solid. Safe and friendly with a kitchen and hot water. ②.

Casa Kaehler, 13 Av 3–33 (☎7612091). Lovely place with spotless rooms around a leafy courtyard; hot showers and some private baths. Very secure, but be sure to book ahead as it's very popular. ②.

Hotel Casa Florencia, 12 Av 3–61 (☎7612811). The lobby isn't going to win any design awards but the nine rooms are comfortable enough and all come with private bath. Cheap breakfasts too. ④.

Hotel Modelo, 14 Av A 2–31 (☎7612529, fax 7631376). Civilized and quiet but a bit gloomy for the price, and decidedly old-fashioned. Nicest rooms face a small garden courtyard or try the separate annexe which is better value. ④–⑤.

Hotel Río Azul, 2 C 12–15 (☎ & fax 7630654). Very reminiscent of an English boarding house, but spotless and friendly and all rooms have private bathrooms. ③.

Pensión Altense, 9 C 8–48 (☎7612811). Just above the budget range, this place has plenty of clean rooms all with private bathrooms. ③.

Pensión Bonifaz, northeast corner of the plaza (☎7612182, fax 7612850). Founded in 1935, the *Bonifaz* offers character and comfort, a decent restaurant and a quirky bar. Very much the backbone of Quetzaltenango society, with an air of faded upper-class pomposity, but still the best place in town. ⑥.

The City

There aren't many things to do or see in Quetzaltenango, but if you have an hour or two to spare then it's well worth wandering through the streets, soaking up the atmosphere and taking in the museum. The hub of the place is the **central plaza**, officially known as the **Parque Centro América**. A mass of mock-Greek columns and imposing banks, it has an atmosphere of dignified calm. The buildings have a look of defiant authority although there's none of the buzz of business that you'd expect.

CENTRAL QUETZALTENANGO

ACCOMMODATION		RESTAURANTS & CAFÉS	
Casa Argentina	7	Bar Tecún	G
Casa Internacional	3	Blue Angel Video Café	H
Casa Kaehler	4	Café Baviera	F
Hotel Casa Florencia	5	Cardinali's	B
Hotel Modelo	1	Deli Crêpe	A
Hotel Río Azul	2	El Rincón de los Antojitos	C
Pensión Altense	8	La Polenesa	D
Pensión Bonifaz	6		

The northern end of the plaza is dominated by the grand Banco del Occidente, complete with sculptured flaming torches. On the west side is Bancafé and the impressive but crumbling **Pasaje Enriquez**, which was planned as a sparkling arcade of upmarket shops. It was derelict for many years but has now been partially revived. Inside you'll find the *Salon Tecún Bar*, the hippest place in town, and a good place for meeting other travellers.

At the bottom end of the plaza, next to the tourist office, is the **Casa de la Cultura museum** (Mon–Fri 8am–noon & 2–6pm, Sat 9am–1pm; US$1), the city's most blatant impersonation of a Greek temple, with a bold grey frontage. The main part of the building is given over to an odd mixture of local exhibits. On the ground floor, to the left-hand side, you'll find a display of assorted documents from the liberal revolution and the State of Los Altos, sports trophies, and a museum of marimba. Upstairs there are some interesting Maya artefacts, a display about local industries and a fascinating collection of old photographs.

Along the other side of the plaza is the **Cathedral**, with the new cement version set behind the spectacular crumbling front of the original. There's another piece of classical grandeur, the **Municipalidad** or town hall, a little further up. Take a look inside at the courtyard, which has a neat little garden set out around a single palm tree. Back in the centre of the plaza are rows and circles of redundant columns, a few flowerbeds, and a monument to Rufino Barrios, president of Guatemala from 1873 to 1885.

Away from the plaza, the city spreads out, a mixture of the old and new. 14 Avenida is the commercial heart, complete with pizza restaurants and neon signs. At the top of 14 Avenida, at the junction with 1 Calle, stands the **Teatro Municipal** (undergoing some restoration), another spectacular Neoclassical edifice. Further afield, the city's role as a regional centre of trade is more in evidence. Out in Zona 3 is the **Mercado la Democracia**, a vast covered complex with stalls spilling out onto the streets. There's another Greek-style structure right out on the edge of town, the **Minerva Temple**. It was built to honour President Barrios's enthusiasm for education and makes no pretence at serving any practical purpose. Beside the temple is the fairly miserable **zoo** (Tues–Sun 9am–5pm; free) where there is also as a children's playground. Below the temple are the sprawling **market** and **bus terminal**, and it's here that you can really sense the city's role as the centre of the western highlands, with indígena traders from all over the area doing business.

Eating, drinking and entertainment

There are more than enough **restaurants** to choose from in Quetzaltenango, with four reasonable pizza places on 14 Avenida alone. Note that almost nowhere opens before 8am in the morning, so forget early **breakfasts**. Xela is very sleepy after dark and **nightlife** is not easy to come by. Hedonists will have to catch a taxi to the best **clubs**, which are all out of town.

Cafés and restaurants

Artura's Restaurant, 14 Av 3–09, Zona 1. Dark, cosy atmosphere, with traditional, moderately priced food and a separate, fairly civilized bar for drinking.

Blue Angel Video Café, 7 C 15–22, Zona 1. A popular gringo hangout with a daily video programme. An intimate, friendly place where you can eat great vegetarian food. Daily 2.15pm–11pm.

Café Baviera, 5 C 12–50, Zona 1, a block from the plaza. Spacious pine-panelled coffee house dripping with photographic nostalgia. Quality cakes and unquestionably the best coffee in town. Daily 8am–8pm.

Cardinali's, 14 Av 3–41, Zona 1. Without doubt the best Italian food outside the capital, at reasonable prices. Make sure you are starving when you eat here because the portions are huge.

Deli Crepe, 14 Av, Zona 1. Looks a bit gloomy from the outside but wait till you try the licuados, pancakes, and delicious sandwiches.

Pan y Pasteles, 18 Av and 2 C, Zona 1. The best bakery in town, run by Mennonites whose fresh pastries and breads are used by all the finest restaurants. Tues & Fri only, 10am–4pm.

Pensión Bonifaz, corner of the plaza, Zona 1. The hotel is always a sedate and civilized spot for a cup of tea and a cake, or a full meal, and for rubbing shoulders with the town's elite. Expensive.

La Polonesa, 14 Av 4–55, Zona 1. An unbeatable selection of set lunches (with daily specials) all at under US$2, served at solid wooden tables.

El Rincón de los Antojitos, 15 Av and 5 C, Zona 1. Despite being run by a French–Guatemalan couple, this friendly little restaurant has a purely Guatemalan menu, with specialities such as *pepian* (spicy chicken stew) and *hilachas* (beef in tomato sauce).

Shanghai, 4 C 12–22, Zona 1. Some of the best Chinese food in town, and not too expensive.

Drinking and nightlife

There's not much to do in the evenings in Quetzaltenango, and the streets are generally quiet by about 9pm. A couple of **bars**, though, are worth visiting. At the popular *Tecún*, on the west side of the plaza, you can down cuba libres, sip the beer on tap and listen to the latest sounds imported by the gringo bar staff. At the more sedate but classy *Don Rodrigo*, 1 C and 14 Av, you'll find leather-topped bar stools, draught beer and good but pricey sandwiches. The *Greenhouse Café Teatro,* 12 Av 1–40 (☎7630271), has a lively cultural programme including theatre, dance and poetry readings.

Quetzaltenango is a good place to catch movies, with a number of **cinemas** including the new screen inside the shopping mall, Plaza Polonco, just off the central plaza for pure Hollywood; and Cadore, 7 C and 13 Av, for violence, horror and soft porn. For art house films, the brand new Paraíso on 14 Av, close to the Teatro Municipal, is excellent.

Listings

Banks and exchange Banco Inmobiliario, Banco del Occidente and Banco del Café (with the longest opening hours – Mon–Fri 8.30am–8pm, Sat 10am–2pm) are all in the vicinity of the plaza and will change travellers' cheques. Banco Industrial, also in the plaza, has an ATM that takes Visa.

Bookstore Vrisa, 15 Av 3–64, opposite Telgua and the post office, has over 3000 used titles, plus a newsroom with *Newsweek*, *The Economist*, a message board, espresso coffee and bike rental.

Car and bike rental Guatemala Unlimited, 12 Av and 1 C, Zona 1 (☎7616043). Mountain bikes are around US$6 a day; or try the Vrisa bookstore (see above).

Consulate Mexican consulate is at 9 Av 6–19, Zona 1 (Mon–Fri 8–11am & 2.30–3.30pm). A Mexican tourist card costs US$1. Hand in paperwork in the morning and collect in the afternoon.

Laundry MiniMax, 4 Av and 1 Zona 1 (Mon–Sat 7am–7pm).

Medical care Doctors Cohen and Molina at the Policlinica, A C 13–15, speak some English. For emergencies, the Hospital Privado is at C Rudolfo Robles 23–51, Zona 1.

Photography For camera repairs try Fotocolor, 15 Av 3–25, or one of several shops on 14 Av.

Post office At the junction of 15 Av and 4 C.

Telephone The Telgua office (daily 7am–10pm) is just opposite the post office. Maya Communications, above *Tecún Bar* on the central plaza (daily 10am–7pm; ☎ & fax 7612832), offers all communication services, including email.

Around Quetzaltenango

It's easy to spend a week or two exploring this part of the country – making day-trips to the markets and fiestas, basking in hot springs, or hiking in the mountains. Quetzaltenango (Xela) is the obvious place to base yourself, with bus connections to all parts of the western highlands. The valley is heavily populated and in the surrounding hills are numerous smaller towns and villages, mostly indigenous agricultural communities and weaving centres. The area also offers excellent **hiking**. The most obvious climb is the **Volcán Santa María**, towering above Quetzaltenango itself. But there's also **Laguna Chicabal**, a small lake set in the cone of an extinct volcano, and **Tajumulco**, the highest peak in Central America. Casa Iximulew, 15 Av and 5 C, Zona 1, run **organized trips** to most of the volcanoes around Xela and to Zunil and Fuentes Georginas, or try Guatemala Unlimited, 12 Av and C 35, Zona 1 (☎ & fax 7616043). Quetzaltrekkers, based inside the *Casa Argentina* (see p.193) run regular hikes to Volcán Tajumulco, Central America's highest mountain and an amazing three-day trek between Todos Santos (see p.202) and Nebaj (see p.178).

To the south, straddling the coast road, is **Zunil** and the hot springs of **Fuentes Georginas**, overshadowed by volcanic peaks. To the north are **Totonicapán**, capital of the department of the same name, and **San Francisco el Alto**, a small town perched on an outcrop overlooking the valley. Beyond that lies **Momostenango**, the country's principal wool-producing centre and a centre of Maya culture.

Volcán Santa María

Due south of Quetzaltenango, the perfect cone of **Volcán Santa María** rises to a height of 3772m. From the town only the peak is visible, but seen from the rest of the valley the entire cone seems to tower over everything around. The view from the top is, as you might expect, spectacular, and if you're prepared to sweat out the climb you certainly won't regret it. It's possible to climb the volcano as a day-trip, but to really see it at its best you need to be on top at dawn, either sleeping on the freezing peak, or camping at the site below and climbing the final section in the dark by torchlight. Either way you need to bring enough food, water and stamina for the entire trip; and you should be acclimatized to the altitude before attempting it.

Zunil and Fuentes Georginas

Heading south to the Pacific, after 10km you come to the traditional village of **ZUNIL**, a vegetable-growing market town surrounded by steep hills and a sleeping volcano. The plaza is dominated by a beautiful colonial church with an intricate silver altar protected behind bars. The women of Zunil wear vivid purple *huipiles* and carry bright shawls, and for the Monday market the plaza is awash with colour. Just below the plaza is a **textile cooperative** where hundreds of women market their beautiful weavings. Zunil is also one of the few remaining places where **Maximón** (or San Simón), the evil saint, is still worshipped. In the face of disapproval from the Catholic Church, the Maya are reluctant to display their Judas, who also goes by the name Alvarado, but his image is usually paraded through the streets during Holy Week, dressed in Western clothes and smoking a cigar. Virtually any child in town will take you to his abode for a quetzal.

In the hills above Zunil are the **Fuentes Georginas**, a spectacular set of luxurious hot springs. A turning to the left off the main road, just beyond the entrance to the village, leads up into the hills to the baths, 8km away. You can walk it in a couple of hours, or rent a truck from the plaza in Zunil for about US$5, though if you're not staying the night you'll have to arrange the return trip (another US$5) a few hours later with the driver. The baths are surrounded by fresh green ferns, thick moss and lush forest, and to top it all there's a restaurant and bar beside the main pool. You can swim in the pool for US$1 or rent a **bungalow** for the night (②) complete with bathtub, double bed, fireplace and barbecue. In the rainy season it can be cold and damp, but with a touch of sunshine it's a fantastic place to spend the night.

Buses to Zunil run from Quetzaltenango's Minerva bus terminal every half-hour or so, with the last bus back from Zunil leaving at around 6.30pm. Most buses will travel via the rotunda on the east side of town.

San Francisco el Alto

From a magnificent hillside setting, the small market town of **SAN FRANCISCO EL ALTO** overlooks the Quetzaltenango valley. It's worth a visit for the view alone, with the great plateau stretching out below and the cone of Volcán Santa María on the horizon. But another good reason for visiting the village is the **Friday market**, which is possibly the biggest in Central America. Traders from every corner of Guatemala make the trip, many arriving the night before, and some starting to sell as early as 4am, by candlelight. Throughout the morning a steady stream of buses and trucks fill the town to bursting; by noon the market is at its height, buzzing with activity.

The town is set into the hillside, with steep cobbled streets connecting the different levels. Two areas in particular are monopolized by specific trades. At the very top is an open field used as an **animal market**, where everything from pigs to parrots changes hands. The teeth and tongues of animals are inspected by the buyers, and at times the scene degenerates into a chaotic wrestling match, with pigs and men rolling in the dirt. Below this is the town's plaza, dominated by textiles. On the lower level, the streets are filled with vegetables, fruit, pottery, furniture, cheap comedores, and plenty more. These days most of the stalls deal in imported denim, but under the arches and in the covered area opposite the church you'll find a superb selection of traditional cloth. For a really good **photographic** angle and for views of the market and the surrounding countryside, pay the church caretaker a quetzal and climb up to the **church roof**. By early afternoon the numbers start to thin out, and by sunset it's all over – until the following Friday.

There are plenty of **buses** from Quetzaltenango to San Francisco, 16km away, leaving every twenty minutes or so from the rotunda; the first is at 6am, and the last bus back leaves at about 5pm (45min).

Momostenango

A further 22km from San Francisco, down a dirt road that continues over a ridge behind the town then drops down through lush pine forests, is **MOMOSTENANGO**, a small, isolated town and the centre of wool production in the highlands. Momostecos travel throughout the country peddling their blankets, scarves and rugs. Years of experience have made them experts in the hard sell and given them a sharp eye for tourists. The wool is also used in a range of traditional costumes, including the short skirts worn by the men of Nahualá, San Antonio Palopó and the jackets of Sololá. The ideal place to buy Momostenango blankets is in the **Sunday market**, which fills the town's two plazas.

A visit at this time will also give you a glimpse of Momostenango's other feature: its rigid adherence to tradition. Opposite the entrance to the church, people make offerings of incense and alcohol on a small fire, muttering their appeals to the gods. The town is famous for this unconventional folk-Catholicism, and it has been claimed that there are as many as three hundred Maya **shamans** working here. Momostenango's religious **calendar**, like that of only one or two other villages, is still based on the 260-day *Tzolkin* year – made up of thirteen twenty-day months – that has been in use since ancient times.

As a visitor it's best to visit Momostenango for the market, unless you can coincide your visit with the start of the Maya new year or the fiesta on August 1. If you decide to stay for a day or two then you can take a walk to the *riscos*, a set of bizarre sandstone pillars, or beyond to the **hot springs** of Pala Chiquito, about 3km away to the north.

The best place **to stay** in Momostenango is the *Hotel Estiver*, 1 C 4–15, Zona 1 (☎7365036; ②). It has clean rooms, some with private bathrooms, great views from the roof and safe parking. For **eating**, there are plenty of small comedores on the main plaza. Momostenango is also home to ADIFAM, a development agency that concentrates on educating children in the municipality. Volunteers with good Spanish are needed; you can contact them at the *Hotel Estiver*.

Buses run here from Quetzaltenango, passing through Cuatro Caminos and San Francisco el Alto on the way. They leave the Minerva terminal in Quetzaltenango every hour or so from 10am to 4pm (1hr 30min) and from Momostenango between 6am and 3pm. On Sunday, special early-morning buses leave Quetzaltenango from 6am: you can catch them at the rotunda.

Totonicapán

Capital of one of the smaller departments, **TOTONICAPÁN** is reached down a direct road leading east from Cuatro Caminos. Surrounded by rolling hills and pine forests, the town stands at the heart of a heavily populated and intensely farmed little region. There is only one point of access and the valley has always held out against outside influence, shut off in a world of its own. Totonicapán is a quiet place, ruffled only by the Tuesday and Saturday **markets**, which fill the two plazas to bursting. Until fairly recently a highly ornate traditional costume was worn here but this has now disappeared and the town has instead become one of the chief centres of commercial weaving. On one side of the main plaza is a workshop where young men are taught to weave on treadle looms; visitors are always welcome to stroll in and take a look around. This same plaza is home to the municipal **theatre**, a grand Neoclassical structure echoing the one in Quetzaltenango.

Totonicapán is very quiet after dark but if you want to stay, the best **hotel** is the *Hospedaje San Miguel*, a block from the plaza at 8 Av and 3 C (②–③). It is pretty comfortable and some rooms have bathrooms, but beware price-rises before market days. The *Pensión Blanquita* (①) is a friendly and basic alternative, opposite the filling station at 13 Av and 4 C. There are good connections between Totonicapán and Quetzaltenango, with buses shuttling the 24km back and forth every half-hour or so; alternatively, take any bus to Cuatros Caminos and change there.

Huehuetenango

In the corner of a small agricultural plain, 5km from the Carretera Interamericana at the foot of the mighty Cuchumatanes, lies **HUEHUETENANGO**, capital of the department of the same name. Though Huehue is the focus of trade and transport for a vast area, its atmosphere is provincial and relaxed. Before the arrival of the Spanish, it was the site of one of the residential suburbs that surrounded the Mam capital of Zaculeu (see p.133). Under colonial rule, it was a small regional centre with little to offer other than a steady trickle of silver and a stretch or two of grazing land. The supply of silver dried up long ago, but other minerals are still mined, and coffee and sugar have been added to the area's produce.

Today's Huehuetenango has two quite distinct functions – and two contrasting halves – each serving a separate section of the population. The large majority of the people are *ladino*, and for them Huehuetenango is an unimportant regional centre far from the hub of things. Here the mood is summed up in the unhurried atmosphere of the attractive **plaza** at the heart of the *ladino* half of town, where shaded walkways are surrounded by administrative offices. Overlooking it, perched above the pavements, are a shell-shaped bandstand, a clock tower and a grandiose Neoclassical church, a solid whitewashed structure with a facade that's crammed with Doric pillars and Grecian urns.

A few blocks to the east, the town's atmosphere could hardly be more different. Around the **market**, the hub of the Maya part of town, the streets are crowded with traders, drunks and travellers from Mexico and all over Central America. This part of Huehuetenango, centred on 1 Avenida, is always alive with activity, its streets packed with people from every corner of the department and littered with rotten vegetables.

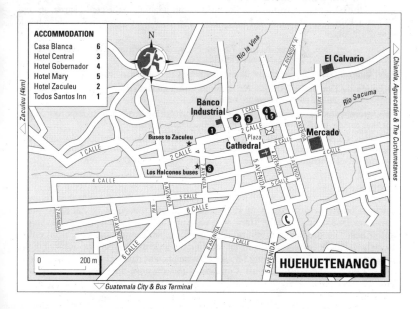

Arrival, information and accommodation

Huehue is fairly small so you shouldn't have any real problems finding your way around, particularly once you've located the plaza. You'll arrive at the purpose-built **bus terminal** halfway between the Carretera Interamericana and town. Minibuses make constant trips between the town centre and the bus terminal. Daily **flights** from Guatemala City land at the airstrip 3km south of the centre of town (50min; approx US$60 one-way).

There's a **post office** at 2 C 3–54 (Mon–Fri 8am–4.30pm) and **Telgua** is at 4 Av 6–54 (7am–10pm), though it may move back to its former location next to the post office.

Virtually all Huehue's hotels are within a short stroll of the plaza and tend to be good value for money, though there's nothing at the top end of the scale.

Casa Blanca, 7 Av 3–41 (☎ & fax 7642586). The town's newest upmarket hotel, built in colonial style. The fine restaurant and spacious garden terrace are well worth a visit too. ⑤.

Hotel Central, 5 Av 1–33 (☎7641197) Classic budget hotel, with large, scruffy rooms in a creaking old wooden building and a fantastic comedor. No singles or private baths. ①.

Hotel Gobernador, 4 Av 1–45 (☎ & fax 7641197). Formerly known as the *Astoria*, this is an excellent budget hotel run by a very friendly family. Attractive rooms come with or without bath; there are hot showers, and a good comedor. ②.

Hotel Mary, 2 C 3–52 (☎7641618, fax 7641228). Centrally located with small but pleasant rooms, some with a private shower and loads of steaming hot water. ②–③.

Hotel Zaculeu, 5 Av 1–14 (☎7641086, fax 7641575). Large, comfortable hotel, something of an institution. Some of the older rooms surrounding a leafy courtyard are a bit musty and gloomy, while in the more expensive new section they are larger and more spacious. All come complete with cable TV and private bathroom. There's also parking and a reasonable restaurant. ④–⑤.

Todos Santos Inn, 2 C 6–74 (☎7641241). The best budget hotel in town. Rooms seem far too attractive for the price and come with bedside lights for reading and reliable hot water. Excellent deal for single travellers. ②–③.

Eating, drinking and entertainment

Most of the better **restaurants** are, like the accommodation, in the central area, around the plaza. **Films** are shown two or three times a week at the cinema on 3 C, half a block west of the plaza.

La Cabana del Café, 2 C, opposite *Hotel Vásquez*. Logwood café with an excellent range of coffees (including cappuccino), great cakes and a few snacks.

Hotel Central, 5 Av 1–33. Very tasty, inexpensive set meals. Particularly good breakfasts.

La Fonda de Don Juan, 2 C 5–35. Attractive place with good if pricey pizzas and a reasonable range of beers but the pasta portions are rather small.

Café Jardin, 4 C and 6 Av. Friendly place serving inexpensive but excellent breakfasts, milkshakes, pancakes and the usual chicken and beef dishes. Open 6am–11pm.

Mi Tierra, 4 C 6–46. Superb new resturant with nice decor including plants and a fountain. Good atmosphere and the flavoursome menu is more imaginative than most – great for house salads, *churrascos* (barbecued meat) and cheesecake. Plus the beer's cheap. Closed Wed.

Zaculeu

A few kilometres to the west of Huehuetenango are the ruins of **Zaculeu** (daily 8am–6pm; US$4), capital of the **Mam**, who were one of the principal pre-conquest highland tribes. The site includes several large temples, plazas and a ball court, but unfortunately it has been restored with an astounding lack of subtlety (or accuracy). Its appearance – more like an ageing film set than an ancient ruin – is owed to a latter-day colonial power, the **United Fruit Company**, under whose auspices the ruins were reconstructed in 1946–7. The walls and surfaces have been levelled off with a layer of thick white plaster, leaving them stark and undecorated. There are no roof-combs, carvings or stucco mouldings, and only in a few places does the original stonework show through. Even so, the site does have a peculiar atmosphere of its own. Surrounded by trees and neatly mown grass, with fantastic views of the mountains, it's also an excellent spot for a picnic. There's a small **museum** on site (daily 8am–noon & 1–6pm) with examples of some of the unusual burial techniques used and some interesting ceramics found during excavation.

The site is thought to have been a religious and administrative centre housing the elite, while the bulk of the population lived in small surrounding settlements or else scattered in the hills. Zaculeu was the hub of a large area of Mam-speakers, its boundaries reaching into the mountains as far as Todos Santos. However, to put together a history of the site means relying on the records of the Quiché, a more powerful neighbouring tribe. According to their mythology, the Quiché conquered most of the other highland tribes, including the Mam, some time between 1400 and 1475. Following the death of the Quiché leader, Quicab, in 1475, the Mam managed to reassert their independence, but no sooner had they escaped the clutches of one expansionist empire than the Spanish arrived with a yet more brutal alternative.

Pedro de Alvarado despatched an army under the command of his brother, Gonzalo, which was met by about five thousand Mam warriors. The Mam leader, Caibal Balam, quickly saw that his troops were no match for the Spanish and withdrew them to the safety of Zaculeu, where they were protected on three sides by deep ravines and on the other by a series of walls and ditches. The Spanish army settled outside the city and besieged the citadel for six weeks until starvation forced Caibal Balam to surrender.

To get to Zaculeu from Huehuetenango, take one of the **pickups** or buses that leave close to the school from 7 Av between 2 and 3 calles – make sure it's a Ruta 3 heading for Ruinas Zaculeu (not Zaculeu Central).

The Cuchumatanes

The largest non-volcanic peaks in Central America, the **Cuchumatanes** rise from a limestone plateau close to the Mexican border and reach their full height of over 3800m above Huehuetenango. This is magnificent mountain scenery, ranging from wild, exposed craggy outcrops to lush, tranquil river valleys. While the upper parts of the slopes are almost barren, scattered with boulders and shrivelled cypress trees, the lower levels, by contrast, are richly fertile and cultivated with corn, coffee and sugar. Between the peaks, in the deep-cut valleys, are hundreds of tiny villages, isolated by the enormity of the landscape.

Despite the initial devastation, the arrival of the Spanish had surprisingly little impact in these highlands and some of the communities here are amongst the most traditional in Guatemala. A visit to the mountain villages, either for a market or fiesta (and there are plenty of both), offers one of the best opportunities to see Maya life at close quarters. In the late 1970s and early 1980s this was the scene of bitter fighting between the army and the guerrillas, a wave of violence and terror that sent thousands fleeing across the border to Mexico. Nowadays, though, with the fighting over, things are much calmer.

The most accessible of the villages in the vicinity, and the only one yet to receive a steady trickle of tourists, is **Todos Santos**, whose horse race fiesta on November 1 is one of the most interesting and outrageous in Guatemala. To the east a road struggles through the mountains past the interesting village of **Aguacatán** on its way to Cobán in Alta Verapaz (see p.232).

Todos Santos

Spectacularly sited in its own remote deep-cut river valley, **TODOS SANTOS** is many travellers' favourite place in Central America. Though the sheer beauty of the alpine surroundings is one attraction, it's the unique culture that is really astounding. The *traje* worn here is startling: the men wear red-and-white candy striped trousers, black woollen breeches and pinstripe shirts, explosively decorated with dayglo pink collars, while the women wear dark blue *cortes* and superbly intricate purple *huipiles*. The Todosanteros are perhaps the proudest of all Guatemala's Maya people – there is a distinctive swagger in the step of the men – and the **fiesta** (on November 1) is one of the most famous in the country. For three days the village is taken over by unrestrained drinking, dancing and marimba music. The whole event opens with an all-day horse race and there is a massive stampede as the inebriated riders tear up the course, thrashing their horses with live chickens, their pink capes flowing out behind them. On the second day, "The Day of the Dead", the action moves to the cemetery, with marimba bands and drink stalls set up amongst the graves. It is a day of intense ritual that combines grief and celebration. On the final day of the fiesta, the streets are littered with bodies and the jail packed with brawlers. The Saturday **market**, although nothing like as riotous, also fills the village.

The village itself is pretty – a modest main street with a few shops, a plaza and a church – but it is totally overshadowed by the looming presence of the Cuchumatanes, insulating Todos Santos from the rest of the world. Above the village – follow the track that goes up behind the *Comedor Katy* – is the small Maya site of **Tojcunanchén**, where you'll find a couple of mounds sprouting pine trees. The site is occasionally used by *brujos* for the ritual sacrifice of animals.

Practicalities

Buses leave Huehuetenango for Todos Santos from the main bus terminal at 12.30pm and 3pm – get there early to mark your seat and buy a ticket. Some carry on through the village, heading further down the valley to Jacaltenango and pass through Todos Santos on the way back to Huehuetenango at 4am and 10.30am. Ask around for the latest schedule.

One of the best places **to stay** is *Hospedaje Casa Familiar* (②), 30m above the main road past *Comedor Katy*, where views from the terrace café are breathtaking. There is another good place, *Hospedaje las Ruinas* (①), further up the track on the right, in a large twin-storey concrete structure that may now be signposted. Turning left just before you reach the *Casa Familiar* brings you to *Hotel Mam* in an orange house; this is another good option with hot showers (①). There are two **hotels** in Todos Santos, both very inexpensive but extremely rough, the *Hospedaje la Paz* (①) and *Las Olguitas* (①).

The best place to **eat** is at the delightful *Comedor Katy*, though you can also find good meals at the *Casa Familiar*. There is a new logwood gringo-geared restaurant/café called *Ixcanac* in the centre of town, where you'll find spaghetti, good barbecued meats, wine and films.

Though most of the fun of Todos Santos is in simply hanging out, it would be a shame not to indulge in a traditional **smoke sauna** (*chuc*) while you're here. Most of the guest houses will prepare one for you. If you want to take a shirt, pair of trousers or *huipil* home with you, you'll find an excellent co-op selling quality **weavings** next to the *Casa Familiar*. Todos Santos is also home to one of Guatemala's most interesting **language schools**, where you can study Spanish or Mam – see p.129 for details.

Walks around Todos Santos

The village of **SAN JUAN ATITÁN** is around five hours from Todos Santos across a beautiful isolated valley. Follow the path that bears up behind the *Comedor Katy*, past the ruins and high above the village through endless muddy switchbacks until you get to the ridge overlooking the valley where, if the skies are clear, you'll be rewarded by an awesome view of the Tajumulco and Tacaná volcanoes. Take the central track from here heading downhill past some ancient cloud forest to San Juan Atitán, four to five hours further on; it's easy to follow. There's a hospedaje (①) if you want to stay and morning **pickups** return to Huehue from 6am (1hr). Market days are Mondays and Thursdays.

Alternatively, you can walk down the valley along the road from Todos Santos to **San Martín** and on to **Jacaltenango**, a route which also offers superb views. There's a basic hospedaje (①) in Jacaltenango, so you can stay the night and then catch a bus back to Huehuetenango in the morning. Some buses from Huehue also continue down this route.

Aguacatán

To the east of Huehuetenango, a dirt road turns off at Chiantla to weave through dusty foothills along the base of the Cuchumatanes to **AGUACATÁN**. This small agricultural town is strung out along two main streets, shaped entirely by the dip in which it's built. The language of Aguateca is spoken only in this village and its immediate surrounds, by a population of around fifteen thousand. During the colonial period, gold and silver were mined in the nearby hills, and the Maya are said to have made bricks of solid gold for the king of Spain, to persuade him to let them keep their lands. Today, the town is steeped in tradition and the people survive by growing vegetables, including huge quantities of garlic, much of it for export.

Aguacatán's huge Sunday **market** gets under way on Saturday afternoon, when traders arrive early to claim the best sites. On Sunday morning, a steady stream of people pour down the main street, cramming into the market and plaza, and soon spilling out into the surrounding area. Around noon the tide turns as the crowds start to drift back to their villages, with donkeys leading their drunken drivers. Despite the scale of the market, its atmosphere is subdued and the pace unhurried: for many it's as much a social event as a commercial one.

The traditional costume worn by the women of Aguacatán is unusually simple: their skirts are made of dark blue cotton and the *huipiles*, which hang loose, are decorated with bands of coloured ribbon on a plain white background. This plainness, though, is set off by the local speciality – the *cinta*, or headdress, in which they wrap their hair, an intricately embroidered piece of cloth combining blues, reds, yellows and greens.

Aguacatán's other attraction is the source of the Río San Juan, which emerges fresh and cool from beneath a nearby hill, making a good place for a chilly dip. To get there, walk east along the main street out of the village for about a kilometre, until you see the sign. From the village it takes about twenty minutes.

Eight daily **buses** run from Huehuetenango to Aguacatán between 6am and about 2.45pm (1hr). There are two small and very simple places to stay: the *Nuevo Amanecer* (②) and the *Hospedaje Aguateco* (①). **Beyond Aguacatán** the road runs out along a ridge, with fantastic views stretching out below, eventually dropping down to the riverside town of **Sacapulas**.

West to the Mexico border

From Huehuetenango the Carretera Interamericana runs for 79km to the Mexican border at **La Mesilla**. There are hourly buses between 5am and 6pm (2hr). If you get stuck at the border there's **accommodation** at the new *Hotel Maricruz* (②–③), a clean place with private bathrooms and a restaurant, or the cheaper *Hospedaje Marisol* (②). The two sets of customs and immigration are 3km apart. There are taxis, and on the Mexican side you can pick up buses running through the border settlement of **Ciudad Cuauhtemoc** to **Comitán** or even direct to **San Cristóbal de las Casas**. Heading into Guatemala, the last bus leaves La Mesilla for Huehuetenango at around 4pm.

travel details

BUSES

Antigua to: Chimaltenango (every 20min 5am–7pm; 40min); Esquintla (2 daily; 2hr 30min); Guatemala City (every 15min Mon–Fri 4am–7pm, Sat & Sun 7am–7pm; 1hr); Panajachel (1 daily; 2hr 30min).

Chichicastenango to: Guatemala City (every 30min 5am–4.30pm; 3hr); Quetzaltenango (7 daily; 2hr 30min); Santa Cruz del Quiché (every 30min; 30min).

Huehuetenango to: Aguacatán (8 daily; 1hr); Guatemala City (14 daily; 6hr); La Mesilla (12 daily; 2hr); Todos Santos (2–3 daily; 2hr 30min).

Panajachel to: Antigua (1 daily; 3hr); Chichicastenango (7 daily Thurs & Sun, less frequent at other times; 1hr 30min); Cocales (5 daily; 2hr 30min); Guatemala City (9 daily; 3hr 30min); Quetzaltenango (6 daily; 2hr 30min); Santa Catarina and San Antonio Palopó (hourly; 30min/45min). There are also tourist shuttles to Antigua and Guatemala City and to Chichicastenango on market days.

Quetzaltenango to: Chichicastenango (7 daily; 2hr 30min); Guatemala City (19 daily; 4hr); Huehuetenango (20 daily; 2hr); to Momostenango (hourly; 1hr 30min); Panajachel (6 daily; 2hr 30min); San Francisco el Alto (every 30min; 45min); Totonicapán (every 30min; 1hr); Santa Cruz del Quiché (7 daily; 3hr); Tecún Umán (10 daily; 2hr 30min); Zunil (every 30min; 25min).

Santa Cruz del Quiché to: Guatemala City (every 30min; 3hr 30min); Nebaj (6 daily; 4hr); Quetzaltenango (7 daily; 3hr); Sacapulas (4 daily; 2hr); Uspantán (4 daily; 5hr).

FLIGHTS

Huehuetenango to: Guatemala City (daily; 50min).

Quetzaltenango to: Guatemala City (daily; 30min).

Santa Cruz del Quiché to: Guatemala City (daily; 25min).

CHAPTER 8

THE PACIFIC COAST

Beneath the chain of volcanoes that marks the southern side of the highlands is a strip of sweltering, low-lying land some 300km long and on average 50km wide, known by Guatemalans simply as **La Costa Sur**. This featureless yet supremely fertile coastal plain – once a wilderness of swamp, forest and savannah – is today a land of vast fincas, scattered with indifferent commercial towns and small seaside resorts.

The **Pacific coast** was once as rich in wildlife as the jungles of Petén, but while Petén has lain relatively undisturbed, the Pacific coast has been ravaged by development. Its large-scale agriculture – sugar cane, palm oil, cotton and rubber plantations – accounts for a substantial proportion of the country's exports. Only in some isolated sections, where mangrove swamps have been spared the plough, can you still get a sense of the way it once looked: a maze of tropical vegetation. The **Monterrico Reserve** is the most accessible protected area, a swampy refuge for sea turtles, iguanas, crocodiles and an abundance of bird life.

As for the archeological sites, they too have largely disappeared, though you can glimpse the extraordinary art of the **Pipil** (see p.133) around the town of **Santa Lucía Cotzumalguapa**. Here, a few small ceremonial centres, almost lost in fields of sugar cane, reveal a wealth of carvings; some of them are still regularly used for religious rituals. The one site that ranks with those elsewhere in the country is **Abaj Takalik**, whose ruins are well worth a detour on your way to or from Mexico, or as a day-trip from Xela or nearby Retalhuleu.

The main attraction should be the **beach**, but as nature has cursed the coast with mosquitoes and unpredictable sea currents, and man has added filthy palm huts, pig pens and garbage, it's not. The hotels are also some of the country's worst, so if you're desperate for a dip and a fresh shrimp feast, it's best to visit a day-trip from the capital or Quetzaltenango. The one glorious exception to this rule is the nature reserve of **Monterrico**, which harbours an attractive village and what may be the country's finest beach, with a superb stretch of clean sand.

The main route through the region is the **Carretera del Pacífico**, which runs from the border with Mexico at Tecún Umán into El Salvador at Ciudad Pedro de Alvarado. It's the country's swiftest highway and you'll never have to wait long for a bus. Venture off the Carretera del Pacífico, however, and things slow down considerably, bus services are irregular and the roads in poor condition.

Some history

Before the arrival of the **Ocós** and **Iztapa** tribes from the north, little is known of the history of the Pacific coast. By 1500 BC, however, these Mexican tribes had developed village-based societies with considerable skills in the working of stone and pottery. Between 400 and 900 AD, the whole coastal plain was again overrun by Mexicans; this time it was the **Pipil**, who brought sophisticated architectural and artistic skills which they used in building ceremonial centres.

The first Spaniards to set foot in Guatemala did so on the Pacific coast, arriving overland from the north. Alvarado's first confrontation with the Maya happened here, in the heat of the lowlands, before the Spanish moved north to Quetzaltenango. Once established there, they despatched a handful of Franciscans to convert the Pipil coastal

For an explanation of **accommodation price codes**, see p.123.

population. In **colonial times**, the land was used for the production of indigo and cacao and for cattle ranching, never becoming anything more than a miserable disease-ridden backwater. It was only after **independence** that commercial agriculture began to dominate this part of the country.

Today this coastline is the country's most intensely farmed region, where entire villages are effectively owned by vast cotton- and sugar-cane-growing fincas, and coffee is grown on the volcanic slopes. Much of the nation's income is generated here and the main towns are alive with commercial activity, and dominated by the assertive machismo of *ladino* culture. In the past, the highland Maya were forcibly recruited to work the plantations here; even today many thousands come to the coast for seasonal work and continue to be exploited by the fincas.

From the Mexican border to Coatepeque

The coastal border with Mexico is the busiest of Guatemala's frontiers, with two crossing points, Talismán and Tecún Umán, open 24 hours. The northernmost of the two posts is the **Talismán Bridge**, also referred to as **El Carmen**, where there's little more than a few huts, a couple of basic pensiones (both ①) and a round-the-clock flow of buses to Guatemala City. If you're heading towards Quetzaltenango or the western highlands, take the first bus to Malacatán and change there. On the Mexican side, over the bridge, there's a constant flow of minibuses leaving for Tapachula.

The **Tecún Umán** crossing is favoured by most Guatemalans and all commercial traffic. It has an authentic frontier flavour, with all-night bars frequented by lost souls,

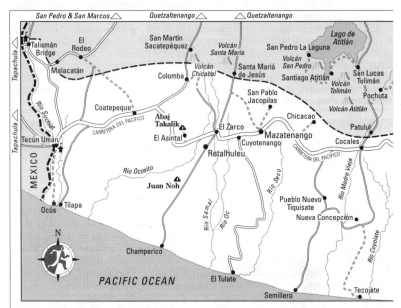

contraband and moneychangers. There are some cheap hotels: the *Hotel Vanessa 2* (②) and the *Hotel Don José,* 2 C 3–42 (☎7768164; ②) are two of the best, but it's probably a much better idea to get straight out of town – everyone else does. Once again, there's a steady stream of buses to Guatemala City along the Carretera del Pacífico via Coatepeque and Retalhuleu. If you're Mexico-bound, once you're over the border, there are very frequent bus services to Tapachula (30min).

Heading east from the Mexican border, **COATEPEQUE** is the first place of any importance you come to, a town that's in many ways typical of the coastal strip. A furiously busy, purely commercial centre, this is where most of the coffee produced locally is processed. The action is centred on the **bus terminal**, an intimidating maelstrom of sweat, mud and energetic chaos. Buses run every thirty minutes from here to the two border crossings, and hourly to Quetzaltenango and Guatemala City. The town is also connected with Guatemala City by daily **flights** (1hr; US$55 one-way), arriving at the airstrip about 3km southwest of the centre.

The best place to **stay** in Coatepeque is the *Hotel Villa Real*, 6 C 6–57 (☎7751308, fax 7751939; ④), a modern hotel with clean rooms and secure parking. A bit cheaper is the family-run *Hotel Baechli*, 6 C 5–35 (☎7751483; ④), which has plain rooms with fan and TV, plus secure parking. There are two **banks** that will change your travellers' cheques on the plaza and a **Telgua** office (daily 7am–10pm) at 5 Av and 7 C.

Retalhuleu to Cocales

About 40km beyond Coatepeque is the largest town in the region, **RETALHULEU**, usually referred to as **Reu**, pronounced "Ray-oo". Set away from the highway and surrounded by the walled homes of the wealthy, Retalhuleu has managed to avoid the worst excesses of the coast and has a relaxed easy-going air. It was founded by the

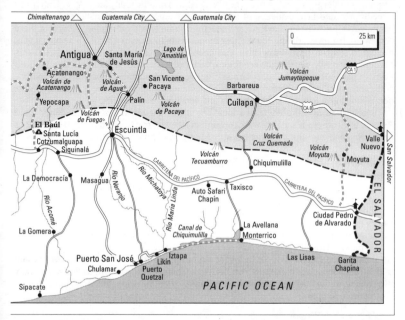

Spanish in the early years of the Conquest and remains something of an oasis of civilization with a plaza of towering Greek columns and an attractive colonial church. If you have time to kill, pop into the local **Museo de Arqueología y Etnología** in the plaza (Tues–Sun 9am–noon & 2–6pm; US$1), where you'll find an amazing collection of anthropomorphic figurines, mostly heads, and some photographs of the town dating back to the 1880s.

Budget **accommodation** is in short supply in Retalhuleu. The cheapest place in town is the *Hotel Pacífico* (☎7711178; ①) at 7 Av 9–29 which is scruffy and fanless. Otherwise rates go up steeply: *Hotel Astor*, 5 C 4–60 (☎7710475; ③), has rooms with fan, TV and bath, set around a pleasant courtyard, and is very good value for money; or across the road there's the *Hotel Modelo*, 5 C 4–53 (☎7710256; ③). If you want a bit more luxury, try the modern *Hotel Posada de Don José*, 5 C 3–67 (☎7710180; ④), which has good rooms, a reasonable restaurant and a pool.

The **plaza** is the hub of activity. Here you'll find three **banks**, including the Banco del Agro and, close by, the Banco Industrial with a 24-hour Visa ATM, the **post office** (Mon–Fri 8am–4.30pm), and the Cine Morán; the **Telgua** office (daily 7am–10pm) is just around the corner. The best **restaurants** are also on the plaza. Try the *Cafetería la Luna*, or for cakes and pastries, *El Volován*.

Buses running along the coastal highway almost always pull in at the Retalhuleu terminal on 7 Av and 10 C, a ten-minute walk from the plaza. There's an hourly service to and from Guatemala City, the Mexican border and Quetzaltenango, plus regular buses to Champerico and El Tulate. Inter airlines **fly** daily to and from the capital (35min; US$40 one-way), using the airstrip about 10km southwest of the town centre on the Champerico road to the coast. Retalhuleu has the only **Mexican consulate** on the Pacific coast, at 5 C and 3 Av (Mon–Fri 4–6pm).

Abaj Takalik

Currently undergoing excavation, the site of **Abaj Takalik** (daily 9am–4pm; US$4) has already provided firm evidence of an **Olmec** influence reaching this area in the first century AD. Excavations have so far unearthed some enormous stelae, several of them very well preserved, dating the earliest monuments to around 126 AD. The remains of two large **temple platforms** have also been cleared, and what makes a visit to this obscure site really worthwhile are the carved sculptures and stelae found around their base. In particular, you will find rare and unusual representations of frogs and toads – and even an alligator (monument 66). The finest carving, though, is a giant Olmec head, showing a man of obvious wealth and great hamster cheeks.

To **get to Abaj Takalik**, take a local bus from Reu 15km east to the village of El Asintal, from where it's a 4km walk through coffee and cacao plantations. If using your own transport, take the highway towards Mexico and turn right at the sign.

Champerico, Mazatenango and Cocales

Some 42km south of Retalhuleu, a paved road reaches to the beach at **CHAMPERICO**, which, though it certainly doesn't feel like it, is the country's third port. The town enjoyed a brief period of prosperity when it was connected to Quetzaltenango by rail but there's little left now apart from a rusting pier. The **beach** is much the same as anywhere else, although its sheer scale is impressive (watch out for the dangerous undertow). Delicious fried shrimp and fish **meals** are widely available; try the *Restaurant Monte Limar*. The best place to stay is the friendly, Spanish-owned *Miramar* at 2 C and Av Coatepeque (☎7737231; ②), a lovely old building with a fantastic wooden bar and dark windowless rooms. **Buses** run between Champerico and Quetzaltenango every two hours or so passing through Retalhuleu. The last bus for Retalhuleu leaves Champerico at 6pm.

Back on the highway, heading east, the next place of any size is the unremarkable town of Cuyotenango, where a side road heads off to the featureless beach of El Tulate. The next stop on the highway is **MAZATENANGO**, another seething commercial town which also has a quieter, calmer side centred on the plaza. *Maxim's*, at 6 Av 9–23, serves excellent Chinese food and barbecued meats, or try *Croissants Pastelería* on the plaza for coffee and cakes. There are also a couple of cinemas, plenty of **banks**, a few run-down pensiones and, on the main highway, the decent, clean *Hotel Alba* (☎8720264; ④), which has secure parking.

About 30km beyond Mazatenango is **COCALES**, a crossroads from where a road runs north to Santiago Atitlán, San Lucas Tolimán and Lago de Atitlán. If you're head-ing this way you can wait for a connection at the junction, but don't expect to make it all the way to Panajachel unless you get here by midday. The best bet is to take the first pickup or bus for Santiago and catch a boat from there to other points on the lake. The last transport to Santiago Atitlán leaves Cocales at around 5pm.

Santa Lucía Cotzumalguapa and around

Another 23km brings you to **SANTA LUCÍA COTZUMALGUAPA**, another uninspir-ing Pacific town a short distance north of the highway. The main reason to visit is to explore the **archeological sites** that are scattered in the surrounding cane fields. You should bear in mind, though, that getting to them isn't easy unless have your own trans-port or hire a taxi.

As usual, the **plaza** is the main centre of interest. Santa Lucía's shady square is dis-graced by possibly one of the ugliest buildings in the country (in a very competitive league), a memorably horrific green and white concrete municipal structure. Just off the plaza you'll find several cheap and scruffy **hotels**, the *Pensión Reforma*, 4 Av 4–71 (①), and the *Hospedaje el Carmen*, around the corner on 5 C (①). The nearest upmar-ket place is the *Caminotel Santiaguito* (☎8825435; ④), a slick motel on the highway, which has a swimming pool and restaurant.

Back in town at least three **banks** will change your travellers' cheques. Try Banco Corpativo in the plaza, which accepts most varieties. For **food**, the *Comedor Lau* on 3 Av does reasonable Chinese meals, or there's a huge new *Pollo Campero* on the north side of the square; the *Sarita* ice cream parlour is on 3 Av. For a drink, *Cevicheria la Española* on 4 Av, south of the plaza, is the best bet.

Pullman **buses** passing along the highway will drop you at the entrance road to town, ten minutes' walk from the town centre, while second-class buses from Guatemala City go straight into the terminal, a few blocks from the plaza. Buses to the capital leave the terminal hourly until 4pm, or you can catch a pullman from the highway.

Pipil sites around Santa Lucía Cotzumalguapa

A tour of the three Pipil sites around Santa Lucía can be an exhausting and frustrating process, taking you through a sweltering maze of cane fields. Doing the whole thing on foot is certainly the cheapest way – you can find children who'll guide you in the plaza or by asking in your pensión. It's far easier, though, to hire a taxi in the plaza; reckon on US$10 to visit all the sites. If you want to see just one of them, choose Bilbao, just 1km or so from the centre of town, which features some of the best carving. If you get lost at any stage, ask for "las piedras", as they tend to be known locally.

In 1880, more than thirty Late Classic stone monuments were removed from the Pipil site of **Bilbao**, and nine of the very best were shipped to Germany. Four sets of stones are still visible in situ, however, and two of them perfectly illustrate the magnif-icent precision of the carving, beautifully preserved in slabs of black volcanic rock. To

get to the site, walk uphill from the plaza, along 4 Av, and bear right at the end, where a dirt track takes you past a small red-brick house and along the side of a cane field. About 200m further on is a fairly wide path leading left into the cane for about 20m. This brings you to two large stones carved in bird-like patterns, with strange circular glyphs arranged in groups of three: the majority of the glyphs are recognizable as the names for days once used by the people of southern Mexico. In the same cane field, further along the same path, is another badly eroded stone, and a final set with a superbly preserved set of figures and interwoven motifs.

The second site is about 5km further afield in the grounds of the **Finca el Baúl**, reached by following 3 Av, the only tarmacked road that heads north out of town. The hilltop site has two stones, one flat and carved in low relief, the other a massive half-buried stone head, with wrinkled brow and patterned headdress. The site itself is still actively used for pagan ceremonies particularly by women hoping for children or safe childbirth. In front of the stones is a set of small altars on which local people make animal sacrifices, burn incense and leave offerings of flowers.

The next place of interest is the **finca** itself, a few kilometres further away from town, where the carvings include some superb heads, a stone skull, a massive jaguar and many other interesting pieces jumbled together. Alongside all this antiquity is the finca's old steam engine, a miniature machine that used to haul the cane along a system of private tracks. As the finca has its own bus service you may be able to get a ride. Buses leave from the tienda El Baúl, a few blocks uphill from the plaza, four or five times a day, the first at around 7am and the last either way at about 6pm.

On the other side of town is the third site, at **Finca las Ilusiones**, where there's another private collection of artefacts and some stone carvings. To get there, walk east along the highway for about 1km, and turn left by the second Esso station. Here there are several original carvings, including some fantastic stelae, plus some copies and a small museum crammed with literally thousands of small stone carvings and pottery fragments.

La Democracia

Continuing down the highway to Siquinalá, a run-down sort of place, there's another branch road that heads to the coast. Nine kilometres south, **LA DEMOCRACIA** is of particular interest as the home of another collection of archeological relics. To the east of town lies the site of **Monte Alto**, many of whose best pieces are now spread around the town plaza under a vast ceiba tree. These so-called "fat boys" are massive stone heads with simple, almost childlike faces. Some are attached to smaller rounded bodies and rolled over on their backs clutching their swollen stomachs. It seems likely that they predate almost all other archeological finds in Guatemala and could well be as much as four thousand years old. Also on the plaza, the town **museum** (Tues–Sun 8am–noon & 2–5pm) houses carvings, ceremonial yokes worn by ball-game players, pottery, grinding stones and a few more carved heads.

Escuintla and south to the coast

At the junction of the two principal coastal roads from the capital, **ESCUINTLA** is the largest and most important of the Pacific towns. There's nothing to do here, but you do get a good sense of life on the coast, its pace and energy and the frenetic commercial activity that drives it. Escuintla lies at the heart of the country's most productive region, both industrially and agriculturally, and the department's resources include cattle, sugar, cotton, light industry and even a small Texaco oil refinery.

Below the plaza a huge, chaotic **market** sprawls across several blocks, spilling out into 4 Av, the main commercial thoroughfare, which is also notable for a lurid blue mock-castle that functions as the town's police station.

There are plenty of cheap **hotels** near 4 Av, most of them sharing in the general air of dilapidation. The *Hospedaje Oriente*, 4 Av 11–30 (①), is cheap and pretty clean; or for a/c and secure parking, head for the recommended *Hotel Costa Sur*, 4 Av and 12 C (☎8881819; ③). As for **banks**, there's a Banco Industrial at 4 Av and 6 C, and Lloyds at 7 C 3–07. For somewhere to **eat**, the best deal is at *Pizzeria al Macarone*, 4 Av 6–103, which has bargain lunch specials. There are also two **consulates** in town, Honduras at 6 Av 8–24 and El Salvador at 16 C 3–20.

Buses to Escuintla leave from the Treból junction in Guatemala City frequently until 7pm, returning from 8 C and 2 Av in Escuintla. For other destinations, there are two terminals: for places **en route to the Mexican border**, buses run through the north of town and stop by the Esso station opposite the Banco Uno (take a local bus up 3 Av); buses for the **coast road and inland route to El Salvador** are best caught at the main terminal on the south side of town, at the bottom of 4 Av (local bus down 4 Av). From the latter, buses leave every thirty minutes for Puerto San José, hourly for the eastern border, and daily at 6.30am and noon for Antigua, via El Rodeo.

Puerto San José

South from Escuintla the coast road heads through acres of cattle pasture to **PUER-TO SAN JOSÉ**, which, in its prime, was Guatemala's main shipping terminal, funnelling goods to and from the capital. It has now been made virtually redundant by Puerto Quetzal, a container port a few kilometres to the east. Today both town and port are somewhat sleazy and the main business is local tourism: what used to be rough sailors' bars pander to the needs of the day-trippers from the capital who fill the beaches at weekends.

The shoreline is separated from the mainland by the **Canal de Chiquimulilla**, which starts near Sipacate, west of San José, and runs as far as the border with El Salvador, cutting off all the beaches in between. Here in San José, the main resort area is on the other side of the canal, directly behind the beach. This is where all the bars and restaurants are, most of them crowded at weekends with big *ladino* groups feasting on seafood. The **hotels** nearby are not so enjoyable, catering as they do to a largely drunken clientele, but try *Casa San José Hotel*, Av del Comercio (☎7765587; ③), where you'll find a pool and restaurant. Or, for a really cheap option, *Hospedaje Viñas de Mar* (②), which is basic but right by the beach.

Buses between San José and Guatemala City run every hour or so all day. From Guatemala City they leave from the terminal in Zona 4 (the new Zona 12 terminal when operational) and in San José from the plaza.

Monterrico

The setting of **MONTERRICO**, further east along the coast, is one of the finest on the Pacific coast, with the scenery reduced to its basic elements: a strip of dead straight sand, a line of powerful surf, a huge empty ocean and an enormous curving horizon. The village is friendly and relaxed, separated from the mainland by the waters of the Chiquimulilla canal, which in this case weaves through a fantastic network of mangrove **swamps**. Mosquitoes can be a problem during the wet season.

Beach apart, Monterrico's chief attraction is the **nature reserve**, which embraces the village, the beach – an important **turtle** nesting ground – and a large slice of the swamps behind, forming a total area of some 28 square kilometres. Sadly, however, the protected status the reserve officially enjoys does not stop the dumping of domestic rubbish and the widespread theft of turtle eggs. That said, this is certainly the best place on the coast to spend time by the sea.

The **Biotopo Monterrico-Hawaii** comprises a mangrove swamp with dark, nutrient-rich waters and four distinct types of mangrove that form a dense mat of branches, interspersed with narrow canals, open lagoons, bulrushes and water lilies. The tangle of roots acts as a kind of marine nursery, offering small fish protection from their natural predators, while above the surface the dense vegetation and ready food supply provide an ideal home for hundreds of species of bird and a handful of mammals, including raccoons, iguanas, alligators and opossums. The best way to explore is in a small *cayuco*; ask around at the dock for a boatman.

Getting to Monterrico

The best way to **get to Monterrico** is via the coastal highway at **Taxisco**, where trucks and buses run the 17km paved road to **LA AVELLANA**, a couple of kilometres from Monterrico on the opposite side of the mangrove swamp, which is crossed by frequent boats shuttling passengers and cars back and forth. There's a steady flow of traffic between Taxisco and La Avellana, the last bus leaving Taxisco at 6pm and La Avellana at 4.30pm. There are several direct buses between La Avellana and the Zona 4 bus terminal in Guatemala City, or you can get on any bus heading for Taxisco and change there. Hourly buses also continue from Taxisco along the Carretera del Pacífico to the border with El Salvador at Ciudad Pedro de Alvarado, just over an hour away. The border is a fairly quiet one, as most traffic uses the Valle Nuevo post to the north, but there are a couple of basic hospedajes (①–②) and some comedores if you get stuck there.

Accommodation

There's a pretty good range of accommodation in Monterrico, with almost everything concentrated right on the beach. As there are **no phones** it isn't easy to book in advance; you'll do best if you try those that have reservation numbers in Guatemala City. As elsewhere on the coast, prices can increase by around fifty percent at weekends.

Johnny's Place (Guatemala City ☎3374191). Turn left when you reach the ocean and it's the first place you'll come to. Self-catering bungalows sleeping four. Three small pools. ④–⑥.

Kaiman Inn, the next place east down the beach. Large rooms with mosquito nets and fans; there's also a pool and a variable Italian restaurant. ④.

Hotel Baule Beach, next door to the *Kaiman* (Guatemala City ☎4736196, fax 4713390). The most enduring gringo guest house on the entire Pacific coast, run by American Nancy Garver, a former Peace Corps volunteer. All rooms have their own bathroom and mosquito net; there's a pool and decent food. Good deal for single travellers. ③.

Hotel el Mangle, behind the *Baule Beach* (Guatemala City ☎3603336). Five simple rooms all with private bathroom. No pool or food. ④.

Pez de Oro, the last place heading east down the beach (Guatemala City ☎3683684). The nicest cottages in Monterrico – well-spaced, comfortable and tastefully decorated with a small swimming pool and a good Italian restaurant with excellent pasta and wine by the glass. ⑤.

Pig Pen, 20m on the right when you reach the beach. Excellent budget base with the cheapest beds in town. Rooms are bare but clean and you can also cook your own food. Alternatively, hook up a hammock for a dollar a night. ①.

Paradise Hotel, 2km outside the village, on the road to Iztapa (Guatemala City ☎4784202, fax 4784595). Best reached with your own transport. Spacious bungalows with two double beds and private bath. Swimming pool too but the restaurant, though decent, charges silly prices. ⑦.

Eating and drinking

When it comes to **eating** in Monterrico, you can either dine at the several hotels on the beach, or at one of the comedores in the village, the best of which is the *Divino Maestro*, where they do a superb shark steak with rosemary. For a **drink** and relaxed socializing with great music, head for the *Pig Pen*, a good hangout run by Michael, a friendly Canadian. He can also point you in the right direction if you want to rent surfboards and boats or find a guide.

travel details

BUSES

Coatepeque to: Guatemala City (hourly; 4hr); Retalhuleu (every 30min; 50min); Quetzaltenango (hourly; 2hr); Talismán and Tecún Umán (12 daily; 40min).

Cocales to: Escuintla (14 daily; 30min).

Escuintla to: Antigua (2 daily; 2hr 30min); Ciudad Pedro de Alvarado (hourly; 2hr 30min); Guatemala City (18 daily; 1hr 15min).

Guatemala City to: La Avellana (4 daily; 3hr 30min); Taxisco (hourly; 3hr); Tecún Umán and Talismán via all towns on Pacific Highway (19 daily; 5hr); Tapachula, Mexico (2 daily; 6hr); Puerto San José (8 daily; 2hr).

La Avellana to: Guatemala City (4 daily; 3hr 30min).

Retalhuleu to: Champerico (8 daily; 1hr); Cocales (14 daily; 50min); Guatemala City (18 daily; 4hr); Mazatenango (12 daily; 30min); Quetzaltenango (10 daily; 1hr 15min).

Talismán to: Guatemala City (10 daily; 5hr).

Tecún Umán to: Guatemala City (14 daily; 5hr); Quetzaltenango (10 daily; 2hr 30min).

FLIGHTS

Coatepeque to: Guatemala City (daily; 1hr).

Retalhuleu to: Guatemala City (daily; 35min).

CHAPTER 9

EAST TO THE CARIBBEAN

T he land to the **east of Guatemala City** is some of the most varied in the entire country, ranging from the cacti-spiked near-desert around the El Rancho junction to the permanently lush Caribbean coast. Although the coastal area was fairly densely populated in Maya times, it was largely abandoned until the end of the nineteenth century. Its revival was due to the arrival of the United Fruit Company, who cleared the land for the banana plantations that still dominate the area. Fruit-laden trucks thunder along the road to the coast, following the **Motagua valley**, a broad river corridor dividing two high mountain ranges. A couple of hours before you reach the coast, the route passes the ruins of **Quiriguá**, a small site with some of the finest stelae and carvings in the entire Maya world. At the end of the road is the faded, slightly seedy port of **Puerto Barrios**, a steamy, largely ladino town, from where it's possible to cross the border into Honduras, via the jungle route.

For an explanation of **accommodation price codes**, see p.123.

To the north of the Motagua valley is **Lago de Izabal**, a vast expanse of fresh water ringed by lonely villages, swamps, hot springs, waterfalls and caves. Its largely unpopulated shores are home to a tremendous variety of **wildlife** (most of it threatened), including alligators, iguanas, turtles, toucans and manatee. The best base for exploring this region is sleepy one-street Mariscos, or the bigger settlement of Río Dulce. Sailing towards the Caribbean from here, you pass through El Golfete and the spectacular, towering gorge systems of the **Río Dulce**, richly coated with jungle. At the end of the river is **Lívingston**, a very funky coconut-and-ganja town, home to Guatemala's black Garífuna people.

Also included in this chapter are the **eastern highlands** – dry *ladino* territory, scarred intermittently by ancient, eroded volcanoes and hot, dusty towns. Though the scenery is superb, there is little for the traveller here, save the beautiful isolation of the **Ipala volcano** with its stunning crater lake, and the curious holy town of **Esquipulas** whose huge basilica containing an image of the black Jesus is the focus for Central America's largest annual pilgrimage.

The Motagua valley

Leaving the capital, the Caribbean highway passes through the hilly, infertile terrain of the upper **Río Motagua**. As you head further down the valley, the land rapidly becomes bleak, dry and distinctly inhospitable, until you come to the first place of any note: the **Río Hondo junction**. Here you'll find a waiting army of food sellers swarming around every bus that stops, and a line of blue and red Pepsi-sponsored comedores. If you need refreshment, there are usually fresh coconuts for sale, too. The road divides here, with one arm heading south to Esquipulas and the three-way **border** with Honduras and El Salvador, and the main branch continuing on to the coast. There are a number of motels scattered around Río Hondo which, bizarre as it may seem, is viewed by middle-class Guatemalans as something of a weekend retreat, due to the presence of the large *Valle Dorada* waterworld park-motel (☎9412542, fax 9412543; ⑥), close by at Km 146.

On down the valley the landscape starts to undergo a radical transformation: the flood plain opens out and the cacti and scrub are gradually overwhelmed by a profusion of tropical growth. It was this supremely rich flood plain that attracted both the Maya and the United Fruit Company, to the great benefit of both.

The ruins of Quiriguá

Set splendidly in an isolated pocket of rainforest, surrounded by an ocean of banana trees, **Quiriguá** may not be able to match the enormity of Tikal, but it does have some of the finest Maya carving anywhere. Only neighbouring Copán (see p.380) offers any competition to the magnificent stelae, altars and so-called zoomorphs, covered in well-preserved and superbly intricate glyphs and portraits.

The **early history** of Quiriguá is still fairly vague, but during the Late Preclassic period (250 BC–300 AD) migrants from the north, possibly Putun Maya from the Yucatán peninsula, established themselves as the rulers here. Later, in the Early Classic period (250–600 AD), the centre was dominated by Copán, just 50km away, and doubtless valued for its position on the banks of the Río Motagua, an important trade route, and as a source of jade, which is found throughout the valley.

It was the during the rule of the great leader **Cauac Sky** that Quiriguá challenged Copán, captured its leader 18 Rabbit in 737, and was able to assert its independence and embark on an unprecedented building boom: the bulk of the great stelae date from this period. For a century Quiriguá dominated the lower Motagua valley and its highly prized resources. Under **Jade Sky**, who took the throne in 790, Quiriguá reached its peak, with fifty years of extensive building work, including a radical reconstruction of the acropolis. From the end of Jade Sky's rule, in the middle of the ninth century, the historical record fades out, as does the period of prosperity and power.

Entering the site beneath the ever-dripping ceiba, jocote, palm and fig trees, you emerge at the northern end of the **Great Plaza**. To the left-hand side of the path is a badly ruined pyramid and dominating the site at the southern end of the plaza is the untidy bulk of the **acropolis**. Liberally scattered amidst the luxuriant grass of the plaza are the finely carved **stelae** for which Quiriguá is justly famous. The nine stelae in the plaza are the tallest in the Maya world, and all are similarly studded with portraits and glyphs covering the sides. The figures represent the city's rulers, with Cauac Sky depicted on no fewer than seven (A, C, D, E, F, H and J). Two unusual features are particularly clear: the vast headdresses, which dwarf the faces, and the beards. Largest of the stelae is E, which rises to a height of 8m and weighs 65 tons.

As you head down the path towards the acropolis you can just make out the remains of a **ball court** on your right, before you reach the other features that have earned Quiriguá its fame. Squatting at the base of the ruined acropolis are the **zoomorphs**: six bizarre, globular-shaped blocks of stone carved with interlacing animal and human figures – look out for the turtle, frog and jaguar. The best of the lot is P, which shows a figure seated in Buddha-like pose, interwoven with a maze of other detail.

Practicalities

The **ruins** (daily 7.30am–5pm; US$4) are situated some 70km beyond the junction at Río Hondo, and 4km from the main road, reached down a dirt track that serves the banana industry. All **buses** running between Puerto Barrios (2hr) and Guatemala City (4hr) pass by. There's a fairly regular bus service from the highway to the site itself, plus assorted motorbikes and pick-ups. You shouldn't have to wait too long to get a ride back to the highway.

There are a couple of good, simple places to **stay** in the village of **QUIRIGUÁ**, 5km away, reached either by following the old railtrack west for 3km or heading back to the highway and getting a ride from there. Alongside the old hospital for tropical diseases is the *Hotel y Restaurante Royal* (②) and, next to the old station, just off the tracks, is *Hotel el Eden* (②), another excellent budget option – the friendly family owners also serve tasty **meals**.

Puerto Barrios

Founded in the 1880s by President Rufino Barrios, the port of **PUERTO BARRIOS** soon fell into the hands of the United Fruit Company, who used their control of the railways to ensure that the bulk of trade passed this way. Puerto Barrios was Guatemala's main port for most of this century, and the Fruit Company were exempt from almost all tax.

These days the boom is over and the town distinctly forlorn, with a sleazy array of strip clubs, all-night bars and brothels. The streets are wide, but they're poorly lit and badly potholed, and the handful of fine old Caribbean houses are now outnumbered by grimy hotels and hard-drinking bars. The reason most travellers come here is to get somewhere else: to Honduras via the jungle route (see p.218) or to Lívingston (see p.218) or Punta Gorda in Belize (see p.110) by boat.

Arrival and information

There is no purpose-built bus station in Puerto Barrios. Litegua **buses**, which serve all destinations along the Caribbean Highway, have their own terminal in the centre of town on 6 Av, between 9 and 10 C. All second-class buses – to Chiquimula for Honduras and Esquipulas for El Salvador – arrive and depart close by from several bays grouped around the central market opposite. **Taxis** seem to be everywhere in Barrios; drivers toot for custom as they drive through the streets. The new daily **flight** from Guatemala City lands at the airstrip about 3km northeast of the town centre (call Inter on ☎3347722 for details).

As there is no Inguat tourist office in town, check at the Litegua terminal for bus schedules and at the **dock** at the end of 12 C for boat departures to Lívingston and to Punta Gorda in Belize. You have to clear **immigration** before you can buy a ticket, which is best done the day before departure: the immigration office is at the end of 9 C, two blocks north of the dock (daily 7am–noon & 2–5pm). The **Telgua** office is at the junction of 8 Av and 10 C (daily 7am–midnight) and the **post office** at 6 C and 6 Av (Mon–Fri 8am–4.30pm). There are a number of **banks** in Puerto Barrios; you'll find Lloyds Bank on the corner of 7 Av and 15 C (Mon–Fri 9am–3pm, Sat 9am–1am), Banco G&T (for Mastercard) at 7 C and 6 Av (Mon–Fri 9am–7pm, Sat 9am–1pm) and Banco Industrial (with a 24hr Visa-friendly ATM) at 7 Av and 7 C.

Accommodation

Cheap **hotels** are plentiful in Puerto Barrios and there is a slice of Caribbean charm in amongst the squalor. This is a very hot and sticky town, so you'll definitely want a fan if not air conditioning.

Hotel del Norte, 7 C & 1 Av (☎ & fax 9480087). An absolute gem of a hotel – a magnificent colonial building that seems to be in a time-warp. The clapboard rooms aren't especially comfortable or very private but there is a nice swimming pool and the location, overlooking the Caribbean, is magnificent. Perhaps best of all is the incredibly classy, mahogany-panelled restaurant and bar – though the food doesn't quite match the decor. ③–⑤.

Hotel Europa 2, 3 Av & 12 C (☎9481292). Ideally placed for the ferry to Lívingston, this is a clean, safe, friendly place – all rooms have fans and private showers. Good prices for single travellers. An almost identical twin, *Hotel Europa 1*, is at 8 Av and 8 C (☎9480127). Both ③.

Hotel Xelajú, 9 C, between 6 & 7 Av (☎9480482). Reasonable budget place. It looks a little rough from the outside but the rooms are clean and it's safe. No visiting señoritas are allowed. ②–③.

Hotel Lívingston, 7 Av between 8 & 9 C (☎9482124). Above a small shopping mall, this funky marine-green painted hotel is fair value for money, safe, and the rooms all have TV and private bathrooms. Not so well priced for solo travellers. ③.

Hotel Caribeña, 4 Av between 10 & 11 C (☎9480384). This large friendly place has very good value rooms, with doubles, triples and quadruples available. Top-notch seafood restaurant attached (and cheap breakfasts). ②.

Hotel Internacional, 7 Av and 16 C (☎9480367). Very well priced motel-style set-up with a small swimming pool. Rooms all have private showers and TV and come with a choice of either a/c or fan. ③–④.

Hotel Cayos del Diablo, across the bay, reached by regular free boat service from the jetty (☎9480361 or 9480362, fax 9482364). Lovely hideaway hotel, discreetly set above a secluded beach. Beautiful thatched cabaña accommodation, swimming pool and good restaurant. The definitive luxury option on this stretch of coastline. ⑧.

Eating, drinking and nightlife

There is an abundance of cheap **comedores** around the market, such as *Cafesama* and *El Punto*. The best place in town, however, is the *Rincon Uruguayo*, where meat is cooked on a giant *parrilla* (grill), South American style, prices are reasonable and there are also vegetarian dishes like barbecued spring onions and *papas asados*. It's ten minutes' walk south of the centre at 7 Av and 16 C and closed on Mondays. Another popular place is the *Safari*, which specializes in fish and seafood, ten minutes north of the centre, right on the seafront at the end of 5 Av. Also worth trying is *Restaurant La Caribeña*, 4 Av, between 10 and 11 C, which does good fish and a superb *caldo de mariscos* (seafood soup); or, in the centre of town, the upmarket *La Fonda de Enrique* on 9 C, right opposite the market/bus terminal, where you'll also find great seafood, a nice relaxed atmosphere and air-conditioning. Finally, there is the unique period charm of the *Hotel del Norte* restaurant (see above).

Puerto Barrios also has more than its fair share of **bars**, pool halls and nightclubs, offering the full range of late-night sleaze. None of these is hard to find, though a lot of the action centres around 6 and 7 Av and 6 and 7 C. **Reggae** and **punta rock** are the sounds on the street in Puerto Barrios. You'll catch a fair selection at weekends in *La Canoa* (5 Av and 2 C), a small club popular with Garífuna. It's a bit of a hike from the town centre, so you may want to take a taxi.

The jungle route to Honduras

Heading into Honduras from Puerto Barrios, there are two very different options: either the long haul by bus via Chiquimula (see p.223), or the adventurous **jungle route**, involving a combination of buses, pick-ups and boats through swamps and banana plantations.

If you set out early from Puerto Barrios, you'll certainly get to San Pedro Sula (see p.393) the same day, and it's even possible to make the late afternoon flight out to one of the Bay Islands. The route is actually pretty straightforward: the first stage involves taking an early bus (6am, 7.45am, then every 45min) from Puerto Barrios to **Finca la Inca**; buses leave from a bay next to the market on 8 C, between 6 and 7 Av, and take two hours. After an hour you pass **immigration** at the village of **Entre Ríos** (unofficial exit "tax" of around US$1.80). After another hour trundling slowly through the banana plantations, the driver will pull over by the Río Motagua, where there should be a **boat** ready and waiting, plus the odd moneychanger lurking. The twenty-minute boat ride takes you to a tiny village just inside Honduras, from where a Honduran *lancha* will take you on the fifty-minute trip up the Río Tinto; look out for kingfishers and terrapins on the way. Some sections of this river trip are difficult in the dry season. Finally a pick-up will drive you to the village of **Tegucijalpita** (20min) where there is a basic comedor and the simple *Hospedaje Rosita* (①) if you get stuck.

From Tegucijalpita there are regular buses to **Puerto Cortés** (2hr) via the pretty Caribbean town of Omoa (1hr 30min); both have **immigration** posts. San Pedro Sula is extremely well connected with Puerto Cortés by Citul buses (every 30min 5am–7.30pm; 1hr 15min); Citul are located just across the plaza from Immigration.

If your route doesn't follow the exact pattern described above, don't panic – it's probably because there is insufficient water to make the river route to Tegucijalpita. In this case, you may well end up travelling via the Honduran village of **Cuyamelito**, a little further on from Tegucijalpita on the same road.

Lívingston, the Río Dulce and Lago de Izabal

At the mouth of the Río Dulce and only accessible by boat, **LÍVINGSTON** is a very funky town that not only enjoys a superb setting but also offers a unique fusion of Guatemalan and Caribbean culture in which marimba mixes with Marley. Along with several other villages in Central America, Lívingston provides the focus for the displaced **Garífuna** or black Carib people, who are now strung out along the Caribbean coast between southern Belize and Honduras. Their history begins on the island of St Vincent, where their African slave ancestors intermarried with shipwrecked sailors and native Carib islanders. In 1795 they rebelled against British rule, and resettled on the island of Roatan, off Honduras, from where they migrated to the mainland (see p.423).

Lívingston is undoubtedly one of the most fascinating places in Guatemala and many visitors find the languid rhythm of life here hypnotic. The town is as popular with week-ending Guatemalans as it is with international travellers, and offers a welcome break from mainstream Guatemalan culture. Carib **food** is generally excellent and more varied than the usual comedor dishes, and Garífuna punta rock and reggae make a pleasant listening diversion from the standard merengue beat. While certainly not unaffected by the pressures of daily life in Central America (crack cocaine use is growing), the atmosphere is in general very chilled.

While there's not really that much to do in town itself, other than relaxing in local style, there are a few places nearby that are worth a visit. The Garífuna **museum** (in theory, Mon–Fri 8am–noon & 2–4pm) is worth a look for its collection of Garífuna art, handicrafts and cultural information; it's in a lovely wooden house just of the main drag to the dock, close to the *Bahía Azul* restaurant. Sadly, the local **beaches** are not of the Caribbean dream variety but swimming is safe at least. It is not safe for women to walk alone along the beaches, however, as a number of **rapes** have been reported in recent years.

The most popular trip out of town is to **Las Siete Altares**, a waterfall about 5km away, but as there have been **attacks on tourists** walking to the falls, you should ask about the current situation before setting out. The safest option is to hire a local guide or visit as part of a tour – try Exotic Travel in the *Bahía Azul* restaurant. If you do decide to go it alone, continue down the street past the *Ubafu* bar and turn right by the *African Place* hotel to the beach, then follow the sand away from the town. After a couple of kilometres, wade across a small river and, just before the beach eventually peters out, take a path to the left. Follow this inland and you'll soon reach the first of the falls. To reach the others, scramble up, and follow the water: all of the falls are idyllic places to swim, but the highest one is the best of all.

Arrival and information

The only way to get to Lívingston is **by boat**, from Puerto Barrios, the Río Dulce, Belize, or Omoa in Honduras. Lívingston is a small place with only a handful of streets, and you can see most of what there is to see in an hour or so. You'll arrive at the main dock on the south side of town. Straight ahead, up the hill, is the main drag with most of the restaurants, bars and shops. The **immigration office** (daily 7am–9pm) is on the left as you walk up the hill, a block or so before the *Hotel Río Dulce*, where you can get an exit stamp if you're heading for Belize or an entrance stamp if you've just arrived. Exotic Travel, in the *Bahía Azul*, is the best **travel agent** in town: the helpful owners will arrange a variety of **trips** around the area – up the Río Dulce to a lovely white sand beach called, appropriately enough, Playa Blanca (US$8); to the Cayos Sapodillas off Belize for **snorkelling** (US$30); and to the Punta Manabique reserve for game **fishing** (US$14). As these trips only take place when there are enough people, sign up early and be prepared to wait a day or two.

For **changing money**, try the Banco de Comercio (Mon–Fri 9am–5pm, Sat 9am–1pm), in the road to the left as you walk up the hill from the docks, or the Almacen Koo Wong in the centre of town. **Telgua** is on the right of the main street up from the docks (daily 7am–midnight), and the **post office** is next door.

Scheduled **boats** leave for Puerto Barrios daily at 5am and 2pm (1hr 30min), supplemented by **speedboats**, which leave when full – roughly half-hourly. There are also boats to Punta Gorda in **Belize** on Tuesdays and Fridays at 8am (1hr) and to Omoa in **Honduras** on the same days at 7.30am (minimum 4 or 5 people; 2hr 30min). You can buy tickets at Exotic Travel.

Accommodation

There's a pretty decent selection of hotels in town, though little in the mid-range bracket. Rooms fill up at weekends and during holidays, but you should always be able to find a bed.

Hotel California, turn right just before the *Bahía Azul* restaurant. Clean hotel painted vivid green with reasonable rooms all with private bathroom. ②.

Hotel Caribe, along the shore to the left of the dock as you face the town (☎9481073). Basic, budget hotel with bare rooms, some with private showers and fans. Doubles only. ①–②.

Hotel Casa Rosada, about 300m left of the dock (☎ & fax 9027014). Cabins right on the water, with nice hand-painted details, beautiful views and an intimate relaxed atmosphere. Bathrooms are shared but are immaculate. Very friendly management and excellent vegetarian meals. ③.

Hotel Garifuna, follow the main street, turn left towards the *Ubafu* bar, then first right (☎9481091). Safe and squeaky-clean with spotless rooms all with fans and private shower. ②.

Tucán Dugú, first on the right uphill from the jetty (☎ & fax 9481073). Livingston's only luxury hotel, with great views of the bay, a pleasant bar and swimming pool (small fee for non-residents). ⑦–⑧.

Hotel el Viajero, turn left after the dock, past the *Hotel Caribe*. Small but safe budget hotel. Slightly shabby rooms with fans and some with private bathrooms. ①.

Eating and drinking

There are plenty of places to **eat** in Livingston, one of the best being *The African Place*, past the *Ubafu* bar in a Moorish-style building, which serves superb seafood and Spanish dishes. For a memorable **vegetarian** meal, check out the *Casa Rosada* (see above), though it's not priced for budget travellers. The *Bahía Azul* on the main street is probably the most popular place in town, with a terrace perfect for watching (and photographing) Livingston streetlife. There are also plenty of cheap, small comedores on the main street, all selling decent **fried fish.** Try *Comedor Coni* or the *Livingston*.

For evening **entertainment** there are plenty of funky bars, of which *Ubafu* is usually the most lively. There's also a disco on the beach where you'll hear the deep bass rhythms of Jamaican reggae and pure Garífuna punta rock.

The Río Dulce

Another very good reason for coming to Livingston is to venture up the **Río Dulce,** a truly spectacular trip that leads eventually to the town of the same name about 30km upriver. From Livingston the river heads into a system of **gorges** between sheer rock faces 100m or so in height. Clinging to the sides is a wall of tropical vegetation and cascading vines, and here and there you might see some white herons or flocks of squawking parakeets. Along the way you'll pass an excellent place for a swim, where warm sulphurous waters emerge from the base of the cliff, and also the **Biotopo de Chocón Machacas** (daily 7am–4pm; US$5), a nature reserve designed to protect the manatee – though the huge seal-like mammals are extremely timid and you'll be very lucky to see one.

The reserve also protects the forest that still covers much of the lake's shore, and there are some specially cut trails where you might catch sight of a bird or two, or even, if you've plenty of time and patience, a tapir or jaguar. Heading on upstream, across the small **Golfete** lake, the river closes in again and passes the marina and bridge at the squalid town known as **Río Dulce** (or sometimes El Rellano). This part of the Río Dulce is a favourite playground for wealthy Guatemalans, with boats and hotels that would put parts of California to shame. Here the road for Petén crosses the river and the boat trip comes to an end, although you should certainly include a stop at the castillo, on the other side of the bridge.

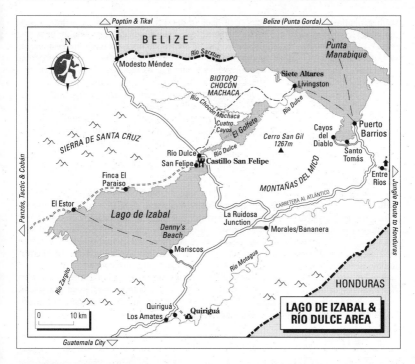

LAGO DE IZABAL & RÍO DULCE AREA

Río Dulce town: practicalities

The town of **RÍO DULCE** itself is little more than a truck stop, where traffic for Petén pauses before the long stretch to Flores. Río Dulce is actually the new name for a couple of older settlements, El Rellano to the north and Fronteras to the south, connected by a monstrous concrete road bridge. The road is lined with cheap comedores and stores, and you can pick up buses here in either direction.

If you're heading towards Guatemala City or Puerto Barrios, take the first minibus to La Ruidosa junction (every 30min) and pick up a connection there. There are frequent buses to Petén until 5pm, and then hourly until 11pm (4hr to Flores), but as travelling at night is not recommended you may want to sleep in Río Dulce and move on in the morning. Before the year 2000 it should also be possible to travel along a new road on the north side of the lake: this route will connect Río Dulce with the Finca el Paraiso, heading on to El Estor (see p.222) for the trip up the Polochic valley towards Cobán and the Verapaces. Finally, Inter **fly** between Guatemala City and the Río Dulce at weekends (US$60 one-way; 1hr, returning via Puerto Barrios 1hr 20min).

An excellent **place to stay** for those on a tight budget is *Hotel Backpackers* (☎2081779, fax 3319408; ①–③), a new setup underneath the bridge, on the south side, where there are dorm beds, private doubles and hammock space. Marie, the manager, is a great source of information and there's a noticeboard with lots of good stuff about yacht crewing opportunities and sailing courses; they also rent canoes. *Hotel Río Dulce*, on the north side of the bridge (③), is a comfortable place with nice, clean double rooms with fans and showers. At the *Hacienda Tijax* (☎9027825; ①–②), two minutes by water-taxi from the bridge, you can pitch a tent or stay in one of the rustic self-catering lodges which comfortably sleep up to eight. This is a working tropical farm with a large-scale rubber plantation and reforestation project underway. For something a little more upmarket, try *Suzanna's Laguna*, on the southwestern waterfront (fax in Guatemala City 3692681; ⑤), which has beautiful polished wood rooms, an open-air bar and a restaurant; or *Hotel Vinas del Lago*, near the castillo (☎9027505, fax 4763042; ⑦), which offers great views across the lake from several terraces and also has its own private beach. Both the above need to be reached by a boat taxi from the jetty in Río Dulce town.

As for **restaurants**, *Bar/Restaurant Hollymar*, on the north side of the bridge, is a great place to meet other travellers (and yachties), eat good food and drink the night away. You can also make radio contact to most places around the river and lake from here. *Bruno's*, a couple of minutes' walk from the *Hollymar*, offers the chance to catch up with the latest news, watch movies and North American sports events – it's very popular with the American sailing fraternity.

Castillo de San Felipe

If you have an hour or so to spare then it's worth heading out to the **Castillo de San Felipe**, 1km upstream from the bridge (daily 8am–5pm; US$1), which looks like a miniature medieval castle. The castle, which marks the entrance to Lago de Izabal, is a tribute to the audacity of British pirates, who used to sail up the Río Dulce to raid supplies and harass mule trains. The Spanish were so infuriated by this that they built the fortress to seal off the entrance to the lake, and a chain was strung across the river. Inside there's a maze of tiny rooms and staircases and panoramic views of the lake.

A kilometre from the castle, close to the village of **SAN FELIPE**, is the *Rancho Escondido* (☎ & fax 3692681; ②–③), a friendly American-Guatemalan guest house and backpacker's retreat (with hammock space), plus restaurant. If you call or radio from the *Hollymar*, they'll come and pick you up.

Lago de Izabal

Beyond the castillo, the broad expanse of **Lago de Izabal** opens up before you, with great views of the highlands beyond the distant shores. Local boatmen run trips from Río Dulce town to various places around the lake, including Denny's Beach (see below) where there's good swimming. On the north shore about 25km from Río Dulce is **Finca el Paraiso**, where there's plenty to explore, including an amazing hot waterfall cascading into pools cooled by fresh river water, and a series of caves whose interiors are crowded with extraordinary shapes and colours – made even more memorable by the fact that you have to swim by torchlight to see them. At the finca itself there are six beautiful cabañas on the waterfront (sleep up to four; ⑤). To book, either radio them on VHF73, or phone Guatemala City on ☎2532397 and speak to Mrs Gabriella de la Vega Rodriguez. The finca is due to be connected by a new bus or pick-up service from Río Dulce and El Estor; if not, you can hire a boat or hitch a bumpy ride on a tractor-drawn trailer.

MARISCOS is the main town on the south side of the lake. The main reason that people head this way is to catch the ferry across the lake to **El Estor**, from where early morning buses run to Cobán in Alta Verapaz. In its day, Mariscos was an important stopping-off point for travellers but nowadays it's no more than a one-street town, with three cheap, pretty scruffy **hotels**, a police station, a pharmacy, and of course the passenger **ferry** that leaves at noon – returning at 6am (1hr). Small *lanchas* supplement the ferry service at other times when there are enough passengers. There's one bus a day here from Guatemala City and one from Puerto Barrios; both return after the arrival of the boat from El Estor at 7am. At other times take any bus along the Caribbean Highway, ask to be dropped at La Trinchera, and a pick-up will take you from there to Mariscos. The best place to stay in Mariscos is *Hotel Karinlinda* (②–③), where some rooms have private bathrooms; *Hospedaje los Almendras* (①) is more basic but reasonably clean.

The other reason to head this way is to reach *Denny's Beach* (☎ & fax in Guatemala City 3692681; VHF 09; ④), a hotel/resort that's perfect for getting away from it all. As well as pleasant cabañas overlooking the sandy beach, there's camping space and room to sling a hammock. The open-air bar and restaurant are a bit expensive, so bring as many provisions as you can from the well-stocked supermarket at Mariscos pier. Hire a *lancha* from the pier for the fifteen-minute trip, or call or radio Dennis Gulck, the owner, and someone will come and get you. On the other side of the lake from Mariscos is another attractive, usually deserted beach, Playa Dorada. It's a 4km hike away, or you can get there by water taxi from the dock at Mariscos.

The eastern highlands

The **eastern highlands** southwest of the capital have to rank as the least-visited part of Guatemala. The population is almost entirely Latinized, speaking Spanish and wearing Western clothes, although many are by blood pure Maya. The *ladinos* of the east have a reputation for behaving like cowboys and supporting right-wing politics, and violent demonstrations of macho pride are not uncommon. Not surprisingly, the military recruits much of its personnel here.

The landscape lacks the immediate appeal of the western highlands: the peaks are lower and the volcanoes less symmetrical. The region's towns are almost all pretty featureless and perennially hot and dusty, so you're unlikely to want to hang around for long. **Esquipulas** is certainly worth a visit, though, for its colossal church, the most important pilgrimage site in Central America. It's also positioned very close to the border with Honduras and El Salvador, though if you're heading into Honduras, you're most likely to end up spending the night in **Chiquimula**, a dull town that's the gateway to the ruins of Copán just over the border (see p.380). Finally there's the spectacular crater lake of on top of the **Ipala Volcano**, an idyllic spot whose isolation adds to its appeal.

Chiquimula

Set to one side of the broad San José river valley is the town of **CHIQUIMULA**, an unattractive, bustling *ladino* stronghold. If you've just arrived from Honduras, things only get better from here. Though the town has long been an important transport terminal, there is little else of note save a massive ruined colonial church on the edge of town beside the highway. Most travellers are in town on their way to or from the Maya ruins of Copán, just over the border in Honduras (see p.380).

Everything you're likely to need in Chiquimula is east of the **plaza** and close to the bus terminal, on 3 Calle, which leads towards the main highway. Of the **hotels** in town *Pensión Hernandez* at 3 C 7–41 (☎ & fax 9420708; ②) is the first place to try, with plenty of very clean, simple rooms, safe with fan and some with private shower, safe parking, and even a small pool. The owner speaks good English and is helpful to travellers; you can also send **email** from here. A little further down the same road, at 3 C 8–30, Zona 1, *Hotel Central* (☎9420118; ④) has five pleasant rooms all with with private bathroom and cable TV. Still on the same street, *Pensión España* at 3 C 7–81 (①) is very cheap and basic. *Hotel Victoria*, half a block west of the bus terminal at 2 C 9–99 (☎9422238; ③), is reasonable value and all rooms have private shower and cable TV.

When it comes to **eating** there are plenty of good, inexpensive comedores in and around the **market** which is centred on 3 C and 8 Av, as well as *Magic Burger* and *Cafe Paiz*, both on 3 C, for predictable fast food and good fruit juices. For something a little more ambitious, try *Bella Roma*, 7 Av 5–31, which specializes in pizza and pasta. *Las*

Vegas, on 7 Av off the plaza, with fairly high prices and garish decor, is where the town's upwardly mobile gather – you can forget the cocktails here but the food's reasonable. Otherwise the only evening entertainment in Chiquimula is the *Cine Liv* on the plaza. For **changing money** there's a branch of the Banco G&T at 7 Av 4–75 (Mon–Fri 9am–7pm, Sat 10am–2pm), or try the largest of the sombrero shops in the market. Telgua is on the corner of the plaza (daily 7am–midnight).

The **bus terminal** is at 1A C, between 10 and 11 Av, midway between the plaza and the highway; walking one and a half blocks south will get you to 3 Av. There are frequent **buses** from here to Guatemala City, Esquipulas, Jalapa via Ipala and to Puerto Barrios (see Travel Details). For Copán catch one of the eight daily buses to the border at El Florido (2hr 30min).

The Volcán de Ipala

Reached down a side road off the main highway between Chiquimula and Esquipulas, the **Volcán de Ipala** (1650m) may at first seem a little disappointing – it looks more like a rounded hill than the near-perfect conical peaks of the western highlands. However, it's well worth heading for if you yearn for some real solitude: extremely few visitors make it out this way and the chances are that if you visit on a weekday you'll have the place to yourself. The cone, inactive for hundreds of years, is now filled by a beautiful little **crater lake** ringed by dense tropical forest, similar in many ways to the cone of Chicabal near Quetzaltenango (see p.191). The lake itself is said to contain a unique species of fish, the *mojarra*, which apparently has six prominent spines on its back. It's beautifully peaceful up here and the lake makes a wonderful place to **camp**, though you'll have to bring all your own supplies as there are no shops or other facilities. You can walk round the entire lake in a couple of hours. To **get to** the lake it is possible to climb the volcano from the village of Ipala itself, a distance of around 10km, but the easiest ascent (2hr) is from the south, setting out from close to the village of Agua Blanca (see below). If you have your own transport, head for the tiny settlement of Sauce, at Km 26.5 on the Ipala–Agua Blanca road, park close to the small store and follow the dirt track up to the summit.

AGUA BLANCA is a *ladino* moustache-and-cowboy-hat kind of place, with a good little hospedaje, the *Maylin* (①), and a couple of comedores, the best of which is the *El Viajero*. It's a pretty straightforward route to the lake; ask the way to the Finca el Paxte and continue to the top from there. The village of **IPALA**, 20km to the north of Agua Blanca, down a fast sealed road, is connected by bus with Jutiapa to the south, Jalapa in the west, Chiquimula to the north and Esquipulas to the east. The village itself is a pretty forlorn place with a few shops and three **hotels**, the best of which is the basic *Hotel Ipala Real* (☎9237107; ②) where rooms have en-suite showers and toilets, plus cable TV if you want it.

Esquipulas

The final town on this eastern highway, **ESQUIPULAS**, has a single point of interest: it is the most important Catholic shrine in Central America. It's a beautiful ride from Chiquimula through the hills, beneath craggy outcrops and forested peaks, emerging suddenly at the lip of a huge bowl-shaped valley with Esquipulas itself below.

The town is entirely dominated by the four perfectly white domes of the **church**, which are brilliantly floodlit at night. Beneath these the rest of the town is a messy sprawl of cheap hotels, souvenir stalls and restaurants. The year-round pilgrimage has generated numerous sidelines, creating a booming resort where people from all over Central America come to worship, eat, drink and relax, in a bizarre combination of holy devotion and indulgence.

The principal day of **pilgrimage**, when the religious significance of the shrine is at its most potent, is January 15. Even the smallest villages will save enough money to send a representative or two on this occasion, filling the town to bursting point. As a religious shrine, Esquipulas probably predates the Conquest. When the Spanish arrived, the Maya chief surrendered rather than risk bloodshed; the grateful Spaniards named the town in his honour and commissioned the famed colonial sculptor Quirio Cataño to carve an image of Christ for the church. Perhaps in order to make it more appealing to the local Maya, he chose to carve it from balsam, a dark wood. Things really took off in 1737 when the bishop of Guatemala, Pardo de Figueroa, was cured of a chronic ailment on a trip to Esquipulas. The bishop ordered the construction of a new church, which was completed in 1758, and his body was buried beneath the altar.

Inside the church today there's a constant scurry of hushed devotion amid clouds of smoke and incense. In the nave, pilgrims approach the image on their knees, while others light candles, mouth supplications or simply stand in silent groups. The image itself is approached by a side entrance: join the queue to shuffle past beneath it and pause briefly in front before being shoved on by the crowds behind.

Back outside you'll find yourself among swarms of souvenir and relic hawkers, and pilgrims who, duty done, are ready to head off to eat and drink away the rest of their stay.

Practicalities

When it comes to staying in Esquipulas, you'll find yourself amongst hundreds of visitors whatever the time of year. **Hotels** probably outnumber private homes but bargains are in short supply – the bulk of the budget places are grubby and bare. Prices are rarely quoted in writing and are always negotiable, depending on the flow of pilgrims. Avoid Saturday nights, when rooms cost double.

Many of the **budget** options are clustered together in the streets off the main road, 11 C. The family-run *Hotel Villa Edelmira* (②–③) is one of the best, or look for a room at *La Favorita* on 10 C and 2 Av (②). For a touch more luxury, head for 2 Av, beside the church, where you'll find the *Hotel los Ángeles* (☎9431254; ③), some of whose rooms have private bathrooms, and the *Hotel Esquipulas* (④), a cheap annex to the *Hotel Payaqui* (☎9431143, fax 9431371; ⑤), which has a pool, and TV and fan in all the rooms.

There are also dozens of **restaurants** and **bars**, most of them overpriced by Guatemalan standards. Breakfast is a great deal in Esquipulas: you shouldn't have to pay more than US$1.50 for a good feed, with a decent range of lunch specials later on, though dinner can be expensive. The *Hacienda Steak House*, a block from the plaza at 2 Av and 10 C, is one of the smartest places in town, while many of the cheaper places are on 11 C and the surrounding streets. Banco Industrial have a branch with a 24-hour ATM at 9 C and 3 Av, and there's a Banco G&T (Mon–Fri 9am–7pm, Sat 10am–2pm) and a lone cinema, the Cine Galaxia.

Rutas Orientales run a superb hourly **bus** service between Guatemala City and Esquipulas; their office is on the main street at 11 C and 1 Av. There are also buses across the highlands to Ipala and regular minibuses to the borders with **El Salvador** (every 30min 6am–4pm; 1hr) and **Honduras** at Aguacaliente (every 30min 6am–5.30pm; 30min). If you want to get to the ruins of Copán, you'll need to catch a bus to Chiquimula and change there for the El Florido border post (see p.224). There's a **Honduran consulate** (Mon–Fri 9am–5pm) in the *Hotel Payaqui*, beside the church.

travel details

BUSES

Chiquimula to: El Florido for Copán (8 daily 6am–4.30pm; 2hr 30min); Esquipulas (every 15min; 1hr); Guatemala City (14 daily; 3hr 30min); Ipala (8 daily; 1hr); Puerto Barrios (10 daily; 3hr).

Esquipulas to: Aguacaliente for Honduras (every 30min; 30min) and El Salvador (1hr); Chiquimula (minibuses every 15min; 1hr); Guatemala City (hourly 2am–6pm; 4hr).

Mariscos to: Puerto Barrios (1 daily at 7am; 2hr); Guatemala City (1 daily at 7am; 4hr 30min).

Puerto Barrios to: Chiquimula (10 daily; 3hr); Esquipulas (4 daily; 4hr); to Finca la Inca for Honduras (12 daily; 2hr); Guatemala City (19 daily; 5hr); Mariscos (1 daily at 3pm; 2hr); Quiriguá (19 daily; 1hr 30min).

BOATS

Agua Blanca to: Guatemala City (3 daily; 5hr).

Lívingston to: Río Dulce (daily; around 3hr); Puerto Barrios (ferries 5am & 2pm; 1hr 30min); Punta Gorda, Belize (2 weekly; 1hr);   Omoa, Honduras (Tues & Fri 7.30am; 2hr 30min).

Mariscos to: El Estor (daily at noon, 1hr; plus frequent speedboats).

Puerto Barrios to: Lívingston (2 ferries daily at 10.30am & 5pm, 1hr 30min; plus speedboats every 30min, 45min); Punta Gorda, Belize (3 daily; 1hr 30min).

FLIGHTS

Puerto Barrios to: Guatemala City (1 daily; 1hr).

Río Dulce to: Guatemala City (1 daily Fri, Sat & Sun; 1hr 20min).

CHAPTER 10

COBÁN AND THE VERAPACES

The twin departments of the **Verapaces** harbour some of the most spectacular mountain scenery in the country, yet presently they attract only a trickle of tourists. Though the Verapaces border the western highlands, the climate is distinctly different. In the south, the low altitude terrain of **Baja Verapaz** gets very little rainfall and much of the land is sparsely populated cactus country. To the north, the contrast could not be greater: the increasing altitude gradually traps more moisture and the mist-soaked hills around Cobán in **Alta Verapaz** are the wettest, greenest mountains in Guatemala. Locals say it rains for thirteen months a year.

Perhaps the reason so few tourists make it out this way is that there's less obvious evidence of Maya tradition and costume than in other areas, but if you've time to spare you'll find these highlands are astonishingly beautiful, with their unique limestone structure, moist, misty atmosphere and boundless fertility. The hub of the area and the capital of Alta Verapaz is **Cobán**, an attractive mountain town with some good accommodation, coffee houses and restaurants. It is a little subdued once the rain really settles in but it's still the best base for exploring the area, particularly in August, when it hosts the National Folklore Festival. In **Baja Verapaz**, the towns of **Salamá, Rabinal** and **Cubulco** also have famous fiestas, where incredible costumes no longer part of everyday dress are worn and traditional dances performed. Heading out to the north of Cobán you can reach the exquisite natural bathing pools of **Semuc Champey**, surrounded by lush tropical forest and fed by the azure waters of the Río Cahabón.

The **history** of the Verapaces is quite distinct from the rest of Guatemala. Long before the Conquest, local **Achi Maya** had earned themselves a unique reputation as the most bloodthirsty of all the tribes, said to sacrifice every prisoner that they took. Their greatest enemies were the **Quiché**, with whom they were at war for a century. So ferocious were the Achi that not even the Spanish could contain them by force. Alvarado's army was unable to make any headway against them, and eventually he gave up trying to control the area, naming it *tierra de guerra*, the "land of war".

The church, however, couldn't allow so many heathen souls to go to waste, and under the leadership of **Fray Bartolomé de las Casas**, they made a deal with the conquistadors. If Alvarado would agree to keep all armed men out of the area for five years, the priests would bring it under control. In 1537 Las Casas and three Dominican friars set out into the highlands, befriended the Achi chiefs, learnt the local dialects and translated

MARKET DAYS IN THE VERAPACES

Monday: Senahú, Tucurú.

Tuesday: Chisec, El Chol, Cubulco, Lanquín, Purulhá, Rabinal, San Cristóbal Verapaz, San Jerónimo.

Saturday: Senahú.

Sunday: Chisec, Cubulco, Lanquín, Purulhá, Rabinal, Salamá, San Jerónimo, Santa Cruz, Tactic.

devotional hymns. By 1538 they had made considerable progress and had converted large numbers of Maya. At the end of the five years, the famous and invincible Achí were transformed into Spanish subjects, and the king of Spain renamed the province Verapaz (True Peace).

Since the colonial era the Verapaces have remained isolated and, in many ways, independent. All their trade bypassed the capital by taking a direct route to the Caribbean, along the Río Polochic and out through Lago de Izabal. The area really started to develop with the **coffee boom** at the turn of the century, when German immigrants flooded into the country to buy and run fincas, particularly in Alta Verapaz, around Cobán. The Germans quickly prospered and exported huge quantities of coffee back to Europe, only to be expelled during World War II, when the USA insisted that Guatemala remove the enemy presence. Today, the Verapaces are still dominated by the huge coffee fincas and the wealthy families that own them, and there are also hints of the Germanic influence here and there. Taken as a whole, however, the Verapaces remain very much *indígena* country: Baja Verapaz has a small Quiché outpost around Rabinal, and in Alta Verapaz the Maya population is largely **Pokomchí** and **Kekchí**. The production of coffee and more recently the spice **cardamom** for the Middle Eastern market has cut deep into their land and their way of life, the fincas dri-

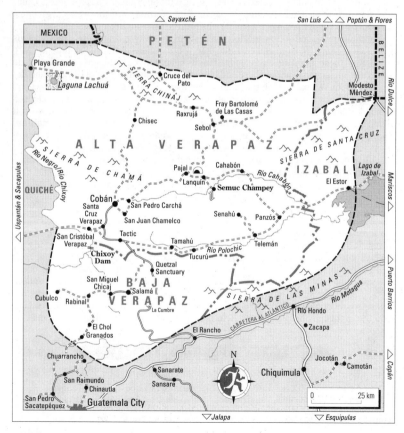

For an explanation of **accommodation price codes**, see p.123.

ving many people off prime territory and on to marginal plots. Traditional costume is also worn less here than in the western highlands.

The northern, flat section of Alta Verapaz includes a slice of Petén rainforest, and in recent years Kekchí Maya and landless *mestizos* from the south have expanded into this region. Here they carve out sections of the forest and attempt to farm, a process which offers little security for the migrants and also threatens the future of the rainforest.

The main **transport** route into the Verapaces climbs up from the El Rancho junction on the Carretera al Atlántico, past the turnoff at La Cumbre, and skirts the Quetzal Sanctuary before arriving at Cobán – a journey very well served by frequent pullman buses. As all other routes in the region are unsealed and only covered by a limited service of second-class buses and pick-ups, the going can be slow.

Baja Verapaz

The main approach to both departments is from the Caribbean Highway, where the road to the Verapaz highlands branches off at the **El Rancho** junction. As this road, lined with scrub bush and cacti, climbs steadily into the hills, the dusty browns and dry yellows of the Motagua valley soon give way to an explosion of greens as dense pine forests and alpine meadows grip the mountains. Some 48km beyond the junction is **La Cumbre de Santa Elena**, where the road for the main towns of Baja Verapaz turns off to the west, immediately starting to drop towards the floor of the **Salamá valley**. Surrounded by steep hillsides, with a level flood plain at its base, the valley appears entirely cut off from the outside world.

Salamá

At the western end of the valley is **SALAMÁ**, capital of the department of Baja Verapaz. The town has a relaxed and prosperous air and, like many of the places out this way, its population is largely *ladino*. There's not much to do other than browse in the Sunday market, though the crumbling colonial bridge on the edge of town and the old church, with its huge altars, darkened by age, are worth a look. The **fiesta** in Salamá runs from September 17 to 21. If you decide **to stay**, the pick of the hotels is the *Hotel Tezulutlan* (☎9400141; ④), a gorgeous old building just off the parque, with rooms set around a leafy courtyard. *Pensión Juarez* (☎9400055; ②), a basic budget hotel at the end of 5 C, past the police station, is cheaper and provides hot water. For **eating**, try one of the places around the plaza; *El Ganadero* is the best restaurant and *Deli-Donus* scores for coffee and snacks. There's also a Banco del Café (Mon–Fri 9am–5pm, Sat 10am–2pm) and a post office (Mon–Fri 8am–4.30pm) in town.

There are hourly **buses** from Guatemala City to Salamá, Rabinal and Cubulco, returning from Cubulco until 2.30pm. If you're only going as far as Salamá there's a steady shuttle of minibuses to and from La Cumbre for connections with pullman buses between Cobán and Guatemala City.

Rabinal

An hour or so from Salamá you arrive in **RABINAL**, another isolated farming town that's also dominated by a large colonial church. Here the proportion of *indígena* inhabitants is considerably higher, making both the Sunday market and the fiesta well worth a visit. Founded in 1537 by Bartolomé de las Casas himself, Rabinal was the first of the settlements in his peaceful conquest of the Achi nation: about 3km northwest are the ruins of one of their fortified cities, known locally as **Cerro Cayup**.

Rabinal's **fiesta**, running from January 19 to 25, is famous for its dances. The most renowned, an extended dance drama known as the *Rabinal Achi*, was last performed in 1856, but many other unique routines are still performed. The *patzca*, for example, is a ceremony calling for good harvests, using masks that portray a swelling below the jaw, and wooden sticks engraved with serpents, birds and human heads. If you can't make it for the fiesta, the Sunday market is a good second-best. Rabinal has a reputation for producing high-quality *artesanía*, including carvings made from the *arbol del morro* (the wood of the calabash tree), and traditional pottery. There are several fairly basic **hotels** in Rabinal, the best of which is the excellent *Posada San Pablo* (②), a superb budget hotel with spotless rooms. If you can't get in there, try the *Hospedaje Caballeros*, 1 C 4–02 (①).

Cubulco

Another hour of rough road brings you down into the next valley and to **CUBULCO**, an isolated *ladino* town, surrounded on all sides by steep, forested mountains. Cubulco is again best visited for its **fiesta**, this being one of the few places where you can still see the **Palo Volador**, a pre-Conquest ritual in which men throw themselves from a thirty-metre pole with a rope tied around their legs, spinning down towards the ground as the rope unravels, and hopefully landing on their feet. It's as dangerous as it looks: most of the dancers are blind drunk and deaths are not uncommon. The fiesta still goes on, though, as riotous as ever, with the main action taking place on January 23. The best place to stay is in the large *farmacia* (①) in the centre of town, and there are several good comedores in the market.

If you'd rather not **leave** the valley the same way that you arrived, there is another option. One bus a day, leaving Cubulco at around 9am, heads back to Rabinal and then, instead of heading for La Cumbre and the main road, turns to the south, crossing the spine of the Sierra de Chuacús and dropping directly down towards Guatemala City. The trip takes you over rough roads for at least eight hours, but the mountain views and the sense of leaving the beaten track help to take the pain out of it all.

The Biotopo de Quetzal

Back on the main highway towards Alta Verapaz and Cobán, the road sweeps around end-less tight curves below forested hillsides. Just before the village of Purulhá (Km 161) is the **Biotopo del Quetzal** (daily 6am–4pm; US$5), an 11.5-square-kilometre nature reserve designed to protect the habitat of the endangered bird. The forest is also known as the Mario Dary Reserve, in honour of one of the founders of Guatemala's envi-ronmental movement. Mario Dary, a lecturer from San Carlos University in Guatemala City, pioneered the establishment of nature reserves in Guatemala and campaigned for years for a cloud forest sanctuary to protect the quetzal. He was murdered in 1981, pos-sibly as a result of his upsetting powerful timber interests. The reserve he instituted is a steep and dense rain and cloud forest, pierced by waterfalls, natural pools and the Río Colorado, which cascades through the reserve towards the valley floor.

Paths through the undergrowth from the road complete a circuit that takes you up into the woods and around above the reserve headquarters (maps available). There are reasonable numbers of quetzals hidden in the forest but they're extremely elusive. The **best time** to visit is at sunrise, just before or just after nesting season (March–June). A favoured feeding tree is the broad-leaved *aguacatillo* which produces a small avoca-do-like fruit. Whether or not you see a quetzal, the forest itself, usually damp with a per-petual mist the locals call *chipi-chipi*, is well worth a visit: a profusion of lichens, ferns, mosses, bromeliads and orchids, spread out beneath a towering canopy of cypress, oak, walnut and pepper trees.

THE RESPLENDENT QUETZAL

The **quetzal**, Guatemala's national symbol – and with the honour of lending its name to the currency – has a distinguished past but an uncertain future. The feathers of the quetzal were sacred from the earliest of times, and in the strange cult of Quetzalcoatl, whose influence spread throughout Mesoamerica, the quetzal was incorporated into the plumed serpent, a supremely powerful deity. To the Maya the quetzal was so sacred that killing one was a capital offence, and the bird is also thought to have been the *nahual*, or spiritual protector, of the Indian chiefs. When Tecún Umán faced Alvarado in hand-to-hand combat his headdress sprouted the long green feathers of the quetzal; when the conquistadors founded a city adjacent to the battleground they named it **Quetzaltenango**, the Place of the Quetzals.

In modern Guatemala the quetzal's image saturates the entire country, appearing in every imaginable context. Citizens honoured by the president are awarded the Order of the Quetzal, and the bird is also considered a symbol of freedom, since caged quetzals die from the rigours of confinement. Despite all this, the sweeping tide of deforestation threatens the existence of the bird, and the sanctuary is about the only concrete step that has been taken to save it.

The more resplendent of the birds, and the source of the famed feathers, is the male. Their heads are crowned with a plume of brilliant green, the chest and lower belly is a rich crimson, and trailing behind are the unmistakeable oversized, golden-green tail feathers, though these are only really evident in the mating season. The females, on the other hand, are an unremarkable brownish colour. The birds nest in holes drilled into dead trees, laying one or two eggs at the start of the rainy season, usually in April or May. Quetzals also can be quite easily identified by their strange jerky, undulating flight.

A kilometre or so past the entrance is the rustic *Hospedaje los Ranchitos del Quetzal* (☎3313579; ②–③), where you can **stay** in wooden cabins or stone houses. There's no electricity and the comedor's menu is usually limited to eggs and beans, but a major compensation is that quetzals are often seen in the patch of forest around the hotel; staff sometimes insist on charging an entrance fee even if you just want to come in and look around. **Camping** at the reserve is no longer permitted. If you're after more luxurious accommodation, try the *Hotel Posada Montaña del Quetzal* (☎3351805; ⑤), 4.5km before the reserve on the way from Guatemala City, which offers pleasant rooms with warm water and private showers and has its own restaurant, bar and pool.

Buses from Cobán pass the entrance hourly, but make sure they know you want to be dropped at the reserve, as it's easy to miss.

Alta Verapaz

Beyond the quetzal sanctuary, the main road crosses into the department of Alta Verapaz, and another 13km takes you beyond the forests and into a luxuriant alpine valley of cattle pastures, hemmed in by steep, perpetually green hillsides. The first place of any size is **TACTIC** – a small, mainly Pokomchí-speaking town adjacent to the main road, which most buses pass straight through.

The colonial church in the village is worth a look, as is the Chi-ixim chapel, high above the town. If you fancy a cool swim, then head for the *Balneario Cham-che*, a crystal-clear spring-fed pool, on the other side of the main road, opposite the centre of town. The simple *Pensión Central* (①), on the main street north of the plaza, is a reasonable budget bet, or try *Hotel Villa Linda* (☎9539216; ③) for a little more comfort.

Continuing Cobán-bound, about 10km past Tactic is the turn-off for San Cristóbal, a pretty town almost engulfed by fields of coffee and sugar cane, set on the banks of the Lago de Cristóbal. From here a rough road continues to **Uspantán** (in the western highlands; see p.177), from where buses run to Santa Cruz del Quiché, via Sacapulas, for connections to Nebaj and Huehuetenango. To head out this way you can either hitch from San Cristóbal or catch one of the buses that leaves San Pedro Carchá (see p.235) at 10am and noon, passing just above the terminal in Cobán ten minutes later, and reaching San Cristóbal after about another half-hour.

Cobán and around

The heart of this misty alpine land and the capital of the department is **COBÁN**, where the paved highway comes to an end. If you're heading up this way, stay in town for a night or two and sample some of the finest coffee in the world in one of Cobán's genteel cafés. Cobán is not a large place; suburbs fuse gently with nearby meadows and pine forests, giving the town the air of an overgrown mountain village. When the rain settles in, Cobán can have something of a subdued atmosphere and in the evenings the air is usually damp and cool. That said, the sun does put in an appearance most days, and the town makes a useful base to recharge, eat well and sleep well. Cobán also acts as a hub for all kinds of **ecotourism** possibilities in the spectacular mountains and rivers nearby.

Arrival, information and tours

Transportes Escobar Monja Blanca, one of Guatemala's best **bus** services (their latest *especiales* have onboard TV and video), operate hourly departures between Guatemala City and Cobán, a journey of four to five hours; their office is on the corner of 2 C and 4 Av, Zona 4. Buses to **local destinations** such as Senahú, El Estor, Lanquín and Cahabón leave from the terminal, down the hill behind the town hall. There are also regular long-distance and local departures to and from **San Pedro Carchá** (see p.235), a few kilometres away. It's also possible to **fly** between Guatemala City and Cobán: Inter run a daily service (30min) to and from the capital from the small airstrip a few kilometres southeast of the town centre.

Inexcusably, Inguat currently choose not to grace Cobán with a tourist office, but luckily a couple of hotels more than adequately fill the **information** gap. First place to try is the *Hostal d'Acuña* (see below), who have helpful staff, a good folder with maps and bus times and also a useful noticeboard. *Hostal Doña Victoria* also provides useful information. Another source is Access, in the same complex as *Café Tirol*, where both the owners are bilingual and you can send **email. Telgua** has its main office in the plaza (daily 7am–midnight), and the **post office** is at 2 C and 2 Av (Mon–Fri 8am–4.30pm). For **changing money**, try Banco Industrial, 1 C and 2 Av, for Visa (Mon–Fri 8.30am–7pm, Sat 8.30am–5.30pm), or Banco G&T, 1 C and 2 Av (Mon–Fri 9am–7pm, Sat 9am–1pm). There's a **laundry**, *La Providencia*, at the sharp end of the plaza on Diagonal 4 (Mon–Sat 8am–noon & 2pm). Cobán is becoming a more popular place to **study Spanish**; recommended language schools are listed on p.129.

Epiphyte Adventures, 2 Av & 2 C (☎9522213), offer highly informative **tours** around Alta Verapaz, including Semuc Champey (see p.236), Laguna Lachuá, and a French-owned eco-lodge near the remote Candelaria caves (for both see p.239). The *Hostal d'Acuña* and *Hostal Doña Victoria* both run trips to Semuc Champey and other destinations. **Car rental** is available from Tabarini, 7 Av 2–27, Zona 2 (☎ & fax 9521504), and the local company Geo Rentals, in the same building as *Café Tirol* and Access (☎9521650).

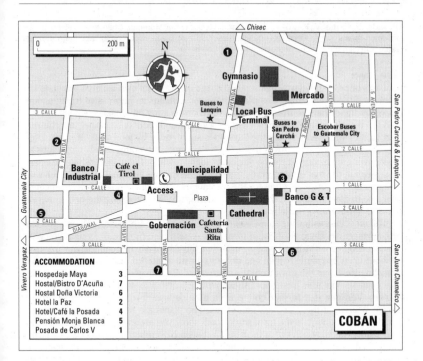

ACCOMMODATION

Hospedaje Maya	3
Hostal/Bistro D'Acuña	7
Hostal Doña Victoria	6
Hotel la Paz	2
Hotel/Café la Posada	4
Pensión Monja Blanca	5
Posada de Carlos V	1

Accommodation

Unless you're here for one of the August fiestas you'll probably only pause for a day or two before heading off into the hills, out to the villages, or on to some other part of the country. There are, however, plenty of **hotels** in town, and there's free **camping** at the Parque Nacional las Victorias on the northwest edge of town, which lacks showers, though there are toilets and running water.

Hostal d'Acuña, 4 C 3–17, Zona 2 (☎9521547). Undoubtedly the most popular budget choice, offering spotless rooms with comfortable bunks. Dorms are built in the garden of a colonial house and guests can enjoy excellent home-cooking on the veranda. Highly recommended. ②.

Hostal Doña Victoria, 3 C 2–38, Zona 3 (☎9522214, fax 9522213). Beautiful refurbished colonial house dripping with antiques and oozing character. Commodious bedrooms are individually furnished and all come with hot water and private bathroom; the streetside rooms are rather noisy, though. Lovely garden, good café/bar and restaurant. ⑤.

Hospedaje Maya, 1 C 2–33, Zona 4, opposite the Cine Norte (☎9522380). Large, basic hotel used by local travellers and traders. Bargain rates, warm showers and friendly staff but smelly toilets. ①.

Pensión Monja Blanca, 2 C 6–37, Zona 2 (☎9521358). Has a wonderfully old-fashioned atmosphere and a variety of rooms, all set around a stunning courtyard garden. The older ones are a little run-down but the others have been nicely refurbished and come with private bath; all are very quiet. ②–③.

Hotel la Paz, 6 Av 2–19, Zona 1 (☎9521358). Safe, pleasant budget hotel run by a very vigilant *señora*. Some rooms have private bathroom. ②.

Hotel la Posada, 1 C 4–12, Zona 2, at the sharp end of the plaza (☎ & fax 9521495). Probably the city's finest hotel, in an elegant colonial building, with a beautiful, antique-furnished interior. The rooms, many with wooden Moorish-style screens and some with four-poster beds, are set around two leafy courtyards and offer all the usual luxuries. Excellent restaurant and café. ⑤.

Posada de Carlos V, 1 Av 3–44, Zona 1 (☎ & fax 9521780). Mountain chalet-style hotel with pine-trimmed rooms and modern amenities but sited close to the market. Comfortable but not memorable. Check out the lobby photographs of old Cobán. ④.

The Town

Cobán's imperial heyday, when it stood at the centre of its own isolated world, is long gone, and the glory faded. The **plaza**, however, remains an impressive triangle, dominated by the cathedral, from which the town drops away on all sides. Check inside to see the remains of a massive, ancient, cracked church bell. A block behind, the **market** bustles with trade during the day and is surrounded by food stalls at night. Life in Cobán revolves around **coffee**: the sedate restaurants, tearooms, trendy nightclubs and overflowing supermarket can be attributed to the town's affluent elite, while the crowds that sleep in the market and plaza, assembling in the bus terminal to search for work, are migrant labourers heading for the plantations. Hints of the days of German control can also be found here and there in the architecture, incorporating the occasional suggestion of Bavarian grandeur.

The most interesting sight in Cobán is the church of **El Calvario**, a short stroll from the town centre. Head west out of town on 1 Av and turn right up 7 Av until you reach a steep cobbled path. You'll pass a number of tiny **Maya shrines** on the way up, crosses blackened by candle smoke and decorated with scattered offerings. There's a commanding view over the town from the church and also the green expanse of the Parque Nacional las Victorias next door. Another place worth a look is just outside town: the **Vívero Verapaz** is a former coffee finca now dedicated to the growing of orchids, which flourish in these sodden mountains. The plants are nurtured in a wonderfully shaded environment, and a farm worker will show you around and point out the most spectacular buds, which are at their best between November and January. The farm is on the old road to Guatemala City, which you reach by leaving the plaza on Diagonal 4, the road that runs past the *Pensión Familiar*, and at the bottom of the hill you turn left, go across the bridge and follow the road for three to four kilometres. Any taxi driver will be able to take you.

Eating, drinking and entertainment

When it comes to **eating** in Cobán you have a choice between fancy European-style restaurants and very basic, cheap comedores. For really cheap food, your best bet, as always, is the **market**, but remember that it's closed by dusk, after which street stalls set up in the plaza selling barbecued meat and warm tortillas.

Bistro Acuña, 4 C 3–17. The most relaxed place to eat in town – stunning period setting, uplifting classical music, attentive service and a good place to meet other travellers. A full-scale blow-out will cost around US$8 a head but there are many cheaper options, including great cannelloni. Make sure you leave room to sample something from the cake cabinet.

Kam Mun, on the entrance road to Cobán, coming from the capital. Excellent, hyper-hygienic Chinese restaurant. Good line-up of economical oriental choices. Daily noon–9.30pm.

Hotel la Posada, 1 C 4–12, at the sharp end of the plaza. The smartest restaurant in town with traditional Guatemalan specialities as well as international cuisine. The café on the verandah outside serves superb breakfasts, coffee, tea and snacks.

Cafetería Santa Rita, 2 C, on the plaza, close to the cathedral. Good comedor with friendly service and decent nosh. Very Guatemalan, in the unlikely event you're sick of all those European-style cafés.

Café Tirol, 1 C on the north side of the plaza. Relatively upmarket by Guatemalan standards, though cheaper than the *Posada*. Serves 22 different types of coffee, pretty good breakfasts, hot chocolate, pancakes and sandwiches. Service can be distracted. Tues–Sun 7am–8.30pm.

NIGHTLIFE

Generally speaking Cobán is a pretty quiet place, particularly so in the evenings, although behind closed doors people do indulge in some very metropolitan pleasures. There are two **cinemas**, the CineTuria in the plaza, and the Cine Norte, on 1 C. In addition to the usual cantinas, there are two half-decent **bars**: *La Tasca* in the *Hostal Doña Victoria*, which has a good happy hour, and *Kikoe's* on 2 Av, close to the *Hostal d'Acuña*. Strange though it may seem, the town also has several **nightclubs**. Try *Oasis*, on 6 Av, just off 1 C, or *Le Bon* on 2 C and 3 Av. Both serve up the usual disco soup of cheesy merengue and handbag house, laced with a dash of salsa.

San Pedro Carchá

A few kilometres away, connected by a regular shuttle of buses, **SAN PEDRO CARCHÁ** is a smaller version of Cobán, with silver instead of coffee-money firing the economy and a stronger Maya character. These days the two towns are merging into a single urban sprawl, and many of the buses that go on towards Petén, or even over to Uspantán, leave from Carchá. Local buses between the two leave from the terminal in Cobán and from the plaza in Carchá.

If you've an hour to spare, the **regional museum** (Mon–Fri 9am–noon & 2–5pm), in a street beside the church, is worth a look. Alongside a collection of Maya artefacts are dolls dressed in local costumes, and a mouldy collection of stuffed birds and animals, including the inevitable moulting quetzal. A little further afield, the **Balneario Les Islas** is a stretch of cool water that's popular for swimming; you can also **camp** here. It's a couple of kilometres from the town centre: walk along the main street beside the church and take the third turning on the right, then follow the street for about 1km and take the right-hand fork at the end.

If you're planning a speedy departure then you might prefer **to stay** here; the *Hotel la Reforma*, 4 C 8–45 (☎9521448; ②), is a good option. For **changing money**, there's a branch of the Banco del Ejercito on the plaza (Mon–Fri 9am–1pm & 2.30–5.30pm, Sat 10am–2pm). **Buses** to local destinations such as Senahú, El Estor, Lanquín and Cahabón leave from the plaza. Two buses a day (10am & noon) leave from beside the *bomberos* **to Uspantán**, for connections to Sacapulas, Nebaj and Quiché.

San Juan Chamelco

A few kilometres southeast of Cobán, easily reached by regular local buses from the terminal, **SAN JUAN CHAMELCO** is the most important Kekchí settlement in the area. Most of your fellow bus passengers are likely to be women dressed in traditional costume, wearing beautiful cascades of old coins for earrings, and speaking Kekchí rather than Spanish. Chamelco's focal point is a large colonial **church**, whose facade is rather unexpectedly decorated with a Mayanized version of the Hapsburg double eagle – undoubtedly a result of the historic German presence in the region. Inside the belfry is hidden the village's most significant treasure, a church bell that was given to the Maya leader Juan Matalbatz by the Holy Roman Emperor Charles V.

The best time to visit the village is for its annual **fiesta**, on June 16. Participants in the wild processions dress up in a variety of outfits, including pre-Conquest Maya costumes and representations of local wildlife, in celebration of the local Kekchí culture and environment.

Not far from Chamelco is a great **place to stay**, *Don Jeronimo's* (⑤ including full board), a vegetarian guest house/retreat run by an eccentric American, who has been living off the land for a good twenty years. You'll find him either by walking 5km from Chamelco to the Aldea Chajaneb, or by catching a bus from outside the Tienda Maranatha, on the street running behind the church. Ask to be dropped off at the appropriate footpath.

Lanquín and Semuc Champey

Northeast of Cobán, a rough, badly maintained road heads off into the hills, connecting a string of coffee fincas. The road soon drops down into rich land to the north as the valleys open out – precipitous sides are patched with cornfields and the level central land is saved for the all-important coffee bushes. As the bus lurches along, clinging to the sides of the ridges, there are fantastic views of the valleys below.

The road divides after 43km at the **Pajal** junction, three hours from Cobán, where one branch turns north to Sebol and Fray Bartolomé de las Casas and the other cuts down deep into the valley to **LANQUÍN**, 12km away (45min), a very sleepy, modest Kekchí village superbly sheltered beneath towering green hills. Don't count on practising your Spanish here – the language has yet to gain much influence. There's a good, cheap hospedaje-cum-store-cum-comedor, the *Divina Providencia* (①), which offers good grub, steaming hot showers and the only cold beers in town. The clapboard-built rooms are comfortable enough, though you'll probably get to know all about your neighbours' nocturnal pursuits. More luxurious is the *Hotel El Recreo* (☎9522160, fax 9522333; ④), on the entrance road, with a choice of rooms in wooden huts, a restaurant, a pool, but electricity only between 6 and 9pm; prices rise at weekends.

Just a couple of kilometres from the village on the road back to Cobán are the **Lanquín caves** (US$2), a maze of dripping, bat-infested chambers, stretching for at least 3km underground. An illuminated walkway, complete with ladders and chains, cuts through the first few hundred metres, but it's slippery, so take care. Before you set out from the village ask in the *municipalidad* (town hall) if they can turn on the lights. It's also well worth dropping by at dusk, when thousands of bats emerge from the mouth of the cave and flutter off into the night. A small car park near the entrance to the caves has a covered shelter where you're welcome to **camp** or sling your hammock.

Semuc Champey

The other attraction around Lanquín, the extraordinary pools of **Semuc Champey** (US$1), are a great deal more spectacular than the caves. The problem can be **getting there**. If you're very lucky and there are enough tourists in town, you can catch a pickup at about 8am, returning around noon. Easiest is to book a tour from Cobán (around US$30 per person) or take the *Hotel d'Acuña* shuttle bus (Wed & Sat, when sufficient demand). Hiring Rigoberto Fernandez's pickup for US$10 return trip is another option: you can find him in the unnamed shop painted vivid green by the parque central. The hard way is to walk – it takes nearly three hours and can be extremely tough going if the sun is shining; take plenty of water. Leave the village along the gravel road that climbs the hill to the south, then drops into another valley. From here the track wanders through thick tropical vegetation where bananas, coffee and the spear-leafed cardamom plants grow beside scruffy thatched huts. After crossing a suspension bridge, the road climbs uphill again to the car park where you may be asked for the entry fee. Finally, follow the muddy track that brings you, at long last, to the pools.

The effort of getting here is rewarded by a natural staircase of turquoise waters suspended on a limestone bridge, with a series of idyllic **pools** in which you can swim. The bulk of the Río Cahabón runs underground beneath this natural bridge and by walking a few hundred metres upstream down a slippy obstacle course of rocks and roots you can see the aquatic frenzy for yourself. The river water plunges furiously into a cavern, cutting under the pools to emerge downstream. If you have a tent or a hammock it makes sense to **stay** the night – there's a thatched shelter, and the altitude is sufficiently low to keep the air warm in the evenings. Be warned, though, it is not safe to leave your belongings unattended.

Beyond Lanquín

Beyond Lanquín the road continues to **Cahabón** (which has a basic pensión), another 24km to the east, and from there a very rough road heads south to Panzós (see below), cutting high over the mountains through superb scenery. In the unlikely event of the road being in a good enough state of repair, there's an occasional bus between these two places, but normally transport is by pick-up – although even these are increasingly rare.

Buses to Cahabón, passing through Lanquín, leave Cobán four times daily (6am, 12.30pm, 1pm & 3pm; 4hr), returning at 5am, 7am and 3pm. On Sundays there may only be the 3pm service to Cobán and it will be packed. Buses pass Pajal for **Fray Bartolomé de las Casas** and **Raxrujá** (see p.239) twice each morning (around 6.30am & 8.30am).

The Polochic valley

If you're planning to head out towards the Caribbean from Cobán, or simply interested in taking a short trip along back roads, then the **Polochic valley** is an ideal place to spend the day being bounced around inside a bus. Travelling the length of the valley's dirt road on one of the hourly services from Cobán to El Estor, you witness an immense transformation as you drop down through the coffee-coated mountains to emerge in the lush, tropical lowlands. The scenery is pure Alta Verapaz: V-shaped valleys where coffee commands the best land and fields of maize cling to the upper slopes wherever they can. The villages along the road are untidy-looking places where the Kekchí and Pokomchí Maya are largely latinized and seldom wear the brilliant red *huipiles* that were traditional here.

The first village in the upper end of the valley is **Tamahú**, and below it is **TUCURÚ**. High above Tucurú in the mountains to the north is the **Chelemá Reserve**, a large protected area of pristine cloud forest which contains one of the highest concentrations of quetzals anywhere in the world, not to mention an array of other birds and beasts, including some very vocal howler monkeys. The forest is extremely difficult to reach; to visit, contact the reserve's office in Cobán at 6 Av, Zona 1 (☎9513238), opposite the *Hotel la Paz*.

Beyond Tucurú the road plunges abruptly and cattle pastures start to take the place of the coffee bushes. Both the villages and the people here have a more tropical look about them. Next comes La Tinta, and then Telemán, the largest of the squalid trading centres in this lower section of the valley. From Telemán a side road branches off to the north to **SENAHÚ**, climbing high into the lush hills past row upon row of neatly ranked coffee bushes. Set back behind the first ridge of hills, Senahú is a small coffee centre set in a verdant, steep-sided bowl and an ideal starting point for a short wander in the Alta Verapaz hills. Three **buses** a day run from Cobán to Senahú, the first returning at 4pm (check with the drivers for the latest times); or you could easily hitch a ride on a truck from Telemán. There are a couple of simple pensiónes, and also the *Hotel Senahú* (☎9522160; ④), in the centre of the village, with six pleasant rooms. It's possible to **trek** to Semuc Champey and Lanquín from here in two to three days – ask around for a guide in Senahú (try *Hotel Senahú*). Another stunning hike takes you to Cahabón; a four-wheel-drive can also sometimes make this trip.

Panzós

Heading on down the Polochic valley you reach **PANZÓS**, the largest of the valley villages. Its name means "place of the green waters", a reference to the swamps that surround the river, swarming with alligators and bird life. In 1978, Panzós made the international headlines when a group of campesinos attending a meeting to settle land disputes were gunned down by the army and local police, in one of the earliest and most brutal massacres of General Lucas García's military regime. García had a personal interest in the matter, since he owned over 300 square kilometres of land around Panzós. The event is generally regarded as a landmark in the history of political violence in Guatemala, after which the situation deteriorated rapidly. Over 100,000 people attended a protest rally in Guatemala City after news of the massacre broke.

El Estor

Beyond Panzós the road pushes on towards Lago de Izabal, passing a huge and deserted nickel plant, yet another monument to disastrous foreign investment. A kilometre or so further, **EL ESTOR** had settled back into provincial stupor after the nickel boom but is now undergoing a revival as a centre of a regional development. Fresh farmlands are being opened up all the time and a new road will open shortly connecting the town with the Río Dulce along the north shore of Lago de Izabal. The town's name is thought to have derived from the English pirates who came up the Río Dulce to buy supplies at "The Store". Now the only boat that drops by is the **ferry for Mariscos**, which leaves daily at 6am, returning at noon. On the other side, the ferry is met by two buses, one to Guatemala City and the other for Puerto Barrios.

The best **hotel** in El Estor is the *Hotel Vista del Lago* (☎9497205; ②), a beautiful colonial-style wooden building beside the dock, which the owner claims was the original "store" that gave the village its name. All rooms have private bathrooms, and second-floor rooms have superb views of the lake. A little cheaper, but still very pleasant, is the *Hotel Villela* at 6 Av 2–06 (②), a block up from the *Vista del Lago*, which is surrounded by a beautiful garden and has private showers. Simpler still, the *Hospedaje Santa Clara*, 5 Av 2–11 (☎9487244; ②), has basic, clean rooms, some with their own shower. For a delicious and not too expensive French **meal**, check out *Restaurante el Dios del Sol*, on the eastern side of town, or try *Hugo's Restaurant*, on the main plaza.

There's not a lot to do in El Estor, although it does have a friendly, relaxed atmosphere, particularly in the warmth of the evening when the streets are full of activity. Don't miss the pool in the plaza, which harbours fish, turtles and alligators. You could, however, spend a few days exploring the surrounding area, much of which remains undisturbed. If you find yourself with an afternoon to spare, you could hike out of town to the **El Boquerón canyon**, 8km away in the hills to the east, which is an excellent place for a swim. There are **bikes** to rent at 6 Av 4–26, or you can arrange to have someone take you there by boat. The delta of the **Río Polochic** (which has recently been given wildlife reserve status) is particularly beautiful – a maze of swamp, marsh and forest which is home to alligators, monkeys, tapirs and an abundance of bird life, while the lake itself abounds with fish, including tarpon and snook.

The best place to enquire about **tours** around El Estor is *Hugo's Restaurant*, whose owner will take you up the river to the canyon for around US$10 a person (minimum two people). In addition, the irrepressible Oscar Paz, who runs the *Hotel Vista del Lago*, is an enthusiastic promoter of the area and will arrange a boat and guide to explore any of the surrounding countryside, go fishing in the lake or visit the hot springs at *Finca Paraiso*.

North towards Petén

In the far northern section of Alta Verapaz, the lush hills drop away steeply onto the limestone plain that marks the frontier with the department of Petén. At present, two rough roads head north: the first from Cobán via **Chisec** and the second from San Pedro Carchá via Pajal, which passes the turnoff for Lanquín and Semuc Champey. From the **Pajal** junction it's a very slow, very beautiful journey north through typical

Verapaz scenery – a verdant green landscape of impossibly green mountains, tiny adobe-built hamlets, pasture and pine forests. After three hours or more of twists and turns, you'll reach **Sebol**, a beautiful spot on the Río Pasión where tributary waterfalls cascade into the main channel and a road heads off for Fray Bartolomé de las Casas and Poptún. The next stop is the small settlement of **Raxrujá**, where the buses from Cobán finish; currently only pick-ups and trucks head north for **Cruce del Pato** and onwards, either up to Sayaxché and Petén or west into the Ixcán.

Just 8km from Sebol is **FRAY BARTOLOMÉ DE LAS CASAS** where there are three **hotels** – the best is *Pensión Ralíos* (①) – and buses to San Pedro Carchá (8hr) and Cobán. For some reason the village has been left off most maps.

Raxrujá and the Candelaria caves
RAXRUJÁ is the best place to get a pick-up, a truck or, if you're very lucky, a bus north to Sayaxché and Flores or west to Playa Grande and the Ixcán. Little more than a few streets and an army base straggling round the bridge over the Río Escondido, a tributary of the Pasión, it has the only **accommodation** for miles around and you may end up staying here. *Hotel Raxruha* (①), next to the Texaco garage, is the best on offer and there are plenty of quite reasonable places to **eat** in town. Buses leave for Cobán at 4am and 8am. Heading north, it's pick-ups only. There's no timetable, they just leave when the driver has enough passengers, but you shouldn't have to wait more than a hour or so.

The limestone mountains to the west of Raxrujá are full of caves. Some of the best are the **Candelaria caves**, 10km west. The most impressive cave mouths are on private property, a short walk from the road, jealously guarded by Daniel Dreux who has built the **Complex Cultural de Candelaria** conservation area. There is wonderful **accommodation** here but it's often block-booked by French tour groups. One of the Cobán travel agents (see p.232) may be able to organize a trip.

The area beyond Raxrujá, where the rolling foothills of the highlands give way to the flat expanse of southern Petén, is known as the **Northern Transversal Strip**, dubbed the "Generals' Strip" as huge parcels of land, complete with their valuable mineral resources, were dispensed to military top brass instead of needy campesinos.

Playa Grande
Continuing west from Raxrujá, trucks make the 90km journey over rough roads to **PLAYA GRANDE** (at least 6hr), the bridging point of the Río Negro. The town is an authentic frontier settlement with cheap hotels, rough bars and brothels. If you need to **stay**, the best option is the basic but clean *Hospedaje Reyna* (①).

One point of interest in this area is the **Parque Nacional Laguna Lachuá**, a beautiful little lake, 4km off the main road east of Playa Grande. One of the least visited national parks in Central America, this is a beautiful, tranquil spot, the clear, almost circular lake completely surrounded by dense tropical forest. Though it smells slightly sulphurous, the water is good for swimming, with curious horseshoe-shaped limestone formations by the edge that make perfect individual bathing pools. You'll see otters and an abundance of birdlife, but watch out for mosquitoes. There's a large thatched *rancho* (shelter) by the shore, ideal for camping or slinging a hammock (available for rent). Though fireplaces and wood are provided, you'll need to bring food and drinking water. There are canoes for rent.

You can get to Playa Grande **from Cobán** on one of a stream of trucks and pick-ups setting out from the corner of the bus terminal – a journey of at least eight hours. Heading south **from Sayaxché** you need to catch a bus or pick-up to Playitas via Cruce del Pato and take another pick-up or truck from there. There are also regular **flights** from the airstrip in Cobán.

Into the Ixcán

The Río Negro marks the boundary between the departments of Alta Verapaz and Quiché; the land to the west is known as the **Ixcán**. This huge swampy forest, some of which was settled in the 1960s and 1970s by peasants migrating from the highlands, became a bloody battleground in the 1980s. In the past few years the Ixcán has become a focus for **repatriado** settlement as refugees who fled to Mexico in the 1980s are resettled in a string of "temporary" camps west of the river.

Travelling further west across the Ixcán and into northern Huehuetenango, though no longer hazardous, is still very arduous – it takes at least two or three days to get from Playa Grande to Barillas. **Veracruz**, 20km (1hr 30min) from Playa Grande, is the first place of note, a settlement at the crossroads beyond the Río Xalbal. Some buses continue to Mayalan, 12km away, across the presently unbridged Río Piedras Blancas. Here the road ends and you'll have to walk 15km (4–5hr) to **Altamira** on the far bank of the Río Ixcán, past several tiny villages; the path is easy to follow. At the last village, **Ranch Palmeras**, ask for directions to the crossing point on the Ixcan, where boys will pole you across the flowing river. Once across, Altamira is still a few kilometres away, up the hill. From here a regular flow of trucks make the 30km (4hr) journey to Barillas, over some of the worst roads in the country. It's a spectacular journey, though, especially as you watch the growing bulk of the Cuchumatanes rising ever higher on the horizon. You can also get trucks over the border in **Mexico**, taking you to Chajul on the Río Lacantún in Chiapas, but you need a Guatemalan exit stamp first, probably best obtained in Cobán or Flores.

travel details

BUSES

Cobán to: Cahabón (4 daily; 4hr); El Estor (11 daily; 8hr); Guatemala City (14 daily; 4–5hr); Lanquín (4 daily; 3hr); San Cristóbal Verapaz (hourly; 45min); San Pedro Carchá (every 15min; 20min); Senahú (3 daily; 7hr); Tactic (hourly; 45min). Also pickups to: Playa Grande via Laguna Lechuá (early morning most days; approx 8hr); Chisec (most days; 5hr).

Cubulco to: Guatemala City via El Chol (1 daily; 9hr); Guatemala City via La Cumbre (hourly; 5hr 30min); Rabinal (hourly; 1hr 30min); Salamá (hourly; 2hr 30min).

Rabinal to: Cubulco (hourly; 1hr 30min); Guatemala City via El Chol (1 daily; 8hr) and via La Cumbre (hourly; 4hr); Salamá (hourly; 1hr).

Raxrujá to: Cruce del Pato (pickup to Canleche, 1hr, then pickup to Cruce del Pato, 20min).

Salamá to: Cubulco (hourly; 1hr 30min); Guatemala City (hourly; 3hr); Rabinal (hourly; 1hr).

San Pedro Carchá to: Cobán (every 15min; 20min); Fray Bartolomé de las Casas (3–4 daily; 6hr); Raxrujá via Sebol (2 daily; 7hr); Uspantán via Cobán (2 daily; 5hr).

FLIGHTS

Cobán to: Guatemala City (daily; 30min); irregular flights to Playa Grande.

CHAPTER 11

PETÉN

T
he vast northern department of **Petén** occupies about a third of Guatemala but
contains less than three percent of the population. This huge expanse of
swamps, dry savannahs and tropical rainforest forms part of an untamed
wilderness that stretches into the Lacandón forest of southern Mexico and
across the Maya Mountains to Belize. Totally unlike any other part of the country,
much of it is all-but-untouched, with ancient ceiba and mahogany trees that tower
50m above the forest floor. Undisturbed for so long, the area is also extraordinarily
rich in **wildlife**. Some 285 species of bird have been sighted at Tikal alone, including
a great range of hummingbirds, toucans, blue and white herons, hawks, buzzards,
wild turkeys, motmot (a bird of paradise) and even the elusive quetzal, revered since
Maya times. Beneath the forest canopy are many other species that are far harder to
locate. Among the mammals are the massive tapir or mountain cow, ocelots, deer,
coatis, jaguars, monkeys, plus crocodiles and thousands of species of plants, snakes,
insects and butterflies.

Recently, however, this position of privileged isolation has been threatened by moves
to colonize the country's final frontier. Waves of **settlers**, lured by offers of free land,
have cleared enormous tracts of jungle, while oil exploration and commercial logging
have cut new roads deep into the forest. The population of Petén, just 15,000 in 1950, is
today estimated at 350,000, a number which puts enormous pressure on the remaining
forest. Various attempts have been made to halt the tide of destruction, and in 1990 the
government declared that forty percent of Petén would be protected by the **Maya
Biosphere Reserve**, although little is done to enforce this. In late 1997 a new move
was made to highlight the threat to the remaining jungles, with a series of conferences
and concerts by an all-star international cast including Bianca Jagger and backed by
President Arzú.

The new interest in the region is in fact something of a reawakening, as Petén was
once the heartland of the **Maya civilization**, which reached here from the highlands
some 2500 years ago. Maya culture reached the height of its architectural, scientific
and artistic achievement during the Classic period (roughly 300–900 AD), when great
cities rose out of the forest. The ruins at Tikal and El Mirador, among the most spectacular of all **Maya sites**, represent only a fraction of what was once here. At the close
of the tenth century the cities were mysteriously abandoned, and many of the people
moved north to the Yucatán where Maya civilization continued to flourish until the
twelfth century.

By the time the Spanish arrived, the area had been partially recolonized by the **Itzá**,
a group of Toltec-Maya who inhabited the land around Lago de Petén Itzá. The forest
proved so impenetrable that it wasn't brought under Spanish control until 1697, more
than 150 years after they had conquered the rest of the country. The Spanish had little
enthusiasm for Petén, however, and under their rule it remained a backwater.
Independence saw no great change, and it wasn't until 1970 that Petén became genuinely accessible by car. Even today the network of roads is skeletal, and many routes
are impassable in the wet season.

The hub of the department are the twin lakeside towns of **Flores** and **Santa Elena**.
You'll probably arrive here, if only to head straight out to the ruins of **Tikal**, Petén's
prime attraction, though the town is also the starting-point for adventures to more

distant ruins – **El Mirador, El Zotz** and **Río Azul. El Remate** is a tranquil alternative location, halfway between Flores and Tikal. The caves and scenery around **Poptún**, on the main highway south, justify exploration, while down the other road south, **Sayaxché** is surrounded by yet more Maya sites. From Sayaxché you can set off down the Río Pasión to **Mexico** and the ruins of **Yaxchilán**, or take an alternative route back to Guatemala City – via Cobán in Alta Verapaz.

Getting to the Petén

Many visitors arrive in Petén by bus or plane directly from **Guatemala City**: **by air** it's a short fifty-minute hop to Flores; **by bus** it can take anywhere between ten and fifteen gruelling hours. A number of internal airlines fly the route daily and **tickets** can be bought from virtually any travel agent in the country; a cutthroat price war means you can get there and back for a bargain US$60 or so at present, though if tariffs return to previous levels you can expect to pay double that. Flights are heavily in demand and overbooking is common. Six **bus companies** provide around twenty services a day from Guatemala City to Flores. If you don't want to do the 554km trip in one go, it's easy enough to do it in stages – the best places to break the journey are at **Quiriguá** (see p.215), **Río Dulce** (see p.220) and **Poptún** (see p.243).

Coming from the Guatemalan highlands, you can reach Petén along the backroads **from Cobán** in Alta Verapaz, a long, adventurous route (see p.238). **From Belize or**

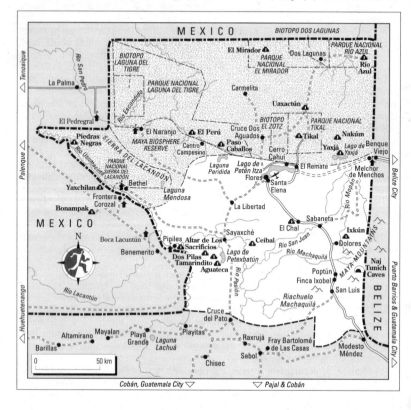

For an explanation of **accommodation price codes**, see p.123.

Mexico, you can enter the country through Petén. The most obvious route is from Belize through the border at Melchor de Mencos, but there are also two river routes that bring you through from Palenque or Tenosique in Mexico. All of these are covered later in this chapter.

Poptún and around

Heading north from the Río Dulce, the main route to Flores (which should be completely sealed in 1999) cuts through a degraded landscape of small milpa farms and cattle ranches that was jungle a decade or two ago. Some 95km from Río Dulce, at an altitude of 500m, the first settlement of any interest is the small town of **POPTÚN**. For many travellers this dusty frontier settlement is the embodiment of rustic bliss and organic food – thanks to the proximity of the *Finca Ixobel* (see below). There's no particular reason to stay in the town itself, but you may well stop by to use the Telgua office or banks. If you do get stuck here, **stay** at the friendly *Hotel Posada de los Castellanos* (②), where you get hot water and a bathroom. The best food in town can be had at the *Fonda Ixobel 2*, which bakes good bread and cakes.

For a more rural setting, head 4km north of Poptún, to *Cocay Camping* (①), set in peaceful isolation on the banks of the river just past the village of Machaquilá. The site provides camping space, very simple huts, and vegetarian and European food. Over the bridge to the right, set nicely in a patch of forest, are the new cabañas of the *Villa de los Castellanos* (☎9277541, fax 9277542; ⑤ – check also for special backpacker rates), offering a comfortable base for adventurous visitors to explore the forests, rivers and caves of central Petén. Carlos, the owner, is an excellent source of information – botanical, historical and logistical.

Finca Ixobel

A couple of kilometres' walk north of Poptún, surrounded by aromatic pine forests in the cool foothills of the Maya Mountains, is the *Finca Ixobel* (☎9277363), a working farm that provides **accommodation** to passing tourists. The farm was originally run by Americans Mike and Carole DeVine, but on June 8, 1990, Mike was murdered by the army. This prompted the American government to suspend military aid to Guatemala, and after a drawn-out investigation which cast little light on their motives, five soldiers were convicted of the murder in September 1992. Others involved have managed to evade capture and their commanding officer, Captain Hugo Contreras, escaped from jail shortly after his arrest. Carole fought the case for years and remains at the finca.

Finca Ixobel is a supremely beautiful and relaxing place, where you can swim in the pond, walk in the forest, dodge the resident "attack" parrots and stuff yourself stupid with delicious home-grown food. There are **hikes** into the jungle, horse-riding trips, rafting, 4WD jungle jaunts, and short excursions to nearby caves. As there was an armed attack on a group visiting the caves in late 1997, check the current security situation with finca staff. Accommodation is in attractive bungalows with private bathroom (④), regular rooms (②–③) or dorms (②), and there's also camping and hammock space (①) and tree houses (②). You run up a tab for accommodation, food and drink, paying when you leave – which can be a rude awakening. To get to the finca ask the bus driver to drop you at the gate (marked by a large sign), from where it's a fifteen-minute walk.

Flores and around

FLORES, the capital of Petén, has an easy pace and a sedate, old-world atmosphere diametrically opposed to the commerce and hustle that typify most of Petén's towns. Its genteel cobbled streets, ageing houses and twin-domed church are set on a small island in Lago de Petén Itzá, connected to the mainland by a short causeway. The frontier

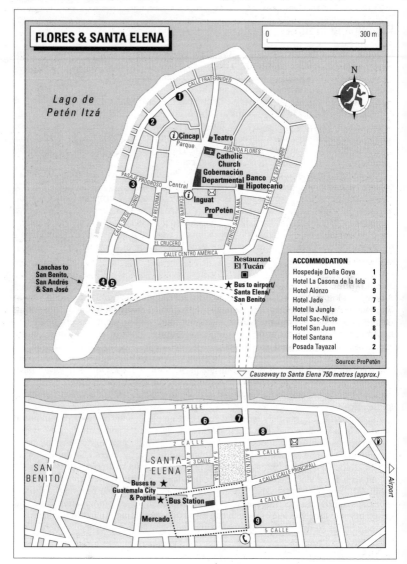

FLORES & SANTA ELENA

0   300 m

N

Lago de Petén Itzá

CALLE FRATERNIDED

❶

❷

ⓘ Cincap   ★ Teatro

Parque   AVENIDA FLORES

Catholic
Church

Gobernación

Departmental   Banco
Hipotecario

PASAJE PROGROSO   Central

❸

ⓘ Inguat

ProPetén

EL CRUCERO

CALLE CENTRO AMÉRICA

Restaurant
El Tucán

Lanchas to
San Benito,
San Andrés
& San José

❹❺

★ Bus to airport/
Santa Elena/
San Benito

ACCOMMODATION

Hospedaje Doña Goya	1
Hotel La Casona de la Isla	3
Hotel Alonzo	9
Hotel Jade	7
Hotel la Jungla	5
Hotel Sac-Nicte	6
Hotel San Juan	8
Hotel Santana	4
Posada Tayazal	2

Source: ProPetén

▽ *Causeway to Santa Elena 750 metres (approx.)*

1 CALLE

❻   ❼

❽

SANTA
ELENA

SAN
BENITO

2 CALLE

3 CALLE   3 CALLE

Buses to
Guatemala City ★
& Poptún ★ Bus Station

4 CALLE (CALLE PRINCIPAL)

4 CALLE

4 CALLE A

Mercado

❾

5 CALLE

Airport

mentality lies just across the water in **SANTA ELENA**, a chaotic, featureless town which is dusty in the dry season and mud-bound during the rains.

The **lake** was a natural choice for settlement, and its shores were heavily populated in Maya times, with the capital of the Itzá, **Tayasal**, occupying the island that was to become modern Flores. Cortes passed through here in 1525, on his way south to Honduras, and left behind a sick horse which he promised to send for later. A horse-worshipping cult started as a result, and later visitors were sacrificed to the equine deity. Tayasal was eventually destroyed by Martín de Ursúa and an army of 235 in 1697. For the entire colonial period (and indeed up to the 1960s) Flores languished in virtual isolation, having more contact with neighbouring Belize than with the capital.

Today, despite the steady flow of tourists passing through en route to Tikal, the town retains an urbane air. It has little to detain you and is small enough to explore in an hour or so, but it does offer some attractive places to stay and spectacular lake views.

Arrival and information

Arriving by **bus** from Guatemala City or Belize, you'll be dropped a block or two from the causeway to Flores. The **airport** is 3km east of the causeway, a US$2 taxi-ride into town per person. **Local buses** cover the route but entail a time-consuming change halfway. They cross the causeway about every ten minutes. Returning to the airport, local buses leave from the Flores end of the causeway every twenty minutes or so.

The staff at the Inguat desk in the arrivals hall at the airport (Mon–Sat 6–10am & 3–6pm, sometimes also on Sun) can give you reasonable maps and **information**. There's another office on the plaza in Flores (Mon–Fri 8am–4pm; ☎9260669), where the helpful staff will most likely direct you across the plaza to the resource centre, CINCAP (Tues–Sat 9am–1pm & 2–8pm, Sun 2–6pm), to examine their more detailed maps, books and leaflets about northern Petén. If you're planning to go on a trip to remote parts of the **Maya Biosphere Reserve**, check with ProPetén on C Central (Mon–Fri 8am–5pm; ☎9261370, fax 9260495) for current information on route conditions, accommodation and guides. They also organize trips, including the "Scarlet Macaw Trail", a five-day expedition by truck, horse and boat along rivers and through primary forest, taking in the remote ruins of **El Perú** and the largest concentrations of scarlet macaws in northern Central America.

Accommodation

Accommodation in Flores/Santa Elena has undergone a boom in recent years and the sheer number of new **hotels** keeps prices competitive. There are several good budget places in Flores itself, making it unnecessary to stay in noisier and dirtier Santa Elena unless your budget is extremely tight or you have a really early bus to catch – even then you can arrange a taxi.

Flores

La Casita de Flores, on the right across the causeway (☎3600000, fax 9260032). Small, attractive rooms with very good rates in the low season. ③.

Hotel la Casona de la Isla, C 30 de Junio (☎9260692, fax 9260593). The one with the arresting citrus and powder-blue paint job. Attractive, modern rooms with private bath and a/c, swimming pool and spectacular sunset views from the terrace bar-restaurant. ⑤.

Hospedaje Doña Goya, north end of the island (no phone). Excellent family-run budget guest house, with the best prices on the island. Clean, light rooms with fans, some with private baths; the ones at the front have balconies. Good rates for single travellers. Can organize trips to nearby caves. ②.

Hotel Jungla, southwest corner of island (☎9260634). The best value in this price range, with gleaming tiled floors and private baths with hot water. Also rooftop views over the town and lake, plus a good restaurant. ③.

Hotel Santana, southwest corner of Flores (☎9260492, fax 9260662). Recently modernized three-storey building with a small pool and patio overlooking the lake. Very comfortable, spotless rooms with fan and private bath; first-floor rooms have private lakeside terraces and a/c. ⑤.

Posada Tayazal, C la Unión, near the *Doña Goya* (☎ & fax 9260568). Well-run budget hotel with decent rooms, some with private baths. Shared bathrooms have hot water. Roof terrace, information service, and tours to Tikal. Best budget bet if *Doña Goya* is full. ②–③.

Santa Elena

Hotel Alonzo, 6 Av 4–99 (☎9260105). Clean rooms, some with balcony, and a few with private bathrooms; the shared bathroom is a little grubby. Public telephone and reasonable restaurant. On the Fuente del Norte bus route from Guatemala City. ②.

Hotel Jade, 6 Av. A backpackers' stronghold: shambolic but the cheapest place in town. ①.

Hotel Sac-Nicte, 1 C 4–45 (☎ & fax 9260092). Clean rooms with fans and private shower; second-floor rooms have views of the lake. Breakfast possible before the 4am trip to Tikal. ②.

Hotel San Juan, 8 C, a block from the causeway (☎ & fax 9260042). Conveniently doubles as the Pinita bus terminal and travel agent, organizing trips to Tikal, but not particularly good value, and distinctly unfriendly. Most guests are captives straight off the bus.

Eating and drinking

Flores unquestionably offers the most cosmopolitan dining scene in Petén and there are a number of good restaurants, many with delightful lakeside views, though prices are a little higher than elsewhere in Guatemala. **Santa Elena** has a very limited selection of comedores, so even if you're staying there you may want to cross the causeway for an evening out.

Flores

La Canoa, C Centro America. Popular, good-value place, serving pasta, great soups, and some vegetarian and Guatemalan food, as well as excellent breakfasts.

The Chaltunhá, opposite *Hotel Santana,* right on the water. Great spot for lunch, snacks and sandwiches, and not too expensive.

Restaurant Gran Jaguar, Av Barrios. Guatemalan restaurant geared up for tourists. Good value meals include soup, salad, tea, coffee and a pastry.

Pizzeria Picasso, across the street from the *Tucán* and run by the same family. Serves great pizza under cooling breezes from the ceiling fans.

Las Puertas, signposted on C Santa Ana. Paint-splattered walls, live music as well as very good pasta and healthy breakfasts. Worth it for the atmosphere.

El Tucán, a few metres east of the causeway, on the waterfront. Excellent fish, enormous chef's salads, Mexican food and the best waterside terrace in Flores.

Santa Elena

Restaurant Petenchel, 2 C, past the park. Simple, good food: the nicest place to eat within two blocks of the main street and you can leave your luggage here.

El Rodeo, 2 C & 5 Av. It's not going to win any Michelin stars but it's good value even if the service is slow.

Listings

Banks Banco de Guatemala, two blocks west of the plaza in Flores; in Santa Elena, Bancafé, Banco G&T (for Mastercard) and Banco Industrial (with Visa ATM) are all on 4 Av.

Car and bike rental Several firms, including Budget, Hertz, San Juan and Koka, operate from the airport. All offer cars, minibuses and jeeps, with prices starting at around US$70 a day for a jeep. Bikes can be rented from Cahuí, 30 de Junio, Flores (daily 7am–7pm; ☎ & fax 9260494) for US$0.80 per hour.

Laundry Lavandería Amelia, behind CINCAP in Flores; Lavandería Emanuel on 6 Av in Santa Elena.

Post office Two doors away from the Inguat office in Flores; at 2 C and 7 Av, two blocks east of the *Hotel San Juan*, in Santa Elena (Mon–Fri 8am–4.30pm).

Telephone office Guatel is in Santa Elena on 5 C, but you're better off using one of the private telephone and fax services: at the *Hotel Alonzo* in Santa Elena, or *Cahuí*, 30 de Junio in Flores (daily 7am–7pm; ☎ & fax 9260494). For email, check out *C@fénet* on Av Barrios (daily 9am–9pm) and *Arpa* on C Centro América, both in Flores. Make sure the messages are sent while you're there.

Travel agents The most helpful is Arco Iris (☎9260786), C Centro América, Flores. They sell flights, and have the best prices for tours to the ruins and around the lake. Expedicion Panamundo, 2 C 4–90, Santa Elena (☎ & fax 9260501), sells more pricey tours than some but the guides have archeological expertise. Explore, C Centro América, Flores (☎9260665, fax 9260550), have specialist knowledge of the Petexbatún area.

Around Flores: Lago de Petén Itzá

If you have a few hours to spare, the most obvious excursion is a **trip on the lake**. Boatmen can take you around a circuit that takes in a *mirador* and small ruin on the peninsula opposite and the **Petencito zoo**, 3km east of Flores (daily 8am–5pm), with its small collection of sluggish local wildlife, pausing for a swim along the way (beware the concrete waterslide by the zoo – it's caused at least one death). Boatmen loiter with intent behind the *Hotel Yum Kax*, or around the start of the causeway. If you'd rather paddle around under your own steam you can rent a canoe for around US$2 an hour.

Of the numerous **caves** in the hills behind Santa Elena, the most accessible is **Aktun Kan** (daily 8am–5pm; US$1.20) – simply follow the Flores causeway through Santa Elena, turn left when it forks in front of a small hill, and then take the first right. Otherwise known as *La Cueva de la Serpiente*, the cave is the legendary home of a huge snake; the guard may explain some of the bizarre names given to the various shapes inside.

San Andrés and San José

Though accessible by bus and boat, the traditional villages of **San Andrés** and **San José**, across the lake from Flores, have until recently received few visitors. Sloping steeply up from the shore, the streets are lined with one-storey buildings: some of palmetto sticks and thatch, some coated with plaster, and others brightly painted concrete. Pigs and chickens wander freely.

Getting to the villages is best achieved by using the *lanchas* that leave regularly from the beach next to the *Hotel Santana* in Flores and from **San Benito**, a suburb of Santa Elena. A chartered *expreso* from Flores or San Benito will cost around US$8. Regular morning **buses** leave for San Andrés from the market in Santa Elena (if they don't continue to San José, it's an easy 2km walk downhill). **Returning** in the mornings is simple, with *lanchas* at 6am, 7am and noon, and there are regular buses throughout the day.

Most outsiders in **SAN ANDRÉS** are students at the only **language school** in Petén, the Eco-Escuela. Since nobody in the village speaks English, a course here is an excellent opportunity to immerse yourself in Spanish without distractions, though it may be daunting for absolute beginners. See p.129 for more details.

There are currently no hospedajes in the village, but 3km to the west is the luxurious *Hotel Nitún* (☎9288132, fax 9288113; ⑤ including transport from Flores), which offers thatched stone cabañas with hardwood floors and private bathrooms; the restaurant serves superb food. *Hotel Nitún* is the base for Monkey Eco Tours, organizing well-equipped expeditions to remote archeological sites (☎ & fax 9260494).

Perched above a lovely bay, just 2km east along the shore from San Andrés, **SAN JOSÉ** is even more relaxed than its neighbour. The village is undergoing something of a cultural revival: Itzá, the pre-conquest Maya tongue, is being taught in the school, and you'll see signs in that language dotted all around. Over the hill beyond the village is a secluded rocky beach where there's a shelter to sling a hammock and a couple of cabins to rent.

Beyond San José a signed track on the left leads 4km to the Classic period **ruins of Motúl**. The site is fairly spread out and little visited (though there should be a caretaker about), with four plazas, stelae and pyramids. It's a secluded spot, ideal for bird-watching, and probably best visited by **bicycle** – borrow one from either of the villages or rent one in Flores.

El Remate

On the eastern shore of Lago de Petén Itzá, 30km from Santa Elena on the road to Tikal, **EL REMATE** offers a pleasant alternative to staying in Flores. It's a quiet, friendly village, growing in popularity as a convenient base for visits to Tikal. **Getting to El Remate** is easy: every minibus to Tikal passes through the village, or catch any bus heading for the Belize border, get off at the village of **Puente Ixlú** (also called El Cruce) and it's a 2km walk down the Tikal road. **Returning to Flores** local buses pass through El Remate at 5.30am, 7.30am and 8am and a swarm of minibuses from Tikal ply the route from midday onwards.

On the north shore of the lake, 3km along the road from the centre of El Remate, the **Biotopo Cerro Cahuí** (daily; US$5) is a 6.5-square-kilometre wildlife conservation area comprising lakeshore, ponds and some of the best examples of undisturbed tropical forest in Petén. The smallest and most accessible of Petén's reserves, it contains a rich diversity of plants and animals, and is especially recommended for birdwatchers. There are hiking trails, a couple of small ruins and two thatched *miradores* on the hill above the lake; pick up maps and information at the gate where you sign in, close to the *El Gringo Perdido* hotel.

Accommodation and eating

All the places listed here have a distinctive charm and they're well spaced, with no sense of overcrowding. There are no private **phone numbers**: to book ahead you need to leave a message (in Spanish) on the community telephone (☎9260269). There are no restaurants per se in El Remate, but the hotels provide meals; *Don David's*, in particular, is highly recommended. The following hotels are listed in the order you approach them from Puente Ixlú.

El Mirador del Duende, high above the lake, reached by a stairway cut into the cliff. An incredible collection of globular whitewashed stucco cabañas, decorated with Maya glyphs, plus space for hammocks and tents. The owner is an expert on jungle lore, leading hikes to all Petén's archeological sites, and the restaurant serves cheap vegetarian food. ①–②.

La Mansión del Pajaro Serpiente, just below *Mirador del Duende* (☎ & fax 9260065 in Flores). The most comfortable accommodation on the road to Tikal. Stone-built and thatched two-storey cabañas in a tropical garden and smaller cabañas at about a third of the price, all with superb lake views. Good food. ④–⑦.

La Casa de Don David, 300m beyond *La Mansión*, right on the junction. Probably the most atmospheric place in El Remate. Great home-cooking and near-legendary after-dinner "tarantula tours" and "Tikal tips" lectures – owner David Kuhn is a mine of information about Petén. New restaurant premises next door (book ahead for dinner). If you need a lift from Puente Ixlú, send a kid on a bicycle and David will come and pick you up. ③.

Casa Mobego (formerly *Casa Roja*), 500m down the road to Cerro Cahuí on the right. Good budget deal right by the lake. Simple, well-constructed stick-and-thatch cabañas, plus camping, canoe rental, a good, inexpensive restaurant and swimming. ②.

El Gringo Perdido, on the north shore, 3km from *Don David's* (contact Viajes Mundial in Guatemala City: ☎2320605, fax 2538761). Long-established place offering rooms with bath, a mosquito-netted bunk and some excellent value basic cabañas, as well as camping and a fine restaurant. The setting is supremely tranquil, and they offer guided canoe tours. ②–⑤.

Hotel Camino Real Tikal, beyond Cerro Cahuí, 4km from the highway (☎9260209; in Guatemala City ☎3334633, fax 3374313). Luxury option in extensive lakeside grounds. The rooms are a bit unimaginative and corporate and there are attendant luxury trappings like buggies and a souvenir shop, but views of the lake are excellent. Private beach and guests have free use of kayaks and a guided tour of the Biotopo Cerro Cahuí. US$132 for a double. ⑨.

Tikal

Towering above the rainforest, **Tikal** is possibly the most magnificent of all Maya ruins. The site is dominated by five enormous temples, steep-sided granite pyramids that rise up to 60m from the forest floor, while around them are literally thousands of other structures, many semi-strangled by giant roots and still hidden beneath mounds of earth.

The site itself is deep in the jungle of the **Parque Nacional Tikal**, a protected area of some 370 square kilometres, on the edge of the even larger Maya Biosphere Reserve. The trees around the ruins are home to hundreds of species including howler and spider monkeys, toucans and parakeets. The sheer scale of the place is overwhelming, and its atmosphere spellbinding. Whether you can spare as little as an hour or as long as a week, it's always worth the trip.

Plane schedules are designed to make it easy to visit the ruins as a day-trip from Flores or Guatemala City, but if you can spare the time it's well worth **staying overnight**, partly because you'll need the extra time to do justice to the ruins themselves but, more importantly, to spend dawn and dusk at the site, when the forest canopy bursts into a frenzy of sound and activity. The air fills with the screech of toucans and the roar of howler monkeys, while flocks of parakeets wheel around the temples, and bats launch themselves into the night. With a bit of luck you might even see a grey fox sneak across one of the plazas.

Arrival and information

The best way to reach the ruins is in one of the **tourist minibuses** that meet flights from the capital and are operated by just about every hotel in Flores and Santa Elena, starting at 4am to catch the sunrise. In addition a **local bus** (Pinita) leaves the market at 1pm, passing the *Hotel San Juan* and arriving at Tikal about two hours later; it then continues to Uaxactún (see p.255), returning at 6am.

If you're travelling from Belize to Tikal, there is no need to go all the way to Flores; get off instead at **Puente Ixlú** – the three-way junction at the eastern end of Lago de Petén Itzá – to change buses. The local bus from Santa Elena to Tikal and Uaxactún passes at about 2pm, and there are passing minibuses all day long, at their most frequent in the mornings.

Entrance to the national park costs US$8.50 a day and you're expected to pay again if you stay overnight, although this is not always strictly enforced. If you arrive after dusk you will automatically be issued with a ticket for the next day. The ruins themselves are **open** daily from 6am to 5pm, and extensions to 8pm can be obtained from the *inspectoría* (7am–noon & 2–5pm), a small white hut on the left at the entrance to the ruins.

Accommodation, eating and drinking

There are three **hotels** at the ruins, all of them fairly expensive and not especially good value, though they offer discounts out of season. The largest and most luxurious is the *Jungle Lodge*, which offers bungalow accommodation (⑥), some "budget" rooms (④), which are often booked up, and a pool; reservations can be made in Guatemala City

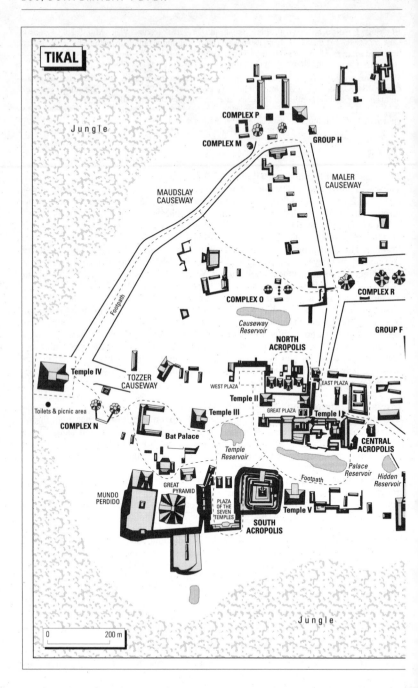

TIKAL

Jungle

COMPLEX P

COMPLEX M

GROUP H

MALER
CAUSEWAY

MAUDSLAY
CAUSEWAY

Footpath

COMPLEX O

COMPLEX R

Causeway
Reservoir

GROUP F

NORTH
ACROPOLIS

Temple IV

TOZZER
CAUSEWAY

WEST PLAZA

EAST PLAZA

Temple II

Toilets & picnic area

COMPLEX N

Temple III

GREAT PLAZA

Temple I

Bat Palace

Temple
Reservoir

CENTRAL
ACROPOLIS

Palace
Reservoir

Hidden
Reservoir

Footpath

MUNDO
PERDIDO

GREAT
PYRAMID

PLAZA
OF THE
SEVEN
TEMPLES

Temple V

SOUTH
ACROPOLIS

Jungle

0   200 m

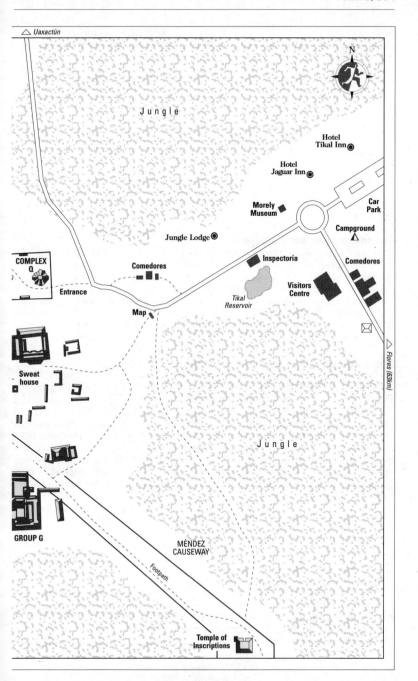

(☎4768775, fax 4760294). Next door is the overpriced *Jaguar Inn* (☎9260002; ⑥), and close by the better *Tikal Inn* (☎ & fax 9260065; ⑤–⑥), where there are thatched bungalows, pleasant rooms and a heat-busting swimming pool.

Alternatively, for US$6 you can **camp** or sling a **hammock** under one of the thatched shelters in a cleared space used as a campsite. Hammocks and mosquito nets (essential in the wet season) can be rented either on the spot or from the *Comedor Imperio Maya* opposite the visitor centre. At the entrance to the campsite there's a shower block, but water is sporadic. The *Jaguar Inn* also has some tents, complete with mattresses and drinking water (②). It is possible to camp within the ruins, although this is, strictly speaking, against the regulations.

The three simple **comedores** at the entrance to the ruins and a couple more inside offer a limited menu of traditional Guatemalan specialities – eggs, beans, grilled meat and chicken. For more extensive and expensive menus, there's an adequate restaurant in the *Jaguar Inn* and an overpriced café in the new visitor centre. It's essential to buy some water before setting out, though cold drinks are sold at a number of spots within the ruins.

The site museum and other facilities

Between the *Jungle Lodge* and *Jaguar Inn* hotels is the one-room **Tikal Museum** (Mon–Fri 9am–5pm, Sat & Sun 9am–4pm; US$1.80), which houses some of the artefacts found in the ruins, including tools, jewellery, pottery, obsidian and jade, and the remains of Stela 29. There's also a **post office**, shops and a **visitor centre** containing a selection of some of the finest stelae and carvings from the site, a scale model of Tikal and a café. Two **books** of note are usually available: the best guide to the site is Coe's *Tikal, A Handbook to the Ancient Maya Ruins*, while *The Birds of Tikal*, although by no means comprehensive, is useful for identifying some of the hundreds of species.

The rise and fall of Tikal

According to archeological evidence, the first occupants of Tikal arrived around 700 BC, probably attracted by its position above the surrounding seasonal swamps and by the availability of **flint** for making tools and weapons. The first definite evidence of buildings dates from 500 BC, and by about 200 BC the first ceremonial structures had emerged, including the first version of the **North Acropolis**. Two hundred years later, at around the time of Christ, the **Great Plaza** had begun to take shape and Tikal was already established as a major site with a large permanent population. Despite development and sophisticated architecture, Tikal remained very much a secondary centre, dominated, along with the rest of the area, by **El Mirador**, a massive city about 65km to the north (see p.257).

The closing years of the **Preclassic** era were marked by the eruption of the Ilopango volcano in El Salvador, which smothered huge areas of Guatemala in a thick layer of volcanic ash. Trade routes were disrupted and the ensuing years saw the decline and abandonment of El Mirador, creating a power vacuum disputed bitterly between the cities of Tikal and Uaxactún. Tikal eventually won under the inspired leadership of Great Jaguar Paw, probably with the aid of the powerful highland centre of **Kaminaljuyú** – on the site of modern Guatemala City – which was itself allied with **Teotihuacán**, the ancient metropolis that dominated what is now central Mexico.

The victory over Uaxactún enabled Tikal's rulers to control central Petén for the next three centuries, growing into one of the most elaborate and magnificent of all Maya city states. This extended period of prosperity saw temples rebuilt, the city's population grow to somewhere between 50,000 and 100,000, and its influence reach as far as Copán in Honduras.

In the middle of the sixth century, however, Tikal suffered a major setback. In the Maya mountains of Belize, **Caracol** was emerging as a major regional power, and conquered Tikal in 557 AD, under the ambitious leader Lord Water. The effect of Caracol's assault was to free many smaller centres throughout Petén from Tikal's influence, creating fresh and disruptive rivalry. By the middle of the seventh century, however, Caracol's stranglehold had begun to relax and Tikal embarked upon a dramatic renaissance under the formidable leadership of **Ah Cacaw**, Lord Chocolate (682-721 AD). During his reign the main ceremonial areas, the East Plaza and the North Acropolis, were completely remodelled, reclaimed from the desecration suffered at the hands of Caracol. Tikal regained its position under Ah Cacaw and, as a tribute, his son Caan Chac had the leader's body entombed in the magnificent Temple 1. Ah Cacaw's strident approach gave birth to a revitalized and powerful ruling dynasty: the site's five main temples were built in the hundred years following his death, and magnificent temples were still under construction at Tikal as late as 889 AD.

What brought about Tikal's final **downfall** remains a mystery, but what is certain is that around 900 AD almost the entire lowland Maya civilization collapsed. Possible causes range from an earthquake to popular uprising, but the evidence points in no particular direction. We do know that Tikal was abandoned by the end of the tenth century.

Little is known of Tikal again until 1848, when it was **rediscovered** by a government expedition led by Modesto Méndez. Later in the nineteenth century a Swiss scientist visited the site and removed the beautifully carved wooden lintels from the tops of Temples 1 and 4 – they are currently in a museum in Basel – and in 1881 the English archeologist Maudslay took the first photographs of the ruins. The site could only be reached on horseback and the ruins remained mostly uncleared until 1951, when the Guatemalan army built an airstrip, paving the way for a cultural invasion of archeologists and tourists. The gargantuan project to excavate and restore the site started in 1956, and involved teams from the University of Pennsylvania and Guatemala's Institute of Anthropology. Most of the major work was completed by 1984, but thousands of minor buildings remain buried in roots, shoots and rubble. A five-year project to restore Temple 5 (the second highest structure at Tikal) is currently being coordinated with help from the Spanish government.

The ruins

The sheer scale of the ruins at Tikal can at first seem daunting. The **central area**, with its five main temples, forms by far the most impressive section; if you start to explore beyond this you can wander seemingly forever in the maze of smaller, **unrestored structures** and complexes. Compared to the scale and magnificence of the main area, they're not that impressive, but armed with a good map (the best is in Coe's guide to the ruins), it can be exciting to explore some of the rarely visited outlying sections. Tikal is certain to exhaust you before you exhaust it.

From the entrance to the Great Plaza

Following the path to the right of the **map** you pass **Complexes Q and R**, twin pyramids built by **Chitam**, Tikal's last known ruler, to mark the passing of a *katun* (twenty 360-day years). Set to one side is a copy of the superbly carved Stela 22 (now in the visitor centre). Bearing to the left after Complex R, you approach the **East Plaza**; in its southeast corner stands an imposing temple, beneath which were found the remains of several severed heads, the victims of human sacrifice. Behind the plaza is the **sweat house**, which may have been similar to those used by highland Maya today. It's thought that Maya priests would take a sweat bath in order to cleanse themselves before conducting religious rituals.

From here a few short steps bring you to the **Great Plaza**, the heart of the ancient city. Surrounded by four massive structures, this was the focus of ceremonial and religious activity at Tikal for around a thousand years. Beneath the grass lie four layers of paving, the oldest of which dates from about 150 BC and the most recent from 700 AD. **Temple 1**, towering 44m above the plaza, is the hallmark of Tikal – it's also known as the Jaguar Temple because of the jaguar carved in its door lintel (now in a museum in Basel). This is the temple built as a burial monument to contain the magnificent tomb of **Ah Cacaw** (Lord Chocolate, 682–721 AD) by his son and successor Caan Chac. Within the tomb at the temple's core, the skeleton was found facing north, surrounded by an assortment of jade, pearls, seashells and stingray spines, the last a symbol of human sacrifice. A reconstruction of the tomb is on show at the site museum. Standing opposite, like a squat version of Temple 1, is **Temple 2**, known as the Temple of the Masks for the two grotesque masks, now heavily eroded, that flank the central stairway. As yet no tomb has been found beneath this temple, which now stands 38m high, although with its roof comb intact it would have equalled Temple 1. It's an easy climb up the staircase to the top.

The **North Acropolis**, which fills the whole north side of the Great Plaza, is one of the most complex structures in the entire Maya world. In true Maya style it was built and rebuilt on top of itself, and beneath the twelve temples that can be seen today are the remains of about a hundred other structures. As early as 100 BC the Maya had constructed elaborate platforms supporting temples and tombs here. Archeologists have removed some of the surface to reveal these earlier structures, including two four-metre-high **masks**. One facing the plaza, protected by a thatched roof, is clearly visible; the other can be reached by following the dark passageway to the side – you'll need a torch. In front of the North Acropolis are two lines of **stelae** with circular altars at their bases, all of which were originally painted a brilliant red.

The Central Acropolis and Temple 5

On the other side of the plaza is the **Central Acropolis**, a maze of tiny interconnecting rooms and stairways built around six smallish courtyards. The buildings here are usually referred to as palaces rather than temples, although their precise use remains a mystery. Possibilities include law courts, temporary retreats, administrative centres, and homes for Tikal's elite. Behind the acropolis is the palace reservoir, which was fed with rainwater by a series of channels from all over the city. Further behind the Central Acropolis is the 58-metre-high **Temple 5**, which supports a single tiny room at the top thought to be a mortuary shrine to an unknown ruler. The temple is currently the subject of a huge restoration project, due to be completed by the year 2000, when the view from the top will be superb, with a great profile of Temple 1 and a side view of the central plaza.

From the West Plaza to Temple 4

Behind Temple 2 is the **West Plaza**, dominated by a large Late Classic temple on the north side, and scattered with various altars and stelae. From here the Tozzer Causeway – one of the raised routes that connected the main parts of the city – leads west to **Temple 3** (55m), covered in jungle vegetation. A fragment of Stela 24, found at the base of the temple, dates it at 810 AD. Around the back of the temple is a huge palace complex, of which only the **Bat Palace** has been restored. At the end of the Tozzer Causeway is **Temple 4**, the tallest of all the Tikal structures at a massive 64m. Built in 741 AD, it is thought by some archeologists to be the resting place of the ruler Coon Chac, whose image was depicted on wooden lintels built into the top of the temple. To reach the top you have to scramble over roots and rubble, and finally up a metal ladder around the side of the pyramid. Slow and exhausting as this is, one of the finest views of the whole site awaits. All around you the forest canopy stretches out to the horizon, interrupted only by the great roof combs of the other temples.

The Mundo Perdido, Plaza of the Seven Temples and Temple of the Inscriptions

To the south of the Central Acropolis, reached by a trail from Temple 3, you'll find the **Plaza of the Seven Temples**, which forms part of a complex dating back to before Christ. There's an unusual triple ball court on the north side of the plaza, and to the east is the unexcavated South Acropolis. To the west, the **Mundo Perdido**, or Lost World, is another magical and very distinct section of the site with its own atmosphere and architecture. Little is known about the ruins in this part of the site, but archeologists hope that further research will help to explain the early history of Tikal. The main feature is the **great pyramid**, a 32-metre-high structure whose surface hides four earlier versions, the first dating from 700 BC. The top of the pyramid offers awesome views towards Temple 4 and the Great Plaza and makes an excellent base for the visual dramatics of sunrise or sunset – minus the crowds.

Finally, there's the **Temple of the Inscriptions**, reached along the Méndez Causeway from the East Plaza behind Temple 1. The temple (only discovered in 1951) is about 1km from the plaza. It's famous for its twelve-metre roof comb, at the back of which is a huge but rather faint hieroglyphic text.

The far north

Away to the north of Tikal, lost in a sea of jungle, are several other substantial **ruins** – unrestored and for the most part uncleared, but with their own unique atmosphere. Twenty-four kilometres north of Tikal, strung out by the side of a disused airstrip, are the village and ruins of **UAXACTÚN**. With a couple of places to stay, several comedores and a daily bus to Santa Elena, the village is an ideal jumping-off point for the more remote sites of **El Zotz, Río Azul** and **El Mirador**, where the bulk of the temples are coated in an anarchic tangles of roots and shoots and only the tallest roof combs are visible. Doubtless in a year or two they'll be reached by road – today **dirt tracks** go as far as Río Azul and El Zotz – but for the moment they remain well beyond the reach of the average visitor. Perfect if you're in search of an adventure and want to see a virtually untouched Maya site.

Uaxactún

Substantially smaller than Tikal, the ruins at **Uaxactún** are thought to date from the same era. During the Preclassic period Uaxactún and Tikal coexisted in relative harmony, dominated by El Mirador, but by the first century AD, with El Mirador in decline, a fierce rivalry ignited between Tikal and Uaxactún. The two finally clashed in 378 AD, when Tikal's warriors conquered Uaxactún, forcing it to accept subordinate status.

The overall impact of Uaxactún may be a little disappointing after the grandeur of Tikal, but for a sense of the forest this is an excellent spot to make for. You'll probably have the site to yourself, giving you the chance to soak up the atmosphere. The most interesting buildings are in **Group E**, east of the airstrip, where three reconstructed temples, built side by side, are arranged to function as an observatory. Viewed from the top of a fourth temple, the sun rises behind the north temple on the longest day of the year and behind the southern one on the shortest day. Beneath one of these temples the famous **E-VII** was unearthed, the oldest building ever found in Petén, probably dating back to 2000 BC. The original pyramid had a simple staircase up the front, flanked by two stucco masks, and post holes in the top suggest that it may have been covered by a thatched shelter. Over on the other side of the airstrip is **Group A**, a series of larger temples and residential compounds, some of them reconstructed, and some impressive stelae.

PRACTICALITIES
A **bus** from Flores passes through Tikal en route for Uaxactún at around 3.30pm; alternatively, you could take one of the **tours** run by a number of companies based in Flores. **Staying overnight** you have three options. The *EcoCampamento* (☎9260077 in Flores) has tents and hammocks, protected by mosquito nets, under a thatched shelter (①–②). The welcoming *Hotel El Chiclero* (③) offers clean rooms without bath; owner Antonio Baldizón organizes 4WD trips to Río Azul, and his wife Neria prepares excellent food. You can camp or sling a hammock for US$2.50 a head. *Tecomate* (①–②) is a similar camping, cabaña and hammock place at the entrance to the village, run by Manuel Soto, who can guide you to any of the more remote Maya sites.

Uaxactún's **guide association** has a small **information office** at the end of the airstrip and will organize **camping trips** to any of the remote northern sites, into the jungle or east to Nakúm and Yaxha. Equipment is carried on horseback and the price (US$30 per person per day for a group of three or more) includes a guide, horses, camping gear and food. Contact CINCAP or ARCAS in Flores for advice.

El Zotz

Thirty kilometres west of Uaxactún, along a rough track not always passable by jeeps, is **El Zotz**, a large Maya site set in its own nature reserve. To **get there** you can rent vehicles in Uaxactún, or hire a pack horse, guide, food and camping equipment from Uaxactún's guide association. After about four hours – almost halfway – you come to **SANTA CRUZ**, where you can camp if necessary. At the site itself you'll be welcomed by the guards who look after the reserve headquarters. You can camp here and, with permission, use their kitchen and drinking water; remember to bring some food to share with the guides.

Totally unrestored and smothered by vegetation, El Zotz has been systematically looted, although there are guards on duty all year. Zotz means "bat" in Maya and each evening at dusk you'll see tens, perhaps hundreds of thousands of **bats** of several species emerge from a cave near the campsite. It's especially impressive in the moonlight, the beating wings sounding like a river flowing over rapids – one of the most remarkable natural sights in Petén.

Walking on, it takes about four and a half hours to get to **CRUCE DOS AGUADAS**, a crossroads village on a bus route to Santa Elena (bus leaves at 7am), where you'll find shops and the *Comedor Patojas*, where they'll let you sling a hammock or camp. Northwards, the road goes to Carmelita for El Mirador and west towards El Perú; not possible in the rainy season).

Río Azul

The remote site of **Río Azul**, almost on the border where Guatemala, Belize and Mexico meet, was discovered in 1962. The city and its suburbs had a population of around five thousand and probably reached a peak in the Preclassic era. Although totally unrestored, the core of the site is similar to a small-scale Tikal, with the tallest temple (AIII) standing some 47m above the forest floor, surfacing above the treetops and giving magnificent views across the jungle.

Several incredible **tombs** have been unearthed here. Tomb 19 is thought to have contained the remains of one of the sons of Stormy Sky, Tikal's great expansionist ruler. Nearby tombs contained bodies of warriors dressed in clothing typical of Teotihuacán in central Mexico – further supporting evidence of links between Tikal and the mighty ancient city. Extensive **looting** occurred after the site's discovery, with a gang of up to eighty men plundering the tombs and removing some of the finest murals in the Maya world once the archeological teams had retreated to Flores in the rainy season. Today there are two resident guards.

The **road** that connects Tikal and Uaxactún continues for another 95km north to Río Azul. This route is only passable in the dry season, and even then it's by no means easy. The three-day round-trip by **jeep** (a day each way and a day at the site) involves frequent stops to clear the road. **Walking** or on **horseback** it's four days each way – three at a push. Trips (around US$300 per person) can be arranged through a number of agents: check with Inguat, CINCAP or ProPetén in Flores, or *Hotel el Chiclero* in Uaxactún. Once you arrive at Río Azul you'll be welcome to **stay** at the guard's camp (bring some supplies) and you may even encounter a lonely group of archeologists.

El Mirador

El Mirador is perhaps the most exotic and mysterious of all Petén's Maya sites. Still buried in the forest, this massive city matches Tikal's scale, and may even surpass it. Rediscovered in 1926, it dates from an earlier period than Tikal, flourishing between 150 BC and 150 AD, and was almost certainly the first great city in the Maya world. It was unquestionably the dominant city in Petén, occupying a commanding position above the rainforest, at an altitude of 250m, and was home to tens of thousands of Maya. Little archeological work has been done here but it's clear that the site represents the peak of Preclassic Maya culture, which was perhaps far more sophisticated than was once believed.

The core of the site covers some sixteen square kilometres, stretching between two massive pyramids that face each other across the forest. The site's western side is marked by the massive **Tigre Complex**, made up of a huge single pyramid flanked by two smaller structures, a triadic design that's characteristic of El Mirador's architecture. The base of this complex alone would cover around three football fields, while the height of the 2000-year-old main pyramid touches 70m, equivalent to an eighteen-storey building and making the structure the tallest anywhere in the Maya world. Heading away to the east, the Puleston Causeway runs to the smaller East Group, the largest of which (about 2km from the Tigre Complex) is the **Danta Complex**. This is another triadic structure, rising in three stages to a height just below that of the Tigre pyramid, but with an even better view since it was built on higher land.

The area **around El Mirador** is riddled with smaller Maya sites, and as you look out across the forest from the top of either of the main temples you can see others rising above the forest canopy on all sides – including the giant Calakmul in Mexico. Among the most accessible are **Nakbé**, 10km south, where a huge Maya mask (5m by 8m), was found in September 1992, and **El Tintal**, around 21km southwest, which you'll pass on your way in from Carmelita.

Getting to El Mirador is a substantial undertaking, involving an arduous 60km pick-up or truck ride north from San Andrés to **Carmelita**, a *chicle* and *xate* gathering centre, followed by two days of hard jungle hiking – you'll need a horse to carry your food and equipment. The trip offers an exceptional chance to see virtually untouched forest, and perhaps some of the creatures that inhabit it. It's essential to bring some supplies for the guards, who spend forty days at a time in the forest, subsisting on beans and tortillas. The journey, impossibly muddy in the rainy season, is best attempted from mid-January to August; February to April is the driest period. Whether you take a tour or go independently, you're advised to examine the information and maps in ProPetén and CINCAP first. ProPetén offers five-day **tours** (around US$200 for two people) from Carmelita to El Mirador, including guide, packhorse and digs in Carmelita – you need to bring your own food and water purification system. It's also possible to travel **independently**, arranging a guide and horse in Carmelita (about US$30 a day), and bringing your own food, water and camping gear. To get to Carmelita, take a bus from Santa Elena to San Andrés (see p.247), then hitch via Cruce Dos Aguadas (see p.256). Check with ProPetén in Flores before setting out – they often have vehicles going to Carmelita. When you arrive at Carmelita ask for Luis Morales, president of the Tourism Committee; he'll arrange guides for the trip.

Sayaxché and around

Southwest of Flores, on a bend in the Río Pasión, the easy-going frontier town of **SAYAXCHÉ** makes an ideal base for exploring the surrounding forest and its huge collection of archeological remains. The town is the supply centre for a vast surrounding area that is being steadily cleared and colonized. The complex network of rivers and swamps that cuts through the forested wilderness here has been an important trade route since Maya times, and there are several interesting ruins in the area. Upstream is **Ceibal**, a small but beautiful site in a wonderful jungle setting; to the south is **Lago de Petexbatún**, on the shores of which are the small ruins of **Dos Pilas** and **Aguateca**. Both sites offer great opportunities to wander in the forest and watch the wildlife.

Sayaxché practicalities

Getting to Sayaxché from Flores is very straightforward, with several Pinita **buses** (6am, 9am, 10am, 1pm and 4pm; 2hr) and one Del Rosio service (5am) plying the fairly smooth 62km dirt road. At other times hitching a ride in a **pick-up** is not too difficult. A ferry takes you over the Río Pasión, directly opposite Sayaxché.

Hotels in Sayaxché are on the basic side. The *Guayacan* (☎9268777; ②), right beside the river, is the best, with lovely sunset views from the terrace. For a cheaper room, head left down the street above the *Guayacan* to the cleanish *Hospedaje Mayapan* (①), where you may be able to rent a **bike** for visiting Ceibal. There are plenty of reasonable places to **eat**, the best being the *Restaurant Yaxkin* which is a little pricey though the portions are huge (closes 8pm). There is also a restaurant at the *Guayacan*. *La Montaña* is another option, owned by the knowledgeable and helpful Julián Mariona, who can arrange **trips** to the nearby ruins. Plenty of **boatmen** are eager to take you up or downriver, though they tend to see all tourists as walking cash-dispensers and quote prices in dollars. Try Pedro Mendez Requena, of Viajes Don Pedro (☎ & fax 9286109), who offers **tours** of the area from his office on the riverfront. You can change travellers' cheques at Banora, a block up from the *Guayacan*.

The ruins of Ceibal

The most accessible and impressive of the sites near Sayaxché is **Ceibal**, which you can reach by land or river. It's easy enough to make it there and back in an afternoon **by boat**; haggle with the boatmen at the waterfront and you can expect pay around US$40. The boat trip is followed by a short walk through towering rainforest. **By road**, Ceibal is just 17km from Sayaxché. Any transport heading south out of town passes the entrance track to the site, from where it's an 8km walk through the jungle to the ruins.

Surrounded by forest and shaded by huge ceiba trees, **the ruins** of Ceibal are a mixture of cleared open plazas and untamed jungle. Though many of the largest temples lie buried under mounds, Ceibal does have some outstanding carving, well preserved by the use of hard stone: the two main plazas are dotted with lovely **stelae**, centred around two low platforms. During the Classic period Ceibal was a relatively minor site, but it grew rapidly between 830 and 930 AD, apparently after falling under the control of colonists from what is now Mexico. Outside influence is clearly visible in the carving here: speech scrolls, straight noses, waist-length hair and serpent motifs are all decidédly non-Maya. The monkey-faced Stela 2 is particularly striking, beyond which is Stela 14, another impressive sculpture straight ahead down the path. If you turn right here and walk for ten minutes you'll reach the only other restored part of the site, set superbly in a clearing in the forest – an unmissable massive circular stone platform which was either an altar or **observation** deck for astronomy.

Lago de Petexbatún: Aguateca and Dos Pilas

A similar distance to the south of Sayaxché is **Lago de Petexbatún**, a spectacular expanse of water ringed by dense forest and containing plentiful supplies of snook, bass, alligator and freshwater turtle. The shores of the lake abound with wildlife and Maya remains and, though the ruins themselves are small and unrestored, their sheer number suggests that the lake was an important trading centre for the Maya. **Aguateca**, perched on a high outcrop at the southern tip of the lake, is the furthest away from Sayaxché but the most accessible site, as a boat can get you to within twenty minutes' walk of the ruins. Surrounded by dense tropical forest and with superb views of the lake, it has a magical atmosphere. You can clearly make out the temples and plazas, dotted with well-preserved stelae. The carving is superbly executed, the images including rulers, captives, hummingbirds, pineapples and pelicans. The guards that live here may give you a well-informed tour of the site.

A slightly closer (and therefore cheaper) option is **Dos Pilas**, another unreconstructed site, buried in the jungle a little way west of the lake. Dos Pilas was the centre of a formidable empire in the early part of the eighth century, with a population of around ten thousand. The ruins, while exhausting to reach, are quite unusual, as the major structures are grouped in an east–west linear pattern. Around the central plaza are some tremendous stelae, altars and four **hieroglyphic stairways** decorated with glyphs and figures.

From Sayaxché, you need to take a 45-minute speedboat trip to *Rancho El Caribe*, at the northern tip of the lake, from where it's a further 12km on foot to the ruins. About 7km from the lake you pass the small site of **Arroyo de Piedra**, where you'll find a plaza and two fairly well preserved stelae. It's cheapest to **stay** at the sites themselves, camping or sleeping in a hammock, although the *Posada Caribe* (☎ & fax 9286114; full board ⑦) offers an alternative of clean, screened cabins, reasonable food and boat trips to Aguateca; negotiate rates in advance. It may be possible to get to both sites **by mule** (or even truck) during the dry months.

Routes to Mexico and Belize

There are a number of possible routes **into Mexico** from Petén, all of which offer a sense of adventure, a glimpse of the rainforest and involve shuttling between buses, boats and immigration posts. It's worth noting that, in mid-1998, Mexican border officials were only giving two-week visas to travellers entering the state of Chiapas from Guatemala, due to the armed conflict in the region. Getting to **Belize** is much more straightforward, with numerous daily buses connecting Flores with the border at Melchor de Mencos and good bus services onward on the Belizean side.

From Sayaxché to Benemérito

Downriver from Sayaxché the **Río Pasión** snakes its way through an area of forest, swamp and small settlements to **Pipiles,** which marks the point where the rivers Salinas and Pasión merge to form the Usumacinta. All boats stop here for **immigration** and you can get your exit stamp. Not far from Pipiles is the small Maya site of **Altar de los Sacrificios**, commanding an important river junction. This is one of the oldest sites in Petén, but these days there's not much to see beyond a solitary stela. Following the Usumacinta downstream you arrive at **BENEMÉRITO** in Mexico, a sprawling frontier town at the end of a dirt road from Palenque. The eight-hour trip costs around US$8–10, though cargo boats can take a couple of days to get this far. There are basic hotels and restaurants in Benemérito and you can head on to Yaxchilán from here directly by boat or, much cheaper, by bus to Frontera Corozal (where there are basic beds and camping) and then by boat. **Buses** leave Benemérito for Palenque (9hr) at least five times a day; make sure you stop at **Mexican immigration** for your tourist card.

From Bethel to Frontera Corozal

Currently the cheapest and most straightforward route to Mexico is along the rough road to **BETHEL** on the Río Usumacinta, where there is a new Guatemalan **immigration** post. Two buses a day leave Flores for Bethel (5am & 1pm; 4hr), passing the junction north of Sayaxché about a couple of hours later. At Bethel it's relatively easy to find a *lancha* heading downstream, or you can rent one (US$25 to Frontera Corozal; 30min). If you need to stay, Bethel itself is a pleasant village where you can **camp** above the riverbank and there are several **comedores** and shops. The **Bethel ruins**, 1.5km from the village, are today little more than tree-covered mounds, but there's an excellent **eco-campamento** here called the *Posada Maya*, with tents (including mattresses and clean sheets) under thatched shelters (②) or hammocks (①) on top of a wooded cliff high above the river. Over the border in Frontera Corozal there is an **immigration post**, plus comedores and very basic hotels. From Frontera Corozal there are fairly regular **buses** and shared minibuses to Palenque until 3pm (4hr).

For further adventure, the spectacular ruins of **Yaxchilán**, grouped around a great loop in the Usumacinta are 15km away; **hiring a boat** for the beautiful trip costs around US$60 return. Even further downstream from Yaxchilán are some of the most remote and inaccessible ruins in all Guatemala, **Piedras Negras**. Despite being possibly as extensive as Tikal, this is one of the least visited of all Maya sites. The official tour operator for **rafting trips** down the Usumacinta to Piedras Negras is the highly recommended Maya Expeditions, based in Guatemala City (☎3634955, fax 3374666; *mayaexp@guate.net*).

El Naranjo to La Palma

Another popular route into Mexico takes you from Flores by a bad road to **EL NARANJO** (several buses a day until 2.30pm; 4–5hr). El Naranjo is a rough spot, consisting of little more than an army base, an **immigration** post where you'll be asked for a US$5 "leaving tax", stores (offering poor exchange rates), comedores and basic hotels. The best place to stay is the friendly, family-run *Posada San Pedro*, across the river (☎9261276 in Flores; ④). The other places in town are pretty filthy. The river trip down the San Pedro starts here; there's usually a **boat** (US$25 per person; 4hr) for Mexico at around 1pm, returning from La Palma at 8am. Your first port of call is the Mexican immigration post, about an hour away, and beyond that is the small riverside village of **LA PALMA** in Mexico. La Palma is a a good transport hub with basic rooms to rent at the *Parador Turistico* and bus connections to Tenosique (last bus 5pm). Entering Guatemala from La Palma, the bus to Flores leaves from immigration in El Naranjo at about 2pm.

From Flores to Belize

The hundred kilometres from Flores to the Belizean border at Melchor de Mencos (3hr) takes you through another sparsely inhabited section of Petén. **Buses** leave from the *Hotel San Juan* in Santa Elena at 5am, 8am and 11am, and *Rosita* buses from the market at 5am, 7am, 9.30am, 11am, 2pm, 3pm and 6pm. Set out early in order to get to San Ignacio or Belize City the same day (at 5am to reach Chetumal, in Mexico). All the buses pass the Puente Ixlú junction halfway between Tikal and Flores. Linea Dorada/Mundo Maya also operate a 5am **express service** to Belize City (5hr; US$20) and on to Chetumal (8hr; US$30), leaving from their offices on C Principal in Santa Elena. More than twice as expensive as the public bus, this service is quicker and connects with services in Chetumal to Cancún. The *Hotel San Juan* operates a similar service.

Lago de Yaxhá and the ruins of Nakúm

About halfway between Puente Ixlú and the border is **Lago de Yaxhá**, a shallow limestone depression ringed by dense rainforest and home to two Maya sites. The lake is a sweltering two-hour walk from the main Flores–Belize road. The track heads to the right towards a *finca*, but to make it to the atmospheric **ruins of Yaxhá** you want to bear off to the left, along a smaller track. The ruins, rediscovered in 1904, are spread out across nine plazas. Clearing and restoration work has only recently begun, so don't expect any of the manicured splendour of Tikal. **Topoxte**, another small site on the lakeshore, is not particularly impressive, but very unusual in that everything is built on a miniature scale, including tiny temples and stelae. You can **stay** at the wonderful *El Sombrero Eco-Campamento* (☎9265299, fax 9265198; in Guatemala City ☎4482428; in San Ignacio, Belize ☎092/3508; ④), on the south side of the lake is a solar-powered jungle lodge with space for **camping** (①). Boat and horseback trips can be organized and there's a library of books on wildlife and the Maya, though meals are on the pricey side. There's also free camping on the far side of the lake beneath a thatched shelter.

The unrestored **ruins of Nakúm**, a somewhat larger site, are about 20km north of Lago de Yaxhá, though the road is rarely passable so you'll probably have to walk. The most impressive structure is the residential-style palace, which has forty rooms and is similar to the North Acropolis at Tikal. There are two guards here who will show you where to camp or sling a hammock. It's also possible to **walk to Tikal** in a day from Nakúm (around 25km) though you'll need to persuade a guard to act as a **guide**, or bring one with you – speak to Inguat or see CINCAP in Flores.

The border: Melchor de Mencos

Despite the differences between Guatemala and Belize, border formalities are fairly straightforward; you have to pay a small departure tax on leaving Guatemala. **Money changers** will pester you on either side of the border and give a fair rate. There's also a **bank** (Mon–Fri 8.30am–2pm) just beyond the immigration building, next to the *Hotel Frontera Palace* (☎ & fax 9265196; ④), which has rooms in pleasant thatched cabins, hot water and a restaurant.

Buses leave **for Belize City** every hour or so (3hr) right from the border. Indeed, most actually begin their journey from the market in Melchor; for other destinations you may have to take a shared taxi to Benque Viejo or to San Ignacio (US$2 per person; 20min).

travel details

BUSES

Flores to: Belize City (2 daily; 5hr); Bethel (2 daily; 5hr); Chetumal (2 daily; 9hr); Cruce del Pato (2 daily; 4hr); El Naranjo (8 daily; 4–5hr); Guatemala City (around 20 daily; 10–15hr); Melchor de Menchos, Belizean border (10 daily; 3hr); Río Dulce (around 20 daily; 10–15hr); Sayaxché (7 daily; 2hr); Tikal (1 daily at 1pm, 2hr; plus innumerable private minibuses, 1hr); Uaxactún (1 daily; 3hr).

Poptún to: Flores (around 20 daily; 2hr); Río Dulce (around 20 daily; 2hr 30min).

Sayaxché to: Cruce de Pato (2 daily; 2 hr); Flores (7 daily; 2hr).

Tikal to: Flores (1 daily, 2hr; plus minibuses, 1hr). Uaxactún (1 daily; 3hr).

BOATS

From **Flores/San Benito** to San Andrés, boats leave when full, in daylight hours only (25min).

From **El Naranjo** to La Palma in Mexico there's a daily boat at 1pm.

From **Sayaxché** to Benemérito, Mexico, a trading boat leaves most days (at least 12hr); rented speedboats take 2hr 30min–3hr. There's also a daily boat to Rancho el Caribe on the Río Petexbatún (2hr).

FLIGHTS

From **Flores** there are at least 5 flights a day to Guatemala City (50min), plus international services to Belize City (daily), Cancún (5 a week) and Palenque and Chetumal (both 3 a week).

You can also charter flights to Uaxactún, Dos Lagunas, El Naranjo, Sayaxché, Poptún, Río Dulce, Lívingston and to the Honduras border.

PART FOUR

EL SALVADOR

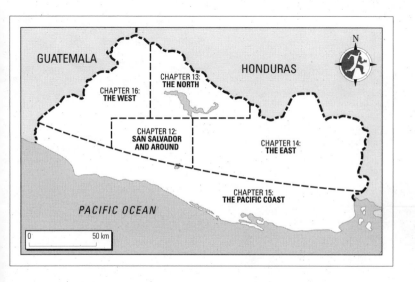

Introduction

The smallest country in Central America, tucked along the Pacific edge of the isthmus, **El Salvador** is chiefly remembered for the devastating civil war of the 1980s, when streams of harrowing news brought this tiny country to the attention of the world. Throughout the lost decade, atrocity followed atrocity in a seemingly unstoppable rise. Then in 1992, with both sides having fought each other to a standstill, peace accords were signed, and the attention of the world's press moved elsewhere. Left behind was a country faced with the immense task of rebuilding itself.

Today, few tourists visit El Salvador, most would-be visitors deterred by the half-remembered headlines and the country's reputation for violence, danger and difficulty. Those that do make it here, however, are well rewarded by the sheer **physical beauty** of the place. There are relatively few museums or buildings of note to visit. Those that have survived numerous earthquakes and the ravages of civil war – such as San Salvador's Palacio Nacional – are currently, interminably, under repair and closed to the public. It's the impact of El Salvador's awesome landscape and its vivid colours and forms that stays in the memory: lush, tropical Pacific lowlands sweeping up through fertile hills to rugged mountain chains, and the majestic cones of towering extinct volcanos, their lower slopes densely shrouded with the glistening green leaves of coffee plantations.

As in Nicaragua, another country both pulled apart and defined by a decade of civil war, travelling in El Salvador brings you into contact with some of the most engaging and interesting **people** in the region. With a well-deserved reputation for hard work and business acumen, El Salvadoreans – predominantly *mestizo* – live life with a vigour that's hard to match. That said, however, as the people here slowly find ways to come terms with their brutal past and uncertain future, some residual hostility to foreigners – particularly Americans – remains, and initial reactions to tourists can be, on occasion, cool. If you persist, however, in the face of what may seem like outright hostility, and make an effort to speak Spanish, you will find that people begin to unbend and bring you into their lives. They may or may not be willing to talk about the civil war. Many aren't. What is important now is the future, and this El Salvadoreans approach with an infectious sardonic humour, designed to lessen the travails of daily life, the corruption of government and everything else that seems insurmountable.

Perhaps unsurprisingly, **tourist infrastructure** is at times sorely lacking. This is not the country for those who like everything on tap, and there's little luxury outside the cities. One feature particular to El Salvador is its network of government-run tourist centres or **turicentros**. Aimed more at locals than tourists, these provide bathing, eating and recreation facilities in areas of natural beauty. Some, like Los Chorros, just outside San Salvador, provide a convenient way to take advantage of natural facilities safely and comfortably. Others, however, such as the one on the beach at La Libertad, are run down and pale in comparison to the stretches of beach that can be enjoyed for free a few kilometres up and down the coast.

Travelling around El Salvador is a lesson in humility. Contrasting with the vibrant colour and sweep of the landscape the overwhelming evidence of the endemic **poverty** and social divisions that sparked the conflict in the first place hits you right between the eyes. While economic growth has stabilized since the peace accords, its benefits have yet to trickle down to the majority of the population. From the muddy shanty towns of San Salvador to the broken down shacks in the countryside, many people live in squalor, eking out a living selling fruit, sweets, household goods and sundry odds and ends on the street. In addition, the ever-growing population – at 5.7m, the highest density in Central America – is placing unprecedented pressure on the country's **natural resources**; hillsides that only a few decades ago supported dense woodlands are being stripped bare at an alarming rate. And while political violence is now a thing of the past, **civil violence** is growing to alarming proportions. Guns are common, and people use them. The casual visitor is unlikely to be directly affected by this, but you can't ignore the underlying sense of tension.

■ Where to go

San Salvador is for many among one of the worst cities in Central America, with a high crime rate and tangible sense of menace. On the plus side are a thriving nightlife, easily matching that to be found in more amenable cities, and facilities and services unavailable elsewhere in the country. For beaches, swimming and sun you don't have to stray too far from the capital, to the

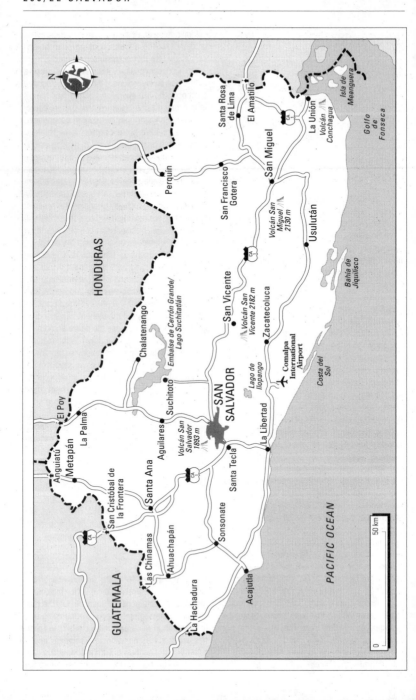

crater lake of **Ilopango** or, an hour's journey away, the small Pacific coast resort of **La Libertad**. Also within easy reach are the small Maya ruins of **San Andrés** and **Joya de Ceren**, which, although they pale visually in comparison to sites in Guatemala – El Salvador was at the furthest fringe of the Maya culture – are nonetheless important. Joya, in particular – a World Heritage Site – gives the most complete picture yet of what daily village life was like in Maya times.

Western El Salvador is the most relaxing and perhaps most scenic part of the country, with the lovely, faded old colonial city of **Ahuachapán** making a convenient entry point from Guatemala, and the laid-back city of **Santa Ana** making a good alternative to San Salvador as a place to stay a few nights. In addition to the Maya ruins of **Tazumal** there are the exquisite cloud forests of **Cerro Verde** and **Montecristo**, bursting with exotic plants and wildlife.

For something slightly more energetic, the volcanic peaks of **Izalco**, **Volcán Santa Ana** and **Cerro Verde** provide great hiking in a variety of geological environments; nestling at their base is the crater lake of **Coatepeque**, whose deep blue waters are perfect for snorkelling or swimming.

The **north** and **east** of El Salvador, though rough and wild, and less accommodating to travellers, hold a number of attractions to make the effort of a trip worthwhile: chiefly the moving and thought-provoking civil war museum at **Perquín**, and what is considered to be the finest colonial town in the country at **Suchitoto**. **La Palma** and **Concepción Quezaltepeque** are famous for their artesenías, producing wooden handicrafts and hammocks, while the small city of **San Vicente** is an enjoyable base for trips to the volcano of **Chinchontepec** and the lagunas of **Apastepeque** and **Ciega**. The larger city of **San Miguel** hosts one of the largest carnivals in Central America each November, drawing visitors from all over the country and beyond.

Up and down the glorious sweep of the **Pacific coast** lie long, palm-fringed stretches of beach, the most beautiful (and remote) of which are **Barra de Santiago** and **Los Espinos**. As you head east down the Pacific shore you come to the mangrove swamps and islands of the beautiful **Bahía de Jiquilisco**, while still further down the coast lie the untouched and idyllic islands of **Meanguera** and **Conchagüita** in the Golfo de Fonseca.

■ When to go

The best time to visit El Salvador is during the **dry season** from November to February. Though temperatures reach a high of around 30°C – and in the coastal lowlands, it feels much hotter because of the humidity – it's easiest to get around at this time and even the backroads are accessible. Towards the end of the dry season, however, in March and April, temperatures increase to around 34°C and, in the lowlands, can feel unbearable. During the **wet season** – May to October – the heat and humidity are relieved by daily downpours, though these rarely last for more than a couple of hours, and there are spectacular lightning storms in the mountains around San Salvador. Travel is difficult, as mud roads in the back country become successively more impassable. Sometimes, between September to November, El Salvador is affected by the tail end of **hurricanes** out in the Pacific; when this happens, the rain can last for days, and cities begin to flood. Whatever the season, the climate is coolest in the **mountains**, where temperatures are moderated by altitude, being far fresher by day and cool at night.

Getting around

The best way to get around El Salvador is **by bus**. Short distances (the longest journey you're likely to take in one stretch, from San Salvador to La Palma for example, is around four hours), and relatively good main highways mean that the few **internal flights** that do exist (on private or military flights) are far more trouble than they're worth.

■ Buses

Though hundreds of companies operate **buses** to everywhere from everywhere every few minutes during daylight hours, on the back roads you do have to plan ahead a little to avoid getting stuck in the middle of nowhere for hours (or even overnight). Though ideally you should confirm what time the buses leave as soon as you get to a place, printed **timetables** – if they exist at all – are only adhered to if the weather is good. If roads are bad because of rain, everything gets delayed. Except for routes to the cities in the east there is only one **class** of bus – and everyone travels on it. It's much easier to cope if you have small bags; larger luggage gets thrown in a heap at the back or, occasionally, on the roof. Buses can

GETTING AROUND EL SALVADOREAN CITIES

Orientation in El Salvadorean cities is initially confusing but logical. Streets running north–south are **avenidas**; those running east–west are **calles**. The main avenida and calle will be named (along with a few of the others) and the heart of any city is at their intersection. North or south of this intersection avenidas are Norte or Sur, while east or west calles are Oriente or Poniente. Avenidas lying to the east of the main avenida are numbered evenly, increasing the further out you go; west of the main avenida, the numbers are odd. Similarly, calles have even numbers south of the main calle and odd numbers to the north. Named avenidas/calles sometimes (not always) change name either side of the intersection.

Addresses can be given either as the street name/number, followed by the building number, or as the intersection of two streets. So: "12a C Pte #2330, Col Flor Blanca" is number 2330, 12a Calle Poniente in the district (colonia) of Flor Blanca, while "10a Av Sur y 3a C Pte" is the intersection of 10a Avenida Sur and 3a Calle Poniente.

be **hailed** at the side of the road, and you can get off at virtually any point. Tickets are bought on board; at stations simply turn up a few minutes before it's due to leave, longer if you want to guarantee a seat. Buses are extremely **cheap**; from San Salvador to Santa Ana (2hr 30min), costs just US$0.80, while San Salvador to Santa Rosa de Lima by fast bus (around 3hr 30min), will cost around US$2.20.

Virtually every town has departures to San Salvador; if you're trying to reach somewhere small *from* the capital, however, it's usually quicker to go to the nearest major town and change. Heading **east** to San Miguel, Santa Rosa de Lima and La Unión the direct ("directo") buses are marginally more comfortable and make fewer stops, knocking about an hour off the standard journey.

■ Taxis

Taxis in El Salvador are yellow, painted with black numbers and a "taxi" sign. They can be hailed anywhere on the street – in fact, they usually see you and honk before you see them – and also tend to congregate in the main square and around bus stations in towns and cities. **Fares** should be fixed before you set off. Expect to pay US$2–5 in a city. Anything anything upwards of US$30 might be considered suitable for a half-day driving around the countryside, which is a good way to see some of the remoter spots if you're in a hurry or don't want to wait for a bus. **Tipping** is not usual unless you've rented the taxi for the day.

■ Driving and hitching

Driving in El Salvador is relatively straightforward on the major roads and a perfect way to reach some of the more inaccessible beaches along the Pacific coast. There are **filling stations** in every town and at most major highway junctions, and no road is so long that you should have to worry about running out of fuel. Finding parts for US and Japanese models is not usually a problem if you have your own car. However, some back roads become impassable at times during the rainy season, even to 4WD; ask locally about conditions before you set off. More worrying is the recent increase in **hold-ups** of private cars on quieter roads; keep an eye on the latest news if in doubt seek police advice. In cities thefts, particularly of newer models, are common, and it's wise to leave your car in a guarded or locked car park. **Car rental** prices are on a par with those in the west; from US$35 a day for a small, family car and from US$90 a day for a jeep. See p.294 for a list of **rental companies** in San Salvador.

Hitching is common in remote areas where any passing vehicle is fair game. However, it should not be done unless you feel extremely comfortable with the area you're in. Armed hold-ups are not unknown, especially in the northern departments of Chalatenango and it is automatically assumed that foreigners have something of value to steal. If you do hitch, it is polite to offer payment – about the same as the bus fare – for the journey.

■ Cycling

Cycling is an extremely common way of getting around and even the smallest of places usually has a repair shop. Mountain bikes, in particular, can take you to places that even the buses don't reach. The main highways, however, can be more than slightly nervewracking for those on two wheels; you might want to consider putting them on top of a bus for sections of your journey. Unfortunately there are no formal places to **rent bicycles** from; your only option is to do a private deal with someone local.

Costs, money and banks

El Salvador's currency is the **colón**, occasionally called the **peso**, and divided into 100 centavos. There are coins of 5c, 10c, 25c and 1 colón and banknotes of 5, 10, 25, 50 and 100 colones.

■ Exchange and banks

Outside the top end hotels and restaurants, the best way to pay is in **cash**. Travellers' cheques are not widely recognized, especially outside the capital, and can only be changed in banks. You must have your proof of purchase. Cash dollars are accepted pretty much everywhere. **Banks** and casas de cambio give the same rate of exchange; the cheapest way to get money is to withdraw colones on a credit or debit card (Visa or Mastercard). There are no ATMs for foreign-issued cards. **Opening hours** for banks are 8.30 or 9am until 4 or 5pm, and some of them close for an hour at lunch. Casas de cambio, which exist in San Salvador, Santa Ana and San Miguel are open daily from 9am until about 5pm. Now that there is no longer a black market, **money changers** are only really in evidence at borders, where you should change only enough to see you through until you can get to a bank.

■ Costs

Day to day living is, for foreigners at least, very cheap in El Salvador. With an **exchange rate** of 8 colones to US$1, a cup of coffee will cost US$0.25–60, while a soft drink will be US$0.50 and fresh juice US$1. Cigarettes are around US$1.40, while a meal in an ordinary cafe will set you back around US$2–3. Also very good value are **bus fares** (see above).

In expensive hotels and restaurants, service charges and **taxes** are added to the bill automatically; room taxes are 13 percent while service charges are 7 to 10 percent. If you're spending less than around US$30 a night for a room however, the tax is usually not charged. There is no entry tax, and **exit tax** (US$20) only applies when flying out.

Information

The helpful government organization **Corsatur**, at Blvd del Hipodrome #508, Col San Benito, San Salvador (Mon–Fri 8am–noon & 1.30–5pm; ☎243 7836) has a useful bi-lingual guide *Destination El Salvador* which gives an overview of what there is to see. They can also provide information (Spanish only) on archeological sites in the country.

The **Instituto Salvadoreño de Turismo** (ISTU), C Ruben Darío, 9a–11a Av Sur, San Salvador (Mon–Fri 8am–4pm, Sat 8am–noon; ☎222 8000) has responsibility for some of the national parks and the network of turicentros.

There are no tourist offices **outside the capital**, and the concept of independent tourism is little understood. If you have any questions, head for the largest and most expensive hotel, or strike up a conversation with a taxi driver.

Accommodation

The widest choice of **accommodation** is, inevitably, in San Salvador. Elsewhere, the choice narrows and, occasionally you'll find nothing between extreme luxury and total dives. Many hotels will be busy **around Easter Week** and **Christmas** and/or at the time of a large festival; at these times it's worth ringing ahead to confirm there is a room. When you turn up, always ask to see more than one room, and if you're staying for a few days ask if there is a discount. Many hotels also have multi-bed rooms, which can cut costs a lot if you're travelling in a group.

Almost all places, however simple, that offer private baths will also provide towels and soap. Spend a little more, and you'll be amazed at the number of places that start offering extras like TV, although hot water for the large part remains wishful thinking. An essential in any part of the country is a fan to keep the heat and insects at bay; mosquito nets are not provided, so especially when travelling along the coast, carry some coils with you.

In **San Salvador**, where the cheapest rooms are located in the worst and most dangerous part of town, you'll need to pay at least US$10, probably more, for somewhere clean and secure. The top of the range places – the Camino Real, the Alameda and others – have everything you would expect; soft lighting, room service, cocktail bars and piped music swirling along the carpeted corridors.

Outside the capital, top of the range hotels are relatively few and far between, although there are a good number of comfortable places to stay. In general, expect to pay at least US$5 for an acceptable double room, rising to around US$10 with private bath.

Camping (and hammock-slinging) is possible on many beaches, but the only formal provision elsewhere is in the parks of Cerro Verde and Montecristo. Hiking in the mountains may also throw up some possibilities, but ask for local advice on safety in the area before you go, and get permission from the landowner. Note, too that sudden downpours are common and, in the winter, can last for hours.

Eating and drinking

Refined cooking is not one of El Salvador's strong points, although there are a few exceptions, with gourmet cuisine available in San Salvador and smart restaurants serving excellently prepared local dishes in the provincial cities. Most local people, however, eat in **comedores**, the ubiquitous café, where you can get a nutritious and substantial meal for around US$2–3. The cleanliness of these places varies, as does the quality of the food; if in doubt, choose one that's busy.

The main meal of the day is **lunch**; generally, unless it's a fiesta, people do not eat out a lot and places close relatively early; around 9pm. Only in the cities, and mostly at weekends, will restaurants be full and stay open late.

■ What to eat

Everywhere you will find the mainstay of life, the *pupuseria*, serving **pupusas**, the national snack. These are small tortillas filled with cheese, beans, meat or a mixture, cooked on a hot plate and served with chopped, pickled cabbage and carrots. *Pupuserias* range from the humble street corner grill to huge, barn-like places filled with families at the weekends;

most of them, however, only start serving from the late afternoon onwards.

In addition to pupusas, other El Salvadorean **specialities** include *mariscada*, seafood in a creamy base; *tamales*, maize dough surrounding meat or chicken and boiled in a leaf; and *ceviche*, raw, marinated fish. *Panes con pavo* are bread-rolls filled with turkey and served with salad; many restaurants specialize in these alone, and *sopa de frijoles* is black or red bean soup, often a meal in itself. *Bocas* are small appetizers – often meat and/or pickles and vegetables – served with drinks or before a meal.

Everywhere across the country are US-style **fast-food** outlets or the Central American equivalents. **Chinese** and **Tex-Mex** restaurants are reasonably common, as well as **Italian** places in the larger cities; the authenticity of these, however, varies.

So far, El Salvador has not been struck by the cholera epidemic. If freshly cooked in front of you, **street food** is generally safe to eat. However, street cleanliness is generally far lower than elsewhere, and there is a lot of dust and dirt in the air – so be warned.

■ Drinking

As for **drinks**, locally-produced **coffee** is very good, usually drunk black and strong at breakfast and with an afternoon snack of *tamales*. In small villages it will be served *lista*, boiled up with sugar cane and surprisingly tasty. El Salvador's abundance of tropical fruits go to make delicious **juices** in the form of *jugos*, *licuados* and *frescos*. *Jugos* are pure juices, most commonly made of orange, papaya, pinapple and melon. *Licuados* (sometimes called *batidos*), blend the fruit juice with milk and ice, while *frescos* are a fruit-based, sweet drink, made up in bulk and served with lunch or dinner. Unless you ask otherwise, sugar will be added to *jugos* and *licuados*. **Horchata**, another favourite, is a rather heavy milk drink with a base of rice, sweetened with sugar and cinnamon.

The usual international brand **soft drinks** are available as well as local alternatives, the most popular of which is the El Salvador-made *Kolashanpan*. **Water** is safe to drink in San Salvador only; elsewhere check that the water and ice used in drinks is purified. Bottled mineral water is available almost everywhere, as are bags of pure spring water and most hotels provide drinking water. The three locally-made **beers** are *Pilsener* (light), *Golden Light* (very light) and *Suprema*, while *Aguardiente* is sugarcane **liquor**, production of which is controlled by the government, sold through licensed outlets called *expendios*.

Opening hours, holidays and festivals

Opening hours throughout the country tend to vary, but the big cities and major towns generally get going quite early in the morning with government offices working from 8am to 4pm and most banks and businesses from 8.30/9am to 5/5.30pm. Some close for an hour at lunch, some don't; **archelogical sites** are usually closed on Monday. Generally, **banks** are open from 8.30 or 9am until 4/4.30/5pm; some close for an hour at lunch.

On **national holidays**, everything will be shut, with some businesses also closing on the day of local fiestas.

PUBLIC HOLIDAYS	
Jan 1	New Year's Day
Mar–Apr	Easter (3 days)
May 1	Labour Day
Aug 3–6	El Salvador del Mundo
Sept 15	Independence Day
Oct 12	Discovery of America Day
Nov 2	Day of the Dead
Dec 25	Christmas Day

All towns and villages have their **fiestas patronales**, commemorating the local saint. The quality of these varies wildly, with some lasting only a day and some, like those at San Miguel (see p.309) and Sonsonate (see p.320) lasting weeks and encompassing a programme of arts and other events. Most commonly, the fiesta is a time for relaxation and holiday-making; large amounts of alcohol are consumed and towards the late evening things can get rather wild. Generally the last day will be the main event.

Mail and telecommunications

Letters from San Salvador generally take about one week to the US and nine or so days to Europe. The **main post office** in San Salvador (see p.295)

LOCAL FIESTAS

Jan 8–15
Cristo Negro, Juayúa

Jan 12–21
La Inmaculada Virgen de Concepción, Cojutepeque

Jan 25–Feb 2
Virgen de la Candelaría, Sonsonate

1st week of Feb
Dulce Nombre de Jesús, Ahuachapán

3rd week in Feb
Dulce Nombre de María, La Palma

2nd Sun in May
Las Palmas, Panchimalco

July 1–26
Nuestra Señora de Santa Ana, Santa Ana

Aug 1–6
Fiesta al Divino Salvador del Mundo, San Salvador; on Aug 5 a carved image of El Salvador

del Mundo winds through the city at the head of a large procession that ends up at the cathedral

Sept 12–14
Santa Cruz de Roma, Panchimalco

Sept 15
Independence Day, San Salvador; civil and military parades, flypasts and fireworks

Nov 14–30
Virgen de la Paz, San Miguel

Nov 26
Nuestra Señora de los Pobres, Zacatecoluca

Dec 12
Virgen de Guadalupe, San Salvador; processions around the Basílica de Guadalupe to honour the Virgin Morena

Dec 12–31
San Vicente Abad y Mártir, San Vicente

is open Mon–Fri 8am–5pm and Sat 8am–noon; it does offer a parcel service, but if sending anything of value it's recommended to use one of the **courier services**. The safest place to **receive letters** is at the *Lista de Correos* (window 12) of the main post office; alternatively, there is the *American Express* office (see p.294) and some embassies hold mail addressed to their citizens. Post offices in **smaller cities** and towns keep the same hours as in the capital, but letters take longer to get to their destinations from these, and they are not recommended as places to receive mail.

Antel, the national phone company, has an office in every town from where it is possible to make local, long-distance and international calls; all offices are open daily from 6am to 10pm. Reverse charge (collect) calls are possible to the US, but not to the UK. A three-minute minimum call to Europe costs about US$8, and direct dial services are available to the US (AT&T, MCI, Sprint). The **telephone area code** for the whole of El Salvador is ☎503.

Public phone booths (with blue hoods) are common, although they don't always work and you can't make international calls from them. Rates for local calls are the same at Antel offices; they take 25 centavo and 1 colon pieces.

Faxes can be sent from Antel offices, and all hotels with a fax will usually transmit one for you, though at a considerable premium. They also may charge for receiving faxes.

The only public access to **email** is the *Cyber Café*, Av Río Lempa 18, Jardines de Guadalupe, San Salvador (*flara@enlinea.com.sv*).

The media

There are four daily **national newspapers** in El Salvador, plus a couple of smaller regional ones. *La Prensa Graficia* and *El Diario de Hoy* are morning papers, both very widely read and both very conservative, although with full coverage of regional and international affairs; their Sunday supplements (which come out on Saturday) are good on arts and cultural events. *El Mundo* and *Diario Latino* are smaller afternoon papers with a moderate stance; *CoLatino*, which also comes out in the afternoon, is the most left-wing. *Tendencias* is a liberal monthly magazine with in-depth analysis of political and social affairs. Daily papers are sold everywhere on the streets. The bigger hotels stock US newspapers and magazines, and the embassies have copies of papers from their particular country.

There are seven national **television stations** and numerous cable channels, showing programmes from South America, CNN and CNN En Español, and films. Over 70 **radio stations**, including Radio Venceremos (owned by the FMLN), transmit rock, Latin sounds and religious programming. The BBC World Service can be picked up in El Salvador on 15220, 12095 and 9915 kHz (shortwave).

Shopping

El Salvador produces a number of instantly recognizable **artesanías**: chiefly the brightly-painted, naive style wood and ceramics from La Palma; hammocks from Concepción Quezaltepeque, and interesting ceramics at Ilobasco. These are far cheaper in their place of origin, but the **Mercado des Artesanías** in San Salvador has an extensive selection of goods from across the country at reasonable prices; a number of more expensive shops around town also carry smaller selections. Hammocks are usually also for sale in the parque central in San Salvador every day.

For everyday goods, almost anything you could want to buy is available. The outlets in the **malls** of San Salvador and San Miguel sell US clothing at US prices. For something a little more down to earth, look no further than the local **market**; each town has one, usually every day, selling clothing, fresh fruit, vegetables and hundreds of things more besides. Larger towns also usually have a **supermarket**, the two biggest chains being *Multi Mart* and *Superselectos*, which are good for imported toiletries, again at a price.

Safety and the police

Sadly, given the beauty of the country and the character of the people, El Salvador can be – if you are extremely unlucky – a **dangerous** place to travel. Since the signing of the peace accords in 1992 **street crime** and delinquency have risen; more alarmingly, levels of **civil violence** continue to spiral upwards. Carrying weapons is commonplace and holidays and festivals particularly can act as flashpoints when alcohol, tensions and bullets collide. While the chances of witnessing, or being caught up in something are low, basic rules should be followed.

EMERGENCY NUMBERS
Police ☎121
Cruz Roja (ambulance) ☎222 5155
Fire ☎271 2227

In **San Salvador**, very few people are on the streets after dark, particularly in the centre, and the streets themselves are generally poorly lit. Outside the centre, the intimidation and threat is usually more potential than actual, but do not walk around alone (this especially applies to women), and take taxis if you have to go any distance – particularly if you arrive in the city after dark. Outside the capital things are more relaxed, but when walking around cities stick to the main roads and take taxis at night. On the street don't flash large amounts of money or obviously expensive cameras or jewellery. Try not to look too obviously lost and walk with confidence; if you think you've inadvertently strayed into the wrong part of town simply retrace your steps. The **civil police** are plentiful in San Salvador and other city centres, and a pilot **tourist police force** has recently been set up in the Zona Rosa and richer parts of the capital.

Bus hold-ups occasionally occur and there is nothing much you can do about it; keep a close eye on the latest news about various areas before you decide where to travel. Generally hold-ups are still comparatively rare and affect the local population far more than tourists; whatever happens, your life is far more important than anything you might be carrying.

Work and study

Unlike Guatemala or Costa Rica, El Salvador is not well equipped with **language schools**, although the government tourist organization *Corsatur* (see p.269) is aware of the potential of this business. There are vague plans to set up schools in the more touristy areas like Apaneca and Panchimalco, with profits going to local communities; contact them to see how far things have progressed. The *Academia Europea*, 99a Av Nte #639, Col Escalón, San Salvador (☎ & fax 224 6492) has private classes for US$12 an hour and group classes starting at US$50 for a course of thirty hours; classes are aimed at business residents and accommodation is not arranged. If you're looking to **teach English**, contact the school direct or check the listings for *Academias de Idiomas* in the yellow pages.

Of more lasting benefit may be **voluntary work**, particularly if you have specific skills. **CIRES** (Committee for the Integration and Reconstruction of El Salvador), 2a C Pte #2137 at 41a Av Sur, San Salvador (☎298 9410) is a nongovernmental agency with a remit to set up development programmes in the wake of the peace accords. It works in fifty areas around the country, with national and international funding, on credit loans, agricultural cooperatives, housing, potable water schemes and primary health care schemes, particularly for women and children; they are always interested to hear from foreigners with relevant medical, technical and administration skills or experience.

History

The first settled peoples of El Salvador were the **Maya**, who arrived in the territory from Guatemala by at least 1200 BC. By 500 BC they had developed several large settlements in the west and centre, the most important of which was Chalchuapa – close to where present-day Santa Ana now stands – trading in ceramics and obsidian across Mesoamerica. A catastrophic eruption of **Volcán Ilopango** around 250 AD, spreading ash over ten thousand square kilometres, all but wiped out many of these settlements, forcing their inhabitants to flee north. Over the next two hundred years, during the early Classic Period (300–900 AD) the land began to repopulate, with important cities at San Andrés, Tazumal, Cara Sucia and in the east Quelepa. West of the Río Lempa the **Maya-Quiché** predominated with the Chortís (Chortí being a dialect of Quiché) settling around Santa Tomas and Tejutla in what is today the department of Chalatenango. To the east of the river the **Lenca** – a mix of the early nomadic tribes and groups of Maya-Quiché, with linguistic links to the South American Chibchan group – established themselves and developed in overall isolation from their neighbours.

Around 900 AD, when – for reasons still unclear – the Classic Maya Culture began to crumble, these cities were abandoned. During the early Postclassic period (900–1200 AD), waves of Nahuat-speaking groups began to migrate south from Mexico, seeking land and power. These settlers, who established themselves in west and central El Salvador and in the northwest around Metapán, came to be known as the **Pipils**. New seats of power were built at Cihuatán, Tehuacán and Cuscatlán; unusually, the deserted Maya city of Tazumal was also reoccupied. The new settlers planted maize, beans, cocoa and tobacco, lived in highly stratified societies under a hereditary system of military rule, had highly developed arts and sciences and worshipped the sun and the idols of Quetzalcoatl (man), Itzqueye (woman), Tlaloc (rain) and Mictlanteuctli (god of the underworld). Trade links with the west and north were strong, based on the exchange of cocoa, extensively cultivated, to buy goods and services.

Final waves of Nahuat speakers arrived in the thirteenth and fourteenth centuries, threatening and occasionally displacing the already established communities and disrupting the network of trade, possibly contributing to the abandonment of Cihuatán and Tehuacán. Chief among the new immigrants were the **Nonualcos**, who settled around what is now the city of Zacatecoluca and the **Pok'omans** who moved in around Chalchuapa.

■ The Conquest of El Salvador

The first **conquistador** to set foot on El Salvador was Andrés Niño who, exploring the Pacific coast of the isthmus, landed on the island of Meanguera in the Golfo de Fonseca on May 31, 1522. The Spanish returned in June 1524 when **Pedro de Alvarado**, commanding a force of around 250 Spanish troops and 5000 indigenous people entered what is now the department of Ahuachapán from Guatemala. The region was fertile and densely populated, with two rival city-states, Cuscatlán, more or less where the city of San Salvador now stands, and Tecpa Izalco, around the Sonsonate area. The Spanish called all of this new territory **Cuscatlán**, a name which is still used today in presidential speeches, stirring newspapers and the like to evoke national pride.

Defeating the Pipils at Acajutla and then at Tacuxcalco, Alvarado advanced up the Zapotitán valley to the city of Cuscatlán, only to find it deserted, its army having fled to the mountains. Wounded, and forced to return to Guatemala, Alvarado reported that the region would take time and effort to conquer. No doubt he exaggerated, but it is thought that the Pipil forces were up to twice as large as those of the Spanish, with the population of the territory as a whole put variously at between 130,000 and one million. Not until April 1528 did a third Spanish force under **Diego**

de Alvarado succeed in subduing the Pipils and establishing the foothold of Villa San Salvador near present day Suchitoto.

Once established, the Spanish almost immediately began to think about advancing east, motivated both by the persistent belief that the undiscovered territories would yield riches and by the need to remain dominant to the rival group of conquistadors advancing up the isthmus from Panamá under Pedrarias Davila. In 1530 Alvarado dispatched Luis de Moscosco from Guatemala to finalize the conquest of the east. Ten years later, despite a number of indigenous uprisings, the most serious of which was in 1537, the Spanish hold upon the territory was secure.

■ Colonial rule

Though the new territory never yielded the fabled riches of the mythical El Dorado, the fertile lands provided sufficient wealth for those Spanish who chose to take advantage.

The **encomienda** system was established and haciendas developed, producing for export primarily balsam and cocoa. This latter proved to be a particular source of wealth, with an ever-increasing demand for the delicacy from Europe. Cattle were also introduced and flourished – the indigenous farming method of slash and burn had created fertile pastures for grazing – providing a firm source of food and income, mainly for domestic use.

As across Latin America the impact of the Spanish arrival was **catastrophic** for the indigenous inhabitants. Susceptible to European diseases, cut off from food sources as lands were enclosed by the *encomenderos*, forced into a different system of beliefs, the indigenous population of El Salvador went into free fall. By the end of the sixteenth century at least half had perished. The Lencas and other groups living east of the Río Lenca, considered by the Spanish to be more primitive and less malleable than the Pipils in the west were particularly badly affected.

The decline in the indigenous population posed a significant problem for the Spanish *encomenderos* – how to secure labour to work the land? Initially, in the early years of the seventeenth century **black slaves** were imported; this came to a halt in 1625, when during Semana Santa, two thousand slaves gathered in the centre of San Salvador, apparently to foment rebellion. The plans came to nothing, but the slaves were henceforth considered too dangerous to use. Thereafter, the *encomienda* system was gradually abandoned, largely replaced by the end of the seventeenth century with a system of **peonage**. Work on the haciendas was rewarded by payment in vouchers, redeemable only in the hacienda shop, whose prices were set significantly higher than on the open market. Money for daily expenses, however, was advanced by the landowner, creating over time a debt that the worker, the peon, was unable to repay and which, moreover, devolved upon his family and heirs.

Haciendas became enclosed, self-sufficient worlds; the workers found all their needs provided for but in return became reliant upon the landowner for everything and unable to leave. Workers could get ahead by serving their patron in all areas, legal or illegal, while he in turn boosted his power by commanding such resources. Such patterns were to continue in El Salvadorean society in later years – not least in the private armies, raised by landowners, that developed into the death squads of the 1970s and 1980s.

From the early eighteenth century, landowners switched from the production of cocoa to that of *añil* (**indigo**). Although long cultivated, it was not until protection measures in the European markets were removed that it became viable to produce the crop on a large scale. Growing demand for the superior dye produced in Latin America ensured that by the mid-1700s indigo had become the primary export crop. The principal beneficiaries of this were – despite the efforts of the Spanish crown to ensure small-scale production – the hacienda owners and *comerciantes,* the middle-men handling the sale and shipping of the crop.

By the end of the eighteenth century El Salvador was a rigidly stratified society, whose European elite consisted of the small number of Spanish-born Crown functionaries and priests and a few hundred Creole (Latin American-born) hacienda owners and *comerciantes*; these last two groups were allocated some responsibility in the management of local affairs on behalf of the Crown. Of available agricultural land, around half was held in private haciendas. The vast majority of the population, *mestizo* and indigenous, existed at subsistence level, cultivating maize.

■ Independence

Following the deposition of Mexican leader Augustín Iturbide in 1822, which brought an end to the hopes of a Mexican Empire, the Salvadorean Manuel José Arce was elected first president of the **Federal Republic of Central America** in April 1825. Beset by the deep divisions between

ANASTASIO AQUINO AND THE INDIGENOUS REBELLION

The most serious challenge to the nascent government of El Salvador came in 1833 with the indigenous uprising led by **Anastasio Aquino**. Ostensibly a protest against the practice of forced conscription among hacienda workers, the month-long rebellion was also a response to the instabilities in society generated by the new state of independence. In particular it focused resistance against a new decree stating that all land not in use should be converted into private property. The hacienda owners expanded their estates; the indigenous and other groups living on subsistence agriculture found that much of the land needed for slash and burn cultivation had been incorporated into private hands.

A worker on an indigo planation near Santiago Nonualco, Aquino rebelled following the arrest and detention – and presumed conscription – of his brother by the hacienda owner. He and his followers, the so-called **"Army of Liberation"** attacked army posts, releasing and arming the forced conscripts and sacked haciendas; according to legend the spoils from these were distributed among the poor. The well-disciplined forces of the rebellion were successful in early confrontations with government troops and at one stage looked capable of advancing on, and taking, San Salvador. Instead, Aquino chose to march on the nearby cities of Zacatecoluca and San Vicente, giving the government time to marshall its forces. On February 16 Aquino arrived in San Vicente and had himself crowned **"Emperor of the Nonualcos"** with a crown taken from the statue of San José in the Iglesia Nuestra Señora del Pilar.

He then returned to Santiago Nonualco where on February 28 he was defeated by the resurgent government forces. Finally captured on April 23, Aquino was **executed** in San Vicente in July. His head was put on public display, a primitive act in accordance with the status of "primitive rebel" which the government accorded him.

Conservatives and Liberals, Arce attempted to unite the rival groups by force. Though himself a Liberal, he allied with the Conservatives of Guatemala and almost immediately plunged the federation into civil war, the first of a series of many to plague the five states during the short-lived union (it dissolved in 1839) and on into full independence. Between 1825 and 1876 El Salvador was in an almost perpetual state of turmoil as rival Liberals and Conservatives battled for power, aided more often than not by similar groupings in the surrounding states. Not until the presidency of **Rafael Zaldívar** – in power between 1876 and 1885 – did the country achieve any measure of stability.

■ A coffee oligarchy: 1860–1931

Commercial production of **coffee** became widespread from 1860 onwards, fuelled by the collapse in demand for indigo following the development of synthetic dyes – and the growing popularity of coffee in Europe and North America. Other exports – sugarcane, beef – also expanded, but it was coffee which came to dominate and be seen as the "best hope" for the Salvadorean economy. Unusually, compared to El Salvador's neighbours, finance for the boom was provided and controlled domestically. Government encouragement for and promotion of a coffee boom created the conditions for development of a **"coffee elite"**. The most significant piece of government policy was the privatization, in 1882, of lands worked under the *ejido* system, that is communally. Growing numbers of small-scale farmers and families dependent upon subsistence agriculture were displaced, with no access to land. Over time, as small-scale producers found themselves unable to compete profitably in the world market, land became concentrated into fewer and fewer hands, creating a tiny but powerful **oligarchy**. This trend became particularly apparent from the early twentieth century onwards, with three-quarters of all land eventually held by less than two percent of the population.

Descended mainly from the original colonial European elite, the oligarchy monopolized coffee production and trade, extending its interests into other agricultural sectors, industry and finance. As the interests became more firmly entrenched, so did the oligarchy's willingness to take action to defend them. The first example of this came in 1885, when President Zaldívar was forced from office. Over the next decades, until a military coup in 1898, private interests were the motivating force behind all changes in government.

■ The early twentieth century

On the back of the profits from the coffee boom, the first decades of the twentieth century were a period of relative **economic stability** and development for El Salvador. Transport links, including railways, and a communications system were put into place, education expanded and a functioning civil judicial system established. It was, however, also a period of deepening **social polarization**. The elite dominated business and the state machine, working alongside a small, mainly urban, middle class. The vast majority, however, lived in the most basic of conditions, marginalized both in the countryside and, increasingly, in the urban centres. Despite regular elections, democracy existed in name only, with the bulk of the population denied access to both the political process and the coffee profits. Despair and anger at conditions was reflected in growing civil and criminal **violence**, in turn dealt with by increasing repression; the *Guardia Nacional* (National Guard) formed in 1912 soon became a professional and highly feared instrument of this repression.

The surprise election of Liberal president **Pío Romero Bosque** in 1927 was, for the majority, a sign that things could change for the better. Vowing to make El Salvador a truly democratic society, Romero took steps to restrain the worst excesses of the police and *Guardia Nacional* and – to the alarm of the oligarchy – ensure that civil rights were observed for all. Romero's successor Arturo Arujo, winning what was possibly the first truly democratic election in 1931, also vowed to continue on the same course.

■ 1932 and "La Matanza"

Despite some initial success, Romero's and Arujo's plans for democratic consolidation were brought to an abrupt end by international events. The **Wall Street crash** in November 1929, and the great depression that followed, were catastrophic for El Salvador. Virtually all – 95 percent – of her exports were coffee. As the market for this collapsed after 1929, so did the country's economy. All were affected, in particular the landless poor for whom living conditions deteriorated appallingly. Unrest, amongst both the destitute masses and the elite grew, and in December 1931 Arujo's brief period in office was ended by a **military coup**, engineered by the vice-president General Maximiliano Hernández Martínez.

Social unrest over the deteriorating conditions suffered by campesinos and the urban poor grew, exacerbated by growing repression meted out by the new government. On the night of January 22, 1932, thousands of campesinos – the majority indigenous – led by the Communist Party, **rebelled**. Armed mainly with machetes they attacked military installations and haciendas in the west of the country, assassinating hundreds of civilians including government functionaries and merchants. Mainly because plans to rebel had been widely known in the days before the event, the rebellion itself was rapidly quashed by superior government forces. The ringleaders, including Augustín Farabundo Martí, were arrested and later executed.

The scale of **government repression** in the wake of the failed rebellion was unprecedented in the history of the country. The army, the police, the *Guardia Nacional* and the private forces of the hacienda owners engaged in a week-long orgy of killing. During **"La Matanza"** ("the massacre") as it became known, anyone suspected of connections to the rebellion, anyone wearing indigenous dress or anyone simply perceived to be guilty was shot out of hand. In some cases, whole villages disappeared. Exact figures have never been known, but the death toll is estimated at up to 30,000 people although the government itself insisted that only 2000 were killed. For El Salvador's indigenous population, the effects of the massacre went far beyond the immediate death toll. As it became increasingly dangerous to be identified as *indio* (indian), traditional dress, language and customs largely disappeared.

■ **Military government 1932–80**

The rebellion and its bloody aftermath ushered in a era of **military rule** as the oligarchy, desperate to defend its interests, handed political power to the army while retaining economic control. For the next fifty years the two groups worked together in a symbiotic relationship. Successive groups of **tandas**, cliques of military officers, assumed power, felled by coups and counter-coups as factions within the military itself fought for supremacy. The economic business of state was handled by the oligarchy, who relied on the army to protect its interests. Depending on the faction in power, occasional limited concessions were made in **social reform**, although leaving the fundamental structures unchanged. A number of political parties were allowed to operate, but elections were widely perceived as a sham.

After World War II, economic interests diversified into production of sugar, cotton and beef for export. During the 1960s and 1970s, some limited industrialization also occurred. Needless to say, profits and benefits deriving from this expansion remained firmly in the hands of the oligarchy, with social inequalities unchanged. The vast majority of the population had no access to land and – at best – a tenuous link to means of survival. The census of 1971 recorded that 64 percent of agricultural land was held by 4 percent of landowners, while two-thirds of rural families had either no land or worked plots that were insufficient to provide daily needs.

A downturn in export markets in the 1970s again led to a steep deterioration in conditions, with a subsequent increase in militant pressure for change. The elections of 1972, won by the Christian Democratic Party (PDC) led by **José Napoleón Duarte**, should have signalled a mandate for democratic change. The PDC, the largest opposition party and, moreover, supported in the elections by a coalition of opposition parties, advocated a peaceful road to reform. Following the election, however, the army installed its own candidate, **Colonel Arturo Molina**, as president. Duarte and other opposition leaders were exiled, the National University closed down and trade union and reform activists persecuted and killed.

The cycle of repression continued throughout the 1970s as Molina's successor, **Carlos Humberto Romero**, took power in elections, again rigged, in 1977. Shortly after Romero took office, news programmes around the world showed footage of the army firing upon unarmed civilians during a protest in front of the cathedral in central San Salvador on February 28; as many as three hundred people died. In 1979 the ineffectual Romero was himself deposed in a coup, replaced initially by a civilian military junta and then by a group of hard-line army officers in January 1980. The army accepted an offer from Duarte to form a provisional government on condition that certain reforms be introduced, yet repression continued, culminating in the **assassination of Archbishop Oscar Romero** on March 24, 1980; the assassination was planned by a serving army officer, Roberto D'Aubuisson. Though preliminary reforms were implemented and agreement secured for a transfer of power from military to civilian hands, these were insufficient to halt a deepening cycle of extra-judicial violence.

The development of the 1970s and continuing military domination of power had convinced many that change could only come through violence. Far-right paramilitary death squads waged campaigns of terror in the countryside and against those advocating reform. At the opposite end of the spectrum, left-wing guerrilla groups were mobilizing and advocating radical change. Archbishop Romero's assassination signalled the point from where descent into civil war was inevitable.

■ The 1980s

In October 1980 the formal integration of all left-wing guerrilla organizations led to the foundation of the **Frente Faribundo Martí de Liberación Nacional (FMLN)**. Three months later, in January 1981, the FMLN launched its first general offensive, gaining territory in the eastern and northern departments of the country and forcing the government into defensive action.

Events within El Salvador were watched closely abroad, particularly in the White House. The newly installed Reagan administration, paranoid about communist insurgency in the region, began to pump aid to the government, to expand and equip fighting forces. Between 1980 and 1992 this aid totalled over US$1 billion, while aid channelled through covert sources is estimated to be at least a further US$500 million. The money flowed despite concerns over the army's *modus operandi* and close connections between government security forces and the death squads. The **El Mazote massacre** in December 1981 – when US-trained troops systematically murdered more than a thousand people – was first denied then ignored by both Salvadorean and US authorities and only fully investigated in the early 1990s. Despite US support, the army remained hampered by insufficient organization, leadership and endemic corruption, unable to confront with success the guerrillas' organized ambush tactics and targeted attacks against strategic infrastructure and economic installations. Army response, tending towards the blanket attack of large areas of "free fire" zones, rebounded most heavily upon the civilian population. During the course of the war eighty thousand people were killed and more than 500,000 fled the country as refugees.

Against a background of continued fighting, the promised transfer of power from military to civilian hands was completed, with **parliamentary elections** in 1982 and a new constitution introduced in 1983. In 1984 presidential elections brought Duarte to power on a mandate for continuing reform, although the FMLN remained outside the political process, disrupting ballots in this and subsequent local and national elections. Sporadic attempts at peace talks foundered upon the seemingly irresolvable demands for fundamental changes in the role and structure of the army and for incorporation of the FDR (the political wing of the FMLN) into political life.

Widely perceived as incompetent and corrupt, Duarte was succeeded in 1989 by **Alfredo Cristiani**, candidate of the right-wing ARENA party founded by Roberto D'Aubuisson. Regarded internationally as a moderate leader, Cristiani began to unpiece economic reforms achieved over the previous decade. The response of the FMLN was to renew offensives against the government, most spectacularly during its **"last offensive"** of November 1989 when areas of major cities, including San Salvador, were occupied. In turn, the death squads and the military intensified their activities. Suspected FMLN sympathizers, trade unionists and Church activists were intimidated and assassinated. Thousands died when San Salvador and other cities were indiscriminately bombed by the air force and – in an incident that caused international outrage – six Jesuit priests, their housekeeper and her daughter were massacred in their rooms on the campus of the Universidad de Centroamerica on November 16, 1989.

■ Steps towards peace

At the close of 1989, an end to the fighting seemed a remote and unlikely dream. Yet in April 1990, representatives of both the FMLN and the government, under the chairmanship of the UN, met and talked in Geneva in the first of a series of **negotiations** that would lead to peace. In large part this was achieved due to international changes; the end of the Cold War reduced Central America's importance as a strategic tool and both the US and USSR switched policy to an active encouragement of resolution of conflicts. Increasingly isolated and drawn into deadlock against each other, both the government and the FMLN bowed to US and UN pressure for a negotiated solution and agreed to talk.

A lengthy and problem-ridden negotiating process resulted in a UN-brokered agreement, the **Chapultepec Accords**, signed on January 16,

1992, followed on February 1 by a formal cease-fire. The FMLN agreed to disengagement and demobilization of its forces, the government to a purge of the armed forces and reduction in its size. In addition, a number of civil institutions were to be created, including a new civilian police force (the PNC), a human rights institution and a Truth Commission. The UN set in place a resident observer mission (ONUSAL) to verify compliance within a set time limit. A land transfer programme, expected to transfer ten percent of agricultural land to demobilized combatants and refugees, was inaugurated and a tripartite commission, including the government, workers and private sector, set up to formulate further social and economic policies. On December 15, 1992, the day the FMLN registered as a formal political party, the civil war was formally ended.

■ El Salvador today

The **elections** held in March 1994, monitored by ONUSAL, resulted in Armando Calderón Sol of the ARENA party assuming the presidency. The FMLN participated fully in the electoral process, gaining 31.6 percent of the vote against ARENA's 68.2 percent. The new government pursued a liberal, free-market economy policy while IMF loans helped to stabilize the currency and encourage real growth in GDP.

However, dissatisfaction has increased – primarily with the government's perceived failure to comply with the Chapultepec Accords – and disquiet over alleged corruption has grown. Members of the armed forces alleged to have participated in human rights atrocities have more often been offered amnesty or early retirement than prosecution. The civilian police force, widely supported, has been hampered since inception by lack of funds. Ex-combatants allege that they are still waiting for financial and other compensation designed to re-integrate them into civilian life, while the land transfer programme remains incomplete. Although a genuine desire for reconciliation and reconstruction is still widespread, the majority of Salvadoreans still fight daily against the deeply ingrained divisions that sparked the original conflict. And while political violence and violation of civil rights have declined dramatically, the growing problem of intensifying civil violence has emerged in their place.

CHAPTER 12

SAN SALVADOR AND AROUND

S prawling across the Valle de las Hamacas (named after its frequent earthquake activity), **SAN SALVADOR**, with its chaos, pollution and dilapadation, makes an ignominious introduction to the country. Earthquake-damaged buildings, lacking funds for repair, deteriorate a little further every day, while shanty towns colonize whatever space is available, housing refugees and the otherwise dispossessed. The crumbling dereliction of the centre seethes with crowds of vendors, traffic and noise, with a tangle of cranes and scaffolding on the skyline marking the slow process of rebuilding since the traumas of the 1980s. The contrast with the quiet streets and shopping malls of the wealthy western suburbs couldn't be more dramatic. Still, a stay, however short, in El Salvador's capital is probably inevitable and many people find it easier to get used to the place than they imagined, appreciating the diversions and services it offers – restaurants, shopping, cinemas – that are simply unavailable in the rest of the country.

San Salvador is also a surprisingly green city, with a canopy of lush vegetation shrouding even the most unlikely of neighbourhoods, and a ring of encircling mountains that seem at times to be close enough to touch. Dominating the skyline to the north is **Volcán San Salvador**, accessible via the pleasant town of **Santa Tecla**, 13km from the city, while in the hills to the south lies the lush, extensive **Parque Balboa**, giving access to vistas across to the Pacific coast. Beneath the park to the east is the predominantly indigenous village of **Panchimalco**, with a rather splendid colonial church. Fifteen kilometres east from the city is the country's largest crater lake, **Lago de Ilopango**, stunningly beautiful and with views on a clear day aross to the peaks of Volcán San Vicente (see p.308) whilst to the west are the natural gorge, waterfalls and pools of **Los Chorros**, a favourite weekend refuge for harrassed city dwellers.

Some history

There has been a city in the vicinity of the present capital since around 1054, when the Pipils founded the city state of **Cuscatlán** in the Zalcuatitán valley, stretching between what are today the towns of San Jacinto and Santa Tecla. Although the Spanish first arrived in the area in June 1524, they did not succeed in establishing a settlement until 1528. This **Villa San Salvador,** to the south of where Suchitoto (see p.302) now stands, is thought to have been named after the day of Transfiguration of the Saviour of the World (El Salvador), the date of a conclusive victory against the Pipils. For reasons which are not clear, the settlement was moved to its present location in 1545, and granted the title of city in September 1546. By 1570, according to Spanish chronicler López de Velasco, there were 150 Spanish inhabitants, of whom sixty or seventy were *encomenderos*, a specific type of landholder.

Rapid growth came only in the **late eighteenth century**, after San Salvador was named the first *intendencia* within the Reino de Guatemala in 1785, stimulating trade

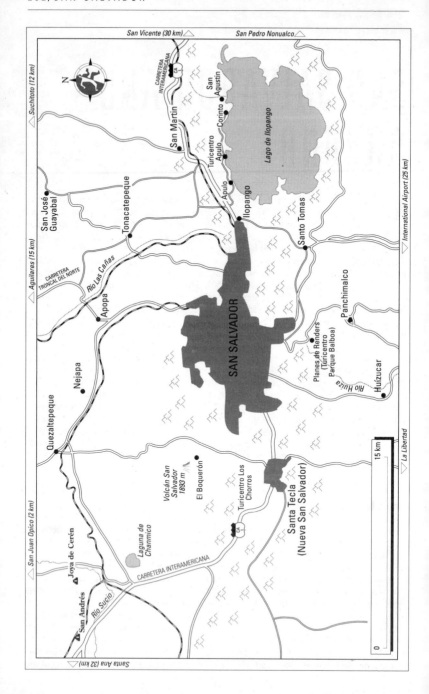

For an explanation of **accommodation price codes**, see p.270.

and commercial development. Growing pressure, within the country and across the isthmus to break away from Spain was particularly evident here; Delgado's first call for independence was issued from San Salvador, and the city became the first capital of the **Central American Federation** in 1824. The city continued to grow slowly and steadily, becoming capital of the Republic of El Salvador in 1840.

A series of destructive **earthquakes** throughout the nineteenth and twentieth centuries successively levelled most of the centre and ensured that virtually nothing remains of colonial San Salvador; today, the oldest buildings date back only to around the end of the nineteenth century. In 1986, as the effects of the **civil war** were beginning to encroach on the capital, another earthquake, measuring 5.4 on the Richter scale, hit on October 10, destroying around 60,000 houses and buildings and leaving six hundred dead and thousands injured and homeless. As if this were not enough, the air force bombed areas of the city thought to be hotbeds of guerrilla support in November 1989, in response to the FMLN's "last offensive" on the country's major cities. While recovery and rebuilding has continued in the decade since then, the scars of this history are still painfully evident in some sections of the city.

Arrival and city transport

Though initially daunting, San Salvador's **layout** is easily grasped with the aid of a map. The central intersection of the city is the northwest corner of the Catedral Metropolitana. The main **avenida** is Avenida España to the north of this and Avenida Cuscatlan (south); the main **calle** is Calle Delgado (east) and Calle Arce (west). It's essential to get to know how the bus system works – the heat, pollution and danger of some neighbourhoods makes walking a bad idea, and crossing the road can be hazardous, to say the least.

The heart of the capital, **El Centro**, centres on a point just north of the Catedral Metropolitana and encompasses several important buildings and churches and the major markets. North, just outside El Centro is the **Centro de Gobierno**, with a major bus station, **Terminal de Oriente**, to the east. To the west/northwest of El Centro are business and residential districts linked by a major throughfare, the **Alameda F. D. Roosevelt**. Running due west of El Centro to Plaza de las Americas, this changes to **Paseo General Escalón**, fringed by quiet, wealthy residential districts. Many of the foreign embassies are located at the far end of the Paseo, as are a number of luxury hotels. A major road, **49a Avenida** intersects with the Alameda just outside El Centro; running northeast this changes to **Boulevard de los Héroes**, lined with restaurants and two major shopping malls. To the **west/southwest** of El Centro are further business and residential areas and the second major bus station, **Terminal de Occidente**. The **Carretera Interamericana** branches out southwest through the city; to the north of this lies the "Zona Rosa", a suburb of secluded houses, upmarket restaurants and nightclubs.

Points of arrival

San Salvador is an **intimidating** city to arrive in for the first time, particularly after dark. If arriving with luggage, take a taxi and do not walk around El Centro at night. The international airport, **Aeropuerto Internacional Comalpa**, is 44km from El Centro. The easiest option into the city is to take a **taxi** – well-run radio cabs wait outside (US$12–18; about 1hr). *Taxis Acaya* also have a **colectivo** service (9am, 1pm & 5.30pm; US$3) to their office close to El Centro at 19a Av Nte 1107 at 3a C Pte (☎271 4937). You could also flag down any passing **bus** for the city at the stop in front of the terminal on the highway (5am–8pm; 45min–1hr; US$0.50).

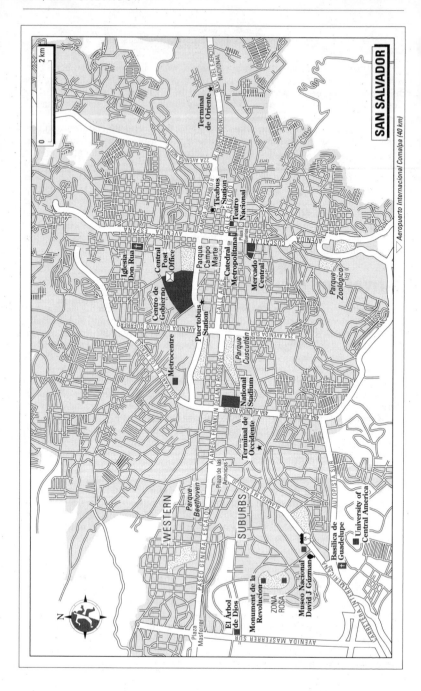

SAN SALVADOR

△ Aeropuerto Internacional Comalpa (40 km)

Terminal de Oriente

Ticabus Station

Teatro Nacional

Iglesia Don Rúa

Central Post Office

Parque Campo Marte

Catedral Metropolitana

Centro de Gobierno

Mercado Central

Parque Zoológico

Puertobus Station

Metrocentre

Parque Cuscatlán

National Stadium

Terminal de Occidente

Parque Beethoven

WESTERN SUBURBS

Plaza de las Américas

University of Central America

Basílica de Guadelupe

El Árbol de Dios

Monument de la Revolucion

ZONA ROSA

Museo Nacional David J Gúzman

2 km

N

USEFUL ROUTES

#30B – along Blvd de los Héroes, up Alameda Roosevelt and part of Paseo Escalón, turning west to run past the Zona Rosa.
#34 – from Terminal de Oriente through El Centro to Terminal de Occidente and out along Carretera Interamericana, past the Mercado de Artesanías.
#44 – along Blvd de los Héroes, onto 49a Av Sur close to the Terminal de Occidente, past the Universidad de Centroamerica and out past the US Embassy to Santa Elena.
#101 A/B/C/D – from El Centro up Alameda Roosevelt to Playa de los Americas and then by a variety of routes, depending on the service, to Santa Tecla.

International buses arrive either, depending on the company, at the PuertoBus terminal on Alameda Juan Pablo II (from Guatemala and Honduras), or at the Terminal de Occidente, Blvd Venezuela in the southwest of the city (from Guatemala). *Ticabus* have their own terminal at C Concepcion 121 in El Centro.

For details of **buses from San Salvador**, see p.295.

City transport

Bus services in San Salvador are comprehensive, frequent and fast. Newer city buses are red and white or green and white; these, however, are vastly outnumbered by the legions of older buses and minibuses in all shapes, colours and sizes that ply the same routes. There is a **flat fare** of about US$0.20 to anywhere in the city, which should be paid to the driver; minibuses are slightly more expensive. There are some marked **stops** (*parada de buses*), generally outside large public buildings, shopping centres and so on. Otherwise look for groups of people waiting by the road; drivers will usually let you board at red lights and the minibuses tend to hoot anywhere along a route to alert you to their presence. Services trail off after around 7pm, finishing altogether at around 9pm – at which time you should be thinking of taking taxis everywhere in any case.

City taxis ply the streets and wait around bus terminals, markets and major shopping areas. **Fares** should be settled before you get in – a trip around the city should be US$3.50–5 depending on distance and time of day.

Accommodation

Although **prices** in San Salvador are substantially higher than in, say, Guatemala or Honduras, choosing **budget accommodation** – most of it in or east of El Centro – is not conducive to peace of mind or a pleasant stay. The area east of Plaza Barrios and along C Concepción towards the Terminal de Oriente is distinctly unpleasant after dark, although we have listed below the better hotels along here. The streets west of Plaza Barrios are more sane, although dimly lit and virtually empty after nightfall. For peace of mind, it's worth investing a few dollars more to stay in the **western suburbs** where the standards of service – and prices – are everything that you would expect at home.

If arriving for the first time, wherever your hotel, take a **taxi**.

El Centro

Hotel American Guest House, 17a Av Nte 119, between C Arce and 1a C Pte (☎271 0224, fax 271 3667). Gloomy rooms with a choice of private or shared bath. Helpful management; hot water and baggage storage. The cafe in front serves all meals. ③–④.

Hotel Custodio, 10a Av Sur 109 across from Mercado Ex Cuartel (☎221 5810). A bit stark but clean and friendly; rooms with bath cost more. ②.

Hotel Family Guest House, 1a C Pte Bis 925, between 15a and 17a Av Nte (☎222 9252, fax 221 2349). Clean, sizeable rooms, with hot water and a friendly atmosphere. A cafe serves all meals. Good for solo women. ③–④.

Hotel Fénix, 17a Av Nte at 1a C Pte (☎ & fax 271 1269). Big, old, clean rooms, some with private bath and hot water. ③–④.

Hospedaje Izalco, C Concepción 666 (☎222 2613). One of the best in this area, with clean rooms, good beds and a luggage storage service. The hotel itself is secure but the area is not nice after dark. ③.

Hotel Leon, C Delgado 621 between 10a and 12a Av Nte (☎222 0951). Basic, acceptable rooms with bath, slightly more expensive on the lower floors or with fan. ②.

Hotel Pasadena II, 3a C Pte 1075, between 17a and 19a Av Nte (☎221 4786). Clean simple rooms, all with bath, in this safe place just behind the Puertobus terminal. ③.

Hotel Ritz Continental, 7a Av Sur 219, by C Darío (☎222 0033, fax 222 9842). Slightly past its prime, but the big rooms are affordable semi-luxury, with hot water and a/c. Also has a pool, restaurant and bar, and is in the nicer end of El Centro. ⑤.

Hotel San Carlos, C Concepción 121 between 10a and 12a Av Nte (☎222 8975). Given the area, which is a nightmare, the only reason to stay here is to catch an early Ticabus from the terminal next door; clean and secure. ③.

Western suburbs

Hotel Alameda, Alameda Roosevelt 2305, at 43a Av Sur (☎260 0299, fax 260 3011). Accessible luxury, with swimming pool, sauna, bars and restaurant and a private beach on the Costa del Sol (see p.322) for guests' use. ⑦.

Amate Guest House, 25a C Pte 1302 at 23a Av Nte (☎ & fax 225 7616). Very quiet and friendly; three light, airy rooms, all with bath, in an old house set in a beautiful garden; breakfast is included and other meals available on request. ④.

Camino Real, Blvd de los Héroes, opposite the Metrocentro (☎279 3888, fax 223 5660). Concrete monolith – something of a landmark – the haunt of the rich and those travelling on expenses, with all the comfort and facilities you would expect. ⑨.

Casa Blanca Bed and Breakfast, 89a Av Nte 719 at 11a C Pte, Col Escalón (☎ & fax 263 2545). Quiet, clean, comfortable big rooms with TV, sparkling bathrooms and hot water. ⑥.

Clementina's Casa de Huespedes, Av Morazan 34 at C Washington, Col Libertad (☎225 5962). Peaceful, friendly place; a good source of information on political and cultural affairs. ④.

Hotel Florida, Pasaje los Almendros 115, off Blvd de los Héroes, Urb La Florida (☎260 2540, fax 260 2654). Business hotel convenient for El Centro and the western suburbs although the rooms are somewhat small. The roof terrace has nice views over the city. ④.

Hotel Good Luck, C Los Sisimiles 2943, Pasaje 5, Col Miramonte (☎260 1655, fax 260 1677). Large, bright rooms and very clean; private bathrooms have hot water. The restaurant next door serves all meals. ⑤.

Hotel Grecia Real, C Los Sismiles 2922, Col Miramonte (☎ & fax 260 1820). A good deal for good-sized rooms with bath, TV and phone; slightly more expensive with a/c. ⑤.

La Hacienda Hotel, Alameda Roosevelt 2937, Urb Santa Monica (☎245 2463, fax 245 2464). Good sized, clean rooms all with bath, though the front ones tend to get noisy; there is also a pool and disco at weekends. Cafe at the front serves breakfasts. ④.

Happy House Hotel, C Los Sisimiles 2951, Col Miramonte (☎260 1568). Slightly dilapated but friendly, with clean rooms, courtyard and communal area; breakfast available on request. ④.

Hotel Miramonte, C Talamanca 2904 at Pasaje No 4, Col Miramonte (☎ & fax 260 1880). Large comfortable rooms all with bath, some with balcony, in a quiet neighbourhood. Friendly place to indulge yourself a little. Breakfast on request. ⑤–⑧.

Hotel Occidental, 49a Av Nte 171, between Alameda Roosevelt and 1a C Pte, Col Flor Blanca (☎260 5724). Good-sized but dark rooms, with TV. Bathrooms are basic and rooms at the front get very noisy from the traffic. En-suite rooms are more expensive. ③.

Hotel Ximena Guest House, C San Salvador 202, Col Centro América (☎260 2481, fax 260 2427). Probably the only real "traveller's" hostel in the city, in a residential area. Big, smelly dorm and some overpriced private rooms; communal TV area and courtyard. English spoken. ②/⑤.

The City

San Salvador is never going to win any prizes for elegance, and the rough edge to life here can come as a shock to those used to a more tranquil, colonial atmosphere in other Central American cities. There is a singular lack of museums and galleries, and little to actually do other than people-watching and soaking up the unique atmosphere. If you can stand it – though many can't – **El Centro** gives a vivid snapshot of El Salvadorean daily life and character, as well as containing some churches and other buildings of interest.

Towards the **west** things get easier, with a number of parks, including **Parque Cuscutlán**, providing acres of green relief from the traffic and noise, and the **Paseo General Escalón** and the **Zona Rosa** offering modern cinemas, bars, clubs and upmarket restaurants. The best museum in the city, commemorating those killed in the years of conflict, is based in the **Universidad de Centroamerica**, in the far southwest.

El Centro

El Centro is traffic-ridden, noisy and hot, its pavements jammed with street stalls and pedestrians, ruinous buildings collapsing into weed-filled empty lots and a tangible air of pollution and decay. Despite the noise, dirt and crowds, however, there is a sense of real life, not always apparent in the more upmarket suburbs to the west. At the heart of the city, teeming with street hawkers and itinerants, is the disappointing **Plaza Barrios**, whose scrubby trees don't succeed in alleviating the heat of the sun. On the northern edge sits the **Catedral Metropolitana**, dating back to 1888 but severely damaged on a number of occasions, most recently by fire in 1951. Repairs after this were suspended by Archbishop Oscar Romero, who argued that funds should be used for more pressing needs such as feeding the hungry. Renovations, resumed in the early 1990s however, are expected to be completed by the millennium; the new facade is strikingly decorated with contemporary murals by Salvadorean artist Fernando Llort.

On the west edge of the plaza is the imposing bulk of the renaissance-style **Palacio Nacional**, the seat of government until the devastating earthquake of 1986. This incarnation dates back to 1905, replacing an earlier edifice destroyed by fire. Repairs to the damage caused by the 1986 earthquake are still underway. When completed, by the new millenium, the building will house the national archives and a national history museum. Facing the cathedral on the southern edge of the plaza is the **Biblioteca Nacional**, moved here after 1986. A large part of the collection was destroyed in the earthquake; the remaining books seem a little forlorn in their new home, a concrete, former bank building.

East of Plaza Barrios along 4a C Ote is **Parque Libertad**, previously the heart of colonial San Salvador; the stained concrete church here is **El Rosario**, built over the tomb of José Matías Delgado, father of independence. (The **Iglesia la Merced**, rebuilt from the original, from where Delgado first called for independence in 1811, is a couple of blocks southeast.) There's an impressive vista, in San Salvadorean terms, from the Plaza Libertad looking north, where the dome and facade of the cathedral rise majestically, with the volcano as a backdrop.

One block northeast of the cathedral is the compact **Plaza Morazan**, bounded on its southern edge by the renaissance-style **Teatro Nacional**. Built with the profits of the coffee plantations and reflecting the impact of French culture in the early twentieth century, the restored interior – all red plush and marble and scrolled, decorative plaster work – harks back to grander times. Regular musical and theatrical events are hosted here, advertised in the newspapers. If you walk east from the theatre along C Delgado you come to the **Mercado Ex Cuartel**, a hangar-like building on the site of a former

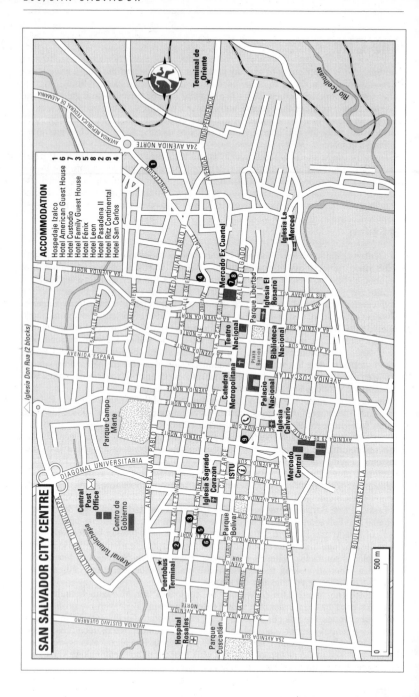

SAN SALVADOR CITY CENTRE

ACCOMMODATION

Hospedaje Izalco	1
Hotel American Guest House	6
Hotel Custodio	7
Hotel Family Guest House	3
Hotel Fénix	5
Hotel Leon	8
Hotel Pasadena II	2
Hotel Ritz Continental	9
Hotel San Carlos	4

Terminal de Oriente

Río Acelhuate

Iglesia Don Rua (2 blocks)

Iglesia La Merced

Mercado Ex Cuartel

Parque Libertad

Iglesia El Rosario

Teatro Nacional

Biblioteca Nacional

Plaza Barrios

Catedral Metropolitana

Palacio Nacional

Iglesia Calvario

Parque Campo Marte

Mercado Central

DIAGONAL UNIVERSITARIA

Central Post Office

Centro de Gobierno

ISTU

Iglesia Sagrado Corazón

Parque Bolívar

Puertobus Terminal

Hospital Rosales

Parque Cuscatlán

AVENIDA GUSTAVO GUERRERO

BOULEVARD VENEZUELA

0   500 m

military barracks, selling a reasonable range of handicrafts from El Salvador and Central America; the quality and selection of local crafts, however, is wider at the Mercado de Artesanías (see below). East from the market, the city begins to disintegrate rapidly, with earthquake-damaged buildings barely managing to remain upright. A major road, C Concepción, lined with cheap comedores and a few budget hotels runs out to the very far corner of the Terminal de Oriente bus station.

Five blocks north from El Centro, at the intersection of Av España and Alameda Juan Pablo II is the green expanse of the **Parque Campo Marte**, popular with workers from the nearby Centro de Gobierno on their lunchbreaks and for family weekend picnics. Continue north along the eastern edge of the Parque Campo Marte and you come to perhaps the most commanding church in the city – and its largest functioning one – the **Iglesia Don Rua**. Built in the nineteenth century, the white bulk of the church towers above the surrounding houses; the stained glass windows are stunning, and a particularly nice time to visit is late on Sunday afternoons as taped choral music is played and the pews begin to fill for evening mass.

South of Plaza Barrios and two blocks west is the sprawling **Mercado Central**, whose ever-expanding street stalls are a constant irritation to the city authorities. Anything and everything can be bought in its ruinous and cluttered alleys, even on a Sunday. Looming behind the market building is the **Iglesia Calvario**, whose dark, gothic-style bulk remains impressive, despite its dereliction.

West along Calle Ruben Darío and Calle Arce

The two major commercial streets of **Calle Ruben Darío** and **Calle Arce** are choked in El Centro with stalls, wandering peddlers and black traffic fumes. The whole racket is overlaid with competing music cassette sellers. Struggle past the stalls and you'll find the entrance to small businesses and shops selling anything you might not have been able to find on the stalls, at a higher price, and cheap, fast-service restaurants and cafés. A few blocks west, however, and things begin to calm down.

Beyond **Antel** and the **ISTU** office on C Ruben Darío is **Parque Bolívar**, usually swarming with street children and the underemployed; more useful as a point for orientation than a respite from the city. Three blocks south of Parque Bolívar, on 17a Av Sur, is the government printing press with a small bookshop selling Spanish-language works on the history and culture of El Salvador. One block north of the parque, on C Arce, is the nineteenth-century **Iglesia Sagrado Corazón**, under repair since earthquake damage. C Arce ends a few blocks west of here, in front of the nineteenth-century **Hospital Rosales**, constructed in Belgium, transported in pieces and put together in the city.

South of the hospital, **Parque Cuscatlán**, a large expanse of green and shady walkways and grass lawns, offers respite from the heat and noise for office workers on their lunch break, and weekend amateur football teams. At this point C Darío becomes the Alameda Roosevelt, heading out towards the richer western suburbs.

The western suburbs

From Parque Cuscatlán, **Alameda Roosevelt** runs west to a major intersection at 49a Av Sur/Blvd de los Héroes. This latter is lined with fast-food restaurant chains, more upmarket restaurants and reputedly the largest shopping mall in Central America, the **Metrocentro**, three storeys of expensive boutiques, sports goods outlets selling mainly US brands at US prices and a couple of well-stocked, though pricy, souvenir shops. The Bookshop on the second level has a decent selection of English-language fiction and general interest books, as well as US magazines. The mall is the target of some disgust in the left-wing press, who argue that the country's problems will be solved by building new homes, schools and hospitals rather than rushing to indulge an alien, foreign-inspired consumerism.

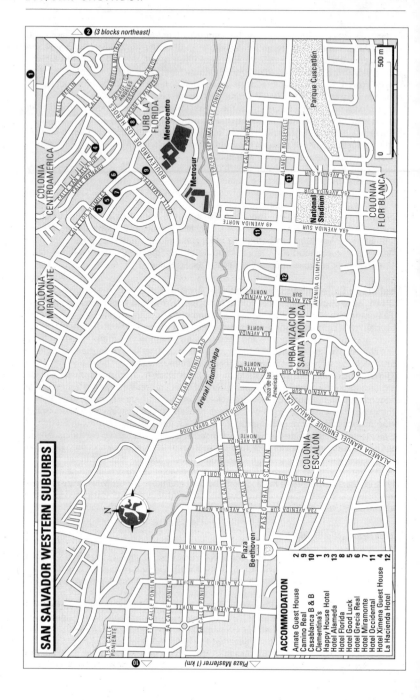

SAN SALVADOR WESTERN SUBURBS

N

(3 blocks northeast)

URB LA FLORIDA

Metrocentro

Metrosur

Parque Cuscatlán

National Stadium

COLONIA FLOR BLANCA

COLONIA CENTROAMERICA

COLONIA MIRAMONTE

URBANIZACION SANTA MONICA

COLONIA ESCALON

Arenal Tutunichapa

Plaza de las Americas

Plaza Beethoven

Plaza Masferrer (1 km)

Plaza Masferrer (1 km)

0 500 m

ACCOMMODATION

Amate Guest House	2
Camino Real	9
Casablanca B & B	10
Clementina's	1
Happy House Hotel	3
Hotel Alameda	13
Hotel Florida	8
Hotel Good Luck	5
Hotel Grecia Real	6
Hotel Miramonte	7
Hotel Occidental	11
Hotel Ximena Guest House	4
La Hacienda Hotel	12

Alameda Roosevelt continues west to the **Plaza de las Americas**, isolated amid eight lanes of traffic. Here stands the national symbol, the **Monumento al Salvador del Mundo**, a statue of Jesus standing on the globe. Small grassy lawns and benches surround the monument, but few people brave the roaring traffic to take advantage of them. From here, the road changes its name again, to **Paseo General Escalón**, and continues west to **Plaza Masferrer** and the rich suburbs of **Escalón** and **Lomas Verdes**. Ritzy restaurants, banks and upmarket businesses line the Paseo, with side roads fringed with secluded houses. The **El Árbol de Dios** art gallery (Mon–Sat 9am–6pm), south of Plaza Masferrer, on Av Masferrer Sur at C la Mascota, has a large collection of paintings and sculptures by Salvadorean artist Fernando Llort, renowned in particular for his *naif* style; there is also a pricy restaurant.

Southwest along the Carretera Interamericana

The Interamericana branches west from the Plaza de las Americas, running through the southwest quarters of the city and out to Western El Salvador. About 2km from El Centro on this road is the **Mercado des Artesanías**, with a wide selection of handicrafts from all over the country; good buys include hammocks, painted, wooden crafts from La Palma and bright hand-towels woven with Llort's *naif*-style paintings; prepare to bargain, although prices will be around fifty percent higher than in the villages of origin. Turn into Av la Revolución, just past the market, and a couple of hundred metres up is the **Museo Nacional David J. Guzmán**, named after the eminent Salvadorean biologist. It's closed indefinitely. The small collection of pre-Columbian carved boulders outside – sadly lacking any kind of written explanation – originated from Lago de Güija. Av la Revolución continues uphill for another kilometre or so, into the heart of the leafy Col San Benito, and ends in front of the **Monumento de la Revolución**, a vast, curved slab of concrete bearing a mosaic of a naked goliath with head thrown back and arms uplifted. Built to commemorate a revolutionary movement of 1948, the monument's location in one of the wealthiest areas of the city and overlooking its best hotel, the *Presidente*, is supremely ironic. East of the monument, along the Blvd del Hipódromo, stretches the **Zona Rosa** entertainment district, with expensive restaurants, nightclubs and boutiques.

Further along the Carretera Interamericana, on the left, is the elegant white mansion and lush gardens housing the Foreign Ministry and, where the road meets the Autopista del Sur, what is possibly the most beautiful church in San Salvador, the **Basilica de Nuestra Señora de Guadalupe**. Built after World War II and consecrated in 1953, the basilica is dedicated to the Virgen Morena, or Black Virgin, patroness of the Americas. Inside are beautiful stained glass windows and a 1950s mural of the Virgin and angels over the altar. Stretching behind the basilica is the campus of the **Universidad de Centroamerica** ("La UCA", also known as the Jesuit University) pleasantly laid out amid shady grounds.

The extremely moving **Centro Monseñor Romero** at La UCA commemorates both the assassinated Archbishop Romero and the six Jesuit priests, their housekeeper and her daughter, murdered here by the security forces in November 1989. The small museum houses clothing, photographs and personal effects of Romero and the priests, along with those of other human rights workers killed during the years of conflict. There are diagrams and explanations of the campus massacre, as well as eye-witness descriptions of other low points during the war, such as the massacres at Río Sumpul (May 1980) and El Mozote (December 1981; see p.315). Outside, a small rose garden has been planted in tribute; the circle of six bushes is for the six priests, the white rose in centre is for Monseñor Romero. Volunteer students act as guides explaining the exhibits and their history (Mon–Fri 8am–noon & 2–5pm; free).

A short distance south of the university, the tranquil **Jardín Botanico la Laguna** (Tues–Sun 9am–5.30pm), sits incongruously at the edge of an industrial park and at the foot of old volcanic cliffs. The gardens contain plants from all over the world, set among shady trees and small streams, and are a good place to escape the city for an hour or two. Bus #101D or #44 will drop you off about five minutes' walk from the entrance.

Eating, drinking and entertainment

The best **restaurants**, **clubs** and **bars** are concentrated in the western suburbs, catering to those with the money and time to indulge. In El Centro and in the less wealthy areas of the city, places tend to shut relatively early. There are lots of **cinemas** scattered around the city, mostly showing subtitled Hollywood releases.

Eating and drinking

The cheapest **places to eat** are the comedores in El Centro, although the richer suburbs occasionally throw up a few surprises; the **Plaza Masferrer** has a number of roadside eateries that stay open until quite late and the unnamed comedor opposite *Ay Jalisco*, off the Blvd de los Héroes, caters to local workers with cheap, quick and good local food. The **Blvd de los Héroes** area has a few good restaurants, while the **Paseo Escalón** and **Zona Rosa** are more cosmopolitan, with pricy international cuisine; at these it is advisable to book at the weekends. Anywhere in the city, however, you are bound to stumble over a *pupusa* stall sooner or later, whilst the markets and bus stations are full of stands selling cheap meals and snacks, and there are numerous international and local fast food chains. The prices quoted below are for a meal in the low-to-mid range of the menu, with a beer or juice.

El Centro

Actoteatro, 1a C Pte between 13a and 15a Av Nte. Laid-back place attached to a small theatre, offering excellently priced *comidas a la vista*, with juices and live music thrown in for free. Packed with the arty set, and policemen from the station around the corner. Lunch only; US$2–3.

Cafe Don Pepe, 4a C Pte and 9a Av Sur. Sodas, juices, pastries and snacks in a lively atmosphere; daytimes only.

Koradi, 9a Av Sur 225, at 4a C Pte. One of the few places to cater to vegetarians, with soy burgers, wholewheat pizzas and great juices. Mon–Fri 8am–5.30pm, Sat 8am–3pm; US$4–7.

Mister Donut, C Arce and 21a Av Nte (and branches around the city). Nominally a donut and coffee-shop chain, with excellent full breakfasts and light evening snacks. US$2–4.

Pan Latino, C Arce at 9a Av Sur. Welcome break from the maelstrom outside, serving coffees, cakes, tamales and sodas.

Around Blvd de los Héroes

Ay Jalisco, Pasaje los Almendros. Moderately priced Mexican and Central American food, although the portions are a little on the small side. US$5–9.

Dallas, Blvd de los Héroes by Pasaje las Palmeras. Seafood and steaks at moderate prices with very attentive service. Try the ceviche. US$7–12.

El Pueblo Viejo, Metrosur mall. El Salvadorean dishes, steaks and seafood a little more expensive than you'd find elsewhere; popular for lunch. Closes at 8pm; US$9–14.

Hang Ly, C Lamatepec behind the Camino Real. Almost authentic, large portions of Chinese food. US$4–8.

La Luna, C Berlin 228, Urb Buenos Aires. Arty restaurant and nightspot serving a good range of vegetarian and meat dishes and a special dish of the day. US$5–8.

La Ventana, C San Antonio Abad 2335, Col Centroamerica. European-run restaurant and bar with an interesting selection of dishes inspired by cuisine from around the world. Very popular at the weekends with resident foreigners and moneyed San Salvadoreans. US$5–9.

Las Tinajas, Blvd de los Héroes 1140, in Edificio F.Q. Good, cheap breakfasts and set lunches; quick service. US$1–3.

Panes Con Pavo, Av Pasco at C Lampatepec (behind Camino Real). Good *panes* and huge juices; more of a lunch than evening spot. US$4–6.

Señor Tortuga, C Sisimiles at C Lamtepec. Mariscos and beer at reasonable prices. US$5–9.

Waldo's, C Lamatepec behind the Camino Real. Well-prepared Spanish dishes in a friendly atmosphere; gets lively at night as regulars drop by to chat with the owners. US$3–7.

Paseo Escalón and the Zona Rosa

Chili's, Blvd Hipódromo 131, Col San Benito. Tex-mex in a fun atmosphere. US$4–7.

Fruity Snacks, Av Olímpica 2930 at 57a Av Sur. Great little place for cheap breakfasts and lunch and superlative juices, if you happen to be in the area. US$1–3.

Kreef, Paseo Escalón at 77a Av Sur. German-style bockwurst, steaks and big sandwiches, served at a price. The attached delicatessen is a favourite for ex-pats. Mon–Sat 10am–10pm, Sun 10am–4pm; US$7–13.

Pizzeria Vesuvio, 79a Av Sur 10, Col La Mascota. Although a little way from the Zona Rosa, this is well worth making the effort to get to for the superb wood-oven baked pizza; also has a wide range of pasta. Very popular in the evenings. US$7–12.

Punto Literario, Blvd del Hipódromo 326. Arty cafe in the rarefied Zona Rosa, serving coffees, drinks and light meals. US$3–6.

Ultima Alucinacion, 7a C Pte 5153 at Av Masferrer Nte. Belgian-owned place serving good, pricy European cuisine. Or have a drink at the attached *Le Rendevous des Artistes* bar. Closed Sunday evenings and Mondays; US$10–16.

Nightlife

The entire population of the city appears to disappear at nightfall, and even in the Zona Rosa, the action takes place inside, rather than on the street. Many of the restaurants have **live salsa/merengue** music and dancing at the weekends; two of the best are *Villa Fiesta*, Blvd de los Héroes opposite the Hospital Bloom and *Quinto Sol*, 15a Av Nte and 1a C Pte, Col Centroamerica. *La Luna*, C Berlin 228, Col Centroamerica, and *Los 3 Diablos* (next to *La Ventana* restaurant) are relaxed bars with a more European feel, popular with local professionals and foreigners; *La Ventana* itself is also a poular drinking spot at the weekends.

In the **Zona Rosa**, *Mario's* and the *Reggae Bar* are both patronized by a lively mixed crowd. Blvd del Hipódromo, around C la Reforma, has a number of loud, street-side bars which start getting full from around 10pm; many appeal to a younger, moneyed set. *Sr Cactus*, on C la Reforma, is more mellow, with a pleasant garden, attracting an older crowd. *Lapsus*, at the Paseo Escalón, is a nightclub playing local music and Euro-bop until late.

There are a couple of **cinemas** in El Centro and four modern, multi-screen complexes on the Paseo Escalón, with a few more scattered around the city; the daily newspapers list programmes. *La Luna* (see above) shows a different film on video every weekday night, starting around 7pm, while *Alianza Française* on 51a Av Nte 152 (☎223 8084) runs French film seasons.

Listings

Airlines Many of the airlines are based around the Alameda Roosevelt/Paseo Escalón districts. Aerolineas Argentinas, Alameda Roosevelt 3006 (☎260 5464, fax 260 5450); Air France, Edificio Edim-Lama, Blvd del Hipodromo 645, Col San Benito (☎245 0781, fax 245 0780); Alitalia, Edificio Credomatic, 55a Av Sur at Alameda Roosevelt (☎ & fax 223 8025); American Airlines, Edificio La Centroamericana, Alameda Roosevelt 3107 (☎298 0777, fax 298 0762); Avianca, Fountainblue Plaza,

Modulo B, Apto 3, 87a Av Nte (☎263 2992, fax 263 2991); Aviateca, Edificio Caribe (by Monumento al Salvador del Mundo), Alameda Roosevelt (☎279 4335, fax 223 3737); British Airways, 43a Av Nte 216 (☎260 9933, fax 260 6576); Continental, Torre Roble (Metrocentro), Blvd de los Héroes (☎260 2180, fax 260 3331); Copa, Alameda Roosevelt and 55a Av Nte 2838 (☎260 3399, fax 260 5481); Iberia, Centro Comerciale Plaza Jardin, Local C, C a Santa Tecla at Av Olímpica (☎223 2711, fax 223 8463); KLM, Centro Comerciale Feria Rosa, local 218-B (☎243 2513, fax 243 2514); Lacsa, 43a Av Nte 216 (☎260 9933, fax 260 6576); Lan Chile, Edificio Imcolinas, Blvd del Hipodromo 253 (☎298 4067, fax 223 2525); Lufthansa, Fountainblue Plaza, Modulo B 1, 87a Av Nte (☎ & fax 263 2850); Mexicana, *Hotel Presidente*, Av la Revolución, Col San Benito (☎243 633, fax 243 3636); Sam, Fountainblue Plaza, Modulo B 3, 87a Av Nte (☎263 2992, fax 263 2998); Taca, Edificio Caribe, Paseo Escalón (☎298 3145, fax 223 3757); United Airlines, Centro Comerciale Galerias, local 14, Paseo Escalón 3700 (☎279 3900, fax 298 5536).

American Express Centro Comerciale La Mascota 1, Carretera Interamericana at C la Mascota (☎279 3844, fax 223 0035). Take bus #101B (to Santa Tecla) which passes the building.

Banks and exchange Most banks ask for the original receipt when cashing travellers' cheques; an exception is Banco Hipotecario, Av Cuscatlan between 4a and 6a C Ote and branches around the city. All banks change cash dollars, including Banco Cuscatlan and Credisur. You can get Visa and Mastercard cash advances from Credomatic, 55a Av Sur and Alameda Roosevelt. Casas de cambio include the Multicambios chain, with central branches at Paseo Escalón 3563 at 69a Av Sur and C Rubén Darío 432; some branches of the attached BMV bank do cash advances on Visa cards. There are also casas de cambio on Alameda Juan Pablo II opposite the Parque Campo Marte, and at the Puerto Bus terminal, giving more or less the same rates as banks; they also sell dollars.

Bookstores The Bookshop in the Metrocentro mall has a selection of English-language books, and some US magazines. Punto Literario, Blvd del Hipódromo 326, has English, French, German and Spanish literature (Mon–Sat 10am–7.30pm). Centro Cultural La Mazorca, C Antonio Abad 1447, Col El Roble, has a small range of Central American literature and political texts (Spanish only) and a small craft shop, while *La Ventana* restaurant (see p.292) has a small selection of political and social texts (in English and Spanish) and US magazines and newspapers.

Car rental Renting a car is a good way to get to the more inaccessible parts of the country; expect to pay around US$40 a day for a small car and up to US$100 a day for a Space Wagon or jeep. Check that the price includes insurance and that emergency assistance is available. Companies include Avis, 43a Av Sur 137, Col Flor Blanca (☎260 7456, fax 260 7165; branch at airport ☎339 9056); Budget, Condominio Balam Quitze, Paseo Escalón (☎263 7174, fax 263 7166); Hertz, C Los Andes, Block J-16, Col Miramonte (☎260 1728, fax 260 1101; branch at airport ☎339 9481); Tropic, Av Olímpica 3597, Col Escalón (☎279 3236, fax 279 3235); Uno Rent-a-Car, Edificio Sunset Plaza, Av Jerusalen and C la Mascota, Col Maquilishuat (☎263 9366, fax 263 9371).

Embassies Most embassies are located in or around the Escalón and Zona Rosa districts – except for the US embassy which is on the road to Santa Elena (#44 bus). Argentina, 79a Av Nte and 11a C Pte 704, Col Escalón (☎263 3674, fax 263 3687; Mon–Fri 8am–noon); Belize, Condominio Medico B, Local 5, 2nd Floor, Blvd Tutunichapan, Urb La Esperanza (☎226 3682, fax 225 3540; Mon–Fri 8am–noon & 1–5pm, Sat 8am–2pm); Canada, Av las Palmas 111, Col San Benito (☎279 4659, fax 279 0765; Mon–Fri 8am–noon); Costa Rica, Av Albert Einstein 11-A, Col Lomas de San Francisco (☎273 3111, fax 273 1455; Mon–Fri 9am–noon & 1–3pm); Germany, 7a C Pte 3972 at 77a Av Nte, Col Escalón (☎263 2089, fax 263 2091; Mon–Fri 9am–noon); Guatemala, 15a Av Nte 135, Col Bloom (☎222 2903, fax 221 3019; Mon–Fri 8am–1.30pm); Honduras, 3a C Pte 3697, between 69a and 71a Av Nte, Col Escalón (☎223 4975, fax 223 2221; Mon–Fri 8am–1pm); Mexico, C Circunvalacion at Pasaje No 12, Col San Benito (☎243 2037, fax 243 0437; Mon–Fri 8.30am–5pm); Nicaragua, 71a Av Nte 164 at 1a C Pte, Col Escalón (☎224 1223, fax 223 7201; Mon–Fri 8am–12.30pm & 2–4pm); Panamá, Edificio Copa, Alameda Roosevelt 2838 at 55a Av Nte (☎260 5453; Mon–Fri 8.45am–1pm); UK, Paseo Escalón 4828, Col Escalón (☎263 6527, fax 263 6516; Mon–Thurs 8am–1pm & 2–4.30pm, Fri 8am–1pm); US, Blvd Santa Elena, Antiguo Cuscatlan (bus #44) (☎278 1188, fax 278 6011; Mon–Fri 8.30am–4.30pm).

Immigration office Ministerio del Interior, Centro de Gobierno, Alameda Juan Pablo II (☎221 2111; Mon–Fri 8am–4pm) for extension of stamps, tourist cards or visas.

Laundry Most hotels will either provide a laundry service – for slightly more than the *lavanderías* – or will let you wash clothes in the laundry sink. For laundry service try Lavandería Lavapronto, C los Sismiles 2944 (near Camino Real; Mon–Sat 7am–7pm) or the nearby Lavapronto, C los Sismiles 2926. An average load should cost US$2–3.

Libraries and cultural institutes La UCA has a very good library with some international works. Opposite the Metrocentro, on C los Sisimiles, the Centro Cultural Salvadoreño has an ageing collection of El Salvadorean and English-language works (Mon–Fri 8am–noon & 2–5pm). The Biblioteca Nacional is open to the public, but you have to show ID (Mon–Fri 8am–5pm).

Medical care There's a 24-hour pharmacy at Farmacia Internacional, Edificio Kent, Local 6, Av Juan Pablo II at Blvd de los Héroes. Embassies have lists of recommended doctors in various fields, and the Medicentro at 27a Av Nte and 21a C Pte has a number of doctors specializing in different fields. Hospital Rosales, 25a Av Nte at C Arce (☎222 5866) provides emergency medical cover.

Police The main station is the unmissable Scottish-castle-like building taking up an entire block on 10a Av Sur at 6a C Ote (☎271 4422).

Post office Behind the Centro de Gobierno on Blvd Centro de Gobierno; look for the large building with UPAE on the side. The *Lista de Correos* is at Window 12 in the main section (Mon–Fri 8am–5pm, Sat 8am–noon). There are smaller offices in the lower level of the Metrocentro mall and by the *Europa* supermarket on Plaza Beethoven.

Telephone office Antel, the state phone company, is at C Ruben Darío and 5a Av Sur, with a smaller branch in the Metrocentro (daily 6am–10pm).

Travel agents Plenty along the Alameda Roosevelt/Paseo Escalón for booking or changing flights.

Moving on from San Salvador

To get to the **airport**, *Taxis Acaya* leave from their office in El Centro (see p.283) at 6am, 7am, 10am and 2pm (about 1hr; US$3). Remember that there is a departure tax on international flights.

Scores of companies run **domestic buses** from a number of different terminals. Heading **west**, they leave from the **Terminal de Occidente** on Blvd Venezuela, west of El Centro; all of these also pick up and drop off on the Carretera Interamericana at the Basílica de Guadalupe. Buses **east** and **north** leave from the **Terminal de Oriente** on Blvd del Ejército Nacional, east of El Centro. Buses to **Usulután**, **Zacatecoluca** and **San Pedro Nonaulco**, however, leave from the **Terminal del Sur**, about 8km from El Centro on the airport highway; city buses #26 and #11b run past the terminal. To the cities and towns further **east** a number of faster "directo" buses leave from the **Terminal de Oriente**, run by a number of companies. These are pullman-style, stop less often and are slightly more expensive. For **San Miguel** and **La Unión**, buses leave every hour on the hour between 6am and 4pm; for **Santa Rosa de Lima**, they run every hour on the half-hour. **Tickets**, however – as on standard buses – are not normally bought in advance; to be sure of getting a seat, turn up well before the bus leaves.

Tours

The agents listed below all arrange **set tours**, starting from around US$30 per person. Though these can save a lot of hassle, especially if you're short of time, they can be rather rushed, whisking you on and off the tourist bus at a rapid rate. All (apart from *El Salvador Divers*) offer similar tours: to archeological sites (primarily Joya de Cerén and San Andrés), and areas of scenic beauty (Bosque Montecristo, Cerro Verde, etc), along with some activity trips.

Amor Tours, 73a Av Sur at Av Olímpica (☎223 5130, fax 279 0363).

El Salvador Divers, 3a C Pte 5020-A, at 99a Av Nte (☎264 0961). PADI courses, equipment rental and diving trips in the Los Cóbanos/Los Remedios stretch of the Pacific coast.

Rios Tropicales, C el Boquerón 6-A Cumbres de la Escalón (☎ & fax 223 9480).

Set Adventure Tours, Av Olímpica 3597 (☎279 3470, fax 279 3235; *tropic@es.com.sv*).

INTERNATIONAL BUS SERVICES FROM SAN SALVADOR

DESTINATION	DURATION	COMPANY	TERMINAL	FREQUENCY
Guatemala City	5–6hr	Puertobus (☎222 2158)	Puertobus Terminal	12 daily
		El Condor (☎224 6548)	Terminal de Occidente	3 daily
		Comfort Lines (☎221 1000)	Puertobus Terminal	2 daily
		Mermex (☎279 3484)	Terminal de Occidente	2 daily
		King Quality (☎222 2158)	Puertobus Terminal	2 daily
		Ticabus (☎222 4808)	Ticabus Terminal	1 daily
Talisman (Mexican/ Guat border)	9hr	El Condor (☎224 6548)	Terminal de Occidente	3 daily
Tegucigalpa	7hr	King Quality (☎222 2158)	Puertobus Terminal	2 daily
		Cruceros del Golfo (☎222 2158)	Puertobus Terminal	1 daily
		Ticabus (☎222 4808)	Ticabus Terminal	1 daily
Managua (connections the following day for San José and Panamá)	11hr	Ticabus (☎222 4808)	Ticabus Terminal	1 daily

Around San Salvador

One good thing about San Salvador is that a number of destinations offer immediate relief from the heat and crowds. Head in any direction and in well under an hour the harshness of the city gives way to lush, rolling countryside.

Santa Tecla, Los Chorros and Volcán San Salvador

Heading **west**, the Carretera Interamericana runs 14km through light industrial and residential districts to the small, busy town of **SANTA TECLA**, briefly the capital in 1854 and also known as Nueva San Salvador. Although considerably more relaxed than the capital, there is little reason to linger here. Six kilometres beyond, just off the highway is the *turicentro* of **Los Chorros** (daily 7am–5pm; US$0.90) beautifully situated in a natural gorge. Small waterfalls cascade through mossy volcanic slopes into a series of landscaped pools, suitable for bathing; there are public changing rooms and showers and a couple of comedores provide meals. Come on a weekday, unless you prefer your scenery with crowds. If you're in a group and feel brave enough to ignore the warnings about robbers, the surrounding hills provide pleasant walks. **Buses** for Los Chorros (#79) leave from 11a Av Sur and C Darío (every 15min; 40min).

From Santa Tecla, a road heads north, up and around the heavily cultivated slopes of **Volcán San Salvador**, about 10km from town. At 1960m it's the fifth-highest volcano in the country; the 540m-deep crater, **El Boquerón**, contains a smaller cone created in the last eruption in 1917. Though, due to frequent robberies, it is not safe to walk up – or down – the volcano, you can get to the top by public transport and then walk around the crater (about 2hr). There is also a marked path down wooded slopes to the base of the crater. To the east of the crater lies **El Picacho** peak; seek local advice as to the best way to reach this, through the coffee plantations. **Bus** #103 (hourly) and pickups run from 4a Av Sur and C Hernández in Santa Tecla to Boquerón; the bus drops you off about thirty minutes' walk from the crater, with the last bus leaving in mid-afternoon. Bear in mind that **taxi** and pick-up drivers are reluctant to make the journey up to the crater in the afternoon, warning of frequent robberies – in any case, early morning is the **best time** to go, when the views from the summit are clearest.

Maya sites: Joya de Cerén and San Andrés

Continuing west, the Carretera Interamericana runs through the flat and fertile Zapotitán Valley. Some 15km past Santa Tecla, a road branches off to the north and immediately splits; the left-hand fork here leads past the Maya site of **Joya de Cerén** (daily 9am–4pm; US$3), 5km south of the town of San Juan Opico. Designated a World Heritage Site in 1993, Joya de Cerén will disappoint those accustomed to the imposing, ceremonial edifices of the sites in Guatemala and Honduras. Its importance, however, lies in the wealth of detail provided about the daily lives of the Maya. To date, eighteen structures have been discovered of a village destroyed in a volcanic eruption around 600 AD. Lava from this and subsequent eruptions buried the site under up to six metres of ash until its accidental discovery in 1976.

Ten structures have so far been excavated, including houses, storage rooms and one believed to be used for religious rituals or communal events; not all are open to the public, however. Artefacts found at the site, including jars containing petrified beans, utensils and ceramics, as well as the discovery of gardens for growing a wide range of plants including maize, beans, agave and chilli peppers have helped to confirm a picture of a well-organized and stable society, relatively wealthy and with trade links throughout the Central American isthmus. A small, informative museum at the site details the development of the Maya culture and outlines the course of excavations (Spanish-language only).

Five kilometres west along the Carretera Interamericana is another important Maya ceremonial centre, **San Andrés** (daily 9am–4pm; US$3), set among rolling fertile agricultural land. Much smaller than sites in Guatemala or Honduras, San Andrés is nonetheless one of the largest pre-Columbian sites in El Salvador, originally covering more than three square kilometres and supporting a population of about 12,000. The site reached its peak in the Late Classic era, around 650–900, establishing itself as the regional capital for the settlements in the Zapotitán Valley.

Only sections of the ceremonial centre have been excavated and the remains of seven major structures are visible; sadly, much of these are today preserved with the help of concrete, spoiling their beauty somewhat and visibly driving home the message that large amounts of cash are a necessity in the preservation of sites like this. Ruins from what would have been the surrounding residential districts, still visible up to fifty years ago, have now also been lost to farming activity. However, you can wander freely around the site, and it is a popular spot for picnicking family groups at the weekends. The informative museum (Spanish-language only) has a small replica of what the site would have looked like in its prime.

Of what is on view, the **Acropolis** (or south plaza) forms the major part of the centre, a raised platform supporting a number of pyramids and annexes. Structure 1 on the south edge was a temple; on its north face are the remains of an altar. Access to these pyramids was restricted to the governing elite, whose living quarters (Los Aposentos) lay along the northern and western edges of the Acropolis; the bases of two of these have been reconstructed. The pyramids along the eastern edge of the Acropolis were possibly burial chambers. North of the Acropolis lay another plaza, used for markets and communal events. The largest pyramid (Structure 5) lies on the eastern edge of this plaza, but has not yet been excavated. Following the collapse of the Maya Empire from around 900 AD, San Andrés was not taken over by incoming Pipils, although the remains of a small farm dating from the Early Postclassic era (900–1200 AD) have been found close to Los Aposentos.

Any Santa Ana-bound **bus** will drop you off on the highway at the access road to the site, from where it is about five minutes' **walk** to the site entrance. It is also possible to walk between San Andrés and Joya de Cerén, but *not* alone. A path leads across the fields behind San Andrés, coming out about 4km northeast at an old railway track and abandoned station, just off the San Juan Opico road. From here it is another 3km or so to Joya de Cerén. From San Andrés you can also continue on to Santa Ana (see p.330) about another hour away – buses can be flagged down on the highway – or return to San Salvador.

East to Lago de Ilopango

Heading **east** from San Salvador, the Carretera Interamericana runs through a succession of dismal slums and dreary suburbs, once independent towns, now incorporated into the city. A couple of kilometres past the domestic airport at Ilopango, a road branches south and winds down to **Lago de Ilopango**, offering stunning views across the water to the mountains on the other side. The country's largest and deepest crater lake, Ilopango is a contrast of blue waters and dramatic, thickly vegetated cliffs tumbling into the water, surmounted to the east by the peaks of San Vicente volcano.

At the weekends, the city crowds pour in, most of them heading for the **turicentro** (daily 8am–6pm; US$0.90) at the poor,dusty hamlet of **APULO**, on the northern shore of the lake. Here there are small restaurants, a swimming pool, changing rooms and a section of beach, although the water is slightly grimy. A number of small boats ply for trade (US$8 an hour); drifting around the Isla de Amor, Isla de los Patos and the Cerros Quemados (created in an 1880 eruption) is a pleasant way to spend an hour or so. From Apulo a road heads round the shore, past the grounds of the private *Club Salvadoreño* to the hamlets of **CORINTO** and **SAN AGUSTÍN**; shortly before Corinto, where it drops closer to the water's edge, there is access to small rocky **beaches** and cleaner stretches of water. If you're tempted to **stay** the night, the *Hotel Vista del Lago* (④) sits about 2km above the lake, on the access road from the highway. The views are stunning, but the rooms – all with bath and a/c – are run-down.

South to Planes de Renderos

Heading **south**, a narrow, paved road clears the city surprisingly quickly and winds up through the low mountains of the Planes de Renderos. Twelve kilometres from San Salvador is the **Parque Balboa**, a somewhat trashy *turicentro* and (daily 8am–6pm; US$0.90) but still a pleasant getaway. About forty minutes' walk within the park is the **Puerto del Diablo**, a split rock formation at the summit of the Cerro Chulo, with spectacular views to the coast and across to San Vicente volcano.

Just before the entrance to Parque Balboa, a road branches off to wind down to the coast; a turning after about 2km leads to the small town of **PANCHIMALCO**, spectacularly set at the foot of the lush slopes of Cerro Chulo, with the Puerto del Diablo overlooking the town to the west. The area is inhabited by the Panchos, descendents of the Pipils, although traditional dress is rarely seen nowadays. The colonial church, built in 1725, is a national monument, and there's a huge ceiba tree in the main square. Usually a sleepy, quiet place, things become livelier during the town's annual **festivals** (see p.271).

travel details

BUSES

San Salvador to: Joya de Cerén (#108, Terminal de Occidente; every 30min; 1hr); Lago de Ilopango (#15, 3a C Pte at 1a Av Nte; every 10min; 45min); Panchimalco (#17, Av 29 de Agosoto; every 15min; 45min); Parque Balboa (#12, Av 29 de Agosto, south of the mercado central; every 15min; 30min); San Andrés (#201, Terminal de Occidente; every 10min; 1hr).

For details of **international services** from San Salvador, see p.296.

CHAPTER 13

THE NORTH

orth of San Salvador, hilly pastures and agricultural land give way to the remote, rugged and sparsely populated **Chalatenango** and **Cuscatlán provinces**, a region of poverty and pride, all but closed to outsiders. The Spanish found few natural riches to attract them this far north, and the wealth generated by the indigo and coffee plantations of the lowlands never reached here. Successive generations of campesinos have struggled to make a living in this harsh terrain, separated from the capital by distance and mind-set. The sustained underdevelopment of the area created fertile ground for dissent and support for the **FMLN**, who controlled large parts of the department of Chalatenango for significant periods during the 1980s. Both army and guerrillas struggled to take control, leaving communities devastated in their wake and refugees fleeing across the border to Honduras. The scars of this are still evident, as – helped by various international aid agencies – villages struggle to repopulate and rebuild, against a background of continuing economic hardship and growing civil violence.

Understandably, then, the welcome extended to foreigners can be initially rather cool; tourism is not a widely understood concept and travelling here is neither easy nor comfortable and – in rare instances – can be **dangerous**. Although so far no foreigners have been killed, the murder rate is high, particularly in Chalatenango, where many locals have been hijacked, held up with guns and shot. Though this usually happens to people in cars, it is not recommended to walk in the countryside in Chalatenango, especially alone, and never carry anything of value. A little common sense, however, along with persistence, does bring results. Quite apart from the breathtaking mountain views and clear, fresh blue skies, there are a couple of genuinely appealing places to see: chiefly the tranquil and friendly **Suchitoto**, considered to be the finest colonial town in the country, set on the shores of **Lago Suchitlán**; and the mountain village of **La Palma**, with its cottage handicraft industry. The Pipil ruins of **Cihuatán**, though somewhat specialist in appeal, are an easy trip from the capital. In addition, the glorious **Metapán Alotepeque** mountain range offers walking and hiking possibilities.

Cihuatán

The main highway north, CA-4, or the **Troncal del Norte**, runs the 95km or so from San Salvador to the Honduran border at El Poy. A favourite target of the guerrillas during the war, the road is still under repair, although most of the work is now complete. Some 35km from the capital, just off the highway, the workaday town of **AGUILARES** has little of interest for visitors but is conveniently close to the ruins of **Cihuatán**, 4km north. Though it's the most important Postclassic site in the country, a visit here is probably only for real archeology buffs; most of the buildings remain unexcavated and there is very little by way of information.

For an explanation of **accommodation price codes**, see p.270.

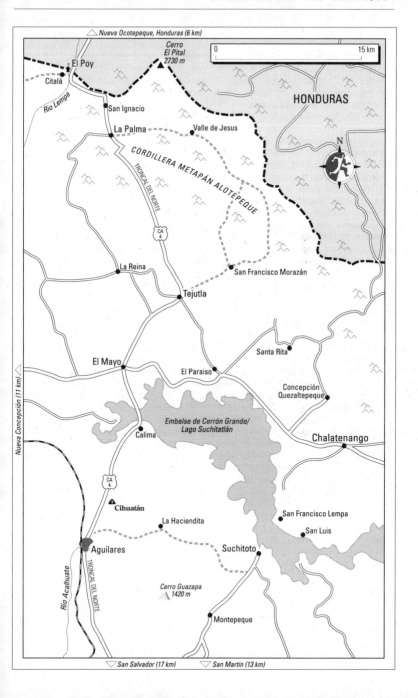

Nueva Ocotepeque, Honduras (6 km)

Cerro
El Pital
2730 m

0   15 km

El Poy

Citalá

Río Lempa

San Ignacio

HONDURAS

La Palma

Valle de Jesus

CORDILLERA METAPÁN ALOTEPEQUE

N

TRONCAL DEL NORTE

CA 4

La Reina

San Francisco Morazán

Tejutla

Santa Rita

El Mayo

El Paraiso

Concepción
Quezaltepeque

Embalse de Cerrón Grande/
Lago Suchitatlán

Chalatenango

Nueva Concepción (11 km)

Calima

CA 4

Cihuatán

La Haciendita

San Francisco Lempa

San Luis

Aguilares

Suchitoto

TRONCAL DEL NORTE

Río Acalhuate

Cerro Guazapa
1420 m

Montepeque

San Salvador (17 km)   San Martin (13 km)

Although sporadic excavations have been carried out over the last hundred years, the true dimensions of the site did not become fully apparent until felling of tree cover began in the 1950s. Sadly, the area is now acutely deforested, and nothing remains of the extensive woods amid which the site stood. Originally covering an area of around four square kilometres, Cihuatán (meaning "Place of Women" in Nahaut) was founded sometime after the first waves of Pipils (or Toltecs) began arriving in El Salvador in the tenth century. There is no evidence of occupation prior to this and the site was abandoned and destroyed around 1200, for reasons unknown. Residential areas surrounded two ceremonial centres, divided by a natural depression and covering an area of about half a square kilometre. Most of the excavations to date have been of the so-called West Ceremonial Centre, stretching west from the Río Acelhuate, where around twenty structures have been identified, including stepped pyramids and an I-shaped pelota court, bearing a clear Mexican influence, reflecting the origins of the Pipils. Artefacts found – including remains of ritual jars, some in the shape of human heads, ceramics and representations of the gods Tlaloc (rain) and Mictlanteuctli (underworld) – indicate trading and other links with settlements in Guatemala, the Gulf Coast and high ground of Central Mexico.

The site is now administered by Concultura (Edificio A-5, Centro de Gobierno, San Salvador; ☎221 4364). There are no set **opening hours**; take a taxi from Aguilares and ask the resident guard for permission to look round. All **buses** running from the capital to Chalatenango or La Palma pass through Aguilares.

Suchitoto and Lago Suchitlán

Some 18km east of Aguilares, near the site of a pre-Columbian Pipil town, **SUCHITO-TO** lies on a small ridge above the southern edge of **Lago Suchitlán**, more properly known as the Cerron Grande dam. The town's height of glory came when the original Villa San Salvador was located near here in 1528. In the many years since the capital was relocated, life has generally been quiet, except during the 1980s, when both the dam and the Cerro Guazapa, looming to the west of the town, were the scene of bitter fighting as the army struggled to dislodge the guerrillas from their strongholds in the area. The roads up and around the Cerro still bear the crumbling remains of the trenches and dugouts used by both sides, now quietly submerged beneath green vegetation.

Today, Suchitoto, set amid beautiful rolling countryside, makes for a relaxing getaway for a couple of days. It's a small, quiet, friendly place, with some of the finest remaining examples of colonial architecture in the country, with low, red-tiled adobe houses stretching along largely unpaved roads. In the centre, the **Iglesia Santa Lucia** – now being restored – is worth a look, with a particularly fine wooden altar. The friendly **Casa de Cultura**, opposite the church, has displays on local history and can give information on walks in the area. A small park, a couple of blocks east of the church, commands stunning views across the blue waters of the **lake**; from the east and north ends of town, paths lead down to the lake shore, where swimming is possible. If the boat services to the villages around the lake shore are not up and running, local fishermen may be persuaded to take you out.

Nothing remains of the pre-Columbian settlement, but the countryside where it stood is tranquil and scenic; further afield, paths also lead up Cerro Guazapa.

Practicalities

Of the limited **accommodation**, the *Posada Suchitlán* on 4a C Pte, a couple of blocks north of the lookout, is a very comfortable place to pass a few days. Large, well-furnished rooms are set around small patios, and the attached restaurant serves until 9pm (☎335 1064; ⑤; reservations recommended at weekends). The Swedish owner is a mine of information on the area and its history. The only other accommodation in town, *El Viajero*, 3a C Pte, two blocks up from the market building (①), has very basic, dark and dirty rooms. For **eating**, *La Fonda* at the eastern end of town on Av 15 de Septiembre has great views over the lake, and serves well-prepared, fresh fish, meat and chicken. Near the church, *El Obraje* is simpler, but good, and there are a couple of small comedores on the main plaza near the market.

You can get to Suchitoto by **bus** via Aguilares, along a dirt road that branches east off the highway, but it is much quicker to take a direct bus from San Salvador via the small town of San Martín (every 15min; 90min). The last service to the capital is at 5.30pm. Returning to Aguilares, buses (hourly; 1hr 30min) use the extremely rough, but serviceable dirt road that connects with the Troncal del Norte and transport to Chalatenango and La Palma.

Northeast to Chalatenango

From Aguilares, the highway continues north 19km to **El Mayo**, a collection of scrubby comedores and bus shelters that form a major road junction. From here, paved highways run west to the small town of Nueva Concepción, and east through agricultural and pasture lands along the fringes of the lake to **CHALATENANGO**. An important commercial centre, capital of the department of the same name, Chalatenango – established as a Spanish settlement in the seventeenth century – has the rough-and-ready feel of a frontier settlement, an atmosphere enhanced by the raised wooden walkways fronting the buildings of the centre. During the early 1980s this was a stronghold of the FMLN, who at one point claimed to have control of 26 of 33 towns in the department and attacked the town on several occasions, the last in 1989. Today, much of the physical damage has been repaired, but the huge military garrison still looms over the central plaza, next to the church, and both the city and department have the reputation of being the most lawless areas of the country. Casual visitors are likely to be unaffected by this, but in recent years there has been a rising trend in car-jackings, armed **burglaries** and – very rare – bus hold-ups.

Incongruously, Chalatenango lies in a beautiful setting, southeast of the La Peña Mountains and overlooking the distant Cerron Grande to the west. **Walks** in the surrounding hills are possible, but seek local advice and don't go alone; in addition to dangers from humans, some of the surrounding areas were mined. Just outside town to the east is the **Agua Fria turicentro** (daily 7am–5pm; US$0.90) with swimming pools filled by the nearby Río Armulasco. Twelve kilometres northwest of Chalatenango, the village of **CONCEPCIÓN QUEZALTEPEQUE** is chiefly noted for its **hammock** industry. Workshops and homes around the village turn out colourful items in nylon and, less commonly, cotton and *mezcal* fibre. Prices are about half those in San Salvador; the hammocks are also sold in the market at Chalatenango at roughly the same prices as here.

There is no earthly reason to stay in Chalatenango; neither atmosphere nor amenities are conducive to a pleasant stay. If you get stuck, **accommodation** is limited to the unmarked *Hospedaje La Inez* (opposite the Antel office on C San Martín, one block west of the central plaza; look for the pink door and the purple *Uva* sign; ①). The none-too-clean rooms and basic washing facilities are somewhat redeemed by the friendliness of the owners. Similarly, there is a dearth of **places to eat**; try *Comedor Portalito* opposite *Banco Cuscatlan* on 4a C Pte and *Comedor Carmary* on 3a Av Sur for comida a la vista. **Buses** arrive and depart from 3a Av Sur and 6a C Pte, a couple of blocks from the parque central.

La Palma

From the El Mayo junction, Highway CA-4 begins its climb up into the mountains of the Cordillera Metapan-Altotepeque, passing through the small, unexciting town of Tejutla, before making the slow, winding ascent to the Honduran border. The tortuous bus journey is compensated for by the views, with pine-clad mountains falling away to either side, and distant, hazy ranges seeming to stretch on forever.

LA PALMA, supposedly named after the indigenous custom of building houses out of palms, is a sleepy mountain village founded in 1915 under the name Dulce Nombre de la Palma. Its calm is really only broken during the annual **fiesta of Dulce Nombre de María**, in the third week of February. Today the village is chiefly famous for its **artesenías** – naïf-style wooden and ceramic handicrafts and toys, brightly painted with representations of people, villages and farming life, sold all over the country. This cottage industry, instituted by Salvadorean artist Fernando Llort in the 1970s, is now the economic mainstay of the village, with workshops turning out hundreds of pieces a week. Most workshops sell their goods on the spot and are pretty relaxed about visitors turning up to watch the work; prices are somewhat cheaper than in San Salvador. Just above *Antel* on the main road through the village is the **gallery** of Salvadorean artist Alfredo Linares (Mon–Sat 9am–noon & 1–4pm) displaying his fine watercolours and pen-and-ink representations of the area and its peoples. Prices for the originals are not particularly low, but postcards and prints are also sold.

North of La Palma are several **hiking trails**, including, for the adventurous, El Salvador's highest mountain **Cerro Pital** (2730m), 10km away on the border. A rough road branches east just before La Palma to run to Las Pilas on the lower slopes of the mountain; a dirt road also leads up from the village of **San Ignacio** (see below). Hiking to the summit will be a 2–3 day adventure, for which you need to be fully equipped. If you don't mind not reaching the top, the trails provide day hikes of varying lengths; the gradients are reasonably steep. The owners of the *Hotel La Palma* are a good source of information on walks and guides.

Practicalities

Accommodation in La Palma is limited to the *Hotel La Palma* (☎335 9012; ⑤), a rustic-style and comfortable but rather over-priced place; the similarly over-priced restaurant serves all meals. Other **places to eat** are the comedor/*pupusería* at the entrance to the hotel; the *La Estancia* restaurant on the main road through village, near the hotel; and La *Terraza*, one block past the church. Both these last tend to shut early in the evening.

To the Honduran border

The highway continues past La Palma to the Honduran border at El Poy, 11km away, a thirty-minute journey by bus. The village of **SAN IGNACIO**, 6km from La Palma, also has a few craft **workshops** and two **places to stay**. The rather basic *La Posada* (②) stands on the central square, while the upmarket *Hotel Entrepinos* is on the highway just before the village (☎335 9370; fax 335 9382; ⑦). The large, very comfortable rooms, all with fireplaces, have beautiful views; horses are available for hire and the hotel arranges tours.

Just short of El Poy, a road branching to the left crosses the Río Lempa and runs to the village of **CITALÁ**, 1km away. From here a daily bus leaves at 5am, running west along a rough but scenic mountain road to **Metapán**, for access to Bosque Montecristo (see p.336) and the Guatemalan border at Anguiatú; the journey takes three to four hours. There is a basic *posada* (①) close to the centre of the village.

El Poy

EL POY itself is a drab, dusty village with a collection of small comedores and general stores. Crossing the border here is straightforward and quick; there is a US$1.50 entrance charge for Honduras, but no entry or exit charges for El Salvador. A lot of trucks use this route, but private traffic is light; crossing early in the day is advisable. The last **bus** from the border for La Palma and San Salvador leaves at 4.30pm. On the Honduran side buses run the 10km to Nueva Ocotepeque (see p.380) every forty minutes or so until 5pm.

travel details

BUSES

San Salvador to: Chalatenango (#125, Terminal de Oriente; every 15min until 5pm; 2hr 30min); El Poy (#119, Terminal de Oriente; every 30min until 4pm; 4hr 30min); La Palma (#119, Terminal de Oriente; every 30min until 4pm; 4hr); Suchitoto (#129, Terminal de Oriente; every 15min; 1hr 30min).

CHAPTER 14

THE EAST

The rough and wild terrain of **eastern El Salvador** remained, in the main, unexplored territory for the pre-Columbian Pipils, who did not venture far beyond the natural frontier of the Río Lempa into this "land that smokes" of lofty volcanoes, hot plains and mountain ranges. Its Lenca inhabitants developed their society in isolation from the west, and it was with some reluctance and difficulty that the Spanish conquered this frontier. Today, the region still remains separated from the capital by distance and experience, with the wealth of the coffee plantations around San Vicente and San Miguel contrasting cruelly with rural poverty. Refugees from communities devastated by the civil war – eastern El Salvador saw the worst of the fighting – have in the last decade returned to try and pick up the pieces in this wild and beautiful area, but their struggle against poverty and underinvestment is painfully apparent. Travelling here, while difficult, is thought-provoking and moving; expect some reservation, even hostility, from locals and be prepared to understand and accept the difficulties – of continual poverty, poor infrastructure and growing civil violence – that people still face.

The charming city of **San Vicente** makes a convenient base for hiking up the lofty peaks of **Chichontepec**, or San Vicente volcano, and swimming in **Lago Apastepeque**. Bustling **San Miguel**, the third-largest city in the country, is a transport hub, and a good place to recuperate from life on the road, with the largely unexcavated archeological site of **Quelepa** and the wetlands reserve of **Laguna el Jocotal** within easy reach. Buses head north from here to the tranquil mountain village of **Perquín** and the moving **Museo de la Revolución Salvadoreña**.

East to San Vicente

From San Salvador, the Carretera Interamericana edges its way through industrial units, shanty towns and the grimy suburbs on the edge of the city, before arriving at **COJUTEPEQUE**, 32km from the capital. There's little to see here other than the shrine of the **Virgen de Fátima** of Portugal; the statue was brought here in 1949. Housed at the top of the Cerro de las Pavas, about thirty minutes' walk from the centre of town, the shrine attracts worshippers and petitioners on Sundays particularly. The summit also gives wonderful views over Lago de Ilopango. Some 6km beyond Cojutepeque, a road branching north leads through beautiful rolling countryside to the small town of **ILOBASCO**, noted for its brightly painted earthenware decorated with animals and daily scenes. Look out for the town speciality known as *sorpresas* (surprises) – detailed scenes of village life contained in small, egg-shaped shells. Regular direct **buses** run to both these towns from San Salvador's Terminal de Oriente (see p.295).

Further along the Carretera Interamericana, some 25km from Cojutepeque, a junction marked by ramshackle cane bus shelters gives on to the branch road for the attractive city of **San Vicente**, set in the Jiboa valley at the foot of **Volcán Chichontepec**.

For an explanation of **accommodation price codes**, see p.270.

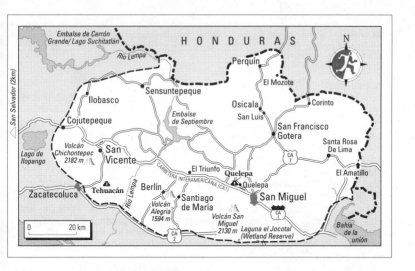

The approach is perhaps one of the most spectacular in the country; the road sharply descending to the valley floor on one side, while across on the other rises the conical bulk of the twin-peaked volcano, dwarfing everything in sight, particularly the white spires of the city nestling below.

San Vicente

SAN VICENTE was founded in 1635 by fifty local Spanish families in accordance with the 1600 Law of the Indies, prohibiting the Spanish from living among the indigenous people. Gathering under the shade of a tempisque tree near Río Alcahuapa on December 26, 1635, the families formally inaugurated San Vicente de Lorenzana, in honour of the Spanish martyr San Vicente Abad.

Until the 1980s, the biggest threat to the stability of San Vicente came on February 16, 1833, when the forces of Anastasio Aquino, leader of the Nonualco indigenous uprising, arrived in the city. "Inebriated with alcohol and success", they removed the crown from the statue of San José in the **Iglesia Nuestra Señora del Pilar** and crowned Aquino "Emperor of the Nonualcos". The rebels then returned to Santiago Nonualco, some 30km away; here, Aquino was captured by government forces on April 23 and later sent back to San Vicente and hanged.

Today, San Vicente is a calm, low-slung city, in a rich agricultural area producing sugar cane, cotton and coffee. It was attacked several times by guerrillas during the 1980s, and there remains an overt military presence, with a huge barracks near the centre. The central **Parque Cañas** acts as focus of the city, dominated by the **Torre Kiosko**, an eye-catching open-work clocktower. On the eastern edge of the parque is the rather bare city cathedral; walk down its side, along C Daniel Diaz, and you come to the original tempisque tree, under which the city was founded, and which was declared a historic monument in 1984. Two blocks south of the parque on Av Mirondo Sur is the **Iglesia el Pilar**; the statue of San José – complete with crown – remains in the church. Classified a historic monument, the church has a beautiful carved wooden altar; a plaque by the entrance honours José Simeon Cañas, the man who abolished slavery in El Salvador.

The military barracks takes up an entire block between El Pilar and the parque; a walk west up the side of the barracks brings you to the extensive **market**, stretching over several streets. On Saturday afternoons, they hold **bingo** games here, in an open-sided hall.

Practicalities

Buses coming from the highway run through the parque and south to the bus station on Av Canónigo Lazo at C Indalecio Miranda; stand with the cathedral on your immediate left and Av Canónigo Lazo is straight ahead. Buses run from San Salvador every ten minutes, with the last leaving for the capital at 6.30pm. For phone calls the **Antel** office is on Av Canónigo Lazo, two blocks from the parque along its eastern edge whilst the **post office** is on C 1 de Julio, one block down from the barracks. There's a **Banco Hipotecario** on the parque.

The best of the **accommodation** is the new and very clean *Villa Españolas* on Av José Maria Cornejo, a block north of the parque (☎333 1445; ③); all rooms have private bath. On the parque itself is *Central Park* (☎333 0383; ②–③), which has some rooms with TV and a/c. The on-site restaurant serves adequate meals. Friendliest of the bunch is the *Casa de Huéspedes el Turista* on C Indalecio Miranda and Av Maria de los Angeles, one block southwest of El Pilar (☎333 0323; ②), where all the rooms have bath, TV and hammocks.

Of the **places to eat**, first choice is *Casa Blanca* at C Alberto de Merino 13 (daily 11am–9pm), for its reasonably priced meat and fish dishes. *Restaurante Taiwan*, on the parque next to *Hotel Central*, has average comidas a la vista, but, despite its name, no Chinese food. The restaurant at *Hotel Central*, serves simple meals and is a good place for people-watching; both these close at around 8.30pm, depending on how many diners there are. *Comedor Rivoly* on Av Maria de los Angeles has good breakfasts and comidas a la vista (daily 7am–8pm), whilst *El Cuco*, next to the bus station on Av Canónigo Lazo, serves tacos and sandwiches (daily 11am–8.30pm). For ice cream *Pops* is on the parque, next to the Alcaldía.

Around San Vicente

Everywhere in San Vicente is dominated by the towering bulk of **Volcán Chichontepec** (or Volcán San Vicente) to the southwest. Meaning "Hill of Two Breasts" in Nahuatl, the twin peaks rise to 2182m, making it the second-highest volcano in the country. It's considered to be dormant, with cultivated lower slopes and the steep summit left to scrub and soil. A number of **paths** lead up the slopes, from the village of **San Antonio** on the east side, or from **Guadelupe** on the northwest flank. From either, it is a stiff, two-hour minimum walk to the top; good walking shoes are essential, as is strong sun protection and lots of water. From the summit there are panoramic views north across the Jiboa valley, with San Vicente nestling distant at the bottom, and west across to Lago de Ilopango. **Buses** to San Antonio and Guadelupe leave every hour or so until mid-afternoon from San Vicente's market.

Laguna de Apastepeque, 3km northeast of the city, is a small, well-maintained *turicentro* (daily 8am–6pm; US$0.90) set round a crater lake, with clear, clean blue waters and shady banks. The good swimming makes this an extremely popular spot with families at weekends. Nearby is the more secluded Laguna Ciega. Bus #156 to Apastepeque leaves from the bus station regularly until 6pm. Near Verapaz, 10km east of San Vicente, are the natural hot-springs **Los Infernillos**, used for years as a medicinal retreat because of their high sulphur content; buses (from the station) leave all day for the village.

Eight kilometres from San Vicente on the road to Tecoluca, the ruins of **Tehuacán** (daily; free) lie on the eastern slopes of Chichontepec. A former Pipil settlement, the site covers an area of about three square kilometres, but unless you're a real archeology buff, there is very little to see. Excavations have uncovered the remains of a series of terraces oriented north–south, a central plaza, walls and roads and a pyramid. In the plaza are what are thought to be the foundations for the elite residences and a temple. Stone and earthenware artefacts of taken from the site bear a clear resemblance to Mexican artefacts from the same era, indicating the common heritage of the Mexican Toltecs and migratory Pipils.

San Vicente to San Miguel

Beyond San Vicente, the Carretera Interamericana continues through low mountains and coffee plantations before crossing the **Río Lempa**, 30km from the city. This formidable, natural boundary once afforded the Lenca inhabitants of the eastern territories some measure of protection, first against the Pipils and then against the Spanish. The Pipils called the area east of the river Popocatepetl or "the land that smokes", presumably because of the number of active volcanos.

Traffic slows crossing the river, as buses creep over the temporary bridges set up in place of the **Puente Cuscatlán**. Once a symbol of El Salvador's modernity, the bridge was bombed by the FMLN in January 1984, and the truncated end supports, daubed with FMLN graffitti, are a sobering reminder of the country's recent past.

At the village of Mercedes Umaña, about 45km from San Vicente, a road heads south to the rough, uncomfortable town of **Berlín**, the scene of much activity during the war and today the location of an important geo-thermal power plant. From here, hourly buses run along a road around the **Volcán Tecapa** to the more pleasant town of **SANTIAGO DE MARÍA**, which has a couple of simple hotels. Halfway between the two towns is Alegría, from where paths lead up the volcano to the sulphurous crater lake **Laguna de Alegría**, an energetic walk of about about one hour. This area is predominantly coffee-growing country, with plantations lining the slopes of the rolling mountains. From Santiago, buses run up to **El Triunfo** on the Carretera Interamericana, to continue on to San Miguel; from both Berlín and Santiago there are also regular connections south to Usulután.

Beyond El Triunfo the scenery changes; the coffee pastures give way to dry plains dotted with the cones of volcanos; to the south the land falls away to pasture lands and the coastal mangrove swamps. A major crop in this area is henequen (sisal); fields of serried ranks of the distinctive, spikey grey-green plants line the highway into the distance.

San Miguel

SAN MIGUEL is a bustling, hot and flat place, the commercial hub for the east of the country. More relaxed than San Salvador and with less claim to grandeur than Santa Ana (see p.330), the city itself does not offer much by way of tourist attractions. It is, however, a pleasant enough place to spend a couple of days resting up between bus journeys and exploring the nearby Lenca archeological site of **Quelepa** or the wetland reserve of **Laguna el Jocotal**. And no one should pass up the chance to eat at *La Pema*, El Salvador's most famous restaurant, just outside the city.

San Miguel really comes alive in November, particularly during **Carnival** on the 29th. A relatively recent affair, instituted in 1958, it has grown to be the largest carnival in Central America (or so they say), attracting visitors from all over the country, and ex-pats returning especially for the event. The music, fireworks, street dancing and general merriment are the climax to two months of celebrations for the festival of **Virgen de la Paz**, the city's patroness (see p.312).

Some history

Shortly after founding Villa San Salvador in 1528, the Spanish began to turn their minds to the territory east of Cuscatlán, motivated by the need to consolidate their gains against both the hostile indigenous population and against rival conquistador forces, based in Nicaragua under Pedrarias Davila. Exasperated by the capture of an expedition led by Diego de Rojas by these forces in 1530, Pedro de Alvarado dispatched **Luis de Moscosco** to finalize the conquest of the east. Around May 8, 1530, the day of San Miguel Arcángel, de Moscosco founded **San Miguel de Frontera**, on a site thought to have been in the vicinity of the Lenca city of Chaparrastique ("place of beautiful gardens"). Surviving a number of ferocious uprisings, the settlement thrived after **gold** was found in the area in 1537, being granted the title of city in 1574. A fire in March 1586 destroyed much of the town, however, and it was moved the few kilometres to its present location at the northern base of Volcán Chaparrastique.

Initially the least important of the Spanish cities, San Miguel soon began to grow wealthy, at first on the profits of gold and trade, and then on the coffee, cotton and henequen grown on the surrounding fertile land. A number of **religious order**s also attracted a certain prestige – by 1740, the city boasted two convents and two friaries – and in 1812 it was granted the title of "most noble and faithful city". Another nickname, sometimes still used, was "pearl of the east", because of its great wealth.

Guerrillas were active in the city and surrounding area during the 1980s and the city's barracks and electrical installations were attacked on several occasions. Today, however, there is a less visible military presence than in other towns in the east and north, and the city's flat streets hum and rattle self-importantly with commerce and trade.

Arrival and information

All **buses**, coming from San Salvador or points east and south of San Miguel, arrive at the main terminal on 6a C Ote and 8a–10a Av Nte, four blocks (or ten minutes' walk) east of the centre. **Antel** is on the corner of Parque Guzmán next to the Alcaldía whilst the **post office** is on 4a Av Sur at 3a C Ote, south from the cathedral. **Banks** cluster around the west side of the parque, including BanCo, Banco Cuscatlán and Banco Multivalores which gives Visa cash advances. For shopping, there is a new Metrocentro on the highway at the edge of town, also with banks and a cinema. A Multi Mart supermarket is on 4a Av Sur just past the cathedral.

Accommodation

San Miguel's handful of upmarket **hotels** lie along the Carretera Interamericana (Av Roosevelt) to the west of town, about fifteen minutes' walk from the centre. Most of the other choices are around the bus terminal, inevitably a rather sleazy area. Given its daytime bustle, San Miguel is very quiet at night; there isn't any unusual amount of danger, but if empty, ill-lit streets make you nervous, staying in a hotel along the highway is your best bet.

AROUND THE BUS TERMINAL

Hotel del Centro, 8a C Ote 505 at 8a Av Nte (☎661 5473). A beacon of light in the surrounding sleaze; very friendly, helpful and spotlessly clean; the comfortable rooms all have bath and TV. ③.

SAN MIGUEL

ACCOMMODATION

Hotel del Centro	1
Hotel Hispanamericano	4
Hotel San Rafael	3
Hotel Terminal	2

Hotel Hispanamericano, 6a Av Nte bis at 8a C Ote (☎661 1202). Has definitely seen better days. The rooms are large but dingy; some have a/c. ②.

Hotel San Rafael, 6a C Ote 704, turn right out of the bus terminal (☎661 4113). Friendly, secure place with clean rooms with bath and hammock and a communal TV area; there's a café on site (6am–8pm) and a nice view from the roof. ②.

Hotel Terminal, 6a C Ote immediately opposite the terminal (☎661 1086). Clean and pleasant, with restaurant service until late; all rooms have bath, TV and a/c. ④.

IN TOWN AND ON THE HIGHWAY

Hotel Caleta, 3a Av Sur 601 between 9a and 11a C Pte (☎661 3233). Clean and quiet with hammocks and a small courtyard; some rooms with bath. ②.

Hotel El Mandarin, Av Roosevelt Nte 407 (☎669 6969). Luxury, San Miguel style; all rooms with bath, phone and TV. The restaurant on the premises stays open until 9pm. ⑥.

Hotel Milian, Av Roosevelt Nte at 10a C Pte (☎669 5052). Comfortable rooms with bath; the hotel also has a pool. ④.

Hotel Oasis, 11a Av Nte between 6a and 8a C Pte (☎661 2126). Clean rooms with bath; a small café serves basic meals. ③.

El Viajero, 7a Av Nte 405 at 6a C Pte (☎661 1716). Rather basic rooms surrounding a grassy courtyard; those with bath are slightly more expensive. ③.

The City

The heart of San Miguel is the shady **Parque David J. Guzmán**, named after the eminent nineteenth-century Migueleño biologist and member of the French Academy of Science. On the east of the parque sits the **Cathedral**, built in the 1880s, and on the south is the Alcaldía. The city is laid out in the usual quasi-grid system, with the main avenida (Av Gerardo Barrios/Av José Simeón Cañas) and the main calle (C Chaparrastique/C Sirama) intersecting at **Parque Barrios** two blocks southwest of Parque Guzmán. Parque Barrios itself is mostly overrun by the extensive market, a sprawling affair stretching back to 3a Av Sur and south, in whose narrow warrens upfront traders encourage you to buy all manner of food, clothes and other goods.

Just south of the cathedral is the **Antiguo Teatro Nacional**, a renaissance-style building completed in 1909; performances occasionally take place here, particularly during fiesta time. Seven blocks west of the centre, the appealing **Iglesia Capilla Medalla Milagrosa**, set in pretty gardens, was built by French nuns who also worked in the hospital that used to stand next door.

Restaurants and cafés

There isn't an overabundance of **places to eat and drink** in San Miguel, although there are a few reasonable places for well-prepared standard meat and chicken dishes. For quick and simple meals, the area around the bus terminal has a number of cheap comedores and there are a few more up-scale places in the centre.

La Barrita, 4a C Ote, two blocks up from the cathedral. Well-prepared and reasonably priced meat and chicken dishes in an informal setting. Daily except Sun.

Comedor Esmeralda, 8a Av Nte between 4a and 6a C Ote. Good, basic breakfasts and comidas a la vista. Daily except Sun 6am–7pm.

Gran Tejano, 4a C Ote just up from the parque. Reasonably priced, large steaks and meat dishes. Daily 11.30am–9pm.

NUESTRA SEÑORA DE LA PAZ

San Miguel's imposing cathedral, while rather disappointing inside, holds the cherished statue of **Nuestra Señora de la Paz**, the city's patroness. Accounts differ as to how she arrived in the city. One version relates that in 1683, San Miguel and San Salvador gathered together an army to fight the English pirates then attacking coastal villages and advancing inland. On seeing the massed forces, the pirates chose to retreat, leaving behind them, in the small port of Amapala, a statue of the virgin, which was then taken to San Miguel. Another version has it that a fisherman, discovering a sealed casket on the beach, loaded it onto a donkey and began to walk to the city. The beast struggled on for fourteen days, before collapsing on the spot where the cathedral now stands. On opening the casket and seeing the contents, it was decided to build a temple to venerate the miraculous image. The statue was christened La Paz because of the cessation of bitter intercine fighting on her arrival.

Regardless of how she arrived, the statue's true moment of glory came during the eruption of Volcán Chaparrastique on September 21, 1787. On seeing a glowing river of lava advancing on San Miguel, the terrified citizens praying to the virgin to save them took the statue to the door of the cathedral and presented her to the volcano. The lava changed course and the city was saved. In honour of these events, San Miguel holds two months of fiesta, beginning with the virgin "descending" the volcano on September 21 and culminating in a procession through the streets, attended by thousands, on November 21. A more recent coda to the fiesta is the annual carnival held on November 29.

Oasis, 4a C Ote, opposite *Pizza Hut*. Possibly the juices and *licuados* in the country; huge glasses go for around US$1.50. Daily except Sun 9am–6pm.

La Pema, 5km from town on the road to Usulután (☎667 6055). El Salvador's most renowned restaurant is not cheap, but the huge servings of *mariscada*, a creamy soup with every conceivable type of seafood, and the jugs of fruit salad served as an accompaniment will mean you won't feel like eating again for a while. Come here and treat yourself. Daily 11am–5pm.

Pizza Hut, 4a C Ote between Av Barrios and 1a Av Nte. Standard dishes and authentic-tasting pizza.

Pupuseria Chilita, 8a C Ote at 6a Av Nte. A barn of a neighbourhood *pupuseria*, particularly popular at the weekends. Three or four *pupusas* and a fruit juice make an adequate meal. Open until around 9.30pm.

Around San Miguel: Quelepa and Laguna el Jocotal

A short distance northwest of San Miguel, about 1.5km from the highway, is the pretty little village of Quelepa, beyond which lie the **Ruinas de Quelepa**. Though there isn't much to see of this predominantly Lenca site dating back to around 300 BC – there has been very little excavation – the walk there and around makes for an enjoyable half day or so.

Quelepa was a flourishing city which reached its peak between 625 and 1000 AD; its I-shaped pelota court and small pyramids have been dated from this time. A jaguar head altar, fragments of ceramics and other artefacts – now in storage in San Salvador – indicate that the inhabitants had trade links with cultures to the west; most of the finds are of the style of – or possibly from – Maya sites in Honduras and Mexico, signifying trade contact. Absence of Toltec-influenced artefacts also suggests that Quelepa was exclusively Lenca, rather than Pipil. Around forty structures have been identified at the site, which was abandoned around 1000 AD, amongst them a series of tombs, in sufficient numbers to form a cemetery. A paved road – parts of which still exist – through the site would have led to the summit of the 300m Cerro Grande, to the south; this is believed to have been a principal monument at the time the city was inhabited, possibly containing the main altar. The friendly **Casa de Cultura** in Quelepa displays a collection of artefacts from the site – fragments of household utensils, ceramic figures and small ceremonial heads.

The **site** itself lies about 2km northeast of the village, between the Río San Esteban and a low range of hills. Follow 4a C Ote out of the centre and down to the river, cross over and ask for directions at the white house on the other side. At first glance there appears to be nothing but fields of henequen and the odd herd of cows; the area has long been under cultivation. The small mounds in the fields, however, are the remains of the pyramids, and close searching may bring to light the remnants of some walls. A nice way to return, if you don't mind getting your feet wet, is by wading up the shallow river itself.

Bus #90 leaves the central parque in San Miguel frequently, dropping you off on the highway, fifteen minutes' walk from the village. Bus #90G, which runs directly to the village, leaves the city less often.

Laguna el Jocotal, a small wetlands reserve supported by the World Wildlife Fund, lies around 18km southwest of San Miguel, just off CA-2, on the road to Usulután. This peaceful, clear stretch of water, surrounded by reed beds with low hills in the distance, is the nesting and feeding ground for numerous species of birds including snow herons and the blue-winged zarzeta, which can be seen year-round. Sadly, this admirable attempt at conservation of an irreplaceable resource comes up daily against the needs of local residents living in the rather depressing hamlet on the shore, who have to use the lake as a source of water and fish for food and to sell. The best time to visit is in the early morning; a helpful warden is usually around the small dock to explain the conservation work, and you can rent a boat to explore the waterways. **Buses** running between San Miguel and Usulután pass the access road to the reserve, from where it is a walk of about ten minutes to the lake shore.

North to San Francisco Gotera and Perquín

East from San Miguel, highway CA-7 runs 18km to an unnamed junction in the middle of nowhere; from here, it heads north, while the Ruta Militar continues east to Santa Rosa de Lima and the Honduran border. **SAN FRANCISCO GOTERA**, the first town of any importance north of the junction, is an edgy and unfriendly place, although set in a beautiful location. The only reason to stay here is if you're heading for the village of **Corinto**, 20km east along a rough road, where rock overhangs bear faint traces of pre-Columbian paintings. Of the two **hotels** in town, the *San Francisco* on Av Morazán at 3a C Pte, just up from the market, is by far the nicest (①–③). Across the street is a friendly little **comedor**, good for breakfasts and lunch.

Beyond Gotera, the road begins to climb into the mountains, with henequen fields and cattle pastures giving way to pine forests and superb mountain vistas, and the air becoming pleasantly fresh. This area was one of those most affected by the war; although war damage and poverty are still very much evident, a surprising and encouraging amount of new building is evident along the roadside. About 20km north of Gotera, the road passes the fringes of **Ciudad Segundo Montes**, a collection of new villages housing repatriated refugees, named after one of the six assassinated Jesuit priests. The main village, **San Luis**, lying along the highway, has a reception office (closed Sun) where staff can explain community projects that are underway. Respectful visitors are welcome to tour the communities and talk with the residents; **accommodation** is available in dormitory rooms in San Luis (①).

Perquín and the Museo de la Revolución Salvadoreña

After passing through the small town of Osicala, the road begins its final climb for the 20km or so to **PERQUÍN**, a small and – given its history – surprisingly friendly mountain town, set in the middle of glorious walking countryside. During the war the town was the FMLN headquarters, from where they broadcast to the nation on the (literally) underground station Radio Venceremos (We Will Triumph). Attempts by the army to dislodge the guerrillas mostly failed, leaving the town badly damaged. Today, however, sitting in the small central square watching the men play dominoes and with the noise of the schoolchildren's football games rising through the air, it is difficult not to feel a sense of renewal and optimism. Much of the damage has now been repaired with the help of foreign donations and the shiny jeeps of international aid agencies are very much evident on the roads around town.

Perquín's main draw is the moving **Museo de la Revolución Salvadoreña** (Tues–Sun 9am–4pm; US$1.25) set up by ex-guerrillas in the wake of the 1992 peace accords. The curators travelled throughout the country collecting photographs and personal effects of those who died during the fighting, and notices request that visitors donate more in order to expand the collection. There is a succinct summary (in Spanish) of the process leading to the beginning of the armed struggle, displays of arms confiscated from the army and weapons – including missile launchers, guns and grenades – disabled after the signing of the Peace Accords. Outside is the bomb crater left by a 1981 explosion and a mock-up of a guerrilla camp; the crude bent-wood and palm leaf shelters offered little shelter but could be erected and dismantled quickly. Behind the museum you can see the remains of the helicopter that was carrying Domingo Monterrosa (architect of the El Mozote massacre; see opposite) when it was shot down by the FMLN in 1984. The most moving exhibits are perhaps the anonymous transcripts of witnesses of the massacre, and drawings by refugee school-children, depicting events as they saw them.

A separate room contains the transmitting equipment and studio used by **Radio Venceremos**. With its subterranean sound rooms to evade detection, the station aired every afternoon throughout the war on a number of frequencies, broadcasting the guerrillas' view of events, as well as interviews and music. After the peace accords, the station received an FM licence in August 1992, and is now based in San Salvador – iron-ically in offices rented from a member of the Arena Party – some distance geographi-cally and ideologically from its former home. Now a commercial, mainstream station playing a mixture of Latin American sounds and US rock Venceremos has been heavi-ly criticized by some of its former listeners for accepting all manner of commercials as well as electoral advertisements from all political parties.

If you decide to **stay** in Perquín, the friendly *El Gigante* (①), five minutes' walk from town back down the road to Gotera, has clean, communal rooms with shared bath and a small comedor. Other **places to eat** in town are limited to two small comedores, *Blanca* and *Las Palmeras*, both just off the main square. When leaving, bear in mind that only three or four buses a day head south to Gotera and San Miguel, the last of which leaves in the early afternoon; occasional pick-ups also make the journey to Gotera.

El Mozote

Southeast of Perquín, past the village of Arambala, the village of **EL MOZOTE** was the setting for the lowest of many low points during the war. In the week of December 11–18, 1981, the elite, US-trained, Atlacatl army battalion attacked the village, burning or burying the 1000 dead bodies in mass graves. The few eye-witness testimonies to the events were ignored for years and only fully investigated in the early 1990s, and the bodies of the victims were exhumed in 1992. Today, what remains of El Mozote is vir-tually a ghost town, although families are slowly moving back; a moving monument to the victims features a iron sculpture of the silhouette of a family and boards carrying the names of those killed.

East to the Honduran border

From the junction with CA-7, the Ruta Militar continues through hot, low hills to **SANTA ROSA DE LIMA**, 40km from San Miguel. Santa Rosa is a relaxed, thriving place, with a large daily market and a well-maintained church. There's not much to do here, but it makes a useful stopover if coming from Honduras. The best of the few **places to stay** is *Hotel el Recreo* on 4a Av Nte between C Giron and 1a C Ote (☎664 2126; ②) which has clean rooms with bath. The basic but adequate *El Tejano* on C Giron between 6a and 8a Av Nte (☎664 2459; ①) is slightly cheaper, but has a 7am checkout. For **eating**, the very clean *Comedor Chayito*, at the corner of C Giron and 1a C Ote, does a good cheap comida a la vista (7am–6pm), while for something with a bit more splash try Taqueria Tex Mex on Av G Arias between 1a and 3a C Ote. Banks, including Banco Multivalores and Banco Cuscatlán, cluster around the plaza at the cen-tre of town, although during the day when the market is in swing it's a bit difficult to spot that there is a plaza. **Antel** is on C Giron, just down from the church.

Beyond Santa Rosa, the road continues for a further 10km before connecting with the Carretera Interamericana to run to the border at **EL AMATILLO**. Formed by the Río Goascoran, the border crossing is easy but busy, used by international buses and teeming with money changers and opportunistic beggars. On the Honduran side, buses leave regularly until late afternoon for Tegucigalpa and Jícaro Galán, 42km from the border; there are also direct buses to Choluteca, for onward connection to the

Nicaraguan border, along the Carretera Interamericana. A bank on the El Salvadorean side changes dollars, colones and lempiras, though the rates are slightly better with the money changers. There is a US$1.55 fee to enter Honduras.

travel details

BUSES

San Miguel to: El Amatillo (#330, every 10min until 5.30pm; 1hr 30min); San Francisco Gotera (#328, every 10min until 5.30pm; 1hr); Perquín (#332A, 3 daily via Gotera; 3hr); Santa Rosa de Lima (#330, every 10min until 5.30pm; 1hr 20min); La Unión (#324, every 10min until 6pm; 1hr); Usulután (#373, every 10min until 5.30pm; 1hr).

San Salvador to: San Miguel (ordinary service, #301, every 15min until 6pm; 4hr; "directo" service hourly; 3hr); San Vicente (#116, every 10min until 6pm; 1hr 30min); Santa Rosa de Lima (#306, every 30min until 2.30pm; 5hr; "directo" service 4 daily; 3hr).

San Vicente to: Usulután (#417, 5 daily until early afternoon; 2hr); Zacatecoluca (#117, every 15min until 6pm; 1hr).

CHAPTER 15

THE PACIFIC COAST

E l Salvador's **Pacific coast**, stretching from the Río Paz in the west to the Río Goascorán in the east, is a 300km sweep of sandy tropical beaches, dramatic cliffs, mangrove swamps and romantic islands. The **Carretera Littoral**, running along the coast, links the towns and villages, and public transport runs regularly to many places, but it is worth renting a car for a few days to reach some of the more remote and beautiful beaches. While there are clusters of **tourist facilities** here and there, don't expect the facilities of international resorts. Instead, the beauty of this part of the country lies in relaxing on clean, wide beaches or spending time in the relatively untouched fishing villages of the coast.

The most accessible stretch of coast near San Salvador – and thus very crowded at weekends – is the small fishing town of **La Libertad**, set amid good surfing beaches. Head west up the coast, towards Guatemala, and there are more untouched beaches including **Los Cóbanos** and **Barra de Santiago**, and the tranquil forest reserve at **Bosque el Imposible**. To the east, the small city of **Zacatecoluca** is a main jumping-off point for the El Salvadorean playground of the **Costa del Sol**; just down the coast are the green waterways and islands of the mangrove swamps of the **Bahía de Jiquilísco** and what is held by some to be the finest beach in the country, **Playa el Espino**. In the east lie the faded port of **La Unión** and the tranquil **islands** of the Gulf of Fonseca.

La Libertad

Just 34km south of San Salvador, **LA LIBERTAD**, once a major port and still an important fishing town, is re-inventing itself as a tourist spot, neatly set between the beaches of the Costa del Balsamo in the west and the Costa del Sol in the east. It's a popular place, particularly crowded at the weekends, when hordes of city dwellers pour in to join the local and international surfing bums, waiting for the right break.

Arrival and accommodation

Buses from San Salvador arrive in La Libertad at C Barrios, by the market, two blocks in from the sea and one block east from the parque. Returning to the capital, the buses leave from 2a C Ote just beyond the *turicentro*. **Antel** is on 2a C Ote at 2a Av Sur, the **post office** is just round the corner. **Credisur** on C Barrios at the east end of town changes cash dollars.

The more upmarket **hotels**, some with their own pools, are generally at the western end of town. If you're hoping to get a room on a holiday weekend, it's best to give them a call first. The more decent of the cheaper alternatives are listed below; if these are full, there are a couple of basic hotels around 2a C Ote and 1a Av Nte. Some of the restaurants also advertise rooms.

For an explanation of **accommodation price codes**, see p.270.

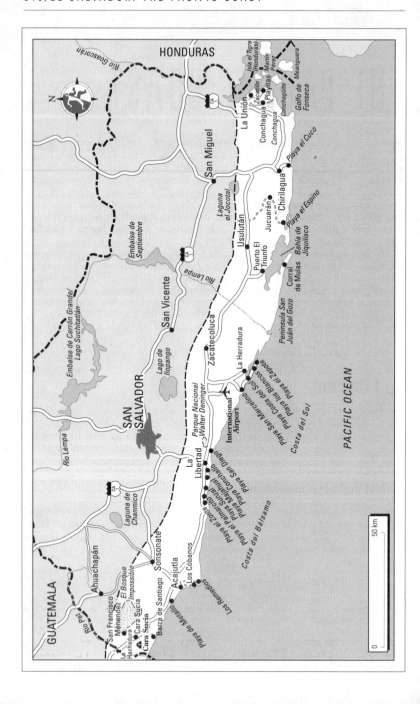

Hotel Amor y Paz, 4a C Pte between 1a and 3a Av Sur (☎335 3187). Basic but adequate rooms, although none has bath. ③.

Hacienda de Don Lito, 5a Av Sur at the end of 4a C Pte (☎335 3166). Very comfortable rooms, although slightly over-priced. All have bath, and there is a restaurant, bar and swimming pool. ⑥.

La Posada de Don Lito, next door to the *Hacienda de Don Lito* (☎335 3166). Same owners and similar accommodation to the hacienda. ⑥.

La Posada Familiar, 3a Av Sur at 4a C Pte (☎335 3252). A very friendly and clean place; the basic rooms, some with bath, are a good deal; a small comedor serves meals. ②.

Hotel Rick, 5a Av Sur 30, at the end of 4a C Pte (☎335 3033). Friendly, if a bit grubby; a favourite among the visiting surfers. ②.

The town and beaches

Set on a small bay, whose curve is bisected by the main wharf jutting out to sea, La Libertad is a rather dusty, crumbling old place. The main action occurs around the **wharf** when the fishing fleet comes in and sells its catch; when not in use, the boats are hauled onto the wharf for repair. There is a small **turicentro** here (daily 7am–5pm; US$0.90), with showers and changing rooms and a picnic area. The shady **Parque Central** sits two blocks back from the sea front; 2a C running along the southern edge of the parque, one block back from the seafront, is where you find the police station, Casa de Cultura (with an interesting, if limited, collection of pickled marine creatures) and buses for the capital.

The beaches: east

The **town beach** itself gets rather dirty, although the waves are good; surfers wait for the right break at the western end by the rocks. A short distance either direction from town, however brings you to much cleaner and welcoming expanses. To the **east** lie the small and crowded playas of Flores and Obispo and, 5km from La Libertad, the gem of **Playa San Diego**, its clean, white sand virtually deserted during the week. A dirt road turns off the Carretera Littoral a couple of kilometres from town (two restaurants here allow use of their swimming pools for the day) to run parallel along the length of the beach; views to the sea are blocked by the ranks of private homes behind locked gates, but paths between the properties lead down to the sand. Buses run the length of this road to the far end of the beach, where a ramshackle collection of **comedores** serve (naturally) fish. Very basic accommodation can also be had in concrete **cabañas** with no facilities for $4 a night.

A little further along the main road, past the turnoff for the beach, is the entrance to **Parque Nacional Walter Deninger**, 1041 manzanas of dry forest, supporting a range of flora and fauna. Over half the park was destroyed by fire in 1986; since then ISTU have been working on reforesting the area and encouraging the return of wildlife. Check with the ISTU office in San Salvador about the park's imminent opening.

The beaches: west

West of La Libertad, the Carretera Littoral winds up and around the thickly wooded hills to palm-fringed and uncrowded **Playa Conchalío**, 3km from town; *Hotel Los Arcos* sits on the highway at the road leading down to the beach, with a restaurant that serves all meals (☎335 3490; ④). Continuing west, the highway passes the turnoff for the small **Playa Majahual**, which gets very crowded, and, about 10km west of town, **Playa Sunzal** (or Zunzal), held to be the best surfing beach in the country. A few kilometres further on is **Playa El Palmarcito**, overlooked by the relaxing and comfortable *Atami Beach Club* resort (reservations necessary at office in San Salvador, 69a Av Sur 164, Col Escalón; ☎223 9000; ⑤), and the smaller and usually empty **Playa El Zonte**. From here, the highway runs for 35km or so through the dramatic, green landscapes of the **Costa del Bálsamo**, named after the now defunct balsam industry, before swinging inland to Sonsonate.

Eating and drinking

Eating in La Libertad is not a problem, unless you don't like fish. The Salvadorean spe-ciality **mariscada**, a creamy seafood soup, is available everywhere and should be tried at least once. The more expensive **restaurants** are gathered at the western end of town. *El Viejo Alta Mar, Sandra* and *Karla*, all on 4a C Pte between 1a and 3a Av Sur, are reasonably priced, all serving the catch of the day along with meat and chicken standards, and offering glimpses of the beach from the dining tables. The slightly more expensive US-owned *Punta Roca*, towards the far end of 4a C Pte, has a great sea view and a range of well-prepared fish and meat dishes; the restaurant at *Posada de Don Lito* attracts a slightly more formal crowd. The **beach comedores** all serve fish, but at much lower prices. For huge **juices** and basic meals try Comedor *Paty* in town on 2a Av Sur just down from the parque.

Moving on from La Libertad

Heading **east**, the town bus #80 leaves from 4a Av Sur every thirty minutes for Playa San Diego, whilst #540 runs every two hours inland to Zacatecoluca (p.322) and con-nections to the Costa del Sol (p.322). **West**, local buses #80A and #80B run past Playas Conchalío and Majahual to Sunzal; to reach Playa Palmarcito, #192 leaves every two hours. For a direct route to Sonsonate (see below), #287 leaves daily at 6am.

West to Guatemala

The section of coast west of the Costa del Bálsamo on the way to Guatemala contains a number of good beaches, best reached by car. The hub of the region is the small, flat, hot, city of **SONSONATE**, not on the coast itself, but a place you will invariably pass through. Set in tobacco and cattle-ranching country, the city is a bustling, com-mercial place. There is little of tourist interest here, except during festival time – chiefly the annual **Verbena de Sonsonate**, held at the end of January, when there's a host of music and drama performances, and the more colourful **Semaña Santa**. During Holy Week crowds flock to join the street processions and intricate pictures are drawn in coloured sawdust on the pavements. Sonsonate is also the **transport hub** for connections to the western beaches and the mountain towns of Juayúa and Apeneca.

Buses arrive at the main terminal, on C 15 de Septiembre, seven blocks east of the centre, and fifteen minutes' walk to the parque central. Of the limited **accommodation** in the centre, the *Hotel Orbe* on Av Fray Mucci Sur and 4a C Ote, two blocks east of the parque, has reasonably clean rooms with private bath (☎451 1416; ②). Much nicer, is the *Hotel Agape*, set in beautiful gardens on the outskirts of town on the road to San Salvador, with comfortably furnished rooms (☎451 1456; ④). Across the road is the cheaper but acceptable *Hotel Fontana* (☎451 2631; ②). There are a number of **restau-rants** along this road, and in the centre a row of comedores overlooks the river by the rather attractive white bridge, on 4a Av Nte.

Los Cóbanos and Los Remedios

Los Cóbanos, 25km due south of Sonsonate, is a favourite beach for Salvadorean hol-iday makers, and somewhat crowded at the weekends. Although rather rocky, this pret-ty, gently curved beach makes a nice contrast to the palm-fringed expanses further down the coast. A couple of places have **cabañas** for rent; *Solimar* (②) is the nicer, although closed during the week. Set slightly back from the seafront the *Mar y Plata*

(②) is slightly run-down. A number of small shacks serve fresh fish and other **meals**. Walk round the headland at the west end of the small bay and you come to the quieter beach of **Los Remedios**. **Buses** leave Sonsonate every hour for Los Cóbanos until early evening and there are also occasional direct buses from San Salvador; the last bus leaves the beach at 5pm.

Acajutla to Cara Sucia

The major town on the coast here is the port of **ACAJUTLA**, the site of Pedro de Alvarado's first encounter with the Pipils in 1524, but today a hot, seedy and distinctly edgy place; it's better to stay at Sonsonate. Acajutla lies 4km from the Carretera Littoral, which from here runs the flat 46km or so to the Guatemalan border at La Hachadura, a beautiful journey with the slopes of the Cordillera Apaneca rising to the north and rolling pasture-lands to the south. After 10km, the highway passes the access road to **Playa de Metalío**, a quiet, palm-fringed beach, whose beauty is somewhat marred by the refuse washed up from Acajutla. More remote, **Playa Barra de Santiago** lies 15km further up the coast, across a small estuary by the fishing village of Barra de Santiago. A rough road leads the 7km from the highway to the estuary; one bus a day in the morning runs along it from Sonsonate. At the estuary, bargain with a fishing boat to take you across to the village and the beach.

A further 10km west, the dusty village of **Cara Sucia** lines the highway just east of the Río Cara Sucia. Nearby, the **archeological site** of Cara Sucia was a Maya settlement made wealthy by trade in salt. Initial excavations uncovered a number of structures including two pelota courts, but today there is not much to see, though it's a peaceful place for a picnic. There is no public **transport** to the site; from the crossroads 50m past the bridge at the end of the village take the road leading left, opposite *Comedor Nohemy*, for about twenty minutes until you reach the Cooperativa Cara Sucia buildings on the right; ask the guard to let you through and follow the track round the buildings, taking the right-hand fork to the ruins.

From Cara Sucia the highway continues the last few kilometres to **La Hachadura**, a busy border crossing used by the international buses heading for Mexico. There is a small hospedaje on the Guatemalan side and buses to Esquintla and Guatemala City.

Bosque el Imposible

The road leading right at the crossroads in Cara Sucia provides access to one of El Salvador's greatest hidden glories, the forest reserve of **Bosque el Imposible**, so called because of the difficulty of traversing the mountain tracks to get into it. Covering over 31 square kilometres and rising through three climatic zones across the Cordillera de Apaneca, the reserve contains more than 400 species of trees and 1600 species of plants, some of which are unique to the area. Birdwatchers may glimpse some of the more than 200 species, including the emerald toucan, trogons, hummingbirds and eagles, while the park provides a secure habitat for a diverse range of animals, including anteaters, the white-tailed deer, ocelots and the tigrillo.

Getting to el Imposible without a private vehicle is time-consuming; the operators listed on p.295 all run tours here. There is an **entrance fee** of US$6 to enter the reserve, which is managed by a non-governmental organization, **SalvaNatura** (77a Av Nte and 7a C Pte, Col Escalón, San Salvador; ☎263 1111), from whom you need to ask permission to enter. They also have a small office in the nearby village of San Francisco Menéndez, the main point of access for the reserve, and if you're very persuasive, you may be able to get permission to enter the reserve from there. The turning for San Francisco Menéndez is on the highway 4km past Cara Sucia. As yet, there is no formal provision for **staying** in the reserve – though SalvaNatura are planning to build a hotel in a nearby village; call them for details.

Zacatecoluca and the Costa del Sol

Heading east from La Libertad, the Carretera Littoral swings inland, running north of the international airport to the small city of **ZACATECOLUCA**, with its impressive **Catedral Santa Lucia**, in front of which stands a monument to the city's most famous son, José Simeon Cañas. Zacatecoluca was a pre-Columbian Nonualco city with about two thousand inhabitants when the Spanish first arrived. No records of conflict exist and in 1594, Don Juan de Pineda reported to the Spanish court that "there are three pueblos next to each other that are good, called San Juan and Santiago Nonualco and Zacatecoluca. In Zacatecoluca there is a corregidor who administers in the name of your majesty." In 1833, however, the indigenous revolt led by Anastasio Aquino from the nearby village of Santiago Nonualco posed one of the most serious threats to the newly independent country. Supported by both local tribes and poor *mestizos* and meeting with little effective resistance, Aquino at one point looked capable of marching on and taking the capital. Instead his army contented itself with sacking Zacatecoluca before moving on to San Vicente, giving government forces time to consolidate.

Apart from its big daily **market**, there is little of interest to Zacatecoluca except its proximity to beaches south, but it's a pleasant enough place, with a couple of acceptable **hotels**. Just across the street from the bus terminal, *Motel Primavera* at Av Juan Viacortez 23 (☎334 1346; ②) has tidy rooms with bath and hammock, while round the corner *Hotel Brolyn* at 7a C Ote 25 (☎333 8410; ②) is similar but slightly more expensive. **Buses** run every few minutes from San Salvador's Terminal del Sur to Zacatecoluca.

The Costa del Sol

Due south of Zacatecoluca lies El Salvador's premier beach playground, the **Costa del Sol**, a 15km-long strip of palm-fringed beaches running between the ocean and the Jaltepeque Estuary. The place seethes at the weekends as the crowds pour in and the owners of the secluded beach houses come to air their residences. From the highway, an access road runs the 20km south to the beginning of the beach strip and east along its length to La Puntita at the end. Another road branches off 8km before the coast to the fishing town of La Herradura; from here, boats can be rented to explore the mangrove swamps of the estuary and the small islands, some of which are inhabited.

Behind the first beach along the strip, **Playa San Marcelino**, the grounds of the rather plush *Costa del Sol Club* offer swimming pools, sports facilities and a restaurant; you can try negotiating at the gate to be allowed in for the day. Head east another 3km or so and you come to **Playa Costa del Sol**, where a *turicentro* (daily 7am–6pm; US$0.90) rents cabañas for the day and has a couple of small restaurants, while about 5km further is **Playa Los Blancos** and towards the end of the strip **Playa el Zapote**. These three beaches have firm, clean expanses of sand, merging seamlessly into one another, and are good for swimming.

Upmarket **accommodation** is on offer at the *Izalco Cabaña Club* (☎223 6764; ⑤) and the *Tesoro Beach Hotel* (☎334 0600; ⑨) at the far end of Playa Costa del Sol and the *Pacific Paradise* (☎334 0601; ⑦) past Los Blancos. **Buses** run down the Costa del Sol from Zacatecoluca, taking around an hour and a half; there are also direct buses from San Salvador.

Bahía de Jiquilísco

Just east of Zacatecoluca, the Carretera Littoral crosses the Río Lempa at San Marcos Lempa, over a temporary structure replacing the Puente de Oro bombed by the FMLN in 1981, to begin a run through lush, green coffee country. The city of **USULUTÁN**, on the southern slopes of the volcano of the same name, is of little interest to tourists except as a convenient **transit point**; *La Posada del Viajero* on 6a C Ote between 2a and 4a Av Nte, close to the centre, is a clean and friendly place to **stay** (☎662 0217; ②). The bus station is about six blocks east of the centre, on C Grimaldi, a main drag which leads down to the parque central.

About 20km southwest of Usulután, down a road lined with sugarcane fields, is **PUERTO EL TRIUNFO**, a small village and port set on the shore of **Bahía de Jiquilísco**, separated from the ocean by the **San Juan del Gozo peninsula**. Formed by coastal mangrove swamps, this beautiful bay features 12km of waterways and a number of **islands**, the largest of which is **Espíritu Santo**. Passenger boats cross to hamlets on the islands and to the village of **Corral de Mulas** on the peninsula; if you miss these – they tend to leave early in the day – boats can be rented for a return crossing or for a few hours navigating the waterways around the **smaller islands** of Tortuga, Madre Sal, Los Cedros and San Sebastian. A long, fine sandy beach forms the ocean-side of the peninsula; a road runs its length, branching off the highway at San Marcos Lempa. You can **camp** on the islands and the peninsula, and there is a small, basic **hotel** (①) with a restaurant serving huge fish dishes in Puerto el Triunfo.

At the far eastern end of Bahía de Jiquilísco is one of El Salvador's remotest, and finest, beaches, **Playa el Espino**, where the wide expanse of soft sand backed by coconut palms is virtually deserted, even at the weekends. Inevitably, access without private transport is rather difficult; an unpaved road branches off the highway about 10km east of Usulután to run south across the low coastal mountains, passing through the village of **Jucuarán**. The road runs to the coast but unless you have a car you may find the beach difficult to get to; though pickups run along the road they're pretty infrequent. If you're prepared to spend a little more, it's worth coming to an arrangement with a boat owner Puerto el Triunfo.

Eastern beaches

Thirty kilometres beyond Usulután the Carretera Littoral turns south; at the junction here, you can connect with buses north to San Miguel (see p.309). After passing the small, unexciting town of Chirilagua, 14km away, a side road winds over the low mountains to another popular beach, **Playa el Cuco**, which, when the dusty, rather unfriendly little village is cleared, stretches endlessly into the distance, empty of tourists during the week. **Hospedajes** *Vasquez*, *Buenos Aires* and *Ricamar* (①) in the village are subtle variations on the theme of windowless, concrete boxes, for which you should pay no more than US$5. Walk out of the village along the dirt road, or along the beach, for five minutes, however, and you come to the cheerfully decaying *Hotel Leones Marinos* (☎619 9015; ④), which has its own restaurant. Fifteen minutes beyond is the more basic *Cucolindo* (③) and a further fifteen minutes brings you to the isolated luxury of *Trópic-Club* with its own pool and restaurant (☎619 9006; ⑤).

Beyond Chirilagua, the highway parallels the coastline, running through the tidy little town of Intipuca before turning north again, around the western slopes of Volcán Conchagua and up to La Unión. Some 5km past Intipuca, a side road gives access to **Playa el Icacal**, 7km south. An untouched expanse of wide soft sand fringed by coconut palms, the beach has good swimming and is perfect for a day doing nothing. There is no **accommodation**, although a few **comedores** serve meals. Unless you're up very early to connect with the morning buses running from San Miguel to the beach, however, you'll need private transport.

La Unión and around

The port town of **LA UNIÓN** sits in a stunning location on a bay on the edge of the Gulf of Fonseca. Though it's not really a tourist town – faded since its glory days as El Salvador's largest commercial port, the streets of low, white houses, bleached by the sun, crumble a little further every day, and the ferocious heat puts some people off – it's the jumping off point to the **islands** of the Gulf, and worth using as a base for a day or so. There are a number of reasonable places to stay and eat, and the Honduran border crossing at El Amatillo (see p.315) is an easy journey away.

Practicalities

The **bus terminal** is on 3a C Pte, 4a–6a Av Nte, three blocks west from the parque central; most buses run through the parque, on the southern edge of which is the market, before terminating here. **Antel** is on 1a C Ote at 5a Av Nte, two blocks east of the parque, whilst *Banco Multivalores* is on 1a C Ote at 3a Av Nte.

The best of the **accommodation** is the *Portobello* on 4a Av Nte at 1a C Pte, which has clean rooms with a/c and bath (☎664 4113; ②). *Hotel San Francisco* on C Gral Menéndez, 9a–11a Av Sur, five blocks east of the parque, is also good, with clean rooms with bath; some have a/c (☎664 4159; ②–③). Of the **places to eat** the airy *Restaurant El Sinai*, next door to the *Portobello* has good, moderately priced seafood (daily until 8pm) while *Restaurant El Marinero* on 3a C Pte at Av Gral Cabañas is the closest you'll come to a pavement café; its huge, covered verandah is perfect for idling away a few hours watching the street activity. Down by the sea at the end of 11a Av Nte, *Miramar* and *Amanacer Marino* are more expensive seafood restaurants, with great views from the dining tables.

Around La Unión

PLAYITAS, 8km southeast of La Unión, is a small fishing village, with a somewhat dirty beach, whose main attraction is its proximity to the **islands** in the Golfo de Fonseca. The views across the gulf, which on clear days stretch to the mainland of Honduras and, in the far distance, the mountains of Nicaragua, are stunning, with the darker humps of the islands looming offshore from the calm, shimmering blue waters. The smallest of the islands, Zactillo and Martín Pérez (to the left looking out to sea) seem almost close enough to touch, while ahead and to the right are the larger Conchagüita and, beyond, the island of Meanguera, both of which have small villages. Irregular **passenger launches** leave for the larger islands; a little bargaining will secure a private vessel to drop you off for a few hours, free to enjoy the secluded beaches and clean waters, before returning to pick you up.

The whole Gulf region has long been associated with the fable and lore of the European corsairs, who regularly made incursions along this coastline in the seventeenth and eighteenth centuries. **Conchagüita** was sacked by English pirates in 1682, who used it as a strategic base from which to attack ships sailing to the old world; the original inhabitants moved to the mainland and the island remained deserted until the 1920s when settlers began moving back. In the centre of the island, on the Cerro del Pueblo Viejo, are the remains of a tiny pre-Columbian church; a path to the north of the ruins leads up to a large rock bearing engravings, which some believe represent a map of the gulf, used strategically to plan defence.

Behind Playitas looms **Volcán Conchagua** (1243m), with beautiful views across the gulf to Nicaragua and Honduras and out across the Pacific. The friendly village of **CONCHAGUA**, sitting on its northern slopes, was founded by the inhabitants of Conchagüita at the end of the seventeenth century. The climate is fresher here, a pleasant relief from the heat of La Unión, and walks around the village give on to views across the Gulf. From Conchagua to the summit of the volcano is a strenuous, hot walk of around two or three hours. As in most places in El Salvador, walking alone is not recommended.

Eight kilometres west of La Unión is the junction with the Carretera Interamericana, which here swings north to run 27km up to the Honduran border at **El Amatillo** (see p.315). There are no direct buses to the border from town; instead take any of the frequent buses to Santa Rosa de Lima and change there.

travel details

BUSES

San Salvador to: Costa del Sol (#495, from Terminal del Sur, every 30min until 4pm; 2hr); La Libertad (#102, every 15min; 1hr); La Unión (#304, every 30min until 2.30pm, via San Miguel; 4hr); Los Cóbanos (#207, via Sonsonate, a few times daily; 2hr 30min); Sonsonate (#205 or #207 every 10min until 6pm; 1hr 30min); Usulután (#302, every 10min until 4pm, via Zacatecoluca; 2hr 30min); Zacatecoluca (#133, from Terminal del Sur, every 15min until 6.30pm; 1hr 30min).

Sonsonate to: Barra de Santiago (#285, 1 daily; 1hr 30min); La Hachadura (#259, every 10min until 5.30pm, passing the access roads for Metalío and Barra de Santiago; 2hr; or #286, via San Francisco Menéndez; 4 daily; 2hr 30min); Los Cóbanos (#257, hourly until 5pm; 45min).

La Unión to: Conchagua (#382, every 30min until 6pm; 30min); Playitas (#418, hourly until 4pm; 30min); San Miguel (#324, every 10min until 6pm; 1hr 30min); Santa Rosa de Lima (#342, every 15min until 5.30pm; 1hr 30min).

Usulután to: El Cuco (bus to San Miguel, then pick up the #320, every 30min; 1hr); El Icacal (#373; every 10min; 30min to junction and pick up #385, 2 daily at 6am & 8am; 1hr); Puerto El Triunfo (#363, every 10min until 5.30pm; 1hr); San Miguel (#373; every 10min, 45min); Zacatecoluca (#171, every 90min until 5pm; 1hr 30min).

Zacatecoluca to: Costa del Sol (#193 every 30min until 5.30pm; 1hr 30min).

CHAPTER 16

THE WEST

M ore muted than in the north, the landscapes of **western El Salvador** offer in many ways a perfect introduction to the country. Soft mountain chains edge back from the valleys, dominated by the dull, green expanses of coffee plantations from which the area gains its wealth. Spared from the most violent hardships of the conflict of the 1980s, the friendly towns and cities here are more amenable to visitors than in many places, and a relatively well developed tourist infrastructure makes travelling easier than in other regions.

The joy of this part of the country consists largely of soaking up the atmosphere. The mountain towns of **Apaneca** and **Juayúa** and the tranquil city of **Ahuachapán** are perfect for a few days spent relaxing, perhaps taking a gentle hike through the countryside – conveniently situated near the border with Guatemala, Ahuachapán in particular is a great little place to acclimatize yourself to El Salvador. The larger city of **Santa Ana** is a mellow contrast to the capital, with the nearby peaks of **Cerro Verde**, **Volcán Santa Ana** and **Volcán Izalco**, and the pre-Columbian site of **Tazumal**, short hops away. Nearer the Guatemalan border, the accommodating little town of **Metapán** gives access to the **Bosque Montecristo**, where hiking trails weave through unspoilt cloudforest amid some of the most remote mountain scenery in this part of the world.

The Cordillera Apaneca to Ahuachapán

Stretching east for more than 70km from the Guatemalan border, the **Cordillera Apaneca-Ilamatepec** is a glorious range of mountains, patchworked coffee plantations and acres of pine forests set under a clear, golden light. The population of the village of **NAHUIZALCO**, set on the southern edge of the range about 10km north of Sonsonate (see p.320), are mostly descended from the region's indigenous peoples, although few wear traditional dress any longer. The town thrives on the manufacture of wicker, with workshops lining the main street. Some of the pieces, such as baskets, are small enough to take home; gentle bargaining is acceptable.

Beyond Nahuizalco, the air cools and freshens as the road winds its way up into the mountains proper; there are superb vistas down to Sonsonate and across the plains to the coast. Fourteen kilometres from Sonsonate is **SALCOATITÁN**, a sleepy little mountain village with the small clean *Hotel Oasis* (②) and a couple of simple places to eat. Along with the beautiful walking in the area, the village is the nearest place to spend the night to the neighbouring town of **JUAYÚA** (pronounced "wai-u-a"), 2km further on down a spur road. Here the magnificent **Templo de Señor de Juayúa**, built in 1955 in colonial style, and with stained-glass windows depicting the saints, houses the **Black Christ of Juayúa**, carved by Quiro Cataño, sculptor of the Black Christ of Esquipulas in Guatemala (see p.224). Consequently the town is something of a pilgrimage site, particularly during the January festival, which makes it all the more surprising that there is no accommodation.

For an explanation of **accommodation price codes**, see p.270.

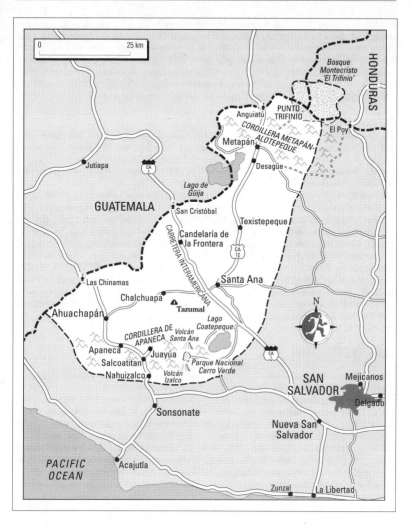

Apaneca and the Laguna Verde

A short leg further along the road from Salcoatitán is another quiet, charming mountain town, **APANECA**, founded by Pedro de Alvarado in the mid-sixteenth century. Popular with weekend visitors, and home to one of the best-known restaurants in the country, drawing wealthy San Salvadoreans and foreign residents alike, the town nonetheless retains an air of friendly tranquillity. During the week, you're likely to have the place – and the surrounding mountain scenery – to yourself. The only **accommodation** is the *Cabañas de Apaneca,* which has six comfortable wood cabins set in lush gardens overlooking the mountain slopes, and a good on-site restaurant (☎450 5106; ⑥; reserve restaurant at weekends and holidays). The best place to **eat**, however, is *La*

Cocina de mi Abuela (Sat & Sun only 11.30am–5pm; ☎450 5203, ext 301), housed in a beautifully decorated colonial-era house. The nicest tables are on the covered verandah at the back, where scenic views come with your meal. Fresh lake fish will set you back about US$8, and you can also get lasagne, meat and chicken. Otherwise, eating options in town are limited to the row of friendly little comedores opposite the church.

The town is easily accessible by **bus** from both Sonsonate (see p.320; 1hr 30min) and Ahuachapán (1hr) if you decide to come for the day or just for a meal.

Laguna Verde

There is little to do in Apaneca itself, but it's an enjoyable, not too strenuous walk through woods and fincas to the **Laguna Verde**, a small crater lake 4km to the northeast of town. Fringed by reeds and surrounded by mist-clad pine slopes, the lake is a popular destination, and at the weekends you're likely to share the path with numerous families and walking groups.

From the highway on the edge of town, follow the dirt road to the right of the *Jardín de Flores* garden centre, which winds up and round the mountain, passing several fincas and a couple of small hamlets, overlooked by the weekend retreats of wealthy San Salvadoreans. An enjoyable shortcut is to walk up the dried-up stream bed through the woods, which links the bends of the road; this is more of a scramble and it's quite easy to get lost – ask directions from anyone you meet. The hamlet just above the lake, reached after about ninety minutes, has sweeping views on clear days; the white city sheltering in the valley below is Ahuachapán, while to the north is the peak of Cerro Artilleria on the Guatemalan border. The grassy slopes around the lake make a good spot for a picnic and you can swim. Closer to town to the north, the smaller, less impressive **Laguna Las Ninfas**, is an easy forest walk of about 45 minutes.

Ahuachapán

From Apaneca the road winds 10km down through the scrubby little town of Ataco to the city of **AHUACHAPÁN**. This area, and the lands further north, are some of the oldest inhabited regions of what is today El Salvador, due in large part to the extremely fertile soil. Artefacts found in the region date back to 1200 BC and the first early Maya. Ahuachapàn is also one of the oldest Spanish settlements in the country, made a city in 1862, and has generally been a place of quiet bourgeois comfort; two attacks by Guatemalan troops – in 1863 and 1864 – were both firmly rebutted. The early twentieth-century British visitor Percy Martin noted: "The people as a whole seemed to me to be very well-to-do and evidences of refinement and solid comfort were to be met with on all sides. . . I was also impressed with the absence of the usual number of drinking shops, of which I counted scarcely more than six in the whole town. The town is a quiet, sleepy and eminently peaceful place of residence where one might dream away one's life contentedly enough."

Today the city's main industry is geo-thermal electricity generation, at one time supplying seventy percent of the country's grid; consequently there are usually a number of European and Japanese technicians stationed here.

Arrival and accommodation

Buses arrive at the terminal on Av Commercial, 10a–12a C Pte, eight blocks from the parque central. **Antel** is 3a C Pte and 2a Av Sur by the parque, while the **post office** is at 4a C Ote and 1a Av Nte. Banco Salvadoreño on C Barrios at 1a Av Nte changes cash dollars.

Of the **accommodation**, *La Casa Blanca*, on 2a Av Nte at C Barrios a couple of blocks from the parque, is housed in a well-decorated colonial building; the large, clean rooms all have bath, hot water and TV. The restaurant, set around a small courtyard is slightly overpriced but good for sitting with a coffee or a beer (☎443 1505, fax 443 1503; ④). For those on a budget, *Hotel San José* on 6a C Pte between Av Commercial and 2a Av Nte, close to the market, has clean, dark rooms (☎443 1820; ③). The nicest place to stay, however, is *Hotel el Parador,* 2km out of town on the road to the Guatemalan border post (Las Chinamas). All rooms have bath, hot water and TV; there's a restaurant (10am–9pm) and a small pool open to the public (☎443 0331; ⑤). About 500m further down the road, *Auto Hotel Los Amigos* (②) has bare but adequate rooms.

The city and around

Apart from its quiet, gently fading streets, and the lively daily **market** around the bus station, the only things to see in Ahuachapán are its **churches**. The imposing white edifice of the **Iglesia Parrocia de Nuestra Señora de la Asuncíon** on the parque central, dominates the centre of the city and acts as the focus for the annual fiesta in the first week of February. The spare, 1950s-built **El Calvario**, with a fine, carved Christ on the cross, is on 6a C Pte at 2a Av Nte.

Immediately south of the city, the hump of **Cerro Ataco** is a not too difficult, safe climb of about two hours; follow 2a Av Sur out of town and pick any one of the small paths going up to the summit. The body of water visible to the northwest, off the road to Las Chinamas, is the **Lago de Llano**, a small, lily-fringed lake fished extensively by locals. It's a thirty-minute stroll along the main road from the centre of town to the lake, or you can catch bus #60 to the rather depressing village of Las Brisas, 500m from the lake; it leaves regularly from the market.

Some 5km east of town near the hamlet of El Barro, **ausoles** (geysers), form the basis of the local geo-thermal industry. The plumes of steam forced up from the earth hang impressively over the lush green vegetation and red soil and are particularly stunning in the golden light of the early morning sun.

Eating and drinking

Like most Salvadorean provincial cities, Ahuachapán is not overly blessed with **places to eat**. All restaurants tend to close relatively early, around 9pm, except for the *El Parador*, *El Paso* and *La Posada* restaurants, in a row on the Las Chinamas road. These serve meat and seafood standards, and occasionally have live music at the weekends. In the centre, *Tacos el Zocalo* and *Jardín de China*, next door to each other on 1a Av Sur at 1a C Ote and with the same owner, offer Ahuachapán's version of Mexican and Chinese cuisine respectively; both are relaxed places, good for a drink as well as a meal. *La Estancia*, housed in a rather run-down white building on 1a Av Sur at C Barrios, has well-prepared standards at average prices. *Pizza Attos* on Av Menendez Nte at 2a C Ote serves big pizzas, while *Las Mixtas*, 2a Av Sur by the parque, is more of a fast-food place with a range of simple meals and snacks. For sitting and people-watching, stands in the parque serve coffee and snacks.

To Las Chinamas and Guatemala

From Ahuachapán, a reasonably good and very scenic road runs the 20km or so to the **Guatemalan border** just past **Las Chinamas**. Local buses leave for the border every fifteen minutes, taking about an hour. International buses, from Santa Ana (see p.330), also pass through at about 5.30am. There is no ticket office – stand on 6a C Pte more or less opposite the *Hotel San José* and flag them down. On the Guatemalan side, at Valle Nuevo, buses run to Guatemala City.

Chalchuapa and Tazumal

Heading northeast from Ahuachapán, the road winds down through the last spurs of the Cordillera onto a scenic broad plain, running to **CHALCHUAPA**, which in addition to its faded but beautiful colonial church contains the archeological site of **Tazumal** (Tues–Sun 9am–5pm; US$3). The most important site in El Salvador, the ruins are – by comparision with sites in Honduras and Guatemala – rather small, although they do have their own, impressive beauty. An informative (Spanish-language) museum at the site explains the development of the civilizations and displays artefacts discovered during excavations. There is not much else to the town and **nowhere to stay**, but Tazumal is an easy trip from Ahuachapán or Santa Ana. Buses drop off at a small plaza a few blocks from the centre of town; from here walk uphill for about four blocks and turn left at the sign.

The site

What is now the town of Chalchuapa was the seat of power for a strong and thriving Maya population from 900 BC onwards. The inhabitants produced "Usulutan" ceramics, key items of commerce in the Maya zone, and also controlled the trade in obsidian from Guatemala. This early society was literate – evidence suggests that they had both calendar and writing systems – and highly stratified, and artefacts indicate strong links with Olmec civilizations in Mexico. The catastrophic eruption of Volcán Ilopango in around 250 AD, covering an area of ten thousand square kilometres in ash, did not affect Chalchuapa as badly as the central zone of the country; the area quickly repopulated and **Tazumal** gradually became the main settlement.

Of the nine structures identified here, only two remain in reasonable condition, with a third partially excavated; the rest have been destroyed by the expansion of the town. The central, largest structure – a stepped ceremonial platform, influenced by the style of Teotihuacan (Mexico) – dates back to the Classic period (300–900 AD). Altogether, however, thirteen different building stages took place over 750 years, mostly during the Late Classic period (600–900 AD); beneath the structure are traces of a platform dating back to between 100–200 AD. Originally a number of smaller temples were attached to the main structure. At the base of its northern edge, a number of tombs (Late Classic period) have yielded artefacts such as Tiquisate ware from Guatemala, jade jewellery, items for religious rites and a flask containing powdered iron-oxide. The last was used for decorating a ceremonial stone *hacha* or head, used during games of pelota. The pelota court itself lay on the southern edge of the structure.

Tazumal as a Maya city was abandoned around the end of the ninth century, at the collapse of the Classic Maya culture; unusually, Pipils moved in and occupied the site. Structure 2, to the west of the main platform, is a Pipil pyramid dating back to the Early Postclassic period (900–1200 AD). The new residents also constructed another pelota court, to the northwest corner of the site. Tazumal was finally abandoned, around 1200 AD, with the focus of settlement in the area moving towards the centre of the current town.

Santa Ana

Self-possessed **SANTA ANA**, the second most important city in El Salvador, lies in a superb location in the Cihautehuacán valley. Surrounded by green peaks, with the slope of Volcán Santa Ana rising to southwest, the gently decaying colonial streets exude a certain bourgeois complacency. Far mellower than San Salvador and regarding itself above the unseemly commercial bustle of San Vicente, it's a good place to relax, admiring the handful of grandiose buildings or simply walking the streets soaking up the atmosphere. Easy day trips away are the natural attractions of **Lago Coatepeque**, the forest reserve of **Cerro Verde** and the summit of the volcanoes **Santa Ana** and **Izalco**.

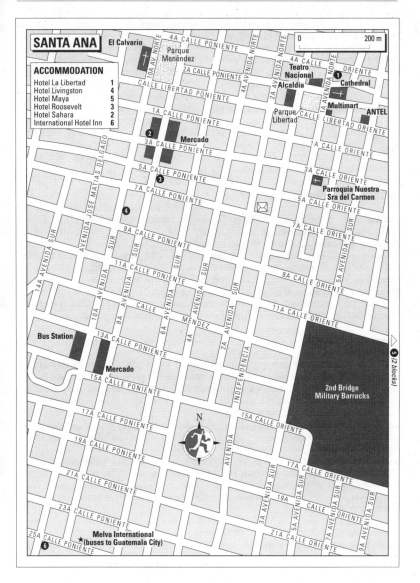

Some history

The conquistadors passed through the valley soon after their arrival in El Salvador, discovering a Pipil town of about three thousand inhabitants more or less where Santa Ana now stands. A Spanish settlement, however, was not founded until July 1569, when the disgraced Bishop Bernardino de Villapando arrived in the valley, en route from Guatemala. Commenting on the beauty and fertility of the area, he ordered work to begin on a church dedicated to **Nuestra Señora de Santa Ana**, the saint of the day of his arrival. This, completed in 1576, was on the site where the cathedral now stands, being destroyed in the early twentieth century to make way for the new building. The settlement grew relatively quickly; a census of 1770 records that the population was almost as large as that of San Salvador at the time, made up of 589 Spanish and *ladino* families, and 138 indigenous families.

Agriculture, particularly sugar cane and latterly coffee, and ranching contributed to the city's wealth, and by the end of the nineteenth century Santa Ana was secure in its position of second most important city in El Salvador, numbering around 30,000 inhabitants. Buildings that befitted the city's perceived status, such as the theatre and cathedral, sprang up. Today, with a population of over 200,000, the city retains an air of restrained, provincial calm, generally only ruptured during the **July fiesta**, with a host of events bringing the streets to life.

Arrival and information

Buses arrive at the main terminal on 10a Av Sur between 13a and 15a C Pte, nine or so blocks southwest of the central district; city bus #51 runs to the centre from the terminal, or you can walk it in about fifteen minutes.

Antel is on C Libertad at 5a Av Sur, just down from the parque central and the **post office** on 7a C Pte between Av Independencia and 2a Av Sur. **Banks**, which cluster around 2a Av Nte behind the Alcaldía, include BanCo, Credisur and Banco Hipotecario; there are also a couple of casas de cambio around here. There's a small, mainly fruit and vegetable market around the bus terminal, and a larger general market on 8a Av Sur, 1a–3a C Pte; there is also a Multi Mart supermarket on the parque.

Accommodation

Santa Ana's title of second city is not reflected in its range of **accommodation**, although there are a couple of reasonably comfortable hotels, one convenient for the bus terminal and the other closer to the general market. This area, around 8a and 10a Av Sur, has a concentration of cheap and basic places to stay; it is not recommended to walk around here alone at night.

International Hotel Inn, 25a C Pte and 10a Av Sur (☎440 0810, fax 440 0804). Convenient for the bus terminal and international buses. The rooms are rather small but comfortable, all with TV and bath. Watch out for the cockroaches. ④.

Hotel La Libertad, 4a C Ote at 1a Av Nte (☎441 2358). Perhaps the nicest budget place in the city with clean, basic rooms, some with bath, and in a great location right by the cathedral; bring your own padlock for the doors. ②.

Hotel Livingston, 10a Av Sur between 7a and 9a C Pte (☎ 441 1801). Safe, but rooms are small and box-like with shared baths. ①.

Hotel Maya, 11a C Ote at 11a Av Sur (☎441 3612). Another good, secure place, with motel style rooms, some with bath; a 20min walk from the centre. ④.

Hotel Roosevelt, 8a Av Sur between 5a and 7a C Pte (☎441 1702). Clean and safe, although the rooms, all with bath, are rather dark. ③.

Hotel Sahara, 3a C Pte between 8a and 10a Av Sur (☎ & fax 447 8865). The city's best, with large comfortable rooms, good service, bar and a restaurant open until 10pm. ⑥.

The Town

The heart of Santa Ana is the **Parque Libertad**, a neatly laid out plaza with a small bandstand, where people gather to sit and chat in the early evenings. The main intersection (Av Independencia Sur/Nte and C Libertad Pte/Ote) skirts its southwest corner. On the eastern edge of the parque is the **cathedral**, an imposing neo-gothic edifice completed in 1905. Inside, brick arches soar upwards and naves, some containing images dating back four hundred years and originally contained in the first church on the site, line the walls to the altar. Inset into the walls are plaques from local worshippers giving thanks to various saints for miracles performed. On the northern edge of the plaza, the **Teatro Nacional**, completed in classic renaissance style in 1910, was funded by taxes on local dignitaries. Once the proud home of the country's leading theatre companies, the building became a movie theatre before falling into disuse. Facing the cathedral on the western edge of the plaza is the **Alcaldía**, another fine renaissance-style piece of architecture. At the time of building the largest of its type, the facade is lavishly built in what travel writer Paul Theroux noted as the "colonnaded opulence of a ducal palace".

Another important church, **El Calvario**, lies five blocks west of the parque on 10a Av Nte by Parque Menéndez. Completed in 1885, the building has since been destroyed and rebuilt twice; the letters D.O.M. on the doric-style facade stand for "Dios Omnipotente and Misericordioso" (God, omnipotent and merciful). A magnificent carving of Christ under the cross stands behind the altar. South of the central parque, on 1a Av Sur, sits the **Parroquía de Nuestra Señora del Carmen**, built in 1822; in 1871 it was briefly occupied by peasants from the area around Volcán Santa Ana, who, spurred on by Guatemalan president Rafael Carrera's calls for the indigenous peoples to reclaim their land, ran riot through the city. After the uprising fizzled out, those who refused to give themselves up were hunted through the mountains and killed.

Eating and entertainment

Santa Ana has a reasonable number of moderately-priced places to eat, around the centre; nightlife, however, is not high on the city's list of priorities. Most restaurants tend to shut around 10pm, even at the weekends. The **cinema** on C Libertad at 3a Av Sur is virtually the only place to go after nightfall; it shows standard first-run Hollywood films, subtitled.

Adriana's, 25a C Pte, one block down from *International Hotel Inn*. Simple place, serving well-prepared steak, meat and seafood.

Cafe Cappuchino, Av Independencia at C Libertad Pte. A relaxed, leafy cafe just off the plaza, serving coffees, good juices, beers and simple meals (daily until 8pm).

Cafe Centro, 2a Av Sur between 1a and 3a C Pte. Good for large breakfasts and cheap lunches.

K'y'Jau, C Libertad between 4a and 6a Av Sur. Popular restaurant, serving large portions of authentic Chinese food.

Los Horcones, next to the cathedral on Parque Libertad. The best views in the city, with seats on the open terrace facing over the cathedral and the plaza. The usual standards are well prepared and the juices are great.

Los Patios, 21a C Pte between Av Independencia and 2a Av Sur. One of the smartest places in the city. Good meals in a nice courtyard setting at reasonable prices.

Kiko's Pizza, Av Independencia between 7a and 9a C Pte. Huge pizzas: the regular size is more than enough for two.

Around Santa Ana – the three peaks

West from Santa Ana, the three **volcanic peaks** of Cerro Verde, Santa Ana and Izalco together form a concise, living example of geological evolution. The oldest, **Cerro Verde**, is now a softened, densely vegetated mountain harbouring a national park. **Santa Ana**, nominally active, has cultivated lower slopes giving way to the bare lava of the summit, whilst juvenile **Izalco**, one of the youngest volcanoes in the world, is an almost perfect, bare lava cone of unsurpassed natural beauty.

Cerro Verde

From the El Congo junction, 15km southeast of Santa Ana, a narrow road winds up through the coffee plantations, maize fields and pine woods of the ancient volcano Cerro Verde to the **Parque Nacional Cerro Verde**. Lying 2000m above sea-level on what was the crater of the long-extinct volcano, this is the most accessible reserve in the country; consequently you're unlikely to be able to walk the short trails in solitude, particularly at the weekends. The dense, mature forest shelters numerous species of **plants**, including pinabetes and more than fifty species of orchids. Animal life tends, wisely, to stay out of sight; most likely to be spotted are **birds**, including the native xara – with a shimmering blue body and black head – hummingbirds and toucans. Armadillos, deer and cuzuco also shelter in the park.

Cerro Verde is very well managed with clear trails and lookouts over Volcán Santa Ana and, far below, Lago de Coatepeque. From the entrance gate (daily until 5.30pm; US$0.60) a short track leads up to the car park, to the left of which is a small orchid garden. The main **trail**, the **sendero natural**, leads from the top of the car park, looping clockwise through the reserve. Despite the weekend crowds this is an enjoyable walk of around forty-five minutes through the green calm of the forest. Smaller trails branching through the trees are variously closed off for conservation work.

By the car park are basic **cabañas** (①), although you have to bring your own food and water; check with the wardens as to where you can pitch a **tent**.

Unless coming by private transport, **getting to Cerro Verde** requires a bit of planning; it's worth renting a taxi for a few hours. Three buses at day run directly from Santa Ana to the car park, the last leaving the city in mid-afternoon (1hr 30min). The last bus from the car park leaves at 5pm and runs to El Congo only. Buses to Sonsonate pass the turnoff to the park, 14km from the entrance, from where you have to walk.

Volcán Santa Ana

From a signed turn about ten minutes into the sendero natural, a path branches down to the left, leading eventually to the summit of the **Volcán Santa Ana**, known also "Llamatepec" or "father hill". The highest volcanic peak in the country, at 2365m, Santa Ana is still considered active, although it hasn't erupted since the early twentieth century. The process of forestation is far less advanced here than in Cerro Verde, and the outlines of the volcano far starker. The walk to the summit takes two or three hours altogether.

Heading downhill from the signed turn for about twenty minutes brings you to the Finca San Blas; the path continues past here and begins to wind up though woodlands. After about 45 minutes, the gradient gets steeper, woodland cover gives way to rock and, towards the summit, lava. Three newer craters sit inside the larger older one – which takes about one hour to circumnavigate; at the bottom of the newest crater is a small, green sulphur lake.

Volcán Izalco

Just below the Cerro Verde is a lookout west over the visually stunning **Volcán Izalco**. Beginning as a small hole in the ground in 1770, the volcano was formed when lava began to pour continously over the next two centuries. Clearly visible from the ocean, the "lighthouse of the Pacific" was used by sailors to navigate by until the volcano finally stopped erupting in the 1960s. Looming up from the breast of a hill, the bleak, black volcanic cone of the 1900m Izalco is a startling contrast to the green slopes on which you're standing. It is possible to walk up Izalco, although locals advise against it, particularly alone, and robberies are not unknown. A marked trail leads from the lookout down for about thirty minutes to a saddle between the two volcanoes. From here it takes at least an hour to climb the completely bare slopes of volcanic scree to the summit.

Lago Coatepeque

East from the El Congo junction, a winding branch road descends 3km to the crater of **Lago Coatepeque**, shadowed by the three peaks. There are great views of the stunning deep blue waters, fed by natural hot springs. Inevitably the lake is a popular weekend destination, both for the rich and not so rich; much of the shore is bounded by private houses and access to the water is difficult. Follow the road round to the left when it reaches the lake and you come to *Hotel Torremolinos* (☎446 9437; ⑤), which charges a small fee for day use of a semi-public beach; you can also rent boats. The rooms in the hotel are large and clean, but much nicer is the *Hotel de Lago* (☎446 9511; ⑤) just up the road, with large, shady gardens and a restaurant overlooking the lake. **Buses** leave Santa Ana every thirty minutes for the lake, running past the two hotels.

To San Cristóbal and the Guatemalan border

From its junction with the road to Chalchuapa, the Carretera Interamericana heads northwest for 30km, through the small town of **Candalería de la Frontera** and on through gentle, green rolling countryside to the Guatemalan border at **San Cristóbal**. There are frequent buses from Santa Ana (1hr) to the crossing, which is efficient and not too busy, and has no exit or entry charges. There is no bank at the border, but numerous moneychangers offer reasonable rates for dollars, colones and quetzales. On the Guatemalan side, buses run to Asunción Mita, with connections to Guatemala City.

From Santa Ana to Metapán

Leaving Santa Ana, CA-12 heads north through agricultural plains and badly deforested hills, becoming wilder after it passes through the dusty town of **Texistepeque**, once a pre-Columbian Pok'oman settlement, and a Spanish town from 1556. Sixteen kilometres further on, at the hamlet of Desagüe, a dirt road leads 2km or so to serene **Lago de Güija**, surrounded by low hills; Río Ostúa, flowing through the lake, forms the border with Guatemala. On the **Las Figuras** arm of land – accessible on foot during the dry season – stretching out on the left side of the lake shore are a number of faint pre-Columbian rock carvings; the area around the lakeshore was populated exclusively by indigenous groups until well into the seventeenth century. You can rent boats from here to the small island of **La Tipa** in the lake.

Ten kilometres beyond the lake the small, friendly town of **METAPÁN** is scenically set on the edge of the mountains of the Cordillera Metapan-Alotepeque, which run east along the border with Honduras. Having survived a number of setbacks, including two devastating fires which nearly destroyed the town, Metapán was one of only four communities which supported Delgado's first call for independence in 1811; rioting citizens opened the jail and attacked representatives of the Spanish crown. The **Iglesia de la Parroquía**, completed in 1743, is considered to be one of El Salvador's finest colonial churches, with a beautifully preserved facade. Inside, the main altar is flanked by small pieces worked in silver from a local mine while the ornately decorated cupola features paintings of the San Gregorio, San Augustín, San Ambrosio and San Jéronimo.

Long gone are the days when its citizens were forced to defend themselves against Guatemalan troops sweeping through the town. Today Metapán is a charming, friendly place, slumbering for the most part beneath the sun. Luckily for the casual visitor, someone decided to build the comfortable *Hotel San José* (☎442 0556; ④) on the edge of town by the bus terminal, a few blocks from the centre, where comfortable **rooms** all have bath and TV. The restaurant is open until 9pm. Accommodation is otherwise limited to the basic *Hospedaje Central* on 2a Av Nte at C 15 de Septiembre in the centre of town (②). For **eating**, *El Rincon de la Pelon* on C Benjamin Mancia, in the centre, is a casual little place in the front room of a private house, serving delicious chicken and meat (until around 8.30pm).

Around Metapán: Bosque Montecristo

The main reason for staying in Metapán is for access to the international reserve of **Bosque Montecristo**. Established in 1986, with funding received from, among others, the European Union, the reserve rises through two climatic zones and is managed as part of the **El Trifinio international biosphere**, administered by the governments of El Salvador, Honduras and Guatemala. The reserve centres on the **Cerro Montecristo** (2418m), at whose summit the borders of the three countries converge.

In the higher reaches of Montecristo, beginning at around 2100m, is an expanse of **virgin cloud forest**. Orchids and pinabetes, typical of cloudforests, thrive in the climatic conditions of an average annual rainfall of 2m and 100 percent humidity. Huge oaks, pines and cypresses, some towering to over 20m, swathed in creepers, lichens and mosses, form a dense canopy preventing sunlight from reaching the forest floor. The numerous species of **wildlife** – which tend to be shy of humans – include mountain foxes, howler and spider monkeys and the occasional jaguar. The abundant birdlife includes quetzals, hummingbirds, striped owl and Elliot's colibri. On the lower slopes of the reserve, the forest cover is mainly mixed pine and broadleaf woods. Much of this is secondary growth, replanted since the early 1970s; acute deforestation and consequent severe flooding provided the impetus for creation of a reserve in the first place. This lower zone is inhabited, with a fragile equilibrium being reached between the demands of the inhabitants and those of conservation.

Getting to Montecristo

The untouched beauty of the upper heights of Montecristo is due in large part to its remoteness; the only road in is a dirt track running northeast from Metapán. All the **tour operators** listed on p.295 can organize trips here; the more people in a group the cheaper it will be. If coming **independently**, the road from Metapán branches right off the highway just before the *Hotel San José*. If you're not in a private vehicle (4WD necessary), occasional pick-ups make the journey, otherwise you have to come to a private arrangement – ask at the hotel or around the market. Montecristo is managed by the **National Parks and Wildlife Service** at MAG (Col Santa Lucía, El Matazano, Ilopango; ☎227 0622), from whom authorization should be sought to enter. You're not allowed to enter on foot. Note that the cloudforest is **closed** to visitors from May to October, and that there is an **entrance fee** of US$1.

The park entrance is 4km from Metapán; after another 2km you come to the Hacienda San José, or *Casco Colonial* where the wardens are based. The right hand fork just before this leads to **Los Planes** (1890m), 18km inside the park, a well-organized recreation area with a small restaurant, camping area and orchid garden. If **camping**, bring food and water.

From Los Planes a marked trail leads to **Punto Trifinio**, the summit of Cerro Montecristo, where the three countries meet. Walking straight to the summit will take around three hours; the path leads through the cloudforest, however, and you can branch off in any direction (be careful not to get lost). You must bring warm clothing and good footwear. Trails also lead from just below Los Planes to the peaks of Cerro el Brujo and Cerro Miramundo.

Crossing into Guatemala: north to Anguiatú

Regular buses (around 30min) make the 13km trip from Metapán along CA-12 to **Anguiatú** and the **Guatemalan border**. This is the most convenient crossing if you're heading for Esquipulas in Guatemala (see p.224), and the formalities are straightforward. If coming in the other direction, note that the last bus to Metapán leaves at 6.30pm. There are no banks, but lots of moneychangers.

travel details

BUSES

Ahuachapán to: Chalchuapa (#210, every 15min until 6pm; 1hr); Las Chinamas (#263, every 15min until 5.30pm; 1hr); Santa Ana (#210, every 15min until 6pm; 1hr 30min).

Metapán to: Anguiatú (#211A, every 30min until 6.30pm; 30min).

San Salvador to: Ahuachapán (#202, #204, from Terminal de Occidente every 10min until 6pm; 3hr 30min); Santa Ana (#201, from Terminal de Occidente, every 10min until 5.30pm; 2hr; *directo* service every 20min; 1hr 20min).

Santa Ana to: Cerro Verde (#248 to Sonsonate runs via the car park; 3 daily; 1hr30min); Chalchuapa (#277, #218, every 10min; 40min); Lago Coatepeque (#220 ("El Lago"), every 30min until 5.30pm; 1hr);

Metapán (#235, every 30min until 6.30pm; 1hr30min); San Cristóbal (every 15min until 5.30pm; 50min).

Sonsonate to: Ahuachapán (#249, every 30min until 5.30pm; 2hr 30min); Apaneca (#249, every 30min until 5.30pm; 1hr 45min); Cerro Verde (the Santa Ana bus (see below) passes the turnoff after 1hr 30min); Juayúa (#249, every 30min until 5.30pm; 1hr30min); Nahuizalco (#249, every 30min until 5.30pm; 30min); Salcoatitán (#249, every 30min until 5.30pm; 1hr15min); Santa Ana (#216, every 15min until 5.45pm; 2hr).

INTERNATIONAL BUSES

Santa Ana to: Guatemala City (*Melva International*, 25a C Pte, 6a–8a Av Sur; ☎440 1608) hourly from 5.30am to 2.30pm; 6hr.

PART FIVE

HONDURAS

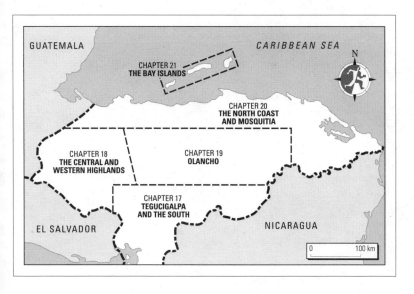

GUATEMALA

CARIBBEAN SEA

N

CHAPTER 21
THE BAY ISLANDS

CHAPTER 20
THE NORTH COAST
AND MOSQUITIA

CHAPTER 18
THE CENTRAL AND
WESTERN HIGHLANDS

CHAPTER 19
OLANCHO

CHAPTER 17
TEGUCIGALPA
AND THE SOUTH

EL SALVADOR

NICARAGUA

0   100 km

Introduction

The original Banana Republic, a byword for corruption and poverty, **Honduras** is all too often overlooked by foreign tourists. Many of those who do make it here head straight for the ruins of **Copán**, one of the finest Maya sites in the region. Some even miss that, in the rush to get to the palm-fringed beaches and clear Caribbean waters of the **Bay Islands**. Beyond these prime tourist sites, however, is a land of inspiring, often untouched natural beauty.

The second-largest country in Central America after Nicaragua, Honduras sprawls from the Atlantic to the Pacific coast, from Caribbean flatlands through the cooler mountainous interior, and south to the sun-baked shores of the Golfo de Fonseca. West to east, the forested highlands on the border with Guatemala give way to the vast, undeveloped savannahs and wetlands of the Mosquitia. While ecotourism is a relatively new concept here, more and more Hondurans are becoming aware of the role the country's extensive network of **national parks and reserves** plays in protecting irreplaceable natural resources. Almost a quarter of Honduran territory is protected, but a lack of funding and growing pressure on the land mean this status often exists more on paper than in reality. Nonetheless, the remoter reaches of the parks still host an astonishing array of flora and fauna, amid some of the finest stretches of virgin **cloud** and **tropical forest** in Central America.

Honduras's close alliance with the US, while preventing the bitter conflicts that beset its neighbours in the 1980s, has not alleviated the country's acute **social** and economic problems. After Nicaragua, this is Latin America's second poorest nation, with levels of poverty that can be disturbing to witness: some eighty percent of Hondurans live in poverty and forty percent are unable to read or write. Exacerbating the pressure on economic and environmental resources is a rapidly growing population, predicted to reach seven million by the turn of the century, much of it absorbed by the ever-increasing shantytowns ringing the main cities.

It is in the cities that the pressures are most evident: life is fast and harsh and social intercourse conducted at times with gratuitous rudeness. Move out into the rural areas, however, and the open generosity and genuine friendliness displayed by those who have little else are what leave an enduring impression. On the north coast, where the population is more ethnically diverse, the heat and sunshine combine to create a way of life that's more Caribbean than Latin.

■ Where to go

Most visitors pass through the capital, **Tegucigalpa**, at some stage, where a stay, however short, is enlivened by the generally relaxed ambience, and the presence of facilities and services you won't find elsewhere. Though small, the city has a reasonable range of places to eat, drink and make merry. From Tegucigalpa just a couple of hours on the bus brings you to the peaceful mountain towns of **Santa Lucía** and **Valle de Angeles**; for the more energetic, there is hiking close by in the cloud forest of **La Tigra**. Further away, though still an easy day's journey, is the little-visited getaway of **Isla el Tigre**, in the warm waters of the Golfo de Fonseca, perfect for a few days spent doing nothing much at all.

Many travellers head straight for the western highlands and the Maya ruins of **Copán**, one of the finest archeological sites in Central America. Though it's an arduous trip from the capital, there are some worthwhile places to break the journey, notably **Comayagua**, the former colonial capital, a couple of hours from Tegucigalpa, which has a wealth of historic churches and a couple of good museums. The equally charming colonial city of **Santa Rosa de Copán** also makes a logical destination on the way to or from Copán.

In the east of the country, the rugged, sparsely populated region known as Olancho is home to the rarely visited national parks of **La Muralla** and **Sierra de Agalta**. The latter contains the most extensive stretch of virgin cloud forest remaining in Central America, best explored with a guide.

Heading towards the Caribbean you're almost certain to pass through Honduras's energetic second city, **San Pedro Sula**, the commercial centre of the country and a useful transport hub. Just an hour or so south of town is one of Central America's premier spots for ornithologists, the placid, blue, fresh waters of **Lago de Yojoa**.

Frequent buses fan out from San Pedro to the **north coast**, with its pristine white beaches, warm clear waters and endless sun. **Tela**, **La Ceiba** and **Trujillo** are all lively towns with thriving nightlife, while the fishing village of **Omoa** moves at a quieter pace. For a glimpse of a different way of life, make for the friendly **Garífuna** villages dotted

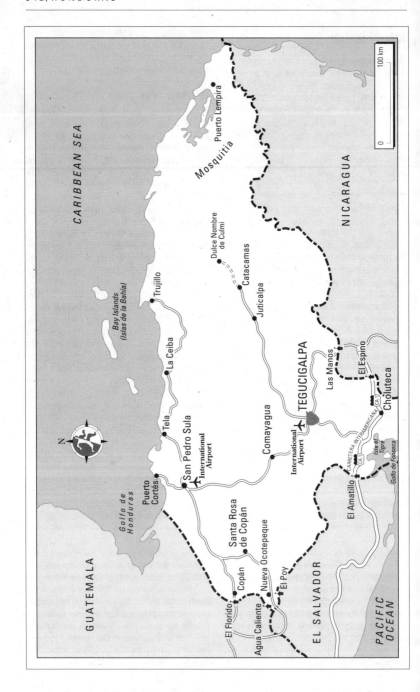

along the coast. Also within easy reach is the coastal wetland reserve of **Punta Sal**, near Tela, sheltering a multiplicity of bird and marine life amid mangrove swamps and marshes. **Pico Bonito**, a reserve near La Ceiba, requires more planning to get to but the effort is spectacularly rewarded.

The jewel in the crown of Honduras's natural resources, however, is the biosphere reserve of the **Río Plátano** in Mosquitia. Encompassing one of the finest remaining stretches of virgin tropical rainforest in Central America, as well as savannah flatlands, the region is largely uninhabited – a trip here really does get you off the beaten track.

Finally, for the ultimate in beach holidays, the **Bay Islands**, though growing more popular each year, continue to provide world-class snorkelling and diving.

When to go

As in much of Central America, the **climate** in Honduras is dictated more by altitude than by season. In the central highlands, the weather is temperate, pleasantly warm in the daytime and cool at night. It's hardly surprising that the Spanish focused their attention here, abandoning the flatlands and the northern coast, which can be unpleasantly hot at any time of year. While the Pacific and Caribbean coasts at least offer the relief of breezes and cooling rainshowers, San Pedro Sula and other lowland towns can be positively scorching in summer.

Honduras's **rainy season**, known as winter (*invierno*), runs from May to November, though how much it will affect your trip depends on where you're travelling. In much of the country it rains for only a few hours in the late afternoon, while along the northern coast and in Mosquitia rain is a constant feature all year round. October and November are perhaps the only months you might want to avoid these parts: this is hurricane season, when heavy rains can cause serious flooding, washing away roads and cutting off all transport.

Getting around

There are a number of alternatives for **getting around** Honduras, depending on how fast you want to travel and where you want to get to. Buses are the cheapest way to go, but occasional flights cut down on the long, often tedious journeys through the country's mountainous terrain. Driving allows you to take things at your own pace and to reach the more remote areas that are

rarely served by buses, while boats are the most atmospheric way of reaching the Bay Islands. A passenger railway service, connecting Puerto Cortés, San Pedro Sula and Tela, was supposedly due to start operating again in 1998; whether it actually does is open to conjecture.

Buses

There are frequent **bus** departures to all points across Honduras from the major transport hubs of Tegucigalpa, San Pedro Sula and La Ceiba, backed up by networks of local services. On the longer intercity routes there are both direct and stopping services, and often a choice of bus. Compared to El Salvador or Guatemala, however, departures are less frequent and timetables more strictly observed. Planning ahead and double-checking departure times are essential if you want to avoid getting stuck. **Fares** are extremely low, the most expensive ticket on the longest routes – between Tegucigalpa and the north coast – costing under US$7. Very roughly, most journeys work out at less than a dollar per hour of travelling. For intercity trips, which tend to get crowded, it's worth buying a ticket well in advance; you'll usually be issued with a seat number. Even direct buses stop to pick up passengers at certain points along the route and, if there are no seats left, you stand.

Taxis

Taxis operate in all the main towns, tooting as they cruise by anyone who looks remotely like a tourist. Meters are nonexistent, so you should always agree a price before getting in. For trips further afield, it can be worth hiring a taxi for a few hours, or even the whole day. Fares are negotiable, but bargaining hard will get you a reasonable deal, particularly if you are in a group.

Driving and hitching

Renting a **car** is the simplest way to get to the more isolated national parks, without having to rely on inconveniently timed buses. Well-maintained highways connect the main cities, running between the north and south coasts and along the coasts themselves. There are also numerous dirt roads connecting the isolated villages of the highlands. Bear in mind, however, that these can be in quite appalling condition for large parts of the year, and at times completely impassable; check local advice on conditions before setting out. **Rental** starts at around US$45 a day for a small car, US$60 for larger models and 4WDs. Check the rental agreement carefully to ensure that insurance and emergency assistance are included.

Hitching is very common in rural areas, and generally safe. Keep an eye out for pick-up trucks with lots of people in the back, and stick out your thumb. You are expected to offer payment at the end of the ride, usually the same as the bus fare – though it may be refused.

■ Cycling

Cycling is a scenic way to travel around under your own steam, although negotiating the main highways can sometimes be a hair-raising experience. You'll need to bring your own bike, preferably a mountain bike to cope with the terrain. Since bicycles are a common form of transport in rural areas, there are repair shops in most places, although it's wise to anticipate potential problems and come equipped with your own tools and spares.

■ Boats

A fast scheduled **boat** service – the *MV Tropical* – operates between La Ceiba and the Bay Islands, running in both directions daily. Tickets are slightly cheaper than the airfare and the journey takes one to two hours. The boat is comfortable, with an air-conditioned lounge, video service and snack bar. There are also unscheduled **cargo boat** departures for Mosquitia from La Ceiba and Trujillo – the only way to find out about these is to go to the dock and ask.

■ Planes

Faced with a six- or seven-hour bus journey from Tegucigalpa to the north coast, many people prefer to **fly**; flying is also the easiest way to reach the Bay Islands and the only practicable way to get to the Mosquitia. A small number of domestic airlines offer competitive prices, with frequent departures between Tegucigalpa and San Pedro Sula, La Ceiba and the Bay Islands. A one-way ticket between Tegucigalpa and San Pedro will cost around US$20, whilst La Ceiba to the Bay Islands is US$11–17 and La Ceiba–Mosquitia around US$34. There is a **departure tax** of US$1.50 for internal flights and US$7.50 for international flights.

Costs, money and banks

Honduras's currency is the **lempira** (L), which consists of 100 centavos. Coins come as 5, 10, 20 and 50 centavos and notes as 1, 2, 5, 10, 20, 50 and 100 lempiras. Oddly, you'll often be quoted prices for which no coinage exists, for example L15.96 – in these cases, change is always rounded down. For day to day living, Honduras works out extremely cheap for foreigners. At the current **exchange rate** of L13 to US$1, a cup of coffee will cost around US$0.30, a soft drink around US$0.40 and fresh juice US$1. Local cigarettes are US$0.50, imported brands slightly more. A meal in an ordinary café will be around US$2–3.

Honduras has a number of national **banks**, of which the biggest are Banco Atlántida, Bancahsa, Banco de Occidente and Ficensa. All of these change travellers' cheques. Banco Atlántida offers cash advances on Visa cards, while Credomatic, with branches in Tegucigalpa, San Pedro Sula and La Ceiba, advances on Visa and Mastercard. At present Honduran ATMs don't accept foreign cards. Banks in Tegucigalpa and San Pedro Sula are usually open Monday to Friday 9am to 4pm and Saturday 9am to noon; in smaller towns, however, most shut for an hour at lunchtime and close up to an hour earlier in the afternoons. All banks are closed on public holidays and on the Monday following an election.

Information

The **Instituto Hondureño de Turismo**, in the Edificio Europa, Av Ramon Cruz and C República de Mexico, Tegucigalpa (☎238 3974, fax 222 6621), is a well-meaning organization that can provide general **information** about where to go and what to see in the country; they also have booths at Tegucigalpa and San Pedro Sula airports. Bear in mind, however, that the concept of independent travel is not readily understood and they are more than likely to try and sell you organized trips through a tour operator.

National parks and reserves are administered by the government forestry agency, **COHDEFOR** (Apdo Postal #1378; ☎223 7703, fax 223 2653). If you intend spending much time in any of the parks, it's worth visiting the COHDEFOR headquarters in Tegucigalpa for detailed information on flora and fauna. The office is a little difficult to find, just off the Carretera al Norte in Comayagüela.

Accommodation

The choice of **accommodation** is widest in Tegucigalpa, San Pedro Sula, Copán and along the north coast, where there's a range of rooms to suit all pockets; outside these areas, the choice begins to narrow. Except in very remote regions, you'll always find a room, but don't count on it being particularly comfortable or even clean. Of the Bay Islands, Utila is the cheapest, with prices not much higher than on the mainland, while Roatán has a couple of places catering to backpackers and a good selection of mid-range and luxury hotels, and Guanaja is geared heavily towards the luxury, all-inclusive package holiday market.

On the mainland, expect to **pay** around US$3 per person for a basic, acceptable room outside the capital and big cities, more if you want a private bath. Paying US$10 and above will secure you a reasonably well-furnished room, with extras such as TV, a/c and hot water. A seven-percent tax is sometimes – not always – added to the bill. In Tegucigalpa and San Pedro Sula, prices are higher: US$3 rooms do exist but they are invariably located in the worst areas; decent budget rooms begin at around US$6 and mid-range at US$20, while those in the top hotels go for around US$70. Normally the only time you need to reserve in advance is at Semana Santa or during a big local festival, such as the May Carnival in La Ceiba.

The only formal provision for **camping** is in some of the national parks. Elsewhere, pitching a tent is very much an ad hoc affair. Tempting though they may seem, the north coast beaches are **not safe** to be on after dark and camping is highly inadvisable. Elsewhere, if you intend to camp, make sure you ask permission from the landowner first.

Eating and drinking

The range of **places to eat** in the big cities is wide and increasing all the time. Smart restaurants serving European, Latin American and Honduran cuisine abound in Tegucigalpa and San Pedro Sula, and the more touristy places, such as Copán and the Bay Islands, generally boast one or two excellent restaurants. Elsewhere, the choice narrows to comedores serving set lunches and dinners, consisting of the usual mix of beans, rice, tortilla and meat, and – very often – a Chinese restaurant, although the authenticity of these is variable.

■ What to eat

Honduran **specialities** worth trying include *anafre* and *tapado*. The former is a fondue-like dish of cheese, beans or meat, or a mixture of some or all of these. The latter is a rich vegetable stew, often with meat or fish added. North coast cuisine has a strong Caribbean influence and fresh fish and seafoods feature heavily. *Guisado* (spicy chicken stew) and *sopa de caracol* (conch stew with coconut milk, spices, potatoes and vegetables) are dishes that should be tried at least once. *Pan de coco* (coconut bread) is often served with meals in the north and makes a delicious snack in itself; Tela in particular is famed for its coconut rolls, sold on the beach by women and children. Probably the most common street snack, sold all over the country, is the *baleada*, a white flour tortilla filled with beans, cheese and cream; two or three of these constitute a decent-sized meal.

■ Drinking

As for **drinks** to go with your meal, the usual brands of fizzy drink are ubiquitous, as is good, local coffee. **Fruit juices** are available everywhere, most commonly in the form of *licuados* or *batidos* (blended with milk), or *frescos* (blended with water). Orange and other fruit juices are widely sold in cartons, but invariably have sugar added. Tap **water** is unsafe to drink; bottled, purified water is sold everywhere and many hotels supply it free to guests. Honduras produces five brands of **beer**, all of them made by the same company. *Salvavida* and *Imperial* are heavier lagers, *Port Royal* slightly lighter and *Nacional* and *Polar* very light and quite tasteless. **Rum** (*ron*) is also distilled in the country as is the Latin American gut-rot, *aguardiente*. In the more expensive restaurants, imported European and South American wines are available, at a price.

Opening hours, festivals and holidays

Business hours are generally Monday to Friday 9am to noon and 2 to 4.30 or 5pm, and sometimes from 9am to noon on Saturdays. Government offices work Monday to Friday 8.30am to 4.30pm, often with an hour's break for lunch. Government offices, post offices and many other businesses close on national holidays and the first Monday after an election. The major **public holidays** are listed in the box below.

All towns and villages have an annual **fiesta patronale** to commemorate the local saint. Some last only a day, some for a week or more, with a variety of events attracting people from far and wide. One of the largest is Carnaval in La Ceiba, more correctly known as *La Feria de San Isidro*. Held during the week leading up to the third Saturday in May, the festivities culminate in a street parade through the centre of the city, followed by performances of live music on sound stages until the early morning. The celebrations in San Pedro Sula in the last week of June, culminating on June 29 (a holiday in the city), and in Punta Gorda (Roatán), from April 6 to 12, celebrating the arrival of the Garífuna, are both worth making an effort to get to. The biggest festival of all, however, is that of the *Virgen de Suyapa* – patron saint of the country – in the first week of February, when pilgrims from around the country flock to Tegucigalpa to worship and celebrate.

PUBLIC HOLIDAYS

Jan 1 New Year's Day
March/April Semana Santa: Thursday, Friday and Saturday before Easter Sunday
April 14 Day of the Americas
May 1 Labour Day
Sept 15 Independence Day
Oct 3 Birth of Francisco Morazán
Oct 12 Discovery of America
Oct 21 Armed Forces Day
Dec 25 Christmas Day

Mail and telecommunications

Letters posted from Honduras generally take around a week to get to the US and nine or so days to reach Europe. Receiving letters poste restante, however, is more hit and miss: mail may take weeks to work its way through the system and there's always the chance it won't be given to you when it does arrive. The main **post offices** in Tegucigalpa and San Pedro Sula are open Monday to Friday 8am to 7pm and until 1pm on Saturdays; smaller offices open from Monday to Friday 8am to 5pm, with a lunch break, and on Saturdays until noon.

In every town there's a **Hondutel** telephone office, where it's possible to make collect calls. The offices in Tegucigalpa and San Pedro Sula are open 24 hours; elsewhere, offices are open daily from 7am to 9pm. There are also public phone booths scattered around the major towns, which take 20 and 50 centavo coins. There are no area phone codes; the international country code for Honduras is ☎504.

Fax services are available at Hondutel in Tegucigalpa and San Pedro (daily 7am–5pm), and at an increasing number of mid-range and upmarket hotels – although beware that these charge a considerable premium for either sending or receiving pages.

The number of **email** connections in Honduras is growing slowly, but aside from a couple of Internet cafés – *Shakespeares Books* in Tegucigalpa and the *Online Cafe* in West End, Roátan – access is most likely to be through business contacts or local friends.

The media

There are six daily **newspapers** in Honduras: *El Periódico, La Tribuna* and *El Heraldo* are published in Tegucigalpa, *La Prensa, El Tiempo* and *El Nuevo Día* in San Pedro Sula. Of these, *El Tiempo* is the most liberal, regularly critical in the past of the activities of government and the armed forces. *La Tribuna*, owned by the family of the current president, is also moderate in its political stance; *El Heraldo* and *La Prensa* – which has the highest circulation at around 42,000 – are both conservative but with good international coverage. While the situation has improved of late, all the print media impose a certain level of self-censorship, particularly when reporting the actions of the armed forces and government.

Probably the most useful publication for travellers is *Honduras This Week*, a weekly **English-language paper** with in-depth coverage of Honduran events, as well as tourist and business information. It's available from English-language bookshops in the capital and in the big hotels in Tegucigalpa, San Pedro Sula, La Ceiba and Roatán.

Honduras's airwaves are filled with over 150 **radio stations**, most in private ownership, which broadcast to some 3.5 million listeners weekly; Radio Honduras is the government-owned station. All the six terrestrial **television** networks are in private hands, with around one-third of households owning sets; in addition there are numerous cable networks, broadcasting films, news and light entertainment from Latin America and the US. Programmes on US channels are usually in English with Spanish subtitles.

Shopping

While the **artesenías** available in Honduras may not be as wide-ranging or as colourful as those in Guatemala, there are a number of crafts that are instantly recognizable as Honduran. The range of **carved wooden goods**, particularly those produced around Valle de Angeles, is extensive, from simple bowls and dishes to elaborate chests and doors, while in the highlands and around Copán **ceramics**, including replicas of Maya pottery and artefacts, are produced. On the north coast the speciality is cotton **hammocks**, along with **Garífuna** handicrafts, music and paintings. Good quality **cigars** are sold in Tegucigalpa, Santa Rosa de Copán and Copán, and a number of companies in Tegucigapla and San Pedro Sula sell high-quality **leather goods** at around half European prices.

For everyday goods, the general **markets** in every town usually provide a bewildering range of cheap clothing, food and household goods. More expensive boutiques and supermarkets are limited to Tegucigalpa and San Pedro Sula.

Safety and the police

Given the overall level of poverty, Honduras is still a remarkably safe country for tourists and travel in rural areas is generally an informative exercise in mutual trust and respect. In the cities, however, **street crime** is undoubtedly rising; pickpocketing and bag or jewellery snatches are ultimately opportunistic and can be prevented by exercising basic caution. While the centre of Tegucigalpa is reasonably safe at night, consider taking a taxi if it's late or you're on your own; Comayagüela, particularly around the market area, is not considered safe to walk around at all at night.

On the north coast **drugs** enter the equation: San Pedro Sula has a thriving gang culture and the highest crime rates in the country, while in the north coast towns, Tela particularly, muggings and physical attacks (including rape) on tourists have increased. Once again, the chances of anything occurring can be reduced by using some common sense: don't flash around money or valuables, and try to remain aware of where you are and how you are returning to your hotel. None of the beaches around the towns is considered safe at night.

The **police**, though now separate from the armed forces, are unlikely, overall, to be of much help if something does happen, but any incidents should be reported for insurance purposes.

Work and study

Honduras is waking up to the demand for **language schools**, though it's by no means in the same league as neighbouring Guatemala, with just a few schools operating in Tegucigalpa, Copán and La Ceiba. A couple with excellent reputations are listed in the box below. Courses can be taken for any length of time you choose and always include the option of staying with a family.

LANGUAGE SCHOOLS

La Ceiba

Centro Internacional de Idiomas, Barrio El Iman #1162 (☎ & fax 440 0547; Apdo. Postal #537; email *cii@tropicohn.com*). A small, friendly school offering weekly courses of four hours a day one-to-one tuition for US$200 with homestay, US$135 without. Transfer credit available from US universities.

Copán

Escuela de Español Ixbalanque, 2 blocks west of parque (☎ & fax 651 4432; email *ixbalan@gbm.hn*). A one-week course including homestay, twenty hours of classes and afternoon activities, costs US$155.

Schools generally also arrange cultural and social activities.

Opportunities for paid employment are few and far between in Honduras. Perhaps easiest to come by are jobs **teaching** English at one of the small language schools – try under listings for *Academias de Idiomas* in the yellow pages.

History

When the Spanish arrived in the sixteenth century, Honduras was populated by a number of different tribes. In the northeast – the Mosquitia, parts of the north coast and Olancho – were the **Pech** and **Sumu**, related to the South American Chibchans, while the north-central region was occupied by the **Tolupan**, migrants from possibly as far away as the present United States. Western Honduras was home to the **Maya**, while the **Lenca**, also believed to be descended from the Chibchans, inhabited the centre of the country. The **Pipils**, migrants from present-day Mexico, lived to the south, along the Gulf of Fonseca, with the Toltec-speaking **Chorotega**, also from Mexico, inhabiting the area around Choluteca.

Of these, it is the **Maya** about whom most is known. Archeologists believe that settlers began moving south into the Río Copán valley from around 1000 BC; construction of the city of **Copán** began around 100 AD. By the time of the founding of the royal dynasty in 426 AD, Copán exerted control as far north as the Valle de Sula, east to Lago Yojoa and west into what is now Guatemala. Home to the governing and religious elite, and supporting a total population of around 24,000, the city was the pre-eminent Maya centre for scientific and artistic development; today it is one of the world's foremost archeological sites. When, for reasons which are not entirely clear, Maya civilization began to collapse around 900 AD, Copán was abandoned, although the area it previously controlled remained inhabited.

Following the collapse of the Maya empire, the **Lenca** became the predominant group in Honduras, absorbing other indigenous cultures and settling in small, scattered communities, supported by subsistence agriculture and hunting and gathering. The Lenca established trade links as far north as Mexico and interacted peaceably with the Maya and Pipil.

■ Discovery and conquest

On July 30, 1502, on his fourth and final voyage, **Columbus** arrived off the island of Guanaja. Naming it the *Isla de Pinos* (Island of Pines), he then continued in exploration of the Central American coastline visible on the horizon, accompanied by a Pech trader encountered coming from the direction of Guatemala. Sailing east along the coast, the fleet first stopped at Punta Caxinas, close to present-day Trujillo, where the first Catholic mass in Latin America was held on August 14, 1502. Sailing on into harsh storms, the fleet rounded a cape where, encountering calmer waters, Columbus is reputed to have exclaimed "Gracias a Dios que hemos salido de estas honduras" (Thank God we have now left these depths), christening both the cape – Cabo Gracias a Dios – and eventually the country. Initially, however, the Spanish called these new lands Higueras, the name used by the indigenous groups they encountered.

Twenty years elapsed before the conquistadors returned to take possession of the new territory, the nominal conqueror being **Gil González Dávila**, who sailed up the Pacific coast from Panamá and partially explored the lands that now form Nicaragua and Honduras. In 1524, however, **Hernán Cortés** dispatched his lieutenant **Cristóbal de Olid** to claim the whole of the isthmus on Cortés's behalf. Olid landed on the north coast in May 1524 and founded the first Spanish settlement, Triunfo de la Cruz on the Bahía de Tela; his own claims on the territory were abruptly ended by assassination later that year. Cortés himself, desperate to stamp his ownership on the new lands, left Mexico for Honduras in 1525, arriving on the north coast in the spring and ordering the founding of Puerto Caballos (now Puerto Cortés) and Trujillo. Aware that his absence from Mexico was undermining his position, however, Cortés returned there in April 1525. Five years later **Pedro de Alvarado**, dispatched from Guatemala, arrived to govern the territory. Under Alvarado, the city of San Pedro Sula was founded, in 1536, and control of the inland regions was secured.

■ The Lempira Rebellion

There was sporadic but persistent **resistance** to the Spanish advance by the indigenous groups they encountered, although the power of these was lessened by the dispersal of the tribes across the land, and the lack of a single powerful group.

No significant threat to the Spanish was posed until **Lempira's rebellion** in 1536. A Lenca *cacique* (chieftain) from what is today Erandique in southwest Honduras, Lempira was a charismatic leader, popularly believed to be invincible. Persuading the tribes of the centre and western highlands to unite in rebellion, he amassed a force of up to 30,000 men, retreating with them to the natural mountain redoubt of Peñol de Cerquín. From here he signalled the outbreak of hostilities by killing three Spanish passers-by. The mass insurrection that followed was at first impossible for the Spanish to control; at one point Comayagua was burnt down and Gracias, San Pedro de Puerto Caballos and Trujillo besieged. Outright rebellion continued for three years, before the Spanish, having lured Lempira down to participate in peace talks, shot and killed him in 1539. With no leader at their head, Lempira's forces were easily overcome and the Spanish hold on the land assured.

■ The colonial period

With Honduras under control, the Spanish increasingly focused their attention on the interior of the country, in large part because of the inhospitable climate of the coastal settlements and their vulnerability to pirate attacks. Discovery of **gold** in the Valle de Comayagua in 1539, and of **silver** at Goascorán and around Tegucigalpa over the following forty years, seemed to promise untold riches. The designation of Comayagua as capital in 1573 reflected the displacement of economic activity away from the coast.

For the indigenous inhabitants, the consolidation of Spanish power was catastrophic. Contemporary population records are notoriously inaccurate, but from an estimated 400,000 in 1524, the population probably fell to as low as 15,000 by 1571. Those who survived the diseases of the Old World were initially enslaved and shipped either overseas or into the mines. Social structures collapsed and communities were forcibly dispersed, with the most affected peoples being the highland tribes, since they had most contact with the colonists. Incredibly, considering their impact, the number of colonists numbered fewer than 300 throughout the seventeenth century.

For the Spanish the steep **decline in population** was above all else a severe hindrance to economic development. Though at their peak the mines provided a comfortable living for their owners, from the seventeenth century onwards the labour shortage made working deeper seams impracticable, and profits dropped sharply as a result. The depopulation of the countryside also hindered the development of a sustainable agricultural sector. *Encomienda*, the system of demanding labour and tribute from the indigenous population, theoretically ensured a supply of workers; in practice, labour scarcity meant that food production rarely rose above subsistence levels, capable only of supplying immediate local needs.

By the early 1800s, Honduras was an **economy in crisis**. Mining was virtually defunct and a series of severe droughts hit both agriculture and livestock. Society was sharply divided, with a narrow layer of the relatively wealthy – state functionaries, merchants, a handful of mine and hacienda owners – above the poor mass of *mestizos* and indigenous peoples. A middle class was nonexistent and any kind of unifying national infrastructure absent; by independence in 1821, Honduras still had no national printing press, newspapers or university.

■ Independence

News of **independence** from Spain reached Honduras on September 28, 1821. While the Liberals of Tegucigalpa celebrated, the Conservatives of Comayagua declared their intention to join the American monarchy under the Mexican Agustín Iturbide. Following Iturbide's deposition, the provinces of Central America declared themselves an independent republic on July 1, 1823. In the civil war that followed almost immediately, the Honduran **Francisco Morazán** – Liberal and sometime soldier – succeeded in defeating Conservative forces in Guatemala and, elected president of the republic in 1830, tried to institute a series of far-sighted reforms in government, the Church, the judicial system and education. Opposed by Conservatives across Central America, his vision of the potential of a united republic was not enough to persuade even his own countrymen. There were sporadic uprisings and eventually civil war broke out again; Morazán failed to crush the Conservative-backed 1837 rebellion of Rafael Carrera in Guatemala, and – when Honduras and Nicaragua went to war against El Salvador – resigned in 1839. The Central American Republic was finished.

In the newly independent **Republic of Honduras**, rivalry between Liberals and Conservatives was as strong as ever. Rallying various bastions of local power to their respective flags, they plunged the country into an almost permanent state of conflict, political and military. The economy, too, was deeply unstable: subject to financial mismanagement by governments of both colours, lacking an export sector to secure foreign revenues and a national infrastructure to push growth, and undermined by flourishing corruption. The effects of this were clearly illustrated in the ill-fated venture to construct a national railway system. Sensing the opportunity to make a quick profit, British banks loaned a desperate government £6 million in 1867–70. Of this, only around £100,000 was ever received and barely 90km of track laid. The resulting debt – which over the next fifty years rose to £30m – was not fully paid off until 1953.

■ **Marco Aurelio Soto and the Liberal Reform**

The man credited with beginning the modernization of Honduras was **Dr Marco Aurelio Soto**, a Liberal, elected president in 1876. He and his successor Luis Bográn reformed the powers of judiciary and Church, professionalized the armed forces and put into place communications and education infrastructures. What was created, in short, were all the elements, above a common language and religion, necessary to make Honduras a unified state capable of taking its place in the world. Recognizing the need to participate in the international economy, Soto also instigated agricultural reforms, in order to develop the coffee and sugar cane industries for export.

Believing that foreign capital was the key to economic development, he encouraged **foreign investment** by US, British and European companies on extremely favourable terms, conversely laying the basis for the country's enduring economic problems. In the mining industry, for example, investors had an obligation to do little more than employ workers, while the government undertook to build roads, ports and any infrastructure necessary to get equipment in and the finished product out. At the El Rosario mine near Tegucigalpa – at one point the most productive mine in the western hemisphere – which accounted for 45 percent of the country's export income at the turn of the century, ninety percent of shares were in foreign (mainly US) hands.

■ **The banana republic**

The same thinking lay behind the development of the **banana industry** in the late nineteenth century, the industry that was to become the dominating factor in Honduras's future. More than happy to accept government concessions, which included exemption from customs duties and ownership of mineral rights, US fruit companies began to move into the rich agricultural lands of the north coast. Three companies – United Fruit, Vacarro Bros (later Standard Fruit) and the Cuyamel Fruit Company (bought out by United Fruit in 1929) – soon became dominant, all but wiping out small-scale producers. Further concessions, granted in return for promises to build railways, allowed the companies to steadily increase their holdings, which, by 1924, amounted to two thousand square kilometres on the north coast and control of seventy percent of Honduras's total exports. Through expansion of interests, the companies also gained control of the country's railways, principal factories and major energy and telegraph companies, set up banks and acted as intermediaries in negotiations over foreign loans.

Political power and influence followed economic might. Cuyamel cultivated strong links with the Liberal Party, while United Fruit – whose support extended to instigating armed uprisings – bankrolled the Conservatives, now known as the National Party. A succession of weak and short-lived governments struggled to keep control in the face of the dominant interests of the fruit companies and, behind them, the United States, as the virtually autonomous north coast spun away from the impoverished centre and south.

■ **The development of modern Honduras: 1932–1963**

With the 1932 election of National Party president **Tiburcio Carías Andino** were laid the foundations for the modern state of Honduras. A virtual dictator for sixteen years, until forced to step down in 1948, Carías strengthened the armed forces and cracked down on political opposition, the press and trade unions. Conversely, his economic austerity programme succeeded in balancing the economy and his authoritarian leadership forged a new national cohesion. His successor, **Juan Manuel**

Gálvez, set up a central bank, a public service sector, and expanded the nascent export industry of coffee, sugar and light manufacturing.

A thus strengthened government was better placed to deal with the worst excesses of the banana companies, reflected in the **Banana Strike** of May 1954. Originating with Puerto Cortés dockers, the strike spread to 35,000 United and Standard Fruit workers, and then to workers in other industries. Ended by a settlement in early July, thrashed out between government, employers and unions, most demands went unrecognized. The two main achievements of the strikers, however – legitimization of labour unions and the drafting of an enduring framework of labour protection laws – made the strike a watershed in Honduran history.

A **coup** in October 1956 introduced the **military** as a new element into the hierarchy of power. Though civilian government resumed in 1957, with the election of Liberal Ramón Villeda Morales, a new constitution the same year gave the armed forces the right to disregard presidential orders they perceived to be unconstitutional, strengthening vastly the position of the military and affecting the development of the state over the next twenty years.

■ **Military influence – and the Football War**

In October 1963 a second coup installed **Colonel Oswaldo López Arellano** as provisional president. Though elected constitutionally in 1965, López remained a ranking officer – eventually rising to Brigadier General – forging an unhealthily close alliance between the military and the National Party, in effect his personal political vehicle. During twelve years in power he decimated the Liberal opposition and reversed most of his predecessor's social reforms. Free-market economic policies led to an increase in unemployment and landlessness, while the profits to be creamed off government development projects fuelled unprecedented corruption. In an attempt to counter growing unrest over land, López introduced limited agrarian reform in 1967, in the form of rural co-operatives, which were far more acceptable to the fruit companies than trade unions. Above all, however, his first period of office is remembered for one of the more bizarre conflicts of modern Central America, the so-called "**Football War**".

On July 14, 1969, war broke out on the Honduras–El Salvador border. Ostensibly caused by a disputed result in a soccer match between the two countries, the conflict stemmed from tensions generated by a steady rise in illegal migration of campesinos from El Salvador into Honduras in search of land. In April 1969 the Honduran government gave settlers thirty days to return to El Salvador and began forced expulsions; sporadic violence broke out, with cynical manipulation of the situation in the press by right-wingers on both sides of the border.

In June, the two countries began a series of **qualifying matches** for the 1970 World Cup, the first of which, held in Tegucigalpa, was won 1–0 by Honduras. At the second game, won 3–0 by El Salvador, spectators at the San Salvador ground booed the Honduran national anthem and attacked visiting Honduran fans. The third and deciding match was pre-empted by the El Salvadorean army bombing targets within Honduras and advancing up to 40km into Honduran territory. After three days, around two thousand deaths and a complete rupture of diplomatic relations, the Organization of American States (OAS) negotiated a ceasefire. A three-kilometre-wide demilitarized zone was set up along the border; tensions and minor skirmishes continued, however, until 1980 when a peace treaty, brokered by the US, was signed. Only in 1992 did both sides accept an International Court of Justice ruling demarcating the border in its current location.

An experiment in democratic government, under Ramón Cruz in 1971–72, was marked by economic chaos and civil unrest, and ended abruptly with a second coup restoring López to power in December 1972. A new programme of industrialization, with the government responsible for investment and accumulation of capital, was – given the by now endemic corruption at senior levels of government, in the military and in business – a recipe for disaster; millions of dollars of national and international loans and aid money were siphoned off to private bank accounts. Limited agricultural reform succeeded to a degree in redistributing under-utilized land, but not enough to contain rural unrest and too much to placate the fruit companies and landowners.

The "**Bananagate**" scandal, the payment of US$1.25m to government officials by United Brands (previously United Fruit) in return for reducing the taxes on fruit exports, eventually forced López to leave office in April 1975. Under his successors, **Colonel Juan Melgar Castro** (1975–78) and **General Policarpo Paz García** (1978–81), agrarian reform slowed to a trickle, repression of civil rights and freedom of speech increased, and corruption among military and government personnel grew to almost laughable levels. In a society sharply divided between rich and poor, almost seventy percent of rural households were unable to meet essential consumption costs, while five percent of the population controlled over half the land.

■ The lost decade – "USS Honduras"

Following the Sandinista revolution in Nicaragua in July 1979 and the election of Reagan to the US presidency in November 1980, Honduras found itself at the centre of US geo-political strategy – the "fourth border of the US", a state of affairs with which the government was only to happy to comply. The **elections** of November 1981, held under US diplomatic pressure, brought **Roberto Suazo Córdova** to power. Though a Liberal, Suazo was closely allied to the rabidly anti-Communist **Colonel Alvarez Martinez**, head of the police force (the FSP), then under military control, and later Commander in Chief of the armed forces. These two men allowed Honduras to become the focus for the US-backed Contra war in Nicaragua, accepting in return over US$1.5bn of direct economic and military aid from the US during the 1980s. US-funded training camps along the border were used on occasion to launch Contra attacks into Nicaraguan territory, while the Honduran army provided logistical support and participated in manoeuvres with the steadily growing numbers of US troops based in the country.

Domestically, the relationship between the military and government grew ever closer. **Human rights** violations rose alarmingly, with the army implicated in at least 184 "disappearances" of activists from labour organizations and peace movements. Forced conscription was common, and lengthy jail sentences were introduced for activities deemed subversive, including street demonstrations. In 1984, army officers, increasingly anxious over Alvarez's actions, forced him into exile. Though repression eased somewhat, the relationship between the military and government continued to be close, with corruption at senior levels in both institutions positively encouraged by the endless flow of dollars from the US.

■ To the present day

Honduras's role as a geo-political lynchpin diminished after Reagan left office and both the Contra war and the civil war in El Salvador were resolved. As the military became less obvious in day to day life, forced conscription was ended and most of the US troops stationed in Honduras were recalled, the country's endemic economic and social problems were thrown into stark relief.

National Party president **Rafael Leonardo Callejas**, winning office in 1989, introduced a neo-Liberal austerity programme, floating exchange rates, privatizing the state sector and cultivating foreign and private investment. Successful in the short term, particularly in forging relations with international lenders, the programme led to a sharp rise in poverty levels and failed ultimately to secure significant investment. Jurisdiction over legal and government affairs was slowly wrested back from the military by a resurgent judiciary, but monitoring groups reported that human rights abuses were still common. Callejas also singularly failed to tackle the issue of corruption, and was himself formally indicted for misappropriation of public funds in 1994.

In 1993, the widely respected Liberal candidate, businessman turned politician **Carlos Roberto Reina**, was elected president. Faced with an economic recession and rapidly devaluing Lempira, Reina put his claims to be capable of engineering moral renewal to the test by taking action on most overt cases of high level corruption. He was not able, however, to prevent the economy sliding further into recession, or to halt a steadily worsening spiral of social instability. This last, fuelled by growing poverty and greater involvement with drug-smuggling between South and North America, affected the north coast in particular.

Reina's successor, Liberal **Carlos Flores Facussé**, took office in November 1997, in elections marred by allegations of corruption and vote-rigging on both sides. Continuing with the free-market economies of his predecessor, Flores also promised a programme of national conciliation, with investment to reverse the cycle of deepening poverty and social despair. The potential for growth remains uncertain, however. As throughout Honduras's history, economic development is still tied to foreign investment. The economic and political power of the fruit companies has to a certain extent diminished – only to be supplanted by the growing influence of Far East *maquiladora* plants and the tourist industry.

CHAPTER 17

TEGUCIGALPA AND THE SOUTH

N estled in a mountain valley 1000m above sea level, **Tegucigalpa** is one of the more enjoyable Central American capitals, thanks to a combination of faded colonial charm, a refreshingly tolerable climate and streets that feel conspicuously safer than those elsewhere. This is a city built on a human rather than a monumental scale: from the small colonial core, home to many of the museums and churches, wealthy residential and embassy districts spread out to the south and east, while across the Río Choluteca to the west lies **Comayagüela**, Tegucigalpa's shabbier, more industrial twin – together the two comprise the administrative **Distrito Central**. Although the nation's economic focus has long since shifted to San Pedro Sula, Tegucigalpa continues to preside as the political and governmental centre of Honduras.

The city sights might keep you busy for a day or two, but it's worth planning a longer stay in the capital in order to venture out into the pine forests and mountain ranges that encircle the city. To the east, the colonial mining villages of **Santa Lucía** and **Valle de Angeles**, both easily reached by local buses, evoke a time when this was a rough frontier, and rich seams of silver provided the wealth on which Tegucigalpa was built. Just a short distance further north is one of the country's most accessible cloud forest reserves, the **Parque Nacional la Tigra**; though commonly visited on a day-trip from the capital, an overnight stay allows time to see more of the forest.

South of Tegucigalpa stretches the stark, sun-baked coastal plain of the Pacific. Tourists are few and far between in this region, whose only real attraction is **Isla el Tigre**, a little-visited volcanic island set in the calm waters of the Golfo de Fonseca. The most likely reason for travelling here is to cross the border into Nicaragua or El Salvador; heading east into Nicaragua, you may well have to change buses in the regional capital, **Choluteca**, whose well-preserved colonial centre makes it an appealing stopover.

Tegucigalpa

Much of **TEGUCIGALPA**'s appeal is understated, with its main pleasure to be found in wandering the winding, narrow streets of the old centre, which meander haphazardly up the lower slopes of **Cerro Picacho**, the dramatic backdrop to the city. Along these streets, crumbling colonial buildings give way to gently decaying nineteenth-century mansions and modern, airy homes, forming the watermarks of the city's history. Even the constant cacophony, gridlock and pollution of the traffic-choked centre doesn't detract entirely from the charm, and the comings and goings of hordes of vendors, beggars, idlers and passers-by provide entertainment for free. More concrete attractions include several well-preserved colonial **churches**, in particular the

For an explanation of **accommodation price codes**, see p.345.

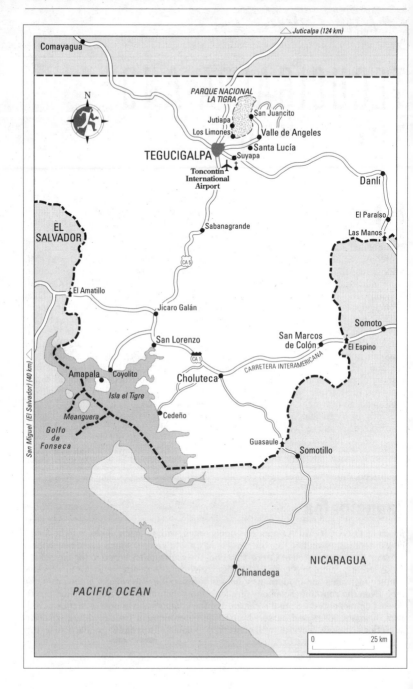

eighteenth-century cathedral on the Plaza Morazán, a handful of national **museum and art collections**, and several small, well-patronized parks.

Cross one of the bridges in the centre and you're in **Comayagüela**. Newer and more down-at-heel than Tegucigalpa proper, the oldest buildings here date back only to the nineteenth century and the place feels distinctly less relaxed. Most visitors come here to visit the sprawling market, or are simply passing through one of the city's **bus terminals**, which are dotted around Comayagüela's streets. Just outside the city proper, around 6km east, is the white bulk of the **Basilica de Suyapa**, site of a pilgrimage and week-long festival in early February.

Some history

Before the arrival of the Spanish, the Tegucigalpa valley was inhabited by small Lenca groups who gradually moved south and settled along the Río Choluteca, as far as what is today Comayagüela. Exactly when the conquistadors first arrived in the valley is unclear; records make no mention of the area until the 1560s, when silver deposits were found in the hills to the east, around Santa Lucía (see p.365). The discovery of further deposits in the surrounding hills attracted growing numbers of settlers, who pushed the indigenous inhabitants out to what are now the outlying barrios of Comayagüela. **Real de Minas de San Miguel de Tegucigalpa** was founded on September 29, 1578, and in 1608 granted the status of *alcaldía*, with authority over a rash of mining settlements in the valley and surrounding hills. Town status came in 1768 and that of city in 1807, with profits from the silver mines aiding the construction of fine colonial churches and houses.

Its mining wealth and location at the centre of cross-country trade routes made Tegucigalpa an increasingly clamorous rival to the then capital Comayagua. Following **independence** – initially spurned by both cities through fear that the other might be named capital – it was decided to alternate the seat of government between the two, a plan that was riddled with shortcomings but nevertheless staggered on until 1830, when parliament was permanently restored to Comayagua. Fifty years later, however, the Liberal President Soto shifted power back to Tegucigalpa, enraged by the failure of Comayagua's innately conservative leaders to support him. In 1932, the city and its poor relation to the south, Comayagüela, were united under the title **Distrito Central**.

Since the late nineteenth century, when the economic focus of the country began to shift to the bountiful fruit plantations of the north coast, Tegucigalpa has become somewhat eclipsed by San Pedro Sula. In essence a chaotic small town grown large, an outpost of what some would call variable political power, the business of government remains the city's main industry. In the words of a local saying, "Tegucigalpa thinks, San Pedro works".

Arrival, information and city transport

Both international and domestic flights arrive at **Toncontín International Airport**, 7km south of the city. **Taxis** wait outside the terminal, but you can save a couple of dollars by walking the 50m down to the highway and hailing one there; the journey to the centre should cost around US$4. City bus #24 ("Río Grande–Lomas") passes the airport frequently, running through Comayagüela and into the centre of Tegucigalpa in around forty minutes, depending on the traffic. At the airport there is a **bank**, a small **Hondutel** telephone office and a number of **car rental** agencies.

Tegucigalpa has no central **bus terminal**; each international or intercity bus line has its own terminal, most of them scattered around Comayagüela. The main exception are buses to and from Danlí and the Nicaraguan border at Las Manos, which run from the Mercado Jacaleapa, Col Kennedy, a long bus ride from Tegucigalpa's centre.

The helpful **Instituto Hondureño de Turismo**, in the Edificio Europa, Av Ramon Cruz and C República de México (Mon–Fri 8.30am–4.30pm; ☎238 3974, fax 222 6621), provides maps of the country and major cities, as well as bilingual information on the

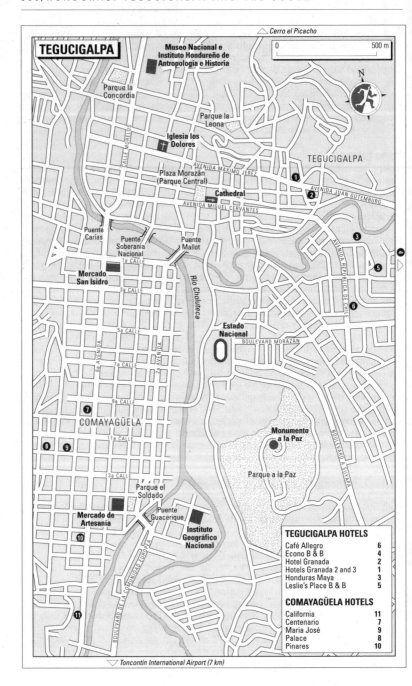

Cerro el Picacho

0   500 m

TEGUCIGALPA

Museo Nacional e
Instituto Hondureño de
Antropología e Historia

N

Parque la
Concordia

Parque la
Leona

TEGUCIGALPA

CALLE MORELOS

Iglesia los
Dolores

AVENIDA MÁXIMO JEREZ

Plaza Morazán
(Parque Central)

AVENIDA JUAN GUTEMBURG

Cathedral

AVENIDA MIGUEL CERVANTES

Puente
Carías

Puente
Soberanía
Nacional

Puente
Mallot

1a CALLE

AVENIDA REPÚBLICA DE CHILE

Mercado
San Isidro

3a CALLE

Río Choluteca

5a CALLE

7a CALLE

Estado
Nacional

BOULEVARD MORAZÁN

2a AVENIDA

3a AVENIDA

9a CALLE

COMAYAGÜELA

Monumento
a la Paz

11a CALLE

BOULEVARD A SUYAPA

13a CALLE

Parque a la Paz

Parque el
Soldado

Mercado de
Artesanía

Puente
Guacerique

Instituto
Geográfico
Nacional

BOULEVARD DE LA COMUNIDAD EUROPEA

TEGUCIGALPA HOTELS

Café Allegro	6
Econo B & B	4
Hotel Granada	2
Hotels Granada 2 and 3	1
Honduras Maya	3
Leslie's Place B & B	5

COMAYAGÜELA HOTELS

California	11
Centenario	7
Maria José	9
Palace	8
Pinares	10

Toncontín International Airport (7 km)

TEGUCIGALPA STREET NAMES

Rather confusingly for visitors new to the city, the authorities recently took the inexplicable decision to **change all the street names** in Tegucigalpa; official maps have not been updated, however, and addresses are still quoted using the previous system. Locals customarily give directions in terms of landmarks, rather than street names. Currently, streets running roughly east to west are avenidas and streets running north to south are calles. In Comayagüela, though, the opposite is the case.

---

main tourist attractions, such as Copán. No English is spoken, however. Keep an eye out for *Honduras Tips*, a privately published, quarterly magazine, available in many of the better hotels and some gift shops, which gives a good overview of sights, hotels and restaurants across the country. For more detailed **maps**, try the Instituto Geográfico Nacional, 15a C off the Blvd de Comunidad Europea, Comayagüela (Mon–Fri 8.30am–noon & 2–4pm).

City transport

City buses are frequent and extremely noisy, generally old US school buses, though unfortunately not painted in the glorious colours seen elsewhere in Central America. Urban routes start running at around 6am and finish around 9pm. Route names and numbers are painted on the front and fares are extremely cheap (US$0.06 anywhere within the city). During rush hour, however, it's usually quicker to walk if you're in the centre. Useful **routes** around the city include buses #20 and #21, both signed "Tiloarque", which run from the centre of Tegucigalpa down to the end of 6a Av in Comayagüela. Bus #02, signed "Carizal–La Sosa", and #21 "Tiloarque–La Sosa", run east from the centre up Av Gutemberg/C la Paz, past the US embassy and Bolívar monument.

Taxis come in a range of shapes and colours, but are easy to identify by the numbers painted on their sides. They announce their availability by incessant honking and are often shared, with passengers dropped off in turn. There are no meters but a trip in the city should be around US$2, more at night and slightly less for a shared ride.

Accommodation

The central and eastern parts of **Tegucigalpa** contain a reasonable range of upmarket **hotels** and pleasant, less expensive accommodation, convenient for museums, restaurants and enjoying the bustling evening street life. A nice alternative, though not particularly cheap, is to stay in one of the **B&B guest houses**, which are mostly located outside the centre. **Comayagüela** contains the bulk of the **budget** places. While these are undeniably cheap, and convenient for early-morning buses, the often drab buildings and small, dingy rooms can be depressing. Bear in mind, also, that much of Comayagüela, particularly the market area, is unsafe at night. All accommodation is marked on the map opposite or on p.359.

Tegucigalpa

Café Allegro, Av República de Chile 360, Col Palmira (☎232 8122). A café and eating place that also has clean dorms with shared bathrooms. The only drawback is the thirty-minute walk to the centre. ②.

Econo B&B, Av San Carlos 437, Col Palmira (☎236 5196, fax 236 5925). A very pleasant and friendly place in a quiet residential area, close to the US embassy. All rooms have TV, phone and hot water, and there's an outdoor pool with a shady terrace. Take a taxi on arrival; otherwise it's half-an-hour's walk or a ten-minute bus ride from the centre. ⑦.

Hotel Boston, Av Maximo Jeréz 321, between C el Telegrafo and C Morelos (☎237 9411). This well-run, perennial favourite is a great place for meeting people. The friendly management keep everything spotlessly clean and offer free coffee, a communal TV area and inexhaustible supplies of hot water. The large, old rooms at the front are nicer, despite the traffic noise. ③.

Hotel Granada, Av Gutemberg at Av Cristóbal Colón (☎237 2381). Rooms are basic but clean, some with bath. Hot water and a communal TV area. Very good value and consequently popular. ①–②.

Hotels Granada 2 & 3, Subida Casa Martín, Barrio Guanacaste (☎237 4004 or 237 0812). Just round the corner from the original *Hotel Granada* and offering a similar deal. All rooms have private bath. ②.

Hotel Honduras Maya, Av República de Perú, Col Palmira (☎232 3191, fax 232 7629). This luxury, modern hotel is something of a city landmark. The upper rooms have great views over the city; facilities include a restaurant, café, pool, souvenir shops, car rental and a travel agency. ⑨.

Hotel la Ronda, Av Jeréz at C las Damas (☎237 8151, fax 237 1454). Centrally located and offering comfortable if slightly small rooms, all with hot water, a/c and TV; price includes breakfast. Downstairs there's a good restaurant and a relaxed bar. ⑥.

Hotel MacArthur, Av Lempira 454, Barrio Abajo (☎237 9839, fax 238 0294). Convenient for the centre and popular with business travellers, but the service is impersonal; smallish rooms all have hot water, fan and TV. Downstairs the small café serves expensive breakfasts. ⑤.

Hotel Maya Colonial, C Palace, just north of the parque central (☎237 2643). A great air of faded charm and a good central location. Rooms are adequately furnished, but there's no hot water. ②.

Leslie's Place B&B, Calzada San Martín 452, Paseo República de Perú, Col Palmira (☎239 0641, fax 239 5912). Comfortable and friendly, but perhaps slightly overpriced. Rooms all have a/c, hot water, TV and phone. ⑦.

Comayagüela

Hotel California, 6a Av, 23a–24a C (☎225 4664). Secure, clean rooms, all with private bath. Not the best of areas but convenient for early-morning buses south. ①.

Hotel Centenario, 6a Av, 9a–10a C (☎237 7729). Safe, clean and friendly. All rooms have TV and hot water and some have private bath. ②.

Hotel Maria José, 12a C, 7a–8a Av (☎237 7292). Rooms in this family-run establishment are clean and pleasant, with private bath, hot water, TV and fan. The café downstairs is open for breakfast through to dinner, closing mid-evening. Good value. ②.

Hotel Palace, 12a C 839, 8a–9a Av (☎237 6660). A new place offering well-furnished rooms, all with private bath. Handy for many of the bus terminals. ③.

Hotel Pinares, 6a Av at 17a C (☎238 4663). Adequate, if basic rooms, some with bath; the only reason to stay here is for the Ticabus terminal across the road. ①.

The City

The heart of Tegucigalpa's **old city** is the pleasant Plaza Morazán, bordered on one side by the **cathedral**; a number of the more interesting churches and museums, plus many of the hotels, lie within easy walking distance of the square. East from the centre, two major roads, **Av Jeréz** (which becomes Av Gutemberg and then Av la Paz) and **Av Miguel Cervantes** (changing its name to Av República de Chile), run out through the richer suburbs and embassy district. A main artery, **1a Avenida**, splits the city in two from north to south, paralleling the Río Choluteca; as the Blvd de la Comunidad Europea, it continues out past the **airport** and to destinations south. Across the river, west from central Tegucigalpa, lies **Comayagüela**, the place to head for cheap hotels and buses out of town.

Around the old centre

Plaza Morazán, Tegucigalpa's parque central, functions as a meeting point, marketplace and site of general entertainment. Hawkers vend, beggars beg, people stop and

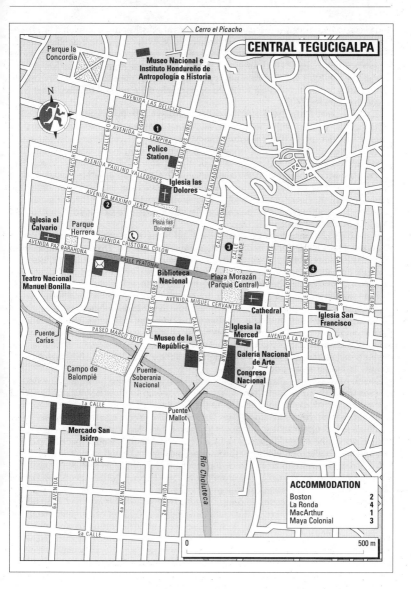

△ Cerro el Picacho

CENTRAL TEGUCIGALPA

Parque la Concordia

Museo Nacional e Instituto Hondureño de Antropología e Historia

AVENIDA LAS DELICIAS

CALLE MORELOS

AVENIDA EL TELEGRAFO

AVENIDA

LEMPIRA

CALLE BUENOS AIRES

❶

Police Station

CALLE SALVADOR MENDIEZA

AVENIDA PAULINO VALLEDORES

Iglesia las Dolores

CALLE LA CONCORDIA

AVENIDA MAXIMO JEREZ

❷

CALLE A LEONA

Iglesia el Calvario

Parque Herrera

Plaza las Dolores

AVENIDA CRISTÓBAL COLÓN

❸

AVENIDA PAZ BARAHONA

CALLE PALACE

CALLE MATUTE

CALLE ADOLFO ZUNIGA

CALLE SALVADOR CORLETO

CALLE AS DAMAS

❹

CALLE PEATONAL

CALLE GUTIERREZ

Teatro Nacional Manuel Bonilla

Biblioteca Nacional

Plaza Morazán (Parque Central)

AVENIDA MIGUEL CERVANTES

CALLE LOS DOLORES

Cathedral

Iglesia San Francisco

Puente Carías

PASEO MARCO SOTO

Museo de la República

CALLE MENDIOLA

Iglesia la Merced

AVENIDA LA MERCED

CALLE EL TELAR

Campo de Balompié

Puente Soberania Nacional

Galería Nacional de Arte

Congreso Nacional

1a CALLE

Puente Mallot

Mercado San Isidro

3a CALLE

Río Choluteca

6a AVENIDA

4a AVENIDA

2a AVENIDA

5a CALLE

ACCOMMODATION

Boston	2
La Ronda	4
MacArthur	1
Maya Colonial	3

0   500 m

chat, and on Sundays the place mills with workers enjoying their day off. As busy after dark as during the day, the plaza makes a pleasant place to while away the time and people-watch. The statue at the centre commemorates the national hero **Francisco Morazán**, a soldier, Liberal and reformer, elected president of the Central American Republic in 1830. The house where he was born, two blocks west on Av Cristóbal Colón, is now the **Biblioteca Nacional** (Mon–Fri 8.30am–4pm). On the east edge of the plaza, the blinding white facade of the **Catedral San Miguel**, completed in 1782, is one of the best preserved in Central America. Inside, look out for the magnificent hand-worked silver Baroque-style altar, and the baptismal font, carved in 1643 by indigenous artesans from a single block of stone. Three blocks east from the plaza, on Av Paz Barahona, the **Iglesia San Franciso** is notable for being the oldest church in the city, first built by the Franciscans in 1592, although much of the present building dates from reconstruction in 1740.

Running **west from the plaza**, the pedestrianized **Calle Peatonal** (literally "pedes-trian street") is lined with shops, cafés and street vendors. Walk west along here for twenty minutes or so, dodging the moneychangers, and you'll come to the small, shady **Parque Herrera** and, opposite, the **Teatro Nacional Manuel Bonilla**. Completed in 1915, the theatre was originally intended to honour Miguel de Cervantes; within the grey-stone renaissance-style shell is an ornately plaster-worked interior, based on the Athenée Comique in Paris. Check the local press or ask at the box office for details of current shows. Five blocks north from the theatre along C la Concordia is another welcome patch of green, the **Parque la Concordia**, dotted with replicas of Maya sculptures.

A couple of blocks northwest from the central plaza, set on the small, newly pedes-trianized Plaza los Dolores is the white, domed **Iglesia los Dolores**, completed in 1732. Its Baroque facade is decorated with a representation of the Passion of Christ, fea-turing a crowing cock and the rising sun; inside, the ornately worked gold altar dates from 1742. Just beyond the church, turn right onto C Morelos and a fairly steep fifteen-minute walk brings you to the Villa Roy, an eighteenth-century mansion – formerly the home of President Lozano Diaz – that's now home to the **Museo Nacional e Instituto Hondureño de Antropología e Historia** (Tues–Sun 8.30am–4.30pm; US$1.50). Inside, a comprehensive exhibition covers the political, economic and social develop-ment of the republic, alongside a display of less interesting presidential artefacts. The institute below the villa has a small reference library with books and information on Copán and other archeological sites.

North of the central plaza, older suburbs – previously home to the wealthy middle classes and rich immigrants, now long gone – edge up the lower slopes of **Cerro el Picacho**. Decent views can be had from the **Parque la Leona**, about twenty minutes walk uphill from the centre along C las Damas, but if you can, it's worth continuing (or catching a bus) up to the top, where the **Parque de las Naciones Unidas** commands a view across the whole of the city and valley beyond. There's ample space for picnick-ing and strolling among the trees; the cramped zoo, near the entrance, is best avoided. On Sundays **buses** run there every half-hour from behind Los Dolores church; on other days, take an El Hatillo bus from the Parque Herrera to the access road, from where it's about fifteen minutes' walk to the entrance.

Just to the south of the parque central, next to the Iglesia la Merced on C Bolivar, the **Galería Nacional de Arte** (Tues–Sun 9am–5pm; US$0.75) is home to an extensive collection of Central American art. Displays on the ground floor range from prehistoric petroglyphs and Maya stone carvings to colonial paintings and religious art, while upstairs rooms are devoted to the gallery's surprisingly ambitious twentieth-century collection. Originally a convent and then the national university, the building's Neoclassical facade sits rather uncomfortably alongside the stained concrete hulk of the **Congreso Nacional**, the seat of government, next door.

One block west, at Paseo Marco Soto and C Mendieta, the late nineteenth-century Presidential Palace has, since 1992, housed the **Museo Histórico de la República** (Wed–Sun 8.30am–noon & 1–4pm; US$1.50), a comprehensive but rather dull exhibi-tion tracing Honduran development since independence. Only those with excellent Spanish and an unquenchable thirst for Honduran history are likely to find much of interest here, since the displays rely heavily on long chunks of text.

South and east of the centre

East from the centre, **Av Máximo Jérez/Gutemberg** skirts the northern edge of **Colonia Palmira**, an upmarket district containing most of the capital's foreign embassies, luxury hotels and wealthy residences. The **US embassy**, a common reference point, lies along Av Gutemberg, about thirty minutes' walk from the plaza. Another city landmark, the modern **Hotel Honduras Maya**, can be found on the Av República de Chile, just south of Col Palmira, fifteen minutes' walk east from the centre. Continue past the hotel for about a kilometre and an overpass gives access to eastward-bound **Blvd Morazán**, Tegucigalpa's major commercial and entertainment artery – for some reason no city buses run along here. At its western end, the boulevard terminates at the **Estadio Nacional**, home to both international and domestic soccer games. The vaguely Greek temple-like monument visible to the south of here on the low Cerro Juana Laínez is the **Monumento a la Paz**, built to commemorate the treaty ending the 1969 Soccer War (see p.351). A road up to the monument starts from the fire station behind the stadium.

Comayagüela

The surging brown waters of the polluted Río Choluteca form a suitable border to Tegucigalpa's twin, **COMAYAGÜELA**, which sprawls away through down-at-heel business districts into industrial areas and poor barrios. There's little to see here and the workaday streets, invariably choked with traffic, have a much less relaxed feel than than those of Tegucigalpa. At night, when there's an undeniably rough edge to the place, even the inhabitants of Tegucigalpa prefer not to venture here.

San Isidro, the capital's main **market**, sprawls around 6a Av and 1a C, just across the Puente Carías river bridge from C Morelos in Tegucigalpa. Stalls jostle for space along the narrow alleys and pavements, sometimes spilling over into the streets themselves, and buses crawl through the crowds, sometimes only inches from the vendors. The atmosphere is hot and frenetic, with the smell of raw meat rising in hot weather. Keep an eye on your possessions while walking around here. About ten minutes' walk past the market, at the intersection with 12a C, is the Banco Central de Honduras building; check in the newspapers for details of the occasional **exhibitions** hosted in the art gallery here.

In the heart of Comayagüela, at 3a Av and 15a C, is the small **Mercado de Artesanía**, housed in a rather gloomy building that never seems to get very busy. Stands sell handicrafts from around the country at prices lower than in Tegucigalpa's shops, although the selection is narrower.

Out from the city: the Basilica de Suyapa

Six or so kilometres east of the centre, the stretch of flat plain is broken by the monolithic white bulk of the **Basilica de Suyapa**. Built in colonial style in the 1950s, to provide a new home for the **Virgen de Suyapa**, the patron saint of Honduras, the church's lofty, bare interior serves to highlight the striking blue stained-glass windows; formal gardens are currently being laid out in front of the building. According to legend, however, the the Virgin has resisted all attempts to place her permanently in the new edifice, each time mysteriously returning to her original home, a simple chapel behind the church. According to legend, the tiny 6cm-tall statue of the Virgin was discovered in 1743 by two campesinos returning to Suyapa from working on Cerro del Pilingüín. Finding themselves still a distance from the village as dark fell, they decided to pass the night in the open air. One of them noticed he was lying on something that felt like a stone and threw it to one side, without looking at it. Within a few minutes, however, the object had returned to the same place. The next day, the two carried the little statue down to Suyapa where, placed on a simple table adorned with flowers, the Virgin began to attract increasing numbers of worshippers. A certain Captain José de Zelaya y Midence built the chapel to house the statue in thanks for recovery of his health.

You can see the statue behind the wooden altar in **La Pequeña Iglesia**, the much simpler, original eighteenth-century chapel, sheltered behind the Basilica. These days it is only moved to the new building temporarily, during the February festival of the Virgen de Suyapa, when thousands of pilgrims from across the country come to worship. City buses to Suyapa run regularly from the Mercado San Isidro in Comayagüela.

Eating, drinking and entertainment

Great culinary experiences and nightlife are not what Tegucigalpa is noted for, although a fairly wide selection of cuisines is available in a reasonable number of **places to eat**. The more expensive restaurants are generally found in the eastern colonias and along the Blvd Morazán, while the centre boasts a number of cheap and cheerful café-style eateries; quality varies but the portions are generally large. Unless otherwise stated, all the places listed below are open daily.

With a few exceptions, **bars** in the centre are fiercely local hangouts, and as a visitor you may get a frosty reception. The atmosphere is more relaxed in the upmarket spots on the Blvd Morazán and along **Blvd Suyapa** towards the university. While nothing like on the scale of most European capitals, this is also the place to come for clubs and **discos**, especially at weekends.

For films, there are a few **cinemas** around the centre, with more modern complexes in the outer suburbs. All show first-run Hollywood movies, generally with subtitles. Closest to the centre are **Aires Tauro** on the Subida Casa Martín, off Av Gutemberg, and **Cine Variadades**, C Mendieta at Av Cristóbal Colón.

Restaurants and cafés

Al Natural, behind the cathedral on C Hipolito Matute. A green, leafy oasis from the city streets, although the quality of the food is not what it was. Generous portions of vegetarian and meat snacks, soups and full meals, plus fresh juices, served in a tranquil courtyard setting. Mon–Fri 7.30am–8pm, Sat 8am–3pm.

Café Allegro, Av República de Chile 360. A pleasant place with a leafy patio serving good, if slightly pricey pasta and meat dishes, coffees and snacks. A main dish plus drinks costs around US$7.

Café Paradiso, Av Paz Barahona at C la Plazuela. A quiet place serving good coffees and snacks; attached is a well-stocked Spanish-language bookshop. Closed evenings and Sun.

Duncan Mayan, Av Cristóbal Colón, 2 blocks west of parque central. Busy barn of a place with large helpings of local food, burgers and snacks from US$1.50. A popular stop for workers on their way home.

El Arriero, Av República de Chile 516, just past *Hotel Honduras Maya*. Expensive but excellent steak and seafood restaurant, where a substantial meal goes for around US$12.

La Posada de Don Chema, Blvd Morazán. A rather upmarket place serving well-prepared Mexican and Spanish dishes in a sedate atmosphere.

La Terraza de Don Pepe, Av Cristóbal Colón, opposite the Biblioteca Nacional. Family restaurant dishing up large portions of local and Chinese-style food, as well as snacks. The tables on the roadside terrace are nicer if you can stand the fumes.

Marbella, C Mendieta, near C Peatonal. Friendly place serving Spanish and Honduran light meals. Also good for a drink and chat. Excruciating live music is sometimes played in the evenings.

Restaurante Nan Kin, in the *Hotel Nan Kin*, Av Gutemberg at Calzada San Miguel. Large, tasty and reasonably priced Chinese standards, and good service.

Romani Restaurante Italien, Blvd Morazán. Acceptable pasta, meat and chicken dishes, in a pleasant atmosphere. The prices are good, though, at around US$10 for a meal with drinks.

Salman's Panaderia, C Peatonal and other locations. Baked goods, including savouries, biscuits and reputedly the best bread in the city – to eat on the spot or take away.

Super Donuts, C Peatonal and other locations. Donut shop, which also does good-value breakfasts of local dishes, or pancakes and fruit, from around US$1. Closed Sun.

Todo Rico, Av Cervantes at C Morelos. Inexpensive vegetarian comedor whose only drawback is the slightly barren eating area; the huge set meals, including soup, a daily special and dessert, are a bargain at around US$3. Closed evenings and Sun.

Nightlife

In the centre, the relatively new **Tobacco Road Tavern**, on Av Paz Barahona at C las Damas, has achieved the feat of gaining popularity with both backpackers and locals. The atmosphere is very relaxed, with regular performances of Garífuna and Honduran folk music, and it's a good place to pick up information from other travellers. Along Blvd Morazán, **Taco Taco** and **Confetti** are both bars popular with Honduran students, while the latter also functions as a disco. **Piano Bar la Hacienda**, Blvd Morazán, goes for a little more sophistication, serving cocktails and hosting variable live music. For dancing, **Plaza Garibaldi**, also on Blvd Morazán, stays open all night, playing Latin American rhythms. **Tropical Port** and the **Backstreet Pub**, both on Blvd Juan Pablo 11, attract a good mix of locals, students and resident foreigners.

Listings

Airlines Air France, Galería la Paz 116, Av la Paz (☎237 0216, fax 237 0189); Alitalia, contiguo Diario la Prensa, Av la Paz (☎221 2099, fax 239 4246); American Airlines, Ground Floor, Edificio Palmira, Col Palmira (☎232 1712, fax 232 1414); British Airways, Edificio Sempe, Barrio la Granja (☎225 5102, fax 225 0341); Continental Airlines, Edificio Palic, Av República de Chile (☎220 0997, fax 220 0990); Copa, Floors 2–4, Edificio Europa, Col San Carlos (☎231 2469, fax 231 2479); Iberia, Edificio Palmira, Col Palmira (☎232 7760, fax 239 1729); Isleña Airlines, Galerías la Paz 105, Av la Paz (☎237 3362, fax 237 3390); Japan Airlines, Galerías la Paz 312, Av la Paz (☎238 0425, fax 237 9914); KLM, Edificio Cicsa (☎232 6414, fax 232 6320); Lacsa, Edificio Interamericana, Blvd Morazán (☎231 2469, fax 233 4075); Lufthansa, 2nd floor, Centro Comercial Plaza del Sol, Av la Paz (☎236 7560, fax 236 7580); Taca International, Edificio Interamericana, Blvd Morazán (☎239 0148, fax 231 1517); Varig, Edificio Sempe, Barrio la Granja (☎234 3916, fax 233 5108).

American Express Local agent is Mundirama Travel Service, Edificio Cicsa, Av República de Panamá, close to the *Hotel Honduras Maya* (Mon–Fri 8am–noon & 1–5pm, Sat 8am–noon).

Banks and exchange All banks will change dollars cash and travellers' cheques. The Coin SA Casa de Cambio on C Peatonal may offer better rates for cash than the banks, whilst the moneychangers on the street invariably offer rates slightly better than the official one. Banco Atlantida, on the parque central and elsewhere, gives advances on Visa cards, whilst Credomatic, C Mendieta at Av Cervantes, gives advances on Visa and Mastercard.

Bookstores Metromedia, C República de Colombia, near the *Econo B&B*, has a wide range of English-language fiction, non-fiction and travel, as well as secondhand books, US newspapers and magazines. Shakespeares Books, at the *Tobacco Road Tavern*, Av Paz Barahona at C las Damas, has stacks of secondhand fiction. Librería Guaymuras, Av Cervantes at C las Damas, is good for Spanish-language fiction and political, economic and social texts whilst the bookshop at *Café Paradiso* also has a reasonable range on contemporary Honduran politics, history and economics. The *Hotel Honduras Maya* and other luxury hotels have US newspapers and magazines and *Honduras This Week*.

Car rental Avis, Av República de Perú, in front of *Hotel Honduras Maya* (☎239 5711, fax 239 5710; airport ☎233 9548); Budget, *Hotel Honduras Maya* (☎232 6832; airport ☎233 5161, fax 233 5170); Hertz, Centro Comercial Villa Real, in front of *Hotel Honduras Maya* (☎239 0772, fax 232 0870); Molinari, 1a Av, 10a C 1002, Comayagüela (☎237 5335, fax 238 0585; airport ☎233 1307); National, *Hotel Honduras Maya* (☎232 3191 ext 2157; airport ☎233 4962).

Embassies Argentina, Col Rubén Darío 417 (☎232 3376, fax 231 0376; Mon–Fri 8am–1pm); Brazil, C la Salle 1309, Col Reforma (☎236 5223, fax 232 2010; Mon–Fri 8am–2pm); Canada, Edificio los Castaños, 6th floor, Blvd Morazán (☎231 4538, fax 231 5793); Chile, Edificio CIA Interamericana, 6th floor, Blvd Morazán (☎231 3703, fax 232 8853; Mon–Fri 8am–2pm); Colombia, Edificio Palmira, 4th

Floor, Col Palmira (☎232 5131, fax 232 8133; Mon–Fri 8am–2pm); Costa Rica, Colonia el Triangulo (☎232 1768, fax 232 1876; Mon–Fri 8am–4pm); Ecuador, Av Juan Lindo, Col Palmira (☎236 5980, fax 236 6929; Mon–Fri 8.30am–1.30pm); El Salvador, 2a Av 205, Col San Carlos (☎236 8045, fax 236 9403; Mon–Fri 8.30am–noon & 1–3pm); Guatemala, 4a C at Av Juan Lindo 2421, Col las Minitas (☎232 9704, fax 231 5655; Mon–Fri 9am–4pm); Mexico, Av República de México 2402, Col Palmira (☎232 6471, fax 231 4719; Mon–Fri 8–11am); Nicaragua, C11, Block M1, Col Lomas del Tepeyac (☎232 7218, fax 231 1412; Mon–Fri 8.30am–noon); Panamá, Edificio Palmira 200, Col Palmira (☎ & fax 231 5441; Mon–Fri 8am–1pm); Peru, C Ruben Dario 1902, Col Alameda (☎231 5261, fax 232 0145; Mon–Fri 8.30am–1.30pm); UK, Edificio Palmira, 3rd Floor, Col Palmira (☎232 0612, fax 232 5480; Mon–Thurs 8am–noon & 1–4pm, Fri 8am–3pm); USA, C la Paz (☎236 9320, fax 236 9037; Mon–Fri 8am–5pm); Venezuela, C Arturo Lopez, Col Rubén Darío (☎232 1886, fax 232 1016; Mon–Fri 8.30am–3.30pm).

Immigration Dirección General de Migracíon, Av Máximo Jérez, just east of *Hotel Ronda* (Mon–Fri 8.30am–4.30pm; ☎238 1957).

Laundry Mi Lavanderia, 2a Av, 3a–4a C, Comayagüela, has coin-operated machines and a laundry service (Mon–Sat 7am–6pm, Sun 8am–5pm); Super Jet, Av Gutemberg, just past the *Hotel Nankin*, offers a laundry service and dry-cleaning (Mon–Sat 8am–6.30pm).

Library The Biblioteca Nacional is open to the public for reference use only, on production of a passport (Mon–Fri 8.30am–4pm); you'll need to be very specific about what you're after.

Medical care Contact your embassy for a list of recommended doctors. Emergency departments (24hr) at Hospital Escuela, Blvd Suyapa (☎232 6234), and Hospital General San Felipe, C la Paz by the Bolívar monument.

Photography Kodak on Av Cervantes by the central plaza and Konica on the C Peatonal do a rapid and reliable developing service and sell film.

Police Go to the FSP office on C Buenos Aires, behind Los Dolores church, with any problems.

Post office C Peatonal at C el Telegrafo, 3 blocks west of the main plaza (Mon–Fri 8am–7pm, Sat 8am–1pm). Window 1 on the ground floor deals with the *Lista de Correos*.

Supermarkets Más Por Menos on Av la Paz, just past the river bridge, has a wide selection of canned and packaged goods and household items.

Telephone office Hondutel is at Av Cristóbal Colón at C el Telegrafo. Phone services operate 24hr; reverse-charge calls to Europe are available. Fax office open Mon–Fri 7am–5pm.

Travel agents Numerous agents around the central plaza and in Col Palmira can book or change flights. Alhambra Travel in the *Hotel Honduras Maya* is quick, friendly and efficient (☎220 1700).

Moving on from Tegucigalpa

Tegucigalpa is the transport hub of the nation, with regular **bus departures** for all the major towns and numerous smaller ones. Departures **south** (to the Golfo de Fonseca), **north** (San Pedro Sula) and **east** (Olancho) are frequent and the roads good; however, unlike many other Central American countries, Honduran bus services tend to run every hour or half-hour rather than every few minutes, and you need to buy tickets before boarding if you're taking an intercity bus. Getting to destinations that lie off the main highways – Copán, the west, and the north coast, for example – is not as straightforward, but in most cases there's no option but to endure a slow and tiring bus journey on bad roads; **flying** to the north coast is one alternative. Leaving Tegucigalpa by bus can be bewildering initially; routes are generally operated by several companies, all broadly similar in terms of price and comfort, out of their own terminals. Listed in the box opposite are the major companies, with terminal addresses and phone numbers.

Tours

A number of companies run **organized tours** to Copán and the Bay Islands, amongst other destinations, usually for a minimum of two people. This can be an easy – if not particularly cheap – way to see the main sights. Copán Tours, in the Edificio AID, just

BUSES FROM TEGUCIGALPA

Unless otherwise stated, all terminals are in Comayagüela.

DESTINATION	COMPANY	DEPARTS FROM
All Central American capitals	Ticabus	16 C, 5–6 Av (☎220 0579)
Choluteca	Mi Esperanza	6 Av, 24 C (☎238 2863)
Comayagua	Transportes Colonial	13 C, 9 Av (☎220 1242)
Danlí/Las Manos	Discua Litena	Mercado Jacaleapa, Col Kennedy, Tegucigalpa (☎231 0470)
North Coast	Empresa Cristina	8 Av, 12 C (☎220 0117)
	Empresa Etrusca	12 C, 8–9 Av (☎220 0137)
Olancho	Discovery	7 Av, 12–13 C (☎222 4256)
	Empresa Aurora	8 C, 6–7 Av (☎237 3647)
San Pedro Sula	Cotraibal	8 Av, 12–13 C (☎237 1666)
	Hedman Alas	11 Av, 13 C (☎237 7143)
	Transportes Norteños	12 C, 6–7 Av (☎237 0706)
San Salvador	King Quality	Barrio Guacerique, Blvd de la Comunidad Europea (☎233 7515)
	Cruceros del Golfo	Barrio Guacerique, Blvd de la Comunidad Europea (☎233 7415)

up from the US embassy (☎236 8769, fax 236 5686), and UTS, on Av Ramón Cruz at Blvd Morazán (☎236 7756, fax 236 7757), are among the more reliable operators. La Moskitia Ecoaventuras, Apdo Postal 3577, Col Walter 1635, Barrio la Leona (☎ & fax 237 9398), is recommended for organized tours to Mosquitia (see p.413).

Around Tegucigalpa

Tegucigalpa's excellent local transport links make for easy day-trips to a number of destinations in the surrounding countryside. Set in the pine-clad mountains to the east are the tranquil colonial former mining villages of **Santa Lucía** and **Valle de Angeles**. To the north, charming **San Juancito** is a point of access for the cloudforest of **Parque Nacional la Tigra**, one of the most accessible national parks in the country. It is possible to visit the park in a day, but it's worth planning to spend at least a night there, to fully enjoy the forest and wildlife. Finally, overland travellers may well make use of the Las Manos **border crossing**, the closest entry point into **Nicaragua** from the capital.

Santa Lucía

Twelve kilometres east of the capital, set amid the pine-clad mountain slopes so characteristic of the central highlands, **SANTA LUCÍA** is a legacy of the days when the riches to be gained from silver mining brought settlers to the area in droves. Built by the Spanish in the late sixteenth century, the fortunes of this archetypal colonial village – all whitewashed houses and red-tiled roofs set on a steep hillside – rose and fell with those of the mines. Its citizens' finest hour came in 1572, when King Felipe II, in gratitude at the stream of riches being produced, presented them with a carved wooden

Crucifix. Now residing in the church, this is honoured annually during the fiesta of the **Cristo Negro** in first two weeks of January. The scenic views from Santa Lucía, over the mountains and down to Tegucigalpa, make for a relaxed half-day or so spent ambling around the steep, cobbled streets and surrounding forest. **Buses** for Santa Lucía leave Tegucigalpa's Mercado San Pablo, Col Reparto, every 45 minutes until 6pm; the last bus back leaves around 5.30pm.

Valle de Angeles

Beyond Santa Lucía, the road continues to rise gently amid some magnificent scenery, winding through forests of pine whose slender trunks reach up towards clear blue skies. Eleven or so kilometres from Santa Lucía is **VALLE DE ANGELES**, another former mining town, now reincarnated as handicraft centre and scenic getaway for capitalanos. Perched on the edge of a valley, surrounded by green, wooded mountains, the town slumbers during the week, in preparation for the weekends of hard business when the tourists pour in. Buses from Tegucigalpa run through the centre of town, passing the parque central and terminating a couple of blocks away. Given its size, everything in Valle de Angeles is only a few minutes' walk from both the parque and the bus terminal.

The town is chiefly noted for its high-quality, carved wooden goods – including bowls and households items, trunks and ornaments – but there is also a wide range of leather and ceramics. Numerous small shops around town sell crafts, and gentle bartering is possible if you are serious about buying. Lessandra Leather, close to the bus stop, is the outlet for a workshop producing very high-quality leather goods – bags, belts, purses and so on – at decent prices. The covered **Mercado Municipal de Artesanías**, by the bus stop, offers an overview of the range and quality of handicrafts on offer.

Although many people visit Valle de Angeles as a day-trip, combining shopping with a walk in the surrounding woods, there are a couple of **places to stay**. The *Posada de Angel* (☎ & fax 766 2233; ④) in the centre of town was, until recently, the only accommodation. Its comfortable rooms, all with bath, are set around a courtyard, where the newly installed pool is open to day visitors. Ten minutes' walk north of town is the new *Los Tres Pinos* (email *Rubio@david.intertel.hn*; ②), which has three very comfortable rooms set in a garden; the American owner arranges horse-riding and tours of the area. Reservations for both places are usually necessary for weekends and recommended during the week. For **eating**, try *Restaurante Epocas* (closed Mon) on the parque central, which also functions as an antique shop. In the dark, candle-lit interior, a range of excellently prepared Honduran dishes are served. *El Anafre*, next door, serves large portions of spaghetti (Wed–Sun 9am–8pm).

Direct **buses** for Valle de Angeles (1hr) leave Tegucigalpa every hour until 6pm, from an open lot near the Hospital General San Felipe. To get there, follow Av Gutemberg/La Paz past the Bolívar Monument and turn right at the Esso petrol station; the terminal is about 100m further on the left. The last bus back to Tegucigalpa is at 5pm.

San Juancito

Heading north from Valle de Angeles, a dirt road curves round the mountains, eventually linking up with the highway to Olancho. The tortuously slow progress of buses along this bumpy, winding route allows you plenty of time to gaze at the raw beauty of the mountain scenery. **SAN JUANCITO**, 10km from Valle de Angeles and set about 1km below the road, down a unmetalled side road, is a charming, shabby village of wooden houses, set in the narrow Río Chiquito valley. Most visitors pass through quickly on their way to the cloudforest of Parque Nacional la Tigra (see opposite), but this friendly little place makes for a pleasant stopover before returning to Tegucigalpa. The only **accommodation** is the *Hotelito San Juan* (①), with an attached café, close to where Tegucigalpa buses stop; the affable owner also runs the nearby pulpería. There's good home cooking at the *Mesa del Minero* comedor, just above the village on the road to the park, and its verandah offers great views across the valley and village.

Direct **buses** to San Juancito leave from the Mercado San Pablo, Col Reparto in Tegucigalpa every morning at 8am, with an extra service on Saturdays at 10am and sometimes at 1pm too; get there early as buses tend to get very crowded. The journey takes up to two hours, calling at Valle de Angeles on the way. Returning to Tegucigalpa there's a bus daily at 8am, with a second supposedly departing at 1pm on Saturdays. Hitching from Valle de Angeles is a possibility, though traffic is usually light.

Parque Nacional la Tigra

The oldest reserve in Honduras, **Parque Nacional la Tigra** (daily 8am–3pm; US$10) was given protected status in 1952 and designated a national park in 1980. Only 14km from Tegucigalpa, its accessibility and good system of trails make it a popular destination; by the same token, however, the diversity of flora and fauna is not as great as that found elsewhere. Previously owned by the El Rosario mining company, the slopes above San Juancito were almost completely denuded through heavy logging earlier this century; the company also cut a road through the heart of the forest to provide easier access to Tegucigalpa, destroying much of the original cloud forest in the process. What can be seen in the central sections of the park open to visitors, therefore, is secondary growth. Nonetheless, La Tigra shelters **wildlife** such as deer, white-faced monkeys, ocelots, quetzals and toucans, and the oak trees, bromeliads, ferns, vines and orchids typical of **cloud forests** are abundant. Any chance of seeing animals is slight, since the creatures wisely stick to the parts of the park that are out of bounds to visitors. Early mornings are the best time for seeing some of the estimated 200 species of **bird**. The well-laid **trails** across La Tigra provide some easy hiking, either on a circular route from the visitor centre or across the park between the two entrances; if you want to see everything in the park you should aim to spend up to two nights at the visitor centre.

PRACTICALITIES

From San Juancito, a dirt track, accessible only by 4WD, winds up the mountainside to the abandoned mining village of **El Rosario**. Though only a couple of kilometres long, the track is very steep and exposed. On foot, it takes one hot hour to reach the **entrance** to the park, where an enterprising family with a fridge sells cold drinks; with notice they will also cook meals. A further ten minutes' walk from the park entrance brings you to the wooden buildings of the mining company, perched above the road on a steep hillside. One of these houses the **visitor centre**, which has boards describing the geography and wildlife of park; the friendly warden is usually around to answer questions and can provide trail maps. Guides are also available for a better understanding of what you're seeing when walking through the park. **AMITIGRA**, a private organization based in Tegucigalpa (Edificio Italia, Col Palmira, ☎232 6771, fax 232 0758), runs the park and can provide information. Theoretically you are supposed to contact them to reserve space in the simple, clean **dormitory** that occupies the former mine hospital, behind the visitor centre, before you enter the park, but in practice this doesn't seem to matter. Dorm beds cost US$5 per night, as do camping spots. Nights can get very chilly, so bring a sleeping bag.

There is a second **entrance** on the western side of the park, reached via the village of Jutiapa, 17km east of Tegucigalpa. Though slightly easier to get to from the capital, this is a less popular entry point with very few facilities. To get there, take a **bus** from Parque Herrera in the city centre to the village of Los Limones (3 daily; 1hr), from where it is a stiff 5km walk uphill, passing through the village of Jutiapa (2km) on the way.

THE TRAILS

All the **trails** branch off the old logging road, which heads up from El Rosario (just under 1600m) over a 2200m pass and back down to the western entrance at Jutiapa. The most pristine patch of forest is around the two highest peaks, **Cerro la Peña de Andino** (2290m), on the southern side of the park, and **Cerro el Volcán** (2270m); both of these, unfortunately, are out of bounds to visitors.

One of the more interesting routes, **La Cascada**, branches left off the logging road about twenty minutes past El Rosario, to head north, around the curve of the mountain, to a waterfall; about halfway, the path passes the old mine workings of Peña Blanca. It takes around an hour to reach the waterfall along a mostly flat trail. From the waterfall, follow the path signed for Jutiapa which, after a relatively strenuous half-hour rejoins the logging road. Turn left here and after a few minutes take another trail on the left, which curves downhill through the thick canopy of the cloudforest. Take your time to admire the gnarled tree limbs, hung with vines and bromeliads, above the carpet of spongey mosses. A gentle pace along here brings you out, around thirty minutes later, just above the Jutiapa entrance.

East to Nicaragua: Las Manos

For overland travellers, the **Las Manos** border crossing, some 120km from Tegucigalpa, is the most convenient place to enter **Nicaragua** from the capital. Buses run regularly to the border and, with an early enough start, it is possible to reach Managua the same day.

Discua Litena runs two direct **buses** to Las Manos (3hr) daily, from its terminal at the Mercado Jacaleapa, Col Kennedy, in the southeast suburbs of Tegucigalpa, a fifteen-minute taxi ride from the centre. Coming the other way, direct buses leave Las Manos at 9.30am and 4.30pm. The same company also runs a more frequent service to the regional capital of **Danlí**, some two hours from Tegucigalpa. From here, local buses take an hour to reach the border, passing through the town of El Paraíso, 12km from Las Manos and the closest accommodation on the Honduran side.

The border post itself is a collection of huts housing the immigration and customs officials. Both sides are open daily until 5pm and crossing is generally straightforward. There are no banks, but eager moneychangers accept dollars, lempiras and Nicaraguan córdobas. No exit tax is charged for leaving Honduras. On the Nicaraguan side, trucks leave every hour for Ocotal, from where you can pick up buses to Estelí and Managua.

Southern Honduras

South of the capital, the pine-clad mountain ranges drop down through rolling green pasture lands to the arid heat of the Pacific coastal plains. A world away from the clear air and gentle climate of the highlands, this region nonetheless has its own particular, stark beauty, defined by the dazzling light and ferocious temperatures. Traditionally this is a poor region, and in recent years many of the campesinos and cattle ranchers who struggled to eke a living here have moved north to swell the barrios of Tegucigalpa and San Pedro Sula.

Tourists are scarce hereabouts, since there are relatively few attractions to make the journey worthwhile. For a change of pace from the capital, however, the shrimping town of **San Lorenzo** and the colonial city of **Choluteca** make convenient stopovers on the longer route to Nicaragua. And, with time to spare, the island of **Isla el Tigre** in the Golfo de Fonseca is a perfect, deserted getaway.

The main transport junction in this part of the country is at the village of **Jícaro Galán** on the intersection of Highway CA-5 and the Carretera Interamericana, some 100km south of Tegucigalpa. Buses heading in all directions stop here to exchange

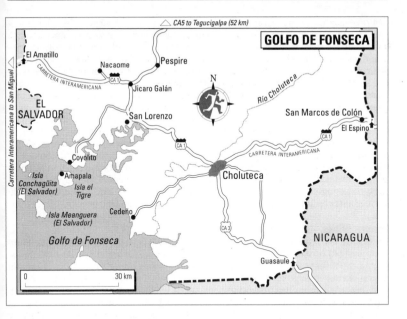

passengers before continuing **west** to the border with El Salvador at **El Amatillo**, 42km away, or **east** across the coastal plain to **Nicaragua**.

West to El Salvador

Seedy, steamy and hot **El Amatillo**, point of entry for **El Salvador**, teems with border traffic, extrovert moneychangers and opportunistic beggars. Crossing here is straight-forward, however, with the border post open daily until 5pm. There's no fee to enter El Salvador. A bank on the El Salvadorean side changes dollars cash, lempiras and colónes, but you'll get slightly better rates from the moneychangers.

The quickest way to El Amatillo by **bus** is to take an express service running between Tegucigalpa and Choluteca, changing at Jícaro Galán onto the Choluteca–El Amatillo service. Over the border in El Salvador, buses leave for Santa Rosa – 18km away and the closest place offering accommodation – and San Miguel (58km; see p.309) every ten minutes until around 6.30pm.

The Golfo de Fonseca: Isla el Tigre

Forty or so kilometres from Jícaro Galán, boats depart the fishing village of Coyolito for the volcanic **Isla el Tigre**, whose conical peak rises sharply against the sky across the sparkling Golfo de Fonseca. So far, tourist development on the island has been minimal, and its beaches, calm waters and constant sunshine make for a perfect getaway. A dirt road runs all the way around the island, giving access to some glorious deserted beach-es and a couple of hotels. From the southern side of the island there are stunning views across the gulf to Volcán Cosiguina in Nicaragua and in some places to Isla Meanguera and the mainland of El Salvador beyond. The island's peak can be climbed in a steep and very hot two- to three-hour walk; ask for directions to the start of the trail, about fif-teen minutes' walk southwest of Amapala, the island's only town.

Previously the country's major Pacific port and now a cheerfully decaying, nineteenth-century relic, **AMAPALA** was founded by special decree in October 1833. A brief stint as capital of the country in 1876 heralded a long slide into obscurity, exacerbated when port activities were transferred to Puerto de Henecán, further east along the coast, in the early twentieth century. Today the town is a sleepy place where nothing much happens, even during the annual **fiesta de Santa Cruz** on May 5. Wooden houses, some still brightly painted, cluster up the hillside from the main dock, a picture that's completed by a large, plain wooden church, a small parque central and an even smaller market building. The economy of both the town and the island is now based on small-scale agriculture and a small shrimp plant.

It takes four or more hours to walk the 22-kilometre road round the island, and half that time by mountain bike (not available to rent). Transport is otherwise limited to taxis; drivers hang around at the end of the dock and charge US$4–5 for a one-way trip around the island. Around twenty minutes west from Amapala is **Playa Negra**, a pretty, curving volcanic sand beach, with the secluded white-sand **Playa Gualora** fifteen minutes further on; both beaches have accommodation (see below).

Practicalities

To **get to the island**, you need to reach **COYOLITO**; the turnoff is around 12km southeast of Jícaro Galán on the Carretera Interamericana, marked by a Dippsa fuel station; local buses wait on the highway to collect passengers for the slow but beautiful 30km journey through agricultural land and mangrove swamps to the village. There's a steady flow of **launches** between Amapala and Coyolito from 7am until late afternoon, although frequency tends to drop off after lunch; alternatively, fishermen can ferry you across to the island and – if you're willing to bargain hard – through the mangrove swamps east of Coyolito to **San Lorenzo** (see below).

Accommodation in Amapala is limited to two basic hospedajes. The unsigned *Hotel Internacional* (①), just to the left of the dock, has large, airy rooms above a family home, with a balcony overlooking the water. A couple of streets back from the seafront, the *Hotel Ritz* (①) charges similar prices, but rooms are smaller and there is no view. For **eating**, the *El Faro Victoria* restaurant by the dock serves fish and chicken dishes and snacks; the family at the *Hotel Morazán* (which doesn't rent rooms), two blocks to the right from the dock, cook meals on request; there are also comedores in the market.

Outside town, the recently renovated *Hotel Playa Negra*, set on rocks above Playa Negra, has a pool and restaurant and rents out motorbikes; comfortable rooms all have private bath (☎237 8822, fax 238 2457; ④–⑤). Much more atmospheric are the *Villas Karissa* on Playa Gualora, a collection of clean cabañas that sleep up to five people (☎237 9281, fax 232 6288; ④–⑤).

San Lorenzo to Choluteca

Dusty **SAN LORENZO** stretches for two or so kilometres between the highway and the coastal mangrove swamps, 2km east of the Coyolito turnoff. This is a lively, friendly town, and a reasonable stopover en route to or from Choluteca and Nicaragua. For **accommodation**, you could try the basic but clean *Perla de Pacifico* (①–②), on the main street. Down by the waterfront, past the town's shrimp packing plant, the *Hotel Miramar* (☎881 2038, fax 881 2106; ⑤) has somewhat overpriced rooms, although the view from the restaurant over the mangroves and beyond to Nicaragua is spectacular, particularly at sunset. The hotel also has a swimming pool open to non-residents. Beyond the *Miramar* is a row of clean, seafood restaurants open for lunch and dinner; in the centre of town, the unnamed restaurant just down from the *Perla de Pacifico* prepares excellent fish and chicken dishes.

Just off the main highway, San Lorenzo is served by hourly **buses** from Coyolito. These stop on the highway at the fuel station, where you can pick up intercity services heading west, or east to Choluteca, 55km away.

Choluteca

Honduras's fourth-largest city, with a population of slightly under 100,000, **CHOLUTECA'S** main attraction is that it boasts one of the finest colonial centres in the country. This amounts to several carefully restored blocks around the parque central, a pleasant place to enjoy the cooler evening air. On the southwest corner of the parque, the building now housing the Biblioteca Municipal was the birthplace of **José Cecilio del Valle**, one of the authors of the Central American Act of Independence in 1821 and elected President of the Federation in 1834, though he died before taking office.

Choluteca makes a convenient stopover en route to or from the Nicaraguan border, but once you've seen the centre, there's not much reason to hang about in the stifling heat. The main **bus terminal** is about ten blocks northeast of the parque central, a twenty-minute walk or US$0.40 taxi ride. Buses run regularly along the Carretera Interamericana in both directions: west to El Amatillo and east to San Marcos de Colón, for El Espino and the Nicaraguan border. From the Mi Esperanza terminal, one block north, there are also direct buses to Tegucigalpa.

Should you need **to stay**, try the *Hotel Pierre* on Av Valle, two blocks east of the parque central (☎882 0676; ③–④), which is comfortable if not overwhelmingly friendly; rooms all have bath and TV. Further down Av Valle, *Hotel Bonsai* (☎882 2648; ①) is one of the better cheap hotels, basic but very clean. There isn't much in the way of **places to eat** but the *Café Colonial* on 4 C SO, a couple of blocks from the parque, and the *Comedor Central* on the parque itself, both serve good-value meals.

Routes to Nicaragua

From Choluteca, the Carretera Interamericana runs northeast along the valley of the Río Choluteca, before beginning a gentle ascent into the mountains. **San Marcos de Colón**, 110km from Choluteca, is a friendly little town, with basic accommodation and banks (cash dollars only). Buses terminate here and to get to **El Espino** and the border, 10km away, you need to take one of the frequent colectivo taxis (US$0.75). The border post itself is quiet and straightforward, with moneychangers on both sides. On the Nicaraguan side, regular buses run to Somoto, 20km from the border.

An **alternative route** to Nicaragua is to take Highway CA-3 from Choluteca, which swings south then east for the 38km to **Guasaule** on the Río Negro. Buses for Guasaule leave from the Mercado Nuevo in Choluteca, a few blocks east of the parque central, calling in at the bus terminal on the way; the journey takes about 45 minutes. There's regular transport from Guasaule on to Chinandega, Managua and León.

travel details

The main domestic and international bus routes from Tegucigalpa are covered in the box on p.365.

Tegucigalpa to: Choluteca (3 daily; 3hr); Danlí (6 daily; 2hr); Las Manos (6am & noon; 3hr).

Choluteca to: El Amatillo (every 30min; 1hr); Guasule (hourly; 45min); San Lorenzo (hourly; 30min); San Marcos (every 30min; 2hr).

CHAPTER 18

THE CENTRAL AND WESTERN HIGHLANDS

I n their haste to reach the archeological site at Copán, or the palm-fringed beaches on the north coast, all many travellers see of the **central and western highlands** is the view from a bus window. To hurry through from the capital to San Pedro Sula – Honduras's second city and the gateway to the coast – would be to miss much, though, as this is the heartland of the country, an expanse of rugged, pine-clad mountain ranges, split by fertile valleys and scattered with villages and a handful of colonial towns. The highlands are home to the country's highest concentration of indigenous peoples, many likely to be descendants of those who fought with Lempira in fierce resistance to the Spanish conquistadors (see p.348). Perhaps because it is so little-visited, this is one of the friendliest parts of the country, and you're likely to be received with genuine warmth wherever you go.

From the capital, the main **CA-5** highway is the direct route through the highlands to San Pedro Sula and the north coast. Along this road, the first place you might want to stop is **Comayagua**, formerly the capital and still boasting some beautiful churches and other remnants of colonial architecture. Not far to the north lies Honduras's biggest lake, the vast blue **Lago de Yojoa** – an ornithologist's paradise, though Hondurans are more likely to come here for a weekend of fishing and boating.

With a little patience, you can take a bus along the painfully slow route that leaves the CA-5 at Siguatepeque, curving northwest towards Copán. Huddled beneath the jungle-covered escarpment of the **Montaña de Celaque**, the cobbled town of **Gracias**, another colonial centre built on the wealth provided by local silver mines, is a relaxing base for hikes in the pristine cloudforest reserve of the **Parque Nacional Celaque**. Beyond here the road improves and it's an easy trip northwest to the region's main town, **Santa Rosa de Copán**. Long the centre of the highland tobacco-growing industry, Santa Rosa has no particular sights to speak of, but is a supremely relaxing place to stay, unspoilt by a growing popularity with tourists.

Chief of the attractions of western Honduras – and, in fact, the country – is the ancient Maya site of **Copán**. Though smaller than the major sites in Guatemala or Mexico, Copán is equally impressive thanks to its wealth of fabulous carvings, most of which remain barely touched by the centuries.

Comayagua

The conquistadors' first city and the capital of Honduras until independence, faded **COMAYAGUA** lies just 85km north of its rival, Tegucigalpa, at the northeast end of the

For an explanation of **accommodation price codes**, see p.345.

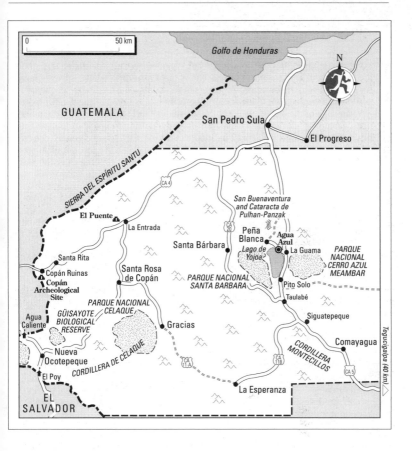

fertile Comayagua valley. Today, the main reason to visit is the architectural legacy of the colonial period, in particular the dramatic cathedral overlooking the parque central. The first Spanish settlement was established here on December 8, 1537, and destroyed soon afterwards during the Lempira rebellion (see p.348). Swiftly rebuilt in 1539, Santa María de Comayagua, as it was first known, rapidly became wealthy thanks to the discovery of **silver** in the vicinity. King Felipe II of Spain bestowed on Comayagua the title of city in December 1557, and in 1573 it became the administrative centre for the whole of Honduras. Following independence, however, the city's fortunes began to decline, particularly after Tegucigalpa was designated alternate capital of the new republic in 1824, an ignominy compounded by sacking and burning at the hands of Guatemalan forces during the civil war in 1827. Backwater status was sealed conclusively in 1880, when President Soto permanently transferred the capital to Tegucigalpa, supposedly because Comayagua was too conservative for his liking. Although Comayagua is today a relatively rich and important provincial centre, its rivalry with Tegucigalpa has barely wavered over the centuries.

The Town

Most sights of interest are within a few blocks of the large **parque central**. Few of the streets are numbered, but the centre is relatively compact and orientation straightforward. On the southeast corner of the parque is the **Cathedral**, whose intricate facade consists of tiers of niches containing statues of the saints. More properly known as the **Iglesia de la Inmaculada Concepción**, the cathedral is home to the twelfth-century Reloj Arabe, one of the oldest clocks in the world. Formerly housed in the Alhambra in Granada, Spain, the clock was presented to the city by King Felipe II in 1582 and now resides in the cathedral's bell tower, built between 1580 and 1708 and considered to be one of the outstanding examples of colonial Baroque architecture in Central America. The highlight amongst a wealth of Baroque artwork inside the church is the elaborately carved seventeenth-century Retablo del Rosario altarpiece; go early if you want to see it, as the doors are normally locked in the evenings and from noon to 2pm. Across the road to the south of the cathedral, the **Museo Colonial** (Mon–Sat 9.30–11.30am & 2–5pm, Sun 10am–noon & 2–5pm; US$0.75), housed in the Casa Cural, holds an exhibition of religious art, statues, chalices and documents from the city's churches. The building was originally constructed for Comayagua's **university**, the first to be established in Central America, in 1678.

Two blocks north of the parque central, on the **Plaza San Francisco**, the **Museo Arqueológico** occupies a rather dilapidated single-storey building that used to be the government palace (Wed–Fri 8am–noon & 1–4pm, Sat & Sun 9am–noon & 1–4pm; US$0.75). Small but interesting exhibits display pre-Columbian ceramics, jewellery, jade and other artefacts, many of the items brought here from the El Cajón valley north of the city, before the area was flooded to create a dam. On the same plaza is one of the city's oldest churches, **Iglesia de San Francisco**, originally established by Franciscan monks in 1574, although rebuilt following an earthquake in 1809.

Head south from the parque central for four blocks and you come to another colonial church, **Iglesia de la Merced**. Built between 1550 and 1558, though its facade dates back only to the early eighteenth century, this was the city's original cathedral, holding the Reloj Arabe until 1715, when the new cathedral was consecrated. Several blocks further south, the **Iglesia de San Sebastián**, completed in 1585, was built specifically for indigenous worshippers.

Practicalities

Highway CA-5, the road from Tegucigalpa, runs 1.5km southwest of the centre, to which it's connected by the broad road known as "the Boulevard". **Buses** between Tegucigalpa and San Pedro Sula drop off on the highway at the top of the Boulevard, a US$0.50 taxi ride or twenty-minute walk from the parque central. Transportes Colonial direct buses to and from Tegucigalpa use a terminal behind the Centro Comercial Plaza, midway along the Boulevard.

There are several **banks** on or just off the parque central, including Banco de Occidente and Bancahsa. **Hondutel** and the **post office** are alongside each other on the street behind the cathedral. An extensive **general market** runs along 1 Av NO, 2–3 C NO, starting three blocks south of the cathedral.

Unfortunately for the visitor, the range of places to both stay and eat in Comayagua is quite narrow. Of the small number of **hotels** in and around the market area, the *Hotel America Inc*, 1 Av NO at 1 C NO (☎772 0360; ②), has rather spartan but clean rooms, all with bath. *Hotel Emperador*, on C Central at the Boulevard (☎772 0332; ②), is of a similar standard and some of the rooms have a/c, while the *Hotel Norymax Colonial*, at the other end of C Central, in front of the school (☎772 1703; ③) is perhaps the nicest place in town, with clean comfortable rooms and flower-filled balconies.

For **eating**, *Restaurante Palmeras*, at 4 C NO on the parque central, serves substantial breakfasts, daily lunches and snacks at low prices. One block down, *Fruity Tacos* does excellent licuados, plus burgers and tacos. More substantial fare can be had from *Kan-ju*, 1 Av NO, 1–2 C NO, whose cook produces large portions of authentic Chinese dishes, as well as steak and other meat dishes. *La Torre Latina*, on the Boulevard, has the reputation of being the best place in town, with a more formal atmosphere and a wide menu of seafood, chicken and steak dishes.

Lago de Yojoa and around

North of Comayagua, the Carretera del Norte (CA-5) rises up to cross the Sierra de Montecillos, a expanse of extensive pine forests, reaching **Siguatepeque**, about halfway between Tegucigalpa and San Pedro Sula, after 30km or so. Beyond Siguatepeque, the highway begins to descend from the mountains and the air becomes appreciably warmer. Some 35km north of Siguatepeque is the spectacular, sparkling blue **Lago de Yojoa**, a natural lake around 17km long and 9km wide. Its reed-fringed waters, sloping away to a gentle patchwork of woods, pastures and coffee plantations, are overlooked by the sharp planes of the mountains of Cerro Azul Meámbar to the east and Santa Bárbara to the north and west. Both of these contain small but pristine stretches of cloudforest and are protected as **national parks**.

An ornithologist's dream, the waters and marshes of the lake attract over 350 species of **bird**, the highest concentration in the country. In a previous incarnation in the 1960s, the lake was a magnet for sports fishermen from all over Central America, who came here to fish for the predatory **black bass**, introduced into the lake in 1954. Stocks of these depleted rapidly, due to overfishing during the 1970s; recent judicious management has succeeded in encouraging regrowth and obtaining a fragile equilibrium between humans and nature.

A favourite with middle-class Hondureños at the weekends, when the peace and quiet is likely to be shattered by the buzz of jetskis, during the week the waters – and surrounding hotels – are virtually empty. Supremely relaxing, Yojoa makes a great base for a couple of days spent rowing on the lake, observing the bird life and exploring the surrounding countryside. Ecolago, in Edificio Midence Soto, by the parque central in Tegucigalpa (☎237 9659), is an independent organization set up to monitor the health of Lago de Yojoa, and can provide **information** on the lake and its environs.

The eastern and northern shores

CA-5 from Tegucigalpa runs along the lake's eastern shore, passing through the small village of **PITO SOLO**, at its southeast tip, and the hamlet of **LA GUAMA**, 10km further north. The *Los Remos* hotel (☎557 8054; ④) in Pito Solo, the only accommodation at this end of the lake, is somewhat shabby and overpriced and it's better to continue to the villages further on (see below). Fresh lake fish is served up at the row of comedores in the village, and at another cluster about 2km further along the highway.

From La Guama, a dirt road runs east for 5km to the entrance to **Parque Nacional Cerro Azul Meámbar** (daily 8am–4pm); there's no public transport along here. Named after its highest peak, the blue-hued Cerro Azul Meámbar (2047m), this is one of the smaller reserves in the national network, with a core of untouched cloudforest. Anyone planning to hike here should be prepared for precipitously steep gradients in the upper reaches of the reserve, with sheer rockfaces, dense vegetation and tumbling waterfalls. With luck, you might spot quetzals, and spider and white-faced monkeys. Cerro Azul is managed by a private organization, PAG, based at 3 C, 1–2 Av NO, Siguatepeque (☎773 2741), with another office in Tegucigalpa (☎232 8287); they can provide information on hiking and hiring guides. The park's **education centre** at the entrance, 5km from La Guama, occupies the old coffee finca of Los Piños, and has **accommodation** in the form of cabins with bunks (①), and information on a number of short walking trails that are being opened up.

A paved road heads west from La Guama along the northern shore of the lake, reaching the town of **PEÑA BLANCA**, the commercial focus for the area, after around 12km. Four kilometres along this, the *Hotel Agua Azul* (☎550 5982; ④) is the most accommodating of the hotels in the area. Comfortable wooden cabins are set among wooded grounds sloping down to the waterside and the restaurant's verandah has fabulous views across the lake; there is also a pool, and the hotel rents boats and organizes horse-riding on request. In **AGUA AZUL** village, just past the hotel, there are some basic stores and a couple of restaurants – the only eating places around here outside the hotels. *Finca las Glorias* (☎556 0736, fax 556 0553; ⑤), about 2km before Peña Blanca, is equally characterful but more pricey; fishing trips and tours of the surrounding coffee finca are available. In Peña Blanca itself the basic, clean rooms at the *Hotel Maranata* (①) comprise the only budget accommodation in the area. **Buses** running along the highway will stop at Pito Solo and La Guama if requested; from the latter there's an hourly service to Peña Blanca.

North to the Catarata de Pulhapanzak

North of Peña Blanca is one of the highlights of the lake region, the **Catarata de Pulhapanzak** (daily 8am–6pm; US$0.40 plus US$0.40 for camping), a stunning 43-metre-high cascade of churning white waters on the Río Lindo. Claimed to be the prettiest waterfall in the country, the cascade with its backdrop of dense, dripping vegetation is at its most stunning in the early mornings, when rainbows form in the rising sun. A narrow trail on the right-hand side – very steep and wet – descends past several viewpoints to the riverbank at the bottom of the falls. The area immediately around the falls has been designated a public park, with comedores and a swimming spot. Right by the entrance, a grassy expanse is identified as the "ceremonial plaza" of a centre of Lenca culture believed to have been sited here, although no excavation has been carried out.

Pulhapanzak is an easy fifteen-minute walk from the village of **San Buenaventura**, 10km north of Peña Blanca; buses ply the dirt road between the two every hour.

The western shore

Access to the western shore of the lake is more limited and the shoreline far less developed. The towering peak of the **Cerro Santa Bárbara** (2740m), encircled by the dense, green cover of the **Parque Nacional Santa Bárbara**, forms a superb backdrop to the waters of the lake. As yet undeveloped for tourism, the reserve consists of virgin cloud forest, with thick stretches of pine and mixed broadleaf forest on the lower slopes. Guides for the reserve can by found by asking in the lakeside hotels; there are no organized facilities for visitors. Nestling at the base of the reserve, by the water's edge, is the archeological site of **Los Naranjos**. Once an extensive Maya settlement, at present there's little to see other than earth-covered mounds.

Taking the junction to the left at Pito Solo brings you onto Highway CA-20, heading west along the lower fringes of the park. Fifty-three kilometres along this road is **Santa Bárbara**, a friendly town situated amid coffee plantations. Buses run to the central plaza and there are a couple of decent hotels in the surrounding blocks.

La Esperanza to Gracias

West of the Tegucigalpa–San Pedro Sula highway lie Lempira and Intibucá, the departments that make up the **western highlands** of Honduras, a stunningly beautiful landscape of pine forests, sparsely inhabited mountains and remote villages. These two departments contain the highest concentration of indigenous peoples in the country and the small, lively town of **La Esperanza**, 68km or so southwest of the highway, is – despite increasingly rapid absorption into mainstream culture – the place where you're most likely to see traditional dress being worn.

The drawback to travelling around here is the state of the roads: most are unsurfaced and can become impassable during the wet season. Private vehicles are infrequent, and public transport frustratingly slow and uncomfortable. If you are prepared to put up with the delays, however, you can take a cross-country route through La Esperanza to the colonial town of **Gracias** and the stunning cloudforest of **Parque Nacional la Celaque**. At this point the infrastructure begins to improve, and it's an easy journey to Santa Rosa de Copán (see p.379).

La Esperanza

Three kilometres north of Siguatepeque, a good paved road leaves the main CA-5 high-way and heads west to **LA ESPERANZA**, 68km away; the route is served by buses every couple of hours until mid-afternoon. Centre of commerce and trade in the region and capital of the department of Intibucá, the town livens up during the **weekend market**, a colourful and noisy affair, when farmers from surrounding villages pour into town. While there's nothing of much interest to buy, it's worth hanging around to observe the intensive bartering and socializing that goes on. Should you need to stay, *Hotel Solis* (☎598 2080; ②), one block east of the market, has clean rooms, some with private bath.

Gracias

Up to five hours from La Esperanza on the one daily bus, **GRACIAS** lies in the shadow of the **Montaña de Celaque**, the peak that forms the centrepiece of the nearby **Parque Nacional Celaque**. This is one of the oldest colonial towns in Honduras and served briefly as the seat of the *Audiencia de los Confines*, the centre of government under the Spanish, until this honour was transferred to Antigua, Guatemala, in 1548. Life since then has been a spiral of gentle decline with little happening today to disturb the town's sleepy rural charm. Around the parque central, a handful of run-down build-ings give off a faint reflection of former glories, among them the building that housed the *Audiencia*, now used by the Church.

Castillo San Cristóbal (daily 8am–5pm; free), a restored fort on a small hill, five minutes' walk above the western edge of town, provides wonderful views over the town and west across to Celaque, particularly in the late afternoon. The fort was built, but never ultimately used, to defend the area against Guatemalan troops during the nine-teenth-century civil wars; the walls contain the tomb of Juan Lindo, president of Honduras from 1847 to 1852. About an hour's walk south of Gracias are a set of natur-al **hot springs** (daily 6am–8pm; US$0.50), with small purpose-built pools for bathing in the 36–39°C waters; a comedor at the site serves basic meals, snacks and drinks. The path to the springs starts on the right just after the first river bridge on the road to La Esperanza, at the southeast edge of town.

PRACTICALITIES

The **bus terminal** is an empty lot three blocks west of the parque central; buses con-tinuing west arrive and depart from here, while local buses from La Esperanza stop at the southeast edge of town. There's a fairly regular service to Santa Rosa de Copán, supplemented by private pickups. Banco de Occidente, one block west of the parque, changes dollars cash and travellers' cheques. **Hondutel** and the **post office** are next to each other, one block south of the parque. The local **COHDEFOR** office, which sells photocopied maps showing the trail through Celaque, is five blocks north of the par-que. Provisions for hiking in the park can be bought at the small general **market**, on the same street, south of the bank.

Best of the limited **accommodation** on offer is *Hotel Colonial*, just off the parque central (①–②); it's clean and some of the rooms have bath and TV. *Hotel Erik*, one block north of the parque (☎656 1066; ①–②), is similar but not as friendly. A third option is the small *Posada del Rosario*, four blocks west of the parque on the edge of town (☎656 1219; ②), which has three comfortable rooms to rent. For **eating**, the European-run *Restaurant Guancascos* on the parque central serves well-prepared meat, chicken and vegetarian dishes, as well as snacks and drinks; it also has information on the Parque Nacional Celaque. *Café Colonial* in the *Colonial* hotel, does good local breakfasts and daily set lunches, as well as snacks, while *Reposteria y Pizzeria la Exquisita*, a block west of the parque, serves the sort of pizza you would expect in rural Honduras, plus rather better ice cream.

Parque Nacional Celaque

Parque Nacional Celaque (daily 7am–3pm; US$2, plus US$1 per night), best approached from Gracias, contains one of the largest and most impressive expanses of virgin cloudforest in Honduras. The focus of the park is the **Montaña de Celaque**, a volcanic escarpment and the source of eleven rivers – "Celaque" means "box of water" in the Lenca language – which boasts the highest mountain in Honduras, the Cerro las Minas (2849m), at its centre. Thick forests coat the slopes of the escarpment, rising from pine through to the cloudforest covering the escarpment plateau.

The park entrance is 6km west of Gracias; take the unmetalled road that runs through the village of Mejicapa, 2km away, from where a marked track leads uphill to the entrance. Few private vehicles run along here, and the walk can get very hot. From the entrance, a track leads for another 2km or so through the pine forest to the **visitor centre**. Here there are bunk rooms, showers and cooking facilities; you'll need to bring plenty of food and water with you, though the warden's family can provide meals on request. It gets cold at night and the trails are invariably wet and muddy, so sleeping bags, decent boots and a change of warm clothing are essential. *Restaurant Guancascos* in Gracias (see above) functions as an unofficial **information centre** for the park. As well as selling booklets and maps and renting some camping gear, they can also arrange lifts up to the visitor centre.

Gentle rambles are possible through the woods surrounding the visitor centre. A more adventurous option is the six-kilometre marked trail through the forest up to the peak of Cerro las Minas. It is not really necessary to hire a guide for the trail, though you definitely need one if you're planning to undertake one of the more difficult treks on the southern slopes: ask at the COHDEFOR office in Gracias. In the upper reaches of the park much of the main trail consists of forty-degree slopes, so this is not a hike for the unfit. Plan on spending at least one night camping, if the summit is your aim; there are two designated camping spots along the way.

THE TRAIL

Starting behind the visitor centre, **the trail** follows the river for about five minutes, then crosses over and heads steeply uphill, before running southwest along and up the slope of the mountain, through pine forest. It's at least an hour's walk from the visitor centre to the nuclear zone of the park, at 1800m, and the first of the camping sites, **Campamento Don Tomás**, is another hour and a half away. Here there's a shack to sleep in (check with the warden at the centre that it will be unlocked), a stream (not suitable for drinking from), and space for tents.

From the campsite, the path, marked with tags, continues very steeply upwards for around two hours before levelling out on the plateau (2560m); **Campamento Naranjo** is at the edge of the plateau by a stream (potable water), and has room for a few tents. Here begins the cloudforest proper, wrapped in a hushed, cathedral-like calm, dripping wet at any time of year. Oaks and liquidambars loom overhead, draped in vines and bromeliads and banked by mosses and ferns. Thousands of years of geographical isolation has resulted in several endemic species of flora, including the abundant *oreopanax limpiriana* and Globus Yew. Sit quietly for a while and you may be lucky enough to catch a rare glimpse of the shimmering green and red quetzal, though hearing the characteristic rattle of a woodpecker echoing from somewhere nearby is more likely. Sightings of animals are even rarer, but you might want to keep an eye out for spider monkeys, pumas, tapirs, coyotes and white-tailed deer.

From Campamento Naranjo to the peak is another two hours, much of it an easier climb, except for the last half-hour or so. The ancient tree cover is more stunted at the summit, a result of almost continual cloud cover and temperatures that frequently drop below freezing. Generally the clouds and vegetation combine to limit the views, but when it is clear there are breathtaking vistas southwest, down the densely covered dark green slopes of the escarpment.

Santa Rosa de Copán and southwest to the border

It's an easy ninety-minute bus ride 45km northwest from Gracias to **SANTA ROSA DE COPÁN**, a wonderfully preserved, cobbled colonial relic built on the tobacco industry. Tourists are relatively few, mainly because the view across the Río Chamelicón valley is about all there is to see here. Nevertheless, Santa Rosa's location, along the main north–south transport route, usually makes a stop here inevitable.

Santa Rosa was once home to the Crown Tobacco Office, which regulated the cultivation of the crop, set official prices and handled sales, and today the golden weed is still central to the local economy. These days the old Tobacco Office, in the centre of town, houses the **Flor de Copán Cigar Factory** (Mon–Sat 8–11.30am & 1–4.30pm), which produces around 20,000 hand-rolled cigars a day, mostly for export. You can observe the process on a free tour, or simply by glancing through the windows of the rolling room, which face the street; boxes of cigars can be bought at the small on-site shop.

At the centre of town is the delightful, shady **Parque Contreras**, with the cathedral on its eastern side. **Calle Centenario**, lined with shops and restaurants, runs along the southern edge of the parque; the cigar factory is a couple of blocks west and the **market** a couple of blocks east.

Practicalities

All **buses** arrive at the new terminal on the highway, about 2km north of the centre, at the bottom of the hill. There are several services a day to Ocotepeque for El Salvador and Guatemala (see p.380), and a constant stream north to San Pedro Sula (see p.393) via La Entrada, and Copán. From the terminal it's a stiff twenty-minute walk into town, or a US$0.50 taxi ride. **Hondutel** and the **post office** are on the western edge of the parque, with Banco Atlántida to the south. The **Casa de Cultura**, two blocks south of the parque, has limited information about the area.

Santa Rosa has a moderate range of **places to stay**, none of them particularly luxurious. By far the nicest place in town is the *Hotel Elvir* on C Centenario at 2 Av SO (☎662 0103; ④), which has large rooms, all with bath and TV. The *Hotel Continental* at 2 C NO, 2–3 Av NO (☎662 0801; ③), is slightly cheaper, and the family-run *Hotel Castillo* at 3 Av NO, 1–2 C NO (☎662 0368; ②), compensates with character for what it lacks in amenities. *Hotel Grand Mayaland*, opposite the bus terminal (☎662 0233; ④), offers modern, impersonal rooms but is convenient for transport.

Santa Rosa's small number of **eating and drinking** places is increasing with the growing number of tourists. One of the newest outfits is the French-owned *Paris*

Restaurant and Bar on C Centenario, two blocks west of the parque, which offers a well-priced menu that changes daily. Both the courtyard dining area and wooden bar are also good for a quiet drink. One block south is *Chiky's Antijitos Mexicanos*, 1 C SO at 1 Av SO, serving inexpensive burgers, tacos and Honduran food in a relaxed atmosphere. Three blocks away, to the east of the parque central, *Restaurant Well*, 2 C SE, 2–3 Av SE, is a friendly place serving large portions of authentic Chinese food at reasonable prices; a couple of blocks further on, the US-owned *Pizza Pizza*, C Centenario, 5–6 Av NE, cooks up good pizza and pasta and its helpful owners are a good source of local information.

The route to Nueva Ocotepeque and the border

From Santa Rosa de Copán, highway CA-4 heads southwest through low valleys before rising up to run through the eastern flanks of the Cordillera de Merendón. **El Portillo**, a small, shabby roadside hamlet, marks the highest stretch of paved road in the country, at 2010m. Fifteen kilometres beyond the pass is **NUEVA OCOTEPEQUE**, the last town in Honduras before the border with both El Salvador and Guatemala and served by several buses a day from Santa Rosa. Modern and unremarkable, founded after a flood destroyed the colonial village of Ocotepeque in 1934, the town is redeemed by its setting at the base of the towering Cerro el Sillón (2310m). Most visitors pass straight through en route to El Salvador or Guatemala, but if you need **to stay** the best option is the comfortable *Hotel Sandoval*, two blocks from the bus station (☎653 3098; ③), which has an attached restaurant. The Banco de Occidente, just up from the hotel, changes dollars cash and travellers' cheques, but you'll get better rates for Guatemalan quetzales and Salvadorean colónes at the borders.

Southeast of town lies the **Reserve Biológica la Fraternidad**, or the **Bosque Montecristo**. Cerro Montecristo, at the centre of the reserve, is the precise meeting point of El Salvador, Guatemala and Honduras. Access from the Honduran side is extremely difficult; the visitor centre and few tourist facilities that exist are reached through **Metapán** in El Salvador (see p.335)

The border: El Salvador and Guatemala
Buses run 10km south to the El Salvadorean border at **El Poy** regularly until early evening. El Poy itself is a drab, dusty little place but the crossing is straightforward; it is as well to cross as early in the day as possible, since public transport onwards within El Salvador is infrequent, stopping altogether after mid-afternoon. There are no banks but a profusion of moneychangers – change enough to keep you going until you reach San Salvador. There's no fee to enter El Salvador.

El Poy has no **accommodation**, but there are basic hotel facilities in El Salvador at the village of Citalá, 1km away, and more upmarket places at San Ignacio, 5km from the border, and La Palma, the nearest town, 11km south of the border (see p.304). Buses to La Palma and on to San Salvador leave every thirty minutes until 4.30pm.

Some 18km west of town is the **Guatemalan** border crossing of **Agua Caliente**. Buses make the thirty-minute trip to the border every half-hour or so until 4pm; the last bus back from the border leaves at 6pm. There are no banking or accommodation facilities on the Honduran side. Over in Guatemala, buses leave regularly for Esquipulas (see p.224).

Copán and around

In the serene, rolling landscape of the the western highlands, 45km from Santa Rosa, lies the Maya site of **Copán**. One of the most impressive of the Maya sites, its pre-eminence is not due to size – in scale it's far less impressive than sites such as Tikal or

Chichén Itzá – but to an overwhelming legacy of artistic craftsmanship that has survived over hundreds of years. Not surprisingly, the site is heavily promoted by the Honduran government and tour operators and now ranks as the second most visited spot in the country after the Bay Islands.

Copán Ruinas: the town

The archeological site of Copán lies one kilometre south of the small town of **COPÁN RUINAS**, generally simply referred to as Copán, a charming place of steep cobbled streets and red-tiled roofs set among green hills. Despite the weekly influx of hundreds of visitors, which now contributes a large part of the town's income, it has managed to remain largely unspoilt and genuinely friendly.

A thirty-minute stroll around Copán, drinking in the clean air and soaking up the relaxed atmosphere, encompasses virtually all the town's attractions. Somewhat eclipsed by the new Sculpture Museum at the site itself, though still worth a visit, is the **Museo Regional de Arqueología** (Mon–Sat 8am–noon & 1–4pm; US$1.50) on the west side of the parque central. Displayed inside are statuettes, sculptures and other Maya artefacts. The small municipal **market** is in the block behind the museum; turn right beyond Hondutel. For a view over the town and surrounding countryside, walk north from the parque central for about five blocks, to the old military barracks up the hill.

Catering to the growing tourist trade are a number of **souvenir shops** on or close to the parque central, selling ceramic, wood and leather crafts from the region and elsewhere in the country. All are broadly similar in terms of price and range. Tabacos y Recuerdos, next to the *La Posada* hotel, has a wide selection of Honduran cigars.

Arrival and information

Most **buses** enter town from the east, by a small football field, with some continuing up the low hill to circle the parque central; buses from Guatemala enter town from the west. Banco Atlántida on the parque changes dollars, travellers' cheques and Guatemalan quetzales, and advances cash on Visa cards. **Hondutel** and the **post office** are next door to each other, just off the southwest corner of the parque. A block further southwest is Justo a Tiempo Lavandería (Mon–Sat 7.30am–5.30pm), a laundry equipped with an English and German book exchange.

Two blocks west of the parque, next door to the Spanish school (see p.347), Go Native Tours arranges day-trips in the area, plus excursions further afield to the Mosquitia and cloud forests.

Accommodation

Many of the town's **hotels** have recently undergone refits to compete for the ever-booming organized tour market. Prices, consequently, are higher than in much of Honduras, though there's still enough of a range to suit most budgets.

Hotel Brisas de Copán, 1 block north of the parque central (☎651 4118). Clean, good-sized rooms, all with bath, hot water and TV. ④.

Casa de Café B&B, at the southwest edge of town, overlooking the Río Copan Valley (☎552 7274). A charming place, with a fabulous garden where you could lie in a hammock and look at the views all day. Comfortable, airy rooms all have bath and hot water. Breakfast is included, there's free coffee all day, plus a library and TV. ⑤.

Hotel California, 1 block northeast of the square (no phone). A new, laid-back place with clean rooms around a courtyard. Free drinking water. ②.

Hotel Camino Maya, southwest corner of parque central (☎651 4446, fax 651 4518). Newly renovated, adequately sized rooms, all with bath and hot water; some have a balcony overlooking the parque. ⑥.

Iguana Azul, next to the *Casa de Café* and under the same ownership. Newly refurbished and nicely decorated dormitory or private rooms, communal area and laundry facilities; all shared bath. Dorms ①, doubles ②–③.

La Posada, just north of the parque central (no phone). Recently renovated large, comfortable rooms, some with bath; good value. ②–③.

Hotel Los Gemelos, across from the *California* (☎651 4077). The backpackers' favourite, still going strong. Very friendly place, very basic but spotless rooms, all with shared bath. The owners provide hot water if enough people ask. ①.

Hotel Marina Copán, east side of the parque central (☎651 4070, fax 651 4477). The most luxurious place in town by a long shot. Stylish rooms have a/c and TV and there's a small pool, sauna, gym and bar on site. ⑧–⑨.

Eating and drinking

Copán has a wide range of places to **eat** and **drink**, some of them catering specifically to the tourist market. Virtually all the restaurants stop serving at 10pm.

Café Elisa, in the *Hotel Camino Maya*. Excellent local and European-style breakfasts, including fruit salads and waffles.

Café Isabel, 1 block west of the parque. Unpretentious place serving a range of well-prepared local dishes; the vegetable soup is particularly good.

Café Welchez, northwest corner of the parque. Pleasant European-style café, serving fairly pricey coffees, juices, alcoholic drinks and light meals. The tables upstairs by the window are the best spot for people-watching.

Llama del Bosque, 2 blocks west of the parque. Wide menu including local breakfasts, meat and chicken dishes, baleadas and snacks.

Tres Locos Bar, at the *Hotel California*. A fun bar and a good place to catch up on local news and information (closes at 9pm).

Tunkul Bar and Restaurant, across from the *Llama del Bosque*. Popular, foreign-owned restaurant, serving large portions of meat, pasta and vegetarian dishes for reasonable prices. The bar stays open until midnight.

Vamos a Ver Café, 1 block south of the parque. Delicious European-style soups, sandwiches, cheeses and snacks. The courtyard eating area is always busy. Shows English-language videos every night.

A brief history of Copán

Once the most important **city state** on the southern fringes of the Maya empire, Copán was largely cut off from all other cities except **Quiriguá**, 64km to the north in Guatemala (see p.215). Archeologists now believe that settlers began moving into the Río Copán valley from around 1000 BC, although construction of the city is not thought to have begun until around 100 AD.

By the sixth century Copán had emerged as a powerful centre, although information on its early history and rulers is sparse. A stela discovered in the Papagayo temple in 1988 refers to **Yax K'uk Mo'**, the first ruler and founder of the dynasty, who governed from at least 426 to 435 AD; the stela itself was erected by the third ruler, **Mat Head**. Little is known about the six subsequent rulers, although both the third and fourth are mentioned on Monument 26 at Quiriguá.

The **golden era** of Copán began with the accession to the throne of **Moon Jaguar**, the tenth ruler, in 553 AD, and continued through the reigns of **Smoke Serpent** (578–628), **Smoke Jaguar** (628–695) and **Eighteen Rabbit** (695–738). This period of stable, long-lasting government allowed for unprecedented political, social and artistic growth: the carved relief style for which Copán is famous developed during the reign of Eighteen Rabbit, who also oversaw the construction of the Great Plaza, the final version of the Ball Court and Temple 22 in the East Court.

Following Eighteen Rabbit's capture and decapitation by Cauac Sky, ruler of an ascendant and increasingly threatening Quiriguá, Copán entered a long decline, halted briefly during the rule of **Smoke Shell**, the fifteenth ruler (749–763 AD), who was responsible for the construction of the **Hieroglyphic Stairway**, one of the most impressive pieces of Maya architecture. Smoke Shell's son, **Yax Pac** (763–820 AD), constructed **Altar Q**, which illustrates the dynasty from its beginning, yet during his rule the city continued to decline; skeletal remains indicate that the main pressure came from inadequate food resources. The seventeenth and final ruler, **U Cit Tok'**, took the throne in 822 AD – two years after Yax Pac is thought to have died – but the date and reason for the ending of his reign are unknown.

The site was known to the Spanish, although they took little interest in it. A court official, Don Diego de Palacios, in a letter written in March 1576, mentions the ruins of a magnificent city "constructed with such skill that it seems that they could never have been made by people as coarse as the inhabitants of this province". Not until the nine-teenth century and the publication of *Incidents of Travel in Central America, Chiapas and Yucatán* by **John Lloyd Stephens** and **Frederick Catherwood** did Copán become known to the wider world. Stephens, the then acting US ambassador, had suc-ceeded in buying the ruins in 1839 and, accompanied by Catherwood, a British archi-tect and artist, spent several weeks clearing the site and mapping the buildings. The instant success of the book on publication and the interest it sparked in Mesoamerican culture ensured that Copán became a magnet for **archeologists**.

British archeologist **Alfred Maudsley** began a full-scale mapping, excavation and reconstruction project in 1891, under the sponsorship of the Peabody Museum, Harvard. A second major investigation was begun in 1935 by the Washington Carnegie Institute, which involved diverting the Río Copán to prevent it carving into the site. A breakthrough in understanding of not only Copán but the whole Maya world came in 1959 and 1960, when Heinrich Berlin and Tatiana Proskouriakoff first began to decipher **hieroglyphics**, leading to the realization that the glyphs record the history of their cities and succession of dynasties. Since 1977 the Instituto Hondureño de Antropología e Historia has been running a series of projects with the help of archeologists from around the world.

The site

The ruins lie one kilometre north of town, a fifteen-minute walk along a raised footpath. Entrance to the site is through the **visitor centre** (daily 8am–4pm; US$10), on the left-hand side of the car park, where a small exhibition explains Copán's place in the Maya empire; 200m beyond the centre is the warden's gate, the entrance to the site proper. On the right-hand side of the car park is the **Museum of Mayan Sculpture** (daily 8am–4pm; US$10), opened in the summer of 1996 and dominated by a full-scale, brightly painted replica of the **Rosalila Temple**, built in 591 and discovered intact under Structure 16 only in 1989. The ground-floor exhibition explains aspects of Maya beliefs and cosmology, whilst the upper floor houses many of the finest original sculptures from the site in a com-prehensive display of the ability and skill of Maya craftsmen. Opinions vary on whether the museum should be visited before or after the site itself; visiting it first enables you to then witness how the carvings have withstood the test of time.

The East and West courts

Turn right after passing through the warden's gate and a short walk takes you into the **West Court**, a confined area that forms part of the main acropolis. **Altar Q**, at the base of Pyramid 16, is the most famous feature here. Carved in 776 AD, it is thought to cel-ebrate **Yax Pac**'s assension to the throne on July 2, 763. The top of the altar is carved with six hieroglyphic blocks, while the sides are decorated with sixteen cross-legged figures, all seated on cushions. These are believed to represent previous rulers of

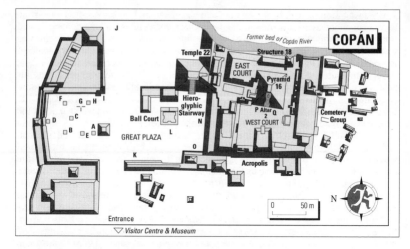

Copán, all pointing towards a portrait of Yax Pac receiving a ceremonial staff from the city's first ruler, Mah K'ina Yax K'uk Mo', thereby endorsing Yax Pac's right to rule. Behind the altar is a small crypt, discovered to contain the remains of a macaw and fifteen big cats, possibly sacrificed in honour of Yax Pac.

Pyramid 16, behind Altar Q, contained the intact facade of the Rosalila Temple, apparently purposely buried within it. The temple served as a centre for worship during the reign of Smoke Serpent, or Butz'Chan, Copán's eleventh ruler, the apogee of political, social and artistic growth. Generally, it was Maya custom to ritually deface or destroy obsolete temples or stelae, so the discovery of the Rosalila has been one of the most exciting finds of recent years. Once scientific studies are completed, the temple will be re-sealed against the outside world.

Climbing the stairs behind Altar Q brings you into the **East Court**, slightly larger than the West and bearing more elaborate carvings. Surrounding the central dip are life-sized jaguar heads; the hollows in the eyes would once have held pieces of jade or polished obsidian. In the middle of the staircase, flanked by the jaguars, is a rectangular Venus mask, carved in superb deep relief.

At the southern end of this court is **Structure 18**, a small square building with carved panels. The floor of this structure has been dug up to reveal a magnificent tomb, possibly that of Yax Pac; empty when excavated by archeologists, the tomb is thought to have been looted on a number of occasions. South of Structure 18 the **Cemetery Group** was once thought to have been a burial site, although current thinking is that it was a residential complex, possibly home to the ruling elite. To date, however, little work has been done on this part of the site.

To the north, one of Copán's most impressive buildings, **Temple 22**, separates the East Court from the Great Plaza. Some of the stonework is astonishingly simple, other sections – particularly around the door frames – superbly intricate and decorated with outlandish carving. Above the door is the body of a double-headed snake, its heads resting on two figures which in turn are supported by skulls. The corners of the temple bear portraits of the long-nosed rain god **Chaac**, a favourite Maya deity. The quality of the carving on this temple has led archeologists to suggest that the East Court may have been Copán's most important plaza. The decoration here is unique in the southern Maya region, with only the Yucatán sites such as Kabáh and Chicanna having carvings of comparable quality.

The Great Plaza

Beyond Temple 22 lies the **Great Plaza**, strewn with the magnificently carved and exceptionally well-preserved stelae that today are Copán's outstanding features. The style of carving is similar to that of Quiriguá, and at both sites the portraits of assorted rulers dominate the decoration, with surrounding glyphs giving details of events during their rule.

Pressed up against the Central Acropolis, at the southern end of the plaza, is the **Hieroglyphic Court**, on the left-hand side of which is the famed **Hieroglyphic Stairway**, perhaps the most astonishing work of all at Copán. Made up of some 63 stone steps, every block is carved to form part of the glyphic sequence – a total of between 1500 and 2200 glyphs. It forms the longest known Maya hieroglyphic text, but, sadly, attempted reconstruction by early archeologists left the sequence so jumbled that a complete interpretation is still some way off. The easiest part to understand is the dates, and these range from 544 to 744 AD. At the base of the stairway, **Stela M** records a solar eclipse in 756 AD.

The **Ball Court**, one of the few Maya courts to still have a paved floor, lies just north of the stairway. Originally the entire plaza would once have been paved like this and probably painted as well. The court dates from 775 AD; beneath it are two previous versions. The rooms that line the sides of the court, overlooking the playing area, were probably used by priests and members of the elite as they observed the ritual of the game.

Facing the ball court is the **Temple of the Inscriptions**, a towering stairway. **Stela N**, at its base, is another classic piece of Copán carving with portraits on the two main faces and glyphs down the sides. The depth of the relief has protected the nooks and crannies, and in some of these you can still see flakes of paint; originally the carvings and buildings would have been painted in a whole range of bright colours, but for some reason only the red has survived.

Dotted all around the Great Plaza are Copán's famed **Stelae**, made from andesite, a fine-grained, even-textured volcanic rock, particularly suited to retention of intricate detail in carvings. Most of the stelae represent **Eighteen Rabbit**, Copán's "King of the Arts" (Stelae A, B, C, D, F, H and 4). **Stela A**, dating from 731 AD, has incredibly deep carving, although much is now eroded. Its sides include a total of 52 glyphs, better preserved than the main faces. **Stela B** is one of the more controversial stones, with a figure that some see as oriental in appearance, supporting theories of mass migration from the east. **Stela C** (730 AD) is one of the earliest stones to have faces on both sides; like many of the central stelae it has an altar at its base, carved in the shape of a turtle. Two rulers are represented: Eighteen Rabbit's father, who lived well into his eighties, is facing the turtle (a symbol of longevity), while the other side depicts Eighteen Rabbit himself.

Las Sepultras

Two kilometres northeast of Copán is the smaller site of **Las Sepultras** (daily 8am–4pm; entrance on the same ticket as for Copán), the focus of much archeological interest in recent years because of the information it provides on daily domestic life in Maya times. Eighteen of some forty residential compounds at the site have been excavated, yielding one hundred buildings that would have been inhabited by the elite. Smaller compounds on the edge of the site are thought to have housed young princes, as well as concubines and servants. It was customary to bury the nobility close to their residences and around the compounds more than 250 tombs have been excavated, allowing insights into the Maya way of life. Given the number of women found in the tombs it seems likely that they practised polygamy. One of the most interesting finds – the tomb of a priest or shamán, dating from around 450 AD – is on display in the museum in Copán Ruinas.

Around Copán

Within easy reach of Copán are a couple of places that make an extra day or so's stay worthwhile. Closest is the small Maya site of **Los Sapos**, a delightful walk south from town. Ten kilometres or so in the opposite direction, the picturesque waterfall of **El Rubí** is the perfect spot for a picnic. Copán is also a convenient spot to cross over into Guatemala, with the **El Florido** border crossing just 12km to the west.

Los Sapos, dating from the same era as Copán, is set in the hills to the south of town, less than an hour's gentle walk away. The site, whose name derives from a rock carved in the shape of a frog, is thought to have been the place where Maya women came to bear children. The walk to the site is more interesting than the ruins themselves, since time and weather have eroded much of the carving. Follow the main road south out of town, turn left onto a dirt track just past the river bridge and follow this as it begins to climb gently into the hills. The views across the tobacco fields of the river valley are beautiful, and there are plenty of spots for swimming along the way.

Pickups leave Copán regularly throughout the day for the peaceful town of **Santa Rita**, 9km north. At the river bridge just before entering the town, a path leads up to **El Rubí**, a pretty double waterfall on the Río Copán, about 2km away. Surrounded by shady woods, this is the perfect spot for a swim in the clear, cold water, followed by a picnic. Follow the path as it climbs along and above the right-hand bank of the river for about twenty minutes; just past a steep stretch and small bend to the right, the narrow path running down through the pasture on the left leads to a pool and high rock, on the other side of which is El Rubí.

Into Guatemala: El Florido

The Guatemalan border is just twelve bumpy kilometres west of Copán and crossing here at the **El Florido** border post – usually busy with backpackers coming to and from the ruins – is straightforward. There is no bank, but the ever-present moneychanges handle dollars, lempiras and quetzales, though not at particularly good rates. **Buses** run both ways every thirty minutes, taking around half an hour; the last leaves Copán at 3pm and the border at 4pm. It's sensible to cross as early in the day as possible to ensure onward connections in Guatemala. On the Guatemalan side there are regular services to Chiquimula, the nearest town, 50km away (see p.223).

North to La Entrada: El Puente

North from Copán, highway CA-11 winds its way through lightly wooded mountains, fertile pasture lands and tobacco fields for 55km to the dusty, hot and distinctly unlikeable junction town of **La Entrada**. The journey is wonderfully scenic but can be painfully slow by bus. This is the route to take if you're heading for San Pedro Sula (see p.393) and the north coast: there are some direct buses from Copán to San Pedro, but it's easy to change at La Entrada on to any bus running along highway CA-4 from Santa Rosa. Should you get stuck here, *Hotel San Carlos* (☎898 5228; ④), at the junction of highways CA-11 and CA-4, is the best of the available accommodation.

Four kilometres before La Entrada, a signed turn marks the way to the archeological site of **El Puente** (daily 8am–4pm; US$3.80), 6km away. Opened in 1994, the site receives comparatively few visitors, which makes its location – amid the grassy fields flanking the Río Chinamito – all the more enjoyable, although after the glories of Copán, the scale of the site is inevitably disappointing.

Once a sizeable **Maya** settlement, dating back to the Late Classic period and under the authority of Copán, El Puente contains over two hundred structures. To date, only a small number in the centre have been excavated, including religious buildings and buildings for the use of the elite, built around what was the main plaza. The most important of these (Structure 1) is an eleven-metre-high, six-stepped pyramid oriented east–west, thought to be a funerary temple; the long, lower pyramid along its lower edge contains burial chambers. The small **museum** at the entrance to the park, about 1km from the restorations, has an informative exhibition on the site itself and on Maya culture in general.

No public transport runs up the road to the site, but hitching is considered safe; traffic is more frequent in the mornings. A round-trip taxi fare from La Entrada will cost around US$10.

travel details

BUSES

Comayagua to: Tegucigalpa (Transportes Colonial, 11 daily; 1hr 30min); Siguatepeque (10 daily; 1hr).

Copán to: La Entrada (every 45min; 1hr 30min); San Pedro Sula (4 daily, all early morning; 2hr).

Gracias to: Santa Rosa de Copán (hourly until 6pm; 1hr 30min).

La Entrada to: San Pedro Sula (every 30 mins; 1hr30mins)

La Esperanza to: Gracias (1 daily; 4–5hr).

Nueva Ocotepeque to: Agua Caliente (every 30min until 4pm; 1hr); El Poy (every 40min; 30min).

Santa Rosa de Copán to: Copán (3 daily; 3hr); La Entrada (8 daily; 1hr 30min); Nueva Ocotepeque (6 daily; 2hr); San Pedro Sula (every 30min, 3hr; 3 direct services a day, 2hr).

Siguatepeque to: La Esperanza (every 2hr until mid-afternoon; 2hr).

CHAPTER 19

OLANCHO

S tretching east to the Nicaraguan border and into the emptiness of the Mosquitia, the sparsely populated uplands of **Olancho** are widely regarded as Honduras's "wild east", an untamed frontier region with a not totally undeserved reputation for lawlessness and violence. Tradition has it that Olanchitos hold little respect for authority and it's true that rebellion has played a large part in their history – first against the Spanish, who settled here to exploit the gold discovered in the rivers, and later against the new, centralized government of the nineteenth century. Though communications have improved vastly in recent years, there is still the sense travelling here that you've entered a very different country. The relatively few visitors who do pass through will receive a brusque yet genuine welcome.

Although, geographically, Olancho makes up almost a fifth of Honduran territory, tourist attractions are few, and the high, forested mountain ranges interspersed with broad valleys make travelling all too often difficult and slow. However, these same ranges harbour some of the country's last untouched expanses of tropical and cloud forest: the national parks of **La Muralla** and **Sierra de Agalta** are awe-inspiring, while the smaller, more accessible reserve of **El Boquerón** offers ample opportunity for gentler hikes. Along the valleys, now given over to pastureland for cattle, are scattered villages and towns. Both **Juticalpa**, the department capital, and **Catacamas**, at the eastern end of the paved road, are good bases for exploring the region, while the friendly mountain settlement of **La Unión** acts as both gateway to La Muralla and a convenient stopover en route to the north coast.

Olancho's **climate** is generally pleasant, with the towns at lower altitudes hot during the day and comfortably cool at night; up in the mountains it can get extremely cold after dark. Once off the main highway, **travelling** becomes arduous, with the dirt roads connecting the remoter villages served by infrequent, invariably slow public transport.

Juticalpa and the east

Olancho's main **transport** artery, Highway CA-15, runs east through mountain passes and across flat valleys to Catacamas, a journey of about four hours from Tegucigalpa. Many people get no further than **Juticalpa**, the region's main centre, which makes a convenient base for expeditions into the national parks. North and east of Catacamas stretch the remote, impassable peaks of the Sierra de Agalta, part of which is protected as the magnificent **Parque Nacional Sierra de Agalta**. Difficult to reach at best, the reserve is easiest approached from the north.

Juticalpa

Situated towards the southern end of the Valle de Catacamas, about 170km from Tegucigalpa, **JUTICALPA** is a thriving, pleasant little city with a number of reasonable

For an explanation of **accommodation price codes**, see p.345.

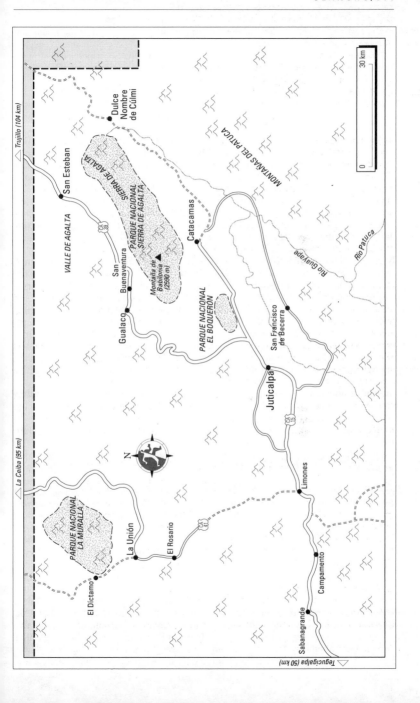

hotels and restaurants. Capital of the department, its streets are busy night and day with provincial bustle and commerce.

Juticalpa's **bus terminals** are just off the highway, on 1 Av SE, which leads straight to the centre, a fifteen-minute walk north. Local buses – including departures east to Catacamas and northwest to La Unión – run from the terminal on the right side of the road (facing town); Empresa Aurora's Tegucigalpa services use the other side.

At the other end of 1 Av SE is the leafy **Parque Banderas**, the city's heart, busy with food stalls in the evenings. The majority of hotels and restaurants, along with the banks, post office and other facilities, are on the streets around the parque. The general **market** stretches for a few blocks to the west, along C Perulapan. The local COHDE-FOR office (☎885 2253), with **information** on the national parks, is in a green house at the very far end of 1 Av SO, about two blocks west of the Empresa Aurora terminal.

Don't expect too much in the way of cosseted luxury in Juticalpa, or indeed any-where in Olancho. The best of the **places to stay** are a couple of comfortable, reason-ably priced hotels and a handful of more basic places, all within a couple of minutes' walk of the parque. The new *Hotel Honduras*, 1 Av, 1 C NO, one street west of the par-que (☎885 1331; ③), is the best on offer, a friendly place with large rooms, all with bath and TV. The similar *Apart Hotel La Muralla*, nearby at 1 C, 2 Av NO (☎ & fax 885 1270; ②), has smaller rooms. There's a range of clean if rather gloomy rooms, some with bath, at the long-standing *Hotel Atuñez*, 1 C, 1 Av NO (☎885 2250; ①–②); finally, there's the *Hotel Rivera,* 2 Av, 1–2 C SO (☎885 1154; ①), which is cheap and clean and makes up for in friendliness what it lacks in comfort.

The range of **restaurants** is similarly modest. *Dirro's*, on the parque, doesn't sell pizza, despite its sign, but does serve some great spaghetti. Try *Restaurante Asia* next door for cheap and cheerful Honduran-style Chinese. Behind the cathedral on 2 Av NE, *El Rancho* has a nice courtyard setting, serves a good range of meat and seafood dishes and soups and is popular with locals for a quiet beer and snack. For wholesome and filling breakfasts, head for *Cafeteria Regis* on 1 C NO, one block from the parque; alternatively, *Tropical Juices*, with branches on the parque and on 1 Av, halfway to the bus terminal, offers truly inspired juices and licuados. For when the attractions of eat-ing and people-watching have worn thin, the **cinema** at 1 C NO, 2–3 Av NO shows subtitled US releases.

El Boquerón

Twenty kilometres east of Juticalpa, **El Boquerón** is one of the last remnants of dry tropical forest in Honduras, and home to a wide variety of wildlife, including over 180 species of bird – quetzals, toucans and taragones have all been spotted here. It's easily accessible as a day-trip from the city, though there are facilities should you want to camp. To see the forest properly, you need to follow the moderately strenuous track through the reserve, which cuts through a small patch of cloudforest.

Any of the buses running along the highway between Juticalpa and Catacamas will drop you at the marked **entrance** to the reserve, a journey of about twenty minutes. From here, the reserve stretches back along the **Canyon de Boquerón**, a kilome-tre-deep natural rift. The path takes you through forest and into the canyon along the left-hand bank of the **Río Olancho**, where there are plentiful opportunities for swim-ming. After around an hour, the path crosses the river and heads uphill away from the canyon through open pastureland to the hamlet of **LA AVISPA**; getting here takes about three hours in total. Beyond the village, the path loops steeply uphill around Cerro Agua Buena (1433m) and through the **cloudforest** section; here you've the greatest chance of seeing elusive bird and animal life, though the trees are stunted and the vegetation less dense than in other reserves. From this point on it's all down-hill, the path emerging after a couple of hours on the highway at Tempisque, a few kilometres west of the main entrance. An early start would allow you to complete the walk in one day; alternatively, use the designated camping spots at the main entrance and at La Avispa – bring food and water. It's an easy matter to flag down **buses** to Juticalpa or Catacamas along the highway.

Catacamas

CATACAMAS, situated midway along the Valle de Catacamas beneath the southern flanks of the Sierra de Agalta, is a much smaller version of Juticalpa, 41km away. Very few tourists come here – Catacamas marks the end of the paved road – which no doubt contributes to the affable, small-town charm of the place. It has a more spectacular setting than its larger neighbour: a short walk up to the **Mirador de la Cruz**, fifteen minutes from the centre on the northern side of town, gives superb views over the town and valley, and across to the Montañas del Patuca.

Buses terminate on the parque central, from where it is pretty easy to find your way around. The banks, post office and other essentials lie on the couple of streets north of the parque, hotels to the west. Of the very limited **accommodation** available, *Hotel Colina*, 1 Av SW, just down from the parque (☎899 4191; ②), is by far the best, with reasonably comfortable rooms, all with bath, set round a courtyard. The *Hotel Rapallo* (①), one block down, is spartan and dingy, but would do in an emergency. For **eating**, *Restaurante Pollo Rico* and *El Riconcito Típico*, both a block north of the parque central, serve unexceptional meat and chicken dishes.

Parque Nacional Sierra de Agalta

Draped across the sweeping ranges of the Sierra de Agalta, the vast **Parque Nacional Sierra de Agalta** shelters within its boundaries the most extensive stretch of **virgin cloudforest** remaining in Central America. Since the establishment of the reserve in 1987, pressure on the land has remained acute, and large swathes of the lower forest of pine and oak have been cleared to provide pasture for ranching. There have, however, been encouraging signs in recent years that the environmental message is getting through, not least because the reserve is the watershed for the region, the source of the rivers Sico and Patuca, among others. It's a different story in the higher reaches of the mountains, where the fifty-kilometre core of the reserve is so remote that both vegetation and wildlife have remained virtually untouched. Typical cloudforest cover of majestic oaks, liquidambar and cedar, draped in epiphytes, vines and ferns, densely cloak the higher slopes, giving way, above 2000m, to an almost primeval dwarf forest, where the trees grow only to a height of around five metres.

This isolation ensures a protected, secure environment for a biologically diverse range of **animals and birds**, many of them extremely rare. Tapirs, jaguars, ocelots, opossums and three species of monkey are among the 61 recorded species of mammal, although to spot them you'll need a great deal of luck. More evident are the birds, of which over four hundred species have been recorded, including 33 species of hummingbird. There are also numerous different butterflies and reptiles.

Its remoteness makes **independent access** to the reserve difficult. There's no accommodation other than official camping spots, for which you'll need to bring all equipment and supplies. The easiest points of entry are along the northern edge of the Sierra, via the small towns of **Gualaco** and **San Esteban**, which you can reach off Highway C39 between Juticalpa and Trujillo. Hiring a **guide** is pretty much essential for hiking on the often difficult trails: ask at the CODEHFOR offices in Gualaco, San Esteban or Juticalpa. A daily bus to Trujillo, passing through both towns, leaves Juticalpa at 4am.

La Unión and La Muralla

Some 110km from Juticalpa in the west of the department of Olancho, **LA UNIÓN** is a pleasant mountain town, the most convenient point of departure for **Parque Nacional La Muralla**, 15km north. Its location, around halfway along the Tegucigalpa–La Ceiba bus route, also makes it a handy stopover between the capital and the north coast.

Accommodation in La Unión is limited to the *Hotel La Muralla* and *Hotel Karol* (both ①), both very basic. There are a couple of comedores around the parque central for meals. If you intend to visit La Muralla, you need to register at the **COHDEFOR** office (Mon–Fri 8am–5pm), three blocks from the parque central; the office can also help with organizing transport into the park.

Parque Nacional la Muralla

La Muralla (daily 8am–4pm; free) takes its name from the appearance of the reserve when viewed from a distance – "the wall" of a high, bulky massif, densely covered with leafy forest, forming an island of incredible biological diversity amid the surrounding low-level mountain ranges. Cocooned in the centre of the reserve is an extensive stretch of virgin cloudforest which, despite the remoteness that has contributed to its pristine state, is more accessible to visitors than the Sierra de Agalta. The park's dazzling array of **bird life** and its well-planned visitor facilities make a visit here very rewarding.

Forest cover in La Muralla ranges from pine woods at the level of the entrance (1400m) through to cloudforest from around 1800m. The mountains slope steeply, rising to the peak of **Las Parras**, at 2064m the highest point. For birdwatchers, quetzales, humming-birds, kites and toucanets are among the species likely to be spotted; the aguacatillo tree in front of the visitor centre is a major food source for quetzals and, if you're lucky, they can be seen feeding there in the early mornings. More evasive are the white-tailed deer, jaguars, pumas, grey foxes and howler monkeys that inhabit the park.

It is possible to visit La Muralla as a day-trip from La Unión, although since bird-spotting is best done in the very early morning, it's wise to plan on spending the night here. The shortest **trail**, El Pizote, swings from the visitor centre in a two-hour loop up through the damp hush of the cloudforest and back down again. Though steep, wet and slippy, this can be done unguided and benches are provided at the best points for birdwatching; guides are recommended, however, for greater understanding of what you're seeing. Longer trails run across the reserve to the **Cascada de Mucupina** (8hr return) and to **Monte Escondido**, a two-day hike.

Access to La Muralla is via the **visitor centre** at the southwest end of the reserve, about 15km north of La Unión on the road to El Díctamo village. Here you can pick up trail maps and information on wildlife; there are also dorm **beds** (reservations through COHDEFOR in Tegucigalpa; ☎223 7703) and **camping space**, with two more camping spots further into the reserve. Bring plenty of food and water and some warm clothes.

travel details

BUSES

Catacamas to: Juticalpa (hourly; 1hr).

Gualaco to: Trujillo (1 daily; 5hr).

Juticalpa to: Catacamas (hourly; 1hr); Gualaco (1 daily; 2hr); La Unión (1 daily; 3hr); San Esteban (1 daily; 3hr 30min); Tegucigalpa (Empresa Aurora, 12 daily; 3hr).

La Unión to: La Ceiba (3 daily; 7–8hr); Tegucigalpa (Cotraibal, 3 daily; 5hr).

San Esteban to: Trujillo (1 daily; 3hr 30min).

CHAPTER 20

THE NORTH COAST AND MOSQUITIA

A world away from the forested mountain ranges of the interior, Honduras's **north coast** stretches for 300km along the azure fringes of the Caribbean. A magnet for Hondurans and foreign tourists alike, most are drawn solely by the prospect of sun, sea and entertainment, provided in abundance by the coastal towns of **Tela**, **La Ceiba** and **Trujillo**, with their broad expanses of isolated beach and clean warm waters, their dozens of restaurants and buzzing nightlife. Dotted in between the main towns are a number of laid-back **Garífuna** villages blessed with unspoilt beaches, where a stay is likely to be more peaceful. **San Pedro Sula**, the region's major city and transport hub, provides amenities of a strictly urban kind.

When beach life loses its appeal, there are several natural reserves in the region to visit. The national parks of **Cusuco**, **Pico Bonito** and **Capiro y Calentura**, whose virgin cloudforest shelters rare wildlife, offer hiking for all levels of fitness; the wetland and mangrove swamps at **Punta Sal** and **Cuero y Salado** require less exertion to explore. Occupying the eastern corner of Honduras is the remote and undeveloped expanse of the **Mosquitia**, at whose heart lies the **Río Plátano Biosphere Reserve**, an extensive swathe of pristine tropical rainforest. Travelling here requires a spirit of adventure and the ability to lose track of time, but the effort is takes is well rewarded.

The two **dry** seasons – December through to April, and August to September – are the best times to visit the north coast. Temperatures rarely drop below 25–28°C, but the heat is usually tempered by ocean breezes. Outside the Mosquitia, **transport** is reasonably good, with frequent buses along the fast, paved highway that links the main coastal towns; as usual, reaching the remoter villages and national parks requires some forward planning. **Accommodation** to suit all price levels is in abundant supply – the only time it's necessary to book is around Semana Santa, when hordes of Hondurans head for the beach and prices often rise.

San Pedro Sula

Honduras's second city, and the country's economic focus, **SAN PEDRO SULA** sprawls across the fertile Valle de Sula, at the foot of the Merendón mountain chain, just an hour from the coast. Flat and uninspiring to look at, and for most of the year uncomfortably hot and humid, this is a city for getting business done rather than sightseeing. What's more, it's the transport hub for northern and western Honduras, making a stay

For an explanation of **accommodation price codes**, see p.345.

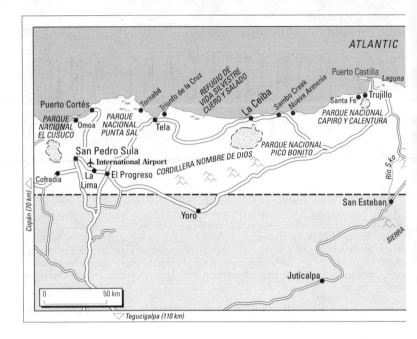

here, however short, usually unavoidable. On a more positive note, in terms of **facilities** San Pedro rates alongside Tegucigalpa, with its own international airport, foreign consulates, and a wide range of hotels, restaurants and shopping outlets – travellers coming from the north rarely need to visit the capital. If you do choose to stick around for a day or two, it's not difficult to organize a trip out to one of the country's finest **cloudforest reserves**, the Parque Nacional el Cusuco (see p.400).

One of the first Spanish settlements in the country, founded by Pedro de Alvadaro in 1536, today's San Pedro bears almost no trace of its pre-twentieth-century incarnation. Burnt out by French corsairs in 1660 and virtually abandoned during a yellow fever epidemic in 1892, the city struggled to maintain a population of more than five thousand, and today only a few wooden buildings remain as proof of its long past. Fortunes began to rise with the growth of the **banana** industry in the late nineteenth century, and the city rapidly cemented its role as Honduras's commercial centre. With its outer reaches continuing to sprout factories, many of them foreign-owned, and a population now in the region of 500,000, San Pedro ranks as one of the fastest-growing cities in Central America.

Arrival and information

The **Aeropuerto Internacional Villeda Morales**, point of entry for both domestic and international flights, lies 12km southeast of the city. As yet, there is no public transport between the airport and the city centre; **taxis** charge around US$8. **Buses** arrive at their own separate terminals, most within a few blocks of each other in central San Pedro (see p.400 for addresses).

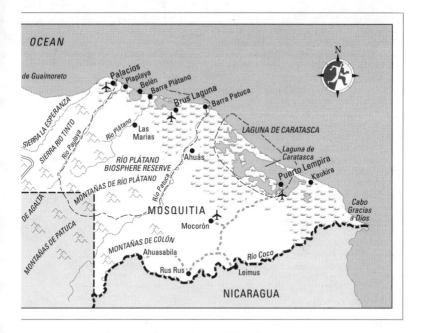

San Pedro's regular grid layout makes navigation easy: avenidas run north–south and calles east–west, numbered in ascending order from the central 1 Avenida and 1 Calle, which intersect two blocks east of the cathedral. The city is further divided into quadrants, whose labels – southwest (SO), southeast (SE), northwest (NO) and north-east (NE) – are always used in directions. The bus terminals, many hotels and the main commercial area are in the southwest sector, close to the centre. Running west from the parque central, 1 Calle is also known as the Blvd Morazán for the twelve blocks until it meets the **Av Circunvalación** ring road, which separates the city centre from San Pedro's wealthier residential districts; this is where many of the more upmarket restaurants are located. Beyond the Circunvalación, 1 Calle becomes Blvd los Próceres.

Accommodation

San Pedro's **accommodation** ranges from the five-star luxury of the *Gran Hotel Sula*, a city landmark, to sleazy, dollar-a-night dives. Expect to pay at least US$10 for an acceptable room with bath in a secure hotel. Double that and TV and air-conditioning become standard. The area south of the market can get rough at night, and although foreigners are unlikely to be targeted, it is not really a place to be wandering around after dark.

Ambassador, 7 C, 5 Av SO (☎557 6825). Reasonably comfortable rooms, all with bath. Not a particularly pleasant area at night, but convenient for many of the bus terminals. ②–③.

Bolívar, 2 C, 2 Av NO (☎553 3224, fax 553 4823). Good-value hotel with an upmarket feel about it. The large rooms all have bath, a/c and TV. Downstairs there is a small pool and terrace, and a rather characterless bar and restaurant. ⑤.

Conquistador, 2 C SO, 7–8 Av (☎552 7605). Small and very friendly place, four blocks west of the parque central. Rooms are small but clean and all have bath, a/c and TV. ④.

Ejecutive Real del Valle, Edificio Maria Emilia, 6 Av, 4–5 C SO (☎553 0366). A comfortable place with a welcoming atmosphere; the front door is always kept locked. All rooms have a/c, bath, hot water and TV. ④.

Ejecutivo, 10 Av, 2 C SO (☎552 4289, fax 552 5868). Friendly, well-run hotel set in a quiet residential area – fifteen minutes' walk from the centre, five minutes in a taxi. Rooms all have a/c, bath and TV and the price includes breakfast. ⑤.

Gran Hotel Sula, 1 C O at the parque central (☎552 9999, fax 552 7000). A city landmark and at present the only real luxury option, though soon to face competition from a number of international chains. Rooms have everything you would expect for the price, including balconies with views over the city. ⑨.

Internacional Palace Hotel, 8 Av, 3 C SO (☎550 3838, fax 550 0969). Recently refurbished hotel offering high-level accommodation at reasonable prices. All rooms have bath, hot water, a/c and TV. The rooftop pool and bar are a good place to cool off. ⑤.

San José, 6 Av, 5–6 C SO (☎557 1208). One of the better hotels in the lower price range; clean, good-sized rooms with bath and a choice of fan or a/c. ②.

San Pedro, 3 C, 1–2 Av SO (☎553 1513, fax 553 2655). Large, rambling and popular with travellers. The choice of rooms ranges from basic ones with shared bath to some with large beds, private bath, a/c and TV. ①–③.

Terraza, 6 Av, 4–5 C SO (☎550 3108). Good value and convenient for the centre and bus terminals; rooms all have bath and hot water and the café downstairs serves decent breakfasts. ③.

The City

Parque Barahona, large and recently re-paved, is the focus of the city centre, teeming with vendors, shoe-shine boys, moneychangers and general malcontents taking the air. On its eastern edge, the colonial-style **Catedral Municipal** was actually only completed in the mid-1950s; facing it across the parque is the unremarkable Palacio Muncipal, home to the city adminstration.

San Pedro has few tourist attractions, but one place that is worth a visit is the first-class **Museo de Arqueología e Historia** (Tues–Sun 10am–4.15pm; US$0.40), a few blocks north of the parque, at 3 Av, 4 C NO. The museum's collection of pre-Columbian sculptures, ceramics and other artefacts, the majority recovered from the Sula Valley, outline the development of civilization in the region from 1500 BC onwards; weaponry and paintings from the colonial period continue the theme. While you're in this area, check out what's on at the **Centro Cultural Sampedrano**, 3 C, 3–4 Av NO (☎553 3911), which regularly hosts concerts and plays. Continue north away from the centre along 3 Av to reach the exhibition hall run by the ecological foundation **Fundación Ecologista Hector Rodrigo Pastor Fasquelle**, at the junction with 11 C NO (Mon–Fri 9am–4pm). Displays feature pictorial and written explanations of the development of cloudforests and the wildlife encountered in the country's varied habitats, including the nearby Parque Nacional Cusuco (see p.400).

San Pedro has a good selection of places to buy **handicrafts** produced throughout the country. Ten or so blocks northwest of the parque central, the **Mercado Guamilito**, 9 Av, 6–7 C NO, is an indoor market with numerous stalls selling hammocks, ceramics, leatherwork and wooden goods. If you can carry them, the cotton hammocks are a good buy; gentle bartering should get you better prices. A couple of shops on the Calle Peatonal, just off the parque central, sell similar stuff, though prices are higher and the range not as wide. For the more eclectically minded, Le Merendon, a taxi ride out of the centre at 18 Av, 6 C SO, is a thatch-roofed display area-cum-beer garden, with an offbeat selection of works from artesans around the

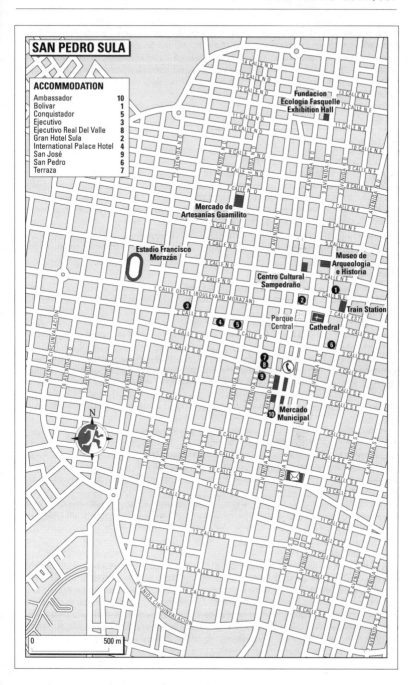

SAN PEDRO SULA

ACCOMMODATION

Ambassador	10
Bolívar	1
Conquistador	5
Ejecutivo	3
Ejecutivo Real Del Valle	8
Gran Hotel Sula	2
International Palace Hotel	4
San José	9
San Pedro	6
Terraza	7

Fundación Ecología Fasquelle Exhibition Hall

Mercado de Artesanías Guamilito

Estadio Francisco Morazán

Museo de Arqueología e Historia

Centro Cultural Sampedraño

Train Station

Parque Central

Cathedral

Mercado Municipal

0   500 m

N

country; look out for the huge straw animals and the ceramic garden decorations. Danilo's, a couple of streets away at 18 Av B, 9 C SO, is an outlet for one of the best leather-goods producers in the country, selling excellent-value bags, purses and belts, among other items. Finally, the vast general market, the **mercado municipal**, is between 4–5 Av SO and 5–6 C SO, though stalls spill onto the streets around for several blocks.

Eating, drinking and entertainment

As you'd expect in such a business-oriented, wealthy city, there's a good selection of **places to eat** and a diverse range of evening entertainment. The more down-to-earth places can be found in the centre, while the Av Circunvalación, south of 1 C, is the so-called Zona Viva, the place to go for upmarket restaurants, bars and clubs. A couple of modern two-screen **cinemas**, the Cine Tropicana, at 2 C, 7 Av SO, and the Cine Geminis, 1 C, 12 Av NO, are within easy walking distance of the centre; both show new US films, and the occasional Latin American offering.

Cafés and restaurants

Cafetería Mayan Way, 6 Av, 4–5 C SO, next to *Hotel Terraza*. Good breakfasts and set lunches at down-to-earth prices.

Café Pampelona, parque central. Always crowded with locals, the menu is extensive and the prices reasonable; don't expect too much in the way of service but soak up the noisy atmosphere (closes 8pm).

Café Skandia, in the *Gran Hotel Sula*. Air conditioned and open 24 hours, the *Skandia* is something of a San Pedro institution. Sandwiches, light meals and snacks are not as expensive as you might expect.

Don Udo's, 1 C, 20 Av SO (☎553 3106). Held to be one of city's finest, offering a broad range of European and local dishes and a decent wine list. Prices are not cheap but worth it for a splurge; expect to pay from US$15 a head for a full meal with wine. Sunday brunches are less formal. Mon–Sat evenings, Sun 10am–2pm.

Italia y Mas, 1 C, 8 Av NO. Excellent pasta, risotto and other Italian dishes for lunch or dinner, with tables inside and in a back courtyard. Prices reflect the upmarket clientele.

Pizzería Italia, 1 C, 7 Av NO. Cosy little place serving good pizza and a small selection of pasta dishes. The service is informal, and prices fairly low.

Restaurante la Tejana, Av Circunvalación, 9 C SO. Popular place for lunch and dinner, with a wide selection of well-prepared seafood, as well as meat and chicken dishes.

Restaurante Shanghai, Calle Peatonal. Reasonably authentic Chinese food served in huge portions.

Shauky's Place, 18 Av, 8 C SO. Now moved from the outskirts of the city, this easy-going bar and restaurant has has tables set around an open-air gravelled garden. Delicious steak and meat dishes cost around US$7; a few vegetarian choices, too. Mon–Sat from 4pm.

Bars and clubs

After dark, the *Café Internacional*, Blvd Morazán, 14–15 Av SO, attracts a young, mon-eyed crowd; the drinks are reasonably priced and there is a small restaurant. The three bars at *Frog's Sports Bar*, Blvd los Próceres, 19–20 C SO, have pool tables and giant TV screens. Later in the evening, *Johnny's*, by the market, is an idiosyncratic spirits-only bar where locals go to shoot the breeze to the accompaniment of 1950s be-bop. The nearby *Black and White* disco, a local favourite, is hot and frenetic at the weekends; *Henry's* and *Confetti's* on Av Circunvalación in the Zona Viva play Latin American and Euro-disco rhythms for a younger crowd.

Listings

Airlines American Airlines, Centro Comercial Firenze, 16 Av, 2 C (☎558 0518 or 558 0521, fax 558 0527); British Airways, Edificio Sempe, Carretera a Chamelecon (☎556 6952 or 556 3942, fax 556 8764); Continental, *Gran Hotel Sula*, 4 Av, 1–2 C (☎557 4141, fax 557 4146); COPA, Centro Comercial Prisa, 1 C, 9–10 Av (☎550 9654, fax 550 8641); Iberia, 3 C, 4–5 Av (☎557 5311, fax 553 4297); Isleña, Edifico Trejo Merlo, 7 Av, 1–2 C (☎552 8322); Lacsa, Edificio Romar, 8 Av, 1–2 C (☎550 6649, fax 550 8641); Taca International, Centro Comercial Prisa 1 C, 9–10 Av (☎550 5649, fax 550 8641).

American Express Agencia de Viajes Mundirama, Edificio Martinez Valenzuela, 2 C, 2–3 Av SO (☎553 0192, fax 557 9092).

Banks and exchange Banco Atlantida has a number of branches in the downtown area for exchange and visa advances; Banco de Occidente, 6 Av, 2–3 C SO, changes cash and travellers' cheques; Credomatic, 5 Av, 1–2 C NO, advances cash on Visa and Mastercard.

Bookshops The cigar shop in the *Gran Hotel Sula* has a small collection of English-language fiction as well as US magazines and newspapers.

Car rental Avis, Blvd Morazán 58 (☎552 2872); Budget, Aeropuerto Villeda Morales (☎566 2267, fax 553 3411); Dollar, 3 Av 3–4 C NO (☎552 7626); Molinari, *Gran Hotel Sula* (☎553 2639, fax 552 2704) and at the airport (☎566 2580).

Consulates Belize, Km 5, road to Puerto Cortés (☎551 0124, fax 551 1740); Colombia, 6 C, 18–19 Av SO, 139 (☎553 2052; Mon–Fri 6–7pm); Costa Rica, 11 C, 22 Av SO, No 126 (☎552 8564; Mon–Fri 2.30–6pm); El Salvador, 12th floor, Edificio Bancatlan (☎557 5851; Mon–Fri 9am–noon & 2.30–3.30pm); Guatemala, 8 C, 5–6 Av NO (☎553 0653; Mon–Fri 8am–2pm); Mexico, 2 C, 20 Av SO, 205 (☎553 2604; Mon–Fri 8.30–11.30am); Nicaragua, 6 C, 16 Av 36, Barrio los Andes (☎552 9069; Mon–Fri 9am–noon & 2–4pm); UK, 13 Av, 11–12 C SO, No 62 (☎557 2046; Mon–Fri 9am–noon).

Immigration Dirección General de Migración, Calle Peatonal, above the Moreira Honduras souvenir shop (Mon–Fri 8.30am–4.30pm).

Laundry Lavanderia Express 9 Av, 3 C NO (Mon–Sat 8am–5pm).

Medical care Emergency department at Clínica Bendaña, Av Circunvalación, 9–10 C SO (☎553 1618).

Police ☎552 3128.

Post office At 9 C, 3 Av SO.

Telephone office Hondutel, at 4 C, 4 Av SO, is open 24hr; fax service is available 8am–5pm.

Travel agents Agencia de Viajes Mundirama, Edificio Martinez Valenzuela, 2 C, 2–3 Av SO (☎553 0192, fax 557 9092) are efficient and well-organized for booking or changing international air tickets. Transmundo de Sula, 5 Av, 4 C NO (☎550 1140), are also a reputable company.

Moving on

San Pedro Sula is a the main transport hub for this part of Honduras, with frequent **bus departures** for Tegucigalpa, Santa Rosa and all destinations along the north coast. Bus companies operate out of their own terminals, most conveniently located within a few blocks of each other in the centre of the city (see below for addresses). At the time of writing, the old **train** service between Puerto Cortés, San Pedro and Tela was due to restart operations; check at the station, 1 Av, 1 C E–2 C NE.

To La Ceiba and Trujillo: Cotraibal, 1 Av, 7–8 C SO (☎552 3822).

To Puerto Cortés: Impala, 2 Av, 4–5 C SO (☎553 0070); Citul, 6 Av, 7–8 C SO (☎553 0070)

To Santa Rosa de Copán: Toritos, 11 C, 6–7 Av SO (☎553 4930).

To Tegucigalpa: Hedman Alas, 3 C, 8–9 Av NO (☎553 1361); Saenz, 8 Av, 5–6 C SO (☎553 4969); El Rey, 7 Av, 5–6 C SO (☎553 4969).

Tours

One of the most reputable **tour companies** is Cambio CA, Edificio Copal, 1 C, 5–6 Av SO (☎552 0496; email *cambio@mayanet.hn*), which runs tours to Mosquitia, Cusuco and Pico Bonito, plus other destinations. Explore Honduras, Edificio Posada del Sol, 1 C, 2 Av SO (☎552 6242, fax 552 6093), also do recommended trips to Mosquitia and the Bay Islands.

Around San Pedro: Parque Nacional el Cusuco

Only 20km or so west of San Pedro in the Sierra del Merendón, the stunning **Parque Nacional el Cusuco** (daily 6am–5pm; US$10) supports an abundant range of animal and plant life, much of it rare and threatened. Though inevitably affected by the proximity of human settlement, Cusuco is still a joy to visit and not too difficult to reach from San Pedro. To see as much as possible, the best plan is to arrive in the afternoon, camp overnight and walk the trails early in the morning.

The lower reaches of the park have long been settled by humans and were heavily logged during the 1950s, contributing to disastrous floods during the 1970s. Here the mixed pine and broadleaf forest is secondary regrowth. At around 1800m the **cloud-forest** begins, its dense oaks and liquidambars reaching to 40m in some places, stacked over avocados and palms, all supporting mosses, vines, orchids and numerous species of heliconias, recognizable by the red or orange brackets holding the blossoms. Studies carried out in the park in 1992–95 revealed the existence of at least seventeen species of plant hitherto unknown in Honduras.

Four **trails**, ranging between 1km and 2.5km, have been laid out among the lower sections of cloudforest (there is no access to the highest, steepest sections of the reserve), taking you through a hushed world of dense, dripping, multi-layered vegetation. If you're incredibly lucky, you might spot the reserve's namesake, the *cusuco* (armadillo), as well as salamanders, monkeys and even a jaguar, but the dazzling range of birdlife is likely to be more rewarding in terms of sightings. Quetzals can be spotted from April to June, and trogons, kites and woodpeckers are among the more numerous of the 100-plus species of bird living here.

Practicalities

Cusuco is managed by the Fundación Ecologista Hector Rodrigo Pastor Fasquelle, whose office is above the *Pizzería Italia*, 1 C, 7 Av NO, in San Pedro (☎552 1014). Information leaflets are usually available and they can also advise on getting to the reserve. The main point of **access** is via the small town of **COFRADÍA**, 18km southwest of San Pedro off highway CA-4. From here, a dirt road continues for another 26km to the village of **BUENOS AIRES**, 5km beyond which is the park **visitor centre**. Getting there independently is time-consuming: you need to take a westbound bus to Cofradía (buses to and from La Entrada or Santa Rosa pass through) and then wait for onward transport. Other options include renting a car – a 4WD can make the whole journey in about two hours, depending on the state of the road – or taking a tour from San Pedro (see opposite). At the visitor centre there are displays on the wildlife, trail maps, a dormitory (①) and a camping site.

The northwest coast: Omoa

North of San Pedro, Highway CA-5 clears the edges of the city to run through the flat agricultural lands of the Sula valley, amidst lush, tropical scenery. After 60km the road reaches the coast at **PUERTO CORTÉS**, Honduras's main port, where the unstinting heat and dilapidated wooden buildings merely add to the rough and ready feel of the place. There is nothing here to entice you to stop, but *Hotel y Restaurante Mr Ggeerr*, 9 C and 2 Av Este (☎555 0444; ④), has the best rooms in town should you need to stay. Incidentally, it's possible to travel from here by fast skiff to **Belize**, a weekly trip that takes around three hours to get to Dangriga (see p.101; for information, call Belize ☎05/23227).

It's in Puerto Cortés that you need to change buses for the excruciatingly slow 14km ride west to Omoa, one of the most peaceful of the north coast beach settlements. Buses leave hourly from the corner of 3 Av and 2 C Este, two blocks west of the parque central.

Omoa

Spreading inland from a deep bay, at the point where the mountains of the Sierra de Omoa meet the Caribbean, the fishing village of **OMOA** has become increasingly popular in recent years, with travellers coming here for a couple of days' total relaxation. At one time strategically important in the defence of the Spanish colonies against marauding British pirates, today the village dozes lethargically under the heat of the Caribbean sun. Its one outstanding sight, the restored **Fortaleza de San Fernando de Omoa** (Mon–Fri 8am–4pm, Sat & Sun 9am–5pm; US$1.50), stands mute witness to this colourful history. Now isolated amidst tropical greenery a kilometre from the coast, beached as the sea has receded over the centuries, the triangular fort was originally intended to protect the port of Puerto Barrios in Guatemala. Work began in 1759 but was never fully completed, due to a combination of bureaucratic inefficiency, problems with materials and labour shortage. The steadily weakening Spanish authorities then suffered the ignominy of witnessing the fortress temporarily occupied by British and Miskito military forces in October 1779.

The rather narrow village **beach**, lined with colourful fishing boats, offers stunning views west across the curve of the bay and the mountain backdrop. At weekends hordes of day-trippers turn up and it's often too crowded for comfort. Better swimming can be had by walking five minutes or so out of the village in either direction, while fifteen minutes around the headland to the east is a much wider, usually emptier expanse of beach.

Practicalities

Buses from Puerto Cortés enter the village at its southern end, before turning down to the beach front, about 2km away, passing the fortress and the **Hondutel** office on the way.

Rising numbers of foreign tourists have led to the opening of a handful of reasonably comfortable **places to stay**. Heading towards the beach from the Puerto Cortés road, you'll come to the comfortable, a/c *Hotel Geminis B* (②), and the Swiss-run *Rolli's and Berni's* (②), which offers rather more basic rooms with shared bath. By the waterfront, the *Bahía de Omoa* (④) has large, modern rooms, all with private bath and a/c, while the *Botin del Suizo* (①) restaurant rents out cheap and cheerful "backpacker rooms" with shared facilities. Eating is best done at the row of **champas** on the beachfront – small, palm-thatched restaurants serving well-cooked seafood and other dishes. Try the clean and friendly *Fisherman's Hut*, or *Champa Virginia*, where a substantial meal costs US$2–4.

Moving on from Omoa, adventurous souls can make the two-hour, invariably very wet boat journey over to Lívingston in **Guatemala**. Launches leave from the dock near the *Fisherman's Hut* every Tuesday and Friday, allegedly at noon, though only in good weather. Check the latest schedule at the *Botín del Suizo* and be sure to get there early; launches take up to ten passengers and the fare is US$25 one-way. Buses heading back to Puerto Cortés run until 6pm.

Tela and around

East of San Pedro, as highway CA-13 runs through fertile lowlands, serried ranks of banana trees extend for mile after endless mile. **La Lima**, 15km from San Pedro, is the definitive company town, headquarters for United Fruit ("Chiquita" brand) operations in Honduras. At **El Progreso**, a dusty town a further 15km east, the highway swings north to enter the stunning scenery of the **coast**.

With its magnificent natural setting, midway round the Bahía de Tela, **TELA** should be a dream getaway. Surrounded by sweeping beaches, the town is indeed a magnet for Hondurans and young European travellers alike; but this is no longer the safe, sleepy town it once was, and there's something of an undercurrent about the place that can either add to its charm or bring a sense of unease, depending on your point of view. However you feel about Tela itself, the wealth of fantastic natural reserves within just a few kilometres of town make it well worth a visit.

Arrival and information
There are no direct buses between San Pedro and central Tela; Cotraibal buses bound for La Ceiba and Trujillo stop along the highway outside town, from where taxis ferry passengers into the centre, five minutes away. The alternative is to take a bus to El Progreso, where you can change onto a local bus. Most local services, including the half-hourly buses to and from La Ceiba, use the terminal at 9 Av, 9 C NE, near the market; buses to the surrounding villages use the terminal close by at 8 Av, 10 C NE.

Hondutel and the **post office** are next to each other at 4 Av, 7–8 C NE, two blocks south of the parque central. For **changing money**, both Banmer and Banco Atlántida are right by the parque, with a casa de cambio, La Teleña, at 9 C and 4 Av NE. Garífuna Tours, 9 C and 5 Av NE (☎ & fax 448 2904), has a limited amount of **information** on what to do around Tela; it also runs good-value day **tours** to the nearby national parks and reserves, and has **bikes** for rent. **Prolansate**, the organization that manages Punta Sal and other reserves in the area, can help with information and advise on access; they're based at at 9 C, 3 Av NE (☎ & fax 448 2042).

Accommodation
Given Tela's resort status, there's an unexpectedly wide range of accommodation to choose from, including a couple of prime examples of the Honduran "beach front"

CRIME AND DRUGS ON THE NORTH COAST

Increasing use of drugs has led to a significant rise in crime rates in Tela and all along the north coast. Muggings, bag snatchings and personal attacks have all been reported and while chances are that nothing will happen to you, it's sensible to take some precautions. Make sure you are never visibly carrying large amounts of cash, or expensive looking bags or cameras; avoid walking around the centre of town late at night; and don't go onto the beach after dark – advice that holds for the whole of the north coast. Finally, in Tela particularly, you may well be approached by one of a small number of highly visible and persistent drugs "salesmen" – best advice is to steer well clear.

genre of architecture, where all the rooms face inland or onto internal corridors.

Bahía Azul, 2 Av, 11 C NE (☎448 2381). On the beach just west of the centre; you pay for the location but not the sea views (there aren't any). Rooms, some with TV, are comfortable, but lacking in character and rather overpriced. ④.

Mi Casa es su Casa B&B, 6 Av, 10–11 C NE. French-Canadian run place with well-furnished rooms in a private house. Shared bath and communal TV area, and the breakfasts (available to non-residents) make a welcome change from eggs. At the time of writing, the owners were due to open a second place. ④.

Presidente, 6 Av, 9 C NE (☎448 2821). Just off the parque central, this is one of the nicer hotels in town; spacious, amply furnished rooms, all with bath, a/c and TV. ④.

Puerto Rico, 5 Av, 11 C NE (☎448 2413). Another seafront special, where only six or so of the small, clean rooms, all with private bath, face the beach. Friendly management and Mickey Mouse sheets go some way to compensate. ③–④.

Tia Carmen, 8 C, 5 Av NE (☎448 2606). The best of the cheaper places in town; rooms are bright and the staff welcoming. ②.

Tela, 9 C, 4 Av NE (☎448 2150). A delightful, rambling, wooden building in the centre, probably slightly older than its owners, with large, clean rooms all with bath and fan. ②–③.

Villas Telamar, Tela Nueva (☎448 2196, fax 448 2984). Occupying what used to be executive housing for United Fruit employees, this idiosyncratic piece of luxury has wooden houses spread across shady grounds, a stretch of beautiful beachfront and facilities including a pool, tennis courts and 9-hole golf course. Individual rooms, plus villas sleeping up to 14. ⑦–⑨.

The Town

Today's Tela is a product of the banana industry. In the late nineteenth century United Fruit nominated what was then a backwater as its headquarters, and set about building a company town – **Tela Nueva** – on the west bank of the Río Tela; the old village became known as **Tela Vieja**. When the company removed its headquarters to La Lima in 1965, the town began to slip back into its former somnolence, although fortunes today have been somewhat restored by the growth in tourism.

The centre of Tela, encompassing the **parque central** and main shopping area, lies about 2km north of the highway and two blocks from the beach. To the west the seafront is lined with hotels, to the east with discos. Five blocks west from the parque central, the **Río Tela** divides the old town from Tela Nueva. A ten-minute stroll covers practically all the delights of downtown. One target to make for is the small **Museo Garífuna**, by the river on 8 C NE (Mon–Sat 8am–6pm; US$0.40), where lively exhibits covering all aspects of the Garífuna way of life, music and traditions are supplemented by a gift shop and a restaurant serving Garífuna food. However, it's the **beaches** that most people come for; those in Tela Vieja, though wide, are more crowded and consequently less clean than the stretch of pale sand in front of the *Villas Telamar*. Much better beaches can be found along the bay outside town.

Eating, drinking and nightlife

Tela has an interesting mix of **places to eat**, with foreign-run restaurants catering to the steady flow of European and North American visitors competing with locally owned seafood places. Most of the hotels along the beach also have terrace restaurants, facing out across the water. One staple that should not be missed is the delicious and addictive *pan de coco* (coconut bread) sold by Garífuna women and children on the beach and around town.

Tela has a thriving weekend **nightlife**, when the cluster of discos by the beach at the east end of the town boom out salsa, reggae and Euro-bop until the small hours; be aware, though, that the atmosphere has been known to get rather rough at times. Out on the beachfront road, east from the parque, *Caribbean Port* and *La Gaviota* are both popular dance halls; more relaxed is *El Submarino*, where you can eat as well as drink; nearby, the *Happy Port* puts on regular live music. For a more tranquil drink with a view, try the *Delfín Telamar* at the *Villas Telamar*, or the restaurant at the *Hotel Puerto Rico*. Finally, check out details of events at the Museo Garífuna, which regularly organizes evenings of Garífuna music and dancing.

Cesar Marisco's, on the beach at 3 Av NE. Renowned for the quality of its seafood, in particular the *sopa de caracol* (conch soup), of which a more than adequate serving costs US$5. The outdoor eating area makes a nice place to relax in the evenings.

Jardín Corona, on the parque central. Cheap and straightforward Honduran fare; breakfasts are particularly good value. Closes at 7pm Mon–Sat, 3pm on Sun.

Luces del Norte, 11 C, 5 Av NE. Very popular with foreign tourists, the menu has a good range of seafood dishes. Food can be slow in coming, so while away the time reading a book from the book exchange.

Restaurante Casa Azul, 11 C, 6 Av NE. Snug place tucked into the ground floor of an old house. The Italian menu features pasta and meat dishes, and there's also a small bar serving drinks. A substantial meal and drinks will set you back about US$9.

Restaurante Puerto Rico, in the *Hotel Puerto Rico*. Large covered terrace with views across the beach and water. The usual range of Honduran standards and seafood dishes, well-prepared.

Tuty Tuty, 9 C NE, just off the parque central. Huge breakfasts and excellent juices; worth the inevitably long wait. Closes 7pm.

Around Tela

Even for those whose initial reaction to Tela is aversion, the town redeems itself with an abundance of places to visit in the vicinity. On either side of town, along the bay, are **Garífuna villages**, more relaxed and friendly than Tela itself and sited along pristine beaches. The **wildlife reserves** of Punta Sal, to the west, and Punta Izopo, to the east, shelter a range of wildlife and flora, whilst Lancetilla, 5km south of town, is probably the finest **botanical reserve** in Latin America. For getting to all of these places you can take taxis or rely on local buses, but renting a bike is probably the most enjoyable way to get around.

The Garífuna villages

Heading **west** from Tela, a dirt road edges along the bay between the seafront and the Laguna de los Micos, forming the eastern edge of Punta Sal (see opposite). Seven kilometres along this road is the sleepy Garífuna village of **TORNABÉ** and, beyond, **MIAMI**, set on a fabulous stretch of beach at the mouth of the lagoon. Miami in particular is unique, consisting of nothing other than traditional palm-thatched huts; Tornabé has a few brick-built houses. Formal accommodation is limited to *The Last Resort* in Tornabé (☎ & fax 448 2545; ⑥), an idyllic getaway with small, comfortable cabins and an excellent restaurant; the hotel rents boats for exploring the lagoon. **Buses** run from Tela's marketplace to Tornabé several times a day until late afternoon; from here, catch one of the three daily (Mon–Sat) pick-ups that continue up to Miami, where asking around will secure a place to camp or sling a hammock. Weekends are the best time to visit, when you'll get to witness performances of Garífuna music – haunting and melodic drum-driven rhythms clearly reflecting an African influence.

Some 7km **east** along the bay from Tela, the village of **TRIUNFO DE LA CRUZ** occupies the site of the first **Spanish settlement** on the mainland. Cristóbal de Olid landed here on May 3, 1524, but the colony was abandoned within a few months and the area not resettled until the Garífuna began arriving at the end of the eighteenth century. Basic accommodation is available, and a couple of small restaurants serve good seafood. The scenic walk along the beach from Tela takes around two hours, passing the smaller village of **LA ENSENADA** on the way; it is not advisable – especially for women – to walk alone or to take anything valuable with you. Intensive tourist development is mooted for the area around the village, but as yet the expanses of palm-fringed beach stretching away to either side remain untouched.

Punta Sal and Punta Izopo

The **Parque Nacional Janet Kawas** (daily 6am–4pm; free), commonly known as **Punta Sal**, is a wonderfully diverse reserve encompassing mangrove swamps, coastal lagoons, wetlands, coral reef and tropical forest, which together provide habitats for a extraordinary range of animal, bird and plant life. Lying to the west of Tela, curving along the bay to the headland of Punta Sal, the reserve covers three lagoons: Laguna de Micos, Laguna Tisnachí in the centre of the reserve and the oceanfront Laguna el Diamante, on the western side of the headland. Over one hundred species of bird are present here, including herons and storks, with seasonal migratory visitors bumping up the numbers; amongst the animals inhabiting the reserve are howler and white-faced monkeys, wild pigs, jaguars and, in the marine sections, manatees and marine turtles. **Boat trips** along the Río Ulúa and the canals running through the reserve offer a superb opportunity to view the wildlife at close quarters. Where the headland curves up to the north, the land rises slightly to the point of Punta Sal (176m); a trail over the point leads to small, pristine beaches at either side.

It is possible to visit parts of Punta Sal **independently** by renting a boat in Miami to explore the Laguna de los Micos and surrounding area. There is also a scenic eight-kilometre walk from the village to the headland, along the beach. For information on the reserve and getting there, contact **Prolansate**, 9 C, 3 Av NE in Tela (☎ & fax 448 2042), the non-governmental organization that manages Punta Sal and other reserves in the area. Janet Kawas, after whom the reserve is named, was a former president of Prolansate, instrumental in obtaining protected status against intense local opposition. Her murder, in April 1995, has never been solved. Garífuna Tours in Tela run reasonably priced **guided day-trips** to Punta Sal, and also to the **Refugio de Vida Silvestre Punta Izopo**, the much smaller wetlands reserve facing Punta Sal at the eastern end of the Bahía de Tela.

Jardín Botánico de Lancetilla

The extensive grounds of the **Jardín Botánico de Lancetilla** (Mon–Fri 7.30am–3pm, Sat & Sun 8am–3pm; US$3.80), 5km south of Tela, started life in 1925 as a United Fruit species research and testing station, handling initially bananas and later fruit and plants from all over the world. Now managed by COHDEFOR, the reserve has grown into one of the largest collections of fruit and flowering trees, palms, hardwoods and tropical plants in Latin America. Within Lancetilla's boundaries are an arboretum, a still-functioning research station and a biological reserve, the last – covering two-thirds of the total grounds – containing one of the only remaining stretches of virgin, tropical wet forest on the Atlantic coast. The stability of the environment has also encouraged numerous species of birds to make their home here.

To **get to** Lancetilla, take the San Pedro highway for a couple of kilometres to the signposted turnoff heading south, from where it is a further 3km. Guided tours of the arboretum are available, and visitors are also free to wander at will along the marked trails; maps are available at the visitor centre. You need a whole day to visit the arboretum and then cross the reserves, through bamboo groves to some small **swimming holes** on the Río Lancetilla. At the visitor centre there's a comedor and a small **hostel** (①); beds should be reserved through Prolansate in Tela.

La Ceiba

One hundred kilometres east along the coast, **LA CEIBA**, the lively capital of the department of Atlántida, is a far more appealing prospect than Tela. Set beneath the green, thickly forested slopes of the Cordillera Nombre de Dios, this is the largest city on the north coast, bustling and self-assured by day, while at night townsfolk and visitors alike gather to sample the excellent nightlife for which the city is renowed across the country. Things really come to a head during La Ceiba's **Carnaval** in May, when 200,000 revellers descend on the town.

Like Tela, La Ceiba owes its existence to the **banana** industry: the Vaccaro Bros (later Standard Fruit and now Dole) first laid plantations in the area in 1899 and set up their company headquarters in town in 1905. Although fruit is no longer shipped out through La Ceiba, the plantations are still important to the local economy, with crops of pineapple and african palm now as significant as bananas.

Though for many travellers La Ceiba is no more than a stopoff en route to the Bay Islands (see p.417), there are some good beaches just ten kilometres or so outside town. Alternatively, with more time and a little planning – or the services of a tour operator – you can explore the cloudforest of the nearby Parque Nacional Pico Bonito or the mangrove swamps of the Refugio Vida Silvestre (see p.410).

Arrival and information

Long-distance and local **buses** arrive at the main terminal, 2km west of the centre; taxis downtown, usually shared, charge US$0.50 per person. Those arriving by **air** will find themselves at **Aeropuerto Internacional Golosón**, 9km west of the centre, off the highway to Tela. From the airport, the taxi fare into the centre is US$3, around half that if you flag one down on the highway, where you can also pick up buses heading into the city. La Ceiba is the main jumping off point for the Bay Islands (covered in the following chapter): the ferry service to and from Roatán and Guanaja uses the **Muralla de Cabotaje** municipal dock, about 5km to the east of the city – taxis charge US$2 per person.

If you're contemplating a trip to the Mosquitia (see p.413), it's worthwhile visiting the La Ceiba office of **Mopawi**, the Mosquitia development organization. Based in the line of shops at the end of Av República, just south of the old dock, the office has leaflets on projects being run in the region. Several **tour operators** organize trips to Mosquitia and Pico Bonito, both of which require considerable time and effort to reach independently; see the listings on p.409 for recommended companies. **FUCSA**, which manages the Refugio de Vida Silvestre Cuero y Salado (see p.410), has an office in the Edificio Ferrocarril Nacional, two blocks west of the parque central (Mon–Fri 8–11.30am & 1.30–4.30pm, Sat 8–11.30am; ☎ & fax 443 0329).

Accommodation

Given La Ceiba's status, both as provincial and party centre, there is a wide range of **places to stay**. The only problem will be in deciding whether you want to be near the centre, or closer to the nightlife along 1 C. Prices inevitably tend to rise around Carnaval time in May, when reserving ahead becomes essential.

Colonial, Av 14 de Julio, 6–7 C (☎443 1953, fax 443 1955). One of the more upmarket places and a good deal for the price. Rooms all have bath, TV and phone, and facilities include a good restaurant, a bar and a sauna. ④.

Dan's Hotel, C 3, Barrio la Isla (☎ & fax 443 4219). Very friendly and quiet family-run place in a private house. The rooms, all with bath, are comfortable and some have TV. The owners cook breakfasts and other meals on request. ③–④.

Gran Hotel Paris, parque central (☎443 2391, fax 443 1614). A central landmark and still considered to be the classiest place in town, although now a little past its heyday. Rooms all have a/c, phone and TV and there is a pool, a quiet bar and restaurant. ⑤.

Iberia, Av San Isidro, 5–6 C (☎443 0401). A very friendly place and a bargain for the price. The rooms with a balcony overlooking the street are the nicest, but all have bath, a/c and TV. ③.

Italia, Av 14 de Julio next to the *Colonial* (☎443 0150). Rooms are large and clean, but somewhat sparsely furnished; all have bath, however, and the place is secure. ②.

Partenon Beach, 1 C, Av Bonilla, Barrio la Isla (☎443 0404, fax 443 0434). A somewhat eclectic place with a great beachfront location at the eastern edge of town. Room prices vary depending on whether they're a/c or not and in the old or new building. There is a good restaurant, outdoor bar and a pool, though the water is not changed with great frequency. ④–⑤.

Plaza Flamingo, 1 C, Av 14 de Julio (☎443 3149). Modern place with a friendly management, right in the centre of the Zona Viva. The large rooms have well-kept bathrooms, a/c, TV and fridge, but only a few have seaviews. ④.

Rotterdam, 1 C, Av Barahona, Barrio la Isla (☎443 2859). New Dutch-run hotel, just up from the beach. Adequate rooms, all with bath, are good value for the price. ②.

The Town

Most things of interest to visitors lie within a relatively small area of the city, around the shady and pleasant **parque central**, six or so blocks back from the seafront. The unremarkable cathedral sits on the southeast corner, the *Gran Hotel Paris* on the northern edge. Running north from the parque almost to the seafront Av San Isidro, Av Atlántida and Av 14 de Julio form the main commercial district, lined with shops, banks and a couple of supermarkets. The main general **market** sprawls along the streets around the old wooden market building on Av Atlántida.

Night action takes place along 1 C, which parallels the length of the seafront. Nicknamed the "Zona Viva" due to the preponderance of bars and clubs, 1 C extends west from the old dock and over the river estuary into **Barrio la Isla**, a quieter residential district, mainly home to Garífuna, once it leaves the seafront.

All the **beaches** within the city limits are, sadly, too polluted and dirty for even the most desperate to want to brave the rough water. Better by far is to head east to the much cleaner beaches a few kilometres out of town (see overleaf).

Eating, drinking and entertainment

Not for nothing does La Ceiba have a reputation as the place to party. The **Zona Viva** hums every night of the week, with a profusion of places to drink, dance and be merry. A steady trickle of tourists and a growing number of resident ex-pats, both in front of and behind the bar, have helped to create a buoyant, distinctly non-threatening, international atmosphere. While the range of **places to eat** is not quite as extensive, excellently prepared Honduran and European food is not hard to find; restaurants generally stop serving at around 10pm. For nominally more cerebral entertainment, the **cinema**, just off the parque central, shows the usual subtitled Hollywood fare.

If you can make it, the most exciting time to be in La Ceiba is **Carnaval**, a week-long bash held every May to celebrate the city's patron saint, San Isidro. Dances and street events in various barrios around town culminate in an afternoon parade on the third Saturday of the month. Led by a float carrying the Carnaval Queen, the parade moves slowly down the gaudily decked Av San Isidro. Bands on stages placed along the avenida then compete to outplay each other throughout the evening and into the early hours.

The 200,000 or so partygoers who attend Carnaval every year flock between the stages and the clubs on 1 C where the dancing continues until dawn.

RESTAURANTS AND CAFÉS

Café Cobal, 7 C, Av San Isidro. A fast-turnaround place serving breakfasts and lunch, mainly to office workers. The food is good, as are the juices, and the portions large.

Café Le Jardín, Av la Bastilla 767, near the Esso station. French-run bistro with seating in the garden, serving what's possibly the best food in Honduras. Steak and the chicken in cream sauce are particularly recommended. The wine list, featuring plenty of South American wines, is equally good. Two courses with wine cost around US$16 per person.

Café Tropical, Av Atlántida, 4–5 C. Cheerful café serving from early morning to around 10pm. Good pollo frito features heavily in the daily set menus.

Centro Cultural Satuye, 4 C, Av Herrera, Barrio la Isla. Light-hearted and informal Garífuna restaurant. Loud live music in the evenings.

Cri Cri Burger, Av 14 de Julio, 3 C. Good burgers, steak sandwiches and other snacks to the accompaniment of at times deafening music; the side tables are a good place to watch comings and goings in the street.

Expatriate's Bar and Grill, 12 C, 2 blocks east of Av San Isidro. Airy, North-American owned thatched bar with a good range of vegetarian, chicken and meat dishes. Popular with resident foreigners and a good source of local information. Mon & Thurs–Sun 4pm–midnight.

Restaurante Elvir, Av San Isidro beneath the *Iberia*. New place tucked away in a little courtyard and serving reasonably good pizza and pasta, as well as burgers and sandwiches. Closed Sun.

Restaurante Palace, Av 14 de Julio, 8 C. Big barn of a place serving deliciously authentic Chinese dishes.

La Casa, 9 C, Av San Isidro–Av 14 de Julio. One of the nicest restaurants in the centre, with tables set around an open courtyard. Wide range of Honduran food, with main courses costing around US$6.

La Concha, 1 C, 3 blocks east of the river. Laid-back German-owned restaurant with a meat-heavy menu; the potato soup is excellent.

Pupuseria Salvadoreña Tonita, Barrio la Isla opposite the *Parthenon Beach*. Unpretentious and friendly; a good place to grab a few quick *pupusas* – small Salvadorean tortillas filled with cheese, beans or meat, or a combination – and chat.

BARS AND CLUBS

African Dani's, 1 C, 2 blocks east of the river, Barrio la Isla. A Garífuna dance hall, with live music and dancing most nights of the week.

Bar el Canadiense, Av 14 de Julio at 1 C. A relaxed French-Canadian-owned bar attracting a good mix of locals, resident foreigners and tourists. The pool table is always popular and the music is eclectic.

Cherry's, on the beach at the end of Av 14 de Julio. A popular club, open all week and packed at the weekend. Plays a mixture of Latin American rhythms, reggae and country music.

Deutsch Australien Club, Av 14 de Julio at the beach. A quiet bar for mellow drinking and conversation.

D'Lidos, on 1 C just east of the river in Barrio la Isla. Just as loud and just as popular as *Cherry's*.

Safari, opposite *D'Lidos*. Another popular club, attracting a predominantly local crowd.

Zanzibar, 1 C at Av 14 de Julio. The dark interior of this bar plays European rock turned up high; the stools on the street in front are good for people-watching.

Listings

Airlines On the parque central are Isleña (☎443 2683), Sosa (☎443 1399) and Taca (☎443 1915); all three also have ticket desks at the airport, as do Rollins Air (☎443 4181) and Caribbean Air (☎445 1933).

Banks Banco Atlántida and Credomatic, among others, are located on Av San Isidro and Av Atlántida.

Car rental Molinari, *Gran Hotel Paris* (☎443 2391, fax 443 0055).

Immigration Av 14 Julio, 1–2 C.

Laundry Lavandería Plaza Copán, Av San Isidro, and Lavandería 2001, Barrio la Isla.

Police ☎448 0241.

Post office Av Morazán and 13 C, south of the parque.

Telephone office Hondutel, at Av Ramón Rosa, 5–6 C, is open 24hr.

Tour operators For trips to Pico Bonito and La Mosquitia, try one of the following: La Moskitia Ecoaventuras, Av 14 de Julio at 1 C (☎442 0104); Euro Honduras Tours, Av Atlántida at 1 C (☎443 3893, fax 443 0933); La Ceiba Eco Tours, Av San Isidro at 1 C (☎443 4420). La Moskitia Eco-Lodge, Plaza Aurora (☎440 0076, fax 440 0077), has 3- to 7-day packages to Mosquitia. Harry's Horse Back Tours, contacted through the *Bar el Canadiense*, organizes horse-riding in Pico Bonito.

Around La Ceiba

Easy to reach as day-trips from the city are the broad sandy **beaches** and clean water at Playa de Perú and the village of Sambo Creek, both a short distance east along the coast. A trip to explore the **cloudforest** within the Parque Nacional Pico Bonito requires more planning, although the eastern edge of the reserve, formed by the Río Cangrejal, is more easily accessible, offering opportunities for swimming and white-water **rafting**.

The beaches: Playa de Perú and Sambo Creek

Ten kilometres east of the city, **Playa de Perú** is a wide sweep of clean sand that's pop-ular at weekends. Any bus running east up the coast will drop you at the turnoff on the highway, from where it's a fifteen-minute walk to the beach. About 2km past the turning for Playa de Perú, on the Río María, there's a series of **waterfalls** and **natural pools** set in lush, shady forest. A path leads from Río Maria village on the highway, winding through the hills along the left bank of the river: it takes around thirty minutes to walk to the first cascade and pool, with some sections muddy and a bit of a scramble during the wet season.

There are further deserted expanses of white sand at the friendly Garífuna village of **SAMBO CREEK**, 8km beyond Río Maria. You can eat excellent fresh fish at a couple of restaurants in the village; there's also a small, basic hotel (①). Olanchito or Jutiapa buses from La Ceiba will drop you at the turnoff to Sambo Creek on the highway, a cou-ple of kilometres from the village; slower buses run all the way to the village centre from La Ceiba's terminal every 45 minutes.

Parque Nacional Pico Bonito

Directly south of La Ceiba, the Cordillera Nombre de Dios shelters the **Parque Nacional Pico Bonito** (daily 6am–4pm; US$2.30), a remote expanse of tropical broadleaf forest, cloudforest and – in its southern reaches, above the Río Aguan valley – pine forest. Taking its name from the awe-inspiring bulk of Pico Bonito (2435m) itself, the park is the source of twenty rivers, including the Zacate, Bonito and Cangrejal, which cascade majestically down the steeply, thickly covered slopes, and provides sanctuary for an abundance of wildlife including armadillos, howler and spi-der monkeys, pumas and tigrillos. Inevitably this abundance is due in large part to the inaccessibility of much of the park. The lower fringes are the most easily penetrable, with a small number of trails laid out through the dense greenery. Best is the four- to five-hour circular walk that winds, steeply in sections, up through the tree cover to a lookout over the Caribbean. Tour companies in La Ceiba operate day and overnight trips to Pico Bonito, from around US$40 per person (see p.409).

The **Río Cangrejal**, forming the eastern boundary of the park, boasts some of the best Class III and IV rapids in Central America; **whitewater rafting trips** are organized by some the tour companies listed on p.409. For the adventurous, there are also some magnificent swimming spots, backed by gorgeous mountain scenery along the river valley. About 2km east of La Ceiba, a dirt road turns off the highway and heads south along the valley. *Balneario las Mangas*, about 12km from the highway, has small cabins for rent (③); there are a couple of buses a day but it's quicker to hitch.

Refugio de Vida Silvestre Cuero y Salado

Thirty kilometres west from La Ceiba, the **Refugio de Vida Silvestre Cuero y Salado** (daily 7am–4pm; US$10) is one of the last substantial remnants of wetlands and mangrove swamps along the north coast. The reserve is home to a large number of animal and bird species, many endangered, including manatees, jaguars, howler and white-faced monkeys, sea turtles, hawks, along with seasonal influxes of migratory birds. Though nominally protected since 1987, the edges of the reserve are under constant pressure from local farmers wishing to drain land for new pastures.

The best way to see the reserve is to take a **guided tour**, not least because the guides know the spots where you're likely to see some wildlife. **FUCSA**, the body that manages the reserve, has an office in La Ceiba (see p.406) and runs regular tours (US$10 per boat), which you need to book in advance. There is also a small hostel at the reserve if you wish to stay (reserve through FUCSA; ①).

To get to the reserve **independently**, catch an hourly bus from La Ceiba's terminal to the village of La Unión, 20km or so west. From here, you can either make your way on foot through the fruit plantations – it takes around an hour and a half to walk the 8km – or travel by *burra*, a flat, poled railcar, along the railway tracks. The last bus back to La Ceiba leaves La Unión mid-afternoon.

Trujillo

Perched above the sparkling waters of the palm-fringed Bahía de Trujillo, with the green backdrop of Cordillera Nombre de Dios rearing up behind, **TRUJILLO** immediately seduces the small number of tourists who make the 90km trip here from La Ceiba. Though you'd never guess it from the town's sleepy demeanour, this is an important city, capital of the department of Colón. All the elements for a relaxing stay are in place – warm, sheltered waters, clean beaches, and a good range of hotels and restaurants – and having endured the four-hour journey from La Ceiba, few are in a hurry to leave.

The area around Trujillo was settled by a mixture of Pech, Tolupan and Maya groups when Columbus first disembarked on the American mainland here, on August 14, 1502. Trujillo itself was founded by Cortés's lieutenant, Juan de Medina, in May 1525, though it was regularly abandoned due to attacks by European pirates. Not until the late eighteenth century did repopulation begin in earnest, aided by the arrival, via Roatán, of several hundred Garífuna from the island of St Vincent. In 1860, a new threat appeared, in the shape of the US filibuster William Walker, who in June of that year briefly took control of the town; executed in September 1860 by the Honduran authorities, he is buried in Trujillo's cemetery. The twentieth century has been distinctly less eventful; there's far more activity these days at **Puerto Castilla**, at the eastern end of the bay, the busy port through which passes the produce of the region's plantations.

Arrival and information

Buses enter Trujillo from the east, passing an airstrip, crossing over the Río Negro at the bottom of the hill and terminating at the top in the parque central. The town proper stretches south up the hill from here; north, a sloping path leads down to the seafront, which is lined with palm-thatched *champas*. Very few of the streets are signposted. Bancahsa and Banco de Occidente have branches one block west of the parque, with the small general market just to the south. **Hondutel** and the **post office** are next to each other three blocks south from the southeast corner of the parque and there is a small **immigration office** one block south and three blocks west of the parque. One kilometre south of town, up the hillside, Turtle Tours (☎ & fax 434 4431), based in the *Villas Brinkley*, organizes day tours to local attractions.

Accommodation

There's plenty of **accommodation** to choose from in the town centre, close to the restaurants and bars, plus a couple of excellent places in glorious settings just outside town. However, since Trujillo has never really featured on the tourist trail, there are fewer rock-bottom cheapies than in La Ceiba or Tela.

Campamento Hotel & Restaurant, on the beach 4km west of town (☎434 4244, fax 434 4200). Comfortable, wooden cabañas are scattered through extensive grounds reaching down to the beach; an idyllic setting, with an open-air restaurant serving well-prepared seafood and other dishes. ④–⑤.

Hotel Colonial, just south of the parque (☎434 4011). Well-situated hotel, with big beds and bath, a/c and TV in all rooms, though the downstairs ones are rather dark. The management could do with a little customer service training. ④.

Cristopher Colombus Hotel, on the beach by the airstrip (☎434 4966, fax 434 4971). A large, green architectural curiosity, redeemed by its location – though from the outside you might say it ruins the beach. Patronized by wealthy Hondurans, its facilities include a pool and tennis courts. ⑥–⑧.

Hotel Emperador, by the market (☎434 4446). One of the nicest cheaper places, with clean rooms set round a courtyard; all have bath and fan. ②.

O'Glynn, 3 blocks south and 1 east of the parque (☎434 4592). Recently refurbished, friendly place; large clean rooms, all with bath and TV. ④.

Villas Brinkley, on the hillside, 1km south of town (☎434 4444 or 434 4545). Possibly the nicest hotel in Honduras, with a relaxed, welcoming ambience. A variety of tastefully furnished rooms all have bath and some have a/c; there are superb views from the terrace over the whole stretch of the bay and its glistening waters. The hotel also has a pool and the restaurant is a good place to come for a meal even if you're not staying here. ③–④.

The Town

The town proper stretches back five or so blocks south of the **parque central**, which is just fifty metres from the sea cliffs. On the northeast edge of the parque is the sixteenth-century **Fortaleza de Santa Bárbara** (daily 8am–noon & 1–4pm; US$0.07), the site of Walker's execution. Low-lying and built of dark stone, it hangs gloomily on the edge of the bluffs, overlooking the coastline it was singularly unsuccessful in defending against pirate attack.

Much of Trujillo's charm lies in meandering through the rather scruffy streets of the town, where the heat of the sun is alleviated by a constant breeze. Southwest from the centre, a couple of blocks past the market, is the **cementerio viejo**. Here, amid at times floridly decorated memorials to the town's dead, you can find Walker's grave. Turn right past the cemetery and a ten-minute stroll brings you to the privately run **Museo Arqueológico de Trujillo** (daily 7am–5pm; US$0.75), a somewhat eccentric collection of junk, amongst which are buried a few interesting pre-Columbian ceramics. Behind the building are a couple of small, moss-surrounded river pools in which to bathe. Back at the parque central, walk west for ten minutes and you'll reach the **Barrio Cristales**, the site of the first mainland Garífuna settlement, founded in 1797. The Gari Arte shop here stocks Garífuna handicrafts and music tapes.

Trujillo's outstanding feature by far are its **beaches**, long stretches of almost pristine sand. The glorious sweep of the Bahía de Trujillo is as yet unaffected by excessive tourist development and its calm, blue waters are perfect for effortless swimming. The beaches below town, lined with *champas,* are clean enough, but the stretches to the east, beyond the airstrip, are emptier. It is possible to walk east along the beach to the reserve of **Laguna de Guaimoreto** or west to the Garífuna village of **Santa Fe** – see opposite.

Eating, drinking and entertainment

First choice of **places to eat** are the informal *champa* bar-restaurants on the beach, where you can dine in the warm evening air, listening to the waves. The main cluster is on the beach below town, with another group to the east by the airstrip, about twenty minutes' walk away – note that it's highly inadvisable to walk back along the beach after dark.

Later on in the evening, *Disco Tropical* in the centre of town heaves at the weekends to Latin American rhythms, while the *Black and White* on the beach in Barrio Cristales attracts a mainly Garífuna crowd. Both venues are generally pretty relaxed, although trouble is occasionally reported.

Bahía Bar, on the beach by the airstrip. Long-established, foreign-owned beach *champa* with a wide menu of seafood, good juices and sandwiches.

Café Oasis, southwest off the parque. The leafy courtyard setting and the welcome relief of a vegetarian menu, as well as good juices, don't quite excuse the occasionally appalling service. The book exchange gives you something to do until your food arrives.

Gringo's Bar, next to the *Bahía*. Everything a tropical beachside bar should be; the breakfasts are good, the food well cooked and the atmosphere easy-going.

Papa Jack Café and Salon, 2 blocks southwest of the parque. A place to have a quick drink more than anything, but the sandwiches and other snacks are reasonably priced.

Restaurante Lempira, at the *Villas Brinkley* above town. Fabulous views, while you feast on well-cooked European and Honduran dishes; walk it off on the stroll back to town.

Pizza Pantry, 2 blocks southwest of the parque. As well as reasonable pizza, the broad menu includes seafood, steaks and breakfasts.

Rincón de los Amigos, on the beach below town. A friendly *champa* serving excellent seafood in a relaxed atmosphere. Live Garífuna music at weekends.

Around Trujillo

Expanses of white-sand **beach** stretch for miles around the bay from Trujillo, all clean, wide and perfect for gentle swimming; don't take anything valuable with you, though, and don't venture onto them after dark. Walking east from town along the beach, for 5km or so, you come to the **Laguna de Guaimoreto**, a small reserve of mangrove swamps that is home to thousands of migratory birds, monkeys and other wildlife. Heading **west** from Trujillo, a two-hour, 10km walk brings you to the

Garífuna village of **SANTA FE**. Even more relaxed than Trujillo, its beach is not as attractive, but the *Comedor Caballero*, a simple place serving exquisite local seafood, is a good enough reason to come here; there is also a very basic hotel (②) in the village. A dirt road connects Santa Fe with Trujillo, travelled by three buses a day in either direction.

On the other side of the mountain peaks directly above Trujillo lies the dark green swathe of **Parque Nacional Capiro y Calentura** (daily 6am–5pm), a reserve of tropical and subtropical rainforest. Huge cedars and pines tower amid the thick canopy of ferns and flowering plants and vines, many of them used for medicinal purposes. Following the devastation brought by Hurricane Fifi in 1974, much of the cover is secondary growth, but it still provides a secure habitat for howler monkeys, reptiles and a colourful range of birdlife and butterflies. You can walk into the reserve following the dirt road past the *Villas Brinkley*, which winds, increasingly steeply, up Cerro Calentura to the radio towers just below the summit, a total of 10km. The walk's best done in the relative cool of early morning; alternatively, you could negotiate with a taxi driver to take you to the top and then walk down.

Taking a hot bath in the heat of the Caribbean may not strike everyone as an appealing thought, but soaking in the clean and very hot mineral waters of the **Aguas Calientes** springs (daily 7am–9pm; US$2.30), 7km inland from Trujillo, feels delightfully decadent. The experience can be topped of with a drink at the bar of the rather slick *Agua Caliente* hotel in the grounds (☎434 4249; ⑤). Any bus heading to Tocoa will drop you off at the entrance to the springs; buses stop running at around 6.30pm.

The Mosquitia

Honduras's northeast corner is made up of the remote and sparsely populated expanse of La Mosquitia. Bounded to the west by the mountain ranges of the Río Plátano and Colón mountain ranges, with the Río Coco forming the border with Nicaragua to the south, this vast region comprises almost a fifth of Honduras's territory. With just two peripheral roads, and a tiny population divided among a few far-flung towns and villages, entering the Mosquitia really does mean leaving the beaten track.

To the surprise of many who come here expecting to have to hack their way through jungle, much of the Mosquitia is composed of marshy coastal wetlands and flat savannah – likened by some to the landscape of South Carolina. The small communities of **Palacios** and **Brus Laguna** are access points for the **Río Plátano Biosphere Reserve**, set up to protect one of the finest remaining stretches of virgin tropical rainforest in Central America. **Puerto Lempira**, to the east, is the regional capital.

The largest ethnic group inhabiting the Mosquitia are the **Miskitos**, numbering around 30,000, who speak a distinct language. There are much smaller indigenous communities of **Pech**, who number around 2500, and **Tawahka** (Sumu), of whom there are under a thousand, living around the Río Patuca.

Some history

Before the Spanish arrived, the Mosquitia belonged to the Pech and Sumu. Initial contact with Europeans was comparatively benign, the Spanish showing slight interest in the area, preferring to concentrate on the mineral-rich lands of the interior. Contact with Europeans intensified when the **British** began seeking a foothold on the mainland in the seventeenth century, establishing settlements on the coast at Black River (now

Palacios) and Brewer's Lagoon (Brus Laguna), whose inhabitants – the so-called "shoremen" – engaged in logging, trading, smuggling and fighting the Spanish.

Britain's claim to Mosquitia, nominally to protect the shoremen, but more profitably to ensure a transit route from the Atlantic to the Pacific, supposedly ended in 1786, when all Central American territories, except Belize, were ceded to the Spanish. In the 1820s, however, taking advantage of post-independence chaos, Britain again encouraged settlement on the Mosquito Coast and by 1844 had all but formally announced a protectorate in the area. Not until 1859 and the British-American Treaty of Cruz Wyke did Britain formally end all claims to Mosquitia.

The initial impact of *mestizo* Honduran culture on Mosquitia was slight. Since the creation of the administrative department of Gracias a Dios in 1959, however, indigenous cultures have become gradually diluted: Spanish is now the main language and the government encourages *mestizo* settlers to migrate there in search of land. Pech, Miskito and Garífuna communities have become more vocal in recent years in demanding respect for their cultural differences and in calling for an expansion of health, education and transport infrastructures.

Planning a trip

A number of companies, based in San Pedro, La Ceiba and Tegucigalpa (see the relevant sections for details), offer a variety of **tours** to Mosquitia. The advantages of an organized tour are that all the planning is done for you and you can count on being accompanied by knowledgeable guides. Travelling independently is by no means impossible, though, so long as you're prepared to go with the flow. **Transport** to and within the area is mainly by air or river: the main centres of **Puerto Lempira**, **Palacios**, **Brus Laguna** and **Ahuas** are connected to La Ceiba by regular flights, while launches ply the waterways connecting the scattered villages. **Accommodation** and facilities are basic; if you're making an independent trek, bring enough food with you for your party and guides. Finally, bear in mind that all schedules are subject to change and delay; transport on the rivers and channels, in particular, is determined by how much rain has fallen.

Air fares to the Mosquitia are standardized. From La Ceiba, a return ticket to Palacios costs US$35, to Puerto Lempira US$45 and to Brus Laguna US$50. Once in the Mosquitia, **boat** fares are relatively high, reflecting the need to import all fuel. Hiring a boat to get from the coast to Las Marías will cost at least US$100, not including food for the guides.

Visiting the reserve: Palacios, Las Marías, Brus Laguna and Ahuas

Sited on what was the British settlement of Black River, **PALACIOS** lies just west of one of the reserve's three coastal lagoons, Laguna Ibans. Served by regular flights to and from La Ceiba, this is frequently the starting point for organized trips to the Río Plátano Biosphere Reserve and a logical place for independent travellers to set out from. Adequate **rooms** (②) can be had in the hotel run by local whizzkid Don Felix Marmol, who is also the Isleña agent.

Getting to the heart of the Río Plátano reserve requires travelling up the Río Plátano to the small village of **LAS MARÍAS**, about seven hours upstream from the coast, where the virgin jungle cover begins. There are two basic hospedajes in the village (both ①), both serving meals. Boats to Las Marías can be hired in the coastal villages of **Belén**, on the outer edge of Laguna Ibans, a one-hour launch ride from Palacios, and in **Barra Plátano**, a two-hour walk east from Belén along the beach. Rooms can be found in either village by asking around. In Las Marías you can hire a guide to explore the river and surrounding jungle for US$5–10 a day.

Thirty kilometres east along the coast from Palacios, on the southeastern edge of the Laguna de Brus, is the friendly Miskito town of **BRUS LAGUNA**. A basic hospedaje here serves for the relatively few visitors who make it this far. Regular **flights** connect the town with La Ceiba. Guides and boats can be hired for multi-day trips, exploring up the Río Sigre (or Sikre), into the southern reaches of the Río Plátano reserve.

A little under 40km from Brus Laguna as the crow flies is the Miskito village of **AHUAS**, scattered across the savannah. The village is only a kilometre from the Río Patuca, which forms the border of the Río Plátano reserve, and narrow cargo boats take passengers on the four-hour trip upriver to Barra Patuca on the coast. Rooms can be found by asking around near the airstrip.

The Río Plátano Biosphere Reserve

The **Río Plátano Biosphere Reserve** is the most significant reserve in Honduras, sheltering an estimated eighty percent of all the country's animal species. Visitors usually come here to experience the jungle, a swathe of tropical rainforest; yet within its boundaries – from the Caribbean in the north to the Montañas de Punta Piedra in the west and the Río Patuca in the south – the reserve also covers huge expanses of coastal wetlands and flat savannah grasslands. Sadly, even international recognition of the importance of this diverse ecosystem, signalled by its World Heritage status, hasn't prevented extensive destruction at the hands of settlers. Up to sixty percent of forest cover on the outer edges of the reserve has disappeared in the last three decades.

Travelling inland to Las Marías, the Río Plátano snakes first through **savannah** lands and secondary forest growth. Upstream from the village begins the primary forest cover, pressing in against both banks of the river. Few experiences can match the initial impression of entering the **rainforest**, as towering trees – mahogany, tamarind, oak – reach up to 50m or more, breaking through the dense canopy to the sunlight. Reaching shorter heights, up to 30m or so, are palms, ceiba and avocados, hung with vines and epiphytic ferns, whilst banked closer to ground level are sprays of brilliantly coloured magnolias and lush ferns. Periodically shattering the cathedral-like calm are the raucous screams of troops of howler and spider **monkeys**. Also hidden among the trees are tapirs, white-faced coatis, pacas, anteaters and squirrels. Sightings of most animals, however, are frustratingly rare. Flashes of the brilliant plumage of **macaws**, **parrots** and **toucans**, a bright contrast against the dim light, are easier to come by.

Puerto Lempira

Capital of the department of Gracias a Dios, **PUERTO LEMPIRA** is the largest town in Mosquitia, with a population of 35,000. Set on the southeastern edge of the biggest of the coastal lagoons, Laguna de Caratasca, some 110km east of Brus Laguna, the town survives on government administration and small-scale fishing and shrimping. The best of the available **accommodation** is *Hotel Flores* (②–④) in the centre of town, close by several small restaurants. **Mopawi** (☎598 7460), the Mosquitia development organization, has its headquarters in the town.

Puerto Lempira is hardly a transport hub, but the only traffic-frequented roads in Mosquitia lead west from here across the savannah to the village of Ahuasbila, an eight-hour drive, passing through Morocón and Rus Rus on the way. A side road shears off to Leimus on the Nicaraguan border; a truck leaves Puerto Lempira early each morning for Leimus, taking around five hours.

°travel details °

BUSES

La Ceiba to: Tegucigalpa (8 daily until 12.30pm; 7hr); Trujillo (7 daily until 2pm; 4hr).

Puerto Cortés to: Omoa (hourly; 1hr).

San Pedro Sula to: Copán (4 daily until 7am; 3hr); La Ceiba (Catisa-Tupsa, 12 daily; 3hr); Puerto Cortés (at least every 30min; 1hr); Tegucigalpa (El Rey, 14 daily; 4hr); Trujillo, via La Ceiba and Tela (Cotraibal, 3 daily until 3pm; 6hr).

Tela to: El Progreso (every 30min; 1hr 30min); La Ceiba (every 30min; 2hr).

Trujillo to: La Ceiba (every 1–2hr until 2pm; 4hr); San Pedro Sula (Cotraibal and Cotuc, 7 daily until 2pm; 6hr); Tegucigalpa (3 daily until 9am; 9hr).

FLIGHTS

Brus Laguna to: La Ceiba (Sosa, 2 weekly).

La Ceiba to: Ahuas (Sosa, 2 weekly); Brus Laguna (Sosa, 2 weekly); Palacios (Isleña, 1 daily Mon–Sat); Puerto Lempira (Isleña, 4 weekly; Sosa, 3 weekly); Tegucigalpa (Taca, 2 daily; Isleña, 2 daily).

Palacios to: La Ceiba (Isleña, 1 daily Mon–Sat).

Puerto Lempira to: La Ceiba (Isleña, 4 weekly; Sosa, 3 weekly).

San Pedro to: La Ceiba (Isleña, 2 daily); Tegucigalpa (Taca, 2 daily; Isleña, 2 daily).

CHAPTER 21

THE BAY ISLANDS

S trung in a gentle curve less than 60km off the north coast of Honduras, the **Bay Islands (Islas de la Bahía)**, with their clear, calm waters and abundant marine life, are the country's main tourist attraction. Resting along a coral reef, the islands are a perfect destination for cheap diving, sailing and fishing, while less active visitors can sling a hammock and relax in the shade on the many palm-fringed, soft sand beaches. Composed of three main islands and some 65 smaller cays, this sweeping 125km island chain lies on the **Bonacca Ridge**, an underwater extension of the Sierra de Omoa mountain range that disappears into the sea near Puerto Cortés. **Roatán** is the largest and most developed of the islands, while **Guanaja**, to the east, is an upmarket resort destination with some wonderful dive sites, and **Utila**, the closest to the mainland, is a target for budget travellers from all over the world.

Even old hands get excited about **diving** the waters around the Bay Islands, where lizard fish and toadfish dart by, scarcely distinguishable from the coral; eagle rays glide through the water like huge birds flying through the air; and parrotfish chomp steadily away on the coral. Meanwhile, barracuda and harmless nurse sharks circle the waters, checking you out from a distance. In addition, the world's largest fish, the whale shark, which can reach up to 16m long, is a regular visitor to the channel between Utila and Roatán in October and November; dive shops on both islands run trips to look for the marine giant.

The best **time to visit** the islands is from March to September, when water visibility is best; October and November are the wettest months, with less heavy rainfall from December to February. Daytime temperatures range between 25 and 29°C year-round, though the heat is rarely oppressive, thanks to almost constant east–southeast trade winds. **Mosquitoes** and **sandflies** are endemic on all the islands, and at their worst when the wind dies down; lavish coatings of baby oil help to keep the latter away.

Some history

The Bay Islands' history of conquest, pirate raids and constant immigration has resulted in a society that's unique in Honduras. The islands' original inhabitants are thought to have been the **Pech**, recorded by Columbus on his fourth voyage in 1502 as being a "robust people who adore idols and live mostly from a certain white grain from which they make fine bread and the most perfect beer". Post-Conquest, the indigenous population dropped rapidly as a result of enslavement and forced labour. The islands' strategic location, as a provisioning point for the Europe-bound Spanish fleets, ensured they soon became the targets for **pirates**, initially Dutch and French and latterly English. The Spanish decision to evacuate the islands, eventually achieved in 1650, left the way open for the pirates to move in. Port Royal, Roatán, became their base until the mid-eighteenth century, from where they launched sporadic attacks on ships and against the mainland settlements.

After the pirates left, Roatán was deserted until the arrival of the **Garífuna** in 1797. Forcibly expelled from the British-controlled island of St Vincent following a rebellion,

For an explanation of **accommodation price codes**, see p.345.

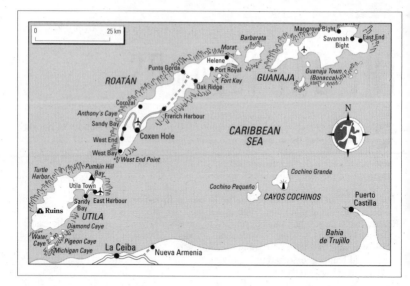

most of the 3000-strong group were persuaded by the Spanish to settle in Trujillo on the mainland, leaving a small settlement at Punta Gorda on the island's north coast. Further waves of settlers came after the abolition of slavery in 1830, when white Cayman Islanders and freed slaves arrived first on Utila, later spreading to Roatán and Guanaja. These new inhabitants fished and built up a very successful fruit industry, which exported to the US – until a hurricane levelled the plantations in 1877.

Honduras acquired rights to the islands following independence in 1821, yet many – not least the islanders themselves – still considered the territory to be British. In 1852, Britain declared the islands a Crown Colony, breaking the terms of the 1850 Clayton–Bulwer Treaty, an agreement not to exercise dominion over any part of Central America. Forced to back down under US pressure, Britain finally conceded sovereignty to Honduras in the Wyke–Cruz Treaty of 1859.

The islands retain their **cultural** distinction from the mainland, although with both Spanish-speaking Hondurans and North American and European expats settling in growing numbers, there is ongoing re-shaping and adaptation. A unique form of **Creole English** is still spoken on the street, but thanks to the increasing number of mainlanders migrating here, Spanish – always the official language – is becoming just as common. This government-encouraged migration engenders mixed feelings, as does the huge growth in tourism since the early 1990s, a trend that shows no signs of abating. The islands' income has traditionally come from fishing or working on cargo ships and oil rigs, but the local economy is coming to rely more and more on tourism. Meanwhile, concern is growing about the environmental impact of the industry and the question of who, exactly, benefits most from the boom.

Getting to the islands

The growth in tourism to the islands over the past few years means that all three are served by regular air and boat connections. Most flights and the scheduled ferry service leave from the coastal city of **La Ceiba** (see p.406), from where there are also occasional unscheduled boats.

RESPONSIBLE TOURISM IN THE BAY ISLANDS

While tourism has given the Bay Islands a higher standard of living than exists on the mainland, it's impossible not to notice the substantial gap between the level of facilities provided by the luxury resorts and the local way of life. Over the last three or four years the islands' resources have been put under growing strain but, fortunately, ways in which visitors can help are relatively simple. Tourists on average use three times as much **water** as locals, so try not to run taps or flush toilets needlessly. To conserve **power**, switch off lights, fans and other electrical appliances when not in your room. **Waste** disposal facilities tend towards the primitive, so if you can, use water purifiers instead of repeatedly buying plastic bottles for drinking water, and reuse plastic bags.

Flying to the islands is uncomplicated, with locals treating the twin-propellor light aircraft almost like buses. From La Ceiba the flight to Guanaja takes around forty minutes, to Roatán around thirty minutes and to Utila about twenty minutes. There are also some direct flights to Roatán from San Pedro Sula (1hr) and Tegucigalpa (1hr). Schedules change at short notice and flights are sometimes cancelled altogether: bear in mind there might be delays to your arrival and, more crucially, departure. There are over twenty flights a day to Roatán, so outside peak season (Dec–April) you can usually buy tickets on the spot at the airport; reservations are required for Utila and Guanaja, which are served by a smaller number of flights – see p.430 for details of flight schedules. The domestic **airlines** Isleña, Taca and Sosa have offices on the central square in La Ceiba and at the airport; Isleña and Taca both also fly to San Pedro Sula and Tegucigalpa. Two further carriers, Rollins Air and Caribbean Air, have offices at the airport.

The scheduled **ferry service** from La Ceiba to Roatán and Utila runs twice a day Monday to Saturday and once on Sunday. There's no need to buy tickets in advance but it's wise to turn up at least an hour before the departure time.

Utila

Smallest of the three main Bay Islands, **UTILA** is a key destination for budget travellers intent on learning to **dive** at some of the cheapest prices in the world. And even if you don't want to don tanks, the superb waters around the island offer great swimming and snorkelling possibilities. Utila is still the cheapest island, with the cost of living only slightly higher than on the mainland, although prices are gradually rising. Life is laidback and people are on the whole friendly, although opportunistic crime is on the increase. As elsewhere, respect local customs in dress and don't walk around in your bathing suit. Note also that drinking from glass bottles on the street is prohibited.

Arrival and information

The **airstrip** is at the southeastern end of the island, at one end of the large, curved harbour around which the main settlement, **East Harbour**, is built. Jutting out into the sea, the main dock neatly bisects the bay: the area around the airport is known as **The Point**, while the west part of town, on the other side of the dock, is called **Sandy Bay**. A paved road runs right the way through town, from the airstrip to Sandy Bay, a distance of around 2km. **Cola de Mico Road**, the island's only other paved road, heads north from the dock across the width of the island.

Wherever you arrive, you'll be met by representatives from the dive schools armed with **maps** and information on special offers. Many schools include free accommodation with their courses, but it's worth checking out the various options before signing up. For more objective **information**, the Utila branch of BICA (Bay Islands' Conservation Association) has a visitor and information office on the main street between the airstrip and the dock, though its opening hours are erratic (usually Mon–Fri 9am–noon and a couple of hours in the afternoon). Since 1996 they have been operating a **Visitor Pass** programme, with the proceeds funding community and conservation projects; the US$5 fee is supposed to be paid on arrival, although no one seems to check. For information on events and an insight into local feelings, pick up a copy of the monthly *Utila Times*, available from the office near BICA.

Everything in town is within easy walking distance; it takes around twenty minutes to stroll from the airstrip to the far western end. **Bikes** can be rented from the house next to Henderson's Grocery store, just west of the centre, and from other places around town – look out for the signs. Current rates are around US$2 a day. Some locals use four-wheeled motorbikes to get around and occasionally pick up hitchers.

Accommodation

There is a profusion of hotels, guest houses, rooms and self-contained houses for rent, some very basic, some of excellent quality. Many places offer discounts for monthly stays. Electricity on the island is provided by two main generators, which supply power from 6am until midnight, with occasional cut-outs in the evening. This doesn't mean it's impossible to run a fan at night, since most hotels now have their own generators, but it's worth checking before taking a room. All the places reviewed below are on one of the two roads in town, listed in the order you come to them when walking from the airstrip.

FROM THE AIRSTRIP TO THE MAIN DOCK

Sharkey's Cabins, behind *Sharkey's Restaurant*, close to the airstrip (☎425 3212). Set in a peaceful garden with a/c, private bath, big beds and a deck with views over the lagoon. ④.

Trudy's, about 200m down from the bridge (☎425 3103). A very popular place, with large, clean rooms. At the back there's a large deck to swim from. ③.

Cooper's Inn, next to the *Utila Times* office (☎425 3184). One of the best cheap places on the island, with airy, clean rooms. *Delaney's Kitchen* downstairs serves good food. ①.

Rubi's Inn, next to the *Mermaid* restaurant (☎425 3240). Very clean, with airy rooms and views over the water; kitchen facilities are available. ②.

COLA DE MICO ROAD

Blueberry Hill, across from Thompson's bakery. Characterful cabins with basic cooking facilities and friendly owners. ①.

Mango Inn, about 300m up from the crossroads (☎425 3335). A new, well run place, where the accommodation, set around a shady garden, ranges from dorms to doubles with private bath. There is a book exchange and laundry service, and the attached *Mango Café* serves good food. ①–③.

SANDY BAY

Utila Lodge, behind Hondutel (☎425 3143). This dive resort is the best hotel in town, offering daily rates as well as weekly packages. Fishing trips can be arranged. ⑦.

Hotel Utila, just past Hondutel (☎425 3340). Rooms with bath and TV, and some with a/c, in a large, modern building. ③–⑤.

Seaside Inn, opposite Gunter's, about 100m past the *Hotel Utila* (☎425 3150). Very popular with younger travellers and often full. The rooms are reasonable, and a good deal. Those in the newer section have private bath. ①–②.

Margaritaville Beach Hotel, about 200m out of town (☎425 3266). It's a bit of a walk to get here, but there are ample rewards in the large airy rooms and breezy seafront location. Very quiet. All rooms have bath and there's free coffee. ②.

Diving

Most visitors come to Utila specifically for the **diving**, attracted by the low prices, clarity of water and abundant marine life. Even in winter, the water is generally calm and common sightings include nurse and hammerhead sharks, turtles, parrot fish, stingrays, porcupine fish and an increasing number of dolphins. On the north coast of the island, Blackish Point and Duppy Waters are both good sites; on the south coast the best spots are Black Coral Wall and Pretty Bush. The good schools will be happy to spend time talking to you about the merits of the various sites.

Rather than signing up with the first dive school representative who approaches you, it's worth spending a morning walking around checking out all the schools. **Price** is not really a consideration, with the dozen or so dive shops all charging US$125–140 for a three- to five-day PADI course; advanced and divemaster courses are also on offer, as are fun dives, from US$25. **Safety** is a more pertinent issue: for peace of mind, you should make sure that you understand – and get along with – the instructors, many of whom speak a number of languages. Also, before signing up, check that classes have no more than six people, that the equipment is well-maintained and that all boats have working oxygen and a first-aid kit. Anyone with asthma or ear problems should not be allowed to dive. A worthwhile investment is the diving **insurance** sold by BICA for US$2 a day, which covers you for medical treatment in an emergency.

The coral reef dies every time it is touched, a fact that should be borne in mind at all times. BICA has been installing buoys on each of the sites to prevent boats anchoring on the reef and all the reputable schools will use these. **Recommended schools** include Alton's (☎425 3108), just over the bridge from the airstrip; Underwater Vision (☎425 3103), based in *Trudy's Hotel*; and Gunter's Dive Shop (☎425 3113), about 300m past the dock in Sandy Bay. Salty Dog's (☎425 3363), just past the dock in Sandy Bay, offers underwater photography equipment rental and instruction. Many of the dive shops also have snorkelling equipment for rent, and Gunter's rents out sea kayaks. West of town and only accessible by boat, the *Laguna Beach Resort* (☎425 3239) and, further down the coast, the *Utila Reef Resort* (☎425 3254), run weekly dive packages including all meals and daily dives.

Swimming, snorkelling and walking

The best swimming near town is at the **Blue Bayou**, about thirty minutes' walk west round the bay, where you can bathe in chest-deep water. Hammocks are slung in the shade of coconut trees and there's a food stand selling burgers and beers; snorkelling gear is also available for rent. East of town, **Airport Beach** at the end of the airstrip offers good snorkelling just offshore, as does the little reef beyond the **lighthouse**. The path from the end of the airstrip up the east coast of the island leads to a couple of small coves, the second of which is good for swimming and sunbathing, though piles of dumped garbage dilute the pleasure somewhat. Five minutes beyond the coves, you'll come to the **Ironshores**, a mile-long stretch of low volcanic cliffs with lava tunnels cutting down to the water, which make for an interesting if tiring walk.

Cola de Mico Road deteriorates into a dirt track as it continues across the island, all the way to **Pumpkin Hill** and beach, about an hour's walk from town. Here, the 82m hill gives good views across the island while down on the beach lava rocks cascade into the sea, forming underwater caves. There is good snorkelling here when the water is calm, although it's not safe to enter the caves. On clear days any point on the southern edge of the island offers great views across to the mainland and the dark bulk of Pico Bonito (see p.410).

The Cays

Eleven tiny outcrops strung along the southwest edge of the island, **Utila Cays** have been a designated wildlife refuge since 1992. Only **Suc Suc (Jewel) Cay** and **Pigeon**

Cay, connected by a narrow causeway, are inhabited, and the pace of life here is slower even than on Utila. Small launches regularly cross the 8km from Utila, or can be privately hired to take you across for a day's snorkelling. *Vicky's Rooms* (①) on Suc Suc is the only **accommodation** at present; for **eating**, there are a couple of restaurants, and a good fish market. Most of the other cays are privately owned, though houses on Morgan and Sandy Cays can be rented through George Jackson (Pigeon Key; ☎425 3161). Camping is allowed on **Water Cay**, however, an idyllic stretch of white sand, coconut palms and a small coral reef, which is a popular spot for weekend and full-moon parties. A caretaker turns up every day to collect a nominal US$1 fee; he also rents hammocks, though you'll need to bring all food and water with you.

Eating

Lobster and **fish** are obviously staples on the islands, along with the usual rice, beans and chicken. With the tourists, however, have also come **European** foods – pasta, pizza, pancakes and granola. Since most things have to be brought in by boat, **prices** are higher than on the mainland: main courses start from around US$4, and beers cost US$1. For eating on the cheap, head for the evening stalls on the road by the dock, which do a thriving trade in baleadas. Note that many of the restaurants stop serving at around 10pm.

Bahía del Mar, just before the bridge by the airstrip. Good steaks and fish dinners, and a popular bar.

Bundu Café, opposite the *Utila Times* office. Big European-style breakfasts, light snacks and lunches, and a book exchange. Mon–Wed, Fri & Sat 9am–3pm.

Golden Rose, just past the 7–11 store, 150m west of the dock. Held by dive instructors and locals to be the best on the island. Large portions of the usual chicken, fish and meat staples are served in a friendly atmosphere.

Island Café, about 50m west of the dock. Good coffee, large sandwiches and light meals. The street-side balcony eating area is good for people-watching.

Jade Seahorse, 200m up Cola de Mico Road. A popular gathering spot for travellers. Large plates of lobster, shrimp and other seafood for around US$5. Good licuados, too.

Mango Café, in the *Mango Inn*. A friendly, open-sided bar-restaurant in the courtyard of the hotel. The menu is heavy on European-style dishes, such as burgers, fishcakes and fries. The bar is popular in the evenings. Closed Mon.

Mermaid's Corner, next to the *Utila Times*. A popular, noisy pasta and pizza restaurant, where service can sometimes be slow. Dishes cost around US$3–4.

Sharkey's Reef Restaurant, opposite the *Bahía del Mar*. The nearest Utila gets to gourmet cuisine, with an eclectic selection of Californian- and Caribbean-style daily specials. Expect to pay around US$9 for an excellent meal with drinks. Wed–Sun, dinner only.

Thompson's Bakery, 50m up Cola Mico Road. An institution among foreign tourists. Large cooked breakfasts of eggs and toast, plus a wide choice of baked goodies. Daily 6am–noon.

Utila Reef, about 200m past the bridge. A small restaurant with tables set on an upstairs deck, overlooking the water. Large portions of local food with a European twist; the lobster and rice is delicious.

Utila's Cuisine, 50m before the dock. An unpretentious place catering to locals. Chicken and meat dishes are well-cooked and cheap.

Nightlife

Utila has a thriving weekend **nightlife**, with a mellower feel during the week when there are fewer visitors in town. Most days, the waterfront *Seabreaker* bar, just past the *Bundu Café*, is good for a quiet drink, but on Tuesday, Thursday and Saturday nights there's a cocktail hour, happy hour and loud Euro-indie and reggae until 11pm. On Saturdays the party continues at *07*, next to the *Mermaid* restaurant, whose happy hour runs from midnight to 1am, accompanied by disco and techno. *Casino*, by the dock, is more of a local hangout, playing reggae and a dash of salsa and merengue. Halfway up Cola de Mico Road, *The Bucket of Blood* is an island institution with regular happy hours and late-night drinking; more relaxed is the *Mango Café*, which closes at 10pm. Should you fancy a game of pool, there's a hall behind *The Bucket of Blood*, which stays open until 11pm. English-language videos are shown nightly at the *Bundu Café*.

Listings

Banks and exchange Banco Atlántida and Bancahsa, on the main road by the dock, exchange money and advance cash on Visa cards until 3pm.

Bookstores The *Bundu Café,* on the main street, east of the dock, has a book exchange.

Immigration office Next to Hondutel, in Sandy Bay.

Medical care There's a clinic just across from Immigration and Hondutel in Sandy Bay; open weekday mornings only.

Post office In the large building on the dock.

Telephones Hondutel is 200m along from the dock in Sandy Bay.

Travel agents Book flights back to the mainland at Utila Tour Travel Centre (agents for Isleña), close to the airstrip, or Tropical Travel, further along the road to the dock.

Roatán

Some 50km from La Ceiba, **Roatán** is the largest of the Bay Islands, a curving ridged hump almost 50km long and 5km across at its widest point. Geared towards tourism at the upper end of the scale, the island's accommodation mostly comes in the form of all-in luxury resort packages, although there are some good deals to be found. Like Utila, Roatán is a suberb **diving** destination, but also offers some great hiking, as well as the chance to do nothing except laze on a beach. **Coxen Hole** is the island's commercial centre, while **West End** is the place to head for absolute relaxation.

Arrival and getting around

Regular flights from La Ceiba and San Pedro Sula – and some from further afield – land at the new **international airport**, 3km east of Coxen Hole, the island's main town. Collective taxis into the centre charge US$1.50; alternatively, walk to the main road just outside the terminal building and wait for one of the public minibuses. In the airport there's an information desk, a hotel reservation desk, car rental agencies and a bank. Coming by **ferry** from the mainland, you'll arrive at the main **dock**, in the centre of Coxen Hole.

A paved road runs west to east along the island, connecting all the major communities. **Minibuses** leave regularly from the main street in Coxen Hole, running west to **Sandy Bay** and **West End** every thirty minutes until late afternoon. East up the island, buses run to **Brick Bay**, **French Harbour**, **Oak Ridge** and **Punta Gorda**, where the paved road ends, every hour or according to demand, until late afternoon. Fares are US$0.50–1.15, depending on distance.

To thoroughly explore, you're best off **renting a car**. In addition to the rental agencies at the airport, Sandy Bay Rent a Car has offices at Sandy Bay and West End, charging from US$45 per day. Hiring a **taxi** for the day is likely to be expensive, but it's worth bargaining to get a better rate. In and around West End village you can also rent **bicycles**; take care cycling on the main routes, since the road is narrow and drivers can be reckless.

Coxen Hole

Dusty and run-down **COXEN HOLE** is the island's main town, and departmental capital. Most visitors come here to change money or to shop, and unless you're on a very early flight there's really no reason **to stay**. If you do need to, try the *Hotel Cayview* on the main street (☎445 1222; ⑤), which has comfortable rooms with a/c and bath. For **eating** there are a number of cheap comedores around the centre, and the friendly *Pava Pizza* on the main street serves decent pizzas and sandwiches. The new *Que Pasa Café* in Librería Casi Todo II, on the western edge of town, ten minutes' walk from the centre, does European-style breakfasts and snacks.

All the town's facilities can be found on a 200-metre stretch of the main street, near where the buses stop. The four-storey Cooper Building holds the headquarters of **BICA**, the islands' conservation organization, where you can pick up leaflets on the flora and fauna of the islands and information on conservation projects. In the same building is the office of the *Coconut Telegraph*, an informative **magazine** about Roatán and its events, which comes out sporadically. Of the **banks** along here, Bancahsa changes travellers' cheques and offers cash advances on Visa; Credomatic also handles Visa transactions. Both the **post office** and **immigration** are by the small square halfway along the main street, while **Hondutel** is behind Bancahsa. For shopping, H.B. Warren is the largest **supermarket** on the island with a wide stock of groceries and foodstuffs, and a basic range of cheap clothes. Yaba Ding Ding and Mahchi are souvenir shops, selling postcards, T-shirts and jewellery.

Sandy Bay

About 7km west of Coxen Hole, halfway to West End, **SANDY BAY** is an unassuming village community, set between the road and the sea. There isn't as wide a choice of places to stay as in West End, but there are a couple of interesting attractions in the village, as well as some excellent snorkelling, since the water around here is protected as the **Sandy Bay Marine Reserve**.

The **Institute for Marine Sciences** (9am–5pm, closed Wed; US$4), based in *Antony's Key Resort*, has exhibitions on the marine life and geology of the islands and a museum with information on local history and archeology. You can also watch daily bottle-nosed **dolphin shows** (daily except Wed 10am & 4pm, Sat & Sun also 1pm; US$4), or dive or snorkel amongst the dolphins: a half-hour dive (for qualified divers only) costs US$115, and half an hour's snorkelling US$75. Across the road from the institute, several short nature trails weave through the jungle of the **Carambola Botanical Gardens** (daily 8am–5pm; US$3), a riot of thick, lush vegetation, trees, flowers, ferns and orchids. A twenty-minute walk from the gardens up Monte Carambola brings you to the Iguana Wall, a section of cliff that serves as a breeding ground for iguanas and parrots.

The cheapest **accommodation** in Sandy Bay is *Beth's Place*, a large wooden building located off the dirt road to the beach (☎445 1266; ②); all the rooms are non-smoking, with shared bath and use of the kitchen. By the sea is the *Oceanside Inn* (☎445 1552; ⑥), with large, comfortably furnished rooms and an attached restaurant. If you can afford it, the nicest place to stay is *Antony's Key Resort* (☎445 1003, fax 445 1140), where the cabins are set among the trees on the hillside above the water and on a small cay offshore; bookings are restricted to all-inclusive dive packages, starting at US$600. For **eating**, *Rick's American Café*, on the hillside above the main road, is a popular bar and restaurant, open daily for dinner and for Sunday brunch.

West End

Curving round a shallow bay at the southwest corner of the island, 14km from Coxen Hole, **WEST END** makes the most of a glorious setting. Though its calm waters and soft, white beaches are drawing a steady flow of foreigners and mainlanders alike, the village has retained its laid-back charm and the gathering pace of tourist development seems to have done little to dent the friendliness of the villagers.

The paved road from Coxen Hole finishes at the northern end of the settlement, by **Half Moon Bay**, one of the best **beaches** in the village. A sandy track runs down along the water's edge, ending in a small bridge at the far end of the village, beyond which is another lovely beach. The Coconut Tree store, just by the end of the paved road, has the best selection of groceries; 50m beyond, Librería Casi Todo is both a book exchange and a **travel agency**, where you can book or change flights. The little stall under the trees just beyond **rents bicycles**, motorbikes, inflatable boats, snorkelling gear and anything else needed for a good time in the water, while Joanna's Gift Shop, towards the far end of the village, has handicrafts and swimwear for sale. The *Online Café* (closed Sun), about ten minutes' walk along the road to Coxen Hole, can send and receive **faxes** and **email** and has a small book exchange.

ACCOMMODATION

The range of **accommodation** in West Bay has widened considerably in recent years, with many more places catering for the budget market. During low season (May–Nov) it's worth negotiating for a discount, particularly for longer stays. Accommodation is listed in the order you come to it entering the village from the main road.

Coconut Tree Cabins, on the paved road at the entrance to the village (☎445 1648). Comfortable, spacious cabins all with covered porches, fridges and and hot water. ⑥.

Chilie's, about 100m to the right at the end of the paved road (no phone). A new, English-owned place with dorm beds and private rooms in a two-storey house, with a kitchen at the back for guests' use. There's also camping space in the garden. ②.

Half Moon Bay Cabins, at the northern edge of Half Moon Bay, across from the village; follow the track for about 300m past *Chilie's* (☎445 1075). One of the original upmarket places to stay, with a lively restaurant attached. Secluded cabins are scattered around the wooded grounds, close to the water's edge, and all have fan or a/c. ⑥.

Valerie's, about 100m to the left down the dirt track, behind Tyll's Dive Shop (no phone). Good budget option, with a relaxed atmosphere. Clean dorm beds or double rooms and use of the kitchen. ①/③.

Dolphin Resort, about 100m past *Valerie's* (no phone). Small but clean rooms in a new brick building; all have a/c, private bath and hot water. ④.

Trish's Wish, about 150m past the *Dolphin Resort*, up the hill – follow the signed turn on the left (☎445 1205). A breezy wooden house, with apartments for 2–5 people. ④–⑤.

Pinocchio's, turn left at the signed turn for *Stanley's Island* restaurant, 150m past the *Dolphin Resort* (fax only 445 1841). This new wooden building, set on the hillside 100m above the village, has clean and airy rooms with bath and hot water. The owners are very friendly and there's a good restaurant downstairs. ④.

Jimmy's Lodge, at the far end of the village, 10min walk from the paved road (no phone). Extremely basic backpackers' institution, with mattresses on the floor in a large dorm and a hose shower; hammocks can also be slung, if there's space. Fantastic beach location. ①.

Keifito's Beach Plantation, about 10min walk along the beach past *Jimmy's* (fax 445 1648). Quiet and secluded, set on the hillside just above the shoreline. There is a small dock to swim off, and the restaurant serves reasonably priced meals.

DIVING AND WATER SPORTS

Diving courses for all levels are on offer, at slightly higher prices than on Utila. An open-water PADI course costs around US$200, with fun dives for around US$30. Optional dive insurance, at US$2 per day, is also available – see p.421 for more on safety precautions. A couple of the more popular shops, with good safety records, are Tyll's Dive, about 100m down from the end of the paved road, and West End Divers, virtually next door. Native Sons, on the beach at the end of the village, is a newer, locally owned school, while Sueño del Mar, 50m beyond West End Divers, rents underwater filming equipment.

The reef just offshore presents some superb **snorkelling** spots, the best being at the mouth of Half Moon Bay and just offshore from *Jimmy's Lodge*. You can rent out **sea**

kayaks from Sea Blades, at the Librería Casi Todo (half-day US$12, full-day US$20). Belvedere's, on the waterfront about 30m south of Librería Casi Todo, runs hour-long glass-bottomed boat tours for US$8 per person, while Flame & Smoke, on the beach past *Jimmy's Lodge*, charters boats for **fishing trips**.

EATING AND DRINKING

There is a more than adequate range of **places to eat** in West End, with fish featuring heavily on many menus, although pasta and pizza are increasingly popular. Eating here is not particularly cheap, with main courses starting at US$5–6. Drinking can also drain your pocket fast in West End – best seek out the half-price **happy hours** at many of the restaurants and bars. The new *Blue Mango Bar*, on the seafront about 200m down from Librería Casi Todo, has a nightly happy hour from 5pm to 7pm. *Foster's Restaurant/Bar*, built over the sea opposite Joanna's Gift Shop, is the scene for a party every Thursday night, and at other times a good place for a quiet drink with superb views over the ocean. The *Cool Lizard*, on the beach past *Jimmy's*, is also perfect for watching the sunset. On Saturdays the *Online Café* organizes a weekly "Utila Party Boat", returning on Sundays.

Cannibal Café, in front of the *Dolphin Resort*. One of the cheapest places to eat, albeit mostly snacks. The baleadas and quesadillas are good value and filling.

Pinocchio's, below the hotel of the same name. Serves an eclectic range of meat, fish and pasta dishes at reasonable prices. Try the chicken or vegetable risotto. Closed Wed.

Rudy's Coffee Stop, on the road just before Joanna's Gift Shop. Great breakfasts of banana pancakes, omelettes, fresh coffee and juices. Closed Sun.

Salt and Pepper, above the Coconut Tree Store. A wide-ranging gourmet menu featuring French, Italian, Indian and Mexican cuisine, plus daily specials. US$10 and upwards for a meal with wine, but worth every penny.

Seaview Restaurant, about halfway along the main drag. A popular joint, with a nicely laid out eating area. Large, thin crust pizzas with a range of toppings are good value, through service can be slow.

Stanley's Island Restaurant, up the hill behind *Pinocchio's*. A locally owned restaurant serving good food at reasonable prices. The *tapado* (fish stew) and coconut bread are delicious.

West Bay

About 4km west of West End, towards the tip of Roatán, is **West Bay**, a stunning, white sand beach, fringed by coconut palms. Its waters are crystal clear, and there's great snorkelling at the southern end of the beach, where the reef meets the shore. Both beach and water come under the protection of the Sandy Bay and West End Marine Reserve, though this hasn't been able to prevent a rash of cabañas and restaurants being built in the vicinity over recent years. Most are low-key, however, only slightly detracting from the tranquillity of the place, and, provided you avoid the sandflies by sunbathing on the jetties, you'll be as near to paradise as you can get.

West Bay beach is a pleasant 45-minute walk from West End, along the sand and over a few rock outcrops; small launches also leave regularly from *Foster's Restaurant*, with the last one back at around 9pm. A dirt road, accessible to cars, has also been opened up; take the first right turning off the road to Coxen Hole.

At West Bay itself, the *Bite on the Beach* (Wed–Sun only) and *Neptuno's Seafood Grill* serve good, seafood **meals** for around US$8 a main course. About halfway along the beach, the Bananarama Dive School has pleasant **cabins** for rent (no phone; ⑤), while those at *Cabaña Roatana* are equipped with hot water and microwave ovens (☎445 1271; ⑥–⑦).

Eastern Roatán

From Coxen Hole, the paved road runs east along the shore, offering occasional glimpses of wrecked ships, and passing the small, secluded cove of **Brick Bay**. After about 10km it reaches **FRENCH HARBOUR**, a busy port and fish-packing town. More attractive than Coxen Hole, it offers accommodation right in the centre of town: try *Harbour View Hotel*, about ten minutes' walk down from the bus stop, which has reasonable rooms with bath and hot water (☎455 5390; ④). A further five minutes down the road, the more upmarket *Buccaneer Hotel* has a pool, a large wooden deck overlooking the water and a disco at the weekends (☎455 5032; ⑦). The best place to eat is *Gio's*, on the harbourfront close to the *Harbour View*, where you can feast on excellent, if pricey, seafood and soups.

From French Harbour the road cuts inland, running along a central ridge with superb views of both the north and south coasts. Much of the original forest cover has gone, however, giving way to pasture and farmland and secondary growth. About 14km past French Harbour the road heads south to **OAK RIDGE**, a quaint fishing port with wooden houses built up the hillsides. There are some lovely unspoilt beaches to the east of town, accessible by launches from the main dock. The best place to stay is the *Hotel San José*, on a small cay just offshore from the dock (☎435 2328; ④). Rather pricey meals are served up at the terrace restaurant in the nearby *Reef House Resort*, along with fabulous sea views. Launches run to the cay on demand (US$0.50).

About 5km from Oak Ridge on the northern coast of the island is the village of **PUNTA GORDA**, the oldest Garífuna community in Honduras and the oldest settlement on Roatán. The best time to visit is for the anniversary of the founding of the settlement (April 6–12), when Garífuna from all over the country attend the celebrations. If you want to **stay**, *Ben's Dive Resort* on the waterfront (☎445 1916; ⑤) has comfortable cabins, while *Los Cincos Hermanos* (no phone) in the centre has basic, clean rooms (①). Nearby, *Hello Hello* serves the standard rice, beans and meat or fish at good prices, while the *Paradise Bar* at the entrance to the village is the place to come for Sunday lunch barbecues.

From the end of the paved road at Punta Gorda, a dirt track, accessible to vehicles, continues east along the island, passing the turn-off for the secluded **Paya Beach** after around 1.5km. A further 5km or so along here is **Camp Bay Beach**, an unspoilt stretch of white sand. The road ends at the village of **PORT ROYAL**, on the southern edge of the island, where the remains of a fort built by the English can be seen on a cay offshore. The village lies in the **Port Royal Park and Wildlife Reserve**, the largest refuge on the island, set up in 1978 in an attempt to protect endangered species such as the Yellow-Naped Parrot, as well as the watershed for eastern Roatán.

The eastern tip of Roatán is made up of mangrove swamps, with a small island, **Morat**, just offshore. Beyond is **Barbareta**, another cay, and one that has retained much of its virgin forest cover. The *Barbareta Beach Resort* runs inclusive packages from US$230 (minimum 3 nights), with diving, windsurfing and fishing tours available (☎445 1255). The reef around Barbareta and the nearby **Pigeon Cays** offers good snorkelling; launches can be hired to reach these islands from Oak Ridge, for around US$10 for a return trip.

Guanaja

The easternmost Bay Island, declared a nature reserve in 1961, **Guanaja** is the most beautiful, undeveloped and expensive of the islands, still heavily forested with hardwoods and the Caribbean pines that led Columbus, landing here on his fourth voyage in 1502, to name it Isla de Pinos. More than 50km long, and about 6km wide, Guanaja actually consists of two main islands, separated by a narrow canal, with the main settlement – **Bonacca** or Guanaja Town – on a small cay a few hundred metres offshore from the larger island. It's here that you'll find the island's shops and main residential area, as well as the bulk of the reasonably priced accommodation. All the houses in Bonacca are built on stilts above the water – a style that harks back to early settlement by Cayman islanders – and the only way to get around is by water taxi. Other, smaller settlements are **Mangrove Bight**, on the west coast of the main island, and **Savannah Bight**, on the east coast.

Arrival and information

Guanaja's **airstrip** is on the main island, by the canal; aside from a couple of dirt tracks there are no roads, the main form of transport being small **launches**. All flights are met by launches bound for the main dock in Bonacca. From here there are scheduled services to Savannah Bight at 7am and 11am; to get to Mangrove Bight, you can hitch a ride on a private boat for a nominal fee. The Capitania de Puerto on the main pier has **information** on unscheduled boat departures for the other islands and points on the Honduran mainland.

Bonacca itself is built on wooden causeways over the canals, many of which have now been filled in. The main causeway, running for about 500m east–west along the cay, with a maze of small passages branching off it, is where you'll find all the shops, **banks** and businesses. You can change dollars and travellers' cheques at Banco Atlántida (left from the dock) and Bancahsa (right from the dock); Bancahsa also gives cash advances on Visa.

Accommodation

Most of the hotels on Guanaja are luxury all-inclusive **dive resorts** offering weekly packages that need to be booked in advance. Bonacca has a small number of more reasonably priced **hotels**, and there's a private house, just before the *Hotel Alexander*, which rents out a couple of rooms for under US$10 per person.

BONACCA

Casa Sobre el Mar, on Pond Cay, just south of Bonacca (☎453 4269). Three bright and breezy rooms, with all meals included in the price of US$85 per person.

Hotel Alexander, at the eastern end of the main causeway, right from the dock (☎453 4326). The best location in Bonacca; large, comfortable rooms have private bath and balconies overlooking the water. ⑤.

Hotel Miller, midway along the main causeway (☎453 4327). The building is slightly run-down, but the rooms are OK. Hot water is available, and, for slightly more, a/c. ③.

Hotel Rosario, opposite the *Hotel Miller* (☎453 4240). Modern building, with comfortable rooms, all with private bath, a/c and TV. ⑤.

LARGE ISLAND

Unless otherwise stated, all prices are per person for a week-long package.

Bahía Resort, on the south side of the island across from Bonacca (☎453 4212). One of the smaller resorts, with a pool; accommodation is in comfortable bungalows. Packages from US$800.

Bayman Bay Club, on the north side of the island (☎453 4179). Well-furnished cabins set on a wooded hillside above the beach. Packages including dives, all meals and other facilities are US$700–750.

Hillton Hotel, by the airstrip (☎453 4299). Clean rooms all have private bath and TV. This is the cheapest option on the main island, though not scenically located as some of the resort. ⑤.

The Island House Resort, on the north side of the island (☎453 4196). A very pleasant resort, close to expanses of beautiful beach. Packages from US$590.

Posada del Sol, on the south side of the island (☎453 4186). Cabins are scattered across 60 acres of ground and amenities include a pool, tennis court, sea kayaks and snorkelling equipment. Packages from US$340 for three nights.

SMALL ISLAND

West Peak Inn, towards the western tip of the small island (fax 453 4219; email *david@vena.com*). Relaxed place with comfortable cabins close to beautiful, deserted beaches and a trail up to the 94m West Peak. Price includes all meals. ⑥.

Around the island

The larger island boasts the highest point of the entire chain, **Michael's Peak** (412m), covered with Caribbean pine forest and hardwoods. A superb trail leads from Mangrove Bight up the peak and down to Sandy Bay, affording stunning views of the island and surrounding reef; fit walkers can do the trail in a day, although it is possible to camp at the summit, provided you bring all food and water with you.

Launches can be hired privately from local fishermen to go **snorkelling** on the reef, though you'll need to bring your own equipment. On the main island, **Michael's Rock**, west of *Island House*, is a small rocky headland surrounded by stretches of beautiful white beach, with good snorkelling close to the shore. **Soldado Beach**, between the canal and the *Bayman Bay Resort*, is the supposed site of Columbus's landing; an unfinished memorial marks the spot. Off the south edge of the island lies the wreck of the *Jado Trader*, 28m below the surface, surrounded by coral.

Diving is excellent all around Guanaja, but can quite difficult to arrange if you're not signed up to a resort package. Dive Freedom, in the *Coral Café* building in Bonacca, can rent equipment for dives and runs courses for PDIC certification, a newer, North American rival to PADI.

Eating and drinking

There are several restaurants in Bonacca, most of which stay open until around 9pm and close on Sundays. Nowhere is particularly cheap, though, since most supplies have to be shipped in. Any truly gourmet eating experiences, however, are likely to be restricted to the package resorts on the large island.

In Bonacca, *Bonacca's Garden*, about halfway along the main causeway, and the restaurant at the *Hotel Alexander*, both serve reasonably priced local dishes. Decent pizza and pasta can be had at the *Up and Down Restaurant*, close to *Bonacca's Garden*, while the *Coral Café* is a good place for snacks and drinks.

Cayos Cochinos

Lying 17km offshore from the mainland, the **Cayos Cochinos (Hog Islands)** comprise two, thickly wooded main islands – **Cochino Grande** and **Cochino Pequeño** – and thirteen cays, all of them privately owned. The small amount of effort it takes to get here is well worth it for a few days' utter tranquillity. Fringed by a reef, the whole area has been designated a marine reserve, with anchoring on the reef and commercial fishing both strictly prohibited. The US Smithsonian Institute, which manages the reserve, has a research station on Cochino Pequeño. On land the hills are studded with hardwood forests, palms and cactus, with Cochino Grande having a number of trails across its interior, and a small peak rising to 145m.

Organized **accommodation** on the islands is limited to the *Plantation Beach Resort* on Cochino Grande (☎442 0974; email *hkinett@hondutel.hn*), which does weekly dive packages for around US$800, including all meals and three dives a day; they collect guests by launch from the Muralla de Cabotaje in La Ceiba (Saturday; US$30 one-way). It can be more rewarding, however, to stay in the Garífuna fishing village of **CHACHAUATE** on Lower Monitor Cay, south of Cochino Grande. Here, the villagers have allocated a hut for visitors to sling their hammocks for a minimal charge, and will cook meals for you. Basic groceries are available in the village, though you should bring water and your main food supplies with you from the mainland.

The only way to get to the islands is by **boat** from the village of **Nueva Armenia**, 40km east of La Ceiba, which leaves for Chachauate early in the morning. One bus a day runs to Nueva Armenia from La Ceiba (11am; 2hr); more frequent buses to

Trujillo, Tocoa and Olanchito all pass through Jutiapa, 8km inland from Nueva Armenia, from where you can hitch or walk. There is a basic hotel (①) in Nueva Armenia and a few simple eating places.

travel details

FLIGHTS

La Ceiba to: Roatán (Isleña, 8 daily Mon–Sat; Sosa, 4 daily; Rollins Air, 7 daily; Caribbean Air, 4 daily); Utila (Isleña, 2 daily Mon–Sat; Rollins, 2 daily Mon–Sat; Sosa, 3 daily Mon–Sat); Guanaja (Isleña, 2 daily Mon–Sat, 1 on Sun; Sosa, 1 daily Mon–Sat; Caribbean, 1 daily).

San Pedro Sula to: La Ceiba (Isleña, 2 daily; Taca, 2 daily; Sosa, 1 daily; Caribbean 1 daily); Roatán (Isleña, 2 daily).

BOATS

MV Tropical runs between La Ceiba and Roatán (2hr), stopping at Utila on weekdays (1hr); fares to both are around US$10 one-way.

La Ceiba to Roatán Mon 5am & 3.30pm, Tues–Fri 3.30pm, Sat 11am, Sun 7am.

Roatán to La Ceiba Mon 7.30am, Tues–Fri 7am, Sat 7am & 2pm, Sun 3.30pm.

La Ceiba to Utila Mon–Fri 10am.

Utila to La Ceiba Mon 11.30am, Tues–Fri 11.30pm.

The *MV Starfish* cargo supply boat runs between La Ceiba and Utila; passages can be bought at the dock.

La Ceiba to Utila Tues 11am.

Utila to La Ceiba Mon 5am.

PART SIX

NICARAGUA

N

HONDURAS

CHAPTER 26
THE ATLANTIC COAST

CHAPTER 23
THE NORTH

CHAPTER 22
**MANAGUA
& AROUND**

CHAPTER 24
**THE
SOUTHWEST**

CHAPTER 25
LAGO DE NICARAGUA

*Lago de
Nicaragua*

CARIBBEAN
SEA

PACIFIC OCEAN

COSTA RICA

Introduction

Wedge-shaped **Nicaragua** may be the largest country in Central America, but it is also the least-travelled in the isthmus – and on the surface it's not hard to see why. Even after nearly a decade of peace, Nicaragua is synonymous in the minds of many with civil war; this reputation, when coupled with the dilapidated infrastructure of a country that has fought its way not only through a bloody conflict but also an American economic blockade, scares many off. Still, many travellers who spend any time there find – much to their surprise – that Nicaragua is their favourite country in the isthmus. Perhaps because it doesn't cater for the tourist experience, Nicaragua is an incorrigibly vibrant and individualistic country, with plenty to offer travellers prepared to brave Nicaragua's superficial obstacles of economic chaos, cracked pavements and crammed public transport.

Cuba aside, Nicaragua is unique in Central – and Latin – America in having pulled off a bona fide revolution of the people. The **revolution** of 1978–79 and the civil war that followed in the 1980s, while ravaging the country, has also given it one of the most dramatic of recent histories. At times it seems that every Nicaraguan has both horrifying and uplifting personal stories to tell. Even though Nicaragüenses would rather forget many aspects of the war, the political past of the country informs every minute of its present and every inch of its landscape.

At the moment Nicaragua is working to develop its **tourism industry**. In the 1980s the country was the destination of choice in Central America for young socialist-minded *internacionalistas* – foreign volunteer workers who came to the country to aid the revolution by working in the education and health sectors. Because the Sandinistas are no longer in power and the country's present government has discontinued many of the programmes that brought the *internacionalistas*, Nicaragua is these days relatively empty of foreign visitors; while this is an advantage for travellers hoping to immerse themselves in the local culture, it's bad business for the budget hotel owners and tour operators. In the capital city a sizeable foreign community of long-term aid workers and embassy officials is in permanent residence, and many travellers find it worthwhile hooking up with this expat community and its activities, especially if they are in Managua for any length of time.

In comparison with the Maya ruins of Guatemala or the national parks of Costa Rica, Nicaragua offers few traditional tourist attractions – almost no monuments or ancient temples remain, and earthquakes, revolution and war have laid waste to museums, galleries and theatres. For years the country has suffered from a chronic lack of funding, and high inflation and unemployment have joined the fray to impoverish Nicaragua's infrastructure. However, no one visits Nicaragua and remains immune to the country's extraordinary **landscape** of volcanoes (17 in all), lakes, mountains and vast plains of rainforest. A smattering of **beaches** – the majority of them on the Pacific Coast – continues to attract the budget **surfing** and backpacking crowd, while culture and **the arts** are very much alive in Nicaragua, and it is here you can buy some of the best-value high-quality crafts in the isthmus.

More than anything, though, the pleasures and rewards of travelling in Nicaragua come from interacting with the inhabitants of a complex society, one that has so eloquently and heroically combined thought and action through literature and music, and, of course, in its struggle to rid itself of generations of dictatorship and economic and social feudalism. Its **people** are well-spoken, passionate, engaged and engaging – Nicaraguans tend to be witty and exceptionally hospitable. The best thing you can do to enjoy Nicaragua is to arrive with an open mind, some patience and a willingness to practise your Spanish.

■ Where to go

Most of Nicaragua's population lives in the hot, relatively dry and **fertile Pacific lowlands**, where much of the country's agriculture is centred. This region is also the political and cultural centre of the country – nearly everything thought of as being inherently Nicaraguan, whether food, music, dress or dance – comes from this area. Virtually every traveller passes through the capital, **Managua**, if only to catch a bus; but there's little to detain the tourist in the capital and many quickly make tracks for colonial **Granada**, with its splendid lakeside setting and beautiful if dilapidated architecture. The town of **Masaya**, 26km southeast of the capital, is the **arts and crafts** centre of the country; both Nicaraguans and foreign tourists descend upon its mercado de artesanía for some of the best crafts in Central America.

In the **Lago de Nicaragua** area, ecotourism is beginning to have some impact, with more and more travellers visiting Ometepe and the Solentiname Islands. Volcano-viewing and hiking are the attractions of Ometepe, whose stirring landscape of twin volcanoes rising out of the freshwater lake has awed travellers for centuries. Further south in the lake, near the Costa Rican border, the Solentiname archipelago and the Río San Juan are some of the most pristine areas in Central America, where flora, fauna and a unique tradition of primitive naif painting prevail.

Nicaragua's mountainous **central region** is distinctly other, with a cooler climate and a reputation for fiercely independent peoples. Much of the country's rich mellow export-grade **coffee** is grown here, and farms dominate the landscape of blue-green pines and mountains. Hiking and birdwatching near the mountain town of **Matagalpa** is the main tourist attraction.

Physically cut off from the rest of the country by a lack of roads, the Caribbean lowlands – called the **Atlantic Coast** in Nicaragua – actually make up nearly fifty per cent of the country's land mass. Hot, humid and perpetually rainy, this area is sparsely populated and little-visited. Most of its inhabitants gain a living from fishing and subsistence agriculture. Politically and culturally separate from the centre and west of Nicaragua, the region – divided into north and south – governs itself autonomously. Descended from escaped African slaves and from the indigenous peoples, the Miskito, Rama and the Suma, who account for the majority of Atlantic Coast inhabitants, speak **English** – a legacy from the days when British pirates patrolled the coast, resulting in the land of the Miskitos becoming, for a time, a British protectorate. Food, dance, music and religion on the Atlantic Coast are West Indian rather than Spanish: rice-and-beans is cooked with coconut milk, the radio play is strictly reggae, and picturesque Protestant and Moravian churches dot **Bluefields** and **Puerto Cabezas**, the two hot, ramshackle jungle towns on the Coast.

■ When to go

Nicaragua has two distinct seasons, the dry and the wet. The **rainy season** is called *invierno* – winter – and corresponds roughly with the Northern Hemisphere summer, from May to November. *Verano* – **summer** (December–April) – is hot and often uncomfortably dry; dust covers everything, and the heat seems to rise to a kiln-like intensity. Fewer travellers come in the rainy season; this alone could be a reason for choosing to put up with the daily downpour. The seasons are most pronounced on the Pacific coast, where from May to November rain is likely in the afternoons, although the mornings will be dry. Influenced by the Caribbean trade winds, the central mountain region has sporadic rainfall all year, although it is drier in the "summer". Its climate is cooler year-round, with misty clouds covering the blue-green summits of its mountains. The Atlantic Coast is wet – *very* wet – year-round and almost unbelievably hot and humid. Whenever you come you should expect rain. As in the rest of the Caribbean region, September and October are the height of the tropical storm season.

Getting around

Finding your way around Nicaragua, whether on crowded school buses, sturdy old lake-boats, or in little single- and double-engined planes, is at least half the fun of travelling in the country. Most journeys, with the exception of the trip to or from the Atlantic Coast, are relatively short and manageable. Public transport, especially buses, is geared toward the domestic population, and is very cheap.

■ Buses

Everywhere you go in Nicaragua you see packed **buses** careening down the highway, dodging the occasional pothole, their knock-off Ray-Ban-wearing drivers grinning, roof racks full of luggage and insides packed to the hilt. For the vast majority of Nicaraguans the bus is the only affordable way to travel, and despite the crush the service is good;

people are friendly and will help you with your bags and with directions. The standard bus in Nicaragua is an old American or Canadian Blue Bird school bus – not uncomfortable, unless you have long legs.

Managua is the **transport hub** of the country, and from here you can get virtually anywhere by bus. The most popular routes are Managua–Masaya–Granada; Managua–Rivas; and in the north, Managua–Leon, and Managua–Matagalpa or Estelí. With some Spanish and a little fancy footwork, you can get from almost any Nicaraguan town to another. These local services tend to be far less frequent, however, and stop more often than the inter-town "express" services.

Most **intercity buses** begin running at either 5am or 7am and the last buses leave about 5 or 6pm. Fares are very cheap – it used to be said you could cross Nicaragua by bus for less than US$1. That's not the case anymore, but most trips cost no more than US$1–2. If you are carrying luggage you may be charged half-fare – sometimes even full fare – for it. This is standard practice and there's no point arguing. Luggage is either put on the roof rack or at the back of the bus; the latter is a bit safer. You can tip the driver's helper a córdoba or two to keep an eye on it. Luggage is unloaded from the back door – try to watch the proceedings to make sure your pack is not stolen. Pickpocketing attempts are also frequent; best to carry valuables in a money belt or inside pocket, and to keep any small backpacks on your front.

Departure times are frequent, usually every thirty minutes, or when the bus is full. Bus **stops** are never marked, but are usually located at the local market. Otherwise buses can be flagged down on the highway, but this means they'll be full and you'll have to stand. Drivers have helpers who collect the money once your journey is underway; they may not have change for big bills, in which case he'll will take your money and return when he has collected enough fares to give you your change.

Camionetas

Adventurous travellers can try the Nicaraguans' cut-rate transport of choice, the **camioneta**. During your time in Nicaragua you'll doubtless see pickup trucks loaded with people hurtling down the highway. A kind of collective transport, cheaper even than the bus, camionetas run on almost all routes, but you have to ask around to find the departure point.

■ Taxis

Although you will mostly see **taxis** in cities, in the form of Ladas in various states of disrepair, taxis also make long-distance journeys in Nicaragua. Although a taxi from, say, Granada to Rivas, will cost several times the bus fare, it is still a bargain, especially if you are in a group, since drivers charge by the distance travelled. Another option is to hire a taxi to take you around for the day; this tends to be more expensive – at least double the price of a town-to-town journey, costing up to US$45 per carload or more. In all cases, when taking a taxi in Nicaragua you must negotiate the fare before getting into the car.

■ Driving and hitching

Renting a car in Nicaragua is only possible in Managua (for a list of companies, see p.467). You need a valid licence, passport and a credit card. Make sure you take out full-cover **insurance**, as road accidents in Nicaragua are on the increase. Throughout the country road signage is quite poor, and your Spanish will certainly get a workout, since you'll frequently need to ask directions. Most roads are now paved, at least, although fuel remains expensive by Central American standards. As with other Central American countries, don't drive at night – it's less a question of crime than the lack of streetlighting disguising potholes, sudden deviations in the road, or even the road disappearing altogether, as well as cattle straying onto the road.

Nicaraguans are a little surprised to see foreigners **hitching**, although it's very common for locals to do so. You'll only see women hitching when accompanied by men, however, and it's wise to follow this rule as a traveller. You will be expected to pay for your lift, but usually no more than US$1–1.50, even for trips of a couple of hours. There is much competition for lifts out of Managua and other large towns. Most hopefuls stand under a patch of shade on the highway just outside of the city; if the competition is tough or drivers unresponsive they give in and take the bus.

■ Boats

For the many people who live around Nicaragua's numerous waterways and two large lakes, **boats** a provide vital link. Travellers, however, tend not to use boats much, since in most cases good bus

or plane connections are also available. The longest boat journey in the country, from Granada on the west side of Lago de Nicaragua to San Carlos on the southeast corner of the lake, is a cheap, although slow (up to 9hr) way to cross this enormous inland sea. The trip is choppy, however, and subject to delays – one reason why a **hydrofoil** service was begun a few years ago, with tourism in mind. The hydrofoils are unfortunately subject to many problems – mostly mechanical – and often the lake is too rough for them. When they do run they make the trip between Granada and Ometepe Island, and on to the Solentiname Islands in the southern corner of the lake. The Nicaraguan boat trip you're most likely to experience is the hour-long ride in the **lancha** – a motorized medium-sized wooden craft – running between San Jorge, near Rivas, and Moyogalpa, the port of Ometepe island.

The trip from Managua and the Pacific lowlands to the Atlantic Coast can be made partly by boat, using the public **ferry** that runs from the hamlet of El Rama at the head of the Río Escondido to the coastal town of Bluefields (a 6hr journey). On the eastern side of the country nearly all travel is by boat along the complex network of rivers and lagoons of **Mosquitia**. All these services are private, and geared towards locals. Journeys are unscheduled, long and unpredictable, and you'll have to ask around in Bluefields and Puerto Cabezas for connections.

■ Planes

Faced with a ten-hour bus trip, followed by six hours on a slow river jungle-cruise, many people heading to Nicaragua's Atlantic Coast from Managua choose to **fly** at least one way. The private domestic airline La Costeña operates the most reliable (and very scenic) flights between Managua, Bluefields and the Corn Islands for about US$60 one-way. La Costeña also flies to Puerto Cabezas in the northeast corner of the country, which is inaccessible by road at least half the year, and to San Carlos de Nicaragua, near the border with Costa Rica, another relatively inaccessible location.

Costs, money and banks

Nicaragua's **currency** is the **córdoba**, officially the Córdoba Oro, written as C$. The córdoba is divided into 100 centavos. Notes come in denominations of 100, 50, 20, 10, 5 and 1 cór-dobas, as well as much smaller 25- and 10-centavo notes. Coins come in 10 and 25 centavos. There is a new 5-centavo note, and some new coins in circulation now: 5 and 1 córdoba coins along with 50, and 5 centavos. The centavos and the one-córdoba notes come in very handy, whether for bus fares or to give to begging kids; you'll learn quickly to get rid of the 100 and 50 notes, as in most places they're about as welcome as a stack of Russian roubles and no one – except maybe bus drivers – ever seems to have change.

Nicaragua is no longer as cheap as it used to be. The IMF and World Bank policies have had their effect, and **prices** have risen accordingly. In general bus transport, food bought at markets and some accommodation are still bargains; restaurant meals, petrol, car rental and more upscale hotel accommodation, especially in Managua, are surprisingly expensive. As a rule, the budget traveller in Nicaragua, staying in hospedajes, taking buses instead of taxis, and eating in markets or at food stalls, can get by on as little as US$10 a day, although US$15 is a more comfortable aim.

■ Banks and exchange

The banking system in Nicaragua is improving, with more **banks** offering better service. Still, one of the main hassles of travelling in Nicaragua is the country's refusal to acknowledge the existence of **travellers' cheques**; what it means for travellers is that you'll always be carrying a huge wad of grubby córdobas with you.

The state banks – Banco Nacional de Desarollo, Banco Popular – are still found in almost every Nicaraguan town. In larger places like León and Granada, private banks are cropping up. These offer more or less the same service to the traveller – they won't cash travellers' cheques either – but in slightly less totalitarian surroundings. For the most part banks are open from 8.30am to 4.30pm and may close for an hour or more over lunch (12.30–1.30pm); many are also open on Saturday mornings. All will change US dollars easily, but no other currency.

To change travellers' cheques you can go to private currency exchange houses, called **casas de cambio**, at present only found in Managua. You will need both your passport and, as a rule, the purchase receipts with the serial numbers. Changing cheques into dollars rather than córdobas incurs a fee of around US$5. The rate for changing dollar travellers' cheques at casas de cambio is slightly worse than the bank rate.

Credit cards such as Visa and Mastercard are accepted in some of the more expensive hotels and restaurants and you can often use them to pay for car rental, flights and tours. Also some casas de cambio in Managua will advance cash on major cards. However, it's as well not to rely on being able to use them.

Moneychangers operate in the street, usually at the town market, but avoid changing dollars in the street – it's too easy to get ripped off. If you must, avoid dealing with more than one person at a time, and watch out for sleights of hand (like replacing a US$100 bill with a US$1). Take a taxi after changing money.

The **rate** of exchange between the dollar and the córdoba fluctuates each day; at the time of writing it was 10.17 córdobas to the dollar.

Information

Managua's **Inturismo** office (see p.456) is the country's only real tourist information centre. Though the staff are friendly, they can't offer much practical help and you're unlikely to come away with much more than a bunch of colourful leaflets. Ask for a copy of the bimonthly *Guía Fácil Nicaragua* (US$1), a useful publication packed with countrywide events listings and features. If Inturismo don't have it, you should be able to pick it up in the bigger hotels.

Accommodation

Most travellers will at some point find themselves in a Nicaraguan **hospedaje** – a pension-type small hotel, most often family-owned and run. Hospedajes are basic but characterful, usually with shared bath, a ceiling or floor fan, but rarely hot water – which on the Pacific and Atlantic coasts is not much missed. Some hospedajes, especially those in old Spanish-colonial-style houses, go far beyond this brief and are truly characterful places to hang out, with big rocking chairs ringing plant-filled patios, laundry facilities, and a lively family life going on around. As a rule, basic hospedajes in Nicaragua still charge under US$5, although with inflation prices are moving into the US$5–10 range; most require payment in cash, and in córdobas, although many will accept dollars. Breakfast is not normally included in the price, so when it is it can be a real bargain, especially in the lower price ranges. Only the most basic of hospedajes will not provide toilet paper and towels. Occasionally a more upscale hospedaje will offer the option of **air conditioning**; since electricity is so expensive this can double the price of the room. Nicaraguan units tend to be old and noisy and in most places a/c is not really necessary – you can get by with ventilation and a ceiling fan.

Hotels tend to be fancier, with air-conditioning, possibly cable television, and other services like tours and rental cars. Outside Managua they are very thin on the ground, although a few, like the characterful *Europa* and *Colonial* in León and Granada's *Alhambra*, merit spending the US$25 or so they charge for a room. You can pay by credit card – although not with travellers' cheque – and a good restaurant is usually attached.

In Nicaragua, as in the rest of Central America, "**Motels**" and "Auto Hotels" are not used for sleeping. Better described as love (or sex) motels, they advertise an amazing array of comforts, including a/c, hot water, cable television, security and "privacy".

Throughout the country **camping** is problematic; unlike in Costa Rica, say, there is little tradition of camping in Nicaragua. Sand flies, mosquitoes, rain and theft are only a few of the deterrents to setting up a tent. If you're determined, the most promising areas in which to camp are beach towns like San Juan del Sur.

Eating and drinking

Nicaraguan **food**, like that in many Central American countries, is based around the ubiquitous **beans, rice and meat** – and plenty of it. Everything is cooked with oil; even the rice is fried, often with a little onion and some finely sliced red chiles or small capsicums. If this sounds like gastronomic hell, take heart – *comida nica* grows on you and you may find yourself craving a plate of gallo pinto (beans and rice) once you have left the

country. Homegrown Nicaraguan beef is very tasty; the downside is that **vegetarians** will have to stick to a rice-and-beans diet.

■ What to eat

Nicaraguan meals are very much centred on meat, usually **chicken**, **beef** or **pork**, most deliciously cooked *a la plancha*, on a grille or griddle, and served spitting on a hot plate. **Seafood** is equally good: on the coast you'll be offered ocean fish such as snapper and bass, with freshwater fish on the menu around Lago de Nicaragua. Fish are usually served whole, deep fried and served with a rich tomato or garlic sauce. Weekends are traditionally the time to eat **nacatamales**, parcels of corn dough filled with either vegetables, pork, beef or chicken, which are wrapped in a banana leaf and boiled for a couple of hours.

On the Atlantic Coast the cuisine becomes markedly more **Caribbean** and sweeter, spicier tastes invade the recipes. Although rice and beans is still a staple dish, often you will find the rice has been cooked in delicious mild coconut milk. **Ron don** – "run down"; in local parlance "to cook" – is a stew of local yucca, chayote and other vegetables, usually with meat added, which is simmered for at least a day and traditionally eaten at weekends.

Nicaragua's secret national treasure is the Eskimo **ice cream** company, which produces an extraordinary range of home-grown flavours, embracing many local fruits and nuts, including chocolate with almonds, coconut, pistachio, star fruit, rock melon and mango. For the more exotic flavours you may have to go to an Eskimo shop or the supermarkets.

■ Where to eat

Throughout Nicaragua **streetside kiosks** sell hot meals, usually at lunchtime. You will soon become familiar with the ubiquitous plastic tablecloths, paper plates and huge bowls of cabbage salad set beside small barbecue grills. The food is generally well prepared and safe to eat: most Nicaraguans have their lunch this way, or in small **comedores**, restaurants with ten or so seats that do a lunchtime *comida corriente*, a good-value set plate of meat, rice and salad. Proper **restaurants** are rare outside Managua, and even León and Granada have only a smattering. In these places a ten percent service charge is usually added on to the bill.

■ Drinking

Nicaragua has two local brands of **beer**, Victoria and Toña, both lagers. Each has its aficionados who refuse to drink the other, but really they taste quite similar – Toña is a little darker and nuttier. You can buy them in cans, but to get them from your local shop you will need to exchange some "empties" – Nicaragua operates a strict recycling program for beer bottles and with no empties to exchange you'll pay double the price.

Local Flor de Caña **rum** comes in both dark and white, gold, old, dry and light. For US$4–7, it is an excellent buy. It is usually brought to the table with a large bucket of ice and some lemons, but you can mix it with soft drinks for something a little less potent.

Given that it is so hot in Nicaragua it is just as well there is a fascinating range of cold drinks, or **refrescos** (usually shortened to *frescos*) to choose from. These are made from a large range of grains, seeds and fruits, which are liquidized with milk, water and ice. *Cebada en grano* is a combination of ground barley and barley grains mixed together with milk and coloured pink – like most drinks it is flavoured with cinnamon and lots of sugar. *Pinolillo* is a maize drink with spices, served in large, carved, oval containers made from the seed of the jickory tree; the *semilla de Jicaroa* itself is made into a delicious drink that looks and tastes rather like chocolate. *Cacao* is also widely available, and often sold in small sealed plastic bags at traffic lights. You can now buy these drinks in powdered form in the supermarket, ready to mix with milk and a little ice in the blender. Just about every fruit imaginable is made into a *fresco*, including watermelon, star fruit, papaya, rock melon – a small, local variety of melon – and oranges. During the rainy months, keep your eye out for *pitahaya* juice. Made from the fruit of a cactus, it's a virulent purple in colour and incredibly tasty. You can also eat the fruit raw, but be warned that your hands and mouth will be stained a deep purple. Some drink stands and street vendors specialize in **raspados**,

a cup full of ice scraped off a large block and topped with flavouring, anything from milk and chocolate to currants (*grosellas*).

Opening hours, festivals and holidays

Shops and **services** in Nicaragua still observe Sunday closing: otherwise you'll find most things open from 8am to 4pm, with the exception of **banks**, which normally close at 3pm. Some **museums** and **sites** close for lunch, normally shutting their doors between noon and 2, to reopen again until 4pm. Supermarkets, smaller grocery shops and the small neighbourhood shops called *ventas* generally stay open until 8pm. **Bars** and **restaurants** tend to close around 11pm, except for nightclubs and dance clubs – most of which are in Managua – which stay open until 2am or later.

Christmas and Easter are still the biggest **holidays**. At **Easter** especially the whole country packs up and goes to the beach: buses are packed, hotel rooms on the coast at a premium, and flights to the Corn Islands booked well in advance from Holy Thursday until the following Monday, and usually for a few days before and after. **Christmas** and New Year are mainly celebrated in the home, but you'll certainly find most things closed between December 23 and 25 and on January 1. The holiday marking the **Revolution**, July 19, is still celebrated ardently by Sandinistas and is usually accompanied by parades and marches. In addition, each town in Nicaragua has its own **patron saint** and will observe the saint's day with processions and celebrations called Toro Guaco, when you might catch a glimpse of old customs inherited from the Aztecs mixed with *mestizo* figures like the masked *viejitos* (old ones – masks of old men and

---

PUBLIC HOLIDAYS
January 1 New Year's Day
Semana Santa Easter Week
May 1 Labour Day
July 19 Anniversary of the Revolution
September 15 Independence Day
November 2 All Soul's Day
(Día de los Muertos)
December 7 & 8 Inmaculada Concepción
December 25 Christmas Day

women worn by young and old alike). In all cases Nicaraguans love to dance, and you will probably see folkloric dances in the streets, usually performed by children.

Mail and telecommunications

Mail service in Nicaragua is fairly fast: though letters to Europe can take up to two weeks, they reach North America in about eight days. Theft from letters is an increasing problem, especially with mail sent into Nicaragua, so it's wise not to trust cash or anything valuable to the postal service. You can send **international** mail from any Nicaraguan town, although outside Managua, León and Granada have the best service. Mail sent from the Atlantic Coast will probably take the longest to reach the rest of the world.

Every Nicaraguan town of any size has a **Telcor** building, which functions as the telecommunications hub for the entire population. Since it began to be privatized in 1995, Telcor has changed its name to Enitel – another acronym – but everyone still refers to it as Telcor. While the service is more reliable than it used to be, calling out of the country can still be a hassle.

In the major towns like Managua, León and Granada, you can buy phone cards that can be used with the new Publitel phones. These cards work by code, not magnetic strip (do not insert them in the telephone), and are useful for making **domestic** calls (and calls to neighbouring countries). Elsewhere, domestic telephone calls have to be placed at the Telcor office.

Calling abroad, you'll have to pay a visit to a Telcor office and wait in line with huge numbers of Nicaraguans. You can ask to reverse the charges or pay for your call afterwards in córdobas – tell the operator how long you wish to talk and they'll calculate the approximate cost for you. You'll then be sent to a numbered booth, where you wait for your call to be patched through – a sometimes frustrating process. Most Telcor offices are open long hours, from 7am until 10pm Monday to Friday, with reduced hours on weekends. Alternatively, many countries have **direct-dial numbers** that get you through to either a member-card operator (AT&T, Sprint or MCI) or your home country operator for a reverse-charge call. Calling Nicaragua from abroad, the country code is ☎505.

Fax machines are common in Nicaragua although Telcor do not provide public fax service. If you stay at a mid-range or upscale hotel you will be able to send a fax abroad for a fee; otherwise, and especially outside Managua, you are out of luck.

The media

The Sandinistas were widely criticized for **censoring** Nicaragua's media during much of the 1980s, when the chief characteristic of Nicaraguan newspapers, especially, was their virulently partisan tone. Nicaragua's press is now technically free, but despite the changes in government, Sandinista dominance in the media continues. According to the Nicaraguan Center for Human Rights, censorship of the media is again on the increase.

Of the national **newspapers**, the organ of authority is *La Prensa*, founded in 1926. During the Chamorro years it was criticized for being too supportive of that government (Violeta Chamorro was on the editorial board, her daughter the paper's editor). Now it walks a slightly more independent line, but is still considered pro-government. No longer the house paper of the FSLN, *La Barricada* remains leftist in tone, and partial to the Sandinistas; it's worth reading for its quite different perspective on local events and world news. The best paper, though, is the new, "independent" *La Tribuna*, which has good foreign coverage. Finally, you'll see the black and white *El Nuevo Diario* being sold on buses; it is leftist but more sensationalistic and populist in tone than all the others.

The only **English-language newspaper** is the monthly *Nica News*, which often prints features on tourist destinations and reproduces flight schedules and the like. The problem is getting hold of it; try the *Casa del Cafe* in Managua, which also sells the Spanish-language Latin American edition of *Newsweek*. Foreign newspapers, even those readily available in other Central American countries, such as the *Miami Herald* or the *New York Times*, are virtually impossible to buy in Nicaragua.

While cable **television** is becoming more widespread in Nicaragua, providing access to a range of international news, sports and movie channels, **radio** remains the most important medium, since very few people can afford to buy a daily newspaper and televisions are still fairly scarce. Most Nicaraguans get their news from the radio and certain stations are so influential that they are singled out for attacks by political opponents. Right-wing **Radio Corporación** was twice attacked by the Sandinistas, and during the first years of the Chamorro government Sandinista **Radio Ya**, established by staff who had been sacked from the official national radio station, was broken into by unknown assailants. Radio Ya is still the most popular station, offering a mix of music, left-wing news, current affairs, and plenty of sport; Radio Corporación runs a close second.

On the FM band, most stations play music, generally a mix of English and Spanish; you can also hear the US Top 40, broadcast live from the States at 10am on a Sunday morning. It is also worth checking out **Radio Sandino**, the official voice of the Sandinista party, and two **community stations**, La Primerísima and Radio Universidad.

Safety and the police

Poverty and unemployment in Nicaragua have contributed to a rising crime rate. **Petty theft** is the most common form, especially on buses. Nicaraguans suffer from this as well as tourists, and locals take the usual precautions of not carrying anything valuable in an outside pocket, and spreading valuables and money over several pockets or purses; travellers should do the same. Opportunistic forms of theft aside, Managua is the only place where you need to worry about assault. Precautions to take are not to walk around at night or to go out alone to bars or nightclubs; be alert when leaving banks or casas de cambio, where thieves have recently targeted both foreigners and Nicaraguans. Never leave anything of value on the beach, even for a few minutes, as it is almost guaranteed to be stolen. Larger hotels will have safes where you can leave your passport and other valuables.

Women need to be wary of going out alone or even in a group at night – the chief threat is harassment by drunken men spilling out of bars in groups.

The police in Nicaragua are generally reliable, except perhaps the traffic police *(policía de transito)* who are infamous for their opportunistic targeting of foreigners – they look for any chance to give you a *multa*, or fine. To report a crime you must go to the nearest police station. If you need a police report for an insurance claim, the police will ask you to fill out a *denuncia* – a full report of the incident. If the police station does not have the denuncia forms,

ask for a *constancia*, a simpler form, signed and stamped by the police. This should be sufficient for an insurance claim. Visitors to Nicaragua must carry their passport on them at all times. A photocopy is acceptable; police checks are not as common as they used to be. Keep passports secure in an inside pocket all the time; when travelling keep a photocopy separately.

In an **emergency**, dial ☎128 for the Red Cross (Cruz Roja); ☎115 for Fire (Bomberos); ☎118 for Police; or ☎119 in the case of a traffic accident.

Work and study

Gone are the heady days of the 1980s, when *internacionalistas* (foreign voluntary workers) came from Europe, North America and other Latin American countries to help the revolution. By all accounts this was a rewarding experience for the mostly young people who found **voluntary work** placements in Nicaragua, doing anything from road-building to picking organic coffee.

Now, with the Sandinistas' loss of office and the political shift to the right, *internacionalistas* still come to Nicaragua, but in tiny numbers compared to those of ten or fifteen years ago. As overseas NGOs and aid agencies take over, it is becoming increasingly difficult to find good voluntary positions in Nicaragua. One place you can try is the Casa Ben Linder in Managua (3 blocks south and 1 and a half blocks east of the Monseñor Lezcano statue; ☎266-4373), the Nicaraguan base for a number of primarily US voluntary groups and agencies. Most towns have a local IXCHEN **women's centre** (casa de la mujer), whose work is largely based on health, family welfare and community issues. Women are always welcome to visit and if your Spanish is good and you have some qualifications, they may be able to advise you regarding voluntary (unpaid) work with women.

Unless you are sponsored by an overseas government, agency or voluntary organization, however, opportunities for work are few and what does it exist is likely to be unpaid. In a country where unofficial unemployment figures hover around seventy percent, foreigners will only find casual work as **teachers** of English. Even so, the Nicaraguan government is strict in its immigration policy and to undertake any paid work you need a long-stay working visa; if you are sponsored by an overseas company they will probably take care of this for you. The address of Managua's immigration office is given on p.467.

History

In comparison with its neighbours to the north, in Nicaragua you can have the impression that history began only with the arrival of the Spanish. Few traces of Nicaragua's pre-Conquest history remain; certainly there are **no major monuments** of the likes of Tikal or Copán, and historians and archeologists are doubtful whether cities of such size and complexity ever existed here. Statues and ornamental objects are quite abundant, though, if you know where to look, and modern Nicaragua retains aspects of its ancient history in its language, food and customs.

Events far to the north in Mexico determined the future of the country that would come to be called Nicaragua. After the fall of the Aztec city of Teotihuacán in 1000 AD, displaced **Mexica** (Aztec) peoples undertook a diasporic migration south. They headed ever southward through the isthmus on the strength of a prophecy that they were to settle where they saw a lake with two volcanoes rising from the water – which they found in the striking form of Isla de Ometepe in Lago de Nicaragua.

Two groups of pre-Columbian peoples settled on the shores of the lake. Roughly divided into the **Chorotegas** and the **Nahuas**, it is still possible to tell who settled where by place names – Momotombo, Masaya, Niquinohomo and Nandaime come from the Chorotegan language, while Managua, Masatepe, Tipitapa and Chinandega are Nahuatl words. The food – maize, beans, chiles and chocolate – and culture of these people closely resembled that of the Aztecs, even after centuries of settlement so far away from metropolitan Aztec culture.

These people called themselves the **Niquirano** and were governed by chief **Nicarao**, who came to be called Nicaragua by the Spanish, so giving a name to the country. A rich cacique (chief) from near present-day Rivas, Nicarao welcomed the first penetrations of the Spanish, made in 1522 by **Gil González de Avila**, an intrepid explorer who made his way north to Nicaragua on foot and by boat from Panamá and Costa Rica. Nicarao allowed his people to be baptized and to mix interracially with the Spanish conquerors.

The inhabitants of the central zone of Nicaragua, the **Chontales**, **Matagalpas** and **Populucas**, were a different ethnic group, related to the Maya of Honduras, and offered far more resistance to the

Spanish. Their language and peoples did not survive the Conquest. On the Atlantic coast the pre-Miskito people (of whom little is known), **Sumus** and **Ramas** made up the indigenous population. Nearly all the coastal peoples, except the Rama, mixed racially with Afro-Caribbean population who came to its shores as freed or escaped slaves from British West Indian colonies.

■ The colonial era

Although the very first Spanish conquistadors glimpsed the eastern coast of Nicaragua as early as 1508, it was not until 1522, three years after Hernán Cortez landed on the coast of Mexico, that a Spanish expedition sailed the Río San Juan into the Lago de Nicaragua. Two years later an expedition led by **Francisco Fernandez de Córdoba** founded the first cities, Granada and León, after suppressing local indigenous groups.

The story of colonial Nicaragua is a familiar one of rapacious looting of resources, exploitation of indigenous peoples as slave labour, and active genocide – in part caused by new diseases to which the pre-Columbian peoples had no immunity. On the Atlantic Coast, where the Europeans did not settle, diseases did not decimate the indigenous population to the same extent. Throughout the colonial period the Spanish crown did not concern itself much with its new hot, volcanic wedge of territory – the gold of Mexico and Peru was far more absorbing. Instead Nicaragua was used as a source of **slave labour** and many indigenous Nicaraguans were sent to work in Peruvian mines. The Spanish did not make much of an effort to penetrate remote parts of the country or to establish other towns, and by the end of the 1500s León and Granada were still the only settlements. Social development in Nicaragua was slow to the point of being stagnant; the country remained poor, the central mountains unexplored through fear of the fierce indigenous peoples who still lived there, the Atlantic coast plagued by pirates. Not much would change in Nicaragua for nearly three hundred years.

■ Independence

By the beginning of the nineteenth century Spain had begun to lose its grip on power in Nicaragua. As in other New World colonies, in Nicaragua only *peninsulares* – those born in Spain – could hold positions of influence. Fuelled by the frustrations of the local-born elite, a revolt staged in 1811 in El Salvador ignited aspirations of independence throughout the region. Along with the other Central American countries, in 1821 Nicaragua gained independence from the Spanish crown as part of the **Central American Federation**, before becoming a fully independent nation in 1838.

In search of a ship-accessible route through the isthmus, the United States showed new interest in Nicaragua, where the Río San Juan and Lago de Nicaragua represented a possible route for transporting goods and passengers between the Atlantic and the Pacific. In 1849, an American, **Cornelius Vanderbilt**, went into business with the Nicaraguan government to form the **Accessory Transit Company**, which was granted the exclusive right to build a canal across the isthmus within twelve years. The contract also gave Vanderbilt a transit route across Nicaragua to move passengers and mining equipment from the east coast of the US to the west to fuel the Californian Gold Rush. This was a period of relative prosperity for Nicaragua – and for Vanderbilt, who made a fortune – with giant steamboats plying the choppy waters of Lago de Nicaragua, filled with overdressed east coast ladies in crinolines sweating under the fierce sun alongside rough Gold Rush hopefuls.

■ **William Walker**

A man who would come to have a disastrous impact on Nicaragua, **William Walker** was an ambitious and megalomaniacal – or mad, depending on your interpretation – American adventurer. A native of Tennessee, schooled in law and journalism, Walker had vast political ambitions. The Liberals of León foolhardily handed him the chance to fulfil them by inviting him to Nicaragua to help them gain power over their arch-rivals, the Conservatives of Granada.

In 1855 Walker set foot on Nicaraguan soil with only sixty mercenaries, but nevertheless managed to gain control of Granada and, by default, the entire country. The Liberals had unleashed a maelstrom upon their country: Walker took matters into his own hands and installed a puppet government, but the real power remained with the American soldier of fortune.

In 1856, alarmed by the situation, Costa Rica declared war on Walker, but an epidemic of cholera forced the Costa Ricans to withdraw. The same year Walker held a rigged election and declared himself President of the Republic. By

making English the country's official language and **legalizing slavery**, Walker managed to alienate all Nicaraguans; Cornelius Vanderbilt, still a force in Nicaragua, was determined to have him out, and the other Central American countries, fearing Walker's activities might spark rebellions in their own countries, began plans to topple him.

Nicaragua paid dearly for the eventual overthrow of Walker, which eventually came only with help from Guatemala and Costa Rica. During his various sieges many Nicaraguans lost their lives, and on his retreat Walker ordered the beautiful colonial city of Granada burned. The final battle of 1856–57, in Rivas, near the Costa Rican border, would come to be known as the **"National War"**. Intervention by the United States forced the issue and on May 1, 1857, Walker and his remaining followers were escorted by marines out of Rivas and onto a ship back to the United States.

Walker was eventually captured by the British and handed over, as a wanted man, to the Americans. In 1860 he was executed in Trujillo, Honduras, aged 36.

■ **The Thirty Years**

For the next thirty-odd years power see-sawed, not always peacefully, between Liberals and Conservatives. But the period from 1857 to 1893 was one of such unusual stability and prosperity that Nicaraguan historians often refer to it, somewhat nostalgically, as **"The Thirty Years"**. These years coincided with the growth of what was to become Nicaragua's most important export – **coffee**. Europe and America's seemingly insatiable desire for coffee and bananas vaulted Nicaragua's coffee growers into the established elite of the cattle ranchers, as more and more land was devoted to the crop. In the first year of the twentieth century the new feature on the economic landscape was the overwhelming presence of US companies in Nicaragua: much of the banana and lumber industries, for example, were controlled from abroad. This alliance between US multinationals and local landowners in Nicaragua was to characterize economic relations for most of the coming century.

■ **The United States invades**

Angered when the United States chose Panamá for the site of the **Transisthmian Canal**, a decison that was ratified in 1904, **José Santos Zelaya**, the president of Nicaragua, countered by inviting Germany and Japan to construct a rival canal across Nicaragua, which never happened. The subsequent worsening of relations with the United States prompted a **civil war** in October 1909, with the nationalist Liberals and the US-friendly Conservatives again at each others' throats. In response, the US inaugurated a precedent in Nicaragua – and in the region as a whole – by intervening in domestic affairs. Four hundred **US marines** were landed on the Caribbean coast the same year; Zelaya resigned soon after.

From 1912 until 1933 the US kept a token number of troops in Nicaragua, more as a reminder of US influence than any real military threat. Pro-US Conservatives held on to power until a further outbreak of unrest between the Conservatives and Liberals in 1926 prompted the US to send more marines, ostensibly to protect United States citizens.

One of the opponents of the US presence in Nicaragua was **Augusto César Sandino**, a socialist who waged independent guerrilla activity, manned by his own personal army of peasants and workers. He eventually joined the Liberals' fight against the Conservatives and their US allies. In response to Sandino's activities – their excuse was the maintenance of "internal security" – in the first years of the 1930s the US took over the country's military and developed the Nicaraguan National Guard, which was to become such a significant force under the next political figure looming on Nicaragua's horizon – Somoza.

■ The Somoza years

The long era of **Somocismo**, or Somoza-family rule, began in 1934. In his role as head of the country's National Guard, **General Anastasio "Tacho" Somoza García** ordered the **assassination of Sandino**, by then the liberal candidate for the upcoming election. With Sandino dead, rigged elections were held and Somoza was sworn in as president of Nicaragua in 1937.

Well-educated in the US, where he attended a school run by the US marines, fluent in English and Americanized, Somoza was also well-connected in Nicaragua through the kind of network of family influence that has always been so significant in Central American political life. Perhaps his privileged lifestyle and reliance upon his family's influence were responsible for Somoza's exceptionally cynical character; in any case, it was clear he had little sympathy for the majority of his compatriots.

Indeed he ruled in typical Latin American strongman fashion as a *caudillo*, or dictator, as he ruthlessly pursued the enrichment of himself, his family and his coterie of associates. He cultivated the National Guard as his own personal army and gave it power far beyond the usual sphere of a military force, until it virtually controlled the radio stations, the postal services and even the health system.

For the Somoza family, at least, the **1940s** were prosperous. Somoza supported the Allies, at least in name (intimates of Somoza during this time recall Somoza replacing his office portrait of Hitler with one of Churchill). For most of the decade Somoza busied himself with accumulating a personal fortune, buying up land, the national airline, even the national dairy.

Somoza remained in power through continuously rigged elections and re-elections, or appointments of puppet governments. In 1955 the Nicaraguan Congress amended the constitution to allow Somoza to be re-elected again. But by then political opposition was growing. Somoza's end came unexpectedly, both for him and the country, brought about by the independent action of **Rigoberto López Perez**, a 27-year-old poet, who shot the dictator dead in the streets of León in 1956. The National Guard responded by shooting Perez some fifty times. His poignant letter to his mother justifying his actions is kept as an historical document in Nicaragua.

As it turned out, little changed, despite Perez's dramatic and passionate action. Somoza's son, **Luis Somoza Debayle**, also US-educated, took the position of interim president. At the same time his younger brother **Anastasio "Tachito" Somoza Debayle** assumed command of the National Guard. Following in their father's footsteps, they stayed in power through manipulation of the constitution and electoral process. A long period of repression followed, when dissidents were regularly tortured and imprisoned.

Opposition grew, however, and in the 1967 elections the Conservatives and Christian Social Party banded together to create the **National Opposition Union** (Unión Nacional Opositora, or UNO). Nonetheless, vote rigging and harassment of voters ensured Somoza's election as president. Luis Somoza died of a heart attack soon after and power was left concentrated in the hands of Anastasio Somoza – now both president and head of the National Guard.

Somoza's term of office should have ended in 1971, but he managed to have the term extended to 1972. The emerging opposition was now led by Pedro Joaquín Chamorro, the editor of the newspaper *La Prensa*.

■ Growing opposition

At a few minutes past midnight on December 23, 1972, Managua was rocked by an incredible seismic disturbance, causing the near total collapse of the city. By the time the ground stopped rumbling – just thirty seconds later – some 10,000 people were dead and about 50,000 families homeless.

Every Nicaraguan recognizes the **earthquake of 1972** as a national turning point – and not just because it brought Bianca Jagger back to her native homeland for a spell of relief work. The earthquake was followed by the looting of the shattered shops of Managua's former commercial core, in which poor Managuans were joined by soldiers of the National Guard. Much of the emergency earthquake relief supplies sent from abroad were also intercepted by the Guard, acting on Somoza's orders, and then sold off to victims in the street. Businesses and homeowners were unable to claim compensation on damaged property because the Somoza-owned insurance companies refused to recognize their claims. All classes of Nicaraguans were appalled by the epic cynicism and greed behind Somoza's actions; by 1974 his personal wealth was estimated at some US$400 million. Even businessmen and the elite, both traditionally loyal to Somoza, deserted camp.

Although the downtown core of Managua was never reconstructed, an effective opposition to the dictator was built out of the rubble of the 1972 earthquake. The **Frente Sandinista de Liberación Nacional** (FSLN), named after Sandino, became a rallying point for dissidents. Founded in the late 1950s by law students at the National University in León as a Marxist-Leninist response to the dictatorship, by the early 1970s the FSLN had gained widespread support, especially in the countryside and among students.

The FSLN's first major success took place on December 27, 1974, when guerrillas raided the home of a government official and held to ransom several relatives of Somoza, gaining a US$1 million payout. The guerrillas fled abroad, and, though the opposition was buoyed by the success of the rebels' audacity, in response Somoza stepped up the repression, surveillance, torture and murder of suspected dissidents.

Opposition to the Somoza regime accelerated in 1977, both within Nicaragua and in the United States, whose new president, Democrat Jimmy Carter, made continuing military assistance to the Somoza regime contingent on the improvement of human rights. In October of that year a group of Nicaraguan intellectuals met secretly in Costa Rica to form the first coherent anti-Somoza alliance, and to work out a plan of action. The catalyst that began the revolution was engineered by the dictator himself when, on January 10, 1978, **Pedro Joaquín Chamorro**, opposition leader and editor of *La Prensa*, was assassinated by the National Guard, acting on Somoza's orders. Mass demonstrations and a general strike followed, crippling the country and galvanizing the opposition. Meanwhile, in response to attacks on civilians and increasing reports of torture and murder, the US cut off the Somoza regime by suspending military aid. Unrest had its effect on the national economy and inflation and unemployment reached new heights.

The most dramatic event staged by the FSLN took place on August 22, 1978, when guerrillas stormed the National Palace while Congress was in session. After 2000 government members had been held hostage for two days, President Somoza was forced to meet the demands of the FSLN. A humiliation for Somoza, the audacity of the guerrillas once again inspired the population. By the end of 1978, demonstrations and outbreaks of fighting had spread around the country.

■ Revolution

As 1979 opened, Somoza's declaration that he would stay in power until 1981, two years past his mandate, sparked a national crisis. As guerrilla attacks by the opposition increased, the Nicaraguan economy nosedived. By now, though, the FSLN was in a stronger position, having acquired arms from sympathetic countries like Cuba. In May the FSLN launched its main offensive in Estelí and Jinotega. No longer merely a group of guerrilla insurrectionists bent on staging dramatic stunts, the **Sandinistas** were now a formidable **fighting force**: their influence had spread to the provinces, and their military strategy was centrally organized.

In June a Nicaraguan **government-in-exile** was established in Costa Rica. Among the five-member governorship of the country were two people who would be key in the political future of

Nicaragua – **Daniel José Ortega Saavedra** of the FSLN and **Violeta Barrios de Chamorro**, the widow of the assassinated *La Prensa* editor. By June the country was largely in the hands of the Sandinistas, although Managua remained under the control of Somoza and his National Guard. Isolated, Somoza was forced to resign and soon after boarded a plane to Miami. He eventually moved to Paraguay, where he was assassinated by South American leftist guerrillas in 1980.

Triumphant, the government-in-exile ceremoniously entered the city of León the day after Somoza's departure. A day later the FSLN forces entered Managua, and the revolution was won, officially, on July 19, 1979.

With the revolution ended a long – perhaps even 500-year-long – era of feudalism in Nicaragua. However, the price had been high: around 50,000 were dead and over 120,000 had fled the country into exile.

■ The Sandinista years and the Contra War

As the 1970s became the 1980s, the challenge facing the **new Sandinista government** was enormous. The country's infrastructure was in ruins: food was scarce, health care nonexistent and diseases like cholera and malaria rampant. But the mood of the country – among the leadership as well as the general population – was buoyant, even ecstatic. By all accounts, the Sandinistas' energy for reconstruction was enormous. Within days new ministers took over buildings formerly owned by Somoza companies, set up government offices, and got down to the business at hand.

First on the agenda for the Sandinistas was the resuscitation of the **economy**, severely damaged by Somoza's appropriation and by war. Foreign debts had to be renegotiated, loans secured, and economic aid directed. Somoza's properties were nationalized – some 2000 farms accounting for twenty percent of Nicaragua's agricultural land.

Operating under emergency measures, the governing junta suspended all the mechanisms of Somocismo, including the constitution, presidency, Congress, and all courts. A new army, the Sandinista People's Army (**Ejército Popular Sandinista** or EPS), was formed along with a Sandinista-controlled police force. With the help of training by Cuban and Soviet armed forces, the EPS soon developed into the most powerful standing army in Central America.

Another task facing the Sandinistas was the construction of a civil society, which had never really existed in Nicaragua. They set about forming various unions and interest groups, of which the largest still exist in some form: the Sandinista Workers' Federation (Central Sandinista de Trabajadores–CST) and the Luisa Amanda Espinoza Nicaraguan Women's Association (Asociación de Mujeres Nicaragüenses Luisa Amanda Espinoza or AMNLAE). In transforming the civil, military and judicial arms of Nicaragua, the Sandinistas made themselves ubiquitous, and within only a year of taking over the country they were in control of most aspects of Nicaraguan society.

The first democratic elections held under the Sandinistas, in 1984, were won by Daniel Ortega with a 67 percent majority. This was the first time most Nicaraguans had ever voted, and the first time since 1928 that the United States did not have a hand in the electoral process. The Sandinistas were not universally popular, however, particularly in the **Atlantic Coast** region. Independent, traditionally suspicious of anyone of Spanish descent and not of a leftist bent, the Miskito, Rama and Creole peoples of the Atlantic Coast never really got behind the revolution, especially after the Sandinistas made attempts to forcibly relocate indigenous groups and to impose leftist ideology upon them. Many coastal dwellers – the Miskito especially – were so disenchanted by the Sandinistas that they would make easy recruits in the civil war that was to come.

The main blow for the Sandinistas came in the form of **Ronald Reagan's** election to the presidency of the US in November 1980. Convinced that Nicaragua's leftist policies and its friendship with Cuba and the Soviet Union meant the spread of Communism in the United States' back yard, the Reagan administration **suspended aid** to Nicaragua in 1981 and thereafter waged an open campaign against the Sandinistas. The **Contra War** – "contra" being short for *contrarevolucionarios* – was launched with nearly $20 million of US military assistance. The troops, based in training camps in Honduras, were mostly made up of former National Guard soldiers who had fled the country on Somoza's departure, though they were soon joined by other groups, namely Miskitos. Although it's true that a certain sector of the population was disgruntled with the Sandinistas, the presence of the universally hated ex-National Guard in the Contra forces caused most Nicaraguans to distrust the Contra movement.

By the mid-1980s the Contra War was causing widespread disruption in the country. What with open US support for the movement, as well as the ambivalent positions of Honduras and Costa Rica – both used as launching pads by the Contras – the Sandinistas felt increasingly isolated, and began to clamp down on political opposition. Revoking their promises for an open political society, they banned opposition in the media – including *La Prensa*, ironically an organ of dissent during the Somoza years – and prevented rival political parties.

Arguably it was the five-year-long **US trade embargo** that succeeded in strangling the Nicaraguan economy and undermining the Sandinistas. Within a few years, though, US support for the Contras was shaken by the **Irangate** scandal, which most people remember as the endless televised proceedings of Oliver North being pseudo-interrogated by Congress; it emerged he was the lynchpin in a CIA scheme to sell weapons to Iran illegally, using the proceeds fund the activities of the Contras.

The first serious initiative for peace in Nicaragua was taken by neighbouring Costa Rica's president, Oscar Arias Sánchez. The **Arias Plan** for peace in Central America, launched in February 1987, had the backing of the United States and was signed by the presidents of the five Central American republics. An initiative to stop conflict within Nicaragua and El Salvador, and to repair relations between Nicaragua and Honduras, the Plan was welcomed as the first serious attempt to solve by diplomatic means the political problems between nations in the region. In March 1988 the FSLN and the Contras signed a cease-fire agreement.

■ 1990–1996: The Chamorro goverment

Elections were scheduled for February 1990. This would be the test for the Sandinistas' staying power as a political force: opposition was gathering strength and in 1989 no fewer than fourteen political parties, with nothing in common except their opposition to the leftists, formed a coalition, the **National Opposition Union** (Unión Nacional Opositora, UNO), and appointed Violeta Barrios de Chamorro, then-publisher of *La Prensa*, as their presidential candidate. Head of a coalition of opposition forces that had the support of the US government and Nicaraguans living in Miami, **Doña Violeta**, as she is known in Nicaragua, had all the ingredients of a leader. Her status as the

widow of a murdered hero of the revolution also gave her a moral authority that few, other than Daniel Ortega himself, could match.

Ortega ran again for the Sandinistas, who adopted an anti-US stance, condemning the UNO as a puppet of US foreign policy. The UNO was fractured and disorganized, fighting what seemed to be, at least on the surface, a less charismatic campaign, which concentrated on promises of peace and reviving the national economy.

The international community and neighbouring Central American countries watched the elections carefully, expecting the Sandinista organizational know-how and showmanship to win through. Perhaps no one was more deeply shocked than Daniel Ortega when on February 25, 1990, Violeta Barrios de Chamorro emerged victorious with 55 percent of the vote against Ortega's 41 percent. Both international observers and Nicaraguan commentators could only conclude that the Nicaraguan people had voted for peace, fearing that another Sandinista government would bring continuing war and poverty. By the end of the 1980s the more well-to-do echelons of society (at least, the ones who had not fled to Costa Rica or Miami) had the distinct impression they had been better off under Somoza. Death had hit at nearly every family, and many people felt the Sandinistas had brought further hardship on the country by inviting the scrutiny of the US and the subsequent blockade. One way or another, Nicaraguans had decided it was time for a change.

Although there were extreme right-wing forces in her coalition, Violeta was seen as an acceptable moderate and with Chamorro's election victory came peace: the US lifted their embargo and cut off supplies to the Contras. After some delay, both sides were disarmed and plans were drawn up to re-integrate soldiers into society, a process that later came to grief as small bands of Contras and Sandinistas re-armed to fight for better conditions for veterans.

However you feel about their politics, the **achievements** of the Sandinistas were enormous. When they took over after Somoza's departure, about sixty percent of Nicaragua's population was illiterate. Literacy workers were dispatched to every corner in the country, armed only with a chalkboard and a gas lamp, and by the end of the Sandinista years the figure had been reduced to thirteen percent. They also transformed the role of women: several women led battalions into combat during the revolution, and women made up about twenty percent of soldiers in the Sandinista army. Because the war effort ate up around half the national budget for many years, basic programmes in health education and culture were heavily reliant on foreign funding and international volunteers. These *internacionalistas*, as they were called, for many years made up an important part of Nicaraguan society. As a result of this contact, Nicaraguans are generally more aware of what is going on in the rest of the world than other Central Americans of similar background, and display a remarkable cosmopolitanism, even in very remote areas. In many ways, the Sandinistas effected a near-total transformation of Nicaraguan society

With Chamorro's victory, the World Bank and the International Monetary Fund began negotiations to relieve Nicaragua's debt burden in exchange for a programme of **economic restructuring**. The government initiated a plan to rein in the inflation rate in the first 100 days – during the first few years of the decade inflation was running at about 410 percent. The honeymoon didn't last long; the country was in a shocking state, the result of a drawn-out war, a crippling US embargo and falling production. Nicaraguans were tired of the constant state of crisis and the steady deterioration of the standard of living. For them, things only got worse.

The new government's plan to halt inflation failed and the economic restructuring, without any of the cushioning in place under the Sandinistas, resulted in two paralyzing **general strikes**, which forced the government to alter much of its programme. Violeta Chamorro's inner circle, the members of the cabinet who effectively decided policy, managed to resolve the crisis by working with the Sandinista leadership during the months of the strikes; in doing so, they alienated the extreme right-wing element in the coalition, which wanted to crush Sandinismo once and for all.

To her credit, Violeta Chamorro managed to hold the government together during the six-year term, but during the **1996 election campaign** right-wing forces gathered around the former Mayor of Managua, **Arnoldo Alemán**. His party, the Liberal Constitutionalist Party (PLC), was a splinter group of the larger National Liberal Party (PLN), the political vehicle of Anastasio Somoza.

The Sandinistas' chances of defeating the Liberals suffered a blow a year before the election when there was a damaging split in the party. A moderate faction led by ex-Vice President Sergio Ramirez broke away leaving Sandinista leader Daniel Ortega in charge of the remnants. The result was that Alemán and the PLC won the election – narrowly – and formed another coalition government, this time more openly committed to the destruction of Sandinismo and more closely aligned with the Catholic Church and the US policy of global integration.

■ The Alemán government and Nicaragua's future

Many Nicaraguans saw the **Alemán victory** as proof that the counter-revolutionary movement had not only won, but had welcomed Somocismo back into Nicaragua. For many Sandinistas, this was a dispiriting, even heartbreaking, conclusion. However, a year or so on, it seems unlikely that Alemán's administration will lead to such a stark reversal. Although the new capitalist ethic in Nicaragua is fuelled by IMF and World Bank structural adjustment programmes and pro-US sentiment, so far Alemán has practised the Nicaraguan art of political deal-making; his style is more likely to involve political cronyism – his mayoral administration of Managua was many times accused of corruption – rather than the right-wing repression of the Somoza years.

The current situation in Nicaragua is both better and worse than it has been for a long time. The papers are full of stories of **lawlessness** – street gangs in Managua, delinquents stealing televisions in Jinotepe, and more than twenty armed bands working in Boaco. Most statistics put Nicaragua as the second poorest country in the Americas, after Haiti. Two million Nicaraguans live in extreme poverty, with an income of less than a dollar a day. Nicaragua has fallen to the 127th poorest country out of 175 studied by the UN Program for Development.

These are not the kind of pronouncements the neo-Liberals of Alemán's administration want to hear and long meditations on the Gross Domestic Product appear regularly in the national press. Whereas in many Latin American countries the military remains a force of repression, the army created by the Sandinistas has managed the transition from a partisan to a professional organization reasonably well. Many sectors of the labour force are well-organized and able to defend workers' rights and, despite all the complications, much of the arable land in Nicaragua is still in the hands of small- to medium-sized producers. These are all good signs for a fledgling democracy. In 1996 Nicaragua also had the fastest rate of growth of any Central American nation and between 1990 and 1996 had the highest per capita aid levels in the world, apart from Israel. The problem is that most of this **wealth** is concentrated in the hands of the rich: the top twenty percent own sixty percent of the wealth, the bottom twenty percent a meagre three percent; shops are full of imported goods and the per capita income is no greater than it was in 1945.

One of the most intractable problems facing the Alemán government today is the **dispute over land**. During the revolution the Sandinistas took over property and industries belonging to the Somocistas and nationalized or redistributed them to peasants, farming cooperatives and veterans of the war, under a variety of systems. When they lost the election in 1990 the Sandinistas had to scramble to pass legislation protecting the redistribution. In the process, they also distributed the gains of the revolution to party members. This giveaway – known as the "piñata", after the hollow papier-mâché form filled with sweets – seriously undermined the party's reputation. In turn, the Chamorro government made use of land grants to persuade Contra fighters to disarm. Little care was taken in any of these redistributions to observe the legal requirements of a land transfer. Ownership became the subject of complex and often violent **disputes** when relatives of Somoza and others who had lost land when they fled to the US returned to claim their former holdings.

The far right was hoping that the Chamorro government would act quickly to return much of that property and was disappointed when instead it sought to recognize the rights of thousands of small landholders. Today the land issue is in many ways the key to Nicaragua's future. If the land is returned to former land owners it will signify a significant shift to the right, alienating many of those who voted for Alemán. If the rights of small landholders are quickly recognized it will perhaps enable Nicaragua to progress towards a stable, democratic and prosperous society. If nothing is done there will be a gradual redistribution of the land as small farmers, starved of credit through lack of title and unsympathetic government policies, sell it off at bargain basement prices.

The irony is that Nicaraguans are tired of conflict and more than anything want peace, but in some ways – faced with poverty, unemployment, uncertainty over land ownership and perhaps even the economic survival of the country – the country seems once again ripe for revolution. Just what happens depends on how President Alemán handles the situation. His government is vulnerable, based on a coalition which can disintegrate at any time; and without the promised social improvements for the average person, his electoral support will disappear. Alemán has the backing of the rich Miami exiles, the US government and the Nicaraguan oligarchy, as long as he responds to their demands for an open economy and return of nationalized property. He can't rely, as other governments might in Central America, on a loyal army and police force. He has to juggle the demands of all these interest groups against the demands of the International Monetary Fund and the World Bank. Even while Nicaraguans sincerely hope for stability, it is not clear how long he can keep these forces from spilling over.

CHAPTER 22

MANAGUA

H otter than an oven and crisscrossed by anonymous highways, there can't be a more tourist-unfriendly city than **MANAGUA**. Less a city in the European sense than a conglomeration of neighbourhoods and commercial districts, Managua offers few sights or cultural experiences of the type you can have in other Central American cities. In fact, most visitors are so disturbed by the lack of street names or any real centre to the city that they get out as fast as they can. Being a tourist in Managua requires some tenacity, but if you can see beyond its lack of elegance, you'll find there are some things to enjoy. Like Nicaragua itself, Managua throbs with life: there is a kind of ragged energy to its streets, which are full almost any hour of the day or night, be it with flocks of schoolchildren, neighbours chatting on street corners, cheery taxi drivers, or sidewalk tamale and refresco sellers.

As Nicaragua's largest and capital city, home to a quarter of the population, Managua occupies a key position in the nation's economy and psyche, and most travellers interested in understanding Nicaragua stay at least a few days. The country's few national **museums** and **cultural organizations** are all found here, most of them in the city's old ruined centre, whose historic cathedral is worth visiting, along with the Palacio Nacional, a museum of Nicaragua's culture and the home of its national library.

Set on the southern shore of **Lago de Managua**, or Lago Xolotlán as it was known to the Chorotega peoples who inhabited the lakeshore before the Conquest, the city is hot, low-lying and swampy. Several kilometres inland, a few eroded volcanoes and dead volcano craters – like Laguna de Tiscapa, just above the old city centre, and Laguna de Xiloa to the north – relieve the city's flatness.

Founded as a new capital city by the Spanish in 1858 as a foil to the warring political factions of León and Granada, from the beginning Managua was intended to represent the political middle ground. But the ground itself proved the problem: Managua sits smack on top of no fewer than eleven **seismic faults**, and the ground by the lakeshore is sandy and unstable. The earthquake of March 1931 destroyed most of the city; what Managuans managed to rebuild was largely razed by a fire only five years later. Again the city was rebuilt, with modern commercial buildings of four or five storeys, wide streets, traffic lights and shops, only to be completely trashed by another **earthquake** on **December 23, 1972**. This one claimed over ten thousand lives and left many more homeless. For a variety of reasons – the greed of the Somoza dictatorship governing the country at the time, who intercepted foreign emergency aid and sold it to victims at inflated prices, the refusal of insurance companies (mostly Somoza-owned) to pay out disaster damages, and the Revolution – the old centre of Managua has never been rebuilt and lies in ruins. There is talk of establishing a new city centre in what is now the south of the city, just over the hill of Laguna de Tiscapa, and ground has already been broken on new hotels and shops.

Managuans fought on the Sandinista side during the **1978–79 Revolution**, which brought fighting to the streets and further damage to buildings. The Sandinista government wanted to **rebuild** the centre, using donated foreign funds, but this never happened and today "downtown" Managua remains a ruined shell of scruffy fields, concrete skeletons of fashionable shops and old parking lots turned into graffiti-sprayed basketball courts. Squatters, the poor and the homeless have colonized the derelict spaces and constructed makeshift homes among the ruins.

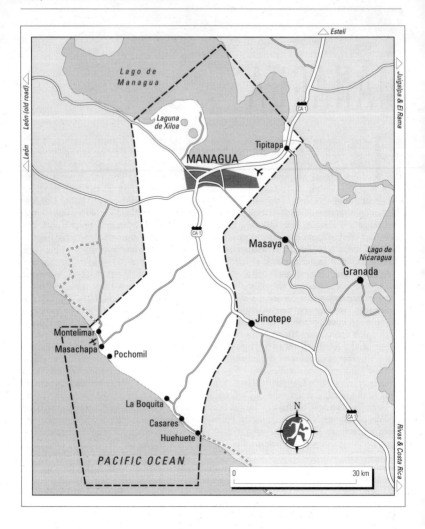

Managua's two million inhabitants now live in the random agglomeration of the city's many barrios, with well-to-do areas side by side with shantytowns. One of the main features of post-earthquake Managua is the proliferation of *centros comerciales*, mostly low-slung North American-style **shopping malls**, with banks, supermarkets and secure parking. During the first half of the 1990s, when current president, the right-of-centre Arnoldo Alemán, was mayor of Managua, he erected costly fountains and had many of the famous murals of the Sandinista era painted over, thereby losing forever many of the best examples of Latin American political street art.

During the Contra war many people fled violence in rural areas and migrated to Managua, creating new **neighbourhoods** and expanding the city's perimeter. The wealthy tend to live in neighbourhoods called *repartos* and *residenciales; colónias* were

> For an explanation of **accommodation price codes**, see p.438.

largely created by the Sandinistas in order to house specific professions, like teachers, and the *barrios* tend to be the poorer areas, where squatters and rural migrants try to eke out a living. In the mid-1990s Managua's culture changed with the return of some of the "Miami boys" – businessmen and influential families who had fled revolutionary Nicaragua to settle in Miami. The current political climate has enticed some to return, and with them have come their American values, air-conditioned four-wheel drives, and alarm-studded mansions. New bars and restaurants catering to the tastes of these **nicas ricas** have sprung up, and even if the cover charges are high, the drinks expensive and the clientele more South Floridan than Nicaraguan, they have improved the nightlife scene.

Still, the reality of the city is that there are few sights of interest. The good news is that most of the old buildings, museums, theatres and cultural centres are within a few blocks' walk of each other – an advantage in the draining heat. And even if the few tourist attractions have been given a lick of paint (for the most part paid for by the Dutch, Austrian or Chinese governments), the majority of Managuans are still very poor. This begs a mention only because **street crime** is on the rise, and Managua has developed a reputation as a dangerous city – not so much for foreigners as for Managuans, since gang warfare is an increasing problem. But it's best to travel by taxi, even in the daytime, and not to walk around at night; in general, be on your guard. In Managua in particular, it is difficult, as a tourist to enter into "real" Nicaraguan life unless you have a local contact; this is due both to a lack of public spaces and meeting places like cafés or galleries and the fact that Managuans' social scene is based in their neighbourhoods, in churches, discos and playgrounds.

Arrival and information

The majority of travellers arrive in central Managua on the **international** Ticabus services from either Honduras or El Salvador in the north or from San José in Costa Rica to the south. Buses from within Nicaragua arrive at one of several crowded, noisy and generally chaotic **urban marketplaces** that also serve as bus terminals. For **drivers** Managua is a disconcerting city in which to arrive; the lack of definable centre and landmarks – not to mention road signs or directions – make driving into the city a stressful experience, especially coupled with zealous traffic cops and aggressive Managuan drivers.

The good news about arriving by air or bus is the abundance of **taxis**. If you know where you are going to stay, it is helpful to have the address given to you in terms of neighbourhood and distance from a well-known **landmark**; no one uses street addresses in Managua, and taxi drivers will find places by its relation to a well-known city fixture. Distances are measured in metres as much as in blocks – in local parlance 100m is a city block or *cuadra*. Sometimes an archaic measure, the *vara*, is also used: one *vara* is roughly equivalent to a metre. To confuse the issue still further, many Managuans do not use the **cardinal points** as directions: in Managua north becomes *al lago* – towards the lake; *al sur* is south; *arriba* – literally, "up", is to the east; *abajo*, "down", is to the west. So, "*del Hotel Intercontinental una cuadra (cien metros) arriba y dos cuadras (doscientos metros) al lago*" means one block east and two blocks north of the *Hotel Intercontinental*. For clarity, we've used blocks and the cardinal points in addresses throughout.

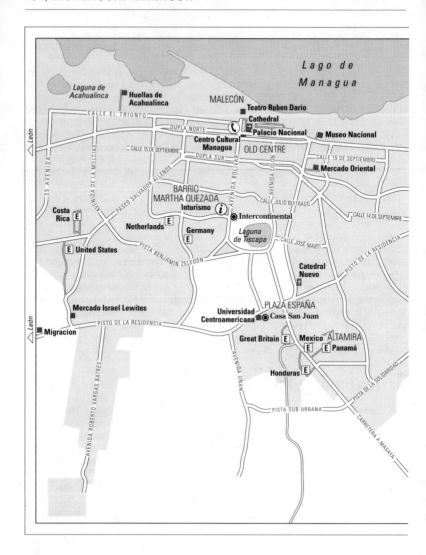

By air

All international flights and the vast majority of domestic ones arrive at Managua's **Aeropuerto Internacional Augusto César Sandino**, 12km east of Managua. The one bank there, Banpro (Mon–Fri 8.30am–noon & 1–4pm, Sat 8.30–11.45am), changes US dollars and gives cash advances at a reasonable rate but won't change travellers' cheques. You can pay for everything (including a taxi to the centre) in dollars, but if you really want **córdobas**, outside banking hours you'll have to hike across the Carretera Norte outside the airport and try the *Hotel las Mercedes*. Local and international

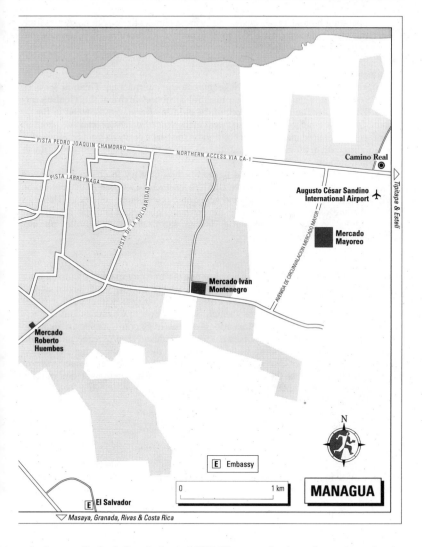

PISTA PEDRO JOAQUIN CHAMORRO

NORTHERN ACCESS VIA CA-1

Camino Real

PISTA LARREYNAGA

PISTA DE LA SOLIDARIDAD

Augusto César Sandino
International Airport ✈

▷ *Tipitapa & Estelí*

Mercado
Mayoreo

AVENIDA DE CIRCUNVALACIÓN MERCADO MAYOR

Mercado Iván
Montenegro

Mercado
Roberto
Huembes

N

E Embassy

0 1 km

MANAGUA

E El Salvador

▽ *Masaya, Granada, Rivas & Costa Rica*

telephone calls (including Sprint and USA Direct services) can be made at the airport's Telcor/Enitel office (daily 7am–6.45pm).

You'll find **car rental** agencies in the arrivals hall at the northern end of the airport (there's also an Eskimo ice-cream bar). If you're not in a hurry it might be worth stopping at the kiosk in the central hall for a **cappuccino**, as there aren't too many opportunities elsewhere in Nicaragua.

The **buses** that ply the Carretera Norte into town are constantly crowded; should you manage to squeeze onto one, you'll be a tempting target for the many practiced thieves operating on Managua's buses – taxis are definitely the way to go. A **taxi** from the arrivals gate into town costs US$7; walking out to the Carretera Norte can save you at least two dollars on the fare.

By international bus
The majority of travellers arrive in Nicaragua on the international **Ticabus** services from San Salvador, Tegucigalpa or San José. All Ticabuses arrive at the **Ticabus terminal** (2 blocks east and 1 block south of the old Cine Dorado; ☎222-6094) in Barrio Martha Quezada, a neighbourhood just west of the *Hotel Intercontinental* and about as central as you get in Managua. If you come in on the **Sirca** services from San José, you arrive in the south of the city, near the Universidad Centroamericana, four blocks north of the Shell station.

Taxi drivers wait for the Ticabus to arrive; they may try to charge innocents a **gringo fare** (currently anything above US$1.20 for a journey within Managua), so be ready to argue for a reasonable fare and agree on a price before you get in. There's a Publitel **phone** on the corner outside the terminal; queues of arriving Managuans mean that savvy telephone touts offer instant satisfaction with **mobile phones** (US$0.50–0.70 for a local call).

By domestic bus
Buses from elsewhere in Nicaragua arrive at one of three **city markets**. Coming from Masaya, Granada, Rivas or other destinations in the **south**, you'll arrive at the **Mercado Roberto Huembes** near the Carretera Masaya. Buses from the **north** and **east** – Estelí, Matagalpa, Jinotega, Ocotal, Somoto, Boaco, Chontales and Rama – arrive at a new terminal in the **Mercado Mayoreo** in Barrio Concepción, near the Pista Mayoreo. The Mayoreo is somewhat more organized than other terminals with re-sold tickets, plenty of seating while you wait for the bus, and a general ban on vendors, making it safer than other terminals. Buses from the **northwest** towns of León and Chinandega use the busy **Mercado Israel Lewites** in the north of the capital. No matter which market you arrive at, keep an eye on your belongings, especially at night.

At each market there is a constant supply of **taxis** waiting to whisk you into town (US$1–1.25). As always, agree on a fare before you get in.

Information

The only place in Managua equipped to provide information is Managua's **Inturismo** office, one block west of the *Hotel Intercontinental* (Mon–Fri 8.30am–12.30pm & 1.30–5pm; ☎222-2962). Taxis will know it as the Ministerio de Turismo. If there is no one there, ask the security guard at the corner entrance to phone for you and someone will come and open the door. The staff are well-intentioned and some speak English, but they are only able to dispense **pamphlets** – the series of pastel-coloured ones in Spanish are well-written but contain nothing of any practical use. It's worth asking for a **city map** of Managua, although these are not always available. The most useful publication is the bimonthly *Guía Fácil Nicaragua* (US$1), which lists cultural events and entertainment throughout the country, with features on regions and tourist activities; sometimes transport schedules are also included and there's usually a helpful map of Managua on the inside back cover. The Inturismo office may be able to sell you one; otherwise you can find it in the *Casa del Café* (see "Eating", p.463) and at the larger hotels.

City transport

Managua's heat and incoherent layout make it a disconcerting city for travellers to negotiate and some form of transport is essential. Buses are the cheapest way to get around, but taxis are more straightforward to use and safer, particularly at night.

Buses

If your confidence and Spanish are up to it, it's worth taking the **bus** at least once, for an insight into how most Managuans live. While the bus service is incredibly **cheap** (US$0.15) and fairly comprehensive, the amazing crowdedness and notorious **pickpockets** – the two are obviously related – are a real deterrent. The crush makes it hard to avoid theft; keeping your money in an inside pocket or clutching your bag on your front are wise precautions. The lack of bus route maps, signed bus stops, or destinations marked on the bus itself – buses are labelled only with numbers – make anything other than a simple trip

---

USEFUL BUS ROUTES

#108 Santa Clara – Socrates Sandino
Carretera Norte, Migración, Mercado Oriental, Nueva Rotunda Santo Domingo, Pista de la Resistencia, Máximo Jeréz, Centro Comercial Managua, Mercado Huembes.

#109 Socrates Sandino – Malecón
Malecón, Teatro Nacional Ruben Dario, Centro Cultural, Palacio Nacionál, Hotel Intercontinental, Largaespada, El Dorado, Mercado Huembes.

#110 Las Piedrecitas – Mercado Mayor
US embassy, Siete Sur, Pista de la Resistencia (or San Juan 11, as it has been renamed), Mercado Israel Lewites, the UCA (University of Central America), Altamira, Centro Comercial Managua, Huembes, Mercado Ivan Montenegro.

#112 Miraflor – Via Libertad
Carretera Sur, Linda Vista, Carretera Norte, Malecón, Teatro Nacional Ruben Darío, Mercado Ivan Montenegro.

#113 Las Piedrecitas – Buenos Aires
Batahola Sur, El Carmen, Martha Quezada.

#117 Villa Jose Benito Escobar – San Juan
Carretera Norte, Villa Revolución, Rubenia, Mercado Huembes, Colonia Centroamérica, Centro Comercial Camino de Oriente, Av UNAN.

#118 Siete Sur – Manuel Fernandez
Siete Sur, Pista de la Resistencia, El Recreo, Plaza España, Martha Quezada, Ciudad Jardín.

#119 Las Brisas – 19 Junio
Las Brisas, Linda Vista, Monseñor Lezcano, Plaza España, Pista de la Resistencia, Metro Centro, Los Robles, Carretera a Masaya, Mexican embassy, British embassy, Altamira, *Casa de Café*, La Colonia, Colonia Centro America, Mercado Huembes.

hopelessly confusing. However, locals know the routes, and will help you find the right stop. Services start at 5am and continue until 10pm, becoming less frequent from about 6pm onwards. For a rundown of the main city bus routes, see p.457.

Certain parts of the city are **dangerous** and should be avoided by foreigners. If a bus breaks down or you get off in the wrong place and find yourself in an unfamiliar neighbourhood, do not walk around looking lost; approach a friendly-looking local and ask them to stay with you until you are safely in a taxi.

Taxis

Managua **taxis** are heroic old Ladas spiffed up by their proud owners with all manner of stickers, banners, religious iconography and sparkly plastic gear-stick tops. Generally **cheap** and with friendly, talkative drivers, they are however not always in good supply – one reason why **sharing** is the usual way to go in Managua. If you see a taxi with one or two people already in it, it's worth flagging it down; drivers will usually honk at you if they are looking for custom. **Detour** time is minimal, though, as drivers will accept an additional fare only if everyone is headed in vaguely the same direction. Fares range from US$0.75–1.25 per person, depending on distance. Drivers may be open to negotiation if you are in a group going to the same destination.

Driving

Driving in Managua itself is not recommended. The city can seem like one endless freeway, with no street signs – confidence and a good city map are both essential. Should you get lost and find yourself in one of the various rough parts of the city, roll up your windows and lock doors, especially at traffic lights. It's not safe to leave your car on the street, but most upscale hotels have secure **car parks**. For exploring outside of Managua, however, a car is a definite bonus; see p.467 for a list of **rental** agencies.

Accommodation

Site of the Ticabus terminal, the **Barrio Martha Quezada**, a neighbourhood twelve blocks south of the old ruined city centre and just west of the *Hotel Intercontinental*, is the place for cheap hospedaje-type accommodation, aimed at both nationals and foreigners – having said that, some of the best hotels and guest houses in Managua are also located here. Directions and **addresses** in the barrio use the local landmarks of the *Hotel Intercontinental*, the Ticabus station, and the closed Cine Dorado, west of the Ticabus station.

During the Revolution years most foreigners were confined to this eight-by-five block area and it became something of an international community, filled with cafés and restaurants where politics and literature were debated over beers by visitors from all over the world. These days the barrio is definitely not the hopping place it used to be. A mixture of upper-middle-class homes and very poor dwellings, some with only corrugated iron for doors, the barrio's hot eventless streets have a forlorn look, as if they miss the activity of past years. There's nothing much to do here except sleep, though a number of good **restaurants** remain in the area, none of them particularly cheap.

Accommodation in Martha Quezada is scattered in a two-block radius on either side of the Ticabus terminal. Arriving at the terminal, you will be met by touts, usually children, offering to take you to a hospedaje. They receive a percentage from the hotel owner for bringing people off the Ticabus and there is no harm in going with them, since you're under no obligation to stay if you don't like the hospedaje they take you to. Most hospedajes in Martha Quezada do not have signs (hospedajes with signs have to pay hotel taxes; those without them are less likely to come under scrutiny).

There's no real concentration of hotels **elsewhere** in the city: several upscale air-port-type hotels are located on the Carretera Norte near the international airport, with a few hotels located in the residential neighbourhood of Bolonia, immediately south of Barrio Martha Quezada. One or two places can be found near the Universidad Centroamericana (UCA), towards the south of the city.

As elsewhere in Nicaragua, Managua accommodation tends to be spartan, with water and light given to interruptions or cuts. Because of the city's amazing heat and humidity, Managua is one place in the country where you might want to shell out for a noisy old **air-conditioning** unit, though this can cost up to double the price of a room with a fan. Many hospedajes in Barrio Martha Quezada are open to discounts of a couple of dollars for groups or for long stays – it's worth asking.

Barrio Martha Quezada

Hospedaje el Bambú, 1 block east of Ticabus (look for the bamboo door). Friendly Marie-Elena and family run a hospedaje with six rather dark rooms with fan and shared bath, set around a pleasant covered patio area. Meals on request. For reservations, call Marie-Elena's sister Nubia on ☎222-3180. ②.

Hospedaje Dorado, 2 blocks west of Ticabus. Very cheap and quiet family-run hospedaje set back from the street. Friendly and secure, but rooms are stuffy, grouped around a small interior patio. Some rooms with private bath, all with ceiling fan. ①.

Hospedaje Quintana, 1 block north and 1 block west of Ticabus. For many years a popular place with solidarity workers, a spotlessly clean and friendly, family-run hospedaje, owned by Paulina. Big rooms with fans and sturdy beds. Some are quite dark, so look before choosing. Toilet paper and towels are provided and there's also a laundry service. ①.

Hospedaje Santos, 1 block north and 2 blocks west of Ticabus (☎222-3713). Sprawling and ramshackle, this hospedaje is a good place to meet other travellers. Piles of atmosphere and revolution art on the walls; also an an indoor patio full of backpackers glued to the cable TV. Rooms, however, are dark and none too clean – try to get one upstairs where ventilation is better. Rooms have ceiling fan and come with a private or shared, basic bath. ①.

Hospedaje Yolanda, half block north of Ticabus. Pleasant yellow building with courtyard and friendly atmosphere; a favourite with Ticabus travellers. Even though all have a fan, the inside rooms are sauna cells – ask for one with a window. Shared bath. Price includes dinner. ②.

Intercontinental (☎228-3592, fax 228-5208). Managua's dowager hotel, an historic sight in its own right, is outrageously overpriced and offers poor service. However, new Taiwanese owners have given it an attractive facelift and first-world amenities, including a pool, chilly a/c, TV and room service. ⑨.

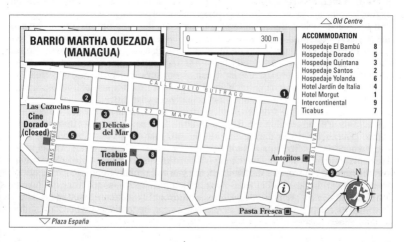

Jardín de Italia, 1 block east and 1 block north of Ticabus (☎222-7967). Five comfortable, very clean and well-ventilated rooms with private bath; a/c rooms cost twice the price of those with fans. ③–④.

Ticabus Hotel, in the Ticabus terminal. The bus company runs its own popular hotel in the station itself, a basic establishment of 40 rooms with shared bathrooms. It's noisy and lacks privacy, but is probably bearable for a single night between buses. ②.

Elsewhere in the city

Casa de Fiedler, near Plaza España; 2 blocks south and 2 blocks west from the CST building (☎266-6620). Rooms are dark and unappealing but the management is friendly and knowledgeable – the guest house has long been popular with visiting solidarity workers. Good breakfasts. Price varies according to room – ask to see several. Accepts travellers' cheques. ③.

Casa de Huéspedes San Juan, C Esperanza 560, behind the Universidad Centroamericana – known locally as "La UCA" (☎278-3220, fax 278-0419). Welcoming guest house in a large suburban house in quiet neighbourhood. Spacious rooms are arranged around a flower-filled patio. Rooms have either shared and private bath; all have fans. Meals available with advance notice. The hotel is popular with visiting academics and solidarity workers, so reserve in advance if possible. ④.

Hotel Camino Real, Carretera Norte Km 9.5, about 10min from Managua, 2min from airport (☎263-1381). The competition to the *Intercontinental*, the *Camino Real* is a pleasant upscale hotel offering better service for not quite as idiotic prices. All rooms have cable TV and a/c. Large swimming pool and a car rental service. ⑨.

King's Palace Hotel, Carretera Masaya Km 5 (☎277-4548, fax 278-2456). Unpretentious hotel located on a busy road not far from Centro Comercial Managua and the Huembes Market – not a bad alternative to Barrio Martha Quezada if you can afford a bit more. Sixteen comfortable rooms, some a/c. Good breakfasts in the attached cafeteria with an outside terrace and bar. ⑤.

Hotel Morgut, in Bolonia, 3 blocks east, 1 and half blocks south from the Teatro Cabrera (☎222-2166, fax 222-3543). Small comfortable hotel in relatively well-to-do area of Managua. Used to catering to visiting foreign professionals, helpful staff can arrange tours and car rental. All seven rooms have TV. Advance reservations needed. ⑤.

The City

For the visitor, sprawling Managua can be thankfully divided into a few distinct areas. The **old ruined centre** on the lakeshore is the site of the city's tourist attractions, such as they are, including the few impressive colonial-style buildings that survived the 1931 and 1972 earthquakes, though several of these – like the old municipal **cathedral** and the **Palacio Nacional** – are more notable for their historical importance than their beauty or cultural heritage. **Lago de Managua**, which forms such a pretty backdrop to the old centre, is severely **polluted** from raw sewage and regular dumpings of garbage, chemical waste, and mercury. The air doesn't seem any cleaner; the rate of increase in car ownership in Nicaragua is the highest in Central America and old buses, school-buses and Ladas belch fumes into an increasingly crowded city.

Twelve blocks south from the old centre, most of Managua's hospedajes and restaurants are clustered in the **Barrio Martha Quezada**, a district that was home to the *internacionalistas* during the Revolution. Just to the east, but visible from everywhere, is the city's main landmark, the **Hotel Intercontinental**, whose white Maya-pyramid form sails above the city. About 1km south of the ruined old city centre, the hotel is not worth a visit in itself, but you will probably end up there anyway, as it stands at the junction of Av Bolívar, which goes north–south from the lake to Plaza España, and C Julio Buitrago, a major thoroughfare running east–west. Many of the city's casas de cambio and airline offices can be found a further 2km south, around **Plaza España**.

The ruined centre

Most of Managua's "sights" are concentrated in the **old city centre**, completely trashed in the 1972 earthquake and now a haunting maze of fields, concrete skeletons of buildings, the odd burnt-out car and a few reclaimed spaces made into basketball courts. Maps and literature put out by the municipal government sometimes refer to these places, euphemistically, as "green areas" or "spontaneous neighbourhoods".

If you don't mind the heat, you can walk the twelve blocks from Barrio Martha Quezada or from the *Intercontinental* to the old centre, or take bus #109 north from the corner of Av Bolívar and C Julio Buitrago. A day is sufficient to take in most of the sights covered below, depending on your tolerance for heat and 100 percent humidity.

Despite its promising name, the **Plaza de la Revolución** is no more than a (usually empty) parking lot, except on July 19, the day the Sandinistas commemorate the Revolution, when its baking expanse fills with thousands of flag-waving faithfuls. On the west side of the plaza is a square of trees and colourful concrete benches known optimistically as the **Parque Central**, but actually a scruffy park filled with hangers-out and overpriced soft drink kiosks.

A monument to a destroyed city, the wrecked ash-grey **Catedral Santiago de los Caballeros** (Mon–Sat 8am–4pm, Sun 8am–8pm; US$0.50), known as the Old Cathedral, stands on the eastern side of the plaza. Funds donated from foreign governments have enabled the cathedral to be re-roofed with a transparent fibreglass cap, and for cut stone to be laid on the formerly grass floor. The old clock, which used to front the right-hand tower and which still bore the time that the big earthquake struck (12.32am on December 23, 1972) has been taken down for cleaning. **Inside**, birds fly through the ruined interior, where the facelift has continued, with the stone cleaned and restored to its original light pink hue. Some semi-exposed murals still line the walls, as do leaning stone angels and saints, some of them with their wings cracked. If your Spanish is good enough, the ticket seller can tell you some frightening earthquake stories. On Sundays at 7pm there is a very tasteful **sound and light** (*son y luz*) display with taped or sometimes live Renaissance music or Gregorian chants; if you can't make it, try to go at dusk when they turn the multicoloured interior floodlights on and warm breezes from Lago de Managua filter through the wrecked walls and open windows.

Since its blue marble and yellow stucco renovation it's hard to believe that the **Palacio Nacional** (daily 8am–4pm; US$1), next to the cathedral, was the scene of a cinematic **coup d'état**. On August 22, 1978, Sandinista commandos disguised as National Guard soldiers ran through these cool corridors and, in an audacious storming operation, captured the deputies of the National Assembly, effectively bringing to an end the rule of the dictator Somoza. This Roman-columned building was the seat of power during the long years of Somoza rule: the Colombian writer Gabriel García Márquez called it *el partenón bananero* – the banana parthenon – alluding to how the dictatorship had turned the country into a banana republic. The Palacio is still a functioning government building but has had much of its interior turned into a **museum and art gallery**. Many of its walls are covered with colourful murals by foreign artists that run the gamut from Mexican Arnold Belkin's socialist-realist depiction of the Mexican and Nicaraguan revolutions to Russian surrealism. As well as rooms showing dark and derivative religious paintings, there are **modern Nicaraguan art** exhibits, and a rather good display of Nicaraguan handicrafts, plus a few pre-Columbian artefacts. Upstairs is the new home of the **Biblioteca Nacional**, which has been beautifully furnished and decorated with funds donated from the government of China.

The distinctive green wooden building on the southwest corner of the Palacio Nacional is the **Centro Cultural Managua** (☎228-4045, fax 228-4046). Renovated and restored, before the earthquake the structure used to be the Gran Hotel, and the low-slung, tasteful wooden structure gives you a bit of an idea of how pre-earthquake Managua looked. Downstairs is a space given to sporadic exhibitions and seminars. Of most interest to tourists is the **Sábado de Artesanía**, a craft fair held here on the first Saturday of each month. Prices are higher than in the Mercado Roberto Huembes, the outdoor Managua market which has the largest selection of crafts, but still lower than in the *galerías* and art shops. The centre's upper floors house many of the country's arts organizations and it's worth going upstairs just to see the **historic photographs** lining the corridor. Some are very rare images of Managua before the 1931 earthquake; others show the pre-1972 quake Managua as an attractive city of palm trees and some colonial architecture, with a commercial downtown and the shops, cinemas and side-walks intact. Other images are from the *La Prensa* edition on the day following the quake, showing crumpled buildings, crushed cars and gaping holes in the road – the juxtaposition of the two Managuas, the past and the post-earthquake, is sobering.

The lakefront and the malecón

Perched like a huge white futurist bird 200m north of the Plaza de la Revolución, near the swampy shores of Lago de Managua, is the **Teatro Rubén Darío**, the cultural venue for the country. Foreign orchestras and dance troupes on tour perform here, along with Nicaraguan theatre groups. Check the *Guía Facíl*, or the newspapers *La Prensa*, *La Barricada* or *La Tribuna* for details of events – though bear in mind that the-atre performances are in Spanish only. If the building is open, it's worth going inside even if there's no performance going on, to see the massive chandeliers, marble floors, and the stirring view out to the lake from the enormous second-floor windows.

Across from the theatre is a derelict area of **fields** where cows graze – there is even a barn, more or less where the old commercial centre used to be. A hundred metres further north brings you to the lakeshore boardwalk, or **malecón**. Erected as a place for Managuans to enjoy the lakeside, the malecón is usually deserted except for stray kissing teenage couples. During the week, most of the small kiosks that line the lakeshore selling refrescos, peanuts and other snacks are closed. On the weekends it's a little more lively, with a few families coming to promenade, but there's really not much to see: a rather fetid shore of the very polluted lake, with hardly a breath of breeze coming off the lake's glass-like surface.

There are pleasant views across the lake to the north, where **Volcán Mombotombo** and little **Mombotombito** sit side by side against the horizon, on the shore of the lake 50km away. Momotombo's capacity for destruction is evoked in the **Museo Huellas de Acahualinca**, Barrio Acahualinca (take a taxi or bus #112; theoretically Mon–Fri 8am–noon & 1pm–3pm; US$2), a shabby little monument to a sort of Managuan Pompeii. On display are animal and human footprints from prehistoric unfortunates fleeing one of the volcano's frequent eruptions. Preserved in volcanic ash, the foot-prints date to between 10,000 and 6000 years ago. In any other context this little display would not merit a visit. Given that it's Managua, however, you might want to take a look if you have some time on your hands.

South of the old centre

About 5km south of the old city centre is Managua's biggest concentration of **residen-tial and commercial neighbourhoods**. The main thoroughfare through the south-ern part of the city is the Carretera Masaya, bordered to the west by the university area and to the east by residential and shopping districts.

Halfway between Plaza España area and the southern limits of the city lies the embassy neighbourhood of **Altamira**, where there are a number of restaurants popu-lar with the district's expat residents. A few kilometres further south on the Masaya road is the campus of the Universidad Centroamericana or UCA, a tranquil place by Managua standards, just off the major road to León and points north. East of here, about 1km south of the Laguna de Tiscapa on Av Rubén Darío, you can't fail to spot the **new cathedral**, the Catedral Metropolitana de la Purísima Concepción, designed by an Italian architect. Sitting in the middle of an empty field, from the outside it looks like a Sixties concrete monstrosity crossed with a mosque; if you wade across the field to get to it, the interior is unimpressive.

Several kilometres further south is the **Centro Comercial Managua**; other centros comerciales – complexes of shops, supermarkets and banks – line this major route. One of Managua's most interesting **markets**, the Mercado Roberto Huembes, is located just off the Carretera Masaya in the south of the city. Huembes, as it is known, has the best **crafts** section of any market in Managua and it attracts a few more tourists than the others for this reason, although the majority of market-goers are still Managuans shopping for avocados, cut flowers, plastic watches or ladies' underwear – you can get literally anything in the main market or in the stall-like shops in the surrounding streets. See the box on p.457 for a list of buses that run to the market.

Eating and drinking

Wherever you walk in Managua – on the street, at the bus stop or even under a shady tree – you will find someone selling a drink or a comida corriente. Good, cheap food on the hoof is also easy to get in any of Managua's major **markets** – Roberto Huembes, the Oriental or Iván Montenegro. A favourite of market sellers is *papusas* – a Salvadoreñan concoction of cheese, tortillas, sauce and meat. Hygienically speaking, the food is safe to eat, and you can get a decent meal for as little as a dollar. Managua also has a surprisingly cosmopolitan selection of **restaurants** catering to many tastes: Chinese, German, French, Italian, Peruvian, North American – even Arabic. **Cafés** are not thick on the ground, though, and the ones that do exist tend to be frequented by expats and wealthier Managuans. The *Casa del Café* in the diplomatic district of Altamira is by far the most popular of these, and is worth going to simply for its selection of magazines and foreign newspapers, and because it is, perversely, the only place in Managua you can buy well-packaged Nicaraguan export-grade coffee.

Cafés and bakeries

Alemana, 1 block west of Antojitos. Good spot for a quick sandwich or piece of cake – there's also a large choice of rye and dark bread you can buy to take away. Closed Sun.

Panadería La Baguette, half block west of the *Sorbet Inn* on the Carretera Masaya. The only place to eat genuine French-style baguettes and a range of other delicacies. The shop itself is a place to eat, but their baguettes are also sold in Colonia supermarkets.

Restaurants

Antojitos, Av Bolívar, in front of the *Hotel Intercontinental* (☎222-4866). The expensive Mexican-Nicaraguan food is OK, but another reason to come are the famous photographs of neon-lit downtown Managua before the 1972 earthquake. Daily noon–midnight.

Casa del Café, in Altamira (ask for it by name; ☎278-0605). A favourite of wealthy Managuans and travellers, this open-air café serves good sandwiches, wonderful cakes and pies – try the torta de limón – and the best coffee in town. You can also buy some English-language magazines and books downstairs, plus Nicaraguan export-grade coffee. US$10–20 for a two-course lunch. Mon–Sat 7.30am–10.30pm, Sun noon–6pm.

Cocina de Doña Haydée, Km 4 on the Carretera Masaya, near the British embassy (☎278-7336). A well-established restaurant offering the usual Nica food but better presented than usual. The only place in Managua to go for breakfast on a Sunday morning – everything else is closed, even the *Casa del Café*.

Delicias del Mar, 1 block west and half block north of Ticabus. Rather upscale for Martha Quezada, this is a popular lunchtime choice for nearby office workers. The *arroz marinero* with shellfish and squid is good value at US$2.50, or try the *filete a la plancha* at US$4.

Fritz, 1 block west of the main entrance to Residencial los Robles (☎278-2459). A classy restaurant serving expensive German cuisine but it's the history of the place that is the real attraction: in 1974 this was the site of the famous 1974 kidnapping of diplomats and senior figures from the Somoza government by Sandinista guerrillas. Daily noon–3pm & 6–11pm.

El Kaliffa, at the *Kings Palace Hotel*, Km 5 on the Carretera a Masaya (☎267-0015). Authentic Middle Eastern food, right down to the hoummus and the baba ganoush. Possibly the only place in Nicaragua to have some tasty pitta bread and lamb dishes, all relatively cheap. Daily noon–midnight.

La Hora del Taco, in Los Robles, 1 block east and half block north of Lacmiel (☎277-0949). A comfortable if characterless air-conditioned Mexican restaurant with good food; not too expensive considering the upscale area.

Nacatamales el Dorado, in Residencial el Dorado, over the Pista Radial, 3 and half blocks south from the traffic lights (☎244-2755). A small place famous for authentic Nicaraguan *nacatamales*, which is pretty much all they serve. Everyone agrees this place makes the best, and one of the banana-leaf parcels washed down with a refresco will fill you up for US$0.75.

Pasta Fresca, near the *Hotel Intercontinental*, 2 blocks north and 1 block west of the Hospital Militar Davila Bolaños (☎266-8545). The sizeable pasta dishes are nothing to write home about, but you can dine by candlelight in a lovely plant-filled courtyard. Try the pasta with basil and shellfish. No Italian wine, only horrible *Concha y Toro*. Entrees start at US$5. Daily noon–3pm & 6–11pm.

Pizzeria Valenti's, in Altamira, 1 block east from Lacmiel, house no. 6 (☎277-5744). The outside patio, an ice-cold mug of draft beer and one of Valenti's excellent thin-crust pizzas, make this unpretentious place one of the best in Managua. Of the several pizza options, anchovies and pepperoni is the best; not particularly cheap, but good value considering the area. US$5 for a pizza and a beer.

Pollo La Radial, Col Maximo Jeréz, 20m south of the main entrance to Radial Santo Domingo on C Principal de Altamira (☎278-1114). Managuans say the best chicken in town can be had in this budget family restaurant – chicken is roasted over a grill and served with rice, beans, plantains and salad. A relaxed place complete with swings and pets to keep children entertained.

Los Ranchos, Km 3.5 on the Carretera Sur (☎266-0526). Popular steak joint which deserves its reputation. Excellent brochettes and filet mignon of tasty Nicaraguan beef come in huge portions. US$10 for a full meal with dessert and a beer. Daily noon–11pm.

Rincón Catalan, 1 block west of the *Hotel Intercontinental*. A favourite with well-to-do guests of the *Intercontinental*, this newish restaurant offers Spanish food with a focus on seafood and paella. A big meal with drinks costs around US$10.

Tacos Charros, Col Centroamerica, on the road going to Mercado Huembes, in front of the Farmacia Vida (☎278-2337). Tasty and cheap Mexican food in a busy, noisy atmosphere; good for a quick meaty taco if you are on your way to the Huembes market.

Nightlife and entertainment

There are plenty of places to **drink** and **dance** in Managua. Some of them are crowded with the young and reckless teenagers of the Nica rich. Others have grandmothers and adolescents alike dancing to the same music. The venues are often large ranchos, or palm-covered shelters, open to the warm Managua night air and whatever cooling breeze there happens to be. Most Nicas are fans of either rancho music (not unlike "country" – fairly unsophisticated and raucous) or merengue, but you can also hear plenty of salsa, disco and occasionally reggae.

Women generally do not go out dancing without a male escort as it can be dangerous on the street at night. Beware of overcharging in the shadier places – keep the bottles on the table and keep track of the bill if in doubt. While there have been reports of travellers being stung with outrageous bills and ending up in jail for non-payment, all the venues listed here should be OK. A beer that costs US$0.50 at the *venta* will cost you US$0.70–1.50 in a bar.

Bars and clubs

Bar Amatl, 1 block south of the *Intercontinental* (☎266-2486). The student crowd tends to hang out here because the outdoor ambience is nice, the food is pretty cheap (US$1.50) and the music good. Cover charge of US$1.50 if there's a a live band.

La Bodeguita del Centro, on the southeast corner in the Centro Cultural Managua. Run by a Cuban, this small venue has café concerts on the weekends. By day a lunch bar, try the healthy brown-bread sandwiches and refrescos, all for about US$2.50. Just outside the bar is a rare clean public washroom.

La Buena Nota, Km 3 on the Carretera Sur (☎266-9797; US$6) Famous throughout Nicaragua for being the home base of Luis Enrique and Carlos Mejía Godoy, two popular guitar-playing and song-writing brothers who dominate the Nicaraguan music scene. Norma Helena Gadea sings here, often on a Thursday night, and is well worth seeing for the extraordinary power of her voice.

Cats Club, 1 block north and 2 blocks east of the *Hotel Intercontinental* (☎222-3232). Stylish club with a small but attractive dance floor and traditional salsa and merengue playlist, with a few American tunes thrown in. Expensive.

La Cavanga, on the northeast corner of the Centro Cultural Managua. A microcosm of Nicaraguan culture, this little bar plays traditional Nicaraguan music and is decorated with black and white photos of Old Managua and a few paintings by Ernesto Cardenal. It's one of the best bars in Managua, packed in the early evening with government workers and students having a beer or two.

Coro de Angeles, Km 5.5 on the Carratera a Masaya (☎267-0398). Less a bar than an arts venue, this hive of activity hosts irregular book readings and cultural nights; there's a small cinema showing Latin American art-house films, too.

Intercontinental Bar, in the *Hotel Intercontinental*. An expensive and thoroughly a/c North American-style bar, the *Intercontinental* at least has a good bar stock and mixed drinks. The multi-lingual eavesdropping and people-watching – visiting dignitaries, staff from various aid organizations – are the real reasons to go.

Light City, next to Cinema 1 and 2. A big disco scene, crowded with wealthy teenagers from the nearby posh district of Las Colinas. Steep cover charge – US$4.

Mirador Tiscapa, overlooking Laguna de Tiscapa (☎222-3452). Great atmosphere at night with a large dance floor, often with live music. The food is exceptional; stays open till 2am.

El Quetzal, in Col Centroamerica, in front of Registros Públicos. A barn-like dance joint where everybody gets up and dances to the wee hours. Firmly off the tourist trail, there's a neighbourhood atmosphere; the typical Nicaraguan food is cheap and filling and the spangled live salsa bands are hot. Friday and Saturday only.

Reggae City, Km 6 on the Carretera Norte (☎289-3803). The best Afro-Caribbean music venue and one of the best nightlife experiences in Managua, *Reggae City* has a family ambience with kids and grandparents getting up for a dance. The fried chicken and cheap beer are a bonus. US$4 cover.

Ruta Maya, 150m east towards the fire station from the statue of Montoya (☎222-5038). Famous music venue for the band of the same name. If you can handle the Rolling Stones, Santana and rest of the 1960s, you'll feel very comfortable here. Mon–Sat 5pm–2am.

Arts and entertainment

Cinema is a popular diversion for rich Nicas and the large foreign population in Managua – at US$3 and up, most other Managuans can't afford the price of a ticket. There are two cinema complexes in the Centro Comercio Camino del Oriente, reached on any bus (except expresses) heading to Masaya or Granada: Cine 1 and 2 and the Alhambra both screen the latest Hollywood movies, usually in English with Spanish subtitles, but it's wise to check. Food in the cinemas is overpriced but there are plenty of restaurants nearby where you can get a good meal and a few beers. Prices are slightly cheaper at the Cinemateca Nacional de Nicaragua in the Palacio Nacional de la Cultura (see p.461), where you can often see European or Latin American films. Occasional screenings of art films are held at the *Coro de Angeles* (see above).

The **theatre** scene in Nicaragua is small but active. It is particularly strong in children's theatre, puppetry and folk dancing – good news for non-Spanish speakers –

while adult theatre tends toward the Brechtian style that has been such a dynamic part of the theatre tradition throughout Latin America. The nation's main venue is the Teatro Nacional Rubén Darío. One of the few buildings in Managua to survive the 1972 earthquake, it is today recognized as one of the best theatres in Central America, with a main auditorium seating 1200 people, an exhibition space on the second floor, and an experimental theatre in the basement. Events are scheduled there most weekends and it's easy to get to, with bus #109 stopping right in front. Check the *Guía Fácil* or the listings in the *Siempre Joven* section of Friday's *La Prensa*.

Shopping and markets

In these post-revolutionary days you can buy anything you want in Managua. There are now plenty of large **supermarkets** with good selections of imported goods: pasta, wine, chocolates, fruits, cheese, frozen foods and plenty more. You can also buy a lot of the basics at local *ventas*, small shops set up in people's houses, which are never more than a couple of blocks away. **Fruit** and **vegetables** are cheapest at the weekend markets, when the growers come into town to sell their produce. It tends to be more expensive elsewhere, unless you go to some of the bigger markets like the Oriental and the Mayoreo.

The **Mercado de Mayoreo** in Barrio la Concepción, near the airport, is divided into separate areas or buildings for different types of produce: onions, lettuces, seafood, eggs, chickens, plantains and so on. Its atmosphere is less aggressive than, say, the Mercado Oriental, and you can get a cheap meal at the comidería while waiting to board buses heading north. In contrast, the famous **Mercado Oriental**, a few blocks southeast of the old centre, is a small, lawless city-within-a-city, where you can buy just about anything, but need to keep a close eye on your pockets – take someone with you to watch your back and help carry your stuff. In the streets around the entrance to the market are several shops selling furniture and electrical goods. If you can carry it, it's worth buying a rocking chair here: beautifully made, they cost around US$25, and can be bought disassembled for carrying onto the plane.

Near the Carretera a Masaya in the south of the city, the **Mercado Roberto Huembes** is somewhat safer to wander around than the Oriental and has an excellent crafts section. You can find rocking chairs here, too, and some of the best hammocks in the world – everything from a simple net hammock, lightweight and perfect for the beach (US$3), to a luxury, two-person, woven cotton hammock with wooden separators and beautiful tassels (US$30). Products made of leather and skins are in abundance, but choose carefully as many of the species used are endangered. Traditional clothing is cheap, finely embroidered and perfect for the tropics. **Paintings** in the style of the artists' colony on the Solentiname Islands are available here, along with many fine pen and ink drawings and abstract works. You can buy Nicaraguan cigars (*puros*) as well as wicker products (*mimbre*) such as baskets, mats, chairs and wall hangings. Much of the artesanía is produced using methods dating back to pre-Columbian times.

A community of **Salvadorean** artists is based at the Flor de Izote, in Plaza Bolónia, a block north of the Parque las Madres (☎266-5792). Earrings and necklaces made from fruit and tree seeds are on sale here.

Listings

Airlines Air France, 2 and half blocks south of Rotonda Guegüense (☎266-2612 or 266-6615); Alitalia, 1 and half blocks west of Los Pipitos (☎266-7030); American Airlines, Plaza España (☎266-3900); Aviateca, Plaza España (☎266-2898 or 266-2364); British Airways, in front of the old Hospital el Retiro (☎266-8268); Continental, Plaza el Sol y Aeropuerto Sandino (☎263-1030); Copa, Planes de

Altamira (☎267-5438 or 267-0045 or 267-5597); Iberia, Plaza España, Edificio Málaga (☎266-4440 or 266-4756); KLM, in front of the west side of the Plaza España (☎266-8052/3); LACSA, Plaza España (☎266-3136); Lan Chile, Plaza España (☎266-7011 or 266-1381); Nica, Plaza España (☎266-3136); Taca, Plaza España (☎266-3136); United, Costado Este, Plaza España (☎266-6663).

Banks and exchange Central branches that do foreign exchange are Banco Nacional de Desarrollo, Plaza España (☎266-8788); Banco Popular, Centro Comercial Managua (☎278-1225); Banco Mercantil, Plaza España (☎266-8228 or 266-8024); Bancentro, Centro Comercial Managua (☎278-0977).

Car rental Auto Express, 1 block north, 20m west of the Simón Bolívar statue (☎228-4144 or 222-3816); Budget, 1 block west, 1 block south of Montoya (☎266-6266); Hertz, Edificio Lang (☎266-8300 or 266-8400); Hyundai, Km 5 Carretera a Masaya (☎278-1249 or 278-1382); Toyota, Casa Pellas, 2 blocks west of Gadala Maria (☎266-1010).

Embassies and consulates Canada, north side of Telcor, Zacarias Guerra (Mon–Thurs 9am–noon; ☎228-7574, fax 228-4821); Costa Rica, 2 blocks north, 1 block east of Montoya (daily 9am–3pm; ☎266-5719); El Salvador, in Las Colinas, Pasaje los Cerros, Avenida del Campo, Casa #142 (Mon–Fri 8am–2pm; ☎276-0160, fax 276-0712 or 276-0711); Guatemala, Km 11.5 Carretera a Masaya (Mon–Fri 9am–1pm; ☎279-9609, fax 279-9610); Honduras, Km 12.5 Carretera a Masaya (Mon–Fri 9am–2pm; ☎279-9231, fax 279-8228); Panamá, 1 block north and half a block east from the *Hotel Colón* (Mon–Fri 8.30am–1pm; ☎278-1619); UK, Reparto los Robles (Mon–Fri 9am–noon; ☎278-0014 or 278-0887, fax 278-4085); USA, Cancilleria, Km 4.5 Carretera Sur (Mon–Fri 7.30–9am; ☎266-6010 or 266-6012 or 266-6013, fax 266-3865).

Immigration office Departamento de Inmigración Extranjería, Km 7 Carretera Sur (Mon–Fri 8am–noon & 2–4pm; ☎265-0014 or 265-0020; Web site *www.migracion.gob.ni*).

Libraries and cultural institutes The Casa Ben Linder, 3 blocks south and 1 and a half blocks east of the Monseñor Lezcano statue (☎266-4373), is the Nicaraguan base for a number of primarily US voluntary groups and agencies. They maintain a small library.

Medical care The Hospital Bautista (Baptist Hospital) in Barrio Largaespada, 2 blocks south and 1 and half east of the Casa Ricardo Morales Aviles (☎249-7070 or 249-7277) is a good private hospital with an emergency department. Dr Enrique Sánchez Delgado, in Bosques de Altamira, Casa #417, 2 blocks east and half a block north of the Cine Altamira, speaks English and German and charges around US$30 for a consultation. Natural medicines are available from the Fundación Julie Marciacq in Barrio José Isaías Gómez, 2 blocks east and 2 blocks north from the SINSA hardware store on the C Principal de Altamira, Casa M-153 (☎278-6681).

Post office 3 blocks west of the cathedral (Mon–Fri 8am–4pm, Sat 8am–noon).

Supermarkets The two main chains are La Unión and La Colonia, which both sell everything you might possibly need, at higher prices than the markets. La Unión has branches in the Centro Comercial Ciudad Jardín and the Centro Comercial Belo Horizonte; La Colonia is in the Centro Comercial Plaza España and the Colonia Centroamerica Plaza de Compras.

Telephone office Telcor/Enitel in the airport.

Travel agents Flights can be bought and reconfirmed at the following places; several also run organized tours (see p.470). Aeroamerica Tours, alongside Banco Mercantil (☎266-3487); Aventurismo, half a block north from Restaurante Wok, Los Robles, Casa no. 143 (☎265-2063); Careli Tours, 3 blocks south of Plaza el Sol (☎278-2572); Tours Nicaragua, half a block east of San Francisco church, Bolonia (☎266-8689); Senderos Tours, 1 block south and 2 blocks east of Gimnasio Hercules (☎278-3238); Tropical Tours, 1 block south and 1 west of la casa de Obrero (☎266-1387); Tropical Travel, 1 block west, half a block north of Ciudad Jardín ITR (☎249-7548).

Out from the city

After a few days in Managua's heat and grime, you'll welcome an escape to the **beach**. Beaches around Managua don't have the white sand and clear water of places like the Corn Islands or the beaches of San Juan del Sur and La Flor further south, but the water is warmer and they are easy to reach. Managuans visit on day-trips, particularly on national holidays, when the beaches – and public transport – get amazingly crowded, especially at Easter and Christmas: watch your belongings wherever you go.

The closest beaches to the city are **Pochomíl** and the nearby town of Masachapa, 3km beyond, around an hour and a half by hourly **bus** from the Mercado Israel Lewites. There is a small fee to enter Pochomíl, but once here you can settle in for the day, as there are restaurants all along the sand, and motorbikes and horses for rent. At the northern end of the beach, the *Villa del Mar* charges an extra entry fee of US$5 but has a freshwater swimming pool, toilets, showers, and large, comfortable ranchos where you can hang a hammock. The fee is redeemable in food and drink – a whole grilled fish costs US$7. You can rent rooms here, or at the hotel *Ticomar* (☎265-0210; ④, a/c rooms for four people ⑤) at the other end of the beach. There are several very basic hospedajes (①) in nearby **Masachapa**, or you may be able to string a hammock up in one of the locals' houses along the beach. Masachapa is more of a fishing village and its beach is not as clean as Pochomíl. The **bus** from Managua goes to both places.

Southwest along the coast from Masachapa is the town of **Casares**, which has its own stretch of fairly rough, unshaded beach, and **Hueuete**, which is a bit rougher again. Near Casares is **La Boquita**, another area developed for tourism which charges a small entry fee and offers plenty of places to relax and eat. The beach here can be dangerous with large rocks hidden in the shallows, but the river mouth which opens onto the beach provides a safe place to swim. The only place to stay is at *Las Palmas del Mar* (☎412-3351; ④–⑤). There is a direct **bus** service from the Mercado Israel Lewites to La Boquita, but it's infrequent except on weekends and holidays; during the week, catch the bus to Diriamba and change there for La Boquita.

Montelimar resort

A short distance north of Pochomíl is the number-one – possibly the only – resort in Nicaragua, **Montelimar** (☎269-6752 or 269-6769; email *montelim@ns.tmx.com.ni*; Web site *www.barcelo.co.cr*). Once the beach house of the dictator Somoza, it was turned into a resort by the Sandinistas and is now run by a Spanish company. Like many other properties nationalized during the Revolution, Montelimar is subject to an involved property dispute with Somoza's relations. Nicaragua's only five-star hotel, it has a relaxed atmosphere with a lovely private beach, four restaurants and four swimming pools, a small zoo and casino, and planned activities such as dance classes, horseriding, tennis, windsurfing and volleyball. Most people come on a package but you can book within Nicaragua. A so-called "all-inclusive" resort, prices are between US$110 and US$150 for a double room, including all meals, drinks and snacks; day rates of US$45 are also available.

El Velero

The hilly coast around **El Velero**, around 40km or so north of Managua towards León, is wilder than the beaches further south, punctuated by cliffs and peninsulas. A holiday village of sorts, El Velero is less frequented by day-trippers than Pochomíl or La Boquita, and consequently far more relaxed. Shady huts line the beachfront, along with showers, changing rooms and a number of food stands. The beach itself is excellent for swimming, and children can play safely in a rock pool at low tide. You can **stay** here at the holiday centre, originally set up for goverment workers, and still run by the Instituto Nicaragüense de Seguridad Social. Rooms have a/c and private bath (③) and there's a restaurant and bar within the grounds. Call the INSS ahead to make reservations (Managua ☎222-6994, El Velero ☎311-5413).

To get to El Velero, take a bus to León, alight at Puerto Sandino and from there take a camioneta. All in all, it's a three-hour journey from Managua.

Moving on from Managua

Even if you don't particularly want to go to Managua, it's virtually impossible to avoid: almost all buses go to and from the capital. The main routes of interest to travellers are the **international** routes from Guatemala City, Tegucigalpa in Honduras and San Salvador in El Salvador; operated by Ticabus (☎222-6094), all these services pass through Managua and you may well have to overnight here if you are travelling south to Costa Rica or to Panamá. In addition to Ticabus, Sirca leaves daily for San José from 4 blocks north of the Shell Station in the south of the city, on the Carretera a Masaya (near the UCA). A new luxury service between Managua and San José has recently begun, run by Transnica, departing from in front of the Ramac building daily at 7am and 1pm (de los semáforos de Repuestos La 15, frente a Ramac; ☎ & fax 278-2090).

The busiest **domestic** bus routes are those between the capital and the provincial cities, particularly León in the northwest and Granada in the south. Other main routes run to Matagalpa, Estelí, Masaya and Rivas, the last for connections to the Costa Rican border. You can get most of the way to the Atlantic Coast by bus, a bone-jarring ten-hour trip from Managua to the port of El Rama, from where boats go upriver to Bluefields on the Caribbean. An alternate route is with a private bus company called Empresa Vargas Peña (☎280-1812 in Managua; ☎822-1410 in Bluefields) that provides bus transport to Rama and then a connection by launch to Bluefields: it leaves Mercado San Miguel/Iván Montenegro daily at 11pm and arrives in Rama at 6am, leaving shortly after by launch for Bluefields, arriving at 9am.

Barring international bus services, which usually require advance purchase of one to three days, you can't reserve tickets on buses within Nicaragua. Buses leave when they become full, which is usually pretty quickly – every fifteen or thirty minutes, with less frequent services leaving every hour or ninety minutes. For a rundown of the main bus routes from Managua, see the box below.

BUS ROUTES FROM MANAGUA

DESTINATION	DEPARTS FROM	FREQUENCY	DURATION
Chinandega	Mercado Israel Lewites	every 30min	2hr
Estelí	Mercado de Mayoreo	every 30min	3hr 30min
Granada	Mercado Roberto Huembes	every 15min	1hr 30min
Jinotepe	Mercado Israel Lewites	every 30min	2hr 30min
León	Mercado Israel Lewites	every 15–30min	1hr 30min
Masaya	Mercado Roberto Huembes	every 30min	45min
Matagalpa	Mercado de Mayoreo	every 30min	3hr
El Rama	Mercado de Mayoreo	1 daily	10hr
	Mercado San Miguel	daily at 11pm	7hr
Rivas	Mercado Roberto Huembes	every 30min	3hr
San Carlos	Mercado Ivan Montenegro	3 weekly	9hr
San José	Ticabus terminal	daily at 7am	7–10hr
San Salvador	Ticabus terminal	daily at 5am	8hr
Tegucigalpa	Ticabus terminal	daily at 5am	7hr
Tipitapa	Mercado de Mayoreo	every 15min	45min

Lacsa has daily **international flights** between Managua and San José, while Copa handles flights to and from Panamá. The main **domestic airline** is the private La Costeña, which runs a frequent and reliable scheduled service, mainly to and from the Atlantic Coast. There are daily services to Puerto Cabezas and three flights a week (Tues, Thurs & Sat) to Waspam on the northern Atlantic Coast; flights run to Bluefields several times a day, with two services daily to Corn Island. Advance reservations are essential (☎263-1281, 263-1228 or 263-2142).

Tours

Given the distances and often erratic schedules on Nicaraguan transport, if you're short of time it's worth considering an organized tour, particularly to remote or difficult to reach areas like the Solentiname archipelago or the Río San Juan. There's not much choice of tour operators, but the ones that do exist are established and reputable. All operators listed here are in Managua; for a Granada tour agency see p.489.

Careli Tours, 3 blocks south of Plaza el Sol (☎278-2572).

Senderos Tours, 1 block south and 2 blocks east of Gimnasio Hercules (☎278-3238).

Tropical Tours, 1 block south and 1 west of la casa de Obrero (☎266-1387).

Tropical Travel, 1 block west, half a block north of Ciudad Jardín ITR (☎249-7548).

CHAPTER 23

THE NORTH

Nicaragua's **north** is really two regions, divided by geography and climate as well as – to an extent – the character of their inhabitants. Leaving the capital and heading directly northwest, you enter hot, dry grassy lowlands punctuated by dramatic volcanoes. East of Lago de Managua the environment is altogether different: mountainous, with a cool, fresh climate. Here the hillsides are planted with the bright green of coffee plants, and cows munch in alpine pastures.

Hot and dry, its horizon punctured by a line of arresting volcanoes, Nicaragua's **northwest** is largely an agricultural area, its wide grassy plains given over to cattle farming, peanuts and cotton. Heading northwest from Managua, two routes lead to the colonial city of **León** and agricultural **Chinandega**, the only towns of any significant size in northwest Nicaragua. The **Central American Highway** (CA-3) is a possibility for drivers, although the journey from Managua to León can be at least an hour longer than the old road north out of Managua, the route that buses use. That said, the old road is notorious for accidents; a pile-up seems to happen every week. For most of the 90-kilometre journey to León on the old road, however, the scenery is magnificent, with a good view of Lago de Managua and Volcán Momotombo's perfect cone, with tiny Volcán Momotombito perched alongside.

The only stop of any interest for visitors on the way to León is the ruins of **León Viejo**, which was among the very first settlements in Central America. Once the capital of Nicaragua, the small city of **León** itself is a tourist attraction, largely for its cathedral, the largest in Central America, though those interested in Nicaraguan politics and history will also find a visit here, to the birthplace of the FSLN, interesting. León has a long history as a politically liberal city – its inhabitants have the reputation for being more religiously and politically tolerant than those in other parts.

Few tourists venture further north and west, to the hot agricultural town of **Chinandega**, or on to the Cosigüina peninsula, where it used to be possible to make a boat crossing to La Union in El Salvador. On the way, the forms of active Volcán San Cristóbal, at 1745m the tallest volcano in the country, and smaller Volcán Cosigüina, perched on the peninsula, alleviate a largely flat, dry landscape. Good beaches are scarce on this stretch of the Pacific Coast. **Poneloya**, a weekend and holiday destination for inhabitants of León, is wild and wave-raked and not really safe for swimming.

The journey **north from Managua** to Estelí, some 150km from the capital, is one of the most inspiring in the country. The Carretera Interamericana (CA-1) winds through the grassy plains of the Pacific landscape, skirts the southern edge of Lago de Managua and slowly gives way to a ribbon of blue mountains and the green terraced slopes of **coffee fields**. It's not an epic ascent, but is a pleasant transition to a cooler region. Set within a circle of mountains, the north has a more temperate climate and very productive soil, with plenty of tobacco plantations and an economy based on coffee, grains, vegetables, fruit and dairy farming.

Many travellers coming from the south notice a distinct difference in the people as well as the geography: northerners are poorer and more battle-hardened, and can sometimes seem less forthcoming than Nicaraguans in other areas. In both the Sandinista Revolution years and during the Contra–Sandinista struggles of the 1980s,

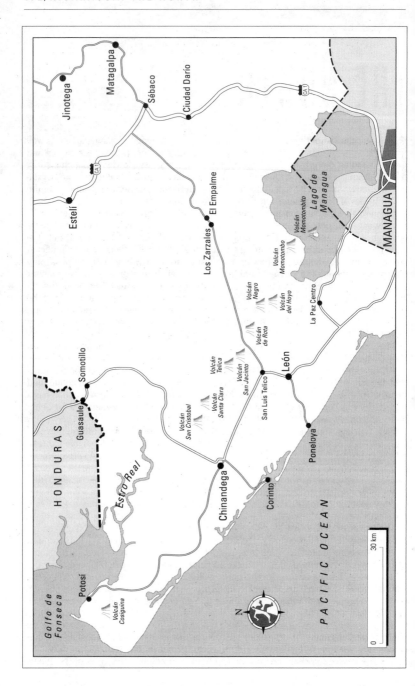

For an explanation of **accommodation price codes**, see p.438.

this region, and particularly **Estelí**, its largest town, saw heavy fighting and serious bloodshed. Because of their staunchly leftist character and legendary tenacity, Somoza bore a particular grudge against the inhabitants of Estelí and waged brutal offensives on the city. Scars have not really healed; not on the bombed-out buildings that still punctuate the streets of Estelí nor in people's minds. The north remains a centre of unflappable Sandinista support, despite the heavy losses in the 1990 election and the Sandinistas' continual waning of influence.

Despite living in a rural and fairly remote area, northerners are used to seeing foreigners, due to the years when many *internacionalistas* flocked here; foreigners still work on aid and environmental programmes in the area. Much cross-border traffic comes through Estelí from Honduras as the route to Tegucigalpa from Estelí is fairly straightforward, although the majority of trans-isthmian tourists these days cross the border some 100km as the crow flies to the west, at Guasaule (see p.477).

León and around

Until 1857 the capital of Nicaragua, **LEÓN**, 90km north of Managua, is these days a quiet, provincial city; it would be even quieter were it not for the presence of the National University, the country's premier academic institution. Founded by Hernández de Córdoba in 1524 as León Viejo – which now lies in ruins at the foot of Volcán Mombotombo – León was moved northwest to its present-day location soon after León Viejo's destruction. Today, the city's main attraction is its **Cathedral**, the largest in Central America. In fact, churches – eighteen in all – seem to spring up on practically every corner.

For all its seeming peace, for nearly two hundred years León has had a **violent history**, with dozens of battles being fought in its streets. In 1824 tensions between the traditional Liberals of the city and the arch-Conservatives of Granada erupted into a total of seventeen battles being fought in the city over the course of the next twenty years; in 1956 the first President Somoza was gunned down by martyr-poet Rigoberto López Perez in the streets of León. During the Revolution in the 1970s the town's streets were again the scenes of several decisive **battles** between the Sandinistas and Somoza's forces, and much of the damage caused – bullet-scarred buildings, cracked sidewalks – is still visible. Also on many walls in León you will see Sandinista **mural art**. The best example is half a block north of the western edge of the plaza, where the Penelas y Sirera department store, wrecked during fighting in 1979, lies in ruins. On the west side of the ruins is a mural of big-hatted Sandino, casting his shadow over the sidewalk. Also mounted on the wall is a reproduction of the letter the poet Rigoberto López Perez wrote to his mother before shooting Somoza.

Many key figures in the Revolution either came from León or had their political start here. The **National University** and the National Law School were (and perhaps still are) hotbeds of revolutionary ferment, and the presence of these institutions has contributed enormously to León's Liberal bent. While the student population livens things up considerably, the town still seems very quiet, with few restaurants and services, but several empty shops where women sit eerily behind vacant glass cases. To the east, near the railroad tracks and market, the town gets tougher, with streetkids darting in and out of darkened adobe houses. The atmosphere improves in the evenings, when mass-goers tumble from the churches, stuffed-animal vendors shuffle across the central plaza and a brick-red setting sun slides a ceramic light across the city's tiled colonial roofs.

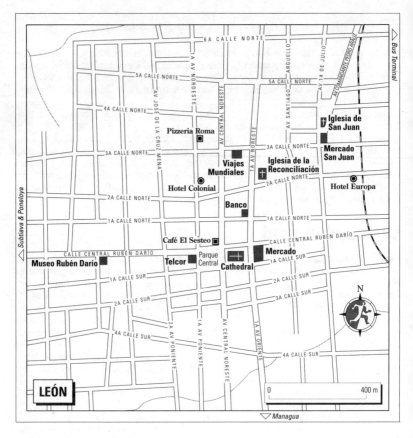

LEÓN

0   400 m

▽ Managua

Arrival and information

Buses from Managua pull in at the new market on C 6 Norte, in the east of town. From there you can hop a taxi (US$0.60) or walk the eight blocks or so west into the centre of town.

A hub of services, the **Telcor/Enitel** office on the west side of the plaza (Mon–Sat 7am–10pm for telephone services) sends **mail**, sells postcards and has USA Direct and Sprint phone boxes from which you can connect to a US operator; otherwise it's a case of slogging it out with the perpetual horde of locals to get the desk where a few harassed staff will place reverse-charge (*a cobrar*) calls for you. The office on the left-hand side as you enter sells phone cards, useful for León's many new Publitel payphones.

Banks are plentiful and will relieve you of your dollars for córdobas at the official rate. Three of the Nicaraguan state banks face each other on the intersection one block north and one block east of the Cathedral. Take your pick: all keep the same hours (8am–noon & 1–4pm) and offer the same rate. Be forewarned that the only place in León you can change **travellers' cheques** is the Viajes Mundiales office (Mon–Fri 8am–12.30pm & 2–5.30pm; ☎311-5920 or 311-6920), just north of the centre, which charges a whopping ten percent commission. This is the place, however, to reconfirm outbound **flights** or book air tickets – they represent all Central American and international airlines.

Accommodation

There are only a couple of comfortable **places to stay** in León, but they're two of the best small hotels in Nicaragua. In the northeast of town, the *Hotel Europa*, 3ra C NO, 4ta Av (☎311-2596 or 311-6040, fax 311-2577; ③–④), is a favourite with visiting academics and foreign aid workers, has professional management, big rooms with comfortable beds and large Nicaraguan rocking chairs, and a plant-filled patio. More central is one of Nicaragua's most welcoming hotels, the *Hotel Colonial*, 50m north of the university (☎311-2279, fax 311-3125; ③–④). An old family home turned into a hotel-cum-hostel for students, the atmosphere at the *Colonial* is very homely, with rocking chairs ranged around a huge inner courtyard, where students watch Mexican *telenovelas* on the cable television and locals chat for hours, all to the creak of rocking chairs. There's a good restaurant attached; the ladies who cook in the student comedor will fix you your meal of choice for a couple of dollars.

The Town

León: ciudad limpia say the street signs, and unlike similar signs throughout the country, here it's the truth: compared to Managua the place is spotless, which makes it a pleasant place to explore on foot.

Towering over León from the rather plain central plaza is the **Cathedral**, a cream-coloured structure of epic proportions. Begun in 1747, it took anything from 70 to 100 years to build, depending on who you talk to. Inside the only things of interest are the large statues of the Twelve Apostles and **Rubén Darío's tomb**, guarded by the statue of a weeping lion. Reportedly the cathedral's safe (to which only the bishop holds the key) houses a shrine covered in white Indian topazes, originally belonging to Philip II of Spain. Masses are held nightly at about 5pm; despite the microphoned drone of the priest echoing in the enormous interior, mass is worth attending, if only to people-watch.

The second tourist attraction in León – and the one that almost every foreigner makes a beeline for, judging from the multinational visitors' book – is the **Museo Rubén Darío** (Mon–Sat 9am–noon & 2–5pm, Sun 9am–noon; free but donation appreciated). This substantial León residence was actually the house of Darío's aunt Bernarda. Inside, the lovingly kept rooms and courtyard garden are home to eloquent and wonderfully frank plaques that narrate the story of Darío's tempestuous personal life and diplomatic and poetic career. Also on display are many of his personal books, family photographs, random personal possessions and commemorative items, such as Rubén Darío lottery tickets.

Four kilometres west of the city centre is the barrio of **Subtiava**, which long predates León and is still home to many of the city's indigenous population. It is also the site of one of the oldest churches in the country, the small adobe **parish church** of Subtiava. Recently renovated, the church is not always open, but worth a visit if you are catching a bus to or from the beach at Poneloya (see p.476).

Eating and drinking

Places to eat well in León are scarce, though if you're fond of pizza you'll probably do all right. Top of the list is *Pizza Roma*, 350m north of the Telcor/Enitel building, on the right-hand side (Tues–Sun noon–11pm). While the pizza and the pasta are nothing to write home about, they serve truck-driver-size portions, the low lighting and checked tablecloths make for a pleasant atmosphere, and you can pay with a credit card. Outside the centre in barrio Subtiava, *Los Pescaditos* is a popular, upmarket outdoor patio restaurant – taxi drivers will know it by name. Try the buttery *camarones con ajillo*, washed down with a cold Victoria beer underneath the night sky. The main **café** in town, the *El Sesteo*, on the northeast corner of the plaza, is currently closed for renovations but offers a very pleasant view of the Cathedral and the plaza and serves good coffee and cakes.

On Friday and Saturday nights sharp-dressed university students head to the only site of nocturnal life in town, the **disco/bar** *El Túnel del Tiempo* – an unthreatening venue playing mostly salsa and merengue. Look for the whitewashed building near the exit to Chinandega on the highway just outside of León – best to come and go in a taxi (around US$1).

Around León: León Viejo and Poneloya

There are a couple of day-trips possible in the León area. The Pacific beach of Poneloya, due west of the city, is a good bet, if only because bus connections are frequent and there are a few places to stay. The mildly interesting historic monument of León Viejo is best reached in a car or taxi; a trip on public transport means some fancy footwork to make your connections and even then entails a long walk.

León Viejo
Founded in 1524, the same year as Granada, **Old León** was destroyed by an earthquake and volcanic eruption on December 31, 1609. The ruins themselves are interesting only for the cathedral (whose walls stand about thigh-high) and the broken stones of the former plaza. Otherwise there's little to see but a pile of rubble and grassy fields. The site is more or less unattended and there are no explanatory plaques. Still, the location is impressive, in view of the lake and under the looming shadow of Momotombo. The only way to get to León Viejo comfortably is by car; there is a local bus from **La Paz Centro**, a hamlet about 60km north of Managua, but the service is irregular – best get to La Paz Centro very early in the day and ask around.

Poneloya
For killer Pacific waves, **Poneloya**, 20km west of León, is the most impressive beach in the country. The water here is notoriously dangerous, due to a combination of powerful waves and rip tides, but it's the only beach within convenient reach of León and many of the city's well-to-do residents have weekend homes here. Outside of peak times like Christmas and Easter, though, Poneloya seems rather run-down and forlorn, with restaurants closed and homes boarded up, and a rather bleak vista out to a sere Pacific. You really must take care if you swim here: waves come ashore with a supernatural force. Ask locals about rip tides (*corrientes peligrosos*) before venturing into the water, and never swim alone. The smaller beach at Las Peñitas, at the south end of Poneloya, is much safer.

Most travellers come to Poneloya for the day and sleep in León: a good option, since accommodation in Poneloya is limited. The only recommended options are the *Posada de Poneloya* (☎0317-377 or 0317-378; ②) which is a bit run-down but serves good meals for about US$2. The *Suyapa Beach* (☎311-6257; ②) is a good deal, and the room price includes a hearty breakfast. **Buses to Poneloya** leave León every hour from the Terminal Poneloya on C Darío, near the Subtiava church in barrio Subtiava (40min). A taxi will cost about US$8 each way – good value for a group.

Chinandega to the Honduran border

The first thing you notice about **CHINANDEGA**, 35km northwest of León, is its extraordinary heat. Set on a plain behind the looming form of Volcán San Cristóbal, the area's dry, kiln-like climate is ideal for cotton-growing, the main economic activity, along with some groundnut cultivation and cattle farming. In Nicaraguan terms Chinandega is a fairly prosperous agricultural town. Many Nicaraguans (and foreigners in the know) recognize Chinandega as their spiritual home, if only because the distillery of Nicaragua's export-grade Flor de Caña rum sits on the outskirts of town.

Buses come and go from the market southwest of the centre – not to be confused with the Mercado Central or the Mercadito, this market/bus terminal is known as the Mercado Bisne – bisne short for "business", as during the years of the Reagan-sponsored embargo much contraband came through here from **Corinto**, Nicaragua's main port, 21km west of the city on a sandy island reached by a bridge. A bizarre combination of the scuzzy and the poignant, Corinto is the only deepwater port in Nicaragua – almost every molecule of shipping commerce passes through the town.

Chinandega's supernatural heat makes it one of the few places in the country where you may seriously want to consider air conditioning. The only comfortable **place to stay** is the *Hotel Cosigüina*, half a block south of the Banco Nacional de Desarrollo (☎341-3636; ④), which has ten rooms with private bath, cable TV, a/c or fan. If you really don't want to shell out, the *Hotel Chinandega*, four blocks east and one and a half blocks south of the parque central (no phone; ②), is not a bad option; the bathrooms could use a scrub but the family which runs it is friendly.

If you are heading to Guasaule and the Honduran border (see below) under your own steam, express **buses** from Chinandega run about every thirty minutes.

Guasaule and the border with Honduras

Most travellers experience **GUASAULE** from the safe capsule of the Ticabus, which whizzes you painlessly through this cumbersome **border post**. If you are travelling by local transport, note that the border tends to close before noon for lunch and open whenever the officials have had their fill and their rest, usually at 2pm. Take a few dollars; the exit tax is currently US\$2, and it must be paid in US currency. There is about a kilometre to walk between the Nicaraguan border post and the Honduran side, and walk you must, unless some kind truck driver takes pity on you, as there are no colectivos.

Crossing from Honduras, don't despair; once you get to the Nicaraguan side a service will get you to Chinandega every thirty minutes or so, arriving at the town's market; this is the nearest place with acceptable accommodation. From there you can pick up an express bus to Managua about every half-hour, or continue by bus to León.

Estelí and around

At first sight **ESTELÍ**, the largest town in the north, can seem downtrodden and poor. It does have its poor barrios, but is an engaging place, and is still – despite the current relatively apathetic political climate – a hotbed of political activity. Of all the towns in Nicaragua, in Estelí you can best get a sense of what the country must have been like during the Revolution and glimpse something of the vision that inspired so many people during the 1980s. Although you can still see the bullet holes in the buildings around the parque central, these days Estelí is a relaxed town, with an elusive charm: the many, mainly young, travellers who come here are attracted by the people and the pleasant setting, and the chance to absorb some quintessential Nicaraguan energy.

Although the war ended with the failure of the Sandinistas in the election of 1990, Estelí has been the scene of fighting as recently as 1994. In what has become known as the **"one-day war"**, former Sandinista and Contra soldiers took up arms together to demand better conditions for veterans. At the same time they robbed a bank and their leader, "Pedrito el Hondureño" reportedly disappeared with the loot. The government responded by encircling the veterans in the centre of town with national police, soldiers and helicopter gun ships. About a dozen veterans were killed along with two civilians.

More recently the town's government has been particularly successful in attracting **overseas aid** and Estelí's streets are chock-full of the offices of international organizations working on projects as diverse as cooperative and organic farming, women's rights and the environment. Estelí is also the site of a US$25 million reforestation project designed to clean up the water supply. Recently, the town provided the location for the Ken Loach movie *Carla's Song*, the making of which no doubt funnelled a few córdobas into the local economy.

Arrival and information

All regional buses – from Managua, Jinotega, Matagalpa or León – stop at the **bus station** in the southern part of town. Local buses ("Urbanos") pass through the parque central in front of the cathedral.

The town is arranged on a narrow north–south grid, with most services clustered together in the small centre along C Transversal: the **post office** is 25m west of Av Central (Mon–Fri 8am–7pm), the **Telcor/Enitel** office between Av 1 and 2 SE (daily 7.30am–9pm, Sat closed noon–1.30pm), and there are four **banks** on the corner with Av 1 NE, a block northeast of the parque – Interbank will change travellers' cheques. You can transfer money, make international phone calls and send faxes at the Western Union office, C 11 SE and Av 1 SE (Mon–Fri 9am–5pm, Sat 9am–noon & 1.30–4.30pm; ☎713-3566).

Although there is no independent tourist information in town, there is a well-resourced **travel agency**, Agencia Viajes Tysey (☎713-3099 or 713-4030), in the *Hotel Mesón*, where you can buy plane tickets, change money and rent cars.

To some extent a leftover from the Sandinista years, when *internacionalistas* flocked here, there are a few **language schools** in Estelí. Los Pepitos, one block south from Teatro Nancy (☎713-2154), does weekly courses including accommodation for around US$130. **Horizonte**, between C 8 and C 9 SE (☎713-3424 or 713-4117), is a cheaper option, run by the Unemployed Women's Movement; it also offers courses in local cooking and crafts.

Accommodation

Because Estelí sees quite a bit of gringo traffic in the form of aid workers, Estelí's **hotels** tend to be a little more expensive than in other parts of the country. Two hotels of the same name and owned by the same management, the *Panorama #1*, C Transversal between Av Central and 1 SE (☎713-3147, fax 713-2386; ④), and the largely undifferentiated *Panorama #2* (☎713-4023; ④), have between them fifteen new, clean rooms, all with private bath. Estelí's dowager hotel, the *Mesón*, a block north of the cathedral (☎713-2655; ③), has something of the feeling of a country inn, with a wood-panelled restaurant and friendly management – the scrappy courtyard inside is a disappointment, but the rooms are comfortable and all have private bath.

Budget travellers should make a beeline for the *Nicarao* on Av Central, just south of C 1 SE (☎713-2490; ②). A small hotel, it's perennially popular with gringos, possibly because of its covered patio where you can relax, dine on the excellent lunch specials (US$2.50) and write your postcards. The *Hospedaje Juares*, C 8 SE, near Av Central (no phone; ①), is a curious place with decent enough rooms set in a ramshackle garden with the standard garrulous bird.

The Town

Although Estelí lacks the stunning mountain views of Matagalpa to the south, the centre of town is clean, well-kept and pleasant to wander around, and the climate refreshingly cool. Much of the pleasure lies in soaking up the atmosphere, particularly along Av

Central, where shops' wares spill out onto the street and the windows display cowboy boots and the local farmers' favourite Western-style hats. Around the Ayuntamiento, on the west side of the parque central, you can sit on a bar stool and chat to a few of the local Sandinistas still running the local government and watch four-wheel drives belonging to numerous international aid organizations doing business around town whizz by. Keep an eye out, too, for Sandinista wall murals.

The south side of the parque is dominated by the **Centro Recreativo las Segovias**, which regularly puts on music and sporting events, particularly basketball. The **cinema** next door was closed in 1997 but there are plans to reopen it. There's another cultural venue around the corner, a block to the south: the **Centro Cultural** hosts art exhibitions, dancing and music events – ask for details of coming events. On the same block is the tiny **Galería de Héroes y Mártires** (daily 9am–5pm; donations), a museum devoted to the Revolution, and to the many residents of Estelí who died in the fight (the women who work at the Galería are, for the most part, mothers and widows of soldiers who were killed). A collection of photographs, maps, newspaper clippings and some personal possessions of those killed, the museum forms a moving, simple monument to the behind-the-headlines reality of war.

Finally, if you want to hear the precocious journalists of tomorrow in training, head down to **Radio los Cumiches**, two blocks south of the Banco Nacional. This extraordinary community radio station is staffed by child journalists, who have been banned from press conferences in the past for asking uncomfortably difficult questions.

Eating and drinking

Estelí's large foreign presence has resulted in an almost cosmopolitan **eating** scene – no small feat for a relatively poor city in the middle of the northern highlands. *Café Palermo*, half a block south of the banks, concocts an inspired pizza for a price (large ones cost US$8), plus pasta and garlic bread, and lunch and dinner specials that you can wash down with wine by the glass. On the Carretera Interamericana, half a block from the turnoff to Concordia, *Do1a Pizza* is another Italian option. Tacos, burritos and other Mexican offerings are dished up by *Taquería Beverley* behind the cathedral on C 1. If you've got that fast-food craving, *Burger Xpress* on the corner of C Transcursal and Av 1 SE will satisfy with a succulent hamburger of Nicaraguan beef. The snack bar *Las Brasas*, west of the parque on C 1 NE, serves fresh juices, fruit salad, toasted sandwiches and tacos for around a dollar.

The real gastronomic surprise in Estelí is the *La Casita* bakery, on the southern outskirts of town (take the local bus to the Nuevo Hospital and walk 500m south). It's run by a Scottish carpenter and his Nicaraguan wife who make and sell their own wooden toys, wholemeal bread and yoghurt – among the best you will taste anywhere – and grow herbs, fruits and vegetables. You can tour the plant nursery and cool gardens.

Nightlife in Estelí is fairly mellow; the one place everyone heads to is the *El Brey*, next to the *Hotel Miraflor,* which is run by musician Ramón Lozano – he performs a couple of times a week. There are two gambling dens in town, best avoided unless your bluffing Spanish is up to par. If you're game enough to play pool with the local lads, head for the Club de Billares, towards the bus station on Av Central between C 9 and C 10 SE.

Around Estelí: Miraflor

Miraflor is a new nature reserve, 28km northeast of Estelí. Managed by the Environment and Natural Resources Commission together with the University of Central America, it covers 150 square kilometres of forest along with some small farms, one of the project's main aims being to find sustainable ways for farming and environmental protection to co-exist. Currently over five thousand locals produce coffee, potatoes and exotic flowers within and around the reserve.

Guides lead visitors along a nature trail around the shore of the Laguna Miraflor, explaining the area's fauna, flora and natural environment. A mix of wet and dry tropical conifers and deciduous species, Miraflor is a great spot to view quetzals, woodpeckers, *guardabarrancos* (the national bird of Nicaragua) and *urracas*, a local type of magpie. It is also home to howler monkeys – which you are likely to hear, if not see, at least at dusk – and reclusive mountain lions.

Plans to build some cabins in the reserve are afoot but currently there is no overnight accommodation for tourists. Visits can be arranged free of charge as part of the management authority's public education program: contact the University of Central America (UCA) at C 9 NE and Av 5 NE in Estelí (email *miraflor@ibw.com.ni*), a few days in advance. Horse riding trips can also be organized to the caves (Las Cuevas), the ancient mountain home of the Yeluca and Cebollal people.

Matagalpa and around

Known as "la Perla del Septentrión" – pearl of the north – **MATAGALPA** is spoken well of by virtually everyone in Nicaragua, principally, you suspect, because of its relatively **cool** climate: at about 21–25°C, it is considered *tierra fría* in this land of 30°C-plus temperatures. Located 130km northeast of the capital on the Carretera Interamericana, Matagalpa is a small, quiet town set among blue-green mountains covered in **coffee plantations**. Most visitors come to the region specifically to visit the *Hotel Selva Negra*, famous all over Nicaragua and one of the country's premier tourism experiences.

Thanks to its climate and coffee-growing potential, there is a significant European **immigrant** presence in the area – mostly Germans, Italians and Americans, whose ancestors moved here in the late 1800s. The town has strong Sandinista credentials, too: Tomás Borge, the former Minister of the Interior under the Sandinista government and the only remaining core member of the FSLN, was born and raised here, as was **Carlos Fonseca**, a key Sandinista gunned down by Somoza's National Guard in 1976.

Matagalpa's services, hotels and restaurants are spread out between the seven or eight blocks that divide the town's two principal **plazas**, and you'll find yourself constantly trekking several blocks between the two. At the northern end, the **Parque Morazán** fronts the **Catedral de San Pedro**, which is relatively new, dating from 1874. Tiny **Parque Darío** in the south is the site of several hospedajes and restaurants.

The town's only museum, the **Museo Casa Cuna Carlos Fonseca**, 100m southeast of the Parque Darío, which documents the life of Carlos Fonseca, is currently closed due to lack of government funds; it may reopen by the time you get here. At the Tienda de Cerámica Negra, two blocks north of Parque Rubén Darío, you can buy examples of the artesanía typical of Matagalpa. The distinctive **black pottery** (*cerámica negra*) is an indication of a Maya link with the indigenous people of the area – this type of pottery is otherwise found only in southern Mexico.

Practicalities

Buses from all destinations – whether from Managua, Jinotega or Estelí – arrive at Matagalpa's **bus terminal** and market, located about 1km southwest of the city centre; it's about a half-hour walk into town, or take one of the taxis that wait at the terminal (US$1).

There is no tourist office in Matagalpa. Bancentro, 50m southeast of the parque Morazán (Mon–Fri 8.30am–4.30pm, Sat 8.30am–noon), **changes dollars** cash but not travellers' cheques. For **post** and **phone** calls, Telcor/Enitel is just a block northeast of Parque Morazán (phones daily 8am–10pm; post Mon–Fri 8am–5pm).

Most tourists head out of town to **stay** at the *Hotel Selva Negra* (see below). If you have to spend the night in Matagalpa, the most comfortable hotel is the *Ideal*, two blocks north and a block west of the cathedral, which has large rooms, private bath and a good restaurant (③). The best budget option in town is the *Hotel Bermudez*, two blocks north of Parque Rubén Darío (①–②); though the rooms are nothing special, there's a large, pleasant courtyard area, facilities for doing laundry, and the manage-ment can provide breakfast.

The quickest and cheapest **eats** in Matagalpa are to be had at the comedores scat-tered around the Parque Darío. The most popular of these is the *Comedor San Martin*, 25m north of the corner of Parque Darío and Av José Benito, where a plate of chicken, rice, chillies and cabbage salad costs about US$2.50. The nicest place to eat in town is the restaurant of the *Hotel Ideal*, where you can sit in the courtyard and feast on meat dishes for about US$6.

The Selva Negra

Named by the area's German immigrants in the nineteenth century, Matagalpa's **Selva Negra** is not just a nostalgic appellation given by homesick newcomers; the dark blue pine-clad mountains really do look like the Schwartzwald. In the sparsely populated, high-altitude pristine tropical forests here, an amazing variety of wildlife flourishes – over 80 varieties of orchids, many birds, including the elusive resplendent quetzal, and sloths, ocelots, margay, puma, deer and howler monkeys are more likely to be spotted here than anywhere else in the country.

Due to the altitude (1311m), the area immediately around Matagalpa has an "eternal spring" climate and a mean temperature of 18°C, which is very refreshing by Nicaraguan standards. As well as the climate, travellers are attracted to the region because of the walking and wildlife spotting opportunities. That said, you can't just head off into the mountains; much of the terrain is farmed or under coffee cultivation, and trails are virtually nonexistent. Because it offers an accessible route to the forest and mountains, nearly everyone who comes here does so expressly to stay in the **Hotel de la Montaña Selva Negra**, 10km from Matagalpa on the road to Jinotega (☎612-3883; rates range from US$50 to US$150, with special US$15 rates for youth hostel members). An establishment of national repute, prices are high by Nicaraguan stan-dards, but worth it. Accommodation is in cabañas, each differently designed and set in beautifully landscaped grounds; there's a good restaurant on site, and apart from hik-ing and touring the hacienda, horseriding is also on offer. The hotel's owners, Eddy and Mausi Kuhl, come from a German family who arrived in Matagalpa in 1891 to grow cof-fee and Eddy's finca still produces some of the best export-grade coffee. In the grounds of the *Selva Negra* hotel are more than fourteen separate trails through the cloudforest vegetation, some of them descending among the coffee plantations. Best to ask Eddy where to walk before you set out – you'll need directions, and take plenty of food and water.

Jinotega

Set amid cool, lush mountains 34km north from Matagalpa, **JINOTEGA** is a non descript but pleasant town, famous in Nicaragua and abroad for the coffee grown near-by. Many foreign solidarity workers have been posted to Jinotega over the years, and the town has a friendly attitude toward strangers. Unless they have a specific reason for coming here, however, most travellers only stop on the way to or from Matagalpa or Estelí. The journey between the two towns is worth doing in itself, as it is the most magnificent trip in the country, winding through mist-washed, perpetually green mountains, although the road is often in bad repair.

If you get caught in between buses and have to **stay**, try Jinotega's friendly hostel, the *Sollentuna Hem*, five blocks north and two blocks east of the cathedral, popular with international travellers and owned by a Swedish woman who will fix you up simple but homely rooms with private or shared bath (①–②). Closer to the centre, the *Hospedaje Tito*, one and a half blocks north of the cathedral (①–②), has similar rooms, kept spotlessly clean. The cafeteria under the same management serves tasty *gallo pinto* breakfasts.

travel details

BUSES

Chinandega to: Guasaule (every 30min; 30min); León (every 30min until 5pm; 1hr 30min); Managua (every 30min until 5pm; 3hr).

Esteli to: Managua (every 45min until 5pm; 3hr); Matagalpa (hourly until 4pm; 2hr); Ocotal, for Honduras (hourly until 5pm; 2hr).

Jinotega to: Matagalpa (every 45min until 5.45pm; 1hr 30min); Managua (5 daily; 3hr 30min).

León to: Chinandega (every 30min; 1hr 30min); Estelí (1 daily; 2hr 30min); Managua (every 30min; buses 1hr 30min, minivans 1hr 10min); Matagalpa (1 daily; 4hr).

Matagalpa to: Estelí (every 30min; 2hr); Jinotega (hourly; 1hr 30min); Managua (every 30min; 3hr).

CHAPTER 24

THE SOUTHWEST

The vast majority of Nicaragua's population lives in the fertile plain that makes up the **southwest** of the country. Bordered by Lago de Nicaragua to the east and the Pacific to the west, the area has been prized since pre-Columbian times for its **agricultural** potential. Studded by volcanoes – Volcán Masaya, Volcán Mombacho just south of Granada, and the twin cones of Ometepe's Concepción and Maderas – the southwest is otherwise a flat, low, grassy plain, ideally suited to cattle, and most of what is left

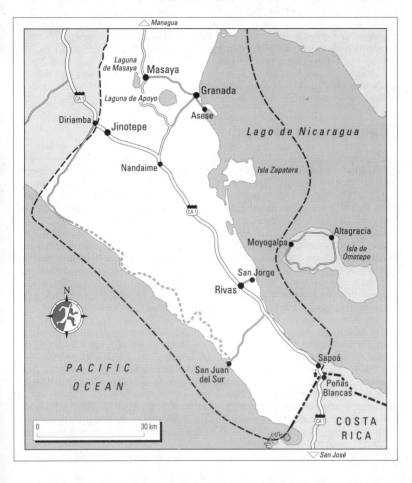

of Nicaragua's beef industry is concentrated here. Where the plain rises to a greater altitude you begin to see carpets of coffee plantations. The area has always been at the hub of the economy and politics of the country, and many of Nicaragua's most prominent political families, including the Chamorros, come from the southwest.

The only two towns of any size are **Masaya**, 29km south of Managua, and Granada, 26km further south, both firmly on the tourist trail. Masaya's colourful history and its enormous craft market attract virtually everyone who comes to Nicaragua. The road connecting Managua, Masaya and Granada passes through one of the most picturesque regions of Nicaragua, the so-called "**Pueblos Blancos**" or White Towns – Nindirí, Niquinohomo, Masatepe, Catarina, Diria and Diriomo – small sleepy settlements considered by Nicaraguans to be at the heart of everything that is authentically *nica*: typical indigenous-influenced food, crafts, and traditions and fiestas inherited from the Chorotgeta and the Mangue groups of native Nicaraguans.

Just outside Masaya, Parque Nacional Volcán Masaya is within easy reach of Managua, and offers the most accessible **volcano-viewing** in the country. Meanwhile **Granada**, with its eventful history, fading classical-colonial architecture and lakeside setting, is undeniably Nicaragua's most beautiful city. Some 75km further south, **Rivas**, the gateway to Costa Rica, is of little interest in itself, but many travellers pass through on their way south or to **San Juan del Sur**, the most pleasant beach town in Nicaragua, where surfing, swimming and seafood are the main attractions.

Masaya and around

Set between the Managua–Granada Highway and the towering form of Volcán Masaya looming to the west, **MASAYA**'s stirring geography would make it an attractive town to visit, even if it weren't the centre of arts and crafts of Nicaragua. For tourists, Masaya's big draw is its colourful **crafts market** and its proximity to Managua, only 29km away. Most visitors know it only as an appealing shopping opportunity; dig deeper, though, and you'll find a rich indigenous culture full of quirky traditions.

Originally peoples from the Chorotega-mangues, the inhabitants of Masaya and the nearby towns are now mostly *mestizo*, or mixed-race. The only remaining seat of real **indigenous culture** is at the southern end of town in the barrio of **Monimbó**, near the San Sebastian church. Monimbó has its own chief (*cacique*), whose authority was recognized under the law in 1991. Other signs of true indigenous culture are scarce: Masaya's church features a gory depiction of the murder of a Spaniard during the colonial period by the local indigenous people, but otherwise Masaya's cultural affinities are expressed only in its crafts and at fiesta time.

The most exciting time to visit Masaya is on Sundays between mid-September and mid-December, when the town experiences a ninety-day period of revelry known as the **Fiesta de San Jeronimo**. One of the most fascinating processions in Central America, the Torovenado, takes place at the beginning of the fiesta; this is an occasion for cross dressing (Monimbó's large gay population comes out in style at this time) that ridicules those in power, pastiching the politicians of the moment. Only quite recently – during the Sandinista years – did Masaya and the Pueblos Blancos develop their crafts tradition into a commodity marketable to foreigners. Masaya remains by far the best place in the country to buy hammocks, rocking chairs, plants, traditional clothing, shoes and souvenirs.

Most visitors come here on day-trips from Managua or Granada – a sensible plan, since hotels in Masaya aren't particularly good and the bus services are fast and efficient.

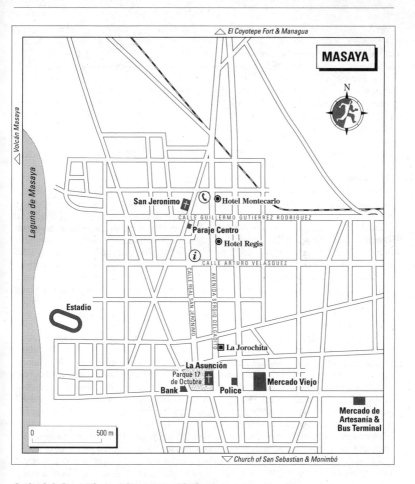

Arrival, information and accommodation

Buses from Managua leave from the Mercado Roberto Huembes every half-hour (45min), ending up at Masaya's Mercado Artesanía, to the east of town; it's a long walk back to the centre from here, so ask to be let off earlier, at the Iglesia San Jeronimo, if you want to explore. Buses between Managua and Granada (plus those heading for Rivas and the Costa Rican border) also stop in town, at the Mercado Viejo (1 and a half blocks east of the Parque 17 de Octubre). Again, it's a long walk to or from town so take a taxi or horse-drawn coach (both US$0.75).

The best thing that can be said about the local **tourist office**, Mintur (Mon–Fri 8am–4pm, Saturday 8am–noon; ☎522-2936), is that it gives a few people a job in a country where unemployment runs at 70 percent. Staff are uninformative and the office is inconveniently located on the highway to Managua, about 1km north of town. As usual in Nicaragua, if you have come to Masaya with travellers' cheques you are out of luck, but several **banks** offer an efficient dollar exchange service: try Bancentro, next to the Telcor/Enitel office; Banco Nacional de Desarrollo, on Av el Progreso; Banco

Popular, two blocks west of the police station; or Banic, in front of the Mercado Viejo. The Telcor/Enitel office on the north side of the parque central (daily 7am–9.30pm) can send telegrams and has public **phones**, including Sprint services to the US. The **mail** service (8am–5pm, ☎522-2631) is on the Parque 17 de Octubre, two blocks north of the Mercado Viejo.

Masaya isn't really the place to bed down for the night; pickings are slim and **hotels** are not used to catering for tourists. Probably the best choices are the *Hotel Regis*, half a block north of Cine González (☎522-2300; ②), which has ten clean rooms, separated by thin partition walls that don't reach the ceiling – you'd better hope your neighbour doesn't snore; and the *Hotel Montecarlo*, two blocks north of *Hotel Regis* (☎522-2166; ②), which has a nice plant-filled courtyard and pokey but good-value rooms.

The Town

Masaya is an attractive town to explore on foot: there is fairly little traffic in the streets, the heat is bearable, and there are destinations of interest on both sides of town – the artisan market to the east, and to the west the volcano, both in easy walking distance.

What little action there is in downtown Masaya takes place in the main square, the **Parque 17 de Octubre**. Bordering the square is the **Catedral de la Ascunción**, with various Central American icons inside, swathed in coloured satin and wilting gold lamé. More plain in its decor is the **Iglesia de San Jeronimo**, a few blocks north. Despite its run-down condition, this church is the best example of colonial architecture in Masaya. The statue of San Jeronimo on the altar depicts an old man wearing a loin cloth and a straw hat, with a rock in his hand and blood on his chest, evidence of self-mortification. For US$0.50 you can climb up to the bell tower for a sweeping view of the town.

Masaya's main attraction is its crafts markets, of which the bigger is the new **Mercado de Artesanía**, a fifteen-minute walk due east from the Parque 17 de Octubre. This is the best place in Masaya – and in Nicaragua as a whole – to buy craft items, many of them produced in Masaya and nearby towns. Goods on sale include **paintings**, many in the naif-art tradition of the Solentiname archipelago, large **hammocks** of the best quality, carved wooden **bowls** and utensils, simple wood-and-bead **jewellery**, cotton shirts, straw hats, and leather footwear, bags and purses. Bargaining is the accepted practice and although prices are generally quoted in córdobas, traders will accept US dollars (small bills are best), though you may get change in córdobas. The mercado is an easy walk from the centre, but if the heat is getting you down, grab one of the many taxis or horse-drawn carriages, which will take you anywhere in town for about US$0.75.

The **Mercado Viejo**, or old market, two blocks east of the parque, is smaller and offers less choice. Another good place to shop is the **Centro de Artesanías de Masaya** at the southern end of town (Mon–Sat 8am–noon & 2–5pm, Sun 8am–noon), an umbrella group representing the craftsworkers of the area, which also acts as a cooperative, selling crafts identical to those you will find in the market, but at higher prices. Check out the giant wall map of the country, which shows the places in Nicaragua where crafts are produced. If your Spanish is up to it, you could ask about visiting artisans at work in their homes and workshops. Just a block to the east are a couple of artisan shops, Los Tapices de Luís and Rincón de las Artesanías – worth visiting but again pricier than the market.

The **Laguna de Masaya** beckons on the western side of town, seven blocks from the Parque 17 de Octubre. However crystalline and inviting it may look, the laguna is actually highly polluted with sewage effluent from the town. The lakeside boardwalk, the malecón, gives a stunning view of the volcano's smoking cone (see opposite).

Eating and drinking

What it lacks in places to stay, Masaya makes up for in its tasty and cheap **eating** establishments. In the centre of town the best choice is the *Nuevo Bar Chegris*, just around the corner to the south of *Hotel Regis* (Mon–Sat 10am–10pm), which is renowned for its "brochettas" (meat on skewers), prawns in garlic sauce and chicken soup. At the southwest corner of Parque 17 de Octubre is the *Restaurante Sandalo* (daily 11am–10pm) where you can have a decent if greasy Chinese meal for about US$4. The surprise award, though, goes to the fabulous Mexican cuisine at *La Jorochita*, on Av Sergio Delgadillo, north of La Asunción, where a *Veracruzano* mom-and-pop operation dish up tacos and fajitas for about US$2. A great unnamed spot for refrescos is located a block north of La Asunción – look for the *Restaurante Alegria* and walk 10m north. The recently opened *Paraje Centro*, opposite the *Hotel Rex*, has an extensive menu including sandwiches and fruit juices (and a payphone). Indigenous food, which comprises mostly pork dishes, is found south of the city centre in Monimbó. Finally, there's a good pizza restaurant, *Pizza Ligabue,* two blocks and a few metres south of the San Sebastian church.

Parque Nacional Volcán Masaya

The only national park of its kind in the country, the **Parque Nacional Volcán Masaya**, between Km 22 and Km 23 on the Managua–Granada highway (Tues–Sun 8am–3pm; ☎522-5415; US$2), offers a glimpse into the smoking cone of the volcano and stunning views of the area around Managua. Trails through the park take you through the hostile, lunar landscape with its own unique selection of flora and fauna, but be warned that walking unguided is not recommended, as it's very easy to get lost.

You can get off any bus between Managua and Masaya or Granada (except the express) at the entrance to the national park, but you will need to hitch a ride up the long road to the crater and back again. Alternatively, you could hire a taxi from Masaya. About 50m before the entrance to the park is the restaurant *Dina #2*, where tables set under little ranchitos offer privacy and a cool breeze; this is a great place to watch the sunset.

About 4.5km before the crater, along the approach road, is the **Centro de Interpretación Ambiental** (Tues–Sun 8am–5pm), which houses an exhibit outlining the agriculture, pre-Columbian history, and geology of the area, along with an interesting three-dimensional display of the country's chain of volcanoes. The centre runs infrequent **tours** (about US$0.50) on the trails around the area, to spot bird and plant life (look out for the stunted bromeliads common to high-altitude volcanic areas). Beside the centre is a shady picnic area and a viewing point on a rickety boardwalk out the back.

There are two **walking trails**, both between about 4.5 and 5km long (at least 2hr round-trip; take water and food), starting at the centre and winding up the side of the volcano. Volcán Masaya last erupted in 1772, but it was a powerful eruption, as the depth of the crater testifies. The fumes coming from the crater are sulphurous and, depending on the level of activity, you might find it difficult to breathe as you get near. Look out for the famous *chocoyos del cráter*, small green parrots that have thrived in an atmosphere that should be poisonous. They live on berries and leaves and seem to have built nests in the walls of the crater. You're likeliest to see them perching on the fence along the perimeter of the parking lot.

The Pueblos Blancos

Scattered within a fifteen-kilometre radius of Masaya are the "Pueblos Blancos" or White Towns – **Nindiri**, **Niquinohomo**, **Masatepe**, **Catarina**, **Diria** and **Diriomo** – small pueblos held dear all over Nicaragua as the embodiment of all things Nicaraguan (or, more precisely, all things from the country's Pacific zone). They get their name from the traditional whitewash used on the houses, *carburo*, which is made from water, lime and salt. The white buildings are pretty, but that said, there is not much more to actually see, few places to sample any cuisine, and, in terms of crafts, nothing obviously on sale.

Although each town has its own specific artisan traditions and fiestas, and local identity is fiercely asserted, to the visitor they seem remarkably similar, sleepy towns with a few hangers-out around nearly identical parques centrales. If you want to visit just one, **CATARINA** is probably the prettiest, with Volcán Masaya looming behind it. All the towns are easily reached in less than half an hour by regular local **buses** from Masaya's Mercado Artesanía terminal.

Granada

Set on the western shore of Lago de Nicaragua some 45km southeast of Managua, **GRANADA** was once the jewel of Central America. It is the oldest Spanish-built city in the isthmus, founded in 1524 by Francisco Hernández de Córdoba, who named it after his home town in Spain. During the colonial period Granada became fabulously rich, its wealth built upon exploitation: sited only 20km from the Pacific, the city was a transit point for shipments of **gold** and other minerals that were mined throughout the Spanish empire, with the help of indigenous slave labour. Laden Spanish galleons would sail from Granada across the lake, down the Río San Juan, out to the Caribbean and then to Europe. The wealth of the city also attracted traffic in the other direction: Granada's gold stores proved tempting to buccaneers and it was sacked several times by English and French **pirates**, until the Spanish built their **Castillo**, a fort on the banks of the Río San Juan (see p.505).

Granada's wealth and its generations of Criollos – people of Spanish descent born in the New World – contributed to its conservative character. The split between liberal León, the only other city of any size in the country, and conservative Granada developed as early as the eighteenth century – and still persists to this day. At the beginning of the nineteenth century, feelings of rivalry between the two cities were ignited by Nicaraguan independence. With the departure of the Spanish, a power vacuum developed and the elite of León decided to fill it by inviting the original troublemaker, the American **William Walker** (see p.443) to fight their cause. Walker attacked and gained Granada, from where he ruled the country as an autocrat for two years, until he was finally driven out. On his retreat from Granada he ordered the city burned and most of

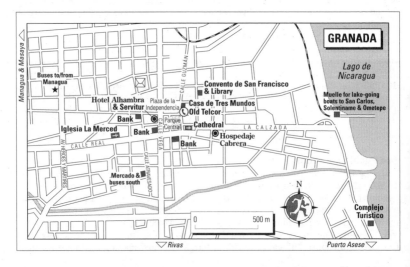

it fell to ruin (you can still see the black carbon on the facade of the cathedral). Granada never recovered its original splendour; nowadays it is certainly more architecturally arresting than any other Nicaraguan town, but it has an overall look of neglect, with empty, eventless streets and ruined houses and churches. Thanks to assistance from the Nicaraguan and some foreign governments, Granada has managed to retrieve some of its colonial character, with its cobblestoned streets, large mansions with distinctive upstairs verandahs, and vistas of tiled roofs stretching toward thick-forested Volcán Mombacho to the south.

Today Granada is central to the Nicaraguan government's **tourism** ambitions. The proximity of the lake, the Zapatera archipelago and Isla de Ometepe, along with the possibility of ecotourism excursions to the Solentiname Islands and San Carlos (all covered in the following chapter, beginning on p.497) suggests that if tourism grows the way the government fervently hopes it will, Granada will be on every visitor's itinerary. For the time being, Nicaragua's only truly beautiful city remains primarily a transport hub for Nicaraguans heading to the south and the east side of the lake, while many travellers on their way to and from nearby Costa Rica stop for a couple of days in Granada to get a last taste of real Spanish colonial atmosphere and architecture.

Arrival, information and accommodation

Buses from Managua and Masaya come into the **terminal** west of town, 700m from the parque central. From here you can grab a taxi into the centre. Arriving from Rivas and points south, buses pull up at the **mercado**, from where it's a short walk, 300m north and 100m east to the parque central. **Ticabus** travellers from Costa Rica can take heart that Ticabus, though destined for Managua, will stop and let you off at its Granada office. The most exciting way to arrive, however, is by **boat** from San Carlos (arrives Tues & Fri; journey time 9–11hr), as the whole of Granada comes out to watch the old chug-tub boat dock.

Although spread out, Granada can be explored comfortably on **foot** – even the 1km walk from the centre to the lakeshore and dock is not arduous, in the shade of floppy mango trees for much of the way. In the heat of midday you will want to follow the example of Granadinos and walk on whichever side of the pavement is in shade. **Horse-drawn taxis** are a picturesque feature of the city; the horses, however, look thin and thirsty. Carriage cabs line up in front of the bandstand on the south side of the parque central. Lada taxis queue just across the street, in front of the *Hotel Alhambra*; if you take them from here it is slightly more expensive than hailing them on the street.

Information

Granada no longer has a government tourist office. Next door to the *Hotel Alhambra* a private operation, **Servitur** (daily 8am–5pm; ☎552-4390, fax 552-2955), has filled the gap; although its primary function is to sell tours, the staff, some of them bilingual, are friendly and will help out if you need information. Among the many **tours** on offer are shopping trips to Masaya, an excursion to Volcán Mombacho just south of Granada, to the Zapatera archipelago in Lago de Nicaragua, and to the Isla de Ometepe. Further afield, they will take you on an "anthropological excursion" to the Solentiname islands, complete with hydrofoil transport and bilingual guide. Tour prices range from US$20 to US$50 and upwards of US$100–150 for the Solentiname archipelago. This might sound steep for Nicaragua, but if you bear in mind the distances and logistical problems involved in getting to some of these places, particularly Solentiname (see p.503), it's not a bad deal. Servitur can also rent cars and sell airline tickets; they also sell tickets for the hydrofoil service to Ometepe, Solentiname and San Carlos de Nicaragua when it is running.

Banks in town will change dollars, but not travellers' cheques. The Banco de Centroamerica (Mon–Fri 8am–3pm), on the south side of the parque central, will give you efficient service in a/c splendour, as will the swish new private bank Bancentro, one block north and one block west of the parque central (Mon–Fri 8am–3pm). The **post office**, 250m north of the Banco Nacional de Desarollo (Mon–Fri 8am–5pm), has a reliable overseas mail service. The old Telcor building (now Enitel), one block north of the cathedral, provides phone services; there are also **payphones** on the street and in the quiet lobby of the *Hotel Alhambra*.

Accommodation

The one good budget hospedaje in town won't thrill those on a super-frugal budget, but if it weren't for the *Hospedaje Cabrera* on C la Calzada, east of the parque central (☎552-2897; ③), it would be the *Hotel Alhambra* or nothing. The friendly *Cabrera*, with a lovely patio stocked with plants and white rocking chairs, and comfortable rooms with fan and clean towels, is one of the best hospedajes in Nicaragua. If you do want to splurge, the upscale *Hotel Alhambra*, on the northwest corner of the parque central (☎552-4486 or 552-6316, fax 552-2035; ④) is very good value for money, considering it is one of the best-designed and friendliest hotels in Nicaragua. For the price, you get the use of a small swimming pool, cable TV (Spanish and English), a room with reasonably quiet a/c and spotless bathrooms with piping hot water.

The Town

Granada has a stately but static feel; the centre of town is the attractive, palm-lined **Parque Central**, where schoolboys goof off under the bandstand and drinks-sellers do a desultory business. If you have time, park yourself under a palm tree and sip a delicious chilled cacao fruit drink at one of the parque's little kiosks. On the east side of the parque is the disappointing **Cathedral**, built in 1712 and damaged when William Walker ordered the city burned (you can still see the burn marks); it has an peeling off-white facade and a rusting tin roof, and is often closed to the public.

Many of the city's most captivating **historic houses** are ranged around the parque central and the **Plaza de la Independencia**, immediately to the north. The palatial red house with white trim on the corner of La Calzada, across from the cathedral, is the **Bishop's Residence**, but once belonged to the prosperous Cardenal family. The columned upstairs verandah is typical of the former homes of wealthy Granadino burghers.

About 200m north of the cathedral on the Plaza de la Independencia is another old stately home, the **Casa de los Leones**. Built in 1724, it has been restored and turned into a cultural centre with help from the governments of Austria and Holland. Now renamed the Casa de los Tres Mundos, it offers workshop space to Granada's musicians and dancers, an auditorium and music classes for schoolchildren. Visitors can wander among its covered and open courtyards and maze-like corridors; the wooden panelling and staircases found within are rare in this concrete-and-adobe country.

Rebuilt in 1867 after Walker's attack, the historic **Convento de San Francisco**, 200m north and 150m east of the cathedral, is a must-see; funds from the government of Sweden have helped restore the former convent and it is in the process of being turned into a municipal museum. It was from the confines of this convent that in 1535 **Frey Bartolomé de las Casas**, apostle of the indigenous peoples of Central America, wrote his historic letter to the Spanish Court condemning the Indians' conversion to Christianity and general maltreatment at the hands of the Spanish. The Convento also houses the city **library**, where those interested in specifics of Granada's history can consult specialist books (in Spanish only). As the Convento is still being renovated, at the moment you can only peruse the outdoor plaza, where about twenty **pre-Columbian statues** stand, some covered in protective plastic. Discovered on Isla Zapatera in Lago de Nicaragua, the statues were hewn from black (volcanic) basalt in about 1000 AD and depict anthropomorphic forms, with the torso and legs of a man but the head and face of lizards, a turtle and a jaguar –

most likely these had ritual significance for the indigenous peoples who inhabited the islands. The statues are dramatically mounted against a view of the slopes of Volcán Mombacho. Inside, there is a small gift shop and very limited exhibit of pre-Columbian artefacts – though it's not really worth the US$1 charged to have a look, entrance fees go towards completing the restoration.

A few blocks southwest of the parque central, activity picks up (at least to a shuffle) at the **market**, a few blocks of indoor and outdoor stalls surrounding the old green market building. You can grab a quick and cheap bite here – the hot tamales and gallo pinto make a good breakfast.

The lakefront

Everywhere in Granada you can feel the welcome breeze off **Lago de Nicaragua**. The shoreline is about 1km east of the parque central; head down the wide dual carriageway boulevard of La Calzada and the wind picks up as the huge vista of the lake stretches across the horizon. In the daytime you may pass a picnicking baseball team having a beer and a hot snack at one of the kiosks on La Calzada; in the evenings Granadinos open the doors of their houses to let in the lake breeze, pull up the rocking chairs, and have a chat on inside patios.

At the lake there's not much going on, unless you happen to arrive as the boat from the other side comes in, when you can watch Granadinos meeting friends and family and see queasy passengers disembark as bananas, chickens and livestock are unloaded along the narrow dock. To the south a small park lines the lake, a few hundred metres beyond which is the entrance to the town's **Complejo Turistico**, a grouping of restaurants and bars, a narrow little beach and grassy areas. Look for the strange little castle that marks the entrance. You walk through the alcove-like door (the drawbridge is for traffic) and cross over the polluted-looking river – warning enough not to swim in this part of the lake. Women walking alone should be aware that even in the afternoons Granada's contingent of permanent drunks may join the love-struck couples lying on benches in the complejo – they may hassle you for money.

Eating and drinking

Despite its increasing tourist traffic, Granada is still very sparse on good **places to eat**. For budget travellers, other than grabbing a quick but basic bite at the town market, the only place to get your fill for under US$2 is the unnamed place next to the *Hospedaje Cabrera* on La Calzada, which serves plain but tasty chicken-and-rice. You could also join the local baseball team at the streetside kiosks further down on La Calzada, opposite the baseball field, for char-grilled meat and chicken, served with chiles and rice on a banana leaf, tamale-style. Washed down with a cold Victoria or Coke, this is one of the better streetside meals you'll have in Nicaragua.

Also on La Calzada, opposite the *Hotel Granada*, is the excellent, if inaccurately named *Drive-in el Ancla*, where a succulent hamburger or lake fish and fries is about US$2.50; friendly staff will point you to the breezier tables, it has long opening hours and even takes credit cards. If you feel like splashing out, the café and restaurant at the swish *Hotel Alhambra* is the place to eat well, while eavesdropping on the Granadino elite and the gringo contingent. The hotel's outside terrace café is a good spot for breakfasts and lunch, while the indoor dining room has several entrees under US$7, and even a wine list. Costa Rican **ice cream** giant *Pops* has a branch in the Centro Comercial one block behind and one block to the south of the *Hotel Alhambra*; it's too pricey for Nicaraguans, but the fruit-flavoured ice creams are worth the gringo guilt.

Granada is peculiarly dead **at night**; down by the lake, the places in the *Complejo Turistico* are much of a muchness and are usually empty, unless it's Friday or Saturday night when locals go out to party. The *Colomar* is slightly classier than others – look for the gates and bamboo shoots outside. Many of these drinking dens advertise happy hours and special "disco" nights. Best to get there and back in taxi at night – local *machos borrachos* (drunk male rowdies) might make the walk back a bit of a hassle.

Around Granada

Although Granada is a convenient jumping-off point for trips to Ometepe and Solentiname (see p.498), there are a couple of worthwhile day-trips closer by.

About 20km south of Granada, in Lago de Nicaragua, **Isla Zapatera** belongs to a group of over three hundred islands scattered about the lake, believed to have been formed from the exploded top of Volcán Mombacho. Many of the pre-Columbian artefacts and treasures you find in museums throughout Nicaragua came from this group of islands, which must have once been of religious significance for the Chorotega-descended people who flourished here before the Conquest. Zapatera is the largest of the islands at 52 square kilometres; it is punctuated by attractive bays and the much-eroded form of an extinct volcano. The island has recently been granted national park status, but that doesn't mean it's easy to get here. Unless you've got some nifty local connections, the only way to go is with a recognized travel agency, such as Servitur in Granada, or one of those in Managua that regularly offer archeological excursions to Zapatera (see p.470). Guides should be able to show you **El Muerto** (The Dead), a site chock-full of the remains of tombs and several **petroglyphs**. You can also see the scant remains – a few grassy mounds and stones – of **Sozafe**, a site sacred to the Chorotegas. Besides these remains there is really very little to see, bar lovely views of the lake. Most of the 300 islands are completely uninhabited and food, drink and lodging are unavailable – hence the necessity for guided tours.

The alternative to a tour is to buzz round the islands in a **hired lancha**. Boatmen in **ASESE**, a fifteen-minute drive south from downtown Granada, beyond the Complejo Turistico, charge around US$12–15 for a boat for up to four people. Ask for Rolando Cruz Salablanca, who runs the Servicio de Transporte Acuatico Turistico (☎522-3845), or negotiate a price with one of the independent boatmen. You don't see much on the standard hour-long trip, so you may want to negotiate a two- or three-hour ride. Make sure the boat is covered, or take a hat and plenty of sunscreen – the sun out on the water is punishing.

LAKE TRANSPORT FROM GRANADA

The sturdy **tub-boat** that plies choppy lake waters between **San Carlos** and Granada has a changing schedule, so you must check either at the docks office (end of La Calzada) or with the Servitur people. At the time of writing, boats depart at 2pm on Mondays and Thursdays and at noon on Saturdays. The trip across the lake to San Carlos takes anywhere from nine to fourteen hours. Some boats stop to let people off at **Altagracia**, on the northeast tip of Ometepe. According to the docks staff, demand for tickets is high at some times of year and people queue from 7am on the day of departure to be assured of a place. At other times you can just show up an hour before the boat is due to leave. Again, best advice is to ask in Granada. Fares are very low: US$1.40 to Altagracia and US$2.20 to San Carlos.

A speedier alternative is the **hydrofoil** service to **San Carlos**, which also stops on the **Solentiname islands**. The only place in town to buy hydrofoil tickets is Servitur; tickets are expensive by Nicaraguan standards (US$20 – most Nicaraguans can't even dream of affording them) but the trip takes only two or three hours. Whether or not the hydrofoils are in service depends upon repairs, weather (if the lake is too rough they can't run) and maybe even demand – nobody seems to know for sure. Best places to ask are the *Hotel Alhambra* and the Servitur office.

Rivas

Most travellers experience **RIVAS** as a dusty bus stop on the way to or from Costa Rica, San Juan del Sur, or Ometepe, unaware that this scruffy town has actually been the site of some decisive events in Nicaraguan – and even Central American – history. Founded in 1736, in its heyday during the California Gold Rush, Rivas was an important stop for gold prospectors looking for their fortune in the gold fields of the western United States. They travelled with Cornelius Vanderbilt's Accessory Transit Company, which ferried goods and passengers between the Caribbean and the Pacific via Lago de Nicaragua. Rivas was never more than a waystation, but there was a time when its languid streets were full of gold-rush hopefuls.

Rivas's dirt-and-stray-chickens **market and bus terminal**, three blocks south and two blocks west of the parque central, is the transport hub of southern Nicaragua. From here you can catch buses north to Granada, Masaya and Managua; west to San Juan del Sur; and south to Sapoá and the Costa Rican border. Bus stops in the market are not marked but everyone knows where buses depart – ask around. If you're headed to San Jorge (for Ometepe), it's best to get a taxi (US$1.50) as buses are infrequent and leave from the highway, a good 1km hike from the market.

Moneychangers frequent Rivas' bus stops, looking for Costa Rican-bound or departing gringos and offering Costa Rican colónes, Nicaraguan córdobas and US dollars at rates more or less the same as at the border. In town, Banco Nacional de Desarollo, two and a half blocks west of the parque central, will change dollars.

Despite its history, Rivas is not a place you want to get stuck in for the night; several of the **hotels** rent beds by the hour. That said, the experience is survivable (earplugs help) and there are far worse dives in Nicaragua. The *Hotel Nicarao*, two blocks west of the parque central (☎463-3234; ②), is better than most, its rooms equipped with private bath and either a/c or fans. For rock-bottom budget travellers, the best bet is the *Hospedaje Internacional* next to the *Hotel Coco* (①), where you will at least get a clean bed and a fan.

A quick, cheap **meal** can be picked up at any of the comedores on the parque central; there are no gastronomic experiences, but good chicken, pork or beef and rice dishes, and tamales. Surprisingly, Rivas has a vegetarian joint: *La Soya*, 50m north of the parque central, offering workaday salads and vegetable dishes.

San Juan del Sur

You would never know it today, but the sleepy fishing village-cum-beach town of **SAN JUAN DEL SUR** was once a lively place. In the mid-1800s this was a crucial **transit point** on Cornelius Vanderbilt's trans-isthmian steamboat line, a scheme whereby people and goods were transported to gold rush-era California. Boats would sail up the Río San Juan, disembark at Granada, and then continue by rail or carriage to San Juan del Sur, from where Pacific-going vessels would head north.

San Juan del Sur's second age of glory was as a popular **holiday spot** for hordes of *internacionalistas* during the 1980s. Today it's the most popular beach in Nicaragua, at least with foreign travellers – European backpackers and American surfers together make up the biggest contingent. The town's setting, in a lush valley with a river running down to the beach, is beautiful; the beach itself is a long wide stretch of fine, dark sand running between two cliffs, with generally calm and shallow waters, suitable for swimming. In the early hours of the morning a range of sea birds hunt along the beach for food, poking around for shellfish in the shallows. With excellent seafood restaurants and plenty of good places to stay, it is the kind of town you could easily spend a few days in. Nearby are some beautiful, less littered beaches, good for surfing or relaxing (although not necessarily swimming – the surf is rough).

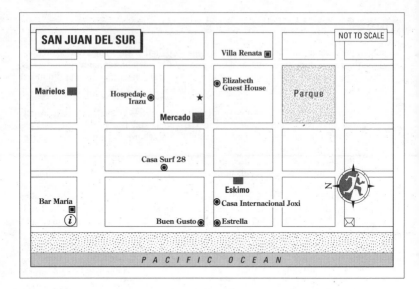

Arrival and information

Regular half-hourly **buses** from Rivas take an hour to reach San Juan del Sur's **bus terminal**, three blocks east from the *Hospedaje Estrella*, beside the market.

There is no tourist office but you can get **information** from the *Joxi* or *Maria's Bar*, the latter run by an English-speaking Austrian/German couple. *Maria's Bar* also rents **bicycles** and can supply you with a map of the town. The Telcor/Enitel office, two blocks south of *Hotel Estrella*, has an international **phone** service (daily 7am–10pm) and mail service (Mon–Fri 8am–6pm). There is **no bank** in town but many establishments take credit cards, travellers' cheques and dollars.

Accommodation

San Juan del Sur has a good mix of accommodation, from well-appointed hotels to surfer's dens; the budget places are mainly located on the road to the beach from the bus terminal.

Hotel Balovento, behind the health centre (☎458-2298 or 458-2374). One of the larger hotels, the *Balovento* has nineteen rooms with an a/c bar and a fairly good restaurant attached. ⑤.

Casa Internacional Joxi, 50m from the beach (☎468-2348). A favourite with backpackers, the *Joxi* is well-run by Norwegian/Nicaraguan management with nice but expensive rooms – check out the spotless dorms with bunkbeds, for US$8. You can receive email here, rent boogie boards and organize sailing trips. ④–⑤.

Casa Surf 28, a block back from the beach (☎458-2441). If you can stand the bargain-basement surfer clientele, *Casa Surf 28* is a good budget option for non-surfers, too. Friendly management will reduce the price for groups of four or more. ①.

Elizabeth Guest House, 75m east of the market (☎458-2270). A small, simple but friendly guest house with twelve rooms with private baths. You can pick up local maps here and rent bicycles. ①–②.

Hotel Estrella, on the beachfront (☎458-2210). The second-storey rooms with balconies have plenty of breeze and character. Unfortunately the owners have all the charm of wrinkled lemons, there are mosquitoes and the rooms are divided only by partitions. ②.

Hospedaje Irazú, 300m from the beach (☎458-2371). Run by a friendly Costa Rican couple – and named after one of the country's volcanoes – the *Irazu* is a clean, if dark budget choice, with fan and private bath. ①.

Hospedaje y Comedor el Buen Gusto, opposite the *Estrella* on the beachfront (no phone). Small rooms but a nice upstairs balcony to relax on. The restaurant is spotless, and serves a good breakfast, included in the price. ②.

Eating and drinking

Seafood is king in San Juan del Sur, and a whole baked fish, big enough for two people, costs only US$7. There are plenty of bars and restaurants serving food along the beach but the same food is considerably cheaper in the market and in *La Soya*, run by the Nicaraguan women's association IXCHEN, which offers good vegetarian food for around US$2. The *Casa Internacional Joxi* does a spot-on breakfast of pancakes (US$4) or eggs (US$3), including coffee and juice. Good Mexican, Italian and Chinese food is served at *Villa Renata*. The seafront restaurants double as a good place to have a beer and shoot the breeze with the surfers at night; for those who'd rather self-cater, you'll find an all-night liquor store strategically located behind *Casa Surf 28*.

Sailing, fishing and surfing

Fast developing a reputation for **water sports**, San Juan del Sur is already well-known as a good spot for **sailing**. All-day cruises, sailing south to Brasilito Beach, are offered on American Chris Berry's boat, *Pelican Eyes* (US$45 per person, including lunch; ☎458 2110, fax 458 2344); you can also take a sunset cruise along the coast (US$15 per person). There is good **deep sea fishing** in this area and trips can be organized on the *Sports Fishing Yvette* (US$180 for six people). On a more modest scale, you can rent **fishing gear** from *Bar Maria* (who will then cook your catch in the restaurant). *Bar Maria* can also arrange a boat for weekend fishing trips for US$25 an hour for up to twelve people.

Diving trips in San Juan del Sur and other locations in Nicaragua can be arranged in advance through the Oceania Dive School in Managua (Bahía Dive Shop, Plaza Barcelona; ☎277-2104; *latincam@tmx.com.ni*). **Surfing**, however, is the real water sport in town. You can rent boards and arrange transport to some of the more remote beaches south of town through *Bar Maria,* who can also set you up for camping. La Flor, 19km south of San Juan del Sur, is an excellent spot to string up a hammock and spend a night. It has good surf, a beautiful white sandy beach and a stand of shady trees. It is now a reserve dedicated to the protection of the sea turtles that nest there in large numbers during October and November. Mosquitoes and voracious sandflies are abundant – take repellent.

South to Costa Rica

Crossing the border at the Sapoá–Peñas Blancas post is a time-consuming process, though leaving Nicaragua is at least faster than entering. Local **buses from Rivas** go as far as the border post at the shantytown of **Sapoá**. The bus pulls up directly in front of the barrier, which you cross (show your passport to soldiers in the little doghouses on either side), and enter the white Nicaraguan immigration building. Inside you must pay an exit tax (US$2) in dollars, and get your exit stamp from Nicaraguan *migración*. **Shuttle buses** leave constantly from the parking lot for the 3–4km trip to the Costa Rican border post (show passport again). From there it is about an 800m walk along the highway to the blue Costa Rican immigration building. Once inside, head for the Entrada window, where the immigration official may ask to see an onward ticket. You will be given a 90-day entrance stamp, and have to pay a fee of US$0.30, after which you pick up your passport from another window when you hear your name called out.

Local buses from **Peñas Blancas**, the name of the Costa Rican border post, run every hour to San José and points between. You can buy your ticket from one of the makeshift tables at the immigration building. Then you must line up for the baggage check, a rudimentary fumble in your bag by Costa Rican customs officials. Once on the bus be prepared for many passport checks in the first few kilometres – best to keep your passport out and handy.

Inside the Costa Rican immigration building is a small Costa Rican tourist office, the ICT (Mon–Sat 8am–8pm, Sun 8am–noon). They are helpful but can only dispense glossy tourist brochures and maps in Spanish only.

travel details

BUSES

Granada to: Managua (almost constant departures 5.30am–5pm; 1hr 30min); Masaya (almost constant departures 5.30am–5pm; 30min); Rivas (every 30min; 1hr 30min).

Masaya to: Granada (every 30min; 30min); Managua (every 30min; 45min); Rivas (hourly; 1hr 30min).

Rivas to: Granada (every 30min; 1hr 30min); Masaya (every 30min; 2hr); Managua (every 30min; 2hr 30min); San Juan del Sur (hourly; 1hr); Sapoá (for Costa Rica; hourly 5.30am–2pm; 1hr).
San Juan del Sur to: Rivas (hourly; 1hr).

BOATS

For a rundown of the services from Granada to San Carlos, Ometepe and the Solentiname islands, see p.492.

CHAPTER 25

LAGO DE NICARAGUA

S tanding on the shore and looking out into its expanse, you can imagine the surprise of the Spanish navigators in 1522 when, nearly certain they were heading toward the long dreamed-for route to the Pacific, they instead came upon **Lago de Nicaragua**. The lake – also known by its indigenous name, *Cocibolca* ("sweet sea") – is the largest **freshwater sea** in the Americas after the Great Lakes, and the tenth largest body of freshwater in the world. Over 177km long, about 58km wide and fed by forty rivers, the lake is not very deep (about 60m at the deepest point) but has a reputation for general choppiness and occasional fierce waves.

Both Lago de Nicaragua and Lago de Managua were most likely once part of the Pacific. **Volcanic eruptions** and earthquakes created the Pacific plain which separates the lakes from the ocean today. Fed by freshwater rivers over millennia, the lake water gradually lost its salinity. Saltwater fish were trapped there and – in a Darwinian case of adaptation – evolved into some of the most unusual types of fish found anywhere on earth: freshwater tarpon, swordfish, even a freshwater shark. Although now thought extinct, this three-metre-long **bull-shark** moves naturally to and from the ocean waters of the Caribbean to the fresh waters of the Río San Juan and the lake, adapting instantly to changes in salinity.

Crossing the lake can be quite an undertaking: Lago de Nicaragua is affected by what locals call a short-wave phenomenon – short, high, choppy waves – caused by the meeting of the Papagayo wind from the west and the Caribbean-generated trade winds

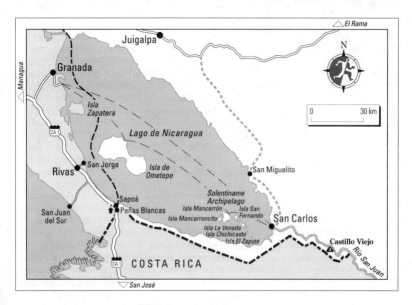

For an explanation of **accommodation price codes**, see p.438.

from the east. Lakegoing craft are notoriously thick-set and slow; the waves require them to advance slowly and in a zigzag pattern – one reason why lake crossings take so long. The lake's choppiness makes crossing it hell for those prone to seasickness and there are occasional dangerous squalls, especially in November.

Travellers who have the patience to cope with erratic boat schedules (and preferably some Spanish, as settlements around the lake are few and isolated) are drawn by the area's unique **culture**. Many are captivated by the natural beauty of the **islands** that dot the southwest sector of the lake – twin-volcanoed **Ometepe** and the scattering of small islands known as the **Archipelago de Solentiname**. Ernesto Cardenal, one of Nicaragua's best-known writers, lived for many years in Solentiname and the islands are also famous for their *pintores primitivos* – naif-style painters who depict lush landscapes where jewel-coloured parrots and red jaguars poke out of hyperverdant jungles. In all, over 400 islands dot the lake – little-visited by travellers, most of these islands are inhabited, while some others are used by well-to-do mainlanders as a place for holiday homes.

On its eastern edge the lake is fed by the 170km-long Río San Juan, which forms Nicaragua's southern border and runs out into the Caribbean. You can take a boat trip down the river to stay in the **Castillo Viejo**, an old Spanish fort on the banks of the Río San Juan. This part of the country is remote, surrounded on all sides by pristine jungle, and offers excellent wildlife viewing. The Río San Juan and the Castillo are reached via the largest town on the east side of the lake, **San Carlos de Nicaragua**, a muddy, dusty town of little interest, used by travellers mainly as a transit point for exploring the river or travelling south to Costa Rica via Los Chiles.

Isla de Ometepe

"Va para la isla?" mainlanders ask you as you head to the San Jorge docks near Rivas to catch the boat to **ISLA DE OMETEPE**. And from the reverential way they say its name, you can tell Ometepe is considered a place apart from the rest of Nicaragua – in fact, it has an almost mystical appeal, not least because of the dramatic way it draws your eye from the mainland as you see two **volcanoes** rising swiftly from the waters of Lago de Nicaragua. The island's name comes from the Nahuatl language of the Chorotegans, the original inhabitants of Nicaragua, who called it *Ome Tepetl* – "the place of two hills". Even on clear days wispy clouds cap the summit of the higher of the two cones, Concepción, which, at 1610m is Nicaragua's second-highest volcano. The dull mauve of its upper slopes, stripped of vegetation by altitude and lava flow, contrasts sharply with the almost shining green of the farms, secondary forest and tilled fields set on Concepción's fertile skirts. To the south is extinct Volcán Maderas, smaller (1394m) and less perfectly conical in shape. Until the last century Ometepe was technically two islands, separated only by a narrow canal until an eruption of Concepción in 1804 filled the gap and sealed the narrow isthmus – Ometepe is now referred to as one island.

The island has likely been inhabited since the first migration of indigenous groups from Mexico arrived in this area of Nicaragua. A few stone sculptures and petroglyphs that attest to their presence remain on the island – some of these can be easily seen if you go on a guided walk. It's not clear if there was any significant population of indigenous people living on the island when the Spanish arrived in around 1600, when criollo farmers and cattle ranchers colonized Ometepe. For hundreds of years Volcán

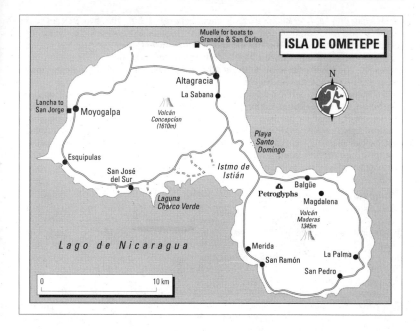

Concepción was dormant, but one morning in 1880 the Spanish-descended settlers awoke to find that they had staked their lives underneath an active volcano. Since then Concepción has erupted seven times, most recently in 1957 there has been no significant activity since. Still, the shadow of the volcano and its lava-scarred slopes looms everywhere on the island.

Ometepe has remained isolated from the outside world; until recently even contact with Granada was sporadic. The island has an amazing **agricultural output**, owing to its unusually fertile volcanic soil, and is more prosperous than much of mainland Nicaragua. Most farms are smallholdings on the skirts of the volcano, growing citrus, bananas, coffee, cacao, watermelon and sesame, as well as dry-country products like tobacco and cotton. Towns on the island are well-kept and schoolchildren and the occasional cow share the dusty graded roads with island traffic.

Almost everyone who travels through Nicaragua comes to Ometepe, if only to sample the island's amazingly lush scenery and tranquil atmosphere. **Walking, hiking and volcano viewing** along with some **horseback riding** are really the only activities on the island and most come specifically to scale the smaller of the two volcanoes, Maderas. The temperature on the island is slightly cooler than the mainland, as the heat is mitigated by lake winds.

Ometepe supports a population of 25,000 – quite large for an island of its size. Most people live in the towns at the foot of Volcán Concepción – this is where the two main towns, **Moyogalpa** and **Altagracia**, are found. A dirt and gravel **road** circles the skirt of Concepción, though in the rainy season one stretch between Moyogalpa and Altagracia can become impassible. On the southwest side of Concepción the road passes a beautiful vista of the isthmus, with tilled fields and pockets of fruit trees in the foreground. There's another, very rough road (4WD only), which goes about three-quarters of the way around Maderas.

Despite only a few kilometres distance between them, the two volcanoes of **Concepción** and **Maderas** have quite different ecosystems. Concepción is the eastern extent of what is known as the **Pacific tropical dry forest** – a dry, grassy and hot vegetation lacking the ebullience of rainforest green. Maderas has an ecosystem very much like the **rainforest** areas of the southeast of Nicaragua, and is the westernmost point where you will find jungle-like vegetation.

On Maderas, as you move from the northeast part of the island further south you can actually see the change taking place with every metre you travel southward. The actual border zone, according to biologists, is around the hamlet of San Ramón. You're likely to spot rainforest **animals** such as the white-faced money (*carablanca*) and howler monkey (*monos congos*), while birdwatchers will want to keep their eyes out for green parrots (*llora verde*) and the commonly sighted blue-tailed birds called *urracas*.

Island transport

The majority of travellers arrive in Moyogalpa via the **lancha from San Jorge**; there are seven or eight daily departures Monday to Saturday, and three on Sunday (see p.506 for detailed schedules). Itineraries sometimes change between the rainy and dry seasons. There are also two boats a week **from Granada** to Altagracia, from where most travellers head straight for Moyogalpa – although it has a smaller population, Moyogalpa has a much better choice of hotels and services. A local bus service leaves Altagracia for Moyogalpa at 5.30pm.

Returning to the mainland, you'll need to take an early-morning crossing if you want to travel on to Peñas Blancas, say, on the Costa Rican border. The 1.30pm crossing will still get you to Granada or Managua before buses stop running. Best to double-check the schedule the day before you plan to leave.

Getting around the island isn't too arduous. A **bus** service circles Concepción, leaving about every ninety minutes from the Parquecito four blocks east (uphill) from the Moyogalpa docks. It heads south initially, passing the entrance to Playa Santo Domingo, and arriving in Altagracia about an hour after leaving Moyogalpa. Buses leave Moyogalpa for Altagracia eight times daily, the first at 6am and the last at 6pm. From Altagracia, the service begins at 4.30am and ends at 4.30pm. A far less frequent bus leaves Altagracia for Balgue, the end of the road on the eastern side of Maderas. Sunday services for all buses are less frequent.

You can rent tough Suzuki Samurai **jeeps** from the *Hotel Ometepetl* for about US$56 for a 24-hour period. Most hotels will rent **bicycles** by the hour (US$2) or by the day (US$8).

An alternative to getting around on your own steam is to hire one of the several local **taxi** drivers/guides to take you around the island. Fares depend on how far you are going, and it's far more economical if you can get a group together. A day's jaunt around Maderas as far as Merida or Balgue, the end of the road, will cost US$40 per carload. Ask at Fundación entre Volcanes (see box opposite).

Moyogalpa

The largest town on the island, **MOYOGALPA** is set on the northwest side of Volcán Concepción. The dock, where the lanchas from San Jorge arrive, is at the bottom of the main street, a steeply rising narrow avenue paved with concrete. Lining it are high sidewalks leading to hardware stores, agricultural supply shops, and Moyogalpa's contingent of lodging and restaurants. Occasional Land Rovers battle up and down Moyogalpa's streets, their front axles hanging loose after too many potholes. Most transport in the town, though, is by tractor, or the thin ragged horses attached to the rubber-wheeled carts driven into town from all over the island.

Moyogalpa is home to nearly all of Ometepe's services, lodgings and restaurants. There are a couple of places to stay in Altagracia, on the other side of Concepción, but Moyogalpa's boat connections and services tend to draw most travellers here. The local Banco Nacional de Desarollo (300m uphill from the dock, on the right; Mon–Sat 8am–5pm) will **change dollars**. Many of the hotels will also oblige if they have enough córdobas on hand – try the *Hotel Ometepetl*. You can make **calls** and send **mail** from the Telcor/Enitel (Mon–Sat 8am–6pm) in the centre, across from the Fundación entre Volcanes.

Accommodation is nearly without exception of the basic, hospedaje variety. Probably the best budget option in town is the *Hotelito Aly*, 100m uphill from the dock, on the left (☎459-4196; ①); a large, comfortable hospedaje with 25 rooms, it's very popular with travellers for its plant-filled courtyard with hammocks, which is a good place to meet people and write postcards. The rooms themselves are basic – beds are narrow and uncomfortable – but the atmosphere makes up for it. There is a restaurant attached, serving a reliably good comida corriente, a bargain at US$2.50, plus tasty traditional breakfasts. One block west, the *Pension Jade* is the cheapest place in town, with lumpy beds and shared cold-water bath (①), but there's a pretty patio and the comida corriente at the little restaurant here is excellent: large plates of delicately cooked chicken or fish with rice and salad for US$2. The only upscale place in town is the *Hotel Ometepetl*, 50m uphill from the dock, on the right (☎459-4276; ②–③), which has large, very clean, soulless rooms with fans. The management is friendly, there's a good restaurant and car rental service.

There are only a couple of places for good **meals**. Best is the *Restaurant Bahía*, 100m uphill from the docks, despite advertising its house speciality as tongue in sauce; it's also the only place, apart from hotels, where you can have a drink in the evening. Taped music draws a small crowd on the weekend and you can choose between snacks like tacos and sandwiches or full dishes of beef and rice for US$5. At the little *Soda Bar el Chele*, 25m uphill from the dock on the left-hand side, owned by Helmut, the friendly "Chele" (foreigner) of the name, you can get inspired bocas.

Altagracia and Volcán Concepción

There's very little to detain the traveller in **ALTAGRACIA**, a sleepy town set slightly inland from the lake on Ometepe's northeastern side. Its **parque central** is nicely ringed by several pre-Columbian statues found on the island and, should you decide to stop here, there are two good **places to stay**. The *Hospedaje y Restaurante Castillo*,

---

FUNDACIÓN ENTRE VOLCANES

In the last few years an indispensable local ecotourism organization has been set up on Ometepe. **Fundación entre Volcanes**, in Moyogalpa, 150m south of the gas station, right in front of the Telcor/Enitel (☎459-4118), operates as the island's **tour** coordination and **information** centre. Founded with help from European governments, the organization's staff are all local people.

Tours offered are nearly all full-day (8hr) excursions, including tours to see the **petroglyphs**, a trip 800m (about halfway) up Volcán Concepción, as well as a ten-hour odyssey up to the lagoon of Volcán Concepción, and an excursion to the lagoon of Volcán Maderas. All tours include a guide but you may have to add on the cost of transport and food. In groups of five or more you'll pay between US$5 and US$12 per person; if there are fewer of you you'll pay between US$12 and US$20 per person. You should bring your own repellent, sunglasses, hat, good hiking boots, water, food and chocolate/nuts (high energy snacks) and sunblock.

100m south and 50m west of the church (☎552-6045; ①), is where most people stay, mainly because the octogenarian owner, Don Ramón Castillo, is a walking oral history of the island. He can also arrange horseback riding trips and guides to take you up Maderas. The hospedaje itself is very basic – rooms have a bed, fan, light and shared bath – but clean. The food at the *Castillo* is good local cuisine and you don't have to stay here to dine. The *Hotel Central*, two blocks south of the parque central, is more upscale and very comfortable. As well as regular rooms, some with private bath, there are good-value little cabañas that sleep up to four people (②); breakfasts, comidas corrientes and sandwiches are served in the little restaurant of the same name.

Hikes up **Volcán Concepción** usually start from Altagracia; the route begins from the back of the town and the ascent is a five-hour trek, all uphill, much of it extremely steep. The upper reaches of the volcano are exposed with lava flows and no vegetation and (the volcano erupted most recently in 1983). The best way to scale Concepción is on one of the various walks of varying difficulty arranged by Fundación entre Volcanes (see box on p.501).

Playa Santo Domingo

On the east side of the isthmus separating Concepción and Maderas, **Santo Domingo**'s narrow grey-sand beach stretches for more than a kilometre. This is the only really swimmable beach on Ometepe, though the lake can be surprisingly rough at times, and many volcano-climbers and hikers spend a day soaking up some sun here. The beach is accessed from the main road circling Concepción, although the first kilometre or so of the road that forks off to Santo Domingo is in exceptionally bad condition (4WD essential). Beyond the beach there's not much to see, other than farmers riding out in the pre-dawn darkness and shy kids playing on the beach. Of the two **places to stay**, the budget choice is the *Finca Santo Domingo*, a lovely rustic building offering simple dark rooms with fans, hammocks strung around the terrace (①), and good food – even if you don't stay here they will cook you large breakfasts and lunch for US$3–4. More upscale is the adjacent *Hotel Villa Paraíso* (☎453-4675, in Managua ☎244-0181; ③–④), run by a Nicaraguan/Austrian couple. Rooms are large, with fans and either shared or private bath, screened windows and rocking chairs on small patios – all in all it's a little overpriced for what you get. The covered restaurant, bordered by hammocks, overlooks the lake, and is a great place to stop for lunch or for a beer. Try the bland but filling grilled lake fish.

Volcán Maderas and around

The hike up the verdant forested slopes of dormant **Volcán Maderas** is a less arduous one than the steep odyssey up and down Concepción. All in all, it takes about nine hours to get to the top and back down, so you need to set out at about 5.30 or 6am. Birds and howler monkeys can be heard if not seen all the way up, and the summit gives stunning views of Concepción and the entire lake – take your camera. The crater itself is eerily silent and still, its lip covered by a mixture of dense rainforest-like vegetation and a few bromeliad-encrusted conifers. In shade, the temperature at the top can be refreshingly cool; it is still very hot and humid in the sun, however, and you must make sure your guide takes plenty of water (and don't forget sunscreen). The clear water in the crater lagoon is good for a chilly swim.

If you have time, it's worth exploring the towns of the lower slopes of Maderas. **Petroglyphs** dot this part of the island, with a group of them located between the hamlets of Santa Cruz and La Palma – you need someone to take you there. Ask at Fundación entre Volcanes for a guide.

In **Balgüe**, on the east side of Maderas, you can visit the *Finca Magdalena* (US$2), a cooperative of producers of organic coffee and livestock. They also serve a good comida corriente lunch for US$2 and you can buy organic honey and coffee produced by the farm. If you find yourself near **Las Pedrecitas** and in need of fuel, Rosa Maria Reyes cooks a comida corriente (US$2) in her house (north side of the primary school). In most of the pueblitos on this part of the island there is a local woman who will cook you lunch in her home – ask around.

The Solentiname archipelago

Lying in the southeast corner of Lago de Nicaragua, the **Solentiname archipelago** is made up of 36 islands of varying size. With the rise of ecotourism, Solentiname is becoming known for its unspoilt natural beauty and remarkable **bird and animal life**. For a long time, though, it was the islands' colony of naif-art **painters** that brought fame to Solentiname. Priest and poet Ernesto Cardenal lived here for many years, writing and preaching liberation philosophy, before becoming the Sandinistas' Minister of the Interior in the 1980s. His poetry and his promotion of the archipelago's primitive art and artisan skills brought Solentiname culture to the attention of the outside world, and it was Cardenal's work that led to the government declaring Solentiname a national monument in 1990.

The largest islands of the group are also the most densely inhabited – **Mancarrón**, **La Venada**, **San Fernando** and **Mancarroncito**. Most people stay on Mancarrón, where the islands' main **hotel** is located, and make trips to San Fernando and other nearby islands. Much of the **wildlife** in the area corresponds to that of northern Costa Rica, just over the border, and the dense jungles stretching from the eastern shore of Lago de Nicaragua to the Caribbean. Birdlife is opulent, including parrots, macaws, egrets, storks and many kingfishers. Much of the vegetation of the islands is pristine tropical forest.

Solentiname's **isolation** keeps all but the most determined off-the-beaten track travellers away. However, tourist traffic from Costa Rica, in the form of organized tours, is increasing. Travellers who give up trying to figure out the confusing and changeable boat schedules often come on a tour organized from Managua or Granada. There's absolutely nothing to do in Solentiname, except make like an anthropologist/art collector and hunt out some of the *pintores primitivos*, if your Spanish is up to it. Make sure you bring plenty of cordóbas with you – there is nowhere to change money on the islands.

Practicalities: Mancarrón

Boats make the two-hour trip to Mancarrón from San Carlos twice a week, on Tuesday and Friday around 7am – although the departure time frequently changes. Unless you come on a tour, this is currently the only way to get here by scheduled transport, although unscheduled private craft make the same trip, leaving constantly – ask around at the San Carlos docks.

Nearly everyone who comes to Solentiname **stays** in the *Hotel Mancarrón* (in Solentiname ☎552-2059, in Managua ☎260-3345), an old tiled-roof building set in grassland on the island of the same name (US$40 per day including three meals). The hotel can fix you up with **boat tours** to nearby islands. A cheaper and potentially more interesting option is to bed down with a local family – even though it runs the hotel, the non-profit-making Solentiname Development Association on Mancarrón can put you in touch with locals; they can also hook you up with local **painters** and craftspeople, advise you on the boat schedule and anything else you need to know about Solentiname. You can call them from Managua (☎260-3345).

Río San Juan

At 170km long, the mighty **Río San Juan** is one of the most important rivers in Central America and the route by which Nicaragua was discovered. Subsequently it has played a key role in the history of the country. In colonial times the nascent cities of Granada and León were supplied by Spain and emptied of their treasure by pirates from the navigable waters of the river.

Nowadays the Río San Juan area has staked its economic hopes on attracting **ecotourism**. The river is relatively pristine, and no settlement of any size exists along the riverbank other than sleepy remote villages home to people who make their living by fishing and farming. If you want to experience the tropical flora and fauna and don't mind being hundreds of miles from civilization of any kind, then a boat ride on the Río San Juan is worth the hassle of getting there. **Wildlife** is abundant along the river, and travellers who venture up or downstream will certainly spot sloths, howler monkeys, parrots and macaws, bats, storks, caimans and perhaps even a tapir.

Most travellers encounter the Río San Juan from the vantage point of a boat sailing from **San Carlos de Nicaragua** on the eastern shore of Lago de Nicaragua to the old Spanish fort of the **Castillo Viejo**, the only real tourist attraction in the area. The southern bank of the river is the border with Costa Rica: although Costa Ricans have right of transit, as soon as you are on the river you are in Nicaraguan territory. See p.640 for trips on the Costa Rican side.

The Río San Juan area is alarmingly **remote** and you have to be prepared to do battle with the elements. Little food and drink is available, not to mention consumer goods, whether it be batteries or toothpaste. There are good hospitals on the Costa Rican side, in Los Chiles and in Ciudad Quesada, but you should be prepared for any emergency. Apart from that, the **basics** you will need are a light raincoat, plastic bags for cameras and other mechanical equipment, sunglasses, repellent, sunscreen, a torch, good boots, a spare (dry) pair of shoes, matches, candles, bottled water, towels and a first aid kid, including, if possible, a snakebite kit.

San Carlos de Nicaragua

Sleepy and slatternly, **SAN CARLOS DE NICARAGUA** has to be one of the most unprepossessing towns in the whole country. An air of lassitude, if not outright stasis, pervades its ramshackle buildings and muddy streets. This could, of course be the fault of the fire which destroyed most of the town in 1984, or the climate of heat and torrential rain, but no one seems to have much civic pride or interest in treating the place to a splash of paint. Travellers come through San Carlos from Los Chiles in Costa Rica in order to make the lake trip to Granada, or specifically to go to Solentiname. Increasingly, more determined **ecotourists** are coming through to pick up a boat to the Castillo Viejo and points further along the Río San Juan.

Getting to San Carlos

San Carlos can be reached by road, boat or air. The **bus** service, which is erratic in the rainy season (always check that it's running) currently leaves Managua's Mercado Ivan Montenegro three times a week at 6am (Mon, Tues & Thurs), arriving about 3pm at the market terminal. If you plan on doing the heroic seven-hour **drive**, get your hands on a sturdy four-wheel drive with high clearance. Leaving Managua, take the Carretera Interamericana to San Beninto and there take the Boaco turnoff. Continue from Boaco – through the small hamlets of San Lorenzo, Camaoapa, Tecolostote and San Patricio – to Juigalpa, 135km from Managua. Then take the road to Rama, and turn off at the 165km point onto the road to Acoyapa. All in all it's 300km from Managua.

Boats leave for San Carlos from Granada on Mondays and Thursdays at 3pm, arriving in San Carlos at 3 or 4am the next day. La Costeña does the **airplane** run from Managua to San Carlos on Monday, Wednesday and Friday at 7am, landing at the airstrip just north of town.

Practicalities

San Carlos's Banco Nacional de Desarollo (Mon–Fri 8am–4pm, Sat 8–11.30am) will **change dollars**; there's also an Telcor/Enitel office (Mon–Sat 8am–5pm), but don't expect mail sent from here to get anywhere quickly.

San Carlos has a lot of transient traffic, which is reflected in the spartan decor and indifferent management of its **hotels**. There are only two reasonable (not bug-ridden, sinister and noisy) places in town. In front of the Plaza Malecón, by the lake, is the *Hotel Azul* (☎283-0282; ②), which is the more expensive option but still doesn't quite convince. The *Hotel San Carlos* in front of the market (②), is the place of choice for the local itinerant crowd, and pretty noisy. With the exception of the stalwart *Hotel San Carlos*, establishments come and go with amazing rapidity in this town; the best strategy is to ask to see a room first and inspect the bathroom.

The best place to **eat** in town is the popular *Restaurante Jaguar*, up the hill from the market, which serves good local steak and big plates of river fish with rice.

Crossing into Costa Rica

To get to **Los Chiles in Costa Rica**, ask at the *muelle* (dock) for boatmen. There is currently no scheduled service, but individuals will do the 14km trip down to the Costa Rican hamlet for a group price – there are always plenty of Nicaraguans going. The actual border post is 3km before you reach Los Chiles. Nicaraguan officials will give you an exit stamp; you get the entry to Costa Rica at the Los Chiles **muelle**. Be aware that Costa Rican officials are rigorous in their checks on Nicaraguans in this area and there is always a chance that a boat will be sent back if you are travelling with Nicaraguans whose paperwork does not satisfy.

Castillo Viejo

The full name of the Río San Juan's historic fort is the **Castillo de la Inmaculada Concepción**, but everyone refers to it as the Castillo Viejo or the Fortaleza (fort). Lying on a hillock perched beside a narrow stretch of the Río San Juan, the Castillo was built by the Spanish to be a bulwark against the pirates who continually managed to sack Granada in the seventeenth century. The fort was more or less effective for over a hundred years, until the British finally took the Castillo in 1780; it was then abandoned for nearly two centuries. The Nicaraguan Ministry of Tourism, with the help of funds from various overseas governments, has renovated and restored the low stone structure with an iron door and an access ramp and has had several floors re-tiled. A library operates from inside the walls, with over a thousand books on the history of the castle and the Río San Juan area. There is also a small **museum** with dusty armaments of the period and a few random artefacts found during the restoration of the castle (entrance US$1).

The Castillo is about an hour and thirty minutes from San Carlos by boat. You can rent a *panga* (motorized dugout boat) in San Carlos for about US$160 shared between eight people (about US$20 each for a return trip). Ask around at the docks and compare prices.

Tourists can **stay** in the Castillo itself – a hot, damp but unusual experience, at least in this castle-less part of the world. The *Albergue el Castillo* (☎552-4635; ④) offers basic rooms with fans; breakfast is included in the price but other meals cost extra (lunch US$10, dinner US$8). All-inclusive packages are also available for US$35 a day.

Beyond the Castillo: Reserva Biológica Indio Maíz

Downstream from the Castillo, heading out towards the Caribbean, the northern bank of the Río San Juan forms part of the 3000-square-kilometre **Reserva Biológica Indio Maíz**, the largest nature reserve in Nicaragua – possibly in Central America. The climate here in the southeastern wedge of Nicaragua is very wet and hot, with the vast expanses of dense rainforest sheltering many species, including the elusive **manatee**, or sea cow, the jaguar, the tapir, scarlet macaws, parrots and toucans. There is no real tourist infrastructure in the area; the usual way to see the Indio Maíz is from a boat on the Río San Juan – travelling toward the Caribbean, much of the left-hand bank of the river is the reserve. The pristine Indio Maíz vegetation stands in sharp contrast with the Costa Rican side, where agriculture and logging have eroded the forest.

travel details

BOATS

Be warned that all boat services are subject to seasonal changes and short-notice cancellations due to weather conditions.

San Jorge to: Moyogalpa, Ometepe (Mon–Sat 9am, 10am, 11am, noon, 3.30pm, 4pm & 6pm, Sun noon, 5pm and 6pm; 1hr).

Granada to: Altagracia, Ometepe (Mon & Thurs 2pm; 3hr); San Carlos de Nicaragua (Mon & Thurs 3pm; 12–13hr).

Moyogalpa to: San Jorge (Mon–Sat 6am, 6.30am, 7am, 1.30pm & 5pm).

San Carlos to: Solentiname (Tues & Fri around 7am; 2hr). Also unscheduled private boats.

BUSES

Managua (Mercado Ivan Montenegro) to: San Carlos de Nicaragua (Mon, Tues & Thurs 6am; 9hr).

FLIGHTS

Managua to: San Carlos (Mon, Wed & Fri 7am).

San Carlos to: Managua (Mon, Wed & Fri 9am).

CHAPTER 26

THE ATLANTIC COAST

L ooking at the map of Nicaragua, the two things you notice first about the east of the country is its sheer size – about half the total landmass – and its remote density of terrain. The **Atlantic Coast** (although in fact the Caribbean, in Nicaragua it is referred to the Atlantic) is low-lying, soaked with mangrove swamps behind which loom near-impenetrable jungles. This area was never destined to appeal to the Spanish, who were in search of fertile agricultural land and gold (not necessarily in that order). Further repelled by disease, inaccessible and endless jungle, dangerous snakes and persistent biting insects, the Spanish conquistadors and the would-be settlers who followed in their wake quickly made tracks for the more hospitable Pacific zone. Spanish influence has never been great in eastern Central America, and it was left to the English to fill that gap.

English, French and Dutch buccaneers had been plying the coast since the late 1500s, and it was they who first made contact with the **Miskito**, **Sumu** and **Rama** peoples who populated the area, trading goods for fish and turtle meat. In turn, the indigenous peoples gave the pirates safe harbour and welcomed them into their settlements. More than any other indigenous group in Central America, it was Nicaragua's fierce Miskito tribe, now thought to number about 70,000, who came under the influence of the English.

From 1687 to 1894 the Atlantic Coast of Nicaragua and Mosquitia as a whole was a **British Protectorate** known as the Miskito Kingdom – named after the indigenous Miskito people (in Spanish, Mosquito). The declaration of this Kingdom in the midst of Spanish territory was the result of a strategic alliance between the English and the Miskito, who had a common interest in keeping the Spanish from gaining influence in the area. Armed by the British, the Miskito became the terror of the Sumu and Rama, who were finally subjugated by the larger group. In turn, from the late 1500s until 1894, when Britain unceremoniously ceded Mosquitia to Managua, the British navy, merchants and privateers gained unlimited rights to fishing and other local products and enjoyed safe conduct along the coast and through the waterways of Mosquitia.

The **ethnicity** of the region today is complex. The Miskito, Sumu and Rama mixed with the slaves brought from Africa and Jamaica to work in the region's fruit plantations, and while many inhabitants are Afro-American in appearance, others have Amerindian features, and some combine both with European traits. For the most part black people from the Atlantic Coast call themselves Creoles; if they acknowledge having Spanish blood, or Spanish is their first language, they may call themselves *mestizos*. **English** is widely spoken on the Atlantic coast, and English travellers may be surprised to be on the receiving end of a very warm welcome and some time-warp nostalgia for Queen Victoria's Britain.

During the years of the **Revolution** and the Sandinista government, the FSLN were met with suspicion on the Atlantic Coast. In part this was due to the area's traditional mistrust of Managua, but also to a lack of sympathy with revolutionary values. During the Revolution the Sandinistas implemented a number of ill-advised socialist-revolutionary programmes that did not mesh with the individualistic values of the region, such as the tradition of making your own way on your own land. In fact, Ortega's administration succeeded in driving many, particularly Miskitos, over to the Contra. Nearly

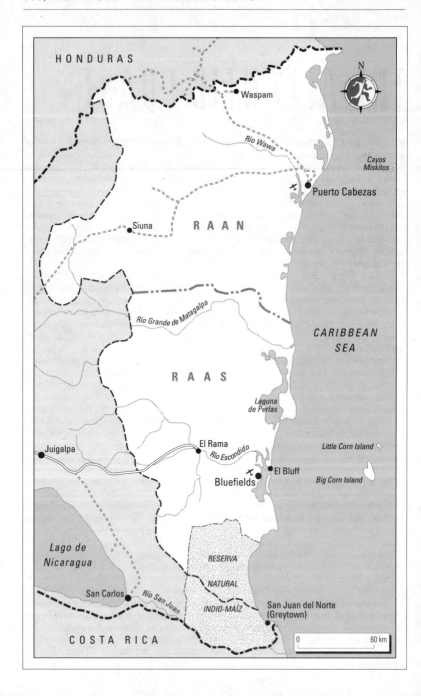

For an explanation of **accommodation price codes**, see p.438.

half the Miskito population went into exile as **refugees** to Honduras; in the south a much smaller number made their way to Costa Rica. In 1985 the Sandinistas tried to repair relations by granting the region political and administrative **autonomy**, creating the self-governing territories **RAAN** (Region Autonomista Atlántico Norte) and **RAAS** (Region Autonomista Atlántico Sur).

The only places that attract visitors in any numbers to the area are **Bluefields**, a quintessential Caribbean port town, whose raffish charm attracts adventurous travellers on their way to the **Corn Islands** (Islas de Maíz). These two small islands off Nicaragua's coast are the country's little corner of the Caribbean, with sandy beaches, swaying palm trees, and a distinctly Caribbean cuisine and atmosphere. As for the rest of the coast, it remains a largely unknown and impenetrable tangle of waterways and rainforests, to be approached with caution and negotiated only by experienced locals. In the northern half of the region, **Puerto Cabezas** is the only town of any size; the area's main industries are mining and logging in the vast, dense forests of the RAAN. Although you can fly to Puerto Cabezas, few travellers make this long trip on a whim, since there's nothing really to interest tourists in or around the town itself.

The Atlantic Coast's extreme isolation and distance from the market economy mean that you can't count on getting **food, water and consumer goods** in most places outside of Puerto Cabezas and Bluefields. If you are intending to travel outside these areas, or to spend any length of time in the region, it's a good idea to stock up on consumer goods – both for yourself and for trade – in one of Managua's markets. Favourite items on the Atlantic are magazines, music tapes, plastic wristwatches, any toys for kids or small electronic goods, sweets or sugar. All these can be bought for a pittance at Managua's Oriental or Huembes market, and will really make you friends along the waterways of Mosquitia.

El Rama and the route to the coast

EL RAMA is a major transit point to the Atlantic Coast and most travellers stop in town only long enough to change from the Managua bus to a boat for Bluefields and vice versa. With a largely transient, edgy population, the town's truck-stop atmosphere is not endearing; the dilapidation of the town itself, its heat and bugginess doesn't help. If you don't manage to make the connection on the same day, then you'll have to stay over. Least frightening of the cheaper options is *Hospedaje El Viajero* (①), an old colonial house one block north of the dock, with dark and stuffy rooms, but fairly friendly management. The *Hotel y Restaurante El Manantial* (①), a couple of blocks beyond, is slightly more expensive but quiet and safe.

Daily **buses** for El Rama leave from the Mercado San Miguel/Ivan Montenegro in Managua. The public **ferry** service between Rama and Bluefields goes out of service from time to time. When it is running, it leaves in the mid-morning on Tuesday, Thursday, Saturday and Sunday. The trip can take five or six hours, so make sure you bring food and drink. If the ferry isn't running, do as everyone else will be doing and hire yourself a motorboat at the dock – the trip takes only two and a half hours and costs US$12–17 per person, depending on the size of the group. An easier alternative is provided by the private bus company Empresa Vargas Peña (in Managua ☎280 1812, in Bluefields ☎822-1410), which takes you by bus from Managua to Rama and then by launch to Bluefields, leaving Managua at 11pm, arriving in Rama at 6am and in Bluefields at 9am.

Bluefields

Despite its romantic name, there are no fields, blue or otherwise, near this steamy little lagoon town. The only town of any size on the Atlantic Coast south of Puerto Cabezas, **BLUEFIELDS** gets its name from a Dutch pirate, Abraham Blaauwveld, who holed up here regularly in the seventeenth century. Perched on the side of a lagoon at the mouth of the Río Escondido, Bluefields has retained the fugitive charm of a pirate-founded town. For most of the year it **rains** torrentially, except in May, when there is a short dry season, although it often rains then too. During these downpours the town – already ramshackle – can look somewhat forlorn.

Blufileños, as the town's inhabitants are called in Spanish, are mainly Creole, descended from Jamaicans. A fiercely proud and independent bunch, they are united in their mistrust of Managua and their delight in anything from the outside world, *de out* – meaning anywhere but the capital. A nostalgia for all things British, harking back to the days when the town imported steel from Sheffield, fabrics from France and dry goods from New Orleans, persists among the older generation. Blufileños speak both English and Spanish, often in the same sentence, although the English is heavily accented patois and takes some getting used to.

There's a lot of activity in town, and most of it takes place on the street, where card table stalls sell batteries, tape players and other contraband goods from Costa Rica. Some examples of English colonial tropical architecture have survived the years: these low-slung wooden buildings, bounded by grilled verandahs, sit alongside Caribbean-style cabañas – small wooden shacks painted in faded reds, greens and blues. You can't see the Caribbean from the town as houses block the view to the sea. To get a sense of being on the shores of a huge ocean you have to get a motorboat (*panga*) from the muelle over to the harbour and administrative hamlet of **El Bluff**, a collection of motley government buildings strung diagonally across the lagoon with the breezy open Caribbean at the end of the finger of land.

Hurricane Joan flattened Bluefields and the surrounding area in 1988; there are still a few signs of the tremendous devastation – the palm trees aren't as tall as they might be, a few planks lie among overgrown grass. The town is occasionally plagued by electricity and water **shortages** – a good reason to bring a torch and batteries, as well as a few candles, and to stock up on bottled water when you can. You have to be on your guard a bit in Bluefields: the atmosphere sometimes seems tense, especially at night, when the several beer halls empty and the local machete-carrying machos tumble drunkenly onto the streets. Petty theft is on the rise, and in this environment tourists stick out painfully. Watch your belongings and be careful walking around at night.

Since 1995 Bluefields has received a shot in the arm in the form of the **URRACAN**, or Universidad de las Regiones Autónomos de la Costa Caribe Nicaragüense, a university set up in the wake of the process for the self-government of the Caribbean coast. The Bluefields campus is the largest of three on the coast – the others are in Puerto Cabezas and Siuna. Although most of the faculty are from the Atlantic Coast region, volunteer professors also come from abroad, mainly Canada and the United States. The small campus is located about 1km from the centre of Bluefields, up the hill that backs the town to the northwest. You can walk up – except at night, when it is considered dangerous – or get a lift in one of the pick-up trucks that ply the "road", really a muddy track.

If you happen to come to town during the last week in May, you're in luck: ¡Mayo Ya!, one of the most exciting **fiestas** in the country, takes place in the streets of Bluefields. Derived from the traditional May Day maypole celebrations of the British, Mayo Ya is now a mixture of reggae, folklore and indigenous dance that young Blufileños pair ingeniously with the latest moves from Jamaica.

MOSQUITOES AND NO SEE'UMS

Bluefields can feel like the mosquito capital of the world, at least at dawn or dusk, when clouds of the creatures descend on any inch of exposed flesh. You need to take precautions: use plenty of repellent and wear long sleeves and trousers (along with socks). **Malaria** is present in the region, and you should fix yourself up with a regime of Chloroquine before you come and take the pills a week before you set foot in the area – see p.20. Coils, a mosquito net and a sleeping bag are useful protection as well.

As if that weren't enough, the **sandflies** that populate the coast are even more virulent than the mosquitoes. Known throughout English-speaking Central America as "no see'ums", sandflies are immune to every repellent known to man except, bizarrely, Avon's Skin-So-Soft body oil. This is not normally available in Nicaragua, but locals in the know may have procured a supply.

Arrival and information

La Costeña **flights** from Managua land at the **airstrip**, 3km south of the town centre. Taxis will take you into town for about US$1. The public **ferry** from El Rama arrives at the El Rama dock, about 150m north of the red-brick form of the town's Moravian Church. From the dock you can walk to all accommodation in Bluefields' "centre" – a three-block by three-block area where all the hotels, restaurants and services are concentrated.

The few streets in Bluefields are named – and even have signs. Calle Central is the main drag and runs north–south alongside the Bahía. Three streets running east–west are Avenida Reyes, Avenida Cabezas and Avenida Aberdeen. However, no one really uses these names, resorting to the usual method of directing from **landmarks**: the Moravian Church, the mercado at the end of Av Aberdeen and the parque to the west of town are the most popular ones.

A Banco Nacional de Desarollo (Mon–Fri 8am–noon & 2–5pm) sits almost opposite the Moravian church on C Central. The bank will change dollars into córdobas, but won't handle travellers' cheques. In general, Bluefields is a dollar-friendly town – restaurants and hotels will be only too happy to accept them. You can send letters from Telcor/Enitel, 50m east of the parque (Mon–Fri 8am–5pm), but don't expect them to arrive swiftly. Telephone calls, both domestic and international, can be made from the same building (Mon–Sat 8am–9pm).

Accommodation, eating and drinking

Budget **lodging** in Bluefields is basic and some establishments attract a raffish local clientele – one reason why many places have a curfew of 10 or 11pm. Nearly destroyed by Hurricane Joan, Bluefields' dependable budget option is the rebuilt *Hotel Hollywood*, 50m south of the mercado (②). The place looks prepossessing, with lovely balconies and friendly proprietors; the shared bathrooms are clean, and the rooms quite large, but the thin partition walls don't reach the ceiling and it can be very noisy. Some rooms get a breeze off the water – ask to see several. A block and a half inland, the *Hotel Dorado* (①) is a little cheaper than the *Hollywood*; while it doesn't have the architecture and the lagoon-side setting, the second-storey balcony is a good place to sip a beer and it's quieter. A jump up in comfort, quality and price is the *Hotel Tía Irene*, signposted 1km north of the centre (☎822-2143; ⑤); run in association with URRACAN, the local university (see opposite), profits from the *Tía Irene* are funelled back into the institution. With a small indoor garden, local art on the walls and well-appointed rooms, not to mention the excellent local breakfasts included in the price, this place is a bargain.

At some point everyone in town ends up at the *Salon Siù*, a **café and restaurant** 50m south of the Moravian church and then 100m west and 75m north, whose time-warped Fifties ice-cream-parlour decor is peculiarly paired with tropicana. The sandwiches are tasty, the ice cream is excellent – for real Fifties reverie, try the *leche malteada*, or milk-shake – and you can sit next to one of the windows, where, if you are lucky, you might even catch a slight wafting breeze. It's open from 8am and tasty eggs-and-beans break-fasts (US$3) are cooked daily. *Los Antojiotos*, 50m east of Telcor, is a friendly bar/restau-rant with a bizarre Central American Asian menu – most dishes come with some form of soy sauce or chop suey. The enormous servings are good value – try the comida cor-riente (US$3.50). Across from the market *Pesca Frita*, true to its name, does some mean if expensive fried fish and lobster in season.

The Corn Islands

Lying 70km off the Atlantic Coast of Nicaragua, the **CORN ISLANDS (Islas del Maíz)** offer white beaches, warm, clear water and even a bit of dreadlocked Rastafarian culture. Although there's not a lot to do, the islands are the epitome of relaxation, espe-cially if the difficult nature of travelling in Nicaragua is grinding you down.

Like many parts of the Caribbean coast, during the last century Big Corn and Little Corn islands were a haven for **buccaneers**, who used them as a base for raiding other ships in the area or attacking the inland towns on Lago de Nicaragua. These days it is drug-runners who sail between the islands from nearby San Andrés, the Colombian drug-running centre. Often, when these ships get boarded the illicit cargo goes into the water and ends up on the beach. The other illegal trade that continues today is in tur-tle flesh. A short walk along the bay in either direction from the main settlement will lead you past houses that are used to store large numbers of turtles on their backs awaiting slaughter. Despite these somewhat shady aspects to island life, they are safe to visit and the beaches are lovely.

Most visitors stay on Big Corn Island, home to all the services and with a decent selection of hotels and restaurants. Easily reached by boat from the bigger island, Little Corn is extremely quiet, with no real tourist infrastructure – most people come on a day-trip, or stay only one night.

Big Corn Island

Big Corn Island (Isla de Maíz Grande) has a fairly heavy population density for an island of its size, at only ten square kilometres and over six thousand inhabitants. The island is still recovering from the **hurricane** in 1988 that destroyed much of the hous-ing. With flattened trees, uprooted flowers and vegetation, and some debris still scat-tered around, it is not as pretty as it once was.

It's possible to walk round the entire island in two or three hours. **Brig Bay** (just south of the fish processing plant) is very tranquil and has a small wreck just off the shore in front of the *Hotel Paraíso Club*. Long Bay, across the air strip heading east, in moderately interesting, and there are plenty of places to swim in either direction. The southwest bay or "Picnic Beach" is the site of a huge party during Semana Santa, when crowds of people come over from Bluefields and the locals set up shady stalls to sell food and drink.

About 1.5km offshore to the southeast is the wreck of a **Spanish galleon** which lies in around 20m of clear water; given the islands' buccaneering past, it's likely that there are other wrecks in the area too. Unfortunately there are no dive facilities on the island for exploring the wreck or the beautiful coral reefs. You can arrange **snorkelling** trips, though, through the *Hotel Paraíso Club* (see opposite).

Arrival, information and transport

The **ferry** to Big Corn Island is the same service that originates in Rama and stops at Bluefields, before heading across the ocean to the island. It departs Rama on Saturday and Sunday at 5am, arriving at Bluefields at 10am, from where it's another four hours to Big Corn. The ocean trip can be choppy and uncomfortable. An express ferry leaves Rama on Tuesday and Bluefields on Wednesday morning. A freight ferry leaves Rama on Thursday or Friday and Bluefields on Saturday, although departures are often delayed and ferry times and schedules in general are always subject to change. A service from Bluefields to Corn Island and back leaves Bluefields on Wednesday at 8.30am arriving at around 1 or 2pm. It returns to Bluefields the same day later in the afternoon. You can buy your tickets (US$4) at the Municipal Port in Bluefields (*muelle municipal*). To verify ferry schedules contact the Empresa Nacional de Puertos (in Rama ☎822-2632, in Bluefields ☎822-2100). Buses and a few taxis make the run from the ferry dock (see below).

A far better way, at least for the seasickness-prone, to reach the Corn Islands is by **plane**, not least because the hour-long flight from Managua gives you an astounding perspective on the country as you fly between the two lakes, over the volcanoes of Ometepe. The plane then rises over the central mountains and, if it's summer, the country changes from the dull brown of the Pacific zone to the perpetual green of the Atlantic Coast, dotted by the small shacks of farmers. The plane crosses over Bluefields and its surrounding waterways before heading out over the Caribbean. Corn Island appears on the horizon, fringed by coral reefs. La Costeña (☎263-1228, 263-2142, on Corn Island ☎505-285-5131) flies to Bluefields and Corn Island from Managua (US$55 one way, US$110 return). Flights land at the airstrip in the centre of the island. It's important to **confirm** your return flight once you arrive, particularly around Easter, when things get very busy. Flight times can change with no notice if there are problems with aircraft or there is heavy demand for seats.

From the airstrip it's ten or fifteen minutes' walk to the beach front at Brig Bay, where you can find some of the hospedajes. If you have a heavy pack it's sensible to take a **taxi** (US$1 per person anywhere on the island, US$2 after 8pm). You can also **rent a car** for US$13 an hour (enquire at the *Paraíso*) or a taxi for US$8 an hour. Otherwise, transport is provided by two local **buses**, which circle the island in opposite directions every forty minutes or so, commencing at 7am – a cheap way to have a look at the island. They pass the airport before heading into town or out to the southwest bay where the ferry comes in.

There is no tourist office but the *Hotel Paraíso Club* has a notice board in their restaurant with some information on things to do. The Caley Dagnall **bank** will change travellers' cheques but does not give cash advances on credit card. It is best to come armed with plenty of dollars or córdobas. You can make **phone calls** (but not send mail) at the Telcor/Enitel office next to the Alcaldía, at the northern end of the island. For accidents and emergencies, go to the **hospital** in the centre near the baseball field. The emergency number for police is ☎285-5201, but don't expect rapid service.

Accommodation

Big Corn has some pleasant **hospedajes**, a number of which now have telephones, making reservations possible; if you can't book in advance, come early if you want accommodation during the Easter period and expect to pay more. Another busy time is August 27, Slavery Day, an occasion for excess in a variety of forms, combined with a festival of crab eating.

All of the hospedajes are scattered along **Brig Bay**, the beach area of the island. At the southern end of the bay, *Hotel Paraíso Club* (☎285-5111; ⑤) has attractive cabinas and a pleasant restaurant under a large rancho. The English-speaking owners provide tourist information and can arrange excursions to Little Corn Island. *Casa Blanca*, right on the beach in Brig Bay, has good, clean rooms with fans, mosquito nets and pleasant verandahs with hammocks (②–③). *Playa Coco* is rather overpriced for dormitory-style accommodation and has a disco downstairs (③). At the northern end of the bay, *Hotel Panorama* has decent rooms with fan for slightly more (④). The only truly budget place on the island is the very basic but friendly *Hospedaje Marisol*, across from the police station (①).

Eating and drinking

More than anywhere else in Nicaragua, seafood lovers are in for a treat on the islands. It is easy to get a good feed of **fish, prawns or lobster** for a reasonable price (US$5–10). You can also order turtle soup in the local restaurants along Brig Bay if your conscience won't be burdened by contributing to their steady extermination.

The Rotonda, just a few metres from the airstrip, is recommended for Creole food. Next to the airstrip, the *Red Lobster* specializes in what its name suggests, and is a rare air-conditioned refuge from the heat. The *Paraíso* restaurant is a shady space, with hammocks strung between the posts, magazines, game boards out on the tables, and attractive gardens. Its menu includes a few European treats like pancakes, and the owners attempt to grow their own vegetables, which are expensive and difficult to get on the island.

Everywhere on the island you should be cautious if approached by locals asking for money to make you "**ron don**", a purportedly potent seafood soup. Your sexual appetite is more likely to be diminished when you realize you have been scammed when the guys take your money but don't show up with the food.

Little Corn Island

Only three square kilometres in size, **Little Corn Island** (Isla de Maíz Pequeña) lies about 9.5km northeast of its larger sister island. Largely undeveloped, the island boasts a beautiful **black-sand beach**. The regular *panga* (a small boat with an outboard motor) leaves the small jetty at the northern end of Brig Bay on Big Corn at 3pm daily, returning from Little Corn at 7am the next morning; the trip takes an hour and a half. Unfortunately, there's no regular morning service from the big island. Enquire at the *Paraíso* about snorkelling expeditions to Little Corn; you can hire a *panga* that carries about a dozen people (US$15 per person, minimum US$60 per day) to drop you off at various spots around the island.

If you don't want to return to the big island at the end of the day, you can arrange accommodation at either of the two hospedajes on the island. *Bridgette's Hospedaje*, on the south side, has eight rather dingy rooms (①) and serves drinks and basic meals. On the northern side, *Hotel Iguana* has two cabins with a small kitchen for cooking but little in the way of food or drink (③). You can camp there as well. To get there, walk across the island from the settlement and turn right, or charter a boat to drop you off at the beach.

The RAAN: northern Mosquitia

The **northern coast** of Nicaraguan Mosquitia is one of the most impenetrable, **underdeveloped** areas of the Americas. No roads connect the area with the rest of the country, and the many snaking, difficult to navigate rivers and lagoons, separated by thick slabs of jungle, prevent the casual traveller – or any non-local, for that matter – from visiting the area.

Bordered at its northern extent by the **Río Coco**, Nicaragua's frontier with Honduras, Mosquitia is dotted by small settlements of the indigenous Miskito peoples. Few of these hamlets show up on any map, but the region is far from empty. The area was highly sensitive during the Contra–Sandinista war years of the 1980s; the Contra bases in Honduras continually sent **guerrilla** parties over the long river border to attack Sandinista army posts and civilian communities in Mosquitia and beyond. The Sandinistas forcibly evacuated many Miskitos from their homes, ostensibly to protect them from Contra attacks, but also to prevent them from going over to the other side.

Few travellers come to **Puerto Cabezas**, the only town of any size and importance in the area: apart from the fact that there is nothing to do, getting around in these parts is difficult, if not dangerous – the RAAN still experiences isolated menacings by groups of re-armed former Contras. Although it has to be said the situation is generally quiet, it's a region where people have very little money but a lot of guns, and it's important to know what you are doing if you venture outside the port town. More than anywhere else in Nicaragua, services are poor, consumer goods nearly nonexistent, and food hard to come by. Make sure you bring plenty of córdobas and perhaps a few dollars too. A detailed map of the area, a compass, and emergency provisions as well as the usual mosquito repellent, sunscreen and first aid kit, are all essential.

Puerto Cabezas

Small and scruffy **PUERTO CABEZAS** is the most important town north of Bluefields and La Ceiba in Honduras. Everyone seems to have come to this town of 30,000 people in order to do some type of business or other, whether it be a Miskito fisherman walking the streets with a day's catch of fish dangling from his hand or a lumber merchant selling planks to foreign mills, or the government surveyors here to work on the long-planned paved all-season road through the jungle that may one day link the town with Managua.

Most travellers arrive by **plane**. The daily La Costeña flight from Managua touches down at the airstrip 2km north of town, from where taxis take you into the centre for about US$1. The town's few amenities are all scattered within a few blocks of the parque central, a few hundred metres west of the seafront. Telcor/Enitel and the Banco Nacional de Desarollo make up the only services in town – the BND will change dollars if they have enough córdobas.

Accommodation in town is slim pickings, unless you are into sleeping with rows of drunken men. The best choice for travellers at the moment is *Cayos Miskitos*, 100m east and 100m north of the parque central; although a little pricey, it's safe and clean, and you can watch Mexican cable TV (③–④). Reflecting the inflationary boom-and-bust economy of the town, **eating** in Puerto Cabezas is very expensive – even though fishing is one of the area's main activities – and a seafood dish will cost you up to US$5. For local fish, try the *Restaurante Costa Brava*, 200m from the parque central. A more upscale option are the passable pizzas at *Pizzeria Mercedita*. *Cayos Miskitos* hotel has a fairly good restaurant attached. **Nightlife** is downright scary; although the nightspots play good Caribeña music, these establishments cater to men, some have weapons checks at the door, and the overall aim is to get aggressively drunk. If you're up for the macho atmosphere, try the salsa at *Disco Scorpio* or the reggae and soca rhythms at the *Blue Beach*.

travel details

BUSES

Managua (Mercado San Miguel/Ivan Montenegro) to: El Rama daily at 11pm (7hr) and connecting with a launch to Bluefields (another 3hr). See p.509 for more details.

BOATS

All boat services are subject to change at short notice. It's always best to check the latest schedules on the spot.

El Rama to: Big Corn Island (Sat & Sun 5am, express Tues morning; 9hr), plus freight ferry on Thurs or Fri; Bluefields (Tues, Thurs, Sat & Sun mid-morning, 5–6hr; motorboats by arrangement, 2hr 30min).

Bluefields to: Big Corn Island (Wed 8.30am; 5hr 30min).

FLIGHTS

La Costeña (☎263-1228, 263-2142, on Corn Island ☎505-285-5131) flies from Managua to Bluefields several times a day and twice daily to Big Corn Island. Advance reservations are essential.

PART SEVEN

COSTA RICA

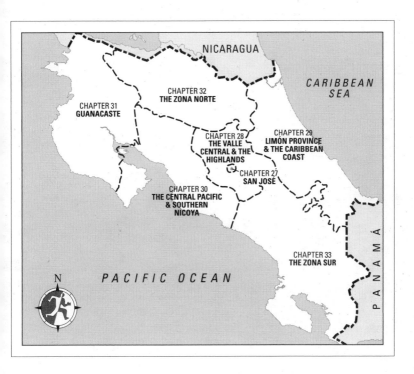

NICARAGUA

CARIBBEAN SEA

CHAPTER 32
THE ZONA NORTE

CHAPTER 31
GUANACASTE

CHAPTER 28
THE VALLE
CENTRAL & THE
HIGHLANDS

CHAPTER 29
LIMÓN PROVINCE
& THE CARIBBEAN
COAST

CHAPTER 27
SAN JOSÉ

CHAPTER 30
THE CENTRAL PACIFIC
& SOUTHERN
NICOYA

PANAMÁ

CHAPTER 33
THE ZONA SUR

N

PACIFIC OCEAN

Introduction

In sharp contrast to the brutal internal conflicts in Guatemala or the grinding poverty of Nicaragua, **Costa Rica** has become synonymous in Central America with stability and prosperity. Costa Ricans enjoy the highest rate of literacy, health care, education and life expectancy in the isthmus. Unlike so many of its neighbours, it has a long democratic tradition of free and open elections, no standing army (it was abolished in 1948) and even a Nobel Peace Prize to its name, won by former president, Oscar Arias, a key architect in the Peace Plan that helped bring an end to the conflicts of the 1980s in the region.

In recent years Costa Rica has also become the prime **eco-tourism** destination in Central America, if not in all the Americas, due in no small part to an efficient promotion machine that trumpets the country's complex system of national parks and wildlife refuges.

Every year hundreds of thousands of visitors – mainly from the United States and Canada – come to walk trails through million-year-old **rainforests**, raft foaming whitewater rapids, surf on the **Pacific beaches** and climb the **volcanoes** that punctuate the country's mountainous spine. More than anything it is the enduring **natural beauty** that impresses. Milk-thick twilight and dawn mists gather in the clefts and ridges divided by high mountain passes; on the Pacific coast, carmine and mauve sunsets splash down into the sea like meteors; vaulting canopy trees and thick deciduous understories carpet large areas of undisturbed rainforest, and vestiges of high-altitude cloudforest offer glimpses into a misty, primeval universe, home to the jaguar, the lumbering Jurassic tapir and the truly resplendent quetzal.

One glib accusation you're almost certain to hear lobbed at the tiny nation is that it has **no culture or history**. It's certainly true that there are no ancient Mesoamerican monuments on the scale of Guatemala or Honduras, and just one percent of the population is of indigenous extraction, so you will see little native culture. However, anyone who has time to spend, and whose Spanish is good enough, will find Costa Rica's character rooted in distinct **local cultures**, from the Afro-Caribbean province of Limón, with its Creole cuisine, games and patois, to the traditional *ladino* values embodied by the sabanero (cowboy) of Guanacaste. Above all, however long you spend

in the country, and wherever you go, you're sure to be left with mental snapshots of *la vida campesina*, or **rural life** – whether it be aloof horsemen trotting by on dirt roads, coffee-plantation day-labourers setting off to work in the dawn mists of the Highlands, or avocado-pickers cycling home at sunset.

■ Where to go

Though everyone passes through it, hardly anyone falls in love with **San José**, Costa Rica's capital city and transportation hub. Often dismissed as an ugly sprawl, lacking in metropolitan ambience, it is much underrated, with a stirring setting amid jagged mountain peaks, some excellent cafés and restaurants, leafy parks, a lively university district and a good arts scene. The surrounding **Valle Central**, agricultural heartland of the country, is generally seen in terms of a series of easy day trips from the capital. Most popular are the **volcanoes**: the huge crater of Volcán Poás, bubbling and simmering, and largely dormant Volcán Irazú, a strange lunar landscape high above the regional capital of Cartago.

Founded as a dairy farming community by American Quaker settlers in the early 1950s, **Monteverde** has become the country's number-one tourist attraction. It's the community-founded **cloudforest** reserve that pulls in the visitors, who flock here to walk trails through some of the only remaining pristine cloudforest in the Americas. Of the many **beaches**, **Manuel Antonio** wins the popularity contest, with its picture-postcard perfect Pacific setting. The steamy **Caribbean** coast holds few good swimming beaches, many of them plagued by strong currents and sharks. However, this is the side of the country where you're most likely to see the seasonal mass-nestings of formerly endangered giant **sea turtles**, at the isolated community of **Tortuguero**, linked by a series of lazy lagoons to the port of Limón.

The **Zona Norte**, stretching up to the Nicaraguan border at the Río San Juan, is often overlooked, despite featuring active **Volcán Arenal**, which spouts and spews over the friendly tourist hangout of Fortuna, affording arresting nighttime scenes of blood-red lava illuminating the sky. It's in the north of the country, too, that you'll find some of Costa Rica's groundbreaking scientific **research stations**, including the tourist lodge and private rainforest reserve

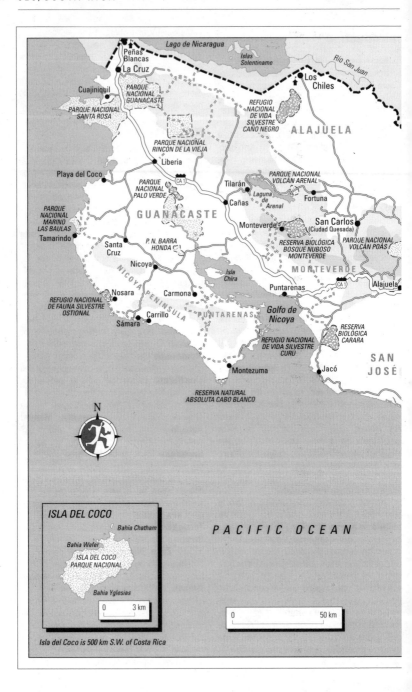

Lago de Nicaragua

Peñas
Blancas

Islas
Solentiname

La Cruz

Río San Juan

Cuajiniquil

PARQUE
NACIONAL
GUANACASTE

Los
Chiles

PARQUE NACIONAL
SANTA ROSA

REFUGIO
NACIONAL
DE VIDA
SILVESTRE
CAÑO NEGRO

ALAJUELA

PARQUE NACIONAL
RINCÓN DE LA VIEJA

Playa del Coco

Liberia

PARQUE
NACIONAL
PALO VERDE

Tilarán

PARQUE NACIONAL
VOLCÁN ARENAL

Cañas

Laguna
de
Arenal

Fortuna

PARQUE
NACIONAL
MARINO
LAS BAULAS

GUANACASTE

Monteverde

San Carlos
(Ciudad Quesada)

PARQUE NACIONAL
VOLCÁN POÁS

Tamarindo

Santa
Cruz

P. N. BARRA
HONDA

RESERVA BIOLÓGICA
BOSQUE NUBOSO
MONTEVERDE

Nicoya

Isla
Chira

MONTEVERDE

REFUGIO NACIONAL
DE FAUNA SILVESTRE
OSTIONAL

Nosara

NICOYA PENINSULA

Carmona

Puntarenas

Alajuela

PUNTARENAS

Golfo de
Nicoya

RESERVA
BIOLÓGICA
CARARA

Carrillo

Sámara

REFUGIO NACIONAL
DE VIDA SILVESTRE
CURÚ

SAN
JOSÉ

Montezuma

Jacó

RESERVA NATURAL
ABSOLUTA CABO BLANCO

N

ISLA DEL COCO

Bahía Chatham

Bahía Wafer

ISLA DEL COCO
PARQUE NACIONAL

PACIFIC OCEAN

Bahía Yglesias

0   3 km

0   50 km

Isla del Coco is 500 km S.W. of Costa Rica

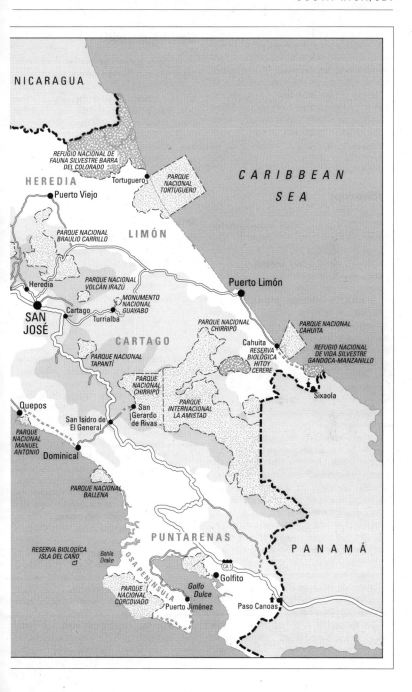

of Rara Avis and the La Selva biological station, both of which are superb destinations for birders and visitors with specialist interests in botany and the life of the rainforest. Off-the-beaten-path travellers and serious hikers will be happiest in the rugged **Zona Sur**, where you can climb to the highest point in the country, Mount Chirripó, in the national park of the same name. Parque Nacional **Corcovado**, probably the best destination in the country for walkers, is tucked away in the extreme southwest, on the outstretched feeler of the Osa Peninsula.

■ When to go

Although Costa Rica lies between 8° and 11° north of the equator, **local micro-climates** predominate and make temperatures and weather unpredictable, though to an extent you can depend upon the **two-season** rule. From roughly May to mid-November you will have afternoon rains and sunny mornings. The **rains** are heaviest in September and October and while they can be fierce, will only impede you from travelling in the more remote areas of the country – the Nicoya Peninsula especially – where dirt roads become impassable to all but the sturdiest 4WDs. In the **dry season** most areas are just that: dry all day, with occasional blustery northern winds blowing in during January or February and cooling things off. Otherwise you can depend upon sunshine and warm temperatures.

In recent years Costa Rica has been booked solid during the **peak season** – the North American winter months – when bargains are few and far between. The crowds peter out after Easter, but return again to an extent in June and July. During peak times you have to plan well in advance, faxing the hotels of your choice, usually pre-paying or at least putting down a deposit by credit card, and arriving armed with faxed confirmations and a set itinerary. Travellers who prefer to play it by ear are much better off coming during the rainy or **low season** (euphemistically called the "green season" in an effort not to scare off the tourists), when many hotels offer discounts. The months of November, April (after Easter) and May are the best times to visit, when the rains have either just started or just died off, and the country is refreshed, green, and relatively untouristed.

Getting around

Costa Rica's **public bus system** is excellent, cheap and quite frequent, even in remote areas. Getting anywhere by bus with a lot of baggage can be a problem, however; many people travel light, leaving the bulk of their baggage somewhere secure (a San José hotel, for example) while on the road. **Taxis** regularly do long- as well as short-distance trips and are a fairly inexpensive alternative to the bus, at least if travelling in a group. **Car rental** is more common here than in the rest of Central America, but is very expensive, at least in US terms.

■ Buses

Buses are by far the cheapest way to get around. The most expensive journey in the country (from Puerto Jiménez on the Osa Peninsula, to San José) costs US$10, while **fares** in the mid- to long-distance range vary from US$2.50 to US$5. **Tickets** on most mid- to long-distance and popular routes are issued with a date and a seat number; you are expected to sit in the seat indicated. Make sure the date is correct; even if the mistake is not yours, you cannot normally change your ticket or get a refund. Neither can you buy **return bus tickets** on Costa Rican buses, which can be quite inconvenient if heading to very popular destinations like Monteverde, Jacó and Manuel Antonio at busy times – you'll need to jump off the bus as soon as you arrive and buy your return ticket immediately to assure yourself a seat.

San José is the hub for virutally all bus services in the country; indeed, often it is impossible to travel from one place to another without backtracking to the capital. Different companies have semi-monopolies on various regions; for a rundown of **destinations and routes**, including international services, see p.551.

Some popular buses, like the service to Golfito, require **advance booking** of three days, though you may be lucky enough to get on without a reservation. Services to popular tourist areas – especially Monteverde – get booked up very fast, so for these you should buy your ticket at least five days in advance.

Though most Costa Rican buses are pretty good, the best of the bunch – arguably the best in Central America – is **Ticabus**, which runs the border routes from San José to Panamá or to

Managua. Old converted US Greyhound buses, they have comfortable seats, adequate baggage space, air-conditioning and very courteous drivers.

■ Driving

You have to exercise caution when **renting a car** in Costa Rica, where companies have been known to try to claim for "damage" they insist you inflicted on the vehicle. It is by far the best policy to rent a car through a Costa Rican travel agent, which costs no more than doing it yourself. If you are travelling on a package, your agent will sort this out. Otherwise, go into an ICT-accredited travel agent in San José.

Car rental in Costa Rica is **expensive**. Expect to pay about US$400 per week for a regular (non-4WD) vehicle, including insurance, and up to US$500 for 4WD. You will need a credit card, either Mastercard or Visa, which has sufficient credit for the entire cost of the rental, both at the beginning and end of the rental period. The majority of companies are based in San José, and you have to return the car there. The exception is Elegante, which has offices throughout the country. For a list of rental companies in San José, see p.550.

If you intend to drive in the rainy season (May–Nov), especially on the Nicoya Peninsula, or want to get to off-the-beaten-track places, or to Santa Elena and Monteverde, you'll need to rent a **4WD**. Indeed, if you intend to go to Monteverde from May through November, some car rental companies will refuse to rent you a regular car.

In recent years a system of hefty **fines** (*multas*) for infractions like speeding has been introduced in Costa Rica. The **speed limit** on the highways is either 75km/hr or 90km/hr; marked on the sidewalk or on signs. If you're caught speeding you could find yourself paying up to US$150. **Fuel** is reasonably priced, positively cheap by European standards; about US$10 a tank on a medium-sized compact or about US$20 for a big 4WD.

■ Cycling

Costa Rica's terrain makes **cycling** a pleasure – indeed, it's easier to dodge the potholes and wandering cattle on a bike than in a car – and the range of places to stay and eat means you don't need to carry a tent. There is very little traffic outside the Valle Central, and Costa Rican drivers tend to be courteous to cyclists. Be warned, however, that if you cycle up to Monteverde, one of the most popular routes in the country, you're in for a slow trip: besides being steep, there's not much traction on these loose gravel roads.

San José's best **cycle shop** is *Mundo del Ciclismo*, at the corner of Paseo Colón and C 26. They have all the parts you might need, can fix your bike, and may even be able to give you a bicycle carton for the plane.

■ Planes

Costa Rica's two **domestic air carriers** offer quite economical scheduled service between San José and many beach destinations and provincial towns. Sansa is the state-owned domestic airline; Travelair is its commercial competitor. Both fly small twin-propeller aircraft, servicing the same destinations.

Of the two, **Travelair**, which flies from Tobias Bolaños airport in Pavas, 7km west of San José, is more reliable, and more frequent on some runs. **Sansa** is cheaper, but less reliable – make your reservations as far as possible in advance and even then be advised that a booking means almost nothing until the seat is actually paid for.

GETTING AROUND COSTA RICAN TOWNS

All Costa Rican towns of any size are intersected by **Avenida Central**, which runs east–west, and **Calle Central**, which runs north–south. From Av Central parallel avenidas run odd numbers to the north and even numbers to the south. From Calle Central, even-numbered calles run to the west and odd numbers to the east. Avenidas 8 and 9, therefore, are actually quite far apart from one another. Similarly, Calles 23 and 24 are at opposite ends of the city. "**0**" in addresses is shorthand for "Central": thus Av 0, C 11 is the same as Av Central, C 11.

If you use street numbers as addresses, locals – and especially taxi drivers – won't have a clue where you are talking about. When possible use directions given in relation to local **landmarks**, buildings, businesses, parks or institutions, or according to the nearest intersection. People use **metres** to signify distance: in local parlance 100 metres equals one city block.

Reconfirm your flight in advance of the day of departure and once more on the day of departure, if possible, as schedules are likely to change at short notice. Sansa also offers good-value packages, usually two or three nights in more popular areas like Manuel Antonio. They fly from Juan Santamaría airport, 17km northwest of San José.

For a rundown of **schedules**, see p.554.

Costs, money and banks

Though prices have dropped from their peak of a few years ago, Costa Rica remains one of the most expensive countries in Central America. Some prices, especially for upper-range accommodation, are similar to those in the US, which never fails to astonish American travellers and those coming from the cheaper neighbouring countries. That said, you can, with a little foresight, travel relatively cheaply.

■ Currrency exchange and banks

Though the **US dollar** is often used, the official currency is the **colón** (plural colones). There are two types of **coin** in circulation: the old silver ones, which come in denominations of 1, 2, 5, 10 and 20, and newer gold coins, which come in denominations of 1, 5, 10 and 25. Public paytelephones do not yet take the new coins, and you will need the silver ones to make a call; otherwise they are interchangeable. **Notes** start at 50, proceeding to 100, 500, 1000 and 5000. You'll often hear colones colloquially referred to as "pesos"; in addition, the 1000 is sometimes called the rojo (red). The colón floats freely against the American dollar, which means the **exchange rate** varies frequently; when this book went to press, it hovered at around 250 colones to US$1.

Changing dollars into colones, try to avoid Costa Rica's **state banks**, Banco Nacional and Banco de Costa Rica (both with branches throughout the country; in many towns they are the only banks). Slow and bureaucratic, they will eat about an hour out of your time. In addition, although they may be able to change cash dollars for colones, some, especially those in remote areas, will balk at travellers' cheques, especially the larger denominations. It's best to carry sufficient colones with you, especially in small denominations – going around with stacks of mouldysmelling notes may not seem safe, but you should be all right if you keep them in a money belt, and

it will save hours of time waiting in line. That said, however, if you are doing a lot of travelling, it's comforting to know that many of even the smallest end-of-the-world towns have a branch of at least one bank.

In sharp contrast to the state banks are the efficient and air-conditioned **private banks**, the majority of which are in downtown San José (for addresses, see p.550). Outside San José you will want to try Bancoop, Banco Popular and, in some places, Banco Lyon. Private banks can legally charge what commission they like; the norm is about US$3 per transaction.

Banking hours change slightly from branch to branch but tend to be Mon–Fri 9am–3pm for state banks and slightly longer – about 8am–3.30 or 4pm – for private ones. Hardly any banks are open on Saturdays. At present few, if any, **ATMs** in Costa Rica accept foreign credit cards, although this is supposed to change soon.

Obtaining colones outside Costa Rica is virtually impossible: wait until you arrive and change some at the airport or border posts. If you miss banking hours then dollar bills in small denominations will do.

You'll find **credit cards** especially useful in Costa Rica for making deposits for hotels via fax and for renting a car. In general, Visa and Mastercard are widely accepted, although retailers tend to accept only one or the other. In outlying areas, however, like the Talamanca coast, Quepos and Manuel Antonio and Golfito, some businesses may levy a six percent charge for credit card transactions; you may be better off taking plenty of cash (see above).

Undeniably the safest way to keep your money, **travellers' cheques** should be brought in US dollars only – Costa Rican banks will only stare blankly at other currencies. However, do not expect to use travellers' cheques as cash except in mid- or upmarket hotels and guest houses that regularly cater to foreigners.

■ Costs

The high cost of living is due in part to **taxes** (18–25 percent), which are levied in restaurants and hotels; and more recently, to the presence of the International Monetary Fund, whose policies, aimed at the restructuring of balance of payments deficit, has raised prices.

Even on a rock-bottom **budget**, you're looking at spending US$25 a day for lodging, three meals and the odd bus ticket. Campers and hardy cyclists have been known to do it on US$15 a day, but this entails sleeping either in a tent or in somewhere pretty dire. You will be far more comfortable if you count on spending at least US$20 a day for accommodation and US$12 for meals.

That said, **bus travel**, geared toward locals, stays cheap – about US$0.25 to US$1 for local buses, around US$4 or US$5 for long-distance (3hr or more), and never rising above US$10. **Eating**, too, needn't be that pricey, while fruit, beer, theatre seats and trips to the movies will all seem very reasonable to visitors from most other countries.

Students with ISIC cards may be entitled to some discounts at museums in Costa Rica. More useful is local student ID, available to visitors on language courses and other education programmes; these may offer discounts at museums and theatres.

Information

The best source of **information** about Costa Rica is the **Instituto Costarricense de Turismo** (ICT) office in San José (see p.539). From abroad you can write to them, although it may take a while to receive a reply, and what you will get will likely be the same glossy pamphlets and brochures handed out at embassies. The postal address is: Instituto de Turismo Costarricense, Aptdo 777, Edificio Genaro Valverde, C 5 y 7, Av 4, San José 1000, Costa Rica (☎506/223-1733, fax 506/255-4997). When you visit the ofice, bear in mind that the most useful information is kept behind the counter – a free map of San José; a complete bus and domestic airline timetable; a full (although not necessarily up-to-date) list of practically all the hotels in the country, along with room rates; a list of museums, and details of many San José restaurants and nightclubs. All are available on request. The smaller ICT offices at the Juan Santamaría international airport and at the Peñas Blancas border crossing (into Nicaragua) don't offer the free timetables, but may have the hotel lists. Otherwise, there are no tourist offices offering independent (unbiased) information outside the capital. As a rule you have to rely on locally run initiatives, often set up by a small business association or the chamber of commerce, or hotels and tourist agencies.

On the Web, **Yahoo** have a countries search, by name, through which you will come to **RACSA** (*www.racsa.co.cr*), Costa Rica's telecommunica-

tions company, which is fully wired, and features news summaries from the leading daily La Nación. Yahoo's country search also gets you through to pages set up by Costa Rica aficionados in the US – more chatty than informative, and spiked with personal opininons.

A number of **tour operators**, based in San José, can offer guidance when planning a trip around the country; see p.555 for details.

Accommodation

Most towns in Costa Rica have a good range of places to stay, and even the smallest settlements have a basic pensión or hospedaje. The best **budget** accommodation tends to be in less touristed areas and caters more for nationals than foreigners. In the **middle and upper price ranges,** though facilities and services are generally of a very good standard, some hoteliers have decided they can pretty much charge what they please. If you don't mind spending US$45–70 a night for a room (especially in San José, and especially in the high season) then you can stay quite comfortably. If you are on a tighter budget, it's going to be more of a struggle.

Along with the ubiquitous hospedajes, casas de huéspedes and pensiones, **cabinas** are common in Costa Rica, usually either a string of hotel rooms, motel-style, in an annexe away from a main building or hotel, or more often separate, self-contained units. Usually – although not always – they are pretty basic, most often frequented by budget travellers.

Few hotels, except those at the upper end of the range, have **double beds**; it's more common to find two or three single beds. Single travellers will generally be charged the single rate even if they are occupying a "double room", though this may not be the case in popular beach towns and at peak seasons.

In the high sèason (Nov–April) and especially at Christmas, New Year and Easter, you should **reserve** well ahead, especially for the good-value hotels in popular spots, and the youth hostels. Although we often give Apartado (post box) numbers, it is far easier to reserve a room with a credit card by **fax** or by **email**. If you want to try to get in touch but don't know the exact email address, it's worth trying the name of the hotel, all in lower case and without any spaces, followed by: *@sol.racsa.co.cr* – this is the email suffix for the vast majority of Costa Rican businesses. Failing that, most hotels in Costa Rica, even some very low-priced budget ones, now have fax numbers.

■ Camping

Though **camping** is fairly widespread in Costa Rica, gone are the days when people could pitch their tents on just about any beach or field. You'll have a far better relationship with locals if you ask politely whether it is OK to camp nearby; if they direct you to a campground, they are doing so not because they don't like the look of you, but in an attempt to keep their environment clean.

In the beach towns especially you will usually find at least one well-equipped private campground, with good facilities. Staff may also offer to guard your clothes and tent while you're at the beach. Sometimes in these same towns you can find a hotelier, usually at the lower end of the price scale, willing to let you pitch your tent on the grounds and let you use their showers and washrooms for a charge. Though not all National Parks have campgrounds, the ones that do usually offer high standards and at least basic facilities – all for around US$2 per person per day. In some National Parks, you may be able to bunk down at the ranger station.

When camping in Costa Rica never leave your tent unattended, or leave anything of value inside it unattended, or it may not be there when you get back. Never leave your tent open except to get in and out, unless you fancy sharing your sleeping quarters with snakes, insects, coati or toads. Finally, take your refuse with you when you leave.

■ Youth hostels

Costa Rica currently has a small network of ten **youth hostels**. While not rock-bottom cheap (many of them cost around US$15–40 per night) these offer a good standard. As ever, if you're coming in the high season, you should ideally book three months in advance. Reserve by fax or

phone with the hostel or through the Toruma hostel in San José (see p.541).

All hostels in Costa Rica follow conservation regulations based on the sustained development principle, working in harmony with nature. Most are in prime locations, near a National Park, beach or main town; more remote hostels provide transport from the nearest town. Most have double, triple and family rooms, and bed linen, towels and soap are included in the price. Contact Red Costarricense de Albergues Juveniles ("RECAJ"), Aptdo 1355-1002, Paseo de los Estudiantes, Av Central, C 29/31, San José (☎ & fax 224-4085).

Eating and drinking

Eating out in Costa Rica can be pricey. Main dishes can easily cost US$7–9, not including the service charge (10 percent) and the sales tax (15 percent). Tipping, however, is not necessary.

■ Where to eat

The cheapest places to dine in Costa Rica, and where most workers eat lunch, their main meal, are the ubiquitous **sodas**, halfway between the North American diner and the British greasy cafe. Sodas offer filling set *platos del día* (daily specials) and *casados*, combinations of rice, beans, salad and meat or fish, for about US$3. Many – at least in San Jose – are **vegetarian**, and in general vegetarians do quite well in Costa Rica. Most menus will have a vegetable option, and asking for dishes to be served without meat is perfectly acceptable.

Because Costa Ricans start the day early, they are less likely to hang about late in restaurants in the **evening**, and establishments are usually empty or closed by 10 or 10.30pm. Wai tend to leave you alone unless they are called for. Non-smoking sections are uncommon, to say the least, except in perhaps the most expensive establishments; if you're looking for a smoke-free environment, try the vegetarian sodas.

ACCOMMODATION PRICE CODES

All accommodation reviewed in this guide has been graded according to the following price scales, which represent the cost of a double room in high season.

① up to US$5	④ US$15–25	⑦ US$60–80
② US$5–10	⑤ US$25–40	⑧ US$80–100
③ US$10–15	⑥ US$40–60	⑨ US$100 and over

■ What to eat

Ticos call their cuisine **comida típica** ("native" or "local" food). Simple it may be, but tasty nonetheless, especially when it comes to interesting **regional variations** on the Caribbean coast (Creole cooking) and in Guanacaste (where there are vestiges of the ancient indigenous peoples' love of maize, or corn).

Dishes you'll find all over Costa Rica usually include rice and some kind of meat or fish, often served as part of a special plate with coleslaw salad, in which case it is called a *casado* (literally, "married person"). The ubiquitous **gallo pinto** ("painted rooster") is a breakfast combination of red and white beans with rice, sometimes served with *huevos revueltos* (scrambled eggs). You should also try **ceviche** (raw fish "cooked" in lime juice with coriander and peppers), **pargo** (red snapper), **corvina** (sea bass), and fresh **fruit**, either by itself or drunk in refrescos (see below). Papayas, pineapple and bananas are all cheap and plentiful, along with some less familiar fruits like mamones chinos (a kind of lychee), anona (which tastes like custard) and marañón, whose seed is the cashew nut.

■ Drinking

Mellow-tasting Costa Rican **coffee** is some of the best in the world, and it is usual to end a meal with a small cup. The best blends are export, which you can buy in stores and are served at some cafés. If you order it with milk (*café con leche*), it is traditionally served in a pitcher of coffee with a separate pitcher of heated milk. Also good are **refrescos**, cool drinks made with milk (*leche*) or water (*agua*), fruit and ice, all whipped up in a blender. You can buy them at stalls, or in cartons – the latter tend to be sugary. You'll find **herb teas** throughout the country; those served in Limón are especially good. In Guanacaste you can get the distinctive corn-based drinks **horchata** and **pinolillo**, made with milk and sugar and with a grainy consistency.

In addition to the many imported American **beers**, Costa Rica has a few local brands, which are not bad at all. Most popular is Imperial (light draught, American-style), followed by Bavaria (sweeter, more substantial and slightly nutty). Of the local low-alcohol beers, Bavaria Light is a good option; Tropical is a bit more watery.

There is an indigenous hard-liquor drink, **guaro**, of which Cacique is the most popular brand. It's a bit rough, but good with lime sodas. For an after-dinner drink, try Café Rica, a creamy **liqueur** made with the local coffee.

Costa Rica has a variety of **places to drink**, from shady macho domains to pretty beachside bars, with some particularly cosmopolitan establishments in San José. The capital is also the place to find the country's last remaining **boca bars**, atmospheric places which serve bocas (tasty little snacks) with drinks. **Gringo grottos** abound, especially in the beach towns, while in many places, especially port cities like Limón, Puntarenas and Golfito, there are the usual contingent of rough, rowdy bars; they advertise their seediness with a giant Impêrial placard parked right in front of the door.

In general Sunday night is dead, with many bars not open at all and others that close at around 10pm or so. Though Friday and Saturday nights are, as usual, the busiest, the **best nights** to go are often during the week, when you can enjoy live music, happy hours and other specials. The **drinking age** in Costa Rica is 18, and many bars will only admit those with ID. A photocopy of your passport page is acceptable.

Opening hours, holidays and festivals

Though you shouldn't expect the kind of colour and verve that you'll find in fiestas in Guatemala, Costa Rica has its fair share of holidays and festivals, or **feriados**, when all banks, post offices, museums and government offices close. In particular, don't try to travel anywhere during **Semana Santa**, Holy (Easter) Week: the whole country shuts down from Holy Thursday until after Easter Monday, and buses don't run. Likewise, the week from Christmas to New Year invariably causes traffic nightmares, overcrowded beaches and a suspension of services.

Provincial holidays, like Independence Day in Guanacaste (July 25) and the Limón Carnaval (the week preceding October 12) affect local services only, but nonetheless the shutdown is drastic: don't bet on cashing travellers' cheques or mailing letters if you're in these areas at party time.

PUBLIC HOLIDAYS

Jan 1 New Year's Day. Celebrated with a big dance in San José's Parque Central.

Feb–March (date varies) Ash Wednesday. Countrywide processions; in Guanacaste horse, cow and bull parades, with bullfights (in which the bull is not harmed) in Liberia.

March–April (date varies) Semana Santa (Holy Week)

March 19 El día de San José (St Joseph's Day). Patron saint of San José and San José province.

April 11 Juan Santamaría Day. Commemorating the national hero who fought at the Battle of Rivas against the American adventurer William Walker in 1856.

May 1 Labour Day.

June 20 St Peter's and St Paul's Day.

July 25 Independence of Guanacaste Day (Guanacaste province only). Marking the annexation of Guanacaste from Nicaragua in 1824.

Aug 2 Virgin of Los Angeles Day. Patron saint of Costa Rica.

Aug 15 Assumption Day and Mother's Day.

Sept 15 Independence Day. Big patriotic parades celebrating Costa Rica's independence from Spain in 1821.

Oct 12 El día de la Raza (Columbus Day). Limón province only, marked by Carnaval, which takes place in the week prior to October 12.

Nov 2 All Soul's Day.

Dec 25 Christmas Day.

Mail and telecommunications

Costa Rica's **postal system**, CORTEL, is reasonably efficient, though you may have problems sending and receiving letters from remote areas. The most reliable place to mail overseas is from San José's **Correo Central**, or main post office (see p.550), which is also the best place to collect General Deli very post. In most cases, especially in Limón province, where mail is very slow, it is probably quicker to wait until you return to San José and mail correspondence from there. **Opening hours** for nearly all Costa Rica's post offices are Monday to Friday from 7.30am to 5 or 5.30pm. Those in San José and Liberia also have limited Saturday hours.

■ Telecommunications

The Costa Rican state electronics company, **ICE** (Instituto Costarricense de Electricidad) provides international telephone, fax and Internet services via **RACSA**, the telecommunications subsidiary.

To make **international calls**, you can **call collect** from any phone or payphone in Costa Rica; simply dial ☎09 or ☎116 to get an English-speaking operator, followed by the country code, area code and number. AT&T, MCI, Sprint, Canada Direct or UK Direct calling-card holders can make credit-card calls from payphones. If you have to pay for the call on the spot, the best thing is to use a private line, perhaps from a hotel (expensive, due to the additional "line" charge the hotel may lay on; anywhere from US$0.75 to US$5) or from the San José Radiográfica office (see p.551) where you can also send and receive faxes, and use directories. It's not a good idea to use a payphone to make international calls with colones. The new microchip telephone cards will allow you to use the new payphones to make **local calls**; you can make international calls with the larger denomination cards but they won't give you much more than 3 or 4 minutes' speaking time.

The **country code** for the whole of Costa Rica is ☎506. There are no area codes. All phone numbers have seven digits, though you may still see numbers on business cards and adverts given in the old six-digit configuration. To check the new number, consult any telephone book; ICE offices also have free phone number conversion tables.

Many Costa Rican hotels and businesses now have **email**. If you don't know an address, it's worth trying the hotel or establishment name, followed by @sol.racsa.co.cr – that's how nearly all email addresses in Costa Rica end.

The media

Though the Costa Rican **press** is free, it does indulge in a certain follow-the-leader journalism. Leader of the pack is the daily *La Nación*, voice of the (right-of-centre) establishment and owned by the country's biggest media consortium. It also comes with a useful daily pull-out arts section, *Viva*, with **listings** of what's on in San José – the classifieds are handy for almost anything, including long-term accommodation.

No less serious, *La República* is slightly more downmarket. *Al Día* is the populist "body count" paper. Alternative voices include *La Prensa Libre*, the very good left-leaning evening paper, and the thoughtful weekly *Esta Semana*, which offers longer, in-depth articles and opinion pieces.The *Semanario Universidad*, the voice of the University of Costa Rica, published weekly, certainly goes out on more of a limb than the big dailies, with particularly good coverage of the arts and the current political scene. You can find it on campus or in San Pedro.

Local **English-language papers** include the venerable and serious *Tico Times*, and the full-colour *Costa Rica Today*, intended for tourists, with articles on activities and holidays. Both can be a good source of information for travellers: the ads regularly feature hotel and restaurant discounts. You can pick up recent copies of the *New York Times*, *International Herald Tribune*, *USA Today*, *Miami Herald*, *Newsweek*, *Time* and sometimes the *Financial Times* in the shop inside the *Gran Hotel Costa Rica* (see p.547) or in selected bookshops in downtown San José (see p.550). Elsewhere they're difficult to find.

There are many **commercial radio stations** in Costa Rica, all pumping out the techno and house tunes-of-the-moment alongside a few salsa spots, commercials, and the odd bout of government-led pseudo-propaganda.

Most Costa Rican households have a **television**, which shows good Mexican/Venezuelan *telenovelas* (soap operas), and some not bad domestic news programmes.

Safety and the police

Costa Rica is generally considered to be a very safe country. Any crime that does exist tends to be **opportunistic**, rather than involving out-and-out assault. The main things travellers have to worry about are street mugging and pickpocketing, and if you take a few common-sense precautions, you should get by unscathed.

In downtown **San José** you need to be wary at all times. Wear a money belt, and never carry anything of value – money, tickets or passport – in an outside pocket. It has also been known for **luggage** to be stolen while you are distracted or while it is being kept supposedly secure in a left-luggage facility. Never hand your baggage to strangers, except the airport porters, who have official identification. If storing your bags in a hotel or guest house while you are travelling around the country, make sure it is locked, has your name prominently written on it, and that you

have left instructions for it not to be removed by anyone but yourself, under any circumstances. **Car theft** – both of cars and things inside them – also occurs. You should not leave anything of value in a parked car – even locked in the trunk – anywhere in Costa Rica, day or night.

In addition, keep copies of your passport, your air ticket and your travellers' cheques, plus your insurance policy at home; and, if possible, keep extra copies in your hotel. In Costa Rica you have to carry **ID** on you at all times, and for foreigners this means carrying your **passport**. A photocopy of your passport – of the first page and the one with your Costa Rican entry stamp – will do (the police understand tourists' reluctance to go about with their passports all the time), but if you are stopped and asked for ID, make sure you can produce the real thing – by going to your hotel, for example – in case the police demand to see it.

■ Reporting a crime

In the past year or so the **police** (*guardia*) presence in San José has increased dramatically. If you have anything stolen you will need to report the incident to the nearest police post: do this right away. In San José, the most convenient method is to head for the Organismo de Investigación Judicial (☎255-0122 or 222-1365) between Av 6 and 8 and C 15 and 19. In rural areas, go to the nearest *guardia rural* who will give you a report (you'll do better if you speak Spanish, or are with someone who does).

Any **tourist-related crime**, such as overcharging, can be addressed to the ICT in San José (see p.539).

> **EMERGENCY NUMBERS**
> **All emergencies** ☎911
> **Police** ☎117
> **Fire** ☎118
> **Traffic police** ☎222-9330 or 222-9245

National parks and reserves

Costa Rica protects 25 percent of its total territory under the aegis of a carefully structured system of **National Parks**, **Wildlife Refuges** and **Biological Reserves**; in all there are currently some 75 designated protected areas. Established gradually over the past thirty years, their role in protecting the country's rich fauna and flora against the expansion of resource-extracting activities and human settlement is generally lauded.

In total the Parks and Reserves protect approximately four percent of the world's total wildlife species and life zones, among them rainforests, cloudforests, páramo – high-altitude moorlands – swamps, lagoons, marshes and mangroves, and the last remaining patches of tropical dry forest in the isthmus. Also protected are areas of historical significance, including a very few pre-Columbian settlements, and places considered to be of immense scenic beauty. Measures have also been taken to protect beaches where several species of marine turtle lay their eggs, as well as a number of active volcanoes.

The **National Parks**, which cover 12 percent of Costa Rica's protected land, provide more services and activities than the Refuges and Reserves, and tend to be more heavily touristed. That said, it's important to remember that none of the protected areas has been set up with tourists in mind – biologists, scientists and researchers make up a large portion of visitors.While we give information as to which **animals** inhabit the specific Parks, keep in mind that you are in no way guaranteed to see them – although you will, most likely, see some of the more common or less shy ones – and you would be very lucky indeed to spot the larger mammals such as the jaguar, ocelot or tapir.

■ Visiting Costa Rica's Parks

All National Parks have entrance **puestos**, or stations, where you pay your fee and pick up a map. Typically the **main ranger stations**, from where the internal administration of the Park is carried out, and where the rangers live, are some way from the entrance *puesto*. It can be a good idea to drop by the main station, where you can talk to rangers (if your Spanish is good) about local terrain and conditions, enquire about drinking water, and use the bathroom. In some Parks, such as Corcovado, you can sleep in or **camp** near the main stations.

Entrance fees are US$6 per person per day. Outside the most visited Parks – Volcán Poás, Volcán Irazú, Santa Rosa and Manuel Antonio – **opening hours** are somewhat theoretical. Many places are open daily, from around 8am to 4pm; where no official times are quoted, these are the times we have given throughout the *Guide*. There are exceptions, however: Manuel Antonio is closed

on Monday and may be closed on Tuesday in the future, while other Parks may open a little earlier in the morning. Unless you're planning on camping or staying overnight, there's almost no point in arriving at a National Park in the afternoon. In all cases, especially the volcanoes, you should aim to arrive as early in the morning as possible to make the most of the day and, in particular, the weather (especially in the wet season).

Since the demise of the excellent National Parks information office in 1997, the ICT has set up a not particularly helpful **information line** (☎192). If you do call this number, the person who answers may or may not speak English, and may not be able to tell you very much at all, and in most cases you will be kept holding for some time. While this lamentable situation may change, for the moment the best advice is to turn up at the parks on spec, or to visit the private organization Fundacion de Parques Nacionales (FPN) (see p.539) who have taken it upon themselves to provide information and a service by which they will contact those parks for which you have to have reservations – chiefly Santa Rosa, Corcovado and Chirripó.

Work and study

There are many **volunteer work and research projects** in Costa Rica, some of which include food and lodging, and most of them can be organized from the US. A good **resource** in the USA for language study and volunteer work programmes is **Transitions Abroad**, a bi-monthly magazine focusing on living and working overseas (write to Dept TRA, Box 3000, Denville, NJ 07834, USA). In Australasia, for current details of student exchanges and study programmes, contact the consul or **AFS**, PO Box 5, Strawberry Hills, Sydney 2012 (☎02/281-0066), or PO Box 6342, Wellington, New Zealand (☎04/384-8066). British travellers should contact the Costa Rican Embassy.

■ Study programmes and learning Spanish

As with most things, you will pay more for a course in Spanish in Costa Rica than in Guatemala. There are so many **schools** in San José that choosing one can be a problem. Though you can arrange a place through organizations based in the US (see opposite), the best way to choose is to visit a few, perhaps sit in on a class or two, and judge the school according to your

VOLUNTEER PROGRAMMES IN COSTA RICA

Amigos de las Aves, 32-4001 Rio Segundo de Alajuela (☎441-2658). Works to establish breeding pairs of scarlet and great green macaws. Volunteers are welcome to help care for the birds; no food or lodging.

ANAI (☎224-6090 or 3570, fax 253-7524). Based in southern Talamanca. Volunteer programme (May–July) to help protect the Gandoca-Manzanillo Refuge and the turtles that come to the Caribbean coast each year. Also work on ANAI's experimental farm; officially a minimum of 6 months, but 3-month stays can be arranged. Lodging and food included.

ANAO (The National Association of Organic Farming; ☎223-3030). Volunteer places on organic farms; lodging and meals provided.

APREFLOFAS (Association for the Preservation of Flora and Fauna), Aptdo 917, 2150 San José (☎240-6087). Accepts volunteers to help protect National Parks and Reserves. The work can be risky, and there's no food or lodging.

ARBOFILIA (Association for Tree Protection), Aptdo 512, Tibas 1100 (☎240-7145). Helps communities to plant native trees; accepts a few volunteers each year.

ASVO (Association of Volunteers for Service in Protected Areas), contact the director of International Voluntary Programmes (☎222-5085). Government-run scheme, enabling volunteers to work in the National Parks. Minimum 2 months; no lodging or food.

CEDARENA (Legal Centre for the Environment and Natural Resources; ☎224-8239). Accepts lawyers or people with experience in the legal area of conservation to help with paperwork. Usually a minimum of 3 months, but some exceptions.

Monteverde Conservation League, Proyecto de San Geraldo, Aptdo 10581-1000, San José (☎645-5053). Volunteer places on various projects in the cloudforests of Monteverde. Lodging not included.

SEJETKO (Cultural Association of Costa Rica), Aptdo 1293-2150, Moravia (☎234-7115). Volunteers needed to help defend indigenous reserves, work in rural development conservation and other projects. Lodging, meals and insurance included. Programmes usually last about a year.

YISKI Conservationist Association, Aptdo 1038-2150, Moravia (☎297-0970). Sponsors various conservation volunteer groups.

VOLUNTEER CONTACTS IN THE US

Caribbean Conservation Corp, PO Box 2866, Gainesville, FL 32602 (☎1-800/678-7853; in Costa Rica ☎225-7516). Volunteer research work with marine turtles at Tortuguero.

Global Service Corps, 1472 Filbert St, #1405, San Francisco, CA 94109 (☎415/922-5538). Service programmes in Costa Rica.

University Research Expeditions, University of California, Berkeley, CA 94720-7050 (☎510/642-6586). Environmental studies, animal behaviour.

Volunteers for Peace, 43 Tiffany Rd, Belmont, VT 05730 (☎802/259-2759). Membership organization which serves as clearing house and organizer of volunteer work projects.

own personality and needs. This is not always possible in high season (Dec–April) when many classes will have been booked in advance, but at other times it should be no problem at the majority of the schools we've listed.

Some of the language schools mentioned in the box above are Tico-run, some are arms of international (usually North American) education networks. Whatever the ownership, instructors are almost invariably Costa Ricans who speak some English. School noticeboards are an excellent source of information and contact for travel opportunities, apartment shares and social activities. Most schools have a number of Costa Rican families on their books with whom they regularly place students for homestays.

History

Archeologists know almost nothing of the various people who inhabited modern-day Costa Rica until about 1000 BC. What is known is that Costa Rica was a corridor for merchants and trading expeditions between the Mesoamerican empires to the north and the Andean empire to the south. Excavations of pottery, jade and trade goods, and accounts of cultural traditions have shown that the **pre-Columbian** peoples of Costa Rica adopted liberally from both areas.

When the **Spaniards** arrived in Costa Rica in the early sixteenth century, it was inhabited by as many as 27 different groups or clans. Most clans were assigned names by the invaders, which they took from the *cacique* (chief) with whom they dealt. Many of these groups had affinities with their neighbours in Nicaragua to the north and Panamá to the south.

■ The arrival of the Spanish

On September 18, 1502, on his fourth and last voyage to the Americas, **Columbus** sighted Costa Rica, and four years later King Ferdinand of Spain dispatched **Diego de Nicuesa** to govern what would become Costa Rica. From the start his mission was beset by hardship, beginning when their ship ran aground on the coast of Panamá, forcing the party to walk up the Caribbean shore. There they met native people who, unlike those who had welcomed Columbus tentatively but politely with their shows of gold, burned their crops rather than submit to the authority of the Spanish. This, together with the impenetrable jungles – and the creatures who lived there – and tropical diseases, meant that the expedition had to be abandoned.

Next came **Gil González** in 1521–22, who sailed from Panamá, where Spanish settlements had already been secured, up the Pacific coast, which offered safer anchorages. The indigenous peoples, meanwhile, began a campaign of **resistance** that was to last nearly thirty years, employing guerrilla tactics, full-scale flight, infanticide, attacks on colonist settlements and burning their own villages. There were massacres, defeats and submissions on both sides, but by 1540 Costa Rica was officially a Royal Province of Spain, and a decade later, the conquest was more or less complete.

■ Early settlers

It seems more appropriate to discuss Costa Rica's *lack* of colonial experience, rather than a bona fide colonization. In 1562, **Juan Vásquez de Coronado** became the second governor of Costa Rica. Coronado has always been portrayed as the good guy, reputed for his favourable, if not benevolent, treatment of the indigenous peoples he encountered in his migration from the Pacific coast to the Valle Central. It was under his administration that the first settlement of any size or importance was established, and **Cartago**, in the heart of the Valle Central, became capital. During the next century settlers confined themselves more or less to the centre of the country. The Caribbean coast was

the haunt of buccaneers – mainly English – who put ashore and wintered here after plundering the lucrative Spanish Main; the Pacific coast saw its share of pirate activity too, most famously when Sir Francis Drake put ashore briefly in the modern-day Bahía Drake in 1579.

This first epoch of the colony is remembered as one of unremitting **poverty**. Within a decade of its invasion Costa Rica was notorious and widely disparaged throughout the Spanish empire for its lack of gold. The Valle Central land was fertile, but there was uncertainty as to what crops to grow. Coffee had not yet been imported to Costa Rica, nor had tobacco, so it was to subsistence agriculture that most settlers turned, growing just enough to live on. In 1719, the governor of Costa Rica famously complained that he had to till his own land. To make matters worse, Volcán Irazú blew its top in 1723, nearly destroying the capital.

■ Independence

The **nineteenth century** was the most significant era in the development of the modern nation state of Costa Rica. Initially, after 1821, when Central America declared **independence** from Spain, freedom made little difference to Costa Ricans. Although status as a republic was granted in the summer of 1823, the news did not reach Costa Rica until well into the autumn, when a mule messenger arrived from Nicaragua to tell the astonished citizens of Cartago the good news. A **civil war** promptly broke out among the inhabitants of the Valle Central, dividing the citizens of Alajuela and San José from those of Heredia and Cartago. This struggle for power was won by the Alajuela-San José faction, and **San José** became the capital city in 1823.

Costa Rica made remarkable progress in the latter half of the nineteenth century, building roads, bridges, and railways and filling San José with neo-Baroque, Europeanate edifices. Virtually all this activity was fuelled by the **coffee** trade, bringing wealth that the settlers just a century earlier could hardly have dreamed of. Today high-grade export coffee is still popularly known as *grano d'oro*. The **coffee bourgeoisie** played a vital role in the cultural and political development of the country, and in 1848 the newly influential *cafetaleros* elected to the presidency their chosen candidate, Juan Rafael Mora. Extremely conservative and pro-trade, Mora came to distinguish himself in the battle against the American-backed filibusterer William Walker in 1856 (see p.443).

■ The twentieth century

The first years of the **twentieth century** represent an unstable route toward democracy in Costa Rica. Universal male suffrage had been in effect since the last years of the nineteenth century, but class and power conflicts still dogged the country, with several *caudillo* (authoritarian) leaders, familiar figures in other Latin American countries, hijacking power. But in general these figures ended up in exile (in contrast to facing the firing squads of the previous century) and neither the army nor the church gained much of a foothold in politics.

With the election in 1940 of the Republican (PRN) candidate **Rafael Calderón Guardia**, a doctor educated in part in Belgium and a devout Catholic, came the social reforms and state support for which Costa Rica is still almost unique in the region. In 1941 Calderon established a new **Labour Code**, which reinstated the right of workers to organize and strike, and a social security system providing free schooling for all. Calderón also paved the way for the establishment of the University of Costa Rica, health insurance, income security and assistance schemes, and thus won the support of the impoverished and the lower classes and the suspicion of the governing élites. One of those less than convinced by Calderón's policies was the man who would come to be known as **"Don Pepe"**, the coffee farmer José Figueres Ferrer, who denounced Calderón and his expensive reforms. Figueres soon formed an opposition party, ideologically opposed to the PRN, calling them "communists". In March, **fighting** around Cartago began, culminating in an attack by the Figueres rebels on San José. Figueres wanted above all to engineer a complete break with the country's past and especially the policies and legacies of the Calderónistas. Seeing himself as fighting both communism and corruption, he not only outlawed the PVP, the Popular Vanguard Party – formerly known as the Communist Party – but also nationalized the banks and devised a tax to hit the rich particularly hard, thus alienating the establishment.

The new **constitution** drawn up in 1949 gave full citizenship to Afro-Caribbeans, full suffrage to women and abolished Costa Rica's army. And to a certain extent, the **abolition of the army** fitted with political precedents.

The **1960s** and **70s** were a period of prosperity and stability in Costa Rica, when the welfare state was developed to reach nearly all sectors of society. In 1977 the **indigenous bill** established the right of aboriginal peoples to their own land reserves – a progressive measure at the time, although indigenous peoples today are not convinced the system has served them well.

■ Storm in the isthmus: the 1980s

Against all odds, Costa Rica in the 1980s and 1990s not only saw its way through the serious political conflicts of its neighbours, but also successfully managed predatory US interventionism, economic crisis and staggering debt.

Like many Latin American countries, Costa Rica had taken out bank and government **loans** in the 1960s and 70s to finance vital development. But in the early 1980s, the slump of prices for coffee and bananas on international commodity markets put the country's current account into the red to the tune of millions. In September 1981, Costa Rica defaulted on its interest payment on these loans, becoming the first third-world country to do so, and sparking off a chain of similar defaults in Latin America that resonated throughout the 1980s and threw the international banking community into crisis. Despite its defaults, Costa Rica's debt continued to accumulate, and by 1989 had reached a staggering US$5 billion, one of the highest per capita debt loads in the world.

To compound the economic crisis came the simultaneous political escalation of the **Nicaraguan civil war**. During the entire decade Costa Rica's foreign policy and to an extent its domestic agenda would be overshadowed by tensions with Nicaragua on the one hand and with the US on the other. Initially, the Monge PLN administration (1982–86) more or less capitulated to US demands that Costa Rica be used as a supply line for the Contras and Costa Rica also accepted military training for its police force from the US. Simultaneously, the country's first agreement for a structural adjustment loan with the IMF was signed. It seemed increasingly clear that Costa Rica was on the path both to violating its declared neutrality in the conflicts of its neighbours and to condemning its population to wage freezes, price increases and other side-effects associated with the IMF dose.

In 1986 PLN candidate **Oscar Arias Sánchez** was elected to the presidency, and Costa Rica's relations with the United States and, by association, with Nicaragua, took a different tack. The former political scientist began to play the role of peace broker in the conflicts of Nicaragua, El Salvador, and, to a lesser extent, Honduras and Guatemala, mediating between these countries and also between domestic factions within them. In October 1987, just eighteen months after taking office, Arias was awarded the **Nobel Prize for Peace**, bringing worldwide attention to this tiny country.

Though Arias had gained the admiration of statesmen around the world, he proved to be less than popular at home. Many Costa Ricans saw him as diverting valuable resources and time to foreign affairs when he should have been paying attention to the domestic agenda. Increasing prices in response to the IMF's economic demands meant that conditions had not improved much in Costa Rica.

■ The 1990s

Until 1994, elections had been relatively genteel affairs, involving lots of flag-waving and displays of national pride in democratic traditions. The elections of that year, however, were probably the dirtiest yet. Costa Rica is a **republic**, with a political power structure resembling that of the United States. The government is divided into legislative, executive and judicial branches, all guaranteed by a formal constitution, which long decreed that no president could rule for more than one four-year term consecutively. In 1969 an amendment added that no president may be re-elected to office once he has served his term. Since 1948 most of the country's elections have been a bipolar fight between the PLN candidate and the opposition party-of-the-moment, with the PLN winning office about once every other four years.

The campaign for the 1994 **elections** opened and closed with an unprecedented bout of mud-slinging and attempts to smear the reputations of both candidates, tactics which shocked many Costa Ricans. The PLN candidate – the choice of the left, for his promises to maintain the role of the state in the economy – was none other than **José María Figueres**, the son of Don Pepe, who had died four years previously. During the campaign

Figueres was accused of shady investment rackets and influence-peddling. His free-market PUSC opposition candidate, Miguel Angel Rodriguez, fared no better, having admitted to being involved in a tainted-beef scandal in the 1980s.

Figueres won, narrowly. A populist, at least in rhetoric, he was also considered to be a charismatic campaigner and continues to appeal to a broad base: visiting outlying areas, recognizing the concerns of campesinos, and winching himself up giant rainforest trees in a show of support for conservation issues.

Costa Rica's **economy** received a shot in the arm in 1996 when the communications giant Intel chose the country for the site of their new factory in Latin America, creating thousands of jobs and foreign investor confidence. As the Costa Rican economy grows, however, so do other indicators: **inflation** runs around 17 percent, and the annual **population** growth is as high as 3.2 percent per annum. Costa Rica has the highest rural population density in Latin America, so there is tremendous pressure on **land**. The prognosis for the campesino, that now nearly-forgotten former backbone of the country, is not good, as peasant agriculture becomes increasingly anachronistic in the face of the big banana, coffee, palmito and pineapple plantations. And external **debts** to service the country's respected system of social welfare remain high – a staggering thirty percent of the government budget goes on keeping up interest payments to foreign banks.

In February 1998 PUSC candidate **Dr Miguel Angel Rodriguez** was elected president. The new government has committed itself to solving Costa Rica's most pressing problems, improvements to the country's dreadful road system being top priority. Increasingly, courting private investment and catering to foreign interests are the order of the day. Plans are afoot to increase the capacity of the Juan Santamaria International Airport in order to bring in more tourists, and while ordinary Costa Ricans struggle under an eroding public health care system, private plastic surgeons cash in on the country's profile as the cut-rate plastic surgery capital of the Americas.

CHAPTER 27

SAN JOSÉ

prawling smack in the middle of the fertile Valle Central, **SAN JOSÉ**, the only city of any size and administrative importance in Costa Rica, has a spectacular setting, ringed by the jagged silhouettes of soaring mountains – some of them volcanoes – on all sides. You're hard pressed to find anyone to say much good about the city's pothole-scarred streets and car dealership architecture, however – not to mention the choking diesel fumes, kamikaze drivers and chaotically unplanned expansion. In the gridlocked **centre** things are wearingly hectic, with vendors of fruit, lottery tickets and cigarettes jostling on street corners and seemingly thousands of shoestores tumbling out onto sidewalks. In general travellers talk about the city as they do about bank line-ups or immigration offices: a pain, but unavoidable. That said, if you've been travelling through the region, you'll find that compared to, say, San Salvador or Managua, San José is not only a reassuringly **safe** place (though street crime is rising) but also vibrant and cosmopolitan, with a sprinkling of excellent **museums**, some elegant buildings and landscaped parks, good cafés and the odd intriguing art gallery. The **theatre** scene is particularly strong, with regular performances by respected national and visiting companies. Which is all to the good: most people find themselves spending considerable time here – it's a major transportation hub, and many journeys involve backtracking through the capital – learning to enjoy it, and even becoming perversely fond of the place.

Arrival

Arriving in San José is relatively stress-free; all the machinery to get you into town is well oiled and there is less opportunistic theft than at other Central American arrival points. San José's compact, frenzied city centre is contained within about fifteen blocks running east–west, and four blocks north–south. To the west, the main approach is the four-lane **Paseo Colón**, lined with car rental agencies, upscale hotels, and office buildings. It turns into **Avenida 2**, a similarly wide avenue that handles most of the traffic passing through town. The centre of town is bisected east–west by the **Avenida Central**, pedestrianized for much of its length and a very pleasant place to stroll. The nondescript **Plaza de la Cultura** is considered to be the centre of town, with most commercial activity concentrated in the streets between Avenida Central and Avenida 7.

Near the post office, in the streets immediately west of Calle 2 is the frantic and sometimes insalubrious area of the **Mercado Central**. The Coca Cola bus station is just four blocks west. The centre is subdivided into little neighbourhoods (barrios) that flow seamlessly in and out of one another: barrios **Amón** and **Otoya**, in the north, are the prettiest, lined with the genteel mansions of former coffee barons, while further out toward San Pedro, **La California**, **Escalante** and **Los Yoses** are full of comfortable homes, the odd embassy, and the *Toruma* youth hostel.

Further east, Avenida Central widens, heading out to the studenty suburb of San Pedro, home of the cool, leafy campus of the **University of Costa Rica** (UCR), one of

For an explanation of **accommodation price codes**, see p.526.

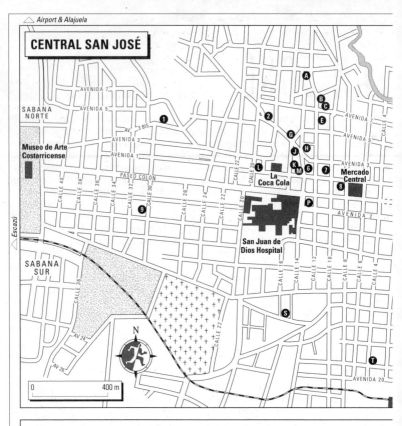

HOTELS

Bellavista	**13**	Galilea	**12**
Bienvenido	**7**	La Gema	**20**
Boruca	**6**	Gran Hotel Imperial	**8**
Cacts	**1**	Grano de Oro	**9**
Casa Leo	**16**	Oak Harbour Inn	**2**
Casa Ridgway	**18**	Pensión de la Cuesta	**10**
Cinco Hormigas Rojas	**4**	Ritz	**19**
Don Fadrique	**17**	Tica Linda	**11**
Edelweiss	**5**	Toruma	**14**
Fleur de Lys	**15**	Vesuvio	**3**

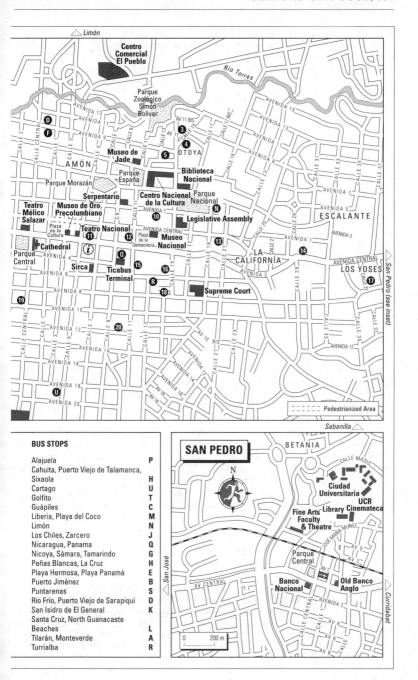

△ Limón

Centro
Comercial
El Pueblo

Río Torres

Parque
Zoológico
Simón
Bolívar

AV 11 BIS

AVENIDA 15

CALLE 1 BIS

AVENIDA 13

CALLE 15

CALLE 17

AVENIDA 13

D
F

AVENIDA 13

AVENIDA 9

CALLE CENTRAL
CALLE 2
CALLE 3
CALLE 5
CALLE 9
CALLE 11
CALLE 13

AV

3
4

AVENIDA 15

AVENIDA 11

AVENIDA 9

CALLE 19

CALLE 23

CALLE 31
CALLE 33
CALLE 35
CALLE 37

AMÓN

Museo de
Jade

5

OTOYA

Biblioteca
Nacional

AVENIDA 7

Parque
España

Parque Morazán

ESCALANTE

AVENIDA 5

Serpentario

Centro Nacional
de la Cultura

Parque
Nacional

N

CALLE 25

CALLE 29

Teatro
Mélico
Salazar

Museo de Oro,
Precolombino

AVENIDA 1

10

Legislative Assembly

AVENIDA 3

CALLE 9

Plaza
de la
Cultura

Teatro Nacional

11

AVENIDA CENTRAL

12

Plaza
de la
Democracia

Museo
Nacional

13

CALLE 27

AVENIDA 1

LA
CALIFORNIA

14

LOS YOSES

△ San Pedro (see inset)

Cathedral

ⓘ

Q

CALLE 19

AVENIDA 2

AVENIDA CENTRAL

Parque
Central

AVENIDA 4

Sirca

15

AVENIDA 6

Ticabus
Terminal

16

CALLE 15

17

CALLE 37

CALLE 7
CALLE 9
CALLE 11
CALLE 3

AVENIDA 8

R

18

Supreme Court

CALLE 29

CALLE 31

CALLE 33

CALLE 35

19

AVENIDA 10

AVENIDA 12

20

AVENIDA 14

AV 10 BIS

CALLE 23

AVENIDA 12

CALLE CENTRAL

AVENIDA 12

AVENIDA 14

AV 12

AV 14

AV 16

AVENIDA 16

AVENIDA 18

U

AVENIDA 20

------ Pedestrianized Area

Sabanilla △

BUS STOPS

Alajuela	P
Cahuita, Puerto Viejo de Talamanca, Sixaola	H
Cartago	U
Golfito	T
Guápiles	C
Liberia, Playa del Coco	M
Limón	N
Los Chiles, Zarcero	J
Nicaragua, Panama	Q
Nicoya, Sámara, Tamarindo	G
Peñas Blancas, La Cruz	H
Playa Hermosa, Playa Panamá	E
Puerto Jiménez	B
Puntarenas	S
Río Frío, Puerto Viejo de Sarapiquí	D
San Isidro de El General	K
Santa Cruz, North Guanacaste	
Beaches	L
Tilarán, Monteverde	A
Turrialba	R

SAN PEDRO

N

BETANIA

CALLE MASIS

Ciudad
Universitaria

UCR

Fine Arts
Faculty
& Theatre

Library

Cinemateca

JOSÉ MARÍA MUNEZ

San José

AV 5

AV 3

Parque
Central

AV 1

AV CENTRAL

Banco
Nacional

Old Banco
Anglo

AVENIDA 2

AV 4

CALLE CENTRAL

CALLE 1

AV 6

AV 8

CALLE 3

Curridabat △

0   200 m

the finest in Central America. The three or four square blocks surrounding the university are lined with some of the liveliest bars and restaurants in San José: in most of them you'll feel more comfortable if you're under thirty.

Many of San José's residents live in the **suburbs** surrounding the city – many shopping malls and embassies are located in the eastern suburb of Curridabat and near Escazu, a mountain town to the north and west of San José. Bus services to suburbs are cheap and frequent, and all leave from the centre of town.

By air

International **flights** arrive at Juan Santamaría International airport (☎441-0744), 17km northwest of San José, and 3km southeast of Alajuela in the Valle Central (see p.558). The **ICT office** (daily 8am–4pm; ☎442-1820 or 8542) can supply maps and give advice on accommodation. There's a **correo** (Mon–Fri 8am–5pm) next to the departure tax window and a **bank** upstairs (Mon–Fri 6.30am–6pm, Sat, Sun & holidays 7am–1pm); colones are not necessary for taxis but you will need them for the bus.

Though the beige/orange Alajuela–San José **bus** (*Station Wagons Alajuela*) stops outside the airport, this is an inter-city service, not really geared up for travellers. Fare is about 100 colones (pay in local currency) and should be paid to the driver (every 3min 5am–10pm, every 15min 10pm–5am; 30min); check before you ride that it is on its way to San José and not Alajuela. The bus drops passengers in town at Av 2, C 12/14. Taxis hang around out front of this small terminus, or can be flagged down on Av 2.

The best way to get into San José is by **taxi** (US$10–12). Drivers will stampede for your business while you're practically still in customs. The ride into town takes about twenty minutes in light traffic.

By bus

International buses from Nicaragua, Honduras, Guatemala and Panamá pull into the Ticabus station, Av 4, C 9/11 (☎221-8954), next to the yellow Soledad church. Ticabus from Managua arrives at about 5pm; the Panamá service arrives at 5am. There's a taxi rank around the corner on the stretch of Av 2 between C 5 and 9. Coming from Managua on Sirca, you will arrive at the terminal at C 7, Av 6/8 (Mon–Fri 8am–5pm, Sat 8am–1pm; ☎223-1464). Taxis can be flagged down on C 7.

The closest thing San José has to a **domestic bus station** is **La Coca-Cola**, so named for an old bottling plant that used to stand on the site. Just west of the Mercado Central at Av 1/3 and between C 16 and 18, the main entrance is off C 16. Buses arrive here from the north and west, including Monteverde, most of the beaches of the Nicoya Peninsula, Liberia and Puntarenas. La Coca-Cola is noisy, hemmed in by small, confusing streets crammed with busy market traders, and invariably prowled by pickpockets. Best to arrive and leave in a taxi. Be especially careful of your belongings

---

SAFETY IN SAN JOSÉ

San José is a relatively safe city, and many travellers walk around without encountering problems. There are dangers, however; mainly **mugging**, purse-snatching or jewellery-snatching. It's worth keeping a tight grip on your belongings around the Coca-Cola bus terminal – roughly from C 12 to 16 and between Av 1 and 3 – as well as around the Parque Central, Av 2, and the Plaza de la Cultura. Other dodgy areas, day and night, include C 12 around Av 8 and 10, and Av 4 to 6 and C 4 to 12, just southwest of the centre. If **driving** in the centre of the city, keep windows rolled up so no one can reach in and snatch your bag.

Also, watch out when **crossing the street**, anywhere in the city; drivers can be aggressive and accidents involving pedestrians are common.

around the **Tilarán terminal**, 200m north of the intersection of Av 7, C 12, which is also used by buses from Monteverde. Many attempted thefts take place while people wait for the 6.30am bus to Monteverde.

Information

San José's **ICT office** is on the 11th floor of the unmissable big ugly building on Av 2 between calles 5 and 7 (Mon–Fri 8am–5pm; ☎222-1090). Entrance is at the back on Av 4. They have free city maps, leaflets and binders in which you can check out photos of hotels before you book, but the crucial information is behind the counter in the form of a computerized printout of the national bus schedule, details of all the hotels in Costa Rica, and lists of restaurants, nightclubs and museums in San José. Look out as well for the free brochure *Espectáculos*, which has fortnightly information on concerts, bars, theatre and films in San José. You can also pick one up at the more upscale hotels.

The only official information on **National Parks** is via the ICT **telephone information line** (☎192). Giving information in Spanish and – though not always – English, the service is understaffed, and waiting times are long. The privately run, unofficial **Fundacion de Parques Nacionales** is more useful; they're 300m north and 175m east of the Santa Teresita church (Mon–Fri 8am–4pm; ☎257-2239).

City transport

Central San José is easily negotiated on foot, though buses are useful in the suburbs. The mountain town of **Escazú** is about twenty minutes' ride to the west, the University of Costa Rica and **San Pedro** about ten minutes' ride to the east. After 10pm the buses stop running and **taxis** become the best way to get around.

Buses

Fast, cheap and frequent, buses reach every one of San José's neighbourhoods and suburbs, generally running from 5am until 10 or 11pm. **Bus stops** in this centre area are clearly marked on metal signs. "*Haga fila*", which you will see on each sign, means "line up". The buses clearly marked with their routes and the fare is also usually written on the windshield. **Fares** are usually between 40 and 60 colones (US$0.25), except for the faster and more comfortable *busetas de lujo* (luxury buses) to the suburbs, which cost about 75 colones and upwards (US$0.35), payable either to the driver or his helper when you board. Buses always have lots of change.

Taxis

Taxis are cheap and plentiful. Licensed vehicles are red with a yellow triangle on the side, and have licence plates which say "SJP" for "San José Publico". A ride anywhere in the city costs between 250 and 350 colones and about double that to get out to the suburbs. The starter fare – about 165 colones – is shown on the red digital read-out. Always make sure the meter is on and running (ask the driver to "toca la maría, por favor"). If the meter really isn't working, best to agree a fare before you start out.

Taxi companies in San José can be phoned from anywhere in the city and will come to your door; if you call from your hotel, though, reckon on paying twice the standard fare, and note that after midnight taxis from the El Pueblo shopping and entertainment centre charge forty percent extra. The larger **companies** are Coopealfaro (☎221-8466); Coopeguaria (☎226-1366); Coopeirazú (☎254-3211); Coopetaxi (☎235-9966); Coopetico (☎221-2552), and Coopeuno (☎254-6667).

Driving

Though it's a bad idea to **rent a car** for getting around San José, you may need one for driving out of the city. Cars should never be left on the street anywhere near the city centre. They are guaranteed to be broken into or stolen. Secure **parqueos** (guarded parking lots) dot the city; some are 24-hour, but most close at 8 or 8.30pm. If you have to leave your car on the street, look for the local security guard (they carry truncheons); and pay him 100 colones for guarding it. For a list of car **rental companies** see p.550.

Accommodation

The last couple of years have seen a hotel boom in San José, though quantity does not necessarily mean quality, especially in the budget to moderate range. Rock-bottom hotels tend, with a few exceptions, to be grim. Staying in the **centre** is convenient, though entails putting up with noise and pollution; avenidas 2 and Central are especially bad for street noise. The very cheapest rooms are in the insalubrious area immediately around La Coca-Cola; staying in these depressing cells makes the city seem far uglier than it is. Within a ten- or fifteen-minute bus ride from the city centre, the suburbs of **Escazú** and **San Pedro** are also worth checking.

Despite the proliferation of hotels, San José does get booked up in **high season**, between December and April, and especially over Christmas and Easter. In general it is best to call or fax ahead for reservations. Almost all hotels listed below do a weekly discount and in the wet season (May–Nov) rates drop considerably.

Central San José

Bellavista, Av 0, C 19/21 (☎223-0095). Retro rooms are a bit dark and musty, but it's a friendly place, with lively murals. Good value but avoid the noisy front rooms. ⑤.

Bienvenido, C 10, Av 1/3 (☎233-2161, fax 221-1872). One of the best downtown budget options, with small clean rooms with private bath. Near La Coca-Cola; great if you want to catch an early bus. The area is a bit dodgy. ③.

Boruca, C 14, Av 1/3 (☎➡23-0016, fax 232-0107). A central and basic if charmless hotel in the Coca-Cola district. Friendly management and a secure atmosphere, although rooms are small and somewhat musty – try for one with a window, although the payoff is noise. ①–②.

Cacts, Av 3 bis, C 28/30 (☎221-2928 or 6546, fax 221-8618; Aptdo 379-1005, San José). Small, quiet, spotless hotel. Some new rooms, but the older rooms, upstairs particularly, are nicer; those with shared bath are best value. All have ceiling fans, hot or heated water. Small café, bar and TV lounge. Friendly owners can help with travel reservation and confirmation. ⑤.

Casa Leo, Av 4 bis, C 15/17 (☎222-9725). Small, friendly guesthouse with dorms and basic private rooms with shared bath. A good alternative to *Casa Ridgway* (see below) and just as near the *Ticabus* stop. The German *dueña* is helpful and will do laundry. Difficult to find, call for directions. ②.

Casa Ridgway, C 15, Av 6/8 (☎233-6168 or 221-8299, fax 224-8910). Affiliated to the adjacent *Friends' Peace Center*, this friendly Quaker guesthouse is San José's best budget option, near the *Ticabus* stop and a great place to meet other travellers. Homey atmosphere, alcohol ban and "quiet time" after 10pm. Try not to arrive after 10pm, except by prior arrangement. Clean single-sex dorms, and private singles and triples, with kitchen, communal bathrooms, laundry and luggage storage. Dorms US$8. Reserve in high season. ②.

Cinco Hormigas Rojas, C 15, Av 9/11 (☎257-8581). *Dueña* Mayra Güell is an artist who has decorated the bright rooms in this small, very good-value B&B with her wonderful paintings. She also offers breakfast, advice and tour information. It's a private house in the quiet barrio Otoya, 200m east of the back of the INS building and 25m north. ④–⑤.

Don Fadrique, C 37, Av 8, Los Yoses (☎225-8166, fax 224-9746). Elegant upscale hotel located in the former home of Don Fadrique Gutierrez, turn-of-the-century architect, general and philosopher. The hotel's halls function as a gallery for Costa Rican art. All 20 rooms have private bath and hot water. ⑦.

Edelweiss, Av 9, C 13/15 (☎221-9702, fax 222-1241). Elegant, heavy dark wood furniture and pretty decor (check the lovely tiles in the shower). They serve an excellent healthy breakfast. Most amenities associated with this price range, but no TV. English and German spoken. ⑤–⑦.

Fleur de Lys, C 13, Av 2/6 (☎223-1206, fax 257-3637). Friendly hotel in an old San José house. Good downtown location near Ticabus and Av 2 but still quiet. Each floor has a sunny, plant filled-atrium. Good restaurant/bar attached. Good discounts in low seasoon. ⑤–⑥.

Galilea, Av 0, C 11 next to Plaza de la Democracía (☎223-6925, fax 223-1689). Clean, if uninspiring, rooms, friendly management, and lots of maritime imagery on the walls (the *dueño* used to be a boat captain). Affordable low season and weekly rates. Popular, so book ahead in high season. ④–⑥.

La Gema, Av 12, C 9/11 (☎257-2524, fax 222-1074). South of the centre in a relatively quiet area, this small hotel is surprisingly light, with an open courtyard planted with leafy trees. Rooms are good, but walls a bit thin: the lighter upstairs rooms are best. ⑤–⑥.

Gran Hotel Imperial, C 8, Av 0/1 (☎222-7899). The spooky entrance (dark stairwell, huge imposing frontage) belies a bare, secure, rock-bottom hotel. For years popular with backpackers, these are some of the cheapest rooms in San José, all with shared bath. There's a restaurant with balcony. Can be noisy. ①.

Grano d'Oro, C 30, Av 2/4 (☎255-3322, fax 221-2782; Aptdo 1157-1007, Centro Colón, San José; in USA: PO Box 025216-36, Miami, FL 33102-5216). Beautiful, individually decorated rooms, all non-smoking with TV and phone, in a quiet area west of the centre, attracting a mainly American clientele. Excellent breakfast served in the restaurant, which is highly respected in its own right. ⑧.

Oak Harbour Inn, Av 3, C 18 bis (☎256-0041, fax 233-0442). Small new hotel owned by a very friendly Chilean family. Large comfortable rooms with bath and hot water and a dizzying array of services: fax, free maps, tour service, kitchen, TV/video lounge, laundry, luggage storage. Near La Coca-Cola, but on a side street so there is minimal bus noise. ③–④.

Pensión de la Cuesta, Av 1, C 11/15 (☎ & fax 255-2896). Italian-owned, pink, colonial-style wooden house, tranquil and tasteful. The previous owner was an artist – hence the gold masks on walls and decorated bedsteads. Decor is bright but some rooms can be gloomy. Laundry, luggage storage, tours and car rental. ④.

Ritz, C 0, Av 8/10 (☎222-4103, fax 222-8849). Very friendly, clean central hotel with its own tour service, frequented by Swiss travellers. Pension rooms (shared bath) are half the price of those with private bath and heated water. Breakfast in the pretty dining area costs extra. ③–⑤.

Tica Linda, Av 2, C 5/7; brown metal door with small sign (☎233-0528). Central hotel that is unusual in being characterful, cheap, clean and respectable, with tiny rooms and dorms. *Bar Esmeralda* next door churns out mariachi all night which, added to the noise of buses and fellow occupants, makes for little sleep. Dorms US$4. Cold water only. Luggage storage. ②.

Toruma, Av 0, C 29/31 (☎ & fax 224-4085). Beautiful hostel with Neoclassical exterior and high ceilings. Good place to meet people, to reserve for hostels and tours, and arrange onward travel. Book at least three months in advance in high season. Luggage storage, safe, laundry, 11pm curfew; non-smoking. Single-sex dorms with shared bath; from US$9 for HI members, US$12 for non-members (membership available at desk). ①–③.

Vesuvio, Av 11, C 13/15 (☎221-7586 or 8325, fax 221-8325). What this place lacks in decor (long, institutional corridors) it makes up for by being quiet and affordable, with friendly family management. Rooms are cosy if a bit claustrophobic, with TV, bath, phone and fan. Bar/restaurant and safe parking. ④.

San Pedro

La Granja, 50m south of the *Antiguo Higuerón* landmark tree, off Av 0 in barrio la Granja, San Pedro (☎225-1073, fax 234-1676). Great HI-affiliated hostel in a pink house with pretty garden, near the university, bars and restaurants. Some singles; most rooms have shared shower. TV lounge, and free breakfast for members. Members pay US$13. ③–④.

Milvia, 100m north and 200m east of Muñoz y Nanne supermarket (☎225-4543, fax 225-7801). Lovely old house in residential area. Beautifully decorated, with fountain, sun terrace and mountain views. TV and fridge in all rooms; restaurant and bar. Free breakfast. ⑧.

Residencia Saint-Pierre, 100m south and 50 east of the Banco Popular, San Pedro. Good, reasonably priced bed and breakfast in quiet, studenty accommodation. Rooms with hot water and private bath; prices include breakfast. ③–④.

Escazú

Casa de las Tias, 100m east of *Restaurant El Che* (☎289-5517, fax 289-7353). Owned by a well-travelled Costa Rican couple, this friendly, atmsopheric place has individually decorated rooms with private bath and hot water. Quiet, although in town; no children under twelve. ⑥.

Posada del Bosque, Aptdo 669-1250 (☎228-1164, fax 228-2006). Very quiet, homey place, in large landscaped grounds. Comfortable no-smoking rooms with shared bath. The friendly owners can arrange tennis and horseback riding. ⑤.

Posada El Quijote, Bello Horizonte de Escazú (☎289-8401, fax 289-8729). Eight spacious rooms, all Spanish colonial style, comfortably furnished with bath, hot water and cable TV, in a private house. Breakfast is included, served on an enclosed terrace with lovely garden and views. ⑤.

The City

Few travellers come to San José for the sights. A city of nondescript buildings, energized by a fairly aggressive street life – umbrella-wielding pedestrians pushing through narrow streets, noisy food stalls, homicidal drivers – San José is certainly not a place that exudes immediate appeal. It has its diversions, however: with plenty of places to walk, sit, eat, meet people, go dancing and enjoy museums and galleries. It's also a manageable city; all the attractions are close together, and everything of interest can be covered in a couple of days. Of the museums, the exemplary **Museo de Oro Precolumbiano**, and the **Museo de Jade**, which houses the Americas' largest collection of the precious stone, are the major draws. Less visited, the **Museo Nacional** offers some interesting archeological finds, while the **Museo de Arte y Deseño Contemporáneo** displays some of the most striking work in the Americas. San José is also a surprisingly **green** city, or at least one with quite a bit of public space, with paved-over plazas and small, carefully landscaped parks punctuating the centre of town.

Around the Plaza de la Cultura

The **Plaza de la Cultura** cleverly conceals one of San José's treasures, the **Museo de Oro Precolumbiano**, or Pre-Columbian Gold Museum (Tues–Sat 10am–5pm; US$5). The bunker-like underground space is unprepossessing, but the gold on display is truly impressive – all the more extraordinary if you take into account the relative paucity of pre-Columbian artefacts in Costa Rica. The exquisitely delicate work on show is almost entirely the work of the master goldsmiths the **Diquis**, ancient inhabitants of southwestern Costa Rica. Most of the pieces are small and unbelievably detailed, with a preponderance of disturbing, evil-looking **animals**. Information panels (Spanish only) suggest that the chief function of these portents of evil – frogs, snakes and insects – was shamanic. The *ave de rapiña*, or bird of prey, seems to have had particular religious relevance for the Diquis: there are tons of them here – hawks, owls and eagles, differing only incrementally in shape and size. Look out, too, for angry-looking arachnids; jaguars and alligators carrying the pathetic dangling legs of human victims in their mouths; grinning bats with wings spread; turtles, crabs, frogs, iguanas and armadillos, and a few spiny, unmistakeable lobsters.

San José's heavily columned, grey-brown **Teatro Nacional** sits on the corner of C 5 and Av 2, tucked in behind the Plaza de la Cultura. The theatre's marbled stairways, gilt cherubs and red velvet carpets would look more at home in old Europe than in Central America, and remain in remarkably good condition, despite the dual onslaught of the climate and a succession of earthquakes. Even if you're not coming to see a performance, you can wander around in the post-Baroque splendour, although you will be charged about US$3 in colones – this is another reason to see the theatre at its best and come here for a show. The elegant cafe attached (see p.547) serves good coffee and European-style cakes.

Around the Parque España

On the north side of the **Parque España**, three blocks northeast of the plaza, rises one of the few office towers in San José: the INS, or Institute of Social Security, building. This uninspired edifice is home to one of the city's finest museums, the **Marco Fidel Tristan Museo de Jade** (Mon–Fri 8am–3.30pm; US$3). This is the largest collection of American jade in the world, ingeniously displayed with subtle backlighting to show off the multi-coloured and multi-textured pieces to full effect. You'll see a lot of **axe-gods**: anthropomorphic bird/human forms shaped like an axe and worn as a pendant. One entire room devotes itself to male fertility symbols, and you'll also see X-shaped objects used to support the breasts of women of standing – a kind of proto-bra. Incidentally, the **view** from the museum windows is one of the best in the city, taking in the sweep of San José from the centre to the south and then west to the mountains.

Sprawling across the entire eastern border of the Parque España, the former National Liquor Factory (FANAL), dating from 1887, today houses the Centro Nacional de Cultura, home to cutting-edge **Museo de Arte y Diseño Contemporáneo** (Tues–Sun 10am–5pm; US$1). Opened in 1994 under the direction of dynamic prize-winning artist Virginia Pérez-Ratton, it's a highly modern space, with a cosmopolitan, multi-media approach. Artists from the region – Guatemala, Colombia, Brazil – are exhibited alongside the work of Costa Ricans; it's definitely worth a visit to see what is going on in the arts in the Americas. There's also a theatre in the complex; a wander around during the day offers interesting glimpses of dancers and musicians rehearsing.

Lurking on the second floor of a nondescript building on the corner of Av 1 and C 9, the **Serpentario** (Mon–Fri 9am–6pm; US$3) is one of Costa Rica's most useful attractions, where aghast tourists and fascinated schoolboys wander amid glass cases of snakes, poison dart frogs and the odd lizard. Species on display include the fer-de-lance, bushmaster and jumping and eyelash vipers. Look out for the rather forlorn-looking Burmese python, who lies curled up in the biggest case.

Plaza de la Democracía

Heading one block south to Av Central, then one block east, you'll come to the concrete **Plaza de la Democracía**, yet another of the city's soulless squares. Constructed in 1989 to mark President Oscar Arias' key involvement in the Central American Peace Plan, this expanse of terraced concrete slopes gently up toward a fountain and the impressive fortress edifice of the **Museo Nacional** (Tues–Sat 8.30am–5pm, Sun 9am–5pm; US$1) which crowns the top of the square. Highlights include petroglyphs, pre-Columbian stonework, and wonderful anthropomorphic gold figures in the **Sala Arqueológica**. This is the single most important archeological exhibition in the country; the grinding tables and funerary offerings, in particular, show precise geometric patterns.

Centro Costarricense de la Ciencia y la Cultura

Near the Centro Comercial El Pueblo, a tourist-oriented shopping centre, at the end of Calle 4 is the new **Centro Costarricense de la Ciencia y la Cultura** (Tues–Fri 9am–noon & 2–5pm, Sat & Sun 10am–1pm & 2–5pm; US$4). Located in a former prison, the complex devotes most of its space to the high-tech **Museo de los Niños** (Childrens' Museum) which educates children about history, culture and science. Also in here, the **Museo Historico Penitenciario** (the Penitentiary History Museum) has restored a number of original prison cells. The avant-garde artwork in the **Sala de Exhibicion** is an eclectic, modern collection of more interest to Ticos than tourists.

Centro Cultural Costarricense-Norteamericano

East of the centre in barrio Dent you'll find the **Centro Cultural Costarricense-Norteamericano**, just 100m north of the Am-Pm supermarket on the corner of Av Central and C 37 (Mon–Fri 7am–7pm, Sat 9am–noon; ☎255-9433 for library). The library holds a huge back stock of English-language publications, and there's an art gallery, the Eugene O'Neill theatre (jazz festivals and English language theatre performances), a good café and CNN beamed out on the communal TV.

San Pedro

First impressions of the student district of **San Pedro** can be offputting: Avenida Central (also called **Paseo de los Estudiantes**) appears to be little more than a strip of gas stations, broken-up sidewalks, and dull malls. Walk just a block off the Paseo, however, and you'll find a lively combination of university student ghettos and elegant old residential houses, home to some of the city's best bars, restaurants and nightlife, catering to students, professors, residents and professionals.

Buses to San Pedro from the centre of town stop opposite the small **Parque Central**, centring on a monument to John F. Kennedy. Walking north from the square, through three blocks of solid sodas, bars, restaurants and abandoned railway tracks, you come to the cool, leafy campus of the **University of Costa Rica** (UCR), one of the finest in Central America, founded in 1940. The university atmosphere is busy, egalitarian and stimulating.

Around the Mercado Central

Northwest of the Parque Central and the commercial centre between Av Central and 1, and C 6 and 8, San José's **Mercado Central** is open from about 5am until 5pm daily except Sunday. Entering its labyrinthine interior, you're assaulted by colourful arrangements of strange fruits and vegetables, dangling sides of beef and elaborate, silvery ranks of fish. It's certainly the best place in town to get a cheap bite, and the view from a counter stool is fascinating, as traders and their customers jostle for *chayotes*, *mamones*, *piñas* and *cas*. Shopping for fruit, vegetables and coffee here is cheaper than in the supermarket.

The surrounding streets, which even in the daytime can look quite seedy are full of noisy traders and determined shoppers. All this activity encourages **pickpockets**, and in this environment *turistas* stick out like sore thumbs. Take only what you need and be on your guard.

Two blocks east and one block north of the Mercado Central, in the *Correo Central*, C 2, Av 1/3, the **Museo Postal, Telegráfico y Filatelico** (Mon–Fri 8am–4pm; free), exhibits old pieces of telegraphic equipment – relics of interest to buffs only. There's a **flower market** in the square opposite, where carnations, orchids, begonias and scores of tropical blooms create a blaze of colour.

Paseo Colón and Parque la Sabana

Clustered around the main entrance to La Coca-Cola, off C 16, shops selling women's underwear, cosmetics and luggage compete for space with a variety of cheap snack bars and drinks stalls. Two blocks south, however, the atmosphere changes, as Av Central turns into **Paseo Colón**, a wide boulevard of upmarket shops, restaurants and car dealerships. At the very end of the *paseo*, a solid expanse of green today known as **Parque la Sabana** was until the 1940s San José's airport, and is now home to the country's key art museum.

The bright orange neocolonial edifice of the old air terminal in **Parque la Sabana** has been converted into the attractive **Museo de Arte Costarricense** (Tues–Sun 10am–5pm; US$2), with a good collection of mainly twentieth-century Costa Rican paintings. The **Salon Dorado** upstairs is remarkable; four full walls of bas-relief wooden carvings overlaid with sumptuous gold, portraying somewhat idealized scenes of Costa Rica's history since pre-Columbian times.

On the southwest corner of Sabana Park, across the road, the quirky natural science museum **Museo de Ciencias Naturales La Salle** (Mon–Fri 8am–3pm; US$1), is in the Ministry of Agriculture and Livestock complex. Walk right in, and after about 400m you'll see the painted wall proclaiming the museum; the entrance is at the back. Displays range from pickled fish and snakes coiled in formaldehyde to some rather forlorn taxidermy exhibits – age and humidity have taken their toll.

Sabana is also the best place in San José to **jog**. The cement track is usually full of serious runners in training, but you can run fairly safely all around the park. There's a small, dank changing hut, shower and lavatory beside the track; you can leave your bag securely with the *señora* who takes the money (10am–4pm only).

Eating

For a Central American city of its size, San José has a surprising variety of **restaurants** (Italian, macrobiotic, Thai). Many of the best places are in the relatively high income and cosmopolitan neighbourhoods of **San Pedro**, along **Paseo Colón**, and in **Escazú**, but wherever you choose, eating out in San José can set your budget back on its haunches. The 23 percent tax on restaurant food can deliver a real death-blow, so it's cheapest to eat in the centre, at the sodas and snack bars, where the tax doesn't apply. A sit-down lunch of the *plato del día* at a **soda** will rarely set you back more than US$5, or for a quick sugar fix you could feast on *churros* dispensed over the counter. Healthier choices include *empañadas* and sandwiches to take out – combine this with a stop at one of the fruit stalls on any street corner and you've got a quick, cheap lunch.

Cafés also abound: some, like *Giacomín*, have old-world European aspirations; others, *Spoon* for example, are resolutely Costa Rican, with Joséfinos piling in to order birthday cakes or grab a **coffee**. Of the major **ice cream** chains – *Pops, Mönpik, Baloons* – *Pops* is the best, with particularly good fruit flavours.

Working Joséfinos eat their main meal between noon and 2pm, and at this time sodas especially can get very busy. Many restaurants close at 3pm and open again for the evening. In the listings below we have given a phone number only for places where you might need to **reserve** a table.

Restaurants

Antojitos Cancun, Los Yoses, in the Centro Comercial Cocorí, 50m before the fountain roundabout. Cheap, filling Mexican food, not wholly authentic, but good for late-night snacks and cheap all-you-can-eat buffets. Draught beer and an outside terrace where you can sit and watch the 4WDs whizz round the fountain. Mariachi Fri and Sat from 10pm. Daily 11am–midnight.

Balcón de Europa, C 9, Av 0/1. City landmark: the food, largely pasta and Italian staples, is nothing special, but great sepia photos of the early days line the wood-panelled wall, along with annoying snippets of "wisdom". Monster cheeses dominate the dining room, as does the game strummer who serenades each table. Closed Sat.

Café 1900, 100m north of La Iglesia de Fatima, Los Yoses. Peruvian restaurant – originally a tea/coffee house – oddly done up in flowery chintz wallpaper. At lunch choose from pisco sours, big salads and crepes; for dinner try a shrimp entrée (about US$7). The fish in spicy sauce is particularly good. Other delicious dinner selections are the *causa limeña, lomo saltado* and the *papas a la huancaina*. Mon–Fri 11.30am–3pm & 6–10pm, Sat 7–11pm, Sun noon–4pm.

Le Chandelier, 100m west and 100m south of the ICE building in Los Yoses. Genuinely exquisite French food cooked by the Swiss owner, who is currently offering an 8-course meal for US$50, which is worth every cent, especially the champagne sorbet to clear your palate.

Cocina de Leña, El Pueblo. *Típico* food, superbly cooked, in rustic, down-homey surroundings (big wooden tables, gingham tablecloths, menus on paper bags). Good for a quiet, upscale night out; dinner costs around US$35 for two.

Fulusu, C 7, Av 0/2. Good Szechuan dishes in a bare restaurant that looks more like a soda, but serves the best Chinese food downtown. Mon–Sat for lunch and dinner.

La Leyenda, in San Rafael de Escazu (☎228-6846). As the name implies, this relatively new restaurant is already a legend. Santa-Fe style decor with indoor or outdoor seating, authentic Mexican cuisine and 28 different types of tequila.

Machu Picchu, C 32, Av 1, 125m north of Paseo Colón (☎222-7384). Great atmosphere; the only truly South American feel in town (kitsch velvet llama pictures on the walls help); the appetizers, including *ceviche* and Peruvian *bocas* are more interesting than the main dishes. Around US$30 for two with beer or wine. Mon–Fri 11.30am–3pm & 6–10pm.

Marisqueria La Princesa, north side of Parque la Sabana. Doesn't look much from the outside but this is one of San José's best restaurants, with seafood at very low prices; the shrimps with garlic (*camarones con ajillo*) are about half the price you find them elsewhere.

Mazorca, 200m east and 100m north of San Pedro church. Macrobiotic restaurant just east of the entrance to UCR. Tasty bread, soups, peanut butter sandwiches and macrobiotic cakes make a welcome change. Also takeout cakes and bread. Mon–Fri 9am–8pm, Sat 9am–2pm.

Pizza Metro, Av 2 next to *Bar La Esmeralda* (☎223-0306). Small place, popular with office workers. Not particularly cheap, but the pasta and pizza are worth it. Dinner only.

Il Pomodoro, San Pedro, 150m east of the entrance to UCR. Sooner or later, everybody ends up at "the tomato", one of the best pizza places in the city. Proper large pizzas, including a great vegetarian special, served in cheerful big restaurant popular with university crowd. Cheap draught beer served in mugs and pitchers. Around US$18 for two.

Tin-Jo, C 11, Av 6/8 (☎221-7605). Quiet, popular and fairly formal Chinese/Thai place; lemongrass soup, bean thread salad in lime juice, and coconut milk curries are particularly recommended. Dinner with wine is around US$40 for two; skip the alcohol, or go for lunch, and you'll get away with half that.

Sodas

La Cocina de Bardolino, C 21, Av 6, 100m east from the Supreme Court. Watch the Argentine owners prepare exquisitely fresh chicken and beef *empañadas* while keeping their eyes glued on the TV soccer game. Images of *La Patria*, including Maradona posters, abound.

El Crillotito, Av 7, C 7/9. Daily about 6 to 8 choices of filling *plato del dias*, which come with a small cup of great ice cream. Still a bargain at US$3 for lunch. Get there just before or at 12 or after 2pm — popular with workers from the local INS building. If it's full you can try the *Soda Pingui* in the same block, similar and also good value.

El Parque, C 2, Av 4/6. Historic soda with real atmosphere; though it's a slightly dodgy area. Serves all the usual specials and good refrescos. Perennial favourite with radio reporters who come here to get *vox populi* for their broadcasts.

La Perla, C 2, Av 2, across from the Parque Central. Pricey and the entire staff suffer from cranky waitress syndrome, but the portions are huge; try the steak sandwich with fries, scrambled eggs on toast, or the great *refrescos*. Streetlife streams by outside; open 24 hours.

La Reina de Pupusas, Av 1, C 5/7, opposite Cine Omni on the corner of Parking Gigante. Salvadorean stand serving great snacks, tortillas with frijoles molidos, cabbage, mixed pickles and chorizo or meat and cheese. A (messy) meal in themselves.

Vishnu, Av 1, C 1/3. Vegetarian pit stop with three other locations in the city. Delicious *platos del día* with brown rice, vegetables and soups. The vegetarian sandwich is a meal in itself and a bargain at US$1.50. Fruit plates and yoghurt are a perennial favourite. A *plato del día*, *refresco* and *café con leche* costs about US$4.

Cafés and bakeries

Café Gourmet, C 3 bis, Av 9. Small, quiet, aromatic café with excellent export-quality coffee, freshly roasted beans, and friendly staff who will answer any questions about the entire coffee process, from bean to cup. Good cappuccino with proper frothed milk, tasty desserts and snacks. Is expanding its menu and also sells souvenirs.

Café la Maga, in Los Yoses, inside Centro Comercial Cocorí, just before the Fuente de la Hispanidad on the way to San Pedro. Currently one of the most popular places in town day or night, this café/bar doubles as an art gallery, and stocks an enormous array of magazines dealing with Latin American and Spanish art, culture and literature. Film club ($21 per annum), with more than 100 videos. Daily 11am–midnight.

Café Parisienne, *Gran Hotel Costa Rica*, Av 2, C 3/5. Wonderful place to sit and have coffee and cake on a sunny day, complete with wrought-iron chairs and trussed-up waiters. San José's closest thing to European street-café elegance, and one of the few establishments in the city that do continental breakfast.

Ruiseñor, *Centro Comercial Casa Alameda*, Los Yoses. Old-world European style and service. If you sit upstairs on the the outdoor terrace you can watch the diplomats come and go. Upmarket, with prices to match.

Teatro Nacional, Av 2, C 3/5. Sandwiches and pastries served in a tranquil mint-green setting – also good for watching the goings-on in the square in front of the *Gran Hotel Costa Rica* although bit heavy on the old world atmosphere.

Drinking and nightlife

San José's nightlife is gratifyingly varied, with scores of **bars** and **live music** venues. That said, a couple of the most popular venues of recent years, including the splendid Casa Matute have had to close because of strict anti-noise regulations (curiously only enforced for live music venues, as opposed to taped salsa blaring at 7am from your neighbour). Many bars change character drastically come Friday or Saturday, when they host jazz, blues, upcoming local bands, rock and roll, or South American folk music. Ticos aren't known for burning the candle at both ends, though people do stay out later on the weekends; with the exception of the studenty bars in San Pedro, most places close by 2 or 3am, earlier on Sunday.

Most young Joséfinos, students and foreigners in the know head to Los Yoses or San Pedro to drink. In **Los Yoses**, Av Central features a well-known "yuppie trail" of bars, starting roughly at the *El Cuartel de la Boca del Monte,* with its mobile phone-wielding contingent, and reaching its peak at *Rio*, a hugely popular American-style bar with an outdoor terrace. **San Pedro** is obviously geared toward the university population, with a couple of very studenty bars.

It's worth experiencing one of the city's **discos**: even if you don't dance, you can watch the Ticos burn up the floor. *Déjà Vu* is the place of the moment; for traditional **salsa**, merengue, cumbia and soca try *La Plaza*, *Cocloco*, *Las Risas* or *Infinito*. DJs at these places intersperse the Latino playlist with reggae and a bit of jungle from Jamaica, the US and the Dominican Republic, and then do a house set, usually playing internationally popular, if somewhat out of date, tunes. In general, the **dress code** is relaxed: most people wear smart jeans and men need not wear a jacket. **Cover charges** run to about 700 colones or US$4, though the big mainstream discos at El Pueblo (see p.548) charge slightly more than places downtown.

You need to be 18 to drink in Costa Rica. Even if you're well over age, if you look even remotely young, bring a photocopy of your passport as **ID**.

Bars and live music

Caccio's, 200m east and 25m north of the San Pedro church. Insanely popular student hangout. Packed tables are great for meeting people: another bonus is the pizza and cheap cold beer. Mon–Sat 11am–midnight.

Chelles Taberna, C 9, Av 0/2 (☎221-1369). More like an English pub than a Latin American tavern, with smooching couples, serious guys in leather jackets and surly waitresses. Good range of drinks and cheap, tasty *bocas*. Open 24 hours.

El Cuartel de la Boca del Monte, Av 1, C 21/23. Indescribably popular with the beautiful young things. Well-stocked bar, great food, and some of the best live music in town from up-and-coming bands (Wed only). Dress hip, take your mobile, and go early, preferably before 8.30pm. There's a door policy of sorts, but the bouncers never seem to turn anyone away. Small cover ($2.50) most nights. Open Wed–Sat 6pm–2am.

La Esmeralda, Av 2, C 5/7. Landmark institution, offering a bit of "local colour". It's the head-quarters of the mariachi bands union, who congregate ready to dash off in a taxi at a moment's notice to serenade or celebrate. In the meantime, they whoosh by your table in colourful swirls of sombreros and sequins. Mon–Sat 11am–dawn.

Bar la Maga, in Los Yoses, inside Centro Comercial Cocorí. For some reason the Maga people abandoned their great San Pedro location in an old house and came to this vapid mall. By day a café, by night a singles/people-watching favourite, this café-bar doubles as an art gallery, and stocks an enormous array of magazines dealing with Latin American and Spanish art, culture and literature. Daily 11am–midnight.

Parillada Los Andes, across the street from the UCR library and cafeteria, San Pedro. University hang-out with low-key atmosphere, cold beer, good snacks and regular acoustic music, including *peñas*. Mon–Sat 11am–midnight.

Las Risas, C 1, Av 0/1. One of the best downtown bars, on three floors. The disco at the top is good, with a small floor and lively young crowd. Bring ID – a copy of your passport in the case of for-eigners – or the bouncers won't let you in.

Shakespeare, C 28, Av 2/4. Quiet, friendly place that attracts a large English-speaking clientele and people on their way to art-house films at the *Sala Garbo*, adjacent, or the *Teatro Laurence Olivier*. Occasional jazz. Daily 3pm–midnight.

La Villa, 125m north and 100m east of the old *Banco Anglo*, San Pedro. San José's best bar for beer and conversation. Atmospheric old house, frequented by students and "intellectuals", and plastered with interesting political and theatrical posters. Mercedes Sosa on the CD player, occasional live *peñas* and tasty *bocas*. Mon–Fri 11am–11pm, Sat 2pm–midnight, Sun 7pm–midnight.

Discos

La Avispa, C 1, Av 8/10. Landmark San José lesbian disco-bar, where men are welcome. Friendly atmosphere, simple dance floor and mainly Latin music. Tues–Sat 8pm–2am, Sun 5pm–2am. Thurs–Sun cover US$5.

Cocoloco, El Pueblo. Smart, well-dressed clientele, small dance floors, and the usual Latin techno-pop/reggae/merengue mix. Mon–Fri 8pm–midnight; Sat & Sun till 2am.

Déjà Vu, C 2, Av 14/16. Gay, lesbian and straight, with a hot and hopping atmosphere. Tunes are mostly house and techno with some salsa. The neighbourhood is pretty scary day or night – take a taxi. Cover varies from US$3 to US$5, and drinks are cheap. Tues–Sat 8pm–dawn.

Dynasty, in Centro Comercial del Sur, Desamparados, south of central San José (next to the old Pacific Railway station). Excellent *caribeña* tunes with reggae, odd sample of garage, soca, merengue and calypso. Young, hard-dancing crowd.

Infinito, El Pueblo. Similar to *Cocoloco*, but with an older, smarter crowd; the DJs here are pretty good. Mon–Fri 8pm–midnight; Sat & Sun till 2am.

La Plaza, across from El Pueblo. Archetypical Latin American disco, playing salsa, merengue, cumbia and soca. Designed like a giant bull ring, the huge round dance floor is packed with merengue danc-ing couples and superb waiters who twirl in their truncated tuxedos when business is slack. There's also a bar with a big TV screen flashing out a steady diet of music and sport. Daily from 8pm.

The arts and entertainment

The quality of the arts in San José is generally high. Joséfinos especially like **theatre**, and if you speak even a little Spanish it's worth checking to see what's on. Prices tend to be very low – from US$2–3 – and the standard very high. Shows usually run only from Thursday to Sunday evening in a single week. The premier venues are the Teatro Nacional, C 5, Av 2 (☎221-1329); and the Teatro Melico Salazar; C Central, Av 2 (☎221-4952), where you'll see performances by the **National Symphony Orchestra** and

National Lyric Opera Company (June–Aug), as well as visiting orchestras and singers – usually from Spain or other Spanish-speaking countries. A number of **cinemas,** often in lovely old buildings, show first-run American films with subtitles. A few are dubbed – watch out for the phrase "hablado en Español" in the newspaper listings or on the marquee posters. For Spanish-language art movies, head for the Sala Garbo, C 42, Av 2/4 (☎222-1034), and the Cinemateca and Faculdad de Derecha Cinema (Faculty of Law; ☎225-9175), at the University.

For **details of performances**, check the *Viva* section of *La Nación* and the listings in the *Tico Times*, which also distinguish between English- and Spanish-language films and productions. There is also a fortnightly brochure distributed to hotels and other tourist haunts called *Info-Spectacles*, which lists much of what is going on in the city.

Shopping and markets

San José's **souvenir and crafts shops** are well-stocked and in general fairly pricey; it's best to buy from larger ones, run by government-regulated crafts co-operatives, from which more of the money filters down to the artisans. You'll see an abundance of **pre-Columbian gold jewellery copies**, Costa Rican liqueurs (*Café Rica* is best known), T-shirts with jungle and animal scenes, weirdly realistic wooden snakes, leather rockers from the village of Sarchí (see p.561), walking sticks, simple leather bracelets, hammocks, and a vast array of wood carvings.

At the bottom of the Plaza de la Democracia, Av 0/2 and C 11/13, a long line of canvas-covered **artisans' stalls** sell hammocks, chunky Ecuadorean sweaters, leather bracelets and jewellery, mostly of the leather-and-beaded type. You'll also find some Guatemalan textiles and decorative textile *molas* made by the Kuna peoples of Panamá (see p.717), all at steeper prices than elsewhere in the isthmus. Traders are low-pressure and friendly, and gentle bargaining is allowed.

ANDA, Av 0, C 5/7. Indigenous crafts including wooden masks, colourful *molas,* and bags and reproductions of Chorotega pottery.

La Casona, C 0, Av 0/1. A large marketplace of stalls selling the usual local stuff along with Guatemalan knapsacks and bedspreads. Jewellery and Panamanian *molas* are the highlights. Quality at some stalls is pretty poor, however, and there's not one good T-shirt in evidence. Great for browsing, though.

Mercado Nacional de Artesanía, C 22, Av 2 bis. One of the largest stocks of souvenirs and crafts in the country, featuring all the usuals: hats, T-shirts, Sarchí ox-carts, jewellery, woodwork including snakes and walking sticks.

Tienda de la Naturaleza, Curridabat, 1km past San Pedro on Av 0. The shop of the private *Fundación Neotropica*, this is a good place to buy the posters, T-shirts and other paraphernalia painted by English artist Deirdre Hyde that you see all over the country. She specializes in the landscapes of tropical America and the animals who live there; her jaguars are particularly good.

Listings

Airline offices In all the following, the first numbers given are downtown offices; a second number refers to the airport office. Aeronica, C 11/13 (☎233-2483; ☎441-1744); Alitalia, C 38, Av 3 (☎222-6138); American, Paseo Colón, C 26/28 (☎257-1266, fax 222-5213; ☎441-1168); Aviateca, at the airport (☎255-4949, fax 223-4238; ☎441-7651); Continental, C 19, Av 2 (☎233-0266, fax 233-4146; ☎442-1904); Copa, C 1, Av 5 (☎223-7033, fax 221-6798; ☎441-4742); Iberia, C 40, Paseo Colón (☎221-3311; ☎442-1932); KLM, C 1, Av 0/1 (☎221-0922, fax 220-3092; ☎442-1922); Lacsa, C 1, Av 5 (☎221-4579); Ladeco (☎641-1444); LTU, Av 9, C 1/3 (☎257-2990); Lufthansa, C 5, Av 7/9 (☎221-7444); Mexicana, C 1, Av 2/4 (☎222-7147 or 1711, fax 222-7847; ☎441-9377); SAM, Av 5, C 1/3 (☎233-3066); Sansa, Av 5, C 1/3 (☎221-5774; ☎441-1064); TACA, C 1, Av 1/3 (☎222-1790; ☎441-5090); United Airlines, Sabana Sur (☎220-2027 or 4844; ☎441-8025); Varig, Av 5, C 1/3 (☎221-3087; ☎441-6244); Viasa, Av 5, C 1/3 (☎231-0033; ☎441-6244).

Banks and exchange Banco de Costa Rica, Av 2, C 4/6 (Mon–Fri 9am–3pm; ☎255-1100); Banco Nacional, Av 0/1, C 2/4. **Private banks** include Bancoop, Av 7, C 3/5 (Mon–Fri 9am–3pm; ☎233-5044); Banco Mercantil, Av 3, C Central/2 (Mon–Fri 9am–3pm; ☎255-3636); Banco Metropolitano, C Central, Av 2 (Mon–Fri 8.15am–4pm; ☎257-3030; Visa only); BANEX, C Central, Av 1 (Mon–Fri 8am–5pm; ☎257-0522; Visa only); Banco de San José, C Central, Av 3/5 (☎221-9911; Visa and Mastercard); Banco del Comercio, 150m north of the Cathedral (☎233-6011; Visa only).

Bookstores San José's best bookstore, the new Libreria Internacional, in barrio Dent, 100m north and 200m east of the Centro Cultural Costarricense-Norteamericano, has the best selection of international fiction, travel books, and fiction in Spanish. Macondo, opposite the entrance to the university in San Pedro, is very good for literature in Spanish, especially from Central America, as well as academic disciplines such as sociology and women's studies. Others include: Book Traders, Av 1, C 3/5, on the second floor in the back of the Omni building (☎255-0528), which has occasional good secondhand finds but is mainly flooded with blockbusters and old *National Geographics*; Chispas, C 7, Av 0/1 (☎223-2240, fax 224-9278), which sells new and secondhand, with the best selection of English-language fiction in town, also a good guide book and Costa Rica section (English/Spanish), plus *New York Times*, *El País* and English-language magazines and a small tour agency in the back; Universal, Av 0, C Central/1 (☎222-2222), which is strong on Spanish books, fiction, titles on Costa Rica (in Spanish), and cartographic maps of the country, and the more downmarket Lehmann, Av 0, C 1/3 (☎223-1212), with a good selection of mass-market fiction and non-fiction in Spanish, with lots of children's books.

Car rental In all the following, the first telephone numbers belong to downtown offices; the last number is the airport office, if it applies. ADA, Av 18, C 11/13 (☎233-7733 or 222-7929; ☎441-1260, fax 233-5555); Adobe, C 7, Av 8/10 (☎221-5425, fax 221-9268); Avis, C 42, Av Las Americas (☎222-6066; in the US ☎1-800/331-1212); Budget, Paseo Colón, C 30 (☎223-3284, fax 255-4966; ☎ & fax 441-4444; in the US ☎1-800/472-3325); Economy, in the Datsun dealership, Sabana Norte (☎231-5410 or 220-1838); Elegante, C 10, Av 13/15, barrio México (☎221-0066 or 233-8605; in the US ☎1-800/582-7432); Hertz, C 38, Paseo Colón (☎223-5959, fax 221-1949; ☎441-9366); National, C 36, Av 7 (☎233-4044, fax 233-2186; ☎441-6533); Prego, Paseo Colón, C 30/32 (☎257-1158 or 221-8689, fax 255-4492); Thrifty, C 3, Av 13 (☎255-4141, fax 223-0660); Tico, Paseo Colón, C 24/26 (☎222-8920, fax 222-1765; ☎443-2078).

Immigration office Costa Rican *migración* is on the airport highway, opposite the Hospital México (Mon–Fri 8am–4pm; take an Alajuela bus and get off at the stop underneath the overhead catwalk). Go early for visa extensions and exit visas. Larger travel agencies can take care of the paperwork for you for a fee (anywhere from US$10 to US$25) – try Tikal Tours (see p.555).

Laundry Burbujas, 50m west and 25m south of the Mas x Menos in San Pedro (Mon–Fri 8am–6pm, Sat 8.30am–5pm; ☎224-9822) is very good, with coin-operated machines; also Lava Más, C 45, Av 8/10, next to *Spoon* in Los Yoses (☎225-1645); Lava y Seca (dry cleaning also), 100m north of Mas x Menos next to Autos San Pedro (☎224-5908); Lavamatic Doña Anna, C 13, Av 16; Sixaola (one of a chain), Av 2, C 7/9 (☎221-2111).

Libraries and cultural centres Biblioteca Nacional, C 15, Av 3; Centro Cultural Costarricense-Norteamericano, 100m north of the Am-Pm supermarket in barrio Dent (Mon–Fri 7am–7pm, Sat 9am–noon; ☎255-9433 for library); Goethe Institut, Av Central across from *Pollos Kentucky* (Mon–Fri 8am–8pm; ☎255-4926); Alianza Francesa, C 5, Av 7 (Mon–Fri 9am–noon & 3–7pm; ☎222-2283) stocks *Le Monde* and some magazines in French. The excellent Friends' Peace Center, C 15, Av 6 bis (☎221-8299) is a wonderful place to drop in and have a cup of coffee and read newspapers. This Quaker-affiliated group works on various fronts for peace in Central America. There are frequent meetings, discussion groups and guest speakers. Drop by and see what is going on.

Photography San José is the only place in the country you should try to get film processed. That said, it's expensive and quality is low: wait until you get home if you can. Bearing in mind these caveats, try Universal, Av 0, C 0/1 (Fuji only, can do 1hr); IFSA, Av 2, C 3/5 (☎223-1444; Kodak only; 1hr).

Post office Correo Central, C 2, Av 1/3, two blocks east and one block north of the Mercado Central (Mon–Fri 7am–5pm, Sat 7am–noon). The *lista de correos* is a safe way to receive mail; they'll hold letters for up to 4 weeks (US$0.20/letter; bring passport).

Supermarkets The best place to buy food, other than the Mercado Central. The excellent Mas x Menos (which means *Mas por Menos* – more for less) stocks mainly Costa Rican brands – cheap towels, umbrellas, plastic containers for storing food and almost anything else under the sun. There are several locations; the best is on Av 0 between C 9 and 11 (open Sun and nightly until 9pm), and there's one in San Pedro, on Av Central. More upmarket is the Muñoz y Nanne complex in San Pedro, where you can buy North American brands at correspondingly higher prices.

Telephone office Radiográfica, C 1, Av 5 (☎287-0087) is a state-run telecommunications shop where you can use directories, make overseas calls, send and receive faxes (☎223-1609 or 233-7932; US$0.75). Unfortunately they now charge US$3 for the use of phones even if you're using a calling card. The ICE (Instituto Costarricense de Electricidad) office next door on Av 5 has the same services at slightly higher prices. Best bet is to buy a telephone card, which can be bought at many stores, Mas x Menos supermarkets, and the like and use it to make international calls from one of the many new card payphones. For more on Costa Rica's telephone system, see p.528.

Travel agents Central American Tours, 150m south of *Aurola Holiday Inn* (☎255-4111, fax 255-4216); is a tour operator (see p.555), and also very good for booking, confirming and changing flights, representing many carriers.

Moving on from San José

San José is the **transportation hub** of Costa Rica. Most bus services, all express bus services, flights and car rental agencies are located here. Wherever you are in the country, technically you are never more than nine hours by highway from the capital, with most places being only four or five hours by road. Eventually, like it or not, all roads lead to San José.

The tables on pp.552–4 deal with **express bus services** from San José. Regional bus information is covered in the relevant accounts. As schedules are given to change, exact departure times are not given here. Details are given where necessary in the accounts of the individual destinations; for a full, current timetable when you arrive, ask at the ICT office (see p.539).

BUS COMPANIES IN SAN JOSÉ

A bewildering number of **bus companies** use San José as their hub: the following is a rundown of their head office addresses, and/or phone numbers and the abbreviations that we use in the tables overleaf.

ALF	Transportes Alfaro, C 14, Av 3/5 (☎222-2750).
BA	Barquero (☎232-5660).
BL	Autotransportes Blanco, C 12, Av 9.
BM	Buses Metropoli (☎272-0651).
CA	CARSOL Transportes, C 14, Av 3/5 (☎221-1968).
CL	Coopelimón, Av 3, C 19/21 (☎223-7811).
CO	Coopecaribeños, Av 3, C 19/21 (☎223-7811).
CQ	Autotransportes Ciudad Quesada, C 16, Av 1/3 (☎255-4318).
EM	Empresa Esquivel (☎666-1249).
ME	Transportes MEPE, Av 11, C Central/1 (☎257-8129).
MO	Transportes Morales, C 16, Av 1/3 (☎223-5567 or 1109).
MRA	Microbuses Rapidos Heredianos, C 1, Av 7/9 (☎238-8392 or 3277).
PU	Pulmitan, C 14, Av 1/3 (☎222-1650; in Liberia ☎666-0458).
S	SIRCA, C 7, Av 6/8 (☎222-5541 or 223-1464).
SA	SACSA, C 5, Av 18 (☎233-5350).
Tica	Ticabus, C 9, Av 4/6 (☎221-8954 or 9229).
TIL	Autotransportes Tilarán, C 14, Av 9/11 (☎222-3854).
TRA	TRALAPA, C 20, Av 1/3 (☎221-7202).
TRC	TRACOPA, Av 18, C 2/4 (☎221-4214 or 223-7685).
TRS	Transtusa, Av 6, C 13 (☎556-0073).
TU	Tuasa, C 12, Av 2 (☎222-5325 or 233-7477).
Tuan	Tuan (☎441-3781).

DOMESTIC BUS SERVICES FROM SAN JOSÉ

The initials in the ☎ column correspond to the bus company that serves this route; see p.551 for telephone numbers. Where advance purchase is mentioned, it is advised, and strongly recommended in the high season (HS), or at weekends; ie from Friday to Sunday (WE). You need buy your ticket no more than one day in advance unless otherwise indicated. NP = National Park; WR = Wildlife Refuge, NM = National Monument.

DESTINATION	FREQUENCY	BUS STOP	DISTANCE	DURATION	☎	ADV. PURCHASE
Alajuela (and airport)	every 5min	Av 2, C 10/12	17km	30min	TU	no
Volcán Arenal *see* Fortuna						
Cahuita	3 daily	Av 11, C 0/1	195km	4hr	ME	yes (HS)
Caño Negro WR *see* Los Chiles						
Cartago	every 10min	C 5, Av 18	22km	45min	SA	no
Los Chiles	2 daily	C 12, Av 7/9	217km	5hr	CQ	no
Playa Coco	2 daily	C 14, Av 1/3	251km	5hr	PU	yes (WE)
Corcovado NP *see* Puerto Jiménez de Osa						
Fortuna	3 daily	C 12, Av 7/9	130km	4hr 30min	BA	yes (HS)
Golfito	2 daily	Av 18, C 2/4	339km	8hr	TRC	yes (3 days)
Guayabo NM *see* Turrialba						
Heredia	every 10min	C 1, Av 7/9	11km	25min	MRA	no
Playa Hermosa	1 daily	C 12, Av 5/7	265km	5hr	EM	no
Volcán Irazú	1 on Sat, 1 on Sun	Av 2, C 1/3	54km	1hr 30min	BM	no (but go early)
Playa Jacó	2 daily	C 16, Av 1/3	102km	2hr 30min	MO	yes (WE)

DESTINATION	FREQUENCY	BUS STOP	DISTANCE	DURATION	☎	ADV/PURCHASE
Liberia	8 daily	C 14, Av 1/3	217km	4hr	PU	no
Limón	14 daily	Av 3, C 19/21	162km	2hr 30min	CL/CO	no
Manuel Antonio NP *see* Quepos						
Monteverde	2 daily	C 14, Av 9/11	167km	3hr 30min	TIL	yes (3–5 days)
Nicoya	8 daily	C 14, Av 3/5	296km	6hr	ALF	no
Nosara	1 daily	C 14, Av 3/5	361km	6hr	ALF	no
Volcán Poás	1 on Sun	C 12, Av 2/4	55km	1hr 30min	TU	no (but go early)
Puerto Jiménez de Osa	2 daily	C 12, Av 7/9	378km	9hr	BL	yes
Puerto Viejo de Sarapiquí	6 daily	Av 11, C 0/1	97km	4hr	check with ICT	no
Puerto Viejo de Talamanca	3 daily	Av 11, C 0/1	210km	4hr 30min	ME	yes
Puntarenas	every 30min	C 16, Av 10/12	110km	2hr	PU	no
Quepos	3 daily	C 16, Av 1/3	145km	3hr 30min	MO	yes (3 days)
Sámara	1 daily	C 14, Av 3/5	331km	6hr	ALF	yes (WE)
San Carlos/Ciudad Quesada	14 daily	C 16, Av 1/3	110km	3hr	CQ	no
Sarchí	34 daily	C 8, Av 0/1	152km	1hr 30min	Tuan	no
La Selva, Selva Verde etc *see* Puerto Viejo de Sarapiquí						
Tamarindo	1 daily	C 14, Av 5	320km	6hr	TRA	yes (WE)
Turrialba	17 daily	C 13, Av 6/8	65km	1hr 30min	TRS	no

INTERNATIONAL BUS SERVICES FROM SAN JOSÉ

Codes given under the ☎ column correspond to the relevant bus company (see p.551). Advance purchase – at least a week in advance, particularly for Managua and Panamá City – is necessary for all routes.

DESTINATION	FREQUENCY	BUS STOP	DISTANCE	DURATION	☎
David, Panamá	2 daily	Av 18, C 2/4	400km	9hr	Tica
Guatemala City (overnight in Managua & El Salvador)	1 daily	Av 4, C 9/11	1200km	60hr	Tica
Managua, Nicaragua	2 daily	Av 4, C 9/11	450km	11hr	Tica
Managua, Nicaragua	Mon,Wed, Fri, Sun	C 7, Av 6/8	450km	13hr	S
Panamá City	2 daily	Av 4, C 9/11	903km	20hr	Tica
Paso Canoas (for Panamá)	7 daily	C 14, Av 5	349km	8hr	TRC
Peñas Blancas (for Nicaragua & Santa Rosa NP)	5 daily	C 16, Av 3/5	293km	6hr	CA
Sixaola (for Panamá)	2 daily	C 0, Av 9/11	250km	6hr	ME
Tegucigalpa, Honduras (overnight in Managua)	1 daily	Av 4, C 9/11	909km	48hr	Tica

DOMESTIC FLIGHTS FROM SAN JOSÉ

Sansa; C 24, Paseo Colón/Av 1
(☎221-9414; reservations ☎233-3258; fax 255-2176).

DESTINATION	FREQUENCY	DURATION
Barra del Colorado	1 daily	30min
Golfito	3 daily	45min
Nosara	1 daily	1hr 25min
Palmar Sur	1 daily	1hr 30min
Puerto Jiménez	1 daily	1hr 15min
Quepos	4 daily	20min
Sámara	1 daily	1hr 45min
Tamarindo	3 daily	40min
Tambor	1 daily	20min
Tortuguero	1 daily	20min

Travelair; Tobías Bolaños airport, Pavas
(☎220-3054 or 232-7883; fax 220-0413).

Golfito	1 daily	1hr 15min
Palmar Sur	1 daily	1hr 30min
Quepos	1 daily (low season)	20min
	3 daily (high season)	20min
Tamarindo	1 daily	40min
Tambor	1 daily	20min
Tortuguero	1 daily	30min

Tours

The Costa Rican tourist boom of the last five years has led to a fast proliferation of **tour operators**. Market research shows that about fifty percent of travellers to Costa Rica arrive with only their return flight and the first few nights of accommodation booked; they then set about planning tours in situ in San José.

Wandering around the city, you face a barrage of tour agencies, and advertisements for tour agencies: if you want to shop around it could take some time to sort yourself out. The operators that we've listed here are experienced, and commendable, offering a good range of services and tours. They are all licensed (and regulated) by the ICT.

Camino Travel, C 1, Av 0/1 (☎257-0107 or 234-2530, fax 257-0243). Young, extremely enthusiastic staff with high standards and a mainly European clientele. Experienced in both upmarket and independent travel; selling individual tours, and booking good-quality accommodation from their range of country-wide contacts. Can also help with bus and transport information and car rental. Convenient downtown office.

Caminos de la Selva, C 38, Av 5, 250m north of Centro Colón (☎255-3486). Contact for serious walkers and birdwatchers, specializing in Volcán Barva, and the other Valle Central volcanos; they also plan itineraries anywhere in the country.

Central American Tours, 150m south of *Aurola Holiday Inn* (☎255-4111, fax 255-4216). Whitewater rafting, hiking, Tortuguero and beach packages. Very friendly, professional staff.

Costa Rica Expeditions, C Central, Av 3 (☎257-0766, fax 257-1665). Longest established of the major tour operators, very often the "ground operators" for overseas tour companies; they have superior accommodation in Tortuguero, Monteverde and Corcovado, superlative guides, tremendous experience and resources. You can drop into their somewhat chaotic downtown office and talk to a consultant about individual tours.

Costa Rica Sun Tours, in Escazú, Av 7, C 3/5 (☎255-3418, fax 255-4410; Aptdo 1195). All-round agency specializing in biking tours in the Valle Central. With good contacts in the Arenal area, including *Arenal Observatory Lodge*, they are also booking agents for *Tiskita Lodge* (near the Panamanian border and Golfito) and surfing contacts in the southwest, near Golfito.

Horizontes, C 28, Av 1/3 (☎222-2022, fax 255-4513). Highly regarded agency known for their intelligent programme concentrating on rainforest walking and hiking, volcanoes and birdwatching, all with an emphasis on natural and cultural history. Specialists in mountain biking and horseback riding also.

OTEC, Paseo Colon (☎255-0554 or 222-6364). Large agency specializing in "adventure" tours including fishing, trekking, surfing and mountain biking, plus hotel reservations and car rentals. One of the few – if not the only – who claim to offer student discounts.

Sansa, C 24, Paseo Colón/Av 1 (☎233-3258, fax 255-2156). Especially good for cheap air/hotel beach package accommodation at Nosara, Sámara, Manuel Antonio and Tamarindo.

Swiss Travel, in the *Hotel Corobici* (☎231-4055, fax 231-3030). Upmarket tour operators with a history of serving European clientele. They also run their own "Banana Train" (see *TAM Travel*, below), that takes you along a section of the old Jungle Train that ran from San José to Limón and back.

TAM Travel, Av 1, C 1/3 (☎222-2642, fax 222-6465). Run the Banana Train (a tourist train from Turrialba to Siquerres). Expensive, catering to an upmarket, mainly North American clientele.

Tikal Tours, Av 2, C 7/9 (☎223-2811, fax 221-1916). Long-standing company with experienced guides, selling packages and individual tours, including trips to Tortuguero, hiking packages and beach holidays. Also diving, surfing, horseback riding, hiking and rafting. Friendly and accommodating; can also help with exit visas.

CHAPTER 28

THE VALLE CENTRAL AND THE HIGHLANDS

C osta Rica's **Valle Central** (literally "Central Valley") is actually an intermountain plateau poised at elevations between 3000 and 4000m. The area covered in this chapter extends to the north, in Alajuela province, to the area around the town of Zarcero, poised nearly at the summit of the Cordillera Central, the central mountain range; to the east it extends to Volcán Barva in Heredia province, and to Turrialba in the southeast and the Orosí valley in the southwest. It's a predominantly agricultural region, with staggered green coffee terraces set in patchwork-quilt fields, loomed over by the blue-black summits of the surrounding mountains. Many of these are **volcanoes**: smoking Poás in the northwest, precipitous Irazú to the southeast and largely dormant Barva and Turrialba in the east. Though there have been no real eruptions since Irazú blew its top in 1963, Poás and Irazú periodically spew, raining a light covering of volcanic ash on the surrounding farmland.

Although it occupies just six percent of the country's total landmass, the Valle Central supports roughly two-thirds of Costa Rica's population. The most fertile land in the country, it is also home to the four most important cities – San José, covered in the previous chapter, and the provincial capitals of **Alajuela**, **Heredia** and **Cartago**. Chief attractions, of course, are the volcanoes, especially **Parque Nacional Irazú** and **Parque Nacional Poás**, and **Volcán Barva**. But there's also **whitewater rafting** on the Río Reventazón near Turrialba.

Most people use San José as a base for forays into the Valle Central; while the **provincial capitals** each have their own strong identity, with the exception of Alajuela – nearer than the capital to the airport – they have little to entice you to linger. If you do want to get out of the city and stay in the Valle Central, the nicest places are the **lodges** and **inns** scattered throughout the countryside.

ALAJUELA AND AROUND

Alajuela province is vast, in Costa Rican terms, extending from **Alajuela** town, 20km northwest of San José, all the way north to the Nicaraguan border and west to the slopes of Volcán Arenal. The account below deals only with that part of the province on the south side of the Cordillera Central, spanning the area from Alajuela itself to the town of Zarcero, 59km northwest, up in the Highlands. **Parque Nacional Volcán Poás** is the area's principal attraction, with some great trails and lakes on its slopes; the ride up to the crater gives good views over the whole densely populated, heavily cultivated province, passing flower-growing *fincas*, fruit farms and the occasional coffee field.

For an explanation of **accommodation price codes**, see p.526.

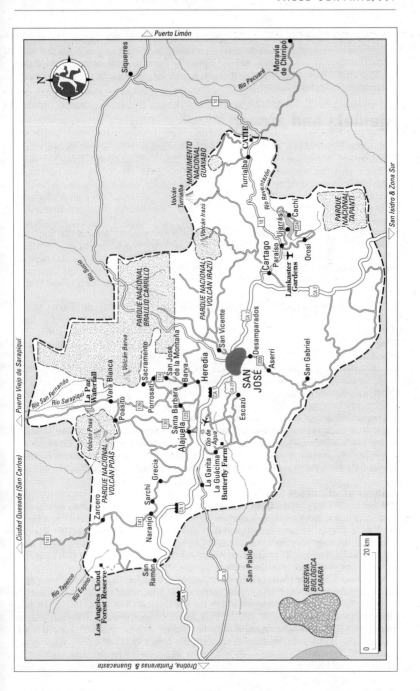

People also head out here to see the crafts factories at **Sarchí**, famous for its coloured wooden ox-carts; **Zoo-Ave**, the exceptional bird sanctuary and zoo just west of town on the way to La Garita; and the **Butterfly Farm** at La Guácima. There's also the little-visited **Los Angeles cloudforest**, a miniature version of the better-known cloudforest at Monteverde (see p.591).

Alajuela and around

With a population of just 35,000, **ALAJUELA**, founded in 1657, is nonetheless Costa Rica's second city. Indeed, on first sight there's little to distinguish it from San José, until the pleasant realization dawns that walking down the street you can smell bougainvillea rather than diesel. The city's few attractions, such as they are, are all less than a minute's walk from the Parque Central. Most impressive is the sturdy-looking whitewashed former jail that houses the **Juan Santamaría Cultural-Historical Museum** Av 3, C Central/2 (Tues–Sun 8am–6pm; free). Alajuela's most cherished historical figure, the drummer-boy-cum-martyr Juan Santamaría, hero of the battle of 1856, sacrificed his life to save the country from the avaricious desires of the American adventurer William Walker (see p.532). The museum's curiously monastic atmosphere is almost more interesting than the small collection, which runs the gamut from mid-nineteenth-century maps of Costa Rica to crumbly portraits of figures involved in the battle of 1856.

Twelve kilometres southwest of Alajuela, **La Guácima Butterfly Farm** (daily 9.30am–4.30pm, last tour at 3.30pm; US$15) breeds valuable pupae for export to zoos and botanical gardens all over the world. The farm also has beautiful views over the Valle Central; in the wet season make sure to go early, as the rain drives butterflies to ensconce themselves, and clouds obscure the views. On a sunny day, however, when the butterflies are active, it's a glorious sight. From Alajuela **buses** marked "La Guácima Abajo" leave from the area southwest of the main bus terminal; the Butterfly Farm is practically the last stop. Buses from San José (2hr) leave from Av 1, C 20/22, daily except Sunday at 11am and 2pm.

The largest aviary in Central America, **Zoo-Ave** (daily 9am–4.30pm; US$4.50), at Dulce Nombre, 5km northeast of La Garita, is just about the best place in the country to see the fabulous and many-coloured birds – especially macaws – of Costa Rica's dense lowland forests and alpine heights. The La Garita bus from Alajuela (15min) passes right by, leaving from the area southwest of the main terminal.

Alajuela practicalities

Red and black Tuasa **buses from San José** arrive at the bus terminus area west of the centre; an inhospitable confusion of stalls, supermarkets and shoe stores. From here, the *Station Wagon Alajuela* drops you off about half a minute's walk from the Parque Central. If **driving**, take the *pista* (General Cañas Highway) to the airport; this is also the road to Puntarenas. The turnoff to Alajuela is 17km from San José – don't use the underpass or you'll end up at the airport.

Alajuela is a quieter place to **stay** than San José, and just 3km from the **airport**; although there is not much choice, the hotels are of good standard. **In town**, *Charly's Albergue*, 200m north and 25m east of the Parque Central (☎ & fax 441-0115; ⑤) has eleven large clean rooms with private bath and hot running water. There is also a lounge with TV and kitchen area; it attracts a mainly gringo crowd. A good budget option is the *Hostel Villa Real*, 100m south of the *correo* (☎441-4022; ③). It's a great place to meet people, rooms are clean and bright with colourful furnishings, and there's a lounge, small kitchen, and library. The only drawbacks are the shared bathroom and noise in the evenings. The friendly *Hotel 1915*, C 2, Av 5/7 (☎441-0495; ④), set in an old house, has rooms arranged around an interior patio with rocking chairs and plants. Though rather dark, they're comfortable, and the private baths, hot water, and free breakfast make this a good mid-range option. The small, friendly *Mango Verde Hostel*, Av 3, C 2/4 (☎ & fax 441-6330; ①–②) has simple rooms, with shared or private bath, and good single rates. There's a shared kitchen and communal TV.

Outside town, a few luxurious country-house style hotels cater to a well-heeled clientele. *La Rana Holandesa*, in Carrizal, 3km from town on the road to San Miguel (☎288-3662, fax 442-1404; ⑤–⑥) has two B&B rooms, with gardens, lovely views, and friendly, knowledgeable owners. *Orquideas Inn*, 5km outside Alajuela on the road to Poás (☎443-9363, fax 443-9740; Aptdo 394, Alajuela; ⑨) is a Spanish hacienda-style country inn with enormous rooms, landscaped gardens, attentive service, and a pool. Children are not permitted. The new, extremely tasteful *Xandari Plantation*, 6.5km north of Alajuela (☎443-2020, fax 442-4847; in US ☎1-800/686-7879; ⑧) is a luxury resort set in an old plantation house near waterfalls just north of town. There is a swimming pool and walking trails on the premises. Low season rates are good value; all include breakfast and airport pickup.

An Alajuela institution, *El Cencerro* on the south side of Parque Central has been around for eighteen years or so and is the only **restaurant** in town with any pretensions, serving succulent beef dishes for US$7. More upscale is *Las Cocinas de Leña*, C 2, Av 6, particularly recommended for filet mignon and chicken cordon bleu, both cooked in a wood stove. For a cheaper meal, try *La Jarra*, C 2, Av 2, a good-value steak restaurant with a nice view from upstairs. The tranquil *Café Alm ibar*, Av Central, C 1/3, is a firm favourite with locals for its pastries and biscuits served with *café con leche*. Located in a 100-year-old adobe house, *Bar la Troja*, Av 3, C 1/3 (☎441-4856) is the most popular **bar** in town, with a courtyard, small garden, gallery area, and even a serpentarium. There's live rock or jazz from Tuesday to Saturday, and they also organize surf and rafting outings.

Moving on, Alajuela's **main bus terminal** is just south of Av 1 between C 8 and 10. Av Central. All services depart from here, including buses to **Naranjo** and **Sarchí** and **local buses** to Grecia and **La Guácima Abajo** for the Butterfly Farm. The terminal is a confusing area, with stops not well marked; ask around to make sure you are waiting at the right place. Buses to **San José** leave from nearby at a stop to the east, close to the corner on C 8 between Av 1 and Central. The fast and frequent red/black Tuasa bus to San José and **Heredia** stops here; even if your bus says "Alajuela–San José", check with the driver if it goes direct to San José or to Heredia first.

Parque Nacional Volcán Poás

PARQUE NACIONAL VOLCÁN POÁS (daily 8am–3pm; US$6) just 55km from San José and 37km north of Alajuela, is one of the most easily accessible active volcanoes in the world, with a history of eruptions that goes back 11 million years. Poás' last gigantic blowout was on January 25, 1910, when it dumped 640,000 tonnes of ash on the surrounding area. At the moment it is comparatively quiet.

You need to get to the volcano before the clouds roll in, which they inevitably do, as early as 10am, even in the dry season (Dec–April). Poás has blasted out three craters in its lifetime: due to more or less constant activity, the appearance of the **main crater** (2704m) is subject to change. At present it's a large area, ripped 1500m wide, filled with murky moss-green water wafting with sulphurous gases. Although it's an impressive sight, you only need about fifteen minutes' viewing and picture-snapping.

The Park features a few very well-maintained, short and unchallenging **trails**, which take you through a strange, otherworldly landscape, dotted with smoking, sizzling fumaroles (steam vents) and tough ferns and trees valiantly holding up against regular sulphurous scaldings. Poás is also home to a rare version of cloudforest called **dwarf** or **stunted cloudforest**, a combination of pine-needle-like ferns, miniature bonsai-type trees, and bromeliad-encrusted cover, all of which has been stunted through an onslaught of cold (it can get down to below freezing up here), continual cloud cover, and acid rain from the mouth of the volcano.

The **Crater Overlook trail**, which, as its name suggests, winds its way around the main crater, is only 750m long, along a paved road. A side trail (1km; 20–30min) heads off through the forest to the pretty, emerald **Botos Lake**, which fills an extinct crater and makes a good spot for a picnic. Named for the pagoda-like tree commonly seen along its way, the **Escalonia trail** (about 1km; 30min) starts at the picnic area (follow the signs), taking you through ground cover less stunted than that at the crater. **Birds** ply this temperate forest: among them the ostentatiously colourful quetzal, the robin, and several species of hummingbird. Although a number of large **mammals** live in the Park, including coyotes and wildcats such as the margay, you're unlikely to spot them. One you probably will come across, however, is the small, green-yellow **Poás squirrel**, which is found nowhere else in the world.

Getting to Volcán Poás

It is possible to get to Poás by public transport, but not ideal; to arrive early enough to be sure of a **cloud-free view** many people rent a car or a taxi, which, added to the admission charge, can hike the price of a visit up to as much as US$60. A weekly private **"tourist bus"** leaves San José at 8am every Sunday from in front of La Merced park on C 12 between Av 2 and 4. This is a small modern minibus, and though theoretically the company – TURASA – puts on another if there is excess demand, in order to secure a seat you should arrive at least an hour (more in the high season) before departure. The **return fare**, which doesn't include the Park fee, is US$4. It arrives at the Park at around 10am, returning to San José at 1.30pm, which theoretically leaves ample time for hiking and crater-viewing – however, as it is common for the crater to be obscured by cloud by 10am, many visitors are left disappointed.

Sunday is by far the most popular day to visit the volcano; to get there mid-week, and avoid the crowds, you'll need to fork out for a **taxi**, as public transport is practically impossible. It will cost between US$25 and US$30, waiting time included; taxis from **San José** charge US$45–50 or so.

The **visitor centre** has an "interpretive exhibit" (videos of the volcano) and a snack shop – hot coffee will be welcome. Better yet is to do as Ticos do and pack a picnic lunch. Bring a sweater and **rain gear** in the rainy season. No **camping** is allowed in the Park.

Accommodation near the park

If you want to get a really early start to guarantee a view of Poás' crater, there are plenty of places to stay in the vicinity. You'll need a car to get to all of them.

Poás Volcano Lodge, 16km from Poás on the road from Poásito, just short of Varablanca (☎482-2194; Aptdo 5723-1000, San José). Working dairy farm, with patches of private protected forest on the grounds and beautifully furnished rooms evoking a combination of English cottage, Welsh farmhouse and American Shaker. ⑥.

La Providencia Ecological Reserve, 1km from the Park entrance on the slopes of Poás (☎232-2498, fax 231-2204). Rustic cabinas on a working dairy farm, near the top of Poás, with spectacular views across to Volcán Arenal and the Talamanca mountains. The owners prepare excellent local food and rent out horses for trots up the volcano. ⑤.

Lo Que tu Quieras ("Whatever you want"), 5km before the Park entrance (☎482-2092). The cheapest option around here. Three small cabinas, with heated water and a restaurant. You can also camp for a small fee. ③.

Sarchí

Touted as the centre of Costa Rican arts and crafts, especially **furniture making**, the village of **SARCHÍ**, 30km northwest of Alajuela, is a commercialized place – firmly on the tourist trail but without much charm. Its setting is pretty enough, between precipitous verdant hills, but don't come expecting to see picturesque scenes of craftsmen sitting in small historic shops; the work is done in factories. The **Sarchí ox-cart** is a kaleidoscopically coloured, painted square cart meant to be hauled by a single ox or team of two oxen. Moorish in origin, the designs can be traced back to immigrants from the Spanish provinces of Andalucía and Granada. Full-scale carts (US$250–300) are rarely sold, but a number of smaller-scale versions are made for tourists (about US$60). Besides the carts, Sarchí tables, bedsteads and **leather rocking chairs** (about US$70) are popular. Besides the shops and factories, the only thing of interest is a bubblegum coloured pink-and-turquoise **church**, looking out from atop the hill in Sarchí Norte (see below).

Practicalities

Sarchí is a spread out place, divided into two halves. Large *fábricas* line the main road from **Sarchí Sur**, in effect a conglomeration of *mueblerías,* to the residential area of **Sarchí Norte**, which climbs the hill. There is really nowhere to **stay** in Sarchí; though you could try the cabinas rented by the hardware store on the main street just above the church in Sarchí Norte: enquire at the "rooms for rent" sign (☎454-4425; ②). For **lunch** or a snack, try the restaurant on the corner of the central plaza; *Soda Donald* beside the soccer field is the only other place for a *refresco* or ice cream. The restaurants in the Mercado de Artesanía are all fine but more expensive than eating in town.

Local **buses** from Alajuela run approximately every thirty minutes from 5am to 10pm. Buses back (via Grecia) can be hailed on the main road. From **San José** an express service (1hr–1hr 30min) runs from La Coca-Cola daily every thirty minutes from 5am to 10pm; the return schedule is the same. You could also take the bus to Naranjo from La Coca-Cola, every hour on the hour, and switch there for a local service to Sarchí. Call the Tuan bus company for information.

The Banco Nacional on the main road beyond the church **changes dollars and cheques** (Mon–Fri 8.30am–3pm), as does a smaller branch in the Mercado de Artesanía. If you need a **taxi** to ferry you back and forth between Sarchí Sur and Sarchí Norte, or to Alajuela or Zarcero, they can be called (☎454-4028) or hailed on the street.

HEREDIA AND AROUND

Heredia province stretches northeast from San José all the way to the Nicaraguan border, skirted on the west by Hwy-9, the old road from San José to Puerto Viejo de Sarapiquí. To the east, the Guápiles Highway, Hwy-32, provides access to Braulio Carrillo and to Limón on the Atlantic coast. The moment you leave San José for **Heredia**, the provincial capital, the rubbery leaves of coffee plants spring up on all sides; in the section of the province covered in this chapter, the land is almost wholly given over to coffee production, and there are a number of popular "**coffee tours**", especially to the *Café Britt finca* near Heredia town.

In the Valle Central, the province's chief attractions are dormant **Volcán Barva**, which offers a good day's climb. Just outside the Park, the **Rainforest Aerial Tram** allows you to see the canopy of primary rainforest from above, causing minimal disturbance to the animals and birds.

Heredia

Just 11km northeast of San José, **HEREDIA** is a lively city, boosted by the student population of the UNA, the Universidad Nacional, at the eastern end of town. The town centre is prettier than most, with a few historical buildings, but that said, Heredia is looking
a bit run-down these days. It's a natural jumping-off point for excursions to the nearby historical hamlet of **Barva** and to the town of **San José de la Montaña**, a gateway to **Volcán
Barva**. Many tourists also come to sample the **Café Britt tour**, hosted by the nation's
largest coffee exporter, about 3km north of the town centre.

Arrival, information and accommodation

From **San José** Microbuses Rapidos Heredianos leave every ten minutes from 5am to
10pm. Another bus runs from C 12, Av 2 (every 20min), and after 10pm a night bus
leaves from the marked stop at Av 2, C 4/6. Buses pull in to Heredia at the corner of
C Central and Av 4, a stone's throw south of the Parque Central.

There is no **tourist office** in town. Banco Nacional at C 2, Av 2/4 (Mon–Fri
8.30am–3.30pm), Banco Interfin Av 4, C 0/2 and Banco Popular Av 0, C 1/3 **exchange
currency** and travellers' cheques. The **correo** is on the northwest corner of the
Parque Central (Mon–Fri 7.30am–5.30pm). **Taxis** line up on the east side of the
Mercado Central, between Av 6 and 8.

Decent **accommodation** in downtown Heredia is pretty sparse. It's unlikely, in any
case, that you will need to stay in town; San José is within easy reach, and nearby there
are some nice **B&Bs** as well as a couple of "**country resort**" type hotels, including one
of the finest in the country. Although they are all accessible by bus, it's easier to drive.

Hotel America, C 0 opposite the San José bus stop (☎260-9292). Probably the best place to stay in
town, with clean, if soulless, rooms. Some are a bit dark, but all have fan, TV, and hot water bathroom. Free local calls and airport pick-up service. ⑤.

Verano, at the western entrance of the Mercado Central (☎237-1616). Downtown budget option;
cheap and very friendly, but the beds and walls are flimsy. ①.

Finca Rosa Blanca, on the road between San Pedro de Barva and Santa Barbara de Heredia
(☎269-9392, fax 269-9555). One of the best hotels in the country, set in the coffee fields. Eight
themed suites; the famous Tower Suite, with wraparound windows and a romantic four-poster, is
continuously booked. Pool in the offing, but no TV (the idea is to relax). Excellent cuisine – Cuban,
Californian and French – by hotel's own chef. Meals and tax included in package rates. ⑨.

Los Jardines B&B, 2km north of the Parque Central, before Barva village (☎260-1904). A good
bet just outside town; comfortable rooms in a modern house with hot water and shared bath. Very
friendly family owners will arrange airport pick-up. ⑤.

La Posada de la Montaña, San Isidro de Heredia, 8km northeast of Heredia (☎ & fax 268-8096;
in USA c/o PO Box 308, Greenfield, MO 65661). Rustic, comfortable rooms at varying prices. Some
are suites with cable TV, kitchen, living room and fireplace (it gets chilly up here). Airport pick-up
on request. ⑥–⑦.

The Town

Heredia's layout conforms to the general Costa Rican pattern, centring on a **Parque
Central** and church. The Parque Central is quiet, draped with huge mango trees and
palms; its plain **Basílica de la Inmaculada Concepción**'s "seismic Baroque" architecture has kept it standing through several earthquakes since 1797. The call of the
country's independence was supposed to have rung out from the bell in its tower.
North of the Parque, the old colonial tower of **El Fortín**, "The Fortress", features odd
gun slats, which fan out and widen from the inside to the exterior, giving it a medieval
look. You cannot enter or climb the tower.

East on Avenida Central, the **Casa de la Cultura**, an old colonial house with a large verandah, displays local art, including sculpture and painting by the schoolchildren of Heredia (daily 9am–5pm; free).

Eating and drinking

Perhaps because of the student population, Heredia is crawling with excellent cafés, patisseries, ice-cream joints and the best vegetarian/health food **restaurants** outside San José. **Nightlife** is low-key, restricted to a few local salsa spots. If you're young or studently inclined, head for the four blocks immediately to the west of the Universidad Nacional – this is where you'll find the best bars in Heredia.

Azzura Italiana, southwest corner of Parque Central. Upmarket café with superior Italian ice cream, excellent *refrescos naturales*, real cappuccino, espresso, and fresh sandwiches.

El Bulevar, C 7, Av 0/2. Although student-oriented, El Bulevar is without a doubt *the* place in Heredia to go out. Open to the street, good for student-watching, cheap beer-and-boca specials.

Restaurante París, C 5, Av 0/2 (☎238-1721). Lovely French place with a daily changing lunch menu (French cuisine, with barbecue on Sunday). Try to sit in the small garden out back. There is a reading corner with some travel literature. Tues–Sun 11am–10pm.

Vishnu's Mango Verde, C 7, Av Central/1. Part of the chain that includes the famous downtown San José vegetarian place, this "green mango" Vishnu has plant-adorned decor, a garden back area and wooden, rustic decor. Good vegetarian food; sandwiches made to order, yoghurt, sweets and coffee. Lunch only Mon–Fri.

Around Heredia

North and east of Heredia the terrain climbs to higher altitudes, reaching its highest point at **Volcán Barva**, at the western entrance of the wild, rugged **Parque Nacional Braulio Carrillo**. Temperatures are notably cooler around here, the landscape dotted with dairy farms and conifers. The towns around here – **Barva**, **Santa Barbara de Heredia** and **San Joaquín de Heredia** – are favoured by expats as pleasant places to live but there's little to detain the visitor.

Rainforest Aerial Tram

The invention of American naturalist Donald Perry, the **Rainforest Aerial Tram** lies just beyond the eastern boundary of Braulio Carrillo (5km east of Río Sucio; Tues–Sun 6am–3.30pm, Mon 9am–3.30pm; US$50). The product of many years' research, most of it carried out at nearby Rara Avis in the Zona Norte (see p.641), the tram is an innovation in rainforest tourism, the first of its kind in the world. Twenty **overhead cable cars**, each holding five passengers and one guide, run slowly along the 1.7km aerial

MOVING ON FROM HEREDIA

Heredia has no central bus terminal. A variety of **bus stops**, marked and signed, are scattered around town, with a heavy concentration around the Mercado Central. Buses **to San José** depart from C Central, Av 4 (about every 10min).

From the Mercado Central, local buses leave for **San Joaquín de Heredia**, **San Isidro de Heredia** and the swimming complex at **Ojo de Agua**. Buses to **San Rafael de Heredia** and on to **San José de la Montaña** depart from near the train tracks at Av 10 and C Central/2. For **Barva** and **Santa Barbara de Heredia** the stop is at C Central, Av 1/3. All leave fairly regularly, about every thirty minutes.

track, skirting the tops of the forest and passing between trees, providing eye-level encounters along the way. The ride affords a rare glimpse of birds, animals and plants, including the epiphytes, orchids, insects and mosses that live inside the upper reaches of the forest and, largely silent, it is less likely to frighten the animals. However don't come expecting to see particular animals. Surrounding the tram track is a 3.5 square - kilometres **private reserve** used by researchers to study life in the rainforest canopy.

Practicalities

Less than an hour from San José, and easily accessible, the aerial tram turnoff is on the northeast border of Braulio Carrillo, 5.3km beyond the (signed) bridge over the Río Sucio, on the right hand side. From the turnoff it's another 1500m. To get there **by bus**, catch the Guápiles service and ask the driver to drop you at the entrance. The return Guápiles–San José bus will stop when flagged down, unless full. It is advisable to wear a hat, insect repellent, and bring binoculars, camera and rain gear.

You can stop by the office in Central San José at the corner of Av 7 and C 7 (☎257-5961, fax 257-6053) to reserve a place. Most San José travel agencies offer **one-day trips** to the tram for about US$60, including pick-up at all the major hotels. Currently this fee allows you as many tram rides as you like (45min each way) and access to the ground trails. Special early-morning birdwatching trips and torchlit night rides (until 9pm) will soon be added – many canopy inhabitants become active and visible only in the dark.

North of Heredia to Volcán Barva

Unique in Costa Rica, the **Museo de La Cultura Popular** (Thurs–Sun 9am–5pm; US$1.50), some 2km north of Heredia, tries to give an authentic portrayal of nine-teenth- and early twentieth-century campesino life. Set in a large verandahed house in landscaped coffee fields, the museum has preserved the kitchen as it would have been on a coffee finca. There you can eat authentic food of the period, including *torta de arroz, pan casero,* and *gallos picadillos.* Otherwise there is little to do other than to wander around the house and the carefully kept gardens.

The colonial village of **BARVA**, about 1km further on, is really only worth a brief stop on the way to Volcán Barva to have a look at the huge cream **Baroque church**, flanked by tall brooding palms, and the surrounding adobe-and-tiled-roof houses. Though Barva was founded in 1561, most of what you see today dates from the 1700s. *Soda Chaporro* sells ice cream and *refrescos* and has a small patio facing the soccer field – **buses** to San José de la Montaña (for the volcano) stop out front.

On the way north from Heredia to Barva, look out for the signs to the **Café Britt finca**, 1km south of Barva (daily tours at 11am & 3pm; US$15). The finca produces one of the country's best-known coffee brands and is the most important exporter of Costa Rican coffee to the world. Costumed guides take you through the history of coffee growing in Costa Rica, demonstrating how crucial this export crop was to the development of the country, with a rather slick multi-media presentation and thorough descriptions of the process involved in harvesting and selecting the beans. It all ends on a free tasting and, of course, the inevitable stop in the gift shop; they can pack and mail coffee to the US. The finca is signed on the road between Heredia and Barva and offers a pick-up from most San José hotels for US$7.

Parque Nacional Braulio Carrillo and Volcán Barva

Since the main trails were recently closed due to mudslide damage and an increasing crime problem, the only way to experience the bulk of **PARQUE NACIONAL BRAULIO CARRILLO**, 20km northeast of San José is from the window of a bus on the way to the Atlantic coast. Named after Costa Rica's third, rather dictatorial, chief of state, who held office in the mid-1800s, the Park was established in 1978, mainly to protect the land from the possible effects of the Guápiles Highway that was then in construction between San José and Limón. This view of Braulio Carrillo's dense forested cover gives you a good idea of what much of Costa Rica used to look like about fifty years ago, when approximately three-quarters of the country's total terrain was virgin rainforest.

The only accessible part of the Park is dormant **Volcán Barva** (daily 8am–3pm; US$6), a popular destination for walkers and climbers. Although it is close to Heredia, it is difficult to reach due to lack of public transport and a bad stretch of road just before you reach the volcano that requires a 4WD, even in the dry season. The **main trail** (3km; about 1hr) up Barva's slopes begins at the village of Porrosatí (also shown on some maps and buses as "Paso Llano"), at the western edge of Braulio Carrillo, ascending through dense deciduous cover, climbing 3000m before reaching the **cloudforest** at the top. Along the way you'll get panoramic views over the Valle Central and southeast to Volcán Irazú; if you're lucky – bring binoculars – you might see the elusive, jewel-coloured quetzal (though these nest-bound birds are usually only seen at their preferred altitude of 3600m or more). It's easy to get lost on Barva. Take a compass, water and food, a sweater and raingear – and leave early in the morning to enjoy the clearest views of the top. Be prepared for serious mud in the rainy season.

Practicalities

Daily **buses** (around 6.30am, 11am & 4pm) run from Heredia to San José de la Montaña, 4km away, and on to Porrosatí, another 16km further. At Porrosatí signs point to the **Barva** *puesto*, gateway to the volcano; it's about 2km from the bus stop. Bus drivers will help with directions – ask before getting off. The only convenient bus from Porrosatí back to Heredia leaves at 5pm, though there is also one at 1pm. Otherwise it's a case of getting a taxi – ask in either of the restaurants mentioned below, or in the village.

Robles Tours (☎237-2116, fax 237-1976) offer a very pretty horse ride in the area around Sacramento, just outside the Park boundary, including a lunch at their own country *posada*. They lay on coffee, naturalist guides and, if the weather is good, will take you up to the pristine crater lake, Lago Barva. **Tours** run when there is enough demand to put a group together – it may be difficult to go during the wet season.

There are a number of good, if pricey, **places to stay** around Volcán Barva; *Cabañas de la Montaña Cypresal*, in San José de la Montaña (☎221-6455, fax 221-6244; ⑦), has rustic, very comfortable rooms, with fireplace and private bath, plus a small pool and restaurant. Bigger is the *Sacramento Lodge*, also known as *Albergue y Restaurante Los Robles* (☎237-2116, fax 237-1976; ④), which is signed as being 2km from the road to Porrosatí. You need a good sturdy 4WD to get up this road. They offer hiking and horseback riding at US$22 a day including guide.

About 4km up the road to San José de la Montaña, *El Refugio de Chef Jacques,* set in a rustic chalet-type building, with stunning views. serves vaguely French food in excellent sauces (rare for Costa Rica). If you want to stock up on energy immediately before climbing, two small Porrosatí **restaurants** serve *típico* food: the *Campesino*, about 3.5km beyond Porrosatí and the *Sacramento* about 500m or so further on. Beyond here the road is in poor shape; any vehicle other than a tough jeep should probably be left at one of the restaurants.

CARTAGO AND AROUND

With land made fertile by the deposits from Volcán Irazú, **Cartago province** extends east of San José and south into the Cordillera de Talamanca. The section covered in this chapter is a heavily populated, farmed and industrialized region, centring on **Cartago** town, a major shopping and transportation hub for the southern Valle Central, and home to Costa Rica's most famous church, the fat Byzantine **Basílica de Nuestra Señora de Los Angeles**. The town itself is seldom used as a place to stay, however, and many of the Valle Central attractions are visited on day trips from San José. Most popular is **Volcán Irazú**, but there's also the mystically lovely **Orosí valley**, the orchid collection at **Lankaster Gardens**, and the wild, little-visited **Parque Nacional Tapantí**.

About forty minutes by car from San José on a good divided toll highway, Cartago has road connections to Turrialba on the eastern slopes of Irazú, Parque Nacional Tapantí and the Orosí valley, and south via the Interamericana over the hump of the Cordillera Central to San Isidro and the Valle de el General.

Cartago

CARTAGO, meaning "Carthage", was Costa Rica's capital for three hundred years before the centre of power was moved to San José in 1823. Founded in 1563 by Juan Vazquez de Coronado, like its ancient namesake the city has been razed a number of times, although in this case by **earthquakes** instead of Romans – two, in 1823 and 1910, conspired to practically demolish the place. Most of the fine nineteenth-century and fin-de-siècle buildings were destroyed, and what has grown up in their place – the usual haphazard assortment – is not particularly appealing, although the town does have a pretty **Parque Central** centring on a ruined church (*Las Ruinas*). Originally built in 1575, **Iglesia de la Parroquía**, destroyed by a number of earthquakes, was stubbornly rebuilt by Cartagoans every time, until eventually the giant earthquake of 1910 vanquished it for good. Only the elegantly tumbling walls remain, enclosing pretty subtropical gardens. From the ruins it's a walk of five minutes east to Cartago's only other attraction: the **cathedral**, properly named **Basílica de Nuestra Señora de Los Angeles**, at C 16 and Av 2. Casualty of a 1926 earthquake, the basilica was rebuilt soon after, in a decorative Byzantine style.

Practicalities

SACSA runs frequent local **buses** to Cartago from San José (40–45 min). You can also pick up a stopping service from any of the stops on Av 2 past C 19 or so – they run along Av Central and out through San Pedro. Like the other provincial capitals in the Valle Central, Cartago has no **tourist office**. Banco de Costa Rica, Av 4, C 5/7 (Mon–Fri 8.30am–3.30pm, with a stop for lunch) and Banco Nacional, C 3, Av 2 (same hours), will change **travellers' cheques** but it's bound to take a while. The **correo** is at C 1, Av 2/4 (Mon–Fri 7.30am–5pm). **Taxis** leave from the rank at *Las Ruinas*.

As for **staying** in Cartago: to put it bluntly, don't. While the widespread claim that Cartago hotels do little but turn over beds by the hour may be overstated, it's not too far from the truth, and there is, at the time of writing, nowhere "suitable" for tourists to stay. Getting stuck in Cartago overnight is an unlikely scenario, however, as there is 24-hour bus service to San José. There are few **restaurants**, and certainly nowhere remarkable. The town does, however, boast several good **pastry shops**, where you can grab something to take out and eat on one of the benches in front of the basilica. *Pastelería el Nido*, C 12, Av 4, 200m west of the basilica is one of the nicest, with superior pastries and pies, plus delicious moist carrot cake. For cheap salad-and-pizza lunches, there's a *Pizza Hut* at C 2, Av 2/4.

To get back to **San José**, hop on whichever bus happens to be loading up in the covered area on Av 4, C 2/4. Buses leave every ten minutes between 5am and midnight, and about every hour otherwise. Local buses are frequent and reliable; for **Paraíso** use the stop on the south side of Las Ruinas; for **Orosí** catch a bus at C 4, Av 1, and for **Cachí** and **Ujarras**, the bus leaves from C 6, Av 1/2 (roughly hourly 5am–4pm).

Around Cartago

Dominating the landscape, **Volcán Irazú**, part of the mighty Cordillera Central, is the most popular excursion in Cartago province. Less visited and fairly off the beaten track, **Parque Nacional Tapantí**, recently upgraded from its former Wildlife Refuge status, is one of the closest places to San José for rainforest hiking; if you have your own transport, it makes a good day excursion or weekend trip.

On the eastern slopes of the Cordillera Central, not officially in the Valle Central, the small town of **Turrialba** is something of a local hub for watersports, with Ríos Reventazón and Pacuaré, two of the best **whitewater rafting** rivers in the country, nearby. Turrialba has also become a small centre for river kayaking – whitewater kayaking, in effect – with one or two specialist tour operators in town. In addition, the town is the gateway to **Monumento Nacional Guayabo**, the most important ancient site in Costa Rica. A good two hours from San José, both are best reached via Cartago.

Parque Nacional Volcán Irazú

The blasted-out lunar landscape of **PARQUE NACIONAL VOLCÁN IRAZÚ** (daily 8am–4pm; US$6) is dramatic, reaching its highest point at 3432m and giving fantastic views on clear days to the Atlantic coast. The inactive **Diego de la Haya crater** is a creepily impressive sight, its deep depression filled with a strange algae-green lake.

Some 32km north of Cartago, a journey that is almost entirely uphill, the volcano makes for a long but scenic trip, especially early in the morning, before the inevitable **clouds** roll in. There is little to actually *do* in the Park after viewing the crater from the mirador; there are no official trails, though it is possible to clamber along the scraggly slopes of a few outcroppings and dip into grey-ash sand dunes.

Practicalities

A visit to Irazú is strictly for **day-trippers** only: there is nowhere to stay within the Park, and camping is not allowed on the slopes. As with Volcán Poás, only one **public excursion bus** runs to the Park, at weekends and on all public holidays, leaving from in front of San José's *Gran Hotel Costa Rica* (information on ☎272-0651 or 551-9795, fax 272-2948). The "Volcano Express", a yellow schoolbus emblazoned with a psychedelic "Irazú", leaves at 8am sharp; get there an hour early to be sure of a seat. The bus picks up passengers at **Cartago** (from *Las Ruinas*) at 8.30am. Return fare is about US$4 from San José and US$2.25 from Cartago, not including the Park entrance fee.

The bus pulls in at the crater parking area, where there are toilets, information and a **snack wagon** serving sandwiches and welcome steaming cups of coffee (it can get cold at the summit – bring a sweater). Tico families bring picnics and set up lunch at the tables provided, determined in the face of the chilly temperatures, but they tend to look pretty shivery. At about 1pm the bus sets off back to San José. You can also get to Irazú on any number of half-day **tours** run by travel agencies in San José; whisking you back and forth in a private modern minibus, they cost around US$45, not including the entrance fee.

Lankaster Gardens

Orchids are the main attraction at **Lankaster Gardens** (daily 8.30am–3.30pm; US$3), a tropical garden and research station 6km southeast of Cartago. While there are always some in bloom at any given time, the wet season (May–Nov) is less rewarding than the dry; March and April are the best months. To get to the gardens by **bus from**

San José, take the Cartago service, get off at *Las Ruinas*, and change to a Paraíso. Get off when you see the very pink *Casa Vieja* restaurant, little more than ten minutes out of town. A gravel road stretches off to your right, with an orange sign for the gardens: it's a one-kilometre walk along this road, turning right at the fork.

Turrialba and around

Though the pleasant agricultural town of **TURRIALBA**, 45km east of Cartago on the eastern slopes of the Cordillera Central, has sweeping views over the rugged eastern Talamancas, there's little to keep you here long. Tourists are most likely to see it as part of a trip to the archeological monument of **Guayabo**, or even more likely, on the way to a **whitewater rafting** or **kayaking** trip on the Ríos Reventazón or Pacuaré. Many of the mountain-lodge-type hotels nearby have guided walks or horseback rides up dormant **Volcán Turrialba**, which, with its lack of trails, is otherwise inaccessible to casual or independent visitors.

Monumento Nacional Guayabo

The most accessible ancient archeological site in Costa Rica, **MONUMENTO NACIONAL GUAYABO** lies 19km northeast of Turrialba and 84km from San José (daily 8am–3.30pm; US$6). Discovered by explorer Anastasio Alfaro at the end of the nineteenth century, Guayabo was only excavated in the late 1960s. It belongs to the archeological/cultural area known as **Intermedio**, which begins roughly in the province of Alajuela and extends to Venezuela, Colombia and parts of Ecuador. Archeologists believe that Guayabo was inhabited from about 1000 BC to 1400 AD; most of the heaps of stones and basic structures now exposed were erected between 300 and 700 AD. The central mound is the tallest circular base unearthed so far, with two staircases and pottery remains on the very top.

Getting to Guayabo by bus entails a stay of two nights. Best to take a taxi from Turrialba ($20 including waiting time). Green Tropical Tours, Aptdo 675-2200, San José (☎ & fax 255-2859) offer a **day-trip** to the monument, including pick-up at a San José hotel, breakfast, guided tour, lunch in Turrialba and a visit to Cartago's basilica.

Accommodation

While Turrialba isn't yet really a tourist town, it has some perfectly decent **places to stay**, from simple hotel rooms in town to the considerably more expensive "mountain lodges" nearby, which offer luxurious rooms, good home-cooked food (which usually costs extra), guided treks and horseriding.

Some of the accommodation listed below is at a **higher altitude** than Turrialba's pleasantly refreshing hillside position; bring a sweater or light jacket.

Albergue la Calzada, 500m before the entrance to Monumento Nacional Guayabo (☎556-0465, fax 556-0427). Large country house, with rustic, very comfortable rooms and excellent local food. The friendly owners know the area well and can advise on excursions. ③.

Albergue de Montaña Pochotel, 2km from Turrialba. Simple accommodation and *típico* food in an astounding situation with volcano views in all directions. Camping also allowed. ③.

Casa Turire, 20km southeast of Turrialba (☎531-1111, fax 531-1075). Country-resort-type place with pool, golf course, horseback riding and tours. Lovely views of the Río Reventazón. ⑧.

Interamericano, southeast edge of Turrialba, near the old train station (☎556-0142). Basic, clean and very friendly, with a kitchen where you can cook snacks. The proprietor can hook you up with sea kayaking tours. The best budget deal in town. ②.

Turrialtico Lodge, 7.5km from Turrialba on the road to Limón (☎ & fax 556-1111; Aptdo 121 7150, Turrialba). An upscale comfortable lodge. The manager, Hector Lezama, runs tours to Volcán Irazú and the Río Reventazon. Twelve rooms in wooden cabinas, all with private bath and hot water. Prices include breakfast and supper. ④–⑤.

Turrialba Volcano Lodge, on the flanks of Volcán Turrialba (☎ & fax 273-4335; Aptdo 1632-2050, San José). Quiet, modern, simply furnished farmhouse, with six rooms with private bath; accessible over a badly rutted road, 4WD only (call for directions). Ox-cart rides, horseback tours to the Turrialba crater with Spanish-speaking guides, and hotel pick-ups from San José. ⑦.

Wagelia, Av 4, Turrialba, just beyond the gas station on the way in from Cartago (☎556-1566, fax 556-1596). Small, clean, comfortable rooms with TV, refrigerator and phone. Popular and often full – ring in advance to reserve. ④.

travel details

BUSES

San José to: Alajuela (constant; 20min); Cartago (constant; 40min); La Guacima Abajo, for the Butterfly Farm (2 express daily except Sun; 40min); Heredia (constant; 15min); San Pedro de Poás (1 weekly; 1hr 30min); Sarchí (17 daily; 1hr 30min); Turrialba (17 daily; 1hr 30min); Volcán Irazú (1 on Sat & Sun; 1hr 30min); Volcán Poás (1 weekly; 2hr); Zarcero (12 daily; 2hr).

Alajuela to: La Guacima Abajo, for the Butterfly Farm (4 daily; 20min); San José (constant; 20min); Sarchí (constant; 1hr); Zoo-Ave (constant; 15min).

Cartago to: Lankaster Gardens (every 30min; 10min); Paraíso (every 1hr 30min Mon–Fri, hourly Sat & Sun; 30min); San José (constant; 40min).

Heredia to: San José (constant; 15min); Volcán Barva, via San José de la Montaña (3 daily Mon–Sat, 2 daily Sun; 1hr).

Sarchí to: Alajuela (constant; 1hr); San José (17 daily; 1hr 30min).

Turrialba to: Guayabo (1 daily Mon–Fri; 1hr+); San José (17 daily; 1hr 30min).

Volcán Barva to: Heredia, via San José de la Montaña (3 daily Mon–Sat, 2 daily Sun; 1hr).

Volcán Poás to: San José (1 weekly; 2hr).

CHAPTER 29

LIMÓN PROVINCE AND THE ATLANTIC COAST

S parsely populated **Limón province** sweeps south in an arc from Nicaragua down to Panamá. Hemmed in to the north by dense jungles and swampy waterways, to the west by the mighty Cordillera Central and to the south by the even wider girth of the Cordillera Talamanca, Limón can feel like a lost, end-of-theworld place. Here you can watch gentle giant sea **turtles** lay their eggs on the waveraked beaches of **Tortuguero**; snorkel coral reefs at **Cahuita** or Punta Uva; surf at **Puerto Viejo**; drift along the **jungle canal** from Tortuguero to Barra del Colorado, a major sportsfishing destination, or try animal- and bird-spotting in the many **mangroves**. The interior is criss-crossed by the powerful Río Reventazón and Río Pacuaré, two of the best rivers in the Americas for **whitewater rafting**.

Although Limón remains an unknown for the majority of visitors – especially those on package tours – it holds much appeal for eco-tourists and off-the-track travellers. The province has the highest proportion of **protected land** in the country, from **Refugio Nacional de Fauna Silvestre Barra del Colorado** on the Nicaraguan border, to **Refugio Nacional de Vida Silvestre Gandoca-Manzanillo** near Panamá in the extreme south – though it has to be said that the Wildlife Reserves and National Parks offer only mitigated resistance to the considerable threats presented by full-scale fruit farming, logging, mining and tourism.

More than anywhere else in Costa Rica, the Atlantic coast exudes a **cultural diversity**, a feeling of community and a unique and complex local history. The only town of any size, **Puerto Limón**, is a lively if jaded port town, with a large (mostly Jamaicandescended) **Afro-Caribbean** population. In the south, near the Panamanian border, live several communities of indigenous peoples from the **Bribrí** and **Cabécar** groups.

There are few options when it comes to **getting around** Limón province. From San José to Puerto Limón you have a choice of just two roads, while from Puerto Limón south to the Panamá border at Sixaola there is but one narrow and badly repaired route (not counting the few small local roads leading to the banana *fincas*). North of Puerto Limón there is no public land transport at all: instead, private *lanchas* ply the coastal canals connecting the port of Moín, 8km north of Puerto Limón, to Río Colorado near the Nicaraguan border. There are also several scheduled **flights** a week from San José to Barra. A good, frequent and quite reliable **bus** network operates in the rest of the province, with the most efficient and modern routes from San José to Puerto Limón and to Sixaola. **English** is spoken widely along the coast, not just in Limón but also in Tortuguero, due to the many Miskito-descended people from Nicaragua who were taught English in school.

For an explanation of **accommodation price codes**, see p.526.

It is very **wet** all year round, with a small dry spell in January and February. South of Limón, September and October offer the best chance of rainlessness.

Puerto Limón

Once the Atlantic Coast's principal port, today **PUERTO LIMÓN**, 165km east of San José, has a somewhat neglected air. There has been little activity at the harbour since the big-time banana boats started loading at **Moín**, 8km up the headland toward Tortuguero; to make things worse, the city was ravaged by the 1991 earthquake, which left a trail of wrecked buildings in its wake. All in all, the place does have the rough edges characteristic of a Caribbean port, and while the scare stories Highland Ticos gleefully tell of the place are a bit exaggerated, it's worth watching your back. Generally speaking, tourists come to Limón for one of three reasons: to get a boat to **Tortuguero** from Moín, to get a bus south to the **beach towns** of Cahuita and Puerto Viejo, or to join the annual Carib-fest and Carnaval-like celebration of **El Día de la Raza** (Columbus Day) during the week preceding October 12.

RESTAURANTS & BARS

Bars	A
Maribú Caribe	B
Pizzería Il Macarrone	G
Restaurante Mares	F
Soda Doña Toda	E
Soda La Estrella	D
Restaurante Tia María	C

ACCOMMODATION

Apartments Cocori	1
Hotel Linda Vista	5
Hotel Nuevo Internacional	2
Hotel/Restaurante Park	3
Hotel Teté	4

PUERTO LIMÓN

Arrival and information

Of the two roads from the capital to Puerto Limón, the **Guápiles Highway** (Hwy-32) is one of the best-maintained in the country, beginning in San José at the northern end of C 3, and climbing out of the Highlands to the northeast. Travelling this way, you're in Puerto Limón in around three hours. The narrower, older route, Hwy-10, often called the **Turrialba road**, runs through Turrialba on the eastern slopes of the Cordillera Central; it's considered dangerous and difficult to drive, and carries very little traffic.

Arriving in Limón can be unnerving at night; best get here in daylight if only to orientate yourself. Coopelimón and Coopecaribeños **buses** do the **San José–Limón** run, starting at 5am and continuing hourly until 7pm (2hr 30min–3hr). You should buy your ticket a day in advance if travelling on a Friday or Sunday; more during Carnaval, when extra buses are laid on. Buses come into town from San José along Av 1, parallel to the docks and the old railroad tracks, pulling in at Limón's main bus station 100m east and 50m south of the mercado. Arrivals **from the south** – Cahuita, Puerto Viejo and Panamá (via Sixaola) – disembark at the Transportes MEPE stop at C 3, Av 4, 100m north of the mercado. Buses from **Moín** pull in at C 4, Av 4, near the landmark *Radio Casino*.

For **information** on the Atlantic coast, you'll need to contact the San José ICT (☎222-1090): there is no official tourist office in the entire province. Tour agencies can provide basic information, however, and you could try the Hellenik souvenir shop, 200m north of the mercado. For **exchange facilities** Banco de Costa Rica, Av 2, C 3/4 (Mon–Fri 8am–noon & 1–5pm), across from the mercado, or Banco de San José, Av 4, C 2/3 (same hours) are open during the week; at weekends try a large hotel like the *Maribú Caribe*. **Mail service** from Limón is dreadful – you're better off posting things from San José. However, if you're desperate, the *correo* is at Av 3, C 3 (Mon–Fri 8am–5pm). If you have a new chip phone card you can use it (for international calls, too) in the **payphones** clustered at the south side of the mercado. Note that during **Carnaval** everything shuts for a week, making banking and posting impossible. Should you need **medical care**, head for Hospital Dr Tony Facio Castro, at the north end of the malecón (☎758-2222).

While Limón is not quite the mugger's paradise it is sometimes portrayed to be in the Highland media, standing on the sidewalk and looking lost is not recommended, nor is carrying valuables (most of the hotels in our list have safes). As opposed to other Costa Rican towns, Limón's avenidas run more or less east–west in numerical order, starting at the docks. Calles run north–south, beginning with C 1 on the western boundary of Parque Vargas, by the malecón.

Accommodation

It's worth shelling out a bit for a **room** in Limón, especially if travelling solo. It's no secret that the diviest places (none listed here) turn over beds by the hour. None of the places listed below is rock-bottom cheap. If this is what you're after, you'll find it easily enough; but always ask to see the room first and make sure to inspect the bathroom. The better places fill quickly at weekends. If you're arriving on a Friday, call or fax ahead.

Staying **downtown** keeps you in the thick of things, and many hotels have communal balconies, perfect for relaxing with a cold beer above the goings on in the street below. If you want to hear waves lapping in the breeze, your best bet is the *Park Hotel*, which stands on a little promontory all its own, quite close to the sea. The most upscale hotels are outside town, about 4km up the spur road to Moín, at **Portete** and the small **Playa Bonita**. In all but the most upscale places, avoid drinking the **tap water**, or use a filter or chlorine tablets.

Hotel prices rise by as much as fifty percent for **Carnaval** week, and to a lesser extent during *Semana Santa*, or Easter week, and between July and October. December, January and February which (confusingly) are elsewhere in the country considered high season, are the cheapest times to come.

In town

Linda Vista, Av 2, C 4/5 (☎758-3359). Rooms are dark and walls flimsy, but this colourful, clean and characterful place is the best choice if you're watching your colones; rooms with bath are only slightly more expensive. Light sleepers will get grief from the bar downstairs. ③.

Nuevo Internacional, Av 5, C 2/3 (☎758-0662 or 0532; Aptdo 288, Limón). Light, bright and scrupulously clean, but with paper-thin partition walls. All rooms have private bath with electric showers. Rooms with fans are about half the price of a/c. ③–④.

Park, Av 3, C 1 and the malecón (☎758-3476, fax 758-4364). Recently renovated, the best choice in town, popular with Ticos and travellers alike. The 30 rooms come in several choices: sea view (most expensive), street view, and *planta turista* (no view, cheapest). Good restaurant, too. Reserve ahead at weekends and in high season. ⑤–⑥.

Teté, Av 3, C 4/5 (☎758-1122, fax 758-0707; Aptdo 401, Limón). Nothing special but clean, friendly, well-cared for and central; the best value downtown in this price range. Rooms on the street can be noisy but have balconies; rooms inside are a little darker. All have private bath, and there's communal TV. ④–⑤.

Portete and Playa Bonita

Apartments Cocorí, Playa Bonita (☎758-2930, fax 758-1670). Friendly family-run place in a beautiful setting; the best value in Playa Bonita. Downstairs rooms have a/c, upstairs have fans. Adequate self-catering facilities, and a lively outdoor bar/restaurant with nice view, right by the sea. ⑤.

Maribú Caribe, Portete (☎758-4543, fax 758-3541; Aptdo 623, Portete). Very luxurious sea-facing complex of round, thatched-roof huts with decor suspended around 1965; a favourite with banana company execs. The pricey restaurant overlooking the sea is not part of the hotel. ⑦.

The Town

Fifteen minutes' walk around Puerto Limón and you've seen the lot, including the vultures which occasionally hang out on street corners. **Avenida 2**, known locally as the "market street", is for all purposes the main drag, touching the north edge of Parque Vargas and the south side of the **Mercado Central**. The market is as good a place as any to start your explorations, and at times seems to be full of the entire town population, with dowager women minding their patch while thin men flutter their hands, clutching cigarettes and gesticulating jerkily to animated chatter. The sodas and snack bars here are good places to grab a bite.

Shops in Limón close over lunch, between noon and 2pm, when everyone drifts toward **Parque Vargas** and the malecón to sit under the shady palms. A little shabby today, the park, at the easternmost end of C 1 and Av 1 and 2, features a sea-facing **mural** by artist Guadalupe Alvarea, depicting colourful and evocative images of the province's tough history. From here the **malecón** (a thin ledge where it is hardly possible to walk, let alone take a seaside promenade) winds its way north. Avoid it at night, as muggings have been reported.

As for other activities in town, forget **swimming**. One look at the water at the tiny spit of sand next to the *Park Hotel* is enough discouragement. There are few **day trips** worth making from Limón. The trip up the *canales* to Tortuguero (see p.576) takes three to five hours (with animal-spotting) one-way; if coming back to town, you'd have to turn round immediately and motor back down without seeing the turtles or the village. A better possibility for a short boat trip is up the **Río Matina** from Moín, but without a guide you are unlikely to spot many animals.

Carnaval in Limón

Though in the rest of the Americas **Carnaval** is usually associated with the days before Lent, somewhat ironically, Limón takes Columbus' arrival in the New World – October 12 – as its point of celebration. The idea was first brought to Limón by a local man named Arthur King, who had been away working in Panamá's Canal Zone and was so impressed with that country's Columbus Day celebrations that he decided to bring the merriment home with him. Today **El Día de la Raza** (Day of the People) is basically an excuse to party.

The carnival features a variety of events, from Afro-Caribbean dance to Calypso music, bull-running, afternoon children's theatre, colourful *desfiles* (parades) and massive firework displays. Most spectacular is the **Grand Desfile**, usually held on the Saturday before October 12, when Afro-Caribbean costumes – sequins, spangles, fluorescent colours – parade the streets to a cacophony of tambourines, whistles and blasting sound systems.

Eating, drinking and entertainment

Limón has pretty good **food**, and variety too, but *Springfield* is the one authentic Creole restaurant in town, serving the food typical to the area – rice and beans cooked in coconut milk, jerk chicken and spicy meat stews. Outside Carnaval most people hang out with a beer in the evenings, but gringos in general and women espe-cially should avoid most **bars** – especially those that have a large advertising placard blocking views of the interior. If you want to drink, stick to places like *Mares* or *Brisas del Caribe*. The only **disco** in town is *Acuarius*, at the *Hotel Acon* (Tues–Sun 8pm–3am) which plays mainly reggae and is all right in groups but not for single (or even double) women. **Playa Bonita** is a great place for lunch or an afternoon beer if you are tired of town.

In town

Doña Toda, southeast corner of the mercado. Cheap and cheerful soda. The usual *casados* and *arroz con pollo* are a good bet, and will set you back just a couple of dollars. Lunch only.

Mares, Av 2, C 3/4. *The* gringo hang-out, exuding café elegance with comfortable cushioned chairs, small glass tables, huge plant-dotted interior and a nice view of the mercado. Varied, reasonably priced menu, featuring sandwiches and burgers.

Pizzería Il Macarrone, C 4, Av 1/2. Excellent Italian pizzeria, somewhat incongruous in this very Caribbean city. Large pizzas, with thin crust and fresh toppings, cost about US$6 and are enough for three; not bad for the best pizza in Costa Rica (and passable red Italian wine!). Credit cards accepted.

Springfield, north of the malecón, across from the hospital. People in the know say it used to be better; but it is still *the* place to get cheap, coconut-flavoured rice-and-beans with chicken, beef or fish (it is also one of the few places to serve turtle, a local delicacy even though turtles are in short supply). Fans labour over gingham tablecloths in the quiet interior. Best arrive early and don't walk along the malecón alone at night. Daily 11am–11pm. Credit cards accepted.

Portete and Playa Bonita

Johnny Dixon's, on the beach. Nice place for fish (ceviche, camarones) and cold beer; music some nights.

Maribú Caribe, Portete. Not cheap but cheerful poolside bar/restaurant for excellent food and *refrescos* (and very friendly waiters).

MOVING ON FROM LIMÓN

Heading north to **Tortuguero**, shallow-bottomed private *lanchas* make the trip up the canals from the docks at Moín. Get to the docks early (preferably 7am) to bargain for a boat; the going prices for groups are around US$65 return for four to six people. If you are travelling alone or in a couple, it's best to try to get a group together at the docks. The bus stop for Moín is at C 4, Av 4/5, 100m north of the mercado, around the corner from *Radio Casino*, but the bus leaves more or less when it wants to, so a taxi (US$2) is a bet-ter option, especially if you've just arrived on the 5am bus from San José.

Buses to San José start running at 5am from the main bus station and continue hourly until 7pm. Buy your ticket a day in advance if travelling on a Friday or Sunday. The tick-et windows for Coopelimón and Coopecaribeños are side by side (both ☎223-7811); Coopetraga (☎758-0618) also has services to **Siquerres** and **Guápiles** from where you can connect with buses to the capital. Destinations **south of Limón** are served from the Transportes MEPE office (☎221-0524) and stop at C 3, Av 4, 100m north of the mercado. There are four buses a day to Cahuita and Puerto Viejo (currently 5am, 10am, 1pm & 4pm). The **Sixaola** bus stops in Cahuita, and at El Cruce – "the cross" – 5km away from Puerto Viejo. Two buses (6am & 2.30pm) go direct to **Manzanillo** village in the heart of the Gandoca-Manzanillo Wildlife Refuge, via Puerto Viejo.

Taxis line up on the north side of the mercado, and also on Av 2 around the corner from the San José bus stop. They regularly do long-haul trips to Cahuita and Puerto Viejo (US$40–50), and to the banana plantations of the Valle de Estrella (US$25). Prices are per carload, so if you are in a group this can be far more convenient than taking the bus.

Parque Nacional Tortuguero

Though isolated – 254km from San José by road and water, and 83km northwest of Limón – **PARQUE NACIONAL TORTUGUERO** (US$6) is extremely popular wtih visitors. It is one of the most important nesting sights in the world for the **green sea turtle**, which, along with the hawksbill, lays its eggs here between July and October. First established as a protective zone in the 1960s, Tortuguero covers a large area – 189.5 square kilometres to be exact – and is 35km long; protecting not only the turtle nesting beach, but also surrounding forests, canals and waterways. Except for a short dry season during February and March, Tortugero receives over 6000mm of rain a year. This soggy environment hosts a wide abundance of species – fifty kinds of **fish**, numerous **birds**, including the endangered green parrot and the vulture, and some 160 **mammals**, some under the threat of extinction. It's the **turtles** that draw people here, however, and the sight of the gentle beasts tumbling ashore and shimmying their way up the beach to deposit their heavy load before limping back, spent, into the dark phosphorescent waves is truly moving.

The most popular way to see Tortuguero is on one of literally hundreds of **packages** that use the expensive "Jungle Lodges" across the canal from the village. These are usually two-night, three-day affairs, although you can certainly go for longer. Accommodation, meals and transport are taken care of, while guides point out wildlife along the river and canals on the way. The main difference between tours comes in the standard of hotels; check the reviews of the lodges on p.578 to help you choose. With a little planning, you can also get to Tortuguero **independently** and stay in cabinas in the **village**, which is a more interesting little place than initial impressions might suggest. Basing yourself here allows you to explore the beach at leisure – though you can't swim – and leaves you in easy reach of restaurants and bars.

Getting to Tortuguero

The journey up the canals from Limón to Tortuguero is at least half the experience. Expect a three- or four-hour trip (sometimes longer) by *lancha*, depending upon where you embark – if on a package tour, it will probably be **Hamburgo de Siquerres** on the Río Reventazón; if travelling independently, you'll find it easier to leave from **Moín** (see below). Either way you'll pass palm and deciduous trees, mirror-calm waters, and small stilt-legged wooden houses, brightly painted and poised on the water's edge – along, of course, with acres and acres of cleared land. Quite apart from the wildlife, the canal is a hive of human activity, with *lanchas*, *botes* (large canoes) and *pangas* (flat-bottomed outboard-motored boats) plying the glassy waters. Package tourists are disgorged at whichever of the lodges, across the canal from the village, they are booked into.

If you're travelling **independently**, you'll need to get to the Moín docks early, ideally by 7am. *Lanchas* leave from behind the large blue-and-white boathouse. Fares currently run at about US$65 to US$75 per group, although if there are eight people travelling it can go down to US$50. Individual travellers or couples are sometimes quoted very high prices – more than US$100. In the high season, though, it's not difficult to get a group together at the dock. You can arrange with your boatman when you would like to be picked up to return (usually not later than 1.30pm, to avoid getting stuck in the dark). Get a phone number from him if possible, so you can call from Tortuguero village if you change plans. The *lanchas* drop you at Tortuguero dock, from where you can walk to the village, or take another *lancha* across the canal to find space at the more expensive tourist lodges. In the turtle-nesting high seasons, accommodation in the village can fill up quickly, so finding a place to sleep should be your first concern.

You can also **fly** to Tortuguero (30min): Travelair leaves San José daily at 6am, flying via Barra del Colorado. Return flights, from the airstrip 4km north of the village, depart at 7am.

The Village

The tiny heat-stunned village of **TORTUGUERO** lies at the northeastern corner of the Park, on a thin spit of land between the sea and the Tortuguero canal. With its exuberant foliage of wisteria, oleander and bougainvillea, the whole place has the look of a carefully tended tropical garden. Tall palm groves and clean, mown-grass expanses are punctuated by zinc-roofed wooden houses, often elevated on stilts. This is classic Caribbean style: washed-out, slightly ramshackle and pastel-pretty, with very little to disturb the torpor until after dark.

A dirt path runs through the village north–south – the "main street", from which narrow paths go off to the sea and the canal. Smack in the middle of the village stands one of the prettiest churches you'll see anywhere, pale yellow and quiet, with a small spire and an oval doorway. At the octagonal ranch-roofed building just north of the Park information kiosk (see below), look out for the semi-naif **jungle murals**, a bright display of sloths lazing on lianas, jaguars pacing and palms swaying. At the north end of the village, the new Caribbean Conservation Corporation-sponsored **Natural History Museum** (daily 10am–noon & 2–5.30pm; US$2) has a small but informative exhibit on the lifecycle of sea turtles and gives a short history of turtling in the area. The CCC, one of the older conservation organizatons in the Americas, was the first to undertake conservation and study of the green turtle back in the 1960s.

Jungle souvenir shop (Mon–Fri 8am–7pm), 200m south of the museum across from the small *muelle*, is very well-stocked with T-shirts, wooden carved souvenirs and cards, sunscreens and hats, with prices more or less in line with those in San José.

Information

The **pulpería** in the centre of the village has details of **boat rental** and **tours**, as well as anything that's happening in the way of nightlife. Though there is a **correo** in the middle of the village, mail may take three or four weeks just to make its way to Limón. If villagers are heading to Limón they might offer to carry letters for you and post them from there; gratifying if you are staying here for any length of time. Tortuguero has only a fortnightly **doctor** service; emergencies and health problems should be referred to the Park's administration headquarters, north of the village, near the airstrip. There is a **pay phone** for outgoing calls at *Miss Junie's* restaurant (see p.579).

For **Park information**, try the kiosk in the centre of town, or the ranger station at the entrance (see below).

Village accommodation

Staying at Tortuguero on the cheap entails bedding down in one of the independent **cabinas** in the village, where accommodation is basic but comfortable, and usually without hot water. **Camping** on the beach is not allowed, though you can set up tent at the Park's central administration headquarters at the very northern tip of the village, as well as at the mown enclosure at the **ranger station** (about US$2 per day) at the southern end of the village, where you enter the Park. It's sheltered, away from the sea breezes, and there is water and toilets. Bring a ground sheet and mosquito net, and make sure your tent is waterproof.

About 6km north of Tortuguero village, Caño Palma Biological Station, run by the Canadian Organization for Tropical Education and Rainforest Conservation (in Canada ☎ 905/683-2116) rents basic rooms with fan. You can get a boatman to run you up there to see if there is room.

TOUR OPERATORS TO TORTUGUERO

A number of operators in San José and Limón offer **packages to Tortuguero**, some with accommodation (in the lodges) and meals included. Though you could usually fix things up more cheaply yourself these save a lot of hassle, and many of them are very good value.

Ecole Travel, in Chispas Books in San José, C 7, Av 0/1 (☎223-2240, fax 223-4128). The best budget option. Transport only to Tortuguero, by bus and boat, for about US$60 per person round trip.

Costa Rica Expeditions, in San José (☎257-0766, fax 257-1665). Upmarket package tours, with accommodation at their comfortable *Tortuga Lodge*. They will also do trips to Barra del Colorado, and will provide transportation by air. Three-day/two-night packages start at US$300.

Cotur, C 36, Paseo Colon and Av 1, San José (☎233-0155, fax 233-0778). This agency uses the *Jungle Lodge* exclusively, and offers fairly good value (about US$250 per person high season) three day tours, including transport by bus and boat, accommodation, meals and guides.

Mitur, Paseo Colon, C 20/22, San José (☎255-2031, fax 255-1946). The bargain basement tour operators to Tortuguero, as far as all-inclusives at the lodges goes; accommodation is at the *Ilan Ilan*.

Mawamba Tours (☎223-2421, fax 255-4039). The best mid-range tour operator, providing superior but affordable tours and accommodation at the lodge of the same name; tours are generally two-day (about US$215 per person, double occupancy) although longer stays can be arranged.

Although many places in Tortuguero now have their own telephone numbers, or a beeper/pager attached to a San José number, several do not, and in this case you can try calling the **public phone** (☎710-6716) in the *pulpería*. This method is not foolproof, however: you need to speak Spanish, and should leave a Costa Rican number where the hotelier can call you back. The phone is usually answered by Sr Olger Rivera, the *pulpería* owner.

Cabinas Aracari, south of the information kiosk and soccer field (☎798-3059). New cabinas set in a lovely garden with majo trees. Run by a friendly local family, all cabinas have private bath, cold water, and fans. A welcome new budget option. ①.

Cabinas Merry Scar, east of the *pulpería*, before the beach (☎290-2804, beeper ☎226-2626, no 125-002). Well-run cabinas with clean small rooms that can get stuffy, and separate, spick-and-span bath. Family atmosphere; the friendly *dueña* or her daughters will cook simple meals on request (about US$4 extra). They will do a small student discount with ID. ①.

Cabinas Sabina, east of the information kiosk, on the beach. Very simple (and very green) cabinas whose attraction is their setting on a nice strip of sand. Rooms are basic and dark; the toilet and shower are outhouse-type, but clean. Upstairs has better ventilation. Rules to vacate by 10am are strictly enforced. Good restaurant and popular bar. ①.

Miss Junie's, at the north end of the village, just before you reach the natural history museum (☎710-0523). Tortuguero's most popular cook (see "Eating" opposite) has built a few well-decorated and comfortable rooms with private bath (although cold water only) and fan. ③–④.

The lodges

Staying at Tortuguero's **lodges**, most of which are across the canal from the village, has its drawbacks. You're pretty much duty-bound to eat the set meals included in your package, and – unless you're at the *Laguna* or *Mawamba* – if you want to explore the village and the beach on your own you have to get a *lancha* across the canal (free, but inconvenient, nonetheless). Prices vary, and though none is officially posted for non-package tours, they hover between US$35 and US$65 per night and it may be possible to stay in them on a room-only basis if they have space.

Ilan-Ilan (☎255-2031 or 255-2262, fax 255-1946). The most basic and cheapest of the lodges. Very prefab looking, cabin-type accommodation in small grounds. Nothing fancy, but private rooms with bath and set meals. Package tours only, through Mitur tour agency. ④–⑤.

Jungle Lodge, owned and operated by COTUR (☎233-0155, fax 233-0778; Aptdo 1818, San José 1002). Friendly, comfortable place in its own gardens, with a not-bad restaurant. Large private baths – this is the only lodge that has running hot water – and your own verandah. Free canoes and foot-path to a lagoon. The second-cheapest tour/accommodation (after *Ilan-Ilan*) and a good deal. ④–⑤.

Laguna Lodge (☎225-3740, fax 283-8031). Small, very attractive hotel with rustic wooden cabins. Peaceful atmosphere and personal service, ideal for those who don't like large *turista* lodges. Convenient village location, with easy access to the beach and full tour services. ④–⑤.

El Manatí, 1.5km north of Tortuguero village across the canal (☎ & fax 239-0911). Basic, comfort-able rooms with private bath, hot water and fans, and several attractive two-bedroom cabinas. The best mid-range option. The owners have started a local initiative to save the endangered manatee, or sea cow, which is endemic to the area. ④.

Mawamba Lodge, 1km north of the village (☎223-2421, fax 255-4039). An upmarket lodge, the best place to go if money is no object. Rooms are cabina-style, with private bath, cold water and ceiling fans, and there's a large pool. The village and ocean are just a short walk away. ④–⑤.

Tortuga Lodge, owned by Costa Rica Expeditions (☎257-0766, fax 257-1665). The plushest lodge in the area, but rather far-flung. Large rooms, with private baths, and elegantly landscaped grounds with lots of walking opportunities. Meals are usually extra and, while of the "all you can eat" variety, are not cheap (US$10 for breakfast). Packages only. ④–⑤.

Eating, drinking and nightlife

Tortuguero village offers downhome food, typically Caribbean, with lots of good fresh **fish**. Prices, however, tend to be high, and there are few places for **breakfast** (though the *dueña* of *Cabinas Merry Scar* has been known to whip up something for a few dol-lars if you ask nicely).

Centro Social la Culebra beside the canal in the village, has a **disco**, but it's general-ly agreed to be a bit rough; *Bar Brisas del Mar* is better, with a large, semi open-air dance floor and a good sound and light system (when it is not visiting Limón). You can hear the sea from your table and atmosphere is low-key and inviting.

Miss Junie's, north end of village path. Sizeable dining room, with gingham tablecloths and cool white walls. Miss Junie is a local who does solid Caribbean food – red beans, jerk chicken, rice, chayote and breadfruit, all on the same plate – with ice-cold beers to boot. She cooks for the Park rangers, so you need to ask a day in advance or in the morning whether she can fit you in. Dinner only.

Pancana Restaurante, on the path to *Cabinas Merry Scar*, east side of the village. A pretty house, otherwise known as *Jacob and Edna's*, this restaurant is famous in the area for succulent baked goods and Caribbean food. Open 6am–8pm.

Restaurant Sabina, east of the information kiosk, on the beach. Great outdoor site next to the sea, with a backdrop of crashing waves and clean breezes. The fresh fish is especially good, but prices are high (twice as expensive as similar dishes in San José, for example), and it can cost more to eat here than to stay the night at the cabinas next door. Daily 6am–11pm.

Soda el Tucan, next to the *pulpería*. Soda staples including rice and chicken and *casados* as well as cool *refrescos* and lunch deals.

Visiting the park

Most people come to Tortuguero to see the **desove**, or egg-laying of the turtles. Few are disappointed, as the majority of tours during laying **seasons** (March–May & July–Oct) result in sightings of the moving, surreal procession of the reptiles from the sea to make their egg-nests in the sand. Most turtles come ashore in the relative safety of night.

Often dozens of turtles emerge from the sea at the same time and march up the sands to their chosen spot. Each turtle lays eighty or more eggs; the collective whirring noise of sand being dug away is extraordinary.

Although Tortuguero is by no means the only place in Costa Rica to see marine turtles nesting (they use the Pacific beaches too), three of the largest kinds of endangered sea turtles regularly nest here in large numbers. Along with the **green** (*verde*) turtle, named for the colour of soup made from its flesh, you might see the **hawksbill** (*carey*), with its distinctive hooked beak; and the ridged **leatherback** (*baula*), the largest turtle in the world, which can easily weigh 300kg – some are as heavy as 500kg and reach 5m in length. The green turtles and hawksbills nest most concentratedly from July to October (August is peak month), while the leatherbacks may come ashore from March to May.

Turtle tours, led by certified guides, leave at 8pm every night from the village. Tickets (US$11 including Park entrance fee) are sold from the information kiosk in the village between 4 and 6pm on the day; if no one's there, go to the **ranger station**, south of the village, where you enter the Park. Guides are instructed to make as little noise as possible so as not to alarm the turtles, allowing them to get on with their business; everyone must be off the beach by 10pm.

During the day, you can walk a single, generally well-maintained, self-guided **trail** (1km), the **Sendero Natural**, which starts at the entrance and skirts a small swamp. As for that long, wild **beach**, you can amble for up to 30km south and enjoy crab-spotting, bird-watching, and looking out for truck-wheel-like turtle-tracks. Swimming is not a good idea, due to heavy waves, turbulent currents and sharks. Remember that you'll need to **pay Park fees** (US$6) to walk on the beach or along the trail.

Other activities around Tortuguero

Almost as popular as the turtle tours are Tortuguero's **boat tours** through the *caños*, or lagoons, to spot animals and birds – dignified looking herons, cranes and kingfishers, for example. For an informative and authentic adventure, take a tour with Mr Damma, a Miskito originally from Nicaragua, who has an assured knowledge of the jungle and its creatures. Damma does an occasional overnight camping trip in the deep jungle (you have to build your own tent) and a 6.30am wildlife-spotting tour paddling along pristine *caños* (4hr; price negotiable). He lives next to the *Cabinas Merry Scar*, on the ocean side of the village. He needs at least a day's notice for an overnight tour, which are not always possible.

Most lodges have **canoes** you can take out on the canal – a great way to get around if you are good with a paddle. In the south of the village, Rubén Aragón, 50m south of the park entrance, right by the water, rents traditional Miskito-style boats for about US$8 an hour, or US$15 with a guide/paddler.

It is also possible to climb **Cerro Tortuguero**, an ancient volcanic deposit looming 119m above the flat coastal plain 6km north of the village. A climb up the gently sloping side leads you to the "peak", from which there are good views of flat jungle and inland waterways (90min round trip). Ask at the village information kiosk or at the ranger station.

Cahuita village and Parque Nacional Cahuita

The tiny village of **CAHUITA**, 43km southeast of Limón, is reached on the paved Hwy-36 from Limón to Sixaola on the Panamanian border. Like other villages on the Talamanca coast, especially Puerto Viejo de Talamanca (see p.585) and Manzanillo (see p.588), it has become increasingly popular with backpackers and surfers for its fabled laid-back atmosphere, forest walking opportunities, and the added appeal of great Afro-Caribbean food and cultural diversity. Near the village, the **Parque Nacional Cahuita** was formed mainly to protect one of the only living coral reefs in Costa Rica, near Punta Cahuita; many people come here to **snorkel** and take glass-bottomed-boat rides.

In many ways, however, Cahuita is a case-study example of the unhappy clash between tourism and local communities; communities that have lost the happy, easy-going veneer that travellers like to assign to them. There's a drugs scene, with crack as well as the traditional ganja around, and some problems with opportunistic theft. Some local men can also be pretty aggressive in their approaches to women, and no woman put in such a situation would agree that, for them, Cahuita is a friendly, easy-going place. That said, with just a bit of common sense – lock your room door and windows, never leave anything on the beach, and avoid walking alone in unlit places at night – it's perfectly possible to enjoy the atmosphere and community in Cahuita. Note that nude or topless bathing is definitely unacceptable, as is wandering though the village wearing no more than a bathing suit.

Though it is mainly wet all year round, the local "dry" season is between March and April, and from September to October.

Arrival and information

The easiest way to get to Cahuita from San José by **bus** is on the modern, comfortable Sixaola service (3–4hr). Taking a bus from San José to Puerto Limón (3hr) and changing there (4 daily) is only marginally cheaper than the *directo* bus and will increase travelling time by an hour, at least. In Cahuita, buses stop at the shelter on the small scruffy park across from the bar-disco *Salon Vaz*, whose walls are painted with the current **bus schedules** to Limón, San José and Sixaola.

Information

If you're coming to Cahuita **from Puerto Viejo**, be sure to pick up a copy of ATEC's *Welcome to Coastal Talamanca* (see p.586), which has good local maps and a directory of local-owned accommodation and businesses. The only sources of **visitor information** in the village itself are the tour companies: Moray's Tours, in the north, on the sea side (supposedly daily 8am–6pm; ☎755-0038) has a small map of the village, while at Cahuita Tours, 200m north of *Salon Vaz* (daily 7am–noon & 1.30–7pm; ☎755-0082), you can get up-to-date national newspapers and occasionally the *Tico Times*. They also sell **stamps**, will **exchange** dollars, and have a phone for **international calls**. They dial for you and keep track of time used, charging about US$0.75 on top of the cost of the call. There's a public **phone** at *Soda Uvita*, next door to *Salon Vaz*.

The nearest banks are in Bribrí, 20km away by road, or Limón, and though established restaurants like the *National Park* and upscale hotels like the *Atlantida Lodge* have been known to **change money**, your best bet is Cahuita Tours (see above). The small **police station** (*guardia rural*) is on the last beach-bound road at the north end of the village; the **correo** next door has erratic hours to say the least (supposedly Mon–Fri 7am–4pm). The **doctor** comes to town every few days: bill posters announce his or her arrival a couple of days in advance.

Accommodation

Though Cahuita is popular with budget travellers, it is not rock-bottom cheap. Groups get the best deal, as most **cabinas** charge per room and have space for at least three or four people. Though accommodation tends to be of the concrete-block cell variety, standards are high, with fans, mosquito nets, clean sheets and bathrooms. Upstairs rooms are slightly more expensive, with sea breezes and occasional ocean views.

The **centre** of the village has scores of options; there is also accommodation in all price ranges along the long (3km or so) road that runs by the sea north along **Black-Sand Beach**. It's quieter here, and the beach is not bad. However, women (even travelling in groups) and those without their own car are better off staying in town, as the Black-Sand Beach road has been reported unsafe at night. Wherever you stay, make sure there are bars on the windows and a sturdy lock on the door. You should **book ahead** on weekends during the Highland dry season (Dec–April).

In the National Park, the Puerto Vargas ranger station has good **camping facilities** (US$2 per day) complete with barbecue grill, pit toilets and showers, but no drinking water. Take water and insect repellent, and a torch. Never leave your things unattended: ask the ranger for advice, as he or she may be able to guard them for you. Be careful, too, not to pitch your tent too close to the high tide line; ask the rangers where it's safest to camp.

In the village

Cabinas Arrecife Reef, 50m north of the school (☎755-0081). Friendly, family-run place, offering a little more comfort than the standard budget concrete cabinas. These are large and shaded, with private bath and hot water, and some have sea views. ③.

Cabinas Jenny, on the beach (☎755-0256). Beautiful rooms, especially upstairs (more expensive) with high wooden ceilings, sturdy bunks, mosquito nets, fans and wonderful sea views, but no hot water. Deck chairs and hammocks provided, and good stout locks on all doors. The owner sometimes offers breakfast. ③–④.

Cabinas Surfside, opposite the school (☎755-0246). Concrete cell rooms, dark and none too special, but very popular with the budget crowd. Good restaurant frequented by locals. ③–④.

Sol y Mar, across the street from *Hotel Cahuita* (☎755-0237). Decor at this hospitable place is nothing special, but upstairs rooms are particularly good: airy, bright and clean, with table fans and pretty sea views from verandahs. ⑤–⑥.

Black-Sand Beach

Atlantida Lodge, next to soccer field on the road to Black-Sand Beach, about 1km from the village (☎755-0115). Best of the pricier options: friendly, with the nicest pool in town, patio, pretty grounds, and good security. Cool rooms, decorated in tropical yellows and pinks, with heated water. Filling breakfasts included. ⑥–⑦.

Cabinas Colibrí Paradise, opposite soccer field (☎755-0055). Charming octagonal-shaped little houses, roomier than most, with hammocks outside. Also a house for rent (US$75 per night) with TV and video. Reached on a narrow, muddy path; bring a torch at night. If driving from Limón, take the first road (unsigned) into Cahuita before the main road. Accepts credit cards. ④–⑤.

Cabinas Iguana, 200m south of *Bar la Ancla* on small sideroad (☎755-0005, fax 755-0054). Some of the best budget accommodation in town; the very friendly Austrian owners have built lovely wood-panelled cabinas set back from the beach. Big screened verandah, laundry service, and a small tourist kiosk (paperback books, some in German). Also two apartments and a three-bedroom house (US$25–40 per night) with kitchen. There is a small swimming pool. ③–④.

Hotel Magellan, 3km up Black-Sand Beach, on small signposted road leading to left (☎755-0054, fax 758-1453; Aptdo 1132, Puerto Limón). Very comfortable hotel, in beautiful gardens dotted with pre-Columbian sculpture and a small pool. Hacienda-style rooms have rattan furniture and running hot water. Continental breakfast, bar and restaurant. ⑥–⑦.

The Village

Cahuita proper comprises just two puddle-dotted, gravel-and-sand streets running parallel to the sea, intersected by a few cross-streets. The main street runs from the Park entrance at Kelly Creek to the northern end of the village, marked more or less by

Moray's Tours. Beyond here it curves round and continues two or three kilometres north along **Black-Sand Beach**. The sea-battered green *Salon Vaz* is the focal point of the village. You don't need to go inside to catch the tunes; by 10.30am, even on Sunday, high-volume reggae and soca blasts from its near-gutted interior, while the snap of pool cues and dominoes can be heard from within.

You can swim on either of the village's two beaches, although neither is fantastic: the first 400m or so of the narrow white sand beach is particularly dangerous on account of rip tides. **Black-Sand Beach** is littered with driftwood, although you can swim in some places. The beach south of Punta Cahuita – in the Park – sometimes called **Playa Vargas**, is better for swimming than those in the village, as it is protected from raking breakers by the coral reef, but is slightly awkward to get to. Backing the shores, a trail leads through the vast area of thick vegetation and mangrove swamps.

A number of people take visitors out on to the coral reef in **glass-bottomed boats**; try Chapan at *Marisquera de Langosta*, near *Cabinas Jenny* (US$20). Moray's and Cahuita Tours run one-day **scuba diving** tours for around US$100 (equipment included) and **snorkelling** expeditions for around US$6 per day plus rental (about US$10); if you go snorkelling on your own, you have to enter the Park from the Puerto Vargas *puesto*, and swim out to the reef from the beach on this side of the point. Note the signs indicating treacherous currents. Wear shoes, as you will have to walk over exposed coral, and watch out for prickly black sea urchins. Though you can **surf** at Cahuita, Puerto Viejo (see p.585) has better waves. Bring your own board; there is nowhere in either village to rent equipment.

Though the tour agencies in Cahuita offer combination "Indian"/beach excursions by jeep, if you are genuinely interested in visiting the **Bribrí indigenous reserves**, including the KéköLdi reserve near Puerto Viejo, the best – most environmentally and politically aware – expeditions are run from Puerto Viejo by ATEC (*Associación Talamanqueña de Ecoturismo y Conservación*; see p.586).

Visiting the park

PARQUE NACIONAL CAHUITA (daily 8am–4pm; "pay what you want" if entering at Kelly Creek; US$6 at the Puerto Vargas entrance, 3km south of Kelly Creek), is one of the smallest in the country, covering the wedge-shaped piece of land from Punta Cahuita back to the main highway from Puerto Limón to Sixaola and, crucially, the **coral reef** about 500m offshore. On land, Cahuita protects the littoral, or coastal, rainforest, a lowland habitat of semi-mangroves and tall canopy cover which backs the gently curving white sand beaches of Playa Vargas to the south of Punta Cahuita and Playa Cahuita to the north. **Birds**, including ibis and kingfishers, are in residence, along with white-faced (*carablanca*) monkeys, sloths and snakes, but the only animals you're very likely to see are howler monkeys, and perhaps coati.

The Park's one **trail** (7km), skirting the beach, is a very easy, level walk, with a path so wide it feels like a road, covered with leaves and other brush, and a few fallen trees and logs. The Río Perzoso, about 2km from the Kelly Creek entrance, or 5km from the Puerto Vargas trailhead, is not always fordable. Similiarly, at high tide the beach is impassable in places: ask the ranger at the Puerto Vargas *puesto* about the *marea*, or tide schedules. Walking this trail can be unpleasantly humid and buggy: best to go in the morning.

Many **snorkellers** swim the 200 to 500m from Puerto Vargas out to the reef. Again, you should ask about currents, although the beach here is calmer than the one next to Cahuita village.

Eating, drinking and nightlife

Cahuita has plenty of places to eat fresh local **food**, and there's a reasonably cosmopolitan selection. As with accommodation, **prices** are not low (dinner starts at US$7). **Service** (with the possible exception of the *National Park*) tends to be laid-back: leave yourself lots of time. **Nightlife** in Cahuita revolves around having a beer, listening to music and slapping those dominoes or mosquitoes, depending on your luck.

Bananas, *Cabinas Algebra*, Black-Sand Beach. Rustic, plant-entwined verandah with great atmosphere. Simple, tasty food from a varied menu; sometimes candlelit at night.

Bar la Ancla (aka *"Reggae Bar"*), 2km up Black-Sand Beach. Lively bar with vivid African tricolour decor. Very popular with locals and tourists alike, with reggae on the sound system, cold beer, and sea breezes. They do pasta and Tico dishes as well as breakfast (US$3–4).

Las Olas, at the northern end of the village, right on the beach. The food is nothing special – the usual rice-and-chicken combinations and some burgers, but there's less of a scene here than in other Cahuita nightspots, and locals come for a quiet beer, despite it being a little more expensive than other places. The ocean breezes and the sound of waves lapping make this a quiet, atmospheric nightime hangout.

Miss Edith's, northern end of village. The *doyenne* of Creole food, Miss Edith is justifiably popular with tourists; get here early, especially on weekend nights, and be prepared for laid-back service. Great rice-and-beans, rundown and *pan bon*, and occasionally home-made ice cream and herbal teas. No alcohol served. Mon–Sat 7am–noon & 3–6pm & 7–10pm.

Pizzeria El Cactus, north end of village, off Black-Sand Beach road. Very popular Italian place dishing out generous pizzas to a mainly gringo clientele. Go for the pizza rather than the pasta; the lemon crepes go down a treat. A great place to hang out late night with a beer. Tues–Sun 5pm–midnight.

Restaurante National Park, at the Kelly Creek Park entrance. Highly recommended, unusual strawberry *refrescos* and tasty *bocas* (try the *patacones* – fried plantains and mashed black beans), along with *casados*, good grilled fish and rice-based dishes. Pleasant situation, and live music most nights.

Salon Vaz, in the village. Ramshackle local bar with history; the place where the locals go to slap dominoes and pool cues. Sweaty backroom atmosphere and good music, mostly reggae. It looks forbidding, but is safe enough; though women will face a bit of cruising.

El Típico Cahuita, off the main road south of the village. Open-air place good for *casados*, served all day; plus their extensive menu of fish, rice and chicken. Tables and stools hewn from tree trunks, with plants and baskets hanging from every conceivable nook. Open 7.15am–10pm.

MOVING ON FROM CAHUITA

All **buses** leave from the park opposite *Salon Vaz*; the **schedule** from Cahuita is painted on the wall of the bar. There are four buses daily to **Limón**, where you can connect for **San José**, but if you're in a hurry to reach the capital, it is faster and easier to take the the (non-stopping) *directo* service (3 daily; 4hr). Call Transportes MEPE in San José (see p.551) for information.

For **Puerto Viejo**, the local bus (9am, 11am & 1pm) takes thirty minutes to one hour and stops right in the village. The express service from San José to **Sixaola**, which stops in Cahuita at around 10am, 5.30pm and 7.30pm, does not go right into Puerto Viejo but drops you at the crossroads (El Cruce; a 5km walk). Whichever bus you take, be at the bus stop about twenty minutes early, as services have been known to leave before the scheduled time.

Puerto Viejo de Talamanca and around

The 12km between the languorous hamlet of **PUERTO VIEJO DE TALAMANCA**, 18km southeast of Cahuita, and Manzanillo village is one of the most beautiful stretches in the country. Though not spectacular for swimming, the **beaches** – Playa Chiquita, Punta Uva and Manzanillo – are the most picturesque on the entire coast; there's plenty of accommodation, and for now, at least, it's a good deal more relaxed than Cahuita.

It's **surfing** that really pulls the crowds; the stretch south of *Stanford's* restaurant at the southern end of the village offers some of the most challenging waves in the country and certainly the best on the Atlantic coast. Puerto Viejo's famous "**La Salsa Brava**" crashes ashore between December and March and from June to July. September and October, when La Salsa Brava goes away to wherever big waves go, are the quietest months of the year.

The **village** itself lies between the thick forested hills of the Talamanca mountains and the sea, where locals bathe and kids frolic with surfboards in the waves. It's a quiet well-cared for place, with pretty hand-painted signs pointing to restaurants and cabinas, and rasta red, green and gold splashed all over the place. Like Cahuita, Puerto Viejo has drawn many Europeans to take up residence here, looking for an easier life and setting up their own cabinas, restaurants and sodas. And, also like Cahuita, most locals are of Afro-Caribbean descent.

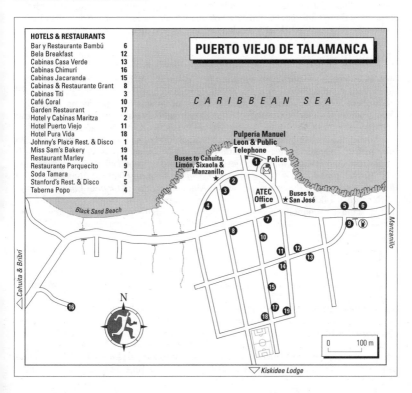

HOTELS & RESTAURANTS

Bar y Restaurante Bambú	6
Bela Breakfast	12
Cabinas Casa Verde	13
Cabinas Chimurí	16
Cabinas Jacaranda	15
Cabinas & Restaurante Grant	8
Cabinas Titi	3
Café Coral	10
Garden Restaurant	17
Hotel y Cabinas Maritza	2
Hotel Puerto Viejo	11
Hotel Pura Vida	18
Johnny's Place Rest. & Disco	1
Miss Sam's Bakery	19
Restaurant Marley	14
Restaurante Parquecito	9
Soda Tamara	7
Stanford's Rest. & Disco	5
Taberna Popo	4

PUERTO VIEJO DE TALAMANCA

C A R I B B E A N   S E A

Pulpería Manuel Leon & Public Telephone

Buses to Cahuita, Limón, Sixaola & Manzanillo

Police

ATEC Office

Buses to San José

Black Sand Beach

△ Cahuita & Bribri

▷ Manzanillo

N

0   100 m

▽ Kiskidee Lodge

ATEC AND TOURS TO THE KÉKÖLDI RESERVE

Skirted by the **Kéköldi** reserve, inhabited by about two hundred Bribrí and Cabécar peoples, Puerto Viejo retains stronger links with **indigenous culture** than Cahuita. The *Associación Talamanqueña de Ecoturismo y Conservación*, or **ATEC** (☎ & fax 750-0191 or 798-4244) is a grassroots organization set up by members of the local community – Afro-Caribbeans, Bribrí indigenous peoples and Spanish-descended inhabitants. As well as being able to tell you where to buy **locally made products** such as banana vinegar, guava jam and coconut oil, and jewellery made from coconut shells, seashells and bamboo, they arrange some of the most authentic and interesting **tours** in Costa Rica. If you're spending even just a couple of days in the Talamanca region, an ATEC-sponsored trip is a must; to reserve a tour, go to their Puerto Viejo office at least one day in advance.

Arrival

Local bus services **from Cahuita** to Puerto Viejo leave at 9am, 11am and 1pm (about 1hr 30min), stopping at *Taberna Popo*, right beside the seafront. **From San José** the 3.30pm bus to Puerto Viejo arrives approximately five hours later. Taking the bus to Limón and changing there for Puerto Viejo (4 daily) is only marginally cheaper, and will increase travelling time by an hour, at least. You can also get to Puerto Viejo on the express service to **Sixaola**. Note that some services – including the Sixaola bus – don't go right into the village, but stop at **El Cruce**, about 5km outside – ask to be sure. You could hitch from El Cruce, but there's little traffic, and it's a hot, dusty walk; instead, call one of Puerto Viejo's two public phones (see below) to book a **taxi** to pick you up (at least US$5).

Information

Puerto Viejo has no **tourist information** per se, but the **ATEC** office on the main road (daily 7am–noon & 1–9pm; ☎ & fax 750-0191) sells a cheap booklet, *Welcome to Coastal Talamanca*, which includes an invaluable list of locals who have particular expertise – from traditional medicine to surfing. Though emphatically not a travel agency, they can arrange exemplary tours or recommend locals to talk to about diving and snorkelling on the Manzanillo reef, or getting to Refugio Nacional de Vida Silvestre Gandoca-Manzanillo (see p.588). They also have a small library of books on the area, plus nature guides, field guides and guidebooks, which, in a gesture of astounding good faith, they may lend you. For **horse rental**, speak to Antonio at *Caballos Antonio*, 500m southeast from the *pulpería* next to *Earl Brown's* restaurant, or Mauricio Salazar at *Cabinas Chimurí*.

Renting a bike is not a bad idea, especially to explore the beaches south of town. For a standard mountain bike by the day or the hour, try *Bela's Bike Rental and Breakfast* (see "Eating", below), or the *Old Harbor's Fresco shop* next to *Taberna Popos*; prices are roughly the same at each (US$9/day).

Resident medic Doctor Rosa León runs a **health clinic** across from *Bela Soda*, about 100m back from the main road. You can get **gas** at the south end of the village, across the road from *Stanford's* in the house next to the billboard sign for the *Las Palmas* hotel. For film and essentials, head for *Pulpería Manuel León*, which also has one of the two public **phones** in town (☎750-0099). The other is at the *Hotel Maritza* (☎750-0199). There is no **bank,** but during the Dec-April high season many hotels will change US dollars cash.

Accommodation

Puerto Viejo's popularity is increasing rapidly, and in recent years there has been a mushrooming of places to stay. Outside high season, or **surfing season** (Dec–March &

June–July) weekends you shouldn't have trouble finding a room on spec; however, now that most places have telephone numbers it is easier to **reserve** in advance. The vast majority of accommodation in the **village** is in simple cabinas, usually without hot water, and sometimes without water altogether. More upscale establishments line the **coast** south of the village. You can **camp** on the beaches, but rock-bottom budget travellers usually foresake their tent for a night and stay at the lovely and very cheap *Kiskidee*.

Cabinas Casa Verde, signed, 100m south and 50m east of *Soda Tamara* (☎750-0047, fax 750-0015). Fantastic value cabinas with very clean showers and communal outside toilets. Also ceiling fans, mosquito nets and space to sling hammocks. Bamboo and plant decor, with shell mobiles and pieces of washed-up coral in each of the twelve rooms. ④–⑤.

Cabinas Chimurí, 20min walk from the village towards the Sixaola–Cahuita road (☎750-0119). Owned by Mauricio Salazar, an indigenous Bribrí, these A-frame hatched huts, set back from the road, have balconies with nice views. Small kitchen and very tasty breakfasts included in highly reasonable price; student discounts with ID. ③.

Cabinas Jacaranda, north of the soccer field (☎750-0069). Basic but very clean budget option, with lively Guatemalan fabrics. Unscreened windows but mosquito nets, table fans, and clean shared bath with cold water only. ②–④.

Kiskidee Lodge, along the path from the soccer field (☎750-0075). Well worth the 15-min trek up the hill – bring a torch at night – this is one of the most beautiful, tranquil lodges in all Costa Rica, and at budget rates. Large verandah, good for bird- and animal-spotting, and spacious bunk accommodation. Room for 8 people, no fans, but mosquito nets and outdoor toilet. Kitchen privileges cost US$1.50 extra (stock up on food at the *pulpería*). ①–②.

Hotel Maritza, 100m southeast of bus stop (☎750-0199). Lots of rooms with private bath and balconies upstairs. A good choice if the others are full or if you're short on cash – accepts credit cards. Also a bar, lounge and tours. ④.

Hotel Puerto Viejo, in the centre of the village (no phone). A large two-storey structure, this budget hotel has more than 30 rooms, which are often full with the surfer and backpacker contingents. Rooms are extremely bare – you get a bed, a light and not much else, but are good value upstairs, where there is ventilation. Downstairs rooms are dark and dank. Can get rowdy. ①.

Hotel Pura Vida, near the soccer field (☎ & fax 750-0002). Popular budget option with seven rooms; it tends to fill quickly. Rooms have sinks, ceiling fans and mosquito nets, and there's a verandah. Toilets are shared and the showers are hot (well, warm) – a Puerto Viejo rarity. Friendly owners (with friendly Rottweiler). ③.

Eating, drinking and nightlife

Puerto Viejo has a surprisingly cosmopolitan range of **places to eat**. Good, traditional **Creole food** is served at *Soda Marley*, and ATEC can put you in touch with village women who cook typical regional meals on request; one such, Miss Dolly, sometimes sells her baked goods at a little shop at the west end of the village.

The village, quiet during the day, begins thumping at **night**; the bass-heavy music usually emanates from *Taberna Popo* and *Stanford's*, probably the most popular place in town, dominated by well-honed surfers. There are also a couple of **discos**, though women, alone and in groups, might find the atmosphere a bit heavy. *Johnny's Place* is good; a restaurant-disco with sea view. A quieter option is to have a beer at *Parquecito* or join the faithful local (mainly male) crowd at *Taberna Popo*. You'll find surfers sipping stiff drinks at *Bambú*, next door to *Stanford's*, which has a narrow verandah facing the sea.

Bela Breakfast, 100m south of the main road (signed). Good *gallo pinto* along with gringo staples such as French toast. Daily 6am–4pm.

Coral, on the road to the soccer field. The tastiest, if pricey, breakfasts in town – traditional Costa Rican as well as healthy yoghurt and granola, or eggs with delicious wholemeal bread, along with an excellent fruit plate and juices. 7am–3.30pm.

Garden Restaurant, near the soccer field. Vegetarian, Asian and Caribbean cuisine cooked by Vera, a Trinidadian/Canadian woman who has an excellent gourmet pedigree from Toronto restaurants *Bamboo* and *Squeeze Club*. Prices are not low (the fantastic breakfasts are cheapest) but the food is exquisite and atmosphere relaxing. Nov–June only, Thurs–Mon 5–10pm.

Parquecito, across the bridge from the gas station. Locally run restaurant with sea view, cross-breezes, cold beer and a fish-oriented menu. Good atmosphere, quieter than *Stanford's* opposite.

Restaurant Marley, south of the main road. Small, locally run place that comes a very close second to the *Garden* for the best food in town. Certainly the nicest for lunch, served on a little terrace. The red snapper is a treat, perfectly cooked with onions and sauce, and the delicate coconut rice-and-beans must be the best in the province. Open 7am–9pm.

Soda Tamara, opposite the ATEC office. The best place in town for cheap and delicious rice-and-beans lunchtime specials. Closed Tues.

Stanford's, opposite *Parquecito*. Lively (or noisy, depending how you look at it) local institution right on the sea, with laid-back good-time atmosphere. Popular with surfers, who keep an eye on the waves and their buddies from the upstairs verandah. The music is reggae but the food is Highland, with rice-and-everything predominating.

South from Puerto Viejo to Manzanillo

The stretch south of Puerto Viejo, dotted by tiny hamlets of **Playa Cocles**, **Playa Chiquita**, **Punta Uva** and **Manzanillo**, the main village, is one of the most appealing on the entire Atlantic coast. Palm trees lean vertiginously over small and little-visited beaches, while purples, mauves, oranges and reds fade into the sea at sunset, heralding the twilight mist that wafts in from the Talamancas. There's a low-hassle atmosphere, and excellent accommodation strung along the Puerto Viejo–Manzanillo road. Bus transport is infrequent, and you'll do best with a car – unless of course you are an ace cyclist and don't mind riding long distances in the staggering humidity.

The little-visited but fascinating **Refugio Nacional de Vida Silvestre Gandoca-Manzanillo**, bordering Río Sixaola and the international frontier with Panamá, incorporates the small hamlets of Gandoca and Manzanillo and covers fifty square kilometres of land and a similar area of sea. It was established to protect some of Costa Rica's last few **coral reefs**, of which **Punta Uva** is the most accessible. You can **snorkel** happily here. There's also a protected **turtle-nesting beach** south of the village of Manzanillo.

Manzanillo Beach, set on a small bay a couple of kilometres before the village, is the least driftwood-strewn of all the beaches on this shore, backed with jungle and mangrove swamps that are home to howler monkeys, toucans and many other birds. Just walking along the sand with a pair of binoculars is rewarding for birders. Bear in mind, though, that it is very swampy, and mosquitoes and sandflies thrive.

MOVING ON FROM PUERTO VIEJO

The bus from Puerto Viejo **to San José** (5hr) leaves at 6.30am, 9am and 4pm, travelling via Cahuita. There are also five buses direct **to Cahuita** (6am, 8.30am, 1pm, 4pm & 5pm; 30min–1hr), and you can get there on the "express" service to Limón (usually the last bus of the day, around 5pm). Note that as this is "express" (actually it stops a lot) you will be asked to pay the full fare to Limón, even if you are getting off along the route.

To get to **Sixaola** and Panamá by bus, you have to flag down the San José–Sixaola service at El Cruce. The bus should get here any time between four and five hours after it has left the capital, but arrival time varies; check with locals. Otherwise get the bus to Cahuita and pick up the San José–Sixaola service there (see p.584). More than anywhere in the country, buses in this area are prone to leave early or late – to be absolutely sure when leaving get to the bus stop half an hour early.

Accommodation

The dirt road from Puerto Viejo to Manzanillo is lined with a number of places to stay, ranging from basic **cabinas**, popular with surfers, through entire vacation houses to a unique **tent camp** near the village.

Aguas Claras, Playa Chiquita (☎284-8616). The best choice for families or groups, these lovely wooden houses, painted in bright Caribbean style, have mosquito nets, sitting area, balcony, clean bathroom, cold water, fully equipped kitchen, and electricity. Set in jungle-like gardens, with a natural path leading 200m to the beach. Weekly rates US$300, or around US$70 per night; can sleep 7 or 8. ⑤–⑦.

Cabinas Garibaldi, 2km south of Peurto Viejo at Playa Cocles. Popular with surfers, these joyless budget rooms at least have private bath and sea breezes. ②.

Lapalapa, 50m north of *Villas del Caribe*. Restaurant (see below) with very basic rooms for rent. ④.

Miraflores, Playa Chiquita (☎750-0038 or 233-2822; Aptdo 7271, San José 1000). Rustic, comfortable lodge opposite the beach, on an old cacao plantation with tropical flower filled-grounds. One of the nicest options in the area, decorated with Bribrí paintings, carvings and objets d'art. Upstairs is better and brighter with mosquito nets, mirrors and high bamboo ceilings. Outside breakfast area. ⑤–⑥.

Selvyn's, Playa Chiquita. Simple, spartan cabinas attached to the restaurant with no fans and cold water only. A short path leads to the beach. ①–②.

Shawandha Lodge, Playa Chiquita (☎233-6613, fax 233-7479). One of the most luxurious lodges on the Atlantic coast. Each chalet-style cabin has private bath and heated water, beautifully decorated with tiles, and the French owners have adorned their place with many beautiful touches. Breakfast included in rates. ⑥–⑦.

Walaba, 8.5km south of Puerto Viejo. Friendly, three-storey rustic lodge, across the road from the beach. Wooden decor and big verandah; fully equipped, bright rooms with fans and cold water, but no cooking facilities. Very good value. ⑤.

Eating and drinking

Elena Brown's, south of *Miraflores Lodge*, 5km south of Puerto Viejo. Established soda/restaurant serving succulent local fish and chicken. Cheap lunchtime specials and snacks.

Lapalapa, 50m north of *Villas del Caribe*. The best place along this coast for a meal or drink. Great fish and French cuisine, Caribbean music and bar snacks. Tree-trunk tables with kerosene lamps and huge dripping candles. Open 9am–1am.

La Paloma Cafe, Playa Chiquita. A small open-air restaurant serving lunch and dinner – the local lobster is wonderful. Gringo-style breakfasts come with fresh wholemeal bread. You can play chess or backgammon, and there are occasional video nights.

Naturales, Old Harbour, 7km south of Puerto Viejo. Excellent, great value, health food. Breakfast with wholewheat bread, 100 percent natural juices, salad, milkshakes and sandwiches, all for less than US$2.

Selvyn's Restaurant, Playa Chiquita. Long-established restaurant that dishes up beautifully cooked local fish, served with coconut-flavoured rice-and beans on weekends.

Soda Aquarius, Playa Chiquita. Healthy, fresh local breakfast, dinner, coffee and *refrescos* kept going all day. Homebaked bread daily.

Bribrí and the Panamanian border

From Puerto Viejo the paved road (Hwy-36) continues to **BRIBRÍ**, about 10km inland southwest, arching over the Talamancan foothills, and revealing the green bowls of valleys from here all the way to Panamá. This is banana country, and there's little to see, even in Bribrí itself, which is largely devoted to administering the affairs of indigenous reserves in the Talamanca mountains. Bribrí does, however, have a **bank** (Banco Nacional – it changes money, but allow half a day). If you are going to Panamá, bring US dollars. There is one basic **place to stay**, *Cabinas Picuno* (☎258-2981; ①), and a couple of simple **restaurants**.

The border and on into Panamá

Sixaola–Guabito is a small crossing that does not see much foreign traffic, and for the most part formalities are simple, but you should get here as early in the morning as possible. At the moment most nationalities need a **visa** or **tourist card** to cross into Panamá for thirty days; the consulate in San José issues them both, or you can get a tourist card from the office of Copa, the Panamanian airline, in San José (see p.549). The crossing is open daily from 7am to 3pm Costa Rica time (Panamá is one hour ahead), with a toll of about US$1.50.

In Panamá, there's nowhere decent to stay before you get to Bocas del Toro – and you should leave time to look for a hotel once there – and bus connections can be tricky.

travel details

BUSES

Puerto Limón to: Cahuita (4 daily; 1hr); Puerto Viejo de Talamanca (4 daily; 1hr); San José (12 daily; 2hr 30min–3hr); Sixaola, for Panamá (1 daily; 3hr).

San José to: Cahuita (3 daily; 4hr); Puerto Limón (12 daily; 2hr 30min–3hr); Puerto Viejo de Talamanca (3 daily; 4hr); Sixaola, for Panamá (3 daily; 6hr).

Sixaola to: Cahuita (4 daily; 2hr); Puerto Limón (1 daily; 3hr); Puerto Viejo de Talamanca (4 daily; 2hr); San José (4 daily; 6hr).

BOATS

Moín docks to: Tortuguero (private *lanchas* only; 4hr).

FLIGHTS

Sansa and Travelair both fly the route below.

San José to: Tortuguero (1 daily Mon, Thurs & Sat; 30min).

Tortuguero to: San José (1 daily Mon, Thurs & Sat; 30min).

CHAPTER 30

THE CENTRAL PACIFIC AND SOUTHERN NICOYA

While Costa Rica's **Central Pacific** area is less of a geographical or cultural entity than the other regions of the country, it does contain several of its most popular tourist spots, among them the number one attraction, **Reserva Biológica Bosque Nuboso Monteverde** (Monteverde Cloudforest Reserve), draped over the ridge of the Cordillera de Tilarán. Along with the nearby **Reserva Santa Elena**, Monteverde protects some of the last remaining pristine cloudforest in the Americas.

The Central Pacific and Southern Nicoya also has a number of **beaches** which, along with those of Guanacaste, are some of the best known in the country, with the advantage of being easily accessible from San José. Each offers a distinctly different experience. A former tiny fishing village near the southwest tip of the Nicoya Peninsula, **Montezuma** is surrounded by a series of lovely coves, perfect for sunbathing and hanging out. On the mainland coast, the rough water and huge waves at **Jacó** make it one of the best places to surf in the country. Further south, **Parque Nacional Manuel Antonio** has several extraordinary beaches, with white sands and azure waters.

With the exception of the cool cloudforest of Monteverde, the **vegetation** is Pacific lowland. The climate is tropical, hot and rather drier than in the south – about 33°C is a dry season average. It's not that much cooler in the wet months, when Quepos and Manuel Antonio, in particular, often receive torrential afternoon rains.

Of the two **routes from the capital** to Puntarenas and points south, the main one is the Interamericana, which climbs over the Cordillera Central before dropping precipitously into the Pacific lowlands, levelling out at the town of Esparza, a few kilometres beyond which is the turnoff for Puntarenas. Buses to Jacó and Manuel Antonio take the slightly shorter old road via Atenas and Orotina. Visiting Monteverde is always a bit of an expedition. Although it is just 170km from San José, the roads along the final 35km or so are unpaved and in difficult condition. In the dry season you can do it with a regular car, but in the wet you need 4WD.

Most people cross over to the southern **Nicoya Peninsula** from Puntarenas on the car ferry to Naranjo or the passenger *lancha* to Paquera, from where you can travel by public transport down to Tambor and Montezuma. From Naranjo you can continue south by car or north to Carmona and then up to Nicoya and Santa Cruz, but you'll need 4WD for either route.

The Monteverde area

Generally associated only with the Cloudforest Reserve of the same name, **Monteverde** is, properly, a much larger area, straddling the hump of the Cordillera de

For an explanation of **accommodation price codes**, see p.526.

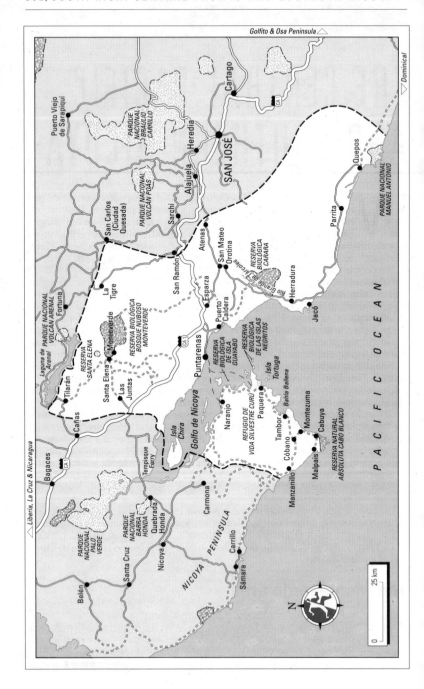

Tilarán between Volcán Arenal and Laguna de Arenal to the east and the low hills of Guanacaste to the west. Along with the Reserve, here you'll find the spread-out Quaker community of **Monteverde**, the neighbouring village of **Santa Elena** – which has a Cloudforest Reserve of its own – and several small hamlets which have not been drawn into any tourism activity.

The area's appeal stems in part from the **Reserva Biológica Bosque Nuboso Monteverde**, and also from the cultural and historical uniqueness of the Monteverde community, which was colonized in the early 1950s by a number of **Quaker** families. Hailing mostly from Alabama, some of them having faced jail for draft-dodging, the Quakers today are completely integrated into Costa Rican society. Many still make their living from dairy farming, producing the region's distinctive **cheese**, sold throughout the country. Abroad, the area is best known as the home of several pioneering **private nature reserves**. Of these, Monteverde is by far the most famous, although the less-touristed **Reserva Santa Elena** is just as interesting, with equally pristine cloudforest cover.

In recent years, Monteverde has become more popular than anyone ever imagined, and strict **rules** govern how many people can enter the Reserve at any one time (see p.598). Apart from the crowds, Monteverde is quite **expensive**, although you can find very good cheap lodging the further away from the entrance you get. Though officially the low season, the **rainy season** (May–Nov) is the best time to visit, to avoid not only the crowds of walkers and fully booked hotels, but also the afternoon fogs of the dry season.

Orientation

Most of the services and the cheaper places to sleep, eat and drink are in **Santa Elena**, 7km southwest of the Monteverde Reserve and 5km south of the Santa Elena Reserve. A major hub for the local farming communities, the village centres on a **triangle** of three (often muddy) streets. There are a few more places to stay at the hamlet of **Cerro Plano**, 1km east, while beyond here comes **Monteverde** proper, essentially a group of dairy farms and smallholdings strung out along a winding, rocky 5km road. Although there are many hotels on this road, it is a much quieter place than Santa Elena, with only the metallic calls of bellbirds and the buzz of the motorcycles and jeeps breaking the silence.

Getting to Monteverde

Getting to Monteverde independently from **San José**, especially in the dry season, entails some pre-planning. You'll need to buy your bus ticket as much as five days in advance, and once you've arrived, buy your return ticket immediately. In the rainy months you can buy your ticket on the day or, better yet, a day in advance. From **Puntarenas** bus demand is less and you can get away with not booking. In the dry months you should **book a room**. In the wet season you can just turn up. Give yourself at least three days in the area; one to get up there, at least one to explore (two is better), and another to descend.

All the major operators offer **tours** to Monteverde from San José; their advantage is a better rate on the more comfortable hotels and transport, but otherwise you can see Monteverde just as well on your own.

By car

Driving from San José to Monteverde takes about four hours via the Interamericana – two hours to the turnoff (there's a choice of three; see below), then another two hours to make the final mountainous ascent. One route, sometimes

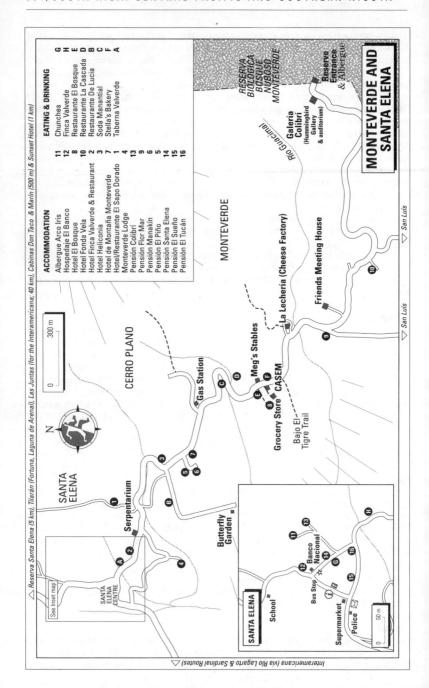

MONTEVERDE AND SANTA ELENA

ACCOMMODATION

Albergue Arco Iris	11
Hospedaje El Banco	12
Hotel El Bosque	8
Hotel Fonda Vela	10
Hotel Finca Valverde & Restaurant	2
Hotel Heliconia	3
Hotel de Montaña Monteverde	7
Hotel/Restaurante El Sapo Dorado	1
Monteverde Lodge	4
Pensión Colibrí	13
Pensión Flor Mar	9
Pensión Manakin	6
Pensión El Piño	5
Pensión Santa Elena	14
Pensión El Sueño	15
Pensión El Tucán	16

EATING & DRINKING

Chunches	G
Finca Valverde	H
Restaurante El Bosque	E
Restaurante La Cascada	D
Restaurante De Lucia	B
Soda Manantial	C
Stella's Bakery	F
Taberna Valverde	A

called the Sardinal route, takes the Interamericana north from Puntarenas towards Liberia, branching off at the **Rancho Grande** turning to Monteverde. Buses go a shorter route, continuing past Rancho Grande to the **Río Lagarto** turnoff – just before Río Lagarto itself – which is signed to Santa Elena and Monteverde. The least well-known route, which local *taxistas* swear is the best, is via **Las Juntas de Abangares**, a small town reached from a small road, labelled 145 on some maps, off the Interamericana. Once you've reached Las Juntas, drive past the main square, turn left and continue over a bridge; turn right, and follow the signs. The first 7km of this 37-kilometre road, via Candelaría, are paved, but have some spectacular hairpin bends – drive slowly. You can also reach Monteverde from **Tilarán**, near Laguna de Arenal. The road (40km) is often very rough, but provides spectacular views over the Laguna de Arenal and Volcán Arenal (see p.635).

Whichever route you take, you'll need **4WD** in the rainy season, when some agencies refuse to rent regular cars for the trip.

By bus

All **buses** stop at Santa Elena. Some then continue along the road to Monteverde, making their last stop at the *Lodge Villa Verde*, one of the closest to the Reserve. Most people arrive on one of the two direct services from **San José**'s Tilarán terminal (3hr 30min minimum – more like 5hr, especially in the rainy season). Be especially vigilant when waiting to board the bus – this service has recently become a magnet for opportunistic thieves. When on the bus, keep everything with you if possible and valuables on your person. Note that taking the afternoon service from San José gets you to Monteverde after dark.

From **Tilarán**, you can catch the 12.30pm bus (3hr), but in the rainy season, this may stop a few kilometres short of Santa Elena, leaving you with no option but to walk the remainder. From **Puntarenas**, a daily bus leaves for Santa Elena at 2.15pm (3hr). And, from Guanacaste, you can pick up the relatively fast service from **Las Juntas**, which goes to Monteverde at 2.30pm (2hr).

The **Santa Elena bus stop** is next to the church, at the top of the "triangle", near the Banco Nacional. From here, all amenities and many *pensiones* are no more than 100m away. *Pensione*/cabina owners will come to the bus and try to entice you to their establishment; most are fine, so take your pick. If you are booked in to one of the hotels on the road to the Reserve, stay on the bus and ask the driver to drop you off, or, if you arrive on the bus from Puntarenas, arrange with your hotel to have a taxi meet you (US$5–6).

Moving on from Monteverde, buses to San José leave Santa Elena at 6.30am and 2.30pm daily. There is sometimes an extra service leaving at 2pm from Friday to Sunday; check the office beside the bus stop. For Tilarán, one bus leaves at 7am; for Puntarenas, at 6am and 2.15pm. There's also a daily service to Las Juntas at 5am, from where you can get to Liberia and points north in Guanacaste.

Accommodation

With the exception of a couple of pensions on the road to Monteverde, the cheapest places to stay are in **Santa Elena**. All accommodation here is basic, but you'll get a bed and heated water at least, and, almost certainly a warm welcome. Many small *pensiones* are run by locals and offer an array of services, from cooking to laundry and horse rental. Some of the hotels in the village triangle, like *Pensión Santa Elena* and *Pensión el Tucán*, are convivial places to meet up and swap information with other travellers. You can also **camp** for a minimal charge on the grounds at the friendly *Albergue Ecológico Arco Iris*.

Hotels in and around the **Monteverde** community tend to be pricey, mainly used by tour groups and older, better-heeled tourists. While you'll certainly be comfortable in these places – large rooms, running hot water, orthopedic mattresses, even saunas and jacuzzis, are the norm – some travellers find the atmosphere a bit dour. You get little sense of a community, partly because Monteverde is not an obvious settlement, and many of the houses are set back in pasture, hidden from the main road.

Santa Elena

Albergue Arco Iris (☎645-5067, fax 645-5022; *arcoiris@sol.racsa.co.cr*). Well-decorated and spacious cabins in peaceful landscaped gardens in the centre of Santa Elena. The best cheap-to-midrange accommodation in the area; they also have bunks (US$10) and camping facilities. Owners Haymo and Susanna are particularly helpful and there's an excellent restaurant. ③–⑥.

Pensión Colibrí (no phone). Family-run, simple accommodation; small rooms, with shared bath and heated water. They cook breakfast, and *casados* for lunch, and also rent horses. ③.

Pensión Santa Elena, 50m south of the Banco Nacional (☎645-5051, fax 645-5147; Aptdo 11689-1000, San José). HI-affiliated (members get ten percent discount), with small basic rooms, right in the centre of things. A good place to meet travellers, with kitchen facilities and laundry. ②–③.

Pensión el Sueño, 25m east of the *correo* (☎645-5021). Basic, clean but rather dark rooms with shared bath, or, for a few colones more, slightly nicer rooms with private bath. TV in a small lounge and friendly *dueños* who cook a good breakfast (US$3) on request. Low season discounts of up to fifty percent. ②–③.

Pensión el Tucán, 100m south of the Banco Nacional (☎645-5017). Doña Rosita has the best rock-bottom rooms in town, most of them above the (good) restaurant of the same name, with shared bath and heated water. Rooms with private bath cost a few dollars more. ②–③.

Monteverde and around

Albergue Reserva Biológica de Monteverde, at the entrance to the Monteverde Reserve (☎645-5122, fax 645-5034). Often packed with researchers and students; tourists have second priority. Cheap, though, and allows you to sleep right in the reserve. Reservations essential; you need to pay half 45 days in advance. ④–⑥.

Hotel el Bosque, about 3km from the Reserve entrance (☎ & fax 645-5129). Best mid-priced option on the road to the Reserve, with large rooms, private baths and views over the hills out towards the Golfo de Nicoya. Discount at the (good) restaurant of same name. ⑤–⑥.

Pensión Flor Mar, about 2km from the Reserve entrance (☎645-5009, fax 645-5008; Aptdo 2498-1000, San José). One of the older *pensiones*, owned by a founder of the original Quaker community. Basic and good value, although rooms are small; some with private bath. Management is friendly and there's a nice restaurant. ③.

Fonda Vela, about 1.5km from the Reserve entrance (☎645-5125, fax 645-5119). Large rooms, though the ones at the back can be quite dark. Has its own trails, plus pleasant grounds with pre-Columbian statuary, and is convenient for the Reserve. Good restaurant, open to public. ⑦.

Pensión Manakín, Cerro Plano (☎645-5080). One of the best budget options, with homely atmosphere, friendly, basic dorms, and rooms with shared or private bath. Use of kitchen facilities. Ten percent discount for students with ID. ②.

Pensión el Piño, Cerro Plano, next to *Pensión Manakín* (☎ & fax 645-5130). Good budget rooms with shared bath and heated water in a small annexe next to a family house. ②.

El Sapo Dorado, 1km east of Santa Elena (☎645-5010, fax 645-5180; Aptdo 09, CP 5655, Monteverde). A good place to splurge – roomy, rustic wooden chalets on a hill, with stupendous views of the Golfo de Nicoya. Some have fireplaces and kitchenettes. Also guided walks on private paths by the Río Guácimal, and one of the best restaurants in Monteverde. ⑦–⑧.

The communities

In recent years **SANTA ELENA** has benefited – economically, anyway – from the influx of visitors to the Monteverde Reserve and, increasingly, to the Santa Elena Reserve, 5km northeast. In the village you'll find the only bank, *correo* and large grocery store for miles. The only unbiased **information** about the area – most hotels and *pensiones* are geared to getting you to use their guides/contacts – is offered by the Unión Turística Autónoma de Santa Elena y Monteverde, known by the acronym **UTaSeM**, who can tell you current bus schedules, advise on transport to the reserves, and give contacts for horse rental, for example. It's in the **Santa Elena Reserve office**, 150m north of the *panadería* in Santa Elena, across from the radio tower (Mon–Sat 9am–noon & 3–7pm; ☎645-5014 or 645-5067).

Gringos hang out at *Chunches* (Mon–Sat 9am–6pm; ☎645-5147), opposite the *Pensión Santa Elena*, which has a laundry, café serving espresso, US newspapers, and a useful noticeboard with details of tours, rooms and just about everything else. Its secondhand bookstore is especially good. Though its better by far to bring plenty of colones, Banco Nacional (Mon–Fri 8am–3pm) can change **travellers' cheques**, a service also offered to guests by many of the upscale Monteverde hotels.

MONTEVERDE proper is a seemingly timeless place, where milk cans are left out at the end of small dairy-farm driveways to be collected, modest houses sit perched above splendid forested views, and farmers trudge along the muddy roads in sturdy rubber boots. The focal points of the community are the **lechería** (cheese factory), the **Friends Meeting House** and school, and the cluster of services around **CASEM**, the women's arts and crafts collective.

Reserva Biológica Bosque Nuboso Monteverde

RESERVA BIOLÓGICA BOSQUE NUBOSO MONTEVERDE (daily 7am–4.30pm; closed Oct 6 & 7; US$8; ☎645-5112) is a large (105 square kilometres) private reserve, holding the last sizeable pockets of primary cloudforest in Mesoamerica. Administered by the Centro Científico Tropical (Tropical Science Centre) based in San José, it's hugely popular with foreigners and Ticos alike, who flock here in droves – especially during Easter week and school holidays – to walk the trails.

Few people fail to be impressed by its sheer diversity of **terrain**, from semi-dwarf stunted forest on the more wind-exposed areas, to thick bearded cloudforest vegetation, and some truly moving **views** of uninterrupted, dense green. The Monteverde Reserve supports six different **life zones**, or eco-communities, hosting an estimated 2500 species of plants, more than 100 species of mammals, some 490 species of butterflies, including the rare blue morpho, and over 400 species of birds, among them the resplendent **quetzal** (best seen Jan–May). The cloudforest cover, however – dense, low-lit and heavy – makes it difficult to see animals.

Plant-spotting, however, is never unrewarding, especially if you take a **guided walk**, which will help you identify thick mosses, epiphytes, bromeliads, primitive ferns, leaf-cutter ants, poison dart frogs and other small fauna and flora. Serious rainforest walkers should plan on spending at least a day in the Reserve; many people spend two or three days quite happily here.

Temperatures are cool: 15° or 16°C is not uncommon. Be sure to carry an umbrella and light rain gear. You should also bring binoculars, fast-speed film and insect repellent. It's just about possible to get away without **rubber boots** in the dry season, but you will most definitely need them in the wet. The Reserve office and some hotels rent them out.

Practicalities

If you don't want to walk the 7km from Santa Elena to the Reserve, hop on the **bus** from in front of the *panadería* (daily 6.20am & 1pm, returning at noon & 4pm). At the entrance, the **Reserve office** (daily 7am–4pm; ☎645-5112) is very well geared up to tourists, with a **visitor centre** where you can pick up maps and buy useful interpretive booklets for the trails. It also has a good souvenir shop, and a small soda, which dishes out coffee, cold drinks and snacks plus vegetarian *casados* at lunchtime. Also at the entrance, the **Galería Colibrí**, or Hummingbird Gallery (Mon–Sat 9.30am–4.30pm, Sun 10am–2pm), named after the birds that buzz in and out to feed at the sugared water fountains, sells nature slides, cards, jewellery and the like, as well as holding slide shows on cloudforest topics.

In an attempt to limit human impact on the Reserve, a number of **rules** govern entrance to Monteverde. Capacity is 250 people per day, but serious birders, wildlife spotters and those who would prefer to walk the trails in quiet, should avoid the **peak hours** of 8am till 10am, when the tour groups pour in. An alternative is to book a ticket a **day in advance** – your hotel can reserve you a place for the following day – and get here by 5.30am (not earlier – it's still too dark), when, even though the visitor centre is closed, you are able to go on the trails. Bookings cannot be made any more than 24 hours in advance.

For overnight and long-distance hikers, there are simple **shelter facilities** along the trails, which cost US$4 per night plus a small deposit. They're not always open, however, so check with the Reserve visitor centre.

Tours and talks

The Reserve organizes a number of **tours** (US$12–15; ☎645-5112), which set off from the office at the entrance. If you're short of time, make a **guided natural history walk** your priority. These are informative, slow-paced affairs, focusing on plants and whatever insect and bird life comes along. They currently leave at 7am, 7.30am, 8am, 8.30am and 9am prompt (maximum 10 people), and take about three hours. **Birdwatching tours** currently run at 5.30am and 8.30am. **Night walks** (7.30pm) are recommended if you want to see a maximum of amphibian, reptile and insect life and don't spook easily. Ask too, about the occasional **orchid walks**, available only at certain times of the year. All walks end with a **slide show**, during which you'll see some of the creatures you encountered in the Reserve and many you did not, including the Monteverde golden toad.

If you can't or don't want to go on the official tours, there are a number of excellent local **guides** who can show you the Reserve and the entire Monteverde area. Check at the visitor centre.

Reserva Santa Elena

Less touristed than Monteverde, the **RESERVA SANTA ELENA** (daily 7am–4pm; US$6), 5km northeast of the village of Santa Elena, offers just as illuminating an experience of the cloudforest. Higher than the Monteverde Reserve – poised at an elevation of 1650m – its three-square-kilometre area consists of mainly primary cover. Trails are steeper and more challenging, and there's a slightly higher chance of seeing quetzals in season. Established in 1992, it strives to be self-funding, assisted by donations and entrance fee revenue, and gives a percentage of its profit to local schools. For maintenance and building projects it depends greatly on **volunteers**, usually foreign students.

Getting to the Santa Elena Reserve from the village entails an arduous 5km walk over a boulder-strewn road, much of it uphill. Best to drop in the **Reserve office** (daily 7am–4pm) in Santa Elena, 400m northeast of the *panadería*, and ask when Eduardo is going in his jeep. He will take passengers for US$2. The Reserve can also telephone a taxi to come and pick you up (US$6).

There's a **visitor centre** at the entrance, with washrooms, a cafeteria (high season only), a small interpretive display, and an information area where staff hand out maps and recommend guides (US$10–15). They also have an excellently succinct six-page leaflet discussing the flora and fauna you might see within the Reserve. **Guided tours** can be arranged for one to four hours; you can rent boots for US$6.50.

Other Monteverde attractions

A number of attractions have sprung up in the Monteverde area. The **Canopy Tour** is based on three static suspended platforms high in the forest canopy southeast of town. Having grappled up strangler figs to reach the top – which gives great views of life in the forest canopy – you can go from platform to platform via pulleys strung on horizontal traverse cables. Dawn and dusk tours, when you're likely to see most animals, are available on request. Prices are steep at US$40, but this is probably the biggest thrill you'll get in tranquil Monteverde. For details contact the "base camp" in Santa Elena (☎645-5243 or 645-5645), or in San José call ☎255-2463 (fax 255-3573). You can get another birds' eye view of the forest from the **Skywalk**, 4km northeast of Santa Elena (daily 7am–5pm; US$8). Built by a resident biologist, five suspension-style footbridges span acres of virgin rainforest, above and below canopy-level, offering some really spectacular views.

Up the hill from Santa Elena on the way to Monteverde, the **Serpentarium** (daily 9am–4pm) has a range of unnerving vipers in residence. The creatures are less menacing at the **Butterfly Garden**, in Cerro Plano (daily 9.30am–4pm; US$5), which, unlike most such places in Costa Rica, is geared to research rather than export of pupae. You can take a guided tour, which illuminates the life-cycle of butterflies, or use the leaflet they hand you to tour by yourself. The best times to visit are between 11am and 1pm, especially on a sunny day – butterflies tend to hide when it's raining. Also in Cerro Plano, near the gas station, the **Bosque Eterno de los Niños** (Children's Eternal Rainforest; daily 7.30am–4.30pm; US$4.50), features the Bajo el Tigre trail, a short, unchallenging trek at lower elevations than in the Cloudforest Reserves. Walks are always guided, geared up for groups, and include a sunset hike between 3pm and 5.30pm. On a rainy afternoon, the **Orchid Garden** in Cerro Plano (daily 8am–5pm; ☎645-5339), run by orchid enthusiast Gabriel Barboza, is a good bet, with over 400 different species of orchids on show, among them the world's smallest. They also show two **rainforest slide shows**.

About 2km from the Monteverde Reserve entrance, **la lechería**, or cheese factory (Mon–Sat 7.30am–noon & 1–3.30pm, Sun 7.30am–12.30pm) sells Monteverde cheese and *cajeta*, a butterscotch spread. Guided tours (☎645-5150 or 5029; US$8) give you a behind-the-scenes glimpse into the world of cheese, but for most people a quick visit to the shop to buy the product is quite enough. Nearby, the women's arts and crafts cooperative **CASEM** (Mon–Sat 8am–5pm, Sun 10am–4pm; free) sells embroidered T-shirts, blouses and dresses, and some hand-painted T-shirts – lovely but expensive.

You can't **ride horses** on the trails in the Monteverde or Santa Elena Reserves, but a number of local outfitters rent them out for trips through the surrounding valleys and on private land. Note that there have been many gruesome stories of mistreatment (and sometimes deaths) of horses on the rides between La Fortuna (see p.635) and Monteverde. This is a nightmarish trek for any horse, especially in the wet season, and should be avoided. There are many shorter treks in the Monteverde and Santa Elena area that do not put such a strain on the animals. In Santa Elena ask at *pensiones Colibrí* and *el Tucán*, both of whom rent good, strong beasts for around US$7 an hour. Emiliano's *Establo La Estrella* rents well cared for horses (US$8/hr; ☎645-5045, or ask at the *Albergue Arco Iris*), and *Meg's Stables*, next to *Stella's Bakery*, is one of the best in the area (US$10/hr; ☎645-5052).

Eating, drinking and nightlife

In **Santa Elena**, most people eat in their **pensions**. The restaurant at the *Pensión el Tucán* (closed Sun), open to non-guests, serves good cheap food, especially *casados*, and is a good bet for breakfast. The *Arco Iris* (open Nov–Easter, July & Aug, open to non-guests but drop by before 4pm to check) has an excellent restaurant with an extensive menu, including shrimp in coconut sauce, succulent red snapper and vegetarian dishes. Doña Laura has a popular kiosk in front of the church serving *casados* – climb up on the wooden stools and chat with the regulars. For espresso, go to *Chunches*. *The Rocky Road Café* above the *panadería* (Mon–Sat 9am–4pm) serves an excellent BLT and fruit shakes.

Cuisine in many of the top-end **Monteverde** hotels is very good indeed, and most of them open their restaurants to the public. Menus are usually fixed, and meals are served at set times. Drop round in person to book for dinner and see what is on the menu.

Being a Quaker community, there is not much **drinking** to be done in the Monteverde area, including gringo-filled Santa Elena. Most restaurants do have alcohol on the menu, but you will notice a whiff of temperance in the air. If it's a **beer** you're after, the relaxed *Bar Valverde* 1km east of Santa Elena is one place where women can feel comfortable. *Bar la Cascada*, opposite *Soda Manantial* midway between Santa Elena and Monteverde, is the only place to **dance** (Thurs–Sun, after 8pm), playing mostly techno. Drinks are not cheap, and food is not served.

The **Monteverde Music Festival**, held in January, February and March, stages a blend of classical, jazz and modern music, from chamber orchestras to big bands. Performances are daily at 5pm and there is a shuttle bus from Santa Elena to the venues – ask at your hotel.

Restaurante el Bosque, Monteverde, about 3km from the Reserve entrance. Good, filling *casados* – not especially cheap – and other *típico* food. Lunch specials are particularly recommended, but watch out if you arrive at the same time as a tour/hotel group; the kitchen puts you at the end of the queue.

Cafe Morpho, Santa Elena (☎645-5818). A new café serving healthy, well-prepared food, some of it macrobiotic, with good large salads for reasonable prices. They show videos some evenings.

Restaurante de Lucia, between Santa Elena and Cerro Plano, 150m from the *Hotel Heliconia*. Don José will set down perfect steak, chicken and pork done just as you like it. Excellent service, varied menu, and a not-bad wine selection.

El Sapo Dorado, 1km east of Santa Elena (☎645-5010). The poshest place in Monteverde, with an excellent changing menu of interesting, expensive, nouvelle-type dishes, such as ink pasta with squid and calamares. Classical music on the stereo, and jaw-dropping views out over the gulf from the open-air terrace in front. Open for dinner daily 6–9pm.

Stella's Bakery, opposite CASEM. Delicious chocolate chip cookies, strudel, brownies and coffee, in a pleasant café-like atmosphere. Daily 6.30am–4.30pm.

Restaurante Valverde, on the road to the *Finca Valverde* hotel, just east of Santa Elena. Rustic restaurant, set in the woods and reached by a lovely floodlit path and a bridge over a stream. Good local food including fish in garlic sauce and grilled steak. Open daily 7am–8pm.

Around Monteverde: Tilarán

TILARÁN, 40km northeast of Monteverde, is a useful stopoff between Guanacaste to the west and the Zona Norte to the east. There are a few **cabinas**, and more in the offing. Good options include *Cabinas Mary,* with large rooms and private bath (☎695-5479; ②), and *Lago Lindo* (☎695-5555; ②), whose basic rooms have communal kitchen facilities. In addition to the service to Santa Elena (see p.595), Tilarán has good **bus** connections with Cañas and the Interamericana, from where you can head on to Liberia and the Guanacaste beaches, or south to Puntarenas.

Puntarenas

Poor **PUNTARENAS**, 110km west of San José, has the abandoned look that haunts so many tropical port cities. What isn't rusting has long ago bleached out to a generic pastel, and the cracked, potholed streets, shaded by mop-headed mango trees, are lined with old wooden buildings painted in faded tutti-frutti colours. Tourists come only to catch a *lancha* or ferry across to southern Nicoya.

Arrival and information

Scores of **buses** arrive from San José every day, stopping on the south side of C 2, near the old train tracks and the old dock that juts out into the gulf. **Local services** from Quepos and Manuel Antonio (3 daily; 3hr) arrive just across the street, as does the daily service from Liberia, which arrives at about 11am, and the daily run from Santa Elena, which currently arrives at about 9.30am.

Walking just one and a half blocks north and a few blocks west of the San José bus stop will get you into the town centre, where you'll find the the very helpful **tourist office** (Mon–Fri 9am–noon & 2–5pm, Sat 9am–2pm; ☎661-1985 or 1169). The office may not always be open, but, when it is, you can pick up town maps. They also have the latest ferry and *lancha* schedules to the Nicoya Peninsula and offer a left-luggage facility. This is the place to come if you want to contact home: an AT&T **phone** connects you directly to the USA, you can call elsewhere at good rates, and there's a **fax**.

The Banco de Costa Rica and the Banco Nacional, virtually next to each other on the north shore near the docks, offer **currency exchange** (both Mon–Fri 9am–3pm). If you get stuck you could try the more upscale hotels too, like the *Tioga*, although these normally change dollars only for their own guests.

Accommodation

The **cheap hotels** around the docks are useful if you want to catch an early *lancha* to Paquera. It's not a great area at night, however. More upmarket options – with the exception of the *Tioga* – congregate just east of the town centre, near the yacht club. Wherever you stay, make sure your room has a **fan** that works.

Ayi-Con, 50m south of the mercado on C 2 (☎661-0164 or 1477). Decent option near the Paquera *lancha* dock. Some rooms with a/c, but those with ceiling fans are fine and better value. Private or shared bath; cold water only. ②.

Tioga, Paseo de los Turistas, C 17/19 (☎661-0271, fax 661-0127). The nicest downtown hotel, with elegant atmosphere, extra-friendly management and a/c rooms – those on the sea-facing side get the best views. Also a soothing interior courtyard and very pretty indoor pool. Rates include breakfast in cafeteria-style restaurant. ⑥–⑦.

Yadran, Paseo de los Turistas, C 35/37 (☎661-2662, fax 661-1944). While somewhat lacking in atmosphere, the rooms here are comfortable enough, carpeted, with TV, a/c and bath. Also a swimming pool and restaurant. ⑦.

Eating, drinking and nightlife

Food, even fish, is pricey in Puntarenas: you'll be lucky to get *casados* or *platos del día* for less than US$4 or US$5. As usual the **mercado** is a good place to pick up a cheap meal and a *refresco*, although you should avoid drinking anything made with the local water. The beachside sodas and kiosks near the **old dock** are more appealing places to linger for a quiet drink or a seafood lunch.

The best restaurants in town, however, are on the Paseo de los Turistas. *Alohas*, on the paseo at C 19/21, has an extensive, expensive menu, and nice breezy tables where you can sit al fresco looking out to sea. It is also the most popular place in town for an evening drink, with live music on Tuesday. *Marisquería el Tabasco*, at C 1/3, offers good surf'n'turf, including black mussels, fish *casados*, burgers, other hunks of meat and French fries. It's not particularly cheap, and service is slow, but the beachside tables, under palms, are the nicest in town. The reasonably priced menu at *La Terraza*, at C 21/23, concentrates on seafood, pizza and pasta, with good marinated mussels and seafood salad.

Moving on from Puntarenas: getting to the Nicoya Peninsula

Puntarenas is a jumping-off point for foot, bicycle and motor vehicle traffic for the southern Nicoya Peninsula. There are two **car ferries**, both of which leave five times daily. The car ferry to **Paquera** (for Tambor and Montezuma; ☎220-2034 for schedules) costs US$12 per vehicle. The **Naranjo car ferry** (1hr 30min), run by *Coonatramar* (☎661-1069, fax 661-2197) currently leaves from the docks at the western end of the estuary side of town. Check at the **tourist office** for the latest schedule. In the summer (Dec–April) especially, get there ninety minutes before sailing to ensure a space. Bear in mind that, though it is possible to drive around the Nicoya Peninsula from Naranjo, the roads are not in great shape, and you'll need 4WD.

The **passenger ferry** (*lancha*) to Paquera currently leaves from behind the mercado, three times daily in the high season (1hr; US$1.50); there are fewer crossings in the low season. Schedules are posted outside the blue kiosk where you buy tickets. You can also store luggage at the kiosk for a minimal fee. Buses for Tambor and Montezuma (2hr; US$4) are timed to meet the Paquera *lancha* and leave once everyone is on board. Rush to get off the ferry when it docks; this way you'll have a better chance of getting a seat.

Puntarenas is also a transportation hub for **buses**. There are services at least every hour on the hour for San José (2hr), while from the other side of the Paseo you can pick up services to Liberia (5 daily; 3hr) and Santa Elena (daily 2.15pm; 3hr 30min). For Manuel Antonio, take the Quepos service (3 daily; 3hr 30min), which will also drop you off just 2km from Jacó.

The southern Nicoya Peninsula

The ninety-minute ferry trip across the Golfo de Nicoya from Puntarenas is soothing: slow-paced, the boat purrs through usually calm waters, passing island bird sanctuaries along the way. In the distance are the low brown hills of the Nicoya Peninsula, ringed by a rugged coastline and pockets of intense jungly green.

Much of the southern peninsula has been cleared for farming or cattle grazing or, in the case of **Tambor**, given over to tourism development. **Cóbano**, 6km inland from Montezuma, is the main town in the southwest of the peninsula, with gas station, *correo*, *guardia rural* and a few bars. Most tourists pass right though on the way to **Montezuma**, one of the most popular beach hang-outs in the country, reached by a reasonable dirt road lined with cattle pasture on both sides.

Montezuma and around

The former fishing village of **MONTEZUMA**, about 25km west of Paquera at the southwestern tip of the Nicoya Peninsula, is in danger of becoming overwhelmed by its popularity. For a place that didn't even have electricity until six or seven years ago, it really has grown extremely quickly, shifting from a haunt for younger, budget tourists to appeal to more upscale visitors.

What brings everyone here is the astounding beauty of the setting. Montezuma and the coast south to Cabo Blanco features some of the loveliest coastline in the country: white sand, dotted with jutting rocks and vertiginous, leaning palms, and backed by lush greenery, including rare Pacific lowland tropical forest.

Some fifteen or twenty years ago a handful of foreigners fell in love with Montezuma and settled here. In recent years, though, the **foreign influx** has been overwhelming. Arriving at night the place can look like the Quartier-Latin-by-the-sea: lights twinkle, music pours out of the bars, and well-tanned, well-honed boys and girls sip cappuccino at cafés. In response to the threats to their community that tourism poses, villagers have formed an articulate **residents' group**, CATUMO, and organize various collective projects, including brigades that regularly clean up the beach. Signs have been erected asking people nicely to use the litter bins, not to cut down trees, and not to park their 4WDs in the *parquecito*.

Arrival and information

From where you get off the bus in Montezuma, at the bottom of the hill, you can see pretty much all there is to see. *Chico's Bar* is straight ahead, as is the grocery store and the souvenir shop. The **information kiosk** is on your left; it is likely to be closed in low season, especially midweek. If you bring a car, respect the wishes of the local community and put it in the village *parqueo* behind the bus stop (US$3 per day).

Monteaventuras (Mon–Sat 8am–noon & 4–8pm; ☎ & fax 642-0025), adjacent to *Hotel el Jardín*, acts as an all-purpose **information** service. As well as organizing tours they have a **fax**, an **international phone** line, and can reserve and confirm **flights** on Sansa and Travelair. Many businesses, including the information kiosk, **close down** for the afternoon, between around noon and 4pm. Bring lots of **colones**, as Montezuma is not really set up to change dollars or travellers' cheques, although the souvenir stores will accept the latter.

If you're heading on **to Puntarenas**, check for current bus/*lancha* schedules at the information kiosk by the parking lot.

Accommodation

Despite Montezuma's popularity, **prices** have tended to remain moderate, as the village still caters to a young, studenty crowd who can't afford the rates of, say, Manuel Antonio. Though there's less of a high season/low season schism here than in most places, some of the upmarket hotels do increase their prices by about US$10 to US$15 in the **high season**; this is less marked in the cheaper lodgings.

It's recommended to **reserve** in the dry season, especially on weekends. If you don't manage to book in advance, make sure you arrive as early as possible to get the best price and choice. Things are easier in the rainy season when it's not quite so dire if you arrive at night without a room.

Staying in the **village** is convenient, saving you from having to walk in the dark back to your lodging, but it can be noisy, due to *Chico's Bar*. Elsewhere it's wonderfully peaceful, with choices out on the **beach,** on the road that heads southwest to the Cabo Blanco Refuge, and on the sides of the steep hill about 1km above the village.

Amor de Mar, 600m southwest of village centre on beach (☎ & fax 642-0262). Seafront hotel, in pretty landscaped gardens set on a rocky promontory, with hammocks swinging between giant mango trees. There's a small restaurant downstairs, and some rooms have kitchenette. Rooms upstairs and facing the sea are best, with nice views and cross-breezes. ⑥.

La Aurora, in the village (☎642-0051, fax 642-0025). Pleasant, environmentally conscious *pensión*, run by friendly Angela Jiménez, one of the driving forces in the local community. All rooms have mosquito nets or screens, fans, communal fridge, coffee- and tea-making facilities. Upstairs rooms, a little more expensive, have ceiling fans, cross-breezes, and hammocks. ⑤.

Hotel el Jardín, in the village (☎ & fax 642-0074). Attractive, spacious rooms with wooden ceilings, tiled bathrooms, verandahs or terraces with Sarchí leather rocking chairs. Some have fridges, and the upstairs rooms have a lovely view over the town and sea. ⑥.

Pensión Jenny, in the village (no phone). Good budget option, with basic rooms with shared bath, in a house on the side of the road, overlooking the beach. Upstairs rooms are quite large, and there's a verandah with a hammock. ②.

Cabinas/Pensión Lucy, in the village (no phone). A Montezuma stalwart that the government once attempted to have torn down, as it violates the *zona marítima*, which says you can't build on the first 50m of beach. Clean and basic, with cold showers, and a nice seaside verandah upstairs. Dorm beds for US$6. ②–③.

Los Mangos, 800m south of *Montezuma*, on the road to Cabo Blanco (☎642-0259, fax 642-0076). Some bungalows, made out of what looks like very expensive wood, which makes them a bit dark, with large (hot water) showers, fan and palm roof. The cheaper rooms – the best are upstairs – in the main building down by the road are good value, particularly for groups of 4 or 6. The only hotel in town with a pool, and a good poolside restaurant (see below). ⑤–⑥.

Hotel Montezuma, in the centre of the village (☎642-0258, fax 642-0058). Popular with budget travellers, the cheapest place in town with shared bath (prices hike significantly for private bath) and ceiling fans. It's not always that friendly, however, and there's noise from *Chico's Bar* next door. Go for the upstairs rooms if you want to sleep. Accepts Visa. ②–③.

Sano Banano Cabinas, 15-min walk northeast of the centre, on the beach – ask for Patricia or Lenny in the restaurant of the same name for directions (☎ & fax 642-0068). Truly wonderful circular cabinas with thatched roof, beachfront balcony, outside shower and kitchenette. This is the place to stay if you want seclusion and don't mind the crabs who do the best to infiltrate your room. Bring a torch. ⑤–⑥.

Cabinas Tucán, in the village (☎642-0284). Good value, adequately clean, basic rooms in two-storey wooden house. Shared cold water baths and ceiling or table fans, but no curtains. Upstairs rooms are marginally better. ③–④.

The village and around

There's nothing much to do in Montezuma itself, and even the swimming isn't that great, hampered by rocks and occasionally heavy surf. The **beach** features a lovely **nature trail** (1500m; 30min), ending at **Playa Grande**, a reasonable swimming beach where people also surf.

There are a number of interesting places to **shop** in Montezuma. Ecofund, run by a local cooperative, sells tiger balm – an all-purpose herbal remedy, especially good for sprains and muscle ache – and condoms, along with the usual T-shirts, sandals, hats and sunblock. The small shop next to Monteaventuras has some beautiful **Indonesian** sarongs and dresses, at better prices than elsewhere. For **crafts** and **jewellery**, head for the streetside stalls between the bus stop and *Sano Banano* cabinas.

Montezuma and its environs is laced with a number of **waterfalls**, the closest of which is about a kilometre walk down the road towards Cabo Blanco and then another 800m on a path through the dense growth (signed). Always take care with waterfalls, especially in the wet season, on account of **flash floods**, and under no circumstances try to climb them: many have been injured in the attempt, and one person even killed. Local tour operators lead **horseback rides** to falls that are otherwise difficult or impossible to reach on foot.

Isla Tortuga off the coast of the peninsula is a popular place to snorkel, swim safely in calm and warm shallow waters, and sunbathe. Local boatmen can take you there and back for quite a bit less than you'd pay with one of the "cruise ship" companies doing the run from San José or Puntarenas, although tours from Montezuma are less

---

TOURS AND TREKS FROM MONTEZUMA

The **information kiosk**, when it is open, can advise regarding guides for the hike to nearby **waterfalls**, **horse rentals** for riding along the beach (US$5–7/hr) and **boat trips** via the local boatmen's cooperative association to Isla Mercadoa, Isla Tortuga, Puntarenas, and around the west coast of the peninsula to Playa Sámara. They will also point you to places that rent **bikes** (US$10/day).

Monteaventuras organize guided **walks** (30–90min) and **horseback** rides (4hr) to the **waterfalls**, snorkelling trips to **Isla Tortuga,** and a wildlife tour to Cabo Blanco (4hr natural history walks with qualified guide cost US$15, transport included). They also rent **snorkelling** gear (US$25/hr) and **scuba** equipment (US$40/hr), **bicycles** (US$12) **motorbikes** and **cars** (from US$40 per day for motorbikes; US$75 for a 4WD).

posh. Drinks may be included, although lunch is usually not. Best to stock up in the village and ask the boatmen if they have a cooler you can use.

The single most popular excursion in town, however, is probably to the **Cabo Blanco** Reserve for a morning's walking (see below). If you like **mountain biking** you could ride the 9km down to Cabo Blanco, walk the trail and bike back in a day. Mind the height of the two creeks en route, though, as you won't get through them at high tide.

Eating, drinking and nightlife

Fresh **fish** has always been very good in Montezuma, which used to be a fishing village before tourism hit. Now there's also vegetarian pizza, granola, mango shakes and paella. Eating three meals a day will set you back a few colones, though.

For one of the **best restaurants** on the peninsula, take a 5km trip to **CABUYA**, the first hamlet beyond Montezuma on the way to Cabo Blanco. Here *El Ancla de Oro* dishes up the most delicious **lobster** in the country, served in garlic butter (around US$10). The red snapper is cheaper and just as good. They also have a few, simple **rooms** (①). The road to Cabuya is very bad, and you can only be guaranteed of getting there in the dry season (Dec–April) – even then, only with 4WD. Transport may be laid on from Montezuma village: ask at the information kiosk.

Nightlife in Montezuma centres around *Chico's Bar*, where the only thing to do is hang out and drink. More retiring types can take in the very popular nightly video shows (in English) at the *Sano Banano* at 7.30pm. You have to spend at least US$2 in the restaurant to watch. The noticeboard outside Monteaventuras announces local dances and events.

Restaurante el Jardín, next to *Hotel el Jardín*. Espresso, good fruit drinks and semi-veggie dishes, including stuffed zucchini and burritos. The spaghetti and shrimp and fish fillet in *ranchera* sauce are good value.

Restaurante Montezuma, in *Hotel Montezuma*. The Spanish chef cooks great paella and seafood, and they also serve delicious fresh bread. Lovely location, upstairs, under palm trees and looking out to sea.

Soda el Parque, fronting the beach. Small soda, underneath the palms, serving great fresh fish – snapper, lobster, bass in garlic and oil – and traditional *gallo pinto* breakfasts. Avoid eating the *cambute* (conch), though, as it's on the verge of extinction and consumption is technically prohibited. Daily 7–10am & 6–9pm.

Sano Banano, in the centre of the village. Filling lunch specials of fish, baked potato, bread with garlic butter and salad, for around US$6. Also crepes, vegetarian pizzas, vegetable *casados* with lentil fritters, yoghurt and beans. If you have nothing else, try a mango shake.

Reserva Natural Absoluta Cabo Blanco

RESERVA NATURAL ABSOLUTA CABO BLANCO (Wed–Sun 8am–4pm; US$6), 9km southwest of Montezuma, is Costa Rica's oldest protected piece of land, established in 1963. At almost twelve square kilometres, Cabo Blanco occupies the entire southwest tip of the peninsula. The natural beauty of the area is complemented by its unique biodiversity, with pockets of **Pacific lowland tropical forest** of a type and mix that are found nowhere else in the country. Animals that live here include howler monkeys, plus sloths and squirrels. Agoutis and coati are common, as are snakes – so watch your step. Sea birds nest down by the shore, using the islands off the very tip of the peninsula as their prime site, and you'll often see clouds of frigate birds hovering above.

The **trail** (5km; 2hr) leads from the ranger station through tropical deciduous forest to **Playa Cabo Blanco** and **Playa Balsitas**; not great for swimming, but two very lovely, lonely spots. Be wary of the high tide – *marea* – ask the ranger at the entrance when and where you are likely to get cut off if walking on the beach. It's very exposed and very **hot**: 30°C is not uncommon, so bring a hat, some water and sunblock.

Practicalities

Colectivo taxis from Montezuma to Cabo Blanco leave from the side of Montezuma's *parqueo* (ask at the information kiosk for schedules). This service may not run in the rainy season if it has been very wet. Though **roads** down to Cabo Blanco are bad, you can drive there with 4WD. Watch the two creeks, however, which are too deep – even for most 4WDs – at high tide.

You pay your entrance fee at the ranger hut, where they can supply you with a map of the trail. There's no real need to take a **guide**, but if you would like one, the information kiosk in Montezuma can recommend locals. No camping is allowed, but there are a number of **places to stay** on the road from Montezuma. Fernando Morales' house, about 5km southwest of Montezuma, and Sr Guevara's house, 500m before you reach the Cabo Blanco entrance, have **rooms** (①–②) and good **campgrounds**.

Playa Jacó

The best thing you can say about **PLAYA JACÓ** is that it's the closest beach to San José. Just three hours away (102km) from the capital, it attracts a mix of surfers, weekenders and holidaying Ticos, from party-hearty students to working-class families. If you've been stuck in San José and are desperate to get to a beach, you might want to take advantage of the weekend specials at larger hotels like *Jacófiesta* and *Jacó Beach*, both of which have swimming pools – but if you have dreams of swimming in the Pacific off pristine white sands, forget it. For one, the water is reported to be polluted near the estuaries; and elsewhere it can be dangerous.

Despite the caveats, it's impossible to overstate Jacó's popularity with surfers (May–Nov), Canadian package tourists (Dec–March) and Joséfinos (all year); be sure to make reservations during the high season (Dec–April), especially at weekends.

Arrival, information and getting around

From San José **buses** leave for Jacó daily at 7.30am, 10.30am and 3.30pm (2hr 30min–3hr). There are extra buses on holidays and holiday weekends but if you intend to travel between Friday and Sunday, especially in the high season or on holidays, buy your ticket three days in advance. Though the bus officially stops at the extreme north end of the village, by *Hotel el Jardín*, it does in fact continue 3km down the main street backing the town. If you know more or less where you want to get off and/or have gear, it's best to stay on until the bus finally terminates. The *Hotel Irazú*, just outside San José on the way to Alajuela has a small bus that goes to Jacó daily at 9am. This doesn't leave you enough time for a day trip, however, as it returns from Jacó at 2pm (☎232-4811; about US$14).

The Banco Nacional (Mon–Fri 9am–3pm) can change **travellers' cheques**. The GAB Casa de Cambio in the centre of town charges slightly higher commission on travellers' cheques but will give you your money much faster. The ICE office (Mon–Sat 8am–noon & 1–5pm) offers a **fax** and **phone** service to Europe and the US. Next door, the self-serve **laundry** has hot water, free soap and coin-operated machines.

Many places **rent mopeds**. More environmentally sound by far is to rent a **mountain bike** for about US$10 a day (though note that no bikes are allowed on the beach). Try Fun Rentals, next to the Restaurante Flamboyant on the main road. You can also rent a car, to get, for example, to Manuel Antonio (although you can get there just fine by bus). ADA (☎643-3207), Budget (☎643-3112) and Elegante (☎643-3224) all have offices here, though prices are higher than in San José.

Accommodation

Jacó's cheapest **cabinas** generally cater to weekending Joséfinos or surfers. Much of the mid-range accommodation is self-catering. In general, be prepared to pay far more than either the town or, in some cases, the accommodation, merits. At the really big hotels you can expect some sort of **discount** – up to fifty percent on the prices we've listed – for low-season (May–Nov) weekends. Keep an eye on the *Tico Times*, and *La Nación* for big splashy adverts. You'll need to **reserve** at holiday times, like Easter and Christmas, and weekends, for any of the places listed below.

The large **campground** at *Tropical Camping* at the north end of Jacó, near the San José bus stop, has toilets, showers and picnic tables (about US$4 per night). It gets crowded during holidays. *Camping Madrigal*, at the southern end of the beach has shade, toilet and showers (US$3). Newer *Camping El Hicaco*, in the centre of town, has nice grounds with picnic tables for about US$3 a night.

Cabinas Antonio, north end of Jacó (☎643-3043). Friendly place with good-value, basic cabinas with private hot bath. Restaurant on site. Low season discounts. ④.

Cabinas Emily, on the main drag (☎643-3513). Friendly hotel, filled with surfers on a budget, with rooms with rickety beds, shared bath and heated water. Also a restaurant. ④–⑤.

Club del Mar, southern end of town (☎ & fax 643-3194). Tastefully-decorated English-owned apartments, good value with a choice of amenities. Some apartments have a/c, sea views and balconies. Pool and restaurant attached. The location means it's quieter than elsewhere. ⑦–⑧.

Estrellamar (☎643-3102, fax 643-3453). Away-from-it-all place with nice touches by French owners. Twenty bungalows in quiet tropical gardens with pool, all with bath, hot water, fan, TV, kitchen and fridge – some extra charges apply for a/c and TV. Excellent low season prices. ⑥.

Gypsy Italiano, end of the street on the first entrance from Puntarenas (☎ & fax 643-3448). Nine cabinas only 250m from the beach in nice grounds with swimming pool. Breakfast included; good mid-price value. ⑤.

Los Ranchos, 50m west of Banco de Costa Rica (☎ & fax 643-3070). Friendly cabinas set around a pool, very popular with surfers and students. A variety of rooms and prices, from upstairs loft rooms, some with kitchenettes, to two-floor bungalows with kitchens. All are well-screened, with fans, and there's laundry service. Good value for groups. ④–⑦.

Zabamar, just off the main drag, north of the San José bus stop (☎643-3174). Nicely equipped, well-screened rooms; choice of cold water and ceiling fans or hot water and a/c (US$10 more). Also a good swimming pool. ⑤–⑦.

Activities and tours

Jacó is very much a beach town; other than sunbathing, surfing and a little cautious swimming, there's little to do. Experienced **surfers** can rent boards at a number of competing places in town; ask at *Los Ranchos* hotel for advice and recommendations. Renting a **mountain bike** (about US$10 a day) affords some opportunity to explore the spread-out town. Some people rent **mopeds** (about US$35 a day) and head out onto the Costañera Sur highway to explore the 10km-long **Playa Hermosa**, 5km south of Jaco, another reputable surfing beach.

A number of operators in town offer tours, horseback riding and surfing. Fantasy Tours (☎643-3211) also run cruises. Horseback Riding Tours, by the Supermarket Rayo Azul (☎643-3248), leads rides into the surrounding forest and on the beach, while Jacó Beach Central Tours (☎643-3510) offers reasonably priced sportsfishing and snorkelling tours, inclusive of gear and beer.

Eating, drinking and nightlife

There's been a recent explosion of **restaurants** in Jacó, and there's lots of variety. *Restaurant Flamboyant* and *Hacienda* are old Jacó favourites, serving good *típico*

MOVING ON FROM JACÓ

For **San José**, buses leave Jacó's *Hotel el Jardín* bus stop daily at 5am and 3pm (2hr 30min–3hr). It's also possible to continue to **Quepos** and the **Manuel Antonio** area by walking the 2km out to the Costañera Sur and flagging down the Puntarenas–Quepos or San José–Manuel Antonio buses that pass on the highway. Buses from Puntarenas to Quepos pass by about ninety minutes after departure (see p.602), while those from San José to Manuel Antonio come by three hours after departure. Just to be sure, get out there on the highway twenty minutes early. Local people can help you out with directions and bus schedules.

---

dishes; the latter is open late. Newer places include the ambitious *La Esperanza*, which serves excellent pizza, pasta and seafood, with outside tables for people-watching, and *Rinconcito Peruvian*, owned by a friendly Peruvian family. *Pizzería Killer Munchies* has a hardcore surfer clientele who chow down on fancy pizzas, including vegetarian and Hawaiian. Similarly popular with gringos is *Bar El Zarpe*, with tasty bocas, Mexican food, and sports on the satellite TV. *El Jardín* offers expensive French food with sea views – you'll need to reserve for dinner on weekends – while *El Gran Palenque* serves good, pricey, Spanish food with flamenco guitar accompaniment (closed Tues). Even more upscale is the *Restaurante Sandalías* in the *Hotel Club del Mar*, serving a small menu of cosmopolitan food – Thai, Indian, seafood – with a changing daily special. **Sodas** frequented by locals include *Restaurante Casita del Maíz*, which serves good *casados* made with fresh ingredients, and *Restaurante Doña Cecilia*, recommended for lunchtime specials.

Sedate during midweek in low season, Jacó transforms itself into beer-drinking-contest hell during the holidays. *Bar y Restaurante Bohio*, right on the beach, has a *típico* menu heavy on the rice, but is a great place for an evening **drink**. They sometimes lay on a – very loud – disco. Other **discos** include those at *Jacófiesta* and *Hotel Jacó Beach*: swanky, and usually open only on weekends. *Disco la Central*, on the beach right in the centre of town, is the most popular with gringos.

Quepos and Parque Nacional Manuel Antonio

With one of the most stunning, picture-postcard backdrops in the country, the small corridor between the old banana-exporting town of **Quepos** and the little community of **Manuel Antonio** outside the **Parque Nacional Manuel Antonio**, has experienced one of the most dramatic tourist booms in the country. In addition to the huge variety of things to do – walking the Park's easy trails, whitewater rafting, ocean cruising and horseback riding, to name but a few – this is one of the lushest places in Costa Rica, with spectacular white-grey sand beaches fringed by thickly forested green hills. The beauty of the area is due in part to the unique **tómbolo** formation of **Punta Catedral**, which juts out into the Pacific from the Park. A rare geophysical phenomenon, a *tómbolo* results when an island becomes joined, slowly and over millennia, to the mainland, through accumulated sand deposits. Other smaller islands, some of them no more than rocky outcroppings, straggle off from Punta Catedral and, from high up in the hills, watching a fantastic sunset flower and die over the Pacific, it does seem as though Manuel Antonio is one of the more charmed places on earth.

That said, the huge tourist input has undeniably taken its toll on the whole area. In the last few years it has been perceived as **overpriced**, and budget travellers searching for cheap beaches have headed instead to Montezuma or to Sámara on the Nicoya peninsula. Consequently, some hotels have had to drop their rates, and many places have gone from being overpriced to being merely expensive. You'll also need to take more precautions against **theft** than in the rest of Costa Rica. Never leave anything on the beach when you are swimming and, if you take the bus, don't let anyone handle your luggage. Wherever you stay, ensure your hotel room is locked at all times, and note that rental cars left on the street have become a favourite target.

Quepos

Arriving at the town of **QUEPOS** from San José, Puntarenas or Jaco, it's immediately apparent that you've crossed into the lush, wetter southern Pacific region. Vegetation is thicker and greener than up north, and you'll notice the proliferation of **sportsfishing** imagery – of all the sportsfishing grounds in Costa Rica, the Quepos area has the most variety and many small tour agencies cater more or less exclusively to sportsfishers. The town itself, backed against a hill and fronted by a muddy beach, can look pretty ramshackle, but it's a friendly place, with plenty of hotels, bars and restaurants. Most important is its proximity to **Parque Nacional Manuel Antonio** and its beaches, 7km south.

Arrival and orientation

Buses from San José's La Coca-Cola to Quepos (currently 7am, 10am, 2pm & 4pm daily; 4hr) are slower than the direct service, also leaving from La Coca-Cola, to Manuel Antonio (daily 6am, noon & 6pm; 3hr 30min). The latter continues beyond Quepos, dropping people off along the seven-kilometre stretch of road between the town and the Park entrance, and is convenient if you are staying at one of the hotels scattered between the two. For weekends, holidays and any time during the dry season, you need to buy your bus ticket for the Manuel Antonio service at least three days in advance, and your return ticket as soon as you arrive. All buses arrive in Quepos at the busy **terminal**, which doubles as the mercado, just one block east of the "centre". The **ticket office** is open daily (Mon–Sat 6–11am & 1–5pm, Sun 7–11am & 1–2pm).

Driving to Quepos is generally discouraged; due to the present condition of the road it can be a five hours' trip from San José. Many locals have given up and simply choose to **fly** – the flight takes only fifteen minutes and there are no potholes. Sansa or Travelair flights are often booked weeks in advance, mainly in the dry season, so check ahead.

The town itself is tiny, three blocks or so by four. "Downtown" consists of the main road along the front (sea side) and the three blocks that run around it. You can stumble off the bus right into a hotel, be in a good restaurant or bar in another two minutes, and then pick up the local bus service to Manuel Antonio in about another thirty seconds.

Information

Quepos has no official **tourist office**. Shock Artesanía, on the south side of the soccer field, sells good **maps** of Costa Rica not found elsewhere, including wildlife guides, maps showing indigenous reservations and protected areas, along with crafts from Costa Rica and the rest of Central America.

For **currency and travellers' cheques exchange**, head for the Banco de Costa Rica, 75m west of the mercado and bus terminal, or the Banco Popular, 25m west and 50m south of the bus terminal (both Mon–Fri 9am–3pm). Many businesses in town will change dollars. Note that there is a trend towards not accepting **credit cards** in the Manuel Antonio area, and where you can use a credit card, it will usually incur a six percent service charge. The **correo** (Mon–Fri 8am–5pm) is on the north side of the soccer field at the far western end of town.

Quepos's excellent **hospital**, the Hospital Dr Max Teran (☎777-0200) is very good for emergency treatment.

Accommodation

Budget travellers will have a hard time around Quepos – especially in the dry season. Plan well ahead, and if you want to come here anywhere near **Christmas**, make sure you have **reserved** and **paid** at least three or four months in advance. Despite the fact that so many hotels are expensive, few take credit cards, so make sure you have plenty of **cash** – colones or dollars – and/or travellers' cheques.

Cabinas Doña Alicia, on the northwest corner of the soccer field (☎777-0419). Basic, clean rooms with comfortable double beds. There are also a few singles, which are good value and scarce in Quepos. All have private bath and cold water only. The friendly owners keep everything spotlessly clean. A good budget choice. ②.

Cabinas Hellen, 50m east of the school (☎777-0504). Clean cabinas in the back of a family home. Large rooms, with private bath, hot water and fridge, fans, small table and chairs, and a small patio; *dueños* will do laundry. Secure, and recommended for those travelling with children. Good single rates also. ②–④.

Hotel Malinche, centre of town, 75m from the bus terminal (☎777-0093). Modern, "American"-style, a/c rooms, with carpet, TV and balcony, and cheaper, older rooms with none of the above. All good value, especially for singles. If you don't like the first room they show you, ask to see another. ③–⑤.

Mar y Luna, near the *Malinche* (☎777-0394). Central, friendly, budget hotel. Rooms have private bath, heated water and fans, and there's a small communal balcony, shared fridge and free coffee. ④–⑤.

Hotel el Pueblo, above the soda of the same name (☎777-1003). Clean new rooms, bright and basic, with private bath and fans. ③.

Hotel Sirena (☎ & fax 777-0528). The only Quepos hotel with a pool; plus poolside bar and restaurant. Simple rooms – the nicest are upstairs – with private bath, hot water and a/c. They can fix up horseback-riding tours. Reserve by fax, and pay 8 days in advance. They'll pick you up at the airstrip. ⑤–⑥.

Villas Verano, 200m north and 100 east of the bus terminal (☎777-1495). Small cabinas arranged near the home of the friendly owner, who will also serve breakfast in her dining room. All have private bath room, cold water only and a few have their own refrigerators. ②–③.

Tours and activities

Though **Bahía Drake and the Osa Peninsula** – including Isla del Caño just off the coast of Osa – are the most popular trips from Quepos, many visitors also had to **Hacienda Barú**, a private hacienda-cum-nature-reserve 2km from Dominical (☎771-1903). They have a canopy observation platform, from where you get a birds' eye view of the upper rainforest canopy, and also offer horseback riding. Lynch Tours across from *Soda el Pueblo* (Mon–Fri 7am–6pm, Sun 8am–noon; ☎777-1170, fax 777-1571) can take you to all these places, as well as organizing horseriding, sportsfishing, and day cruises in the Quepos area. **Rafting** outfitters Ríos Tropicales have an office between Quepos and Manuel Antonio at Centro "Si como No" (☎ & fax 777-1262). They also rent mountain bikes. **Sportsfishing** outfitters include Bluefin Sportsfishing Charters, across from the soccer field (☎777-1676), and Costa Rican Dreams (☎777-0593), next to *Restaurante Ana*.

Eating and drinking

For cheap lunchtime *casados*, head for the **sodas** scattered around the mercado. **Fish** is predictably good – order grilled *pargo* (snapper), and you can't go wrong. You can also eat "**international**", with macrobiotic, American and continental breakfasts at

Restaurante Isabel, and pizzas at *Gabriel's*. *Boquitos*, above Adobe Bike Rentals, is a popular second-storey **bar**, and certainly the best place for a relaxed drink.

La Botánica, northeast of the centre (Mon–Fri 8am–4pm) is dedicated to all things **herbal**, including vanilla and sachets of herbal tea grown on the owner's nearby farm.

Dos Locos, southwest of the mercado. Moderately priced cosmopolitan menu, including large healthy sandwiches and Mexican cuisine, with a nice open-to-the-street dining area.

Gastronomía Langosta, across from *Dos Locos*. Small, classy Italian deli, with four or five tables. This is the place if you're craving fettucini with real gorgonzola cheese (US$6); if you're self-catering, take some fresh bread, pasta, salami and Italian wine back for a fabulous meal.

Pizza Gabriel, west of the mercado. Small, quiet restaurant with gingham tablecloths, serving nice, simple, fairly cheap pizzas.

Restaurante Isabel, on the main street. Pleasant washed-out orange wooden house with soft wicker chairs. Serves macrobiotic breakfasts, salads, pasta and rice dishes. Friendly, fast service, and they give you individual coolers for your beer.

Soda el Pueblo, west of the mercado. Spotless soda, with huge menu and long hours (7am–midnight).

Quepos to Parque Nacional Manuel Antonio

Southeast of Quepos, a seven-kilometre stretch of road winds over the surrounding hills, pitching up at the loop at the entrance to Parque Nacional Manuel Antonio. In recent years there has been a tremendous influx of new **hotels** in this corridor. The most exclusive – and expensive – places are hidden away in the surrounding hills, reached by side roads. The very best overlook Punta Catedral, or Cathedral Point, which juts out so picturesquely into the Pacific.

Though there are some reasonably **affordable** places near the Park entrance, and the occasional low-season discount, prices are likely to rise as the seemingly inexhaustible popularity of the area continues to draw travellers. You should also make sure to **reserve** well in advance.

La Buena Nota souvenir shop, between the *Hotel Karahé* and the *Cabinas Piscis* (☎777-1002), functions as an **information** centre for the area, as well as selling foreign papers and magazines. Here you'll find the best selection of swimsuits, locally made and hand-crafted clothing, film and the *New York Times*.

Taking a **taxi** from Quepos to any of the hotels on the road to the Park is a direct service with a set fare of around US$6. If you are going back to Quepos by taxi, it is cheapest to flag one down on the road. Fares are per person, and the driver may pick up a number of people along the way.

MOVING ON FROM QUEPOS

Buses to Manuel Antonio leave from the terminal at the mercado (15 daily; 20min) between 5.30am and 9.30pm; there are slightly fewer in the rainy season. For bus information, call ☎777-0263. **Taxis** line up at the rank at the south end of the terminal/mercado, or you can ring Quepos Taxi (☎777-0277) who will take you to the Park for US$5.

San José, Puntarenas and San Isidro in the Zona Sur are reached over the new road via **Dominical**, 44km south of Quepos on a terrible but passable road (if driving, best have 4WD). From Quepos the service to **San José** (3hr 30min) currently departs at 5am, 8am, 2pm and 4pm. Be sure to buy tickets for the return to the capital in advance (see "Arrival" on p.609 for ticket office times). To **Puntarenas** buses leave at 4.30am, 10.30am and 3pm (3hr); and to **San Isidro** at 5am and 1.30pm (3hr 30min).

For **plane tickets** (to San José) and schedules, drop by Lynch Tours (see opposite).

The hotels below are listed in the order you encounter them from Quepos. All are well signed from the road. More than anywhere else, the choice is partial, each one representing the best value in its price range.

Accommodation

Cabinas Pedro Miguel, 500m beyond Quepos, on right-hand side (☎777-0035). One of the friendliest places in the area, Costa Rican owned and managed. Rooms in the main complex are nothing special, but comfortable, with balcony/patio and sunset views; go instead for the two little *casitas* backed up against the rainforest, with mosquito nets, kitchenette and basic furnishings. Small pool and great cook-your-own restaurant (see below). Book ahead. Low-season discounts of 25 percent Mon–Wed and 15 percent Thurs–Sun. ④–⑦.

Hotel Plinios, Aptdo 71, Quepos (☎777-0055, fax 777-0558). Rooms vary, some are dark, but all are well-screened, and nicely decorated with Guatemalan prints. The highest rooms give spectacular sunset views from a raised platform bed. Landscaped tropical gardens, pool and very good restaurant, plus 4-km-long nature trail, with stupendous views from top. Good off-season discounts. ⑤–⑦.

Villa Teca (☎777-1117, fax 777-1578; *hvteca@sol.racsa.co.cr*). Rather small, dark bungalows, in a tranquil hillside setting, surrounded by bougainvillea. There's a good sized pool and restaurant, and continental breakfast is included. Prices change dramatically according to season. ⑤–⑥.

Flor Blanca (☎ & fax 777-1633). The only budget option on the road to Manuel Antonio, with friendly Tico management and good off-season discounts; otherwise the plain, sometimes dark, rooms with thin walls are a bit overpriced. ②.

Villas Nicolas (☎777-0481, fax 777-0451). Very friendly, classy accommodation, suspended high above the surrounding landscape, with lovely views. All villas have private bath, hot water and ceiling fans; some have kitchens. Also a small pool. Good value. ⑤–⑦.

El Colibrí, Aptdo 94, Manuel Antonio (☎ & fax 777-0432). Clean, spacious hotel, with a nice atmosphere. Rooms are attractively ranged around a pool, with kitchens, verandahs and hammocks. Well-priced, friendly and efficient. ④–⑦.

Hotel Villa Nina, 2500m from Park entrance (☎777-1628 or 777-1554, fax 777-1497; *vilanina@sol.racsa.co.cr*). Romantic hideaway managed by welcoming Costa Rican family. Rooms have a balcony and terrace – those upstairs have great ocean view. All have refrigerator and coffee-maker, and some are a/c. Rates include breakfast, and there's a pool, rooftop bar and sloths and monkeys in the trees. The best value in this price range. ⑤–⑦.

Cabinas Piscis, just north of Playa Espadilla (☎777-0046; Aptdo 207, Quepos). One of the best budget places in Manuel Antonio, with student and group discounts available. Big, clean, basic cabina rooms, with cement floors and private bath with cold water. The pleasant garden area leads to the beach, where a little restaurant serves juices and sandwiches (high season only). Friendly *dueños*. Very popular, so reserve in advance. ③–④.

Costa Linda, Manuel Antonio village (☎777-0304). The cheapest accommodation around, right on the beach. Small, plain, stuffy rooms, with shared bath and cold water, and an environmentally conscientious owner. The adjacent *Café Relax* is good. ②–③.

Cabinas Espadilla, Manuel Antonio village (☎ & fax 777-0416). One of the best places to stay in the village, although not especially cheap. Each room has private bath; some have a/c and hot water. Rooms shared between four people are good value, with kitchenettes. The friendly, ecologically inclined management is very helpful. ⑤.

Los Almendros, Aptdo 68-6350 (☎777-0225). Good value – if not exactly budget – option close to the beach. Rooms with cold water and fans are cheaper than those with a/c and hot water. Nice restaurant attached. ⑤–⑥.

Eating and drinking

Most of the **hotel-restaurants** along this stretch are very good, if expensive. Cheaper places can be found in Manuel Antonio village right next to the Park entrance, where a cluster of beachside and roadside **sodas** serve Tico food, although there have been complaints about hygiene in some of these unlicensed food stands. Some restaurants, especially the best ones, close or have restricted hours in the rainy season. At popular places – *Plinios*, *Karola's* and *Vela Bar* among them – make reservations in high season.

Barba Roja, next to the *Divisimar Hotel*, on road to Manuel Antonio, about 2500m from the Park entrance. Friendly, popular place for high-quality American food, including burgers and desserts.

Cafe Milagro, midway between Quepos and Manuel Antonio. Great cappuccino and banana-and-carrot cake, and you can buy ground coffee to go.

Karola's, near *Barba Roja*. Mexican cuisine, with burritos, seafood, vegetarian dishes and a macadamia nut pie that has entered local food legend. Closed Wed and in the low season.

Mar y Sombra, Manuel Antonio village, 500m from the Park entrance, on the beach. In a shady palm grove, this sprawling, cheap place is the most popular in the village. You can have a drink on the beach, and eat *típico* food including good *casados*, and there's a disco at weekends. Try fried fillet of fish of the day – simply done in garlic and butter, with fried plantains and salad.

Restaurante Pedro Miguel, signed immediately as you leave Quepos, in *Cabinas Pedro Miguel*. Wonderful, open-air barbecue-your-own steak restaurant with rough-hewn wooden tables and chairs, set right next to the forest. Choose your cut of meat or fish, then cook it to your liking on the big outdoor grill. Extremely popular, and lots of fun. Dec–April only.

Plinios, directly opposite *Pedro Miguel* (☎777-0055, fax 777-0558). Quite simply one of the best restaurants in the country, locally famous for its eggplant parmesan. Also pot roast in red wine, tiramisu, and reasonable Chilean wine. Nice bar, too; relaxed, with good music. Seven percent surcharge on credit cards. Breakfast 6–10am, lunch 11am–1pm, dinner 5–9.30pm.

Vela Bar, Manuel Antonio village. Traditionally the swankiest food in the area, with good grilled fish, some vegetarian choices and paella. Not cheap, though, starting at around US$7.

Parque Nacional Manuel Antonio

By far the smallest Park in Costa Rica's system, **PARQUE NACIONAL MANUEL ANTONIO** (Tues–Sun 7am–5pm; US$6), some 150km southwest of San José, fights it out with Parque Nacional Volcán Poás in the Valle Central (see p.559) for the title of the most popular Park in the country. It is hard not to appreciate the foresight that went into the establishment of Manuel Antonio as a National Park in 1972; considering the number of hotels and restaurants sidling up to its borders, you can just imagine how developed the white sands would be today. Still, the Park is suffering from the numbers it receives, and frequently reaches its quota of six hundred visitors a day.

Covering an area of just under seven square kilometres, Manuel Antonio preserves not only the lovely **beaches** and the unique *tómbolo* formation (see p.608) of Punta Catedral, but also **mangroves** and humid tropical **forest**. Visitors can walk only on the sea-side section of the Park. The eastern *montaña*, or mountain section, off limits to the public, is regularly patrolled by rangers to deter poaching, which is rife in the area, and incursions into the Park from surrounding farmers and *campesinos*.

This forest is one of the few remaining natural habitats for **squirrel monkeys.** Other **mammals** in the Park – you're likely to see many of the smaller ones – are the racoon, the coati, the agouti, the two-toed sloth and white-faced capuchin monkey. **Birdlife** is also abundant, including the shimmering green **kingfisher**, the brown pelican, who can often be seen fishing off the rocks, and the laughing falcon. Beware the snakes that do a mean imitation of a vine, draping themselves over the trails; you may not see them, but they're here.

The **climate** is hot, humid and wet, all year round. Though the rains ease off in the dry season (Dec–April), they never disappear entirely. The average temperature all year is 27°C, and it can easily go to 30°C and above.

Beaches in Manuel Antonio can be confusing, called by a number of different names. Because some are not safe for swimming, it is important to grasp which one is which. **Playa Espadilla**, also sometimes called Playa Manuel Antonio, or playa numero uno, is outside the Park, immediately north of the entrance and of Punta Catedral. One of the most popular beaches in the country – it is very beautiful, with a wide stretch of smooth light-grey sand and stunning sunsets – it is also very dangerous, plagued by **rip**

tides that travel between six and ten kilometres per hour. However, lots of people do swim here – or rather, paddle and wade – and live to tell the tale. Now the professional lifeguards are around, it is considerably safer; in the dry season, at least. Within the Park, follow the rangers' advice and swim only at **Playa Blanca** (also called playa numero dos, or tres), which is where everyone else will be, anyway. Immediately south of Punta Catedral, it is in a protected, deeper bay than the others. Numero dos is very calm – like a swimming pool, say the rangers – but you can still get clobbered by the deceptively gentle-looking waves as they hit the shore.

Practicalities

Buses from Quepos and San José can let you off right in front of the *Restaurante Sol y Mar*, about 500m short of the Park entrance, if you want to grab lunch or stop off at Playa Espadilla. Otherwise it continues round the loop before returning to Quepos. The driver stops on request, so ask him to let you off at your hotel.

If you're driving, note that there isn't much **parking** at the loop at the end of Manuel Antonio village; arrive early in the morning for the best (shady) spot, and pay the kids who guard cars about 150 to 200 colones. To get to the Park entrance from here you have to wade across a creek (shoulder-deep at high-tide). The entrance hut is across the creek and about 50m up a track. Here you can pick up a basic photocopied **map** (US$0.50), which marks the beaches and trails. **Facilities** within the Park are minimal. Beyond the entrance hut and the toilets and showers staked out at close intervals along the trails, the only other buildings are administrative. There are no **guides** for the Park, but you hardly need them. Rangers are often on patrol.

travel details

BUSES

Jacó to: Quepos (via Puntarenas, 3 daily; 1hr); San José (2 daily; 2hr 30min–3hr).

Monteverde/Santa Elena to: Puntarenas (from Santa Elena only, 1 daily; 3hr 30 min); San José (2 daily; 4–5hr); Tilarán (1 daily; 3hr).

Montezuma to: Paquera (for ferry to Puntarenas, 3 daily; 1hr); Tambor (3 daily; 30min).

Paquera to: Montezuma (3 daily; 1hr); Tambor (3 daily; 40min).

Puntarenas to: Liberia (1 daily; 3 hr); Quepos (3 daily; 3hr 30min); San José (14 daily; 2hr); Santa Elena, for Monteverde (1 daily; 3hr 30min).

Quepos to: Dominical/San Isidro (2 daily; 3hr 30min); Puntarenas (3 daily; 3hr 30min); San José (express, 3 daily; 3hr 30min–4hr; stopping service, 4 daily; 5hr).

San José to: Jacó (2 daily; 2hr 30min–3hr); Manuel Antonio (express, 3 daily; 3hr 30min–4hr); Monteverde/Santa Elena (2 daily; 4–5hr); Puntarenas (14 daily; 2hr); Quepos (stopping service, 5 daily; 5hr).

Tilarán to: Santa Elena (1 daily; 3hr).

FERRIES

Naranjo to: Puntarenas (car/passenger ferry, 4–5 daily; 1hr 30min).

Paquera to: Puntarenas (car ferry 4–5 daily, 1hr 30min; passenger ferry, 3–4 daily; 1hr 30min).

Puntarenas to: Montezuma (passenger ferry, via Paquera, 3–4 daily; 1hr 30min; car ferry 4–5 daily, 1hr 30min; car/passenger ferry, via Naranjo, 5 daily; 1hr 30min).

FLIGHTS

Sansa

Quepos to: San José (Mon–Sat 2 daily, Sun 1 daily; 20min).

San José to: Quepos (Mon–Sat 2 daily, Sun 1 daily; 20 min); Tambor (1 daily; 20min).

Tambor to: San José (1 daily; 20min).

Travelair

Quepos to: San José (3 daily high season, 1 daily low season; 20min).

San José to: Quepos (3 daily high season, 1 daily low season; 20min).

CHAPTER 31

GUANACASTE

Guanacaste **province**, hemmed in by mountains to the east and the Pacific to the west, and bordered on the north by Nicaragua, is distinctly different from the rest of Costa Rica. Though little tangible remains of the dance, music and folklore for which the region is famous, there is undeniably something special, affecting even, about the place. Granted that much of the **landscape** has come about essentially through the slaughter of tropical dry forest, it is still some of the prettiest you'll see in the country, especially in the wet season, when wide open spaces, stretching from the ocean across savannah grasses to the brooding humps of volcanoes, are washed in a beautifully muted range of earth tones, blues, yellows and mauves. Its **history**, too, is distinct. If not for a very close vote in 1824, it might have been part of Nicaragua, which would have made Costa Rica very small indeed.

Most tourists come for the **beaches**: specifically those where the **Nicoya Peninsula** joins the mainland (roughly two-thirds of the mountainous peninsula is in Guanacaste, with the lower third belonging to Puntarenas province). Several beaches are also nesting grounds for **marine turtles**. An enormous number of hotels, some all-inclusive resort types, are being built on both coasts, and with the opening of the Liberia airport to international traffic, winter charter tourism has arrived. Inland, however, mass tourism is less evident. Here the dry heat, relatively accessible terrain and panoramic views make Guanacaste the best place in the country for **walking** and **horseback riding**, especially around the mud pots and stewing sulphur waters of **Parque Nacional Rincón de la Vieja**, and through the tropical dry forest cover of **Parque Nacional Santa Rosa**. The only **towns** of any significance for travellers are the provincial capital of **Liberia**, and **Nicoya**, the main town of the peninsula. If you are overnighting on the way to **Nicaragua**, La Cruz makes a useful base.

Much of Guanacaste has long been put under pasture for cattle ranching, and a huge part of the region's appeal is the **sabanero** (cowboy) culture, based around the hacienda (ranch) and *ganado* (cattle). This dependence on cattle culture has its downside, however; much of Guanacaste is degraded pastureland. Although impressive efforts to regenerate former tropical dry forest are under way – at Parque Nacional Santa Rosa and **Parque Nacional Guanacaste**, for example – it is likely that this rare life zone/forest will never recover its original profile.

The province is significantly greener, and prettier, in the "wet" season (May–Nov), generally agreed to be the **best time** to come, with the added benefit of fewer travellers and lighter rainfall than in the rest of the country.

Liberia and around

The spirited provincial capital of **LIBERIA** has a distinctively friendly and open feel, its wide clean streets and blinding white houses the legacy of the pioneering farmers and

For an explanation of **accommodation price codes**, see p.526.

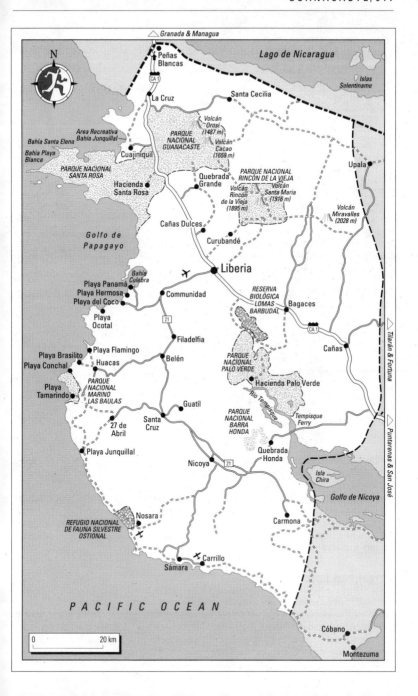

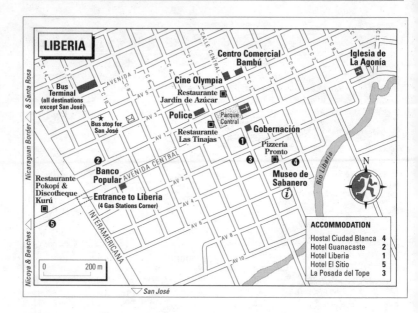

cattle ranchers who founded it. At present most travellers use the town simply as a jumping-off point for **Parques Nacionals Rincón de la Vieja** and **Santa Rosa**, an overnight to or from the **beaches** of Guanacaste, or a stopoff on the way to Nicaragua. It's worth getting to know it better, however, for Liberia is actually one of the most appealing towns in Costa Rica.

Sometimes called the **"Ciudad Blanca"** (white city), with its whitewashed houses, it is the only town in the country that seems truly "colonial". Liberia has everything you might need for a relaxing stay of a day or two – well-priced accommodation (although not much choice), a very helpful tourist office and a couple of nice places to eat and drink. This may all change, of course, when the nearby **international airport** starts pumping in the passengers in the next few years, but for now it's the epitome of dignified (if static) provincialism, with a strong identity and atmosphere all its own.

Several lively local **festivals** take place in Liberia, the most elaborate of which is **July 25**, *El día de la independencia*, celebrating Guanacaste's independence from Nicaragua with parades, horseshows, cattle auctions, rodeos, fiestas and roving marimba bands. If you want to attend, make your bus and hotel reservations as far in advance as possible and buy that straw hat.

Arrival and information

El Pulmitán de Liberia's **buses** from San José arrive at Liberia's clean and efficient bus station on the western edge of town near the exit for the Interamericana. It's at most a ten-minute walk to the centre of town seven blocks northeast (Liberia is set on a **northeast slant**). **Addresses** in Liberia are most often given in relation to the church, the Parque Central, or La Gobernacion, a large white building accoss from the church on the corner of C Central and Av Central.

Information

Liberia's helpful **tourist office** is five minutes' walk south from the Parque Central (Mon–Sat 7.30–11.45am & 1.30–4.45pm, Sun 7.30am–1.30pm; ☎666-1606). Staff have computers showing images of the beaches and hotels, will call to book hotels or ask directions, and will even place international calls and faxes at cost. In the high season especially, they also function partially as a **tour service**: with local operators they arrange group outings such as "Culture of Guanacaste" (rather stagey, including a trip to a working cattle ranch), or crocodile and bird-watching in Parque Nacional Palo Verde. The Cowboy Museum (see below) is in the same building.

The efficient **correo** is 500m west and 100m north of the church (Mon–Fri 7.30am–5.30pm). Bancoop (Mon–Fri 8am–4pm, Sat 8am–2pm), is recommended for fast **dollar exchange**. Just 50m from the entrance to the Interamericana on Av Central, Banco Popular is also good.

Accommodation

Liberia is a convenient place to spend the night if heading north to the border or to the beaches. Because of tourist traffic to and from the beaches, the town is chock-full in the dry season, especially weekends, and it is imperative to have a **reservation** before you arrive. At other times, midweek especially, there's no problem with space.

Hostal Ciudad Blanca, 200m south and 150m east of the Gobernación (☎666-2715). New hotel with twelve modern, comfortable rooms, a/c, TV, private bath and ceiling fans. Spotless, with a lovely breakfast terrace and bar. Liberia's best mid-price option. ④–⑤.

Hotel Guanacaste, Av 1, 300m south of the bus station (☎666-0085, fax 666-2287). Popular, budget HI-affiliated hotel, with a traveller-friendly restaurant where you can start a conversation as well as have a cold beer. Rooms are simple, clean and dark. Reservations recommended. US$20 without HI card, US$12 with. ③.

Hotel Liberia, 75m south of the Parque Central on C 0 (☎ & fax 666-0161). Established, friendly hotel, with secure parking and basic, box-like rooms. Probably the cheapest non-dive in town. ②–③.

Posada del Tope, 150m south of the Gobernación (☎666-3876, fax 385-2383). Sorely needed, friendly new budget option in a beautiful historic house. Only six basic rooms, all a bit stuffy, with fan and shared shower, but the nice big rocking chairs in the courtyard make it a relaxed place to sit in the evening. Accepts Visa and Mastercard. ②–③.

El Sitio, on the Nicoya road, 200m west of the intersection (☎666-1211, fax 666-2059). Good upscale option with over 50 beautifully decorated rooms with a/c, TV, and private bath. Small pool. ⑥–⑦.

The Town

Liberia's wide, clean streets are used more by cyclists and horsemen than motorists. It's pleasant to walk around in the shade provided by the mango trees, though in March and April watch out for the ripe fruit plopping down to your feet full-force. The town is arranged around its large **Parque Central**, properly called Parque Mario Cañas Ruiz. It's dedicated to *el mes del annexion*, the month of the annexation (July), celebrating the fact that Guanacaste is not in Nicaragua. Liberia's parque is one of the loveliest central plazas in the whole country, ringed by benches and tall palms that shade gossiping locals. Its **church** is startlingly modern – somewhat out of place in this very traditional town. About 600m away at the very eastern end of town, the colonial **Iglesia de la Agonía** is more arresting, with a mottled yellow facade like a pocked, washed-out banana. On the verge of perpetual collapse – it has had a hard time from those earthquakes – it's almost never open, but you could try shoving the heavy wooden door and hope the place doesn't collapse around you if it does give way. The tourist office houses the **Museo de Sabanero**, or Cowboy Museum (Mon–Sat 7.30–11.45am & 1.30–4.45pm, Sun 7.30am–1.30pm; free), a fascinating, if small-scale, display of objects that you might have found in the big old ranch houses.

MOVING ON FROM LIBERIA

As well as having good connections with **San José** (8 direct Pulmitan de Liberia buses daily, 4hr 30min), Liberia is also the main regional hub, giving easy access to Guanacaste's Parks and beaches, and the Nicaraguan border.

For **Parque Nacional Santa Rosa**, take a La Cruz or Peñas Blancas (Nicaraguan border) bus (currently 5.30am, 8.30am, 11am, 2pm & 6pm; 2hr) from the Liberia station. Take the earliest bus you can to give yourself more time for walking – though bear in mind that the Park won't be officially open until after 7.30am – and ask the driver to let you off at Santa Rosa. For **Parque Nacional Guanacaste**, take the 3pm bus to Quebrada Grande village, from where it's a walk of at least two hours. If you're heading for Nicaragua, regular buses run to **La Cruz** (hourly; 1hr). Services to **Bagaces** and **Cañas** leave the station at 5.45am, 1.30 and 4.30pm, taking about forty minutes to an hour.

There are direct services to the more northerly of Guanacaste's **beaches**; services may be reduced in the rainy season. For Playa Hermosa buses leave daily (7.30am, 11.30, 3.30pm, 5.30pm & 7pm; 1hr). Playa del Coco is served by three or four services per day (5.30am, 12.30pm, 4.30pm and, high season only, 2pm; 1hr). You can also get to **Santa Cruz** (hourly; 5.30am–7.30pm; 1hr), from where you can hook up with buses to Tamarindo, Junquillal and beaches further south. Buses for **Nicoya** leave at 6am, 8am, 11am, and 4pm (2hr). Buses to **Puntarenas** leave at 5am, 8.30am, 10am, 11am and 3pm (3hr).

Hotel Guanacaste has an occasional **minibus service** (US$8) to Rincón de la Vieja – hotel guests get first refusal. It's supposed to be daily, but drop by and ask if it is going. **Colectivo taxis**, shared between four or five people, can be good value if you're heading for **Parque Nacional Rincón de la Vieja (Santa Maria station)** or the haciendas near **Las Espuelas ranger station**. They line up at the northwest corner of the Parque Central, and charge about US$45.

Eating, drinking and entertainment

Liberia has several **restaurants** that are particularly good for breakfast and lunch. Local treats include **natilla** (soured cream) eaten with eggs or *gallo pinto* and tortillas. For a real feast, try the various **desayunos guanacastecos** (Guanacastecan breakfasts): hearty food, made to be worked off with hard labour. For rock-bottom cheap **lunches**, head for the stalls in the bus terminal, *Las Tinajas* or at a number of fried chicken places. There's little **drinking** to be done in Liberia, though the bar at the *Hostal Ciudad Blanca* is a nice place for a beer, as are *Las Tinajas* or *Pizzería Pronto*. The one **disco**, *Kurú*, next to the *Pokopí* restaurant, is lively with salsa and merengue, especially on weekends and *feriados*. The main Saturday evening activity, however, involves parading around the Parque Central. The **Cine Olimpia**, 100m north of the church shows action-adventure blockbusters.

Restaurants and sodas

Hostal Ciudad Blanca, 200m south and 150m east of the Gobernación. A really nice place, with a good choice of drinks, in a semi-open-air tiled hotel terrace.

Jardín de Azúcar, 100m from Banco de Costa Rica on other side of street. But for the ear-splitting Latinopop, this place would be wonderful. Great breakfasts include *Americano* (ham, egg, toast, plus coffee or tea) and *guanacasteco* (*gallo pinto*, *natilla*, *tortillas* and eggs). Go later for Liberia's cheapest grilled fish in garlic.

Pizzería Pronto, 200m south of the church. The most cosmopolitan place in town for good, cheap pizzas (US$5) beautifully cooked in a wood oven and drinks. In an old tile-decorated adobe house, cool, dark and pleasant inside.

Pókopi, 100m from "four gas stations corner" on the Interamericana, on the road to Nicoya, across from *Hotel el Sitio*. Fastidiously clean (they mop the floor every two seconds) and with Tropico-naif toucans and the like decorating the walls. Good gringo food includes huge, dripping burgers (US$3), and very tasty *pargo en ajillo* (snapper in garlic butter; about US$7).

Las Tinajas, west side of Parque Central. Nice outdoor tables on verandah of old house with park view. Good for a *refresco* or beer, basic *casados* and rice combinations and excellent hamburgers (US$3). Live music on Thrusday and Sunday; sells the *Tico Times*.

Parque Nacional Rincón de la Vieja

The dramatically dry landscape of **PARQUE NACIONAL RINCÓN DE LA VIEJA** (daily 8am–4pm; US$6), northeast of Liberia, varies from rock-strewn savannah to patches of tropical dry forest and deciduous trees, culminating in the blasted-out vistas of the volcano crater. The land here is actually alive and breathing: Rincón de la Vieja last erupted in 1991, and rivers of lava still broil beneath the thin epidermis of ground, while brewing **mud pots** (*pilas de barro*) bubble, and puffs of steam rise beatifically out of lush foliage, signalling sulphurous subterranean springs. This is great terrain for **camping, riding** and **hiking**, with a comfortable, fairly dry heat – although it can get damp and cloudy at the higher elevations around the crater. **Birders**, too, get excited about Rincón de la Vieja, as there are more than 200 species in residence.

Getting to the Park

The park's main entrance and ranger station is at **Santa María**, 25km northeast of Liberia via the village of San Jorge. There are camping facilities here, and the trailheads of the main routes up the volcano. There are no buses to Santa Maria from Liberia: options for getting there include renting a *colectivo* taxi, checking at the *Hotel Guanacaste* to see if they are running their own minibus, or hitching.

A number of **lodges** in the area offer trips to the Park for guests, including *Hacienda Guachepelín* and *Albergue de la Montaña Rincón de la Vieja*, near the village of Curubandé, 16km north of Liberia. They will pick you up from Liberia for an extra charge (US$10–25 return); you can also organize packages from tour operators in San José (see p.555). Staying at *Buenavista* you can walk to the crater without paying the Park entrance fees, as they own the land by which the volcano is accessed. For more on the lodges, see below.

Accommodation

You can **camp** at the Santa María station (US$3 per person per day) where there are lavatories and water. If you have a sleeping bag, and ask in advance, you can also stay inside the rustic **bunk rooms** in the ranger station – though these are a bit musty and the beds have long ago given up the ghost.

Albergue de la Montaña Rincón de la Vieja, 5km northwest from the *Guachepelín*; follow signs (☎ & fax 695-5553). Extremely popular, HI-affiliated large (27 rooms) lodge, offering rooms with private hot water bath (US$50), and dorms with shared cold water (US$19). Meals are filling but not especially cheap. Excellent tours, including guides and horses plus transport from Liberia, cost extra. ③–④.

Buenavista Lodge, 31km northeast of Liberia (☎ & fax 695-5147). Working cattle ranch with stupendous views. Trails lead through the ranch and pockets of rainforest on the flanks of the volcano up to the crater; they also offer reasonably priced guided horseback rides and hikes. Don Gerardo and Doña Amalia will make you feel at home – you can even ride with the cowhands if your horsemanship is up to it. The new bungalows are too close together and too dark; ask for the older rooms, and those with hot water (it's cool up here). To get here, call ahead and ask for transfer from Cañas Dulces (accessible from Liberia by bus); they will send a 4WD. If driving yourself 4WD is essential. ⑤–⑥.

Hacienda Guachepelín (☎442-2818 or 2695, fax 442-1910). One of the nicest places to stay in the country, this unpretentious historic working ranch offers comfortable doubles in the main house and a bunkhouse (US$10, limited water and electricity). Meals cost extra. There's a waterfall 5min away, and well-marked trails; they even have their own mud pots. Guides are available for a variety of tours, including riding/hiking to the volcano. Will arrange pickup from Liberia (costs extra), and packages are available. ④–⑤.

Rinconcito, San Jorge (☎666-0267). The cheapest option close to the park; nice rustic cabins in an annexe on the farm of a friendly local family. Cold water only, and no electricity. Don Gerardo and Doña María Inés give good advice on transport, guides and directions. ③–④.

Visiting the Park

You can walk Rincón de la Vieja's **main trail** to the crater from either the Santa Maria or Las Espuelas ranger stations. Whether on foot or horseback or a combination of the two, this is quite simply one of the best hikes in the country, if not *the* best. A variety of elevations and habitats reveals hot springs, sulphur pools, bubbling mud pots and fields of purple orchids, plus a great smoking volcano at the top to reward you for your efforts. **Animals** in the area include all the big cats, shy tapir, red deer, collared peccary, two-toed sloth, and howler, white-faced and spider monkeys. **Birders** will have a chance to spot the weird-looking three-wattled bellbird, the Montezuma oropendola, the trogon and the spectacled owl, among others.

It's 18km from the **Santa María** ranger station to the top of the volcano, a fairly leisurely hike of around two days. From **Las Espuelas** the summit is much closer, some 7km, and can be reached in in few hours, but you'll probably want to **camp** along the way – most likely at the crater. You see far more by starting out at Santa María, which enables you to follow a number of minor trails to **aguas thermales**, or hot springs, the *pilas de barro* **mud pots**; and the geothermal **hornillas** (literally, "stoves"), mystical-looking holes in the ground exhaling elegant puffs of steam. At the **summit** of the volcano (1916m), Rincón de la Vieja presents a barren lunar landscape, a smoking hole surrounded by black ash, with a pretty freshwater **lake**, Lago los Jilgueros, to the south. You can get hammered by wind at the top; bring a sweater and windbreaker.

For up to date information on conditions in the Park, call the **Area de Conservación de Guanacaste** (ACG) headquarters at the Santa Rosa National Park (☎695-5598 – Spanish only).

Parque Nacional Santa Rosa

Established in 1971, **PARQUE NACIONAL SANTA ROSA** (daily 7.30am–4.30pm; US$6), 35km north of Liberia, and 260km from San José, was the first National Park in Costa Rica's system, established to protect the increasingly rare dry tropical forest. Today it's one of the most popular, due to good trails, great surfing (though poor swimming) and prolific turtle *arribadas*. It's also, given a few official restrictions, a great destination for **campers**, with a couple of sites on the beach.

Santa Rosa has an amazingly diverse topography for its size, ranging from mangrove swamp to deciduous forest and savannah. Home to 115 species of mammals – half of them bats – 250 species of **birds** and 100 of **amphibians** and **reptiles** (not to mention 3800 species of **moths**), Santa Rosa is prime biological investigation territory, attracting researchers from all over the world. Jaguars and pumas prowl the park, but you're unlikely to see them; what you may spot – at least in the dry season – are coati, coyotes and peccaries, often snuffling around watering holes.

The appearance of the Park changes drastically between the **dry season**, when the many streams and small lakes dry up, trees lose their leaves, and thirsty animals can be seen at known waterholes, and the **wet months**, greener but affording fewer animal-viewing opportunities. From August to November, however, you may be able to enjoy the sight of hundreds of **Olive Ridley turtles** (*llora*) nesting on Playa Nancite by moonlight; September and October are best. Though too rough for swimming, the picturesque **beaches** of Naranjo and Nancite, about 12km down a bad road from the administration centre, are popular with serious **surfers**.

Santa Rosa's **casona** (Big House), one of Costa Rica's most famous historical sites, was for many years the centre of a working hacienda until the land was expropriated for the National Park in 1972. Historically, its proximity to Nicaragua made it a prime target for would-be interlopers; **plaques** (in Spanish) outside the house recount the various derring-dos, with resumés of the battles of *20 de Marzo 1856*, of 1919, and of 1955, against the Nicaraguan dictator Anastasio Somoza.

Practicalities

Santa Rosa's **entrance hut** is 35km north of Liberia, signed from the Interamericana. After paying fees, pick up a map and proceed some 6km or so, taking the right fork to the **administration centre** (☎695-5598), which also administers Guanacaste and Rincón de la Vieja Parks. From here two rough roads lead to the beaches, but they're not really passable, even with 4WD. Most people park at the administration centre and walk. If you're without a car, a ranger or fellow tourist will probably give you a ride, but bring **water** just in case – five litres, at least, for two people, even on a short jaunt. You can also buy **drinks** at the administration centre.

Camping facilities at Santa Rosa are some of the best in the country. There are four sites and each charges US$2 per person, payable at the administration centre. The shady **la casona** site has bathrooms and grill pits; **Playa Nancite** has no water or bathrooms (and requires a permit); **Playa Naranjo** has picnic tables and grill pits, and a ranger's hut with outhouses and showers plus, apparently, a boa constrictor in the roof. The **Estero Real** site, next to a mangrove swamp, has no water, but does have grill pits and outhouse toilets.

You need a permit to watch the **arribadas**. Provided there is space (25 is the maximum), there should be no problem; again, call at the administration centre.

Parque Nacional Guanacaste

Some 36km north of Liberia on the Interamericana, much of **PARQUE NACIONAL GUANACASTE** (hours and admission as for Santa Rosa) was not long ago under pasture for cattle. Influential biologist D.H. Janzen, editor of the seminal volume *Costa Rican Natural History*, who had been involved in field study for many years in nearby Santa Rosa, was instrumental in creating the Park virtually from scratch in 1991. Raising over $11 million, mainly from foreign sources, he envisioned creating a kind of biological corridor in which animals, mainly mammals, would have a large enough tract of undisturbed habitat in which to hunt and reproduce. The **Santa Rosa–Guanacaste** (and, to an extent, Rincón de la Vieja) **corridor** is the result of his work, representing one of the most important efforts to conserve and regenerate tropical **dry forest** in the Americas.

With tropical wet and dry forests and a smattering of cloudforest, and covering the slopes of the dormant volcanoes Orosí and Cacao, Parque Nacional Guanacaste also protects the **wellspring of the Río Tempisque**, as well as the Ríos Ahogados and Colorado. More than 300 species of **birds** have been recorded, while mammals lurking behind the undergrowth include jaguar, puma, tapir, coati, armadillo, two-toed sloth and deer. It's also thought that there are about 5000 species of **butterflies** and moths alone.

Few people come to Parque Nacional Guanacaste. The only primary rainforest exists at the upper elevations and, of the three biological stations, you are currently allowed to visit only the one on Volcán Cacao. **Trails** are being cut, however, and there are pre-Columbian **petroglyphs** lying around at El Pedregal, near the Maritza field station at the bottom of Volcán Orosí. Ask the rangers at the entrance about the best way to see them; they are not on any currently existing trail, nor are they marked.

Practicalities

Facilities at Guanacaste are minimal. To get there, take the exit for Potrerillos on the right-hand side of the Interamericana, 10km south of the Santa Rosa turnoff. At Potrerillos turn right for the hamlet of **Quebrada Grande** (on some maps called Garcia Flamenco) and continue for about 8km. Best to have a 4WD for this trip. You can **camp** at the main ranger station and there is a rustic, simple **lodge** at Cacao field station. Call in at Santa Rosa administration to check if it is open and how much they charge for people to stay.

Crossing the border into Nicaragua: Peñas Blancas

Peñas Blancas (8am–noon & 1–4pm), the main crossing point into Nicaragua, is emphatically a border post and not a town, with just one or two basic sodas and no hotels. Aim to get here as **early** as possible, as procedures are ponderous and you'll be lucky to get through the whole deal in less than ninety minutes. In addition, buses on both side of the border are far more frequent in the morning, and fizzle out completely by 2 or 3pm. Things are smoothest if you come with Ticabus – all passengers are processed together and have some priority. Both Costa Rican and Nicaraguan border officials are quite strict, and there are many checks to see that your paperwork is in order. Canadians, Australians and New Zealanders need **visas**, which can be organized in San José (around US$25, or US$15 for a 72-hr transit visa).

Exit stamps and fee (75 colones) are paid on the Costa Rican side, where there is a restaurant and a helpful, organized Costa Rican **tourist office**. Money changers are always on hand and have colones, córdobas and dollars. After getting your Costa Rican exit stamp, it's a short walk north to the barrier, where you can pick up shuttle buses (US$2) 4km north to the Nicaraguan shantytown **Sapoá**, where you go through *migración* (see p.495).

The Guanacaste beaches

Many of the **beaches of Guanacaste**, scattered along a rocky coastline from Bahía Culebra to Sámara on the west of the Nicoya Peninsula, are being aggressively developed for mass tourism. Most controversial is the fits-and-starts **Papagayo Project**, that covers nearly the entire Bahía Culebra. Over the next fifteen years about 14,000 rooms are planned, making it the largest tourism development in Central America (there are currently a total of 13,000 hotel rooms in the whole of Costa Rica). That said, despite all the noise, the project seems to be permanently stalled. The **golf course** craze, however, shows no signs of abating – particularly damaging to this delicate environment, golf courses require an enormous amount of water, which is in danger of being abstracted from wetlands, mangroves and other fragile habitats, never mind the fact that local people may have their water supply curtailed.

Despite the increasing development, the coast here has a lot to recommend it, not least **Parque Nacional Marino las Baulas**, where droves of leatherback **turtles** come ashore to lay their eggs between October and February. If it's a good swim you want, however, best head down to **Tamarindo**, or better still to **Sámara** or **Nosara**, on the Nicoya Peninsula.

It can take a long time to get to the Guanacaste coast from San José (5hr minimum, unless you fly) and in some places you feel very remote indeed. **Getting around** can take time, too, as the beaches tend to be separated by rocky headlands or otherwise impassable formations, entailing considerable backtracking inland to get from one to the other. Unless you're just going to one place, **bus** travel is tricky, although possible if you intercept local services. By far the most popular option is to **rent a car**, which allows you to beach-hop with relative ease. Roads are not bad, if somewhat pothole-scarred, and you'll do best with **4WD**, though this can prove expensive.

Playa Panamá and Playa Hermosa

Sheltered from the full force of the Pacific, the clear blue waters of **Bahía Culebra** on the **Gulfo de Papagayo** are some of the best for swimming and snorkelling in the country. A dark sweep of volcanic sand, **Playa Panamá** is still a nice, quiet spot, despite the encroachment of new hotels: try *Costa Smeralda* (☎670-0044, fax 670-0379; ⑧), an upscale resort-type hotel with air-conditioning, a nice pool and good restaurant. Two **buses** daily arrive from Liberia, arriving noonish and around 8pm. The turnoff for Playa Panamá is 3km north of the more travelled turnoff for Coco, all on a good paved road.

Playa Hermosa ("Pretty Beach"), on the southern edge of Bahía Culebra, 10km north of the nearest beach to the south, Playa del Coco, is calm, clean and good for swimming. Small islets dot the bay, and in the wet season Hermosa is wonderfully quiet, and you may well have it to yourself but for the odd cow that has ambled down from pasture.

If you want to **stay** on the beach, there are two places to choose from. *Cabinas Playa Hermosa*, with private bath and ceiling fans (☎ & fax 670-0136; ③–④) is the most comfortable; next door, the much more basic *Cabinas Vallejo* (☎670-0417; ②), has shared bath and cold water. Fronting the beach, the popular and friendly *Hotel el Velero* (☎670-0330, fax 670-0310; ⑦), with excellent low-season discounts) has a great restaurant, two-storey rooms with balconies and sea view, and a small pool, all in lovely floral gardens with resident birds and lizards. A short path takes you to the beach. The new, good-value *Villa del Sueño* (☎ & fax 670-0026; ⑥) is a small eight-room hotel with lovely large rooms with private bath. There's a small pool and a good open air restaurant.

Playa del Coco

Thirty-five kilometres west of Liberia, with good road connections, **Playa del Coco** was the first Pacific beach to hit the big time with weekending Costa Ricans from the Valle Central. It used to be quite dirty, strewn with litter and streaked with boat motor oil, but has been cleaned up in recent years. Its accessibility, budget accommodation and good restaurants make it a useful place for a couple of days' jaunt or, if you have a car, as a base to explore the better beaches nearby.

Coco has also become a major diving centre, and **snorkelling** and **diving tours** are popular. In town, Mario Vargas Expeditions (☎ & fax 670-0351), is run by a seasoned divemaster; also recommended is Bill Beard's Diving Safaris, based in nearby Playa Hermosa (☎670-0012). The English-speaking staff at Rich Coast Diving, about 300m from the beach on the main road (☎670-0176) organize snorkelling, scuba trips and rent out mountain bikes.

Arrival and information

Direct **buses** (5hr) leave San José for Coco daily at 10am, returning at 9.15am. You can also get to Coco on local services from Liberia (see p.620), returning to Liberia at 7am, 9.15am (high season only), 2pm and 6pm (1hr). The town itself is very small, fronting the beach and focusing on a tiny **parquecito**. Minimal services include a **correo** (Mon–Fri 7.30am–5pm), and public **telephones** on either side of the *parquecito*. The Banco Nacional changes dollars and travellers' cheques.

Taxis gather in front of the *Restaurante Cocos* by the beach.

Accommodation

Coco has lots of fairly basic **cabinas**, catering to weekending nationals and tourists. In the high season, you should make sure to **reserve** for weekends, but can probably get away with turning up on spec mid-week, when rooms may also be a little cheaper. In the low season bargains abound. There's **camping** (US$4) at the Ojo Parqueo, 75m from the beach on the main road; they will keep an eye on your belongings, and also sell water.

Cabinas Catarina, 100m from the parquecito (☎670-0156). The most basic cabinas in town, each with private bath and cold water only. The friendly management will let you do laundry and cook meals in the small kitchen. All round a good deal. ①.

Cabinas Chale, 50m from the beach, 500m beyond the *parquecito* (☎670-0036). Slightly pricier than the others, with big rooms plus fridges (useful if you don't want to walk into town for a beer), and a pool, unusual in this category. ④–⑤.

Cabinas el Coco, on the beach, 200m north of the parquecito (☎670-0276, fax 670-0167). New cabinas right on the beach; comfortable, clean and friendly. Rooms on the second storey are best; on Saturday nights noise from the nearby disco can be troublesome. Shared or private bath, fans and free breakfast. ③.

Flor de Itabo, on the main road coming into town, about 1km from the beach (☎670-0011 or 0292, fax 670-0003). The best, most expensive, hotel in Coco, with good off-season rates. Tastefully decorated rooms have private bath, a/c, hot water and TV. Very friendly; they will change money for non-guests and, even better, you can use the pool for 400 colones. ⑤–⑦.

Hotel Anexo Luna Tica and **Cabinas Luna Tica**, 100m south of where the road ends at the beach (☎670-0279). Rooms in both are about the same price, and good value, but the hotel is a bit breezier than the cabinas, with some fans and a/c. Breakfast included in both. ④–⑤.

Villa Flores, on the road leading to the right before you reach the beach (☎ & fax 670-0269). Quiet and comfortable, the rather dark rooms each have private bath with hot water – some have ceiling fans, others have a/c (about US$10 more). Head for the second-storey balcony, a great place to catch sea breezes. ④.

Eating, drinking and nightlife

Coco has two very distinct types of **restaurants**, **sodas** and **bars**: those catering to nationals and those that make some sort of stab at cosmopolitanism to hook the gringos. Nightlife is generally quiet during the week, but things get livelier at the weekend, when the *Cocomar* **disco** starts up.

Cocomar disco, right on the beach, about 100m north of the parquecito. The town disco, which can be very loud on weekends, when it plays a mixture of salsa and reggae. Weekday evenings it's a quiet bar unless someone decides to crank up the powerful sound system. Open until midnight; later on weekends.

Restaurante Cocos, right by the beach. Popular place in prime position. Good for seafood lunches, but the music is *very* loud; it doubles as a bar in the evening.

Flor de Itabo, in the *Flor de Itabo* hotel. The most ambitious food in town, with prices to match; the fillet of beef and fresh shrimp are recommended if you feel like splashing out. Open 6.15am–9.30pm. The popular *Havana Bar* is open until 11pm.

Pizzería Pronto, 500m north of the beach on the right-hand side as you enter Coco. Green salad and large pizzas for about US$7 – the *jalapeña* is good; the *pequeña* better value at US$4 – served beneath a pleasant canopy. Daily except Tues 11.30am–10pm.

San Francisco Treats, 200m from beach. The Californian crowd who run this cheery melon-coloured restaurant offer treats such as home-made lasagne and roast beef sandwiches.

Parque Nacional Marino las Baulas

On the Río Matapalo estuary between Conchal and Tamarindo, **PARQUE NACIONAL MARINO LAS BAULAS** (US$6) is less a National Park than a Reserve, created to protect from developer speculation the nesting grounds of the **leatherback** turtles (*baulas*), who come ashore in droves from October to February. The largest reptile in the world, the leatherback can reach a truly astounding size (over 5m long) and bulk. They lay their eggs at **Playa Grande**, a beautiful beach with a great wide sweep of bay and light-grey sand. Outside laying season you can surf and dash into the waves, but swimming is a bit rough, plagued by rip tides.

Playa Grande is one of the most important spots for leatherback nesting in the country, and in the past has been a magnet for tour groups from upmarket Guanacaste hotels, as well as day-trippers from Tamarindo and Coco. Nowadays, however, there are **number restrictions** on turtle-viewing. You have to be led by official Park guides to the viewing platforms, leaving the turtles in peace to go about their business. To **drive to Las Baulas**, take the road from Huacas to Matapalo, and turn left at the soccer field. During the wet season, **4WD** is recommended for this stretch. Most people, however, visit the park by **boat** from Tamarindo, entering at the southern end rather than from the Matapalo road.

Playa Tamarindo

Stretching for a couple of kilometres over a series of rocky headlands, **Playa Tamarindo** is one of the most popular beaches in Guanacaste, attracting surfers and weekending Costa Ricans. **TAMARINDO** village, which has a sizeable foreign community, boasts a great selection of restaurants – you'll even find cappuccino and *pain au chocolat* – a lively beach culture and some high-season nightlife.

Arrival and information

You can **fly** into Tamarindo on Travelair and Sansa (see p.554), both of which have offices in town; **buses** arrive inconveniently late, particularly in high season, when you need to have called ahead (the daily direct service currently leaves San José at 4pm, arriving about 6hr later). Buses stop at the village loop, which effectively constitutes Tamarindo's small centre, with a circular *parquecito* populated by pecking chickens and surrounded by restaurants. The small Banco Nacional, about 500m north of the loop, may be able to **change dollars** and **travellers' cheques** (Mon–Fri 8am–3pm); there are **public telephones** on the *parquecito*.

Accommodation

Many of Tamarindo's **hotels** are very good, if expensive. You can **camp** at *Tito's* (US$5) at the south end of the beach; he also rents horses for reasonable prices.

Cabinas Marielos, about 800m north of village loop (☎ & fax 653-4041). Basic rooms; light and clean, with fan, cold water and use of small kitchen, in pleasant colourful grounds. Professional, helpful *dueña*; but a very tough reservation and advance deposit policy. ④–⑤.

Capitán Suizo, south end of beach (☎ & fax 653-0292). Excellent upmarket 22-room hotel with exclusive, quiet atmosphere. Cabin-type rooms all have a balcony or terrace and fridge and ceiling fans or a/c (not really necessary), sunken bathtub, hot water and outside shower. Buffet breakfast, cocktail bar, pool and beautiful beach views. Good discounts in low season. ⑦–⑧.

Dolly's, on main road opposite *Cabinas Marielos* (no phone). Friendly established place, popular with surfers and budget travellers, which fills up fast. Very basic rooms with flimsy beds and fan, or better, quieter upstairs rooms with sea view. All are a good deal, with private bath. Bar and restaurant attached. ③–④.

El Milagro, 1km north of the village loop (☎653-0042, fax 6653-0050). A favourite with Europeans; nicely decorated cabinas with fans, private bath and hot water. Poolside restaurant serves great food, though bar prices are high. ⑥.

Pasatiempo, south of the village loop (☎ 653-0096, fax 653-0275). Popular, small (10 rooms) hotel with spotless rooms, ceiling fans and hot water; larger rooms (sleeping 5) are the best deal. The real advantage is the friendly and attentive management, nice pool, plus lively restaurant and very popular bar (though this can be loud in high season). ⑥.

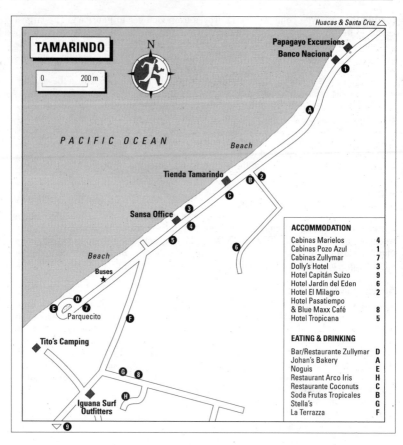

Pozo Azul, at northern end of the village (☎653-0280). Geared towards weekending nationals, this older complex of cabinas offers a small kitchen and a murky pool, and run-down but clean rooms. Rooms with fan are cheap; price rises steeply for a/c. ③.

Sueño del Mar, 1km from Tamarindo on the road heading south to Playa Langosta (☎653-0284). Good value, attractive B&B rooms with whitewashed walls, murals and sea views. There's also a garden that leads directly to the beach, although there's little sand. The friendly owners include a hearty breakfast in the room rate. ⑥–⑦.

Tropicana, 600m north of the village loop (☎ & fax 653-0261). Pleasant new hotel owned by an elderly Italian couple. The 40 spacious rooms come with a/c or fan, at very fair prices for Tamarindo. Good low season rates. ⑤–⑥.

Villa Alegre, 300m south of the *Capitan Suizo* (☎653-0270, fax 653-0287; *vialegre@sol.racsa.co.cr*). Small Californian-owned B&B, in a quiet location on the beach just south of Tamarindo. The four rooms and two suites each have a private garden and patio; you can choose between fans or a/c and between private or shared bath. Each room is designed with furniture from a country where the owners have travelled (Mexico, Guatemala, Russia etc). A good breakfast is served on the verandah, with a lovely view of the Pacific. ⑧.

Zullymar, at the village loop (☎653-0140). Clean, spacious cabinas with carved wooden doors, set in pleasant grounds scattered with reproduction pre-Columbian art. Rooms with fan and cold water cheaper than a/c and heated showers. ③–⑥.

Activities

Swimming is not great around Tamarindo, as the waves are fairly heavy and there are rip tides. Most people are content to paddle in the rocky coves and tide-pools south of the town, while **surfers** ride the waves at adjacent Playa Langosta. Just south of Playa Grande, where the **leatherbacks** lay their eggs, Tamarindo also attracts its fair share of turtles, though they come ashore here in much smaller quantities.

A number of outfitters in Tamarindo rent **surfboards** and windsurfing equipment; among them, Tienda Tamarindo (closed for lunch between 2 and 2.30pm; ☎653-0148). You can rent a **bike** here, too (US$12–15/day), and explore the area, although make sure it is sturdy enough to negotiate the gravel roads. Iguana Surf Outfitters (☎ & fax 653-0148) has a larger selection of surfboards (US$15–20/day), boogie boards and snorkelling gear (around US$12/day). In addition, numerous operators offer **turtle tours** to Las Baulas in nesting season (about US$12 per person); these are not permitted by the Park administration to land on the beach. Contact Papagayo Excursions at the northern end of the village (☎653-0254, fax 653-0227), which also rents windsurfing boards, or Tamarindo Rentals and Tours, further south on the main road.

Eating, drinking and nightlife

Along with plenty of good cheap, seaside places dishing up *típico* meals, Tamarindo offers some of the best food in the country – at a price. **Nightlife** focuses on the restaurants and bars in the centre of the village, many of them geared towards surfers. It can get very quiet in low season, when residents and tourists head to the *Hotel Pasatiempo* bar, the local hangout.

Arco Irís, on the road that leads to the *Hotel Pasatiempo*. Italian restaurant with an innovative, impressively large vegetarian menu. The owner also rents several beautifully decorated cabinas, though these aren't particularly cheap (US$30). Tues–Sun 6–10pm.

Blue Maxx Cafe, in the *Hotel Pasatiempo*. Good American breakfasts served to non-guests from 7am daily, with proper cappuccino and espresso. A nice place for coffee any time of day.

Coconuts, on the main road north of the village. Sandwiches, herb teas, stunning cakes, espresso and cappuccino for breakfast; at night dine by candlelight on pricey Indonesian crossed with Japanese and European cuisine, to a classical music accompaniment. They show videos some evenings. Main courses US$10–12. Breakfast (high season only) 7–10am, dinner 5–10pm.

Jardín del Edén, in the hotel of the same name. Romantic, fairly priced restaurant, serving high-class French and Italian cuisine. Their special menu – which changes daily – is a great deal at about (US$15) per person.

Johan's Bakery, 600m north of the village loop. Small bakery serving delicious fresh croissants, *pan dulce*, *pain au chocolat*, banana cake, pizza, waffles and apple flan for breakfast. Under new French management; the name may change. Daily 6am–8pm.

Milagro, in the *Hotel el Milagro*. Respected restaurant with a changing menu of European dishes and a pleasant poolside setting. Rather expensive bar.

Noguis, right by the village loop. Really good breakfasts, with delicious breads, pastries and coffees – you can also get a breakfast to take away. Breezy seaside tables are a plus.

Soda Frutas Tropicales, on the main road as you come into town. As the name says, there's plenty of tropical fruits in this little snack bar – try the fruit refrescos; otherwise the menu is the usual soda fare, but fairly inexpensive at US$3–4.

Stella's, 500m back from the town; take left road from *Tamarindo Resort Club* and follow signs. One of Tamarindo's best restaurants, with good Italian pasta and fresh fish cooked in excellent, inventive sauces. Main courses US$8–12. Closed Sun.

La Terraza, on the right-hand side of the road heading toward the *Hotel Pasatiempo*. Good, authentic Italian pizzas, with an impressive view of the village and beach from the upstairs dining room.

Bar/Restaurante Zullymar, right in front of the *parquecito*. Popular place for a cold beer to the accompaniment of crashing waves; restaurant serves seafood and *típico* dishes, most of them between US$5 and US$7.

MOVING ON FROM TAMARINDO

A direct bus to **San José** leaves at 5.45 and 6.45am, and one to **Liberia** at 6am (1–2hr), or you could take a bus 30km to sprawling **Santa Cruz** at 6.45am, and from there hook up with **local services** to Liberia or San José (call TRALAPA ☎221-7202 for schedule information).

Continuing down along the west coast of the peninsula is only really possible if you have your own transport, especially **4WD**. It's trickier by bus, although you can pick up occasional services to Sámara or Nosara from Santa Cruz and Nicoya. A more convenient, if expensive, option is to take a **long-distance taxi** from *Dolly's*: destinations include Nicoya, Santa Cruz, Liberia, Nosara and Sámara. Fares run between US$15 (Santa Cruz) and US$80 (Sámara). You can also **fly** back to San José with either *Travelair* or *Sansa*. The airstrip is about 2.5km north of town.

Nicoya

Many bus travellers making connections between, say, Tamarindo and Sámara, might end up spending a night in **NICOYA**, the main settlement of the peninsula. Set in a dip surrounded by low mountains, it's a hot place, but undeniably pretty, with a lovely **Parque Central**, centring on a preserved white adobe church (earthquake-battered, structurally unstable and currently closed).

Practicalities

Eight **buses** a day arrive in Nicoya from San José, a journey of around six hours. Some take the long way round via the road to Liberia, but most take the Tempisque ferry (only slightly shorter). In addition, buses arrive from a number of regional destinations, including Liberia (14 daily), Santa Cruz (17 daily) and Sámara (3 daily). Most buses arrive at Nicoya's spotless new bus station, on the southern edge of town, a short walk from the centre. The Liberia service, however, pulls in across from *Hotel las Tinajas*. As usual, you'll find most **services** around the Parque Central, including the *correo* (Mon–Fri 7.30am–5.30pm), the Banco de Costa Rica (Mon–Fri 7am–3pm), and **taxis**. For the latter you can also call Coopetico (☎658-6226).

The friendly *Hotel Jenny*, 200m south of the Parque Central (look for sign; ②) is the cheapest **place to stay**, with old, basic rooms with a/c, TV and phone. *Las Tinajas*, 100m north and east of the Parque Central, has dark rooms inside the main building, an old house, and lighter cabinas in the back (②). Good **restaurants** include the *Cafetería Daniela*, 100m east of the park, for breakfast and pastries; the sodas by the park for large *casados* and, for Chinese food, the restaurants *Tey-et*, across from the *Hotel Jenny*, and *El Presidente*.

Bus connections from Nicoya are good, with daily services to Sámara (3pm; 2hr) and Nosara (1pm; 2hr). You can also get to San José (6 daily; 6hr), Liberia (14 daily; 2hr) and Santa Cruz (15 daily; 40min).

Playa Sámara

At present, for sheer size and safety for swimming, **SÁMARA**, 30km southwest of Nicoya, is probably the best beach in Costa Rica, especially now that local residents and visitors have tackled the litter problem that once plagued its wide, flat sands. The waves break on a reef about a kilometre out, so the water near the shore is actually quite calm. It's also a great place to relax; its distance from the capital means it's quieter than the more accessible Pacific beaches.

Arrival and information

Sansa and Travelair planes from San José come in at the airstrip 6km south of town at Carrillo, where 4WD taxis can take you to Sámara for about US$6. The express **bus** from San José leaves at noon and gets in about six hours later, stopping about 50m in front of the beach right in the centre of the village. The express bus **back to San José** currently leaves at 4am, and there are buses **to Nicoya** at 6am and 4pm (2hr). You can buy bus tickets for San José services from the *Pulpería Mileth*, which also has the village public **telephone**. Sámara's **correo** (Mon–Fri 7.30am–5pm), a small shack really, 50m before the entrance to the beach, offers minimal services. It's very difficult to **change money** in Sámara; bring plenty of colones, especially in low season.

Accommodation

Staying in Sámara is getting pricier, with few cheap cabinas. Though during the low season most hotels can offer better rates than the ones listed here, at high season weekends you should have a **reservation** no matter what price range you aim for. The best budget option is to **camp**: especially popular on weekends, *Camping Coco*, on the beach, is clean and well-run with cooking grills (US$2.50). At the north end of the beach *Camping Playas Sámara* is also clean, with toilets and showers (US$3).

Cabinas Arena, about 150m from the beach (no phone). The 12 rooms are very basic, but clean, with private bath with good low season prices. In high season the owners operate a restaurant on the grounds. ③–④.

Cabinas Belvedere, first left as you come into town from Nicoya (no phone). Clean, basic cabinas with heated water. One of the cheaper options in town, with breakfast (included) served on a nice terrace. ⑤.

Cabinas Doña Marta, a few metres from the beach (no phone). An excellent budget option: locally owned cabinas, all with private bath for under US$10. ②.

Casa del Mar, set back from beach, 50m north of entrance to beach (☎232-2241). Downstairs rooms are clean and white, but lack light. Better rooms upstairs with shared bath and palm-fringed sea view. Currently changing management, so may change its name. ⑤–⑥.

Giada, about 100m northeast of the beach, on the left (☎222-7553, fax 223-5426). Fairly upscale, with spotless rooms, good beds, overhead fans, private baths and tiled showers. Upstairs rooms are better for views and breeze. Dollar exchange for guests only. ⑤–⑥.

Isla Chora Inn, about 400m along the road to Nosara (☎232-3087, fax 296-1873). The nicest place in town, offering cabins with red tiles or palm-leaved roofs, all attractively set around a swimming pool. Prices vary for cold or hot water, private bath, a/c or fans, and kitchens. The friendly Italian owners can arrange tours and activities, and there's an excellent restaurant (see "Eating", below) with special rates for guests. ⑥.

Eating, drinking and nightlife

There are a couple of very nice places to **eat** in Sámara, where you can enjoy a cold beer or two by the lapping waves. **Nightlife** is quiet, though things can get a little loud on high season Saturday nights when the village's *Tutti Fruti* disco comes into its own. By far the best place to nurse a cold *Imperial* in the evening is the beachside *Bar/Rest Bahía* (to find it from the beach, walk south toward Playa Carillo), with little tables set under palms in the sand.

Colochos, 300m before the beach. Moderately priced (US$4) seafood, starring the usuals: *pargo* (snapper) and *corvina* (bass).

Isla Chora Inn, in the hotel (see above). Without a doubt the nicest place to eat in town, this new Italian restaurant is run by a couple who brought their *gelati*-making skills with them. Try the spectacular *pizza con mariscos* (US$7) or any of the pasta dishes.

Marisquería el Dorado, on the road to Nosara. Daily fresh-caught fish; they specialize (as the name says) in *dorado*, although the *pargo* (snapper) is also very good. Both are a real bargain at around US$3 each with tasty vegetables.

Soda Sindhy, in the middle of the village, about 75m before the beach. Open-air soda; service is slow, but it's clean, and serves generous heaps of *típico* food.

Nosara and around

The drive from Sámara 25km north to the village of **NOSARA** is pretty; a shady, secluded stretch along dirt and gravel roads punctuated by a few creeks – it's passable with a regular car (low clearance) in the dry season but you'll need a 4WD in the wet. The village itself, prettily set some 3km inland between a low ridge of mountains and the sea, is one of the most appealing in the whole of Costa Rica. Usually grouped together as **Playas Nosara**, the three beaches in the area – Nosara, Guiones and Pelada – are fine for **swimming**, although you can be buffetted by the crashing waves, and there are some rocky outcrops. The whole area is great for beachside walks, and the vegetation, even in the dry season, is greener than further north. Some attempts have been made to limit development and to protect land: largely on the initiative of locals and foreign residents, a good deal of the area around Nosara has been designated a **Wildlife Refuge**.

Refugio Nacional de Fauna Silvestre Ostional
Eight kilometres northeast of Nosara, **OSTIONAL** and its chocolate-coloured-sand beach make up the **REFUGIO NACIONAL DE FAUNA SILVESTRE OSTIONAL**, one of the most important nesting grounds in the country for **Olive Ridley turtles**, which come ashore to lay their eggs between May and November. You can't swim here; it's too rough, and there are sharks.

If you're in town during the first few days of the *arribadas* you'll see locals with horses, carefully stuffing their big, thick bags full of eggs and slinging them over their shoulders, kids skipping alongside. This is quite legal; villagers of Ostional and Nosara are allowed to harvest eggs, for sale or consumption, during the first three days of the season only. It takes about fifteen minutes to drive the gravel-and-stone road from Nosara to the Refuge; alternately you can bike it or take a taxi (see below).

Nosara arrival, orientation and getting around
Travelair and Sansa **fly** to Nosara from San José, often via Sámara, landing at the small airstrip. The San José **bus** comes in at the Abastecedor general store. There isn't much to the village itself but a soccer field, a couple of restaurants and a **gas station**. The latter is little more than a shack, with nothing, no pumps even, to show what it is. Gas is syphoned out of a barrel or canister, and they can also change tyres. The Monkey Business **tour shop** nearby sells souvenirs, clothes and Travelair tickets, as well as pizza and *refrescos*. There's a **correo** (Mon–Fri 7.30am–5pm) as you leave the town on the right, and the village phone is between the gas station and *Cabinas Chorotega*.

Ask at the gas station about **taxis** to Ostional to see the turtles (about US$15), or **rent a bike** from Cyclo Nosara, next door – also very useful for getting to the beaches. They also sell Travelair and Sansa tickets.

Nosara accommodation

If you want to stay on the **beach** you've got two options: posh **gringo-run accommo-dation** or **camping**. There's a group of economical cabinas and hotels in the village – but you'll need to rent a bike or count on doing a lot of walking to get to the ocean.

Almost Paradise Cafe and Cabinas, signed from the left turn at *Hotel Playas Nosara* (via the public fax in Nicoya: ☎685-5004, mark fax "attention Apartado 15, Nosara"; *almost@nosara.com*). This pink wooden bungalow perched above town houses five spacious, very comfortable rooms with private bathand hot water. There are stupendous views, howler monkeys and birds in the garden (along with a pool) and a restaurant serving mainly vegetarian food. A really lovely, unpretentious choice. ④.

Cabinas Chorotega, in the village (☎680-0836 – village public phone, leave message). Superb cabinas, owned by friendly enterprising dueña Emiliana Nuñez. Large, spotless rooms with a communal terrace and rocking chairs where you can sit with a beer under the stars. Homely, and very fairly priced. ③.

Estancia de Nosara, set back about 1km from Nosara beach; follow signs (☎ & fax 680-0378). Upmarket, foreign-owned hotel in landscaped grounds, with comfortable rooms with many small details. Quiet and well-run with a restaurant and tennis court. ⑤–⑦.

Lagarta Lodge (☎ & fax 680-0763). Set in a 500,000-square-metre private nature reserve, with excellent birdwatching and stunning coastal views. Rooms have private bath, hot water and handy refrigerators, and there's a pool. ⑦.

Rancho Suiza Lodge, set back from Playa Pelada, copiously signed (☎ & fax 284-9669). One place you won't have trouble finding. Bungalows with hammocks, whirlpool, fan, heated water and fridge, and chattering birds in lovely landscaped grounds. Well-cared-for by friendly Swiss *dueños*. ⑤.

Nosara eating and drinking

Owing to Nosara's relative isolation, food can be pricey, and there's little choice. In the **village** there are a number of places around the soccer field. *Restaurant el Bambú* features the usual rice dishes; more popular for a night out, *Rancho Nosara* has a sound system and serves food and drink at wooden tables. Further down the road, the simple restaurant at *Cabinas Chorotega* dishes up local dishes and very cold beer under a conical roof. Of places on or near the **beach**, *The Gilded Iguana* is an upmarket bar with Mexican food that attracts the sizeable local foreign community. There are great views at the *Almost Paradise Café*, as well as fresh, healthy food. *Olga's*, on **Playa Pelada**, serves cold beer, good *casados* and fish, again with ocean views. The most ambitious restaurant in the area is the *churasscuría* at *Rancho Suiza*; head here for tasty fish, meat and Thai food (daily except Sat). They also do lunch in their very pretty seaside restaurant (daily 11am–5pm). For a **picnic** or budget meal, pick up something in the supermarket across from *Cabinas Chorotega*.

Río Tempisque ferry

The **Río Tempisque ferry** carries cars and passengers across the river between Puerto Moreno, 17km from the Nicoya–Carmona road, and a point 25km west of the Interamericana on the mainland. Crossing here will save you a 110-kilometre drive up and over the cleft of the peninsula, via Liberia, but leave yourself plenty of time on weekends (Fridays and Sundays especially) and holidays, when the line-up of traffic can mean waits of four to five hours. Whatever time you cross, and in whichever direction, be in line about an hour before departure. Unless curtailed by bad weather in the wet season, **eastbound** crossings take place on the half-hour between 6.30am and 8.30pm, **westbound** every hour on the hour from 6am to 8pm – it takes twenty minutes.

travel details

BUSES

Cañas to: Liberia (constantly; 50min); San José (5 daily; 6 on Sun; 3hr).

Liberia to: Bagaces (3 daily; 40min); Cañas (3 daily; 50min); Cuajiniquil (daily; 1hr 30min); La Cruz (14 daily; 1hr); Nicoya (14 daily; 2hr); Peñas Blancas, for Nicaragua (9 daily; 2hr); Playa del Coco (3–4 daily; 1hr); Playa Hermosa (2 daily; 1hr); Playa Panamá (2 daily; 1hr); Puntarenas (5 daily; 3hr); San José (8 daily; 4hr); Santa Cruz (14 daily; 1hr); Parque Nacional Santa Rosa (5 daily; 1hr).

Nicoya to: Liberia (14 daily; 2hr); Nosara (daily; 2hr); Playa Sámara (2 daily; 2hr); San José (6 daily; 6hr); Santa Cruz (15 daily; 40min).

Nosara to: Nicoya (daily; 2hr); Sámara (daily; 40min); San José (daily; 6hr).

Peñas Blancas to: Liberia (9 daily; 2hr); San José (2 daily; 6hr).

Playa del Coco to: Liberia (3–4 daily; 1hr); San José (daily; 5hr).

Playa Hermosa to: Liberia (2 daily; 1hr); San José (daily; 5hr).

Playa Panamá to: Liberia (2 daily; 1hr); San José (daily; 5hr).

Playa Sámara to: Nicoya (2 daily; 2hr); San José (daily; 6hr).

San José to: Cañas (5 daily; 3hr); Junquillal (daily; 5hr); Liberia (8 daily; 4hr); Nicoya (8 daily; 6hr); Nosara (daily; 6hr); Peñas Blancas, for Nicaragua (4 daily; 6hr); Playa Brasilito (2 daily; 6hr); Playa del Coco (daily; 5hr); Playa Flamingo (2 daily; 6hr); Playa Hermosa (daily; 5hr); Playa Panamá (daily; 5hr); Playa Potrero (2 daily; 6hr); Playa Sámara (daily; 6hr); Santa Cruz (5 daily; 5hr); Parque Nacional Santa Rosa (4 daily; 6hr); Tamarindo (daily; 6hr).

Santa Cruz to: Junquillal (daily; 1hr 30min); Liberia (14 daily; 1hr); Nicoya (15 daily; 40min); Playa Brasilito (2 daily; 1hr 30min); Playa Flamingo (2 daily; 1hr 30min); Playa Potrero (2 daily; 1hr 30min); San José (5 daily; 5hr); Tamarindo (1 direct daily; 1hr).

Tamarindo to: Liberia (daily; 1–2hr); San José (daily; 6hr); Santa Cruz (1 direct daily; 1hr).

FLIGHTS

Travelair

Nosara to: San José (daily except Sun; 1hr 25min).

Playa Sámara to: San José (daily except Sun; 1hr 45min).

San José to: Nosara (daily; 1hr 25min); Playa Sámara (daily; 1hr 45min); Tamarindo (daily; 40min).

Sansa

Nosara to: San José (daily except Sun; 1hr 30min).

Playa Sámara to: San José (daily except Sun; 1hr 45min).

San José to: Nosara (3 weekly; 1hr 30min); Playa Sámara (6 weekly; 1hr 45min); Tamarindo (daily; 40min).

Tamarindo to: San José (daily; 40min).

CHAPTER 32

THE ZONA NORTE

Costa Rica's **Zona Norte** ("northern zone") spans the hundred-odd kilometres from the base of the Cordillera Central to just short of the mauve-blue mountains of southern Nicaragua. Cut off from the rest of the country by a lack of roads, the Zona Norte has developed a distinct character, with independent-minded farmers and Nicaraguan refugees making up large segments of the population. Neither group journeys to the Valle Central very often, and many people of the north hold a special allegiance to their area and a pride in its importance.

Geographically, the Zona Norte separates neatly into two broad, river-drained plains (*llanuras*), which stretch all the way to the Río San Juan on the Nicaraguan–Costa Rican border. Less obviously picturesque than many parts of the country, the entire region nonetheless has a distinctive appeal, with lazy rivers snaking across steaming plains scarred by trails of blood-orange soil, and flop-eared cattle languishing beneath the draping limbs of riverside trees.

Most travellers only venture up here to see the perpetually active **Volcán Arenal**, using the nearby town of **Fortuna** as their base. To the east is the **Sarapiquí** area, with its tropical forest "**eco-lodges**" and research stations of **Selva Verde** and **Rara Avis**. Further north, the remote flatlands are home to the increasingly accessible **Refugio Nacional de Vida Silvestre Caño Negro**, which harbours an extraordinary number of migratory and indigenous birds.

The **climate** in the north is hot and wet, more so in the east than in the west near Guanacaste, where there is a dry season. There's a serviceable **bus** network, though if you're travelling outside the La Fortuna or Puerto Viejo areas, you'd probably do better with a car. As for other facilities, the area around Volcán Arenal is best geared up for tourists, even boasting a couple of excellent five-star **hotels**. Between Boca de Arenal and Los Chiles in the far north, on the other hand, there is a real shortage of accommodation, though fuel and food are in good supply.

Volcán Arenal and La Fortuna

That the Arenal region attracts such huge numbers of tourists is largely due to the majestic **Volcán Arenal**, one of the most active volcanoes in the Western hemisphere. Just 6km away, **LA FORTUNA DE SAN CARLOS**, or **Fortuna**, as it is more often called, was until recently a simple agricultural town. Nowadays, true to its name, it's booming, with visitors flocking to watch the lava ooze down the lip of the volcano – a **National Park** – like juice from a squashed fruit.

Now very much geared to the tourist market, Fortuna is a curiously characterless place, although people are friendly enough. There's nothing to do except book tours, bed down and have a meal or a beer, and maybe gaze at the volcano, looming 1633m above town. One popular excursion is to Fortuna's two **cataratas** (waterfalls), just 6km from the south side of the church in town and an easy day's hike (make sure to wear

For an explanation of **accommodation price codes**, see p.526.

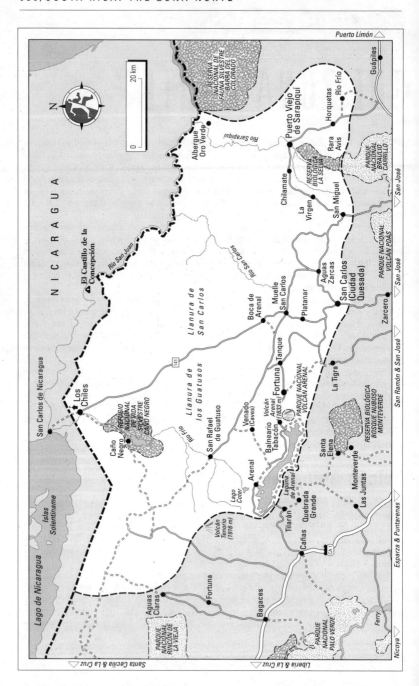

sturdy, waterproof shoes) or half-day horse ride. Fortuna also has excellent **bus** connections, making it one of the main setting-off points for tours to the remote Wildlife Refuge of **Caño Negro** and something of a transportation hub to San José in the south and to Guanacaste in the west.

Note that as Fortuna becomes increasingly popular, opportunistic theft is rising; never leave anything unattended, especially in a car, and be careful about walking around alone late at night. Also be wary of "guides" who offer their services on the street.

Arrival and information

There are three **direct bus services from San José to Fortuna**, currently leaving La Coca-Cola at 6.15am, 8.40am and 11.30am. You could also take a direct bus from **San José to San Carlos**, where you can change for frequent buses to Fortuna (40km; 1hr). From Tilarán get either the 8am or the 1.30pm bus (3hr). Buses from San José and San Carlos stop next to the *Hotel La Fortuna*, around the corner from the *El Jardín* restaurant. If you arrive from Tilarán you will alight in front of the *bomba*.

Fortuna is set on a small grid of four streets criss-crossed by five, centring on the soccer field in front of a modern stucco church. It is never hard to orient yourself – the volcano is west. Most hotels and almost all amenities are on the "main street" that borders the south side of the field.

Change money at the Banco Nacional or at your hotel. There are **payphones** scattered about town; with phone cards you can call anywhere, or try making international calls outside Sunset Tours' smaller office, 50m north of the soccer field just beyond Rancho La Cascada.

Aguas Bravas (see under "Tours from Fortuna", below) sells *La Nación, Tico Times,* and the *New York Times*, and rents sturdy **mountain bikes**.

Accommodation

Though there's plenty of **budget accommodation** in Fortuna, the place does get booked up during the dry season when you should try to call ahead. Note that prices tend to be per person and single rooms are hard to find.

Cabinas Andrea, 100m south and 150m west of the soccer field, on the road beside the Río Burío (no phone). Very basic budget hangout, with adequate rooms with shared bath and cold water for about the cheapest rates in town. ①.

Las Colinas, 50m south of the soccer field (☎479-9107). Clean and comfortable with hot water and fans. Upstairs rooms are airier and some give views of the volcano. This is a popular hotel, and often booked; will accept unpaid reservations if you indicate when you will arrive and turn up on time. There's a 9pm silence rule enforced to discourage the reveller element. ③.

Hotel La Fortuna, next to San José bus stop (☎479-9197). Good value, basic hotel; rooms come with shared or private bath, and the management knows everything there is to know in town. Very popular with budget travellers; book in advance. ②–③.

Cabinas Mayol, 50m south of *Hotel La Fortuna* (☎479-9110). Good budget rooms in an old Fortuna house, all with fans and private bath; luxury rooms with a/c are planned, along with a pool. The well-travelled *dueño* Luis Diego is very helpful. ①–③.

San Bosco, 100m north and east of the soccer field (☎479-9050, fax 479-9109). Good value, big rooms with fans and spacious bath with running hot water. Their low observation platform gives good views of Arenal. Managed by a friendly and informative local family. ④–⑤.

Cabinas Sissy, east of *Cabinas Andrea* (no phone). Good sized rooms with hot water showers. Less basic than the others and fairly priced. ①–②.

Cabinas Las Tinajas, north of the centre of town (☎479-9199). Small complex, with four clean, well-furnished rooms. Friendly, good value, and a step up from the rock-bottom places. ③.

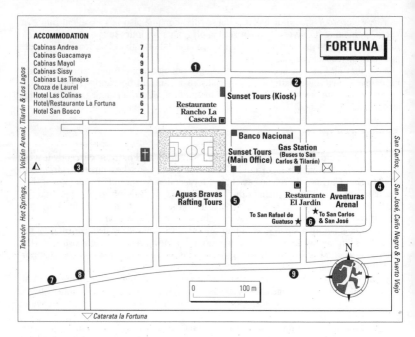

ACCOMMODATION

Cabinas Andrea	7
Cabinas Guacamaya	4
Cabinas Mayol	9
Cabinas Sissy	8
Cabinas Las Tinajas	1
Choza de Laurel	3
Hotel Las Colinas	5
Hotel/Restaurante La Fortuna	6
Hotel San Bosco	2

Parque Nacional Volcán Arenal

Though **Volcán Arenal** is one of the most active volcanoes in the world, whether you will see any lava flow depends very much on the weather. In the rainy season the spectacular night flows are very elusive, hidden by shrouds of mist and cloud. However, if nothing else you'll certainly hear unearthly rumbling and sporadically feel the ground shake – especially at night.

Lava currently pours down the west side of the volcano, which, conveniently, is where the entrance to **PARQUE NACIONAL VOLCÁN ARENAL** (daily 8am–5.30pm; US$6) is located. There's a viewing platform, looking over the volcano and Laguna de Arenal behind it: especially spectacular after dark, when the orange glow of the lava lights up the night. In the dry season **night tours** leave from Fortuna every evening at about 6pm; they may not run when it is wet. None offers you your money back if you **do not see a lava flow**, so you might want to wait for a clear evening before signing up.

Driving to Arenal, you take the first left after Balneario Tabacón (12km west of Fortuna). The park is signed. Taking a taxi costs around US$35 or more including waiting time and return journey, so unless you're in a group, it's cheaper – and less bother – to take an official tour.

Tours from Fortuna

When booking a **tour** from Fortuna, your best bet is to go with one of the official operators, or to book through a hotel – *Hotel La Fortuna*'s are particularly good and cheap. In recent years there have been serious complaints from women travellers about unwanted attention received from some of the uncredited, freelance "guides" who approach visitors on the street; it's best to deal with these with a firm refusal.

By far the most popular excursion, of course, is to **Volcán Arenal**. Note, though, that many of these trips include a visit to soak in the thermal waters at **Balneario Tabacón**, and that the price of the tour generally does not include the admission fee (US$14). Sunset Tours, 50m north of the soccer field (daily 8am–8pm; ☎ & fax 479-9099) runs trips to Caño Negro (see p.640; US$45), and horseback rides to La Catarata de la Fortuna (US$15), and sometimes a (5hr minimum) horseback trip to Monteverde (see p.591). Trips run by the professional Aventuras Arenal, 150m east of the soccer field (☎ & fax 479-9133) are almost identical, and slightly cheaper. They can also transfer you just about anywhere in the country. Aguas Bravas (☎479-9025; fax 229-4837) is a very professional new **rafting** outfit, offering jaunts on the Sarapiquí river. Stop by their office on the southeast corner of the park and talk to friendly Juan Carlos.

Eating and drinking

Considering the number of tourists passing through, **restaurant** prices (US$5–7 per person for dinner) in La Fortuna are quite fair, catering for locals as much as visitors. The food is pretty much the same everywhere: the inevitable *casados*, *platos del día* and *arroz-con*-whatever; for something a bit more varied, head for the *Rancho la Cascada*, on the north side of the soccer field, which is also the place to hang out and have a beer.

The far north

The **far north** of the Zona Norte is an isolated region, in many ways culturally – as well as geographically – closer to Nicaragua than to the rest of the country. Most tourists are here to see **Refugio Nacional de Vida Silvestre Caño Negro**, a vast wetlands area and – at 192km from San José – one of the most remote Wildlife Refuges in Costa Rica. You can visit Caño Negro on a day-trip from the capital or on an excursion from Fortuna or any of the larger hotels in the Zona Norte; getting there independently, as everywhere in Costa Rica, is more complicated.

Los Chiles

LOS CHILES, nearly 200km from San José, is the only town in the region; you can cross the border here into Nicaragua and journey on to San Carlos de Nicaragua (see p.504). Two **buses** per day run from La Coca-Cola in **San José** "direct" to Los Chiles (in reality, they stop frequently, and always in Ciudad Quesada). The journey takes more than five hours. The San José bus stops right outside the Mercado Central, while buses arriving from Ciudad Quesada often stop close to the docks. Nelson Leiton, who runs a small **travel agency**, Servitur, is a good source of **information**. The office is based in the cool and spotless *Cabinas Jabirú*, 200m north of the centre (☎471-1055; ①–②), which offer private bath, hot water and fans, and a laundry service. You can supposedly **change dollars** and travellers' cheques at the Banco Nacional on the north side of the soccer field (Mon–Fri 8am–3.30pm).

Returning from **Los Chiles to Ciudad Quesada**, buses currently leave at 4.45am, 5.15am, 6.15am, 7.45am, 9am, 11am, 12.30pm, 2pm, 3pm and 4pm. From Ciudad Quesada there are ten daily services to San José between 5am and 7pm (2hr 30min).

Crossing into Nicaragua

The boat to Nicaragua usually departs the *muelle* from Monday to Friday at 8am, but it's always worth checking with *migración* (Mon–Fri 8am–5pm; ☎471-1061; note that it often closes early – get there about 3pm to be safe) or at the Nicaraguan consulate in San José.

The **Nicaraguan border patrol** is at the 3km point upriver from Los Chiles. Make sure they stamp your passport, as you will need proof of entry when leaving Nicaragua. There is also a **police check** on the highway south of Los Chiles. From the border control point it is a 14km trip up the Río Frío to the small town of **San Carlos de Nicaragua**, on the southeast lip of huge Lago de Nicaragua. You'll need at least a bit of cash upon arrival; change a few colones for córdobas at the Los Chiles bank. From San Carlos de Nicaragua it is also possible to cross the lake to **Granada** and on to **Managua** (see p.451).

Refugio Nacional de Vida Silvestre Caño Negro

The largely pristine **REFUGIO NACIONAL DE VIDA SILVESTRE CAÑO NEGRO** (US$6), 25km west of Los Chiles, is one of the best places in the Americas to view huge concentrations of both migratory and indigenous **birds**, along with mammalian and reptilian **river wildlife**. Until recently well off the beaten tourist track – partly because of its isolated location, so far from San José – nowadays more and more tours are being offered to an area that has been on the itineraries of specialist birdwatching excursions for years.

Getting to Caño Negro

Though most people come to the refuge on tours from Fortuna (see p.639), you can also get to Caño Negro **independently**. Driving is easy enough in the dry season, while in the wet season a public boat leaves from the Los Chiles docks (Tues & Thurs only 7.30am; for information call ☎460-1301); on other days you can take your pick from several private *lanchas*. Get there early in the morning and ask around for prices: expect to pay at least US$65 per boat for the five-hour return trip. Note that the first 25km of the trip down the Río Frío (taking an hour or more by *lancha*) does not take you through the Wildlife Refuge, which begins at the mouth of the large flooded area and is marked by a sign poking out of a small islet. Make sure your boatman takes you right into Caño Negro. If you take a tour, the **entrance fee** is included. If not, you should pay at the ranger station on the north side of the lake.

Unless you're an expert in identifying wildlife, the most rewarding way to enjoy the diverse flora and fauna of Caño Negro is to use the services of a **guide** who knows the area and can point out animals and other features of river life as you motor down to the refuge. If you come independently, asking at the docks or at Servitur in Los Chiles might turn up someone.

Sarapiquí

Steamy and tropical, carpeted with fruit plantations, the eastern part of the Zona Norte bears more resemblance to the hot and dense Caribbean lowlands than the plains of the north and, despite the toll of deforestation, it shelters some of the best preserved **premontane rainforest** in the country. North by northwest from the Las Horquetas turnoff on the Guápiles Highway, the Sarapiquí area makes a parabolic arc around the top of Braulio Carrillo National Park and stretches west to the village of San Miguel, from where Arenal and the western lowlands are easily accessible by road.

The region's chief tourist attractions are the biological research station **La Selva**, and the eco-lodges of **Rara Avis** and **Selva Verde**, all of which offer access to some of the last primary rainforest in the country. The largest settlement, **Puerto Viejo de Sarapiquí**, is primarily a river transport hub and a place for the fruit plantation workers to stock up on supplies and have a beer or two.

There are two options when it comes to getting **from San José** or the Valle Central to Puerto Viejo. The western route, which takes a little more than three hours, goes via Varablanca and the La Paz waterfall, passing the hump of Volcán Barva. This route offers great views of velvety green hills clad with coffee plantations, which turn, eventually, into rainforest. Faster (1hr–1hr 30min) and less scenic is the route via the **Guápiles Highway**. This region receives a lot of **rain** – as much as 4500mm annually – and there is no real dry season (although less rain is recorded Jan–May), so wet-weather gear is essential.

Rara Avis

RARA AVIS, a private rainforest reserve 17km south of Puerto Viejo de Sarapiquí, and about 80km northeast of San José, offers one of the most thrilling and authentic "ecotourism" experiences in Costa Rica, featuring both primary rainforest and some secondary cover dating from about thirty years ago. Established in 1983 by American Amos Bien, a former administrator of La Selva (see p.643), with Trino, a local squatter campesino, Rara Avis is both a tourist lodge and a private rainforest preserve, dedicated to the conservation, study and farming of the area's biodiversity. Its ultimate objective is to show that the rainforest can be profitable for an indefinite period, giving local smallholders a viable alternative to clearcutting for their cattle. Rara Avis also functions as a **research station**, accommodating student groups and volunteers whose aim is to develop rainforest products – orchids, palms and so forth – as crops.

Rara Avis' **flora** is as diverse as you might expect from a premontane rainforest. The best way to learn to spot different flowers, plants, trees and their respective habitats is to go on a walk with one of the knowledgeable **guides**, who typically have lived at Rara Avis or nearby for some time. Especially interesting plants include the **stained-glass palm tree**, a rare ornamental specimen, and the **walking palm**, whose fingertip or tentacle-like roots can propel it over more than a metre of ground in its lifetime, as it "walks" in search of water. **Orchids** are numerous, as are non-flowering bromeliads and heliconias. A mind-boggling number of **bird species** have been identified, and it is likely that more are yet to be discovered. Among the more common **mammals** are monkeys, tapirs, ocelots and jaguars, though the last three are rarely seen.

Rara Avis also has a network of very good **trails**: there are at least four around *Plástico*, not including the two ("Atajo" and "Catarata") that lead up to the *Waterfall Lodge*. From the *Waterfall* nine or so trails weave through fairly dense jungle cover. All are well-marked, and give walks of thirty minutes to several hours, depending upon the pace. While guided walks are fun and informative, guests are welcome to go it alone: you'll be given a map at the lodge receptions. Just below the *Waterfall Lodge*, a

50m-high waterfall on the Río Atelopus plummets into a deep pool before continuing the river's slide down towards lower ground. **Swimming** in the pool, icy cold and shrouded in a fine mist, is a wonderful experience.

Getting to Rara Avis

Some **packages** to Rara Avis include private transport from San José. If time is short, then this can be worth it, but with some planning it is perfectly possible to get there **independently**, by taking the bus from San José to the turnoff for the small village of Las Horquetas de Sarapiquí, where a tractor-pulled cart makes the final 15km of the journey.

As the tractor for Rara Avis leaves daily at 9am, you have to take the 7am bus to Río Frío/Puerto Viejo de Sarapiquí from San José. Make sure to get the express (*directo*) service via the Guápiles Highway (the bus via Heredia leaves thirty minutes earlier and takes the long western route to Puerto Viejo). If in doubt, ask people at the bus stop or the driver.

It takes between an hour and ninety minutes from San José to get to the turnoff for Horquetas. The *directo* bus does not go through Horquetas, but continues along the highway, so ask the driver to let you off at the *cruce* (cross, or turnoff) for Las Horquetas. From here **taxis** will take you to the Rara Avis office in Horquetas (all accommodation at the lodge is pre-booked, so they will know you are coming, but you should call and double-check that a taxi is waiting for you).

Getting to Rara Avis **from Horquetas** is at least half the fun, though not exactly comfortable. The uphill flatbed-tractor journey to the lodges takes two to four hours depending upon the condition of the "road" (actually a horrendously muddy rutted track). If you have booked ahead to take the tractor and do by any chance miss it, **horses** are available for hire from villagers (US$15) until noon – any time after that is too late as the trip takes several hours. Ask at the Rara Avis office when you arrive. The horses can get as far as the *El Plástico Lodge* (see below); if you are staying at the *Waterfall Lodge*, you'll have to walk the last 3km on a rainforest trail as the road is impassable for horses by that point.

Leaving Rara Avis, the tractor departs at about 2pm. This means that it often arrives in Horquetas too late to connect with the last bus for San José, which passes through at 5.15pm daily. If you miss this bus, the Rara Avis office in Horquetas can arrange for a taxi (about US$25 per carload) to the Guápiles Highway, from where you can flag down a Guápiles–San José bus (passing by hourly until 7pm).

Accommodation

Due to its popularity, you have to **book accommodation** in Rara Avis well in advance, either through Aptdo 8105, San José 1000 (☎ & fax 253-0844; *raraavis@sol.racsa.co.cr*), or a travel agent. Rates include guided walks and meals, as well as transport by tractor from and to Las Horquetas. Although it is quite possible to stay for one night, because of the relative difficulty of access it is best to stay for two or more to get the most out of a trip.

There are three **places to stay** at Rara Avis. Cheapest is the HI-affiliated *El Plástico Lodge* (US$45 per person), in a cleared area 12km from Horquetas. *Plástico*, as everyone calls it, is named after a convicts' colony that used to stand on the site, in which the prisoners slept underneath plastic tarpaulins. It has dirt floors downstairs, bunk-style beds and cold water, a covered but open-view communal dining table and a sitting area. Despite its rusticity, it's all very comfortable, and probably the only way to see Rara Avis on the – relatively – cheap.

The road from *Plástico* to the more comfortable *Waterfall Lodge* (⑧) is only 3km, but it's uphill, through dense rainforest, and takes at least an hour by tractor on a broken corduroy road which looks as if it's been hit by an earthquake. If you are in good shape, however, the best way to get there is to hike the (fairly obvious) trail through the rainforest – you'll have been given a map at the Rara Avis office in Horquetas. This should take about an hour: do not, under any circumstances, leave the trails, which are in good condition despite year-round mud.

A few people stay at the new and quite expensive (US$150 per person) *Treehouse*, a 30-metre-high canopy platform where you can pass a (screened) high-altitude night. You get up there with a special harness on a pulley system, but it's a strenuous climb to and from your bed.

Estación Biológica La Selva

A fully equipped research station, **ESTACIÓN BIOLÓGICA LA SELVA**, 93km northeast of San José and 4km southwest of Puerto Viejo de Sarapiquí (☎766-6565; in San José ☎240-6696; *laselva@ns.ots.ac.cr*; US$20) is owned and operated by the Organization of Tropical Studies (OTS), an international group of institutions dedicated to the study of rainforest and tropical areas. La Selva is probably the best place to visit in the Sarapiquí region if you are a botany student or have a special interest in the scientific life of a rainforest and, like Rara Avis, it is a superb birder's spot, with more than 400 species of indigenous and migratory birds.

Though tourists are secondary to research at La Selva, visitors are welcome, providing there is space – it's impossible to overstate La Selva's popularity, and in the high season it is sometimes booked months in advance, even for day trips. Be sure to **reserve** way in advance by fax (710-1414) if you are coming between November and April. Visiting in the low season (roughly May–Oct) is a safer bet, but even then you should call first.

Visiting La Selva

La Selva is impressively geared up to cope with its many visitors, with a reception, dining room, shop (selling posters, T-shirts, maps and a small selection of books) and visitors' centre. The ground cover extends from primary **forest** through abandoned plantations to pastureland and brush, crossed by an extensive network of about 25 **trails**. Varying in length from short to more than 5km long, most are in very good condition, clearly and frequently marked. Some, however, are pretty rough, with no corduroy, cement blocks or wire netting to help you get a grip, and many become very muddy indeed. Tourists tend to stick to the main trails within the part of La Selva designated as the **Ecological Reserve**, next to the Río Puerto Viejo. These **trails**, the *Camino Circular Cercano*, the *Camino Cantarrana* and the *Sendero Oriental*, radiate from the river research station and take you through dense primary growth, the close, tightly knotted kind of tropical forest for which the Sarapiquí area is famous.

Practicalities

To get to La Selva **from San José**, the least expensive option is to take the 7am Río Frío/Puerto Viejo de Sarapiqui bus (marked "Río Frío"), which, if you ask, drops passengers off at the entrance to the road leading to the station. Note, however, that it is a two-kilometre walk down the road from the junction. The OTS (☎240-5033 or 6696; fax 240-6783) also lays on a thrice-weekly bus from its office in Curridabat, a suburb in the east of San José (US$10); though mainly reserved for researchers and students, it is worth asking if they can fit you in. Taxis make the four-kilometre trip **from Puerto Viejo de Sarapiqui** for about US$5.

If you want to **stay** at La Selva, you *must* book in advance, by calling the office number. The tourist rate (⑥) is not cheap, but proceeds go towards the maintenance of the station. Researchers and students with scientific bona fides stay for less (④). Visiting on a day trip allows you to walk the trails and have a hearty lunch of *típico* food at the station's dining room. A **day visit** costs about US$20 (including lunch); again, you have to reserve in advance, whatever time of the year you come.

Puerto Viejo de Sarapiquí

Just short of 100km northeast of San José, **PUERTO VIEJO DE SARAPIQUÍ** (known locally as Puerto Viejo, not to be confused with Puerto Viejo de Talamanca on the Atlantic coast) is an important hub for banana plantation workers and those who live in the isolated settlements between here and the Atlantic coast. Its only interest to independent travellers is as a jumping-off point to visit the nearby jungle lodges. Facilities are few, inadequate even to cope with the demands of migrant workers, though there are plenty of *licorías* (liquor stores); residents complain about rising levels of drunkenness and prostitution.

Numerous **buses** leave San José for Puerto Viejo and Río Frío (see above). The service that goes **via Las Horquetas** (the fast route, via the Guápiles Highway through Braulio Carrillo) currently departs at 7am, 9am, 10am, 1pm, 3pm and 4pm (1hr 30min). Buses from San José to Puerto Viejo **via Heredia** (ask the driver if you are unsure which bus you're on – there's nothing on the front indicating which route it takes) are more likely to take around three hours. They leave at 6.30am, noon and 3pm, returning from Puerto Viejo at 8am and 4pm – although the last has been known to end up in La Virgen, some 12km west of Puerto Viejo.

Though most people choose to stay in one of the lodges in the countryside outside the town (see below), if you're stuck, *Mi Lindo Sarapiquí*, on the main street (☎760-6281; ③) is the best **place to stay**, with a good restaurant that doubles as a bar at night. Ask behind the counter in the restaurant for rooms, as there is no reception.

Accommodation around Puerto Viejo de Sarapiquí

Although La Selva, Selva Verde and Rara Avis are the prime tourist destinations in this area, there are also a number of very attractive **hotels** and **lodges** dotted around Puerto Viejo that allow you to experience something of the **rainforest**. In general they are reasonably priced and accessible, and some offer **packages** from San José. If you are travelling by bus and the accommodation is west of Puerto Viejo, you should take the San José–Río Frío bus via Heredia (see above). Anything in Puerto Viejo itself or east is faster reached by the service to Río Frío/Puerto Viejo via the Guápiles Highway.

El Gavilán, 4km north of Puerto Viejo (☎234-9507; fax 253-6556; Aptdo 445-2010, San José). A former cattle *finca*, this lovely secluded lodge offers many excursions: hiking, swimming, river trips to Tortuguero (see p.576) and horseback rides. Guides are available. Simply furnished, comfortable rooms have hot water and fan. Packages cost about US$400 for 2 nights/3 days, including transport from San José; all rates include breakfast. No alcohol served. Hard to find, so call for directions or take a taxi. ⑥.

La Quinta, about 7km west from Puerto Viejo, and 5km east of La Virgen (☎ & fax 761-1052). On the banks of the Río Sardinal, near Selva Verde, this comfortable lodge offers swimming, biking, horseback riding and birdwatching. All rooms have ceiling fans and hot water. Meals are extra. ⑤–⑥.

Posada Andrea Cristina, 1km west of Puerto Viejo (☎ & fax 766-6265). Simple rooms with private bath and fan, great breakfasts, and without doubt the best cup of coffee and conversation in the area from the local owners. Many people stay here for the family atmosphere and use it as a base to explore the area, including Tortuguero. ⑤.

MOVING ON FROM PUERTO VIEJO DE SARAPIQUÍ

Puerto Viejo is a hub for the entire Zona Norte and eastern side of the country. From here it's possible to travel back to the **Valle Central**, either by the Guápiles Highway (1hr 30min or more) or via Varablanca and Heredia (3hr or more). You can also cut across country west to **San Carlos** (3 daily; 2–3 hr) and on to **Fortuna** (3–4hr) from where you can easily travel, via Tilarán (see p.600), on to **Monteverde** and **Guanacaste**.

By **river** it is possible to continue from Puerto Viejo north to the **Río San Juan** and **Nicaragua**. To get to Barra or Tortuguero on Costa Rica's Atlantic coast, a pleasant journey along the Ríos Sarapiquí and San Juan can take anywhere between four and seven hours (you're going upstream) by *lancha* and is fairly pricey if you're travelling independently – unless you happen to be with a group of eight or so other people. Ask at the Puerto Viejo dock, or in the soda above it, where local boatmen will be able to advise on availability and will quote about US$300 for the trip (8–10 maximum capacity). For a full rundown of routes along the Río San Juan, see p.504–506.

travel details

BUSES

Fortuna to: San Carlos (7 daily; 1hr); San José (express, 1 daily; 4hr 30min); San Rafael de Guatuso (2 daily; 1hr); Tilarán (1 daily; 1hr).

Los Chiles to: San Carlos (10 daily; 2hr 30min); San José (2 daily; 5hr).

Puerto Viejo de Sarapiquí to: San Carlos (3 daily; 3hr); San José (via Guápiles Highway, 7 daily; 1hr 30min–3hr; via Heredia, 2 daily; 3–4hr).

San Carlos to: Fortuna (7 daily; 1hr); Los Chiles (10 daily; 2hr 30min); Puerto Viejo de Sarapiquí (3 daily; 3hr); San José (14 daily; 3hr); San Rafael de Guatuso (5 daily); Tilarán (2 daily; 2hr).

San José to: Fortuna (3 daily; 4hr 30min); Los Chiles (2 daily; 5hr); Puerto Viejo de Sarapiquí and Río Frío (via Guápiles Highway, 6 daily; 1hr 30min–3hr; via Heredia, 3 daily; 3–4hr); San Carlos (14 daily; 3hr); Tilarán (4 daily; 4–5hr).

Tilarán to: Fortuna (1 daily; 1hr); San Carlos (1 daily; 2hr); San José (4 daily; 4–5hr); Santa Elena, for Monteverde (1 daily; 3–4hr).

BOATS

Puerto Viejo de Sarapiquí to: Trinidad, near Río San Juan (1 daily; 3hr).

CHAPTER 33

THE ZONA SUR

osta Rica's **Zona Sur** (southern zone) is the country's least-known region, both for Ticos and for travellers. Geographically, it's a diverse area, varying from the agricultural heartland of the Valle de el General to high mountain peaks, most notably the mountain pass at Cerro de la Muerte ("Death Mountain"), and **Cerro el Chirripó** – at 3819m the highest peak in Central America. Both of these crown the Cordillera de Talamanca, which falls away quickly into the river-cut lowlands of the Valle de Diquis and the coffee-growing Valle de Coto Brus.

The chief draw for travellers is the **Osa Peninsula** in the extreme southwest, the site of **Parque Nacional Corcovado**, one of the prime rainforest hiking destinations in the country. For those bent on getting to remote places, there are plenty, including the picturesque **Bahía Drake** on the hump of the peninsula. Less off the beaten track, and one of the most recent areas in the country to open up to tourism, there's the **Playa Dominical** area of the Pacific coast, a surfing destination whose tremendous tropical beauty is beginning to draw snorkellers and swimmers especially. **Golfito** is the only town of any size. For years after the pull-out of the United Fruit Company's banana operations in 1985, Golfito received a bad press, painted as a town of ill repute. However, it has been attacting more visitors of late, since being made a tax-free zone (called the *depósito libre*) for manufactured goods from Panamá.

Despite the abundance of budget accommodation in the Zona Sur, you'll find yourself **spending** more than you bargained for simply because of the time, distance and planning involved in getting to many of the region's more beautiful spots. Many people prefer to take a package rather than travel independently; and travellers who stay at the more expensive **"rainforest lodges"** often choose to fly in.

Climatically the Zona Sur has two distinct regions. The Pacific lowlands, from south of Quepos roughly to the Río Sierpe delta at the top of the Osa Peninsula, and the upland Valle de el General and the Talamancas, all experience a dry season (Dec–April), which is not so marked in the Osa Peninsula, Golfito and Golfo Dulce. In these places, from roughly October to December, spectacular seasonal thunder and lightning storms canter in from across the Pacific. In the rainy season, some parts of Parque Nacional Corcovado become more or less unwalkable, local mud roads become undrivable, and everything gets more difficult.

Dominical

DOMINICAL, 44km south of Quepos (see p.609), was until recently relatively undiscovered, due mainly to the lack of a good road. However, since the road has been paved, the once quiet fishing village has been discovered by foreigners, lured by the beauty of the surroundings, the romantic sunsets and the get-away-from-it-all

For an explanation of **accommodation price codes**, see p.526.

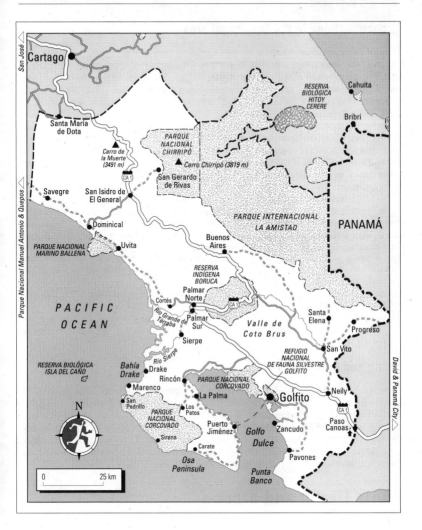

atmosphere. Though it seems poised to become the country's next Manuel Antonio, development remains – for the time being at least – relatively low-key.

Wide and long, Dominical **beach** is postcard-pretty, although its sand is dark, backed by a wall of palms. It is often deserted, and only ever crowded when **surfers** flock to chase the big waves. **Snorkelling** is good here, too, and there are a couple of pretty waterfalls nearby.

From San José the fastest route to Dominical is via the sleepy town of San Isidro de el General, on the Carretera Interamericana, from where there are good bus connections; **from Guanacaste** and the Central Pacific, you'll do best to take the road south from Quepos. **Buses** from Quepos arrive at around 6.30am and 3pm daily, and continue to San Isidro (2hr).

Accommodation in the Dominical area

Though most **accommodation** in the Dominical area is still considered basic – in the past, the area catered mainly to surfers – a number of more upmarket places, usually owned by foreigners, are springing up fast. The most expensive of them are wonderful hideaways, good for honeymoons, romantics and escapists. For the moment, however, it is still possible to find rooms, on the whole owned by locals, in the US$20–30 range.

There are currently just a few private phones installed in this area; most locals communicate via CB radio. However, Jack Ewing, long-time resident and owner of *Hacienda Barú*, has set up a local **reservation service**, Selva Mar, through which you can book any of the acommodation listed below, either in advance or by dropping into their office in the centre of Dominical (☎ & fax 771-1903).

Hacienda Barú, 1km north of Dominical on the road to Quepos (☎ & fax 771-1903). Good-value, comfortable cabinas. With 3.3 square kilometres of rainforest, a fixed canopy platform, mangroves and horseriding tours, this is the largest, most upscale accommodation in the area. Good for birders and orchid lovers (there are 250 varieties scattered around). ⑤.

Finca Brian y Milena, 300m above Dominical, on the road to Escaleras (☎ & fax 771-1903). One of the nicest small-scale family farm operations, doubling as a wildlife sanctuary, experimental fruit farm, botanical garden and guest lodge. You can't drive here, so call Selva Mar and have the owners come and meet you with horses. Most people arrive on packages, which include hikes in the surrounding rainforest and meals. ⑤.

Cabinas Nayarit, Dominical (☎ & fax 771-1878). Comfortable, basic rooms, with private bath, fan, and hammocks strung between palm trees. A/c (not necessary) costs extra. ④–⑤.

Albergue Willdale, Dominical (☎ & fax 771-1903). Also known as *Cabinas Willi*. Very basic but clean cabinas with fan and hammocks; the owner is planning renovations so they may become more fancy (and expensive). ④.

Eating and drinking

There's a *pulpería* in Dominical, but if you're **self-catering**, stock up in the mercado in Quepos or in San Isidro. Many local **hotels** include meals or will cook for you for a small charge. Of the **restaurants**, in Dominical *Marisquería Maui* serves fish and seafood, while the *San Clemente Bar and Grill* has a Tex-Mex menu with a little Italian and Cajun thrown in. The pizzas are highly recommended. The *Restaurante y Cabinas Roca Verde*, 2km south, has the only barbecue in the area, plus a beautiful sea view; its **disco** is a meeting place for surfers, travellers and young locals.

Bahía Drake and around

Bahía Drake (pronounced "Dra-kay") has to be one of the most stunning areas in Costa Rica, especially at dusk, when fire-orange Pacific sunsets plunge like meteors into the water. Bahía Drake and the tiny hamlet of **DRAKE** make a good base for Parque Nacional Corcovado on the northwest of the Osa Peninsula – the San Pedrillo entrance is walkable from here, and hikers can combine serious walking with serious comfort at either end of their trip to the Park by staying at one of the upscale rainforest "eco-lodge"-type hotels that have sprung up in recent years.

Like many other places in the Zona Sur, **getting to Bahía Drake** requires some planning. There are three choices: the tough way, hiking in from Corcovado; the cheap way, by bus from San José and then by boat along the Río Sierpe; and the luxury way, by flying from San José to Palmar or Sierpe, and taking one of the many **packages** offered by hotels in the area, whereby transport to your lodge is taken care of.

Travelling **independently** you will need to get a bus from San José to the banana processing town of Palmar Norte, 120km southwest of San Isidro de el General (6 daily; 5hr 30min); depending on what time you get in, you can then either bed down or get a local bus or taxi to **SIERPE** (about US$12), where there are a few cabinas. In Sierpe, you must find a **boatman** to take you the 30km downriver to Bahía Drake (2hr). You need someone with experience, a motorized *lancha*, and lifejackets. Emiliano González is recommended; he can take you practically anywhere on the peninsula (☎771-2336). You can also hook up with a boatman in *Bar Las Vegas*, a rendezvous for tourists and boat captains – check out the ancient jukebox while you wait. The going rate for a one-way trip to Drake is currently about US$20 per person or around US$70–80 per boat-load (maximum usually 8); ask around for the best rates.

Accommodation in and around Bahía Drake

Virtually all the **eco-lodges** listed below do a range of **tours**, from accompanied excursions to Corcovado to boating in Bahía Drake and trips to Isla del Caño. The larger lodges are accustomed to bringing guests on packages from San José and can include transport from the capital, from Palmar Norte, or from Sierpe. The packages (and the prices we give below) usually include three meals a day – there are few eating options in Drake otherwise. Although hoteliers will tell you you can't **camp** in the Drake area, people do – but you should do your best to be courteous as to where you pitch your tent, and make sure to leave no litter.

Bahía Drake Wilderness Camp, Punta Agujitas (☎ & fax 771-2436; in San José ☎256-7394). The most-established lodge in the area, providing a buffer zone between tourist and wilderness with rustic, comfortable cabinas – or, if you want to rough it a bit, well-appointed tents. Both options are well-screened. Three hearty meals are included, and there's excellent snorkelling and canoeing available. The camp has its own solar heated water supply, generator-fuelled electricity at night, and even a laundry service. It's popular, so book and pay in advance. ⑦–⑨.

Cabinas Jade Mar, in the village (☎284-6681, fax 786-6358). One of the few village cheapies, offering very well-priced, basic cabinas with shared bath with cold water and good cross-breezes. They're kept spotless by Doña Marta, who is from the area, and a font of information. Hearty meals are included – it's a good place to stay if you want to get a taste of local life. They also runs tours – cheaper than many – to Corcovado and Isla de Caño. ④.

Cocalito Lodge, Punta Ajucitas (☎ & fax 786-6150 or 786-6335). Small, family-run Canadian-owned cabinas scattered around the main lodge where delicious candlelit meals are served in their restaurant. They rent mountain bikes and you can swim safely from the small beach in front. There's no evening electricity, but solar-heated water and shared or private bath are available and all accommodation is well-screened. They will also rent you tents and allow you to camp (US$8). ⑥–⑦.

Corcovado Adventure Tent Camp, 7km south of Bahia Drake (☎233-6868, fax 257-4201). A relatively new establishment on an isolated beach on the way to Corcovado. Here you can get a wilderness camping experience, but with a few comforts, including beds, tables and good screening. They also have their own canopy tour, where you can be winched up a 40m-high rainforest tree to a stable platform in order to view life in the forest canopy. It's a relatively easy hike from here to Corcovado. ⑨.

Albergue Jinetes de Osa, between Punta Agujitas and the village of Agujitas (☎253-6909). One of the cheaper options. Simple but comfortable bunk accommodation with shared cold water bath. Prices include three meals. They can connect you with boat, horseriding tours and treks. ⑨.

Marenco Biological Station, 7km south of Drake (☎221-1594, fax 255-1346). Secluded accommodation in an ex-biological station, with thatched-roof cabinas and beautiful views of Isla del Caño. Snorkelling and swimming spots and good birdwatching, too. It's 5km north of Corcovado's San Pedrillo entrance, and a good starting point for hiking the San Pedrillo–Sirena trail (see p.655). Because of limited access (it can take 2hr to walk here from Drake) most guests come on all-inclusive packages. ⑦–⑧.

Rancho Corcovado, in the village (☎786-6462). Another new locally owned initiative with simple cabinas on the beach, or further up the hill, poised over the Pacific with beautiful (and relatively inexpensive) views. All have private bath and cold water. You can also camp within the friendly family's land for US$5 per person. Very reasonable prices include three meals; boat tours to nearby beaches are avialable. ④.

Golfito

The former banana port of **GOLFITO**, 33km north of the Panamanian border, straggles for 2500m along the water of the same name (*golfito* means "little gulf"). The town's **setting** is spectacular, backed up against thickly forested, steep hills on the east, and with the glorious Golfo Dulce – one of the deepest gulfs of its size in the world, formed by volcanic activity – to the west. The low shadow of the Osa Peninsula shimmers in the distance, and everywhere the vegetation has the soft muted look of the undisturbed tropics.

Golfito's **history** is inextricably intertwined with the giant transnational **United Brands** company – locally known as *La Yunai* – which first set up in this area in 1938. What with fluctuating banana prices, a three-month strike by workers and local social unrest, the company eventually decided Golfito was too much trouble and pulled out in a hurry in 1985. The town died, and in the public eye became synonymous with rampant unemployment, alcoholism, abandoned children, prostitution and general unruliness.

Today, at the big old *muelle bananero*, container ships are still loaded up with bananas processed further up toward Palmar Norte. This residual traffic, along with tourism – Golfito is a good base for getting to **Parque Nacional Corcovado** by *lancha* or plane – have combined to help revive the local economy. The real rescue, though, came from the Costa Rican government, who in the early 1990s established in the town a **depósito libre**, or tax-free zone, where Costa Ricans can buy manufactured goods imported from Panamá without the 100 percent tax normally levied. Ticos – but not tourists – who come to shop here have to buy their tickets for the *depósito* 24 hours in advance, obliging them to spend a night, and therefore colones, in the town.

Golfito straggles for ages without any clear centre; in some stretches the main road is hemmed in by hills on one side and the lapping waters of the *golfito* on the other. The town is effectively divided – by the poverty line as well as architecturally – into two parts. In the north is the **zona americana**, where the banana company execs used to live and where better-off residents still live, in beautiful wooden houses shaded by dignified palms. It is the site of the *depósito libre*, an unaesthetic outdoor mall ringed by a circular wall of concrete, with a cattle-auction atmosphere. South of the *parquecito*, the **pueblo civil** (civilian town), is a very small, tight nest of streets; hotter, noiser and more crowded than the *zona*. It's here you'll find the good-value hotels and sodas, as well as the *lancha* across the Golfo Dulce to Puerto Jiménez and the Osa Peninsula.

Arrival and information

Buses from San José currently leave TRACOPA's terminal at 7am, 11am and 3pm (8hr). Buy your return ticket (see below) as soon as you disembark. You can also **fly** here with Sansa; the airstrip is in the zona americana.

Banco de Costa Rica, in the *pueblo civil* next to the gas station, and Banco Nacional, in the *zona americana* next to the TRACOPA terminal (both Mon–Fri 8am–3.45pm) will theoretically change **travellers' cheques** but it's best to bring lots of cash just in case. The **correo** (Mon–Fri 7.30am–5pm) is a few blocks south of the Banco de Costa Rica. **VHF radio**, rather than telephone, is often used to communicate in this area, but there is an ICE office in the *pueblo civil*, across from the *muellecito*.

MOVING ON FROM GOLFITO

Buses to San José leave daily at 5am and 1pm. If you're getting the 5am bus you will need to have bought your return ticket in advance. There are also flights to San José on Sansa. For **Corcovado**, you can take the *lancha Arco Iris* across the Golfo Dulce to Puerto Jiménez (daily 11am; 1hr 30min; ☎735-5036; US$3), or a small plane to Jiménez. The ten-minute flight can cost anywhere from US$20 to a fortune, depending on the number of passengers (5 max). Contact Aeronaves de Costa Rica (☎775-0278) or Aero Taxi (☎735-5178).

Accommodation

Accommodation in Golfito comes in two varieties: swish places in the *zona americana,* catering to businesspeople and shoppers at the *depósito*, and decent, basic rooms in the *pueblo civil.*

Hotel del Cerro, between the *pueblo civil* and the *zona americana* (☎775-0006, fax 775-0551). Good-value, friendly budget option: they can help with tourist information and reservations. Rooms with choice of shared or private bath, heated water and ceiling fans. ③–④.

Hotel Delfina, in the *pueblo civil* (☎775-0043). An older house, converted into a warren of widely varying rooms. Some are good value, others are dark; those at the back are quieter, and overlook the water. Cheap rooms (shared bath, ceiling fan) are better value than those with private bath and ancient, groaning a/c. ③.

Esquinas Rainforest Lodge, La Gamba, 4km from Km-37 on the Interamericana (☎ & fax 284-7196). Friendly, family-owned lodge, about 15min from Golfito. It's set in primary rainforest cover, with animals on the grounds. You can hike the on-site trails yourself or with a guide, and they offer a variety of tours, including to Corcovado and Wilson Botanical Gardens. Member of a local co-op, the lodge shares profits with the small community of La Gamba. Rates include (delicious) meals. Packages available. ⑤–⑥.

Las Gaviotas, at the southern entrance to town (☎775-0662, fax 775-0544). Golfito's most upscale choice – the only one with a pool – with good rooms with private bath and hot water. Set in lovely gardens, with a waterside restaurant serving great local seafood. The best value rooms are without a/c but with good sturdy ceiling fan. ④.

Hotel Golfito, in the *pueblo civil* beside the gas station (☎775-0047). The cheapest deal around; stuffy, dark rooms, with private bath (cold water only) and ceiling fans. Most rooms sleep three, and single rates aren't bad. The back balcony has a nice view. ②.

Cabinas el Vivero, signed, in the *zona americana*. Big, simply furnished rooms, and a friendly family atmosphere with shared kitchen. *Dueño* Don Bob grows orchids and other plants in his nursery next door, and is a walking oral history of the area. Very good value. ②–③.

The Osa Peninsula

In the extreme southwest of the country, the **Osa Peninsula** is an area of immense biological diversity, semi-separate from the mainland. **Parque Nacional Corcovado**, which protects much of the peninsula, is what draws visitors, who base themselves in the tiny, friendly town of **Puerto Jiménez**. Certainly few will fail to be moved by Osa's beauty. Whether you approach the peninsula by *lancha* from Golfito or Bahía Drake, on the Jiménez bus, or driving in from the mainland, you will see what looks to be a floating island, an intricate mesh of blue and green, with tall canopy trees sailing high and flat like elaborate floral hats. You could feasibly "do" the whole peninsula in four days, but this would be rushing it, especially if you want to spend time walking the trails and wildlife-spotting at Corcovado. Most people allot five to seven days for the area, taking it at a relaxed pace, and more if they want to stay in and explore Bahía Drake (see p.648).

Puerto Jiménez and around

Relaxed, environmentally conscious **PUERTO JIMÉNEZ** – known locally as just Jiménez – is a place where it's easy to strike up a conversation. Though not yet over-whelmed by tourism, it has plenty of places to stay and eat and good public transport connections. There's also the possibility of grabbing a lift with a truck to **Carate**, 43km southwest, from where you can enter Corcovado (see opposite). Drivers shouldn't try going further south – including to Carate – in anything less than a 4WD, at any time of year. What looks like a good, patted-down dirt road can turn into a quagmire after a sud-den downpour.

Arrival and information

Two **buses** daily arrive from San José via San Isidro (6am & noon; 8–9hr) returning at 5am and 11am. The ticket office in Jiménez is open daily (7–11am & 1–5pm). There's a **lancha** from Golfito (1 daily; 1hr 30min), and you can **fly** in from San José with Sansa, or from Golfito on the *avioneta*. The *lancha* back to Golfito leaves at 6am (☎735-5036).

The **Corcovado administration and information office** (Mon–Fri 8am–noon & 1–4pm; ☎735-5036, fax 735-5276) is staffed by friendly rangers who can answer ques-tions, arrange accommodation at the *puestos* (if you haven't already done so – in most cases you should have before coming) and radio ahead if you want to eat with the rangers (there's a small charge). For other **tourist information**, try the Osa Tours office, which also doubles as the local Travelair agent, on the main road in town 50m north of the gas station (☎735-5062, fax 735-5043). Besides buying plane tickets, you can make room reservations here, and may be able to pay to use the phone and fax to call elsewhere or abroad. Next door to the Park information office, the tiny Banco Nacional (Mon–Fri 8am–3pm; may close over lunch) may be able to change **travellers' cheques**, and will certainly change dollars, but the accepted wisdom is to come with all the colones you'll need. You can **telephone** from a few hotels.

The **town truck to Carate** leaves daily except Sunday in the dry season at about 6am, but you'd do best to confirm this locally. You could ask staff at *Restaurante Carolina*, its departure point. In the wet season it goes about three times a week. The price is about US$4 per person one way; the driver will also pick you up to take you back to town if you pre-arrange it, and will drop off at any of the hotels between Jimenez and Carate. If you don't get a place on the truck, a number of places **rent 4WD taxis**: Oscar Blanco at *Cabinas Puerto Jiménez* will take you to Carate and return at a fixed day or time to pick you up (about US$50 per carload).

Accommodation

Jiménez's **hotels** are reasonably priced, clean and basic. Though in the dry season it's best to reserve, this may not always be possible, as phone and fax lines sometimes go down. In the rainy season there are far fewer people about and you shouldn't need to worry about booking in advance. **Between Jiménez and Carate**, around the lower hump of the peninsula, are a few comfort-in-the-wilderness places, a couple of which make great **retreats** or honeymoon spots.

IN JIMÉNEZ

Bungalows Doña Leta (☎ & fax 735-5180). Nicely constructed grouping of eight bungalows set on their own small beach. Each has private bath with hot water and a kitchenette and there's a small snack bar run by the friendly expatriate owners, who will also do laundry. Good for groups, as some bungalows will take up to six people. ④.

Iguana Iguana (☎735-5158). Good rooms, with private or shared bath (cold water only), and a small pool. The friendly *dueña* will advise on transport to Corcovado or will drive guests there and back (pre-arrange pick-up time) for about US$30. ③–④.

Cabinas Manglares, towards the airstrip (☎735-5002). The most upscale cabinas in town, in quiet surroundings, next to a mangrove swamp. Private bath (cold water) and ceiling fans, and a restaurant-bar on site. ⑤.

Cabinas Marcelina, right in town, east of the main drag (☎735-5007, fax 735-5045). Big, basic rooms with shelf space, table fan, and private bath (cold water only); owned by friendly family. ②.

Cabinas Puerto Jiménez, next to *El Rancho*. Quiet (unless the adjacent disco is on – ask around) cabinas next to the water. Simple, clean, nicely furnished rooms, well-screened, with bath and fan. Some can be dark, so ask to see a few. ③.

BETWEEN PUERTO JIMÉNEZ AND CARATE
The following are ordered in order of their distance from Puerto Jiménez. The first, *Tierra de Milagros*, is 20km south from Jiménez. The last, *Corcovado Tent Camp*, sidles right up to the Park entrance. All are signed.

Tierra de Milagros (☎735-5075). Rustic lodge in a nature preserve. You sleep in an open (no walls, but a roof) *rancho* in hammocks or sleeping bag. All meals are vegetarian or fish, and no smoking is allowed. Proceeds help fund a local reforestation project. ③.

Lapa Ríos (☎735-5130, fax 735-5179; in USA: PO Box 025216-SJO 706, Miami, FL 33102-5216). One of the most comfortable and impressive "jungle lodges" in the country, set in a private nature reserve of more than four square kilometres. Rooms have big beds and mosquito nets, and blend into surrounding forest. There's a huge thatch-roofed restaurant, complete with spiral staircase, and a swimming pool (you can't swim in the ocean due to sharks and currents). Excellent birdwatching on the grounds. ⑦–⑨.

Bosque del Cabo, above Playa Matapalo, down private road to the left (☎735-5206, fax 735-5043). Very secluded, comfortable bungalows, with stupendous views out to the Pacific. The owners are helping to repopulate scarlet macaws, and there are lots around. Waterfall and swimming hole nearby, and a good restaurant. ⑤.

Corcovado Tent Camp, about 45-min walk along the beach from Carate (book via Costa Rica Expeditions; see p.555). Eight self-contained, fully screened "tent-camps", elevated on short stilts, with bedroom and verandah, in an amazing sheltered, beachside location. Communal baths, and good local cooking served on site (rates include meals). Very good value; packages available, some of which fly you right to Carate. ⑤–⑥.

Eating and drinking

There's not much choice when it comes to **eating** in Jiménez, but you certainly won't starve. Everybody goes to *Restaurante Carolina*, on the main drag, which has a *comida típica* menu. The soda beside the Transportes Blanco bus stop is as good a place as any to have a *casado* or *plato del día*. For **evening meals** try the *Agua Luna*, across the creek on the way to the lancha dock; the seafood is good and the light gulf breezes are welcome.

Parque Nacional Corcovado

Created in 1975, **PARQUE NACIONAL CORCOVADO** ("hunchback"), 368km southwest of San José (daily 8am–4pm; ☎735-5036, fax 735-5276; US$6), protects a fascinating, biologically complex area of land, most of it on the peninsula itself. It also covers one mainland area just north of Golfito, which may soon be made into a National Park in its own right.

It's an undeniably beautiful Park, with deserted beaches, some laced with waterfalls, high canopy trees and better than average wildlife-spotting opportunities. Many people come with the express purpose of spotting **margay**, **ocelot**, **tapir** and other rarely seen animals. Of course, it's all down to luck, but if you walk quietly and there aren't too many other humans around, you should have a better chance of seeing some of these creatures here than elsewhere.

Serious walking in Corcovado is not for the faint-hearted. The **terrain** varies from beaches of packed or soft sand, riverways, mangroves, *holillo* (palm) swamps to dense forest, although most of it is at lowland elevations. Hikers can expect to spend most of their time on the beach trails that ring the outer perimeters of the peninsular section of the Park. Inland, the broad alluvial Corcovado plain contains the **Corcovado lagoon**, and for the most part the cover constitutes the only sizeable chunk of tropical **premontane wet forest** (also called tropical humid forest) on the Pacific side of Central America. The Osa forest is as visually and biologically magnificent as any on the subcontinent: biologists often compare the tree heights and density here with that of the Amazon basin cover – practically the only place in the entire isthmus of which this can still be said.

The coastal areas of the peninsular section of the Park receive at least 3800mm of **rain** a year, with precipitation rising to about 5000mm in the higher elevations of the interior. This intense wetness, combined with a sunny respite, is ideal for the growth and development of the intricate, densely matted cover associated with tropical wet forests. There's a dry season (Dec–March), however, and the inland lowland areas, especially those around the lagoon, can be amazingly **hot**, even for those accustomed to tropical temperatures.

Practicalities

Unless you are coming to Corcovado with *Costa Rica Expeditions* and staying in their tent camp (see p.653), in the dry months at least you have to **reserve** in advance. The best way to do is is to fax the Puerto Jiménez office of Corcovado (☎735-5276) or, if you're already in the country, you can phone the ☎192 number in San José or visit the Fundacion de Parques Nacionales (see p.539), who will contact Corcovado on your behalf. You will need reservations for meals and for camping space or lodging at the *puesto* of your choice (see below); you have to specify your dates and stick to them. Current prices for **staying** at the *puestos* are US$2 per night for camping, or US$4 for sleeping under the attic roof at Sirena. You can either take **meals** with the rangers (US$4 for breakfast, US$6 for lunch and dinner – you pay in colones at the *puesto*) or bring your own food and utensils and use their stove. Food is basic – rice and beans or fish – but filling.

You should **bring** your own tent, mosquito net, sleeping bag, food and water, and plan to **hike** early – not before dawn, due to snakes – and shelter during the hottest part of the day. Corcovado is set up so that the rangers at each *puesto* always know how many people are on a given trail, and how long they are expected to be. If you are late getting back, they will go looking for you. This gives a measure of security, but, all the same, take **precautions**. Incidentally, it's especially important when coming to Corcovado to brush up on your **Spanish**. You'll be asking the rangers for a lot of crucial information, and few, if any, of them speak English. Bring a phrase book if you're not fluent.

Puestos and routes through the park

In the village of **Carate**, about 43km from Jiménez, Sr Morale's *pulpería* sells basic foodstuffs. From here it is a ninety-minute to two-hour walk along the beach to enter Corcovado at the **La Leona** *puesto*. It's then a sixteen-kilometre hike – allow six hours as you have to wind along the beach, where it's slow going – to **Sirena**, where you can stay for a day or two in the simple lodge, exploring the local trails around the Río Sirena. Sirena, the biggest *puesto* in the Park, is also a research station, often full of biologists. Hikers coming from the Bahía Drake area enter at **San Pedrillo** and walk to Sirena from here.

The small hamlet of La Palma, 24km north of Puerto Jiménez, is the starting point for getting to the **Los Patos** *puesto*. It's a twelve-kilometre walk to the Park, much of it through hot lowland terrain. You need to arrive at Los Patos soon after dawn; if you want to stay in La Palma and get up early, *Cabinas Corcovado* (①–②) are a good bet.

The relatively new **El Tigre** *puesto*, at the eastern inland entrance to the Park, is the largest and most comfortable of all the Corcovado *puestos*, a good place to take breakfast or lunch with the ranger(s) before setting off on the local trails. To get there from Jiménez, drive 10km north and take the second left, a dirt track, signed to El Tigre and Dos Brazos.

All puestos have camping areas, drinking water, information, toilets and telephone or radio telephone contact. Wherever you enter, jot down the **marea** (tide tables) which are posted in prominent positions. You'll need to cross most of the rivers at low tide. To do otherwise is dangerous. Rangers can advise on conditions.

Walking the trails

The fifteen-kilometre trail from **La Leona to Sirena** runs nearly entirely upon the beach. You can only walk its full length at low tide; if you do get caught out, the only thing to do is wait for the water to recede. With few tide problems you should be able to make the walk in five hours, although most hikers take six, taking time to look out for birds. The walk can get a bit monotonous, but the beaches are uniformly lovely and deserted, and if you are lucky you may spot a flock of **scarlet macaws** in the coastal trees – a rare sight. You will probably see (or hear) monkeys, too. You need to take lots of sunscreen, a big hat and at least five litres of water per person; it is very hot on this trail, despite sea breezes.

The really heroic walk in Corcovado, all 25km of it, is from **Sirena to San Pedrillo** – the stretch along which you'll see the most impressive trees. It's a two-day trek, so you need a tent, sleeping bag and mosquito net, and must not be worried by pitching in the jungle. Fording the **Río Sirena**, just 1km beyond the Sirena *puesto*, is the biggest obstacle: this is the deepest, with the strongest out-tow current, of all the rivers on the peninsula. It has to be crossed with care, at low tide only. At high tide, sharks come in and out in search of food. Get the latest information from the Sirena rangers before you set out.

All in all, the trail across the peninsula from **Los Patos to Sirena** is 20km long. You may want to rest at the entrance, as this is an immediately demanding walk, continuing uphill for about 6–8km and taking you into high, wet and dense rainforest. After that you've still got 14km or so of incredibly hot lowland walking to go. This is the trail for experienced rainforest hikers and hopeful **mammal**-spotters: taking you through the interior, it gives you a reasonable chance of coming across, for example, a margay, or the tracks of tapirs and jaguars. That said, some hikers come away very disappointed, having not seen a thing. It's a gruelling trek, especially with the hot inland temperatures (at least 26°C and 100 percent humidity), and the lack of sea breezes.

The **El Tigre** area, at the eastern inland entrance to the Park, is gradually becoming more developed, with short walking trails cut around the *puesto*. These provide an introduction to Corcovado without having to slog it out on the marathon trails, and can easily be covered in a morning or afternoon.

Paso Canoas and the Panamanian border

Duty free shops and stalls lining the Interamericana announce the approach to **PASO CANOAS**. As you come into town, either driving or on the TRACOPA or international Ticabus service, you'll pass the Costa Rican customs checkpoint, where everybody gets a going-over. Foreigners don't attract much interest, however; customs officials are far more concerned with nabbing Costa Ricans crossing the border with an unauthorized amount of cheap consumer goods.

Visitors who need tourist cards or visas (see p.16) should collect them from the **Panamanian consulate**, or from the Copa office in San José. The Paso Canoas *migración* is notorious for running out, and you won't be allowed to enter without one. The **migración** is on the Costa Rican side, next to the TRACOPA bus terminal. You'll have to wait in line, maybe for several hours, especially if a San José–David–Panamá City Ticabus comes through, as all international bus passengers are processed together. Arrive early (8am) to get through fastest. There's no problem **changing currency**; on the Costa Rican side there is a Banco Nacional (Mon–Fri 8am–4pm) and, beyond that, plenty of moneychangers.

If you absolutely have to bed down in Paso Canoas, there are about a dozen rock-bottom cheap **cabinas** and hospedajes. These are all extremely basic, with cell rooms, private bath and cold water. They can be full on weekends. One place a cut above the pack is *Cabinas Interamericano*, on a side road to the right after the TRACOPA bus terminal, heading towards the border. Rooms (①) are not bad, and there's a restaurant.

Note that you cannot take any fruit or vegetables across the border – even if they're your lunch. They will be confiscated.

travel details

BUSES

Dominical to: Quepos (2 daily; 2hr); San Isidro (2 daily; 40min–1hr).

Golfito to: Playas Pavones and Zancudo (dry season only, 1 daily; 2hr 30min); San José (2 daily; 8hr).

Palmar Norte to: San José (3 daily; 5hr 30min); Sierpe (5 daily; 30min).

Paso Canoas to: San Isidro (2 daily; 6hr); San José (4 daily; 9hr).

Puerto Jiménez to: San Isidro (2 daily; 5hr); San José (2 daily; 8–9hr).

San Isidro to: Dominical (2 daily; 40min–1hr); Puerto Jiménez (2 daily; 5hr); Quepos (2 daily; 3hr 30min); San Gerardo de Rivas, for Chirripó (2 daily; 40min); San José (12 daily; 3hr); Uvita (1 daily; 1hr 30min).

San José to: Golfito (3 daily; 8hr); Palmar Norte (6 daily; 5hr 30min); Paso Canoas (4 daily; 9hr); Puerto Jiménez (2 daily; 8–9hr); San Isidro (12 daily; 3hr).

Sierpe to: Palmar Norte (5 daily; 30min).

FLIGHTS

Sansa

Golfito to: San José (1 daily Mon–Sat, 2 daily Wed–Fri).

Palmar to: San José (3 daily Mon & Sat, 2 daily Wed, Thurs, Fri – always indirect, via Quepos, Puerto Jiménez or Coto 47).

Puerto Jiménez to: San José (1 daily Mon–Sat).

San José to: Golfito (1 daily Mon–Sat, 2 daily Wed–Fri); Palmar Sur (1 daily Tues, 2 daily Mon, Wed, Thurs, Fri & Sat); Puerto Jiménez (1 daily Mon–Sat).

FERRIES

The *lancha Arco Iris* leaves Golfito daily at 11am (1hr 30min), returning from Jiménez at 6am.

PART EIGHT

PANAMÁ

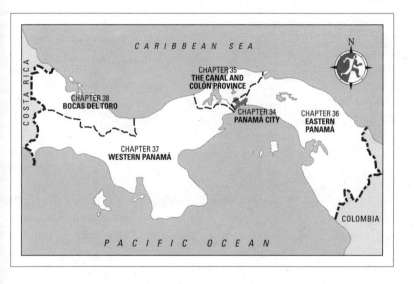

CARIBBEAN SEA

COSTA RICA

CHAPTER 38
BOCAS DEL TORO

CHAPTER 35
THE CANAL AND
COLÓN PROVINCE

CHAPTER 34
PANAMA CITY

CHAPTER 36
EASTERN
PANAMÁ

CHAPTER 37
WESTERN PANAMÁ

COLOMBIA

PACIFIC OCEAN

N

Introduction

Even before the construction of its famous canal, its strategic location at the wasp waist of the Americas and at the meeting place of the Atlantic and Pacific oceans made **Panamá** one of the great crossroads of the world. A narrow, S-shaped isthmus that stretches some 750km between Costa Rica and Colombia, it remains a vital **thoroughfare** of international commerce, but is rarely visited by travellers. In part this is because the land bridge to South America, the Darién Gap, remains virtually impassable; in part because the use of the US dollar and the relatively high level of economic development make it a more expensive country to visit. But above all it seems that Panamá suffers from a serious image problem. To most outsiders, this is an independent republic in name only, a virtual colony of the US artificially created so that they would have somewhere to build the canal, and its culture is seen as a desperately compromised imitation of North America: urbanized, anglicized and Coca-colonized. Yet while it is true that no other country in Central America has been so dominated by the US – Panamá owes its very existence to US intervention, and US military bases continue to stand guard over the canal – in fact the North American cultural influence, though strong, is but one among many. Spanish, African, West Indian, Chinese, Indian, European – all have contributed to a **compelling cultural mix**, creating perhaps the most cosmopolitan, open-minded and outward-looking society in Central America. At the same time, it is also home to some of the most unassimilated and culturally fascinating indigenous societies in Central America – within 30km of the high-rise banking district of Panamá City, for example, the indigenous **Embera** still practise subsistence agriculture in the rainforest and hunt for their supper with blowpipes.

Most travellers who make it down to Panamá are surprised by its outstanding **natural beauty**. With 1600km of coastline on the Pacific and 1280km on the Caribbean side, Panamá boasts unspoiled beaches and coral reefs to match any in the region. And although it is Costa Rica that has achieved world renown as an **ecotourism** destination, in terms of pristine wilderness and ecological diversity Panamá has little reason to envy its neighbour. A biological bridge between continents, Panamá supports an astounding biodiversity - it is home to more than nine hundred species of bird, more than in the whole of North America. Over half the country is still covered by dense tropical rainforest, and large areas are protected by a system of National Parks and nature reserves.

Although the government is keen to promote international tourism, for the moment Panamá remains one of the best-kept travellers' secrets in Central America. Of course, this means that in comparison to, say, Costa Rica, the **infrastructure** for visiting the protected wilderness areas is much more limited. But while this may put some people off, for others it simply adds to the sense of adventure – if you do visit Panamá's National Parks, you are unlikely to have to share them with more than a handful of other visitors. Moreover, wherever you travel in Panamá, the absence of a travellers' "scene" means you will be forced into much more direct contact with local people, an experience which, given the natural warmth and open-mindedness of most Panamanians and the fact that they have not yet become jaded with foreigners due to the impact of mass tourism, is undoubtedly one of the most rewarding aspects of any visit to this underrated and misunderstood country.

■ Where to go

Some two-thirds of Panamá's population live in the narrow corridor on either side of the canal, most of them in the capital, Panamá City, or in the well-developed Pacific coastal plain west of the canal. The rest of Panamá, east of the canal and north of the rugged mountain chain that runs like a spine down the length of the country, is heavily forested and sparsely inhabited, a virtual wilderness.

Cosmopolitan and contradictory, **Panamá City** is perhaps the most exciting capital city in Central America, combining the intrigue and frenetic energy of its international banking centre with the laid-back street-life of its old colonial quarter and the antiseptic order of the former US-controlled Canal Zone towns. Surrounded by some of the most accessible tropical rainforest in the Americas, it is also the best base from which to explore the rest of the country. Without doubt Panamá's biggest attraction for visitors, the monumental **Panamá Canal** can be easily visited from the city; there are visitors' centres where you can watch mighty ships being raised and lowered through the locks, or, best of all, you can take a cruise. Also within

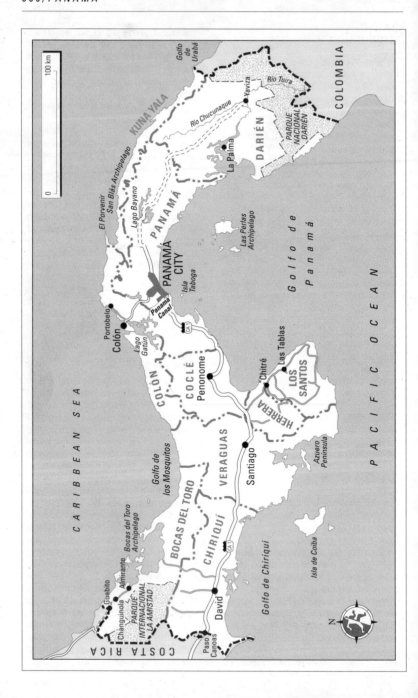

easy reach from the capital are the colonial ruins and pristine Caribbean coastline of the province of Colón. East of Panamá City and the canal stretches **Darién**, the rainforest-covered wild frontier between Central and South America, and stretched out along the length of its wildly beautiful Caribbean coastline is **Kuna Yala**, the autonomous homeland of the Kuna, who live in isolation on the coral atolls of the San Blas Archipelago, accessible by light aircraft from the capital.

West of Panamá City and the canal, the Carretera Interamericana to Costa Rica runs through the Pacific coastal plain, Panamá's agricultural heartland. Densely populated in comparison with the rest of the interior and with a decent road network, the attractions of this region include the folkloric traditions and coastal nature reserves of the **Azuero Peninsula** and the protected cloudforests of the **Chiriquí highlands**, close to the Costa Rican border. The Caribbean coast west of the canal is virtually uninhabited except in the extreme northwest corner, in the isolated province of **Bocas del Toro**. More easily accessible from Costa Rica than from the rest of Panamá, the Bocas del Toro archipelago is one of the last undeveloped frontiers in the Caribbean, a region of virtually unspoiled rainforests, beaches and coral reefs, inhabited by an unusual mix of indigenous groups and English-speaking West Indians.

■ When to go

Lying between 7 and 10 degrees north of the equator, Panamá is set well within the **tropics** and consequently temperatures are constant year-round – around 25–30°C – and vary only with **altitude**: in the Chiriquí Highlands, the average temperature is about 19°C, but this is the only region you are ever likely to feel cold. **Humidity** is always very high. **Rainfall** varies markedly between the Pacific and Caribbean sides of the mountain chain that runs the length of the country: on the Pacific side, the annual average is about 1500mm, on the Caribbean, about 2500mm. The **best time** to visit Panamá is during the dry season between mid-December and April, known as *verano* (summer), though this seasonal variation is really only evident on the Pacific side of the mountains. On the Caribbean side, rainfall is spread more evenly throughout the year. Though heavy, the rainstorms during the May–December

rainy season – *invierno* (winter) – rarely last long, and are no reason not to visit.

Note that Panamá is in the **Eastern Standard Time Zone**, five hours behind GMT and an hour ahead of Costa Rica.

Getting around

Travel within Panamá varies as sharply as everything else in the country. While the **canal corridor** and the **western Pacific** region are covered by a comprehensive road network served by regular public transport, both **eastern Panamá** and **Bocas del Toro** are linked to the rest of the country by single roads. Getting around these areas entails relying on light aircraft and (generally unscheduled) boats.

■ Buses

Where there are roads, **buses** are the cheapest, easiest and most popular way to travel around Panamá. Panamá City is the hub of the network, with regular buses to Colón, Yaviza in Darién, Chiriquí Grande (for Bocas del Toro) and all the cities and towns of western Panamá. Almirante and Changuinola in Bocas del Toro are connected by road to the Costa Rican border, but not to the rest of Panamá.

Buses **vary** in comfort and size, from modern, air-conditioned Pullmans to smaller minibuses and cramped, brightly painted old US school buses. Smaller towns and villages in rural areas are served by less frequent minibuses, pickup trucks and flat bed trucks known as *chivas* or *chivitas*, converted to carry passengers. Most buses are individually owned, and even when services are frequent **schedules** change all the time. The cities and larger towns have bus terminals, otherwise buses leave from the main street or square. You can usually flag down through buses from the roadside, though they may not stop if they are full or going a long way.

Both Colón and David are also served by **express buses**, which are more expensive, more comfortable and faster than the normal service, largely because they stop less frequently. The express bus to David and international buses to Costa Rica are the only ones worth **booking** in advance – generally, just turn up shortly before departure and you should get a seat. **Fares**, as elsewhere in Central America, are good value: the most you'll have to pay is US$11 for the ride from David to Panamá City (7hr) or US$14 for Panamá City to Yaviza (11hr).

■ Driving and hitching

Driving in Panamá is pretty straightforward: roads (where they exist) are pretty good and distances relatively short. **4WD** is a good idea, particularly during the rainy season and if you want to drive to more remote rural areas, particularly Darién; even the paved major roads in the canal corridor and the west can be ill-maintained, and in Panamá City it is useful for negotiating potholes.

At around US$40 a day or US$200 a week (more for 4WD), **car rental** is reasonably cheap. It is also a good way of seeing the country, especially in the canal corridor and areas close to Panamá City. Most rental companies are based in Panamá City (see p.696) but some also have offices at the airport and in David. Always read the small print, make sure you are insured and check the car for damages before you accept it. **Gas** costs around US$2 a gallon, though this increases in the more remote areas. **Filling stations** are easy to find on major roads and in most towns – many are open 24 hours – but there are fewer in rural areas, and in Darién you should carry an extra gas can in the car.

Traffic in Panamá City is fairly chaotic, and both there and in Colón parking and **security** are a problem. Car hijacking is growing, so keep your doors locked and (if you have air conditioning) your windows closed. Most hotels have their own parking lots, but otherwise when parking in the street someone is likely to offer to watch over your car for you in return for small change – though not exactly a demand for protection money, this is worth doing.

Hitching is possible, but private cars are unlikely to stop for you on main roads served by buses. In more remote areas, it is often the only motor transport available, and there is little distinction between private vehicles and public transport – drivers will pick you up, but you should expect to pay the same kind of fares as for the bus.

■ Cycling

Riding a bike in Panamá City is virtually unheard of, but in the west of the country, where roads are generally paved and traffic (away from the Carretera Interamericana) scarce, it is a popular way to get around, and most towns have somewhere for parts and simple repairs. The stretch of road from the continental divide to Chiriquí Grande on the road from David to Bocas del Toro, in particular, is a cyclist's dream – some 40km downhill on a well-surfaced, little-driven road, through rainforest-covered mountains that march down to the Caribbean.

■ Boats and ferries

Scheduled **ferries** run from Panamá City to Isla Taboga and between Chiriquí Grande, Almirante and Bocas del Toro in the province of Bocas del Toro. **Smaller boats** – launches or dugout canoes with outboard motors – are an important means of transport in Bocas del Toro, Darién and Kuna Yala, and often the only way to reach islands or other remote areas. The only scheduled small boat services are the **watertaxis** in Bocas del Toro (more expensive but much faster than the ferry) and between Puerto Quimba and La Palma in Darién. Otherwise you have to either wait for somebody who is going your way, or rent a boat and a boatman yourself. The latter is expensive, largely because outboard motors consume huge amounts of gas, but it becomes more economical the more people there are to share the boat, and it can be the most exciting way to get around. Renting a canoe with an outboard motor and a boatman opens up unlimited possibilities for wilderness adventure – up jungle rivers to isolated villages or to uninhabited coastal islands.

Occasional **boats and ships** that take passengers run along the Pacific coast of Darién from Panamá City and sometimes continue to Colombia, though they have no fixed schedule. Similarly, tramp steamers run the length of Kuna Yala from Colón and often on to Colombia along the Caribbean side, but both Kuna and Colombian-owned ships are generally loath to take foreigners as passengers.

■ Planes

Cities and larger towns are served by regular **flights** by Aeroperlas (☎269 4555), the principal domestic carrier, which also has regular flights to Darién. Other than Bocas del Toro and David, most destinations are so close to Panamá City that it scarcely worth flying, but flights are generally **inexpensive** (the longest flight, from Panamá City to David, costs around US$50) and on some routes (David to Bocas del Toro, for example) the views alone make it worthwhile. In eastern Panamá – Darién and Kuna Yala – on the other hand, light aircraft are the main and often the only way to get around. ANSA (☎226 7891), Aviatur (☎270 1748) and – the most reliable of the three – Aerotaxi (☎264 8644) have several flights a week to most of the major communities in Kuna Yala and towns in Darién.

■ Trains

Sadly the **railway** between Panamá City and Colón, which runs alongside the canal and was the first transcontinental railway in the Americas, has not carried passengers since the 1989 US invasion. There are plans to bring back a passenger service, though, so it's worth checking. The only other trains in Panamá that you might take run along the banana railway from Changuinola in Bocas del Toro up to the Costa Rican border. They are intended for banana workers and are much slower than making the same journey by road, but they will take other passengers.

Costs, money and banks

Panamá is the most economically advanced country in Central America and has the highest GDP per head (although income distribution is so polarized that poverty remains widespread). This, together with the use of the US dollar makes **costs** higher than in other countries in the region Other than the ten percent tourist tax on hotel accommodation, though, taxation is very low.

■ Currency, exchange and banks

Panamá adopted the US dollar as its **currency** in 1904, and has not printed any paper currency since. Dollars are referred to interchangeably as **dólares** or **balboas**. Panamá does mint its own coinage – 1, 5, 10, 25 and 50 centavo pieces – which are the same shape and size as and used alongside US coins. Fifty cents is also referred to as a peso, and five cents as a real, so 35 cents, for example, can also be described as "siete reales". US$100 and US$50 bills are often difficult to spend, for fear of forgeries or simply because change is difficult to come by, so it is best to make US$20 bills the largest you carry.

It is difficult to **change foreign currency** in Panamá, and you should change any cash into US dollars as soon as you can. In Panamá City there are Banco Nacional branches at the airport on Via

España in the El Cangrejo district, or you could try Panacambios, a casa de cambio also on Via España. Foreign banks will generally change their own currencies.

Travellers' cheques are the safest way to carry your money and are easy to change as long as they are issued by major companies (Visa, Mastercard) and are in US dollars. The three major **banks** in Panamá – Banco Nacional, Banco del Istmo and Banco General – will all change these, as will some of the international banks in Panamá City. Most banks are open from 8 or 8.30am to 3 or 4pm Monday to Friday; the Banco Nacional is also often open 9am to noon on Saturday.

Major **credit cards** are accepted in the more upmarket hotels and restaurants in Panamá City and the larger provincial towns. They can also be used to withdraw cash from banks, either over the counter or using an ATM. Visa is the most widely accepted, followed by Mastercard.

■ Costs

Though costs are low compared to Europe and North America, Panamá – along with Costa Rica and Belize – is one of the more **expensive** Central American countries. Sticking to a tight budget you can just about get around on US$25 a day, though you should be prepared to spend more than that in Panamá City and in remote areas where basic goods have to be brought in by sea or air. A **basic double room** in a hotel or pensión will usually cost at least US$10, and you will often have to pay twice that to get somewhere comfortable. Fortunately, **bus transport** is inexpensive – more or less US$1–1.50 an hour – and if you stick to basic local **restaurants** you can eat well on a dollar or two for each meal. Because of low taxes and import duties **imported consumer goods** – electronics, clothing and the like – are often cheaper than in Europe or North America (see p.667 for more on Panamá's duty free status).

Leaving Panamá, there's a US$20 **departure tax**, payable at the airport.

Information and maps

The best source of information in Panamá is the Panamanian Tourist Institute (**IPAT**), which has its main office in Panamá City (see p.676) and several provincial branch offices. Though the government is keen to promote tourism, the idea that some foreign visitors prefer independent travel to package tours is still a novelty to most IPAT workers. However, you can get some useful information at the Panamá City office – advice, free maps, leaflets – though unless you go there with some fairly specific questions you may end up with little more than glossy brochures. The provincial offices are more variable, though even in the most rudimentary of them you should be able to find some useful information – a local map or brochures – and there is usually someone who speaks English. *The Visitor/El Visitante*, a free monthly **tourist promotion magazine** in English and Spanish available at IPAT offices, hotels and restaurants throughout Panamá, lists Panamá's attractions and upcoming events.

Panamá's **national parks** and other protected natural areas are administered by the National Institute of Renewable Natural Resources, **INRENARE**; the main office in Panamá City (see p.676) is an essential stop for information on and permission to visit all but the most accessible of these protected areas. You can also get permission, and some information, at the INRENARE provincial offices, which are definitely worth visiting if you want to spend the night in a refuge (see opposite). Once again they are often unaccustomed to the idea of travellers visiting national parks independently, but are usually very helpful once they realize you are serious. Several **tour operators** based in Panamá City can also give you advice and information on visiting the rest of the country, though of course they will do so in the hope of selling you a tour.

The best **map** of Panamá (1:800,000), available in specialist map shops is produced by International Travel Maps (345 West Broadway, Vancouver, BC, Canada V5Y 1P8). **In Panamá**, large-scale maps are available at the Instituto Geográfico Nacional Tommy Guardia on Vía Simon Bolivar opposite the entrance to the University in Panamá City (Mon–Fri 8.30am–4pm).

Accommodation

Outside Panamá City and some resort areas, few **hotels** in Panamá are designed with foreign travellers in mind, particularly those on a budget. But in most areas there is a wide choice of places to stay. In general, **prices** are relatively high – the cheapest room may cost US$15–20 a night (the price for a single room varies little from that of a double) – but for this you'll usually get television, private bath, and air-conditioning. Cheaper rooms, with a fan instead of **air-conditioning** (you'll need one or the other), are often available, but staff will assume you are not interested in these unless you ask. **Hot water** is not considered a necessity and is usually only available in more expensive places, except in the Chiriquí highlands where it takes the place of a fan or a/c. In **Panamá City** most hotels are aimed at business travellers and prices tend to be even higher, while at the lower end of the market many hotels cater largely for Panamanian couples – some even have hourly rates – and are often full on the weekends, when prices go up.

You don't usually need to **book in advance**, except in the more upmarket hotels in Panamá City and at weekends or during public holidays. A ten percent **tourist tax** is charged on hotel accommodation and usually included in the price quoted.

■ Camping and places without hotels

There are no **official campsites** in Panamá, but it is possible to camp in remote rural areas and national parks, though you should always ask permission or at least let local people know that you are doing so. Other than on uninhabited islands in Kuna Yala or deep in the wilderness it is never really necessary – even in the smallest villages there's almost always somewhere you can sling a hammock or bed down for the night in return for a few dollars. If you do camp, a hammock and a plastic sheet or tarpaulin strung up against the

---

ACCOMMODATION PRICE CODES

All accommodation reviewed in this guide has been graded according to the following price scales, which represent the cost of a double room in high season excluding any taxes.

① up to US$5	④ US$15–25	⑦ US$60–80
② US$5–10	⑤ US$25–40	⑧ US$80–100
③ US$10–15	⑥ US$40–60	⑨ US$100 and over

rain are just as good as a tent. A **mosquito net** or mosquito coils (known as *mechitas* and widely available) are essential, as is a good repellent.

Almost all the national parks have INRENARE (see opposite) **refuges** where you can spend the night for US$5 or so, though this is not always charged. They are usually pretty basic, with bunk beds, cooking facilities and running water.

Eating and drinking

Known as *comida típica*, **traditional Panamanian cooking** is broadly similar to what you will find elsewhere in Central America. Basic, filling meals based on rice and beans or lentils served with a little chicken, meat or fish form the mainstay, though *yuca* (manioc) and plantains are also important staples.

■ Where to eat

The cheapest places to eat are canteen-like **self-service restaurants** serving a narrow but filling range of Panamanian meals for a few dollars, which you will find almost everywhere. Larger towns usually have some more **upmarket restaurants** with waiter service where a main meat or fish dish may cost US$5–15, and in Panamá City there is no shortage of expensive and exotic restaurants. There is no **tax** to pay on meals and **tipping**, though always welcome, is only expected in more expensive places or where service has been particularly good. All towns have US-style **fast-food** places, but **street vendors** are less common than elsewhere in Central America.

In **remote areas** with no real restaurant, there is usually someone in the village who will be prepared to cook you a meal, though it is always best to let them know in advance.

■ What to eat

Panamá's national dish is **sancocho**, a hearty chicken soup with *yuca*, plantains and other root vegetables flavoured with coriander, closely followed by the ubiquitous **arroz con pollo**, chicken with rice. **Seafood** is plentiful, excellent and generally cheap, particularly corvina (sea bass), pargo rojo (red snapper), lobster and prawns – the latter are one of Panamá's biggest exports. Ceviche – a cool, spicy dish of raw fish or seafood marinated in lime juice with onions and hot

peppers – is a popular appetizer, though a disappointment to anyone who has eaten the more substantial South American version. Fresh **tropical fruit** is also abundant, but rarely on the menu at restaurants other than in juice form – you're better off buying it yourself in local markets.

Breakfast for most Panamanians is *fritura*, a combination of fried foods such as sausages, eggs, *patacones* (fried green plantains), *tortillas de maíz* (smaller and thicker than elsewhere in Central America) and *hojaldres* (fried dough – much tastier than it sounds). Popular **snacks** include *carimañolas* or *enyucados* (fried balls of manioc dough filled with meat), *empanadas*, *tamales* (a mix of maize porridge, vegetables and pork or chicken wrapped in a banana-leaf parcel and boiled) and *patacones*.

The diverse **cultural influences** that have passed through Panamá have also left their mark on its cuisine, especially in Panamá City, where there are hosts of reasonably priced French, Greek, Italian, Chinese, Indian, Japanese and American restaurants. Elsewhere, almost every town has at least one **Chinese** restaurant – often the best option for **vegetarians,** as outside Panamá City there is little to choose from other than eggs, rice and beans – and dishes such as chow mein and fried rice often find their way onto the menus of even the most basic Panamanian restaurants. **US influence** is evident in the widespread availability of hamburgers and hot dogs. Perhaps the strongest outside influence on Panamanian food, though, is the distinctive **Caribbean cuisine** of the West Indian populations of Panamá City and the provinces of Colón and Bocas del Toro, which usually involves fish, seafood and rice cooked in hot spices, lime juice and coconut milk. Popular dishes include *saos*, pigs' trotters marinated in lime and chiles, and *fufu*, a stew of fish, plantains and manioc cooked in coconut milk. In Darién and other remote areas you may well be offered wild game – *conejo pintado* (agouti), a large rodent with sweet, greasy meat, is the most common bush meat.

■ Drinking

Coffee is generally good in Panamá, made espresso-style and served black. Weaker coffee is known as *café americano*. Otherwise, everyone drinks **cold drinks**, essential given the heat and humidity. The **drinking water** of Panamá City is so good that it is known as the "Champagne of the Chagres" after the river from which it is drawn, and iced water, served free in restaurants as a matter of course, along with the tap water in most towns and cities, is perfectly safe. Known as **sodas**, bottled fizzy drinks are available everywhere. Cheaper and more refreshing, though, are **chichas**, delicious blends of ice, water and the juice of any one of a dozen tropical fruits, served in restaurants or in paper cones by street vendors everywhere (except, that is, in Kuna Yala, where *chicha* is a ceremonial alcoholic drink made from fermented sugar-cane juice flavoured with coffee or cacao). *Batidos* are thick fruit milkshakes, often made with ice-cream.

Beer is extremely popular in Panamá, though with a strength varying between 3 and 3.5 percent it is more for refreshment than intoxication. Locally-brewed brands include Panamá, Lowenbrau, Atlas, Soberana and Balboa. Imported beers (Budweiser, Guinness) are only widely available in Panamá City. When it comes to intoxication, most Panamanians turn to locally-produced **rum** – Seco Herrerano (known as seco) and Carta Vieja are the most common brands – though imported whiskies and other spirits are widely available. Outside the more upmarket restaurants in Panamá City, wine is hard to come by.

Opening hours, holidays and festivals

Business hours vary from establishment to establishment, but generally **banks** are open from 8 or 8.30am to 3 or 4pm, Monday to Friday, and some also open on Saturday morning. **Businesses** and **government offices** are usually open Monday to Saturday from 8 or 9am to 4 or 5pm; **museums** the same hours from Tuesday to Saturday, and with some opening on Sunday morning. Some or all these close for **lunch** from around 12.30pm or 1pm to 1.30 or 2pm. **Shops** are usually open from Monday to Saturday from 9am to 6pm.

Panamá has ten **national public holidays**, during which pretty much all government offices, businesses and shops close. Panamá City and Colón also each have their own public holiday, and there is one public holiday for government employees only. When the public holidays fall near a weekend many Panamanians take a long weekend (known as a *puente*) and head to the beach or the countryside, so it can be difficult to find hotel rooms.

PUBLIC HOLIDAYS

Jan 1 New Year's Day
Jan 9 Martyr's Day (in remembrance of those killed by US troops in 1964 riots)
Feb-March (date varies) Carnaval
March-April (date varies) Good Friday
May 1 Labour Day
Aug 15 Foundation of Panamá City (Panamá City only)
Nov 3 Independence Day (from Colombia, 1903)
Nov 4 Flag Day (government holiday only)
Nov 5 National Day (Colón only)
Nov 10 First Cry of Independence
Nov 28 Emancipation Day (independence from Spain).
Dec 8 Mothers Day
Dec 25 Christmas Day

Several of these public holidays coincide with **national fiestas** that continue for several days. **Carnaval**, in February or March, is the largest and wildest of these, celebrated with parades, drinking, water fighting and dancing in Panamá City and across the country, most colourfully in Las Tablas. **Holy Week** (Easter) is celebrated with religious processions. In November, known as **"El Mes de la Patria"**, the anniversaries of the first declaration of independence and of both independence days (from Spain and Colombia) are celebrated by a succession of drum band parades.

In addition, **local fiestas** are held by every small town to celebrate its own anniversary and saint's day. The most vibrant of these are the **Fiesta of the Black Christ of Portobelo** on October 21, when up to 50,000 purple-clad pilgrims descend on that town (see p.706), and the numerous religious and folkloric fiestas of the towns of villages of the **Azuero Peninsula** (see p.727). In **Kuna Yala**, the Kuna celebrate their own independence day (the anniversary of the short-lived Dule Republic) in February, as well as several other dates throughout the year.

Mail and telecommunications

Other than in remote areas, **communications** in Panamá are good. Most small towns have a post office and telephone office, so keeping in touch with home is fairly easy.

Letters posted with the Correo Nacional (COTEL) cost US$0.35 to the US and US$0.45 to Europe. They should reach either destination within a week or two, though have been known to take far longer – it's best to post them in Panamá City. Most post offices have an *Entrega General* (Poste Restante, General Delivery) where you can **receive mail** – in Panamá City your correspondent must specify the post office zone: the most central is Zone 5, on Av Central/Via España. Post office **opening hours** are generally from 7am to 6pm Monday to Friday, 7am to 5pm on Saturday.

Panamá's recently privatized **telephone** company is owned by Cable and Wireless (C&W), but is still widely referred to as INTEL. **Local phone calls** are cheap, and there is a wide network of modern payphones that take 5, 10 and 25 cent coins. You can make collect **international calls** from these via the international operator (☎106), and both AT&T (☎109) and MCI (☎108) can place collect or credit card calls to the US. Otherwise, the INTEL/C&W offices are the best place to make international calls or send **faxes** (they will also hold faxes for up to a month for a fee of US$1) - they are listed in the Guide for each town.

Panamá's **country code** is ☎507 and there are no regional codes for internal calls.

Email has yet to take off in a big way in Panamá, though there are a couple of cybercafés in the capital (see p.691).

The media

For a small country, Panamá has an impressive number of newspapers: the **independent press** has flourished since the end of military rule. *La Prensa*, *La Estrella de Panamá*, *El Panamá America* and *El Universal* are all serious broadsheets, while *Critica Libre* and *El Siglo* are the most popular tabloids. **La Prensa** is probably the most effective critic of the present government, has a good international section and publishes entertainment listings. *The Panamá News*, a free fortnightly English-language newspaper covering local news and with an entertainment listings section, is widely available in Panamá City, as is the international edition of the *Miami Herald*. You can also find *Newsweek*, *Time*, *The Economist*, *The Financial Times* and several US papers.

Most Panamanian households have a **television**, and so do most hotel rooms. There are four private television stations – Channels 2, 4, 5 and 13 – offering a mix of Latin American soap opera, sport, US sitcoms, movies and news, as well as a government educational channel, Channel 11. In the canal corridor, you can also tune in to Southern Command Network, the US military station, which is worth checking for amusement value alone. Cable and satellite television is also widely available - particularly in the more upmarket hotels – giving access to CNN, BBC World, and a plethora of US sport and entertainment channels.

There are a massive number and variety of **radio stations** in Panamá and there's almost always a radio within earshot, blasting out anything from music and news to evangelical exhortations and US military broadcasts.

Shopping

For many visitors, **shopping** is the main reason to come to Panamá: it has always been an important trading centre and today people from all over Latin America and the Caribbean come here to buy **consumer goods** – electronics, designer fashion, jewellery – that are available at a lower cost and in greater variety than elsewhere in the region. You can buy almost anything you might want in the bazaars and superstores of Panamá City, often at a lower price than in Europe or the US. Panamá is also home to the second largest **duty-free zone** in the world: the **Colón Free Zone**. Goods from all over the world are traded here in vast quantities, and though most business is in bulk you can find good bargains (remember you may have to pay duty when you return home).

Panamá also produces some beautiful **handicrafts**. The most famous and exceptional are the **molas** – brightly-coloured cotton cloths intricately decorated with abstract designs created by a system of reverse-appliqué – made by the Kuna people (see p.717). The *mola* has become something of a national symbol and are sold all over the country. The Embera-Wounaan in Darién produce exquisite **carvings**, in wood or *tagua* (a palm seed known as "vegetable ivory"), mostly of birds and rainforest animals, while the artisans of western Panamá, and in particular those of the Azuero Peninsula, produce a wide range of handicrafts: pottery, lurid fiesta masks, leatherwork, and straw sombreros. The brightly coloured dresses and fibre shoulder bags (*chacaras*) of the Ngobe-Buglé people also make beautiful and practical souvenirs. Sadly, authentic **Panama hats** come from Ecuador.

Almost all these handicrafts are available in Panamá City, in shops and in cooperative artesania **markets** (listed in the Guide) but of course if you have the time it is much more rewarding (and cheaper) to buy them from the artisans themselves.

Safety and the police

Panamá has something of a reputation as a dangerous place to travel, but though **violent crime** is a problem – most shops, banks and hotels have private armed guards – outside certain areas Panamá is really no worse than elsewhere in Central America. You should take special care in **Colón** and in **Panamá City** (particularly in the San Felipe, El Chorillo and Calidonia districts), where **mugging** is a real threat, and always ask local advice about the relative safety of different areas. Other than your **passport**, which you are required to carry at all times, leave your valuables in your hotel when you can, keep them close to your body when you can't, and carry a few dollars separately so that muggers do not search you for more (or become violent with disappointment). Late at night or when carrying luggage, it's a good idea to take a taxi – think of it as a cheap insurance policy. If you are **driving**, never leave your car unattended and, in Panamá City and Colón, keep your doors locked and windows closed to avoid hijacking (see p.662).

Outside Colón and Panamá City, the only area where there is any particular danger is **Darién** and the easternmost part of **Kuna Yala**. This wilderness frontier with Colombia has long been frequented by Colombian Marxist guerrillas, bandits, and cocaine traffickers, but since 1996 the situation has deteriorated dramatically. Several travellers attempting to cross overland to Colombia have been killed and US missionaries kidnapped. It is still possible to visit Darién, and the situation may well improve, but at present **we do not recommend travel** in this area. Even when the situation has improved, you should check with INRENARE and in the press in Panamá City before going, and register with the police in every town. And if you are planning to travel to Colombia by sea, you should be aware that many of the boats that ply the coast are involved in smuggling.

If you are robbed or otherwise the victim of a crime, you should report it immediately to the local **police** station, particularly if you will later

EMERGENCY NUMBERS
Police ☎104
Fire ☎103
Traffic Police ☎232 5289
Tourist Police ☎226 4021 or 270 2467

be making an insurance claim. If treated respectfully, Panamanian police are generally honest and helpful. In Panamá City the **tourist police** (*Policia de Turismo*) are better prepared to deal with foreign travellers and more likely to speak English. They wear white armbands and are often mounted on bicycles.

Work and study

Although Panamá City teems with foreign workers, without a permit there are few opportunities for **work** in Panamá. There are some **English schools**, but given the US presence there is no shortage of teachers. With patience, luck or charm you may be able to find work crewing on a **yacht**, as a linehandler as it passes through the canal or even onwards into the Caribbean. For details see p.699.

For **Spanish language classes**, contact the *Ileri Spanish School*, Altos de Chase, Via La Amistad, El Dorado (☎260 4424) in Panamá City.

History

Perhaps no country in the world has had its history so thoroughly determined by geography as Panamá. In prehistoric times this was a crucial land bridge in the migration routes by which the Americas were populated, and from the moment the conquistador **Vasco Nuñez de Balboa** emerged from the forests of Darién to become the first European to look out onto the Pacific Ocean on September 25, 1513, the history of Panamá has been the history of the route across the isthmus. Balboa claimed what he called the "Southern Ocean" in the name of the King of Spain, but received scant reward for his discovery – in 1519 his jealous superior **Pedro Arias Dávila** (known as Pedrarias the Cruel), the first governor of what was by then known as Castila de Oro, had him beheaded for his troubles. In the face of appalling losses from disease in the first Spanish settlements on the Caribbean, Pedrarias moved his base across the isthmus to the more salubrious Pacific coast, where he founded **Panamá City** in 1519. The new settlement became the jumping-off point for further Spanish conquests north and south along the coast, and after the conquest of Peru in 1533 began to flourish as the **transit point** for the fabulous wealth of the **Incas** on its way to fill the coffers of the Spanish crown. From Panamá City cargo was transported across the isthmus on mules along the paved Camino Real to the ports of Nombre de Dios and later Portobelo, on the Caribbean coast. A second route, the Camino de Cruces, was used to transport heavier cargo to the highest navigable point on the Río Chagres, where it was transferred to canoes that carried it downriver to the coast. Once a year huge trade fairs lasting several weeks were held at Portobelo, when the Spanish royal fleet arrived to collect the gold and silver that had accumulated in the treasure houses of Panamá and to trade European goods that were then redistributed across the Americas. The vast wealth that flowed across the isthmus was quick to attract the attention of Spain's enemies, and despite ever heavier fortification the Caribbean coast was constantly harassed by English and other European **pirates**. In the most daring attack, the English Henry Morgan sailed up the Río Chagres and crossed the isthmus to sack Panamá City in 1671.

Though the city was rebuilt behind defences so formidable that it was never taken again, the raiding of the Caribbean coast continued until finally in 1746 Spain rerouted the treasure fleet around **Cape Horn**. With the route across the isthmus all but abandoned, Panamá slipped into decline, and settlement of the interior began to increase. Despite fierce resistance from indigenous groups the rest of the isthmus had been progressively conquered in the decades following the foundation of Panamá City. The forests of Darién and the Atlantic coast had been largely abandoned once the early colonial gold mines established there had been exhausted, and provided a refuge for unsubmissive tribes and bands of renegade slaves known as *cimarrones*, while the Pacific coastal plain west of Panamá City was gradually settled by farmers. **Trade** remained the dominant economic activity – whereas in most of the Spanish Empire political power lay in the hands of large landowners, in Panamá it was always held by the merchant class of Panamá City.

In 1821 Panamá declared its **independence from Spain**, but retained its name as a department

of Gran Colombia, which, with the secession of Ecuador and Venezuela, quickly became simply **Colombia**. Almost immediately, though, conflicts emerged between the merchants of Panamá City, eager to trade freely with the world, and the distant, protectionist governments in Bogota, leading to numerous half-hearted and unsuccessful attempts at independence.

Meanwhile, traffic across the isthmus was once again increasing, and exploded with the **discovery of gold in California** in 1849. Travel from the US east coast to California via Panamá – by boat, overland by foot, and then by boat again – was far less arduous than the overland trek across North America, and thousands of "Forty-niners" passed through on their way to the goldfields. In 1851 a US company began the construction of a **railway** across Panamá. Carving a route through the inhospitable swamps and forests of the isthmus proved immensely difficult and thousands of the mostly Chinese and West Indian migrant workers died in the process, but when the railway was completed in 1855, the **Panamá Railroad Company** proved an instant financial success. Panamá's importance as an international thoroughfare increased further, but the railway also marked the beginning of foreign control over the means of transport across the isthmus. Within a year, the first **US military intervention** in Panamá – "to protect the railroad"– had taken place.

■ The French canal venture

In 1869 the opening of the first **transcontinental railway** in the US reduced traffic through Panamá, but the completion of the **Suez Canal** that same year at last made the longstanding dream of a canal across the isthmus a realistic possibility. Well aware of the strategic advantages such a waterway would offer – a ship travelling from, for example, Boston to San Francisco would be reduced from 21,000km to just 8000km if it could cross the continent by passing through Panamá rather than going all the way round Cape Horn – Britain, France and the US all sent expeditions to seek a suitable route. It was the French, though, who took the initiative, buying a concession to build a canal from the Colombian Government. In 1881, led by **Ferdinand de Lesseps**, the architect responsible for the Suez Canal, the *Compagnie Universelle du Canal Interoceanique* began excavations.

But despite De Lesseps' vision and determination, the "venture of the century" proved to be an unmitigated disaster. In the face of the impassable terrain – forests, swamps and the shifting shales of the continental divide – the proposed sea-level canal proved technically unfeasible, and yellow fever and malaria ravaged the workforce, killing as many as 20,000. In 1889 the *Compagnie* collapsed as a result of financial mismanagement and corruption, implicating the highest levels of French society in what the official described as "the greatest fraud of modern times".

But the dream of an interoceanic canal would not die. The US government, never keen on the idea of a canal controlled by a European power and convinced by its 1898 war with Spain of the military importance of a fast passage between the Atlantic and Pacific oceans, took up the challenge. President **Theodore Roosevelt** in particular was convinced that the construction of a canal across Central America was an essential step in pursuit of the control of all the Americas. At first the US favoured building a canal through Nicaragua, but the persuasive lobbying of Philipe Bunau-Varilla, a French engineer anxious to profit from the sale of the French rights and equipment, swung the crucial Senate vote in Panamá's favour. A treaty allowing the US to build the canal was negotiated with the Colombian government in 1903, but the Colombian Senate refused to ratify it. Outraged that "the Bogotá lot of jackrabbits should be allowed to bar one of the future highways of civilization" Roosevelt gave unofficial backing to Panamanian secessionists who had long been seeking independence. The small Colombian garrison in Panamá City was bribed to switch sides and a second force that had landed at Colón agreed to return to Colombia without a fight after its officers had been tricked into captivity by the rebels. On November 3, 1903 the **Republic of Panamá** was declared and immediately recognized by the US, whose gunships standing off shore prevented Colombian reinforcements from landing to crush the rebellion.

Though it is true that Panamá would never have come into existence as an independent republic without the involvement of the US, the independence movement was not a wholly US invention. The Panamanian merchant elite had good reason to seek independence – rule from remote Bogotá limited Panamá's ability to trade and involved it in Colombia's endless civil wars – and had attempted secession thirty-three times in the previous seventy years. The difference, in 1903, was the support of the US, and this, as the Panamanians were soon to discover, came at a high price.

■ The canal

A new **canal treaty** was quickly negotiated and signed on Panamá's behalf by Bunau-Varilla. It gave the US "all the rights, power and authority . . . which [it] would possess and exercise as if it were sovereign", in perpetuity over an area of territory – the **Canal Zone** – that extended five miles either side of the canal. In return, the new Panamanian government received a one-off payment of $10 million and a further $250,000 a year. These conditions were so favourable that even American Secretary of State John Hay had to admit they were "very satisfactory, very advantageous for the US and we must confess... not so advantageous for Panamá." Panamá's newly formed national assembly found the terms outrageous, but when told by Bunau-Varilla that US support would be withdrawn were they to reject it, they ratified the treaty and work on the canal began.

It took ten years, the labour of some 75,000 workers and some $387 million to complete the task, which represented an unprecedented triumph of sanitation, organization and engineering. Chief medical officer Colonel William Gorgas established a sanitation programme that eliminated yellow fever from the isthmus and brought malaria under control, and the US engineers abandoned the idea of a sea-level canal. Instead, a series of locks were built to raise ships to a huge artificial lake formed by damming the mighty Río Chagres, an obstacle the French had never been able to overcome. Together the engineers solved the problems that had defeated the French, excavating over 160 million cubic metres of earth and rock, building the biggest concrete constructions (the locks), the biggest earth dam and creating the largest artificial lake the world had ever seen. On August 15, 1914, the SS Ancon became the first ship to transit the canal, which was completed six months ahead of schedule.

An enormous **migrant workforce**, which at times outnumbered the combined population of Panamá City and Colón, was imported to work on the canal's construction, and many – Indians, Europeans, Chinese and above all West Indians – stayed on after its completion, transforming the racial and cultural makeup of Panamá. They worked under what was effectively an apartheid labour system where white Americans were paid in gold, the rest – the vast majority of whom were black – in silver. Dormitories, mess halls, even toilets and drinking fountains were set aside for the exclusive use of one group or the other, and despite the success of the sanitary programme, mortality amongst black workers was four times higher than among whites.

Meanwhile, though their economy boomed during the construction, Panamanians soon came to realize that in many ways they had simply exchanged control from Bogotá for dominance by the United States. The de facto sovereignty and legal jurisdiction that the US enjoyed within the Canal Zone made it a strip of US territory in which Panamanians were treated as second class citizens, denied the commercial and employment opportunities enjoyed by US "Zonians". And the US agreement to guarantee Panamanian independence came at the price of intervention – inside and outside the Canal Zone – whenever the US considered it necessary to "maintain order", a right they exercised eight times between 1903 and 1936. Though the Panamanian Government, largely controlled by a ruling elite known as the "twenty families", was ostensibly independent, in fact it was little more than a client of the US. "There has never been a successful change of government in Panamá," one US official admitted in 1944, "but that the American authorities have been consulted beforehand."

Despite a new treaty limiting the US right of intervention in 1936, resentment of US imperialist control became the dominant theme of Panamanian politics and the basis of an emerging sense of national identity. Maverick politician **Arnulfo Arias Madrid** led demands for a further renegotiation of the canal treaty, but the US-backed Panamanian National Guard made sure that no president who challenged the status quo lasted long in office. Nevertheless **anti-US riots** in 1959 and 1964 revealed the enduring popular resentment of US domination.

When Arias was deposed by the National Guard after winning the 1968 elections, it appeared to be business as usual in Panamá. But in fact the coup marked a turning point in Panamanian politics. After a brief power struggle Lieutenant Colonel **Omar Torrijos** established himself as leader of the new military government. Described by his friend Graham Greene as a "lone wolf", Torrijos broke the political dominance of the white merchant oligarchy - known as the *rabiblancos*, or "whitearses" - in his pursuit of a pragmatic middle way between social-

ism and capitalism. Over twelve years he introduced a wide range of populist reforms - a new constitution and labour code, limited agricultural reform, nationalization of the electricity and communications sectors, expanded public health and education services – while simultaneously maintaining good relations with the business sector, establishing the Colón Free Zone and introducing the banking secrecy necessary for Panamá's emergence as an international financial centre. At the heart of Torrijos' popular appeal, though, was his insistence on the recovery of Panamanian control over the canal and his nationalistic opposition to US intervention in Panamanian affairs. After intensive negotiations a new canal treaty was signed by Torrijos and US president Jimmy Carter on September 7, 1977. Under its terms the US agreed to pass complete control of the canal to Panamá by the year 2000, and in the meantime it was to be administered by the **Panamá Canal Commission**, composed of five US and four Panamanian citizens. The Canal Zone was handed over to Panamanian jurisdiction and US military bases would remain only until 2000. However, though a memorandum of understanding made it clear that the US had no right of intervention in Panamá's internal affairs, the US maintained the right to intervene militarily if the canal's neutrality was threatened, even after the year 2000.

■ Noriega and the US invasion

With his main aim accomplished, Torrijos formed a political party, the **Partido Revolucionario Democratico** (PRD), and began moving towards a return to democracy in elections scheduled for 1984. In 1981, however, he died in a plane crash in the mountains of Coclé province. Though the crash was officially an accident, many Panamanians now believe that there was some involvement by the CIA or by **Colonel Manuel Noriega**, his former intelligence chief. Whatever the truth, Noriega soon took over as head of the National Guard, which he restructured as a personal power base and renamed the Panamá Defence Forces (PDF). Though fraudulent elections were held in 1984, by the following year Noriega had established himself as effective dictator of Panamá.

Noriega had been on the CIA payroll since the early 1970s and, whereas Torrijos had supported the Sandinistas in Nicaragua, Noriega quickly became an important figure in covert US military support for the Contras. Despite this, the undemocratic nature of his regime and revelations about his involvement in drugs trafficking began to prove embarrassing for his erstwhile employers, and in 1987 the US government began a campaign to drive him from power. Economic sanctions were followed by the indictment of Noriega for drug offences in February 1988, and after a US-backed coup attempt by dissident PDF officers failed in March 1988 the confrontation between Noriega and the US began to slide out of control. On December 20, 1989 US president **George Bush** launched "**Operation Just Cause**", and 27,000 US troops invaded Panamá. They quickly overcame the minimal organized resistance offered by the PDF. Bombers, helicopter gunships and even untested "stealth" aircraft were used against an enemy with no air defences, and over four hundred explosions were recorded in the first fourteen hours. The poor Panamá City barrio of El Chorillo was heavily bombed and burned to the ground, leaving some 15,000 homeless. Noriega himself evaded capture and took refuge in the papal nunciature before surrendering on January 5.

Estimates of the number of Panamanians killed during the invasion vary enormously – from several hundred to as many as 7000 – largely because little care was taken in counting the dead, and many were quickly buried in mass graves. That the invasion was illegal, however, was clear – it was condemned as a violation of international law by both the United Nations and the Organization of American States, both of which demanded the immediate withdrawal of US forces. President Bush gave four reasons for the invasion: "to safeguard the lives of Americans, to defend democracy in Panamá, to combat drug trafficking, and to protect the integrity of the Panamá Canal Treaty." But the defence of democracy in Panamá had scarcely been a US priority in the past, and Bush's concern with Noriega's extensive involvement in drug trafficking was also new. As director of the CIA in 1976 he had increased payments to Noriega, despite the CIA's detailed knowledge of Noriega's drug links. After the invasion and Noriega's arrest and imprisonment in Miami (where he remains), the flow of drugs through Panamá actually increased. The invasion was also in direct violation of the canal treaty provision prohibiting US intervention in Panamanian politics, and though one US soldier had been killed in the build up to the invasion (running a PDF roadblock) this alone was scarcely sufficient reason to invade an entire country.

The real reasons for the US invasion remain unclear. Certainly Bush's desire to appear tough in the domestic political arena played a part, and the invasion set an important precedent for further US military interventions in the post-Cold War world. To many Panamanians, though, the reasons were all too familiar: reassertion of US control over Panamá and its strategic waterway, and the destruction of the PDF. Not that most Panamanians opposed the invasion: unlike Torrijos, Noriega was deeply unpopular, and almost all were relieved to see the back of him. But most were angry at the excessive use of force and felt humiliated by the reassertion of US dominance that Noriega's removal involved. Some likened Operation Just Cause to a brilliant cancer operation by a surgeon who had been pushing cigarettes to the patient for forty years.

After the invasion, the US installed **Guillermo Endara**, winner of elections annulled by Noriega in 1989, as president. In 1994 he was defeated by Ernesto Perez Balladares, leader of the PRD - the party of both Torrijos and Noriega. Since taking office, Perez Balladares has implemented neoliberal economic policies – privatization of state-owned companies, reduction of public expenditure – aimed at meeting the payments on the vast external debt that was the legacy of the Torrijos years: Panamá has one of the highest per capita **debt** levels in the world. As ever, the future of the canal remains the most controversial issue in Panamanian politics. As the end of the millennium deadline for the full **transfer** of the canal to Panamanian control draws near, the last US military bases are gradually being handed over to Panamanian jurisdiction. But controversy is raging over who will bear the cost of the environmental clean-up of the toxic chemicals and unexploded shells on the bases, and the US government seems set to succeed in its efforts to persuade Panamá to establish a multilateral anti-drugs base (CMA) in the US military bases alongside the canal. Some Panamanians see the proposed CMA as a desperate affront to Panamanian sovereignty and an attempt by the US to maintain a military presence in Panamá after 2000, while others welcome its continued presence as the best guarantee of future stability and economic prosperity. Panamá's love-hate relationship with US remains as strong as ever. But whatever the outcome of the CMA negotiations, when Panamá finally becomes a **fully independent** country on December 31, 1999, it promises to be quite a party.

CHAPTER 34

PANAMÁ CITY

If the world had to choose a capital, the Isthmus of Panamá would be the obvious place for that high destiny.

Simon Bolívar, 1826

F ew cities in Latin America can match the diversity, cosmopolitanism and sheer energy of **PANAMÁ CITY**: polyglot and post-modern before its time, in many ways it is closer in atmosphere to the mighty trading cities of Asia – Hong Kong or Singapore – than to anywhere else in the region. Situated on one of the great crossroads of the world, the city has always thrived on commerce, and its unique geographical position and the opportunities it presents have attracted immigrants from all over the globe. Though it is the undisputed political and social centre of Panamá and home to almost half its population, Panamá City's gaze is fixed firmly on the outside world, and its inhabitants pay scant attention to what they refer to rather vaguely as "the interior". Open-minded and outward looking, the population is among the sharpest and most sophisticated in Central America.

With a spectacular **setting** on the Pacific bay of the same name, with the canal on one side and lush, forested mountains rising behind, Panamá City encompasses some startling incongruities. On the southwest end of the bay stands the old city centre of **San Felipe**, a jumble of crumbling colonial churches and nineteenth-century mansions, while 4km or so to the east rise the shimmering skyscrapers of **El Cangrejo**, the modern banking and commercial district. Further east, amid the sprawling suburbs, stand the ruins of **Panamá Viejo**, the first European city to be founded on the Pacific coast of the Americas, while west of San Felipe the former US Canal Zone town of **Balboa** retains a distinctly North American character despite having been returned to Panamanian control in 1979.

Those who find the city's ceaseless commercial energy overwhelming, meanwhile, can easily escape: to **Isla Taboga**, the idyllic "island of flowers"; along the **Amador causeway** that juts out into the Pacific beside the canal; or into the **Parque Nacional Metropolitano**, the only pristine tropical rainforest within the limits of a Latin American capital. Panamá City is also a good base from which to explore the rest of the country – the canal, Colón and the Caribbean coast as far as Portobelo can all be visited on day trips.

Some history

The first European city on the Pacific coast when it was founded by the **conquistador** Pedrarias Davila on August 15, 1519, Panamá quickly flourished as the base for further conquest along the Pacific and as the point of transit for the vast booty so accrued on its way to the treasure houses of Spain. By the mid-seventeenth century it had a population of some 10,000 and boasted some of the grandest constructions in the new world. The opulence of "Panamá the golden" did not escape the notice of the **pirates** then ravaging the Spanish Main. In 1671 Henry Morgan captured the fort of San Lorenzo at the mouth of the Río Chagres, crossed the isthmus and descended on the city with a force

For an explanation of **accommodation price codes**, see p.664.

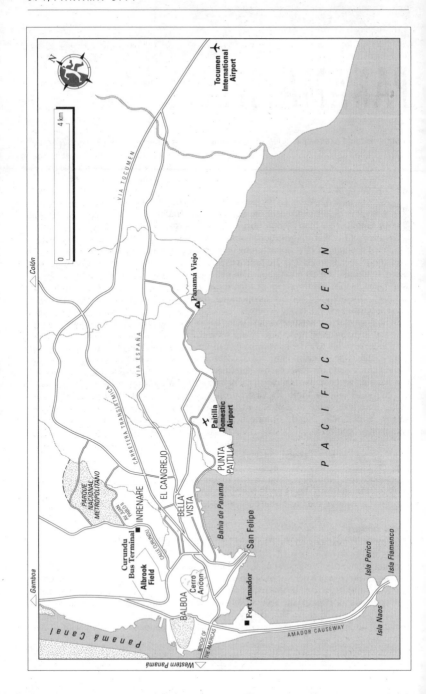

of 1200 corsairs. After a bloody three-hour battle Morgan's desperate band defeated the much larger defending army and seized the city, already in flames after the defenders set light to its gunpowder magazines. They pillaged for three weeks before departing with 600 prisoners and a quantity of loot so vast that 175 mules were needed to carry it back across the isthmus. Known as **Panamá Viejo**, the ruins of Pedrarias' city still stand amid the sprawling suburbs of the modern city.

When the scattered survivors regrouped, they opted to rebuild the city on a rocky peninsula jutting out into the bay 10km to the west, a site deemed easier to defend and more salubrious than its swamp-bound predecessor. Founded in 1673 and today known as **San Felipe**, the new city was heavily fortified against pirate attack, protected by defences built at such enormous expense that the King of Spain was said to scan the horizon from his Madrid palace for a glimpse of the walls of Panamá, saying that given the vast quantity of gold spent in their construction they should be visible from any point on earth.

Though it never matched the glory of its predecessor (and was all but destroyed by fires in 1737 and 1756), the new city slowly prospered, its fortunes rising and falling with the traffic across the isthmus. The decline brought about by the rerouting of the Spanish treasure fleet around **Cape Horn** in 1746 was arrested after **independence**, which made Panamá free to trade with the world, and then reversed with the construction of the **transisthmian railroad** in 1855. The railroad, and subsequently the French and US canal construction efforts, brought immense prosperity and a wealth of new cultural influences that transformed the city and its population. But though the **canal** confirmed Panamá City's importance as a global trading centre, it also restricted its development. Hemmed in to the west and northwest by the US-controlled Canal Zone, the city was only able to expand east along the coast, which it began to do very quickly from about 1920. The introduction of banking secrecy laws in the 1970s led to the rapid expansion of the financial services sector, boosted by a massive influx of narco-dollars from South America, leading the British novelist John Le Carré to describe the city as ". . . like *Casablanca* without the heroes, a hotbed of drugs, laundered money and corruption." This was somewhat harsh, and in the 1990s banking regulations have been tightened enormously, but **El Cangrejo** remains a hive of intrigue and many of its luxury high-rise apartments stand empty, the astronomical rents paid by their fictitious occupants providing a useful means of laundering money.

The **1989 US invasion** devastated the poor neighbourhood of El Chorillo and was followed by widespread looting, but the city recovered quickly, free of the economic sanctions imposed by the US on the Noriega regime. But though the vast amounts of real estate made available by the gradual handing over of the US military bases around the city has opened up room for expansion and looks set to spur another economic boom, the harsh neo-liberal policies that have been implemented since the invasion have hit the poorer sectors particularly hard, leading to an increase in **street crime**.

Arrival, information and city transport

Arriving in Panamá City can be disconcerting, so unless you are travelling very light or are within walking distance of your hotel, it's best to take a taxi. Spread out along the Bahía de Panamá, the city has no real centre, but once you've established your bearings it is relatively easy to find your way around. **San Felipe** and **El Cangrejo** are joined by **Avenida Central**, the city's main thoroughfare, which runs north from San Felipe through the district of Santa Ana then veers northwest, its name changing to **Via España** as it continues through the downtown districts of Calidonia and La Exposición and the residential district of Bella Vista. Several other main avenues run parallel to Av Central: Av Peru, Cuba, Justo Arosemena and, along the seafront, Av Balboa.

Confusingly, most streets in Panamá City have at least **two names**: Av Cuba, for instance, is also Av 2 Sur, and the road known universally as Calle 50 is also Av 4 Sur or Av Nicanor de Obarrio. We have used the most common names in the following accounts.

By air

International flights arrive at Tocumen International Airport (☎238 4322), about 26km northeast of Panamá City. There are several **car rental** offices here and an **IPAT** office (daily 8am–10pm) which has some basic tourist information, can book accommodation and will arrange a **taxi**, by far the best way to get into the city. These cost US$25 to hire individually or US$8 per person if you share with other passengers. You can also take one of the frequent **buses** from the airport that run into the city and along Av Balboa to Plaza Cinco de Mayo and Plaza Santa Ana; a ticket costs only US$0.30, but there's not much room for luggage.

Domestic flights arrive at Paitilla Airport (☎226 1622), near El Cangrejo on Av 6 Sur (Via Israel). Frequent buses run past the airport entrance and along Av Balboa to Plaza Cinco de Mayo, and there are always taxis waiting.

By bus

International buses from Costa Rica and beyond arrive at the Ticabus terminal on C 17, just off Av Central (☎262 6275), next to the *Hotel Ideal*. This is a dodgy area, so unless you're staying there its best to get a taxi to your hotel, particularly if you arrive at night. Most **domestic buses** arrive at the new **Curundu bus terminal** on C Curundu, a short taxi ride west of the city and served by occasional SACA buses to Plaza Cinco de Mayo (see below). The exceptions to this are buses from Colón, David, the former Canal Zone and Paso Canoas on the Costa Rican border. Slow buses from **Colón** pull in on the corner of Calle P with Av Central, express buses on the corner of C 29 and Av Central, opposite the *Hotel Soloy* – either way you're in the middle of the Calidonia district and close to plenty of hotels. Buses from **David** pull in to a terminal opposite the Mercado de Mariscos on Av Balboa. Buses from **Paso Canoas** on the Costa Rican border arrive and depart from outside the *Hotel Roma* on Av Justo Arosemena near the corner with C 33 Este. Finally, buses to **Gamboa** and elsewhere in the **former Canal Zone** leave from the **SACA bus terminal** just off Plaza Cinco de Mayo.

By sea

Irregular boats from Darién and Colombia dock at the **Muelle Fiscal** next to the Mercado Central on the seafront of Santa Ana. If you're heading for San Felipe, it's a short walk along the shore to the southeast. Otherwise, walk two blocks up the hill in front to Parque Santa Ana where you can catch a bus or hail a taxi to anywhere in the city.

Information

The main **IPAT** office is in the Atlapa Convention Centre on Av 6 Sur, out in the suburbs east of El Cangrejo (Mon–Fri 8.30am–4.30pm; ☎226 7000). The staff are generally helpful and enthusiastic, though their brochures tend to be of the glossy, non-specific variety. They are not really used to independent travellers asking for information, but will do their best to answer specific questions in Spanish or English. For details on and permission to visit Panamá's National Parks or other protected natural areas, you should contact the **INRENARE** offices (Mon–Fri 8am–4pm; ☎232 4325 or 232 4083) on C Curundu opposite the Curundu bus terminal.

The **Kuna General Congress** (☎263 3615; see p.718) has an office in El Cangrejo, above an electronics shop in the Edificio Dominó on Via España with Via Argentina, where you can get information on Kuna Yala. **PEMASKY** (☎225 8084), the Kuna organization that manages the Nusagandi Nature Reserve (see p.719), has an office on C 37 between Via España and Av Peru – you must get permission here if you want to stay in the Nusagandi lodge.

City transport

Taking a ride in one of Panamá City's brightly-painted former US school **buses** is an exciting experience, although sadly a recent ban means they no longer bounce along to the impossibly loud reggae and salsa that used to blast from speakers more powerful than their engines. They are inexpensive (US$0.15) and go to almost every corner of the city between 6am and midnight. However, most are individually owned and there are no fixed **routes** or **schedules**: you just have to look for the destination painted on the windscreen. Plaza Santa Ana is the main hub where you can get buses to almost anywhere in the city.

Taxis are plentiful and inexpensive, with **fares** based on a zone system: US$1 a zone plus US$0.25 for each additional passenger. No journey should cost more than US$3 – it's best to agree the fare in advance.

Accommodation

There are three main areas to stay in Panamá City. Most budget travellers opt for the faded splendour of **San Felipe**: the city's historic centre offers low-cost accommodation in run-down but atmospheric hotels that were once the finest in Panamá, but is a long way from most of the city's restaurants and nightlife and is unsafe at night – even during the day you should be careful. The more upmarket hotels are in the safer neighbourhoods of **Bella Vista** and **El Cangrejo**, the centre of the city's nightlife, culture and commercial activity, which has some good mid-range options on the fringes. Between San Felipe and El Cangrejo, and with good access to both along the city's main arteries, the **Calidonia/La Exposicion** area offers a compromise, with a wide choice of unexceptional modern hotels and pensions, including plenty of budget options and good mid-range deals. There's not much of interest in the area itself though, and here, too, you must be careful.

San Felipe

Hotel Central, C 5, Plaza Catedral (☎262 8096 or 262 8044). The grandest hotel in Central America when it was built in 1884, the *Central* housed many of the key figures involved in the canal construction and was for decades the centre of the city's social life. Although rather rundown, it retains much of its former glory and enormous charm. Rooms are well-ventilated with high ceilings, and those at the front, though noisy at night, have balconies looking out across the square to the Cathedral. Good value, and worth a look even if you don't stay. ②–③.

Hotel Foyo, C 6, Av A (☎262 8023). Slightly dilapidated but charming building set around a courtyard and with a communal balcony with rocking chairs overlooking the street. Rooms vary, and some have thin walls, so ask to see a few before you choose. ②.

Hotel Herrera, C 9, Parque Herrera (☎228 8994). Elegant though decaying nineteenth-century neoclassical building with flower-covered balconies overlooking the park. Rooms are basic, and some of the furniture and mattresses seem almost as old as the building itself. Cheaper rates for shared bathroom, more expensive rooms available with a/c and fridge. ③.

Hotel Ideal, C 17 Oeste, Av Central (☎262 2400). Just off Av Central on the way out of San Felipe, halfway between Plaza Santa Ana and Plaza 5 de Mayo, next door to the Ticabus office. Surprisingly

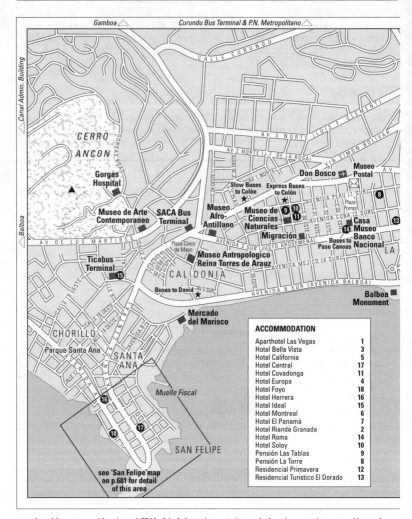

ACCOMMODATION	
Aparthotel Las Vegas	1
Hotel Bella Vista	3
Hotel California	5
Hotel Central	17
Hotel Covadonga	11
Hotel Europa	4
Hotel Foyo	18
Hotel Herrera	16
Hotel Ideal	15
Hotel Montreal	6
Hotel El Panamá	7
Hotel Riande Granada	2
Hotel Roma	14
Hotel Soloy	10
Pensión Las Tablas	9
Pensión La Torre	8
Residencial Primavera	12
Residencial Turistico El Dorado	13

comfortable rooms with a/c and TV behind the grim exterior and chaotic reception area. Always busy and in a dodgy area. Restaurant, 24-hour cafe, swimming pool, discounts for Ticabus passengers. ④.

Calidonia/La Exposicion

Hotel Covadonga, C 29, Av Peru (☎225 3998 or 225 2989, fax 225 4011). Modern and clean with a good 24-hour restaurant and a small rooftop swimming pool. All rooms have a/c, phone, cable TV and intermittent hot water. Extra charge for safety-deposit box. ⑤.

Pension Las Tablas, Av Peru, C 28 (no phone). Small, basic but clean rooms with TV. More expensive at weekends. ②.

Pension La Torre, Av Peru, C 36 (☎225 0172). The upper floor of an incongruously elegant 1913 mansion – the Casa Patterson – on the corner above a cluster of restaurants. Entrance up the stairs behind a row of small trees on C 36. Basic, clean rooms with TV, a/c extra. ③.

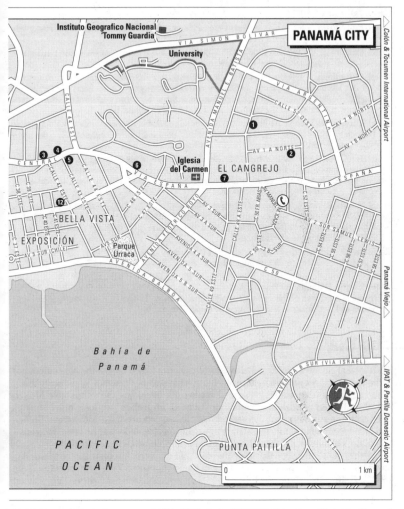

Hotel Roma, Av Justo Arosemena, C 33 (☎227 3844, fax 227 3711). Friendly and helpful with good tourist facilities. Large, comfortable rooms with hot water, a/c, cable TV, fridge. Swimming pool, gym, bar, 24-hour cafe and good Italian restaurant. A little overpriced but cheaper rates may be negotiable. ⑦.

Residencial Turistico El Dorado, C 37, Av Peru (☎227 5767). Basically a short-stay hotel for Panamanian couples and so busy at the weekend, but inexpensive. Most rooms are claustrophobically small and dark, so it's worth paying slightly more for an upstairs room with a window. A/c and TV also cost a few dollars more. ②–③.

Hotel Soloy, Av Peru, C 30 (☎227 1133, fax 227 0884). Enormous Spanish chain-owned hotel with 200 rooms, casino, 24-hour restaurant, swimming pool, bar and lively disco Thurs–Sat. Comfortable, spacious rooms with uninspired decor, hot water, cable TV, a/c, fridge and mini-bar. Excellent value but a bit too classy for the area. ⑤.

Bellavista/El Cangrejo

Hotel Bella Vista, Via España, Av Peru (☎264 1193 or 264 4029). Unspectacular but reasonably priced rooms with a/c, TV, hot water and telephone. ④.

Hotel California, Via España, C 43 (☎263 7736, fax 264 6144). Large, modern and comfortable rooms with hot water, a/c, TV and telephone. ⑤.

Hotel El Panamá, C 49B Oeste, Via España (☎269 5000, fax 223 6080). Formerly the *Hilton*, this five-star Art Deco hotel has plenty of character and is ideally located in the heart of El Cangrejo. Salmon-pink walls, luxurious decor, swimming pool, three bars, two restaurants, casino, gym, indoor tennis courts and all other features of a first-class international hotel. ⑨.

Hotel Europa, Via España, Av Peru (☎263 6369 or 263 6911, fax 263 6749). Friendly, comfortable Art Deco hotel with 24-hour restaurant, bar, swimming pool and bizarre interior decor – the lobby looks like a 1970s disco. Rooms have a/c, TV, hot water and telephone. ⑥.

ApartHotel Las Vegas, Av Eusebio A Morales, C 49B Oeste (☎269 0722, fax 223 0047). Self-contained apartments with kitchen, bathroom, a/c, cable TV, telephone and free coffee and ice. Perfect location two blocks from the centre of El Cangrejo. Smaller, "mini-studio" rooms with kitchenette also available. Good weekly and monthly rates. ⑥–⑦.

Hotel Montreal, Via España, Justo Arosemena (☎263 4422, fax 263 7951). Excellent location – the closest in this price-range to the centre of El Cangrejo – but a lot of noise from Via España traffic. Small, poorly lit rooms with TV, hot water, phone and a/c. Those at the back are quieter. Bar, rooftop swimming pool and modest restaurant. ④.

Residencial Primavera, Av Cuba, C 42 (☎225 1195). Poky, dark rooms but friendly and excellent value given its location: a quiet, residential area on the edge of Bella Vista. Small, and therefore often full. ②.

Hotel Riande Granada, Av Eusebio A Morales, Via España (☎263 7477, fax 264 0930). Luxurious international hotel with excellent service and central location. 24-hour cafe, bar, outdoor barbecue restaurant and swimming pool surrounded by tropical plants. ⑧.

The City

The colonial city centre of **San Felipe** (also known as Casco Viejo – the old compound) is the most picturesque and historically interesting part of Panamá City, home to many of its most important buildings, several **museums** (including the unmissable **Museo del Canal Interoceanico**). Crumbling **colonial churches** overlook quiet squares filled with **monuments** and the narrow, cobbled streets are lined with ornate French and Spanish-influenced nineteenth-century mansions painted white or in the faded pastels of the Caribbean, some with cast-iron balconies draped with flowers.

Northwest of San Felipe the steep, forested hill of **Cerro Ancon** offers commanding views of the city and marks the boundary of the former Canal Zone, while the canalside town of **Balboa**, which retains the feel of a US provincial town is an interesting contrast to the chaotic vitality of the rest of the city. It is also the jumping-off point for the peaceful **Isla Taboga**. North of the city, meanwhile, a stroll through the rainforests of the extraordinary **Parque Nacional Metropolitano** offers an even more fundamental change of scenery.

San Felipe

For centuries the centre of the city's social and political life and still home to the presidential palace, **San Felipe** has been in gradual decline for several decades. Although it was declared a UNESCO world heritage site in 1997 and restoration efforts are underway, this is still a poor, rundown neighbourhood with a relaxed but slightly seedy streetlife. It is dangerous to walk the streets at night, and even during the day you should be careful when out of sight of the tourist police. The best way to see San Felipe is on foot, and **Plaza Catedral**, the main square, is a good place to start – you can reach it from the rest of the city by taxi or by walking down Av Central from Parque Santa Ana.

Plaza Catedral

Plaza Catedral, also known as Plaza de la Independencia – the proclamations of independence from both Spain and Colombia were made here – centres on a bandstand, ringed by benches shaded by trees and by busts of eminent Panamanians. Flanked by white towers inlaid with mother of pearl, the classical facade of the **cathedral** looks out on the square from the west. It was built between 1688 and 1796 using stones from the ruined cathedral of Panamá Viejo (see p.686). Three of its bells were also recovered from its ruined predecessor, and reputedly owe their distinctive tone to a ring thrown by Empress Isabella of Spain into the molten metal from which they were cast. Southeast of the cathedral is the neoclassical **Municipal Palace**, whose small **Museo de Historia Panameña** (Mon–Fri 8.30am–4.30pm; US$1) offers a cursory introduction to Panamanian history that pales in comparison beside its neighbour, the superlative **Museo del Canal Interoceanico** (Tues–Sun 9.30am–5pm; US$2; free guided tours in English or Spanish). The museum lays out clearly and in great detail the history of the transisthmian route, from the first Spanish attempt to find a passage to Asia to the contemporary management of the canal, with many photographs and cinema footage and historic exhibits including the original canal treaties.

Across the square from the cathedral is the **Hotel Central**, built to replace the *Grand Hotel* and in its time the swankiest hotel in Central America. The huge central

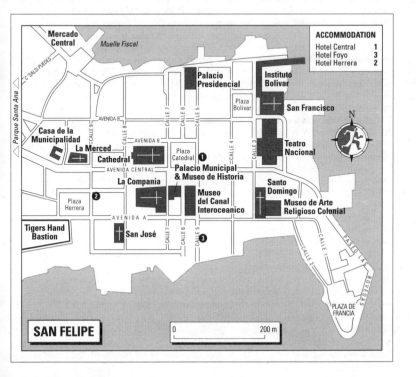

patio was once a chandelier-lit palm garden where glittering balls were held, and it was here that jubilant crowds gathered in 1903 to celebrate Panamanian independence by pouring champagne over the head of General Huertas, the defecting garrison commander, for over an hour. Though rundown today, it retains much of its former splendour and is a characterful place to stay (see p.677).

Palacio Presidencial

On the seafront two blocks north of the square along C 6 the **Palacio Presidencial,** originally built in 1673, was home to successive colonial and Colombian governors before being rebuilt in grandiose neo-Moorish style in 1922 under the orders of President Belisario Porras. It is commonly known as the "Palacio de las Garzas" due to the white Darién herons that were introduced by Porras and have lived free around the patio fountain ever since. Rumour has it that when US president Jimmy Carter visited the palace before the signing of the new canal treaty his security team sprayed the building with a disinfectant that proved fatal to herons, and replacements had to be rushed in under cover of darkness to avoid any embarrassment this inauspicious accident might have caused. The streets around the palace are busy with presidential guards, who may let you in for a glimpse of the interior or at least close enough to photograph the exterior.

Plaza Bolívar and around

Walking a block back down C 6 and then two blocks east along Av B brings you out onto **Plaza Bolívar**, an elegant square dedicated in 1883 to Simon Bolívar, whose statue, crowned by a condor, stands in its centre. Bolívar came here in 1826 for the first Panamerican congress, held in the chapter-room of the old monastery building on the northeast corner of the square. Lined with carved wooden panelling and nineteenth-century portraits, the plush interior was fully restored in 1954 and is now administered by the **Bolívar Institute**, closed to the public unless you arrange a visit in advance (☎262 2947). Next door stands the **church and monastery of San Francisco**, built in the seventeenth century but extensively modified since. The church is usually closed, but if you ask in the parish office on Av B someone will open it up and show you around (no charge, but donations to fund restoration are appreciated). Other than the carved wooden confessional dating to 1736, the interior is unspectacular, but the views across the city from the tower make it well worth visiting.

Just off the square to the south on Av B is the **Teatro Nacional**, designed by Genaro Ruggieri, the Italian architect responsible for La Scala in Milan. Extensively restored in the early 1970s and reopened with a performance by Margot Fonteyn, the British ballerina and long-term Panamá resident, in 1974, the theatre still stages performances in the evening and can be visited during the day (free, but ask the security guards' permission). Built to the most exacting acoustic standards, the neoclassical interior is splendid; richly furnished and decorated in red and gold, with French crystal chandeliers, busts of famous dramatists and a vaulted ceiling painted with scenes depicting the birth of the nation by Panamanian artist Roberto Lewis. Avenida B ends in a parking lot on the seafront. From here it is a 200m walk south along the seafront to the corner of Av A and C 1, past some immaculately restored nineteenth-century houses to the west and, overlooking the sea to the east, the ruined shell of the **Club de Clases y Tropas**, a recreation centre for Norega's National Guard destroyed during the US invasion, with some Noriegista slogans still visible beneath the heavy graffiti on the walls.

Plaza de Francia and around

A 100m walk south along C 1 brings you out onto the **Plaza de Francia**, enclosed on three sides by the seaward defensive walls and site of a monument dedicated to the thousands of workers who died during the disastrous French attempt to build the canal (see p.669). The centrepiece of the monument is an obelisk topped by a proud Gallic cockerel which is ringed by busts of some of the key figures involved, including Ferdinand de Lesseps. There is also a plaque dedicated to Carlos Finlay, the Cuban doctor whose ground-breaking research on the causes of malaria and yellow fever was so important to the later success of the US canal. The neoclassical **French Embassy** overlooks the square from the north, fronted by a statue of Mario Arosemena, a Panamanian politician who gave crucial support to the French venture. The elegant building to the east was formerly the Palace of Justice, badly damaged during the US invasion in 1989 and now home to the National Cultural Institute. In the colonial period the square was a military centre, and the vaults under the seaward walls served as the city's jails – built below sea-level, they would sometimes flood at high tide, drowning the unfortunate prisoners within. Known as Las Bovedas, some of the vaults have been restored: one houses a French restaurant (see p.691). From the square steps lead up to the **Paseo Las Bovedas**, also known as the Esteban Huertas Promenade, which runs some 400m along the top of the defensive wall, all the way around the plaza and back to the corner of C 1 and Av A. Partially shaded by bougainvillea and with panoramic views, this is a popular place for courting lovers.

Along Avenida A

Two blocks west along Av A from the corner with C 1 stands the ruined **Church and Convent of Santo Domingo**, completed in 1678 and famous for the **Arco Chato** (flat arch) over its main entrance. Only 10.6m high, the arch spans some 15m with no external support, and was reputedly cited as evidence of Panamá's seismic stability when the US Senate was debating where to build an interoceanic canal. In the chapel next door the absorbing **Museo de Arte Religioso Colonial** (Tues–Sat 9am–4.15pm; US$0.75) has a small collection of religious paintings, silverwork and sculpture from the colonial era. Four blocks west along Av A is the ruined shell of **La Compania**, a Jesuit church and university completed only eighteen years before the Society's expulsion from all Spanish America in 1767. The walls and ornate facade still stand, but the interior is overgrown, rubbish-strewn and heavily populated by cats.

A block further west on the corner with C 8 is the **Church of San José**, built in 1673 but since remodelled, exceptional only as home to the legendary baroque **Golden Altar**, one of the few treasures to survive Henry Morgan's sacking of Panamá Viejo in 1671 – it was apparently painted or covered in mud to disguise its true value. One block beyond San José, Av A emerges onto **Plaza Herrera**, a pleasant square lined with elegant nineteenth-century houses, some with cast iron balconies imported during the French canal construction. This was originally the Plaza de Triunfo, where bullfights were held until the mid-nineteenth century but was renamed in 1922 in honour of General Tomas Herrera, whose statue stands in its centre. Herrera was the military leader of a short-lived independence attempt in 1840 who went on to be elected president of Colombia but was assassinated before taking office in Bogotá in 1854. Just off Plaza Herrera to the west stands **The Tiger Hand Bastion**, a crumbling and indistinct pile of masonry that is the last remaining section of the city's defensive walls on the landward side. The walls came to symbolize the class divide between wealthy San Felipe residents and the poorer neighbourhood of Santa Ana, and were largely dismantled in the mid-nineteenth century.

Santa Ana

Shaded by trees, the small green **park** in the centre of **Santa Ana** – a busy transport hub – offers an island of tranquillity from the swirling traffic. A few blocks to the west,

under the shadow of Cerro Ancon, is the poor barrio of **El Chorillo**, which was devastated during the US invasion, leaving hundreds dead and thousands homeless. It has
since been rebuilt, but the concrete tenements that replaced the old wooden slum
housing are already rundown and it remains a dangerous neighbourhood even during
the day. Just beyond Parque Santa Ana on Av Central a right turn takes you down Calle
Sal si Puedes ("get out if you can"), a steep, narrow street crammed with market
stalls that runs two blocks down to the seafront and the covered **Mercado Central**,
the lively food market. Beside the market to the southeast is **Muelle Fiscal**, from
where the occasional boats to Darién and Colombia leave (see p.721). The area
between the market and Av B is known as the **Barrio Chino** (Chinatown), the historic
centre of Panamá City's large Chinese population, which began to arrive in the middle
of the nineteenth century to work on the railway. The Chinese community is much
more dispersed now, but the barrio retains a distinct, oriental feel: there are Chinese
supermarkets selling everything from dried shark fins to newspapers; restaurants
where it is difficult to order unless you speak Cantonese; and, at the north end of C
Juan Mendoza, an ornate gate that marks the official entrance to the barrio from Av
Balboa. Just outside the gate, overlooking the sea, is the new, superclean **Mercado
del Marisco**, where you can buy seafood or eat a freshly prepared ceviche at the
stalls. From here, Av Balboa runs 3.5km around the bay to the luxury high-rise
suburb of Paitilla.

From Parque Santa Ana north as far as Plaza Cinco de Mayo, **Avenida Central** is
pedestrianized, the liveliest and most popular shopping district in the city. Blasts of air
conditioning and loud music pour from the huge superstores that line the avenue selling cheap clothing, electronics and household goods as hawkers with megaphones
attempt to entice shoppers inside. Nowhere is the sheer energy of the city and the enormous cultural diversity of its population more evident: stop for a while on one of the
tree-shaded mosaic benches and you will see Hindus in saris, Kuna women in their traditional costumes (see p.717), bearded Muslims in robes and skullcaps, *interioranos* in
sombreros (see p.712), Chinese, Afro-Antillans (see opposite), Latinos, even the occasional group of off-duty US servicemen, all scrambling for bargains in the super-
charged atmosphere of this post-modern bazaar.

Calidonia, La Exposición, Bella Vista and El Cangrejo

Ten blocks down, the pedestrianized section of Av Central ends as it emerges onto
Plaza Cinco de Mayo and the maelstrom of traffic takes over again. In fact, this is two
squares rolled into one: the first has a small monument to the volunteer firemen killed
fighting an exploded gunpowder magazine in 1914 – the *bomberos* occupy a revered
position in a city that has so often been devastated by fire. Opposite the monument a
columned former railway station houses the splendid **Museo Antropologico Reina
Torres de Araúz** (Tues–Fri 9.30am–4.30pm, Sat 9am–3pm; US$0.50), which houses an
extensive collection of pre-Columbian artefacts including some beautiful gold pieces,
and provides a good introduction to Panamá's indigenous societies. Behind the museum is a large, open-air **handicrafts market**. The second square, Plaza Cinco de Mayo
proper, is a little further down, with a black, monolithic monument emblazoned with
the Torrijos slogan: "Ni limosnas, ni milliones, queremos justicia" (neither alms, nor
millions, we want justice).

Across the road, on the corner with Av Justo Arosemena, inside a small fenced garden stands a statue of **Mahatma Gandhi**, erected by the city's Hindu community and
often garlanded in flowers. A block down Av Justo Arosemena on the corner with C 24
an unmarked wooden former church houses the **Museo Afro-Antillano** (Tues–Sat
8.30am–4pm; US$1), dedicated to preserving the history and culture of Panamá's large

West Indian population. It is very small, but its exhibits – photographs, tools, furniture – give a good idea of the working and living conditions of black canal workers. There is also a small library and occasional events, including Afro-Antillano cookery courses and jazz festivals.

Beyond Plaza Cinco de Mayo, Av Central continues to the northeast, the city's main thoroughfare and still a busy shopping street as it runs through Calidonia and La Exposición. Two blocks away from Av Central on Av Cuba between C 29 and C 30, the **Museo de Ciencias Naturales** (Tues–Sat 9am–4pm, Sun 9am–1pm; US$1) offers a basic introduction to Panamá's geology and ecology, with many stuffed animals. Look out for the pickled fer-de-lance which killed the director of Panamá's old zoo in 1931. Four blocks further down Av Central, facing C 34, is the neo-Moorish **Church of Don Bosco**, built in the 1950s with open sides screened by iron grilles and a minaret-like tower. In the post office opposite, the **Museo Postal** (Mon–Fri 9am–4pm; free) has a small collection of old post and telegraph machinery, but no old stamps on display. In the same vein, a little further down on C 34 the **Casa Museo Banco Nacional** (Tues–Fri 8am–4pm, Sat 8am–noon; free) has a varied collection of nineteenth- and twentieth-century coins, banknotes and stamps as well as old banking paraphernalia. A couple more blocks down C 34 brings you out onto Av Balboa on the seafront, and two blocks to the left, set in a small park shaded by palm trees, is the glorious **Balboa Monument**. Erected in 1913 with Spanish help, Balboa stands atop a globe with a sword in one hand and a flag in the other, looking out in perpetual triumph on the southern ocean he "discovered".

THE AFRO-ANTILLANOS

Some five percent of Panamá's population are **Afro-Antillanos** – descendants of the black workers from across the English and French-speaking West Indies that began migrating to Panamá in the mid-nineteenth century to work on the railroad and canal constructions. West Indians, above all from Jamaica and Barbados, formed the vast majority of the labour force in both the French and the US canal construction efforts, living and working in appalling conditions – most of the 20,000 workers who died during the French attempt were West Indians and, despite the vast sanitary improvements, mortality among black workers was four times higher than among whites during the US construction. Despite the racial discrimination – lower wages, poorer conditions, strict segregation – they faced in the US Canal Zone, many West Indians stayed in Panamá City and Colón after the canal's completion, while others migrated to the banana plantations of Bocas del Toro. In Panamá as a whole they were widely considered second-class citizens or undesirable aliens. Populist politician Arnulfo Arias was an undisguised racist, and as president in 1940 pushed through a constitution that prohibited further immigration by blacks and denied the right to own property to those without an adequate knowledge of Panamanian history and the Spanish language. The inclusionary politics of the Torrijos regime eased discrimination: jobs in government and even business were made accessible to Afro-Antillanos and they became more widely accepted, but though today they are more socially integrated than the black communities of several other Central American republics, they remain among the most marginalized sectors of the population.

More than a century after their arrival in Panamá, the Afro-Antillanos maintain a vibrant and distinct **culture** whose influence is apparent in many aspects of contemporary Panamanian society. Many second- and third-generation Afro-Antillanos still speak English, or rather the melodic patois of the West Indies, and the street Spanish of Panamá City and Colón is peppered with Jamaican slang. The Protestant churches they brought with them from the West Indies continue to thrive; heavily spiced Caribbean dishes have permeated Panamanian cuisine; and their music, from jazz in the 1950s through to "reggaespañol" – the compelling combination of Spanish lyrics and hardcore Jamaican dancehall rhythms that has taken Latin America by storm in the 1990s – is popular across the country.

As it continues northeast, Av Central changes its name to Via España and passes through the comfortable residential neighbourhood of **Bella Vista**. On the corner with Av Manuel E. Batista, the twentieth-century neo-gothic wedding-cake **Del Carmen** church marks the beginning of **El Cangrejo**, the high-rise banking district and commercial heart of the city, centred on Via España between the church and Via Argentina and on C 50. Most of the classier hotels and restaurants are here, as well as upmarket stores and shopping centres selling the latest designer fashions and state-of-the-art electronics. This is also where much of the city's nightlife is concentrated, and it is reasonably safe to walk around at night.

Panamá Viejo

On the coast about 6km northeast of El Cangrejo stand the ruins of **PANAMÁ VIEJO**, the original colonial city founded by Pedrarias Davila in 1519 and abandoned in 1671. Although many of its buildings were dismantled to provide stones for the construction of San Felipe and in recent decades much of the site has been built over as the modern city has continued to spread eastward, a surprising numberof the original buildings still stand, testimony to the skill of the Spanish masons who built them and a sharp contrast to the skyscrapers of the modern city visible to the southwest. A walk among the ruins will give you a good impression of the former splendour of the first European city on the Pacific Ocean.

To **get to Panamá Viejo**, either take a taxi or catch any bus marked Panamá Viejo or Via Cincuentenario. The best place to start a visit is the **museum** (Mon–Sat 9am–4pm, Sun 9am–1pm; US$1), on Via Cincuentenario in the centre of the ruins, where a scale-model and audio-tape history gives a good idea of what the city must have looked like. You can also see pottery, ceramic plates and coins recovered during ongoing archeological excavations. The ruins are poorly marked, but a good map with detailed descriptions of each building in English or Spanish is on sale at the museum for US$2.50, and you can arrange a **guided tour** by calling ☎224 2155.

The site

The ruins are spread out either side of Via Cincuentenario, with many trees still scattered among them, remnants of the forest that engulfed the site after its abandonment (some buildings still have gnarled roots embedded in their walls). To the right as you come out of the museum is the former **Plaza Mayor**, overlooked by the three-storey square stone tower of the **cathedral**, built between 1619 and 1629 to replace an earlier wooden structure, and flanked by the square **cabildo** (town hall) to the right and the well-preserved bishop's house to the left. Behind the cathedral, through the grounds of the National Sport Institute, you can still see the foundations of the **casas reales** – the royal treasury, customs house, court and governor's residence that together formed the centre of royal power in Panamá Viejo, originally separated from the rest of the city by a moat and wooden palisade. Returning to the cathedral and turning right brings you to the **church and monastery of Santo Domingo**, the smallest religious structure but also the best preserved, with a tall buttressed tree growing inside. From here, Via Cincuentenario runs 400m north to the **Church of San José**, which survived the fire of 1571 and was the home of the famous golden altar which escaped Morgan's notice and is now in the church of the same name in San Felipe (see p.683). Another 200m brings you to the **King's Bridge**, the beginning of the Camino Real, the treasure route across the isthmus to Nombre de Dios (see p.709). You should be careful if walking alone in this area, though, as the ruins are surrounded by poor barrios and this is a long way from the tourist police who patrol the site.

The major ruins across the road from the cathedral are the **Church of La Compania de Jesus** (Jesuits) and the **Church of La Concepcion**, both of which had their respective monasteries, of which little now remains. Close by, on Via Cincuentenario, only one wall of the **Hospital de San Juan de Dios** still stands. As you walk east along Via Cincuentenario, after 100m you pass the remains of the **Monastery of San Francisco**, where the Franciscan monks were said to have been massacred by Morgan's men while tending to the wounded. Some 200m beyond are the crumbling remains of the **church and monastery of La Merced**, where Francisco Pizarro took communion before embarking on the conquest of Peru. La Merced was considered the most beautiful church in the city and survived the fire in 1571 – Morgan used it as its headquarters – but its ornate facade was dismantled and moved to San Felipe (where it can be seen today: see p.681), the cloisters are no more and the whole structure is sadly cut in two by the road.

The former Canal Zone

To the southwest of Calidonia and El Chorillo, Panamá City now encompasses the former Canal Zone town of **BALBOA**, administered by the US as de facto sovereign territory from 1903 to 1979. Panamanians who lived or worked here were subject to US law and many of the residents, known as Zonians, still maintain a distinct and somewhat exclusive transnational identity. The English writer Graham Greene described the Zone as "an island of prosperity in a sea of poverty", and though the difference has faded after twenty years of Panamanian jurisdiction (and the same is now more true of the modern luxury suburbs to the east), Balboa retains many of the characteristics of a US provincial town; clean and well-ordered in stark contrast to the chaotic vitality of the rest of the city. To the east, the Canal Administration Building looks down on Balboa from the slopes of Cerro Ancon, an enduring symbol of US power in the isthmus, while to the south is the largely derelict **Fort Amador**, a former US military base and barracks of the Panamanian Defence Force until the invasion. Beyond the fort a **causeway** stretches 6km out to sea between the bay and the canal approaches, linking the islands of Naos, Perico and Flamenco.

Ancon and Balboa

Along the border of the former Canal Zone runs Av de Los Martires, named in honour of the 21 Panamanians killed by the US military during the "flag riots" of 1964 (see p.688). Above it to the right rises the heavily forested **Cerro Ancon**, crowned by a huge Panamanian flag that is visible throughout the city. From the entrance on Av de Los Martires it is a steep twenty-minute walk to the summit, well worth it for the spectacular views of the city, the bay and the canal as far as Pedro Miguel locks, 10km away. There are toilets and a drinking fountain at the top, and often a contingent of tourist police – there have been muggings on the hill, so be wary, particularly if walking alone. The forest is surprisingly well-preserved, and deer, agouti and iguanas are frequently seen, as well as plenty of birds. From the summit you have to return the way you came.

Just off the entrance on Av de Los Martires is **Mi Pueblito** (Tues–Sun 10am–10pm; US$0.50), a replica of an early twentieth-century village in the interior, complete with church, telegraph office and barber's shop. It's far less tacky than it sounds, and worth visiting if you are not going to get to the real thing. Folkloric dances are performed on Friday evenings, and two more replica villages, one indigenous and one Afro-Antillean, are being built on a neighbouring site.

Some 200m east of the entrance to Cerro Ancon on Av de Los Martires is a turn-off onto Gorgas Road, which winds round the side of Cerro Ancon to the Canal Administration Building in Balboa Heights, about twenty minutes away on foot. Just off Gorgas road to the right, the **Museum of Contemporary Art** (Mon–Fri 9am–4pm, Sat 9am–noon; free) has a small but unexceptional collection of modern art by obscure national and international artists, housed in a former Masonic temple built in 1936. As you climb Gorgas Road you pass the **Gorgas Military Hospital**, named after the US military doctor William Gorgas who did so much to reduce the death toll from malaria and yellow fever among the canal construction workforce. A formidable stone construction, the hospital was recently handed over to Panamanian administration and its future is uncertain, though one former hospital building has housed the Palace of Justice since 1993. As it continues around Cerro Ancon, the road's name changes to Heights Road, lined with several luxury houses set amid well-manicured lawns, including, at **107 Heights Road**, the residence of the Panamá Canal Commission administrator.

Soon after, Gorgas road reappears to the right and winds down to the three-storey **Panamá Canal Commission Administration Building** (daily 7.15am–4.15pm; free), a classic example of US colonial architecture built during the canal construction and still home to the principal administration offices. Inside, four dramatic murals by US artist William Van Ingen depict the story of the canal construction under a domed ceiling supported by marble pillars, and there are busts of De Lesseps and Roosevelt. In front of the building, looking down over Balboa, stands a monument to the canal workers (a rock blasted from the Gaillard cut), and a broad stairway runs down to the **Goethals monument**, a white megalith with stepped fountains that represent the canal's different locks, erected in honour of George Goethals, Chief Engineer from 1907 to 1914 and first governor of the Canal Zone. Beside the monument is **Balboa High School**, whose ordinary appearance belies the dramatic events it has witnessed. It was here in 1964 that Zonians attacked students attempting to raise the Panamanian flag, triggering the **flag riots** that left 21 Panamanians dead, and during the 1989 invasion the school was used as a detention camp for Panamanian prisoners, some of whom were allegedly executed by US soldiers. From here, the palm-lined El Prado boulevard runs a few hundred metres down to **Stevens' Circle**, surrounded by stalls selling handicrafts from all over Panamá, including good Kuna molas (see p.717). This is Balboa proper, the main residential area of the former Canal Zone, its bilingual road signs, solid white buildings with red-tiled roofs and immaculate lawns still giving it a distinctively North American feel.

Fort Amador and the causeway

From the Balboa YMCA, Calle Amador runs towards the causeway through **Fort Amador**, a former US military base returned to Panamá in the seventies and made a barracks of the Panamanian Defence Forces, retaken during the 1989 invasion and handed back to Panamá again in 1996. Many of the former military buildings and homes were damaged during the invasion and some are abandoned and falling into disrepair while others, occupied by squatters, are draped with banners defying government plans to sell the site off for redevelopment. On the left as you head towards the causeway is the modest **Mausoleum of General Omar Torrijos**, flanked by four life-size statues of National Guardsmen and engraved with one of the revered general's most famous sayings: "No quiero entrar en la historia, quiero entrar en la Zona del Canal" (I don't want to enter the history [books], I want to enter the Canal Zone). In all it's about 25 minutes walk from Balboa to the beginning of the causeway, but SACA buses marked Amador will also take you there from the terminal on Plaza Cinco de Mayo.

From Amador, a 6km **causeway** (Calzada de Amador) (daily 24 hours; US$0.25) runs out in the Bay, linking the tiny islands of **Naos**, **Perico and Flamenco**. Built during the canal construction with spoil from the excavation as a breakwater to prevent silting of the canal entrance, the causeway is a popular weekend escape for the city's residents who come here to jog, swim, stroll or cycle – you can rent bicycles at the entrance; US$2.25/hour), and to enjoy the sea air and the view of the city on one side and the entrance to the canal on the other. In the early years of Panamá City the islands served as deep-water moorings for ships and after the causeway's construction they together formed Fort Grant, heavily fortified for canal defence. The causeway remained a restricted area until 1989, contributing to the conservation of the islands' varied ecology, and some of the military installations can still be seen, including rails that once carried fifteen-inch guns.

On **Naos**, 2km along the causeway, the **Smithsonian Marine Exhibition Centre** (Tues–Fri 1–5pm, Sat & Sun 10am–5pm; US$0.50) offers an excellent introduction to Panamá's marine ecology, including an aquarium where you can stroke octopus, starfish and sea cucumbers. The centre also organizes **guided tours** of the island's different ecological systems, which include mangrove, tropical dry forest and coral reefs (book by calling ☎227 4918, minimum ten people). If you've rented a bicycle, a ticket stub from here gets you a half-hour extension. There are a couple of small beaches on Naos which are popular for swimmers but, given the proximity of the city and the canal, they are not the cleanest. The second island, **Perico**, is so small as to be indistinguishable from the causeway, and the last, **Flamenco**, home to the National Maritime Service, is closed to the public.

Parque Natural Metropolitano

Just a couple of kilometres away from the city centre in an area of the former Canal Zone that reverted to Panamanian control in 1983, the 2.65-square-kilometre **Parque Natural Metropolitano** is an unspoilt tract of primary rainforest home to more than 200 species of birds as well as mammals such as titi monkeys, white-tailed deer, sloths and agoutis. You don't need a permit from INRENARE to visit the park, which is officially **open** from 6.30am to 5.30pm, though there is nothing to stop you coming earlier and, as elsewhere, the best time to see wildlife, particularly birds, is early in the morning. The **park office** (Mon–Sat 8am–4pm; ☎232 5552 or 232 5516) and main entrance are on Av Juan Pablo II, just off C Curundu not far from the Curundu domestic bus terminal – occasional SACA buses from Plaza Cinco de Mayo pass close by. There is a small exhibition centre and library here, and three-hour **guided tours** can be arranged (US$2 per person; book in advance), though you can easily walk the park's three short trails without a guide. The best of these is the 2km **La Cienaguita trail**, which leads to a viewing point 150m above sea-level with fantastic views across the forest to the city.

Around Panamá City: Isla Taboga

Twenty kilometres off the coast and about an hour away by boat, the tiny island of **Taboga** is one of the most popular weekend retreats for Panamá City residents, who come here to enjoy its clear waters, peaceful atmosphere and verdant beauty. Known as the "Island of Flowers" for the innumerable fragrant blooms that decorate its village and forested slopes, Taboga gets very busy on the weekends, particularly during the summer, but is usually quiet during the week and if you stay the night you will have the place largely to yourself.

The island was **settled** by the Spanish in 1524, and served as a deep-water port before such facilities were established on the mainland – it was from here that Francisco Pizarro set sail for the conquest of Peru. Frequent pirate raids led to the fortification of El Morro Island, opposite Taboga, which in the nineteenth century served as the headquarters of the Pacific Steam Navigation Company. In 1882 the French Canal Company built a sanatorium on Taboga for convalescing employees, among whom was the French post-impressionist painter **Paul Gauguin**, who came to Panamá hoping to buy land on Taboga and "live on fish and fruit". However, the canal construction work was too hard and the price of land too high for his meagre wages, so on recovery he took his quest for paradise west across the Pacific to Tahiti.

The island

Taboga's one **fishing village** is very picturesque, with scrupulously clean narrow streets that run between its whitewashed houses and holiday homes, and dozens of gardens filled with bougainvillea and hibiscus. Most visitors head straight for the **beach**, either right in front of the village or in front of the *Hotel Taboga*, to the right of the pier as you disembark, where the water is calmer and the view of Panamá City magnificent. You have to pay US$5 to get on to this one, but in return you get US$5 worth of tokens which you can spend on food, drinks or other services at the hotel.

Behind the village, steep forested slopes rise to the the 300m peak of **Cerro Vigia**, where a viewing platform on top of an old US military bunker offers spectacular 360-degree views. It's about an hour's steep climb through the forest to the mirador – follow the path some 100m up behind the church until you find a sign marked Sendero de los Tres Cruces, beyond which the trail is marked with posts numbered 1 to 8. The other side of the island is home to one of the biggest brown pelican breeding colonies in the world and together with the neighbouring island of Uraba forms a protected **wildlife refuge**.

Snorkelling and diving are also popular activities on Taboga as marine life is abundant, particularly around El Morro, the island opposite the village. The *Hotel Taboga* rents equipment, though for diving it is better to organize a trip with one of the dive companies in Panamá City.

Practicalities

A visit to Taboga is worth it for the **voyage** out alone. Launches leave from Muelle 18 in Balboa (2 daily at about 8.30am, returning at 4pm, more frequently on weekends; 1hr; US$7 return; call Argo tours on ☎228 4348 or Calypso Queen on ☎232 5736 to check schedule) and pass under the Bridge of the Americas and along the canal channel, passing several uninhabited islands before reaching Taboga.

There are two **places to stay** on the island: the modern, family oriented *Hotel Taboga* (☎250 2122 or 264 6096, fax 223 0116; ⑥) has comfortable rooms with a/c, TV and hot water. There's also a pool, tennis court, and snorkel and scuba equipment for rent. In the village the *Hotel Chu* (☎250 2035 or 263 6933; ④) is less expensive and more atmospheric, with well-ventilated, basic rooms and communal bathrooms in a brightly painted wooden structure on stilts on the seafront. At high tide the sea used to come right up under the hotel, but they have built a bar-disco there, *El Galeon*, which is convenient if you want to stay up late drinking rum and dancing, but rather noisy if you don't.

Both hotels have **restaurants**; the *Chu* serves reasonable Chinese food and good seafood on a broad wooden balcony overlooking the sea, while the *Taboga* offers more varied and more expensive international and Panamanian cuisine, and a full buffet on the weekends.

Eating

Panamá City's cosmopolitan nature is reflected in its **restaurants**: pretty much every cuisine in the world can be found here, from US fast food to Greek, Italian, Chinese, French and Indian. Most of the best options are concentrated in **Bella Vista** and **El Cangrejo**, but you're never far from a range of good and inexpensive places to eat. Excellent **fish** and seafood are widely available, and there are a couple of specialist vegetarian restaurants – a welcome change from the rest of Panamá.

Bon Profit, Via Argentina, a block up from Via España (☎263 9667). Cosy Catalan place with excellent service and refined Mediterranean cuisine from about US$10 a head. The lunch menu is good value at US$3.50, as is the low-calorie menu at US$2.50. Small, so worth reserving in the evenings. Mon–Sat noon–3pm & 6–10pm.

Las Bovedas, Plaza Francia (☎228 8068). Exquisite French cuisine from about US$20 a head, under the arched brick ceilings of one of the old colonial dungeons. Excellent service, live jazz on Fri and Sat. Mon–Sat 7–11pm.

Calcutta, Av Federico Boyd, Via España, on the ground floor of the Costa del Sol building. Authentic Indian curry and tandoori restaurant. Curries tend to be a little mild – to Panamanian taste – but they'll add spice if you ask. A bit pricey (about US$15 a head) and the lunch menu, at US$2.50, is pretty meagre. Mon–Sat 11am–10pm.

La Casa de las Costillitas, Via Argentina, two blocks up from Via España. The same menu as *La Cascada* (below) with less outrageous decor and a more central location. Tues–Sun noon–11pm.

La Cascada, Av Balboa, C 24. Enormous, surreal open-air restaurant "like an oasis, a dream, a mini-Disneyland in Panamá", according to its 16-page menu. Tables lit with multicoloured mushroom lights and shaded by avenues of fig trees are set around a waterfall that tumbles over artificial rocks to feed a moat filled with goldfish and floating model ducks. Wide choice of meat and seafood, mostly grilled or fried in breadcrumbs, with the emphasis on quantity rather than quality. Starting at US$6, most meals are enough to feed a family of four for a week. Doggy bags and copies of the menu available on request. Mon–Sat noon–11pm.

Ciber Cafe, Via Venetta, C 49B Oeste, a block up from Via España behind the *Hotel El Panamá*. Internet access for US$2.50/hour. Reasonable coffee, sodas and snacks. Mon–Fri 10am–10pm, Sat 10am–11pm.

Coca-Cola, C 12, Av Central, on Plaza Santa Ana. Self-proclaimed "oldest restaurant in Panamá" and something of an institution for the city's older residents, who gather to drink coffee, read the papers and discuss the news. Good, basic Panamanian meals for about US$3, particularly good for breakfast. Daily 7.30am–11.30pm.

Covadonga, C 29, Av Peru, next to hotel of same name. US-style diner with reasonably priced Panamanian and international food and full bar. Good for breakfast, especially the fruit salad at US$1.75. Daily 24 hours.

Jimmy's, corner of Via España and C Manuel M. Icaza. Busy 24-hour restaurant-cafeteria in the heart of El Cangrejo with a wide choice of Panamanian food from the self-service counter, grilled meat and fish from the outdoor barbecue, good sandwiches prepared to order and strong coffee. Good value, and popular with Panamanians and US servicemen alike.

Kwang Chow, Av B 13-80, just off Sal si Puedes. Excellent, moderately priced Chinese food and a largely Chinese clientele. Come here in the morning and ask for *desayuno chino* and you'll get the best dim sum this side of Shanghai. Daily 6.30am–9pm.

Manolo, C 49B Oeste, a block up from Via España. One of three restaurants so-named, this one offers a broad range of meats, fish and seafood as well as 12" pizzas for US$4. Daily 6am–1am.

Manolo II, Plaza 5 de Mayo. A tranquil haven from the bustle of Avenida Central, this Spanish-run place specializes in meats and seafood, including a delicious sopa de mariscos for US$3. Also sells the finest Havana cigars, though you can't smoke them here. Daily 7.30am–9.30pm.

Mireya, C 50 Este, a block away from the *Hotel Continental* on Via España. Inexpensive self-service vegetarian restaurant with a choice of about twelve different hot dishes and an excellent salad bar. Mon–Sat 6am–8pm.

Mi Salud, C 31, Av Mexico. Vegetarian health-food restaurant with filling meals for about US$2, very good fruit salads, juices and ice-cream. Also home-made bread and dietary supplements. Mon–Sat 7.15am–7pm.

Napoli, C 57, two blocks from Via España (☎263 8799). Large, usually busy upmarket Italian restaurant with reasonable pizza, excellent pasta and immaculate service. Tues–Sun 10am–midnight.

Pizzeria Athens, C 48E, C 50, behind the Delta garage. Very popular fast-food style restaurant with harsh fluorescent lighting and phones on the tables for ordering. Not the best pizza, but very good Greek dishes, including sublaki, gyros, roast aubergines (*berenjena*) and the inevitable Greek salad. About US$4–5 a head. Open daily except Wed 11am–11.30pm. Another branch on C 57, opposite *Ristorante Napoli*, is open the same hours, closed Tues.

Ricuras Colombianas, Via España, C 40. One of several popular self-service restaurants dishing up low-cost comida tipica on this block of Via España. Daily 6am–6.30pm.

Rincon Griego, Av Cuba, C 32. Busy self-service restaurant with good range of comidas tipicas for around US$2. The Greek salad (US$1.75) is the only evidence of the origin of the name. Daily 6am–7pm.

Siete Mares, C Guatemala, Via Argentina (☎264 3032). Expensive seafood restaurant popular with the business community. Excellent food, staid atmosphere, reservations recommended. Mon–Sat 11.30am–11pm.

Drinking and nightlife

Panamá City is very much a **24-hour city**, whose residents like nothing better than to cut loose and eat, drink and dance into the early hours. Most of the upmarket places are around **El Cangrejo**, and it's easy and relatively safe to walk between them at night. Many **bars** also act as **restaurants**, and there are several **discos**, playing a mixture of reggae, salsa, merengue and US and euro dance music. **Cover charges** tend to be high, but often include several (sometimes unlimited) free drinks. The free bi-monthly English-language *Panamá News* has entertainment **listings** including live music and theatre (see below).

At the other end of the market are the **cantinas** and bars around Av Central: hard-drinking dives where women are rarely seen. The wildest nightspots are out in the Afro-Antillan ghetto of Rio Abajo, but it is not a good idea to go there unless accompanied by locals.

Café El Aleph, Via Argentina, Via España. Stylish alternative arts café combining art and sculpture displays, live jazz music on Friday and Saturday (US$6 cover after 9pm), Internet access and good but expensive food and drink. Open daily 6pm–1am.

Balboa Yacht Club, beside the Canal just off Av Amador. Although it looks almost abandoned from the landward side, the club bar is lively and a good place to watch ships passing under the Bridge of the Americas, especially over sundowners during happy-hour (Sat–Thurs 5–7pm; Fri 5–9pm). This is the place to ask about work as a linehandler on private yachts transiting the Canal. There's also a restaurant serving decent but overpriced seafood. Daily 11am–midnight.

Beer House, Via España, Via Argentina. Appropriately named lively drinking dive with loud salsa and merengue and a young crowd. Daily noon–3am.

Boy Bar, Av Ricardo Alfaro, Tumba Muerto. Panamá City's biggest and most popular gay nightclub, with a large dancefloor, impressive lightshow and pumping dance music. Out in the suburbs and difficult to find, so take a taxi. US$5 cover. Fri–Sun 9pm–3am.

Coco Club bar, ground floor of the *Hotel el Panamá*. Classy and expensive even during the 5–8pm happy hour, but with excellent live salsa and merengue bands Thurs–Sat from 9pm. Sun–Wed 5pm–12.30am, Thurs & Fri 5pm–3am, Sat 8pm–3am.

Dreams, Via España, in front of *Hotel el Panamá*. Massive multi-level disco currently the place to be for the city's bright young things. US$5–10 cover, though women usually get in free. Daily 9pm–3am.

Josephines Gold, C 50. One of several upmarket but sleazy erotic dancing bars, which local men consider the highlight of the city's nightlife. US$20 entrance fee gets you free drinks all night. Daily 9pm–4am.

Mangos, C Uruguay, C 50. US-style bar and grill with good food and live rock music on the weekend, currently very fashionable. Daily 10am–1am.

La Maravilla, C 18, Av B. One of several raucous drinking dives on C 18, with pool tables upstairs. Daily 10am–2am.

El Pavo Real, C 51E, C 50. "English" pub with darts, pool tables and live music on Friday and Saturday nights; popular with expatriates and wealthy Panamanians. Good but expensive food, including the inevitable fish and chips served in newspaper. Happy hour Mon–Thurs 3–7pm. Daily noon–1am.

Sahara, C 50. Popular nightclub with live rock and reggae music from 11pm Tues–Sat. US$5 entrance sometimes charged on the weekend. Mon–Sat 5pm–6am.

Sunset Bar, top floor of the *Hotel Costa del Sol*, Via España, Av Federico Boyd. Classy rooftop bar/restaurant with live Panamanian music every evening. Expensive, but a good place to watch the sun set over the city during the 5–7pm happy hour. Daily 6.30am–1.30am.

Las Tinajas, Av 2 Sur (C 51E), Av Federico Boyd (☎269 3840). Restaurant and bar serving traditional Panamanian food. Folkloric dance shows on Tues and Thurs–Sat from 9pm. Reservations recommended; US$5 cover charge. Mon–Sat 11am–midnight.

Entertainment

Panamá City is not renowned for its love of high culture, but there are a couple of good **theatres** featuring national and international productions – check the *Panamá News* for listings. Teatro Balboa, Stephens Circle, Balboa (☎272 0372) features jazz, folkloric dancing and theatre sponsored by the National Cultural Institute, while the splendid Neoclassical Teatro Nacional, Av B, Plaza Bolívar (☎262 3582) also has ballet performances. **Cinema** is far more popular, and there are many places where you can see the latest Hollywood blockbusters, in English with subtitles. *La Prensa* lists current screenings. The Cine Universitario (☎264 2737) shows an eclectic range of films with the emphasis on the arty and obscure.

Panamanians of all social classes love to **gamble**, and as well as the ever-present lottery ticket sellers there are several (soon to be privatized) **casinos**, all located in the major hotels: try the *El Panamá*, *Granada* or *Soloy*. **Cockfighting**, a bloody spectacle feverishly popular throughout the country, can be seen at the *Club Gallistico* on the corner of Via España and Via Cincuentenario (Sat–Mon; ☎221 5652; US$1); and **horse racing** meetings are held three times a week at the Hippodrome Presidente Ramon, out in the eastern suburbs.

Moving on from Panamá City

Panamá City is the **transportation hub** of the country, with scores of domestic and international services converging on a variety of terminals. Other than for the express bus service to David and the international bus to San José, there is no need to **book** bus tickets in advance – just turn up shortly before you wish to travel and you should be able to get a ticket on the next bus.

Tours

There is a growing number of operators in Panamá City offering a range of guided **tours**, from city tours and canal cruises to trans-Darién treks and diving trips.

ANCON, the National Association for the Conservation of Nature, Via Argentina, El Cangrejo (☎264 8100, fax 264 1533). Organizes trips to its five field stations (*centros ambientales*) around the country – in Bocas del Toro; Punta Patiño and Caña in Darién (see p.712); Chagres National Park; and La Pintada, near Penonomé. The trips cost between US$42 and US$80 per person per day all inclusive. They must be booked months in advance, however, and can only be taken by groups of at least six. ANCON also has a small useful library with a wealth of information on Panamá's ecology.

Argo Tours, Balboa (☎228 4328). Regular partial and full canal cruises. They also run one of the ferries to Isla Taboga.

Aventuras Panamá (☎260 0044). Operate the "Chagres Challenge" – whitewater rafting in Chagres National Park – as well as fishing and diving excursions in the Pacific.

Ecotours Panamá, C Ricardo Arias, Via España (☎263 0767, fax 263 3089). The most experienced ecotourism operator in Panamá. They can organize tours to anywhere in the country, but are particularly good for birdwatching tours and expeditions to Darién. Also regular trips to Barro del Colorado (see p.701).

Iguana Tours, Av Porras, Parque Omar (☎226 8738, fax 226 4738). Fishing and diving excursions to Isla Iguana (see p.730) as well as the usual city and canal tours.

Imama Tours, C Ricardo Arias, Via España (☎223 0728, fax 223 0729). Responsible ecotourism operator specializing in trips to indigenous communities.

Panamá Paradise, C 1, Pasadena (☎269 9860). Tours of the canal area and diving trips.

Scuba Panamá, Av 6 Norte, C 62A (☎261 3841, fax 223 2027). Diving trips all over the country, equipment sale and rental, diving instruction.

Listings

Airlines Aeroflot, Unicentro Bellavista Av Justo Arosemena, C 41 (☎225 0587 or 225 0497); AeroMexico, C 58 Urb Marbella (☎264 8320); AeroPeru, Av Manuel M. Icaza, C 51 (☎269 5291); Air France, C Abel Bravo, C 59 (☎223 0204); American, C 50, Plaza New York (☎269 6022 or 269 7666); AVENSA, Edificio Grobman, C Mario M. Icaza (☎264 9906); AVIANCA, Edificio Grobman, C Manuel M. Icaza (☎223 5225 or 264 3120); British, Av Ricardo J. Alfaro, Av Juan Pablo II (☎236 8335); Canadian, C 58 Urb Marbella (☎264 8320); Continental, Edificio Galerias Balboa, Av Balboa (☎263 9177); COPA, Av Justo Arosemena, C 39 (☎227 2522 or 227 5000); Cubana, C 29, Av Justo Arosemena (☎227 2291 or 227 2122); Iberia, Av Balboa, C 45 (☎227 2322 or 227 3966); KLM, Av Samuel Lewis, C 53E (☎223 3747); LACSA, Av Justo Arosemena 31–44 (☎265 7814); LanChile, Via Cincuentenario, Av Sur (☎226 0133); Lloyd Aereo Boliviano, Edificio Bolivia, C 50 (☎264 1330 or 263 6771); Lufthansa, C Abel Bravo, C 50 (☎223 9208); United, C Abel Bravo, C 50 (☎269 8555 or 269 1549); Varig, Edificio Margarita, C 51 (☎264 7666 or 264 2266).

American Express Torre Banco Exterior, Av Balboa, Parque Urraca (Mon–Fri 8.30am–4pm; ☎263 5858).

Banks and exchange Branches of the Banco Nacional de Panamá (BNP) (Mon–Fri 8am–3pm, Sat 9am–noon) and Banco del Istmo (Mon–Fri 8am–3.30pm, Sat 9am–noon) across the city change travellers' cheques and allow cash withdrawals on credit cards – some have ATMs. Both have branches on Via España in the heart of El Cangrejo, where Citibank (Mon–Fri 8.30am–2pm, Sat 9am–noon) performs the same services. The closest to San Felipe is the *BNP* on the corner of Av Central and C 17 Este. Foreign currency is more difficult to change – foreign banks will generally change their own currency and there is one licensed exchange house: Panacambios (Mon–Fri 8am–4pm; ☎223 1800) Plaza Regency building, Via España opposite the *Hotel Continental*.

Bookstores Libreria Argosy, Via Argentina with Via España, has a wide collection in Spanish and English.

Car rental Avis, C 55, El Cangrejo (☎264 0722; airport ☎238 4056); Budget, Via España, C 46 (☎263 9190; airport ☎238 4069); Discount, Via Veneto (☎223 6111); Hertz, C 55, El Cangrejo (☎263 6511; airport ☎238 4081); National, C 50 (☎265 3333; airport 238 4144); Thrifty, Via España, C 46 (☎264 2613; airport ☎238 4955).

Embassies and consulates Belize, C 5 Colonia del Prado (☎266 8939); Canada, Edificio Banco Central Hispano, Av Samuel Lewis (☎264 9731); Colombia, Edificio Grobman, C Manuel M. Icaza

TRANSPORT FROM PANAMÁ CITY

DOMESTIC BUS SERVICES FROM PANAMÁ CITY

DESTINATION	FREQUENCY	DEPARTS FROM	DURATION	DISTANCE
Chitré	hourly	Curundu Terminal	4hr	251km
Colón	every 20min		2hr	76km
Colón (express)	every 20min		1hr 30min	76km
David	hourly	Av Balboa, opposite Mercado de Mariscos	7hr	438km
David (express)	2 daily		5hr	438km
Gamboa	8 daily	SACA terminal, Plaza Cinco de Mayo	45min	26km
Paso Canoas	11 daily	Av J Arosemena, C 33 Este	9hr	494km
Paso Canoas (express)	3 daily	Av J Arosemena, C 33 Este	7hr	494km
Penonomé	every 20min	Curundu Terminal	2hr 30min	150km
Santiago	every 30min	Curundu Terminal	4hr	250km
Las Tablas	every 2hr	Curundu Terminal	4hr 30min	283km
El Valle	every 35min	Curundu Terminal	2hr 30min	134km
Yaviza	3-4 daily (morning only)	Curundu Terminal	9-12hr	276km

INTERNATIONAL BUS SERVICE FROM PANAMÁ CITY

Ticabus, C 17, Av Central (☎262 6275), to **San José, Costa Rica**. One bus daily, 14-15hr.

DOMESTIC FLIGHTS FROM PANAMÁ CITY

DESTINATION	FREQUENCY	DURATION
Aeroperlas, Paitilla domestic airport (☎269 4555).		
Bocas del Toro	1 daily	1hr 40min
Colón	14 daily Mon–Fri	15min
David	2–3 daily	1hr
El Real	1 daily	50min
La Palma	1 daily	45min
Sambú	3 weekly	1hr 20min
Aviatur, Paitilla domestic airport (☎270 1750).		
El Real	3 weekly	50min
La Palma	3 weekly	45min
Sambú	1–2 weekly	1hr 20min

Aviatur (☎270 1750), Aerotaxi (☎264 8644) and ANSA (☎226 7891), all at Paitilla domestic airport

To Kuna Yala: 2–3 flights daily Mon–Fri to (from northwest to southeast, 30min–1hr 15min): Porvenir (also Sat and Sun), Río Sidra, Río Azucar, Corazon de Jesus, Río Tigre, Playa Chico, Tupile, Ailigandi, Achutupo, Mamitupo, Ogobsucun, Mansucum, Mulatupu, Tubuala, Caledonia and Puerto Obaldia.

Phone ☎238 4322 for **international flight** enquiries.

(☎264 9266 or 223 3535); Costa Rica, C G. Ortega, Via España (☎264 2937 or 264 2980); Cuba, Av Cuba, Av Ecuador (☎227 0349); El Salvador, Edificio Citibank, Via España (☎223 3020); Guatemala, Edificio Versailles, Av Federico Boyd (☎269 3475 or 269 3406); Honduras, Edificio Tapia, Av Justo Arosemena, C 31 (☎225 0882); Mexico, Edificio Bancomer, C 50, C 53 (☎263 5021); Netherlands, C Manuel M. Icaza 4 (☎264 7257); Nicaragua, C 50, Av Federico Boyd (☎223 0981); UK, Torre Swiss Bank, C 53E (☎269 0886); USA, Av Balboa, C 40 (☎227 1777).

Immigration office *Migración* is on the corner of Av Cuba and C 29 (Mon–Fri 8am–3pm). Come here to extend your visa or to get permission to leave the country if you have been in Panamá for over a month – for the latter you will also have to visit the office of *Paz y Salvo* in the Ministerio de Hacienda y Tesoro on Av Cuba with C 35 (Mon–Fri 8.30am–4pm). At both offices, it is best to arrive early and be prepared to queue.

Laundry Most upmarket hotels have a laundry service, and there are cheap, coin-operated lavamaticos all over the city, including Lavamatico La Economica, Av Central, C 35 (daily 7am–8pm); and Lavamatic, C 3, Av Central (Mon–Sat 8.30am–4.30pm).

Libraries The Smithsonian Tropical Research Institute, Av Roosevelt, Ancon (☎227 6022) and ANCON, the National Conservation Association (see p.694), both have extensive libraries.

Medical care There are doctors at Centro Medico Bella Vista, Av Peru, C 35 (☎227 4022) and Centro Medico Paitilla, Av Balboa, C 53 (☎263 6060). Hospitals include Hospital Santo Thomas, Av 5 Sur, C 34 E (☎227 4122). Farmacia Arroch, Via España, C 49E is a 24hr pharmacy.

Photography Fujifilm, C Manuel M. Icaza, Via España, is one of many places that sell and develop print and slide film. Plenty of camera equipment shops on Av 2 Norte, opposite the entrance to the *Hotel el Panamá*.

Police Emergencies (☎104); tourist police (☎226 4021 or 270 2467).

Post office The most central post office is on Av Central at C 34, opposite the Don Bosco Church (Mon–Fri 7am–6pm; Sat 7am–5pm).

Telephones Public phonebooths throughout the city take 5-10- and 25-cent coins. For international calls and to send and receive faxes, the Cable and Wireless/INTEL office (daily 7.30am–9.30pm, fax 263 7849) is on Av Manuel M. Icaza, a block down from Via España.

CHAPTER 35

THE CANAL AND COLÓN PROVINCE

R unning some 82km across the isthmus between the Atlantic and Pacific oceans, the **Panamá Canal**, one of the greatest engineering feats of all time, is the country's biggest visitor attraction – and, like most of the province, an easy day-trip from Panamá City. Quite apart from its sheer magnitude, the canal also possesses an unexpected, rugged **beauty**. Though the corridor that surrounds this vital thoroughfare of world trade is home to almost two-thirds of Panamá's population, for much of its length the canal cleaves a narrow path through pristine **rainforest**, large tracts of which are protected within **Parque Nacional Soberania** and **Parque Nacional Chagres** and on **Barro Colorado Island**. These are among the most accessible tropical rainforest preserves in Latin America, all of them supporting an exceptional biodiversity. Soberania and Chagres also offer the opportunity to walk along the remnants of the **Camino de las Cruces** and the **Camino Real** – paved mule trains carved across the forested spine of the isthmus in colonial times, providing a convenient route by which the treasures that the Spanish accumulated could be transported from Panamá City to the Atlantic.

From 1903 to 1977 the strip of land that extends for five miles on either side of the canal was de facto US territory, known as the **Canal Zone**. Though the US presence is now confined to a few military bases, the well-ordered society they established remains in delicious contrast to the wilful tropical disorder and vibrant **Caribbean culture** of Colón and the surrounding coast, inhabited by the descendants of workers brought to build the waterway. At the canal's Atlantic entrance, **Colón** is an infamously poor and dangerous, yet strangely compelling, city, steeped in history. The Caribbean coast of the province of the same name offers a perfect antidote to its sometimes depressing squalor. To the west, along the **Costa Abajo**, the formidable ruins of the colonial **Fort San Lorenzo** still stand guard over the mouth of the Río Chagres amid pristine tropical rainforest; while to the northeast stretches the **Costa Arriba**, a region of deserted beaches, pristine coral reefs and laid-back fishing villages, much of which is protected by the **Parque Nacional Portobelo**, set around the ruins of the colonial ports of **Portobelo** and **Nombre de Dios**.

The canal

Although Panamanians are keen to insist that their country is "much more than just a canal", the truth of the matter is that the **Panamá Canal** remains the country's defining characteristic, the basis of its economy and the key to understanding its history and

For an explanation of **accommodation price codes**, see p.664.

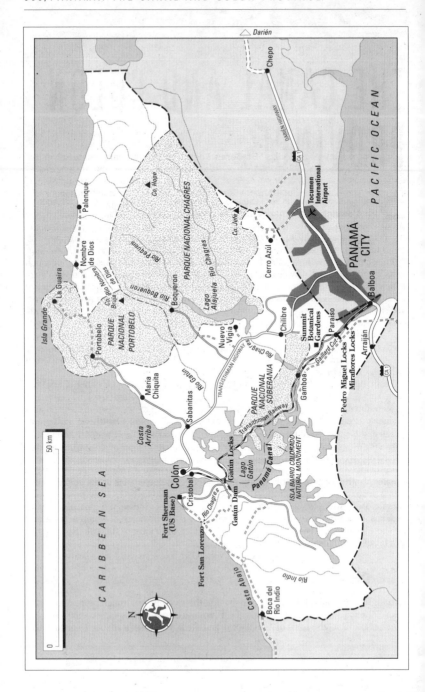

uniquely distorted society. Were it not for the US government's determination to build it, Panamá might never have come into existence as an independent republic, yet it is also at the root of the country's economic dependency and deeply resented US imperialist intervention. The struggle to establish **control** of the canal has been central to the emergence of a Panamanian identity, and though after more than ninety years it should finally be handed over to Panamanian jurisdiction at midnight on December 31, 1999, its future remains the most controversial issue in Panamanian politics.

The canal's **configuration** is such that the Pacific entrance is 43.2km east of the Atlantic entrance. From the Bahía de Panamá on the Pacific side, it passes under the broad sweep of the Bridge of the Americas and alongside the port of Balboa, running at sea-level some 6km inland to the **Miraflores Locks**, which raise ships some 16.5m to Lago de Miraflores. Some 2km further on, ships are raised another 10m to the canal's maximum elevation of 26.5m above sea level by the **Pedro Miguel Locks**, beyond which they enter the **Gaillard Cut** (formerly known as Culebra but renamed in honour of Colonel William Gaillard, the US engineer who was responsible for its excavation). Described by the English Lord Bryce as "the greatest liberty ever taken with nature", Culebra was the deepest and most difficult section of the canal construction, a 13.6km cut through the rock and shifting shale of the continental divide. An enormous amount of excavation was required, and the work was plagued by devastating landslides.

After the confinement of the Gaillard Cut, the canal channel continues for 37.6km across the broad expanse of **Lago Gatún**, the largest artificial lake in the world when it was formed in 1913 by the damming of the Río Chagres. Covering 420 square kilometres, the lake is placid and stunningly beautiful; until you see an ocean-going ship appear from behind one of the densely forested headlands, it is difficult to believe that it forms part of one of the busiest waterways in the world. At the lake's far end ships are brought back down to sea-level in three stages by the **Gatún Locks**, easily visited from Colón, after which they run 3km through a narrow cut into the calm Atlantic waters of Bahía Limón.

Exploring the canal

By far the best way to experience the canal is by **boat or ship** – passing through the narrow confines of the Gaillard Cut or weaving between the forested islands of Lago Gatún is the only way to truly appreciate its awesome scale and beauty. The easiest way is to take an **organized tour** through a Panamá City tour agency (see p.694). A half-day, partial transit of the canal, through Miraflores and Pedro Miguel Locks and into the Gaillard Cut, costs around US$50, while a full-day complete transit, continuing into Lago Gatún and down through Gatún Locks, costs twice that.

The other way is to get taken on as a **linehandler** on one of the private yachts that transit the canal – each yacht must take four linehandlers, who need no experience and are usually paid US$20–30 a day for the one- or two-day trip. The best way to find work is to visit the yacht clubs at Balboa or Christobal and talk with yacht owners; there's a noticeboard at Balboa where you can offer your services, but direct contact is better. You may have to wait several days, though, and be aware that more yachts transit from the Atlantic to the Pacific than vice-versa.

Much of the canal can also be explored from **land**. The transisthmian railway, which runs alongside the canal, has not carried passengers since being damaged during the US invasion, but a road served regularly by SACA buses from the Panamá City terminal on Plaza Cinco de Mayo runs 26km along the side of the canal, past the Miraflores and Pedro Miguel Locks, to the town of Gamboa on Lago Gatún, passing the entrance to Parque Nacional Soberania. This journey is described below. The Gatún Locks, on the Atlantic side, can also be visited via Colón.

Even experienced divers, jaded with the undersea wonders of the Caribbean and Pacific, should make an effort to **dive** in the Panamá Canal. Huge amounts of machinery and entire villages were submerged by the rising waters of Lago Gatún, and now make an unusual underwater attraction for scuba divers. Trips can be arranged through several of Panamá City's dive companies, including Scuba Panamá and Panamá Paradise (see p.694).

The road to Gamboa

The road to Gamboa leaves Panamá City to the north, past Albrook airforce base, which reverted to Panamá in 1997, and Fort Clayton, still US-occupied. Opposite Clayton, 9km from Panamá City, a side road leads to **Miraflores Locks**, a short walk from the road. Miraflores Locks raise or lower ships the 16.5m between sea-level and the Lago Miraflores in two stages, each time using fifty million gallons of fresh water which flows through 5m-diameter tunnels to fill each lock chamber in just ten minutes. Because of the extreme tidal variations in the Pacific, the first lock gates at Miraflores are the biggest in the whole system, each weighing a colossal 700 tons. The gates open in just two minutes, and ships are guided through by electric locomotives known as mules, taking thirty minutes. The **visitor centre** at Miraflores (daily 8am–5pm; free) has a scale model of the canal, a slide show and a viewing platform with a guided commentary in English and Spanish. The **best times** to see ships passing through are betwen 9 and 10.30am, when they come up from the Pacific side, and after 3pm, when they descend from the Atlantic side.

Some 1.5km further up the road, the **Pedro Miguel Locks** raise ships to the level of Lago Gatún. There are no special facilities, but you can watch ships here too. After Pedro Miguel Locks, ships enter the Gaillard Cut, which cannot be seen from land. Instead, the road continues 1km to the small canal town of Paraiso, a little way beyond which on the left is the **French Cemetery**, one of the few remaining traces of the doomed French attempt. There's not much to see other than the graves where a generation of France's finest engineers lie buried, but the place has the solemn atmosphere of a war cemetery. The road then climbs some 5km through dense rainforest to the **Parque Nacional Soberania office** (daily 8am–4pm; ☎276 6370). If you want to walk any of the trails in the park (see below) you'll need a permit fom here; they charge US$3 for admission, and can provide guides for larger groups if arranged in advance. You can also get a permit from the INRENARE office in Panamá City (see p.676).

A little further up on the crest of the continental divide are the **Summit Botanical Gardens and Zoo** (Mon–Fri 8am–4pm, Sat & Sun 8am–6pm; US$2). The gardens were established by the US in 1923 to experiment with the introduction of exotic species, particularly palms, and more than fifteen thousand different plant species are spread out in their ample grounds. Handed over to Panamá in 1979 they are now a popular weekend destination for families from the capital, most of whom come for the zoo. Examples of most of Panamá's large mammals are imprisoned here in the name of environmental education, including pumas, jaguars, several species of monkey and an ocelot. Most have wild relatives in the surrounding forest, but your chances of seeing them there are slim. There is also a captive breeding programme for the Harpy Eagle, Panamá's highly endangered national symbol.

From the summit, the road continues 9km to **GAMBOA**, where the canal channel emerges from the Gaillard Cut and follows the flooded bed of the Chagres into **Lago Gatún**. Gamboa is the headquarters of the Canal Dredging Division, Gamboa is a typical Canal Zone town. There's a small marina where you can rent boats to take you out onto the lake, or back up the Chagres to the Las Cruces trail (see below).

Parque Nacional Soberania

Around Gamboa, the rainforest-covered watershed that is so vital for the canal's continued operation is protected by the 220-square-kilometre **Parque Nacional Soberania**, formerly the Canal Zone Forest Preserve. Just half an hour from Panamá

City by road, Soberania is the most easily accessible national park in Panamá. There are three good **trails** that you can walk, all of which pass over rugged terrain covered by pristine rainforest, with good chances of seeing wildlife: monkeys, innumerable birds, even (if you're very lucky) large mammals such as deer or tapir. You'll need a **permit** from the park office (see above) or from the INRENARE office in Panamá City (see p.676).

The shortest and best marked trail is the **Sendero El Charco**, which begins a few kilometres beyond the Summit Botanical Gardens on the road to Gamboa, stretches for about 4km, and takes about an hour. The second is the old **Pipeline Road**, which begins outside Gamboa and which holds the world record for the highest number of bird species identified in a twenty-four hour period, set by the Audubon Society in 1985. The trail stretches for 24km and ends on the shores of Lago Gatún, and so is too long to walk in a day.

The third trail is a remnant of the **Camino de las Cruces**, the colonial mule trail from Panamá City to the now abandoned village of Venta de las Cruces, where cargo was transferred to boats and taken down the Río Chagres to the Atlantic. The trailhead is marked by an old cannon near the park office along the Gaillard highway, which forks right off the Gamboa Road and cuts across to the village of Chilibre on the Transisthmian Highway from Panamá City to Colón. It is still partially paved and runs about 10km through pristine rainforest to the banks of the Río Chagres, so you can either walk some distance down it and retrace your steps, or rent a boat in Gamboa to take you up the Chagres to Venta de las Cruces and walk back to the highway, which should take about six hours.

Isla Barro Colorado

As the waters of Lago Gatún began to rise after the damming of the Chagres, much of the wildlife in the surrounding forest was forced to take refuge on points of high ground that later became islands. One of these, **Barro Colorado**, is one of the most intensively studied areas of tropical rainforest in the world, administered by the **Smithsonian Tropical Research Institute**. Though the primary aims of the reserve are conservation and investigation, you can visit by contacting the Smithsonian in Ancon (☎227 6022, ext. 2271). If possible call well in advance, as visitor numbers are strictly limited and the waiting list is very long, though there are sometimes cancellations. The eight hour trip costs US$28, which includes lunch, and is worth it for the journey alone, a breathtaking cruise across the placid waters of the lake. **Tours** of the island are conducted in English or Spanish by extremely knowledgeable guides, and provide an excellent introduction to tropical rainforest ecology. The island teems with wildlife – myriad species of bird, monkeys, even tapirs – but as groups arrive after 9am and are a bit too large and noisy (up to fifteen people), you shouldn't expect to see much. If you can't get on a Smithsonian trip, *Ecotours* in Panamá City (see p.694) offer a similar tour to a peninsula that is also part of the Natural Monument. It's a lot more expensive (US$85) but the smaller groups make wildlife sightings more likely.

The Transisthmian Highway and Parque Nacional Chagres

From Panamá City the **Transisthmian Highway** – the *transistmica* – passes through the city's northern suburbs, over the continental divide and across the Río Chagres towards Colón. To the east of the transistmica as it crosses the Chagres is **Lago Alajuela**, an artificial lake formed after the completion of the Madden Dam in 1934 which provides forty percent of the water needed for the operation of the canal as well as all Panamá City's drinking water. The watershed of the lake is protected by the **Parque Nacional Chagres**, 1290 square kilometres of mountainous rainforest comprising four different life zones that are home to over three hundred species of bird as well as several Emberá (see p.712) communities displaced by the flooding of Lago Bayano further east. It is relatively easy to visit the park as a day trip from the capital: ask the bus driver to let you off 29km from Panamá City at the turning for the lakeside village of **Nuevo Vigía** and either walk the few kilometres to the village or wait for one of the irregular local buses. At Nuevo Vigía you can rent a canoe for about US$25 plus gas to take you across the lake and up either the Río Pequeni or Río Chagres into the park. The Emberá communities of **San Juan de Pequeni** and **Parrara Puru** (at the mouth of the Chagres) both accept visitors, and are keen to sell handicrafts (wood carvings and the like) which they produce to supplement the subsistence hunting and agroforestry which are the only other economic activities they are allowed to practise in the park.

When water levels permit you can also visit the park by **whitewater rafting** down the Río Chagres to the lake. It's an exciting one-day trip from Panamá City through level II and III rapids promoted as the "Chagres Challenge"; the primary operator is *Aventuras Panamá* (see p.694), though most Panamá City tour agencies will be able to book it.

It is still possible to walk along the remains of the **Camino Real** through the park to Portobelo (4 days) or Nombre de Dios (2–3 days), though this is only recommended if you have plenty of tropical wilderness experience, and you should inform INRENARE in Panamá City beforehand. The trailhead is at the village of **Boqueron**, 12km off the transistmica from a turn-off just beyond the one to Nuevo Vigía; you may be able to find a guide in the village to take you but don't count on it. You'll need a good map, a compass, a machete and all the food and equipment you may need for several days alone in the rainforest.

Colón and around

In all the world there is not, perhaps, now concentrated in a single spot so much swindling and villainy, so much foul disease, such a hideous dung-heap of moral and physical abomination as in the scene of this far-fetched undertaking of nineteenth-century engineering.
James Anthony Froude, British journalist, 1886

In fact, Froude never visited **COLÓN**, claiming that his curiosity was less strong than his disgust, but his opinion of the city during the French canal construction was widely shared by his contemporaries and were he to visit the city today he would find little to change his mind. Situated at the Atlantic entrance to the canal, with a population approaching 150,000, Panama's second city represents the dark side of the Caribbean that never makes it into the holiday brochures, and to most Panamanians its name is a by-word for poverty, violence and urban decay. To a certain extent, this is fair enough – much of the city is a rundown slum, the streets strewn with rubbish and rife with violent crime. But despite decades of terminal decline, Colón retains the decadent charm of a steamy Caribbean port where pretty much anything goes, its former glory still evident in its many monuments and crumbling turn of the century architecture. Moreover, if you can get past the initial hostility and suspicion, the people of Colón, mostly descendants of West Indians who came here to build the canal, are as warm and friendly as anywhere in the country, and enjoy a lively street culture that helps offset the desperate poverty that most of them face. Most visitors to Colón come here solely to shop at the **Colón Free Zone**, a walled enclave where goods from all over the world can be bought at very low prices – the starkest possible contrast to the rest of the city, which they avoid assiduously.

> ### WARNING
>
> Though exaggerated, Colón's reputation throughout the rest of the country for **violent crime** is not undeserved, and if you come here you should exercise extreme caution – mugging, even on the main streets in broad daylight, is common. Don't carry anything you can't afford to lose, try and stay in sight of the police on the main streets, and consider renting a taxi to take you around, both as a guide and for protection. They charge about US$6 an hour.

Southwest of Colón, a road runs along the Costa Abajo to Gatún Locks, where ships are raised and lowered between sea level and Lago Gatún, and on to San Lorenzo, a formidable colonial fortress overlooking the mouth of the Río Chagres.

Some history

Founded in 1852 on filled-in mangrove swamps as the Caribbean terminal of the transisthmian railway, Colón was originally named Aspinwall after one of the railway's owners. The Colombian authorities' insistence that it be called Colón, after Christopher Columbus, led to a long-running dispute that only ended because letters from the US addressed to Aspinwall never reached their destination. The railway brought many immigrants and a degree of prosperity to the town, and though it slipped into decline in 1869 when the completion of the transcontinental railway in the US reduced traffic across the isthmus, its fortunes revived with the initiation of the French canal construction in 1879. The French founded the neighbouring port enclave of Cristobal, and vast quantities of men and material flowed through Colón, but it remained a poverty- and disease-ridden slum town famed for its depravity. Burned to the ground during an 1885 uprising led by **Pedro Prestan**, a Haitian later hanged in front of huge crowds on **Front Street**, the city was rebuilt by the French and prospered again during the US canal construction effort. Colón's heyday came in the 1950s, when it was among the most fashionable cruise destinations in the Caribbean, but despite its role as Panamá's main port and the success of the Free Zone (founded in 1949), the city slipped into gradual decline and the cruise ships stopped coming. Although the port and Free Zone continue to thrive, little of the money they generate stays in Colón, and in the face of urban poverty as extreme as any in Latin America and unemployment levels approaching fifty percent, it is little surprise that many have turned to **crime**, particularly drug trafficking, as a way to survive. Ambitious plans are underway to revive Colón as a cruise destination by reconstructing the historic heart of the city, and the authorities are considering extending the Free Zone to encompass the entire city, but for the moment it remains desperately poor and rundown.

Arrival and information

The **bus terminal** is on the corner of Av Bolívar and C 13, two blocks away from Front Street. Buses arrive from and leave to Panamá City about three times an hour between 4am and 10pm; to and from Portobelo twice an hour from 5am to 8pm. If you arrive by **ship** from Kuna Yala you'll come in at Coco Solo port, a US$3 taxi ride from the city centre. **Yachts** coming through the canal dock outside the Yacht club in Cristobal. France's Field, Colón's **airport**, is a short taxi ride outside the city: Aeroperlas has fourteen **flights** a day between Panamá City and Colón, used mainly by business people visiting the Free Zone, but you'd have to be in a real hurry to want fly here, given the short distance between the two cities by land.

There is an **IPAT** office in Colón (Mon–Fri 8am–4pm; ☎441 9644), on Av Balboa with C 9 close to the entrance to Cristobal, but they don't have much information and will be very surprised to see you. The **post office** (Mon–Fri 7am–6pm, Sat 7am–6pm) and a branch of the **Banco Nacional** are just around the corner on C 9; there are several more banks in the Free Zone.

Accommodation

There's a wide choice of **places to stay** in Colón, catering mostly to business people, and most of them would be seen as good value in any other city. If you are going to stay overnight, it's worth splashing out on the more expensive hotels, which have armed security guards and restaurants so you won't have to go out at night.

Pension Acropolis, Av Guerrero, C 11 (no phone). Basic, with communal bathrooms; the best budget option in a moderately safe part of town. ②.

Hotel Garcia, C 4, Av Central (☎441 0860). In front of the mosque one block from Av Central, a bad area at night. Clean, well-ventilated rooms with TV, a/c costs extra. ③.

Hotel Internacional, Av Bolívar, C 11 (☎445 2930 or 441 5457). Secure, with clean, spacious rooms with a/c, TV and hot water. Good restaurant and a rooftop bar. ④.

New Washington Hotel, Av Frente, C 2 (☎441 8120). The best place in town. Historic building recently refurbished in a very elegant French style. Comfortable rooms with hot water, a/c and TV; those at the front have balconies overlooking the sea. Very secure with bar, restaurant and casino. ⑥.

Hotel Sotelo, Av Guerrero, C 11 (☎441 7703). Small and dark, with clean rooms with TV and a/c; also bar, restaurant and casino. ④.

The City

From the bus terminal, a left turn takes you north up dilapidated **Front Street** (Av Frente), once the city's main commercial road, which runs along the waterfront of Bahiá Limón. Most of the shops are closed and the elegant two- and three-storey buildings with pillared overhanging balconies are crumbling, their faded pastel paintwork covered in graffiti. Opposite the corner with C 8 is the abandoned **railway station**, built in 1909; beyond here the view of the bay is obscured by the shantytown settlement of La Playita, which is home to two hundred or so families of *precaristas*, as illegal urban squatters are known. How the plans to restore Front Street and turn it into a tourist centre will affect these families is uncertain.

Just off Front Street on C 6, the **Colón Boxing Arena** was built in the 1970s to nurture the mass of local talent. The city has produced numerous world champions, the most famous of whom was "Panama Al" Brown, the first Latin American world champion in the 1930s and one of the greatest boxers of all time. Four blocks down C 8 is the **cathedral**, which was built between 1929 and 1934 with high, neo-gothic arches. Back on Front Street, it's six blocks north to **The New Washington Hotel**, built around 1850 to house railway engineers and rebuilt several times since. Famous guests have included Bob Hope, who entertained troops here during World War II, exiled Argentinian dictator Juan Perón, former British prime minister David Lloyd George and US president George Taft. Inside a palm-filled walled enclosure, its recently refurbished neo-colonial elegance, complete with chandeliers and ornate double staircase, is a reminder of Colón's former splendour as well as a gesture of confidence in the city's future. The seafront verandah is a good place to relax with a drink and watch the ships in the bay.

To the left of the hotel as you look towards the city is a small stone **Episcopal Church** that was the first Protestant church in Colombia when it was built, for West Indian railway workers, in 1865. Seven blocks east along the seafront, a statue of Christ the Redeemer, arms outstretched, faces down **Av Central**, which is lined with monuments, including, on the intersection with C 2, a statue of Columbus with an indigenous girl, donated to Panamá by Empress Eugenie of France in 1866.

Behind the bus terminal is the port enclave of **Cristobal**, formerly part of the Canal Zone and still one of Latin America's busiest ports, handling more than two million tons of cargo a year. Apart from the Yacht Club (see below) there's not much of interest here and most of the port is off-limits to visitors anyway.

The Colón Free Zone

The southeast corner of Colón is occupied by the **Free Zone**, a walled city-within-a-city covering more than a square kilometre. This is the second biggest duty free zone in the world after Hong Kong, with an annual turnover of more than US$10 billion. All manner of consumer goods are imported here and then re-exported across Latin America, and it is visited by thousands of businesspeople every week. The Free Zone is basically a forbidden city for Colón residents unless they work there, but you are allowed in if you present your passport at the gate. Inside, the contrast with the rest of Colón could not be greater – immaculate superstores line the Zone's clean, well-paved streets and the only smell is of money and expensive perfume. Most of the trade is in bulk orders, but you can buy individual items at low prices if you bargain hard or enlist one of the professional hagglers who tout their services at the entrance (they work for commission). Officially, what you buy must be held in bond and given to you at the airport as you leave the country.

Eating and drinking

Though there are several cheap **restaurants** in Colón serving the delicious local cuisine – usually seafood cooked to spicy Caribbean recipes – most are in dangerous parts of the city. In the evening, you are better off eating in or near your hotel.

Restaurante Hotel Internacional, on the ground floor of the hotel. Standard Panamanian and international food from about US$5, particularly good for breakfast. Daily, 8am–midnight. The rooftop **bar** (Mon–Sat 6pm–midnight), open to hotel guests only, is a good place to drink a sundowner and watch the ships lit up in the harbour at night while the city rages below.

Café Nacional, C 11 with Guerrero. Popular, with good, inexpensive food and a convenient location, which is fairly safe during the day. Mon–Sat 7am–11pm.

Cristobal Yacht Club, on the seafront inside the Cristobal port enclosure. The open air restaurant, serving decent seafood, is expensive, but the atmospheric bar, shaped like a ship's prow, is a good place to hang out if you're looking for work as a linehandler on a yacht transiting the canal or heading out into the Caribbean. Daily 10am–2pm.

Gatún Locks

From Colón, a road runs 10km southwest to **Gatún Locks**, where ships are raised or lowered from Lago Gatún to sea-level on the Atlantic side of the canal. Almost 2km long, Gatún Locks raise or lower ships the 26.5m between the lake and sea-level in three stages, and are among the most monumental features of the canal's engineering. The **visitors' centre** (daily 8am–4pm) has a scale-model of the canal, some photos of the locks during construction (their enormous size is most evident when viewed empty) and a viewing platform that offers the best vantage point to watch ships pass through (9–11am and after 3.30pm are the busiest times). There are also good views of the lake surrounded by dark, forest-covered mountains and of the vast **Gatún Dam**. More than 2km long and 800m wide at its base, this was the largest earthen dam in the world when it was built in 1906 to dam the Río Chagres to form the lake.

Occasional **buses** from the bus terminal in Colón can drop you at the locks; the road then goes on to cross the canal via a swing bridge which is only passable when there are no ships passing through (each transit takes about an hour). It then forks, the left branch crossing the dam and following the west bank of the Chagres to the sea, then staggering along the **Costa Abajo** as far as the village of Boca del Río Indio. Costa Abajo is virtually undeveloped, with just a few fishing villages between the forest and the sea, and beyond Boca del Río Indio, the coast is scarcely inhabited, stretching for 200km along the Golfo de Mosquitos to Bocas del Toro. Taking the right fork, not on the bus route, takes you through Fort Sherman to **Fort San Lorenzo**, at the mouth of the Río Chagres.

Fort San Lorenzo

With a spectacular setting on a promontory above the Caribbean overlooking the mouth of the Río Chagres, **Fort San Lorenzo** is the most impressive Spanish fortification still standing in Panamá. Until the construction of the railway, the Chagres was the main cargo route across the isthmus to Panamá City and thus of enormous strategic importance to Spain. The first fortifications to protect the entrance to the river were built here in 1595, but the fort was taken by Francis Drake in 1596 and, though heavily reinforced, fell again to Henry Morgan's pirates in December 1670. Morgan then proceeded up the Chagres and across the isthmus to sack Panamá City (see p.673). Further fortifications were insufficient to prevent English Admiral Edward Vernon from taking the fort again in 1740; and those that remain today, built over seven years from 1760, were never seriously tested, as by the time they were completed the era of the freebooters was coming to an end. Today the fort is well-preserved: a moat surrounds its stout stone walls and great cannons look out from the embrasures. It's an isolated place, surrounded by pristine rainforest, and from it the view of the mouth of the Chagres and of the Costa Abajo is little changed since the days of Drake and Morgan.

Fort San Lorenzo can only be reached by private car or **taxi** – you can rent one in Colón for US$6 an hour. It's a drive of about forty minutes or so from Gatún Locks, and you have to stop and register with the US military police at the entrance to Fort Sherman (access daily 7am–5pm; bring your passport). Fort Sherman is a jungle training base, so take the MPs seriously when they tell you not to stray from the road – you could walk into an ambush.

Costa Arriba

The **Costa Arriba**, stretching northeast of Colón, features beautiful beaches fringed by dense tropical forest, the historic towns of **Portobelo** and **Nombre de Dios**, and excellent diving and snorkelling in the **Parque Nacional Portobelo**.

Portobelo

Named by Christopher Columbus in 1502 after the magnificent bay on which it stands, **PORTOBELO** – "beautiful harbour" – was for centuries the most important Spanish port on the Atlantic coast of the New World, the northern terminus of the Camino Real. Today, it is a sleepy little town that sits amid the remains of the formidable fortifications built to defend the treasure fleets from pirate attack, and makes a good base from which to explore the rugged coastline and underwater treasures of **Parque Nacional Portobelo**. And on October 21 each year Portobelo explodes into life as thousands of pilgrims descend on it from all over Panamá to pay homage to the miraculous **Black Christ** that is its patron saint.

Some history
Portobelo was founded in 1597 to replace Nombre de Dios as the Atlantic terminus of the **Camino Real**, a year after the latter was destroyed by Francis Drake. Set on a

deepwater bay deemed easier to defend from the ravages of pirates, Portobelo was heavily fortified and for 150 years played host to the famous **ferias**, when the Spanish treasure fleet came to collect the riches that came across the isthmus on mule trains from Panamá City and to leave merchandise brought from Seville for distribution throughout the Americas. Unsurprisingly, the wealth concentrated in the royal warehouses here was an irresistible target for the **pirates** that scoured the Spanish Main. Henry Morgan sacked the town for fifteen days in 1668 before moving on to San Lorenzo and thence to Panamá City, and subsequent refortification was not enough to prevent the English Admiral Edward Vernon from seizing Portobelo again in 1739. Vernon destroyed the fortifications and though they were rebuilt at enormous expense, the Spanish treasure fleet was rerouted around Cape Horn and the Portobelo *ferias* came to an end. The Spanish garrison left after independence in 1821, and with the establishment of Colón as Panamá's principal Atlantic port, Portobelo slipped into the tropical indolence that characterizes it today.

The village and ruins

As you walk into Portobelo along the road from Colón, you come to the well-preserved **Santiago Battery**, which was built between 1753 and 1760 to the most exacting military standards of the day. From its stout battlements fourteen rusting cannons still look out to sea. Behind the battery the village itself begins, its ramshackle houses built on top of the ruins of the **Santiago de la Gloria Fort** and the many public buildings and merchants' houses destroyed by Vernon in 1739. The road leads onto the litter-strewn main square, flanked on one side by the colonial **Church of San Felipe**, built in 1776 and exceptional only as home to the famous **Black Christ** (see p.708). Just off the square is the crumbling two-storey **contadoria**, the royal customs house where treasure was stored before the arrival of the fleets from Spain. It is currently undergoing reconstruction, appropriately enough with Spanish funding, and there are plans to establish a museum inside. Behind the church the **San Geronimo Battery** looks out onto the bay, built at the same time as the Santiago battery and equally well-preserved, complete with cannons. There are more ruins largely covered by the forest that descends almost to the road from above the town, and across the bay the twin batteries of **San Fernando** are also in good condition – it's easy to find someone in the town to take you across in a boat for a few dollars, or ask one of the dive companies (see below) to do the same. Portobelo's most formidable defence, the **"Iron Castle" of San Felipe**, stood at the mouth of the bay on the opposite side, but was dismantled during the canal construction to uncover the basalt rock on which it was built, and most of its stones were used to build the breakwater in Colón.

Practicalities

Buses for Portobelo leave from Colón; if you are coming from Panamá City and want to avoid Colón, change at Sabanitas, 14km before Colón. The small **IPAT** office in Portobelo, tucked away behind the contadoria, keeps irregular hours but is very helpful when open. There's no **accommodation** in the village itself, but several of the diving centres on the road towards Colón rent rooms; ask the bus driver to drop you at one of these before heading into town to explore. *Divers Haven* (☎448 2003 or 448 2040; ⑤) has basic concrete cabins with private bathrooms and pleasant patios overlooking the bay. They will also let you camp in safety for US$5 per person. Further along, *Cabanas El Mar* (☎441 9504; ⑤) has more luxurious cabins with TV and a/c, while *Scuba Portobelo* (☎448 2147; ⑤–⑥) has pleasant cabins that sleep up to four people for US$50. All are busy on weekends and charge less on weekdays. Several basic **restaurants** in the village serve fish and seafood cooked to local recipes with coconut

---

THE BLACK CHRIST OF PORTOBELO

There are several different stories as to how the small, unspectacular **Black Christ** figure came to Portobelo. Some say that it was found floating in the sea during a cholera epidemic, which disappeared after the Christ was brought into the town, others that it was on a ship bound for Colombia that stopped at Portobelo for supplies and was repeatedly prevented from leaving the bay by bad weather, sailing successfully only when the statue was left ashore. Whatever its origin, though, the Black Christ is without doubt the most revered religious figure in Panamá and is reputed to possess **miraculous powers**. Every year on October 21 up to fifty thousand devotees, known as *Nazarenos* and dressed in purple robes, come to Portobelo for a huge procession that is followed by festivities that continue through the night – a wild and chaotic celebration of faith.

---

rice – try the *Casa del Marisco* or *Restaurante Miriam*. There are also some more upmarket places on the road towards Colón: *Restaurante el Torre, Rene's Place* and *Restaurante los Canones*. Just before *Los Cañones*, *Bar la Parada del Capitan* serves excellent **cocktails** with sunset views, and sells souvenirs including bottles of Portobelo Gold rum, available exclusively in Portobelo.

Parque Nacional Portobelo

The rugged coast around Portobelo is officially a **National Park**, and although little is done in terms of protection or administration of the area (you don't even need permission from INRENARE to enter) it has good **beaches** and some of the best **diving** and **snorkelling** sites on the Caribbean coast, including coral reefs, shipwrecks and, somewhere in front of Isla de Drake, the as yet undiscovered grave of Francis Drake, buried at sea in a lead coffin after he died of dysentery in 1596. Most of these areas can only be reached by sea; contact the dive shops listed above. At US-owned Divers Haven the friendly and knowledgeable staff take boat excursions all over the park, which cost upwards of US$10 per person. They rent snorkelling equipment for US$7 a day but you have to bring your own diving equipment from Panamá City. Scuba Portobelo do much the same, but they also rent diving equipment for US$20 a day and offer full diving courses through Scuba Panamá in Panamá City (☎261 4064).

Isla Grande

Some 12km beyond Portobelo, a side road branches off the unpaved road to the tiny village of **La Guaira**, where launches can take you across to **Isla Grande**, a very popular weekend resort for residents of Colón and Panamá City.

Though undeniably beautiful, friendly and relaxed, with some good beaches, Isla Grande is no more spectacular than other parts of Costa Arriba. It does, however, have better **facilities** – and higher prices. The best **swimming** beach is around the island to the right as you face the mainland; the beach round the other side is good for surfing. For **snorkellers**, there's plenty to see around the Christ statue in front of the village, though beware of the current beyond the reef and of passing boats.

Practicalities

There are plenty of **places to stay** on Isla Grande, spread out along the seafront path that passes for the main street. The least expensive is *Super Cabañas Jackson* (no phone; ④) which has small, box-like rooms; *Posada Villa Ensueno* (☎269 5819; ⑤) and *Cabañas Cholita* (☎232 4561; ⑤) have spacious cabins with a/c set around gardens.

During the summer and on weekends it's worth booking; on weekdays prices can be lower and you can turn up on spec. There are also several **restaurants** serving mostly fish and seafood (try octopus cooked in coconut milk or *fufu*, a filling fish soup): *La Cholita*, *Candy Rose* and *Villa Ensueno* are all very good. The **social centre** of Isla Grande is the seafont shack in front of *Super Cabanas Jackson*, where locals gather to drink beer, play dominoes and listen to loud reggae. The last **bus** back to Colón from La Guaira leaves at 1pm (Mon–Sat) or 4pm (Sun).

Nombre de Dios

Some 23km from Portobelo along the unpaved road, **NOMBRE DE DIOS** is a small village founded in 1520 that was Portobelo's predecessor as the Atlantic terminus of the Camino Real. Almost nothing remains of the Spanish settlement destroyed by Drake in 1596, and it is difficult today to believe that in 1550 half the trade between Spain and the Americas passed through this tiny port. It is a charming village, though, friendly and laid-back, with the calm waters of San Christobal bay in front and the lush forest descending like a curtain from the mountains behind. Of the beautiful deserted beaches close by, the best is **Playa las Damas**, which can be reached by walking an hour or so along the sands; you'll need to get one of the locals to show you how to wade across the sand bank in front of the Río Nombre de Dios. There are also plenty of good **snorkelling** spots (bring your own equipment). The only **place to stay** is the seafront *Cabañas Chicho Marin* (☎448 2117, ask for Chicho Marin; ②), which offers very basic but clean cabins without fans (there's almost always a cool sea breeze at night). Several simple **restaurants** serve good fish and seafood, though it's best to let them know in advance if you want to eat in the evening. The busiest is *Las Tres Hermanas*.

Beyond Nombre de Dios, the road continues 13km along the unspoiled coast as far as the hamlet of Palenque, 30km short of the frontier of Kuna Yala. If you're heading back to Portobelo, note that the last **bus** usually leaves Nombre de Dios at 1pm, though it's worth checking with the locals in case it leaves earlier.

travel details

BUSES

Colón to: La Guaira (3–4 daily; 2hr); Nombre de Dios (3–4 daily; 2hr); Panamá City (every 20min; express 1hr 30min, local 2hr); Portobelo (15 daily; 1hr).

Gamboa to: Panamá City (8 daily; 45min).

La Guaira to: Colón (3–4 daily; 2hr).

Nombre de Dios to: Colón (3–4 daily; 2hr).

Panamá City to: Colón (every 20min; express 1hr 30min, local 2hr); Gamboa (8 daily; 45min).

Portobelo to: Colón (15 daily; 1hr).

FLIGHTS

Panamá City to: Colón (14 daily Mon–Fri; 15min).

Colón to: Panamá City (14 daily Mon–Fri; 15min).

CHAPTER 36

EASTERN PANAMÁ: DARIÉN AND KUNA YALA

parsely populated by isolated indigenous communities and the descendants of escaped African slaves, the eastern third of Panamá – some 19,000 square kilometres – is perhaps the last great untamed **wilderness** of Central America, the beginning of an immense forest that continues almost unbroken across the border into Colombia and down the Pacific coast to Ecuador. This was the first region on the American mainland to be settled by the Spanish, but though they extracted great wealth from gold-mines deep in the forest, they were never able to establish effective control, hampered by the almost impassable terrain and by the fierce resistance put up by its inhabitants, and harassed at every turn by European pirates and bands of renegade African slaves known as *cimarrones*.

Though historically the whole of eastern Panamá was referred to as Darién, today it is divided into two distinct regions, separated by a low chain of forested mountains that runs the length of the Atlantic coast. The Atlantic side of these mountains is **Kuna Yala**, the autonomous *comarca* (territory) of the Kuna people, one of the most wildly beautiful and culturally fascinating regions of Panamá. Here some forty thousand Kuna live in isolation on the idyllic offshore islands of the **San Blas Archipelago**, connected to the rest of the country only by boat or plane.

The rest of eastern Panamá is **Darién**, the almost impenetrable wilderness frontier between Central and South America and the largest and most isolated province in Panamá. Only one road penetrates Darién: known as the **Darién Highway**, it is the extension of the Carretera Interamericana, intended to connect the road systems of North and South America. But for the moment the 106km gap between the two – the **Darién Gap** – remains unbridged. Here the vast forests remain largely undisturbed, one of the most pristine and biologically diverse ecosystems in the world and home to the semi-nomadic Emberá-Wounaan. Along the border with Colombia huge areas of these forests are protected by **Parque Nacional Darién**, the largest and most important protected area in Panamá.

Eastern Panamá has always been a wild frontier, a haven for rebels and renegades that defies effective government control, and today the *cimarrones*, pirates and insubmissive indigenous tribes of the colonial era have been replaced by drug traffickers, **bandits** and **guerrillas**. In recent years the situation has got markedly worse, with the vicious decades-long Colombian **civil war** spilling over into Panamá. The Marxist guerrillas of the Colombian Revolutionary Armed Forces (FARC) have long maintained bases in Darién, but now right-wing paramilitary groups backed by powerful landowners and drug traffickers have begun pursuing them, terrorizing isolated Panamanian communities they accuse of harbouring the guerrillas. The paramilitaries have also

For an explanation of **accommodation price codes**, see p.664.

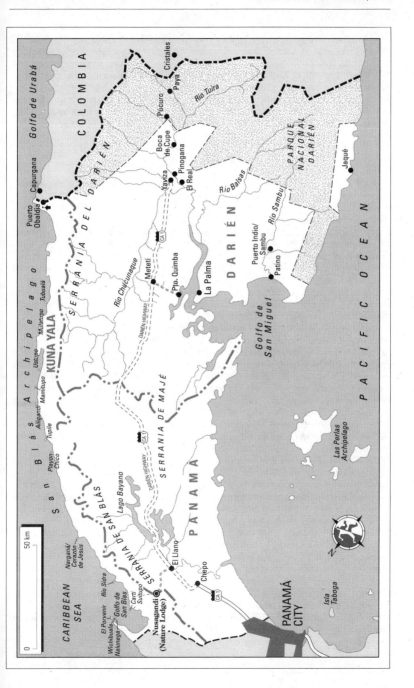

been waging a brutal campaign against poor peasants in Colombia, driving floods of refugees across the border, and unidentified armed groups have begun attacking Panamanian police outposts. Thus a climate of fear and suspicion reigns in Darién and the eastern extreme of Kuna Yala: remote villages have abandoned, locals fear to travel by river, and thousands of extra police have been rushed in. While large areas of the region can still be visited safely, including almost all of Kuna Yala and western Darién, until the security situation improves the Parque Nacional Darién is **best avoided** and crossing the frontier by land, always a risky adventure, would now be crazy.

DARIÉN

With its mighty rivers, rugged mountain chains and vast, impenetrable rainforests, **Darién** is in many ways much closer to South than to Central America, its incredible biological diversity matched only by the cultural diversity of its population, which is made up of three main groups: black, indigenous and colonist. Other than a few Kuna communities, the indigenous population of Darién is composed of two closely related but distinct peoples, the **Wounaan** and the more numerous **Emberá**, classic semi-nomadic South-American rainforest societies characterized by their use of blowpipes for hunting and their encyclopedic knowledge of the rainforest. Easily recognizable by the black geometrical designs with which they decorate their bodies, the Emberá-Wounaan have been migrating across the border from Colombia for the last two centuries. Only since the 1960s have they begun to settle in permanent villages and establish official recognition of their territorial rights in the form of a *comarca* that is divided into two districts: the **Comarca Emberá Cemaco**, in the north, and the **Comarca Emberá Sambú**, in the southwest. The black people of Darién, descended from the *cimarrones* and released slaves, are known as **Dariénitas** or **libres** (the free). Culturally distinct from the Afro-Antillan populations of Colón and Panamá City (see p.685), they are an urban population, acting as intermediaries between the Emberá-Wounaan and mainstream Panamanian society. The **colonists**, meanwhile, are the most recent arrivals, poor peasants driven off their lands in western Panamá by expanding cattle ranches and encouraged to settle in Darién during the construction of the Darién Highway. Also known as **interioranos**, many colonists still wear their distinctive straw sombreros as a badge of identity and maintain the folk traditions of the regions they abandoned.

The **Darién Highway** was built in the seventies and early eighties to open up the region's supposedly empty lands to colonization and to complete the last link in the Carretera Interamericana from Alaska to Tierra del Fuego. At present it goes no further than Yaviza, 276km east of Panamá City, and the 106km **"Darién Gap"** between the road systems of Panamá and Colombia remains unbridged. Both governments are keen to complete the highway, but various factors have conspired to prevent this: the enormous expense; fears that a road link with Colombia would facilitate drug trafficking and the spread of foot-and-mouth disease from South America; and the opposition of environmentalists and indigenous groups. The environmental consequences of the progress that the highway was supposed to bring are sadly evident along its existing length: the lands on either side are heavily deforested, plundered by illegal logging companies and cleared and replaced by low-grade cattle pasture. For the moment the exceptionally rich rainforests that stand in the highway's path along the border are protected by the 5790-square-kilometre **Parque Nacional Darién**.

Given the **security concerns** currently affecting the border area, including the National Park and the Comarca Emberá Cemaco, a visit to **southwestern Darién** is a better option if you want to experience the ecology and culture of the region independently without risking an encounter with armed groups. The provincial capital of **La Palma**, on the Pacific, is a good base from which to rent a boat to take you along the coast and up the Río Sambú into the Comarca Emberá Sambú.

Visiting Darién

Several tour companies in Panamá City (see p.694) run **tours** to Darién – Ecotours are the most experienced but Jungle Adventures and Panamá Paradise are also good – ranging from short trips to two-week trans-Darién treks, but it's easy enough to visit the region **independently**. You'll need equipment and supplies, but you can rent guides and a canoe (gas is the biggest expense) in any of the region's towns to take you up river into the forest and to visit indigenous communities. Though the national park is accessible from Yaviza, this is not currently recommended.

The Darién Highway

East of Panamá City the **Darién Highway** is well-paved as far as the busy cattle ranching centre of **Chepo**, 53km away. Beyond here it's unpaved, getting worse the further east you travel, and is often impassable in the wet season. Some 18km east of Chepo the highway passes through the quiet village of **El Llano**, where a side road leads up to the **Nusagandi Nature Reserve** in Kuna Yala (see p.719). Some 10km beyond El Llano the highway crosses the placid **Lago Bayano**, surrounded by well-preserved rainforest. Formed in 1972 by the construction of the hydro-electric dam that provides most of Panamá City's power, the lake is named after the king of the *cimarrones* that terrorized Panamá's colonial rulers in 1500s. After defeating several armies sent against him, Bayano was captured in 1555 and taken to Seville, where he lived out the rest of his years as an honoured prisoner of the Spanish king. Though the provincial border is still some 90km further east, beyond the lake you are to all intents and purposes in Darién. The highway rolls on for 196km through a desolate, deforested landscape passing Emberá-Wounaan hamlets, with their characteristic open-walled houses raised on stilts, and tin-roofed colonist settlements before ending on the banks of the Río Chucunaque at Yaviza.

Meteti

Fifty kilometres before Yaviza the highway passes through **METETI**, a small *interiorano* settlement. From here a side road leads some 20km down to **Puerto Quimba** on the Pacific coast, where **boats** can be taken across the Golfo de San Miguel to La Palma, the provincial capital (see p.715). Pick-up trucks leave Meteti for Puerto Quimba every 45 minutes or so between 5.30am and 6pm, and there are usually a couple of *chivitas* a day from Meteti to Yaviza and back, when there are enough passengers. You can find **accommodation** at the *Hotel Tres Hermanos Ortiz* (no phone; ②) by the roadside; the **restaurant** next door is simple but good. Meteti is also not a bad place to organize an expedition into the Comarca Emberá Cemaco to the north – you can probably find a guide and a canoe to take you down the Río Meteti to the Río Chucunaque, which forms the southern border of the Comarca and runs parallel to the highway to Yaviza. Expect to pay US$10–20 a day for each guide, much more (for gas) if the canoe is motorized.

Yaviza

Founded by the Spanish in 1638 as a garrison town to establish colonial control over the gold mines further up river, **YAVIZA** thrives as the terminus of the Darién Highway. Beyond here, the only transport is by water, and the river port is always busy with the

---

WARNING

Though crossing the Darién Gap has always been a hazardous undertaking (and one of the most celebrated adventures in Latin America), given the present security situation we **do not recommend travel** in the region – several travellers have disappeared or been **killed** in the attempt in recent years, and at the very least you are likely to be robbed or kidnapped, even if you can find guides willing to take you (many of the villages in the region have been attacked or overrun by bandits and the inhabitants have fled). All the National Park stations are currently affected by **bandits** and **paramilitary violence**.

The information we've given, then, should only be used if the security situation in Darién improves, and even then you should remember that there is a **war** raging across the border in Colombia. *Always* check with INRENARE in Panamá City and with the police in Yaviza before attempting to make this journey.

---

plantain-laden canoes of Emberá from the upriver communities of the Comarca who come here to trade with the town's mostly black population. It is also the jumping-off point for those wishing to cross the Darién Gap into Colombia, a good base for trips into the Emberá Comarca Cemaco, and a short distance from the Parque Nacional Darién office in El Real.

Sadly, though, with the recent upsurge in **bandit** and **paramilitary incursions** from Colombia, Yaviza today is once more beginning to resemble a garrison town, busy with nervous, heavily armed policemen and the thud of military helicopters. You should let the police know of your presence and your plans when you arrive and ask their advice before you continue.

Practicalities

Buses from Panamá City and Meteti arrive and depart from beside the dock at the entrance to town. From here the town's only real street runs down to a small square, just off which the friendly *Hotel Tres Americas* has simple **rooms** (③). There's a basic **restaurant** next door and a few others on the main street, as well as shops where you can buy supplies. There are no telephones in Yaviza.

Crossing the Darién Gap to Colombia

To cross the gap, you must first get permission from INRENARE and the Colombian consulate in Panamá City (make sure you have your exit permission from *migración* if you have been in Panamá for more than thirty days). It takes seven or so days to get from **Yaviza** to **Turbo**, some 70km across the border, where you must register on arrival with DAS, the Colombian immigration agency. The route is by canoe or on foot to Palo de las Letras on the border, from where it is eight hours to Cristales, a park guard station for the beautiful Parque Nacional Los Katios in Colombia where you can get a boat up the mighty Río Atrató to Turbo.

Parque Nacional Darién

Covering almost 5800 square kilometres of pristine rainforest along the border with Colombia, **Parque Nacional Darién** is possibly the most biologically diverse region on earth – over five hundred species of bird have been reported here. Inhabited by scattered indigenous communities, it is the only great forest in Central America that has not been affected by logging, and provides a home for countless rare and endangered species including jaguars, harpy eagles and several types of macaw.

Given its isolation, the Park is surprisingly accessible, especially from the village of El Real (see below), though even once the security situation has improved in the region you should check on whether or it not it is safe to visit at INRENARE in Panamá City (see p.676), and again at the park office in El Real.

There are three **guard stations** in the park. The closest is **Rancho Frio**, a three-hour walk through the forest from El Real, where there are plenty of trails into the forest, including one to the peak of Cerro Pirre (1200m), considered one of the best bird-watching locations in the world. **Cruce del Mono**, a five-hour walk from Boca del Cupe, is considered the best station for seeing mammals. The third station, **Río Balsas**, is about eight hours by boat down the Tuira and up the Balsas – renting a boat from Yaviza or El Real could cost anything up to US$200. There is also an ANCON lodge deep in the park at the old Cana Mine, another excellent birding location – you should contact them in Panamá City well in advance.

Practicalities

To visit the park you should first head to the park office in the small town of **EL REAL**, about half an hour by boat down the Chucunaque and up the Tuira from Yaviza. There's no scheduled boat service, but if you go to the dock in Yaviza in the morning you should find vessels which will take you for about US$4 per person. These boats go to meet the Aeroperlas (☎263 5363) and Aviatur (☎270 1750) **planes** that arrive daily from Panamá City, returning the same day – the El Real airstrip, on the edge of town, serves Yaviza as well. There's basic **accommodation** at the *Hotel El Nazareno* (②–③), a few stores, and a couple of simple restaurants (inform them in advance if you want an evening meal).

To the enter the park you need permission (US$3 per day) from the Parque Nacional Darién office (daily 8am–4pm). They can also inform you on the relative safety and accessibility of the guard stations, and can provide a guide (US$10) to take you to **Rancho Frio**. To reach the **Cruce del Mono** station you must first go to Boca del Cupe, a small village about two hours up the Río Tuira from El Real. INRENARE should be able to help organize a boat. The guard stations all have basic **lodges** where you can stay for US$5 a night. You should take food, bedding, mosquito repellent and nets or coils, a water bottle and purifiers, and a first aid kit. Gifts for the park guards (food, drink, batteries, newspapers) are much appreciated.

La Palma

With a spectacular setting overlooking the Golfo de San Miguel – where the silt-laden waters of the Río Tuira flow into the Pacific Ocean with rugged, densely forested mountains rising on all sides – **LA PALMA** is the capital of Darién province, a lively commercial and administrative centre despite its isolation. There's not much to do here, but it's a friendly place as yet unaffected by the fear gripping much of Darién (though you should still register with the police on arrival) and a good base from which to rent a boat to take you along the coast and up the Río Sambú into the **Comarca Emberá Sambú**. Given the dangers currently involved in going into the forest from El Real and Yaviza, this is the best place to experience the indigenous culture and pristine ecology of Darién independently.

Practicalities

La Palma clings to a steep slope that runs down to the seafront, along which runs its only real street, lined with houses on stilts projected over the water. **Planes** arrive and depart for Panamá City (and occasionally continue to Sambú) from the airstrip at the northwest end of the street – Aeroperlas and Aviatur both have small offices there. **Boats** from Puerto Quimba arrive on the beach below the main street. There are sometimes boats direct to Panamá City, but no scheduled service – this route has largely been superceded by the connection to the Darién Highway, though if you ask around in town you may turn up something. There are two clean and pleasant **places to stay**: the elegant *Hotel Biaquirú Bagará* (☎299 6224; ④), with a beautiful patio overlooking the gulf, and the *Pensión Takela* (☎299 6213; ④). The *Crismary*, opposite the *Takela*, is the most popular **restaurant**, and there are a couple of unnamed places on the main street. For a small town, La Palma has some lively **nightlife** – check out the *Cantina Brisas del Tuira* on the seafront for booming all-night reggae. There's a **telephone office** on the main street (no international calls), and a **Banco Nacional** (Mon–Fri 8am–3pm, Sat 9am–noon) where you can change travellers' cheques and make cash withdrawals on a Visa card.

Comarca Emberá Sambú

From La Palma it is a fantastic one-day boat journey to the **Comarca Emberá Sambú**, passing the forested islands in the mouth of the Golfo de San Miguel, along the wild coastline fringed with mangroves and deserted beaches, and up the tidal estuary of the Río Sambú to the twin towns of **Sambú** and **Puerto Indio**. Sambú is a trading town with a mostly black population, while Puerto Indio is the capital of the Emberá Comarca. The two stand on opposite sides of the river, joined by a footbridge that is effectively a frontier between two different worlds: as you cross, the squat concrete homes of the *libres* are replaced by the open-walled thatched houses of the Emberá, raised high on stilts. The Emberá are keen to promote ecotourism, and Puerto Indio is a good place to find a guide and a canoe to take you upriver, deep into the Comarca. Away from Puerto Indio the Emberá live in dispersed communities along the river banks, hunting, fishing and cultivating small gardens that provide the only break in the otherwise pristine vegetation.

Practicalities
There are no scheduled **boat** services up the Río Sambú, but if you ask around in La Palma you should be able to find a cargo boat that will take you in return for a contribution to fuel costs, though you may have to wait for several days. Midway between La Palma and the mouth of the Río Sambú at **Patiño**, about 30km along the coast, there is a nature reserve with facilities for visitors run by ANCON – you should contact them in Panamá City (see p.694) well in advance if you want to stay there. Sambú also has an airstrip served by Aeroperlas and Aviatur light **aircraft** from Panamá City (usually via La Palma) several days a week, though arriving this way you miss out on the spectacular boat trip.

There are no hotels in Sambú or Puerto Indio and only one restaurant, the *Fonda Ari* in Sambú, but you can find **accommodation** with local families, though you should ask the permission of the headman of Puerto Indio first. Travelling further upriver into the Comarca is a real adventure – there are no facilities and you will have to bring all your own supplies and either camp or stay with local families. Goods such as machetes, batteries and preserved food are often more useful than cash when it comes to paying for accommodation.

KUNA YALA

Stretching some 375km along the northeastern Caribbean coast of Panamá from the Golfo de San Blas to Puerto Obaldía, **Kuna Yala** is the autonomous *comarca* of the Kuna (or Dúle), the only region in the country populated and governed exclusively by indigenous people. Although their territory includes the narrow strip of land between the sea and the peaks of the Serrania de San Blas, almost all the Kuna live on the **San Blas Archipelago**, a chain of coral atolls that runs the length of the forested coastline like a string of pearls. They say there is an island for every day of the year (in fact there are slightly more), some forty of which are inhabited, with populations ranging from several thousand to single families living on narrow sandbanks all but submerged at high tide.

The untamed beauty of its forested coastline, palm-fringed islands, coral reefs and bounteous marine life make Kuna Yala a good destination for a beach holiday, though transportation is difficult and there are few facilities. The real appeal is the opportunity to observe the unique culture and lifestyle of the Kuna themselves.

Some history

Historians still argue over whether the **tribes** the Spanish first encountered on the coasts of Darién were Kuna, but it is clear that by the mid-sixteenth century the Kuna were migrating into Darién from the great Atrató swamp in present-day Colombia. Gradually driven onto the north coast by war with the Spanish and with the Emberá, their historic rivals, they began moving to the relative safety and isolation of the islands in the nineteenth century. A treaty signed with the Spanish in 1787 guaranteed a measure of independence, but in the early twentieth century the authorities of newly independent Panamá initiated efforts to "civilize" the Kuna, sending police and missionaries to the islands. This twin assault on Kuna culture and autonomy and the

KUNA CULTURE

Fishing is the mainstay of the traditional Kuna subsistence economy, but they also cultivate food crops in clearings in the forest on the mainland and collect coconuts to sell to Colombian trading ships. Kuna society is regulated by a system of highly participative **democracy**: every community has a *casa de congreso* where the *onmakket*, or congress, meets regularly. Each community also elects a *sahila*, usually a respected elder, who attends the Kuna General Congress twice a year. The General Congress is the supreme political authority in Kuna Yala, and it in turn appoints three *caciques* and sends representatives to the Panamanian National Assembly. Colonial missionaries struggled in vain to christianize the Kuna, and though some of the Christian sects that have made so much headway elsewhere in Latin America have now established a foothold in Kuna Yala, most Kuna cling to their own **religious beliefs**, based above all on the sanctity of Nan Dummad, the Great Mother, and on respect for the environment they inhabit. The Kuna also have a rich tradition of **oral history**, and the ritual interpretation of their past by poet-historians plays an important part in decision making and in maintaining their collective identity. Though Kuna men wear standard Western clothes, **Kuna women** wear gold rings in their ears and noses and blue vertical lines painted on their foreheads; they don piratical headscarves and bright bolts of trade cloth round their waists, their forearms and calves are bound in coloured beads, and their blouses are sewn with beautiful reverse-appliqué designs known as **molas**. Depicting everything from fish and birds to complex abstract designs and even political slogans, *molas* are the most popular souvenir for visitors to Kuna Yala and are on sale all over Panamá.

Although it is idiosyncratic, it would be wrong to consider Kuna culture as entirely traditional and unchanging – its very strength comes from the Kunas' ability to absorb those aspects of the outside world that suit them and adapt them to their needs. The Kuna have travelled the world as sailors, many work in the US bases, and thousands work and study in Panamá City and Colón. Of course, this integration with the outside world poses some problems – egalitarian traditions are gradually being eroded and some resources, particularly lobster, are being overexploited to satisfy market demand. But if their history is anything to go by, the Kuna are likely to find ways of resolving these problems without losing their culture and their identity.

despoilation of their natural resources by outsiders provoked an explosive reaction. In 1925 the Kuna rose up in what they still proudly refer to as **"the Revolution"**, killing or expelling the Panamanian police garrison and declaring an independent republic. The government sent a punitive expedition but a US warship standing offshore prevented further bloodshed – the Kuna had sent representatives to Washington to request assistance before the uprising – and a settlement was made by which the Kuna recognized Panamanian sovereignty in return for a degree of autonomy. The **support of the US** has never been forgotten: to this day while outsiders in general are referred to as *uaga*, a derogatory term, North Americans are known as **merki**, a superior category, making Kuna Yala one of the few places in the region where it is advantageous to be (or to be mistaken for) a North American. Protracted negotiations in the decades after the revolution led to the final recognition of Kuna Yala as an independent self-governing **comarca** in 1952. No non-Kuna can own land or property in the *comarca* and the Kuna General Congress is responsible for all administration in accordance with the Kuna's own constitution – a degree of political autonomy far greater than that of any other indigenous people in Latin America.

Visiting Kuna Yala

Though the Kuna are generally keen to promote **tourism**, they are are determined to control its development and limit its negative impacts. When in Kuna Yala, particularly in the more remote areas, it is important to remember that you are a guest of the Kuna and must abide by their laws. Always ask **permission** from the local *sahila* when you visit or wish to stay on an island, and ask before **photographing** anybody (expect to pay about US$0.25 per photo, more for group shots). The Kuna are particularly sensitive about the *casas de congreso* and the cemeteries on the mainland – never enter or photograph these without permission. Some islands charge a **fee** for visitors and most will assign a **guide** to take you around and make sure you respect the Kuna's sometimes strict social codes – full or partial nudity and public displays of affection, for example, are frowned upon.

Pretty much every **tour company** in Panamá City (see p.694) can organize trips to Kuna Yala, some to exclusive resort hotels, but it is easy to visit the *comarca* independently. The few islands with any organized tourist **facilities** are concentrated in the western end of the archipelago in the Golfo de San Blas. Here you can stay in basic guesthouses or small hotels where meals and boat-trips – to other islands, beaches and snorkelling spots, or into the forests of the mainland – are included in the price. Away from these islands the possibilities for adventure are endless – there's no reason why you shouldn't fly to any of the other islands or mainland communities where, once you have received permission from the *sahila*, you can find a family to stay with and rent a boat to take you around. You can also – with permission – get a boatman to drop you on one of the many uninhabited islands to camp, though you will need to bring all your own food and water.

If you are planning any kind of research or a **long stay** in Kuna Yala, you need permission from the *onmakket* office in Panamá City (☎263 3615) above an electronics shop in the Edificio Dominó on Via España. They also sell books of Kuna history and poetry, in Kuna and Spanish, and publish a useful pamphlet, "Tourism in Kuna Yala".

By air

The easiest way to reach Kuna Yala is by **plane**. Almost all the forty or so inhabited islands and the twelve mainland communities have airstrips closeby, which are served regularly by ANSA (☎226 7891), Aviatur (☎270 1750) and Aerotaxi (☎264 8644) light aircraft from Paitilla domestic airport. Flights cost between US$25 and US$45 one-way. The airstrips are often bigger than the islands themselves and located on the mainland, and a small arrival and departure fee is usually charged. If you need to return to

Panamá City on a specific day, you should book in advance, as there may not be space on the plane, or, if there are no guaranteed passengers, it may not come at all. The light aircraft are also not a bad way to travel between islands. If you wait at the airstrip you may be able to persuade the pilot to take you on to another island, though sometimes you will have to settle for going where he is going. The fare is flexible and goes direct to the pilot, so feel free to negotiate.

By sea

You can also reach the islands – and travel between them – by **boat**, renting one or asking around and getting a lift. In addition, several Kuna-owned trading ships travel between Coco Solo port in Colón (see p.703) and the islands, but they are generally unwilling to carry outsiders, as are the Colombian ships from Turbo or Cartagena that tramp up and down the archipelago trading basic goods for coconuts. You may be able to get them to take you between islands, but remember that this is a wild coast, and many of the ships that pass along it are involved in smuggling. If you can get on one, they are the least expensive way to travel throught the archipelago – the 3- to 5-day trip from Coco Solo to Puerto Obaldia won't cost you more than US$30, meals included.

On foot

You can **walk** into Kuna Yala across the Serrania de San Blas from the village of El Llano, 70km east of Panamá City on the Darién Highway, a two-day journey passing through the pristine Nusagandi Nature Reserve (see below). There are plenty of other adventurous routes you can walk across the Serrania from the coast of Kuna Yala to the tributaries of the Chucunaque, which you can then descend by canoe to reach the Darién Highway, but for these you will need guides.

Nusagandi Nature Reserve

The semi-abandoned road that runs some 47km from El Llano on the Darién Highway across the Serrania de San Blas to the coast is the **best land route** into Kuna Yala, easy to follow without a guide. Built in the 1970s as part of General Torrijos' planned "conquest of the Caribbean", the road originally extended to the coast opposite the island of Carti, bringing a wave of colonists to the borders of Kuna Yala, clearing the forest for agriculture and cattle-ranching. The Kuna General Congress acted swiftly in response to this threat to the territorial and ecological integrity of the region, establishing a **nature reserve** covering some 1000 square kilometres – the first such reserve in Latin America to be set up and administered by an indigenous people. Today the road is usually passable by 4WD as far as the park guard station and **nature lodge** at **Nusagandi**, 27km from El Llano.

Visiting the reserve

To visit Nusagandi you need **permission** from PEMASKY in Panamá City (see p.676), a Kuna organization set up to manage the reserve. They **charge** US$5 per day plus US$10 per night to stay in the Nusagandi lodge (see below). It is a short drive from El Llano to Nusagandi if you have your own vehicle, or about four to six hours on foot – you may be able to hitch, but don't count on it. As the road climbs the deforested southern slopes of the Serrania de San Blas, the desolate landscape of scrubby cattle pasture and recently planted timber plantations gradually gives way to lush vegetation as it approaches the border of Kuna Yala. Perched just over the continental divide, **Nusagandi** has excellent views of the jagged, forest-covered ridges that march down to the Caribbean, and on clear days you can see the islands laid out in the shimmering waters of the Golfo de San Blas. Set amid the pristine forests, the **nature lodge** sleeps up to forty people in dorms, with a communal bathroom and a kitchen – you should bring all the food you need, plus a little extra for the park guards. The forest around the lodge is rich in wildlife, particularly toucans and various species of monkey. **Trails** pass waterfalls and *miradores*, and the knowledgeable park guards are usually happy to act as guides. Not that you need to go far to see wildlife here – you can simply lounge in the hammock on the patio and watch innumerable bird species flit by while the eerie dawn chorus of the howler monkeys echoes across the treetops.

Beyond Nusagandi, the 20km road down to the **coast** is impassable to vehicles but easy to follow on foot. It's a tough six-to-eight-hour walk through pristine forest, longer if you stop to observe the wildlife, so you should leave early in the morning. For the last two hours the road levels out as it reaches the narrow coastal plain where the Kuna farms are concentrated, but even here you are unlikely to see another soul. The only place where the road is difficult to follow is after it crosses a bridge over the Río Carti Grande – you should veer left here. An hour beyond the bridge you emerge at the coast beside the Carti airstrip, where you can find a boat to take you over to Carti or one of the other islands.

The islands

Set just off the Punta de San Blas on the northern tip of the gulf, **EL PORVENIR** is the administrative capital of Kuna Yala, and the airport for the nearby islands of **Wichubuala** and **Nalunega**, which are the best prepared to receive visitors. You can **stay** here at the *Hotel Porvenir* (⑥) where various boat trips are included but food in the restaurant is not, but there's little reason to do so – apart from the airstrip, the Kuna-controlled *gobernación*, and a small beach, there's nothing much to the place. The hotels on Wichubuala and Nalunega send boats to meet arriving planes, and you are better off heading straight to one of these.

On **Nalunega**, the *Hotel San Blas* (☎262 5410; ⑥) has basic rooms in a modern concrete building and sand-floored cabins on the pleasant beach in front. Bathrooms are shared. Don't leave valuables in the cabins, and if you give your money to the staff for safekeeping, count it in front of them first. You can also rent snorkelling equipment here. On **Wichubuala** there are two hotels: the pleasant *Kuna Niskua* (☎227 5308; ⑦) and the more comfortable *Anai* (☎239 3025; ⑧); the families that run them are the only inhabitants of the island. Rates in these three hotels are good value when you consider they include three decent meals a day, usually with fish and sometimes with lobster, and numerous boat excursions.

Carti Suitupo

One of a cluster of densely populated islands close to the mainland about 10km south of El Porvenir, **Carti Suitupo** (Carti) is a busy community where about 1500 Kuna live on a patch of land not much bigger than a soccer pitch. There's a small, basic *dormitorio* (③), and a *cafeteria* serving basic **meals**. These are not really oriented towards tourists; if you stay here you'll be living in the midst of the community. Though there's no beach, you can easily hire a boatman to take you out during the day. There's even a small **museum** (US$1), which has a collection of Kuna arts and crafts, from day-to-day objects to the miniature carved canoes used in funeral ceremonies. Carti's **airstrip** is on the mainland, where the path down from Nusagandi emerges onto the coast.

Narganá and Corazon de Jesús

For some Kuna the twin islands of **Narganá** and **Corazon de Jesús**, 40km east of El Porvenir, are a nightmare vision of what the future of Kuna Yala might be like if the *uaga burba* – the spirit of the outsiders – continues to spread. Few women here wear traditional

CROSSING INTO COLOMBIA

As well as the hazardous land route through the Darién Gap (see p.714), you can also **cross into Colombia** from the coasts. Occasional boats from Muelle Fiscal in Panamá City run down the **Pacific coast** of Darién to **Jaqué**, 90km due south of La Palma (20hr), and sometimes continue to Jurado and Bahía Solano, in Colombia (3 days), where you can get flights on to Quibdó, Medellin and Turbo. You can get an exit stamp from the *migración* office at the dock in Panamá City, but should check on entry requirements with the Colombian consulate there.

On the **Caribbean** side, you can enter Colombia from **Puerto Obaldia**, a remote border outpost at the far southeastern extreme of Kuna Yala, served by light aircraft from Panamá City. It has a basic pensión and a couple of restaurants. After going through customs and *migración*, you can walk or take a motorboat down to Capurgana, a small fishing village and incipient holiday resort on the Colombian coast. From Capurgana boats head across the Gulf of Urabá to Turbo, where you must register with DAS, the Colombian agency that deals with immigration, and there are also regular light aircraft flights to Medellin and Cartagena. Be warned, though, that the whole border area is busy with guerrilla and paramilitary activity – the police garrison at Obaldia has been attacked several times – and Turbo is the centre of Urabá, the most violent region in Colombia.

dress; the buildings are mostly of concrete rather than cane and palm; there is a **Banco Nacional** but no *casa de congreso*; and whereas most communities do not allow missionaries onto their islands, here five different Christian sects compete for possession of the islanders' souls. In some ways this makes it an interesting place: the frontline in a longstanding cultural struggle. The fiercely traditional community of **Isla Tigre**, close by, offers a profound contrast and the surrounding coastline is very beautiful, with extensive coral reefs and many uninhabited islands with good beaches. You can **stay** at the very basic and dirty *Hotel Cadenita de Oro* (②), and there are several simple **restaurants**.

Ailigandi

Some 60km further southeast, **Ailigandi** is an important regional centre with a population of some two thousand, many of whom are Baptists. You can **stay** at the *Hotel Ikasa* (☎224 8492; ④), a simple, clean concrete construction with a basic restaurant, or you may be invited to stay in someone's home. There's also a small communal **restaurant**. Once again, there is plenty of scope for excursions, and the island is also home to the **Hogar Cultural Kuna**, where wood carving, pottery, weaving and *mola* design are taught. Visitors are welcome, and you may be able to study there.

travel details

BUSES

Panamá City to: Yaviza (3–4 daily; 9–12hr).
Meteti to: Puerto Quimba (every 45min; 30min); Yaviza (1–2 daily; 2–3hr).
Puerto Quimba to: Meteti (every 45min; 30min).
Yaviza to: Meteti (1–2 daily; 2–3hr); Panamá City (3–4 daily; 9–12hr).

BOATS

La Palma to: Puerto Quimba (10 daily; 45min).
Puerto Quimba to: La Palma (10 daily; 45min).

FLIGHTS

Panamá City to: El Real (1–2 daily; 50min); Kuna Yala* (2–3 daily Mon–Fri; 30min–1hr 15min); La Palma (1–2 daily; 45min); Sambú (4–5 weekly; 1hr 20min).

* flights to (from northwest to southeast): El Porvenir (2–3 daily); Río Sidra, Río Azucar, Corazon de Jesús, Río Tigre, Playa Chico, Tupile, Ailigandi, Achutupo, Mamitupo, Ogobsucun, Mansucum, Mulatupu, Tubuala, Caledonia and Puerto Obaldia.

CHAPTER 37

WESTERN PANAMÁ

Western Panamá is divided into two by the rugged **Cordillera Central**, which begins not far west of the Panamá Canal and runs some 400km to Costa Rica. North of the mountains, the undeveloped Atlantic coast is covered in dense rainforest and inhabited by isolated indigenous groups. South of the mountains, meanwhile, the drier and more fertile coastal plain is largely deforested and heavily settled. This agricultural heartland is known as **el interior** (its inhabitants are known as *interioranos*), the homeland of *ladino* rural culture.

Before the arrival of the Spanish, this Pacific coastal region was home to the most sophisticated **indigenous societies** in the country, and it was here that the conquistadors met the fiercest resistance, led above all by **Urraca**, a chieftain whose head now decorates the one cent coin. Gradually these societies were defeated and assimilated or driven into the infertile highlands – where their descendants, the **Ngobe-Buglé**, still live – and the forests were cleared for agriculture and ranching.

Though the towns in this region – **Penonomé**, **Chitré**, **Las Tablas**, **Santiago** and **David** – are dull, provincial market centres, and the agricultural lands that surround them scarcely match the untamed beauty of the wilderness that covers much of the rest of the country, there are several places worth checking out as you head west towards Costa Rica or Bocas del Toro. Close to Panamá City there are some spectacular Pacific **beaches** and the cool mountain resort town of **El Valle**; while near Penonomé the remnants of the pre-Columbian societies that dominated the region can be seen at **Parque Arqueológico el Caño**. Off the Interamericana to the south the **Peninsula de Azuero** is a fascinating agricultural region famed for its religious fiestas where early Spanish folkloric traditions survive almost unchanged; although the peninsula is largely deforested, much of its coastal ecology is well-preserved. Surrounded by coral reefs, **Isla Iguana Wildlife Reserve** is one of the best places in Panamá for divers and snorkellers, while at **Isla Cañas Wildlife Reserve**, to the south, sea turtles arrive every year in their thousands. In the far west, near the Costa Rican border, the Cordillera Central rises to its highest peaks in the **Chiriquí Highlands**, a beautiful region of extinct volcanoes, dense cloudforests and idyllic mountain villages.

West from Panamá City

West of Panamá City the **Interamericana** runs along a narrow plain squeezed between the Pacific and the slopes of the Cordillera Central. The landscape becomes noticeably more **arid** as you travel west – deforestation and *El Niño* have made the crescent formed by the coastal plains of Coclé and Herrera provinces the driest region in Panamá and the sugar-cane fields depend on irrigation water from the rivers that run down from the mountains to the north. At the border of Coclé province 23km beyond Aguadulce and 213km from Panamá City the road forks at Divisa: the Interamericana continues west to Santiago, the capital of Veraguas Province, and another road turns south into the Peninsula de Azuero.

For an explanation of **accommodation price codes**, see p.664.

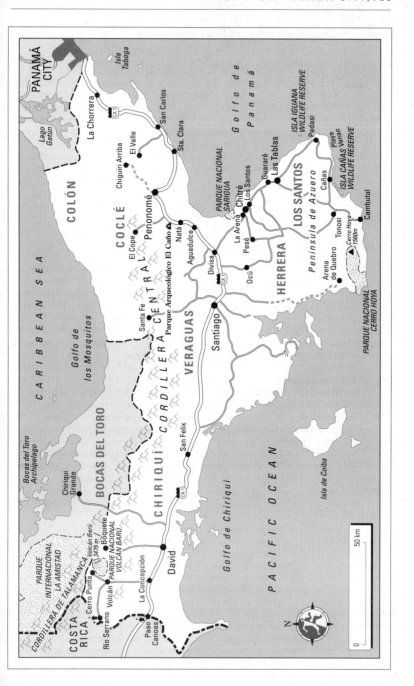

Beaches along the Carretera Interamericana

From Panamá City the Interamericana crosses the Bridge of the Americas, which soars 1600m across the mouth of the canal, and passes through the satellite town of La Chorrera as it heads west towards the province of Coclé. For 50km beyond the village of Bejuco, 29km west of La Chorrera, the coast is lined with some of the most beautiful and popular Pacific **beaches** in Panamá, all just a few kilometres from the highway and accessible by taxi or local buses. From east to west **Playas Gorgona** and **Coronado** are the most fashionable weekend destinations for the wealthy residents of Panamá City, while **Playa San Carlos** is the most popular with surfers.

Playa Santa Clara, 30km east of Penonomé, is probably the loveliest – a seemingly endless stretch of white sand lapped by usually calm waters. There's a **restaurant**, *Las Veraneras* (daily 10am–7.30pm), which serves decent fish and seafood, and locals rent horses close by. They also have four delightful self-catering **cabañas** overlooking the sea, *Cabañas Veraneras* (☎993 3313; ⑥), which sleep up to five, though if you eat at the restaurant they won't mind if you camp on the beach.

El Valle

Just beyond San Carlos, 96km west of Panamá City, a side road climbs up into the cordillera to **EL VALLE**, a small village set in an idyllic fertile valley that was once the crater of a long-extinct volcano. At 600m above sea-level, El Valle is comparatively cool, and the surrounding countryside is good for walking or horseriding. The area is renowned for its flowers and **orchids**, and is a popular retreat for residents of Panamá City at the weekend, when it gets very busy. Otherwise it is a peaceful place, where most people get around by bicycle or on horseback and the only noise is of lawnmowers and of hummingbirds buzzing among the flowers.

The village and around

Everything in El Valle is spread out along Avenida Principal, the main street. Next to the church, a small **museum** (Sun 10am–2pm; US$0.25) run by nuns, has some good exhibits on local history and folklore, while nearby the Sunday **market** sells fruit, handicrafts (including carved soapstone, traditional earthenware pottery and woven baskets) and flowers. Opposite, a side road leads up to **El Nispero**, a plant nursery and zoo (daily 7am–5pm; US$2) where you can see monkeys, the celebrated golden frog that is endemic to the area, and birds ranging from macaws and toucans to such exotic wonders as the *Gallina Inglés* – the English chicken. Beside the church a side road leads to the **thermal baths** (daily 9am–6pm; US$0.25) by the Río Anton. Reputed to have medicinal powers, these make a great place to relax after a day's **walking** in the countryside – one of the joys of a visit to El Valle.

Across the bridge at the east end of Av Principal the road forks three ways. A thirty-minute walk up the right fork takes you up to **El Chorro Macho**, a 35m waterfall set amid the forest of a private ecological reserve and well worth the US$1 admission fee. The reserve also operates cable rides through the forest canopy, the **"Canopy Adventure"** (☎983 6547), costing US$40 for just over an hour. The left fork from the bridge leads to the smaller **Las Mozas** waterfall, while the centre fork leads to **petroglyphs**, fifteen minutes' walk away. Carved on a huge white rock and highlighted with chalk and charcoal, the petroglyphs are pre-Columbian abstract designs, including spirals and anthropomorphic and zoomorphic figures; nobody knows when or by whom they were carved, let alone their significance. Further afield, innumerable trails climb up into the **cloudforests** of the surrounding mountains, which are excellent for birdwatching – try following the road beyond the El Macho reserve.

Practicalities

There's no bus terminal in El Valle, but all **buses** run down Av Principal. Buses from Panamá City arrive every 35 minutes or so between 7.30am and 6.30pm (2hr 30min) and minibuses arrive every 45 minutes from San Carlos (20min). The small **IPAT** office (daily 8am–4pm; ☎983 6474), in a hut next to the market, has lots of information, including good maps. There are no **banks**, so bring all the cash you need and bear in mind that El Valle is relatively expensive. **Accommodation** is no exception. The *Motel Niña Delia* (☎983 6110; ④) on Av Principal has small, clean rooms and a pleasant patio and garden, while the *Santa Librada* restaurant, also on Av Principal, has some rooms (☎983 6376; ③) that vary in size, comfort and price. The best place in town is the *Hotel Campestre* (☎983 6146; ⑥) a country club-style hotel set in lavish grounds on the outskirts of the village at the end of the road that heads off Av Principal opposite the *Niña Delia*. Locals sometimes rent rooms, which can be arranged through IPAT. There are several **restaurants**, though most only open on the weekends. Of those that are open daily, the *Santa Librada* is the best, serving very good *típica* food, while the restaurant at the *Hotel Campestre* is good but overpriced. For basic, filling and inexpensive meals, try the restaurant inside the covered market. You can rent **bicycles** (US$3 an hour) from the Jaque Mate Supermarket, just off Av Principal as you come into the village, and **horses** (US$3.50 an hour) from a little kiosk close to the *Hotel Campestre*. In both cases, you can probably get a better price on weekdays or for a whole day. **Moving on** from El Valle, you can either take a direct bus to Panamá City or a minibus to San Carlos, where you can flag down buses heading in either direction along the Interamericana.

Penonomé

Founded in 1581 as a *reducción de Indios* – a place where conquered indigenous groups were forcibly resettled so as to be available for labour service – and briefly the capital of the isthmus after the destruction of Panamá Viejo, the lively market town of **PENONOMÉ** was named after Nomé, a local chieftain cruelly betrayed and executed here by the Spaniards after years of successful resistance. Now the capital of the province of Coclé, apart from its small museum Penonomé doesn't have much to see, but it makes a good enough base.

From the bus terminal on the Interamericana Penonomé's busy commercial main street, Via Central or Avenida J. D. Arosemena, runs a few hundred metres down to the **Plaza 8 de Diciembre**, which features a statue of Simon Bolivar and the inevitable bandstand. It's flanked by several government buildings and the unspectacular **cathedral**. From the square a short walk down C Damian Carles and a right turn opposite the covered market brings you to the **Museo de Historia y Tradición Penonomeña** (Tues–Sat 9am–4pm, Sun 9.30am–1pm; US$1), which has some good pre-Columbian ceramics and colonial religious art. The streets around the market bustle with the activity of campesinos from local villages selling their agricultural produce and spending much of the proceeds in the city's many bars.

Practicalities

Buses from Panamá City arrive at the **terminal** at the intersection of Via Central and the Interamericana every twenty minutes or so, and it is easy to flag down any through bus going east or west along the Interamericana. The **IPAT** office (Mon–Fri 8.30am–4pm; ☎997 9230), above the Barcelona furniture shop on Via Central, is scarcely worth bothering with. There are two **places to stay**: the *Hotel Dos Continentes* (☎997 9325; ④) opposite the bus terminal has clean, unimaginative rooms; while the newer, friendly *Residencial El Paisa* (☎997 9242; ③) just off the plaza on Av Manuel Amador Guerrero, charges per person. Of the several **restaurants**, the best is *Oasis* (daily noon–11pm), on the Interamericana just beyond the footbridge, which has good steak and pizza. Across the Interamericana *Las Tinajas* (daily 7am–10pm), is a reasonably inexpensive self-service place. There are three restaurants called *Gallo Pinto*, each with menus as original as their name; the best is opposite *El Paisa* (Mon–Sat 7am–7.30pm, Sun 7am–2.30pm). The restaurant of the *Dos Continentes* is also good, particularly for breakfast. The **post office** is on Via Central, as is the Banco del Istmo (Mon–Fri 8am–3.30pm) where you can **change travellers' cheques** or use a Visa card, while the **telephone office** is on the main square.

Around Penonomé: Chiguiri Arriba

From the market area in Penonomé, *chivas* head off to villages scattered in the folds of the cool, forested mountains that rise to the north. One of these, **Chiguiri Arriba**, 29km away, makes an easy day trip (1–2 *chivas* daily; leaving about 10am, returning in the afternoon; 1hr 20min; US$1.50). There are plenty of good hiking trails, spectacular views and a 30m waterfall nearby – local children will happily guide you there for a small tip. Some 2km before the village is *La Posada del Cerro La Vieja* (☎263 7890 or 223 4553; ⑨), a luxurious **eco-resort** set amid beautiful gardens and a private forest reserve. Rates include all meals and guided excursions, on foot or horseback. They can also arrange longer trips across the mountains to El Valle or down through pristine rainforest to the Caribbean coast by trail and canoe along the Río Indio, though there's no reason – with a little Spanish, a local guide and the right supplies and equipment – why you can't do this independently.

El Caño Archeological Park

El Caño Archeological Park (Tues–Sat 9am–4pm, Sun 9am–1pm; US$1) is the most impressive pre-Columbian site in Panamá, but that's not saying very much – compared to the Maya wonders elsewhere in Central America there's very little to see. It was an important ceremonial site from 500 to about 1200 AD, after which it became a cemetery that was still in use after the conquest – horse remains have been found in some of the tombs – but the hundreds of stone statues that formed what was described as the "Temple of the Thousand Idols" were illegally decapitated by US archeologist Hyatt Verril in the early twentieth century, and the best of their zoomorphic and anthropomorphic heads are now in New York. Set amid cornfields and plagued by mosquitoes, the site consists of several funeral mounds, one of which is excavated and open to view, and lines of decapitated standing stones whose significance can only be speculated – some believe they were part of an astronomical observatory. A small **museum** displays ceramics and lesser stone statues, but otherwise there's nothing to delay you for more than half an hour. To reach the site from the marked turn off on the Interamericana, walk ten minutes to the village of El Caño, beyond which it's another 25 minutes' walk.

Natá

Founded by Gaspar de Espinoza in 1522 and officially recognized two years later, **NATÁ DE CABALLEROS** was the forward base for the Spanish conquest of what was then known as Veragua, and faced continuous attack from the indigenous forces led by Urracá. Resistance was finally overcome in 1556, and Natá became an agricultural centre supplying the now long-abandoned gold mines on the Atlantic coast. Today Natá is a quiet backwater, notable only for the **Church of Santiago Apóstol**, built in 1522 and possibly the oldest church on the American mainland still in use. Set on the main square about five minutes' walk fom the highway and still boasting a fine baroque facade, it is currently closed for restoration.

The Peninsula de Azuero

Jutting out into the Pacific Ocean like the head of an axe (or adze – that's what *azuero* means), the largely deforested **Peninsula de Azuero** was one of the earliest regions of Panamá to be settled by Spanish colonists, and is considered the cradle of Panamanian rural tradition and folklore. Predominantly agricultural, the landscape here is dry and scrubby, dotted with small villages little changed from colonial times, its narrow roads often blocked by herds of cattle being led to market by cowboys on horseback or the occasional ox-drawn cart. In many ways visiting the Azuero is like going back to seventeenth-century rural Spain – the peninsula's Spanish heritage is clearly evident in the traditional handicrafts and folkloric costumes, and above all in the vibrant religious **fiestas**. Between fiestas, the principal towns of **Chitré** and **Las Tablas** are sleepy market centres where little happens, but the historic town of **Los Santos** and the eerie desert landscape of **Parque Nacional Sarigua**, both near Chitré, make interesting excursions. Further south, meanwhile, the peninsula's rich coastal ecology is well preserved. The small town of **Pedasí** is surrounded by deserted white-sand beaches, while the nearby **Isla Iguana Wildlife Reserve**, an offshore island surrounded by coral reefs, is one of the best places for snorkelling or scuba diving on the Pacific coast of Panamá. The rarely visited **Isla Cañas Wildlife Reserve**, further west, is an excellent place to observe nesting sea turtles. The mountainous western half of the peninsula is scarcely penetrated by roads, its southern tip protected by **Parque Nacional Cerro Hoya**, among the most beautiful and remote national parks in Panamá, accessible only by boat or by a long, unpaved road from Santiago.

FIESTAS IN THE PENINSULA DE AZUERO

The Peninsula de Azuero is famous throughout Panamá for its many **religious fiestas**, usually honouring a particular patron saint. Many date back almost unchanged to the days of the early settlers, and represent the most obvious expression of the region's Spanish heritage. Religious **processions** are accompanied by traditional music, fireworks and costumed folkloric dances as **pagan** as they are Catholic. Listed below are just a few of the major events; every village and hamlet has its own main fiesta and there is almost always one going on somewhere – IPAT in Los Santos has good information on all these.

Jan 6 Fiesta de Reyes and Encuentro del Canajagua in Macarcas.
Jan 19–22 Fiesta de San Sebastian in Ocú.
Feb (date varies) Carnaval in Las Tablas (and everywhere else in the country).
March/April (date varies) Semana Santa, celebrated most colourfully in La Villa de Los Santos, Pesé and Guararé.
Late April Feria Internacional del Azuero in La Villa de Los Santos.
June (date varies) Corpus Christi in La Villa de Los Santos.
June 24 Patronales de San Juan in Chitré.
June 29–30 Patronales de San Pedro y San Pablo in La Arena.
July 20–22 Patronales de La Santa Librada and Festival de la Pollera in Las Tablas.
Aug 15 Festival del 'Manito in Ocú.
Sept 24 Festival de La Mejorana in Guararé.
Oct 19 Foundation of the District of Chitré, in Chitré.
Nov 10 The "first cry of independence" in La Villa de Los Santos.

Chitré

The capital of Herrera province and the largest town in the peninsula, **CHITRÉ** is a quiet market centre where life is conducted at a leisurely pace. Other than its small museum there's not much to see, but it is the main transport hub of the peninsula. Chitré centres on the Parque Union, with the usual bandstand, benches and trees, flanked on one side by the **cathedral**, which was built at the turn of the century to replace a pre-existing structure dating back to 1578. It has an impressive vaulted wooden roof and a clock that signals the end of the day with a rendition of Beethoven's *Ode to Joy* at 9pm. The cathedral faces down Av Herrera, the town's main street – walk down a block and turn left on C Manuel Correa to reach the **Museo de Herrera** (Tues–Sat 9am–4pm; US$1), three blocks away. The museum has a collection of pre-Columbian pottery from the surrounding area and a good display on local folklore and customs, featuring traditional masks, costumes and musical instruments. Just off Parque Union on C M. Martin, a shop sells regional **handicrafts** – ceramics, sombreros, leather sandles, fiesta masks and costumes, and **polleras**, the painstakingly embroidered colonial-style dresses characteristic of the peninsula that are something of a national symbol.

Practicalities

Buses from Panamá City pull in at the new **terminal** on the outskirts of town, about ten minutes' walk from the centre. The **IPAT** office for the entire peninsula is in neighbouring Los Santos (see below). The best **hotel** is *Rex* (☎996 4310; ④) on Parque Union, which has comfortable rooms with TV and a/c. *Pension Central* (☎996 0059; ③), and *Hotel El Prado* (☎996 4620 or 6859; ③) are both on Av Herrera near the cathedral; the latter is slightly cleaner and has a balcony overlooking the street. Of the many **restaurants**, the best is the *Meson del Rex* (daily 7am–10pm), in the hotel, its Spanish ownership evident in its red checked tablecloths and excellent, reasonably priced cuisine. Also on the parque, the open-air *Restaurante Aire Libre* (daily 6.30am–10pm) has a limited menu but great breakfasts. *Panadería Chiquita* (daily 5.30am–10.30pm) on Av Herrera is good for cakes, sandwiches and huge pizzas, while *Restaurante Andalucia* (daily 6.30am–7.30pm) on C M. Correa serves good-value fish, seafood and *típica* meals. The **Banco del Istmo** (Mon–Fri 8am–3.30pm) is on the corner of C M. Correa and Av Perez. The **post office** and **telephone office** (Mon–Fri 7.30am–5.30pm) share a building a block down Av Perez.

Moving on from Chitré, buses to Las Tablas, Santiago and to villages in the interior of the peninsula leave from the **terminal**, while buses to Los Santos (every 10min; 10min) can be flagged down at any of the stops on the main streets in town.

Parque Nacional Sarigua

Ten minutes north of Chitré, the village of **La Arena** is famous for its pottery, sold on the roadside by the potters themselves. Further north, just before the village of Parita, a side road leads into **Parque Nacional Sarigua**, eighty square kilometres of **salt flats** ringed by dense **mangroves** that constitute one of the strangest landscapes in Panamá – a harsh, arid desert entirely devoid of vegetation due to occasional flooding by high tides. The salt flats have existed for thousands of years, but deforestation and sea winds that carry salt further inland are contributing to their expansion, threatening the livelihoods of local farmers. Not that the flats support no life at all – the area provides an excellent breeding ground for shrimp, which are farmed commercially and attract numerous wading birds. Indeed, archeological remains suggest that these marine resources provided the basis for Panamá's oldest known human **settlements** – pottery, graves and arrowheads from between 5000 and 1500 BC have been found in the area, as well as mounds of discarded shells. There are several other small **wildlife reserves** on this stretch of the coast, which is the best place in Panamá for observing migrating birds – for information go to the INRENARE office (Mon–Fri 8am–4pm; ☎966 8216) on the road to Los Santos.

To **reach Sarigua**, take any bus heading north from Chitré, get off before Parita and walk 4.5km along the marked dirt road or catch the irregular minibus (1 daily) to the village of Puerto Limón, 1.5km from the park. There's a rangers' station at the entrance to the park and a small **visitors centre** (daily 8am–4pm).

La Villa de Los Santos

South of Chitré just across the Río La Villa, **LA VILLA DE LOS SANTOS** is where the first Panamanian declaration of independence from Spain was made on November 10, 1821. A small, quiet town, Los Santos comes alive twice a year: to commemorate the **"Cry of Independence"** on November 10, and during the eight-day rum-fuelled fiesta of **Corpus Christi** in late May or early June.

The **IPAT** office (Mon–Fri 8.30am–4.30pm; ☎966 8037) on Parque Bolívar, the centre of the town, is probably the best in the country, with excellent information on the peninsula. Also on the parque, the **Museo de la Nacionalidad** (Tues–Sat 9am–4.30pm, Sun 9am–1pm; US$1) has a small collection of colonial religious art and documents relating to the independence declaration. The building – a crumbling eighteenth-century house where the declaration was signed – is actually more interesting than its contents, with a garden filled with traditional handicrafts and agricultural tools. Just off the parque, the **Church of San Anastacio**, begun in the eighteenth century, features several intricately carved baroque colonial altars.

Guararé

From Los Santos the road continues 20km south to Las Tablas, passing through the small town of **GUARARÉ**. It's worth stopping here for the **Museo Manuel F. Zarate** (Tues–Fri 8am–4pm, Sat 8am–noon; US$0.75), behind the church on the main square. It has a fascinating collection on the folklore and fiestas of the peninsula, featuring masks, costumes, old photographs and a collection of the finest *polleras*. Manuel Zarate was a local teacher and musician who was dedicated to conserving the rich folk traditions of the Azuero and in 1949 began the **"La Mejorana" National Folkloric Festival**, a competition of traditional music, dance and costumes from all over Panamá that is still celebrated in Guararé every September 24.

Las Tablas

Turn up at any other time of year and it's almost impossible to believe that this quiet colonial market town hosts the wildest **Carnaval** celebrations in Panamá, but for five days in February **LAS TABLAS** is overwhelmed by visitors from all over the country who come here to join in the festivities. The town divides into two halves – **Calle Arriba** and **Calle Abajo** – that fight a pitched battle with water, paint and soot on streets awash with a seemingly endless supply of *Seco Herrerano*, the vicious firewater of the peninsula. The fiesta of the **Santa Librada**, in July, is less raucous but just as colourful, and incorporates the *pollera* fiesta – the town is the production centre for the most exquisite *polleras* in Panamá.

Practicalities

Buses from Panamá City arrive at the Shell station a few blocks from the square, while those from Chitré pull in to the Parque Porras. For **accommodation**, the *Hotel Zapiro* (☎994 8200; ④) on Parque Porras has modern rooms with a/c and TV, and a balcony overlooking the square that makes it good, though noisy, at fiesta time; the *Hotel Piamonte* (☎994 6372; ④), on Av Belisario Porras a couple of blocks from the square, is bigger and older but otherwise similar; while the *Pensión Mariela* (②), opposite, is pretty seedy. Everywhere fills up for the fiestas, when prices go up. There are several basic **restaurants** on the square – *Las Tinajas* is good – and along Av B. Porras, the best of which is the *Jardin Praga*, with local food and a massive dancehall that is the centre of things on Friday and Saturday nights.

Banks include the Banco del Istmo (Mon–Fri 8am–3.30pm) on the square and the Banco Exterior (Mon–Fri 8am–3pm) a block away on Av B. Porras. If you're heading into Cerro Hoya from this side of the peninsula (see below), you should get **information** and permission from INRENARE (Mon–Fri 8am–4pm; ☎994 7313) on the outskirts of town on the road to Pedasi; this is unnecessary for Isla Iguana and Isla Cañas. **Moving on** from Las Tablas, buses for Pedasi (hourly; 45min) and Tonosi (hourly; 2hr 30min) leave from the square or Av B. Porras.

Pedasi and around

From Las Tablas, a road runs 42km south through cattle country to **PEDASI**, jumping-off point for **Isla Iguana**. Pedasi is a friendly, uneventful little village with a couple of **places to stay**, both on the main street: the long-established *Pensión Moscoso* (☎995 2203; ③), has comfortable rooms with a/c and TV, and less expensive ones with shared bath and fans; while the newer *Hotel Dim* (☎995 2303; ④), has large, well-ventilated rooms and a charming garden with hammocks and a patio. Pedasi's two **restaurants**, the *Angela* (daily 6am–6pm) and *Las Delicias* (daily 6am–8pm), on the same street, serve *típica* food; the latter is slightly more expensive. **Buses** from Las Tablas and along the coast to Cañas via Playa Venao pass along the main street. As well as Isla Iguana, there are several good **beaches** near Pedasi – Playas Destilladeros, Las Almendras, El Toro and Punta Mala. Servicios Ecoturisticos Matzuri (☎995 2446), a small **tour agency** on the square, can arrange transport to these and to Isla Iguana, though you can easily organize this yourself – there are a few taxis in town and some of the beaches are within walking distance.

Isla Iguana
Some 7km off the coast of Pedasi lies **Isla Iguana**, an uninhabited wildlife reserve surrounded by the most extensive **coral reefs** in the Bahía de Panamá. The reefs, composed of twelve different species of coral, teem with more than 540 species of fish, making Isla Iguana one of the best sites for **snorkelling** or **diving** in the country (though unless you come here with an organized tour from Panamá City you need to bring your own equipment). Quite apart from this, the island has white sand beaches, crystalline waters and a colony of some five thousand magnificent frigate birds, though, despite its name, iguanas are scarce – their meat remains a local delicacy. Between May and November you may see **whales**, and even the most inexperienced angler has a good chance of catching big game fish.

You can **rent a boat** to the island from **Playa el Arenal**, a short taxi ride or thirty-minute walk from Pedasi down the dirt road to the right just past the gas station on the road out to Las Tablas. Fishermen charge US$40 round trip (25min each way) in boats that carry up to eleven people – on the weekends, you may find other visitors to share the cost. You should take all the food and drink you need. You can **camp** on the island or sling a hammock under a makeshift shelter on the beach – take plenty of drinking water and arrange for a boat to collect you the next day.

Playa Venao
Thirty kilometres west of Pedasi, the beautiful black-sand **Playa Venao** – Venado with a silent "d" – is great for **surfing**. There's an international competition here every

November – come any other time, though, and you'll not find it crowded. *Jardín Vista Hermosa* (☎995 8107), serves inexpensive **fish** and seafood and rents basic concrete **cabañas** on the beach that sleep up to three people for US$16 a day, though if you eat at the restaurant they don't mind if you camp. Unfortunately, they haven't got round to renting surfboards yet.

Isla Cañas Wildlife Reserve

Separated from the mainland by dense mangrove swamp and with a 14km beach on the seaward side, **Isla Cañas** is the most important **sea turtle nesting** site on Panamá's Pacific coast, frequented by four of the world's eight species of sea turtle. Though archeological evidence suggests that people have been coming to the island to hunt turtles and harvest their eggs for many centuries, it was only settled in the 1960s. The settlers, who now number some 400, have cleared most of the land for crops, but the eggs have always been their principal source of income. Since 1988, the hunting of turtles has been prohibited and a cooperative has been established to **control the harvest**. Members watch over the beaches at night and collect the eggs as soon as they are laid, keeping 80 percent for sale and consumption and moving the rest to a nursery where the turtles can hatch and return to the sea in safety. The Reserve was officially declared in 1994, protecting the mangroves as well as the marine life, and the turtle population has made a dramatic recovery. Come here between May and January and you will almost certainly see green, hawksbill or Olive Ridley turtles laying their eggs at night – the latter often arrive in massive **arribadas** of five to ten thousand in one night between August and November, a truly magnificent sight. From December to March there's a good chance of seeing the leviathan-like leatherback turtle, which can weigh over 800 kilos.

Surprisingly, given the popularity of Parque Nacional Tortuguero in Costa Rica (see p.579), there is as yet almost no tourist development at Isla Cañas, so if you make it down here you will almost certainly have the place to yourself. The island is also very beautiful by day – you can rent a horse and ride along the endless white sand or get one of the locals to take you through the mangroves in a canoe.

Practicalities

To **reach Isla Cañas** take a bus heading for the village of **Cañas** from Pedasi or Tonosi and tell the driver you want to go to the island – the port is down a side road a few kilometres from the village but buses go there on request. **Canoes** wait at the port to take people to the island (US$0.50 per person) through channels cut in the mangroves, though at low tide you may have to wade through mud to reach it. Once on the island you should head for the INRENARE office to pay the US$3 **visitors charge** and get information. The cooperative that manages the turtles – Cooperativa Isleños Unidos – has built three rustic but clean **cabañas** (②) with outside bath and mosquito nets. The latter are absolutely essential, as is insect repellent. The cooperative also has a small **restaurant**, though you should let them know in advance if you want to eat, and for a small tip (a few dollars should suffice) they will assign a member to take you out on the beach at night to **see the turtles** – they may even let you eat an egg or two, fresh-laid and still warm. **Buses** to Pedasi (1–2 daily; 2hr) and Tonosi (1 daily; 1hr) from Cañas usually come down to the port to collect passengers.

Tonosi and Parque Nacional Cerro Hoya

From Cañas the road continues 25km west to **TONOSI**, a small town set in a green valley ringed by mountains. There are several basic **restaurants** and you can **stay** at the *Pension Rosyini* (☎995 8106; ④), but there's no reason to do so unless you get stuck on your way to Isla Cañas. **Buses** to Las Tablas cut through the mountainous interior rather than following the coast via Pedasi. West of Tonosi the southwestern tip of the peninsula is covered by **Parque Nacional Cerro Hoya**, pretty much the last remaining area of natural forest in the Azuero. Rainforest-swathed mountains rise from pristine beaches to heights of more than 1500m, encompassing five distinct lifezones.

It is difficult to reach Cerro Hoya from this side, but you can rent a boat from **Cambutal**, a village on the coast south of Tonosi. You can either camp or ask to stay with one of the few families that live on the fringes of the park. This is expensive, but a real adventure – take all the supplies you may need and get permission from INRENARE in Las Tablas (see p.730), where you should also pay the US$3 entrance fee. IPAT in Los Santos (see p.729) know the region well and can advise on how to organize a trip. Otherwise, it is easier to enter the park along a seasonal dirt road that runs 98km down the west coast of the peninsula from Santiago to the village of **Arena de Quebro**, beyond which it's an hour's walk to the park office at **Restingue**. You can **stay** here in a basic refuge (②); and a network of trails head into the park. If you go this way, get permission from INRENARE in Santiago (see below) first.

Santiago and the route west

The easiest way to continue west from the Azuero is to return to the Interamericana at **Divisa**, though it is possible to cut across the interior – via Pesé, Las Minas and Ocú – from Chitré. From Divisa, the Interamericana continues 36km west to **SANTIAGO**, Panamá's fourth biggest city and a busy market centre. It's an incorrigibly dull and provincial place, with little reason to stay except to break a journey. Pretty much anything you might need is on Av Central, which runs from the Interamericana down to the modern cathedral.

Practicalities

Buses to Panamá City and Chitré arrive and leave from the terminal on C 10, while through buses heading for David pull in at the service station close to the *Hotel Gran David* on the Interamericana. The *Gran David* (☎998 4510; ③) is by far the best **place to stay**, with comfortable rooms set around a central garden and a good restaurant. As for **restaurants**, the *Bueno y Bueno* (daily 9am–9pm), below the *Pension Central* on Av Central, serves good, inexpensive Chinese food; the 24-hour *Cafe El Aire Libre*, a little further down, is very popular for snacks, sandwiches, breakfast and excellent coffee. There are several more upmarket restaurants on the Interamericana close to the *Gran David*. **Banco Nacional** (Mon–Fri 8am–3pm, Sat 9am–noon) and **Banco del Istmo** (daily 8.30am–3.30pm) are both on Av Central, as is the helpful **IPAT** office (Mon–Fri 8.30am–4.30pm; ☎998 3929), towards the Interamericana, which has plenty of information on Veraguas' largely neglected tourist attractions. If you are heading to Cerro Hoya (see above), the **INRENARE** office (Mon–Fri 8.30am–4pm; ☎998 4271) is close to the bus terminal on C 10.

West to David

From Santiago the Interamericana continues west into the rich agricultural province of Chiriquí. A large area of the forested slopes of the Cordillera Central to the north, and the Caribbean coast behind, is recognized as the **Comarca Ngobe-Buglé**. Commonly but erroneously referred to as the Guaymi, the Ngobe and Buglé (or Bokata) are two closely related peoples that together form the largest indigenous group in Panamá. Recognizable by the brightly coloured dresses of the women, the Ngobe-Buglé travel widely throughout the provinces of Chiriquí and Bocas del Toro to work on the farms, ranches and banana and coffee plantations – migrant wage labourers on the rich lands that once belonged to their ancestors.

David and around

The only one of three Spanish settlements founded in the area in 1602 to survive repeated attacks from indigenous groups, **DAVID** developed slowly as a marginal and remote outpost of the Spanish empire – as late as 1732 it was overrun and destroyed by British-backed Miskito groups raiding from Nicaragua. Only as settlement of Chiriquí increased in the nineteenth century did David begin to thrive as a marketing and transportation centre. Today, despite being a busy commercial city – the third largest in Panamá – and the focus of Chiriquí's strong regional identity, it retains a sedate provincial atmosphere. Hot and dusty with unexceptional modern architecture spread out on a well-planned grid (the only surviving feature of the original colonial settlement), David has few attractions, but it is a good place to break a journey between Panamá City and Costa Rica, Bocas del Toro or the Chiriquí highlands – these can be visited as a day-trip, but it is much better to stay up in Boquete or Cerro Punta if you have the time.

Arrival and information

Aeroperlas **flights** from Panamá City, Bocas del Toro and San José arrive at the **airport**, about 5km out of town, a US$2 taxi ride away. Aeroperlas (☎775 4389) have an office just off the parque on C A Nte. **Buses** from Panamá City, Chiriquí Grande, Boquete, Cerro Punta and Paso Canoas, and TRACOPA **international buses** from San José all leave from the terminal on Av Cincuentenario. If you are heading to San José or by express bus to Panamá City you should buy a ticket in advance. There's a self-service **restaurant**, *America* (daily 5am–midnight) in the terminal, and a left-luggage office that's open until

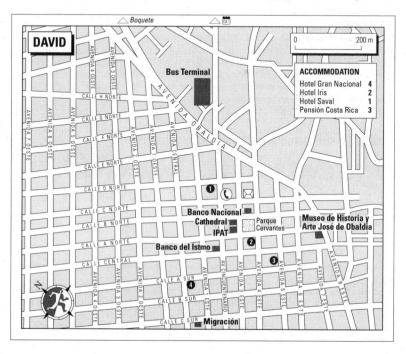

10pm – later than that, the kiosk near the office selling tickets to Panamá City will look after bags for you. The **IPAT** office (Mon–Fri 8.30am–4pm; ☎775 4120), next to the cathedral on the parque, isn't very helpful. If you are heading for Costa Rica and need a visa, the **Costa Rican consulate** (☎775 7725) is on the outskirts of town on the Interamericana, while if you need a Panamanian visa extension or permission to leave the country, **migración** (Mon–Fri 8am–3.30pm; ☎775 4515) is on Calle C Sur.

Accommodation

Accommodation in David is probably the best value in the country. There's a broad range, all in the city centre.

Pensión Costa Rica, Av 5 Este, C A Sur (☎775 1241). Maze-like and ramshackle with rooms of all shapes and sizes, each named after a different Panamanian town. A bit rundown and noisy, but friendly and full of character. ③.

Hotel Gran Nacional, C A Sur, Av Central (☎775 2221 or 2222, fax 775 7729). Recently refurbished and by far the grandest place in town, expensive but good value. Immaculate modern rooms with a/c, phone and TV; bar, pool, casino, and restaurant. ⑥.

Hotel Iris, Parque Cervantes (☎775 2251). Small, clean and comfortable rooms with a/c, TV and hot water. Communal balcony overlooking the parque and a café open 6am–9pm. ④.

Hotel Saval, C D Nte, Av 1 Este (☎775 3543). Quiet and friendly with clean rooms and a pleasant communal patio. More expensive rooms available with a/c. ③.

The Town

David centres on **Parque Cervantes**, a good place to relax with a freshly squeezed sugar-cane juice and get your shoes shined in the shade of its immense trees. Three blocks southeast of the parque down C A Nte on the corner with Av 8 Este, the **Museo de Historia y Arte José de Obaldia** (Tues–Sat 8.30am–4.30pm; US$1) has a small but intriguing collection focusing on local history and culture, ranging from pre-Columbian artefacts and colonial religious art to relics from the Coto War and photographs of David in the early twentieth century. The building is a beautiful colonial mansion that was home to successive generations of the distinguished Obaldia family – José was the founder of the province of Chiriquí and later generations included presidents of both Colombia and Panamá.

Eating, drinking and entertainment.

There are plenty of good value **restaurants** in David, several of which double as nightspots at the weekends. Otherwise, **entertainment** generally revolves around the city's many nondescript bars and poolhalls, and a few discos – the *Brandywine*, a block away from *Pensión Costa Rica* on Av 5 Este, is a current favourite. There are also two **cinemas**: the ageing *Plaza*, just off the parque on C B Nte, and the brand new four-screen *Gran Nacional*, attached to the hotel of the same name.

Cafés and restaurants

Amelia, C D Nte, Av Cincuentenario. Very popular and inexpensive self-service restaurant offering *típica* food. Daily 7am–3pm.

Las Antorchas, C C Nte, Av Central. Upmarket bar and restaurant with good meat, seafood, pasta and Mexican dishes. Excellent service and free snacks with your drinks in the afternoon. Daily 8am–midnight.

Churrascos Place, Av 2 Este, a block from the Parque. A bar and grill with good steaks and a set lunch menu for less than US$2. Open daily 24 hours.

Café Don Dicky, C C Norte, Av Central. Very popular 24-hour café serving basic but good snacks and meals. Excellent sandwiches, fresh orange juice and the strongest coffee in town.

Don Pan, opposite the *Pensión Costa Rica* on Av 5 Este. A bakery that also does sandwiches, snacks, coffee and burgers. Daily 7.30am–10pm.

Café Restaurante Hotel Nacional, Av Central, C A Sur. Decent pizza and meat and fish dishes for US$3–4 and a reasonable set lunch menu, but very slow service. Daily 6am–11pm.

Green House, Av 5 Este, C Central. Small open-air restaurant serving good, inexpensive *típica* food. Particularly popular for breakfast. Daily 7.30am–midnight.

Listings

Banks Banco Nacional (Mon–Fri 8am–3pm; Sat 9am–noon) is on the Parque Cervantes; Banco del Istmo (Mon–Fri 8am–3pm) a block away on the corner of Av Cincuentenario and C Central.

Car rental Avis (☎774 7075); Budget (☎775 1667).

Laundry Lavanderia Panamá (Mon–Sat 7am–7pm), two blocks south of the Parque on Av 3 Este.

Photography The Kodak shop (Mon–Fri 8am–5pm, Sat 9am–5pm) on Parque Cervantes sells and develops films.

Post office The post office (Mon–Fri 7am–6pm; Sat 7am–5pm) is a block away from the parque on C C Nte.

Shopping Deportes Hawaii, two blocks from the parque on Av Cincuentenario sells a wide range of snorkelling, camping and fishing equipment.

Telephone office The INTEL/Cable and Wireless telephone office (daily 8am-4.30pm) is on the corner of Av Cincuentenario and C C Norte.

Tour agencies 4 Tour (☎775 1397) on Via Belisario Porras, and Eco-Tours (☎775 5782) on C A Norte with Av Central can organize excursions throughout Chiriquí and can book whitewater rafting trips (see below).

On to Costa Rica

From David the Interamericana continues west 56km to the Costa Rican border at **PASO CANOAS**, passing through the saddle-making town of La Concepción, from where a side road heads up to Volcán and Cerro Punta (see p.736). The **migración** at the border is open 24 hours, and there's an **IPAT** office (daily 6am–midnight) and a **Banco Nacional** (Mon–Fri 8am–3pm; Sat 9am–noon) where you can change travellers' cheques. Moneychangers will change Costa Rican currency. After passing through *migración* and customs (a formality unless you have anything to declare) you simply walk across the border, though queues for both can be long if international buses are passing through. If you're coming the other way, **buses** for David (every 10min between 5am and 6pm; 1hr 20min) and to Panamá City with PADAFRONT (11 daily; 9hr; express buses at 6.45pm, 9.45pm, 10.45pm; 6–7hr) depart from just beyond the border.

The Chiriquí Highlands

North of David rise the slopes of the **Cordillera Talamanca**, home to **Volcán Barú**, an extinct volcano that at 3475m is the country's tallest peak. These are **the Chiriquí Highlands**, a region of cloudforest-shrouded peaks, fertile valleys and mountain villages. The cool, temperate climate and stark scenery give the highlands a distinctly alpine feel, an illusion reinforced by the influence of the many European migrants who have settled here since the nineteenth century. Sadly, their agricultural success poses a grave threat to the survival of the region's spectacular **cloudforests**, which have been cleared at a devastating rate over the last fifteen years. Large areas are now protected by **Parque Nacional Volcán Barú** and **Parque Internacional La Amistad**, where trails through the cloudforest offer some of the best hiking in Panamá and a chance to see much of its most endangered **wildlife**, including jaguars, pumas, tapirs, harpy eagles and resplendent quetzals.

Two roads wind up into the highlands on either side of Volcán Barú. The first runs from La Concepción through the town of **Volcán** to **Cerro Punta**, the highest village in Panamá and the best base for visiting the cloudforests. The second climbs to **Boquete**, an idyllic coffee growing town that has become a popular resort and is the best place from which to climb Volcán Barú. Between the two, the trail that runs around the back of the volcano through the cloudforests can be walked in a day.

The **tour company** Chiriquí River Rafting (☎236 5218) runs year-round whitewater rafting trips on the rivers that run down from the Chiriquí Highlands through grade III and IV rapids for about US$90 per person per day. Predictably, they are based in Panamá City, but you can book through IPAT or one of the tour agencies in David (see p.735).

The road to Cerro Punta

From La Concepción, the road to Cerro Punta winds up into the mountains through a lush valley with excellent views of the plain and the Golfo de Chiriquí before emerging at **HATO DE VOLCÁN** (known simply as **Volcán**), a small town set on a broad plateau at the foot of Volcán Barú. Spread out along the road with no real centre, Volcán is a resort in its own right, and there are some good **trails** in the surrounding hills, including one to the protected Chiriquí lakes. However, if you want to visit Parque Nacional Volcán Barú you're better off staying in Cerro Punta. If you do choose to **stay** in Volcán, the comfortable *Motel California* (☎771 4274; ④), a US-style motel with hot water close to the crossroads, is the least expensive, and there are several **restaurants**, and a Banco del Istmo (Mon–Fri 8am–3pm), on the main road.

Cerro Punta

Set in a bowl-shaped valley surrounded by densely forested mountains and often swathed in cloud, at almost 2000m above sea-level **CERRO PUNTA** is the highest village in Panamá. In the eighty or so years since it was settled, agriculture has expanded so rapidly that Cerro Punta now produces some 80 percent of the vegetables consumed in Panamá. This has been at the expense of the surrounding forests, and the local population are just beginning to face up to the consequences of **deforestation**, soil erosion and excessive pesticide use. Despite these problems, the village and surrounding fields are still undeniably beautiful, filled with an abundance of flowers buzzing with hummingbirds; and the pristine **cloudforests** of La Amistad and Volcán Barú are within easy reach. This spectacular scenery, together with the cool, crisp mountain air (it even gets cold at night – a rare luxury in Panamá) makes Cerro Punta a perfect base for **hiking**.

Practicalities

Everything is spread out along the main road from David and a side road leading towards Parque Internacional La Amistad. **Buses** from David pull up on the one main street and sometimes do a circuit of the outlying hamlets, which are also served by irregular minibuses. There are a couple of **places to stay**: the *Hotel Cerro Punta* (☎771 2020; ⑤), on the main road, has clean, comfortable rooms with good views; the friendly *Pensión Primavera* (no phone; ④), on the road towards La Amistad, is overpriced, with five musty rooms and a fairytale cottage with its own kitchen (US$40 a night). The newer, non-smoking *Hotel Los Quetzales* (☎771 2182, fax 771 2226; ⑤), in the hamlet of

Guadelupe, has pleasant rooms in a chalet-like building. They can also organize tours with horses and guides into the parks and have three wonderful self-catering cabañas in the cloudforest, where you can watch quetzals and up to ten different species of hummingbird from your balcony while you eat breakfast – an amazing experience, if a bit steep at US$90 a night. All the above have hot water. *Hotel Cerro Punta* has a reasonable **restaurant** (daily 7am–10pm) with meals from about US$5, and there are several places in the village: the *Restaurante Rossmar* (daily 6am–3pm), opposite the *Pensión Primavera*, is best, with very good *típica* food and excellent *batidos de fresa* – creamy milkshakes made with local strawberries. In Guadelupe, *Hotel Los Quetzales* has a great bakery (daily 6.30am–9pm) and there's a supermarket in town.

Parque Internacional La Amistad

Covering 4000 square kilometres of rugged, forested mountains on either side of the border with Costa Rica, **Parque Internacional La Amistad** (PILA) forms a crucial link in the "biological corridor" of protected areas running the length of Central America. Encompassing between seven and nine lifezones, the park supports an incredible biodiversity, including more than four hundred different bird species, making it the most important park in Panamá after Darién (see p.714). Almost all of the Panamanian half of PILA is in Bocas del Toro (see p.741) – from the continental divide its forests sweep down almost undisturbed to the banana plantations on the Atlantic coast around Changuinola – but it is only accessible from this side.

To **get to PILA** from Cerro Punta, walk or take a minibus to **Las Nubes**, a few kilometres away down the well-signposted side road. There's a permanently staffed **park office** here, where you must pay the US$3 **admission charge**; they also have an exhibiton centre and a **refuge** (US$5 per night) – bring your own food and, ideally, a sleeping bag as it gets cold at night. In the early mornings between November and April there's a good chance of seeing quetzals here. There are two well-marked **trails**, with *miradores* offering excellent views of the four highest mountains in Panamá (at least before the cloud descends) and a 55m waterfall, but though it teems with birds, the forest immediately around Las Nubes is secondary growth. The area was heavily deforested in the early eighties when one of Noriega's cronies established an illegal cattle ranch here – the park office was his holiday home – and is only just beginning to recover. Longer trails lead into the virgin cloudforest further away but you will need to get one of the park guards to guide you, which they will usually do if there is more than one of them there. It's a good idea to let them know you're coming in advance by contacting INRENARE in Boquete (see p.738).

The quetzal trail to Boquete

East of Cerro Punta a partially paved road winds 6km up the western slope of Volcán Barú to **Respingo**, a park guard station at the entrance to **Parque Nacional Volcán Barú**, where the US$3 admission fee is rarely charged. There's no refuge, but you can camp. From Respingo **the quetzal trail** runs around the northern flank of the volcano to Boquete, a four- to six-hour hike, mostly downhill, through spectacular cloudforest. For the first hour or so the trail plunges down a steep valley and is difficult to follow, so you should get one of the park guards to guide you as far as a point known as La Victoria, beyond which the trail is easy to follow. It runs along the Río Caldera and eventually becomes a track before emerging at **Alto Chiquero**, another park guard station. From here it is another hour's walk to the tarmac road above Boquete, where you can hitch or walk the last few kilometres into town – take a left turn when you reach the tarmac. Walking the trail in the other direction, from Boquete to Cerro Punta, involves some very steep climbs.

Boquete

Set in the tranquil Caldera Valley 37km north of David at just over 1000m above sea level, **BOQUETE** is the biggest town in the Chiriquí Highlands, the centre of coffee production and a popular weekend resort for the residents of David. The slopes that surround the town are dotted with coffee plantations, flower gardens and orange groves, rising to rugged peaks that are usually obscured by thick cloud that descends on the town in a constant fine mist known as *bajareque*. Only when the cloud clears can you see the imperious peak of Volcán Barú, which dominates the town to the northeast. The town itself is a charming and – except during the annual *feria de las flores y el café*, usually in April – peaceful place, spread out along the road that comes in from David and around two squares, the **Parque de las Madres**, decorated with flowers, fountains and a monument to motherhood, and the **Parque Central**, which bustles with activity during the weekend market. But the real attraction of Boquete is walking or riding in the surrounding countryside and, of course, climbing the volcano – a strenuous day's walk to the summit or a couple of hours by car when the road is in good condition.

Practicalities

Buses from David pull up and depart from the Parque Central, and *transporte urbana* **minibuses** head up to the surrounding hamlets from the streets around the parque – taking one of these and then walking back to town is a good way to see the countryside, and some of them stop near Volcán Barú. As yet there is no IPAT office in Boquete, though plans are afoot to build a massive tourist centre overlooking the town on the road towards David. There's an **INRENARE** office (Mon–Fri 8.30am–4pm) further along the same road in the hamlet of Alto Boquete, where you can get information on trails into PILA, but though technically you should come here to pay the US$3 admission for Volcán Barú, no one does. You can also get information from the hotels or tour companies mentioned below.

There are plenty of **places to stay** in Boquete, though prices are relatively high. All have hot water and tend to fill on the weekends. Most luxurious is the *Panamonte* (☎720 1327 or 1324, fax 720 2055; ⑥), on the way out of town to the north, in an elegant building with a pool, restaurant and a beautiful garden. On the Parque Central, the *Pensión Virginia* (☎720 1260; ④) is charming if slightly delapidated, while opposite each other a few blocks down Av B. Porras the *Hotel Rebequet* (☎720 1365; ⑤) and the *Pensión Marilós* (☎720 1380; ④) are clean and comfortable with kitchens – the latter has less expensive rooms with shared bathrooms. Further down, the *Pensión Topas* (☎720 1005; ⑤) has six rooms decorated with Tintin murals set around a nice garden and small pool with views of the volcano. They serve an excellent breakfast. Its European owners are extremely helpful and knowledgeable and can arrange guided excursions and horse hire.

There's also a wide choice of **restaurants**. *La Conquista* (daily 10am–9.30pm), on the main road, has a hearty set lunch for US$2.25, excellent fresh trout and a glorious selection of thick fruit *batidos*, while the *Casona Mexicana* (daily noon–10pm), as its name implies, offers good Mexican food. *Ristorante Salvatore*, between the square and *Pensión Marilós* on Av B. Porras, serves authentic pizza, and the nameless café (daily 7am–10pm) next door to the *Pensión Virginia* on the square offers burgers, sandwiches and *típica* meals amid classic 1950s US diner decor. On the main road there are a couple of bakeries and a supermarket, a laundry and a **Banco Nacional** (Mon–Fri 8am–3pm, Sat 9am–noon). The **post** and **telephone** offices (Mon–Fri 7am–6pm, Sat 7am–5pm) are both on the main square.

In addition to the *Topas* (see above), Rio Monte Ecological Tours (☎720 1327), at the *Panamonte*, organizes expensive **tours and excursions** – by car to the volcano and to the owner's coffee *finca* where a sight of a resplendent quetzal is almost guaranteed between January and August. Run by young, enthusiastic locals, Expediciones Tierras Altas (☎720 1342), across the bridge to the left as you head out on the road towards David, offers similar tours at much lower prices, with the emphasis on hiking in the forests north of the volcano.

Volcán Barú

Boquete's biggest attraction is undoubtedly the ascent of **Volcán Barú**. A 22km road winds up through spectacular scenery to the peak, from which on clear days (unfortunately few and far between) both oceans can be seen. The volcano receives 5m of rain a year, and is often enveloped in thick cloud, so outside the dry season, your best chance of experiencing the view is to be on the peak at dawn. This is only possible if you walk out, walk all night or drive up a couple of hours before, but even if the view is partially obscured it is still a worthwhile climb.

The first 6km of the road is paved, after which it becomes a rough track passable with 4WD only, and sometimes in the rainy season it becomes impossible even for them –check conditions in town before you set off. To **walk** to the summit it is best to get a *transporte urbana* minibus or a taxi (US$4–5) to the end of the tarmac, beyond which it is a steep and strenuous four- to six-hour hike, and another six hours or so back to Boquete, unless you catch another minibus on the way down. If you are lucky you might be able to hitch a ride on a truck heading to one of the farms on the lower slopes, or even all the way to the summit with a telecommunications vehicle, but otherwise it's a long day's walk and you should take waterproof clothing and plenty of food and water. The road passes coffee plantations tended by Ngobe labourers which soon give way to majestic cloudforest, its tall trees bearded with lichen and covered with orchids and bromeliads. As you climb, the views of the Caldera Valley, the plains around David and the islands of the Gulf of Chiriquí open up, the air gets cooler, and the cloudforest gradually gives way to stunted, elfin forest and finally to bleak high-altitude paramo. Surrounded by seven long-extinct craters and crowned by a cluster of telecommunications aerials, the **peak** is often shrouded in cloud, but don't let this dishearten you – even in the depths of the rainy season the cloud breaks every so often to reveal the sight of at least one of the oceans and of the forest-covered mountains marching west to Costa Rica. Trails lead down the other side to Hato de Volcán and Cerro Punta, but they are difficult to follow without a guide. You can camp on the grassy plateau just below the peak, but it gets very cold at night and there is rarely any water available.

travel details

BUSES

Boquete to: David (every 25min; 1hr).

Cañas to: Pedasi (1–2 daily; 2hr); Tonosi (1 daily; 1hr).

Cerro Punta to: David (every 20min; 2hr 30min).

Chiguiri Arriba to: Penonomé (1–2 daily; 1hr 20min).

Chitré to: Las Tablas (every 10min; 30min); Los Santos (every 10min; 10min); Panamá City (hourly; 4hr); Santiago (every 45min; 1hr 20min).

David to: Boquete (every 25min; 1hr); Cerro Punta (every 20min; 2hr 30min); Chiriquí Grande (8 daily; 3–4hr); Panamá City (hourly; 7hr; 2 express buses daily 10.30pm & midnight; 5hr); Paso Canoas (every 10min; 1hr 20min); San José, Costa Rica (1 daily; 7hr 30min).

El Valle to: Panamá City (every 35min; 2hr 30min); San Carlos (every 45min; 20min).

Las Tablas to: Chitré (every 10min; 30min); Panamá City (every 2hr; 4hr 30min); Pedasi (hourly; 45min); Tonosi (hourly; 2hr30min).

Los Santos to: Chitré (every 10min; 10min).

Panamá City to: Chitré (hourly; 4hr); David (hourly; 7hr; 2 express buses daily 10.30pm & midnight; 5hr); El Valle (every 35min; 2hr 30min);

Las Tablas (every 2hr; 4hr 30min); Paso Canoas (11 daily; 9hr; 3 express buses daily in evening; 7hr); Penonomé (every 20min; 2hr 30min); Santiago (every 30min; 4hr).**Paso Canoas** to: David (every 10min; 1hr 20min); Panamá City (11 daily; 9hr; 3 express buses daily in evening; 7hr).

Pedasi to: Cañas (1–2 daily; 2hr); Las Tablas (hourly; 45min).

Penonomé to: Chiguiri Arriba (1–2 daily; 1hr 20min); Panamá City (every 20min; 2hr 30min).

San Carlos to: El Valle (every 45min; 20min).

Santiago to: Chitré (every 45min; 1hr 20min); Panamá City (every 30min; 4hr).

Tonosi to: Cañas (1 daily; 1hr); Las Tablas (hourly; 2hr 30min).

FLIGHTS

Aeroperlas (☎2694555)

David to: Bocas del Toro via Changuinola (1 daily Mon–Fri; 1hr 10min); Panamá City (2–3 daily; 1hr); San José, Costa Rica (4 weekly; 1hr).

Panamá City to: David (2–3 daily; 1hr).

CHAPTER 38

BOCAS DEL TORO

I solated on the Costa Rican border between the Caribbean and the forested slopes of the Cordillera Talamanca, **Bocas del Toro** (Bocas) is one of the most remote and beautiful provinces in Panamá. Until the road across the cordillera from the province of Chiriquí to Chiriquí Grande was built in the early 1980s, Bocas del Toro was completely cut off from the rest of Panamá, accessible only by sea, air or via Costa Rica. Christopher Columbus explored its coast during his third voyage in 1502, but during the **colonial era** the Spanish had little success in taming the many warring indigenous tribes that populated the mountainous interior, and European pirates often sheltered in the calm waters between its many offshore islands. Only in the nineteenth century did Bocas del Toro begin to develop, and even then it was as an enclave of **US banana corporations**, little related to the rest of the country. Concentrated on the islands of the Bocas del Toro Archipelago, the plantations brought a measure of prosperity – in 1895 they accounted for over half of Panamá's export earnings – and transformed the population. Though the inland forests are still populated by **indigenous groups** – Ngobe-Buglé, Naso and Bribrí – the islands are inhabited by the descendants of **West Indian** workers brought to work on the plantations, and English, or rather *Guari-Guari* – Jamaican patois embellished with some Spanish and Ngobere – remains the lingua franca.

Plagued by disease in the early twentieth century, the banana plantations were relocated to the lowlands around Changuinola, and the islands reverted to the tropical indolence that characterizes them today. It is these islands that form the main attraction for a growing number of visitors – thanks largely to its accessibility from Costa Rica you are likely to meet more travellers here in a day than in the rest of the country in a month.

Described by Dr Charles Hanley of the Smithsonian Institute as the "Galapagos of the twenty-first century", the **Bocas del Toro Archipelago** is the last frontier of the Caribbean, the outstanding natural beauty of its ecosystems – tropical forests, mangroves, deserted beaches, extensive coral reefs, crystalline waters teeming with rare marine life – largely protected by the **Parque Nacional Marino Isla Bastimentos**. An incipient tourist industry is emerging based in the provincial capital, **Bocas del Toro**, and, predictably, land speculation and foreign investment are rearing their heads, but for the moment the region remains scarcely developed.

The coastal banana zone is usually visited only by those heading to Costa Rica, but from Changuinola you can also penetrate into the great wilderness that still covers most of the province by heading up the Río Teribe to **Panajungla**.

Chiriquí Grande

From the village of Chiriquí, 14km east of David on the Interamericana, a spectacular road runs across the continental divide, crossing the Fortuna hydroelectric dam and through the pristine forests that protect its watershed, to **CHIRIQUÍ GRANDE**, the Atlantic terminal of the trans-Panamanian oil pipeline that transports Alaskan oil across

For an explanation of **accommodation price codes**, see p.664.

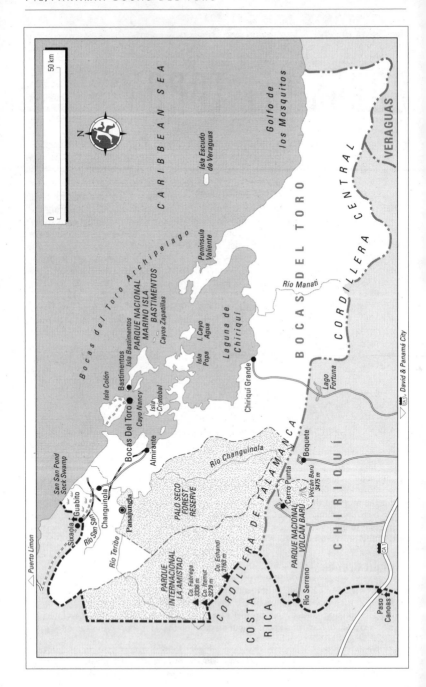

the isthmus. Hemmed in by dark forested mountains, Chiriquí Grande is a ramshackle port town of tin-roofed houses that project on stilts over the calm waters of **Laguna de Chiriquí**. There's a road up the coast to Almirante under construction, much to the consternation of environmentalists and local indigenous groups, but for the moment the only way to continue from here is by boat. A **car ferry** (*palanga*) runs daily to Almirante (4hr) and twice a week to Bocas del Toro (5hr); its schedule changes frequently. Better by far are the fast **water taxis** that leave for Almirante (1hr 20min) from beside the ferry port – the last one to connect with an onward water taxi to Bocas del Toro leaves at about 4pm. There's no reason to **stay** in Chiriquí Grande unless you miss an onward connection, but there are a few options, spread out, like everything else, along the one main street. The a/c *Hotel Emperador* (no phone; ④) is the best, closely followed by the *Marisol* (☎757 9012; ③); the basic *Posada Siquem Inn* (no phone; ②) is the least expensive. Of several **restaurants**, the simple *Marismar-Chinese Food Ji Hai* (daily 7am–9pm) and the more upmarket *Steakmar* (daily 11am–11pm) are the most popular. **Buses** for David leave from the port, where a **Banco Nacional** (Mon–Fri 8am–3pm, Sat 9am–noon) changes travellers' cheques.

Almirante

From Chiriquí Grande water taxis head out across Laguna de Chiriquí, weaving through narrow channels between small islands where stilted Ngobe houses perch above the mangroves to **ALMIRANTE**, an equally ramshackle port from where the Changuinola bananas are exported. The **ferry** to Bocas del Toro and on to Chiriquí Grande (5hr) usually leaves in the morning, and water taxis to Chiriquí Grande (1hr 20min) and Bocas del Toro (25min) leave every hour or so – the last for Bocas del Toro is at 6pm. If you arrive by **bus**, touts from the two **watertaxi** companies, Taxi 25 and De La Tours, will lead you to the port – the services are exactly the same, though you should check which company is leaving first before you buy a ticket. **Buses** for **Changuinola**, where you can get connections for the border, leave from the terminal close to the port. Adjacent to the terminal is the **railway station**, from which a banana workers' train runs to the border each morning – it's much slower, but is the last running passenger train in Panamá and good for leisurely sightseeing.

Once again, there is no reason to **stay** here unless you get stuck heading to Bocas del Toro from Costa Rica. If you do, try the a/c *Hotel Gran Hong Kong* (☎658 3763; ④), two blocks towards the banana port from the railway station. The *Delimar*, by the banana dock, is the best **restaurant**, and there are several basic places near the bus terminal and the water taxi dock. There is a **Banco Nacional** (Mon–Fri 8am–3pm, Sat 9am–noon) opposite the *Gran Hong Kong*.

Bocas del Toro

Connected to the rest of Isla Colón by a narrow causeway, the provincial capital of **BOCAS DEL TORO** is by far the best base from which to explore the islands, beaches and reefs of the archipelago. It is also a charming place, with classically Caribbean rickety wooden buildings painted in faded pastels, and a disconcertingly friendly English-speaking population. There's nothing much to see, but that's hardly a problem – after a hard day in the sea and the sun there's no better place to chill out with a cool drink and the local calypso music while the sun sets behind the forest-covered mountains of the mainland and the air fills with delicious cooking smells.

Arrival, orientation and information

Bocas is a small town and it is easy to find your way around. Most activity is concentrated on C 3, on the seafront. The **ferry** from Almirante docks at its eastern end,

De La Tours water taxis beside *Le Pirate* restaurant on the same street, and **Taxi 25 water taxis** just off C 3 on C 1. Flights with Aeroperlas (☎757 9341) from David, Panamá City and San José arrive at the **airport**, a few blocks away up Av G. The small **IPAT** office (Mon–Fri 8.30am–4.30pm; ☎757 9642), on stilts over the sea in front of C 3, is one of the most helpful in the country. You can get information on the Isla Bastimentos park and on the other, more remote protected areas in the province from **INRENARE** (daily 8.30am–4pm; ☎757 9441) on C 1, though at the moment you don't need to come here for permission to enter the park. A new building to house both IPAT and the INRENARE personnel dealing with ecotourism is under construction on C 3. The **Banco Nacional** (Mon–Fri 8am–3pm, Sat 9am–noon), **post office** (Mon–Sat 8am–5pm) and **migracíon** (Mon–Sat 8am–4pm) are on Av F between C 2 and 3, and there are several public **telephones** in front of Parque Simón Bolívar, also on C 1.

Accommodation

Accommodation in Bocas is among the least expensive in Panamá, with an ever-increasing range, and more and more foreign-owned places. For a more authentic Bocas experience, several families rent rooms in their houses.

Hotel Bahia, at the far end of C 3 by the ferry dock (☎757 9626). Imposing early twentieth-century wooden structure that was formerly the United Fruit Company HQ, with a communal balcony overlooking the sea. Comfortable but musty rooms with ageing funiture. More expensive rooms have a/c, TV and hot water. ④.

Hotel Las Brisas, on the corner of C 3 and Av Norte (☎757 9248). Friendly, with a variety of rooms, including some with a/c. Free coffee in the morning and a floating patio. ④.

Pensión Las Delicias, C 3 opposite the IPAT office (☎757 9318). Large, dark rooms suited to large groups. Cheaper rooms have shared bathroom. Noisy at night at the weekends. ③.

Hospedaje Heike, C 3 facing the square (☎757 9558). Small, friendly, good value place that's often full. One room has a balcony overlooking the square. Shared bath and use of kitchen. ②.

Hotel Laguna, C 3 opposite De La Tours watertaxi dock (☎757 9091, fax 757 9092). The most upmarket place in town, brand new and Italian-owned with a 24-hour bistro. Immaculate rooms with a/c and hot water. ⑤.

Mangrove Inn Eco-Resort, a short boat trip around the west side of the peninsula – book in their office on C 3 (☎757 9594). Purpose built luxury eco-dive resort with comfortable wooden cabins on stilts over the water. Rates include food and boat excursions. ⑦ or ⑧ with diving equipment.

Casa Señora Soya Lopez, C 6, Av Norte (no phone). Classic Caribbean-style private home with a charming owner who rents three comfortable rooms with a shared bathroom. Homely atmosphere and excellent value. ②.

Eating, drinking and nightlife

There are plenty of **restaurants** in Bocas, though the increasing number of foreign-owned pizza and pasta joints compare poorly with the distinctive and delicious **local cuisine** – fresh fish and seafood cooked in coconut milk with sharp Caribbean spices. Several restaurants double as music and drinking venues in the evening, but the nameless shed-like **bar** on the seafront is the place to be on the weekends, with booming bass and free-flowing beer, while *Starfleet Eco-Adventures*, on C 1 (see below), also has a bar with live Bocas-style calypso music on the weekends.

Buena Vista Deli and Bar, C 1, just off C 3. Authentic US burgers, snacks and cocktails and US sports on satellite TV, with only the view of the Caribbean to remind you you are not in San Francisco. Wed–Sun noon–8pm, Mon 4pm–midnight.

Kun Ja, corner of C 3 and C 1. Inexpensive, no-nonsense Chinese food in a neon-lit room. Daily 10am–4pm & 5.30–10pm.

Lako's Place, Av Norte, C 5. Large portions of very good fish and seafood, inexpensive ice-cold beer and loud reggae music in the evenings. Daily 9am–midnight.

EXCURSIONS FROM BOCAS

In addition to the Marine Park (see p.746), there are endless possibilities for boat excursions from Bocas further afield: west around the **Peninsula Valiente** to the **Isla de Escudo de Verguas**, which aficionados consider one of the best diving spots in the whole Caribbean, or up one of the rivers into the rainforests of the mainland to visit isolated Ngobe-Bugle communities. The **Río Manati** which flows into Laguna de Chiriquí and the **San San Pond Sock** swamp, west of Changuinola, both support manatee, the extremely endangered and rarely seen Caribbean sea-cow, as well as turtles and a great variety of bird life. Diving with the gentle, lethargic manatee is an amazing experience, though to visit San San Pond Sock you should check with INRENARE in Bocas first. The price of gas makes excursions expensive, but the relative cost comes down if you can put a group of five or six people together. Most of the tour companies listed below – try Captain Cesar Smith at Transparente Tours – can organize such trips but don't promote them, as they don't think visitors are interested in much beyond sea and sand.

TOUR COMPANIES IN BOCAS DEL TORO

ANCON, the National Conservation Association, office and environmental education centre on Av Norte (☎757 9226). Heavily involved in efforts to protect Bocas' marine turtle population, with occasional excursions to see turtles laying eggs on the beaches of the Marine Park.

Bocas Water Sports, C 3 (☎757 9541). Diving and snorkelling excursions and equipment rental. Professional and US-run.

The Eden Project, C 3 (☎757 9608). Snorkelling excursions and equipment rental, as well as trips into the rainforest on the mainland, in the name of environmental conservation.

Starfleet Eco-Adventures, C 1 (☎757 9630). Diving and snorkelling excursions on a ten-metre catamaran, equipment rental for both and full PADI open water diving courses (about US$250 plus equipment). Friendly, professional team. Canadian-owned.

Transparente Tours, inside *Le Pirate* restaurant on C 3 (☎757 9600). Regular excursions into the Marine Park, along with customized trips. Run by experienced locals.

El Lorito de Don Chicho, C 3 opposite the square. Always busy with a lively atmosphere and good, inexpensive, self-service *típica* food. Daily 6.30am–midnight.

Mondo Taitu, Av Norte, C H. Best of the Italian restaurants in town: Mediterranean sophistication applied to local ingredients with excellent results. Daily noon–11pm.

La Palmita, a few blocks up Av Sur from the ferry dock. Excellent seafood restaurant on a floating platform over the sea decorated with conch shells and red lighting. Very popular with the locals, with loud music and a lively atmosphere at weekends. Happy hours 6–7pm. Mon–Sat 10am–11pm, Sun 6–11pm.

Le Pirate, C 3, beside the De La Tours watertaxi dock. Expensive Italian restaurant more popular as a bar, especially for sundowners during the 4–6pm happy hour. Daily 10am–10pm.

Isla Colón

From Bocas town, a dirt road runs across a narrow isthmus to Isla Colón and forks after about 1.5km – one branch heading across the centre of the island to Boca del Drago, on the north coast, the other 8km up the east coast towards Bluff point. This road passes **Playa Bluff**, a long white sand beach occasionally visited by turtles. The surf here can be powerful and the currents strong, so be careful and don't swim alone. *Camping Guaymi* (②), has several very basic indigenous-style **cabañas** scattered among the palm trees on the beach with mattresses and hammocks but no electric light, and a very laid back roots-reggae surfer vibe. To stay here either make your own way or ask for Kinga, the boss, in *Pensión Las Delicias* in Boca. He also prepares inexpensive meals and usually has cold drinks and *pipas* – drinking coconuts – to sell, as well as a couple of surfboards he sometimes rents.

BOCA DEL DRAGO is a small fishing community set on a broad horseshoe bay with calm waters perfect for swimming and a narrow beach fringed with palmtrees and patches of mangrove and coral. You can stay here at *Cabañas Estefani* (☎774 3168, ext 2020; ③), which has two cosy self-catering cabins; the small restaurant next door (closed Tues) serves simple, delicious fish and seafood.

A **bus** runs from Boca del Drago to the market in Bocas town on Monday, Wednesday and Friday at 6am, returning at 12.30pm, but otherwise the best way to get around is by **bicycle**. The hotels *Las Brisas* and *Laguna* and the *Farmacia Chen* rent bikes by the hour or for about US$7 a day.

Bastimentos and the National Marine Park

Just across the water from Bocas town on the western tip of **Isla Bastimentos** is the small fishing community of **BASTIMENTOS**, one of the few parts of the island not included in the National Marine Park. Though barely developed for tourism, a few places offer **rooms**, the best of which is the welcoming *Mr Wolf's Place* (no phone; ④), which has two very comfortable rooms. The German Mr Wolf is very helpful and lets guests use his canoe, snorkelling equipment, and kitchen for free. *Pensión Bastimentos* (no phone; ②–③), on a floating wooden platform beside the dock, is also pleasant and friendly, with a good restaurant, while *Pensión Archibold* (no phone; ②–③), further up the hill, has basic concrete cabins. From the village a trail leads 1km or so across the island to **Red Frog beach**, which is good for swimming, and it is easy to hire a boatman to take you elsewhere in the Marine Park.

Parque Nacional Marina Isla Bastimentos

Most visitors to Bocas come to explore the pristine beauty of **Parque Nacional Marina Isla Bastimentos**, a 130-square-kilometre reserve that encompasses a range of virtually undisturbed **ecosystems**, including rainforest, mangrove, and coral reef. Deserted white sand beaches and extensive reefs support an immense diversity of **marine life**, including dolphins, sea turtles and a kaleidoscopic variety of fish – a veritable paradise for snorkellers and divers. The easiest way to visit the park is with one of the **tour companies** in Bocas town (see p.745), which offer a variety of excursions for about US$10–15 per person, though you can easily rent a boat yourself from one of the fishermen who wait at the docks on C 3. They usually charge US$30–40 for a day (more if you want to go further – the price of gas determines everything). Haggling is not necessary. The most popular destinations are the wonderful beaches around the north side of Isla Bastimentos, and to **Crawl Cay**, an island off the south side, with excellent snorkelling among mangroves and coral reefs. The best snorkelling is around the **Zapatilla Cays**, two idyllic coral-fringed islands to the east of Bastimentos where Henry Morgan is supposed to have buried his loot – treasure-seekers have so far failed to find it and the pirate's curse is supposed to hang over anyone who does. There is an INRENARE station on one of the cays, the only place where the US$10 **park admission fee** is currently charged.

Changuinola

From Almirante the road to the border runs 29km west through seemingly endless banana plantations to **CHANGUINOLA**, a typically hot and uninteresting banana town where almost everyone works for the Chiriquí Land Company ("The Company", successor to United Fruit) which owns most of the surrounding land. There's no reason to stop unless you get stuck between Costa Rica and Bocas or on your way to the Río Teribe. **Buses** from Almirante and the border at Guabito arrive and leave from the **terminal**, which is usually busy with workers heading to the banana fincas, known by numbers rather than names. If you do end up **staying** here, everything you might need is along the main road that runs alongside the terminal, including, the a/c *Hotel Carol* (☎758 8731; ③), a **Banco del Istmo** (Mon–Fri 8am–3.30pm, Sat 9am–noon) and several **restaurants**: *La Piquera* (daily 7am–10pm) in the bus station is good and inexpensive, while the *Chiquita Banana* (daily 6am–1pm), opposite, is more upmarket.

Crossing the border

From Changuinola the road runs 16km to the border with Costa Rica at **GUABITO**. There's little here except a few shops selling consumer goods to Costa Rican day-trippers and a **migracíon** (daily 8am–6pm), beyond which it's a short walk across a bridge to Costa Rica, where you can change currency. Buses for Guabito are marked "Las Tablas."

Río Teribe

From Changuinola you can make an interesting side trip up the **Río Teribe**, which rushes down from the forested mountains of La Amistad and is home to the **Naso** people, the smallest remaining indigenous group in Panamá apart from scattered comunities of Bribri on the border. Now numbering some three thousand, the Naso cultivate subsistence crops and fruit as well as working on the plantations, and, uniquely among the indigenous peoples of the Americas, are ruled by a hereditary monarchy. With support from IPAT and INRENARE a group of young Naso have set up an ecotourism company, EDEN, and built a basic tourist lodge amid the ruins of **Panajungla**, a jungle warfare training base during the Noriega years.

Panajungla

To reach Panajungla, take a minibus fom the terminal in Changuinola to **El Silencio** on the Río Changuinola (20min), where you can rent a boat to take you up the Teribe for about US\$30 – you might find a boat going anyway that will take you for a few dollars, but don't count on it. The trip up the fast-flowing Teribe takes about an hour, but within minutes the pesticide-drenched monotony of the banana plantations gives way to dense forest. Kingfishers flit overhead; Naso traders, taking oranges to market on precarious bamboo rafts, pole themselves over the rapids; and you may see otters dancing in the rushing white water.

Set on a high bluff overlooking the river, **Panajungla** is the closest Panamá gets to a lost city, with crumbling concrete barracks buildings painted with camouflage and military slogans all but swallowed by the encroaching rainforest. There is an INRENARE station with a small generator, and the EDEN **lodge**. Cooking facilities are available but you will need to bring food, bedding and mosquito nets or coils. Naso guides can take you on **trails** into the forest or to communities further up river. Otherwise you can fish or swim, and, for your return journey, get the Naso to help you build a raft to carry you back to El Silencio on the current. EDEN haven't worked out how much to charge for accommodation, for river transport or for working as guides, and have almost no experience of foreigners, so when you negotiate prices with them remember that your behaviour will shape their future attitude towards travellers. If you want to make this trip, it's a good idea to get in touch with **IPAT** or **INRENARE** in Bocas (see p.744) – they can radio ahead to let EDEN know you are coming, and get them to meet you at El Silencio.

travel details

BUSES

Almirante to: Changuinola (every 30min; 45min).
Changuinola to: Almirante (every 30min; 45min);
Guabito (every 30min; 20min).
Chiriquí Grande to: David (8 daily; 3–4hr).
David to: Chiriquí Grande (8 daily; 3–4hr).
Guabito to: Changuinola (every 30min; 20min).

BOATS

FERRY (*PALANGA*) *
* Only one of the two ferries is currently operating, and the schedule changes frequently.
Almirante to: Chiriquí Grande (1 daily; 4hr 30min).
Bocas del Toro to: Chiriquí Grande (2 weekly; 5hr).
Chiriquí Grande to: Almirante (1 daily; 4hr 30min); Bocas del Toro (2 weekly; 5hr).

WATERTAXI

Almirante to: Bocas del Toro (8 daily; 25min);
Chiriqui Grande (10 daily; 1hr 20min).
Bocas del Toro to: Almirante (8 daily; 25min).
Chiriqui Grande to: Almirante (10 daily; 1hr 20min).

FLIGHTS

Panamá City to: Bocas del Toro (1 daily; 1hr 40min).
Bocas del Toro to: David (1 daily Mon–Fri; 55min); Panamá City (1 daily; 1hr 40min); San José, Costa Rica (5 weekly; 1hr 30min).
David to: Bocas del Toro (1 daily Mon–Fri; 55min).
San José, Costa Rica to: Bocas del Toro (5 weekly; 1hr 30min).

CHRONOLOGY OF CENTRAL AMERICA

15,000 –12,000 BC	First waves of **nomadic hunters** from the north spread down through Mexico and the isthmus.
7500 BC	Evidence of settled agricultural communities throughout Mesoamerica – maize cultivation and domestication of animals – particularly in the northern regions.
1500 BC	Formative period of the **Maya culture** across Mesoamerica. Cultural and trade links with, among others, the Olmecs of Mexico. Southern Central America – present-day Panamá and Costa Rica – has links extending both north and south with settled agricultural communities. Immigrants from South America migrate up the isthmus, reaching as far as Honduras by 1000 BC.
300 AD	**Classic period** of Maya culture in Mesoamerica begins. Emergence of the great city states at Teotihuacán, Tikal, Copán and elsewhere; scientific and artistic development reaches its peak. Trade contact with the various groups living further south along the isthmus.
c. 900	Classic Maya culture begins to **decline**, with many of the great cities abandoned. The influence of Toltec and other **Mexican civilizations** travels down the isthmus; a Toltec–Maya civilization establishes itself in what is now Guatemala. The **Lenca**, descended from South American Chibchan groups, establish themselves in Honduras and El Salvador. Waves of **Nahua**-speaking groups migrate down the isthmus, settling as far south as northern Costa Rica.
1400–1475	**Quiché** overrun much of Guatemala establishing a short-lived area of dominance.
1500	Central America inhabited by a number of different groups, none predominant and none ultimately capable of withstanding the conquest. The Maya region is divided in a shifting pattern of alliances between rival city-states.
1502	**Columbus** lands on the island of Guanaja and first sights the Central American mainland. First Catholic mass said at Punto Caxinas (Trujillo, Honduras); first exploration of the Atlantic coast.
1510	First Spanish settlement founded in Panamá by **Diego de Nicuesa**.
1513	**Vasco Nuñez de Balboa** crosses the isthmus of Panamá to become the first European to look out on the Pacific Ocean.
1519	**Hernan Cortés** lands in Mexico.
1522	**Gil González Davila** sails from Panamá up the Pacific coast, exploring as far north as Honduras.
1523	**Pedro de Alvarado** arrives in Guatemala and defeats the the dominant Quiché tribe at Quetzaltenango. His army explores down into El Salvador.
1524	**Cristóbal de Olid** arrives in Honduras and founds the first Spanish settlement there. **Francisco Hernández de Córdoba** founds the cities of Granada and León in Nicaragua.

1524–40	**Spanish conquest** of the isthmus proceeds, encountering and defeating resistance such as the Lempira rebellion in Honduras. *Audiencia de los Cofines* – essentially the seat of **government of the region** – first founded at **Gracias, Honduras**, in 1539.
1548	Seat of the *Audiencia* moved to **Antigua, Guatemala**; Guatemala becomes the predominant region during Spanish rule.
17th C.	Development of **colonial rule** throughout Central America. Spain claims sovereignty over Belize but never effectively colonizes it. British and other pirates use the Atlantic coast of the isthmus and its islands as a refuge.
18th C.	Colonial Central America remains a backwater, producing no great riches for the Spanish. **British claims** to Belize, Mosquitia and the Bay Islands are denied. Britain cedes all claims to land, except Belize, in 1786.
1773	Series of devastating **earthquakes** destroy Antigua, Guatemala; the capital is moved to **Guatemala City** in 1776.
1797	**Garífuna** forced to migrate to Roatán from the island of St Vincent. Quickly move on to settle along the north coast of **Honduras**.
1821	Mexico and Central America gain **independence** from Spain. Short-lived monarchy under the Mexican **Augustín Iturbide**. Panamá declares independence and becomes part of Gran Colombia, later simply **Colombia**.
1822	Iturbide is deposed.
1823	The Monroe Doctrine is announced, asserting US geo-political interests in Central America. Following Iturbide's deposition, the provinces of Central America (except Chiapas, now part of Mexico) declare themselves an independent republic – the **Central American Federation** – on July 1. First president is Salvadorean **Manuel José Arce**.
1824–39	**Civil war** almost immediately follows the creation of the republic, prompted by rivalry between Conservatives and Liberals. **Francisco Morazán** becomes president in 1830, and tries to institute reform of the church and government. Fighting breaks out again with Morazán failing to crush the 1837 **rebellion** of Rafael Carrera in Guatemala. With Morazán's resignation in 1839 the Central American Federation is finished. The states become independent republics, except for Panamá, which remains part of Colombia.
1820s–1850s	**British** again assert claims to Belize, Mosquitia, Bay Islands and north coast of Nicaragua. **Cruz Wyke treaty** cedes all territories except Belize.
1855	US filibuster **William Walker** elected president of Nicaragua. Announces intention to take over the other republics. Driven out in 1857.
1860	Walker returns, capturing Trujillo in Honduras. Taken prisoner by British navy and executed by the Honduran army.
1862	Belize officially becomes part of the British Empire as the **Colony of British Honduras**.
1870s	Beginning of **coffee** boom in Guatemala, El Salvador and Costa Rica.

1890s   Beginning of **banana** boom in Guatemala, Honduras, Costa Rica and Panamá. Influence of US fruit companies begins to grow.

1903   **Panamá** declares **independence** from Colombia; new government recognized by US, which immediately presents a treaty for construction of the canal.

1904   Work on the **Panamá Canal** begins; completed in 1914.

1912   US responds to a **rebellion in Nicaragua** by landing 2500 marines. Start of domination of Nicaraguan politics by US.

1932   La Matanza (the Massacre): thirty thousand peasants and indigenous people, led by Augustín Farabundo Martí, murdered in El Salvador by security forces following an anti-government rebellion.

1934   Socialist **Augusto César Sandino** assassinated in Nicaragua on orders of US-supported **Anastasio Somoza**. Somoza founds a dictatorship that will last 45 years.

1948   "**Revolution**" in **Costa Rica**; Figueres assumes presidency under the Junta of the Second Republic. The following year a new constitution introduces universal suffrage and abolishes the army.

1954   CIA-backed military coup ends the Guatemalan presidency of socialist Jacob Arbenz. Start of **military rule** in **Guatemala** and a series of military-backed dictators.

late 1950s   Frente Sandinista de Liberación Nacional (**FSLN**) movement formed in **Nicaragua**.

1960   **Guerrilla war** begins in Guatemala's eastern highlands.

1963   Military coup installs **Col. Oswaldo López Arellano** as president of **Honduras**. Beginning of overt military influence on government.

1964   Full internal self-government granted to **Belize**.

1968   **Panamá's** Guardia Nacional deposes the president, suspends the constitution and dissolves parliament. Lieutenant-Colonel (later General) **Omar Torrijos** assumes leadership of country.

1969   Honduras and El Salvador engage in the five-day "**Football War**", essentially over a disputed border but triggered by a soccer match.

1972   **Earthquake** in **Managua** leaves over 10,000 dead and many more homeless. International aid money is appropriated by President Somoza. Opposition to the dictatorship grows.

1972   **El Salvador's President Duarte** exiled by the military, who assume government. Upsurge in guerrilla activity and creation of right-wing paramilitary "death squads". Kidnapping and extra-judicial killing of civilians increase.

1976   **Earthquake** in Guatemala leaves 23,000 dead and 77,000 homeless.

1977   **New Canal Treaty** allows for Panamá to assume control of most of canal zone, with total control to be handed over by the end of 1999, along with phasing out of US bases in the country.

1979	Somoza flees Nicaragua and **Sandinistas** march into Managua on July 19.
1980	In **El Salvador**, Archbishop Romero is murdered whilst saying mass. Armed uprising, led by the **FMLN**, begins and lasts throughout the decade.
1981	**Ronald Reagan** assumes presidency of US. During the "lost decade" of the 1980s, billions of dollars of military aid flows towards the right-wing government of El Salvador; covert aid used to fund the **Contras** and direct attacks on Nicaragua; trade embargo imposed.
1981	**Belize** gains full **independence**.
1982	Gen. **Ríos Montt** becomes president of **Guatemala**; ongoing repression in the country-side as the guerrilla war continues.
1983	**Manuel Noriega** assumes leadership of **Panamá**. Remains in power, despite losing two elections, until forcibly removed in 1989.
1984	"**Irangate**" scandal blows up; US revealed to have funded Contra aid through arms sales to Iran.
1986	**Earthquake** in San Salvador leaves 600 dead and thousands homeless.
1986	Return to **civilian rule** in **Guatemala**, although military influence remains strong.
1988	US indicts Noriega of drug trafficking and involvement in organized crime. **Sanctions** imposed against **Panamá**, while internal repression increases.
1988–89	Costa Rican President Arias presents a **regional peace plan**, signed by Guatemala, El Salvador, Nicaragua and Honduras. Though it is never fully implemented, the departure of Reagan from office and the "end" of the Cold War ensures aid to the Contras slows to a trickle.
1989	El Salvadorean military murder six Jesuit priests and their housekeeper in **San Salvador** and an estimated 4000 die in military offensives on cities.
1989	**US invade Panamá** in "**Operation Just Cause**". Noriega seeks asylum in Vatican Embassy, eventually giving himself up in early 1990 (extradited to the US and convicted of conspiracy to distribute cocaine in 1992). Estimates of the numbers killed during the invasion go as high as 7000.
1990	FSLN lose the Nicaraguan election. **Violeta Chamorro** and her UNO government assume office. Contra fighting stops soon after and US trade embargo is lifted.
1991	**President Serrano** of Guatemala recognizes Belize as an independent state, a decision not acceptable to Congress; the president attempts to govern independently – and is forced into resignation and exile.
1992	UN-negotiated **peace settlement** brings an end to twelve years of civil war in **El Salvador**, in which an estimated 75,000 people were killed. FMLN becomes an opposition party, participating in elections in 1994, won by the right-wing ARENA party.

1996   **Alvaro Arzú** of the centre-right PAN party assumes presidency of **Guatemala**. **Peace accords** with guerrilla groups signed, ending over thirty years of civil war.

1998   Human rights leader Bishop Jean Gerradi is murdered in **Guatemala City** following publication of his investigation into abuses committed by the military during the civil war. Landslide victory for left-of-centre PUP in **Belize** elections.

WILDLIFE

Be it the sinuous spotted jaguar, the technicolour macaw or the banana-beaked toucan, tropical animals are more colourful – even garish – and fabulous than their temperate zone cousins. Nowhere is this more true than with the life forms of Central America.

The immense **geographical diversity** of the Central American isthmus accounts for the vast number of its resident animals, birds, insects and reptiles. And within each species you can observe an enormous variety, according to locality and **habitat**. For example, the freshwater turtles that inhabit mangrove streams are quite different from their larger sea-going cousins, and you won't see a jaguar on the dusty agricultural plains of northwest Nicaragua. Meanwhile, the crested harpy eagle seems to be locally extinct in Guatemala, but is thought to be alive and well in the matted density of the rainforests of Panamá's Darién Gap. You may encounter rare squirrel monkeys, delicate and savant-faced, which are endemic to a small wedge of the Pacific coast of Costa Rica but found nowhere else in the isthmus. Similarly Guatemala's bizarrely fluffy ocellated turkey can be seen only in the jungles of Petén.

The animals of the isthmus do have in common a general **genealogy** – many can be described as mixtures of temperate zone (North America) and tropical (South American) fauna. Some of the animals you are more likely to see – because of their

abundance and diurnal activity – look like outsize versions or variations of temperate zone mammals: the agouti or paca (*tepezcuintle*), a large water-rodent, for example, or the mink-like tayra (*tolumuco*), who may flash by you on its way up a tree. The Neotropical river otter (*nutria*) is a friendly creature, although extremely shy. The coati (often mistakenly called coatimundi; *pizote* in Spanish) looks like a confused combination of a raccoon, domestic cat and an anteater. There is also a tropical racoon (*mapache*) that looks like its northern neighbour, complete with eye mask.

Despite its reputation as a wildlife haven, Costa Rica does not have Central America's most diverse vertebrate fauna – that award goes to Guatemala. However, Costa Rican insects and birds are particularly numerous, with 850 species of birds (including migratory ones) – more than the US and Canada combined. Costa Rica is also home to a quarter of the world's known butterflies – more than in all Africa – about 3000 types of moth, and scores of bees and wasps. Despite all this abundance, you may spot a quetzal more easily in, say, the central mountains of Nicaragua, which are sparsely populated and undertouristed, and where there are still plenty of nesting sites remaining.

Nowhere in Central America – even in Costa Rica's or Belize's national parks – should you expect to see the larger (and shyer) mammals as a matter of course – the tapir, jaguar and ocelot are particularly elusive. Many of the more exotic mammals that inhabit the isthmus are either nocturnal, endangered, or made shy through years of hunting and human encroachment. Although encounters do occur, they are usually brief, with the animal in question fleeing in a haze of colour and fur or dipping quietly back into the shadows from which it first emerged. That said, however, it's quite likely that you'll come into (usually fleeting) contact with some of the smaller and more abundant mammals.

BIRDS (PÁJAROS, AVES)

Bird life, both migratory and indigenous, is abundant in Central America and includes some of the most colourful birds in the Americas: the quetzal, the toucan and the scarlet macaw. The most famous bird of Central America is without doubt the brilliant green and red **quetzal**. With a range historically extending from southern Mexico to northern Panamá, the dazzling quetzal was highly prized by the Aztecs and the Maya. In the language of the Aztecs, *quetzali* means, roughly, "beautiful", and along with jade, the shimmering, jewel-coloured feathers were used as currency in Maya cities. The feathers were also worn by Maya nobles to signify religious qualities and social superiority, and formed the headdress of the plumed serpent Quetzalcoatl, the Aztec overgod. Hunting quetzals is particularly cruel, as it is well known that the bird cannot (or will not) live in captivity, a poignant stance that has made it a symbol of freedom throughout Mesoamerica.

The male in particular, which possesses the distinctive feather train, up to 1.5m long, is still pursued by poachers. The quetzal is further endangered by the destruction of its favoured high altitude rainforest (cloudforest) habitat. These days the remaining **cloudforests** – particularly Monteverde and the mountains of Cartago in Costa Rica and the Biotopo del Quetzal, a protected area of cloudforest in Guatemala's Baja Verapaz – are among the best places to try to see the birds (March–May especially), although they are always difficult to spot, in part due to shyness and in part because the vibrant green of their feathers, seemingly so eye-catchingly bright, actually allows them to blend in well with the wet and shimmering cloudforest.

The increasingly rare technicolour **scarlet macaw** (*lapa*) with its liberal splashes of red, yellow and blue, was once common on the Pacific coast of southern Mexico and Central America; they can also be found in the rainforests of Belize, where the Belize Zoo has started a conservation project aimed at protecting the remaining 300 birds.

Parakeets are still fairly numerous and are most often seen in the lowland forested areas of the Pacific coast. You're also likely to see the chestnut-mandibled and keel-billed **toucans** (*tucanes*), with their ridiculous – but beautiful – banana-shaped beaks. The chestnut-mandibled is the largest; their bills are two-tone brown and yellow. Keel-billed toucans have the more rainbow-coloured beaks and are smaller, which is sometimes taken advantage of by their larger cousins, who may drive them away from a cache of food or hound them out of a particular tree.

In the waterways and **wetlands** of the isthmus, most birds, at least in winter, are migratory species from the north, including herons, gulls, sandpipers and plovers.

The most common bird, and the one you're likely to come across hiking or riding in cattle country, is the unprepossessing grey-white **egret** (*garça*).Of the commonly found **raptors**, the laughing falcon (*guaco*) has the most distinct call, which sounds exactly like its Spanish name. The "laughing" bit comes from a much lower-pitched variation, which resembles muted human laughter. The shrunk-shouldered **vulture** (*zópilote*) is not usually considered of interest to birders. That said, it is the one bird that almost everyone will see at some point, hanging out opportunistically on the side of major highways waiting for rabbits and iguanas to be thumped beneath the wheels of a passing vehicle.

MAMMALS (FAUNA, ANIMALES)

Central America's **mammals** range from the fairly unexotic (at least for North Americans and Europeans) white-tailed deer (*venado cola blanca*) and brocket deer (*cabra de monte*), to the lumbering antediluvian Baird's tapir (*danta*) or the semi-sacred jaguar (*jaguar/tigre*). Now an endangered species, the **jaguar** is endemic to the New World tropics and has a range from southern Mexico to northern Argentina. Although it was once common throughout Central America, especially in the lowland forests and mangroves of coastal areas, the jaguar's main foe has long been man, who has hunted it for its valuable pelt and because of its reputation among farmers as a predator of calves and pigs. It is easily tracked, due to its distinctive footprint. Incredibly, sport hunting of jaguars was allowed to continue into the 1980s, although hampered by the fact that it is illegal to import jaguar pelts into most countries, including the United States.

Though you would be phenomenally lucky (or unlucky, depending on how you see it) to come across a jaguar in the wild, one of the sorriest sights you may come across is a jaguar caged in a hotel or private zoo, where it can do little but pace back and forth. Considered sacred by the Maya, the jaguar is a very beautiful mid-sized cat, nearly always golden with black spots, and very rarely a sleek, solid black. They feed on smaller mammals such as agoutis, monkeys and peccaries, and may also eat fish and birds.

Not to be confused with the jaguar, the **jaguarundi** is a small cat, also very rarely seen, that ranges in colour from reddish to black. Little-studied, the jaguarundi has short legs and a low-slung body, and is sometimes mistaken for the *tayra*, or tropical mink. All the cats have been made extremely shy through centuries of hunting. The one exception, which does not yield a big enough pelt, is the small, sinuous-necked **margay** (*tigrillo*), with its complex black-spotted markings and large, inquisitive eyes. It has been known to peek out of the shadows and even sun itself on the rocks in open view. The **ocelot** (*manigordo*) is similar, somewhere between the margay and jaguar in size, but is another animal you are very unlikely to see. Of all the cats, the sandstone-coloured **mountain lion** (*puma*) is said to be the most forthcoming. It's a big animal, and although not usually aggressive toward humans it can be, and should be treated with respect.

Along with the jaguar, the **tapir** is perhaps the most fantastical beast inhabiting the Neotropical rainforest. Rather homely, with eyes set back on either side of its head, the tapir looks something between a horse and an overgrown pig, with a stout grey-skinned body and a head that suggests an elephant with a truncated trunk. Their antediluvian look comes from their prehensile snout, small ears, and delicate cloven feet. Vegetarian creatures weighing as much as 300kg, they are extremely shy in the wild, largely nocturnal, and stick to densely forested or rugged land: consequently they are very rarely spotted by casual rainforest walkers. The tapir has proved to be very amiable in captivity, and is certain to be unaggressive should you be lucky enough to come upon it. Like the jaguar, its main foe is man, who hunts it for its succulent meat. Nowadays the tapir is protected to a degree, particularly in some of Costa Rica's National Parks.

The **peccary** (*saíno*), usually described as a wild pig or boar, comes in two little-differentiated species in Central America: collared or white-lipped. They can be menacing when encountered in packs, when, if they get a whiff of you – their sight is poor so they'll smell you before they see you – they may clack their teeth and growl a bit. The usual advice, especially in Costa Rica's Corcovado National Park, where they travel in groups as large as thirty, is to climb a tree. However, peccaries are not on the whole dangerous and in captivity have proved to be very affectionate, rubbing themselves against you delightedly at the least opportunity.

One of the oddest, although perversely friendliest-looking animals is the tropical **anteater** (*hormiguero*), which you may well see vacuuming an anthill at some point. Top of the list for gregariousness – and sometimes noise – are the several species of **monkey** inhabiting the tropical lowland forests of the region. Most people can expect to at least hear, if not see, the **howler monkey** (*mono congo*), especially in the lowland forests: the male has a mechanism in its thick throat by which it can make sounds similar to those of a gorilla. Their whoops are most often heard at dawn or dusk. The **white-faced** or capuchin (*carablanca*) monkey is slighter than the howler, with a distinctly humanoid expression on its delicate face. This, combined with its intelligence, often consigns it to being a pet in a hotel or private zoo. The **spider monkey** (*araña*) takes its name from its spider-like ability to move through the trees employing its five limbs – the fifth one is its prehensile tail, which it uses to grip branches. The **squirrel monkey** (*mono tití*) is presently only found in and south of Manuel Antonio National Park on Costa Rica's Pacific coast. Their delicate grey and white faces have long made them attractive to pet owners and zoos, and consequently they have been hunted to near-extinction in Costa Rica.

Two types of **sloths** (*perezosos*) live in the trees of the hotter regions of the isthmus: the three-toed sloth, active by day, and the nocturnal two-toed sloth. True to their name, sloths move very little during the day and have an extremely slow metabolism. They are excellently camouflaged from their main predators, eagles, by the algae that often covers their brown fur. In the first instance, at least they are very difficult to spot, then, when you're used to the familiar hairy clump, you begin to notice them more often.

AMPHIBIANS AND REPTILES (ANFÍBIOS, REPTILES)

If you spot nothing else during your time in Central America, you'll almost certainly see a **frog** or a **toad**. Though they may look vulnerable, many tropical frogs and toads protect themselves by secreting poison through their skin. Using some of the most powerful natural toxins known, the frog can directly target the heart muscle of the predator, paralyzing it and causing immediate death. As these poisons are transmittable through skin contact, you should never touch a rainforest frog. Probably the best-known, and most toxic, of the frogs, is the colourful **poison dart frog**, usually quite small, and found in various combinations of bright red and blue or green and black.

The chief thing you'll notice about the more common frogs is their size: they're much stouter than temperate zone frogs. Look out for the gaudy **leaf frog** (*rana calzonudo*), star of many a frog calendar. Relatively large, it is an alarming bright green, with orange hands and feet and dark-blue thighs. Its sides are purple, and its eyes are pure red, to scare off potential predators.

Travelling along isthmus waterways, in most places you will see **caimans** sunning themselves on riverside logs, and massive **crocodiles** lolling on the mudflats. The crocs look truly fearsome, and usually confine themselves to fresh water – although the reefs off the Belize coast are home to some American saltwater crocodiles.

Pot-bellied **iguanas** are the most ubiquitous of the lizards. Despite their dragon-like appearance, they are very shy, and if you do spot them, it's likely that they'll be scurrying away in an ungainly fashion.

Central America is also home to a vast array of **snakes** (*serpientes*, *culebras*). Many of them are non-venomous, but it's worth knowing about a few of the ones that are in case you have a (statistically very unlikely) encounter. Bear in mind, though, that snakes are largely nocturnal, and for the most part at least as wary of you than you are of them. Of all the snakes it is the **bushmaster** (*cascabela*, *matabuey*) that inspires the most fear. A viper whose range extends from southern Mexico to Brazil, it is the largest venomous snake in the Americas – it can reach a size of nearly 2m. The most aggressive of snakes, it will actually chase people if it is so inclined. The good news is that you are extremely unlikely to encounter one, as it prefers the sort of dense, precipitous and mountainous territory tourists hardly ever venture into.

Once solely the inhabitant of rainforests, the **fer-de-lance** viper (*terciopelo*) has now adapted quite well to cleared areas, grassy uplands, and even some inhabited stretches, although you are far more likely to see them in places which have heavy rainfall (like the Caribbean coast) and near streams or rivers at night. Though it can reach more than 2m in length, the **terciopelo** (as it is most often called, in English or Spanish) is well-camouflaged and very difficult to spot, its grey-black skin with a light crisscross pattern resembling a big pile of leaves. Along with the bushmaster, the terciopelo is one of the few snakes that may attack without provocation.

Considering the competition, it's not hard to see why the **boa constrictor** (*boa*) wins the title of most congenial snake. Often with beautiful semi-triangular markings, largely retiring and shy of people, the boa is one of the few snakes you may see in the daytime. Although they are largely torpid, it is not a good idea to bother them. They have big teeth and can bite (though they are not venomous) but are unlikely to stir unless startled. If you encounter one, either on the move or lying still, the best thing is to walk around it slowly, giving it a good 5m berth.

INSECTS (INSECTOS, BICHOS)

The many climates and microclimates of Central America support an enormous diversity of **insects**, of which **butterflies** (*mariposas*) are the most flamboyant and sought-after. Active during the day, they can be seen, especially from about 8am to noon, almost anywhere in the region. Most adult butterflies take their typical food of nectar – usually from red flowers – through a proboscis. Others feed on fungi, dung and rotting fruit. Best-known, and quite often spotted, especially along the forest trails, is the fast-flying **blue morpho**, whose titanium-bright wings seem to shimmer electrically.

The **lantern fly** (*machaca*) emits an amazingly strong mint-blue light, like a mini lightning streak – if you have one in your hotel room you'll know it as soon as you turn out the light. The **ant** kingdom is well-represented, especially in the humid forests. Chief among the rainforest salarymen are the leaf-cutter ants, who work in businesslike cadres, carrying bits of leaf to and from to build their distinctive nests. Endemic to the Neotropics, carnivorous **army ants** are often encountered in the forest, typically living in large colonies, some of more than a million individuals. They are most famous for their "dawn raids", when they pour out of a hideaway, typically a log, and divide into several columns to create a swarm. In this columnar formation then go off in search of prey – other ants and insects – which they carry back to the nest to consume.

MARINE LIFE

Of all the Central American marine areas, Belize's barrier reef and the Bay Islands of Honduras are probably the best places to spot sealife, whether while diving, snorkelling, or taking a boat trip. Belize, in particular, is home to a particularly rich concentration of marine life. The Caribbean **coral life** on the reef and in the Bay Islands is second to none in Central America, with oysters, the distinctive neon pink chalace sponge, the tentacled fire coral, and the apartment sponge – a tall thin tube with small holes stacked neatly through it.

Among the Caribbean coast's marine mammals, the friendliest has to be the sea-cow or **manatee**, elephantine in size, good-natured and well-intentioned, not to mention endangered. Manatees all over the Caribbean and Florida are declining in number, due to the disappearance and pollution of the fresh or saltwater riverways in which they live. You may come across them in the coastal areas of Belize. In Costa Rica your only reasonable chance of seeing one is in the Tortuguero canals in Limón province, where they sometimes break the surface. At first you might mistake it for a tarpon, but the manatee's overlapping snout and long whiskers are quite distinctive.

Five species of **marine turtle** nest on Central America's shores. Nesting takes place mostly at night and mostly in the context of *arribadas*: giant invasions of turtles who come ashore in their thousands on the same beach (or spot of beach) at a certain time of year, laying hundreds of thousands of eggs. Greens, hawksbills and leatherbacks come ashore on both coasts, while the Olive Ridley comes ashore only on the Pacific.

The strange blunt-nosed **loggerhead** can sometimes be seen in Belize, although they are still hunted for food there and so their numbers are in decline. The **green turtle**, long-prized for the delicacy of its flesh, has become nearly synonymous with its favoured nesting grounds in Tortuguero, northeast Costa Rica. In the 1950s it was classified as endangered, and, thanks in part to the protection offered by areas like Tortuguero, is making a comeback. Some greens make herculean journeys of as much as 2000km to their breeding beaches, returning to the same stretch year after year. *Arribadas* are most concentrated in June and October.

The **hawksbill** (*carey*), so-named for its distinctive down-curving "beak", is found all over the tropics, often preferring rocky shores and coral reefs. It used to be hunted extensively on the Caribbean coast for its meat and shell, but this is now banned. Poaching does still occur, however, and you should avoid buying any tortoiseshell that you see for sale. Capable of growing to a length of 5m, the leatherback (*baula*) is the largest reptile in the world. Its "shell" is actually a network of bones overlaid with a very tough leathery skin. Though it nests most concentratedly on the Pacific beaches, it also comes ashore on the Caribbean coast.

The **Olive Ridley** (*lora, carpintera* – also called Pacific Ridley) turtle nests on Pacific beaches, particularly on their protected grounds at Playa Nancite in Santa Rosa National Park and Ostional near Nosara on Costa Rica's Nicoya Peninsula. They come ashore in massive *arribadas*, and, unusually, often nest during the day.

The **black river turtle** and the **snapping turtle**, about which little is known (except that it snaps), also inhabit rivers and mangrove swamps, and may occasionally be spotted on the riverbanks.

Though **dolphins** (*delfines*) and **whales** thread themselves through the waters of the Pacific coast, it is rare to see them as they usually remain many miles offshore. **Sharks** (*tiburones*) are around on both coasts, and though the vast majority of species are harmless, it's wise to ask around before deciding to swim.

ECOTOURISM

Global **tourism** is a multi-billion dollar industry. With some 567m international tourists per year, the industry was worth, in 1995, some $372bn – figures which are set to more than double by the year 2010. Though notoriously difficult to classify in any commonly accepted form, **ecotourism** (in a very broad sense, encompassing organized nature and wildlife tours) is estimated to account for as much as forty percent of the market. Through sheer numbers alone, such tourism is bound to have an impact even on societies which are sufficiently developed to be able to absorb it. And many of the relatively undisturbed areas that appeal to the ecotourist are located in precisely those societies that may be least able to absorb such an impact and are most vulnerable to the negative consequences such change can bring.

Since the term was coined a decade or so ago, the **rationale** behind ecotourism has been that the relatively large sums of money dispensed by visitors from developed nations could be channelled successfully into protecting the natural resources they come to visit. By enabling local people to earn more by protecting their environment and encouraging visitors to come to it, both sides could benefit. In the words of the London-based Economics for Environment Consultancy, all natural resources have a "rent", or scarcity value. Local management of the resource and the capturing of this rent, in the form of visitor fees, can be used to control the number of people visiting the resource, and allows for greater flexibility in determining and funding the best method of protection. This protection would be in line with local customs and traditions, and the evolution of the local society itself.

DEFINITIONS

Ecotourism is a tricky term to **define**. It is often seen in relation to what it is not: package tourism, wherein visitors have limited contact with nature and with the day-to-day lives of local people. But as more and more organizations and businesses hijack the eco prefix for dubious uses, the authentic ecotourism experience has become increasingly difficult to pin down. For some ecotourism is a way to assure themselves that they are a better tourist, that they are giving something back. Others point to the fundamental **contradiction** between encouraging large numbers of people to visit a resource while ensuring its protection – at heart, perhaps, the best way to be an ecotourist is not to be a tourist at all. Lying somewhere between these different views is the argument that if people are going to travel, they may as well do so in a low-impact manner that minimizes destruction of the visited environment, and promotes cultural exchange.

One of the best attempts to put forward a workable definition has been made by **ATEC**, the Talamancan Ecotourism and Conservation Association in southwest Costa Rica, which

CODES OF CONDUCT

Though well-meaning, ecotourism codes of conduct can seem preachy and presumptuous. Still, in any attempt to define the term, or to go any way towards understanding its aims, it's useful to know what the locally accepted guidelines are. The Asociación Tsuli, the Costa Rican branch of the Audubon Society, has developed its own short code of conduct for "**Environmental Ethics for Nature Travel**":

1 Wildlife and natural habitats must not be needlessly disturbed.

2 Waste should be disposed of properly.

3 Tourism should be a positive influence on local communities.

4 Tourism should be managed and sustainable.

5 Tourism should be culturally sensitive.

6 There must be no commerce in wildlife, wildlife products, or native plants.

7 Tourists should leave with a greater understanding and appreciation of nature, conservation and the environment.

8 Tourism should strengthen the conservation effort and enhance the natural integrity of places visited.

seeks to promote, as it says, "socially responsible tourism" by integrating local Bribrí and Afro-Caribbean culture into tourists' experience of the area, as well as giving residents pride in their unique cultural heritage and natural environment. They say: "Ecotourism means more than bird books and binoculars. Ecotourism means more than native art hanging on hotel walls or ethnic dishes on the restaurant menu. Ecotourism is not mass tourism behind a green mask. Ecotourism means a constant struggle to defend the earth and to protect and sustain traditional communities. Ecotourism is a cooperative relationship between the non-wealthy local community and those sincere, open-minded tourists who want to enjoy themselves in a Third World setting and, at the same time, enrich their consciousness by means of significant educational and cultural experience."

A CASE STUDY: COSTA RICA

Along with Belize, **Costa Rica** has become virtually synonymous with ecotourism in Central America and is widely regarded to be at the cutting edge of worldwide conservation strategy, an impressive feat for a small, cash-strapped Central American nation. At the centre of its internationally applauded conservation effort is a complex system of National Parks and Wildlife Refuges, which protect a full 25 percent of its territory. These statistics are used with great effect to attract tourists, the vast majority of whom still come to see the country's remarkably varied tropical flora and fauna.

However, for years the country has been in danger of being overwhelmed by its popularity, attracting over 700,000 visitors annually – the population of the country itself is only 3.5 million. The question uppermost in the minds of conservationists and biologists who undertook field studies in Costa Rica long before it was "discovered" is: what is the damage being caused by so many feet walking through the rainforests?

In **Manuel Antonio National Park** on Costa Rica's Pacific Coast, visitors can walk seaside trails, one of which circles the stunning Punta Cathedral, which juts out into the sea. As ecotourism experiences go, it's a soft option, easily reachable and sandwiched between beautiful beaches. Here the **squirrel monkeys**, an endangered species, have become too used to people. Ecotourists walking Manuel

Antonio's trails complain about them behaving "as if they were in a zoo", begging for food and being cheeky, or alternately hiding from the stress of having, on popular holidays like Easter, literally hundreds of people trudge through their habitat. Rangers at Manuel Antonio talk openly of the "psychological pressure" large numbers of visitors put on some animals. When the squirrel monkeys began to display symptoms of neurosis, officials took the decision to shut the park on Mondays, to give the animals a rest.

Monteverde and **Santa Elena**, two small farming communities high in the mountains of the Cordillera Central, are home to two reserves that together protect one of the last sizeable pristine pieces of **cloudforest** (high-altitude rainforest) in the Americas. In recent years increasing tourism has transformed the communities, and flotillas of tourist buses rattle up and down the muddy roads connecting the towns to the reserves. In the high season, the Monteverde administrators have had to set a 100-visitor-a-day ceiling, in order to preserve the ecological integrity of the Reserve. Both communities have resisted paving the 40-kilometre stretch of road which links their communities with the Carretera Interamericana, in an attempt to avoid a daytripper culture where visitors would be bussed up to the reserve for the day and then back down to their beach hotels, spending little money and making maximum impact.

It is arguable that an underdeveloped country in need of foreign currency should hardly complain about being too popular, especially when the type of tourism it has developed is so very "green". But Costa Rica highlights what some observers criticize about the concept of ecotourism – at least in Latin America – that it represents not so much as an act of environmental altruism but is merely part of an imperialist, bourgeois agenda: wealthy first-world ecotourists can console themselves that they are saving the environment, but what about the 38 percent of Costa Rica's population who live in poverty and without access to land? And as tourists visit areas previously reserved only for scientific study, many tropical biologists have concluded that, in sum, if you love the rainforest, it would be better to stay at home and donate money to conservation organizations rather than travelling abroad to tramp through the forests and change local economies with the influx of your dollars. Ask any National Park or private reserve administrator in Costa Rica about this and their response is nearly uniform – "People are going to come anyway. You can't stop them. Our job is to make sure the tourism is managed properly."

It's a delicate balance. Many powerful vested interests are lined up to log, mine and prospect for minerals in Costa Rica. As the country with the highest population density in Central America, there is also tremendous pressure on land, and parks are regularly invaded by squatters. There's no doubt that the financial success of ecotourism has guaranteed the survival of many natural places. All you have to do is look at the land *not* protected by the reserves – the lowlands around Monteverde, for example, almost entirely comprising pure pasture-land and clear-cut areas.

ECOTOURISM AROUND CENTRAL AMERICA

While there may be no lack of genuine enthusiasm for ecotourism across Central America, sadly in many cases, a shortage of financial means ensures that little more than paper status is gained for numerous wildlife, nature and marine reserves across the region. Political turmoil during the 1980s and the grinding problems of poverty mean that – with Costa Rica being the notable exception – the questions of environmental preservation and sustainability have only recently had a realistic chance of being addressed.

Honduras, for example, has an extensive national network of parks and reserves, many of them designated protected areas only in 1987. Some, like Celaque in the central highlands and Cusuco, near San Pedro Sula in the north, are extremely well-managed and have ensured the protection of irreplaceable tracts of virgin forest and fragile ecosystems. Others exist as little more than lines on maps. While scant government resources combine with the ongoing need for local people to find more land and the, at times illegal, activities of large landowners, there is little realistic chance of ensuring that any effective change can be made. And as in Costa Rica, the areas bordering Honduras's national parks are a stark contrast to the protected land: just outside the World Heritage site of the Río Plátano Biosphere Reserve, what was once pristine forest has been replaced by pasture and crop land.

In **El Salvador**, a nascent network of national parks is in existence. Perhaps the most advanced – in terms of a comprehensive project for both environmental protection and community development – is the Bosque Montecristo, part of the El Trifinio international biosphere, administered jointly by the governments of El Salvador, Honduras and Guatemala. The work carried out here places as much emphasis on the local indigenous communities as on environmental protection.

Since the mid-1980s the number of foreign tourists visiting **Belize** each year has grown from fewer than 100,000 to well over 300,000 – the result of deliberate decisions taken by successive governments to promote tourism as the way to generate much needed foreign exchange revenues. Moreover, given Belize's abundant natural resources – the second-largest barrier reef in the world, tropical forest, Maya ruins – this promotion has been premised upon the bases of "greenness" and sustainability. Marine, wildlife and archeological reserves have been established, with local groups encouraged to take an active part in developing and maintaining ecotourist facilities. In Central America and the Caribbean, Belize is seen as having paved the way in creating a locally controlled industry that benefits both cultural traditions and the environment.

Certainly the country has benefited, with at least one quarter of the GNP derived from tourist revenues. Underneath the surface, however, things are a little different. There is growing disquiet about the nature of so-called ecotourist development, and there are fears that the industry is now spiralling beyond the control of Belizeans. Deliberate marketing of the country as a "green" destination has created a demand, to which the solution is perceived to be more and larger tourist developments, funded if not managed by foreign capital. A case in point were the proposals to regenerate Belize City's waterfront, drawn up initially under the sponsorship of US aid, aimed at creating a prototype "downtown" area, studded with hotels, shops, restaurants and bars. While seen as appealing to tourists, such a development would be of little benefit to Belizean residents, facing the consequences of a decaying infrastructure, increasing poverty and corresponding increases in crime. Nor was it immediately apparent how much – if any – of the revenues generated by this project would flow directly to the local community. Similarly, plans for the redevelopment of Ambergris Caye sparked a long-running controversy when it emerged that the government proposed to transfer over one-third of the island to a US developer for the creation of a upmarket resort.

NEW INITIATIVES: THE WAY FORWARD

In recent years Mario Boza, a founder of Costa Rica's National Parks System and prominent conservationist, has advocated a strategy of **macro-conservation**. Shifting the emphasis from nation-by-nation projects to united concerns and linking together chunks of protected land, he argues, will allow the creations of larger protected areas for animals that need room to hunt, like jaguars and pumas. Even more importantly, these initiatives will allow countries to make more effective joint conservation policies and decisions.

Macro-conservation **projects** include the Proyeto Paseo Pantera (all of Mesoamerica), El Mundo Maya (Belize, El Salvador, Guatemala, Honduras and Mexico), Si-a-Paz (Nicaragua and Costa Rica) and La Amistad International Park and Biosphere Reserve (Costa Rica and Panamá). The largest conservation project undertaken in the western hemisphere, the **Paseo Pantera** (Path of the Panther) is an interesting example of ecological cooperation between the Central American governments. When completed it is hoped this green corridor will allow unimpeded migration, north and south, of a wide range of animal, bird, and marine life. In some species this could be the answer to long-term survival (the jaguar, for instance, needs about 100 square kilometres as its "patch"; under these conditions jaguars encounter each other and mate with a minimum of stress). Part of the strategy is to implement a tightly controlled ecotourism program, with tourist dollars helping to pay the green corridor's way.

Arguably, however, the most revolutionary change in conservation management, and the one likeliest to have the biggest pay-off in the long term, is the shift toward **local initiatives**. Some projects are truly local, such as the tiny grassroots organization TUVA on Costa Rica's Osa peninsula, which oversees the selective logging of naturally felled rainforest trees,

or the ecotourism co-operative of Las Delicias on Costa Rica's Nicoya Peninsula, which provides professional guides to take tourists into Central America's largest underground caves. Another initiative, even more promising in terms of how it affects the lives of many rural-based Central Americans, is the creation of "buffer zones" around some National Parks. In these zones campesinos and other smallholders can do part-time farming, are allowed restricted hunting rights and receive education as to the ecological and economic value of the forest. Locals may be trained as nature guides, and campesinos may be given incentives to enter into non-traditional forms of agriculture and ways of making a living which are not so distressing to the environment.

In the Talamanca region of Costa Rica, ATEC (source of the "ecotourism definition" offered above) takes tourists on tours of the local **indigenous** KeköLdi reserve. The Bribrí indigenous guides take outsiders into the local villages, on treks through the rainforest pointing out traditional medicinal uses of many plants, and demonstrate how many local products such as banana vinegar, guava jam and herbal teas are made. All tour fees go back into the local community. In the department of La Mosquitia, Honduras, the **Pech** indigenous people live in small villages near the headwaters of the Río Plátano, within the protected lands of the 5000-square-kilometre UNESCO Biosphere Reserve of the same name. Their income is supplemented through offering guide services and by the sale of miniature wooden carvings of *pipantes* (dugout canoes), and of small bags of packaged cocoa. Some tour operators are taking tourists on multi-day jungle excursions in the area, and a fair portion of this revenue goes directly into the pockets of the indigenous Pech, Miskito and Garífuna communities visited.

The inhabitants of Nicaragua's unique twin-volcanoed island, **Ometepe**, have taken ecotourism similarly in their own hands. Natives of the island act as taxi drivers and guides for the growing number of tourists, most of them drawn by the sight of two volcanoes rising vertiginously out of the waters of Lake Nicaragua. Ometepe's ecotourism operation, Entre dos Volcanes (Between Two Volcanoes) is locally managed and all tours, taxi fares and guide's fees go directly to the local person involved.

Despite the problems outlined above, there's no question that ecotourism is the most effective way of preserving the natural environment while allowing it to pay its way – through the contribution of tourists. At present, though, the onus falls on eco-minded visitors to make sure their dollars are going to the right place, at least until a universally accepted definition of the term is arrived at. Probably the most positive sign for the future is the growth in community-based projects, a step forward in the development of an economically viable industry that's committed to protecting the stunning landscapes, wildlife and cultures of Central America.

BOOKS

Following is a list of the books that proved most useful – or enjoyable – in the preparation of this guide. General books are listed first, followed by individual sections on each country. Publishers are given in the format UK/US; where only one publisher is listed, this covers both the UK and US, unless specified.

CENTRAL AMERICA

HISTORY, POLITICS AND SOCIETY

Tom Barry, *Central America Inside Out* (Grove Atlantic, US). Well-informed background reading on the entire region. The same author has also written some of the *Inside* country guides.

James Dunkerley, *Power in the Isthmus* and *The Pacification of Central America* (Norton /Verso). Detailed accounts of Central American politics (excluding Belize) that offer a good study of recent events, particularly the region's civil wars, albeit in academic style. Well researched with plenty of statistics and charts, the style is factual rather than flowing.

In Focus (LAB/Interlink Books). An excellent series of country guides that give concise, highly readable accounts of the people, politics and culture of the region. Titles on Costa Rica and Guatemala are already available, while the Belize and Nicaragua guides will be published in 1999.

Inside (LAB/Resource Center Press). A series of guides covering the history, politics, ecomomy and society of Central America. Packed with accessible facts and analysis, titles cover Belize, Guatemala, Costa Rica, Honduras, Panamá and El Salvador.

Peter Dale-Scott and Jonathan Marshall, *Cocaine Politics: Drugs, Armies and the CIA in Central America* (University of California). Polemical but well-researched exposé of CIA involvement in cocaine trafficking and political oppression in Cental America in the 1980s. Reveals the truth behind the Iran–Contra scandal and gives the lie to the rhetoric of the war on drugs.

William Weinberg, *War on the Land: Ecology and Politics in Central America* (Zed Books/ Humanities Press). The author tells a story of intertwining conflicts and causes between conservation (and to a small extent ecotourism), land rights and politics in the individual Central American countries in a volume that deftly straddles the gap between academic studies of these subjects and the general interest reader.

Ralph Lee Woodward Jr, *Central America: A Nation Divided* (Oxford University Press). More readable than Dunkerley, this is probably the best book for a general summary of the Central American situation, despite its daft title.

TRAVEL AND IMPRESSIONS

Thomas Gage, *Travels in the New World* (University of Oklahoma Press). Unusual account of a Dominican friar's travels through Mexico and Central America between 1635 and 1637, including some fascinating insights into colonial life as well as some great attacks on the greed and pomposity of the Catholic Church abroad.

Aldous Huxley, *Beyond the Mexique Bay* (Flamingo, UK). Huxley's travels, in 1934, took him from Belize through Guatemala to Mexico, swept on by his fascination for history and religion, and sprouting bizarre theories on the basis of everything he sees. There are some great descriptions of Maya sites and indigenous culture, with superb one-liners summing up people and places.

Patrick Marnham, *So far from God* (Penguin). A saddened and vaguely right-wing account of Marnham's travels through the Americas from the United States to Panamá (missing out Belize). Dotted with amusing anecdotes and interesting observations, the book's descriptions are dominated by the civil wars in Guatemala and El Salvador, and the ideological battlelines in Sandinista Nicaragua.

Jeremy Paxman, *Through the Volcanoes* (Paladin). A political travel account investigating the turmoil of Central America and finding solace in the calm of Costa Rica. Paxman's travels take him through all seven of the republics, including Belize, and he offers a good overview of the politics and history of the region.

John Lloyd Stephens, *Incidents of Travel in Central America, Chiapas, and Yucatán* (Dover). Stephens was a classic nineteenth-century traveller. Acting as American ambassador to Central America, he indulged his own enthusiasm for archeology; while the republics fought it out among themselves he was wading through the jungle stumbling across ancient cities. His journals, told with superb Victorian pomposity punctuated with sudden waves of enthusiasm, make great reading. Some editions include fantastic illustrations by Catherwood of the ruins overgrown with tropical rainforest.

Ronald Wright, *Time Among the Maya* (Abacus/Henry Holt). A vivid and sympathetic account of travels from Belize through Guatemala, Chiapas and Yucatán, meeting the Maya and exploring their obsession with time. The book's twin points of interest are the ancient Maya and the violence of the 1970s and 80s. An encyclopedic bibliography offers ideas for exploration in depth, and the author's knowledge is evident in the superb historical insight he imparts through the book. Certainly one of the best travel books on the area.

ARCHEOLOGY AND MAYA CIVILIZATION

Michael Coe, *The Maya* (Thames & Hudson). Now in its fifth edition, this clear and comprehensive introduction to Maya archeology is certainly the best on offer. Coe has also written several more weighty, academic volumes. His *Breaking the Maya Code* (Penguin/Thames & Hudson), a very personal history of the decipherment of the glyphs, owes much to the fact that Coe was present at many of the most important meetings leading to the breakthrough. This book demonstrates that the glyphs did actually reproduce Maya speech.

Joyce Kelly, *An Archaeological Guide to Northern Central America* (University of Oklahoma). Detailed and practical guide to 38 Maya sites and 25 museums in four countries; an essential companion for anyone travelling purposefully through the Maya region of Central America. Kelly's star ratings – based on a site's archeological importance, degree of restoration and accessibility – may affront purists but it does provide a valuable opinion on how worthwhile a particular visit might be.

Linda Schele and David Freidel et al. The authors, in the forefront of the "new archeology", have been personally responsible for decoding many of the glyphs. While their writing style, which frequently includes "recreations" of scenes inspired by their discoveries, is controversial, it has nevertheless inspired a devoted following. *A Forest of Kings: The Untold Story of the Ancient Maya* (Quill, US) in conjunction with *The Blood of Kings*, by Linda Schele and Mary Miller, shows that far from being governed by peaceful astronomer-priests, the ancient Maya were ruled by hereditary kings, lived in populous, aggressive city-states, and engaged in a continuous entanglement of alliances and war. *The Maya Cosmos* (Quill, US), by Schele, Freidel and Joy Parker, is perhaps more difficult to read, dense with copious notes, but continues to examine Maya ritual and religion in a unique and far-reaching way. *The Code of Kings* (Shribner, US), written in collaboration with Peter Matthews and illustrated with Justin Kerr's famous "rollout" photography of Maya ceramics, examines in detail the significance of the monuments at selected Maya sites. It's her last book – Linda Schele died in April 1998 – and sure to become a classic of epigraphic interpretation.

Robert Sharer, *The Ancient Maya* (Stanford University). The classic, comprehensive (and weighty) account of Maya civilization, now in a completely revised and much more readable fifth edition, yet as authoritative as ever. Required reading for archeologists, it provides a fascinating reference for the non-expert.

J. Eric. S. Thompson, *The Rise and Fall of the Maya Civilization* (University of Oklahoma). A major authority on the ancient Maya, Thompson has produced many academic studies, of which this is one of the more approachable.

FICTION

Rosario Santos (ed), *And We Sold the Rain: Contemporary Fiction from Central America* (Ryan Publishing, UK). Put together in the late 1980s, this collection is still one of the best volumes of well-translated short stories from the isthmus, bringing together new contemporary writers of national stature from all the countries (many of them women). The introduction, by Jo Anne Englebert, gives an excellent overview of Central American literature in context.

WILDLIFE AND THE ENVIRONMENT

Catherine Caulfield, In the Rainforest (Knopf, US, o/p). Still, after a decade, one of the best introductory volumes to rainforests, dealing in an accessible, discursive fashion with many of the issues covered in the more academic or specialized titles. Much of the book is directed at the Amazon, but could easily be transposed to Panamá, Guatemala or Costa Rica – the author turns a wry eye on Costa Rica's cattle ranching culture, as well as providing an interesting profile of the farming methods used by the Monteverde community.

Louise H. Emmons, Neotropical Rainforest Mammals (University of Chicago). Supported by François Feer's colour illustrations, this highly informative book is written by experts for non-scientists. Local and scientific names are given, along with plenty of interesting snippets.

Steve Howe and Sophie Webb, The Birds of Mexico and Northern Central America (Oxford University Press). A tremendous work, the result of years of research, this is the definitive book on the region's birds. Essential for all serious birders.

John C. Kricher, A Neotropical Companion (Princeton University Press). Subtitled "An Introduction to the Animals, Plants and Ecosystems of the New World Tropics", this contains an amazing amount of valuable information for nature lovers. Researched mainly in Central America, so there's plenty that's directly relevant.

BELIZE

HISTORY, POLITICS AND SOCIETY

Gerald S. Koop, Pioneer Years in Belize (Country Graphics, Belize). A history of the Mennonites in Belize, written in a style as stolid and practical as the lives of the pioneers themselves. A good read nonetheless.

Assad Shoman, Thirteen Chapters of a History of Belize (Angelus Press, Belize). A long overdue treatment of the country's history written by a Belizean who's not afraid to examine colonial myths with a detailed and rational analysis. Primarily a school textbook, but the style will not alienate non-student readers. Shoman, active in politics both before and since independence, also wrote Party Politics in Belize, a short but highly detailed account of the development of party politics in the country.

ARCHEOLOGY

Byron Foster (ed), Warlords and Maize Men – A Guide to the Maya Sites of Belize (Cubola, Belize). An excellent handbook to fifteen of the most accessible sites in Belize, compiled by the Association for Belizean Archeology and the Belize Department of Archeology.

J. Eric S. Thompson, The Maya of Belize – Historical Chapters Since Columbus (Cubola, Belize). Interesting study of Belizean history in the first two centuries of Spanish colonial rule. It's a little-researched area of Belizean history and casts some light on the groups that weren't immediately conquered by the Spanish.

Rosita Arvigo with Nadia Epstein, Sastun. A rare glimpse into the life and work of a Maya curandero, the late Elijio Panti of San Antonio, Belize. Dr Arvigo has ensured the survival of many generations of accumulated healing knowledge, and this book is a testimony both to her perseverance in becoming accepted by Mr Panti and the cultural wisdom of the indigenous people. Arvigo has also written and co-authored several other books on traditional medicine in Belize, including Rainforest Remedies.

FICTION, POETRY AND AUTOBIOGRAPHY

Zee Edgell, Beka Lamb (Heinemann). A young girl's account of growing up in Belize in the 1950s, in which the problems of adolescence are described alongside those of the Belizean independence movement. The book also explores everyday life in the colony, describing the powerful structure of matriarchal society and the influence of the Catholic Church. In Times Like These (Heinemann) is a semi-autobiographical account of personal and political intrigue set in the months leading up to Belize's independence.

Zoila Ellis, On Heroes, Lizards and Passion (Cubola Productions, Belize). Seven short stories written by a Belizean woman with a deep under-standing of her country's people and their culture.

Felicia Hernandez, *Those Ridiculous Years* (Cubola Productions, Belize). A short autobio-graphical book about growing up in Dangriga in the 1960s.

Shots From The Heart (Cubola Productions, Belize). Slim anthology of the work of three young Belizean poets: Yasser Musa, Kiren Shoman and Simone Waight. Evocative imagery and perceptive comment relate experiences of a changing society. Musa's *Belize City Poem* (pub-lished separately) is a sharply observed, at times vitriolic, commentary on the simultaneous arrival of independence and US dominated tele-vision on Belizean society.

Emory King, *Belize 1798* (Tropical Books, Belize). Rip-roaring historical novel peopled by the characters involved in the Battle of St George's Caye. King's enthusiasm for his country's history results in the nearest thing you'll get to a Belizean blockbuster, yet it's based on meticulous research in archives on both sides of the Atlantic. Wonderful holiday reading.

WILDLIFE

Alan Rabinowitz *Jaguar* (Arbor House, UK). Account of the author's experiences studying jaguars for the New York Zoological Society in the early 1980s and living with a Maya family in the Cockscomb Basin, Belize. Rabinowitz was instrumental in the establishment of the Jaguar Reserve in 1984.

SPECIFIC GUIDES

Kirk Barrett, *Belize by Kayak*. The most detailed book on this increasingly popular activity. Not widely available; contact Reef Link Kayaking, 3806 Cottage Grove, Des Moines, Iowa, USA.

Ned Middleton, *Diving in Belize* (Aqua Quest, US). The most readable book on the subject, expertly written and illustrated with excellent photographs taken by the author. Covers in detail all the atolls and many of the reefs and individual dive sites. Includes a section on Mexico's Banquo Chinchorro, just north of Belize.

GUATEMALA

HISTORY, POLITICS AND SOCIETY

Tom Barry, *Guatemala: A Country Guide* (Resource Centre). A comprehensive and concise account of the political, social and economic situation in Guatemala, with a mild left-wing stance. Currently the best source for a good overview of the situation.

Anthony Daniels, *Sweet Waist of America*. A delight to read. Daniels takes a refreshingly even-handed approach to Guatemala and comes up with a fascinating cocktail of people and politics, discarding the stereotypes that lit-ter most books on Central America.

Jim Handy, *Gift of the Devil*. The best modern history of Guatemala, concise and readable with a sharp focus on the Maya population and the brief period of socialist government. Don't expect too much detail on the distant past, which is only explored in order to set the mod-ern reality in some kind of context, but if you're interested in the history of Guatemalan brutali-ty then this is the book to read. By no means objective, it sets out to expose the development of oppression and point the finger at those responsible.

Rigoberta Menchú, *Rigoberta Menchú – An Indian Woman in Guatemala* and *Crossing Borders* (Verso). Momentous story of one of Latin America's most remarkable women, Nobel Peace Prize winner, Rigoberta Menchú. The first volume is a horrific account of family life in the Maya highlands, recording how Menchú's famly were targeted, terrorized and murdered by the military. The book also reveals much concerning Quiché Maya cultrual tradi-tions and the enormous gulf between ladino and indigenous society in Guatemala. The sec-ond volume documents Menchú's life in exile in Mexico, her work at the United Nations fighting for indigenous people and her return to Guatemala. An astounding tale of a woman's spirit, courage and determination.

Víctor Perera, *Unfinished Conquest.* Superb, extremely readable account of the civil war tragedy, plus comprehensive attention to the political, social and economic inequalities affecting the author's native country. Immaculately researched, the book's strength comes from the extensive interviews with ordinary and influencial Guatemalans and incisive analysis of recent history. The best introduction to the subject.

The Popol Vuh. The great poem of the Quiché, written shortly after the Conquest and intended to preserve the tribe's knowledge of its history. It's an amazing swirl of ancient mythological characters and their wandering through the Quiché highlands, tracing Quiché ancestry back to the beginning. The best version is translated by Dennis Tedlock and published by Touchstone in the US.

Jean-Marie Simon, *Eternal Spring – Eternal Tyranny*. Of all the books on human rights in Guatemala, this is the one that speaks with the utmost clarity. Combining the highest standards in photography with crisp text, there's no attempt to persuade you – the facts are allowed to speak for themselves, which they do with amazing strength. If you want to know what happened in Guatemala over the last twenty years or so there is no better book. Again Simon clearly takes sides, aligning herself with the revolutionary left: there's no mention of any abuses committed by the guerrillas.

FICTION

Miguel Angel Asturias, *Hombres de Maíz* (Macmillan). Guatemala's most famous author, Nobel Prize winner Asturias is deeply indebted to Guatemalan history and culture in his work. "Men of Maize" is generally regarded as his masterpiece, classically Latin American in its magic realist style, and bound up in the complexity of indigenous culture. His other works include *El Señor Presidente*, a grotesque portrayal of social chaos and dictatorial rule, based on Asturias's own experience; *El Papa Verde*, which explores the murky world of the United Fruit Company; and *Weekend en Guatemala*, describing the downfall of the Arbenz government.

Francisco Goldman, *The Long Night of White Chickens*. Drawing on the stylistic complexity of Latin American fiction, this novel tells the tale of a young Guatemalan orphan who flees to the US and works as a maid. When she finally returns home she is murdered. It's an interesting and ambitious story flavoured with all the bitterness and beauty of Guatemala's natural and political landscape.

Gaspar Pedro Gonzales, *A Mayan Life* (Yax Te' Press, USA). Absorbing story of the personal

and cultural difficulties affecting a K'anjobal Maya from the Cuchumatanes mountains. The conflict between indigenous and ladino values becomes acutely evident as the central character seeks a higher education. Rich in ethnological detail and highly autobiographical, the book claims to be the first novel ever written by a Maya writer.

SPECIALIST GUIDES

William Coe, *Tikal: A Handbook to the Ancient Maya Ruins*. Superbly detailed account of the site, usually available at the ruins. The detailed map of the main area is essential for in-depth exploration.

EL SALVADOR

HISTORY, POLITICS AND SOCIETY

Robert Armstrong and Janet Shenk, *El Salvador: The Face of Revolution*. Accessible history of the root causes and development of the civil war of the 1980s.

Tom Barry and Kent Norsworthy, *El Salvador – a Country Guide* (Resource Center). Concise study of contemporary political, economic and social affairs, with historical background, detailing the initiatives made in the years following the 1992 peace accords.

Charles Clements, *Witness to War* (Bantam Press). Fascinating account of a year spent working in the guerrilla zone of Guazapa in the early 1980s by a volunteer US doctor. A vivid portrayal of how the civil war affected a specific area, and by assocation allows the reader a greater insight into what conditions were like across El Salvador.

Larry Dowell, **Mark Deinner**, *El Salvador* (Norton). Evocative and compelling collection of photographs taken during 1986, sharply delinating the progress of the civil war and its impact.

FICTION AND POETRY

Mirrors of War (Zed Books). Wide-ranging collection of modern poetry and prose by Salvadorean writers, focusing on the causes and impact of the civil war.

Salarrué, *Eso y Más*, *Cuentos de Barro* and *La Espada y Otras Narraciones*. Born Salvador Salazar Arrué in 1899, Salarrué was a writer, painter and commentator and is one of the most widely known El Salvadorean writers. His short stories and novellas focus upon the lives and realities of campesinos and non-metropolites.

Roque Dalton, *Taberna y Otras Lugares* and *Poemas Clandestinas; Pobrecito Poeta que era Yo*. Perhaps the most famous El Salvadorean poet, Dalton was also a journalist and revolutionary, and in constant open conflict with successive governments. Born in 1935, he was imprisoned and exiled on various occasions, always returning to the land of his birth. He was a member of the People's Revolutionary Army (ERP) in the early 1970s, along with founder members of the FMLN. After differences of opinion led to his departing the movement he was assassinated on ERP orders in May 1975 near Guazapa; his death remains a landmark in Salvadorean literary history and still remains unsolved. *Taberna y Otras Lugares* and *Poemas Clandestinas* are both collections of poetry, while *Pobrecito Poeta que era Yo* is a novella.

HONDURAS

HISTORY, POLITICS AND SOCIETY

Tom Barry and Kent Norsworthy, *Honduras – a Country Guide* (Inter-Hemispheric Education Resource Center). Concise but comprehensive study of contemporary political, economic and social affairs, with some historical background.

William V. Davidson *Historical Geography of the Bay Islands, Honduras* (South University Press, US). A study of physical and cultural geographical development of the islands. Useful for pieces of interesting background information.

TRAVEL AND IMPRESSIONS

Peter Ford, *Tekkin a Waalk along the Miskito Coast* (Flamingo Press). Ford gives himself the task of walking along the Caribbean coast from Belize to Nicaragua in the mid-1980s. A nice tale, with snippets of information on Garífuna history and contemporary development.

FICTION

Paul Theroux, *The Mosquito Coast* (Penguin). Well-known tale of the collapse of a man in the steaming heat of Mosquitia. Though entertaining, Theroux only touches – literally – upon a remote corner of Honduras and the novel does little to enlighten the reader about the country as a whole. The movie, with Harrison Ford and Helen Mirren, was filmed in Belize.

Guillermo Yuscarán is the pen name of expatriate Willam Lewis, a long time resident of Honduras. His novels and short stories, illustrating contemporary Honduran life can be bought (Spanish and English-language; Nuevo Sol, Tegucigalpa) in bookshops in Tegucigalpa and San Pedro Sula.

SPECIALIST GUIDES

Cindy Garoute, *Diving the Bay Islands* (Aqua Quest, US). Glossy book with lots of great photos outlining the best places to dive off all the islands. Consider it essential if you're going to spend much time diving here.

William L. Fash, *Scribes, Warriors and Kings* (Thames & Hudson). The definitive guide to the ruins of Copán with the complete historical background, superb maps and lavishly adorned with drawings and photographs.

NICARAGUA

HISTORY, POLITICS AND SOCIETY

John Brentlinger, *The Best of What We Are, Reflections on the Nicaraguan Revolution* (University of Massachusetts Press). An attempt to explain that unity of thought and action, of real and unreal, of religion and magic, of life and death that is so present in Nicaragua even today. An interesting journal of the period 1985–92, only published in 1995.

Midge Quandt, *Voices of Sandinismo In Post Election Nicaragua, 1997*. For Sandinista groupies only, this is a booklet of interviews with Sandinista party members, university intellectuals and union organizers. Provides an insight into current struggles and thinking within and about the Sandinista movement.

Holly Sklar, *Washington's War on Nicaragua* (South End Press, Boston). A dissection of US policy on Nicaragua in all its ugly manifestations. Covers the Iran-Contra affair, the years of political double talk that undermined regional attempts to broker peace, the drug running, gun running and espionage that sought to destabilize the Sandinista regime, and the whole saga of the often clandestine US support for the Contras. A fascinating book.

Sandino's Daughters, *Testimonies of Nicaragua Women in Struggle* (revised edition, 1995). Interviews with Sandinista women who participated at various levels in the struggle to liberate Nicaragua and later worked for the creation of a new and just society. Being a book about women it has a dimension that most other books on revolutionary subjects lack. First published in 1981, and later re-issued, it is one of the most popular books written about that period.

David R. Dye, Judy Butler et al, *Contesting Everything, Winning Nothing* (Hemisphere Initiatives, US). A fifty-page booklet that examines the Chamorro period of government in Nicaragua. A fairly dry analysis, but it is useful for putting the post Sandinista period into context.

TRAVEL AND IMPRESSIONS

Salman Rushdie, *The Jaguar Smile, A Nicaraguan Journey* (Picador). The result of a three-week trip to Nicaragua at the height of the Sandinista era in the mid-1980s, Rushdie was impressed – or seduced – by the Sandinista achievement. The only note of criticism he struck was with the lack of freedom of speech – ironically, this would come to be the defining factor in Rushdie's life and work. The real charm of this slim narrative is Rushdie's witty portrait of cosy Managuan political society and its family affcliations.

Penny O'Donnell, *Death, Dreams and Dancing in Nicaragua*, (Australian Broadcasting Corporation). Written by an Australian radio journalist who, in her own words, avoided the "newsworthy" in favour of the "everyday stories of my neighbours and friends". It plods along at times, but for those planning an extended stay it's an excellent insight into the challenges and pleasures of living and working alongside Nicaraguans.

FICTION AND POETRY

Gioconda Belli, *From Eve's Rib* and *The Inhabited Woman* (Curbstone Press). The only translated works available by the well-known Nicaraguan poet and novelist, at first a political activist, an exile and then a member of the Sandinista government (although she has since disassociated herself from the party). Her writing is at the same time political and erotic.

Ernesto Cardenal, *The Cosmic Canticle* (Curbstone Press). Thirty years of work went into the this narrative poem and mythic song –

an epic work spanning the whole of Latin American history.

Ruben Dario, *Cuentos Completos* (Fondo De Cultura Enconimica); *Azul Cantos De Vida Y Esperanza* (Planeta); *Poesia* (Alianza). Like so many Latin American authors, Ruben Dario was a versatile writer, and wrote stories and essays as well as poetry, for which he remains best known. Dario is perceived more as a national hero than a writer, and as a kind of reference point in the Nicaraguan psyche. Perhaps more than any other nation in Central American, Nicaraguans have a great respect for literature and many of their heroes are poets: Dario stood up against US military intervention, notably in his 1904 work "To Roosevelt"; and it was a poet, Rigoberto Lopez Perez, who assassinated the dictator Anastasio Somoza in 1936. During the Revolution priests like Ernesto Cardenal led the Church towards liberation theology by integrating the heroes and martyrs of the revolution into biblical stories, unifying the goals of the church with the goals of the revolution through literature.

Francisco Goldman, *The Ordinary Seaman* (Atlantic Monthly Press, US). Dark and depressing book about the fate of several Nicaraguan men contracted to work on a freighter. Their salvation from the wreck of post-Sandinista Nicaragua turns out to be a rotting hulk in Brooklyn harbour. Flight, exile, death and bittersweet memories form an enormous part of contemporary culture since the revolution and this book captures much of it.

COSTA RICA

HISTORY, POLITICS AND SOCIETY

Marc Edelman and Joanne Kenen (eds), *The Costa Rica Reader* (Grove Atlantic, US, o/p). The best single title for the general reader. The chronologically arranged essays are mainly by respected Costa Rican historians, academic in tone but not inaccessible. See especially Chilean sociologist Diego Palma's essay on current Costa Rican politics and class conflict, which penetrates the picture of Costa Rica as a haven of middle-class democracy.

Silvia Lara and Tom Barry *Inside Costa Rica* (Resource Center/LAB). One title that will bring you up to date with most aspects of the country, although it has little to say about tourism, conservation, and culture. Left-leaning, argumentative and analytical, the authors refuse to toe the party line on Costa Rica, and though the style is factual and somewhat dry, it is enlivened by flashes of humour and apt, well-supported conclusions.

Paula Palmer, *What Happen: A Folk History of the Talamanca Coast* (San José, Ecodesarrolos). The definitive – although now dated – folk history of the Afro-Caribbean community on Limón province's Talamancan coast. Palmer first went to Cahuita in the early 1970s as a Peace Corps volunteer, later to return as a sociologist, collecting oral histories from older members of the local communities. Great stories and atmospheric testimonies of pirate treasure, ghosts and the like, complemented by photos and accounts of local agriculture, foods and traditional remedies. Available in English and Spanish (in Costa Rica only).

TRAVEL AND IMPRESSIONS

Allen M. Young, *Sarapiquí Chronicle: A Naturalist in Costa Rica* (Smithsonian Institute Press). Lavishly produced book on entomologist Young's twenty years off-and-on work in the Sarapiquí area. A fluid and well-written combination of autobiography, travelogue and natural science, centring on the insect life he encounters.

ART AND ARCHEOLOGY

Between Continents, Between Seas: Precolumbian Art of Costa Rica (Harry Abrams, US, o/p). Produced as a catalogue to accompany the exhibit that toured the US in 1982, this is the best single volume on pre-Conquest history and craftsmanship, with illuminating accounts of the lives, beliefs and customs of Costa Rica's pre-Columbian peoples as interpreted through artefacts and excavations. The photographs, whether of jade pendants, Chorotega pottery or the more diabolical of the Diquis' gold pieces, are uniformly wonderful.

FICTION AND POETRY

Fabián Dobles, *Ese Que Llaman Pueblo* (San José, Editorial Costa Rica). Born in 1918, Dobles is Costa Rica's elder statesman of letters. Set in the countryside among *campesinos*, this title is a typical "proletarian" novel.

Carmen Naranjo, *Los perros no ladraron* (1966), *Responso por el niño Juan Manuel* (1968), *Ondina* (1982) and *Sobrepunto* (1985). In keeping with a tradition in Latin American letters but unusual for a woman, Naranjo has occupied several posts of public office, including Secretary of Culture, director of the publishing house EDUCA and ambassador to Israel. She is widely considered an experimentalist. Her novels are accessible in Costa Rica, and her collection of stories *There Never Was Once Upon a Time* (US, Latin American Literary Review Press) is available in English.

WILDLIFE AND THE ENVIRONMENT

Daniel H. Janzen, *Costa Rican Natural History* (University of Chicago Press). The definitive reference source, with accessible, continuously fascinating species-by-species accounts, written by a highly influential figure, involved on a policy level in the governing of the National Parks system. If nothing else the introduction is worth reading, as it deals in a cursory, lively fashion with tectonics, meteorology, history and archeology. Illustrated throughout with gripping photographs. Available in paperback, but still doorstep-thick.

F. Gary Stiles and Alexander F. Skutch, *A Guide to the Birds of Costa Rica* (Black Press/Cornell University Press). All over Costa Rica you'll see guides clutching well-thumbed copies of this seminal tome, illustrated with colour plates to aid identification. Hefty, even in paperback, and too pricey for the amateur, but you may be able to pick up good secondhand copies in Costa Rica.

Philip J. De Vries, *The Butterflies of Costa Rica and their Natural History* (Princeton University Press). Much-admired volume, really for serious butterfly enthusiasts or scientists only, but illustrated with beautiful colour plates so you can marvel at the incremental differences between various butterflies.

PANAMÁ

HISTORY, POLITICS AND SOCIETY

David McCullough, *The Path Between the Seas: The Creation of the Panama Canal* (Touchstone, US). Compelling and authoritative account of the epic struggle to build the Panama Canal. Detailed and well-resarched, it nonetheless reads like a novel.

John Weeks and Phil Gunson, *Panama: Made in the USA* (LAB, London). Detailed exploration of the unanswered questions behind the US invasion of Panamá in the context of the turbulent history of US–Panamanian relations and the struggle for control of the Canal.

TRAVEL AND IMPRESSIONS

Graham Greene, *Getting to Know the General* (Bodley Head, UK). Fascinating personal reminiscences regarding the author's unlikely friendship with General Omar Torrijos, dictator of Panamá from 1968 to 1981.

FICTION

John Le Carré, *The Tailor of Panama* (Coronet, UK). Fast-moving spy thriller by the great master of the genre, set in Panamá on the eve of US military withdrawal. Its satirical depiction of Panamá as a murky world of intrigue and corruption, populated by ambiguous characters, casued great controversy on first publication.

SPECIALIST GUIDES

Michele Labrut, *Getting to Know Panama* (Focus Publications, Panama). Enthusiastic introduction to the country's many attractions, detailed and up-to-date.

LANGUAGE/775

LANGUAGE

Across the whole of the Central American isthmus there is a bewildering collection of languages, probably numbering well above thirty in all; fortunately for the traveller, there are two that dominate – English, primarily in Belize and the Bay Islands of Honduras, but spoken to some extent all along the Caribbean coast; and Spanish everywhere else.

ENGLISH

Belizean English may sound familiar from a distance and, if you listen to a few words, you may think that their meaning is clear. Listen a little further, however, and you'll realize that complete comprehension is just out of reach. What you're hearing is, in fact, **Creole**, a beautifully warm and relaxed language, typically Caribbean and loosely based on English, with elements of Spanish and indigenous languages. A similar dialect, Guari Guari, is spoken in the Panamanian province of Bocas del Toro. Written Creole, which you'll come across in Belizean newspapers, is a little easier to get to grips with. There's an active movement in Belize to formalize the language, and a dictionary is currently in production. Luckily, almost anyone who can speak Creole can also speak English.

To get a taste of the language on the streets in Belize, here are some simple phrases. For more, get hold of a copy of *Creole Proverbs of Belize*, usually available in Belize City.

• *Bad ting neda gat owner* – Bad things never have owners.

• *Better belly bus dan good bikkle waste* – It's better that the belly bursts than good victuals go to waste.

• *Cow no business eena haas gylop* – Cows have no business in a horse race.

In the **Bay Islands** of Honduras things are much simpler. English is English rather than Creole, and immediately understandable, albeit spoken with a unique, broad accent. Influenced by Caribbean, English and Scots migrants over the years, local inflexions turn even the most commonplace of remarks into an attractive statement. English, however, is slowly being supplanted by Spanish as the language heard on the street as growing numbers of mainlanders make the islands their home.

SPANISH

Those new to the region can take heart – **Spanish**, as spoken across Latin America, is one of the easier languages there is to learn and even the most faltering of attempts to speak is greatly appreciated. Apart from the major tourist areas in Guatemala, Costa Rica, and in some parts of Panamá and Honduras, English is not widely spoken; taking the trouble to get to know at least the basics of Spanish will both make your travels considerably easier and reap countless rewards in terms of reception, appreciation and understanding of people and places. And there is no quicker way to learn than having your mistakes laughingly corrected by native speakers.

Overall, Latin American Spanish is crisper, clearer and slower than that of Spain – gone are the lisps and bewilderingly rapid, slurred, soft consonants of the old country. There are, however, quite strong variations in accent across Central America: Guatemalan Spanish has the reputation of being clear, precise and eminently understandable to the worst of linguists, whilst the language as spoken in Honduras – thick and fast – can initially bewilder even those who believed themselves to be reasonably fluent. Nicaraguans in particular take great pleasure in fooling around with language, creating new words, pronouncing certain letters differently and employing different grammar. There are enough Nicaragnismos – words and sayings particular to Nicaragua – to fill a 275-page dictionary. As far as pronunciation goes, the "s" is often dropped from word endings and the "v" and "b" sounds are fairly interchangeable.

For the most part, the rules of **pronunciation** are straightforward and strictly observed. Unless there's an accent, words ending in d, l, r and z are **stressed** on the last syllable, all others on the second last. All **vowels** are pure and short.

A somewhere between the "A" sound of back and that of father.

E as in get

I as in police

O as in hot

U as in rule

C is soft before E and I, otherwise hard; *cerca* is pronounced serka.

G works the same way – a guttural "H" sound (like the *ch* in loch) before E or I, a hard G elsewhere; *gigante* is pronounced higante.

H is always silent.

J is the same sound as a guttural G; *jamon* is pronounced hamon.

LL sounds like an English Y; *tortilla* is pronounced torteeya.

N is as in English, unless there is a *tilde* (accent) over it, when it becomes NY; mañana is pronounced manyana.

QU is pronounced like an English K.

R is rolled, RR doubly so.

V sounds like a cross with B, *vino* becoming beano.

X is slightly softer than in English, sometimes almost like SH, so that *Xela* becomes sheyla; between vowels in place names it has an H sound – México is pronounced Meh-hee-ko.

Z is the same as as a soft C; *cerveza* is pronounced servesa.

FORMAL AND INFORMAL ADDRESS

For English speakers one of the most difficult things to get to grips with is the distinction between formal and informal address – when to use it and to whom and how to avoid causing offence. Generally speaking, the third-person "**usted**" indicates respect and/or a non-familiar relationship and is used in business, for people you don't know and for those older than you. Second-person "**tú**" is for children, friends and contemporaries in less formal settings. (Remember also that in Latin America the second person **plural** – vosotros – is never used, so "you" plural will alway be ustedes). In day to day exchanges, genuine mistakes on the part of an obviously non-native speaker will be well received and corrected with good humour.

One idiosyncrasy is the widespread use of "**vos**" in Central America. Now archaic in Spain, it is frequently used in place of tú, as an intimate form of address between friends and compañeros of the same age. In most tenses, conjugation is exactly the same as for tú. In the present indicative, however the last syllable is stressed with an accent (tú comes/vos comés); in "ir" verbs also in this tense, the final "i" is kept instead of changing to an "e" (tú escribes/vos escribís). In commands, the vos form drops the final "r" of the infinitive, replacing it with an accented vowel (tú come/vos comé). Take your lead from those around you – if you are addressed in the "vos" form it is a sign of friendship which should be reciprocated; on the other hand it is sometimes seen as patronizing to use it with someone you don't know well.

NICKNAMES AND TURNS OF SPEECH

Nicknames are very common in Central America, used in both speech and writing and for any situation from addressing a casual acquaintance to referring to political candidates. Often they centre on obvious physical characteristics – *flaco/a* (thin), *gordo/a* (fat), *rubio/a* (blond) – with a nice juxtaposition between the informal words spoken in a formal tone.

Often, these nicknames will be further softened by **diminution** – the addition of the suffix *ito* or *ita* at the end of nouns and adjectives, a trend used sometimes with a passion in everyday speech. You are quite likely to hear someone talk about their *hermanito* for example, which translates as "little brother" regardless of respective ages, whilst *mí hijita* ("my little daughter") can as easily mean a grown woman as a child.

Also very common are **casual street addresses**, used lightly in brief encounters and to soothe transactions. Heard in virtually every country are *(mí) amor* – used in much the same way as "love" in England and also between friends – as is *jóven* or *jovencito/a*, young one. More specific to each country (often but not always between men) are terms used to make casual questions or remarks less intrusive. *Papa* (literally "father") is used daily in Honduras, for example as in "*¿Qué hora tiene, papá?*" (What time is it?), whilst the Nicaraguans use *primo* (cousin). Panamanian men regularly address each other as *compadre*, often abbreviated to *compa*. In Nicaragua, the local term (a fond one) for foreigners is *chele/a*.

POLITESSE

Verbal courtesy is an integral part of speech in Spanish and one that – once you're accustomed to the pace and flow of life in Central America – should become instinctive. Saying *Buenos días/Buenas tardes* and waiting for the appropriate response is usual when asking for something at a shop or ticket office for example, as is adding *Señor* or *Señora* (in this instance similar to the US "sir" or "ma'am"). The response when thanking someone for a service is more likely to be *para servirle* (literally "here to serve you") rather than the casual *de nada* ("you're welcome"). The *tss tss* sound is commonly employed to attract attention, particularly in restaurants. In this very polite culture shouting is frowned upon.

> **PHRASEBOOKS AND DICTIONARIES**
> It's worth investing in a good **phrasebook** and **dictionary** before you go. One of the best specifically Latin American dictionaries is the University of Chicago *Dictionary of Latin-American Spanish* (Pocket Books). Alternatively, HarperCollins produce the best general range of pocket dictionaries and grammars, which include many Latin American terms. The *Rough Guide to Mexican Spanish* can also come in extremely useful.

On meeting, or being introduced to, someone, Central Americans will say *con mucho gusto*, "it's a pleasure", and you should do the same. On departure you will more often than not be told *¡que le vaya bien!* ("may all go well") a simple phrase that nonetheless invariably sounds sincere and rounds off transactions nicely. In rural areas especially, it is usual to greet even complete strangers met on the path with *!Adiós, que le vaya bien!* Don't be surprised if you're greeted with "*Adiós*", as this can mean both hello and goodbye.

A SPANISH LANGUAGE GUIDE

BASICS

yes, no	*sí, no*	open, closed	*abierto/a, cerrado/a*
please, thank you	*por favor, gracias*	with, without	*con, sin*
where, when	*dónde, cuando*	good, bad	*buen(o)/a, mal(o)/a*
what, how much	*qué, cuanto*	big, small	*gran(de), pequeño/a*
here, there	*aquí, allí*	more, less	*más, menos*
this, that	*este, eso*	today, tomorrow	*hoy, mañana*
now, later	*ahora, más tarde*	yesterday	*ayer*

GREETING AND RESPONSES

hello, goodbye	*¡hola!, adios*	I don't speak Spanish	*(No) Hablo español*
good morning	*buenos días*	What (did you say)?	*Mande?*
good afternoon/ night	*buenas tardes/noches*	My name is...	*Me llamo...*
How do you do?	*¿Qué tal?*	What's your name?	*¿Como se llama usted?*
See you later	*Hasta luego*	I am English	*Soy inglés(a)*
sorry	*lo siento/disculpeme*	...American	*americano(a)*
Excuse me	*Con permiso/perdon*	...Australian	*australiano(a)*
How are you?	*¿Cómo está (usted)?*	...Canadian	*canadiense(a)*
Not at all/ You're welcome	*De nada*	...Irish	*irlandés(a)*
		...Scottish	*escosés(a)*
I (don't) understand	*(No) Entiendo*	...Welsh	*galés(a)*
Do you speak English?	*¿Habla (usted) inglés?*	...New Zealander	*neozelandés(a)*

NEEDS – HOTELS AND TRANSPORT

I want	*Quiero*	Is there a hotel nearby?	*¿Hay un hotel aquí cerca?*
Do you know...?	*¿Sabe...?*	How do I get to...?	*¿Por dónde se va a...?*
I'd like....	*Quisiera... por favor*	Left, right, straight on	*izquierda, derecha, derecho*
I don't know	*No sé*		
There is (is there)?	*Hay (?)*	Where is...?	*¿Dónde está...?*
Give me...	*Deme...*	...the bus station?	*....el terminal de bus?*
(one like that)	*(uno asi)*	...the train station?	*....la estación de ferrocarriles?*
Do you have...?	*¿Tiene...?*		
...the time	*...la hora*	...the nearest bank	*...el banco más cercano (ATM is cajero automático)*
...a room	*...un cuarto*		
...with two beds/ double bed	*...con dos camas /cama matrimonial*	...the (main) post office?	*...el correo (central)?*
It's for one person (two people)	*Es para una persona (dos personas)*	...the toilet	*...el baño/sanitario*
...for one night (one week)	*...para una noche (una semana)*	Where does the bus to... leave from?	*¿De dónde sale el camión para...?*
It's fine, how much is it?	*¿Esta bien, cuánto es?*	What time does it leave (arrive in...)?	*¿A qué hora sale (llegaen...)?*
It's too expensive	*Es demasiado caro*	What is there to eat?	*¿Qué hay para comer?*
Don't you have anything cheaper?	*¿No tiene algo más barato?*	What's that?	*¿Qué es eso?*
Can one...?	*¿Se puede...?*	What's this called in Spanish?	*¿Cómo se llama este en español?*
...camp (near) here?	*¿...acampar aquí (cerca)?*		

NUMBERS AND DAYS

1	*un/uno/una*	20	*veinte*	1999	*mil novecientos noventa y nueve*
2	*dos*	21	*ventiuno*		
3	*tres*	22	*veintidos*	2000	*dos mil*
4	*cuatro*	30	*treinta*	100,000	*cien mil*
5	*cinco*	40	*cuarenta*	1,000,000	*un millón*
6	*seis*	50	*cincuenta*		
7	*siete*	60	*sesenta*	first	*primero/a*
8	*ocho*	70	*setenta*	second	*segundo/a*
9	*nueve*	80	*ochenta*	third	*tercero/a*
10	*diez*	90	*noventa*	fifth	*quinto/a*
11	*once*	100	*cien*	tenth	*decimo/a*
12	*doce*	101	*ciento uno*	Monday	*lunes*
13	*trece*	200	*dos cientos*	Tuesday	*martes*
14	*catorce*	201	*dos cientos uno*	Wednesday	*miércoles*
15	*quince*	500	*quinientos*	Thursday	*jueves*
16	*dieciséis*	1000	*mil*	Friday	*viernes*
				Saturday	*sábado*
				Sunday	*domingo*

GLOSSARY

ABASTECEDOR A general store, usually in a rural area or barrio that keeps a stock of groceries and basic toiletries.

AGUACERO Downpour.

AGUARDIENTE Raw alcohol made from sugar cane.

AGUAS Bottled fizzy drinks; *Coca-Cola, Sprite* etc.

AHORITA Right now (any time within the coming hour).

ALCALDE Mayor.

ALDEA Small settlement.

AYUNTAMIENTO Town hall/government.

BARRANCA Steep-sided ravine.

BARRIO Neighbourhood, area within a town or city; suburb.

BIOTOPO Protected area of national ecological importance, usually with limited tourist access.

BOMBA Gas station.

CABAÑA Usually applies to tourist accommodation. Literally a cabin, but can mean anything from a palm-thatched beach hut to a US-style motel room.

CACIQUE Chief. Originally a colonial term, now used for elected leaders/figureheads of indigenous *comarcas* in Panamá.

CAMIONETA Small truck or van, or in Guatemala a second-class bus.

CAMPESINO Peasant farmer, smallholder, cowboy.

CANTINA Local hard-drinking bar, usually men-only.

CARRETERA INTERAMERICANA Transnational highway that runs 24,400km from Alaska to Tierra del Fuego, broken only by the Darién Gap between Panamá and Colombia.

CARRO Car, equivalent of *coche*.

CASA DE CAMBIO Currency exchange bureau.

CHAC Maya god of rain.

CHICLE Sapodilla tree sap from which chewing gum is made.

CHIQUILLOS Kids; also *chiquititos, chiquiticos*.

CHORREADOR Sack-and-metal coffee-filter contraption, still widely used.

CHURRIGUERESQUE Highly elaborate, decorative form of Baroque architecture (usually in churches).

CLASSIC Period during which ancient Maya civilization was at its height, usually given as 300–900 AD.

COLECTIVO Shared taxi/minibus, usually following fixed route. Can also be applied to a boat – *lancho colectivo*.

COLONIA City suburb or neighbourhood, often seen in addresses as "Col".

COMEDOR Basic restaurant, usually with just one or two things on the menu, always the cheapest place to eat. Literally dining room.

CONQUISTADORS "One who conquers": member of early Spanish expeditions to the Americas in the sixteenth century.

CONVENTO Convent or monastery.

CORDILLERA Mountain range.

CORRIENTE Second-class bus.

CREOLE Of mixed African or Caribbean (and European) descent; also the English patois spoken in Belize and Caribbean towns throughout the region.

CUADRA Street block.

DESCOMPUESTO Out of order.

DON/DOÑA Courtesy titles (sir/madam), mostly used in letters or for professional people or the boss.

EFECTIVO Cash.

EJIDO Communal farmland.

EVANGÉLICO Christian evangelist or fundamentalist, often a missionary. Name given to members of numerous Protestant sects seeking converts in Central America.

FERIA Fair (market).

FINCA Ranch, farm or plantation.

FINQUERO Coffee grower.

GAMBAS Buttresses, the giant above-ground roots that some rainforest trees put out.

GARÍFUNA People of mixed African and Amerindian descent, with unique language and strong African heritage. They live in numerous communities on the Caribbean coast between southern Belize and Nicaragua.

GASEOSA Fizzy drink.

GASOLINERA Gas station.

GLYPH Element in Maya writing and carving, roughly the equivalent of a letter or numeral.

GRINGO/GRINGA Any white-skinned foreigner, particularly North Americans. Not necessarily a term of abuse.

GUACA Pre-Columbian burial ground or tomb.

HACIENDA Big farm, ranch or estate, or big house on it.

HENEQUÉN Fibre from *agave* (sisal) plant, used to make rope.

HOSPEDAJE Very basic pensión or small hotel.

HUIPIL Maya women's traditional dress or blouse, usually woven or embroided.

I.V.A. Sales tax.

INDÍGENA An indigenous person; preferred term among indigenous groups, rather than the more racially offensive *índio:* indian.

INVIERNO Winter (May–Oct).

JORNALEROS Day labourers, usually landless peasants who are paid by the day, for instance to pick coffee in season.

JUEGO DE PELOTA Ball court.

LADINO A vague term – applied to people, means Spanish-influenced as opposed to indigenous, and at its most specific defines someone of mixed Spanish and indigenous blood. It's more commonly used simply to describe a person of "Western" culture, or one who dresses in "Western" style, be they of indigenous or mixed blood.

LICUADO Fresh blended fruit juice, made with water or milk.

MALECÓN Seafront promenade.

MAYA Indigenous people who inhabited Honduras, Guatemala, Belize and southeastern Mexico from earliest times, and still do. Although they also lived in El Salvador, there are none left there today.

MESTIZO Person of mixed indigenous and Spanish blood, though like the term ladino it has more cultural than racial significance.

METATE Pre-Columbian stone table used for grinding corn

MIGRACIÓN Immigration office.

MILPA Maize field, usually cleared by slash and burn.

MIRADOR Lookout point.

MISKITO Native American group living along the area of the Caribbean coast of Honduras and Nicaragua known as the Mosquita.

MUELLE Jetty or dock.

NATURAL An indigenous person.

NEOTRÓPICOS Neotropics: tropics of the New World.

ORIENTE East; often seen in addresses as Ote.

PALACIO Mansion, but not necessarily royal.

PALACIO DE GOBIERNO Headquarters of state/federal authorities.

PALACIO MUNICIPAL Headquarters of local government.

PALAPA Palm thatch. Used to describe any thatched/palm-roofed hut.

PASEO A broad avenue, but also the ritual evening walk around the plaza.

PELOTA Ball, or ball court.

PENSIÓN Simple hotel.

PEÓN Farm labourer, usually landless.

PERSONAJE Someone of importance, a VIP, although usually used pejoratively to indicate someone who is putting on airs.

PLANTA BAJA Ground floor – abbreviated PB in elevators.

PLATERESQUE Elaborately decorative renaissance architectural style.

PONIENTE West; often seen in addresses as Pte.

POPUL VUH The Quiché Maya's epic story of the creation and history of their people.

POSTCLASSIC Period between the decline of Maya civilization and the arrival of the Spanish, 900–1530 AD.

PRECLASSIC Archeological era preceding the blooming of Maya civilization, usually given as 1500 BC–300 AD.

PULLMAN Fast and comfortable bus, usually an old Greyhound.

PULPERÍA General store or corner store. Also sometimes serves cooked food and drinks.

QUICHÉ Largest of the Guatemalan Maya groups, centred today on the town of Santa Cruz del Quiché.

RANCHO Palm-thatched roof, also smallholding.

REDONDEL DE TOROS Bull-ring, used for local rodeos.

REFRESCO Drink, usually made with fresh fruit or water, sometimes fizzy drink, although this can also be called a *gaseosa*.

SABANERO Cowboy.

SACBE Maya road, or ceremonial causeway.

SIERRA Mountain range.

SODA Costa Rican cafeteria or diner; in the rest of Central America it's usually called a *comedor*.

STELA Freestanding carved monument. Most are of Maya origin.

TECÚN UMÁN Last king of the Quiché Maya, defeated in battle by the conquistador Alvarado.

TEMPORADA Season: *la temporada de lluvia* is the rainy season.

TERRENO Land, small farm.

TIENDA Shop.

TÍPICO/TÍPICA Literally "typical". Used to describe food, or in Guatemala, the multi-coloured textiles geared to the Western customer.

TRAJE Traditional costume.

VERANO Summer (Dec–April).

INDEX

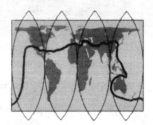

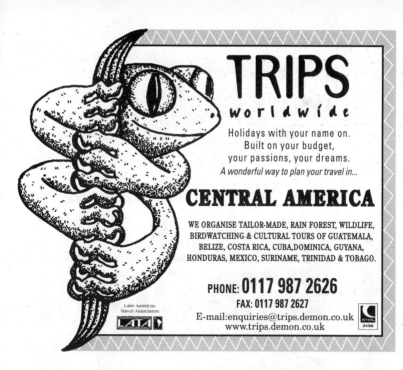